Jacob & Esau

Jacob & Esau is a profound new account of two millennia of Jewish European history that, for the first time, integrates the cosmopolitan narrative of the Jewish Diaspora with that of traditional Jews and Jewish culture. Malachi Hacohen uses the biblical story of the rival twins, Jacob and Esau, and its subsequent retelling by Christians and Jews throughout the ages as a lens through which to illuminate changing Jewish–Christian relations and the opening and closing of opportunities for Jewish life in Europe. *Jacob & Esau* tells a new history of a people accustomed for over two and a half millennia to forming relationships, real and imagined, with successive empires but eagerly adapting, in modernity, to the nation-state, and experimenting with both assimilation and Jewish nationalism. In rewriting this history via Jacob and Esau, the book charts two divergent but intersecting Jewish histories that together represent the plurality of Jewish European cultures.

Malachi Haim Hacohen is Professor and Bass Fellow at Duke University. He serves as the Director of the Religions and Public Life Initiative at the Kenan Institute for Ethics. His *Karl Popper – The Formative Years, 1902–1945* (Cambridge, 2000) won the Herbert Baxter Adams Prize of the AHA and Austria's Victor Adler State Prize.

Jacob & Esau

Jewish European History Between Nation and Empire

Malachi Haim Hacohen

Duke University, North Carolina

CAMBRIDGE UNIVERSITY PRESS

CAMBRIDGE
UNIVERSITY PRESS

University Printing House, Cambridge CB2 8BS, United Kingdom

One Liberty Plaza, 20th Floor, New York, NY 10006, USA

477 Williamstown Road, Port Melbourne, VIC 3207, Australia

314–321, 3rd Floor, Plot 3, Splendor Forum, Jasola District Centre, New Delhi – 110025, India

79 Anson Road, #06–04/06, Singapore 079906

Cambridge University Press is part of the University of Cambridge.

It furthers the University's mission by disseminating knowledge in the pursuit of education, learning, and research at the highest international levels of excellence.

www.cambridge.org
Information on this title: www.cambridge.org/9781316510377
DOI: 10.1017/9781108226813

© Malachi Haim Hacohen 2019

First published 2019

Printed in the United Kingdom by TJ International Ltd. Padstow Cornwall

A catalog record for this publication is available from the British Library.

Library of Congress Cataloging-in-Publication Data
Names: Hacohen, Malachi Haim, 1957– author.
Title: Jacob & Esau : Jewish European history between nation and empire / Malachi Haim Hacohen, Duke University, North Carolina.
Other titles: Jacob and Esau : Jewish European history between nation and empire
Description: New York, NY : Cambridge University Press, [2019]
Identifiers: LCCN 2018022118 | ISBN 9781316510377 (hardback)
Subjects: LCSH: Judaism – Relations – Christianity – History. | Christianity and other religions – Judaism – History. | Jews – Europe – History. | Europe – Ethnic relations – History. | BISAC: HISTORY / Europe / General.
Classification: LCC BM535 .H23 2018 | DDC 940/.04924–dc23
LC record available at lccn.loc.gov/2018022118

ISBN 978-1-316-51037-7 Hardback
ISBN 978-1-316-64984-8 Paperback

For Julie, my love

סיון בת אברהם ושרה שתה׳

Contents

Figures

Acknowledgments

Jacob & Esau is a monograph on two millennia of Jewish European history. The book has gone through several metamorphoses over the years, each expanding, I hope, the opportunities for Jewish history to tell European stories. The history of Jewish–Christian relations converged, via the rabbinic trope of Roman Esau, with the tale of nation against empire, leading from the ancient world to modernity. In modern times, nation-state and pluralist empire represented alternative modes of Jewish emancipation. Jacob and Esau both shaped the intellectual world of Jews and Christians as they struggled with nation and empire and registered the changes in their relations. They have become Jewish European history.

The book first emerged, in my post-tenure sabbatical in Jerusalem and Vienna, as a fairly contained project on Jewish emancipation, seeking to vindicate Enlightenment universalism against illiberal multiculturalism. It quickly expanded into a project on the European Jewish intelligentsia – the abiding concern of all of my work – from the Enlightenment to the Cold War. I progressively recognized, however, that I was arguing at cross-purposes: I was using rabbinic traditions to advance a European cosmopolitan project that left only limited room for traditional Jews and my own Jewishness. No wonder I was encountering difficulty joining Jacob & Esau with the acculturated European Jewish intelligentsia!

Historian Dan Diner's brilliant comments in a December 2004 Haifa conference on Jewish transnational networks became transformative for my project. He suggested that the common view of the Jew as a modernizer was misleading. The nation-state's demand for cultural assimilation confronted Jews with an impossible identity dilemma, and premodern imperial corporatism and postnational European federalism, in contrast, constituted pluralist orders that made allowance for Jewish particularity. The Jewish Question was exemplary of the European nation-state dilemma. In writing its history via Jacob & Esau, Jewish history becomes European, that is, Jewish European history.

It dawned on me that the nation-state represented a paradox: The political idea of the nation, emerging from the French Revolution, made Jewish emancipation and citizenship possible, even necessary, but consummation of the nationalist drive toward cultural uniformity, whether in assimilation or in ethnic exclusion of the Jews, would spell the end of European Jewry. The nation-state's dilemmas made Austrian Jewish imperial patriotism and nostalgia for pluralist Austria-Hungary understandable. A dialectic between nation and empire drove Jewish European history: Imperial Austria guarded pluralism and opened up space for Jewish nationality in ways the nation-state could not, but modern empire was not an emancipatory agent.

As late as 2009, I was still unsure how precisely Jacob & Esau told the Jewish European story. Enlightenment came in the form of a countermodel. In his *Mimesis* (1946), philologist and literary critic Erich Auerbach used a literary and theological trope, typology, to construct a Judeo-Christian European history. Christian typology saw the Old Testament Patriarchs, like Jacob, as presaging Christ. Auerbach argued for the Jews as biblical predecessors of Christianity and founders of the West. I realized that through Jacob & Esau, I was recounting a Jewish European history that, unlike Auerbach's, highlighted rabbinic Jews as European and made them makers of Europe. Jacob & Esau was both a Jewish and a Christian *topos*, and Jewish–Christian exchanges charted two millennia of European history. Jacob & Esau provided continuity between Antiquity and modernity, and constituted a barometer of Jewish–Christian relations, signaling opening and closing opportunities for Jewish life in Europe.

As I was completing the book, the significance of this *longue durée* history for both the Jewish and European future became clearer. *Jacob & Esau* tells the story of a people, regarding itself a nation (אומה), accustomed for over two and a half millennia to forming relationships, real and imagined, with successive empires but eagerly adapting, in modernity, to the nation-state, and experimenting with national integration (emancipation) and Jewish nationalism. Even in modern times, however, the great majority of Jews lived, until 1918, in multiethnic empires and not in nation-states. In such a long history, short episodes of Jewish sovereignty – Ancient Judah, the Hasmonaean Kingdom, and the State of Israel – appear as contingent, lulls in Near Eastern imperial hegemony: the short-term absence of a regional empire. To gain a proper perspective on nation and empire in Jewish history, I realized, modern emancipation and contemporary Jewish sovereignty needed to be projected against longer periods of imperially negotiated Jewish autonomy. In turn, premodern traditions and political configurations may well prove edifying, once the anomalies of European modernity and Jewish power will have run their course. Having relativized modernity, postmodernity must look backward, to the *longue durée*, if it wishes to look forward. Would it be presumptuous to offer the European Jews and rabbinic traditions as particularly instructive examples of life sustenance over the ages?

Lest my secular colleagues – and they are a vast majority – be alarmed that my proposal may encroach on their culture, the book is anchored in liberal pluralism, and its narrative structure should put them at ease. With Jewish acculturation into modern European culture, Jacob & Esau cannot tell the whole story of the liberal intelligentsia. My unified premodern narrative diverges in modernity into two alternate ones: the first focusing on Jacob & Esau, the second on nation and empire. Rabbis, historians, writers, and poets who reconfigured Jacob & Esau to address the Jewish Question are the major protagonists of the first, and the German-acculturated Jewish intelligentsia imagining a pluralist Central Europe are those of the second. A vision of Jewish pluralism, crucial to Jewish European history and the politics of European integration alike, underlies my dual narrative. Historical forms hint at political ones: Multiple narratives and voices, seeking dialogue but refusing uniformity, would ideally characterize Jewish life, European integration, and historiography, all at the same time.

The long period of the making of this book has been edifying for me, and saw the formation of many new friendships. I have become ever more aware of my indebtedness to fellow scholars, friends, and family. I would like to acknowledge some of these debts here.

Duke University and several international research centers provided crucial support. Former Duke Provost Peter Lang and successive chairs of the History Department, from Sally Deutsch to Bill Reddy to John Martin, supported precious research leaves and made sure I stayed at Duke. I thank them for their confidence in my work. My colleagues in the History Department have shown exemplary fairness and commitment to scholarly standards over the years. Among the many whom I call my friends, I would like to mention especially Dirk Bönker: Our friendship is symbolic of the new German–Jewish relationship in the aftermath of the Holocaust – may it last. I am deeply saddened that my dear late colleague Warren Lerner is no longer here to see the book, but am comforted that Martin Miller and Sy Mauskopf are. Jamie Hardy has accompanied the book for a decade, and saw primary sources moving from the print age to the digital one, always making sure that they ended up in my manuscript.

I often joke that a university can do without faculty and administrators but the librarians are indispensable. Duke librarians are the best.

European Studies librarian Heidi Madden and Jewish Studies librarian Rachel Ariel have unfailingly obtained the most obscure literature, and Elizabeth Dunn from Special Collections made sure, in stimulating presentations to my classes, that my students shared in the process of intellectual discovery. Now that the project is done, I promise Heidi that I will cease sending requests in the wee hours of Sunday morning (but if I fail to keep the promise, I know her response will be there within minutes). The Lilly Library personnel – Carson, Danette, Grete, Kelley, Lee, and Yunyi – have likewise proven remarkably adept in making research materials available to me, and they also made sure that the library provided a hospitable space, a beautiful one, for my work. Libraries are the soul of the university. I hope that they will not progressively vanish as a physical space in the digital age.

Duke is embedded in regional intellectual life that is second to none. My work, and this book in particular, has benefited greatly from the Triangle Intellectual History Seminar – an institution I helped found more than twenty years ago, which has meanwhile become a mainstay of contextual intellectual history – and the North Carolina Jewish Studies Seminar. Members of both seminars have seen the book developing and going through its different stages. They responded with valuable feedback and sustained me with social companionship. Among my close friends in both seminars, I would like to mention especially K. Steven Vincent, who has been steadfast in his support and friendship for over two decades, and Yaakov Ariel and Shai Ginsburg, who were always the first to read new chapters and provide insights that drew on their immense erudition. I know my good fortune and am grateful to all.

A fellowship at the *Internationales Forschungszentrum Kulturwissenschaften* (IFK) in Vienna served to launch this project. I want to thank the entire IFK team, but especially the Deputy Director at the time, Lutz Musner, for his support and friendship, and express the hope that this exceptional Austrian institution will retain its original mission and character. This is also a good moment to remember my other Austrian friends who have been part of my intellectual life, from *Metropole Wien* in the mid-1990s to "Empire, Socialism and Jews," reenvisioning Austrian history, today: The late Siegi Mattl and Wolfgang Maderthaner יבדל״א were invaluable readers of the Austrian chapters of this book, and Georg Spitaler has joined my journey from the IFK to "Empire, Socialism and Jews." Conservator Verena Graf of the *Kunsthistorisches Museum*, Vienna, introduced me, at the project's beginning, to Schönfeld's reconciliation paintings, one of which appears on the cover of this book, and conservator Ina Slama told me about the paintings' restoration toward the end.

They have brought the circle to a close, but I look forward to many years of continued collaboration.

An ACLS Frederick Burkhardt Fellowship for "long-term, unusually ambitious projects in the humanities and related social sciences" supported my residence at the National Humanities Center in 2003–2004, and a summer fellowship at the Bucerius Institute for Research of Contemporary German History at the University of Haifa, for which I thank Yfaat Weiss, followed. I am not sure whether either sponsor recognized quite how long-term a project they were supporting, but I hope that I made good on the Burkhardt goal of realizing "a major piece of scholarly work." I also enjoyed hospitality at the Center for Advanced Studies in the Behavioral Sciences in Stanford in 2006–2007. I was warmly received by the Jewish Studies Program at Stanford, where I presented an early outline of the book, and the Stanford librarians, so nicely integrated into the program, made the library's exceptional holdings accessible to me.

I completed the book during my stay as a Polonsky Fellow at the Center for Advanced Hebrew and Jewish Studies at Oxford. I was a member of a research group on "Jews, Liberalism and Antisemitism: The Dialectics of Inclusion." The Oxford group was intellectually exhilarating, and it laid the foundation for rethinking the relationship between race, religion, and national culture, as I move beyond the present study. I would like to thank especially Abigail Green, an organizer of the group, and a wonderful conversation partner, for her special efforts to make my Oxford experience both intellectually and socially rewarding. I am also grateful to the Center, its President, Martin Goodman, and its staff. I cherish the memory of the small institute library, where every book I wanted, in any field of Jewish Studies, was within my hand's reach. I feel privileged to have so benefited.

At the final stage of this book, the Kenan Institute for Ethics at Duke University, at the initiative of the Director, Suzanne Shanahan, organized a book workshop and invited old and new friends to comment on the MS. For years Paul Mendes-Flohr has been my ultimate source for German-Jewish life, and in his inimitably kind fashion, he offered astute observations this time, too. Sociologist John Hall has been a conversation partner on Jews and nationalism from Popper to Jacob & Esau, a loyal reader and a steadfast supporter. Ted Fram challenged my view of medieval Christian Edom, and I only wish I had had more time to deliberate over his questions, and learn more. Hillel Kieval challenged my nation-state paradigm with his superior knowledge of Central Europe, and elicited the audience's sympathy in arguing that I ignore emancipation's success and that the story did not have to end this way. I am grateful to all.

Joseph Agassi, Israeli philosopher and public intellectual, and don of the Popperians, has been a source of stimulating exchanges for a quarter of a century. He is one of the few to whom I can send anything I write and, of course, he will have an informed and decisive opinion on it. Economist and historian Aladár Madarász of the Hungarian National Academy has been likewise a good friend and an inspiring commentator on many topics related to the book. Together with Stanley Hauerwas, I was a member of two working groups at Duke University, "New Beginnings" in 2002–2003 and "Naming Evil," organized by my friend and colleague Ruth Grant, in 2004–2005. I never avowed Hauerwas's wholesale rejection of modernity, but his provocations are echoed in my exploration of premodern traditions as a source for a postmodern liberal polity. Shannon van Wey has been, in recent years, a source of insight and support, as he followed, with some fascination, the project's completion. Medievalist Fred Behrends, an incomparable Latinist and head of a local Talmud study group, has been a loyal friend, a Jewish Studies resource, and an intellectual model for a quarter of a century. I was fortunate to meet him at the tiny local Orthodox Kehillah holding its services on the ground floor of a Conservative synagogue. The OK has accompanied this project from start to finish and has remained a prime site for articulating my postorthodox ambivalence toward modern Orthodoxy, above all my irritation at its effort to retain gender privilege as an identity marker. לא זה הדרך (Wrong Way!), but it remains the *minyan* I complain about (and attend).

Gerald (Shaya) Izenberg is known to many as a brilliant intellectual historian, unique for his ability to march readers through complicated texts and render them lucid. He has been a supportive friend for over two decades and has seen this project through its different stages. He has read and reread the entire MS, encapsulating with his usual brilliance its central theses, offering insightful criticism, and suggesting editorial changes – always on target. By now I have had the good fortune of teaching a few of his students, and have engaged others, who are leading historians, in intellectual exchange. It is no wonder Shaya is universally recognized as the great educator and mentor of his generation. I feel privileged to have been a beneficiary.

The help I have received over the years from scholars in diverse fields has been extensive, and many have generously shared their time and knowledge. I have endeavored to acknowledge all help in my notes, but I fear that I may omit mentioning some; I ask for forgiveness in advance and promise to correct it in any future edition. (I will be asking for forgiveness again before Yom Kippur הבעל"ט.) Among those I would like to thank for reading chapters and offering invaluable comments are Steve Aschheim, Daniel Bessner, Marc Brettler, Dirk Bonker, Matthias Bormuth, Eric Brandom, James Chappel, Shaye Cohen, Yaacov Deutsch, Arie Dubnov, Yedida Eisenstat (who greatly improved chapters 2–3), Ari Geiger, Kata Gellen, Simon Glick, Adi Gordon, Abigail Green, Eden Hacohen, David Halperin, Ari Joskowicz (who greatly improved chapters 5–6), Helmut Konrad, Lloyd Kramer, Jan Kühne, Tony La Vopa, Emily Levine, David Luft, Shaul Magid, the late Ezra Mendelsohn, Michael Miller, Yehudah Mirsky, Hilda Nissimi, Tom (Tevye) Prendergast, David Rechter, Joel Revill, Lucas van Rompay, Alex Rosenberg, Nancy Sinkoff, Martina Steer, Noah Strote, Martin Vialon, and Saskia Ziolkowski.

Members of the Johns Hopkins History Seminar and of the NYC Intellectual History Seminar have both offered excellent critical comments on the Auerbach chapter. The European Studies Seminar at Harvard offered helpful suggestions for chapter 8. Audiences at a Columbia University conference on Jewish internationalism, at my lecture in the Jewish Studies and Contemporary History Departments at the University of Vienna, and in two conferences at Bar-Ilan University responded graciously to presentations of an outline of this book. E. Roy Weintraub and members of the seminar at the Center for the History of Political Economy at Duke alerted me to the role Jewish difference plays in narratives of Western economic development.

I have kept in touch with my teachers at Bar-Ilan University for four decades, and have had the great pleasure of collaborating with my friends there from undergraduate days, above all, with Hilda Nissimi. The author of *Jacob & Esau* is probably not the person they imagined would emerge when they sent the twenty-two-year-old to Columbia University for the Ph.D., but I hope they still take some pride in him. I know they will appreciate the rabbinic phrases I left in the midst of notes in Latin script. While I have made every effort to ease readers' access to Hebrew literature, and provided an English title for virtually every Hebrew work, Hebrew is as much a European language as Latin. If Latin phrases, inaccessible to some, are part of scholarly notes in European history books, so should Hebrew idioms in a book on Jewish European history.

Phyllis Berk was my copy editor for *Karl Popper*. She is also the copy editor for *Jacob & Esau*. She represents standards in copyediting that were always rare and now are disappearing. I am thankful to her for being a partner to my work. An hour meeting with Michael Watson of Cambridge University Press, in a Durham NC coffee house in 2011, was all I needed to change my publication plans. He has since read significant parts of the MS and offered his invaluable editorial advice –

always on the mark. He represents for me old-fashioned scholarly decency and intellectual standards that one would have thought are gone from the publishing world of the digital age. The Cambridge production team, headed by Ruth Boyes and Lisa Carter, made the publication process one any author would envy. I feel fortunate to have collaborated with them.

My daughters, Hadas and Lilach, came into the world as the book was conceived and written, and they have grown up with it, sharing in Dad's rapprochement with rabbinic traditions. They are now both flourishing teenagers, intellectuals of their own, more savvy about the world than their Dad ever was, and American in ways that he will never be. Their Jewish liturgical and scholarly erudition is a source of immense gratification for me. It suggests that the postorthodox convergence of rabbinic and liberal culture that moves this book is not only a prospect but also a reality.

Julie Mell, my spouse, is herself a medieval Jewish history professor, forging new paths in Jewish European history. She fights the myth of the Jewish moneylender, often considered the founder of capitalism and the modernizer of the European economy, a myth that has come to dominate mainstream Jewish history. Her intellectual enthusiasm for the rabbis inspired my own exploration of the heritage of my youth, forging relationships, as a historian, with a mixture of distance and enchantment. Julie has accompanied the making of this book as an insightful and caring companion, repeatedly reading, commenting, and challenging its central ideas, creating a dialogue on Jewish European history, where each of us enriched the other's work without ever taking away the unmistakable stamp of individuality. Neither of us quite recognized it, but this book about the Europeanness of the Jews is also one about our own relationship, and the world that made it possible. Soma Morgenstern, a Galician Jewish writer, could only dream about this world, but it has become a reality in our time, at an anomalous juncture of Jewish history that may not last long. So the book is dedicated to Julie.

My fascination with rabbinic culture may leave some readers wondering why I am not in a *yeshivah*, reasoning that Marx, Popper, and other apostates may be read there more avidly than on most campuses. No way! I have enjoyed the academy too much. The Sages envisioned the time when Judean princes would be teaching the Torah in Roman circuses. I am, as my name attests, from priestly rather than princely descent, but I have always taken great joy in teaching Torah in a well-run (and civilized) Roman circus. So I am here to stay.

Durham NC
October 2017
ק״ק דורהם ע״נ אינו
מרחשוון, תשע״ח לפ״ק

Earlier versions of several chapters of this book appeared in print. A section of chapter 1 was published as "Nation and Empire in Jewish European History," *Leo Baeck Institute Yearbook* (2017). Chapter 8 was published in German as "Kosmopoliten in einer ethnonationalen Zeit? Juden und Österreicher in der Ersten Republik" (Cosmopolitans in Ethnonational Times? Jews and Austrians in the First Republic), in Helmut Konrad and Wolfgang Maderthaner, eds., *Das Werden der Ersten Republik... . der Rest ist Österreich*, 2 vols. (Vienna: Gerold, 2009), I: 281–316. Chapter 11 was published as "Typology and the Holocaust: Erich Auerbach and Judeo-Christian Europe," *Religions* 3: 600–645. Chapter 12 was published as "From *Forvm* to *Neues Forvm*: The 'Congress for Cultural Freedom,' the 68ers and the Émigrés," in *Das Jahr 1968 – Ereignis, Symbol, Chiffre*, ed. Oliver Rathkolb and Friedrich Stadler (Vienna University Press, 2010), pp. 239–74. Chapter 13 was published as "Jacob & Esau Today: The End of a Two Millennia Paradigm?" in *Encouraging Openness: Essays for Joseph Agassi on the Occasion of His 90th Birthday*, ed. Nimrod Bar-Am and Stefano Gattei, Boston Studies in Philosophy 325 (New York: Springer, 2017), pp. 167–90.

A Note on Transliteration from Hebrew to English

This book seeks to speak to audiences broader than Jewish Studies scholars. I have offered English translations for virtually all Hebrew titles. Commonly, a transliterated Hebrew title is followed by an English translation in parentheses. When the English translation substitutes for the Hebrew title, it is followed by the words "in Hebrew" in parentheses.

For proper names, Jewish figures with well-known English names, for example, Ramban, appear under the English Naḥmanides rather than the Hebrew Moshe ben Naḥman. In other cases, I have often preferred to retain the Hebrew name, for example, Shmuel ben Meir for Rashbam rather than Samuel ben Meir.

Conventions of transliteration from Hebrew to English continue to evolve and diverge between academies, and sometimes even between fields and journals. Throughout the book, I have used ḥ rather than ch for the Hebrew ה, and ẓ rather than tz or ts for the Hebrew צ (hence, *Ẓiyon* rather than *Tsiyon* for the well-known Hebrew journal and *Ẓenah u-Renah* rather than *Tsenah u-Renah* for the Yiddish classic). I have used the q for ק to distinguish it from k for כ, and used kh for the כ, hence Rabbi Aqiva and Halakhah. As a rule, seeking to bring transliteration and phonetics closer together, I have used single consonants for Hebrew letters with *dagesh*: b and p for ב and פ, respectively, and v and f for ב and פ, respectively. I have avoided the apostrophe for the ע.

That said, I accepted the commonly used spelling of words, so the Passover *Haggadah*, Ḥanukkah, Kabbalah, *Midrash Rabbah*, and shabbat, and even Kehillah and tractate Gittin it is, but tractate Megilah, *Midrash Tehilim*, and the kabbalistic *tiqun*. Similarly, for proper names, Yaakov has by now become common for Jacob and, for Isaac, commonly rendered as Yitzchak, I duly used the ẓ and ḥ but dared not substitute the q for the k, so Isaac's Hebrew name is spelled Yiẓḥak throughout the book. May the Lord (and scholars jealous for consistency העומדים על קוצו של יוד) have mercy.

The common spelling of authors' names and authors' transliterated titles has always been honored, even when diverging from my own transliterations.

Introduction: Jewish European History

Figure 1: Daniel Cohn-Bendit's portrait with the European Union's emblem and the 1968 rubric: "We are all German Jews now."

The setting was uncannily idyllic: an international conference on German-Jewish émigrés in 2011, held in the beautiful Schloss Elmau, set against the Bavarian Alps near the Austrian border, above the resort town of Garmisch-Partenkirchen. Leading U.S., German, and Israeli historians lectured on the émigrés' abiding legacy.[1] Europe's foremost philosopher, Jürgen Habermas, reminisced about the émigrés' role in his life, and Daniel Cohn-Bendit recounted his journey as a Jewish European public intellectual from 1968 to the Greens of today.[2] The pariahs,

---

[1] "Jüdische Stimmen im Diskurs der sechziger Jahre" (Jewish voices in the German sixties), International Conference of Ludwig Maximilian University of Munich (LMU) and the University of California, June 27–29, 2011. Most conference lectures appeared in the *Journal of Modern Jewish Studies* 13:1 (2014).

[2] Jürgen Habermas, "Grossherzige Remigranten: Über jüdische Philosophen in der frühen Bundesrepublik: Eine persönliche Erinnerung," *Neue Zürcher Zeitung* (2 July 2011);

fugitives of the Holocaust, have come to define European culture, inhabiting as non-Jewish a space as Schloss Elmau.[3] In Garmisch-Partenkirchen below, memories abound of a sixteenth-century witch-hunt, a Marian miracle that saved the town from the plague, and the 1936 Winter Olympics, "Juden sind unerwünscht" (Jews unwelcome), but in Elmau's Europe, "nous sommes tous des Juifs allemands," we are all German Jews now.[4] (See Figure 1.)

"But the majority of émigrés whom you called 'Jewish,' Herr Habermas, were no longer Jewish," queried a participant.[5] Habermas seemed puzzled for a moment, then shrugged his shoulders and gestured with his hand, as if to say "Give me a break!" The émigrés' lives were fashioned by their exile as Jews, he pointed out: "Whatever the émigrés may have thought or believed [about themselves], they could return to Germany after 1945 only as Jews."[6] Habermas was right: Notwithstanding their own frequent disavowal of Jewish identity, racial and national exclusion had shaped the émigrés' existence and their cosmopolitanism. He understood well their investment in Enlightenment traditions and their transformative cultural role in the Federal Republic. His incredulity and his interrogation of their disavowal of Jewish identity were well founded.

Still, Habermas could not quite answer the question about the émigrés' Jewishness. In what sense were émigrés like Karl Löwith, a Protestant Jew, who was equally distant from Judaism and Christianity, or Theodor Adorno, son of an Italian Catholic mother, who refused religion and

---

"Daniel Cohn-Bendit im Gespräch mit Norbert Frei," in *Münchener Beiträge zur Jüdischen Geschichte und Kultur* 6:1 (2012): 19–40.

[3] Inhabiting it for a second time: Immediately after World War II, Elmau served as a sanatorium for tubercular displaced persons and Holocaust survivors. I owe this information to Noam Zadoff of Indiana University.

[4] In the May 1968 Paris street protests, the students chanted "nous sommes tous des Juifs allemands." They were responding to press articles accentuating Cohn-Bendit's foreignness and calling for his deportation. The right-wing *Minute* opined that "ce Cohn-Bendit, parce qu'il est juif et allemand, se prend pour un nouveau Karl Marx" ("Assez de ces enragés rouges: Qu'attend-on pour expulser l'Allemand Cohn-Bendit, chef des Commandos de vandales?" 2 May 1968), and Communist Party Secretary General Georges Marchais inveighed the next day in *L'Humanité* against "'Le Mouvement du 22 mars Nanterre' dirigé par l'anarchiste allemand Cohn-Bendit" ("De faux révolutionaries à démasquer," 3 May 1968). Later in May, student banners appeared, carrying Cohn-Bendit's jovial portrait, with the refrain under it. Decades after, election campaign T-shirts for the European Greens reproduced the banner, and encircled Cohn-Bendit's portrait with a gold-starred European Union emblem.

[5] "Jürgen Habermas im Gespräch mit Rachel Salamander," *Münchener Beiträge zur Jüdischen Geschichte und Kultur* 6:1 (2012): 15. Throughout the book, translations are my own unless a translator is mentioned.

[6] Ibid.: "Jeder von den Emigranten konnte nach 1945 nur als Jude zurückkommen! Egal, was er sonst noch gedacht oder geglaubt hat."

politics, "Jewish"?[7] Habermas has little familiarity with Jewish cultures that could lend him insight into being Jewish, let alone Christian-Jewish. He has great appreciation for Jewish culture but limited understanding of its variability or complexity. The noted German-Jewish and Israeli Kabbalah scholar Gershom Scholem (1897–1982) was Habermas's model of Jewish authenticity, and other émigrés were "non-Jewish Jews," Jews by virtue of Nazi persecution. The philosopher who has repeatedly acknowledged his debt to the Jewish émigrés, a "righteous gentile" who has done much to enshrine their legacy, had no access to their Jewishness.[8]

The conference's inability to confront the Jewishness at its very center became evident in the final session. The non-Jewish Germans watched with dismay as German-Jewish participants sparred over Jewish identity, each bemoaning the vanishing of their favorite Jewish culture.[9] This Jewish sense of irretrievable loss was too much for Cohn-Bendit: "Wir haben gewonnen" (We won), he cried out, mobilizing sentiment against defeatism. Jewish life, he said, has not disappeared from Germany but has been redefined and normalized. His son – "non-Jewish," he insisted – coaches a multiethnic Maccabi team in Frankfurt, embodying a newly integrated Jewry in a multicultural Germany.[10] Bela Cohn-Bendit vindicates the cosmopolitan Jewish European narrative, a story of modernity culminating in supranational Europe, and leading from Marx and Heine to Adorno and Benjamin to Habermas and Cohn-Bendit.

The cosmopolitan narrative is beautiful, and true within limits. It has made Jewish European history possible.[11] More traditional European

---

[7] Ibid., 15–18.

[8] In his earlier "Der deutsche Idealismus der jüdischen Philosophen" (1961), in his *Philosophisch-Politische Profile* (Frankfurt: Suhrkamp, 1971), pp. 37–66, Habermas suggested that German idealism absorbed kabbalistic influences via German Protestantism; hence, German-Jewish philosophers reencountered their tradition in new clothing in idealism. The dubiousness of his Scholem-inspired intellectual history aside, it is too narrow to define the émigrés' Jewishness.

[9] "Gesprächsrunde über jüdisches Leben im Nachkriegsdeutschland," *Münchener Beiträge zur Jüdischen Geschichte und Kultur* 6:1 (2012): 41–60.

[10] Ibid., 56. The text omits the outcry "Wir haben gewonnen" and reads: "My son is not Jewish [according to Jewish law]." Cohn-Bendit was right to emphasize the changing cultural profile of German Jewishness. It is all the more surprising, then, that he would deploy Jewish Orthodoxy to deny his son Jewishness. For both Habermas and Cohn-Bendit, inaccessibility to traditional Jewish culture paradoxically results in falling back on essentialist Jewishness, whether racial or legal.

[11] Dan Diner, "Geschichte der Juden: Paradigma einer europäischen Geschichtsschreibung," in his *Gedächtniszeiten: Über jüdische und andere Geschichten München* (Munich: Beck, 2003), pp. 246–62; Dan Diner, ed., *Synchrone Welten: Zeiträume jüdischer Geschichte* (Göttingen: Vandenhoeck & Ruprecht, 2005). The *Jahrbuch des Simon-Dubnow-Instituts* and the *Enzyklopädie jüdischer Geschichte und Kultur*, ed. Dan Diner (Stuttgart: JB Metzler, 2011–17) have been major sites for

Jewish history has also long broken out of the mold of Jewish national narratives and shown the Jews embedded in European culture, its creators and product at the same time. Jewish European history, as exemplified in the émigrés, has taken the further step of presenting the Jews – a Diaspora struggling to define its relationship to diverse national cultures – as both emblematic of Europe and a catalyst for European self-definition. It has shown Europeans defining their national and European identities in response to the Jews, and, in turn, the Jews negotiating their membership in the nation and in Europe, forming transnational networks, and inventing national and European ideas – the Europeans par excellence. At a time when Europe is struggling to define its identity against multiple national and minority cultures, Jewish history tells edifying European stories.

I admire Jewish European history. This book partakes in the project and pushes it further. In the forms it has assumed so far, however, it bears little relationship to traditional Jews and Jewish culture. Indeed, émigré scholarship has perfected a history that excludes traditional Judaism.[12] It wonderfully deploys the Jews to tell European stories, but limits the stories to Jews whose difference can be made intelligible and inspiring to contemporary Europeans, and these do not include rabbinic Jews. Historians have not yet found ways for traditional Jews to tell European stories. Instead, émigrés who struggled with their Jewishness but were remote from traditional Jewish culture – political philosopher Hannah Arendt (1906–1975), philologist Erich Auerbach (1892–1957), and literary critic Walter Benjamin (1892–1940) – have become the paragons of Jewish European history. Émigrés who no longer regarded themselves as Jewish and professed cosmopolitanism – art historian Ernst Gombrich (1909–2001), jurist Hans Kelsen (1881–1973), and philosopher Karl Popper (1902–1994) – tell the story of Europe fallen and redeemed.

The cosmopolitan émigrés surely belong in the Jewish story, but they cannot stand for all of European Jewry and alone sustain Jewish European history. They leave out too much of Jewish culture. Their Jewishness is devoid of rabbinic culture – of Talmud, *Midrash*, Kabbalah and *responsa* – and of Hebrew and Yiddish literature. Meanwhile, traditional German-Jewish émigrés, like Israeli philosopher

---

experimentation with Jewish European history, but the genre has expanded on both sides of the Atlantic to cover much work in European intellectual history, even when the term "Jewish European" is not used.

12 I use "traditional Judaism" for rabbinic Judaism broadly conceived. It includes Reform rabbis. Readers suggested that the rubric is both a misnomer – this book shows Jewish Orthodoxy, too, to be a modern invention; there is no traditional Judaism – and misleading, as it is used in Israel for Conservative Judaism. But I have no other: Postorthodox Jews, like this author, are traditional Jews conscious of their tradition's historicity.

Yeshayahu Leibowitz (1903–1994), liberal Rabbi Benno Jacob (1862–1945), and Orthodox Rabbi Jeḥiel Jacob Weinberg (1884–1966), barely register in émigré scholarship because they chart alternative European Jewishness. Traditionally, European histories marginalized the Jews, and Jewish historians told exclusively Jewish stories. The émigrés' journeys across cultural boundaries and their cosmopolitan visions have made it possible for historians to tell Jewish European stories, but they have narrowed unacceptably the meaning of "Jewish." History as told via the émigrés excludes those Jews who led traditional Jewish lives. It is thus the task of this book to offer an alternative Jewish European history that integrates traditional Jews and Jewish culture.

In contrast with émigré history, the broader field of European intellectual history resonates with voices of Jewish authenticity. The Prague Zionists and their prophet, Martin Buber (1878–1965), have recently joined Weimar Germany's antiliberal Jewish rebels, from Franz Rosenzweig (1886–1929) to Gershom Scholem to Leo Strauss (1899–1973), as historians' favorite subjects. They are irresistible because they make possible a history that is so obviously both Jewish and European, and one that speaks eloquently to contemporary political concerns.

Yet the limits of the Jewishness emergent from Prague and Weimar histories should be noted, too. The Prague Zionists' reinvention of Jewish ethnicity and religion took place against a background of disengagement from Judaism. Franz Kafka (1880–1924) depicted contemporary Prague Jewish authors as "writing in German to distance themselves from Jewishness ... their hind legs still stuck to their father's Jewishness and their forelegs finding no new ground."[13] Few had as firm grounding in tradition as Buber. Similarly, Scholem spoke of his generational rebellion as postassimilatory, and Paul Mendes-Flohr aptly describes Weimar Jewish intellectuals as having a dual identity, German and Jewish.[14] Notwithstanding the ingenuity they displayed in creating new Jewish philosophy and theology, and the Weimar revival of Jewish learning, few Weimar rebels matched the erudition of nineteenth-century *Wissenschaftler des Judentums* (whom they derided). In explicating their

---

[13] Franz Kafka to Max Brod, June 1921, in *Briefe 1902–1924* (Frankfurt: S. Fischer, 1966), p. 337.
[14] Scholem deployed Kurt Blumenfeld's view of German Zionism as "postassimilatory Judaism": *On Jews and Judaism in Crisis*, ed. Werner Dannhauser (New York: Schocken, 1976), pp. 1–2; Paul Mendes-Flohr, *German Jews: A Dual Identity* (New Haven, CT: Yale University Press, 1999). The "German" in German-Jewish was also European, as Jewish networks crossed national boundaries. See Malachi Hacohen, "From Empire to Cosmopolitanism: The Central-European Jewish Intelligentsia, 1867–1968," *Jahrbuch des Simon-Dubnow-Instituts* 5 (2006): 117–34, and the other essays on Jews in multiethnic networks in this volume.

work, historians pay as much heed to Christian theology as to Jewish philosophy, and as much attention to German culture as to Jewish texts.[15] They find little occasion to refer to rabbinic literature.

Moreover, current political concerns join to diminish traditional Jewish culture. If émigré history tracks the European search for supranational identity, Prague and Weimar intellectual histories reflect the academic pursuit of alternatives to liberal democracy and contemporary Zionism. Heidegger's philosophy and Schmitt's political theology frame the context for scholarly work on Hans Jonas, Emmanuel Levinas, Rosenzweig, Strauss, and Jacob Taubes.[16] *Berit Shalom*, a Palestinian Jewish group of mostly Central European Zionists who pursued binationalism as a solution to the Jewish-Arab conflict in Palestine in the interwar years, confronts Israeli politics with a Zionist alternative.[17] Jacob Taubes was trained in a *yeshivah* and received an Orthodox rabbinic ordination, but it is his Pauline millenarianism that fascinates contemporaries most: In a post-Marxist age, Paul's putative nonviolent messianism appears as a political alternative to liberalism.[18] The burgeoning interest of émigré history is, nowadays, in Christian-Jewish émigrés. With recent debates on

---

[15] Luc Anckaert, Martin Brasser, and Norbert Samuelson, eds., *The Legacy of Franz Rosenzweig* (Leuven, Belgium: Leuven University Press, 2004); Zachary Braiterman, *The Shape of Revelation: Aesthetics and Modern Jewish Thought* (Stanford, CA: Stanford University Press, 2007); Benjamin Lazier, *God Interrupted: Heresy and the European Imagination Between the World Wars* (Princeton, NJ: Princeton University Press, 2008); Eugene R. Sheppard, *Leo Strauss and the Politics of Exile: The Making of a Political Philosopher* (Waltham, MA: Brandeis University Press, 2006). Even Orthodox Rabbi Alexander Altmann felt impelled to create, in the 1930s, a new theology in defense of the *Halakhah* (Jewish law), rather than argue from within Jewish sources: Thomas Meyer, *Vom Ende der Emanzipation: Jüdische Philosophie und Theologie nach 1933* (Göttingen: Vandenhoeck & Ruprecht, 2008).

[16] Peter Eli Gordon, *Rosenzweig and Heidegger: Between Judaism and German Philosophy* (Berkeley: University of California Press, 2003); Nitzan Lebovics, "The Jerusalem School: The Theopolitical Hour," *New German Critique* 35 (2008): 97–120; Heinrich Meier, *Leo Strauss and the Theologico-Political Problem* (Cambridge: Cambridge University Press, 2006); Samuel Moyn, *Origins of the Other: Emmanuel Levinas Between Revelation and Ethics* (Ithaca, NY: Cornell University Press, 2005); Richard Wolin, *Heidegger's Children: Hannah Arendt, Karl Löwith, Hans Jonas, and Herbert Marcuse* (Princeton, NJ: Princeton University Press, 2001).

[17] Steven Aschheim, *Beyond the Border: The German-Jewish Legacy Abroad* (Princeton, NJ: Princeton University Press, 2007); Adi Gordon, ed., *Brith Shalom and Bi-National Zionism* (in Hebrew) (Jerusalem: Carmel, 2008); Zohar Maor, "Between Anti-Colonialism and Postcolonialism: *Berit Shalom*'s Critique of Nationalism and Secularization" (in Hebrew), *Theory and Criticism* 10 (2007): 12–28; Noam Pianko, *Zionism and the Roads Not Taken: Rawidowicz, Kaplan, Kohn* (Bloomington: University of Indiana Press, 2010); Yfaat Weiss, "Central European Ethnonationalism and Zionist Binationalism," *Jewish Social Studies* 11 (2004): 93–117.

[18] The current popularity of Taubes's *Die politische Theologie des Paulus* (Munich: Wilhelm Fink, 1993) owes much to Giorgio Agamben, *The Time That Remains: A Commentary on the Letter to the Romans* (Stanford, CA: Stanford University Press, 2005).

Judeo-Christian Europe, interest in émigrés who contemplated Christian-Jewish civilization, from Auerbach to Carl Friedrich to Löwith to Hans Joachim Schoeps, has surged.[19] Jewish intellectuals are still Europeanized in a manner that makes them accessible to Europeans and usable to academic culture – and diminishes their Judaism.

What is to be done? The horizons of Jewish Studies and European history have been drawing closer in recent years, as national narratives have opened up to border crossing.[20] Jewish Studies scholars now seek to locate their subjects within European history, and European historians recount transnational histories using the Jewish Diaspora. But convergence is still limited. Rabbinic scholars and European historians still seem to inhabit different intellectual universes, as if their concerns did not matter to each other. Divergent training and interests continue to inhibit the extension of European Jewishness to traditional Jews. The painstaking textual labor of Jewish Studies, whether in Talmud, Midrash, rabbinic responsa or Kabbalah, does not make it into European history.[21] Traditional Jewish Studies still do not tell a European story, and European intellectual history does not tell a traditional Jewish one. For traditional Jewish culture to become part of European history, rabbinic discourses must be "Europeanized," and Jewish European history written, at least in part, out of traditional Jewish sources. This book aims to do just that.

---

[19] *Religions* 3: 2/3 (2012), special issue on "Between Religion and Ethnicity: Twentieth-Century Jewish Émigrés and the Shaping of Postwar Culture," esp. essays by Matthias Bormuth, "Meaning and Progress in History – A Comparison between Karl Löwith and Erich Auerbach," 3:2, 151–62; Adi Gordon and Udi Greenberg, "*The City of Man*, European Émigrés, and the Genesis of Postwar Conservative Thought," 3:3, 681–98; and Malachi Haim Hacohen, "Typology and the Holocaust: Erich Auerbach and Judeo-Christian Europe," 3:3, 600–645. See also Udi Greenberg, "The Limits of Dictatorship and the Origins of Democracy: The Political Theory of Carl J. Friedrich from Weimar to the Cold War," *The Weimar Moment*, ed. Rudy Koshar (New York: Rowman & Littlefield, 2012), pp. 443–64.

[20] Moshe Rosman, *How Jewish Is Jewish History?* (Oxford: The Littman Library of Jewish Civilization, 2007), discusses the challenges and opportunities that blurry boundaries and hybrid identities present to the coherence of Jewish history and its subject, the Jew. David Hollinger, "Communalist and Dispersionist Approaches to American Jewish History in an Increasingly Post-Jewish Era," *American Jewish History*, 95:1 (2009): 1–32, does the same for American Jewish history. Hollinger legitimates non-Jewish Jews as subjects of Jewish history; I seek to legitimate traditional Jews as subjects of non-Jewish history. The projects are complementary.

[21] This has been changing for the better. Two examples: Maoz Kahana, *From the Noda BeYehuda to the Chatam Sofer: Halakha and Thought in Their Historical Moment* (in Hebrew) (Jerusalem: Zalman Shazar Center, 2015); Pawel Maciejko, *The Mixed Multitude: Jacob Frank and the Frankist Movement, 1755–1816* (Philadelphia: University of Pennsylvania Press, 2011). Still, émigré historians and Kabbalah scholars study Scholem, but they have little to say to each other and create divergent Scholem profiles. The German-Jewish intellectual and the Kabbalah scholar do not converge.

The challenge is not as formidable as it may seem. Acceptance of the Jewish minority in European Christendom has been an issue from the beginnings of Europe. Medieval religious polemics and disputations between Christians and Jews showed both sides defining their identity against the other. In modernity, the Jewish Question became the ultimate test case for the European nation-state.[22] The debate on Jewish emancipation and the prospects for Jewry's national integration began in the 1780s and continued all the way to the Holocaust.[23] Whether the Jews opted for integration in the nation-state or for autonomy in Central and Eastern Europe's multinational empires, Austria-Hungary and Russia, they exemplified a Diaspora minority negotiating its membership in a nationalizing state or a federalist empire. The debates on Jewish integration and autonomy reverberate today in deliberations on Europe's Muslim communities and on European federalism.

For well over a millennium, Jews and Christians, rabbis, theologians, and secular intellectuals polemicized over the terms of Jewish existence in Europe. Indeed, the debate is older than Europe itself. The Roman Empire's destruction of Jerusalem and devastation of the Palestinian Jewish community constituted the greatest trauma of Jewish history and were permanent *topoi* of rabbinic discourse. As the empire became Christian, and the Christian Empire became, later, definitive of Europe, rabbinic discourse on imperial Rome carried on to Christian–Jewish relations in medieval Europe. Empire and Christendom became the notions against which the Jews defined their European membership. A two-millennia-old rabbinic discourse on Jewish–non-Jewish relations permeates European history.

The rabbinic idiom for Jewish–Christian relations emerged from the biblical story of the rival twins, Jacob & Esau. (I use the ampersand rather than the conjunction "and" advisedly – Jacob and Esau appear in this book as a unit, each defined by the other, deriving their meaning from the polarity.) Genesis tells that the two already began struggling for primacy in their mother's womb. Jacob was born holding onto Esau's heel (*aqev*

---

[22] The term "Jewish Question" entered political discourse in the 1750s with the British debate on the naturalization of Jews, and it became widespread with the German debates on emancipation in the 1840s: Jacob Toury, "The Jewish Question – A Semantic Approach," *Leo Baeck Institute Yearbook* 11 (1966): 85–106.

[23] The term "Jewish emancipation" was first used in 1828 in the course of the debate in England on Catholic emancipation – the removal of the Catholics' civic disabilities: Jacob Katz, "The Term 'Jewish Emancipation,'" in his *Emancipation and Assimilation: Studies in Modern Jewish History* (Westmead, UK: Gregg International Publishers, 1972), pp. 21–46. While Roman law spoke of freeing slaves as "manumission" and not as emancipation, the term also became quickly associated with the abolitionist struggle to end slavery in the colonies and the U.S. South.

עֵקֶב), as if trying to outmaneuver him and come out first, hence his name Yaakov (יַעֲקֹב). A tent dweller, he bought the rights of the firstborn from Esau, a hunter, by feeding his hunger. With the help of his mother, Rebecca, he deceived his father, Isaac, by wearing Esau's clothes and received the firstborn's blessing. A furious Esau conspired to kill him, and Jacob escaped abroad, returning, after two decades, wealthy and mature, and with a large family. He feared that Esau would still seek revenge and decimate his family, but when they met, they fell on each other's shoulders and cried. The Genesis story ends in reconciliation.[24]

Rabbinic Midrash and Kabbalah, and Jewish historiography, rewrote and retold the Jacob & Esau story in innumerable versions over two millennia. The discourse had parallels among Christians and, to a lesser extent, among Muslims. Jews, Christians, and Muslims recognized Patriarch Jacob as the father of the Jewish nation and Esau as the ancestor of Edom, a people who lived on the southern borders of the Israelite Kingdom of Judah. Through a remarkable chain of events, recounted in the following chapters, Esau became first Roman and then Christian, and the rabbis directed biblical prophecies on Edom against the Roman Empire and Christianity. The biblical story became a *topos* for Roman–Jewish and Christian–Jewish relations. The Bible presaged the future: "All that happened to our ancestor Jacob with Esau his brother," opined the medieval Spanish Jewish biblical commentator Naḥmanides (1194–1270), "will always happen to us with Esau's descendants."[25] Jacob & Esau provided the paradigm of the Jews' relationship to Europe.

Christianity developed its own Jacob & Esau typology to speak about Christian–Jewish relations. God's oracle to the matriarch, Rebecca, presaged that of the rival twins she carried in her womb, "the elder shall serve the younger" (Genesis 25:23). "The older people of the Jews," said Augustine, "was destined to serve the younger people, the Christians."[26] The typology was not as central to Christianity as it was to Judaism, but it provides historians with a rare view of Jews and Christians using analogous discourses, vested in shared sources, to discuss their relations. As they deliberate about Jacob & Esau, they

---

[24] *JPS Hebrew-English Tanakh*, 2d ed. (Philadelphia: Jewish Publication Society, 1999); *The New Oxford Annotated Bible*, ed. Michael D. Coogan, Marc Z. Brettler, Carol A. Newsom, and Pheme Perkins, 4th ed. (Oxford: Oxford University Press, 2010). I have occasionally modified the English translations.

[25] Ramban (Rabbi Moses ben Nachman Girondi; Naḥmanides), *Commentary on the Torah*, trans. Charles B. Chavel, 5 vols. (New York: Shilo Press, 1971–76): 1 (Genesis): 32:2; *Perush ha-Torah*, 2 vols. (Jerusalem: Mosad Ha-Rav Kook, 1969): "כל אשר אירע לאבינו עם עשו אחיו יארע לנו תמיד עם בני עשו".

[26] *Concerning the City of God against the Pagans*, trans. Henry Bettenson (Harmondsworth, UK: Penguin Books, 1985), 16:35–38, 18:31, quotation on p. 698.

negotiate, from asymmetrical power positions, the Jews' place in Europe. *Jacob & Esau* tracks the Jews' changing position in Europe over two millennia, from the late Roman Empire to Christianization to the Crusades to late medieval expulsions to early modern modus vivendi to emancipation to racialization and murder to postnational integration. To rectify the exclusively modern focus of Jewish European history, *Jacob & Esau* projects modernity – Jewish emancipation, racial antisemitism, and genocide – against the *longue durée* of a beleaguered European minority, whose oppression and survival alike, simultaneous foreignness and kinship to Europe, had been, until modern times, fundamental premises.

Modernity and its Jewish dilemmas remain, however, this book's focal concern. The European nation-state opened for Jews the unprecedented prospect of national integration, but three multiethnic empires, the Austrian, Russian, and Ottoman, represented, until they collapsed in the aftermath of World War I, the prospect of Jewish autonomy in an imperial federalist structure. Modern Jewry negotiated its political membership between nation and empire. German-speaking Central Europe was the battleground of emancipation and antisemitism, the cradle of Jewish pluralism, and the sphere where Jews were confronted with the competing options of nation-state and empire, represented by Germany and Austria-Hungary, respectively; hence its preeminence in this book.

Contrary to most historical narratives, however, my focus is not solely on Germany but also, and even more so, on Austria, and not on the interplay between nationalism and cosmopolitanism but on the nexus of imperial pluralism that proved capacious enough to accommodate emancipation. Gerson Hundert has not tired of reminding us that the majority of European Jews lived until 1917 in imperial Russia (including former Congress Poland), and experienced modernity without emancipation or secularization.[27] Historians have begun telling the story of Eastern European Jewish modernity, and it will no doubt become a center of future studies. *Jacob & Esau* puts traditional Eastern European Jewry in dialogue with German culture via Austrian Galicia, and shows Yiddish and Hebrew literature to be crossing imperial borders between Russia, Germany, and Austria. But my search for a Europeanism accommodative of Jewish culture, and my insistence that the story of traditional and secular Jews be told together, lead to late imperial Austria rather than to Russia.

---

[27] Gerson David Hundert, "Re(de)fining Modernity in Jewish History," in *Rethinking European Jewish History*, ed. Jeremy Cohen and Moshe Rosman (Oxford: The Litman Library, 2009), pp. 133–45, and *The Jews of Poland-Lithuania in the Eighteenth-Century: A Genealogy of Modernity* (Berkeley: University of California, 2004), pp. 1–20. I am indebted to a conversation with Nancy Sinkoff of Rutgers University.

Marking a postnational turn in historiography, historians have recently declared the nation-state a historical exception and empire normative.[28] Truly, the nation-state, and not empire, was the primary emancipatory agent for Jews, but in late imperial Austria, a federalist constitution and imperial governance encouraged political and cultural pluralism conducive to traditional Judaism and cosmopolitan ideas alike. The empire also gave rise to nonterritorial conceptions of Jewish nationality that left their imprint on Zionism and Diaspora nationalism. Both envisioned solutions to the Jewish Question within an imperial rather than nation-state framework.[29] After the empire's dissolution at the end of World War I, nostalgia for imperial diversity gave rise to cosmopolitan visions of Central Europe distinguished for their pluralism. The "Habsburg myth" was the grounds for alternative visions of Europe that attenuate the disparity of cosmopolitanism and nationalism, and provide historical grounding for contemporary European visions of federalism.[30]

Jacob & Esau informed Jewish discourse on emancipation and nation and empire, and outlined the Other – Christian, antisemite or *Goy* (non-Jew) – with and against whom integration and autonomy were negotiated. Jewish European history must engage them, but if it extends to the nonrabbinic Jewish intelligentsia, as I insist it does, it cannot limit itself to these traditional tropes. Prominent secular intellectuals, both Jewish and non-Jewish, from Heinrich Heine to Else Lasker-Schüler, and from Hermann Gunkel to Thomas Mann, engaged Jacob & Esau, but focusing on the typology still risks producing a lopsided traditionalist view of European Jewish culture, a mirror image of the modernist narratives for which this book serves as a corrective. No unitary narrative can do justice to the plurality of Jewish European cultures.

Jacob & Esau can also not adequately address the alternate options opened by the nation-state and multinational empire. As the Holy Roman Empire dissolved on the eve of emancipation, the nearly two-millennia-old association between Esau and empire was severed. Jewish hostility to empire dissipated, and a space opened up for the modern (one-sided) love story between Jews and imperial Austria. The premodern vision of Jewish

---

[28] Jane Burbank and Frederick Cooper, *Empires in World History: Power and the Politics of Difference* (Princeton, NJ: Princeton University Press, 2010).

[29] Dimitry Shumsky, "Brith Shalom's Uniqueness Reconsidered: Hans Kohn and Autonomist Zionism," *Jewish History* 25 (2011): 339–53; Marcos Silber, "The Metamorphosis of Pre-Dubnovian Autonomism into Diaspora Jewish-Nationalism," in *Homelands and Diasporas: Greeks, Jews and Their Migrations*, ed. Minna Rozen (London: I. B. Tauris, 2008), pp. 235–55, 391–400.

[30] Claudio Magris, *Der habsburgische Mythos in der modernen österreichische Literatur* [1963] (Vienna: Paul Zsolnay Verlag, 2000). Magris criticizes the myth; I emphasize its productive role in the émigré *imaginaire*.

nation versus evil empire changed into Jews as potential members of the German nation or the Austrian Empire. To be sure, traditional Jews thought of Franz Joseph as a Roman emperor all the way to World War I, but, unprecedentedly, nation-state and empire both presented prospects for resolving the Jewish Question. The traditional tropes informed emancipation discourse but did not exhaust it.

In the following chapters, the unified premodern narrative diverges in modernity into two alternate narratives: one focusing on Jacob & Esau, the other on nation and empire. Rabbis, historians, writers, and poets who reconfigured the Jacob & Esau story to address the Jewish Question are the major protagonists of the first, and the German-acculturated Jewish intelligentsia imagining a pluralist Central Europe are those of the second. The narratives converge and diverge intermittently: Figures like the Hebrew writer Asher Barash, the Zionist and then Ultra-Orthodox leader Nathan Birnbaum, Vienna's Chief Rabbi Adolf Jellinek, and Galician German-Jewish author Soma Morgenstern show up in both, but the narratives never merge. They represent alternating yet complementary perspectives on Jewish European history, one more traditionally accentuated, the other more cosmopolitan. Chapters 2–4 narrate Jacob & Esau and nation versus empire from the ancient world to the French Revolution; then the modern chapters, taking the story from emancipation to postwar Europe and Israel, alternate between Jacob & Esau (5–6, 9–10, 13) and nation versus empire (7–8, 12). Chapter 11 provides a biography of Eric Auerbach, author of *Mimesis*, who, in response to the Holocaust, deployed Christian typology to construct a Judeo-Christian European history, against which I offer my own counter-model of Jewish European history.[31]

A vision of Jewish pluralism, crucial for Jewish European history and the politics of European integration, underlies my dual narrative. The Jacob & Esau discourse contains cosmopolitan moments – Heine, Else Lasker-Schüler, Thomas Mann – and the cosmopolitan narrative shows Central European Zionists and Austrian patriots articulating multicultural visions protective of Jewish identities. But constructing a unitary narrative reconciling cosmopolitanism and rabbinic Judaism would fly in the face of the alternative visions of European Jewishness presented by the émigrés and Jacob & Esau. Rabbinic Judaism has, to be sure, cosmopolitan moments, but I do not wish to fold the Open Society into traditional Judaism anymore than I wish to surrender traditional Judaism to Popper

---

[31] *Mimesis: Dargestellte Wirklichkeit in der abendländischen Literatur* [1946], 2d ed. (Bern: Francke, 1959); *Mimesis: The Representation of Reality in Western Literature*, trans. Willard R. Trask (Princeton, NJ: Princeton University Press, 1953).

and likeminded cosmopolitans. I have made my own contribution to the cosmopolitan Jewish European narrative, and I do not retract it.[32] But it has to find its place in a broader vision of historiography and politics that is cognizant and respectful of traditional Jewish culture. Historical forms may hint at political ones: Multiple narratives and voices, seeking dialogue but refusing uniformity, would ideally characterize Jewish life, European integration, and history, all at the same time.

The postwar German reception of Gershom Scholem highlights the blind spots of émigré cosmopolitanism and the antinomies of the Jewish European history that it supports. In the last decade of his life, Scholem became an icon of German Jewishness and Europeanness. Precisely because he had made the Zionist choice, his émigré peers, Herbert Marcuse included, acknowledged him as a prophet, and Habermas and his generation regarded him as *the* authentic Jew.[33] He inspired awe and became arbitrator of the German-Jewish dialogue.[34] Twice in his late years, upon receiving the Reuchlin Prize in 1969 and on opening the *Wissenschaftskolleg* (institute for advanced studies) in Berlin in 1981, Scholem delivered lectures on the European significance of the Kabbalah. Ranging beyond his usual Jewish sources, he masterfully described the Christian discovery of the Kabbalah and its interpretation from Johannes Reuchlin (1455–1522) to the nineteenth century.[35] Remarkably, the Jewish Kabbalists played no role in Scholem's lectures.[36] Jewish and European histories represented

---

[32] Malachi Hacohen, *Karl Popper – The Formative Years, 1902–1945: Politics and Philosophy in Interwar Vienna* (New York: Cambridge University Press, 2000).

[33] Noam Zadoff, "Gershom Scholem: A German Returnee?" paper presented at the Jewish Studies Seminar, Duke University (May 3, 2012); Jürgen Habermas, "Begegnungen mit Gershom Scholem," *Münchener Beiträge zur Jüdischen Geschichte und Kultur* 2 (2007): 9–18. Martin Buber, who had immigrated to Palestine in 1938, had been recognized even earlier as a major German philosopher and as an exemplar of Jewish authenticity. But as master of Ḥasidic tales, Buber represented the vanished Jewish past, Scholem the Zionist future.

[34] Scholem famously protested "Against the Myth of the German-Jewish Dialogue" [1964], in *On Jews and Judaism in Crisis*, ed. Werner Dannhauser (New York: Schocken, 1976), pp. 61–64, but this became a call for opening a new dialogue under Scholem's guardianship. On Scholem's fragmented German and Israeli identity, and his role in shaping the postwar German-Jewish dialogue (by promoting, first, the legacy of his friend, Walter Benjamin), see Noam Zadoff, *Gershom Scholem: From Berlin to Jerusalem and Back*, trans. Jeffrey Green (Waltham, MA: Brandeis University Press, 2017).

[35] Gershom Scholem, "Die Erforschung der Kabbala von Reuchlin bis zur Gegenwart," *Judaica III: Studien zur jüdischen Mystik* (Frankfurt: Suhrkamp, 1973), pp. 247–63, and "Die Stellung der Kabbala in der europäischen Geistesgeschichte," *Judaica IV*, ed. Rolf Tiedemann (Frankfurt: Suhrkamp, 1984), pp. 7–18.

[36] Nineteenth-century Jewish Kabbalah scholars did appear in the 1969 Reuchlin lecture, but they mostly set the stage for the Jewish rediscovery of the Kabbalah in the course of the Zionist national revival, with Scholem implicitly playing the Jewish Reuchlin (which he may well have been). Thanks to Noam Zadoff for conversations and references.

different trajectories. To talk to Germans, Scholem moved from one to the other, but he would not bring them together. Jews had their own history, Europeans theirs.

This book is written to provide an alternative to the cosmopolitan and nationalist antipodes of Jewish European history. Notwithstanding the profound empathy and goodwill that Habermas and likeminded cosmopolitans have shown toward Scholem's history, its premises are incompatible with Jewish Europeanness, and it cannot serve any longer dialogue between Jewish and non-Jewish Europeans. Whether in its cosmopolitan or Zionist version, émigré-inspired Jewish European history does not recognize traditional Jews as Europeans and cannot confront Jewish pluralism: Jews are cosmopolitan émigrés or Zionists. Space must be opened and concepts reshaped for Jewish European history to accommodate traditional Jewry.

The following chapters offer a history, telling a European story, in part, out of rabbinic sources. Rabbis and secular intellectuals, both Jewish and non-Jewish, appear side by side as European figures, inhabiting a shared intellectual universe, often in dialogue, addressing, from divergent perspectives, European problems. This intellectual universe will become, I hope, a shared research field for both European historians and Jewish Studies scholars. Both groups will encounter here a range of Jewish cultures that they normally do not approach, and may become more comfortable with sources that often appear to them uninteresting or inaccessible. Over the last century, Heine, Marx, and Freud became European legends. Historians can now help "Europeanize" the rabbis and set an example for European integration that welcomes cultural pluralism.

1   Writing Jewish European History

In his classic *Mimesis*, philologist and literary historian Erich Auerbach used Christian typology to construct a Judeo-Christian European history.[1] Typology "sees in persons, events, or places the prototype, pattern, or figure of historical persons, events, or places that follow it in time."[2] Christians view the Old Testament Patriarchs like Jacob, for example, as presaging Christ. Auerbach thought of typology as a literary trope connoting realism, and, noting its decline in the Renaissance, tracked realism's modern transmutations. Typology also provides this book's leitmotif, but Jacob & Esau is just as much, if not more, a Jewish *topos* than a Christian one, and it shows greater continuity between Antiquity and modernity. Looser in its rabbinic deployment than Christian theological *topoi*, Jacob & Esau crossed over to the modern age with greater ease and became literary metaphors, retaining a measure of explanatory power, albeit nontheological. The typology provides for a two-millennia-long history of ideas, but it also constitutes a barometer of Jewish–Christian relations, signaling opening and closing opportunities for Jewish life in Europe. Emerging from Jewish culture and, in turn, shaping Jewish horizons, Jacob & Esau comprises a contextual intellectual history.

Esau came to embody the Roman Empire in the second century CE, and Jacob/Israel's struggle with Esau became one of a nation against empire. A two-millennia story of Jews working their way through imperial orders followed, ending in modern Europe, where nation-state and continental empire offered divergent options for Jewish life: acculturation and national integration as against cultural autonomy in a multinational state. Jews were divided in their sympathies: Western European liberals endorsed the nation-state, whereas Eastern European traditionalists – the

---

[1] *Mimesis: Dargestellte Wirklichkeit in der abendländischen Literatur* [1946], 2d ed. (Bern: Francke, 1959); *Mimesis: The Representation of Reality in Western Literature*, trans. Willard R. Trask (Princeton, NJ: Princeton University Press, 1953).
[2] Michael Fishbane. *Biblical Interpretation in Ancient Israel* (Oxford: Oxford University Press, 1988), p. 350.

15

majority – preferred federalist empires. Whether in a national or an imperial context, Jewish emancipation required that Jacob & Esau portray and regulate new forms of Jewish–non-Jewish relations. The book peruses Jacob & Esau's transmutations in Jewish and Christian discourses, reflecting divergent strategies for managing relations with the Other.

Internal contests among Jews and Christians receive as much attention in this book as Jewish–Christian polemics. The modern rabbinic and "secular" Jewish intelligentsia constituted international networks that negotiated between traditional Jewish life and Christian-inflected European national cultures. Jacob & Esau's fate registered the dilemmas of Jewish in-between existence and the infighting on how best to negotiate it. The dialectics of nation and empire, in turn, reflected the Jewish intelligentsia's search for a home. The book begins with hatred of imperial Rome and ends with love for the Habsburg Monarchy, which traditional Jews viewed as carrying the Roman legacy. The European nation-state launched emancipation yet failed to provide a home for the acculturated Jewish intelligentsia. Austria-Hungary's federalist and corporatist structure, constitutional protections, and cultural pluralism provided an increasingly attractive alternative for a wide spectrum of intellectuals, from the Jewish nationalist to the socialist internationalist.

Typology, nation and empire, and the Jewish intelligentsia are the foci of my *longue durée* Jewish European history and this chapter's conceptual introduction. In the final section, I draw their ramifications for the writing of Jewish European history today, in light of some major historiographical questions.

Typology and Jewish European History

"It is a maxim that Esau hates Jacob," was a favorite dictum of Eliezer Shakh (1899–2001), Israel's most eminent Ultra-Orthodox rabbi in the last decades of the twentieth century.[3] He chastised Israeli statesmen repeatedly for engaging in world politics and making enemies and friends, instead of pacifying the powers that be – whoever they may be – and

---

[3] הלכה בידוע שעשיו שונא ליעקב. Midrash *Sifre*, be-haalotkha 11 attributes the maxim to Rabbi Shimeon bar Yoḥai. Shakh used the maxim to urge caution about reliance on any non-Jewish power, even the United States: Elazar Menaḥem Man Shakh, *Mikhtavim U-maamarim*, 2d ed., 6 vols. in 5 (Benei Beraq: E.M.M. Shakh, 1986): 1–2:7, 6:195. (Thanks to Moshe Hellinger for the reference.) The phrase "it is a maxim" (הלכה) probably originates in erroneous explication of a scribal abbreviation (והל') of "but surely" (והלא). Most manuscripts have "but surely" (H. S. Horovitz's notes to *Sifre* 69 [Frankfurt am Main: J. Kauffmann, 1917]), but the foremost medieval Ashkenazi exegete, Rashi, popularized the "maxim" version. It is a testimony to the force of the trope that the awkward elocution became convention. (Thanks to Yehudah Mirsky for the reference.)

fortifying Judaism. His mantra was two millennia old, a tried-and-true postulate for Jews on conducting their relations with non-Jews. The Patriarch Jacob's handling of Esau provided the exemplar. Whether Esau was Roman or Christian, or just a *Goy* (non-Jew), he was to be treated suspiciously – and, yet, never provoked. Shakh stood at the end of a long chain of rabbinic leaders who had turned Jacob into a model for Jewish survival in the Diaspora. Elucidating on Jacob and Esau's reconciliation in the Book of Genesis, the medieval exegete Naḥmanides had counseled readers to take instruction from Jacob in facing adversaries, by offering prayer to God and gifts to enemies or by running away.[4] Shakh thought that Zionism broke with an ancient tradition.

Shakh survived the Holocaust by a thread and thrived under a despised Jewish government for more than half a century. Naḥmanides had not been as lucky. He headed the Jewish delegation to the Disputation of Barcelona (July 1263), where he fended off Christian claims that Scriptures and rabbinic texts alike showed Christ to be the anticipated messiah.[5] He published his version of the debate, and the Dominican Friars pressured the king of Aragon to expel him for having blasphemed Christianity. He emigrated to the Land of Israel and ended his life in Jerusalem. Yet Naḥmanides was forbearing of Christian maltreatment: "The descendants of Esau will not completely erase our name but persecute us in a few countries; one king will rob us of our money or expel us, and another will show mercy and save the refugees in his country" (Genesis 32:9).

Naḥmanides' politics was not one that the Holocaust, or even the worst periods of medieval persecution, could easily let stand. But expulsions and Christian–Jewish disputations, not genocide, characterize the Jewish European history that Jacob & Esau tells. Polemics serves as this history's marker, and both contenders in the polemics must survive.[6] Jacob and

---

[4] (Genesis 32:4): "Let us avail ourselves of the three measures Jacob took: prayer, gift, and salvation by way of war, that is, to escape and save oneself" (נזמין את עצמנו לשלשת הדברים שהזמין הוא את עצמו, לתפילה ולדורון ולמלחמה, לברוח ולהנצל). Jacob actually prepared for war; Naḥmanides' only option was to escape, "לברוח ולהנצל."

[5] The Barcelona Disputation focused on the novel claim of Dominican Friar Pablo Christiani, a Jewish convert, to have discovered Talmudic evidence for the rabbis acknowledging Jesus as the messiah. But the debate digressed to the traditional polemics on biblical prophecies, especially Isaiah's prophecies on the Servant of the Lord, who, to Christians, was Jesus. Nina Caputo, *Debating Truth: The Barcelona Disputation of 1263: A Graphic History* (New York: Oxford University Press, 2017), includes translations of Naḥmanides' Hebrew account (pp. 90–114) and surrounding Latin documents (pp. 114–33).

[6] Israel Yuval, *Two Nations in Your Womb: Perceptions of Jews and Christians in Late Antiquity and the Middle Ages*, trans. Barbara Harshav and Jonathan Chipman (Berkeley: University of California Press, 2006), underlines the cultural interdependence that such polemics

Esau are estranged brothers, but they are brothers all the same. Fratricide, whether feared or threatened, emerges rhetorically as a possibility, and looms darkly at the end limit of Christian–Jewish relations, but it would end the brotherhood, and the story. The Holocaust nearly did, and together with the State of Israel, it undermined the traditional Jacob & Esau typology.

Jewish tradition does have a topos for genocide perpetrators: *Amaleq*, the legendary people who had first attacked Israel in the desert on their way out of Egypt to the Land of Israel. The Israelites were commanded to eradicate Amaleq. Biblical genealogy (Genesis 36:12) designated Amaleq as Esau's grandchild, and recent work has shown the two joined in "the kingdom of Amaleq and Esau," a Jewish appellation for Christendom.[7] Edom and Amaleq's convergence, however, represented only periods of intense persecution, such as the Crusades or the Holocaust.[8] More typically, Naḥmanides distinguished between Amaleq and Edom (Genesis 36:19; Exodus 17:16), insisting, against the foremost medieval Ashkenazi exegete Rashi (Shlomo Yiẓḥaki, 1040–1105), that the injunction to eradicate Amaleq did not apply to Christians.[9] Esau could kill: One of the oldest references to Rome as Edom reads: "Jacob's voice cries out about the deeds of Hadrian the Emperor who killed eighty thousand myriads in Beitar [a city the Romans had subdued in 135 CE]."[10] But, more commonly, Esau oppressed. The story of the brotherhood of Rabbi Judah the Prince (Yehudah ha-Nasi) and the Roman Emperor "Antoninus" would be inconceivable for the Jewish relationship with Amaleq.[11] Genocide is

entailed, and the borrowing and mimicry between the two hostile communities of Jews and Christians.

[7] Elliot Horowitz, *Reckless Rites: Purim and the Legacy of Jewish Violence* (Princeton, NJ: Princeton University Press, 2006).

[8] Rashi, who lived through the First Crusade, read God's promise to eradicate Amaleq as inclusive of Esau (Exodus 17:16): *Miqraot Gedolot ha-Keter* (commentators' Bible, ha-Keter edition), ed. Menaḥem Kohen (Ramat-Gan: Bar-Ilan University, 1992–2013). A similar convergence of Esau and Amaleq returned with Nazi persecution, but Amaleq's use quickly trumped Edom.

[9] Asaf Turgeman, "Mein Bruder ist ein Einzelkind: Die Esau-Darstellung in jüdischen Schriften des Mittelalters," in *Esau: Bruder und Feind*, ed. Gerhard Langer (Göttingen: Vandenhoeck & Ruprecht, 2009), pp. 135–54. Ashkenazi Jews are European Jews north of the Pyrenees and Alps; Sephardi Jews are of Spanish origin.

[10] *Yerushalmi* (Jerusalem/Palestinian Talmud), henceforth *PT*, Taanit 24a. I have occasionally modified the English translation of *The Talmud of the Land of Israel: A Preliminary Translation and Explanation*, ed. Jacob Neusner, 35 vols. (Chicago: University of Chicago Press, 1982–1994).

[11] *Bavli* (Babylonian Talmud), henceforth *BT*, Avodah Zarah 11a. I have occasionally modified the English translations of the *Hebrew-English Edition of the Babylonian Talmud*, ed. Isidore Epstein and Judah J. Slotki, rev. ed., 30 vols. (London: Soncino Press, 1990), and *Talmud Bavli: The Schottenstein Edition*, ed. Hersh Goldwurm et al., 73 vols. (Brooklyn, NY: Mesorah Publications, 1990–).

the end limit of Jacob & Esau, and of Jewish European history, not its essence. Esau and Jacob are warring brothers, not mass murderers.

Both Christians and Jews traditionally claimed to be Jacob's legitimate descendants. Proud of their invented imperial brotherhood with the Romans, Jews refused, throughout Late Antiquity, the Christian claim to brotherhood with Jews, only to see the empire turning Christian, and Christian emperors becoming oppressive brothers. Conversely, Christians claimed Jacob as their own spiritual father but remained ambiguous about the Jews' descent. Spiritually, and typologically, the Jews descended from Esau, but Jewish ethnicity – descent from Jacob – unsettled the typology, and no Christian topos of Jewish Esau emerged. The tables were turned in modern times: Secular Christian intellectuals, notably German liberal scholars, disavowed Jacob and brotherhood with the Jews. With late nineteenth-century racialization of culture, disaffection with the Hebrew Bible grew, and liberal Protestants and antisemites alike wished to have no share in Jacob. Let Jacob be Jewish, they urged. The identities of Jacob and Esau have been shifting over two millennia. Only the polarizing Jacob & Esau typology reigned unchallenged.

Notwithstanding periodic shifts in Jewish–Christian relations, the Patriarch Jacob has endured as a central figure in Jewish life. His biography prefigured the Jewish journey in exile, and he accompanied the Jews in the Diaspora, his travails presaging theirs. The Jewish people are called, after him, "House of Jacob," and after his second name, "Children of Israel."[12] Traditional Jews open the daily Morning Prayer with "how beautiful are your tents, O Jacob, your dwellings, O Israel," and, toward the service's end, express the wish that "a redeemer will come to Zion and to those who turn from transgression in Jacob." Before retiring to sleep, traditional Jews recite Jacob's blessing to his grandchildren: "The angel who has delivered me from all harm will bless the boys."[13] Jacob eases difficult life transitions, major and routine alike. On the departure of the *shabbat*, when one faces the harshness of the coming week, Isaac's blessing to Jacob is recited – "May God give you of heaven's dew and of the earth's richness" – and many communities chant the responsive *piyut* (liturgical poem), "God told Jacob," with the refrain: "Fear not, my servant Jacob."

Jacob is the only patriarch whose life story shows character development. He is the single patriarch to have suffered setbacks: "Few and miserable were the days of the years of my life" (Genesis 47:9), Jacob

---

[12] "House of Jacob" and "Children of Israel" have been occasionally used to refer to Jewish women and men, respectively. See Rashi on Exodus 19:3 (based on Midrash), in *Miqraot Gedolot*.

[13] Singing it to my daughters, I changed "boys" to "maidens," יְרַחֵם זֶה.

tells the pharaoh, Egypt's king. Yet Jacob prevailed. Neither awe-inspiring Abraham, recognized as father of three monotheistic religions, nor his innocent son Isaac, who was bound to the altar as a heavenly offering, have as intimate a presence in Jewish life as the earthly Jacob, who escaped his enemies by a split hair, and by guile. Countless homilies render Jacob's biblical story into *exempla* (moral anecdotes), a source of instruction and comfort. "The Patriarchs' deeds are a sign for their descendants" (מעשה אבות סימן לבנים): Jacob's enemy, Laban, threatened to decimate the Jewish people by harming their ancestor, but acumen and divine help stood by Jacob, and the Jews, in times of trouble.[14] The biblical story conveys the Jewish hope for a happy end to the journey: "And Jacob arrived safely to the city ... in the land" (Genesis 33:18).

Jacob & Esau, said Naḥmanides, "allude also to future generations": "גם לדורות תרמוז זאת הפרשה". Naḥmanides, who in Barcelona confronted Christian typology, that is, views of biblical prophecy as presaging Christ, rendered a robust Jewish typology of the Patriarchs:[15] "Typological interpretation connects a classic literary text with historical events that lie beyond that text – whether in past, present, or future for the interpreter."[16] Early Christians used typology to demonstrate the continuity between the Hebrew Scriptures and the Christian narrative: The Old Testament (the Hebrew Bible) prefigured the New Testament. Typology grounded Christianity's claim to supersede Judaism by revealing the Bible's real meaning. Auerbach saw typology emergent in Pauline and patristic literature, culminating in Dante, and declining in early modern times with secularization. Hans Frei tracked typology's disintegration in the aftermath of modern biblical

---

[14] The idea appears first in *Midrash Bereshit Rabba* 40:6 (*Midrash Rabbah: Genesis*, ed. Chanoch Albeck and J. Theodor, 3 vols. (Jerusalem: Wahrmann Books, 1965); henceforth *Bereshit Rabba*): "Everything you find written [in Genesis] about Abraham, you will find written [later] about his descendants." It is repeated frequently in medieval exegesis. The popular version in the text appears first in Samuel Eliezer Edels (Maharsha, 1555–1631), *Sefer Ḥidushe Agadot* (Frankfurt, 1682), p. 86a (Avodah Zarah 8b), and p. 46b (Ḥagigah 5b), http://HebrewBooks.org/40856. For a list of sources: Yair Ḥarlap, "'The Patriarchs' Deeds Are a Sign for Their Descendants' as Typological Exegesis in the *Rishonim* (medieval exegetes)" (in Hebrew), *Megadim* 41 (2005): 65–92.

[15] Like the Prophets' symbolic acts, the Patriarchs' deeds represented divine decrees that turned later from potentiality into actuality. A symbolic act triggered its own future repetition to complete itself, creating similitude, or a topos (Genesis 12:6, 12:10, 14:1). Naḥmanides spoke of four senses of Scriptures (PaRDeS פרדס): literal, typological, homiletic, and mystical (kabbalistic). The four had Jewish as well as Christian origins, and polemics with Christianity called for their full use. Naḥmanides was adamant that Scripture conveyed, at one and the same time, "two senses, and both of them are true." On Naḥmanides' pivotal role in Jewish typology: Amos Funkenstein, *Perceptions of Jewish History* (Los Angeles: University of California Press, 1993), pp. 98–120.

[16] Marc Saperstein, "Jewish Typological Exegesis After Nachmanides," *Jewish Studies Quarterly* 1:2 (1993–94): 158.

criticism.[17] Contemporary research regards typology as predominantly Christian.[18] The late Amos Funkenstein viewed Naḥmanides as the great Jewish exception and attributed his typological exegesis to Christian influence.[19] "I dislike the trope," says literary critic Harold Bloom. "It urges that one text can fulfill another. That is a Christian argument and, as a Jew, I repudiate it."[20]

Recent Jewish Studies scholarship has recovered a continuous and rich rabbinic tradition of typology, however.[21] To be sure, typology was less essential to the rabbis than it was to Christianity. Rabbinic legitimacy did not hinge on Edom prefiguring Rome the way Christian legitimacy depended on Adam and Isaac prefiguring Christ. Christ had to fulfill biblical prophecies, whereas the rabbis survived without Rome ever fulfilling the Edom oracles. Jewish typology remained looser than the Christian: Individuals, Jacob and Esau, prefigured nations. "The Patriarchs' deeds are a sign for their descendants" could mean just that Jacob's deeds provided testimony of national character or moral instruction for his descendants and not that events that happened once would reoccur. *Midrash* made Esau look Roman, but Romans, or Christians, did not quite embody Esau but were like him. Even more than in Christianity, typology hovered between prefiguration and metaphor. Yet as a bridge between past and present, typology was crucial to rabbinic Judaism. Whereas Christ had already fulfilled biblical prophecies, the Jews were still waiting for the Edom oracles to be realized – and their salvation depended on it. More was at stake in typology for medieval Jews, says Marc Saperstein, than for Christians.[22]

It is a measure of the modern myopia of Jewish European history that no one has yet taken advantage of Jacob & Esau to tell a European story.[23]

[17] *The Eclipse of Biblical Narrative: A Study in Eighteenth and Nineteenth Century Hermeneutics* (New Haven, CT: Yale University Press, 1974).
[18] Friedrich Ohly, *Sensus Spiritualis: Studies in Medieval Significs and the Philology of Culture* (Chicago: University of Chicago Press, 2005); *Typologie*, ed. Volker Bohn (Frankfurt: Suhrkamp, 1988); Kathleen Biddick, *The Typological Imaginary: Circumcision, Technology, History* (Philadelphia: University of Pennsylvania Press, 2003).
[19] *Perceptions of Jewish History*, esp. p. 105.
[20] Email to Avihu Zakai, January 22, 2012. Responding to my argument on typology's Jewish character, Bloom added (February 23, 2012): "They captured the trope from us, and by now they own it. They can have it."
[21] Marc Saperstein, "Jewish Typological Exegesis After Nachmanides," 158–70; Yair Harlap, "The Patriarchs' Deeds Are a Sign for Their Descendants," 65–92. Marc Brettler, *The Creation of History in Ancient Israel* (London: Routledge, 1998), pp. 48–61, shows the working of typology in the Bible's making, and underlines its Jewish character.
[22] "Jewish Typological Exegesis," 169–70.
[23] Israel Yuval, in *Two Nations in Your Womb*, has, but his story ends in the Middle Ages. Modernity remains the territory of cosmopolitans and antisemites.

Jacob & Esau make an alternative Jewish European history possible by telling of long-term Jewish survival in hostile cultures, and of partial and lopsided dialogues between Christians and Jews that contrast with the modern feats of integration and murder, and with openness and constant exchange. The following chapters will suggest that late antique exchanges on Jacob & Esau may have been more limited than generally thought, high medieval ones just as limited, but, in contrast, late medieval Christian biblical exegesis revealed a measure of "Judaization" of European culture, and early modern Europe witnessed a Sabbatean efflorescence of hybrid Christian–Jewish religiosity. I offer an alternative to Auerbach's Europeanization of the Jews as the biblical (i.e., pre-Christian) people, which excludes rabbinic Judaism. Using a typology that goes to the heart of Judaism, yet in dialogue with Christianity, I tell a European story that highlights traditional Jews.

I focus on Jews and Christians, but I recognize the role of another major partner in European history, the Muslims. Europe's boundaries were permeable: The Jewish Diaspora extended beyond them, and Jacob & Esau competed with Isaac & Ishmael, used to describe Jewish–Muslim relations. A comparison between the two typologies is instructive. Like Esau, Ishmael, too, registered the turns in Jewish–non-Jewish relations. His neutral image in pre-Islamic rabbinic literature became negative with oppressive Arab rule. The medieval Yemenite *Midrash Ha-Gadol* joined Ishmael to his nephew Esau and described their collaborative designs against Jacob. Likewise, the early modern Kabbalist Ḥayim Vital spoke of Esau as "robbing soul" (forcing conversion) and of Ishmael as robbing life.[24] Yet Isaac & Ishmael never assumed the central role in Jewish life that Jacob & Esau had, and Ishmael never became a subject of deadly enmity as Esau did. He was crucial, however, to Esau's transformation. Chapter 3 argues that the rise of Islam, and the Christian–Muslim struggle, especially in Spain, triggered Esau's Christianization in Jewish literature: Esau came to stand for Christendom. Jacob & Esau thus track a Muslim role in Europe's making.

"Typologies never let go," says Kathleen Biddick with exasperation.[25] But typologies, however resilient, "do let go." They behave like Foucauldian discourse, changing only rarely but radically and abruptly, their shifts and breakdowns responding to historical crises. Typologies are contingent, malleable, and even ambiguous: Jacob & Esau homiletics

---

[24] *Midrash Ha-Gadol* on Genesis 27:41, 28:8–9, ed. S. Schechter (Cambridge: Cambridge University Press, 1902); *Sefer Eẓ ha-Daat Tov*, 2 vols. (Jerusalem: Ahavat Shalom, 2000), 1: 23a–b, 2: 82a.
[25] *The Typological Imaginary*, p. 2. Biddick highlights the tenacity of Christianity's supersessionist claims over Judaism.

reveals the undercurrents of alternative traditions that question the mainstream interpretation of Jacob's conduct. As this book begins in the late First Temple period, an older typology of Jacob in Ancient Israel – one critical of the patriarch's guile and deceit – has already dissolved, and Esau has recently become associated with Judah's enemy, Edom.[26] The book ends with the dissolution of the two-millennia-old typology in our own time. In between, it portrays several premodern typological transformations in response to Jewish calamities – to the two Temples' destruction, the Crusades, and the 1492 expulsion from Spain – and it highlights the typology's surprising survival in modern Central Europe in the age of Jewish emancipation. Typology enables a long-term history, and its historicity yields Jewish European stories.

Modernity posed formidable challenges to the typology: Jewish emancipation and racial antisemitism undermined its concomitant assumptions of Jewish servitude and Christian–Jewish brotherhood. Emancipation advanced Jewish citizenship and the brotherhood of citizens, and racial antisemitism, in response, dismissed Christian–Jewish brotherhood and renounced Jacob: He was no longer a prefiguration of Christ; he was Jewish, and Jesus was Aryan. With the political nation, nationalism opened up the gates to Jewish integration, and then closed them down by turning to ethno-nationalism. Yet, throughout, nationalism worked against the background of traditional Jewish–Christian relations. Religion offered resistance to both integrationist and racist designs, and limited both Jewish acceptance and exclusion. Nationalism had to work through the tense intimacy of the biblical brothers, Jacob and Esau.

The typology survived modern challenges, and its tenacity testifies to the limits of emancipation and the force of racial antisemitism. To be sure, it lost some of its eschatological force: Until the Holocaust, Edom (and Amaleq) rhetoric became subdued, and the uses of Jacob & Esau in non-rabbinic literature could be metaphorical more than typological. In liberal Jewish polemics, Abraham and Moses often superseded Jacob: Reform Jews claimed them as earlier and better monotheists than Jesus.[27] Jacob became a bourgeois paterfamilias and a Jewish cosmopolitan, and for Orthodox and Reform Jews, Esau was now more a Jewish apostate than a

---

[26] Michael Fishbane, *Biblical Interpretation in Ancient Israel* (Oxford: Oxford University Press, 1988), pp. 376–79, elaborates Hosea's "intrabiblical typology" (also p. 351): Israel's transgressions are reflective of Jacob's character.

[27] Abraham Geiger, *Judaism and Its History*, trans. Maurice Mayer (New York: M. Thalmessinger, 1865), esp. pp. 91–92; Ludwig Philippson, *The Development of the Religious Idea in Judaism, Christianity and Mahomedanism* (London: Longman, Brown, Green and Longmans, 1855), esp. pp. 55–104.

Christian.[28] Still, the paucity of Jacob & Esau reconciliation discourse among Jews and Christians, and the ease with which avowed integrationists, such as Vienna's chief rabbi, Adolf Jellinek (1821–1893), fell back on the traditional view of Esau was surprising, and telling of Jewish integration's limits.[29] With racial antisemitism's rise in the 1880s, Protestant scholars re-Judaized Jacob and made him a Jewish trickster, and in Jewish national literature, Esau emerged as the *Goy*, the ethnic non-Jew, often a violent antisemite.[30] However transformed, for Jews and Christians alike, Jacob & Esau remained explanatory theological or racial types – and the ultimate Other.

When visions of the Jacob & Esau reconciliation emerged before and after World War I, in expressionist poet Else Lasker-Schüler (1869–1945) and dramatist Waldemar Jollos (1886–1953), their beauty and appeal were contingent on their dissociation from history and reality.[31] They were utopias of peaceful brotherhood drawn against the hopelessness of a reality of racialized national enmity. Thomas Mann acknowledged this openly: His dignified Ancient Eastern Jacob in *Joseph and His Brothers*, unmistakably a Jew yet the embodiment of civilization, was a myth he counterposed to the Nazi endeavor to racialize the Jews and exclude them from European civilization.[32] Nineteenth-century writers deployed Jacob & Esau to advance platforms of emancipation but could project no reconciliation. Twentieth-century writers posed an ethereal alternative to a nation-state gone awry. Ethnic portrayals of Jacob & Esau in Jewish national literature, Yiddish and Hebrew alike, likewise registered emancipation's declining fortunes. Liberal Rabbi Benno Jacob passed the final verdict on emancipation in his *Genesis* commentary: Esau's reconciliation, he said, was contingent on Jacob's limping.[33] Only Jacob's weakness evoked Esau's sympathy. Emancipation was never to be fulfilled.

[28] Isaak Noah Mannheimer, *Gottesdienstliche Vorträge*, 2 vols. in 1 (Vienna: Brüder Winter, 1876): 2: 1 ff.; Samuel Holdheim, "Der Name Israel," in *Predigten über die jüdische Religion* (Berlin: Carl David, 1853), pp. 1–12.

[29] Adolph Jellinek, *Predigten*, 3 vols. in 1 (Vienna: Carl Gerold's Sohn, 1862–66): 2: 203–14.

[30] *Genesis*, trans. and interpreted by Hermann Gunkel (Göttingen: Vandenhoeck & Ruprecht, 1901), pp. 281–83; Sholem Aleichem, *The Complete Tevye the Dairyman* (in Hebrew), trans. from the Yiddish by Dan Miron (Jerusalem: Keter, 2005), pp. 161–67, 175–76.

[31] Else Lasker-Schüler, *Hebrew Ballads and Other Poems* (in German and English), trans. and ed. Audri Durchslag and Jeanette Litman-Demeestère (Philadelphia: The Jewish Publication Society, 1980), pp. 60–61; Waldemar Jollos, *Esau und Jakob* (Berlin: S. Fischer, 1919).

[32] *Joseph and His Brothers*, trans. H. T. Lowe-Porter (New York: Alfred A. Knopf, 1948). The first volume of the Joseph tetralogy, "The Tales of Jacob," was written between 1926 and 1930 and published in 1933.

[33] *Das erste Buch der Tora: Genesis*, trans. and interpreted by B. Jacob (Berlin: Schocken Verlag, 1934), p. 645.

Christian and Jewish reconfigurations of Jacob & Esau show emancipation and nationalism endeavoring to transform the fundamental structure of Jewish–Christian relations – and failing. They provide insights into the conflicting Jewish and German strategies for national integration, expose the barriers to the resolution of the Jewish Question in Central Europe, and illustrate Jewish identity dilemmas. They disclose the European nation-state's permanent dilemma: It cannot become diverse enough to accommodate traditional Jewry, and when turning ethno-national, then and now, it undermines the European order. It never overcame the Jewish–Christian rift. Jacob and Esau did not become national brothers.

As Jacob & Esau traveled between empire and nation, "evil empires" and "kingdoms of grace," the tenor of Jewish–Christians relations set the typology's course. Better Christian–Jewish relations gave rise to a softer vision of Esau, while worsening relations produced a darker one; better relations loosened the typology, while worsening relations reaffirmed and hardened it. "And so it is in all ages," affirmed Naphtali Zevi Yehudah Berlin (1816–1893), head of the famed Volozhin yeshiva, in a Torah commentary, reflecting the liberal atmosphere of Tsar Alexander II's years. "Whenever the seed of Esau is prompted by sincere motives to acknowledge and respect the seed of Israel, then we, too, are moved to acknowledge Esau: For he is our brother."[34]

Nation, Empire, and the Jewish Question

"May he who gives salvation to kings and dominion to princes ... bless and protect, guard and help, exalt, magnify and uplift our sovereign, his majesty Wilhelm II, Emperor (*qeysar*) of the kingdom (*malkhut*) of the German Empire (*deutsches Reich*)"; so reads the Jewish prayer for the kingdom's welfare in a 1910 prayer book. (See Figure 2.)[35] Nowadays the prayer is recited weekly on the shabbat in Orthodox Jewish congregations and, in modified versions, also in Conservative and Reform ones. Tradition often enlists the prophet Jeremiah's (29:7) call to Jerusalem's exiles to seek their host city's welfare, and the *Mishnah*'s (Avot 3:2) injunction to pray for the kingdom, as support for the prayer. Truly, the prayer originated in fifteenth-century Spain, and reworked recent

---

[34] *Humash Haameq Davar, Sefer Bereshit* [1879] (Jerusalem: Yeshivat Volozhin, 1999) on Genesis 33:4.

[35] http://he.wikipedia.org/wiki/שיחת_משתמש:תמרה/תמרכיון/ארכיון_28#;mediaviewer/קובץ:Wilhelm_Pr ayer_Prague_1910.JPG. I could not track the source. (The Wikipedia reference to *Tefillot. Mahzor. German. 1910. Prague,* trans. and commentary by Michael Sachs, rev. ed., 4 vols. [Prague: Jakob B. Brandeis, 1910] appears wrong. Tamara Hayardeni and Daniel Zevi Shani, Jerusalem Wikipedia contributors, tried to help.)

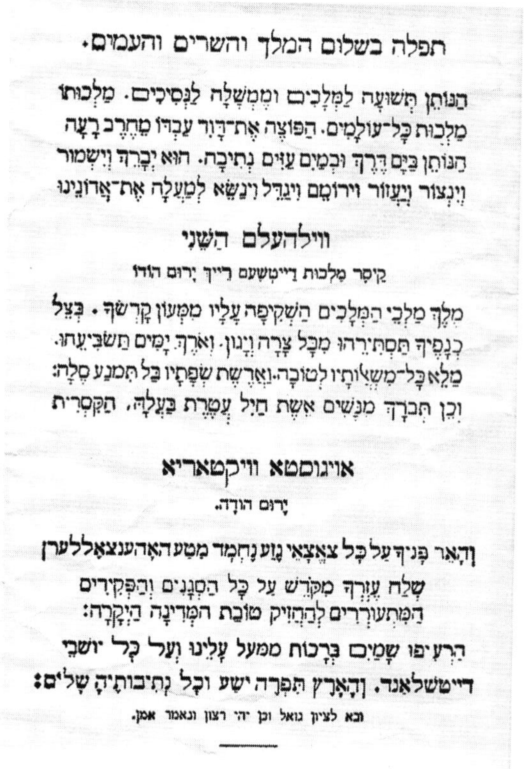

תְּפִלָּה בִּשְׁלוֹם הַמֶּלֶךְ וְהַשָּׂרִים וְהָעַמִּים •

הַנּוֹתֵן תְּשׁוּעָה לַמְּלָכִים וּמֶמְשָׁלָה לַנְּסִיכִים • מַלְכוּתוֹ
מַלְכוּת כָּל־עוֹלָמִים. הַפּוֹצֶה אֶת־דָּוִד עַבְדּוֹ מֵחֶרֶב רָעָה
הַנּוֹתֵן בַּיָּם דֶּרֶךְ וּבְמַיִם עַזִּים נְתִיבָה. הוּא יְבָרֵךְ וְיִשְׁמוֹר
וְיִנְצוֹר וְיַעֲזוֹר וִירוֹמֵם וִיגַדֵּל וִינַשֵּׂא לְמַעֲלָה אֶת־אֲדוֹנֵנוּ

וִוילְהֶעלְם הַשֵּׁנִי
קֵיסֶר מַלְכוּת דַּייטְשְׁעם רֵייךְ יָרוּם הוֹדוֹ

מֶלֶךְ מַלְכֵי הַמְּלָכִים הַשְׁקִיפָה עָלָיו מִפְּעוֹן קַרְשֶׁךָ • בְּצֵל
כְּנָפֶיךָ תַּסְתִּירֵהוּ מִכָּל צָרָה וְיָגוֹן. וְאֶרֶךְ יָמִים תַּשְׂבִּיעֵהוּ.
מַלֵּא כָל־מִשְׁאֲלוֹתָיו לְטוֹבָה. וַאֲרֶשֶׁת שְׂפָתָיו בַּל תִּמְנַע סֶלָה:
וְכֵן תְּבָרֵךְ מְנַשֵּׂם אֵשֶׁת חַיִל עֲטֶרֶת בַּעֲלָהּ, הַקֵּיסְרִית

אוֹיגוּסְטָא וִויקְטָארִיא
יָרוּם הוֹדָהּ..

וְהָאֵר פָּנֶיךָ עַל כָּל צֶאֱצָאֵי נֶוַע נֶחְמָד מַטַע הָאֶהֶנְצָאֶלֶלְעֶרְן
שְׁלַח עֶזְרְךָ מִקֹּדֶשׁ עַל כָּל הַסְּנָנִים וְהַפְּקִידִים
הַמִּתְעוֹרְרִים לְהַחֲזִיק טוֹבַת הַמְּדִינָה הַיְקָרָה:
הַרְעִיפוּ שָׁמַיִם בְּרָכוֹת מִמַּעַל עָלֵינוּ וְעַל כָּל יוֹשְׁבֵי
דֵּייטְשְׁלַאנְד. וְהָאָרֶץ תִּפְרֶה יֵשַׁע וְכָל נְתִיבוֹתֶיהָ שָׁלֹם:

וּבָא לְצִיּוֹן גּוֹאֵל וְכֵן יְהִי רָצוֹן וְנֹאמַר אָמֵן.

Figure 2: Prayer for the welfare of German Emperor Wilhelm II and his family from an early twentieth-century *maḥazor.* (prayerbook for the High Holidays)

medieval versions.[36] It is difficult to imagine late antique Jews praying for anything but the Roman Empire's destruction.

Both Yosef Hayim Yerushalmi and Hannah Arendt saw in the Jews' attachment to the rulers, or the state, a structural feature of Diaspora minority life.[37] Perhaps it was, but the Jewish affinity for rulers appears more typical of medieval and early modern Europe and less of Late

---

[36] The prayer may have originally been subversive: The biblical verses composing it (Psalms 144:10; Isaiah 43:16) are followed by a call not to put trust in foreigners and by a description of God subduing armies. There was not a trace of subversion, however, in Jewish prayers for Wilhelm's and Franz Joseph's welfare.

[37] Hannah Arendt, *The Origins of Totalitarianism* (New York: Harcourt Brace Jovanovich, 1973); Yosef Hayim Yerushalmi, *The Lisbon Massacre of 1506 and the Royal Image in the Shebet Yehudah* (Cincinnati, OH: Hebrew Union College, 1976), and *"Servants of Kings*

Antiquity, and attachment to the state may actually connote affinity for the nation and is, first and foremost, modern. The Holy Roman Empire became popular only in decline, and the great love story between Jews and empire is modern: Austria-Hungary and the Emperor Franz Joseph (1830–1916). Imperial patriotism had resonances in the Ottoman and other European empires, but everywhere it competed with national patriotism. Yerushalmi and Arendt may have created the myths they set out to dissolve.

Germany's cumbersome designation as kingdom and empire in the 1910 prayer book was due, in part, to its federal structure: Wilhelm II was King of Prussia and Emperor of Germany. Yet the poverty of the traditional Jewish political lexicon contributed to the awkwardness, too: Rabbinic Hebrew has only one term for state and government – kingdom (*malkhut* מלכות). The modern Hebrew term for "state," *medinah* (מדינה), traditionally meant a province or a *polis*, and has received its contemporary meaning only with Theodor Herzl's 1896 *Der Judenstaat* (The Jews' state; מדינת היהודים).[38] The ruler, whether of a city or an empire, was traditionally the "king." The Talmudic term *qeysar* (Caesar; emperor) was infrequent, and *qeysarut* (empire) is a recent invention; indeed, the German prayer book transliterated German Reich for the lack of a Hebrew term. Hebrew borrowed the terms "republic" and "democracy." Notwithstanding the recent valiant efforts to construct a Jewish political tradition, the traditional lexicon's poverty tells of the confinement of Diaspora politics.[39] Jews gave careful thought to communal institutions, and terms for the authorities determining Jewish welfare were familiar.[40] When imagining a sovereign Jewish polity, in contrast, ancient governance served as the model and not contemporary politics. Conceptual transition to

and Not Servants of Servants": Some Aspects of the Political History of the Jews (Atlanta: Tam Institute for Jewish Studies, 2005).

[38] Theodor Herzl, *Der Judenstaat* (Leipzig: M. Breitenstein, 1896); *The Jewish State*, trans. Sylvie d'Avigdor (London: Nutt, 1896). Yiddish uses *medine* loosely for country, province, or smaller states but not for larger states, such as the Austrian or Russian empires, which are designated as *imperye*. *Melukhe* and *malchus* are also used in their broad Hebrew sense. Ladino domesticated *estado*. Herzl's use of *Staat* intimated a solution to the Jewish Question in a larger imperial setting. My thanks to the late Ezra Mendelsohn for suggesting that there must be Yiddish and Ladino equivalents, and to Sheva Zucker and Jacob Golan for help in hunting for them.

[39] *The Jewish Political Tradition*, ed. Michael Walzer, Menachem Lorberbaum, Noam J. Zohar, and Yair Lorberbaum, 2 vols (New Haven, CT: Yale University Press, 2000–2003); *Kinship & Consent: The Jewish Political Tradition and Its Contemporary Uses*, ed. Daniel J. Elazar, 2d ed. (New Brunswick, NJ: Transactions Publishers, 1997).

[40] Adi Ophir of Tel Aviv University writes: "Your claim about the absence of rabbinic terminology to differentiate types of political systems is certainly correct. Note, however, that the rabbis recognize well the different authorities within the empire (e.g., *centorium*, *hegmon*), and that they repeatedly distinguish between the divine and earthly kingdoms (*malkhut shamayim* vs. *melekh basar va-dam*)": email, August 10, 2010.

modernity was difficult for all Europeans; for Jews, modern nationalism and the nation-state were outright revolutionary.

The Imperial Longue Durée

Three millennia of Jewish history sustain the historiographical trend under-lining the nation-state's modernity and presenting empire as normative. To be sure, Jews were subject to diverse premodern governments, not only to empires, and recent taxonomies of empire raise doubt about the concept's coherence: "Empire" is capacious enough to include divergent forms of governance that defy generalization (of the sort to which the nation-state is susceptible).[41] Empires can be maritime or continental, global or regional, ancient or modern. In continental Europe, and in this book, empire con-trasts with nation-state, federalism with centralization, and cultural diver-sity with uniformity. From the French Revolution and the late years of the Holy Roman Empire to the continental empires' downfall in the aftermath of World War I, international imperial federalist visions of Europe, both conservative and progressive, contrasted with liberal and democratic visions of Europe as a conglomeration of nation-states and cultures with clearly delineated borders. Yet modern nation-states, like France, were also successful overseas empire builders, and Algerian Jews were declared French citizens (and "European") in 1870. Late nineteenth-century European imperial metropoleis went through nationalization, and it is now common to speak of "nationalizing empires."[42] The European Union eventually emerged as a federation of democratic nation-states. Nation and empire converge as much as they diverge.

All the same, Jewish European history shows the persistence of Jewish concern with empire and the stability of the vocabulary associated with it. Jacob & Esau tells the story of a people regarding itself a nation (אומה), accustomed for over two and a half millennia to forming relationships, real and imagined, with successive empires but eagerly adapting in mod-ernity to the nation-state, and experimenting with national integration (emancipation) and Jewish nationalism.[43] Even in modern times, however,

---

[41] Jürgen Osterhammel, *Die Verwandlung der Welt: Eine Geschichte des 19. Jahrhunderts* (Munich: Beck, 2009), esp. pp. 565–672; Peter Moraw, Karl Otmar Freiherr von Aretin, Notker Hammerstein, Werner Conze, and Elisabeth Fehrenbach, "Reich," in *Geschichtliche Grundbegriffe*, 8 vols. (Stuttgart: Klett-Cotta, 1972–97): 5: 423–508; Richard Koebner, *Empire* (Cambridge: Cambridge University Press, 1961).

[42] Stefan Berger and Alexei Miller, eds., *Nationalizing Empires* (Budapest: CEU Press, 2014).

[43] The Jews viewed themselves as a people (עם) and a nation and were recognized as such by others. Radical discontinuities in Jewish communal life and disparate diasporic cultures challenge a unified Jewish nation and history. But this study is in an easier position than most: Continuity exists where the typology does. For one historian's confrontation with

the great majority of Jews lived until 1918 in multiethnic empires and not in nation-states. In such a long-term history, short episodes of Jewish sovereignty – Ancient Judah, the Hasmonaean Kingdom, and the State of Israel – appear as contingent on Near Eastern imperial lulls: the short-term absence of a hegemonic regional empire. To gain a proper perspective on nation and empire in Jewish history, modern emancipation and con-temporary Jewish sovereignty need to be projected against longer periods of imperially negotiated Jewish autonomy.

At the outbreak of World War I, Galician Jews issued a gold medallion, in the shape of a Star of David, depicting Franz Joseph (1830–1916) as a triumphant Roman emperor crowned with laurels.[44] Traditional Jewry considered the Austrian emperor the inheritor of the Holy Roman Empire's legacy, and the one-sided love affair that Jews had with him reflected a remarkable turn of events in Jewish history and one of its ironies. The Roman Empire represented Jewish history's greatest trauma, the *Ḥurban* – Ancient Rome's devastation of Jerusalem and Jewish Palestine, and the subjection, slaying, and exile of the Jewish people. The Ḥurban created a fifteen-hundred-year-long tradition of relentless Jewish hatred of "the evil empire [that] destroyed our temple, and burnt down our sanctuary, and exiled us from our land." The rabbis reinter-preted the apocalypse of the biblical Book of Daniel to make Rome the last of the Four Empires (ארבע מלכויות) dominating the world before the restoration of the Jewish people and divine rule.[45] In practice, the imperial order proved acceptable to the Jews during certain periods, and the Babylonian Talmud also contains tales of peaceful Roman–Jewish coex-istence. But the overwhelming picture of Rome in rabbinic literature remains one of an implacable enemy, a "kingdom of malice" (מלכות זדון) whose destruction is a precondition to Jewish redemption.

The empire's Christianization from the fourth century on wove the Jewish–Christian and nation–empire relationships together. The rabbis seemed initially to take little notice of imperial power's changing religious character, but the Islamic Caliphate's rise and struggle with the Eastern

---

continuity and coherence in Jewish history: Michael A. Meyer, *Judaism Within Modernity: Essays on Jewish History and Religion* (Detroit: Wayne State University Press, 2001), esp. pp. 87–98.

[44] Lili Arad, "Her Beauty Your Eyes Shall See," in *High above High* (in Hebrew), ed. Yochai ben Gedalia, Uriel Gelman, and Reuven Gafni (Jerusalem: Yad Ben-Ẓevi, 2016), p. 137.

[45] *BT*, Gittin 57b for the "evil empire," and *Mekhilta* be-shalakh 1 and yitro-ba-chodesh 9 (*Mekhilta d'Rabbi Ismael*, ed. and introduction by S. Horovitz and I. A. Rabin [Jerusalem: Bamberger & Wahrmann, 1960]), for Rome's anticipated downfall. (*Mekhilta* intimated Rome rather than mentioned it explicitly.) For the messianic time line: "The world will last six millennia: Two millennia of chaos, two millennia of Torah [Jewish Law from Abraham to the Messiah] and two millennia of messianic time, when the evil empire and Israel's enslavement will end"; Rashi on *BT*, Sanhedrin 97a.

Roman Empire "Christianized" Rome in their eyes, too. Their portrayals of Muslim rule were predominantly negative, but their vision of the caliphate never assumed apocalyptic dimensions comparable to those of Rome. Jewish redemption was made to depend on the Christian empire's downfall more consistently and enduringly than any historical parallel.

With Europe imagined as Christendom in medieval times, the target of Jewish hatred began shifting from the Roman Empire to the Roman Church. A gradual warming of Jewish feelings toward emperors and monarchs began, and it extended, in early modern Europe, even to the Holy Roman Empire itself. All the same, the imperial legacy partially accounts for liberal Jews' enthusiastic response to the modern nation-state, and their willingness to refashion Jewish identity to comply with emancipation's terms and become bona fide citizens. Likewise, the dissolution of the Holy Roman Empire in the aftermath of the Napoleonic Wars freed up the imperial space for Jewish love of late imperial Austria. Criticism of Jewish emancipation and the nation-state's shortcomings, as well as of Jewish nationalism and cosmopolitanism and understandable nostalgia for Austria-Hungary, must be measured against the long-term imperial *modus vivendi et morti* of Jewish European history.

Empire, Nation-State, and the Jewish Question

Late imperial Germany and Austria illuminate the alternatives that nation and empire opened for Jews in modernity. In the 1880s, as antisemites bid to racialize citizenship, German and Austrian Jews alike endeavored to dissociate citizenship from ethnicity and define membership of the nation as political. Philosopher Moritz Lazarus (1824–1903) developed a "multicultural" definition of the German nation, and conceived of the Jews as one of the ethnicities and subcultures contributing to it.[46] He tried to pluralize the nation-state, but a uniformly ethnicized national culture made multiculturalism seem hopeless. Fin-de-siècle German nationalism had no place for Jewish culture. Austria experienced even more virulent German nationalism, and antisemitism played a role in parliamentary life exceeding anything the German Reichstag experienced, but the state served as a bulwark against German nationalism.[47] Austria-Hungary was federalist and pluralist, the Germans were a minority, the Jews were one ethnicity

---

[46] Moritz Lazarus, *Was heißt National?* (Berlin: Ferd. Dümmlers Verlagsbuchhandlung, 1880).

[47] Saskia Stachowitsch and Eva Kreisky, eds., *Jüdische Identitäten und antisemitische Politiken im österreichischen Parlament 1861–1933* (Vienna: Böhlau, 2017). I owe this reference to Abigail Green of Oxford University.

among many, and their Austrian identity did not depend on being German.[48] The Jewish intelligentsia could advance Jewish nationalism: In Austria, unlike Germany (or France), it did not mean seeking "a state within a state."

Pluralist empires in different times and places opened opportunities for Jews. Having provided refuge to Jewish exiles from Spain, the Ottoman Empire became an object of Jewish love in the early sixteenth century. With the 1856 *Tanzimat* reforms, the Ottomans could also be seen to advance emancipation ahead of Austria or Germany.[49] Elsewhere in Europe, Jewish national and imperial patriotism often converged. Nineteenth-century French Jews promoted "universal" French culture among the Jewish Diaspora and fought for recognition of their brethren in North Africa as French nationals. British Jewry exuded imperial pride, enhanced, perhaps, by recognition that Jews were more easily accepted as British in the ethnically heterogeneous dominions than in the metropolis. Well into the World War II, Jewish intellectuals, including émigrés, imagined a liberally reformed British Commonwealth as the largest free community on earth.[50] Yet only in Austria did imperial patriotism constrain rather than promote a hegemonic national identity and provide an alternative to it. The secret of the Habsburg magic for Jews was that, more evidently than elsewhere, empire could not nationalize without undermining its own foundations.

To Jewish socialists and progressives, however, this hybrid seemed obsolete. The nation-state bespoke modernity. Nationalizing empires, whether continental, such as the Austrian, German, and Ottoman, or maritime, such as the French, extended citizenship rights to the Jews as part of their nation building: Austria-Hungary in 1867, Germany in 1871, Turkey in 1908, and France in 1790–91 and, again, in Algeria in 1870.[51]

[48] Marsha Rozenblit, *Reconstructing a National Identity: The Jews of Habsburg Austria during World War I* (New York: Oxford University Press, 2001), outlines the layers of Austrian Jewish identity.

[49] Julia Phillips Cohen, *Becoming Ottomans: Sephardi Jews and Imperial Citizenship in the Modern Era* (New York: Oxford University Press, 2014).

[50] Alfred Zimmern, *The Third British Empire*, 3d ed. (London: Oxford University Press, 1934); Karl Popper, *The Open Society and Its Enemies*, 2 vols. (London: Routledge & Sons, 1945); Arie Dubnov, "Dreaming of the Seventh Dominion in Oxford: Palestine and the British Commonwealth," lecture, October 20, 2016, at St John's College, Oxford.

[51] Ernest Gellner saw empires as inadvertently initiating the drive toward nationalization through the pursuit of administrative uniformity and efficiency. *Language and Solitude: Wittgenstein, Malinowski and the Habsburg Dilemma* (Cambridge: Cambridge University Press, 1998), p. 31. Joseph II of Austria (1780–1790) was the classic example. Not surprisingly, he also issued the *Toleranzpatente*, a series of edicts removing Jewish liabilities. They presaged Jewish emancipation but retained the corporate order. Julia Phillips Cohen, in *Becoming Ottomans*, believes that the Ottomans may have gotten even closer to

Policies aiming to nationalize imperial culture followed suit. Imperial Austria guarded pluralism and opened up space for Jewish nationality in ways that other states could not, but modern empire was not an emancipatory agent.[52] The nation-state was.

The modern nation-state represents a paradox. The political idea of the nation, emerging from the French Revolution, made Jewish emancipation and citizenship possible, even necessary, but consummation of the nationalist drive toward cultural uniformity, whether in assimilation or in ethnic exclusion of the Jews, would spell – and, in the Holocaust, nearly did spell – the end of European Jewry. For a century and a half, European Jewry existed precariously between assimilation and exclusion, its survival dependent on nationalism's inability to drive the logic of national unity to its end. When this did occur, and ethno-nationalism triumphed, the entire European order came crashing down, together with European Jewry. Postwar Europe constituted a mosaic of ethno-national states, and European unity – postnationalism – has been built up on their foundation. Nowadays, the nation-state, challenged by novel forms of globalization and regional collaboration, is changing, but it is not yet quite going away. We had better learn to live with its dilemmas and attenuate them with lessons derived from the imperial legacy.

The Jewish Question highlights the nation-state's dilemmas. The French Revolution pronounced equal citizenship and the nation's indivisibility. Indivisibility implied the end of corporate privileges but also a unified national culture. In what sense could Jews remain Jewish? The nation-state tolerated different confessions, but the idea that Jews were merely another religious community never gained ground, and in any case, national culture continued to carry the Christian imprint: Even civic nationalism had an attenuated Christian character. In France, where the state was successful in melting different regional identities and dialects into a political nation and culture, the majority of Jews, within two generations, went through acculturation and political and economic integration. As the classical case of civic nationalism, France demonstrated that for the sake of citizenship and integration, Jews would thin down traditional Jewish identity and become part of the national culture. The

emancipation with the 1856 *Tanzimat* reforms. For the French, Germans, and Hungarians, however, emancipating the Jews was part of founding the nation.

[52] David Sorkin questions this premise. Presently at work on *Interminable Emancipation: European Jewry and the Quest for Equality, 1550–2000*, he redefines emancipation to include early modern improvement in Jewish conditions, and emphasizes imperial agency and the role of the imperial legacy in shaping modern emancipation. Joseph II's *Toleranzpatente*, the *Tanzimat* (Ottoman reforms), and French improvement of Jewish conditions in Algeria and Morocco adduce evidence to support his view and may require modification of my categorical distinction. צריך עיון.

Jewish elite proved especially resourceful in shaping French-Jewish identities and in forging relations to the Jewish Diaspora as representatives of French culture.[53]

Napoleon's troops first brought civic nationalism to Germany. After eight decades of struggle and reversals, all Central European Jewry was emancipated. Germany remained politically fragmented until 1871, and German conceptions of nationality put a premium on culture rather than on politics. They reflected the legacy of German humanism and the *Aufklärung* (German enlightenment), but they also expressed racially inflected populism, joining religion, ethnicity, and culture to exclude Jews. Protracted unification made the molding of a German national culture an openly contested process and, until the 1870s, more a project of the intelligentsia than of the state. German-speaking Central Europe became the site of intensive emancipation debates. In the aftermath of the *Haskalah* (Jewish enlightenment), *Bildung* (educational and cultural formation) became the key concept in Central European Jewish acculturation. As Germany's boundaries were set only in 1871, belonging in the German cultural sphere (*deutsche Kulturbereich*) seemed as significant as citizenship. In France and Germany alike, however, Jews made claims for their culture's universal character. Loyalty to the nation and humanity was one – "national cosmopolitanism."[54]

The great majority of European Jews inhabited the Pale of Settlement in the Russian Empire, where emancipation remained a distant dream. Russia was a multiethnic empire, and in the second half of the nineteenth century, its minorities went through nationalization, albeit one that was divergent in pace and pattern. A hegemonic Russian nationalism with Pan-Slavic designs emerged, without citizenship becoming a serious prospect until the revolutions of 1905 and 1917. Whereas in Western and Central Europe emancipation, acculturation, and commercialization modernized the Jewish community, and the intelligentsia debated strategies for integration, in Russia the acculturated Jewish intelligentsia confronted a largely traditional Jewry, invigorated by *Hasidism*, the Lithuanian *yeshivot* and new spiritual movements, and a nascent secularizing proletariat that was exploring new class and national identities. Traditionalists, Diaspora nationalists, Zionists, and many socialists viewed the Jews as a separate people, neither

---

[53] Jay R. Berkovitz, *The Shaping of Jewish Identity in Nineteenth-Century France* (Detroit: Wayne State University Press, 1989); Lisa Leff, *Sacred Bonds of Solidarity: The Rise of Jewish Internationalism in Nineteenth-Century France* (Stanford, CA: Stanford University Press, 2006).

[54] Michael Steinberg coined the term in *The Meaning of the Salzburg Festival* (Ithaca, NY: Cornell University Press, 1990) to speak of interwar Austrian Catholic–Jewish cosmopolitanism. It befits currents in liberal Jewry even more.

desirous nor capable of national integration, and sought to redefine the Jews' place in a nationalizing, modernizing, and politically oppressive empire.

Traditional Jews emphasized their loyalty to the state everywhere, but they were suspicious of the modern nation. They rarely opposed emancipation outright, but they objected to Jews fighting for it, reasoning that the pursuit of emancipation amounted to renunciation of hope for divine redemption. Throughout Central Europe, but especially in the Austrian Empire, traditionalists responded to emancipation with "illiberal multiculturalism" (*avant la lettre*): They advocated the peaceful coexistence of closed ethno-religious communities. From Moses Sofer to Joseph Bloch (1850–1923) to Nathan Birnbaum (1864–1937), traditionalists sought to reshape nationalization to recapture a measure of the communal autonomy afforded earlier by the imperial corporate order. Contemporary multiculturalism represents a postnational effort to pluralize the nation-state. Jewish traditionalism was multicultural because it was instinctively prenational, preferring empires to nation-states.

The preference for empire over nation-state was overwhelming among Eastern European Jews. The late Austrian Empire seemed ideal to both traditionalists and nationalists, but they endorsed even the Russian Empire over Western-style national "assimilation." In Russian-controlled Poland and the Baltic, many Jewish liberals and socialists advocated imperial reform rather than Polish, Lithuanian, or Latvian national liberation. The spectrum of Jewish imperial federalists ranged widely from left to right. Rosa Luxembourg and Karl Radek broke with the mainstream Polish socialists on the national question: Both envisioned Polish autonomy in a Russian federation and would not support an independent Poland. The spurious statement attributed to Rabbi Schneur Zalman of Liadi (*Ḥabad Ḥasidism*'s founder, 1745–1812) endorsing the tsar over Napoleon reflected the attitude of the overwhelming majority of Eastern European Jews: Better empire than nation.[55]

The late 1870s and early1880s marked a European watershed on the Jewish Question: a shift from civic to ethnic nationalism that accentuated nationality's ethnic dimensions and reified culture into race. Racial motifs

---

[55] "Should Napoleon be victorious, wealth will abound among the Jews ... but Israel's hearts will be separated and distant from their father in heaven. But if our master Alexander triumphs, though poverty will abound ... Israel's hearts will be tied and joined with their father in heaven." Immanuel Etkes, *Ba'al Ha-Tanya: Rabbi Shneur Zalman of Liady and the Origins of Habad Hasidism* (Jerusalem: Zalman Shazar Center, 2011), pp. 386–413, argues persuasively that the letter to Moshe Meizeles is of mid-nineteenth-century vintage. Like most Russian Jews, Schneur Zalman did support Alexander, but on the assumption that he would improve Jewish conditions and not that he would leave them poor.

had been part of German (and other) concepts of nationality since the eighteenth century, and they coexisted with political, religious, and cultural conceptions of the nation. Recent scholarship has attenuated the boundary between traditional and modern, religious, and racial antisemitism by pointing out the persistence of traditional religious themes in integral nationalism.[56] Still, George Fredrickson's view of racism as postemancipatory and reactive in character remains prescient.[57] Modern antisemitism, a blatant attempt to reverse emancipation, was the epitome of ethno-nationalism. Wilhelm Marr coined the term *antisemitism* in 1879, and, reinforced by scientific discourse, race became the nation's foundation.[58]

In hindsight, the nation-state may have been set on a course that would end with the Jews' exclusion from the polity, and worse. With the crisis of World War I, the collapse of ethnically pluralist empires, and, some would argue, the instruction derived from colonial population management, radical rethinking of the Jewish Question in the context of racialized citizenship and population transfers became possible. The nation-state depended on a delicate balance between civic and ethnic citizenship, and East-Central Europe was "one of the most mixed of all the thoroughly mixed regions of Europe." Ethno-nationalism would end up undermining the nation-state it purportedly sought to secure, and the Jews' exclusion would signal the nation-state's end and the European order's collapse.[59]

All this was in store for the future. For the time, emergent Zionism and Diaspora nationalism denoted the predicament of Jewish emancipation. As long as Jewish integration seemed a real prospect in Western and Central Europe, and even a remote chance in Russia, Jewish nationalism remained subdued. The 1881 pogroms in Russia and German antisemitism in Central Europe problematized Jewish hopes for integration and triggered a Jewish nationalist response. Zionists hoped to build national life and a Hebrew culture in Palestine, and turn Zion into a cultural center that would renovate the Diaspora. Diaspora nationalists opted for Jewish political autonomy and a Yiddish culture, in the Russian and Austrian

---

[56] Helmut Walser Smith, *The Continuities of German History: Nation, Religion, and Race across the Long Nineteenth Century* (Cambridge: Cambridge University Press, 2008).

[57] George Fredrickson, *Racism: A Short History* (Princeton, NJ: Princeton University Press, 2002).

[58] Wilhelm Marr, *Wählet keinen Juden! Der Weg zum Siege des Germanenthums über das Judenthum: Ein Mahnwort an die Wähler nichtjüdischen Stammes aller Confessionen* (Berlin: Hentze, 1879).

[59] The "thoroughly mixed regions of Europe" belong to Karl Popper, *The Open Society and Its Enemies*, 2: chap. 12, n. 53, and the conclusion to Hannah Arendt, *The Origins of Totalitarianism*, pp. 267–90.

Empires first, then in the interwar nation-states established on their ruins. Both Zionism and Diaspora nationalism regarded ethno-nationalism as a threat but also as a Jewish opportunity: Ethno-nationalism revealed the realities of national life, made a mockery of emancipation, integration, and cosmopolitanism, and forced Jews to recognize their own nationality.

Unlike other nationalists, Jewish nationalists had to mobilize a Diaspora without a territorial center. Even Zionists who focused on work in Palestine recognized that European Jewish life required urgent solutions and claimed autonomy for European Jews. They had first envisioned multinational empires, then when the empires collapsed in the aftermath of World War I, pluralist nation-states. Forming a multicultural vision, Jewish nationalists found themselves appealing to civic nationalism and human rights, that is, to universal standards transcending particular groups. For all their homage to ethnicity and scorn for "assimilation," the multiacculturated Jewish nationalists staged the most cosmopolitan ethno-nationalism that Europe had seen.

Zionists shared with other Jews a respect and an affection for imperial Austria. Late imperial Austria was so attractive because it represented a unique balance between premodern and modern politics, pluralism and nationality. German nationalization had progressed just enough to emancipate the Jews, yet imperial pluralism necessitated federative arrangements, protective of minority cultures and opening the gate to Jewish nationalization. Beginning in 1867, Emperor Franz Joseph was also the King of Hungary, and Hungary behaved as a nation-state within the Dual Monarchy, aggressively promoting Magyarization. Yet until World War I, Jews were considered collaborators in the Hungarian national project and part of the liberal elite, and, significantly, they considered Hungarian nationalism compatible with imperial patriotism. Austria-Hungary enjoyed overwhelming Jewish support precisely because it was a hybrid between nation-state and empire.

The Bolshevik Revolution in Russia and the dissolution of Austria-Hungary ended the prospect of an imperial pluralism open to Jewish nationality. The nationalizing state became the European norm. Germany and Austria granted Jews full rights, and other states sharing in the Habsburg territorial legacy signed treaties protecting minority rights. In Russia, the revolutions of 1917 emancipated the Jews, and the Soviets made rapid Jewish integration in communist society a priority. Was this emancipation completed? Hardly. Interwar Central Europe became a national battleground: Multiethnic nationalizing states tried to become ethno-national, and ethnic minorities practiced "homeland nationalism" that sought to undermine their state and join compatriots across the borders. Victims to mounting antisemitism, the Jews turned out to be the great losers everywhere. In Soviet Russia, the policy encouraging minorities to nationalize as part of the imperial federalist organization did not extend to the Jews, and early hopes for a Jewish national culture quickly faded as the *Yevsektsiya*, the Communist Party's Jewish section, led a crusade against traditional culture, the Bund, and Zionism.[60] As the Jews' exclusion from economic and civic life in Central and East-Central Europe increased in the 1930s, Jewish nationalism surged. The majority of European Jews may have remained vaguely integrationist until the Holocaust, but the Zionists' triumph in the 1932 elections to the Viennese Jewish *Kultusgemeinde* (religious community), a last bastion of liberalism in Austria, symbolized the turn in Jewish and European politics.

The predicament of Jewish national integration gave birth in the 1930s to relentless nostalgia for Austria-Hungary among Central European Jewish intellectuals of imperial origin. From Karl Popper to Joseph Roth (1894–1939) to Franz Werfel (1890–1945) and Stefan Zweig (1881–1942), Jewish intellectuals in the 1930s began envisioning cosmopolitan commonwealths in the image of the vanished empire. The Zionists, too, were wistful about imperial Austria: Asher Barash (1889–1952), founder of the Hebrew Writers' Association in Palestine, waxed lyrical about Jewish imperial patriotism. Postwar remigrés who had escaped from Nazism and later returned, like Hilde Spiel (1911–1990) and Friedrich Torberg (1908–1979), portrayed the lost golden age of Central European culture, the major protagonists of which were Austrian Jewish writers. The empire's appeal was never greater than after it had already collapsed, and a Europe of nationalizing states degenerated into warfare.

Postnational Historiography and Late Imperial Austria

American historians of late imperial Austria and its successor states have recently challenged the historiographical convention of Austria-Hungary as living on borrowed time in an age of triumphant nationalism.[61] They

---

[60] Terry Martin, *The Affirmative Action Empire: Nations and Nationalism in the Soviet Union, 1923–1939* (Ithaca, NY: Cornell University Press, 2001); Kenneth Moss, *Jewish Renaissance in the Russian Revolution* (Cambridge, MA: Harvard University Press, 2009). In 1928, the party simultaneously disbanded the Jewish section and decided to establish an autonomous district (Oblast) as a "Jewish homeland" (an alternative to Zionism). Birobidzhan was founded in 1934, and from the 1930s on, Soviet passports designated Jews as a "nationality." Historians have recently begun perusing the logic behind these seemingly contradictory policy and ideology changes.

[61] Two most recent contributions: John Deák, *Forging a Multinational State* (Stanford, CA: Stanford University Press, 2015); Pieter Judson, *The Habsburg Empire* (Cambridge, MA: Harvard University Press, 2016).

emphasize the limits of nationalization in the late Austrian Empire, and the accommodation achieved between divergent nationalisms and the empire.[62] They highlight provincial indifference to nationalism, resistance to nationalism among groups that found their loyalties split across newly established ethnic divides, and, in general, the nation's failure to become the center of people's lives. Nationalism's putative success, they suggest, was due to press manipulation by the intelligentsia, to U.S. President Woodrow Wilson's setting of national self-determination as a guiding principle for state boundaries in Central Europe, and to the post–World War I settlement that created nationalizing states. They search for a new narrative for European history, one moving away from inexorable nationalization and positing the Austrian Empire as an alternative model of modernization.

The postnational historians view ethnicity and nationality as categories devoid of explanatory power. They point out that we cannot revert to prenational ethnicities to explain emergent nationalities: Both formed together, and ethnicity was no less an invention than nationhood. States played a crucial role in nationalization, and they made it deadly. The postnationalists retain religion as a cultural marker, but they foreground political categories, especially constitutional arrangements, as crucial to identity. They deny that Austria-Hungary was multinational, inasmuch as nationalities were only created by the interwar (or even postwar) nationalizing states (if then).[63] At their most radical, they deny that the Dual Monarchy was an empire at all: Hungary behaved like a (liberal) nation-state, and Austrian federalism and constitutional pluralism were sui generis, nonimperial.[64]

This book reflects the postnational turn, but it also suggests its limits.[65] Central European exiles invented the "multinational Habsburg Empire," but the émigré *imaginaire* was not divorced from the realities of imperial pluralism. As the ethnicization of politics in late Habsburg Austria

---

[62] Rogers Brubaker et al., *Nationalist Politics and Everyday Ethnicity in a Transylvanian Town* (Princeton, NJ: Princeton University Press, 2006); Jeremy King, *Budweisers into Czechs and Germans: A Local History of Bohemian Politics, 1848–1948* (Princeton, NJ: Princeton University Press, 2002); Pieter Judson, *Guardians of the Nation: Activists on the Language Frontiers of Imperial Austria* (Cambridge, MA: Harvard University Press, 2006); Tara Zahra, *Kidnapped Souls: National Indifference and the Battle for Children in the Bohemian Lands, 1900–1948* (Ithaca, NY: Cornell University Press, 2008).

[63] The German term for a "multinational state," *vielvölkerstaat*, seems to me free of the critics' objections, as it leaves the "people" undefined, not necessarily a nationality.

[64] Pieter Judson, "L'Autriche-Hongrie était-elle un empire?" *Annales: Histoire, Sciences Sociales* 63:3 (2008): 563–96.

[65] For a more robust critique of the postnational turn, vested in Jewish Diaspora nationalism: David Rechter, "A Nationalism of Small Things: Jewish Autonomy in Late Habsburg Austria," *Leo Baeck Institute Year Book* 52 (2007): 87–109.

constrained Jewish life, imperial pluralism opened new prospects for it. Both the exclusion from the nation to which the Jews aspired to belong (German, Czech, or Polish) and the new opportunities for Jewish culture – not to mention imperial protection – were real: deadly real, as it turned out. Like the postnational historians, liberal Jews wished to foreground political and cultural definitions of nationality against an ethnic one – to no avail. The evidence of increasing exclusion and a hardening of ethnic lines is overwhelming. The nation may have become the center of life for only a few, and provincials may have cared little about the language wars raging in their regions, but at crucial historical moments most answered the nation's call and fell behind the newly forming ethnic lines. Election returns from contested territories sustained radical nationalism. Few, if any, modern inventions proved as successful as nationalism in drawing mass support.

The deconstructive edge of "ethnicity without groups" – Rogers Brubaker's term – is blunted when dealing with the European Jews, a Diaspora long marked by religion, culture, and communal life.[66] For all the Jews' purported lack of indigeneity – were the Saxons more indigenous? – they fulfill the prerequisites of ethnicity and nationality, more easily perhaps than other groups. Through the Jews, we can see non-Jewish ethnicity forming as an exclusionary force, a barrier to Jewish integration. Ethno-nationalism gave rise to Jewish cosmopolitanism, to multinational imperial blueprints, and to the Habsburg *imaginaire* – to postnationalism *avant la lettre*. If we deny nationalism's force, we also lose out on cosmopolitanism. Moreover, we ignore nationalism's emancipatory drive and its paradox: The premise of equal citizenship represented modernity's promise to the Jews and made possible an acculturated Jewish intelligentsia and modern European culture as we know it. Jewish emancipation was the first and most persistent European test of the egalitarian force of nationalism and gave testimony to its Janus-faced character.

The European nation-state was a promise impossible to fulfill, yet a promise without which modern Jewish life could not do. Acculturated Jews usually preferred nation-states to empire, but the majority of European Jews – traditional and Eastern European – preferred empires to nation-states. The threats of domestic chaos and nationalist oppression, should the empire collapse, drove traditional Jews the most. Whereas liberal Jews wagered on nationalism's promise of integration, the traditionalists dreaded populist antisemitism. Remarkably, however, in nation-states in danger of falling apart, such as contemporary Belgium, Jews often appear as the single representatives of the national

---

[66] *Ethnicity Without Groups* (Cambridge, MA: Harvard University Press, 2004).

culture. How is one to square Jews as "the best Austrians," the only people enthusiastically adopting the Austrian imperial idea, with Jews as "the only remaining Belgians," the single devotees of a nation-state dissolving into its multicultural constituents? The fear of the collapse of public authority, national or imperial, is an enduring feature of Jewish life, surpassing the divergent historical experiences of nation and empire: "Thou shalt always be praying for the welfare of the monarchy, for without the fear of the authorities, people would devour each other alive."[67]

The Jewish Intelligentsia and European Internationalism

"I am of Jewish descent, but . . . I abhor any form of racialism or nationalism; and I never belonged to the Jewish faith. Thus I do not see on what grounds I could possibly consider myself a Jew," Popper told *The Jewish Chronicle* in 1969.[68] "I [am] not 'an assimilated German Jew,'" he retorted to a critic; "this is how the *Fuehrer* would have considered me."[69] Notwithstanding his protest, I shall argue shortly that Popper and his ilk do represent the Jewish intelligentsia.[70] For now, I would note how radically Popper dissented from the prevailing nationalist currents, and suggest that his brand of cosmopolitanism has made the Jewish intelligentsia agents and symbols of European internationalism. It also put the Jewish intelligentsia in a paradoxical relationship to the nation-state. Assimilation made sense only as part of the nation-building project, which gave rise to Jewish emancipation, but Popper's cosmopolitanism demonstrated the project's failure: He could not imagine assimilation into German Austria, only into the Open Society.[71] Popper exemplifies the impossible interdependence of the Jewish intelligentsia and the European

---

[67] Mishnah *Avot*, 3:2. This tractate recites sayings and dicta of Jewish sages.

[68] Popper to Michael Wallach, January 6, 1969, Hoover Institute Archives, Popper papers (313, 10).

[69] Popper to M. Smith, August 7, 1982, Popper Archives (407, 17).

[70] The term *intelligentsia* (Intelligenz) is no longer identified exclusively with the alienated Russian-educated class (Isaiah Berlin, "The Birth of the Russian Intelligentsia" [1955], in his *Russian Thinkers*, ed. Henry Hardy and Aileen Kelly [London: Penguin Books, 1994], pp. 114–35), as there are Polish and German versions: Andrzej Walicki, "Polish Conceptions of the Intelligentsia and Its Calling," in *Words, Deeds and Values: The Intelligentsias in Russia and Poland during the Nineteenth and Twentieth Centuries*, ed. Fiona Björling and Alexander Pereswetoff-Morath (Lund: Department of East and Central European Studies, 2005), pp. 1–22. My own use should become clear in what follows. My thanks to Mustafa Tuna for the Walicki reference.

[71] I use "assimilation" to designate those Jews who left the Jewish community by converting to Christianity or declaring themselves atheists (*konfessionslos*) and who no longer wished to be recognized as Jews. I use "acculturation" for the wide spectrum of Jewish immersion in non-Jewish culture, from language to academic study to politics.

nation-state, a paradox that had first doomed this intelligentsia and then made them, in postnational Europe, the symbol of European internationalism.

Acculturation into non-Jewish European cultures in the aftermath of the *Haskalah* and emancipation created the modern Jewish intelligentsia. Until World War II, the hegemonic international culture of Central and East-Central Europe remained German. As Czech, Hungarian, and Polish nationalism arose, Jewish intellectuals increasingly identified with the locally predominant ethnic group and spoke its language, and in Eastern Europe, most also spoke Yiddish. Still, German remained the lingua franca. German acculturation varied among Central Europe's different regions, but in general, it extended wider and deeper than acculturation across the Russian border. In Russia, the intelligentsia thought of itself as a social class, distinguished by its education from the masses but dispossessed of political power, in an adversarial position toward the state and the Jewish leadership. The German acculturated intelligentsia set itself on a mission to "civilize" the Eastern Jews and felt more empowered and less alienated, as emancipation and acculturation made the march of enlightenment seem inevitable.[72]

Widespread German acculturation makes my inclusion of rabbis in the Jewish intelligentsia uncontroversial. The rabbinic networks provide venues for Jewish European history already in premodern times. The *responsa* literature – rabbis' correspondence on Jewish legal cases across and beyond Europe – is rich and remains an unexplored source for European historiography. In modern times, rabbis have addressed the same questions as the liberal intelligentsia – those emerging from Jewish emancipation and nationalism. In German-speaking Central Europe, from the mid-nineteenth century on, most were academically trained. Their omission so far from European intellectual history narrows ideologically the meaning of the European.

The spectrum of the Jewish intelligentsia covered in this book may be gleaned from several generations of the Popper family. Karl Popper's great-great maternal grandfather, Rabbi Akiva Eger (1761–1837), was a famous traditional German rabbi, a contemporary and father-in-law of Moses Sofer. His grandfather, Imperial Councilor (*Kaiserlicher Ratsherr*) Max Schiff (1829–1903), was an entrepreneur and a founding member of the Society of Friends of Music that built the Musikvereinsaal, home to the Vienna Philharmonic Orchestra. His father, Simon Popper (1864–

---

[72] Even in fin-de-siècle Vienna, where the intelligentsia felt dismayed by German antisemitism, imperial obtuseness, and growing Galician Jewish immigration resistant to liberal acculturation, the prevailing mood remained, *pace* Carl Schorske, optimistic and reform oriented.

1932), was an attorney, partner of Vienna's last liberal mayor, a philanthropist, chair of a Masonic lodge, collector of a major library, and author of a political satire. Karl himself, a philosopher, was the first bona fide intellectual in the Popper line, but his uncles and aunts included Walter Schiff (1866–1950), a professor of political economy and socialist reformer, as well as professional pianists and a medical doctor. His cousins included musicians, an engineer, and a physicist. Intellectuals directly engaged in the production and circulation of ideas – rabbis, writers, and scholars – will naturally receive greater attention in this book than professionals and philanthropists, but the distinctions are blurred. My conception of the intelligentsia is broad and inclusive, and network and discourse rather than intellectual production set the boundary.

The Jewish intelligentsia sought engagement in politics and culture as prospective or actual citizens. Even Jews averse to acculturation, like the Orthodox Rabbi Moses Sofer, found themselves reshaping Jewish life in response to emancipation. The intelligentsia coexisted with the nation-state, and depended for its survival on the nation-state's inability to drive the logic of nationalism to its limits. If integration were fully accomplished, the intelligentsia would not be recognizably Jewish. If ethnicity prevailed, the Jews would be pushed out. In fact, Jewish integration remained elusive. The nation-state could neither assimilate the Jews nor accommodate a Jewish culture. The Jewish intelligentsia existed precariously for a century and a half between integration and exclusion. Living the dream of integration in a national culture that could well spell their end, the Jewish intelligentsia were doomed when, on the contrary, the nation-state turned ethno-national in the interwar years and the European order collapsed. In a comic end to a tragic history, commemoration of the Jewish intelligentsia in recent decades has become part of the project of forming European identity.

Life between integration and exclusion contributed to the formation of an international German culture, the major exponents of which were Jews. German-acculturated Jewish intellectuals provided a major constituency for the legendary Central European networks of the fin-de-siècle and interwar years, but they were not alone. Nationalization and internationalization went hand in hand. A modernizing and globalizing Europe experienced, from the 1850s on, the growth of international organizations of every kind, from philanthropic (Red Cross) to professional (engineers) to religious to political (socialist internationals and pan-nationalist movements) to scientific and philosophical (Monists), all testifying to increased communication across national borders.[73] "From the expansion of

---

[73] Michael Geyer, "The Subject(s) of Europe," in *Conflicted Memories: Europeanizing Contemporary Histories*, ed. Konrad H. Jarausch and Thomas Lindenberger (New York:

'international' state and non-state organisations to the extension of trans-national sociability and economic entanglement," the triumph of nationalism and global colonial expansion issued in internationalism aiming, at one and the same time, to coordinate and arbitrate relations among the nation-states and advance particular nationalist claims.[74]

The Jewish networks were unique in that they all responded to ethnic exclusion, reflected solidarities of a Diaspora, and – the Zionists not excluded – sought to expand opportunities for Jewish integration. Many of the networks discussed in this book were not, however, exclusively Jewish.[75] Their non-Jewish members came from groups that did not easily find their place in the mainstream national cultures. They could be progressive Austrians and Germans who broke with antisemitism, socialists and communists organized in the International(s), or monarchists, aristocrats, and clerics who found it difficult to adjust to the nation-state after Austria-Hungary's dissolution. Glenda Sluga and Patricia Calvin have recently argued that "the overemphasis of the utopian dimensions of internationalism has masked and marginalized the (complex) practical and ideological significance of international institutions and laws," but the politics of Jewish internationalism, a product of marginality, had a decidedly utopian dimension, whether in its socialist, nationalist, or liberal cosmopolitan version.[76] Nationalism, internationalism, and cosmopolitanism represented the same political moment and shared a discursive universe, but the appeal of Jewish internationalism was grounded in nationalist rejection of the Jews.

Liberal Jews, committed to German national integration, were a mainstay of the Central European networks. With the rise of German antisemitism, they endeavored to retain enlightenment universalism and cultural definitions of *Deutschtum*. Socialists shared with liberals the

---

Berghahn Books, 2007), pp. 254–80; Wolfram Kaiser, "Transnational Mobilization and Cultural Representation: Political Transfer in an Age of Proto-Globalization, Democratization and Nationalism 1848–1914," *European Review of History* 12:2 (2005): 403–24; Abigail Green and Vincent Viaene, eds., *Religious Internationals in the Modern World* (Basingstoke, UK: Palgrave Macmillan, 2012).

[74] Glenda Sluga and Patricia Calvin, "Rethinking the History of Internationalism," in *Internationalisms: A Twentieth-Century History* (Cambridge: Cambridge University Press, 2017), pp. 3–14. Quotation is on pp. 4–5.

[75] Abigail Green, "Intervening in the Jewish Question, 1840–1878," in *Humanitarian Intervention: A History*, ed. Brendan Simms and D. J. B. Trim (Cambridge: Cambridge University Press, 2011), pp. 139–58, and "Religious Internationalisms," in *Internationalisms*, ed. Glenda Sluga and Patricia Calvin, pp. 15–37.

[76] Glenda Sluga and Patricia Calvin, "Rethinking the History of Internationalism," in *Internationalisms*, p. 8. I am grateful to Abigail Green for pointing out that my conflation of cosmopolitanism and internationalism runs against current historiography. I distinguish between the two but wish to retain the affinity of cosmopolitanism and Jewish internationalism, with the exceptions noted later in this section.

view that the Jews were not a nation and should assimilate, but made the resolution of the social question a precondition to the success of Jewish integration. The leadership of the Central and Eastern European Marxist parties included many Jewish intellectuals. They wagered that the creation of a classless society would reduce national animosities within and among nations, and that the proletariat's redemption would mean both humanity's salvation and authentic Jewish emancipation. Most internationalists regarded Jewish difference as a regrettable historical contingency and believed that the Jewish Question would find its solution in a new world order. Yet the Jewish "anti-cosmopolites" could tell the story of internationalization equally well. Orthodox German and Polish Jewry, in 1912 in Kattowitz, founded Agudat Yisrael, a world alliance of Torah-loyal Jews to combat assimilation and Zionism. The Zionist network extended from Central and Eastern Europe into Russia. Only the socialist network was larger.

Jewish cosmopolitanism did not escape nationalist antinomies. In the Austrian Empire, German-acculturated Jews were persuaded of the mission for German culture among the Slavs, and often supported the 1848 vision of a democratic Greater Germany, virtually a German *Mitteleuropa*. They may have recognized that Austria-Hungary resembled "the international order of humankind in miniature," but they saw no contradiction between the empire and a culturally defined German nationalism. German culture was cosmopolitan, liberal nationalism was emancipatory, and the empire was a vehicle for the spread of both. Yet just as imperial pluralism offered resistance to the aspirations of the German nationalists, so did it also to those of the German-Jewish cosmopolitans. Austrian-Jewish cosmopolitanism could not become outright German nationalist or it would be, like the Pan-Germans, anti-imperial. German-acculturated Jews had to recognize cultural and national Others. They did not give up on the German nation or become, like traditional Jews, whole-hearted imperial patriots, but Austrian pluralism forced them into supranational thinking that was missing elsewhere.

The best example of their supranational visions was the proposed socialist solution to Austria-Hungary's nationalist conflicts. Socialist leaders Karl Renner (1870–1950) and Otto Bauer (1881–1938) suggested federalizing the monarchy and granting individuals nonterritorial cultural autonomy based on their declared national affiliation.[77] This famed "personal national autonomy" did not reflect a celebration of pluralism:

[77] Synopticus [Karl Renner], *Staat und Nation: Staatsrechtliche Untersuchung über die möglichen Principien einer Lösung und die juristischen Voraussetzungen eines Nationalitäten-Gesetzes* (Vienna: Josef Dietl, 1899); Rudolf Springer [Karl Renner], *Der Kampf der Österreichischen Nationen um den Staat* (Leipzig: Franz Deuticke, 1902); Otto Bauer,

Renner and Bauer bemoaned Austria-Hungary's failure to build up democratic nationhood. Nonterritorial nationality was a response to the German Diaspora's predicament, and a counsel of despair in the face of the empire's territorial indivisibility and its unyielding pluralism, which was threatening to fracture the Socialist Party. Ironically, the Socialists' proposed solution to the German Question became, in the short run, a blueprint for Jewish Diaspora nationalism and Zionism and, in the long run, a blueprint for postnational European nationality: Subjective cultural affinity mattered most in determining national affiliation. Here as elsewhere, the challenges and promise of Austria-Hungary were precisely in its liminality – a cross between a traditional continental empire and a modern nation-state.

The continental empires' collapse in the aftermath of World War I, the Bolshevik Revolution, and the triumph of national self-determination reshaped the interwar international networks. Until the Great Purges of 1936–38 in the Soviet Union, the Third International and the Communist Party had many Jewish leaders who put their faith in Jewry's modernization and assimilation, and in world revolution. They had a counterpart in the Menshevik network, which collaborated with the German Social Democrats, in the Trotskyists and other anti-Stalinist socialists, and in networks of nonsocialist Russian exiles.[78] Moscow became the Mecca of communist internationalism and the fallen Jerusalem of Russian exiles.

Nonsocialist Central European networks went through equally radical transformation. To be sure, the Vienna Circle of philosophers carried on the tradition of fin-de-siècle progressivism, and in Vienna's and Prague's literary cafés, Jewish writers still pretended that the Austrian Empire never fell apart. Yet far more influential were new movements, such as *Paneuropa*, intent on creating a European order to supersede the nation-states. Conservative, mostly Catholic networks sought alternatives to the "liberal" nation-state. Internationalists ranged from communists to liberals to Catholic nationalists to pro-Nazi *Volksdeutsche* (ethnic Germans living beyond German borders), all disaffected from the European order, and offering competing schemes for a new Europe that only deepened

---

The Question of Nationalities and Social Democracy [1907], ed. Ephraim J. Nimni, trans. Joseph O'Donnell (Minneapolis: University of Minnesota Press, 2000).

[78] Warren Lerner, *Karl Radek: The Last Internationalist* (Stanford, CA: Stanford University Press, 1970); André Liebich, *From the Other Shore: Russian Social Democracy After 1921* (Cambridge, MA: Harvard University Press, 1997); Marc Raeff, *Russia Abroad: A Cultural History of Russian Emigration 1919–1939* (New York: Oxford University Press, 1990).

their opponents' anxiety, and their determination to transform the present order.

Several European networks, notably Paneuropa, had their headquarters in Vienna. The former imperial capital was the crossroads of Europe, yet also the capital of a nation-state that no one wanted: The Austrian Socialists and the Pan-Germans opted for German unification, the first grounded in civic nationalism, the latter in an ethnic one, while the Catholics dreamed of a Danubian federation. Both Jews and Austrians were Europe's quintessential "internationalists," formerly imperial peoples who could find no place in a Europe of nationalizing states. But others, like the ethnic Germans, were searching for a national home, too. The Jews were unique in having no territorial base, no defender, and no hope for a homeland in Europe.[79] The "Protocols of the Elders of Zion" made the stereotype of the Jewish internationalist global in the interwar years, and it never seemed more compelling. Opening the European Youth League convention in September 1942 in Vienna, Baldur von Schirach, putting an international face on the Nazi racial empire, took pride in Vienna's deporting the Jews, a contribution, he said, to European culture.

The murder of the Jews, the expulsion of the Germans from the Sudetenland and Eastern Europe, and the population transfers of the immediate postwar years, nowadays labeled "ethnic cleansing," turned postwar Europe into a mosaic of ethno-national states as it had never before been in history. The Cold War divided Europe, making a Central European culture impossible. Still, a remnant of the old Jewish intelligentsia survived for another generation. Rémigrés who either returned to Central Europe or chose to settle in Western Europe helped rebuild a new Western European and transatlantic culture.[80] The wave of student rebellions sweeping much of Western Europe and the United States in 1968 signaled the end of this culture. The 68ers' outright rejection of Cold War politics and their tense relationship with many émigrés made the break between the old and young intelligentsia evident. The émigrés had no successors. The old Jewish intelligentsia had reached its end.

Yet 1968 also spelled the beginning of a new European Jewish intelligentsia, and it appropriated the old intelligentsia's legacy. The émigrés were, directly and indirectly, the 68ers' teachers, and, paradoxically, they made 1968 possible by liberalizing postwar culture. The 68ers, in turn, catapulted the émigrés to the center of intellectual life and made them

---

[79] The Roma and Sinti peoples represented a close parallel.
[80] Marita Krauss, "Jewish Remigration: An Overview of an Emerging Discipline," *Leo Baeck Institute Yearbook* 49:1 (2004): 107–20.

spokespersons for Europe. The 68ers' internationalism, however different from émigré cosmopolitanism, relaxed national boundaries and advanced Jewish integration. Postnational Europe offered the young Jewish intelligentsia the integration that the nation-state had denied the old one. It also turned the old intelligentsia and its Central European networks into icons of a new European cosmopolitanism.

The new intelligentsia was (and still is) openly and often proudly Jewish, and even Zionist. In much of Europe, any suggestion that their Jewishness or Zionism is incompatible with national loyalty would, at this time, be considered unacceptable in mainstream politics and the academy. This is a revolutionary development, unlikely to continue for much longer. It reverses not only the modern drive toward assimilation but also two millennia of Jewish–Christian relations. In this world of normative Jewish Europeanness, assimilation makes no sense as a strategy for defusing antisemitism. Popper's denial of his Jewishness jars with contemporary Europe. Yet the urge to vindicate *ex post mortem* the old intelligentsia against Nazi racial persecution is such that historians hesitate to interrogate the émigrés' self-proclaimed identity.

Why do I insist that the cosmopolitan intelligentsia was "Jewish" if Popper and his like severed any tie to Jewish tradition? The intelligentsia's professions of self-identity must be consulted, but they cannot all be accepted. Popper grew up in an assimilated Jewish family and, from childhood to death, his closest friends were assimilated and highly acculturated Jews. Preponderantly Jewish networks were essential to his intellectual growth. In crucial historical moments, he shared the fate of traditional Jews: Antisemitism drove him into exile; emigration saved his life. He partook of a cosmopolitan discourse unique to the Jewish intelligentsia. He retained a special relationship to Judaism and Zionism: He was "always careful not to scorn religion with the exception of Judaism," and he condemned Zionism but felt responsible for it.[81] If this is not convoluted enough, in rebutting antisemites in the postwar years, Popper declared himself a Jew.[82]

---

[81] Malachi Haim Hacohen, "Dilemmas of Cosmopolitanism: Karl Popper, Jewish Identity and 'Central European Culture,'" *Journal of Modern History* 71:1 (1999): 105–49, and *Karl Popper*, pp. 67–69. The apt comment on Popper's scorn for Judaism belongs to Joseph Agassi, email to Arie Dubnov, May 20, 2013.

[82] Joseph Agassi, email to Malachi Hacohen, May 18, 2013: "It was in an informal casual gathering around a huge table [in the Alpbach Summer School in 1954], when two very respectable participants exchanged opinions half privately half publicly … with antisemitic overtones. It was clearly unpleasant but also clearly not requiring any response of anybody.... So it was surprising that Popper responded swiftly and emphatically and with tremendous dignity: He stood up and said, in German, in tone between the conversational and the declarative, 'I am a Jew.' And he sat down. Silence. I was in my twenties and a student of his and a fan of his and very proud of him."

"Collective identities," *pace* Popper, "are products of histories; and our engagement with them invokes capacities that are not under our control." "Once labels [such as 'Jew'] are applied to people, they have social and psychological effects."[83] Racialized citizenship limited the Jewish options, shaped the intelligentsia's projects, and determined their fate. "Assimilated Jew" is an ascribed identity, not a self-identification, but it captures well the social and psychological effects that shaped Popper's life and imagination. Speaking of the "Jewish intelligentsia," and including the assimilated Jews in it, I neither emulate "the Führer" nor deny cosmopolitanism. Rather, I use the dilemmas of national integration to explain Jewish internationalism. The modern nation-state and the anti-semites created a Europe that invoked Jewishness and set limits to cosmopolitanism in ways beyond Popper's or the historian's control. I am happy that in contemporary Europe, such limits no longer exist.

Jewish European History Today

We live in extraordinary times in Jewish history. The State of Israel and the North American Jewish Diaspora provide unprecedented opportunities for Jewish life: independent national life in Israel and integration into multiethnic societies in the United States and Canada. The two options represent an alternative both to the autonomous premodern community, the *Kehillah*, and to integration in the European nation-state. Europe is experimenting with a supranational government, and proponents of European identity speak of a shared Judeo-Christian legacy and lionize the old Jewish intelligentsia. The eternal outsiders have become, for a moment, the quintessential European.

Millennia-old markers have collapsed in recent decades. This book's last chapter recounts the collapse of the Jacob & Esau typology. In contemporary Israel, post-Zionists cultivate Esau, West Bank settlers speak of him as a Jew tragically rebuffed by Jacob, and a modern Orthodox rabbi proposes an alliance between Jacob & Esau against Ishmael.[84] In Europe, *Jakob der Lügner* (1969, Jacob the liar), by the East German–Jewish writer Jurek Becker, signaled a radical reevaluation of Jewish stereotypes: With his lie, Jacob emboldens the doomed Lodz ghetto residents, opening horizons of hope. The British Commonwealth's former chief Orthodox rabbi regularly sermonizes against idealizing Jacob, or rejecting Esau, or

---

[83] Kwame Anthony Appiah, "Liberalism, Individuality, and Identity," *Critical Inquiry*, 27 (Winter 2001): 326, and *In My Father's House: Africa in the Philosophy of Culture* (New York: Oxford University Press, 1992), p.178, respectively.

[84] Binyamin Lau, "Israel vs. Edom – Seventh Round" (in Hebrew), *Haaretz* (4 December 2009), www.haaretz.co.il/literature/1.1293204.

assuming that being "chosen" implies superiority.[85] The Nazis assigned to Germans of Jewish origin the generic names Israel (Jacob's second name) and Sarah to identify them unmistakably as Jews. Jacob and Sarah are nowadays among the most common names in the United States.

The collapse of traditional markers creates opportunities for Jewish European historiography, but they may be short-lived. Commemoration of the Holocaust and celebration of the Jewish intelligentsia were formative for European identity. The process had begun in the 1970s with the cultivation of the surviving émigrés and acquired momentum in the 1990s with the European Union. It has been reinforced by Vatican II and by the Protestant reevaluation of the church's antisemitic legacy. Catholics and Protestants recognize Judaism nowadays as a legitimate religion and expect Jews and Christians to coexist until the messianic time. The Holocaust's role in shaping European identity is diminishing, however. As Europe confronts renewed nationalist challenges, and integration of communities other than the Jews is foremost on the agenda, the moment of opportunity is passing. The task of Jewish European historiography is urgent.

Contemporary European rhetoric and policies toward the Muslim communities suggest that little has been learned from the European Jewish experience. Jewish emancipation revealed permanent tensions between the nation-state's ethnocultural diversity and its drive to nationalize culture. These tensions still effect European responses to Muslims. They may not be impossible to manage, but historically they issued in demands for impossible assimilation. Even civic nationalism presumed a measure of ethno-cultural uniformity. Historians have been slow to draw comparisons between European Jews and Muslims, and there is no Muslim parallel to Jewish European historiography. This book can only gesture toward a Muslim European history, but it provides a historiographical model.

The stakes in Jewish European history may be more European than Jewish: World Jewry's future is not in Europe. But for good and bad, Europe played the leading role in Jewish history for the entire second millennium. Jewish European history expands and loosens Europe's geographic and temporal boundaries. The Jewish Diaspora extends to North Africa and the Middle East and, in modern times, across the Atlantic. This book begins in the Ancient Near East, continues with the Roman and Muslim Mediterranean, and concludes with the State of Israel. The

---

[85] Jurek Becker, *Jacob the Liar*, trans. Leila Vennewitz (New York: Arcade Pub., 1996); Jonathan Sacks, "Chosenness and Its Discontents" (10 November 2007), http://www.rabbisacks.org/covenant-conversation-5768-toldot-chosenness-and-its-discontents/.

origins and telos of my European story are in part non-European. They reflect Europe's non-European making, the Europeanization of the world, and Europe's globalization. Where is Europe? Where the Jews are. Why Europe? Christendom formed in confrontation with the Jews and the Muslims, and provided Europe's original identity. Jacob & Esau and Isaac & Ishmael create an *histoire de la longue durée* of Jewish–Christian and Jewish–Muslim relations that relativizes European modernity and puts the Israeli–Arab conflict and European–Muslim relations in a millennia-long Jewish European perspective.

The case for Europe made, I do wish to offer this Jewish European history as a historiographical model for Jewish history. Rabbinic literature can inform every field of Jewish history and, in turn, rabbinic sources must be embedded in contexts and cultures extending beyond Jewish life. Historicization would amount to "Europeanization." The provenance of yeshivah-trained scholars needs to expand and include other academics and, at the same time, become "European": Jerusalem historian Jacob Katz (1904–1998), educated in Hungarian and German yeshivot and at the University of Frankfurt, may still serve as a model. Neither historicization nor Europeanization conforms to the rabbis' own wishes: Moses Sofer made it a point that Jews were always exiles. But Sofer, who wanted to be a Jew and not a European, was no more in control of his cultural resources than was Popper, who wished to be a European but not a Jew.[86] In historiography, we may complete emancipation on Jewish terms – terms that would enable Sofer and Popper to be, at one and the same time, Jews and Europeans.

These are not the terms prevailing in Jewish European historiography. Historians vindicate *ex post calamitatis* the Jewish intelligentsia's European character, but they leave the rabbis' Europeanness in question by ignoring them. Jewish European history must include the full spectrum of Jewish life and reflect its pluralism. Europeanness need not connote cosmopolitanism. Traditional Jews and Christians inhabited the same territory as the cosmopolitan intelligentsia, and interacted daily, but their cultures crosscut rather than overlapped, and they need to be documented in their divergence and conflict. Historians, especially medievalists, have explored the shared urbanity of Christians and Jews over

---

[86] Describing the advent of Jewish Studies in the U.S. academy, Geoffrey Hartmann expresses the unease lest perusing the Bible as literature infringes on its coherence and sacrality: "Preface" to his *The Third Pillar: Essays in Jewish Studies* (Philadelphia: University of Pennsylvania Press, 2011). Traditional Jews may experience similar discomfort about the historicization of rabbinic literature, but Hartmann's project of legitimizing Jewish Studies as an academic field will only be completed when rabbinic literature crosses over disciplines and traditional Jewish culture becomes academic mainstream.

the last two decades.[87] *Jacob & Esau* does not tell a story of shared urbanity but, rather, one of hostility, polemics, and pogroms. Even in the age of emancipation, the polarity of Jacob & Esau held on, and Esau was vilified. Typology represents the end limit of Jewish European history: It tells a history of a shared culture, but one that divides rather than binds its protagonists, a shared but divergent history.

Highlighting Jewish Diaspora and Europeanness, this book partakes in a recent historiography that has curbed the Zionist narrative in Jewish history, but it parts decisively with several new trends. The pervasiveness of Jacob & Esau discourse throughout the Diaspora in all ages counters recent challenges to the existence of a Jewish people and the possibility of Jewish history. As Leonard Krieger, the previous generation's greatest intellectual historian, suggested, ideas are history's best connectors: Where discourse is continuous, so is history.[88]

Moreover, in their zeal to deprive triumphal Zionism of the moral legitimation provided by a history of Jewish powerlessness, recent historians have belittled the precariousness of Diaspora existence. Quoting Salo Baron's critique of the lachrymose conception of Jewish history has now become de rigueur for any emergent historian.[89] Yet Baron himself regarded emancipation as a Faustian bargain with the nation-state and was anxious about Jewry's fate in the interwar ethno-nationalizing states. As David Engel argues, to deploy Baron to advance liberal diasporic narratives against Zionist ones is to place him in a debate he never entered.[90] In Baron's spirit, this book relativizes modernity and dispenses with "the lachrymose theory of pre-Revolutionary woe."[91] In the tradition of both Baron and Simon Dubnov, this book highlights the

---

[87] Jonathan Elukin, *Living Together/Living Apart: Rethinking Jewish-Christian Relations in the Middle Ages* (Princeton, NJ: Princeton University Press, 2007) (but see also David Nirenberg's furious critique: *The New Republic* [13 February 2008]: 46–50); Julie Mell, "Geteilte Urbanität: Die befestigte Stadt in der deutsch-jüdischen Kunst in der Zeit vor der Entstehung des Ghettos," *Wiener Jahrbuch für Jüdische Geschichte Kultur und Museumswesen* 5 (2001): 25–41; *Jews and Christians in Twelfth-Century Europe*, ed. Michael A. Signer and John Van Engen (Notre Dame, IN: University of Notre Dame Press, 2001), esp. the essays by Jeremy Cohen and Ivan Marcus); Edith Wenzel, ed., "Grenzen und Grenzüberschreitungen: Kulturelle Kontakte zwischen Juden und Christen im Mittelalter," *Aschkenas* 14:1 (2004): 1–7.

[88] Malachi Haim Hacohen, "Leonard Krieger: Historicization and Political Engagement in Intellectual History," *History and Theory* 35:1 (1996): 80–130.

[89] "Ghetto and Emancipation: Shall We Revise the Traditional View?" *Menorah Journal* 14 (1928): 515–26. Baron's critique targeted Heinrich Graetz's intellectual history, a "history of suffering and scholarship (*Leidens-und-gelehrtengeschichte*)." He pleaded for historicization of the Middle Ages and modernity and for attention to social and economic life.

[90] Engel, "Crisis and Lachrymosity: On Salo Baron, Neobaronianism, and the Study of Modern European Jewish History," *Jewish History* 20 (2006): 243–64.

[91] Baron, "Ghetto and Emancipation," 526. See also his " Nationalism and Intolerance," *Menorah Journal*, 16 (1929): 503–14; 17 (1929): 148–58.

protections and opportunities extended to Jews in pluralist imperial orders, especially in Austria-Hungary, as an alternative to national integration. Going beyond the polemics on Zionism, it makes it possible for pre-Holocaust and pre-Israel historiography, grounded in the *longue durée*, to speak to the Jewish future.

Modern Jewish historiography, child of emancipation and, in Baron's case, Austrian and American Jewish life, has "corrected" Jewish memory by balancing the tragedy of exile with Diaspora's normalcy. Baron, who lost his parents and a sister in the Holocaust, upheld the "joy mixed with sorrow" view of Jewish history to the end of his life. But *Jacob & Esau* testifies to the potency of memories of destruction and exile, to perpetual Jewish yearning for redemption and vengeance, and, above all, to a life of eternal waiting. The typology records not the joys of life but the mourning and persecution that were imprinted on Jewish memory. The traditional Jew's daily, annual, and life cycles commemorate Jerusalem's destruction and the calamities that have befallen the Jewish people: "One shall plaster his home ... and leave out a small bit as a remembrance of Jerusalem; one may prepare all the needs of a meal, and leave off a little bit as a remembrance of Jerusalem."[92]

Jewish acceptance in the Western Hemisphere in recent decades has contributed to historiographical euphoria, expressed in the celebration of Jews as successful moneymakers, modernizers, and cosmopolitans.[93] Triumphalist historiography has replaced a lachrymose one, paying little heed to the fragility of acceptance and to the risk in affirming antisemitic stereotypes. Like Yuri Slezkine, I highlight Jewish cosmopolitanism, but unlike him, I view the Jews less as agents leading change and more as a minority whose options are limited by ethno-nationalism.[94] Internationalism is a product of nationalization, not Jewish first but European and global; and Jewish cosmopolitanism is born in despair over national integration. Like the Patriarch Jacob, the Jews, pushed out of the nation and forced into wandering and exile, show ingenuity in adjusting. Contemporary historians may take instruction from Jacob's cautious appraisal of his situation. The rabbis did. This book journeys with him and them.

The dissolution of the Jacob & Esau typology in recent decades left narratives incompatible with improved Jewish–Christian relations either

---

[92] *BT* Baba Batra 60B: "All who mourn over Jerusalem in this world will be joyful with her in the world to come."

[93] For a critique of the literature celebrating (or castigating) the Jews as moneylenders and modernizers, see Julie Mell, *The Myth of the Medieval Jewish Moneylender*, 2 vols. (New York: Palgrave Macmillan, 2017).

[94] Yuri Slezkine, *The Jewish Century* (Princeton, NJ: Princeton University Press, 2004).

to wither away or be transformed into new stories. Rabbinic discourse has always included alternative storylines, and for the traditional Jew, tradition's ambiguity offers a promising opportunity. One subdued narrative emerging from Midrash suggests a path that Jacob did not take. On his way to meeting Esau, so tells *Genesis Rabbah* (80:5), Jacob hid his daughter Dinah in a coffin, lest Esau rest eyes on her and propose a marriage. He missed an opportunity to reform Esau, a brother, and was punished when a foreigner, the prince of Shekhem, forcibly took Dinah. Another midrash goes further (*BT* Sanhedrin 89b). The Patriarchs refused conversion to the Edomite princess Timna, and, wishing to join their tribe, she became the concubine of Esau's son Elifaz and the mother of Amaleq, Israel's future persecutor. Rejection of wayward brothers and benevolent foreigners, refusal to join together in a restorative marriage that would advance amity and resolve conflict, intimates Midrash, is the source of tragedy in Jewish history.

Curiously, the rabbinic homilies on missed opportunities for expansive familial bonds evoke a central motif in Austrian history. The motto of Habsburg policy since the fifteenth century was *Bella gerant alii, tu felix Austria nube*, "Let others wage wars: you, fortunate Austria, marry!" Imperial growth was to occur through dynastic marriage rather than conquest. The Habsburgs, to be sure, waged devastating wars, and after they had expropriated, burned, and expelled Vienna's Jews in 1420–21, Austria was known among Jews as "the land of blood."[95] Yet the motto suggests something of the qualities that made late imperial Austria a better home for the Jews: the retention of premodern imperial institutions in the age of nationalism, protection of pluralism and communal bonds, and a conjuncture of tradition and modernity.

I am tempted to see the late imperial Austrian conjuncture as presaging the postmodern convergence of tradition and modernity represented in this book. In my book on Karl Popper, I endeavored to show how, with critical rationalism, modernity could respond to the postmodern challenge from within. It can, but it requires institutional support to make the response socially viable and an intellectual tradition to make it existentially fulfilling. The exploration of institutional and intellectual resources should not remain confined to the modern. A correct appreciation of modernity can only emerge from exploring premodern possibilities, and this is especially true for Jewish European history.

---

[95] See Maharil's responsa (c. 1360–1427): Jacob ben Moses Moellin, *Sheelot u-Teshuvot Maharil* (in Hebrew) (Cracow: Fischer & Deutscher, 1881): 95, 140, 157, 181; Samuel Krauss, *Die Wiener Geserah vom Jahre 1421* (Vienna: Braumüller, 1920).

Exploration of the premodern cannot mean, of course, going back. Fully historicized rabbinic Judaism can only emerge in the postmodern age, when the truth claims of modern narratives have been so radically relativized that a comparable relativization of tradition no longer does it damage. European Jewishness can only be envisaged in the postmodern age, when the bounds of Europeanness and Judaism have been so relaxed as to become expansive and permeable. Beyond the pursuit of Europeanness on behalf of traditional Jews, the Jewish historian may have a broader mission to the Europeans: to set an example of a dignified postmodernity. The irresponsible, iconoclastic trashing of progressive narratives familiar from the previous century's final decades still expressed modern bravado and hubris, and offered Europeans no attractive alternative. A Jewish European history illuminated by rabbinic sources may display the gentle search for protective traditions that can enrich modern life, sustain communal attachment, and provide comfort that no modern therapy can. Perhaps this is what the rabbis anticipated when they presaged that the day will come when the princes of Judah will teach the Torah in Roman circuses.

2   Rabbinic Jacob & Esau, Pagan Rome, and the Christian Empire

"Remember, O Lord, against the Edomites the day Jerusalem fell, how they said, 'Lay it bare, lay it bare, down to its foundations!'" (Psalm 137:7). The Edom typology arose from a national disaster: the destruction of Jerusalem and the First Temple by the Babylonians in 586 BCE, and the exile of the Judahite people, who, in exile, became the Jews. Consciousness of this catastrophe shaped biblical narratives. Esau became the Edomites' ancestor, and redactors edited the Jacob & Esau stories in Genesis to convey the character and role of the protagonists in the *Hurban* (destruction), Jews and Edomites, and to express Jewish hopes for restoration. Each of the typology's future transformations would reflect a tragedy: the Roman destruction of the Second Temple in 70 CE and the repression of the Jewish rebellion in 135, the Rhineland pogroms of 1096, the 1492 expulsion from Spain, and the Holocaust. Refusing to concede defeat or accept doom, the Edom typology reflected recurring national failures and conveyed Jewish powerlessness, an awareness that Jews could do little to abate the catastrophe. The typology called upon God for vengeance, and drew an eschatological vision of redemption, punishment of the enemies, and national restoration.

The Edom typology's utopianism and messianism remained relatively contained during the Second Temple period (c. 516 BCE–70 CE). To be sure, Psalm 137 charged the Edomites with abetting the destruction of Jerusalem. Apocalyptic prophecies turned the Edomites into a *topos*, a typological enemy whose power and significance far exceeded that of historical Edom: Edom was but a small kingdom during the First Temple period, and a vulnerable province, Idumaea, to the south of Persian and Hellenistic Judea, during the Second. Still, the topos had only a limited reach: The historical Idumaeans still embodied Edom, and eventually Judea subdued Idumaea and incorporated its people. The pseudepigraphic Book of the Jubilees expanded the biblical narrative to account for these events.[1] Jubilees depicted a final war of Jacob & Esau: Jacob and his sons overcame Esau and his descendants, one nation triumphed over another, and the descendants of the elder son (Esau) became servants of the younger (Jacob) "to these days" (38:14). Redeemers may not have climbed Mt. Zion to proclaim a messianic age, but biblical prophecy was partially fulfilled. Edom was gone.

By identifying Edom with the Roman Empire and redirecting the biblical prophecies against Edom to Rome, the rabbis, beginning in the second century CE, globalized the struggle against Edom and virtually assured its failure. Visions of the messianic age were tied to the triumph over Rome. Not only would the empire collapse and Jerusalem be rebuilt, but the rule of Torah would also become universal. Nation (the Jews) would triumph over empire (Rome). In the aftermath of the second *Hurban*, the rabbis' hostility toward imperial rule knew no bounds. Admittedly, rabbinic literature, Talmud and *Midrash* alike, contains traces of more positive views of Rome and more hopeful evaluations of Roman–Jewish relations, but the overwhelming picture of Rome emerging is one of an evil empire (מלכות הרשעה), responsible for the Second Temple's destruction, the Land's devastation, and Israel's exile and servitude.[2] In the messianic age, imperial rule would vanish, and Judah's princes would teach the Torah in Roman circuses.[3] Jews would await this messianic redemption their entire history, and waiting will be seen as shaping Judaism's character.

Remarkably, the rabbis' counterimperial vision depicted the Romans as wayward brothers: Jews and Romans were descendants of Jacob and Esau, respectively, and they represented universal principles that had been in conflict from time immemorial. In Midrash, the rabbis rewrote the biblical story to reflect the struggle with Rome. Esau rebelled against the Torah and conspired to inherit the world. He was a pagan Roman, an apostate – a countermodel of the rabbinic Jew. The rabbis' interest in

---

[1] Pseudepigraphic books are noncanonical Jewish religious works from the third century BCE to the first century CE, which were incorporated into none of the Christian canons. For a full reference, see the section on Biblical Edom.

[2] *Loci classici* for the benevolent view of Rome, good Roman–Jewish relations, and appreciation for orderly rule: *BT* Shabbat 33b, Gittin 56a–b, Avodah Zarah 10b, *Mishnah*, Avot 3:2, respectively. For the evil empire, see the section on Tannaitic Edom.

[3] *BT* Megilah 6a. Judah's governors are cast more as rabbis and less as statesmen. Alexei Sivertsev, *Judaism and Imperial Ideology in Late Antiquity* (New York: Cambridge University Press, 2011), suggests that rabbinic visions of a messianic restoration of the Davidic kingdom were a response to Byzantine imperial eschatology, which presented Christian Rome as the New Jerusalem. If they "envisioned the Jews as the legitimate heirs of the Roman imperial legacy" (p. 13), their vision was counterimperial: *Pace* Sivertsev, future Jerusalem was *not* modeled on Rome. Nothing shows it better than the vision of Judean princes teaching the Torah in Roman circuses.

world politics may have been limited to its impact on rabbinic Jews, but their vision was global. Reading Rome into the Bible, the Edom typology posited Jewish history as universal history.

Rabbinic universalism became historical reality in a roundabout way. Pagan Rome disregarded Jewish history, but Christian Rome took it seriously. Christian Rome's ongoing relationship with the Jews determined the history of the Edom typology and shaped Jewish European history. Interpreting the brotherhood of Jacob & Esau as one of Christians and Jews, Christian polemics against the rabbis made the typology part of European history. If pagan Rome made Jewish victory unlikely, the Christian empire made it impossible. The Talmud occasionally fantasized about the Persians bringing down the Roman Empire and enabling, once again, a reconstruction of the Jerusalem Temple.[4] In 363 CE, Emperor Julian the Apostate ordered the Temple rebuilt, and in the wake of the Persian conquest of Jerusalem in 614, the Jews set up an altar on the Temple Mount: A limited Jewish restoration was not altogether impossible.[5] When the Christian empire, and with it Edom, became European Christendom, all hope was lost. Rome fell several times to its enemies, but Edom as the rabbis imagined it lived on. Jewish European history became a fight, which the Jews could never win – unless they became European.

From History to Eschatology: Biblical Edom

"Two nations are in your womb, and two peoples shall diverge from your body; one people shall be mightier than the other, and the elder shall serve the younger" (Genesis 25:23). Thus begins the biblical story of Jacob and Esau: God tells Rebecca, wife of Isaac, future mother of Jacob and Esau, that the reason for her difficult pregnancy is the struggle of two nations in her belly. When Rebecca gives birth to the twins, the second, Jacob, comes out holding onto the heel (עקב in Hebrew) of the first, Esau, as if wishing to pull Esau back and come out first, hence the name יעקב. Esau is born covered with a plume of red hair (hairy, שעיר), hence his name עשו. As they grow up, Esau becomes a hunter and Jacob an indoor man (tent dweller, יושב אהלים). Isaac loves Esau because he has a taste for game, and Rebecca loves Jacob. One day Esau returns tired and hungry from the

---

[4] *BT* Yoma 10a; *Eichah (Lamentation) Rabbah* (Vilnius and Grodno, 1829): 1:41 (henceforth, *Eichah Rabbah*); *Eichah Rabbah*, ed. Shlomo Buber (Vilnius: Romm, 1899): 1:1 (henceforth, *Eichah Rabbah*, ed. Buber).

[5] Julian hoped to reverse Christian advances. Building was interrupted, and the emperor's untimely death brought it to naught. The Persian conquest was short-lived. The Byzantines were back in 629, and the Arabs conquered Jerusalem in 638. See chapter 3.

field to find Jacob cooking a lentil potage. Feed me, he demands. Sell me your birthright, answers Jacob. I may die any day; what is my birthright good for, says Esau, and the deal is concluded under oath. Curtain down: Biblical scene one ends here.

Their father, Isaac, must not have known: At the beginning of scene two (Genesis 27), preparing for his approaching death and wishing to confer upon Esau the customary blessing of the firstborn, Isaac sends him to hunt for game in order to inspire the blessing. Rebecca overhears him, calls Jacob, and orders him to bring her two choice lambs, which she cooks to Isaac's liking. Overcoming Jacob's reluctance, she dresses him in Esau's clothes, puts the lambs' skins on his smooth hands so that they become as hairy as Esau's, and has him serve Isaac the food. Isaac senses that something is amiss: "The voice is Jacob's voice, yet the hands are Esau's hands" (Genesis 27:22). All the same, he proceeds with the blessing, granting Jacob the heavenly dew and the fat of the earth, abundance of grain and wine – and lordship over his brother. No sooner has Jacob left than Esau enters, asking for his blessing. Isaac recognizes that he was duped, but Esau's bitter cry and tears notwithstanding, he can do no more than grant him a lesser blessing: Esau will have to serve Jacob, but when he revolts, he will overthrow Jacob's yoke (27:40).

Esau hates Jacob for stealing his blessing and conspires to kill him. Rebecca learns of his designs and convinces Isaac to send Jacob to her relatives in Ḥaran (in today's southeastern Turkey, on the Syrian border) so that he can marry within the family: Esau's marriage to native Canaanite women was a source of aggravation to both parents. Scene two ends with Isaac calling for Jacob, commanding him to take a wife from their family abroad, and giving him the blessing of Abraham. Jacob leaves for Ḥaran, where he marries Leah and Rachel (and their two maidservants) and has twelve sons and one daughter with them over two decades. He grows in wealth and matures in character, showing resourcefulness in overcoming the treachery of his uncle and host, Laban the Aramean.

In scene three, Jacob, returning to his homeland, hopes to reconcile with his brother and sends him messengers. He hears that Esau is coming toward him with four hundred men. He is frightened and prays to the Lord: "Deliver me, I pray, from the hand of my brother, from the hand of Esau, for I fear him, lest he come and smite me, the mother with the children" (Genesis 32:11). He sends elaborate gifts to appease Esau but also prepares for war. The night before meeting Esau, Jacob, having crossed the Jabbok River, finds himself alone, and he wrestles with a mysterious stranger – whose identity has preoccupied Jewish and Christian interpreters for millennia – until the dawn breaks. Unable to overcome Jacob, the stranger wrenches his hip and strains it, but then, asking Jacob to let him off, he blesses Jacob and changes his name to Israel, "for you have striven [שרית] with God and with men, and have prevailed" (32:28).

The day after, the two brothers meet. Esau falls on Jacob's shoulders, embraces and kisses him, and both weep. Esau offers to escort Jacob to Seir, Esau's land, but Jacob declines and they each go their own way, Jacob arriving safely – "shalem, שלם" (whole; also meaning perfect) – to the city of Shekhem, and later to his father Isaac in Hebron. When Isaac dies, Esau and Jacob together bury him. The Genesis narrative ends in reconciliation.

The biblical narrative shows the redactive marks of divergent stories, dating from different periods, being made into a coherent whole.[6] The story of Jacob stealing the blessings may have been the ancient core of the Jacob & Esau story cycle, and it may have started as a legend about the conflict between hunters and shepherds. Esau's nonendogamous marriages and Isaac's exhortation to Jacob to marry within the tribe, in contrast, may be late Priestly additions, dating to the early Second Temple period, perhaps the fifth century BCE, a time when fights over intermarriage raged in the postexilic community in the Jewish province of Persian Judea. Recent scholarship has tended to push the redaction of the Jacob & Esau story into the exilic (597–538 BCE) and postexilic periods and to interrogate the association between Esau and historical Edom.

Esau's association with Mount Seir (שעיר) in the northern Negev (נגב), south of Judea, appears less tenuous than the one between Esau and Edom: Seir (hairy) is etymologically and visually related to Esau; the site appears twice in the narrative of Jacob and Esau's final meeting; and Israel's encounter with Esau's descendants on their way to the Promised Land from Egypt speaks of "our brothers, sons of Esau who dwell in Seir" (Deuteronomy 2:1–8). Edom, in contrast, seems precariously grafted onto Esau through the red (אדם) color of the lentil potage that Esau coveted and of his hair, אדמני (Genesis 25: 30, 25, respectively). The redactors, it appears, made an effort to link Esau of Seir with Edom.

---

[6] Scholarly conventions about the Bible's formation have been in transition in recent decades. A broad scholarly coalition (labeled "Minimalists" by critics) defers the composition of the Pentateuch (the five books of Moses, the Torah) into the Hellenistic period, challenges the previously regnant view of sixth-century exilic redaction, and questions the importance of the Babylonian Exile as a formative event for Judaism. See Marc Brettler, "The Copenhagen School: The Historiographical Issues," *AJS Review* 27:1 (2003), 1–22; David Vandehooft, ed., "In Conversation with Oded Lipschits, *The Fall and Rise of Jerusalem* (Winona Lake, IN: Eisenbrauns, 2005)," *Journal of Hebrew Scriptures* 7:2 (2007): 1–49, www.jhsonline.org/Articles/article_63.pdf. My account is inclined toward the more conservative approach.

We know exceedingly little about the Edomites, a western Semitic people who may have settled in the southern plains of Transjordan as early as the fourteenth century BCE, down from the Dead Sea to the Bay of Eilat (or Aqaba). Most scholars no longer lend credence to biblical accounts in Samuel, Kings, and Chronicles, which describe the Edomites as coming under the control of David's United Kingdom in the tenth century BCE, claiming their independence in a rebellion against the southern Israelite Kingdom of Judah in the middle of the ninth, and remaining in a protracted conflict with Judah until the Assyrian Empire weakened Judah and imposed a new order on the Middle East in the final third of the eighth century BCE.[7] Rather, the emergence of Israel's Transjordanian neighboring kingdoms, Moab, Ammon, and Edom – all with languages close to Hebrew and the first two with a religious cult the Bible regards as competitive – is presently dated to the ninth and eighth centuries BCE, with Edom quite possibly the last state to form. Living off of copper mining and trade on their mostly nonarable land, the Edomites became, in the late eighth century, a thriving vassal state under the Assyrians and later, in the late seventh century, under the Babylonians. They lost their autonomy and suffered destruction, the extent and source of which is still under debate, in the middle of the sixth century BCE, probably at the hands of the Babylonian King Nabonidus in 553 BCE – that is, a few decades after the Babylonians had destroyed the First Temple in Jerusalem.[8]

Of great significance to the Edomites' enduring relationship with Judea was their migration across the Wâdi Aravah into the Negev and southern Judah. The migration began in the late eighth century BCE, grew strong in the seventh, and reached its peak in the first half of the sixth century. Whether the result of pressure from nomadic tribes, especially the Nabataeans, or of the lure of the commercial route passing from the Mediterranean to Arabia through the northern Negev, the migration brought Arabic-Edomite (or Idumaean) culture into close contact with the Jews. The newly settled territory, just south of Judea, became, in the

---

[7] Biblical archaeologist John Bartlett, the previous generation's leading Edom scholar, considers the biblical narrative historically valuable: *Edom and the Edomites* (Sheffield, UK: JSOT Press, 1989). Even if the historicity of the biblical narrative is rejected, it may explain, by way of internal reference, Isaac's blessing to Esau (Genesis 27:40), "but when you grow restless you shall break his yoke from your neck," as an allusion to the (mid-ninth-century) rebellion against the Judean King Jehoram that overthrew David's yoke (2 Kings 8:20–22).

[8] Piotr Bienkowski, *"New Evidence on Edom in the Neo-Babylonian and Persian Periods,"* in *The Land That I Will Show You: Essays on the History and Archaeology of the Ancient Near East in Honor of J. Maxwell Miller*, ed. J. Andrew Dearman and M. Patrick Graham (Sheffield, UK: Sheffield Academic Press, 2001), pp. 198–213.

Hellenistic period (333–63 BCE), officially a province, Idumaea, the northern boundary of which reached deep into original Judean territory, halfway between Hebron and Jerusalem.[9]

Why was Edom singled out from all neighbors to be Israel's brother, and when did Esau become father of Edom? John Bartlett suggests that this had happened already in the "early monarchic period" because of similarities between Edomite and Israeli religious cults.[10] In a more recent, and provocative, interpretation, Bert Dicou suggests that Edom did not become a brother until early in the sixth century BCE, and that the Edomites' migration, which made them Judah's southern neighbors, residents of "Esau's land," Seir, was the primary reason. He argues for radical late-exilic redaction of the Jacob–Esau narrative in Genesis. To realize one of the projects of Genesis and define the Jewish nation's territory against its neighbors, the redactors foregrounded the struggle between Israel and Edom.[11]

Biblical attitudes toward the Edomites seemed ambivalent from the start. "You shall not abhor an Edomite – he is your brother," instructs Deuteronomy (23:8), recognizing third-generation progenies of marriages with Edomites as Israelites, while excluding Moabites and Ammonites. The Israelites are warned against attacking "your brothers, Esau's descendants" on their way from Egypt to Israel, "because I have given Mount Seir to Esau as his inheritance" (Deuteronomy 2:4–5). Shortly thereafter (2:29), we learn that Esau's descendants permitted the Israelites to pass through their country and provided food and water in exchange for money. But brotherhood could turn to animus. The same story, as told in Numbers (20:14–21), presents a belligerent Edom refusing passage to the Israelites and threatening war.[12] The Jacob & Esau narrative in Genesis likewise conveys an ambivalent message: Edom is a wild and impetuous brother, living by the bow and sword, yet one who is capable of generosity and forgiveness and may reconcile.

[9] Aryeh Kasher, *Jews, Idumaeans, and Ancient Arabs: Relations of the Jews in Erez-Israel with the Nations of the Frontier and the Desert during the Hellenistic and Roman Era (332 BCE–70 CE)* (Tübingen: J. C. B. Mohr [Paul Siebeck], 1988); John Lindsay, "Edomite Westward Expansion: The Biblical Evidence," *Ancient Near Eastern Studies* 36 (1999): 48–89.

[10] *Edom and the Edomites*, pp. 175–84.

[11] Bert Dicou, *Edom, Israel's Brother and Antagonist: The Role of Edom in Biblical Prophecy and Story* (Sheffield, UK: JSOT Press, 1994).

[12] The traditional commentators are at pains to reconcile the conflicting accounts. See Rashi, Rashbam, and Ibn Ezra (the first two French, the last a Sephardi medieval commentator) on Deuteronomy 2:29 (and Rashbam also on 2:4), in *Miqraot Gedolot ha-Keter*, ed. Menaḥem Kohen (Ramat-Gan: Bar-Ilan University Press, 1992–2013). For a modern effort: David A. Glatt-Gilad, "The Re-Interpretation of the Edomite-Israelite Encounter in Deuteronomy II," *Vetus Testamentum* 47:4 (1997): 441–55.

All ambivalence seems to disappear after Jerusalem's destruction by the Babylonians in 586 BCE: The Bible turns downright hostile to Edom. The Prophets charge the Edomites with collaboration with the Babylonians and allege that they rejoiced at Jerusalem's fall. We may never know what role the Idumaeans actually played in Judah's destruction, but they benefited from it, as their expansion into Judah accelerated and they inhabited the territory, the population of which went, in part, into exile. Other neighbors abetted the Babylonians and also benefited from Judah's destruction, but the Prophets singled out Edom, their "brotherhood" now counting against them. "Because of the violence against your brother Jacob, you will be covered with shame," chastised Obadiah; "On the day you stood aloof while strangers carried off his wealth and foreigners entered his gates and cast lots for Jerusalem, you were like one of them" (Obadiah 1:10–11). Isaiah (34:1–17), Jeremiah (49:7–22), and Ezekiel (25:12–14, 35:1–14) professed destruction and annihilation for Edom.[13]

The tenuous link between Esau and the Edomites turned out to have momentous significance. It gave the Jacob & Esau story in Genesis an apocalyptic meaning. Throughout the Jewish Diaspora, lamentation rituals (Eichah 4:21–22) commemorating Jerusalem's destruction helped turn the Edomites into a typological enemy of Israel, a leitmotif that will never again vanish from Jewish history.[14] Esau and Edom became a symbol for Israel's enemies, their punishment a messianic expectation, their demise an apocalyptic event integral to Judah's restoration: "And saviors shall go up on Mount Zion to judge the mountain of Esau, and the Kingdom will be the Lord's" (Obadiah 1:21).

---

[13] See also Amos (1:11–12, 9:12), Ezekiel (36:5), Isaiah (63:1–6), Joel (4:19), Eichah (4: 21–22), Malachi (1:1–4), and Psalm (60:1–12; 137:7: "Remember, O Lord, against the sons of Edom the day Jerusalem fell, who said, 'raze it, raze it, to its very foundation'"). Bert Dicou, *Edom, Israel's Brother and Antagonist*, traces how Edom became the typological enemy. He views Genesis and the Prophets as providing alternative late-exilic narratives, one suggesting a peaceful division of the Land among Israel and its neighbors, the other the annihilation of Israel's enemies (pp. 202–4). The expansion of Edom prophecies in later centuries may or may not reflect growing Jewish–Idumaean tensions, as Edom had already become a typological enemy, symbol of all hostile foreign nations. For Isaiah 63:1–6, "Who is this coming from Edom, from Bozrah, with his garments stained crimson? . . . I [the Lord] trampled the nations in my anger . . . their blood spattered . . . and I stained all my clothing," Edom and Bozrah were no longer geographical locations, else the prophet would have found them inhabited mostly by Nabataeans.

[14] *Piyut* scholar Eden Hacohen questions the idea of a pre-Rome typological Edom (conversation with author, summer 2009). He points out that postexilic biblical texts as Haggai, Zechariah, Ezra, Neḥemiah, and the Chronicles show no trace of hostility to Edom: Malachi (1:2–4) appears to be the exception. They view other neighbors as threats to Judah's welfare.

Jerusalem's fall also reshaped the Patriarch Jacob. Ancient Israelite ambivalence toward the cunning patriarch disappeared. In Genesis, Laban shortchanges Jacob on wages and exchanges Leah, his older daughter, for the younger one, Rachel, as a bride for Jacob. Jacob's own sons deceive him about Joseph's fate. Genesis implied that Laban's treachery and the brothers' deceit were in retribution for Jacob's trickery in obtaining Esau's birthright and blessings. The Israelite prophet Hosea (12:3–5) suggested that the Israelites' treachery reflected their ancestor Jacob's character deficiencies: He cheated his brother and, instead of trusting in God – the angel promised Jacob that God will shortly meet him (בית אל ימצאנו ושם ידבר עמנו) – extorted his blessing and his new name, Israel, from the angel.[15] Jeremiah (9:3) intimated that the Judahites' dishonesty mimicked Jacob's: "Every brother is a deceiver" (literally, will completely supplant, *aqev yaaqov*; כי כל אח עקב יעקב).[16] The Prophets' remonstrations with Israel and Judah had also extended, in the First Temple period, to their ancestor, Jacob.

The critical attitude toward the patriarch did not survive Esau's transformation into a national enemy. Consolation prophecies assured the house of Jacob, Israel, of a future restoration of their covenant with God. These prophecies reveal no ambivalence toward Jacob: "For the Lord will have compassion on Jacob and will again choose Israel, and will set them in their own land" (Isaiah 14:1). "Jacob will take root, Israel will blossom and sprout" (Isaiah 27:6). "Many nations will come and say, 'Come and let us go up to the mountain of the Lord and to the house of the God of Jacob, that He may teach us about His ways and that we may walk in His paths'" (Micah 4:2). To be sure, Jacob's transformation was not as radical as Esau's: "Perfect Jacob" would only emerge with the rabbis. Deceptive Jacob, however, was gone. "'Was not Esau Jacob's

---

[15] Medieval interpreters, who did their best to create a picture of perfect Patriarchs, could not let the typology of crooked Jacob and corrupt Israel stand. Rashi (Hosea 12:5; Genesis 32:29) used *Bereshit Rabba* 78:2 to explain the two divergent reports for the name Israel and how Jacob got it: the angel's blessing (Genesis 32:29) and revelation in Beth El (Genesis 35:10). The Sepharadi commentators interpreted Hosea as creating contrasting models of Jacob and the people of Israel: the patriarch positive, the people negative. Meira Polliack, "Medieval Oriental Exegesis on the Character of Jacob in Hosea 12," in *Jewish Studies at the Turn of the Twentieth Century*, ed. Judit Targarona Borrás and Ángel Sáenz-Badillos, 2 vols. (Leiden, NL: Brill, 1999): 1: 177–87.

[16] Yair Zakovitch, *Jacob: Unexpected Patriarch* (New Haven, CT: Yale University Press, 2012), pp. 109–10, suggests that the Prophets' use of an alternative etymology for Israel – *yashar* (upright) – censured the Israelites for deceit and testified to the strength of the repressed "crooked Jacob" tradition (Michah 2:7; Isaiah 48:1). He also points (pp. 133–34) to a single trace (Genesis 48:22) of Jacob as a fighting patriarch, conqueror of the Land.

brother?' declares the Lord. 'Yet I have loved Jacob; but Esau I have hated'" (Malachi 1:2).

The relationship between historical and typological Edom became ever more complex during the Persian Achaemenid (538–333 BCE) and Hellenistic periods. Jewish–Idumaean interaction increased. The Apocrypha suggest increasing hostility between Jews and Idumaeans in the late Hellenistic period, but nowhere do we hear an outcry against fraternizing or intermarrying with the southern neighbors.[17] The Aramaic-speaking Idumaeans, no longer inhabiting their original realm, seemed to have absorbed Arab, Jewish, and Hellenistic influences. They were a people whose hybrid cultural identity seemed ever fluid, whereas theology turned them into an intractable enemy.

When Judea rebelled against the Seleucid (Hellenistic-Syrian) Empire in 167 BCE, and reclaimed first its autonomy, then, in 140 BCE, its independence, the Jewish leader, Judas Maccabeus (יהודה המכבי), temporarily seized Idumaean territory and apparently destroyed the cities of Hebron and Marissa (Maresha). The war made Esau again a concrete historical enemy. The pseudepigraphic Book of the Jubilees (37–38) rewrote the biblical Jacob & Esau story so that it ended not with reconciliation but with war, death, and the enslavement of Esau's descendants. Jubilees recounted that Esau and his sons violated the peace, and attacked Jacob and his family. Jacob killed Esau, and his sons seized Esau's territory and reduced his descendants to slavery: "And, up to this time, Esau's descendants have not removed the yoke imposed on them by Jacob's twelve sons."[18]

---

[17] A caveat: Shaye Cohen alerted me (December 2015) that most modern scholars emend the last word of Ezra 9:1, protesting against intermarriage, to read Edomi, instead of Emori.

[18] Jubilees 38:14: *The Old Testament Pseudepigrapha*, ed. James Charlesworth, 2 vols. (Garden City, NY: Doubleday, 1985), 2: 128; Cana Werman, *The Book of Jubilees: Introduction, Translation, and Interpretation* (in Hebrew) (Jerusalem: Yad Izhak ben-Zvi Press, 2015), esp. pp. 467–77. Composition date for Jubilees is controversial, and Werman (pp. 44–48) delays it to the late second century BCE, until after the Idumaeans' incorporation in Judea. Werman sees Esau becoming already in *Jubilees* a *topos* for foreigners in general and not just for Edom. Testaments of the Twelve Patriarchs, a later apocryphal book, repeats the story in brief: Judah's Testament 9:1–8, in *Old Testament Pseudepigrapha*, 1: 797. Rabbinic Midrash has Judah's or Dan's son Ḥushim killing Esau (*Sifre* Deuteronomy, ve-zot ha-berakhah 7 and *BT* Sotah 13a, respectively), but the context is Esau's endeavor to prevent Jacob's burial and not war. Esau wished to be buried, instead of Jacob, next to his ancestors in the Cave of the Patriarchs in Hebron. Other Apocrypha convey intense hostility to the Idumaeans: The deuterocanonical I Esdras 4:45 and the pseudepigraphic I Enoch 89:66 blame the Edomites for burning the First Temple, and the deuterocanonical Ecclesiasticus (Ben-Sira) 50:25–26 professes hatred of "the nation of Seir": *Old Testament Pseudepigrapha*, 1: 68 (I Enoch); *Outside of the Bible: Ancient Jewish Writings Related to Scripture*, ed.

Forty years later, in 125 BCE, the Jewish King John Hyrcanus, of the Hasmonaean dynasty, completed the conquest of Idumaea and converted the population to Judaism, expelling those who refused circumcision.[19] Idumaean integration in Judea followed. Less than a century later, in 37 BCE, Herod the Great, son of an Idumaean court official, Antipater, and a Nabataean mother, became King of the Jews under Roman auspices. In 6 CE, the Romans made Idumaea part of the province of Judea. We last hear of the Idumaeans during the Great Jewish Revolt against the Romans (66–70 CE), when their troops joined the Jewish Zealots in defending Jerusalem against the Romans: An Idumaean legion defended Judean independence to the last. After the Second Temple's destruction in 70 CE, the Idumaean remnant must have assimilated among the Jews. The "Idumaean Question" was solved in a manner in which the Jewish Question refused to be: conversion and assimilation.[20] In rabbinic times, historical Edom was gone.

Louis Feldman, James Kugel, and Lawrence Schiffman, 3 vols. (Philadelphia: Jewish Publication Society, 2013): 1: 172 (I Esdras), 3: 2347 (Wisdom of Ben Sira). Marc Brettler directed me to this recent edition.

[19] The Roman-Jewish historian Josephus remains our main literary source for Jewish–Idumaean relations – Flavius Josephus, *Antiquitates Judaicae* (in English and Greek), trans. H. St. J. Thackeray, 9 vols. (Cambridge, MA: Harvard University Press, 1930–98): esp. 5: 13:257 – but there are other short reports of the Idumaeans' incorporation in Judea, all discussed in Shaye J. D. Cohen, *The Beginnings of Jewishness: Boundaries, Varieties, Uncertainties* (Berkeley: University of California Press, 1999), pp. 109–39. Cohen insists that the Idumaeans' incorporation was political – they became Judean citizens – rather than religious, but he also shows the contemporaneous emergence of a concept of religious conversion. A Jewish state religion was emerging.

[20] Jewish historians have shown great unease about the Idumaeans' forced conversion. German-Jewish historian Heinrich Graetz (1817–1891), who inveighed against German pressure on the Jews to assimilate, denounced the Hasmonaeans: "In John Hyrcan Judaism evinced religious intolerance for the first time; but it learned soon enough … what a fatal error it is" (*Popular History of the Jews*, 5 vols. [New York: Hebrew Publishing Company, 1919]: 1: 424–25). Other historians sought to minimize the coercion, suggesting that the Idumaeans had already been inclined to assimilate, or ignored the episode as best they could. Joseph Klausner, *Yehudah ve-Romi* (Judah and Rome) (Tel Aviv: Umah u-Moledet, 1946), p. 32, speculated that the Idumaeans had forced indigenous Jews to assimilate; Hyrcanus "returned" them to Judaism. Aryeh Kasher, *Jews, Idumaeans, and Ancient Arabs*, insists that the conversion was voluntary and the integration successful. Shaye Cohen, *The Beginnings of Jewishness*, pp. 109–39, believes that, at least for the rural Idumaeans, the incorporation in Judea was neither forceful – they had affinities with Judean anti-Hellenism – nor religious. He conjectures that they had already practiced circumcision, and they kept their ethnic God and culture. They were neither converted nor assimilated. The Hellenized Idumaean urbanites were the only ones to protest and leave.

The Evil Empire: Tannaitic Edom

The disappearance of historical Edom set the stage for the main drama: Rome as Edom.[21] The first cluster of *midrashim* explicitly identifying Rome with Edom is attributed to the rabbinical generation of the Bar-Kokhba rebellion against the Romans (132–35 CE). "A star (*kokhav* כוכב) shall come out of Jacob, and a scepter shall rise out of Israel," says Balaam's oracle in Numbers (24:17–18), "and Edom shall be dispossessed, and Seir, his enemies, shall also be dispossessed, and Israel shall do valiantly." Rabbi Aqiva explicated the oracle as referring to Shimon bar Kosiba, the rebellion's military leader (hence Bar-Kokhba, son of star, fulfilling the Numbers oracle): "When rabbi Aqiva beheld Bar Kozba, he exclaimed: 'This one is the King Messiah (מלך המשיח).'"[22] Bar-Kokhba was to fulfill biblical prophecy against Edom by liberating Judea from the Roman Empire.

Scholars have become cautious about the historicity of homilies attributed to particular rabbis in noncontemporaneous sources, and the one on Rabbi Aqiva recognizing Bar-Kokhba as the Messiah exemplifies scholarly doubt.[23] Gerson Cohen and Mireille Hadas-Lebel associate the rise of the Edom-Rome typology specifically with Aqiva and his school.[24]

---

[21] Friedrich Avemarie, "Esaus Hände, Jakobs Stimme: Edom als Sinnbild Roms in der frühen rabbinischen Literatur," in *Die Heiden: Juden, Christen und das Problem des Fremden*, ed. Reinhard Feldmeier und Ulrich Heckel (Tübingen: J.C.B. Mohr, 1994), p. 179, argues eloquently for the disappearance of historical Edom as a precondition for the emergence of the Rome typology. Following Leopold Zunz (*Zur Geschichte und Literatur* [Berlin: Veit und Comp, 1845], p. 845), many scholars, until the mid-twentieth century, surmised that resentment toward Herod, "an Idumaean slave" ruling under Roman auspices, was the origin of the Rome-Edom typology, but there is no evidence for it. However, Josephus's benevolent portrayal of Jacob & Esau's brotherhood in *Jewish Antiquities* 1:257–346 led Louis Feldman to propose, unconventionally, that the identification of Esau with Rome may predate the Roman–Jewish wars: "Josephus' Portrait of Jacob," *Jewish Quarterly Review* 79:2/3 (1988–89): 101–51.

[22] *PT* Taanit 24a. Compare *Eichah Rabbah* 2:4; *Eichah Rabbah*, ed. Buber 2:9.

[23] Peter Schäfer suggests that we read Rabbi Aqiva out of this Midrash altogether (but does not question its contemporaneity with the rebellion): *The Bar Kokhba War Reconsidered: New Perspectives on the Second Jewish Revolt Against Rome*, ed. Peter Schäfer (Tübingen: J.C.B. Mohr, 2003), pp. 2–5. On the problem of rabbinic attribution, see Marc Bregman, "Pseudepigraphy in Rabbinic literature," in *Pseudepigraphic Perspectives*, ed. Esther Chazon and Michael Stone (Leiden: Brill, 1999), pp. 27–47.

[24] Gerson Cohen, "Esau as Symbol in Early Medieval Thought," in *Medieval and Renaissance Studies*, ed. Alexander Altmann (Cambridge, MA: Harvard University Press, 1967), esp. pp. 22–23; Mireille Hadas-Lebel's *Jerusalem Against Rome*, trans. Robyn Fréchet (Leuven, Belgium: Peeters, 2006), pp. 496–511. Rabbinic traditions on Aqiva, especially on his martyrology, have been recently subjected to critical scrutiny. Saul Lieberman shows how Jewish martyrology became embellished in the third century in response to the Christian one: Saul Lieberman, "The Martyrs of Caesarea," *Annuaire de l'Institut de philology et d'histoire orientales et slaves* 7 (1939–40): 395–446. The late *Midrash Mishle* (9B) shows Aqiva dying peacefully in prison. But whatever position one

Jacob Neusner, in contrast, regards the rabbinic Edom typology as Amoraic and delays its emergence to the fourth century.[25] He suggests that the typology emerged in the aftermath of the Roman Empire's Christianization, and the rabbinic identification of Esau with Rome responded to Christianity's claim to Jacob's heritage. I shall address later Christianity's role, or its absence, but the Tannaitic evidence for the typology is significant. The conjecture that a failed messianic rebellion triggered a typological transformation, the identification of the Roman Empire with the old enemy, Edom, remains attractive. This transformation set the typology for almost two millennia of Jewish history. This section tracks its formation in Tannaitic sources in the century subsequent to the Bar-Kokhba rebellion.

Bar-Kokhba did not dispossess "Edom"; instead, the Romans suppressed his rebellion, devastated Judea, and imposed draconian restrictions on Jewish practice. An eschatology explaining the catastrophe, and promising redemption and revenge, became imperative for both supporters and detractors of the rebellion. The Edom-Rome typology provided it. "The voice is Jacob's voice but the hands are Esau's hands," says Genesis (27:22). "Jacob's voice," explicates the Palestinian Talmud, "cries out about what Esau's hands did to him in Beitar," the last fortress city to fall to the Romans.[26] "And the hands are Esau's hands," adds the

---

takes on Aqiva's martyrology does not impinge on the Bar-Kokhba rebellion as the trigger for Edom-Rome.

[25] The Tannaim were the rabbinic sages whose views were recorded in the *Mishnah*, 70–220 CE. The Amoraim were the legal scholars who followed the Tannaim, 220–500 CE. The Palestinian and Babylonian Talmuds assembled Amoraic discussions. Neusner discerns a *Gestalt* change between the Tannaitic *Tosefta* (*Mishna* supplements), which he finds indifferent to history, and the eschatology of the Amoraic Midrash, *Bereshit* (Genesis) *Rabba* and *Va-yiqra* (Leviticus) *Rabbah* (turn of the fifth century CE): "From Enemy to Sibling: Rome and Israel in the First Century of Western Civilization," in *Neusner on Judaism*, 3 vols. (Aldershot, UK: Ashgate, 2004–5): 1: 435–63. Neusner's historicization of Midrash is vital, but the evidence for Tannaitic Edom-Rome seems decisive to me. A comparison of a Tannaitic Midrash, as *Sifre*, with Amoraic Midrash would seem more appropriate than a comparison of the *Tosefta* with Midrash.

[26] *PT* Taanit 24a continues: "Rabbi Yoḥanan said: [Jacob's] voice [cries out about] Hadrian the Emperor killing eighty thousand myriads in Beitar." *PT* attributes the midrash to rabbi Yehudah bar Ilai (Aqiva's student), who relates it in the name of his (unknown) teacher, Barukh. *Bereshit Rabba* 65:21 attributes it to Yehudah bar Elai, who says it in his own name. *Eichah Rabbah*, ed. Buber 2:9 attributes it to Rabbi (Yehudah ha-Nasi; Judah the Patriarch); *Eichah Rabbah* 2:4 has only Rabbi Yoḥanan; *BT* Gittin 57b relates it anonymously. Schäfer may insist that this homily, quoting in some sources Rabbi and Rabbi Yoḥanan, is late Tannaitic or early Amoraic, and may excise Barukh and Yehudah bar Ilai, as he excised Aqiva and Shimon bar Yoḥai in the Bar-Kokhba homily. But Harry Sysling, *Teḥiyyat Ha-Metim* (Tübingen: J.C.B. Mohr, 1996): pp. 106–14, persuasively argues for Aqiva and Yehudah bar Ilai. Tannaitic tradition on Esau's hands as connoting murder (if not in the Beitar context) seems old. See *Sifre* on Deuteronomy 33:2 in this section.

Babylonian Talmud; "this refers to the evil empire that destroyed our temple, and burnt down our sanctuary, and exiled us from our land."[27] But the evil empire's destructive power, the rabbis emphasized, did not mean that God broke his Covenant with Israel. "Wherever Israel went into exile," says the Tannaitic Midrash *Mekhilta*, "the Divine presence (*Shekhinah*) went with them: to Egypt . . . Babylonia . . . Elam [Persia] . . . [and] Edom. . . . And, when they shall return, the Divine presence (as if) will return with them."[28] The Persian–Roman wars gave rise to periodic speculation about when the time will come: "Rabbi Joshua ben Levi said in the name of Rabbi: Rome is destined to succumb to Persia."[29] Visions of Rome's end were many. On the side of vengeful apocalyptic prophecies, the Babylonian Talmud also tells of the day when "the governors of Judah will teach the Torah publicly in the theaters and circuses that were in Edom."[30]

The Romans had no historical or ethnic affiliation with the Edomites, and Rome was thousands of miles away from Idumaea. A three-century-old Jewish tradition associated Rome with Kittim (Genesis 10:4), the people inhabiting the islands of the Mediterranean, descendants of Yefet (Japheth) and his son Yavan (the Hebrew name for Greece, יון), not with Edom.[31] Moreover, Edom had typological competition. As Jewish tradition commemorated the destruction of the First and the Second Temples together, the Babylonians, who had destroyed the First Temple, became, in the generation after 70 CE, an emblem for Rome. Unlike Edom, Babylon was an empire. In apocrypha of the turn of the first century CE, Babylon was subject to apocalyptic prophecies of revenge and doom.[32] The Christian vision of the "whore of Babylon,"

---

[27] Gittin 57b.

[28] *Mechilta d'Rabbi Ismael*, ed. and introduction by S. Horovitz and I. A. Rabin (Jerusalem: Bamberger & Wahrmann, 1960): bo 14 (henceforth, *Mekhilta*). Compare *Midrash Sifre* (Jerusalem: Mosad Ha-Rav Kook, 1948): Bamidbar (Numbers), be-haalotkha 26 and masei 3, and *PT* Taanit 3a. *Mekhilta* and *Sifre* attribute the midrash to Rabbi Aqiva, and the *PT* attributes a similar one to his contemporary Rabbi Shimon bar Yoḥai.

[29] *BT* Yoma 10a continues: "As it is said (Jeremiah 49:20): 'Therefore hear the plan that the Lord has made against Edom. . . . Surely the least of the flocks shall drag them away' [the Persians are the flocks]." Compare *BT* Sanhedrin 98b. For the sighting of a Persian horse in Palestine as presaging the Messiah (attributed to Shimon bar Yoḥai): *Eichah Rabbah*, ed. Buber 1:43; *Eichah Rabbah* 1:1; *Shir Hashirim Rabbah* 8:13 (*Sefer Midrash Rabbah*, 2 vols. [Vilnius: Romm, 1884], henceforth, *Shir Hashirim Rabbah*).

[30] Megilah 6a. This midrash is attributed to Rabbi Yosi bar Ḥanina (late third-century Palestine).

[31] Daniel's "ships of Kittim" (11:30), especially in the Septuagint (Greek) translation, the Qumran sect's writings (Dead Sea scrolls), such as *Pesher Habakuk*, and the *Targumim* (the Bible's Aramaic translations), all designated Kittim as Rome: Mireille Hadas-Lebel, *Jerusalem Against Rome*, pp. 23–26.

[32] *Old Testament Pseudepigrapha*, 1: 623–25, 644 (pseudepigraphic II Baruch 10:1–3, 11: 1–2, 67:7); 1: 528–29 (deuterocanonical IV Ezra [II Esdras] 3:1–2, 28–31); 1: 396–97

emerging from the Book of Revelation (17–18) and persisting for millennia, demonstrated the potential of an alternative model to Edom.[33] How could Edom become Rome, Esau's hands become Caesar's?

Bar-Kokhba, appearing as the messiah prophesied by biblical oracles to dispossess Edom, represented the turning point from Babylon to Edom. The correlation between Roman symbols – the eagle and boar – and biblical and apocryphal prophecies about Edom may have facilitated the transition, as did the similar Hebrew spelling of the names, אדום and רומא, אדומי and רומי (Edomite and Roman).[34] But most crucially, Edom proved irresistible because it was already a typological enemy associated with the destruction of the First Temple, a symbol for all of Israel's foes, the subject of emotionally charged chiliastic prophecies. Edom made the Roman–Jewish struggle the center of a universal history in ways that Babylon could not. It joined biblical narrative and contemporary events to portray an eternal struggle between Jacob and Esau, God's people and the universal empire. Within two to three generations – at most a century – the impossible happened: Edom became synonymous with Rome.

One can trace the emerging typology in the Apocrypha, Tannaitic and Amoraic Midrashim, the Palestinian and Babylonian *Talmudim*, and the *Targumim* (the Bible's Aramaic translations). The apocryphal IV Ezra (II Esdras), composed about 100 CE, reinterpreted the apocalypse of the biblical Book of Daniel to make Rome the last of the Four Empires dominating the world before the coming rule of the holy.[35] Viewing Rome as the Fourth Empire was not unusual, but IV Ezra also suggested,

---

(pseudepigraphic Sibylline Oracles 5:143, 155–61); *Outside the Bible*, 2: 1610–12 (IV Ezra 3:1–2, 28–31).

[33] Revelation 17:1–18, 18:1–24: *The New Oxford Annotated Bible with the Apocrypha* (New York: Oxford University Press, 1977).

[34] Jeremiah 49:16: "'Though you build your nest as high as the eagle's, from there I will bring you down,' declares the Lord"; I Enoch 89:66: "the wild boars [Edom] ... burned the tower and destroyed the house"; Jubilees 37:24: "Jacob saw that [Esau] was wickedly disposed towards him and ... had come springing like the wild boar": *Old Testament Pseudepigrapha*, 1: 68, 2: 127, respectively. If the tradition that the Edomites burned the First Temple was widespread, as M. D. Herr, "Edom," *Encyclopedia Judaica* (Jerusalem: Ketter, 1971): 6:379 suggests, it must have reinforced the Edom-Rome typology. *PT* Taanit 3a: "In Rabbi Meir's book, they found written: 'The oracle concerning Dumah (דומה)' [means] 'the oracle concerning Rome (רומי)' [and continuing] 'one is calling me from Seir' (Isaiah 21:11)." *Pesikta de-Rav Kahana* (fifth-century Palestinian Midrash), ed. Bernard Mandelbaum, 2 vols. (New York: JTS, 1962), 1: 7:12: "He who punished the first [the Egyptians] will punish the latter [Edom-Rome]: ... Just as in Egypt He killed the big one [the firstborn child], so also in Edom, 'the wild oxen (ראמים) will come down with them' (Isaiah 34:7). Rabbi Meir said: 'The Romans (רומיים) will come down with them.'" Of course, these homilies may represent only ex post facto justification for the typology.

[35] IV Ezra 12:10–12, *Old Testament Pseudepigrapha*, 1: 550.

opaquely, that the present age of Esau will be followed imminently by Jacob's rule.[36] The book however, made no connection between Esau and Rome: Elsewhere in IV Ezra, Babylon represented Rome. Tannaitic Midrash developed, in the second century CE, a rabbinic vision of the Four Empires (ארבע מלכויות) that anticipated Rome's fall.[37] It is replete with Edom-Rome allusions, but they are rarely explicit.[38] *Sifre* on Deuteronomy 33:2, a series of homilies on "the Lord came from Sinai, and dawned on them from Seir," may be the single incontrovertibly Tannaitic Midrash to openly identify Esau (Seir) with Rome. These *Sifre* homilies brought together major components of the emergent Edom-Rome typology and may reflect its state in biblical exegesis toward the end of the Tannaitic period. They deserve a closer look.

Sifre relates that God gave the Torah to Israel "not in one but in four languages. 'Dawned on them from Seir' [means that the Lord spoke to them] in Rome's language." (Rome and Esau are thereby joined.) God revealed Himself in Sinai to all nations but chose to give the Torah to Israel alone because they represented the first perfect people ever. The first two patriarchs' lineage was still tainted with other nations' ancestors: Abraham begot Ishmael, and from Isaac came forth "the pollution of Esau and all of Edom's chiefs." But Jacob's lineage, the twelve tribes of Israel, was without blemish; hence Genesis 25:27 says: "and Jacob was a perfect man (איש תם)." No other nation partakes in God's Covenant with Israel. The nations first offer assimilation to Israel and are mystified by the refusal and the Jewish martyrs. Then, when they find out about Israel's special relationship with God, they wish to join, too, but Israel tells them: "I am my beloved's and my beloved is mine" (Song of Solomon 6:3). The nations had missed their chance when they declined the Torah.

---

[36] IV Ezra 6:8–10, *Old Testament Pseudepigrapha*, 1: 534.

[37] *Mekhilta* be-shalakh 1 and yitro-ba-chodesh 9. *Mekhilta* intimated Rome rather than mentioned it explicitly. On the Four Empires in rabbinic literature, see Rivka Raviv, "The Shaping of Daniel's Four Empires Prophecies in Rabbinic Literature" (in Hebrew), *JSIJ* 5 (2006): 1–20, www.biu.ac.il/JS/JSIJ/5-2006/Raviv.pdf.

[38] E.g., *Mekhilta* be-shalakh-shira 2 on Exodus 15:1: סוס ורכבו: "When the day comes and the Lord will exact vengeance from the the different empires, he will exact it first from their rulers, as it is said: ... 'behold, [my sword] will descend in judgment upon Edom' (Isaiah 34:5)"; *Sifre* naso 40 on Numbers 6:24 (*Sifre de-ve Rav*, ed. Ḥayim Shaul Horovits [Jerusalem: Sifre Varman, 1966–69]): וישמרך [The Lord shall keep you]: "Keep for you the end [of days]. As he says: 'The oracle concerning Dumah. Someone calls to me from Seir [Esau's land]: Watchman, what is left of the night [before the dawn of redemption]?' (Isaiah 21:1)"; *Sifre* haazinu 27 on Deuteronomy 32:42: מדם חלל ושביה: "[The Lord will have] 'a great slaughter in the Land of Edom' (Isaiah 34:6) ... for what they did to the slain [and captive] of my people." See also references to the Four Empires in *Mekhilta* in my previous note.

When God offered the Torah, He first approached Esau's descendants. They refused the Torah on account of the prohibition against murder and exclaimed: "Lord of the universe, the very essence of [our] ancestor [Esau] is murder, for it is said: 'the hands are Esau's hands,' and [moreover] his father [Isaac] reassured him: 'By your sword you shall live' [Genesis 27:40]." At the end of days, God will exact vengeance from Esau's descendants, and will shake the whole world just as he did when he gave the Torah, "as it is said: 'When you, Lord, went out from Seir, when you marched from the land of Edom, the earth shook, the heavens poured' [Judges 5:]." The messianic age was at the gate. Genesis 25:26 says: "'Afterward his brother came out with his hand holding Esau's heel, so his name was called Jacob.' The Eternal One promised [Israel] that no nation will come in between them," and Jacob's rule will follow immediately upon Esau's demise.[39] Just as God revealed Himself when He first redeemed Israel from Egypt and gave them the Torah in Sinai, so he will reveal Himself in the final battle for the world (גוג ומגוג) and in the messianic age.

The relative coherence of this cluster of midrashim reflects the *Sifre* redactors' global vision of Israel and the nations, as well as their eschatology. They pulled together homilies previously not associated with Rome, such as the ones about the nations' refusal of the Torah and Jacob's pure lineage, and used them to elucidate Edom-Rome's place in history and the Sinai Covenant's significance for the confrontation with Rome.[40] Their stark vision of Esau-Rome is unusual for Tannaitic discourse. While Esau, Edom, and Rome each incurred rabbinic animus, stretches

---

[39] It is interesting, to note that this midrash corresponds to IV Ezra 4:8–10; II Esdras 6: 8–10, and the marginal glosses to *Targum Neofiti*: C. T. R. Hayward, "A Portrait of the Wicked Esau in the Targum of Codex Neofiti 1," in *The Aramaic Bible: Targums in Their Historical Context*, ed. D. R. G. Beattie and M. J. McNamara (Sheffield, UK: JSOT Press, 1994), pp. 297–98.

[40] For Edom's rejection of the Torah free of association to Rome, see *Mekhilta* on Exodus 20:2: אנכי ה' אלקיך; *Targum Pseudo-Jonathan* on Deuteronomy 33:2 (*Targum Pseudo-Jonathan of the Pentateuch: Text and Concordance*, ed. E. G. Clarke [Hoboken, NJ: Ktav Pub. House, 1984], henceforth, *Pseudo-Jonathan*, possibly the story's oldest version: No reason is given for Edom's rejection of the Torah. Esau may not yet have been associated with murder: Joseph Heinemann, *Agadot ve-Toldotehen* [Jerusalem: Keter, 1974], pp. 156–62). For Jacob's pure genealogy, see *Sifre* on Deuteronomy 32:9: כי חלק ה' עמו; *Va-yiqra Rabbah* 36:5 (*Midrash Va-yiqra Rabbah*, ed. Mordechai Margaliot, 5 vols. [Jerusalem: Ministry of Education, 1953–60], henceforth, *Va-yiqra Rabbah*). Israel Yuval, *Two Nations in Your Womb*, pp. 16–18, thinks that *Sifre* on Jacob's pure genealogy represented anti-Christian polemics ואין גורסים כן. Steven Fradde, *From Tradition to Commentary* (Binghamton, NY: SUNY Press, 1991), pp. 25–46, closely analyzes the *Sifre* cluster on Deuteronomy 33:2 and likewise notes the redactors' use of intrabiblical interpretation to extend Sinai's meaning over history and the redrafting of *Mekhilta* homilies to shape an eschatology that responds to historical exigencies. My thanks to Yedida Eisenstat for this last reference.

of Tannaitic Midrash on Esau, and even on Edom, seem free of Rome in a way inconceivable for later Amoraic Midrash.[41] Certain homilies, such as those in *Mekhilta* about Esau living by the sword, virtually cry out for Roman association, and the association is absent, just as it is absent in the *Mishnah*, *Tosefta*, *Sifra* (halakhic Midrash on Leviticus), and the Babylonian and early Palestinian *Targumim*.[42] *Mekhilta* intimates Rome as the Fourth Empire, rather than spells it out, and even in *Sifre*, Rome is explicitly mentioned only as "the language of Seir." Fear of censorship and persecution cannot alone explain this reticence and tentativeness. Rather, refocusing Midrash traditions on Rome was a century-long process. Violent, rebellious Esau had probably been a Midrash figure before Edom became Rome: He was a murderer and a fratricide who had been barred from the genealogy, the territory, and the heritage of Israel.[43] The second-century rabbis embellished existing Esau and Edom traditions and affixed them onto Rome, first loosely and then firmly.

The Edom-Rome typology became paradigmatic in rabbinic discourse in the Amoraic period, and the Amoraim projected it back to Rabbi Aqiva and his disciples and created a unitary vision of Midrash, centering on the Roman Esau. Significantly, in *Sifre*, typological Edom still retains association with historical Edom: The homilies highlight Seir, Edom's territory. That said, the fundamentals of the typology are all present in *Sifre*, and its origins seem to me incontrovertibly Tannaitic. By the mid-third century CE, at the latest, the typology was in place. Esau and his descendants became Roman, distinguished, above all, by their proclivity to wield the sword, undeterred by the universal law prohibiting murder.[44] Edom had migrated from Seir to Rome.

---

[41] Carol Bakhos, "Figuring (out) Esau: The Rabbis and Their Others," *Journal of Jewish Studies* 58:2 (2007): 250–62, points out that even in later Midrash, Esau may represent the Other with no particular reference to Rome. Edom, in contrast, became virtually synonymous with Rome.

[42] Missing Rome: *Mekhilta* be-shalaḥ 2 on Exodus 14:10: וייראו מאד: Israel's art of prayer (Jacob's voice) against Edom's profession of the sword (Esau's hands); yitro-ba-ḥodesh on Exodus 20:2: אנכי ה' אלקיך: Esau lives by the sword, hence his descendants reject the Torah. The Babylonian *Targum Onqelos* *(The Bible in Aramaic,* ed. Alexander Sperber, 5 vols. [Leiden: Brill, 1959]: 1, henceforth *Targum Onqelos)*, identifies Rome with Kittim (Numbers 24:24), and C. T. R. Hayward, "A Portrait of the Wicked Esau," pp. 291–309, points out the absence of Edom-Rome from the Palestinian *Targum Neofiti.*

[43] C .T. R. Hayward tracks a tradition associating Esau with Cain already in the Hellenistic Jewish philosopher Philo (20 BCE–50 CE), and retained in the early Palestinian *Targumim* as *Neofiti:* "A Portrait of the Wicked Esau," pp. 303–9.

[44] *Sifre* ve-zot ha-berakha 2: "'I will exact vengeance in anger and wrath upon the nations that have not obeyed me' (Micah 5:15) and could not keep even the seven Noahide laws, which they discarded and gave to Israel."

Rabbinic Jacob and Pagan Esau

Roman Esau became central in rabbinic discourse just as rabbinic Judaism arose to hegemony, becoming normative Judaism. The Amoraim received from the Tannaim a diffused Esau discourse, casting a negative but incomplete and, at points, faint Esau figure, and they unified the discourse by drawing Esau's portrait as the ultimate rabbinic Other. They attributed to Esau every Roman crime, as well as transgressions of their other opponents, past and present. Esau had already been a murderer and a robber; now he also became an adulterer and a rapist, and, above all, an apostate who worshipped idols and denied the afterlife and the resurrection of the dead: "That wicked [Esau] committed five sins on the day [he sold his birthright]. He raped a betrothed maiden, he committed a murder, he denied God, he denied the resurrection of the dead, and he spurned the birthright."[45] The rabbis rewrote the biblical story in Midrash. Their Jacob & Esau reflected less the biblical narrative and more their fears and hopes for the future of Judaism. Esau became the antithesis of the rabbinic Jew.

Rabbinic Jacob and Roman Esau acquired a universal, and even cosmic, significance that transcended the bloody episodes of the Roman Jewish wars that gave rise to the typology. "'The voice is Jacob's voice': [this means that] no prayer is effective unless the seed of Jacob has a part in it. 'The hands are Esau's hands': [this means that] no war is successful unless the seed of Esau has a share in it."[46] The Beitar massacre withdrew into the background as the eternal divergence between Israel's Covenant with God and Roman worldly dominion took center stage. The rabbis expanded the early tradition identifying Cain and Esau as fratricides into a universal genealogy of evil, leading down from Cain to Esau to Pharaoh to Haman to Gog and Magog, all of whom conspired against Israel and sought worldly dominion. Each of Israel's enemies sought to learn from his predecessor's failure, but God contravened their designs, and, at the end of days, fighting the nations, He will emerge triumphant and be recognized by all.[47] Against this evil genealogy, the rabbis posited Israel,

---

[45] *BT* Baba Batra 16b; *Bereshit Rabba* 63:12; *Targum Pseudo-Jonathan* on Genesis 25:29; *Tanḥuma*, ed. Buber, toledot 3 63ab; *Pesikta de-Rav Kahana* 3:1; *Pesikta Rabbati* 12 (*Pesiqta rabbati: A Synoptic Edition*, ed. Rivka Ulmer [Atlanta: Scholars Press, 1997]); *Shemot Rabbah* 1: 1 (*Midrash Shemot Rabbah:* Parashot 1–14, ed. Avigdor Shinan [Jerusalem: Devir, 1984]); *Midrash Tehilim* 9: 7 (*Midrash Tehilim Known as Shoḥer Tov*, ed. Shlomo Buber [Vilnius: Romm, 1891], henceforth *Midrash Tehilim*).

[46] Gittin 57b. This homily built, however, on the Tannaitic tradition in *Mekhilta* be-shalaḥ 2 on Exodus 14:10: וייראו מאד.

[47] *Va-yiqra Rabbah* 27:11; compare *Esther Rabbah* 7:23 (*Midrash Esther Rabbah*, ed. Joseph Tabory and Arnon Atzmon [Jerusalem: Schechter Institute, 2014]); *Tanḥuma*, ed. Buber, emor 18; *Pesikta de-Rav Kahana* 1 9:12; *Midrash Tehilim* 2:4.

descendants of the Patriarchs, keepers of the Covenant, from which the nations – Esau and, for the most part, also Ishmael – were excluded.[48] From time immemorial, Jacob-Israel, praying to God and fulfilling the commandments, struggled against violent rebellious Esau, the representative of cosmic evil. The rabbinic Jew and Roman Esau were shaped together, one staged against the other.

The polarization of the Jacob & Esau typology purged earlier ambiguity in the brothers. Rabbinic views of Jacob's perfection left room neither for Jeremiah's deceptive Yaakov nor for Hosea's critique of Jacob's actions.[49] The rabbis whitewashed his questionable conduct and made him a model of piety.[50] As to Esau, Amoraic Midrash allowed but one anomaly in its portrayal of the rabbinic Other: It conceded that Esau honored his father in an exemplary fashion.[51] This anomalous tradition could still not overcome the rabbis' conviction that Esau had a design on the family's fortune: He conspired to kill Isaac and take his place as head of the family.[52] Jacob and Esau's reconciliation, the happy end in Genesis, became incomprehensible. The Tannaitic *Sifre* still contravened the view that Esau's reconciliation was disingenuous: "Although it is a maxim that Esau hates Jacob," says Rabbi Shimeon bar Yoḥai, "at that hour, feelings of mercy welled in him, and he kissed [Jacob] with all his heart."[53] Amoraic Midrash did not allow for genuine reconciliation. *Genesis Rabbah* 78:9 depicted a grotesque scene, humorous and horrific at the same time: Esau sought to bite Jacob (*va-yishakehu*, 'and he kissed him' = *va-yishakhehu*, 'and he bit him'; וישקהו = וישכהו), yet Jacob's neck turned as hard as marble, and Esau's teeth were blunted. Hence, the two

---

[48] Tannaitic-Amoraic continuity seems pronounced here: *Sifre* va-ethanan 6: שמע ישראל, haazinu 7 on Deuteronomy 32:9: כי חלק ה' עמו, ve-zot ha-berakhah on Deuteronomy 33:2: משעיר ה' בא; *Va-yiqra Rabbah* 36:5; *BT* Sanhedrin 59b, Nedarim 12a, 31a; *Midrash Tehilim* 81:1, 117:20.

[49] See the discussion of the Prophets' Jacob in this chapter's first section.

[50] But see *Bereshit Rabba* 70:19 and *Devarim Rabbah* 1:14 (*Sefer Midrash Rabbah*, 2 vols. [Vilnius: Romm, 1884], henceforth *Devarim Rabbah*) for caveats: Jacob's deceptiveness is highlighted, but softly.

[51] The Roman reputation for honoring parents, the authority of the particular Tannaitic tradition about Esau honoring Isaac, and the pedagogical opportunity that the rabbis saw in this example may have assured this midrash's survival as an anomaly in Esau's otherwise negative portrayal. *Sifre* Haazino 31 רק דבר לא כי: Esau's one *miẓvah* was honoring his father. *Bereshit Rabba* 65:16: Rabban Shimon ben Gamliel found Esau's honoring of his father superior to his own, as Esau served his father in his best clothes, befitting royalty. *Devarim Rabbah*, 1:14: Esau's merit in honoring Isaac explains Edom-Rome's worldly success. Rome is rewarded for Esau's observance of one single *miẓvah*.

[52] Whereas the biblical text (Genesis 27:41) suggests that Esau, not wishing to aggravate Isaac, determined to wait for his death before killing Jacob, *Bereshit Rabba* 75:9 opined that Esau conspired to kill his father first, and *Va-yiqra Rabbah* 27:11 saw a demonic plan to eradicate Jacob's lineage.

[53] Be-haalotkha 11.

brothers cried, one over his neck, the other over his teeth.[54] There was no respite in the two brothers' war.

Jewish–Roman coexistence, suggested these midrashim, was impossible. "Caesarea and Jerusalem: If one says to you that both are destroyed [or] that both are flourishing, do not believe him."[55] Only Rome's downfall would bring forth Israel's regeneration, Esau's downfall Jacob's redemption. The Babylonian Talmud conjured scenes of Jewish martyrology – Jewish youth committing mass suicide to avoid Roman enslavement and prostitution – and the rabbis fantasized revenge against Edom.[56] Claims of mercy or pardon for Esau were summarily rejected. "Let Esau be pardoned" (יוחן עשו), pleaded Isaac with God, and God answered: Esau is irredeemably wicked and will devastate the Land of Israel.[57] Apocalyptic scenes imagined a dramatic power reversal between Israel and Rome, but most striking was the quiet confidence in the empire's ephemerality, expressed by a rare *Deuteronomy Rabbah* midrash, attributed to Rabbi Meir: "The day will come when Israel will be saying: 'Here was [Esau's] palace, here his theatre, here his court stage.' And you shall look around and find they have vanished."[58]

---

[54] *Bereshit Rabba* attributes this view to Rabbi Yannai. Rabbi Abahu ben Yoḥanan derives it from "your neck is like an ivory tower" (Song of Solomon 7:4). Rabbi Shimon ben Elazar is cited for Yoḥai's view (in *Sifre*) of a sincere kiss. In *Shir Hashirim Rabbah* 7:9, Shimon ben Elazar expresses Yannai's view and derives it from "your neck is like an ivory tower." See also *Tanḥuma va-yishlaḥ 4* (*Midrash Tanḥuma* [Jerusalem: Makor, 1971], henceforth *Tanḥuma*): "Esau cries because Jacob's neck turned into marble and Jacob cries lest Esau bite him again." The peculiar orthography of *va-yishakehu* in the Masoretic text – the points (*nequdot*) added above the word by the *soferim* who set the precise letter-text (indicating doubt as to the correct version) – gave grounds to these midrashim. See Saul Lieberman, *Hellenism in Jewish Palestine*, 2d ed. (New York: JTS, 1962), pp. 43–46; Emanuel Tov, *Textual Criticism of the Hebrew Bible*, 3d ed. (Minneapolis, MN: Fortress Press, 2012), pp. 51–52.

[55] *BT* Megilah 6a: "If he says that Caesarea is waste and Jerusalem is flourishing . . . you may believe him." Caesarea is called "daughter of Edom, a metropolis of kings." See also *BT* Pesaḥim 42b; *Pesikta de-Rav Kahana* 1 5:21: "As long as wicked Esau's light shines in the world, Jacob's light is hardly noticed; once wicked Esau's light diminishes, that of Jacob spreads."

[56] Martyrology: Gittin 57b. Daniel Boyarin, *Dying for God* (Stanford, CA: Stanford University Press, 1999), emphasizes the multivalence of such texts and their role in forming counter-Christian martyrology. Revenge: *Bereshit Rabba* 78:14; *Va-yiqra Rabbah* 13:5; *Tanḥuma*, ed. Buber ẓav 4, devarim 3; *BT* Makot 12a, Gitin 56b.

[57] Megilah 6a. See also Sanhedrin 104a.

[58] *Devarim Rabbah* devarim 19 (*Midrash Devarim Rabbah*, ed. Saul Lieberman [Jerusalem: Bamberger and Wahrman, 1940], henceforth *Devarim Rabbah*, ed. Lieberman). The midrash does not appear in other manuscripts. Lieberman suggests that it completes a midrash in *Avot de-Rabbi Natan* 21. Burton Visotzky, *Golden Bells and Pomegranates: Studies in Midrash Leviticus Rabbah* (Tübingen: Mohr Siebeck, 2003), pp. 154–72, and Carol Bakhos, "Figuring (out) Esau," 250–62, have correctly suggested that midrashic Esau can sometimes best be explained by the rabbinic desire to shape an Other, rather

For the time being, however, the Romans were the rulers, and the rabbis made Jacob a guide on relations with them. His multivalent, perhaps inconsistent, counseling testified to the complexity of the task the rabbis saw themselves facing. Jacob's entreaties to Esau on his return to the Land, calling Esau repeatedly "my master," became *exemplum* for relations with the Roman authorities, and his artful rebuff of Esau's offer to join him on a trip back to Seir was a model for snubbing collaboration with non-Jews.[59] Yet in their moral *exempla*, the rabbis also imagined lost opportunities for brotherhood and were critical of Jacob for failing to protect it. If non-Jews were to be rebuffed, brothers in danger of going astray had to be saved, and genuine converts accepted. *Genesis Rabbah* tells of Jacob's punishment for denying his daughter Dinah to Esau.[60] *BT* tells of the patriarch's wrongfully refusing conversion to the Edomite princess Timna.[61] She so badly wanted to join Israel that when rebuffed, she consented to become the mistress of a relation, Esau's son Elifaz, and gave birth to Amaleq, Israel's worst enemy. These stories, and the passing suggestion that the Amaleqite Haman's genocidal design on the Jews was divine retribution for the injustice Jacob had done Esau, would for many centuries remain rarely used resources for an alternative Jacob & Esau discourse.[62] They would emerge periodically and sink quickly, until our own time, when we see them appear frequently in progressive Orthodox discourse.

How long will Esau's dominion last? Rabbinic Bar-Kokhba stories show the rabbis wavering on messianism, playing apprehensively yet persistently, with chiliastic prophecies, torn between messianic

---

than as a rhetorical strategy against Rome. Jacob and Esau's emergence as ideal types, the rabbinic Jew and his Other, respectively, made it indeed possible for Midrash to leave Esau often without a historical referent, but even such cases can rarely be read apart from the Roman background. The imperial trauma cut the lenses for the rabbis' reading of the biblical story and shaped their understanding of history.

[59] *Bereshit Rabba* 75:5: Rabbi Judah the Patriarch signed his letters to the emperor with "your servant Judah," supporting himself with Jacob's missive to Esau: "Thus said your servant Jacob." (See also *Bereshit Rabba* 78:15.) But *Bereshit Rabba* 75:3 and 75:11 use Jacob's conduct as negative exempla: He should not have engaged Esau or prostrated himself. On collaboration with non-Jews: *BT* Avodah Zara 25b: "A Jew overtaken by an idolater while on the road [and asked] whither he is going, should say toward a place beyond his actual destination, just as our ancestor Jacob acted toward the wicked Esau."

[60] *Bereshit Rabba* 76:9: Here, Esau is a brother to be reformed, rather than a recalcitrant enemy who has broken the brotherhood bond. This is an alternative vision easily overwhelmed by the hatred of Rome.

[61] *BT* Sanhedrin 99b; compare *Sifre* haazinu 31; *Bereshit Rabba* 82:14.

[62] *Bereshit Rabba* 67:4. "God may delay punishment but eventually exacts his retribution. Jacob made Esau cry out but one loud and bitter cry, as it is said: 'When Esau heard his father's words, he burst out with a loud and bitter cry' (Genesis 27:34). Where did God exact retribution? In the capital city of Shushan, as it is said: 'When Mordekhai learned all that had been done ... he cried out with a loud and bitter cry' (Esther 4:1)."

expectation and everyday life. They shrank from declaring Bar-Kokhba a false messiah, but they would not recognize him as Messiah son of Joseph, presaging Messiah son of David and destined to fall in war.[63] In the midst of deliberation of cosmo-historical periodization, Rabbi Shmuel bar Naḥmani, a noted turn-of-the-fourth-century CE Palestinian Amora, opines (in the name of his master, Rabbi Yonatan): "Blasted be the bones of those who calculate the end. For [people] would say, since the predetermined time has arrived, and yet he has not come, he will never come. But [even so], wait for him, as it is written, 'though he tarry, wait for him.'"[64] Setting parameters for two millennia of Jewish life, the rabbis lived its abiding dilemma – retaining, yet containing, messianic expectation by fortifying the Torah rule.

We do not know enough about the Jewish communities in Palestine and Babylonia in the late antique period to historicize fully the Edom-Rome discourse, but like rabbinic Judaism, Edom-Rome triumphed against the background of a Christianizing empire, the simultaneous formation of orthodox Christianity and rabbinic Judaism, and the shaping of Jewish communal institutions that would endure to modernity.[65] The rabbis knew Christianity foremost as *minut*, a "deviating sect." With Constantine's Edict of Tolerance (313 CE) and Theodosius's proclamation of Christianity as state religion (380), "the Empire became minut," that is, a sect of Jewish origin took hold of the empire.[66] Roman–Jewish brotherhood now seemed all the more obvious, but the rabbis gave no indication that they noticed. They continued their relentless attack on the empire and kept silent on its emergent Christian character. They had envisioned imperial and not religious brotherhood. They could not but have been aghast about the turn that history had taken.

---

[63] *PT* Taanit 24a–b; *Eichah Rabbah*, ed. Buber 2:9. Bar-Kokhba does not cast a rabbinic figure. The rabbis describe him as incredibly strong, ruthless, and quick-tempered, but they attribute Beitar's successful resistance of the Roman siege to the prayers of a sage, the Tanna Rabbi Elazar ha-Modayi. Bar-Kokhba suspects Rabbi Elazar of collaboration with the Romans and kills him, and immediately Beitar falls. All the same, Bar-Kokhba does not fall into the Romans' hands but is divinely killed by a snake. This is consummate rabbinic ambivalence. Compare *Ruth Rabbah* 2:3–4 (*Sefer Midrash Rabbah*, 2 vols. [Vilnius: Romm, 1884]); *Shir-Hashirim Rabbah* 2:20. On Messiah son of Joseph and Bar-Kokhba, see Joseph Heinemann, *Agadot ve-Toldotehen*, pp. 131–41.

[64] *BT* Sanhedrin **97**b; see also Avodah Zarah 8b–9a.

[65] Seth Schwartz, *Imperialism and Jewish Society, 200 B.C.E to 640 C.E.* (Princeton, NJ: Princeton University Press, 2001), and "The Political Geography of Rabbinic Texts," in *The Cambridge Companion to the Talmud and Rabbinic Literature*, ed. Charlotte Elisheva Fonrobert and Martin S. Jaffee (New York: Cambridge University Press, 2007), pp. 75–96.

[66] *BT* Sotah 13a.

The Christianizing empire may help explain the rabbis' unremitting hostility to Rome, which seems incongruent with Late Antiquity's less combative Roman–Jewish relations. The third and fourth centuries knew nothing as traumatic as the Temple's destruction or the devastation and persecutions that ensued after the Bar-Kokhba war. In 212 CE, the Jews, like all imperial subjects, became citizens; in the fourth century, Palestinian Jews enjoyed economic growth; and after the mid-fourth century, the empire increasingly recognized the rabbis as communal leaders. The Land of Israel's landscape and population would not become preponderantly Christian until the sixth century, but the rabbis could already see that the minut was disinheriting Hellenistic Judaism and taking over the empire. Rabbinic claims to represent Judaism were becoming tangible, yet the empire showed no sign of retreating. The rabbis' fears and hopes focused on Rome's imperial power, not on its religious character, but the empire's increasingly Christian profile excluded the possibility of rapprochement and normalization of Roman–Jewish relations.

Later in the fourth century, and at greater pace in the early fifth, imperial legislation began excluding the Jews from civic life, and threatened rabbinic Judaism with provincialization. Confident in their Torah and growing authority, indifferent to Hellenistic Judaism's demise, and sustained by their local academies, a measure of wealth, and diasporic networks spreading from Egypt to Palestine to Sassanid Babylonia, the rabbis took marginalization in stride. But Christianization assured that the traumatic Roman–Jewish past would not go away. On the contrary, rabbinic Judaism would continue and deploy the past to affirm its universal history, the staging of the Jewish nation against the Roman Empire.

With Edom-Rome, the rabbis struck back against marginalization, first by pagan, then by Christian Rome. They did so most ingeniously in their tales of the friendship of Rabbi Judah the Patriarch, the leader of the Jewish Palestinian community at the turn of the third century CE, and the "Roman Emperor" – an ideal type called "Antoninus." The Babylonian Talmud presents the Jewish patriarch and Roman emperor as having a relationship of equals: "'Two nations in your womb' (Genesis 25:23) ... this refers to Rabbi and the [Emperor] Antoninus."[67] "Once [Antoninus] asked [Rabbi]: 'Shall I enter the world to come?' 'Yes!' said Rabbi. 'But,' said Antoninus, 'is it not written, "There will be no remnant

---

[67] *BT* Avodah Zarah 11a: "'Two nations (*goyim*) are in your womb': Rav Yehudah (a mid-third-century Amora) said in the name of Rav: 'Read not *goyim* (nations) but *geyim* (lords). This refers to Antoninus and Rabbi.'" Compare: *BT* Berakhot 57b; *Bereshit Rabba* 63:7. On the significance of this midrash in the context of rising Christianity, see the next chapter.

to the house of Esau?" 'That,' replied Rabbi, 'applies only to those whose evil deeds are like those of Esau.'"[68] Imagining a moment of grace in Roman–Jewish relations, and hinting at good relations between the empire and the emergent rabbinic Palestinian Patriarchate, the story also provides a clue to the Jacob & Esau typology's irresistible attraction. By turning their enemies into wicked brothers, the rabbis declared themselves equal to the emperors and converted Jewish history into universal history. Ironically, only Christian Rome's claim to religious brotherhood, a claim the rabbis studiously avoided, assured the credibility of the rabbinic narrative, and made the Jews, a small nation, as historically significant as the evil empire.

Thunderous Silence? Rabbinic Edom and Christianity

"Two nations in your womb": In recent decades, scholars have shown that the biblical metaphor was historical reality – rabbinic Judaism and Christianity emerged in the late Roman Empire as twin religions competing for the Jewish legacy. With the Roman Empire's Christianization in Late Antiquity, Christianity and imperial power became entangled, the source of Jewish fear and hatred for millennia. Through the Christian Empire, Jacob & Esau became a major *topos* of Jewish European history, but contrary to some scholars, Esau's Christianization in Jewish thought appears to me to have been primarily a response to European "Christendom," and, as such, medieval rather than late antique in character.

My postdating of rabbinic "Christian Esau" by at least half a millennium, according to some scholarly views, is grounded in a reconsideration of Christianity's role in the formation of rabbinic Edom, a reassessment of Jacob & Esau in patristic culture, and an examination of the Islamic Caliphate's place in the Four Empires eschatology. I argue that the Roman Empire and not Christianity was crucial to rabbinic Edom; that there was asymmetry in Jacob & Esau's role in rabbinic and patristic literatures; that the late antique Christian–Jewish dialogue may have been more limited than some imagine; and that European Christendom's formation in confrontation with Islam first fixed the Jewish gaze on the Roman Empire's religious character and triggered the Christianization of Edom and Esau. The first three arguments are elaborated in this section and the next, and the last argument concerning the Muslim role in the next chapter.

---

[68] *BT* Avodah Zarah 10b.

In recent decades, scholars from Allan Segal to Israel Yuval to Daniel Boyarin to Peter Schäfer have drawn a picture of rabbinic Judaism forming in response to Christianity.[69] For Yuval and Boyarin, rabbinic Judaism was the younger religion of the two, truly a Jacob.[70] They view late antique discourses as a shared, if contested, Christian–Jewish terrain, see rabbinic Judaism as apologetic, and emphasize the blurry and shifting boundaries of minut. Together with Jacob Neusner, they argue that the Edom-Rome typology makes sense only in the context of the Christian claim to Jacob's heritage.[71] The rabbis, they say, found themselves in an awkward position: Judaism was perceived as the older-brother religion, and Christianity as the younger, Jacob's inheritor. The only alternative was to identify their enemies, Rome, with the older brother, a formula that received special poignancy when the empire became Christian. Otherwise, the claim of brotherhood with Rome makes no sense.

Against the centrality of Christian polemics to rabbinic Jacob & Esau, older and younger scholars from Avigdor Shinan to Robert Goldenberg to Burton Visotzky to Carol Bakhos insist that the force of rabbinic *topoi*, such as "the Other," and of internally referential hermeneutics, lend rabbinic discourse a measure of autonomy from historical reality, with the concern with Christianity marginal.[72] Most recently, Adiel Schremer has argued that Christianity provides the wrong context for understanding the rabbinic quandary, which centered on the Roman imperial triumph and the Temple's destruction.[73] It is an anachronism, they all agree, to persistently discern rabbinic anxieties about Christianity where

---

[69] Alan Segal, *Rebecca's Children: Judaism and Christianity in the Roman World* (Cambridge, MA: Harvard University Press, 1986); Daniel Boyarin, *Dying for God* (Stanford, CA: Stanford University Press, 1999); Israel Yuval, *Two Nations in Your Womb*; Peter Schäfer, *Jesus in the Talmud* (Princeton, NJ: Princeton University Press, 2007).

[70] Boyarin, *Dying for God*, esp. pp. 1–6; Yuval, *Two Nations*, pp. 1–30. Yuval's and Boyarin's approaches are, however, diametrically opposed. Yuval's explanatory model requires polarization of Jewish–Christian relations, whereas Boyarin's shared discursive universe undermines it. Blurred borderlines seem to me more helpful than polarities in understanding rabbinic anxieties, but when borderlines dissolve, so does the explanatory power of social groups as well. Diversity of minut can no longer be ascribed to particular groups, and their interaction can no longer explain historical development. In "Beyond Judaisms," *Journal for the Study of Judaism* 41:3 (2010): 323–65, Boyarin draws this conclusion: He proposes archaeology of discourse; history is no longer possible.

[71] Jacob Neusner, "From Enemy to Sibling," *Neusner on Judaism*, 1: 435–63.

[72] Avigdor Shinan, *The Aggadah in the Aramaic Targums to the Pentateuch* (in Hebrew), 2 vols. (Jerusalem: Maqor, 1979): 2: 345–52; Robert Goldenberg, "Did the Amoraim See Christianity as Something New?" in *Pursuing the Text*, ed. John C. Reeves and John Kampen (Sheffield, UK: Sheffield Academic Press, 1994), pp. 293–302; Burton Visotzky, *Golden Bells and Pomegranates*, pp. 154–72; Carol Bakhos, "Figuring (out) Esau."

[73] *Brothers Estranged: Heresy, Christianity, and Jewish Identity in Late Antiquity* (Oxford: Oxford University Press, 2010).

the rabbis suggested that they were concerned with other issues. To the extent that the rabbis were familiar with Christian beliefs and practices, they saw them as minut, a sectarian challenge to rabbinic Judaism, divergent communal practice rather than heterodoxy, insists Schremer.[74] Christianity did not define minut, at least not initially, and minut itself was only one challenge to rabbinic rule, not the one the rabbis viewed as most threatening.

Moreover, the *minim* were many, and vast stretches of Midrash are free of Christian allusion. No hermeneutic of suspicion (or presumption of later-day censorship) can undo the absence of Christian reference. Living under the Sassanid Empire, Babylonian Jewry confronted Zoroastrian dualism. In Palestine, the Samaritans appear to be of greater concern than the Christians. The old Sadducees make the most frequent appearance of all. They form an ideal-type Other, a conglomerate of deviations from rabbinic practice and belief, having but a tenuous relationship, if any, to the historical Sadducees. They may disguise contemporary opponents, but their heterodoxy is hardly Christian. The question of internal versus contextual interpretation of Midrash aside, the historicity of the Christian context for rabbinic discourse seems dubitable.

Late antique Christian discourse on Jacob & Esau suggests that Christian–Jewish polemics played only a limited role in shaping rabbinic visions of Esau and Rome. The Church Fathers developed a Christian Jacob & Esau typology to claim Israel's heritage, but they did not use it as extensively as the rabbis used theirs.[75] For Christians, Esau never assumed a place equivalent to Rome in Jewish discourse. The Church Fathers showed greater interest in rabbinic Judaism than the rabbis did in Christianity – a few, notably Jerome (340–420), had knowledge of Hebrew and Midrash – and public exchanges between Jews and Christians over biblical interpretation appear to have taken place at least in third-century Caesarea.[76] There is little doubt that the Christian

---

[74] John Gager focuses on the foremost site for discerning Jewish anxieties that may not have found expression in rabbinic literature: He tracks the origins of *Toledot Yeshu* (Life story of Jesus), an early medieval Jewish counter-gospel. Significantly, Gager presupposes the Jewish Christians as the original interlocutors, and shows the counter-gospel using fissures in the Gospel story to reconfigure Jesus within shared Jewish discourse. *Toledot Yeshu* remains an internal Jewish story until the ninth century. A Jewish Jesus and not a Christian Jacob aroused rabbinic anxieties. "Simon Peter, Founder of Christianity or Saviour of Israel?" in *Toledot Yeshu ("The Life Story of Jesus") Revisited*, ed. Peter Schäfer, Michael Meerson, and Yaacov Deutsch (Tübingen: Mohr Siebeck, 2011), pp. 221–45.

[75] Klaus Thraede, "Jakob und Esau," *Reallexikon für Antike und Christentum*, ed. Theodor Klauser et al., 26 vols. (Stuttgart: A. Hiersmann, 1994): 14: 1118–1217.

[76] Louis Ginzberg exhaustively mined the Church Fathers for Midrash references: "Die Haggada bei den Kirchenvätern VI," in *Jewish Studies in Memory of George A. Kohut*, ed. Salo W. Baron and Alexander Marx (New York: The Alexander Kohut Memorial

typology served as background knowledge for both sides in such disputations. The Church Father Origen (c. 185–254) spoke of the triumph of Church over Synagogue – "the elder serves the younger" – as common knowledge to everyone.[77] But short of brief summary dismissals of rabbinic Edom in Jerome, we have no record of Church Fathers confronting the Jewish typology.[78] Jacob & Esau did not figure as highly as we might expect in late antique Christian–Jewish polemics. Why?

The Church Fathers had plenty of metaphors and figures, and several biblical pairs (e.g., Leah & Rachel), to describe their relationship to Judaism, and their homiletic strategies often carried them away from the typology.[79] If they claimed Jacob's legacy, they had little interest in defending imperial Rome, even after it had turned Christian. They regarded rabbinic Judaism as a challenge, but they also had Christian and pagan enemies whom they often needed to address first. As for the rabbis, in the late antique universe of amorphous minut that Boyarin vividly describes, they appeared more anxious about blurred boundaries than about binary Christian typologies setting borderlines between Christians and Jews. The Christian group of greatest concern to the rabbis, the Jewish Christians, viewed the rejection of Jacob's Jewishness as threatening – this was no bone of contention with the rabbis.[80]

Foundation, 1935), pp. 289–314. (Page 289 lists the five earlier parts, published 1899–1933.) For the classic overview of Christian–Jewish exchange: Marcel Simon, *Verus Israel: A Study of the Relations Between Christians and Jews in the Roman Empire AD 135–425* [1948] (London: The Littman Library of Jewish Civilization, 1996). For exchanges in Caesarea: N. R. M. de Lange, *Origen and the Jews* (Cambridge: Cambridge University Press, 1976); Paul Blowers, "Origen, the Rabbis, and the Bible," in *Christianity in Relation to Jews, Greeks, and Romans*, ed. Everett Ferguson (New York: Garland Pub., 1999), pp. 2–22; John A. McGuckin, "Origen on the Jews," in *Christianity in Relation to Jews, Greeks, and Romans*, pp. 23–36.

[77] *Homilies on Genesis and Exodus*, trans. Ronald E. Heine (Washington, DC: Catholic University of America Press, 1982), Homily 12, p. 179.

[78] Jerome, *Commentary on Isaiah* and *Commentary on the Minor Prophets* (Notitia Clavis Patrum Latinorum 584 and 589, respectively; henceforth CPL), Library of Latin Texts – Series A (Turnhout: Brepolis Publishers, 2005), Isaiah 21:11 and preface to Obadiah, respectively. In both cases, Jerome's knowledge seems limited to the interplay of "Dumah" and "Roma" (*PT* Taanit 3A), as in Obadiah: "Judaei frustra somniant contra urbem Romam, regnumque Romanum hanc fieri prophetiam (The Jews dream in vain that this prophecy was made against the city and rulers of Rome)."

[79] For overviews of Christian anti-Jewish polemics: A. Lukyn Williams, *Adversus Judaeos: A Bird's-Eye View of Christian Apologiae until the Renaissance* (Cambridge: Cambridge University Press, 1935); Heinz Schreckenberg, *Die christlichen Adversus-Judaeos-Texte und ihr literarisches und historisches Umfeld (1.–11.Jh)* (Frankfurt am Main: Peter Lang, 1982).

[80] We have no record of a Jewish Christian using the Christian typology. It is interesting to note that Charles K. Barrett, "The Allegory of Abraham, Sarah, and Hagar in Galatians," in *Rechtfertigung: Festschrift für Ernst Käsemann zum 70. Geburtstag*, ed. Johannes Friedrich, Wolfgang Pöhlmann, and Peter Stuhlmacher (Tübingen: Mohr, 1976), pp. 1–16, suggests that Paul was responding to Jewish members of the Jesus

The rabbis may have elliptically responded to Christian claims in Midrash, *Targum*, and *Piyut* (liturgical poems), but their concern with Christian Jacob did not approach their hostility toward Roman Esau.[81] The Christianization of the empire enhanced the existing Edom-Rome typology, but remarkably, it triggered no major transformation. For long centuries, Esau remained a pagan.

Rome and not Christianity was central to the Jewish typology. Were it not for the startling convergence of imperial power and Christian religion under the heading of Rome, Jews and Christians might not have been disastrously entangled for two millennia. Highlighting the Roman Empire and sidelining Christian–Jewish polemics reinforces a historically contingent view of Christian–Jewish relations. In contrast, the Christo-centric context for rabbinic discourse, which recent scholarship has constructed, retains a measure of historical teleology by restricting the late antique protagonists to Christian and Jew (even if their identities are loosened). Christian–Jewish polemics obscures the fortuitousness of the Christian Empire and conceals the ultimate irony of the Jewish typology. Rabbinic Judaism may have wished to treat Christianity as just another minut, but with the Christianization of the empire, the Edom-Rome typology affirmed precisely the Christian brotherhood the rabbis wished to avoid, a relationship that has never since been undone.

The Church Fathers on Jacob & Esau

To the first-century Jesus movement and the early Church Fathers, the prospect of a Christian Rome would have seemed hallucinatory. They shaped the Christian Jacob & Esau typology as they were sorting out their relationship to Judaism. Trying to open Israel's Covenant community to non-Jews and vindicate his mission to the Gentiles, the Apostle Paul argued in the Epistle to the Romans (9:6–13) that genealogy did not define the Israel with whom God had made a Covenant. Not all of Abraham's children inherited the promise – God had elected Jacob and rejected Esau even before the twins were born. Christians who did not descend from Abraham became children of the promise through Jesus. Paul had no intention of suggesting that Jews were Esau's descendants; rather, non-Jews were "grafted" onto Israel's tree. Jacob & Esau served as example, not

movement, arguing that followers must be integrated into Jacob. (Thanks to Joel Marcus.)

[81] Burton Visotzky, *Fathers of the World: Essays in Rabbinic and Patristic Literatures* (Tübingen: Mohr, 1995), especially "Anti-Christian Polemics in Leviticus Rabbah," pp. 93–105. See also the previously mentioned works of Boyarin, Simon, and Yuval and the discussion that follows.

types.[82] But Paul had no more control over Jacob & Esau than over his statements about Jews. Future readers will trace the typology to Paul.

Around the turn of the second century, the *Epistle of Barnabas*, directed against Jewish Christians (or "Judaizers," Christians observing Jewish ritual) and advocating separation from the Jewish community, used the verse "two nations in your womb" and Jacob's blessing to his grandchildren (crossing his hands in preference for the younger) to suggest, obliquely, that "the covenant belongs to us [Christians, and not] to them [Jews]" (Chapter XIII).[83] In "Dialogue with Trypho" (c. 160 CE), the first major work in the *Adversus Judaeos* tradition – Christian disputations against the Jews – Justin Martyr argued that the promise to the Jewish Patriarchs "in your offspring shall all the nations of the earth be blessed" (Genesis 22:18) passed through a restricted genealogy via Isaac, Jacob, Judah, and David to Christ, "so that some of [the Jewish] nation would be found children of Abraham, and . . . in the lot of Christ; but others, who are indeed children of Abraham, would be . . . barren and fruitless" (p. 120).[84] Esau and Reuben, Isaac and Jacob's first sons, were excluded from the promise. Christ circumscribed the community of promise – "Jacob was called Israel; and Israel has been demonstrated to be the Christ" – but unlike the anti-Jewish *Barnabas*, Jews remained Jacob's descendants. Jacob & Esau did not yet prefigure the Christian and Jewish peoples.

Justin reflected Christian puzzlement over Jewish identity. Introducing the topos of Synagogue and Church (Chapter 134) – "Leah is your people and synagogue; but Rachel is our Church" – Justin emphasized that "Christ even now serves both." Jacob's descendants could be found in Synagogue and Church alike, and the Synagogue did not confront the Church, as of yet, as its polar opposite.[85] Yet Justin also likened Esau's

---

[82] In Paul's heated rhetoric against Judaizers in Galatians 4:21–31, the Matriarch Sarah and her servant Hagar, mother of Ishmael, do form types for the two covenants of Sinai and Christ, present-day Jerusalem and Jerusalem above, flesh (law) and spirit, slavery, and the promise. He implies (but does not say) that those under the first Covenant, presumably Jews who refuse Jesus (and possibly even the Judaizers), are "cast away" from the promise, the way Hagar and Ishmael were from Abraham's household.

[83] Trans. Alexander Roberts and James Donaldson, http://www.earlychristianwritings.com/text/barnabas-roberts.html.

[84] Observe the parallel with Midrash on "through Isaac your descendants shall be named" (Genesis 21:12), but in rabbinic genealogy, *all* of Jacob's descendants were perfect. Trans. Alexander Roberts and James Donaldson, http://www.earlychristianwritings.com/text/justinmartyr-dialoguetrypho.html.

[85] The Church vs. Synagogue metaphor, embodied in the two maidens decorating many medieval cathedrals, provides the motif for James Parkes, *The Conflict of the Church and the Synagogue: A Study in the Origins of Antisemitism* [1934] (New York: Atheneum, 1969). In chapter 3, "The Parting of the Ways" (pp. 71–120), he discusses Christian anti-Jewish polemics (but not the metaphor).

persecution of Jacob to Jews' persecution of Christians: "We now, and our Lord Himself, are hated by you and by all men, though we are brothers by nature." Jews could be alternately Jacob or Esau. The ambiguity would become a permanent feature of Christian–Jewish relations. The invitation for Jews to rejoin Jacob, *Verus Israel* (true Israel), would remain, in principle, forever open, but the Jacob & Esau typology would reify Jewish and Christian identities and make rejoining Jacob an ordeal.

Twenty years later, about 180, we find the mature typology in Irenaeus, Bishop of Lyons. In *Against Heresies* (21:2–3), Jacob's character and deeds prefigure Christ, Jacob's twelve sons prefigure the twelve Apostles, Leah and Rachel the Old and New Testaments, and Rachel also the Church. The verse "the older shall serve the younger" speaks to future Jews and Christians: "The latter people has snatched away the blessings of the former from the Father, just as Jacob took away the blessing of Esau."[86] At the turn of the third century, the Latin Church Father Tertullian followed suit in his *Adversus Judaeos* (I): "The prior and 'greater' people – that is, the Jewish – must necessarily serve the 'lesser,' that is, the Christian."[87] His audacity in imagining the persecuted Christians served by Jews matched the rabbis' daring in imagining Jewish rulers teaching Torah in Roman circuses. Tertullian was as hostile to Rome as the rabbis – Rome was the whore of Babylon drunk with martyrs' blood (*Scorpiace* 12) – but the Christian typology had no room for Rome and remained confined to Christians and Jews.

Once the typology emerged, it appears to have circulated rapidly among Mediterranean Christian centers. In his commentary on Genesis, Hyppolitus of Rome (died c. 236) equated Jacob with Christ and the Church, and Esau with the devil and the Jews: "The devil who exhibited the fratricidal Jews by anticipation in Cain, makes manifest disclosure of them in Esau."[88] Cyprian's Books of Testimonies (I:

---

[86] Irenaeus continues: "The [stolen blessings] became a cause for [Jacob's] suffering of [his brother's] plots and persecutions, just as the Church suffers ... from the Jews": *The Ante-Nicene Fathers*, ed. and trans. Alexander Roberts and James Donaldson, revised by A. Cleveland Coxe, 10 vols. (New York: Charles Scribner's sons, 1903): 1: 493.

[87] Translated by S. Thelwall, *The Ante-Nicene Fathers*, 3: 151. See also his *Five Books Against Marcion* (book 3, chap. 25), trans. Holmes, *The Ante-Nicene Fathers*, 3: 343: "[T]he Jews ... were in Esau the prior of the sons in birth, but the later in affection (*Judaeorum enim dispositio in Esau priorum natu et posteriorum affectu filiorum*)."

[88] Hyppolitus (quoted in Jerome, Epistle 36, ad Damasum, number 18) uses Genesis 27:41 as evidence of fratricide. Esau says: "Let the days of the mourning for my father come on, that I may slay my brother." The parallel to the rabbinic genealogy of fratricide (*Targum pseudo-Jonathan* and *Va-yiqra Rabbah* 27:11) is startling, but the Cain-Esau topos is prerabbinic: C. T. R. Hayward, "A Portrait of the Wicked Esau," pp. 303–9. Hyppolite continues: "The robe ... of Esau denotes the faith and Scriptures of the Hebrews, with which ... the Gentiles were endowed.... . As Jacob moves to Mesopotamia to escape his brother's evil designs, so Christ, too, constrained by the

19–20, c. 248) joined the topoi of Jacob & Esau and Church & Synagogue: "[T]he Church ... should have more children from among the Gentiles than the Synagogue had had before."[89] If the typology first emerged in the western empire, in Lyons, Rome, and Carthage, the Alexandrian Origen, in Caesarea, in his *Homilies on Genesis* (12:3), left no doubt as to its wide spread: "How 'one people has arisen above the other,' that is, the Church over the Synagogue, and how 'the elder serves the younger' is known even to the Jews themselves; ... these things are ... commonplace to everyone."[90]

If the Jews were as keenly aware of the Christian challenge as Origen suggested, the rabbinic response seems contained. Rejoining the Christian claim to be the younger nation, the rabbis insisted that the biblical verse "one people (*leom*) shall be mightier than the other – יאמץ ולאם מלאם" actually referred to empires rather than to nations: "the meaning of *leom* is none other than kingdom – אין לאום אלא מלכות."[91] *Genesis Rabbah* 63:6–7 provided a series of homilies on "two nations" that could be an effort to deflect Christian polemics. One suggests that a pair of Jewish and Roman royalties – Hadrian and Solomon – represented the two nations. The biblical story, emphasized the rabbis, was about the struggle of Edom-Rome and Israel and not about Jews and Christians.

Indeed, the apostate Esau never became Christian in Amoraic Midrash. Even Esau portrayals that could be construed as Christian still suggest rabbinic concern with fencing off the Torah against apostasy, rather than with Christianity. Wrapping himself in a *tallit* (prayer shawl), the Palestinian Talmud relates, Esau, in the time to come, will try and sit among the righteous in Paradise, only to find himself dragged out by God.[92] This Esau may be Christian, as some readers suggest, or he may not. Significantly, Rome fails to advance any (Christian) claim of proximity to the Torah in other "Day of Judgment" scenes. As God sits with a Torah scroll in his hand to reward Torah loyalists, and as the Messiah accepts gifts from the nations, Rome presses the cause of brotherhood with Israel but makes no claim for the Torah. Like other empires,

---

unbelief of the Jews, goes into Galilee to take to Himself a bride from the Gentiles, His Church," and so on. "The Extant Works and Fragments of Hyppolitus," trans. S. D. F. Salmond, in *The Ante-Nicene Fathers*, 5: 169.

[89] Trans. Ernest Wallis, *The Ante-Nicene Fathers*, 5: 508.

[90] *Homilies on Genesis and Exodus*, Homily 12, p. 179.

[91] *BT* Avodah Zarah 2b. (Rashi uses it in his commentary on Genesis 25:23.) The *Targumim* all agreed on this translation. The Babylonian Targum had been redacted prior to the typology's triumph, and so an earlier tradition may have already suggested this interpretation, but it gained poignancy in the context of Christian polemics.

[92] *PT* Nedarim 12b. Marcel Simon, *Verus Israel*, pp. 187–88, thinks that this is anti-Christian polemics.

it professes to have used imperial power to facilitate Jewish Torah study.[93] The rabbis contrast empire and Torah; they manifest no anxiety about the empire appropriating the Torah. *Va-yiqra Rabbah* 4:6 says that the Torah speaks of Esau and his family in the plural and of Jacob and his family in the singular, "seventy soul," because Esau worships many gods, Jacob only one. If there is a gibe at the Trinity here, the focus is on Jacob's dedication to One God in the context of polytheistic rituals, of drawing Jewish boundaries against multiple amorphous nations and insisting that Jews may not take part in their cults.

Puzzled by the limited rabbinic response to the Christian challenge, some scholars seek to establish a more robust exchange between the concurrently emergent Jewish and Christian typologies. Yet our ability to track homiletic exchange remains frustratingly inadequate. We rarely have sufficient historical information to venture guesses about the specific challenges that particular homilies addressed, and discern when they were responding to external challenges and when pursuing hermeneutical tasks, when in conversation across communities, or borrowing, and when using communal traditions. The shared background, biblical texts, and homiletic strategies of Christians and Jews make guesses all the more hazardous.[94] Israel Yuval discerns analogies and common topoi in Christian and Jewish discourse and ritual and interprets them as polemical encounters in which both sides defend their legitimacy. But the assumption that Jews and Christians were always struggling over legitimacy is transhistorical. It turns the Jacob & Esau typology into historical explanation, the *explanandum* into the *explanans*.[95] Alternative models of historicization need to be explored.

This book is not the place for such exploration other than to suggest that if we venture guesses, we may do better by trying to locate homilies historically. Origen lived the last decades of his life in Caesarea Maritima, a religiously and ethnically mixed city, with Christian and Jewish academies, the former led by Origen himself and the latter by leading Palestinian rabbis.[96] Origen had some Hebrew and familiarity with Midrash, referred to Hebrew teachers, and expressed anxiety about

---

[93] *BT* Avodah Zara 2a–b and Pesaḥim 118b, respectively.

[94] Shaye J. D. Cohen pursues some of these issues and offers "antipodal texts" as an alternative model of polemics not presupposing dialogue: "Antipodal Texts: B. Eruvin 21b–22a and Mark 7:1–23 on the Tradition of the Elders and the Commandment of God," in *Envisioning Judaism*, ed. Ra'anan S. Boustan et al., 2 vols. (Tübingen: Mohr Siebeck, 2013): 2: 965–83.

[95] Yuval's presupposition of one-sided influence (pp. 18–22) – the Christians challenge, the Jews respond – is particularly objectionable, especially for early exchanges when Christian culture is by no means hegemonic.

[96] Hayim Lapin, "Jewish and Christian Academies in Roman Palestine: Some Preliminary Observations," in *Caesarea Maritima: A Retrospective After Two Millennia*, ed. Avner Rabsan and Kenneth G. Holum (Leiden: E. J. Brill, 1996), pp. 496–512.

Christian ability to hold the line in exchanges with Jews.[97] If the Jewish and Christian typologies were in conversation anywhere, it would be in Origen's Caesarea. Saul Lieberman recognized Caesarea as a promising site for historicization. His model may call today for reduced confidence in rabbinic transmission and greater allowance for rabbinic invention, but it still inspires.[98]

Origen, having alluded to the typology, dropped it and moved on to an allegory dear to him: "Two nations," he said, existed in every soul. The Christian Fathers all believed that the Church inherited Jacob's legacy, but Christian Jacob was less central for them than Jewish Jacob was for the rabbis, and Jewish Esau was marginal compared with Roman Esau. The Greek Fathers Athanasius (c. 293–373) and Cyril (c. 376–444) only infrequently referred to the typology in their homiletic works. Athanasius could be discoursing on Esau and Cyril on Edom without a hint of their Jewish lineage.[99] Among the Latin Fathers, Ambrose avowed that Isaac's blessing to Jacob "revealed that the kingdom was predestined to be bestowed on the Church rather than on the Synagogue," and the Jew "made subject to servitude."[100] But the Jews are an aside; his portrayal of a pious Jacob draws a vision of the Christian happy life. Jerome affirmed the "two nations" typology and elaborated on Esau as Edom, but he wrote

---

[97] Scholars debate the extent of Origen's familiarity with Jewish sources. See the previous references to N. R. M. de Lange, Paul Blowers, and John A. McGuckin, as well as Shaye J. D. Cohen, "Sabbath Law and Mishnah Shabbat in Origen *De Principiis*," *Jewish Studies Quarterly* 17 (2010): 160–89.

[98] "The Martyrs of Caesarea," *Annuaire de l'Institut de philology et d'histoire orientales et slaves* 7 (1939–40): 395–446; "Redifat dat Yisrael (persecution of Judaism)," in *Salo Wittmayer Baron Jubilee Volume*, 3 vols. (Jerusalem: American Academy for Jewish Research, 1974), 3: 213–45. I am aware that Lieberman's view that *Seder Neziqin* of the Palestinian Talmud originated in Caesarea is no longer accepted, and that his faith in rabbinic transmission permitted no open statement that rabbinic traditions of martyrology were shaped in response to Christian ones (which his evidence supports). What I find inspiring in his interpretive model is the agile moves between Church Father Eusebius and Caesarean rabbis, between *Ecclesiastical History* and the Palestinian Talmud, reading both back into the local context. If we are to make mistakes venturing guesses about Christian–Jewish exchange, they are better made in identifying historical context (where they are subject to control) than in devising irrefutable hermeneutical frameworks.

[99] *Select Writings and Letters of Athanasius, Bishop of Alexandria*, ed. Archibald Robertson, vol. 4 of *Nicene and Post-Nicene Fathers of the Christian Church*, ed. Philip Schaff and Henry Wace, 14 vols. (New York: Christian Literature Company, 1892), esp. 4: 258–62, 286; 337, 357, 529–30. St. Cyril of Alexandria, *Commentary on the Twelve Prophets*, trans. Robert C. Hill, 2 vols. (Washington, DC: Catholic University of America Press, 2008): 2: 23–28, 135–36. Hermeneutical principles may explain the Alexandrian Fathers' reticence about the typology. The penchant for allegorical as opposed to figural meaning may have swayed them away from Jacob as the prefiguration of Christ, especially as they were fighting Aryanism (the view of Christ as exclusively human).

[100] St. Ambrose on "Isaac, or the Soul" and "Jacob and the Happy Life," in *Seven Exegetical Works*, trans. Michael P. McHugh (Washington, DC: Catholic University of America Press, 1972), esp. pp. 151–54. Ambrose's interpretation, too, is moral and mystical rather than figural (typological).

his Midrash-informed *Hebrew Questions on Genesis* without mentioning a Jewish Esau.[101] John Chrysostom (349–407) poured his venom on the Jews without deploying the typology.[102] Mining references among the Church Fathers to construct the Christian typology carries the risk of exaggerating its impact. The typology was not central to Christian exegesis and anti-Jewish polemics, certainly not as central as it was to Midrash and Jewish anti-imperial discourse.

The asymmetry of the Jewish and Christian typologies bears highlighting. The Jewish typology sidelined Christianity and the Christian one sidelined Rome. The subject that each community marginalized was of utmost concern to the other, but neither community cared to sort it out in debate. Polemics deflected rather than confronted challenges. Those scholars viewing Jacob & Esau through the prisms of Christian–Jewish polemics not only accept the Christian framework but excluding Rome, also diminish the most painful Jewish experience of classical and Late Antiquity. The rabbis' proclamations against Rome appear as avoidance maneuvers against Christianity. Christianity, a moderate challenge that the rabbis thought they could deflect, substitutes for the empire, which, the rabbis repeatedly told us, wrought devastation on Jewish life and culture. Rome's unique role in shaping a history of Jewish powerlessness vanishes.

The Christianization of the empire, observed Gerson Cohen, turned the Jacob & Esau typology into political theory. The power of empire could now be drafted to ensure that "the older shall serve the younger." Even before the empire went Christian, Christians had highlighted Jewish powerlessness – the Temple's destruction and Bar-Kokhba's defeat – as a sign that God had punished the Jews for rejecting Christ. The force of such arguments now seemed inexorable. In a mid-fifth-century dialogue, the Church tells the Synagogue:

Look at the legions' standards, notice the name of the savior, observe the emperors worshipping Christ, and bear in mind that you are cast out from your kingdom. . . . You pay tribute to me, cannot come near the imperial power, be a prefect [or] a count, enter the senate, . . . get admitted into the army, touch the tables of the rich. You lost your nobility rank. . . . All of it . . . [conforms] to what was said to Rebecca . . . "the elder shall serve the younger."[103]

---

[101] *Saint Jerome's Hebrew Questions on Genesis*, trans. with introduction and commentary by C. T. R. Hayward (Oxford: Clarendon Press, 1995), esp. pp. 196–97.

[102] *Discourses against Judaizing Christians*, trans. Paul W. Harkins (Washington, DC: Catholic University of America Press, 1979).

[103] Anon., *Altercatio Ecclesiae et Synagogae* (CPL 577*)*, Library of Latin Texts. I modified A. Lukyn Williams's translation: *Adversus Judaeos*, p. 328.

Augustine himself was never as sanguine about imperial power marking spiritual superiority. Still, as he was setting the parameters of Christian tolerance of Jews whose blind wandering among the nations and subservient existence gave testimony to Christian truth – "slay them not, lest my people forget; scatter them with your power" (Psalms 59:11) – he rehearsed, in *The City of God*, the Christian Jacob & Esau typology. Here, and elsewhere, he rearticulated what had now become the underpinning of Christian policy: "The older people of the Jews was destined to serve the younger people, the Christians."[104]

Christian Rome encumbered Christianity with the Jewish–Roman past and Rome with the Christian claim to disinherit Israel. Rome disastrously reshaped the Jewish imperial experience. For the rabbis, says Seth Schwartz, Rome abrogated the historical alliance of empire and Jews – an exchange of loyalty and tax for a measure of legal autonomy.[105] Under Sassanid rule, the Babylonian Talmud declared at least some imperial laws valid – דינא דמלכותא דינא.[106] There was no echo in the Palestinian Talmud: The rabbis would owe Rome no allegiance. *Pace* Yosef Hayim Yerushalmi's "Jewish historical alliance with the rulers," it would take more than a millennium to reverse this Roman turn decisively.

Christianity made the imperial threat cultural, menacing a people left with nothing but its Torah, with dispossession of its heritage. Erecting typological barriers between Christians and Jews, imperial policies reinforced late antique provincialization of cultures and delegitimized rabbinic Judaism. The rabbis responded by constructing a counterculture, the universal claims of which relied on eventual settling of scores with the empire. Paradoxically, the imperial brother, Esau, was now Christian, and a two-millennia-long account opened. The deadly irony of the Christian Empire explains the rabbis' fixation on Rome, lessens puzzlement over their "thunderous silence" about Christianity, and renders the history of the Jacob & Esau typology one of endless surprise.

---

[104] *Concerning the City of God against the Pagans*, trans. Henry Bettenson (Harmondsworth, UK: Penguin Books, 1985), 16:35–38, 18:31, quotation on p. 698. (Augustine's rendering of Obadiah 1:21, p. 799, "those who have been saved will go up from Mount Zion to defend Mount Esau" is unusual, due probably to Old Latin Bibles. This makes it possible for him to speak of Zion and Esau-Edom as the Church of the Jews and Gentiles, respectively. The text is remarkable in associating the Church with Edom.) See also Letter to Asellicus (concerning Christians observing Jewish rituals and calling themselves Israel), *Epistulae* (epistles; CPL 262), Library of Latin Texts, epistle 196. Marcel Simon, *Verus Israel*, p. 188, sees in the latter traces of Christian–Jewish polemics.

[105] *Were the Jews a Mediterranean Society? Reciprocity and Solidarity in Ancient Judaism* (Princeton, NJ: Princeton University Press, 2010), pp. 112–29.

[106] *BT* Nedarim 28a; Gittin 10b; Baba Kama 113a; Baba Batra 54b–55a.

3   Esau, Ishmael, and Christian Europe: Medieval Edom

"It is a tradition we possess that Esau's soul incarnated in Jesus the Christian," said Isaac Abravanel in his Isaiah commentary, written shortly after the Jews' 1492 expulsion from Spain.[1] He provided an appropriate epithet for the medieval Jewish view of Esau. Christianity universally marked the Jews as the Other in medieval Europe. In response, the Jews' own Other, Esau and Edom, became Christian. A 1243 Würzburg tombstone for two Jews killed in a brawl with Christians reads: "Esau's descendants rose upon them and killed them."[2] Even Rashbam (Shmuel ben Meir 1085–1158), an Ashkenazi commentator averse to typology, and willing to question the traditional view of unremittingly hostile Esau, could not escape the lore of Esau's Christian identity. "The first came out red, all his body like a hairy shirt, so they called his name Esau" (Genesis 25:25): "Like a hairy shirt (כאדרת שער)" – comments Rashbam tersely – "worn by Christian pilgrims (שלובשים התועים, literally, those wandering in error)."[3] Esau and Edom came to mean Christian and Christianity. They were a living reality to medieval Jews. Jews wrote of Jacob & Esau with the messianic vision of Christian Edom's downfall

---

[1] Commentary on Isaiah 35:10, *Perush al Neviim u-ketuvim* (Jerusalem; Abarbanel, 1960): 3: 172.

[2] קמו עליהם בני עשו והרגום: Avraham (Rami) Reiner, "'Fragment to Fragment (shever qarev el shever)': Discoveries in the Würzburg Jewish Cemetery" (in Hebrew), *Zemanim* 95 (2006): 52–57.

[3] *Miqraot Gedolot ha-Keter*, ed. Menaḥem Kohen (Ramat-Gan: Bar-Ilan University, 1992–2013). (The pilgrim's hair cloak was a form of penance. I am indebted to Julie Mell and Joseph Shatzmiller.) For the Rashbam questioning Esau's malevolent intentions, see his commentary on Genesis 32:7, 32:8, 32:21, 32:23, and 32:29 and the explanatory notes in Martin Lockshin, *Rabbi Samuel ben Meir's Commentary on Genesis* (Lewiston, NY: Edwin Mellen, 1989). The twelfth-century Tosafists insisted that Esau remained uncircumcised. Isaac, apprehensive that Esau's red complexion indicated blood clots, waited to circumcise him, and the mature Esau declined to be circumcised. Genesis 25:25, *Sefer Tosafot ha-Shalem*, ed. Yaakov Gelis (Jerusalem: Mifal Tosafot ha-Shalem, 1984), 3: 19. *Tosafot*, literally, the "Additions," a critical gloss on the Talmud and on Rashi's commentary on it, were printed in all Talmud editions around the text, opposite Rashi. The Tosafists also wrote biblical commentaries. Most were Rashi's students.

foremost on their minds. Overwhelming the biblical story, the medieval narrative assumed a life of its own.

"Christian Esau" became part of the Jewish repertoire all the way to the twentieth century. Modern secularization and racialization would tarnish Esau's Christianity, but it was still evident. *Pace* the medieval Jewish commentators, however, Esau was not Christian from time immemorial; indeed, they made him so. He became Christian when Jews recognized, belatedly, that what they dismissed as another *minut* became the driving force of empire. Jacob and Esau's biblical uncle, Ishmael, brought this recognition. At crucial historical moments, Islam decisively shaped the Jacob & Esau relationship, and European history. The Muslim–Christian struggle, especially in Spain, transformed the Jewish messianic horizons and, with them, the Jacob & Esau typology. Spanish Jews thought of the Jewish Diaspora as living "under Edom and Ishmael." Of the two, the relationship with the first was the more traumatic, but while focusing on Edom, Jewish European history can also track a Muslim role in shaping Europe.

Ishmael and Esau: Islam and the Christian Empire

The Christian Empire remained alive in rabbinic discourse to modernity. The split into eastern and western Roman empires, solidified after Theodosius's death (395 CE), and the disintegration of the western empire in the fifth century, barely registered in contemporary Jewish sources. Whereas Christian polemics harped on Jerusalem's fall, Jewish polemics made no mention of the Vandals' sack of Rome in 410: The event that shook contemporaries and elicited Augustine's *The City of God*, a foundational text of Christendom, had no Jewish echo. The eastern empire, Byzantium, continued to carry the imperial title, and Charlemagne's coronation as a Roman emperor in 800 sustained an illusion of continuous Roman imperial rule. Rabbinic discourse elided the imperial split even after the Great Schism into Latin and Orthodox churches in 1054. Down to the fall of Byzantium to the Ottomans in 1453, Constantinople and Rome continued to stand interchangeably for imperial Edom.[4] In the Jewish even more than in the European imagination, the Roman Empire never fell.

---

[4] See how the *paytan* (liturgical poet) Yannai (*qerova* 158:43), in *The Liturgical Poems of Rabbi Yannai* (in Hebrew), ed. Zvi Meir Rabinovitz, 2 vols. (Jerusalem: Bialik Institute, 1987), 2: 175 (and note), hints at the "divided empire"; *Targum pseudo-Jonathan* to Numbers 24:19, 24, speaks of Constantinople and Caesarea as "the city" that the Messiah will destroy (fragmentary *Targumim* and Rashi mention Rome), and of troops

The Edom typology could elide such a fundamental geopolitical division because universal Christianity came increasingly to define empire. To the Talmud, the Roman Empire's religious character was of minor importance, but for medieval European Jews, it was paramount. With every proclamation of imperial renewal (*renovatio*), the emperor was anointed protector of the universal church, and the empire declared an *imperium christianum*. However diminished imperial authority was in practice, it derived legitimacy primarily from its Christian character. Jewish typology mirrored Christian ideals. Edom-Rome became first and foremost Christendom, and empire only by implication – "*that Rome whence Christ is Roman.*"[5]

Yet Jewish typology also reflected the divisions of imperial authority and the complexity of imperial ideals. In its radical interpretation, Charlemagne's *renovatio* was a *translatio*, displacement, the return of the imperial seat from Constantinople to Rome. The Carolingians answered Byzantine protests by claiming that Byzantium was "the Empire of the Greeks."[6] This comported well with both the Jewish and Byzantine visions of Greco-Roman civilization. For Jews, Rome represented Hellenistic culture, and Rome's descent from Greek lineage had been an established tradition: Kittim, identified with Rome, was son of Yavan (Greece in Hebrew; Genesis 10:4). *Midrash* refers to southern Italy as "Greece's Italy" – *Italia shel Yavan*.[7] Medieval Jewry's most popular history book, the *Josippon* (*Sefer Yosifon*) refers to Byzantium as Yavan.[8] The eastern empire was Greek by descent and Roman (i.e., Christian) by religion, Yavan and Edom at the same time. Rome and Constantinople alike represented Christendom.

The catalyst of Edom's Europeanization was, however, the Arab conquest of the Middle East in the 630s. The Islamic Caliphates dominating the southern Mediterranean all the way to Spain mounted a challenge to the Rome-centered Edom typology. An Islamic empire, identified with Ishmael, now ruled most of the Jewish Diaspora. Remarkably, Jewish hostility to Rome continued unabated, and the Edom-Rome connection

joining from Rome and Constantinople; *Midrash Tehilim* 60:3 speaks of the wars of Rome and Constantinople.

[5] Dante, *Purgatorio* XXXII: 102: " Quella Roma onde Cristo e romano": *Divina Commedia*, ed. Giorgio Petrocchi (Milan: Mondadori, 1966–67).

[6] Robert Folz, *The Concept of Empire in Western Europe from the Fifth to the Fourteenth Century*, trans. Sheila Ann Ogilvie (London: Edward Arnold, 1969), esp. p. 171.

[7] *Bereshit Rabba* 67:6 – Greece is omitted in some printed editions – and Rashi on Genesis 27:39.

[8] *Sefer Yosifon*, ed. with an introduction, commentary, and notes by David Flusser, 2 vols. (Jerusalem: Bialik Institute, 1980–81): 1: *passim*, e.g., p. 7 (*Yosifon* 1:24–25).

was never questioned. No rivaling typology of Islam and Ishmael, equal in power to Edom-Rome, ever emerged. But Jews under Islam needed to work out their own redemption into the Four Empires scheme. Ishmael and the Arabs had to join Esau and Rome. A religious divide, Christian against Muslim, now marked the contenders on the Mediterranean scene. This was clearest to medieval Spanish Jews who lived the *reconquista* wars, the Iberian Christian kingdoms' gradual takeover of Muslim Al-Andalus. The Islamic Caliphates triggered, and reinforced, Esau's and Edom's Christianization.

That said, Esau's Christianization lagged behind that of the Roman Empire. The sixth-century Palestinian *paytan* (liturgical poet) Yannai makes the lag palpable. The signs of Christian triumph were evident all over contemporary Palestine. Yannai lived through Justinian's anti-Jewish legislation and his brutal repression of two Samaritan revolts (in which Jews took part). He acknowledged that Christian oppression was having its effects: "The lamps of Edom shine on the dead [probably Jesus]; the lamps of Zion are forgotten like the dead."[9] But his Edom poetry, vividly envisioning a messianic triumph over Rome while beseeching his congregants not to take up arms, was virtually silent on the empire's Christian character.[10] Jewish powerlessness was central to Yannai, the Christian character of imperial oppression insignificant. Ignoring Jacob and Esau's reconciliation, and mildly rebuking Jacob for prostrating himself before Esau, Yannai pleaded patient waiting for divine redemption and revenge.

Jewish messianic hopes had remained dim since the fiasco of Emperor Julian the Apostate's plan to rebuild the Temple (362–63). But the Persian (Sassanid) conquest of Palestine in 614, which permitted the Jews (who collaborated) to take vengeance upon the Christians and, for a short time, renew sacrifices at the Temple site, reignited messianic expectations. The Byzantines reconquered Jerusalem in 629 and, shortly thereafter, issued an order for forced baptism, ensuring that the Arabs arriving in 634 and entering Jerusalem in 638 would be welcomed as liberators. Jewish liturgy and apocalyptic literature expressed excitement,

---

[9] *Qerovah* 109:22 (to be-haalotkha): 2: 38. For Edom in the *Piyut*: Israel Rosenson, "Edom – Poetry, Sermons and History" (in Hebrew), *Masoret ha-Piyut* 3 (2002): 45–75. For Yannai and the Samaritan revolts: Laura Lieber, "'You Have Skirted This Hill Long Enough': The Tension between Rhetoric and History in a Byzantine Piyyut," *Hebrew Union College Annual* 80 (2009): 63–114. In a Yom Kippur poem, Yannai poured contempt and wrath on Christian beliefs and practices: II: 221–23. Thanks to Eden Hacohen for the Yannai references to Christianity.

[10] His warning, "Do not enter their churches," part of elaborate counseling on limiting exchange with non-Jews, was the only hint that Rome was no longer pagan. *Qerovot* to Va-Yishlaḥ and Devarim, I: 191–201, and II: 123–29.

with the promise that the Arab victory would be but a prelude to the restoration of Israel: "Fear not! God brings Ishmael's empire only to redeem you from the evil one."[11]

Instead, the Jews faced a long economic decline in Palestine and had to settle for the inferior status of *dhimmi* – "people of the contract," a non-Muslim minority, afforded protection and property rights – throughout the Arab empire. Conditions in the Jewish Diaspora from Babylonia to Spain varied greatly over the centuries of Islamic government. There was no Arab or Islamic ordeal equivalent to the Ancient Roman and medieval Christian ones, but late Midrash gave expression to the hope for messianic redemption from Arab rule and engaged in anti-Muslim polemics. Ishmael joined Esau as a wicked and oppressive brother, the end of whose empire, too, Jews anticipated.

Ishmael played a secondary role to Esau in Jewish traditions. In the Book of Genesis, Ishmael is the son of Abraham from his mistress Hagar, and a brother of Isaac. At the behest of Abraham's wife Sarah, Ishmael is expelled from the household, but God assures Abraham that Ishmael, too, will be blessed and become a nation. Ishmael resides in the southern desert, and his daughter becomes Esau's third wife. The association between Ishmael and the Arabs preceded rabbinic literature and appears in *Jubilees* (second century BCE) and Josephus. Christian writers from Eusebius to Jerome to Isidore accepted the association, and so did Islamic traditions.[12]

Pre-Islamic rabbinic literature was ambivalent toward Ishmael. In Tannaitic and Amoraic literature, Israel's identity as Isaac's descendants is defined against Ishmael, who is excluded from the household because, as a boy, playing, he shows a predilection for idolatry and murder and challenges Isaac's inheritance.[13] But he remains blessed, and in contrast with Esau, Midrash also portrays him positively: "'God blessed Abraham with everything' (Genesis 24:1) – this teaches us that Ishmael repented [his bad ways] when Abraham was still alive."[14] There is a fair amount of stereotyping of the Ishmaelites as sexually licentious and as thieves. As Ishmael is often paired with Esau, the halo extends to

---

[11] *Nistarot shel Rabbi Shimon bar Yoḥai* [The mysteries of Rabbi Shimon bar Yoḥai], in *Midreshe Geula* [Homilies of redemption], ed. Yehudah Even-Shmuel (Tel Aviv: Bialik Institute & Masada, 1943), p. 188; Elazar ha-Kalir, "Oto ha-Yom [That day]," *Midreshe Geula*, p. 160: "Edomites and Ishmaelites will be fighting in the Acra valley, . . . and Israel will be coming out of the city, . . . and their Messiah will reveal himself."

[12] John Tolan, *Saracens: Islam in the Medieval European Imagination* (New York: Columbia University Press, 2002): pp. 10–11, 286–87, nn. 24–26.

[13] *Bereshit Rabba* 53:11.

[14] *BT* Baba Batra 16b; *Bereshit Rabba* 47:5 (for Ishmael's blessing).

him. But unlike Esau, Ishmael is not "wicked."[15] Leading pre-Islamic Jewish rabbis were called Yishmael. Both before and after the confrontation with Islam, Jewish exegetes debated the merit of Ishmael's expulsion and questioned Sarah's treatment of Hagar.[16] The contrast with Esau-Edom is stark.

Early medieval *Midrashim – Pirqe Rabbi Eliezer, Exodus Rabbah, Tanḥuma, Midrash Tehilim –* reworked earlier rabbinic material to produce a more hostile picture of Ishmael and the Ishmaelites. *Midrash ha-Gadol* (the Great Midrash), an expansive Yemenite compilation of the thirteenth or early fourteenth century, shows a full picture of medieval Ishmael from the perspective of Jews under Islam. Responding to the Islamic tradition identifying Ishmael as the brother whom Abraham was to sacrifice, medieval Midrashim highlight Ishmael's hatred of Isaac, and his wish to displace, even kill him, and become head of the family.[17] They emphasize Abraham's disapprobation of "wicked" Ishmael and stridently affirm Isaac's election.[18] Ishmael emerges on the side of Esau as a threat to Israel.

Yet medieval Midrashim also reveal a complexity of attitudes toward Arabs and Islam rarely shown toward Christianity. Protesting oppression, and insisting on the Jews' right to the Land of Israel, they also hint that exile may be tolerable.[19] Calling the Ishmaelites "thorns" and

---

[15] Carol Bakhos, *Ishmael on the Border: Rabbinic Portrayals of the First Arab* (Albany: State University of New York Press, 2006), pp. 47–74.

[16] Adele Reinhartz and Miriam-Simma Walfish, "Conflict and Coexistence in Jewish Interpretation," in *Hagar, Sarah, and Their Children: Jewish, Christian, and Muslim Perspectives*, ed. Phyllis Trible and Letty M. Russell (Louisville, KY: Westminster John Knox Press, 2006), pp. 101–25. Christian writers, in contrast, showed no ambivalence. The Arabs' association with Ishmael did not prevent Hagar and her descendants from becoming, among the Church Fathers, an archetype of the outcasts, from Jews to Christian heretics: Elizabeth Clark, "Interpretive Fate amid the Church Fathers," in *Hagar, Sarah, and Their Children*, pp. 127–47.

[17] Reuven Firestone, *Journeys in Holy Lands: The Evolution of the Abraham-Ishmael Legends in Islamic Exegesis* (Albany: State University of New York Press, 1990), pp. 135–52, discusses the competing Islamic traditions on the identity of the son whom Abraham was to sacrifice, and the triumph of the tradition identifying Ishmael. For Ishmael's hatred: *Pirqe de-Rabbi Eliezer* 30–31, ed. C. M. Horowitz (Jerusalem: Maqor, 1972); *Midrash Ha-Gadol* on Genesis 50:21, ed. S. Schechter (Cambridge: Cambridge University Press, 1902).

[18] *Pirqe de-Rabbi Eliezer* 30; *Exodus Rabbah* 1:1; and the discussion in Carol Bakhos, *Ishmael on the Border*, pp. 85–96.

[19] *Pirqe de-Rabbi Eliezer* 32: Ishmael was so named (meaning in Hebrew, "may God hear") as God foresaw that Israel would cry to the heavens on account of his oppression. See also *Midrash Ha-Gadol* Genesis 25:14. Asserting the right to the Land against Ishmael: *Pirqe de-Rabbi Eliezer* 38; *Midrash Ha-Gadol* Genesis 25:5–6. Tolerable exile: *Pirqe de-Rabbi Eliezer* 48: "Israel lived in Egypt safe and carefree." See Joseph Heinemann, *Agadot ve-Toldotehen*, p. 193, for the suggestion that the narrator had life under Arab rule in mind.

"thieves," they offer a softer version of their rejection of the Torah: The Ishmaelites abide by their ancestors' tradition.[20] The stories of Abraham's visits to Ishmael in *Pirqe de-Rabbi Eliezer* (30) seem to be in dialogue with Arab tales. They reveal Abraham's love for Ishmael, show Ishmael listening to Abraham and Abraham blessing his house, and sympathetically depict Ishmael's mother and Arab wife. Esau's portrayal, in contrast, remains negative and apocalyptic – everywhere. In *Midrash ha-Gadol*, Esau marries Ishmael's daughter in a conspiracy to consolidate both families under his leadership: He expects Ishmael to imitate him by committing fratricide, that is, killing Isaac, and then he, Esau, will avenge his father and kill Ishmael. Ishmael's refusal to take part is not very honorable but the lesson is clear: Esau is the greater danger to Israel, and a threat to Ishmael, too.[21]

Esau and Ishmael's dual threat shaped the redemptive vision of Jews under Islam. *Pirqe de-Rabbi Eliezer*, redacted in the late eighth or ninth century, reenvisioned the Four Empires to include Ishmael, but without a clear order of succession.[22] Rabbi Saadiah Gaon (882–954), the intellectual leader of Babylonian Jewry in its golden age, appears to have viewed the Fourth Empire alternately as Roman and Arab.[23] Pointing out that Mount Seir was in Israel and not in Italy, he questioned the genealogy of Edom to Rome.[24] The Spanish-Jewish biblical commentator, poet, and philologist Abraham ibn Ezra (1092–1167) radicalized Saadiah's vision. Wandering most of his life around the Mediterranean as an exile from Muslim Almohad Spain (Al-Andalus), Ibn Ezra insisted that Israel was presently under Ishmael's reign, not Edom's. The Romans descended from Kittim, not from Edom, and biblical Edom prophecies were directed, for the most part, to the days of King David and the Babylonian Empire, not to Rome or the messianic

---

[20] For "thorns": *Midrash Ha-Gadol*, Genesis introduction to *Toledot* (p. 384). Loyalty to tradition: *Pirqe de-Rabbi Eliezer* 41. Heinemann, *Agadot ve-Toldotehen*, pp. 194–95, suggests that "we cannot depart from our ancestors' rite" may also reflect Jewish apologetics – rejection of pressures to convert.

[21] Genesis 27:41, 28:8–9.

[22] 28 (and see also 48). Compare *Midrash ha-Gadol* 15:9. Discussion: Carol Bakhos, *Ishmael on the Border*, pp. 125–27.

[23] The "Eighth Composition on Redemption," *Sefer Emunot ve-Deot* (Book of beliefs and opinions) (Jerusalem: Maqor, 1972), pp. 134–35, focuses exclusively on Edom. *Perush Shir-Hashirim* (commentary on the Song of Solomon), in *Geon ha-Geonim* (The *Geonim's* pride), ed. Shlomo Wertheimer (Jerusalem: n.p., 1925), speaks of Edom as the Fourth Empire (pp. 75–76, 119, 125), with only a hint of Ishmael (p. 129). Saadiah's Daniel commentary, in contrast, refers to Ishmael as the Fourth Kingdom and offers diverse schemes for Edom: 7:6–8, 7:12, 7:23, and 8:9, in *Miqraot Gedolot ha-Keter*, ed. Menaḥem Kohen (Ramat-Gan: Bar-Ilan University, 1992–2013).

[24] *Saadia's Polemic against Ḥiwi al-Balkhi*, ed. Israel Davidson (New York: The Jewish Theological Seminary, 1915), pp. 76–77 (line 67).

age.[25] The Greeks and Romans constituted one Greco-Roman empire, the third in the scheme of redemption, and Ishmael was the fourth.[26] The majority of the Jewish Diaspora, Ibn Ezra noted, were subject to Ishmael (Daniel 12:11). He made them the center of redemption.

Ibn Ezra proved too radical even for Spanish (Sephardi) Jews.[27] The tenth-century poet Dunash ben Lavrat joined the redemption from Edom and Ishmael, beseeching God, in a *shabbat* song, to "tread the winepress in Boẓra [Edom-Rome] and in overpowering Babylonia [Arab Ishmael]."[28] Maimonides, in his *Epistle to Yemen* (1172), articulated the hegemonic Sephardi view of the current exile as joint Roman-Arab domination: "The advent of the Messiah will take place at some time subsequent to the universal expansion of the Roman and the Arab empires."[29] Provençal biblical commentator, scientist, and philosopher Gersonides (Levi ben Gershom, Ralbag, 1288–1344) agreed: "The Fourth Empire ... will be divided, part ruled by the Ishmaelites, part by the Romans."[30] The Spanish Kabbalist and biblical commentator Baḥya ben Asher (c. 1255–1340) likewise followed suit: "'The Lord your God will put all these curses upon your enemies and on your foes who persecuted you' (Deuteronomy 30:7): These are the two nations among whom we are oppressed – Edom and Ishmael.... Your 'enemies' are Esau's descendants and your 'foes' are Ishmael's descendants." By Baḥya's time, however, the *reconquista* made Christian hegemony

---

[25] Genesis 27:40: "Dreamers who have not woken up from their fool's sleep think that we live in Edom's exile"; Numbers 24:17: "It seems to me that ['a star shall come out from Jacob'] is a prophecy on David.... The fools think that those who [so] interpret deny the Messiah. Heavens forbid!"

[26] Commentary on Daniel, introduction, 2:39, 7:14–18, 12:11, in *Miqraot Gedolot*.

[27] The Hebrew names for Spain and France are Sepharad and Ẓarefat. They carry a messianic message. Obadiah's oracle on Edom (1:20) promises that "the exiles of ... Israel ... as far as Ẓarfat, and the exiles of Jerusalem who are in Sepharad shall possess the cities of the Negev." The gathering of the Sephardi and Ashkenazi (Northern European) exiles became Israel's redemption. The term *Sephardi* was extended to all Jews under Islamic rule, the term *Ashkenazi* to all European Jewry under Christian rule.

[28] דרוך פורה בתוך בצרה וגם בבל אשר גברה: *The Koren Siddur* (in Hebrew and English) (Jerusalem: Koren Publishers, 2009), p. 593. This is a play on Isaiah's prophecy about the nations 63:3.

[29] *Epistles of Maimonides: Crisis and Leadership*, trans. with notes by Abraham Halkin (Philadelphia: Jewish Publication Society, 1993), p. 121. *Midrash ha-Gadol* on Genesis 6:15, 15:9, and 27:29 largely concurred with Maimonides' view of dual liberation: "'Be lord over your brothers': These are the sons of Ishmael and Keturah. 'And may your mother's sons bow down to you': These are Esau's sons and his chiefs." (However, 15:9 has Ishmael as the Fourth Empire in one homily and Edom and Ishmael in another.)

[30] *Perush Daniel* (commentary on Daniel) 2:45 (Rome: Obadiah, Menasseh and Benjamin of Rome, 1470). See also Daniel 11:11, the final war between the King of the North (Rome) and the Negev (Ishmael), to be followed by Israel's redemption.

evident, and he added: "The essence of our exile is . . . the evil empire of Edom."[31]

At the height of the Islamic Caliphates, when the majority of Jewry lived under Islam, Esau and Rome continued to haunt the Jewish imagination. Even Ibn Ezra accepted the association between Edom and Rome, and included liberation from Rome in his scheme of redemption.[32] But the invasion of Spain by the radical Muslim Almohads in the 1140s that sent Maimonides and Ibn Ezra fleeing gave rise, among Spanish Jews, to the single consistent expression of preference for Christian over Muslim rule: "[Better to be] under Edom and not under Ishmael (תחת אדום ולא תחת ישמעאל)."[33] Spanish-Jewish intellectuals from Maimonides to Baḥya opined that "there is no nation in the world that hates Israel as much as Ishmael's descendants."[34] Naḥmanides (1194–1270), who was forced into exile from Christian Spain, still preferred Christian to Muslim rule. The preference – never shared by Jews elsewhere – vanished in the aftermath of the 1391 pogroms, and even in its heyday, did not alter the Edom eschatology.[35] "Edom will fall at the Messiah's hands, for our exile today, at the Romans' hands, is Edom's exile," said Naḥmanides (Numbers 24:18).

Yet, Sephardi Jews faced an intellectual dilemma. Ibn Ezra challenged the Romans' Idumaean origins so that he could retain the prospect of liberation from Ishmael. If the Romans had no ethnic or territorial relationship to Edom, how could Sephardi Jews associate the two? "Christianity" was Ibn Ezra's answer.

---

[31] *Kad ha-Qemaḥ* (The flour vase), 2 vols. (New York: Kelilat Yofi Pub., 1960): 1: 57b–58a (under *Geulah*).

[32] Ibn Ezra conceded that Obadiah's concluding prophecy on Edom – "and saviors shall go up on Mount Zion to judge the mountain of Esau" (1:21) – referred to the messianic age. He insisted in an almost modern critical fashion that Daniel directed his prophecies to a succession of Persian Achaemenid and Greek Seleucid kings (chapter 8) and that Daniel could not predict the end of days (9:30), but he extended his prophecies to the Second Temple's destruction (9:25–26, 11:30–34), Constantine (11:36–38), and the end of Rome (11:39–45). The rationalist commentator Yosef ibn Kaspi (1280–1340) rejected any association of Edom and Rome and rendered himself an outsider: *Mishne Kesef*, ed. Yiẓḥak Halevi Last (Jerusalem: Meqorot, 1970), second pamphlet, p. 40. See also the references later in this section to Yosef Albo and Ḥayim Galippa.

[33] Baḥya ben Asher, *Perush Rabbenu Baḥya al ha-Torah*, 5 vols. in 2 (Jerusalem: Mishor, 1994), 5: 137 (on Deuteronomy 30:7). (It was censored in most editions.) Baḥya reworks *BT* Shabbat 11a: "[Better to be] under Ishmael than under any other people (*goy*; גוי)." In medieval times, *goy* came to mean "Edom," and Rashi interprets: "Better serve Ishmael than the more wicked Idumaeans." A century later, Spanish Jews reversed the meaning. See Dov Septimus: "'Under Edom and Not under Ishmael' – Genealogy of a Phrase" (in Hebrew), *Ẓiyon* 47:2 (1982): 103–11.

[34] *Perush Rabbenu Baḥya al ha-Torah*, 1: 114 (on Genesis 21:14), 5: 137.

[35] But Dov Septimus, "Under Edom," 109–11, discerns nostalgia for Christian Spain even among the exiles of the 1492 expulsion.

Rome that exiled us descended from Kittim ... and is the Greek Empire (as I interpreted in [the Book of] Daniel). But a few people believed in the man whom they made god [Jesus]. When Rome converted – in the age of Constantine, who, on the initiative of an Idumaean priest, upheld the new religion and put the cross on his flag – a few Idumaeans were the only ones to follow the new teaching; hence Rome was called the Empire of Edom.[36]

The idea that Idumaeans were the first Christians was as far-fetched as that they were Romans, but it reflected a new consciousness of Roman otherness. With Sephardi Jews witnessing two competing empires holding up cross and sickle, Christianity – not empire – came to define Roman otherness.

Future Sephardi commentators supplemented Ibn Ezra's religious Edom with an ethnic one, but the idea that Christianity was Edom's essence, and Constantine's conversion a major turning point, became commonplace.[37] Maimonides cited it in his *Epistle to Yemen*; biblical commentators David Kimḥi (Radak, 1160–1235) and Naḥmanides highlighted the Christian character of the "Idumaean-Roman emperors"; philosopher Joseph Albo (1380–1444) – the only major figure to accept Ibn Ezra's denial of Rome's Idumaean ethnicity – fancied an Idumaean priest converting Rome; and Isaac Abravanel (1437–1508) cited his predecessors in a grand synthesis of religious and ethnic Edom, composed in the shadow of the 1492 expulsion from

---

[36] Genesis 27:40, *Perush ha-Torah* (Torah commentary) (Istanbul [Kushtandina], 1514); *Miqraot Gedolot ha-Keter* (censored in most editions; Vatican MS Ebr. 38, Jerusalem: Maqor, 1974 includes it). The origins of Ibn Ezra's Christian Edom are mysterious. He says nothing that would suggest that he sees himself as a revolutionary innovator. Additions to the popular *Josippon* recounted stories of Christian Idumaeans inciting the Romans against the Jewish authorities in Jesus' time: *Sefer Yosifon*, ed. David Flusser, 1: 439–42, 2: 54–58. Flusser dates them all to before 1160 (2: 57). He also notes (2: 106) that *Josippon* itself uses a tenth-century model of Christianization from above – a missionary converting a king or tribe chief – to describe an Idumaean initiative with the Egyptians in Herod's time. Could Josipponian stories about Idumaean priests converting Constantine have circulated in the early twelfth century so that Ibn Ezra would take the story for granted?

[37] This is also the case for Spanish-Jewish philosopher Abraham ibn Daud (Ravad I, 1110–1180), whose brief "Zikhron Divre Romi (chronicle of Rome)" diverges from the common Josippian account of Rome's Idumaean origins by attributing Idumaean ethnicity to the Goths ("Bene Uẓ," people of biblical Uẓ, commonly associated with Edom [Lamentations 4:21]). In his account, Constantine had first instituted Christianity. The Goths conquered Spain, married into the imperial Roman dynasty, and later became Roman Christian. Spain is doubly Idumaean, religiously Roman Christian and ethnically Gothian. "Zikhron Divre Romi," in *Seder Olam Rabba ve-Seder Olam Zuta u-Megilat Taanit ve-Sefer Ha-Kabbalah le-ha-Ravad* (Basel, 1580), pp. 80a–83b; Mordechai Klein and Elḥanan Molner, "Ha-Ravad as Historian, II" (in Hebrew), *Hazofeh Quartalis Hebraica* 8 (1924): 24–35; Gerson Cohen, *A Critical Edition with a Translation and Notes of The Book of Tradition (Sefer Ha-Qabbalah) by Abraham ibn Daud* (Philadelphia: Jewish Publication Society of America, 1967), pp. 250–55.

Spain.[38] Among Sephardi Jews, the Christianization of Edom-Rome was a result of the *reconquista*, of the confrontation between Islam and Christianity first, and only later of Christian persecution.

Conditions in medieval Europe north of the Pyrenees converged with Islam to the south to Christianize Edom. In contrast with Late Antiquity, the Jews were the single tolerated religious minority in medieval Europe. Otto I's coronation in 962 as a Holy Roman Emperor (*Imperator Romanus Sacer*) reinforced the Carolingian legacy of *imperium christianum*. The religious divide became definitive of Jews' relations with the empire. The political limits of the medieval empire – the rise of a powerful papacy to challenge the emperor in the eleventh century, the Holy Roman Empire's decentralization in the thirteenth, and the centralizing national monarchies emerging in the late Middle Ages – reinforced the primacy of the Christian–Jewish divide. The empire aspired to universality, but Christendom, not empire, defined Europe, singling out the Jews as the Other.

Unlike their compatriots under Islam, northern European (Ashkenazi) Jews never doubted Rome's Idumaean ethnicity. They cited in support the *Josippon* (*Sefer Yosifon*), a history book edited in southern Italy in the first half of the tenth century and attributed to Yosef ben Gorion, a late Second Temple Jewish leader (whose name was confused with that of the historian Josephus; hence the book's name). *Josippon*'s anonymous editor invented a tale about Rome's origins that tied together the biblical narrative and early Roman history. He added the story, as an introduction, to an existing Hebrew manuscript, which represented a reworking of the Latin Josephus and the Book of the

[38] Maimonides, *Epistle to Yemen*, pp. 98–99; David Kimḥi on Isaiah 34:1, *Perush Radak al Yeshayah* (Kimḥi's commentary on Isaiah), ed. Eliezer Aryeh Finkelstein (New York: n. p., 1926), Part I (censored in most editions); Naḥmanides (Ramban), *Sefer ha-Geula* (Book of redemption), ed. Yehoshua Aharonson (Tel Aviv: Sifriati, 1959), pp. 53, 58; Yosef Albo, *Sefer ha-Iqarim* (Book of principles), ed. Yehoshua Aharonson (Tel Aviv: Sifriati, 1959): 4:42 (Albo quotes Rabbi Ḥayim Galippa's lost "Epistle of Redemption" [fourteenth-century Navarre] as supporting a radical view: Daniel's prophecy was directed to the Second Temple period and the Fourth Empire was Greece); Yiẓḥak Abravanel on Isaiah 35:10, *Perush al Neviim Aḥaronim* (Commentary on the later prophets) (Jerusalem: Torah va-Daat, 1956), pp. 169–70. A Jewish polemicist against the Christian convert Avner of Burgos (1270–1350) proposed that Constantine was himself Idumaean or converted by an Idumaean priest: Yehudah Rozental, "Mi-tokh 'Sefer Alfonso' (Selections from the book of Alfonso)," in *Studies and Essays in Honor of Abraham A. Neuman*, ed. Meir Ben-Horin, Bernard D. Weinryb, and Solomon Zeitlin (Leiden: Brill, 1962), p. 611. Yehudah Rozental, "Ribit min ha-Nokhri II (Taking interest from non-Jews)," *Talpiyot* 6:1/2 (1953): 139–52, provides invaluable references. For medieval European Jews' view of the origins of Christianity: Ram ben Shalom, *Facing Christian Culture: Historical Consciousness and Images of the Past among the Jews of Spain and Southern France during the Middle Ages* (in Hebrew) (Jerusalem: Ben-Zvi Institute and the Hebrew University, 2006), pp. 147–207.

Maccabees.[39] The motives prompting the editor, from anti-Christian polemics (the area was still under Byzantine rule) to local patriotism to literary inspiration, remain mysterious, but the compilation became the medieval Jewish history book par excellence.[40] It was translated into Arabic, repeatedly expanded in the high Middle Ages, and read throughout the Jewish Diaspora. In the early sixteenth century, it provided a major source for another popular history, *Sefer ha-Yashar*, and in 1546, it became the first book to be translated into Yiddish and printed with many illustrations.[41]

The *Josippon* told how Esau's grandson, Zepho (Genesis 36:11), captured by Joseph in the skirmish over Jacob's burial in Hebron, escaped to Carthage, joined their king in his expedition to Italy against the Kittim, and established there his own dynasty. Rome's founder, Romulus, descended from Zepho. An influx of Idumaean refugees from King David joined Romulus, and he reinforced Rome against David.[42] The Romans were thus a Yavan-Edom hybrid, and the two Jewish traditions about Roman lineage were joined together. Sixteenth-century scholars questioned the *Josippon* narrative, but for medieval Jews, it removed any doubt about the historicity of Edom-Rome. From the start, they reasoned, Rome and Jerusalem were at war, and fortunes reversed once could be again reversed. Confronting Christian Rome, medieval European Jews reshaped the Jacob & Esau typology to include both empire and church. The *Josippon* stories, repeatedly told, tightened Christian Rome's historical ties to biblical Edom both religiously and ethnically.[43]

---

[39] *Sefer Yosifon*, ed. David Flusser, 2: 74–120; *The Arabic Josippon*, introd. and trans. Shulamit Sela, 2 vols. (Jerusalem: Ben-Zvi Institute and Tel Aviv University, 2009): 1: 3–84.

[40] Saskia Dönitz, "Historiography Among Byzantine Jews: The Case of Sefer Yosippon," in *Jews in Byzantium: Dialectics of Minority and Majority Cultures*, ed. Robert Bonfil et al. (Leiden: Brill, 2012), pp. 951–68.

[41] *Sefer ha-Yashar*, ed. and introduction by Joseph Dan (Jerusalem: Bialik Institute, 1986).

[42] *Sefer Yosifon*, I: 10–19. Gerson Cohen marvelously recounts the *Josippon* moment in "Esau as a Symbol in Early Medieval Thought," pp. 40–44. David Flusser suggests Christian origins for the Zepho legend: 1: 11, n. 19, but, in his history of prophets and kings, the Persian historian Abū Jaʿfar Muḥammad ibn Jarīr al-Ṭabarī (839–923) provides a genealogy of Job, whom he identifies as Byzantine, that has Esau as his ancestor. It appears that by the turn of the tenth century, stories were circulating around the Mediterranean about Esau's ancestry of both the Romans and the Byzantines (the latter reputed among Muslims for their religious zeal): *The History of al-Ṭabarī*, trans. Franz Rosenthal, 40 vols. (Albany: State University of New York Press, 1984–2007): 2: 140. I owe this reference to Danny Crowther of Oxford University.

[43] While Rome's Idumaean lineage sustained the Edom eschatology, the *Josippon* ironically marked a shift toward a positive Jewish view of the Roman Empire as well. It described the emperors as benevolent (see esp. 1: 404–5, 409–13), and blamed Jerusalem's destruction on the Jewish rebels: Ram ben Shalom, *Facing Christian Culture*, pp. 111–12. Yiẓhak Baer thought that the *Josippon* preached patient submission: "The Hebrew Jossipon," in

The Islamic Caliphates temporarily shifted the Jewish focus from Esau to Ishmael, and an Islamic "fundamentalist" movement, the Almohads, created a two-century Sephardi preference for Christian over Muslim rule. This remained a blip in Edom's – and Jewish – history. Notwithstanding the Sephardi preference, by the high Middle Ages Edom, and Christian Europe, staged a forceful return. For Kimḥi, Naḥmanides, Albo, and Abravanel – not to mention Ashkenazi commentators like Rashi – Ishmael withdrew into the background. They were living, they thought, in Edom's exile, the last one, and they were anticipating Rome's downfall. Midrash's hostility toward Islam never matched its enduring hatred of Rome, and the trauma of Roman imperial experience remained formative of the Jewish relationship with Christianity.

In Islamic countries, where Jews felt free to express hatred of Christianity, *Birkat ha-Minim*, the malediction against the Jewish "sectarians" (understood in medieval times as apostates) recited thrice daily in Jewish prayer, often included an explicit invective against the Christians (*Noẓerim*). The malediction also appealed to God to uproot the "empire of insolence" (*memshelet zadon*). The last rubric was broad enough to include Muslim governments, yet while Christians repeatedly complained that the Jews were cursing them in the synagogue, we know of no similar Muslim complaint.[44] The Jewish grievances against the Christian Empire, enshrined as *memshelet zadon* in *Birkat ha-Minim*, so overwhelmed those against Muslim rule that Muslims recognized the malediction's anti-Christian bent.

The conjunction of empire and Christianity ensured that, short of a messianic intervention, the Jews, beholden to the Edom typology, would have no opportunity for victory. All three metropoleis that stood as surrogates for the Roman Empire in rabbinic literature fell to their enemies in Late Antiquity and the Middle Ages: Rome was sacked in 410 and the western empire dismembered by the Barbarians; the Crusaders' Caesarea – "Caesarea and Jerusalem: If one says to you that both are destroyed [or] that both are flourishing, do not believe him" (*BT*, Megilah 6a) – was laid to ruins by the Mamluks in 1265; and Byzantium saw its

---

Studies and Essays in Jewish History (in Hebrew), 2 vols. (Jerusalem: Israel Historical Society, 1986): 2: 101–27. Flusser denied that the *Josippon* had a coherent worldview but emphasized its nonmessianic character: *Sefer Yosifon*, 2: 169–71. See also Joshua Holo, "Byzantine Jewish Ethnography," in *Jews in Byzantium*, ed. Robert Bonfil et al., pp. 923–49.

[44] Ruth Langer, *Cursing the Christians? A History of Birkat HaMinim* (New York: Oxford University Press, 2012), esp. pp. 40–65. Langer is puzzled (pp. 58, 65) by the malediction's pronouncedly anti-Christian bent under Muslim rule. I hope my account of the Edom-Rome topos allays the puzzlement. In medieval Europe, the *minim* expanded to include Christians in general.

territory progressively taken over by Muslim invaders, with the fall of Constantinople in 1453. Muslim armies repeatedly brought down the symbols of Roman and Christian power, but the Jewish Diaspora had no opportunity to rejoice. First Byzantium stood for Rome, and then Roman pope and empire stood for Christendom. Christian persecution of Jews in medieval Europe would sustain the Jacob & Esau typology, as well as hope against hope for redemption, for another millennium.

From Empire to Church: Christendom and Medieval Edom

Medieval Europe represented the apex of the Edom typology. Christian Edom emerged against the background of the Crusades, burnings of the Talmud, conversion offensives, and the Jews' expulsion from Western Europe in the late Middle Ages. Isaiah's prophecy about the nations (63:1–6), depicting God returning from the battlefield in Edom, attired in crimson clothes soiled with the nations' blood, became central to the Jewish *imaginaire*. In lament liturgy (*qinot*), petitions for mercy (*selihot*), and Crusade chronicles, the memory of the Jewish martyrs of the 1096 and later pogroms fed repeated calls to God to destroy the enemy.[45] Sephardi Jewry entertained a more peaceful messianic vision, anticipating the nations' conversion, but with the *reconquista*, the Ashkenazi vision began leaving its marks on Spanish Jews, too. The gap between Edom and Amaleq, between the wicked brother and the genocide perpetrator, closed down. Rashi (1040–1105) crystallized medieval Esau and Edom in his consummate biblical commentary:[46] "The Holy One, Blessed Be He, swore that His Name shall not be perfect and His Throne shall not be perfect until Esau's name is erased" (Exodus 17:16).[47]

---

[45] Israel Yuval, *Two Nations in Your Womb*, pp. 92–115, discusses the sources in detail and provides references. He tracks a Palestinian-Ashkenazi tradition of "vengeful redemption," diverging from the Sephardi "proselytizing redemption."

[46] Ronen Lubich, "Jacob & Esau and Rashi's Interpretive Method" (in Hebrew), *Shaanan* 13 (2008): 71–107, http://app.shaanan.ac.il/shnaton/13/4.pdf. Yizhak Baer, "Rashi and the Historical Reality of His Time" (in Hebrew), *Ziyon* 15 (1950): 320–32, discusses Jewish–Christian relations as a context for Rashi's anti-Christian polemics. Rashi's portrayals of an evil Esau and a hostile Edom were vested in Midrash. As early Midrash had a pagan Esau, and Rashi also practiced self-censorship, his Christian referents remained opaque.

[47] See also Rashi on Psalms 9:7–8. His conflation of Esau and Amaleq was not uncontroversial. The original homily in *Tanhuma*, ki teze 11 uses Amaleq, as do many Rashi MSS (possibly self-censorship). MS Leipzig 1, considered by many the oldest and most reliable, has Esau: http://alhatorah.org/Commentators:Rashi_Leipzig_1/Shemot_17#cite_note-4. (My thanks to Yedida Eisenstat.) Nahmanides held a midway position between "vengeful" and "proselytizing conversion." He made Amaleq's destruction a precondition to redemption from Edom, but insisted that the command to erase Amaleq did not apply to Esau

The Crusades completed Edom's Christianization. They also shifted the major target of Jewish hatred from empire to church. To be sure, the Holy Roman Empire remained associated with Edom. The Worms tombstone of Rabbi Meir of Rothenburg (c. 1215–1293), who died as a captive of the emperor, carries the inscription: "seized by the Roman King." But the Roman Church, leading Crusades across the Mediterranean against the Muslims and in Europe against heretics, and overseeing the Inquisition, was the one to look truly imperial – Europe's leader and the Jews' mortal enemy. Pope Innocent III (1198–1216) claimed to "alone bear the imperial insignia," the emperor, confirmed and consecrated by him, merely his "minister."[48] Late medieval Jewish sources recognized the pope as "the king of all kings" or "king of the nations."[49] Empire and church were the foundations of European Christendom – of European identity. Medieval Jewish Edom captured both moments, but the church overshadowed the empire.

Indeed, medieval Jewish historiography signaled a change in Jewish attitudes toward imperial rule. In the course of the Crusades and the blood libels, Jews increasingly found themselves reliant on imperial and papal protection against persecution, and the vision of a royal alliance with the Jewish minority that Yerushalmi found exemplified in sixteenth-century historiography began to form.[50] High medieval additions to the *Josippon* embellished its benevolent picture of the Roman emperors, depicting them as friends of the Jews.[51] Following the *Josippon*, Abraham ibn Daud's twelfth-century Roman and Jewish chronicles

---

(Exodus 17:9, 16, Genesis 36:19, respectively). See Asaf Turgeman, "Mein Bruder ist ein Einzelkind: Die Esau-Darstellung in jüdischen Schriften des Mittelalters," in *Esau: Bruder und Feind*, ed. Gerhard Langer (Göttingen: Vandenhoeck & Ruprecht, 2009), pp. 135–54, and Elliot Horowitz, *Reckless Rites: Purim and the Legacy of Jewish Violence* (Princeton, NJ: Princeton University Press, 2006), pp. 125–29.

[48] Robert Folz, *The Concept of Empire in Western Europe from the Fifth to the Fourteenth Century*, trans. Sheila Ann Ogilvie (London: Edward Arnold, 1969), p. 200.

[49] Joseph Kobak, "Jacob of Venice's Epistle of Polemics" (in Hebrew), *Jeschurun* 6 (1868): 30. Joseph Shatzmiller lists a series of Jewish references to the pope as the supreme king, often in connection with his protection of the Jews against the blood libel: "Did the Convert Nicholas Donin Allege the Blood Libel?" (in Hebrew) in *Studies in the History of the Jewish People and the Land of Israel*, 5 vols. (Haifa: University of Haifa Press, 1970–80): 4 (ed. Uriel Rappaport, 1978): 181–82, and 5 (ed. Bustenay Oded, 1980): 167.

[50] Yosef Hayim Yerushalmi, *The Lisbon Massacre of 1506 and the Royal Image in the Shebet Yehudah* (Cincinnati, OH: Hebrew Union College, 1976). References to the pope as the supreme king suggest that Jews imagined him to be a friend, albeit as a political as opposed to a religious leader.

[51] *Sefer Yosifon*, ed. with an introduction, commentary, and notes by David Flusser, 2 vols. (Jerusalem: Bialik Institute, 1980–81): 1: 32–42; Ram ben Shalom, *Facing Christian Culture: Historical Consciousness and Images of the Past among the Jews of Spain and Southern France during the Middle Ages* (in Hebrew) (Jerusalem: Ben-Zvi Institute and the Hebrew University, 2006), pp. 113–14.

described the Emperor Titus – whom the Talmud bedeviled as the Temple's destroyer and the worst of God's offenders – as wise, culturally refined, and just.[52] Ibn Daud laid the blame for the Temple's destruction and the Land's devastation squarely on the Jewish warlords (הפריצים). The view of Rome as an orderly and civilized empire gradually entered Jewish literature and gained eloquent expression in Abravanel, who agilely joined hatred for Christian Rome with appreciation for the Roman polity.[53]

Rabbinic Edom and Josipponian Rome, typology and historiography, coexisted in medieval European Jewish discourse. Chroniclers and commentators skirted the dissonance of rabbinic and Josipponian discourse and pulled typology and historiography together. From Ibn Daud to Abravanel, historiography informed the configuration of the Four Empires, and Edom eschatology set the goal – Jewish redemption – for historiographical narratives.[54] Historiography and rabbinic literature shared in messianism, however quietist, and in animosity toward Christianity. At the same time, Josipponian Rome showed Jews imagining political arrangements that would make it possible for them to partake in European polities and civilization. The rapprochement with empire was a first step, however tentative, to membership in the European community.

Late medieval Christian–Jewish relations rendered such membership impossible. Until the late thirteenth century, Christian culture showed no interest in rabbinic or Christian Edom, but it retained the claim to Jacob's legacy and reworked the Jewish concepts of exile and Jerusalem. With the Crusaders' conquest of Jerusalem in 1099, biblical hymns celebrated the return to Zion; with Jerusalem's fall to Saladin in 1187, they mourned the loss and called for vengeance. *Deus venerunt gentes*, "O God, the nations have invaded your inheritance," wailed Psalm 78:1 (79:1), a centerpiece of Christian liturgy. "Pour out your wrath on the nations that know you not ... for they devoured Jacob and laid his dwelling place to waste." Friday liturgy recited Psalm 82 (83): "The [enemies] conspire ... that the name of Israel be remembered no more.... [T]he tents of Edom and the Ishmaelites ... form an alliance

---

[52] "Zikhron Divre Romi" and "Divre Malkhe Yisrael be-Yeme Bayit Sheni," in *Seder Olam Rabbah ve-Seder Olam Zuta u-Megilat Taanit ve-Sefer Ha-Kabbalah le-ha-Ravad* (Basel, 1580), pp. 81a–b, 120b–129a, respectively.

[53] Ram ben Shalom, *Facing Christian Culture*, pp. 113–46.

[54] Gerson Cohen, *A Critical Edition with a Translation and Notes of The Book of Tradition (Sefer Ha-Qabbalah) by Abraham ibn Daud* (Philadelphia: Jewish Publication Society of America, 1967), pp. 240–62; Yiẓḥak Abravanel, *Maayane ha-Yeshuah: Perush al Daniel* (Fountains of redemption: Commentary on Daniel) (Stettin: R. Grossmann, 1860), pp. 17a–b.

against you (verses 3–6)."[55] Using the same verses, the Christian and Jewish Jacobs beseeched God to protect Israel against the Idumaeans. Ironically, Jewish Jacob feared that Christian Jacob, whom he called Edom, would devour Israel.

As Christians became familiar with rabbinic literature in the thirteenth century, they began engaging Edom and responding polemically to the Jewish concept. However violent, late medieval polemics produced a remarkable convergence of Christian and Jewish biblical commentaries, which was often the work of Jewish converts to Christianity. Edom polemics makes it possible to write Jewish European history as one of partly shared, intersecting Jewish and Christian cultures. The story is one of communities unfamiliar, for long intervals, with each other's texts, then encountering them in conflict, with an overwhelming power disparity between Christians and Jews. Such a history can provide no model for contemporary Europe, but it must be told if its legacy is to be overcome. Medieval Europe shaped Jewish European history as a Christian–Jewish confrontation, hostile and traumatic, in ways quite different from the Jewish encounter with Islam. We are still working out the legacy.

Medieval Christian Jacob & Esau: Biblical Commentary

The Christian passion for Jacob & Esau had waned by the early Middle Ages, when the Christian victory in the struggle over *Verus Israel* seemed long secure. All the same, the patristic typology remained unchanged. Gregory the Great, Isidore of Seville, and the Carolingian bishops reaffirmed it. So did the *Glossa Ordinaria*, the major medieval biblical commentary, arranged by the school of Anselm of Laon (d. 1117). Commenting on Obadiah, the Gloss rejected the Jewish view that his messianic prophecy on Edom (1:18) was directed against Rome: "The Jews foolishly dream that whatever is said against the Idumaeans is meant against the Roman rule" and that it presages a yet-to-come messianic age, "but we understand all these things to have already been accomplished" with Christ, who redeemed Mt. Zion.[56] The Gloss remained unclear on

---

[55] Amnon Lindner, *"Deus venerunt gentes:* Psalms: 78 (79) in the Liturgical Commemoration of the Destruction of Latin Jerusalem," in *Medieval Studies in Honor of Avrom Saltman,* ed. Bat-Sheva Albert, Yvonne Friedman, and Simon Schwarzfuchs (Ramat-Gan: Bar-Ilan University Press, 1995), pp. 145–71.

[56] Genesis 25:23: "Two peoples [gentes] in your womb" = Idumaeans and Jews; "and two nations [populi] shall be divided" = Christian Israel and Idumaean Jews; "and the older shall serve the younger" = those among the Jewish people, older by birth, who did not convert to the true faith will serve the younger Christian people. *Biblia Sacra cum glossis, interlineari et ordinaria: Nicolai Lyrani postilla, ac moralitatibus, Burgensis additionibus & Thoringi replicis,* 6 vols. (Venice: n.p., 1588). My thanks to Fred Behrends (formerly of

the meaning of Christ's triumph and showed neither interest in developing a Christian concept of a Jewish Edom nor awareness that contemporary Jews identified Rome with Christianity and anticipated its downfall. It displayed none of Rashi's urgency about Edom. It allegorized Edom rather than typologized: Edom signified flesh versus spirit, and "the Idumaeans were always hostile to the Israelites just as Esau was to Jacob." Christians inherited Jacob's legacy, but it was difficult to see how the Jews descended from Esau. The Jews remained suspended between Christian Israel and Edom.

The *Bible Moralisée* (moralized Bible), composed by clerics in the French royal court around 1220, exemplified high medieval exposure to Jacob & Esau among the highest social echelons. It consisted of six hundred miniatures accompanied by simple, brief French commentary.[57] Rebecca occupied a central place as the Mother Church, and Jacob & Esau represented, respectively, the good Christians "who stay willingly in the Holy Church and do her will" and "the usurers, malefactors and wicked people who leave their mother, the Holy Church." Isaac's blessing of Jacob "signifies Jesus Christ who gave His Blessing to His disciples," and Esau's forfeiture of the blessings "signifies the Jews and the wrongdoers [both pictured bearded, the Jews with peaked caps, holding bowls filled with coins], who will come on Judgment Day before Jesus Christ for His blessing, and He will say to them: You are too late; the Christians have taken it" (see Figure 3).

Sara Lipton suggests that the *Bible Moralisée* "judaicizes damnation [by absorbing] many diverse sinners within the figures of the Jews," and that it highlights usury rather than the Old Law as the reason for damnation, thereby forewarning Christians of falling into "Jewish" vices.[58] Jacob & Esau divide Christians and wrongdoers, and the Jews represent the wrongdoers. If the *Bible Moralisée* deployed Jacob & Esau to advance a thirteenth-century redefinition of Christian identity, this came at the cost of their typological coherence. Esau appears more a heretic than a Jew. When old and ailing, Jacob signifies the "old Jews," while at other times he signifies Christ. Christian Jacob & Esau emerge from the *Bible Moralisée* diffused, useful but not central to Christian politics and morals.

UNC) and Julie Mell of NCSU, who helped with difficult Latin passages, here and elsewhere.

[57] *Bible Moralisée: Codex Vindobonensis 2554, Vienna, Österreichische Nationalbibliothek*, trans. with commentary by Gerald Guest (London: Harvey Miller, 1995). Production of these picture Bibles was extremely expensive. Fifteen manuscripts remain from this tradition, which lasted two and a half centuries. Horst Wenzel of Humboldt University, Berlin, directed me to the *Biblia Moralisée*.

[58] *Images of Intolerance: The Representation of Jews and Judaism in the Bible Moralisée* (Berkeley: University of California Press, 1999), p. 119.

Figure 3: *Bible Moralisée: Codex Vindobonensis* 2554, folio 6. Courtesy of the Österreichische Nationalbibliothek, Vienna.

On the other side of the social spectrum is the *Biblia Pauperum*, the "Poor Man's Bible," a forty-to-fifty-leaf "block-book," consisting of impressions of carved wooden blocks that produced illustrated plates with brief Latin text in their midst. The books proliferated in the second half of the fifteenth century as a transition to printing, but may reflect earlier manuscript tradition, sustained by mendicant friars using the *Biblia Pauperum* for preaching against heresy. They tell the Gospel story and recall Old Testament episodes as prefiguring the New Testament: Jacob's flight from Esau and return to Canaan prefigures the Holy Family's escape from Herod to Egypt and their return; Jacob sleeping on a stone and receiving assurance of inheriting the Land of Israel signifies that those who die trusting in Christ, the stone, will obtain the Kingdom of Heaven.[59] The *Biblia Pauperum* provides a measure of lay exposure to Jacob, existent but limited.

Christians were more likely to become familiar with Jacob & Esau through vernacular renderings of Genesis – in prose, rhyme, drama, and chronicle, such as the Anglo-Saxon and Middle English Genesis, the eleventh- and twelfth-century Old and Middle German *Wiener* and *Vorauer Genesis*, the fifteenth-century French *Mistére du Viel Testament*, or the thirteenth-century *Legenda sanctorum* (Readings of the saints), a medieval best-seller, translated and printed in English in 1483 as *The Golden Legend*.[60] The vernacular Genesis presented literal-historical readings, relatively free of typology. Jacob could appear all too human, sexually desirous, for example, in his marriages to Rachel and Leah.[61] The church was not happy about the unauthorized reading but, significantly, the popular Genesis did not challenge the Gloss. If Chaucer's *Canterbury Tales* tells of "a trick that Dame Rebecca for Jacob found, by which his father's benison he won," the popular Genesis explains the trickery away in the traditional fashion, as presaged by prophecy and confirmed by character.[62] Popular Jacob stories, likely to circulate in oral culture, reaffirmed a Christian Jacob.

Medieval Christians could encounter Jacob in a few more venues. Easter and Christmas church dramas, recounting Gospel stories – an endeavor to displace popular plays – exhibited Old Testament stories on occasion. A Latin church drama of the late twelfth century on Isaac, Rebecca, and their children provides the conventional typological interpretation, the church chorus singing after each act an "allegory"

---

[59] *The Bible of the Poor [Biblia Pauperum]: Facsimile and Edition of the British Library Blockbook C.9 d.2*, trans. with commentary by Albert Labriola and John Smeltz (Pittsburgh, PA: Duquesne University Press, 1990), pp. 22, 24, 53, 106, 108, 132, 138, 150, 153, 155.

[60] Brian Murdoch, *The Medieval Popular Bible: Expansions of Genesis in the Middle Ages* (Cambridge: D. S. Brewer, 2003), has complete references.

[61] The story of Laban's trickery in the *Wiener* and *Vorauer Genesis*: Ibid., pp. 149–65.

[62] *Canterbury Tales*, rendered into modern English by J. U. Nicolson (Mineola, NY: Dover, 2004), p. 360.

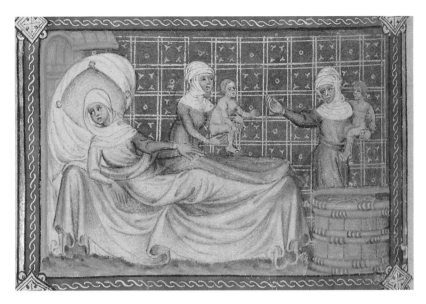

Figure 4: *The Birth of Esau and Jacob* by Master of Jean de Mandeville, Paris, c. 1360. Courtesy of the J. Paul Getty Museum, Los Angeles.

explaining it.[63] It is interesting to note that all actors wore Jewish hats, casting Old Testament characters as contemporary Jews when the allegories purported them to be Christian.[64] Scenes from the Jacob story cycle, especially Isaac's blessing of Jacob, Jacob's ladder dream, and Jacob's struggle with the angel, show up in illuminated psalters (often used by the affluent to learn reading) and in mosaics, frescoes, and altarpieces in churches.[65] Some of the pictures are famous: the fifth-century nave mosaic of Isaac blessing Jacob in Rome's Santa Maria Maggiora. Others are exceptionally beautiful: Master of Jean de Mandeville's miniature of Jacob and Esau's birth (c. 1360; see Figure 4). But like the Christmas

---

[63] Only a fragment survived of "Ordo de Ysaac et Rebecca et Filiis eorum Recitandus": Karl Young, *The Drama of the Medieval Church* (Oxford: Clarendon Press, 1933), pp. 258–66, 484–85. Toni Weber, *Die Praefigurationen im geistlichen Drama Deutschlands* (Marburg: Werner u. Winter, 1919), pp. 1–20 reconstructs the context of contemporary German typology.

[64] Wilhelm Creizenach, *Geschichte des Neueren Dramas*, 2d ed., 3 vols. (Halle: Max Niemeyer, 1911), I: 68. This may suggest that the conventional dating is too early. Friedrich Keinz and K. Bartsch published a short fragment of a twelfth-century Middle German poem, "De esav et iacob," exemplifying a similar typology: "Mittheilungen aus der Münchener Kön. Bibliothek," *Germania* 31 (1886): 57–62. Thanks to Horst Wenzel for the reference.

[65] "Jakob," *Lexikon der christlichen Ikonographie*, ed. Engelbert Kirschbaum, 8 vols. (Rome: Herder, 1974), 2: 367–83, for an overview and references.

play, New Testament scenes predominate overwhelmingly in the iconography. The asymmetry in the Jewish and Christian investments in Jacob & Esau is palpable.

Brotherhood Estranged: Jewish Anti-Christian Polemics

Christians encountered the Jewish Jacob & Esau in exchanges with Jews: conversations, polemics, and, from 1240 on, formal disputations. Both sides had only limited familiarity with each other's literature. At least until the late twelfth century, very few Jews read Latin, and Christian biblical commentators had exceedingly limited Hebrew. Hebrew functioned almost as a "code language."[66] Indirect knowledge of each other's views came through daily exchanges, partial translations, Jewish converts, or, in Spain, through Muslim and Karaite critiques of Judaism.[67] Such knowledge increased in the twelfth century. According to Beryl Smalley, Christian biblical exegetes consulted with Jews and had a proclivity to accept Jewish interpretation.[68] Jews, in turn, appear to have had vernacular translations of Latin polemics but limited their responses to Hebrew.[69] Rashi argued against Christian biblical exegesis without having read much, if any, of it and expected his own commentary to be read by Jews alone.[70] Until the thirteenth century, medieval European Christians and Jews appear not to have had direct access to each other's works.

The high Middle Ages witnessed a turn to literal-historical exegesis, the *peshat*, among both Jews and Christians. A linguistic-contextual approach, using rhetorical and grammatical conventions as principles of

---

[66] Hanne Trautner-Kromann, *Shield and Sword: Jewish Polemics against Christianity and the Christians in France and Spain from 1100-1500* (Tübingen: Mohr, 1993), p. 7. (Professor Anna Abulafia of Oxford University suggests that Herbert of Bosham [d. c. 1194] had direct access to Hebrew commentaries, and my generalization about limited Christian familiarity with Hebrew literature requires attenuation.) This contrasted with the Muslim world, where Arabic was, with Hebrew, the Jews' literary language: Judah Halevi's polemics, *Kitab al Khazari* (c. 1140), was the notable example: *The Kuzari: An Argument for the Faith of Israel*, trans. Hartwig Hirschfeld (New York: Schocken Books, 1964).

[67] The Karaites were a dissenting Jewish movement that recognized the Hebrew Bible alone as a source of Jewish law and rejected rabbinic traditions.

[68] *The Study of the Bible in the Middle Ages*, 3d. ed. (Oxford: Basil Blackwell, 1983).

[69] Hasdai Crescas, *Bittul Iqarei ha-Nozerim* (Refutation of Christian principles, 1397–98) (Jerusalem: Maqor, 1972), written in Catalan (1398) and translated into Hebrew (1451), was the exception.

[70] Esra Shereshevsky, "Rashi's and Christian Interpretations," *Jewish Quarterly Review* n.s. 61:1 (1970): 76–86; Sarah Kamin, "Rashi's Commentary on the Song of Songs and the Jewish-Christian Polemic," in her *Jews and Christians Interpret the Bible* (in Hebrew) (Jerusalem: The Magnes Press, 2008).

interpretation, substituted for or supplemented the *derash*, the noncontextual homily. The peshat became characteristic of Ashkenazi and Sephardi Jewish commentators – Rashi, Rashbam, Ibn Ezra, and Radak – and of the Christian exegetes associated with the Paris Abbey of St. Victor, the Victorines Hugh, Richard, and Andrew. Both showed burgeoning awareness of the historical gap separating text and exegete and criticized Midrash for ignoring it. The Jewish peshat may have reflected, in part, a move against Christology, an effort to explain biblical events and prophecies as referring to historical contexts already elucidated in the Hebrew Bible, rather than as prefiguring the New Testament. But Jews and Christians alike needed to contain the peshat, since the messianic promise depended on typology. There remained key passages – the final verse in Obadiah, "saviors shall go up to Mount Zion to judge Mount Esau," for example – where even the greatest "historicists" found prophecies about Christ and the Jewish Messiah. At the height of the peshat in the twelfth century, all of the Jewish exegetes, Ashkenazi and Sephardi alike, accepted the association of Edom with Christianity and Rome.

Until the mid-twelfth century, polemics on both sides were directed more toward sorting out and firming up one's own position, and less toward proselytizing. Even the vicious anti-Jewish polemics of Peter the Venerable (1092–1156) and Bernard of Clairvaux (1090–1153) did not seek to undermine the Jews as a protected minority.[71] On the Jewish side, Rashi and Jewish leaders, wishing to neither provoke nor risk exposure, advised against disputation, and limited Jewish response – *teshuvat ha-minim*, answer to apostates and Christians – to arguments embedded in Jewish biblical commentary.[72] To be sure, an older counter-gospel, *Toledot Yeshu* (Life story of Jesus), completed no later than the ninth century but containing earlier materials, circulated among European Jews and Christians, but, significantly, we know of no contemporary Jewish polemical work, exegetical or philosophical in character, openly addressing Christianity.[73] By the late twelfth century, however, Jews felt compelled to respond with works of their own. "When they find

---

[71] Jeremy Cohen, "Scholarship and Intolerance in the Medieval Academy," *American Historical Review* 91 (1986): 601–4.

[72] Erwin Rosenthal, "Anti-Christian Polemic in Medieval Bible Commentaries," *Journal of Jewish Studies* 11 (1960): 115–35; Shaye D. Cohen, "Does Rashi's Torah Commentary Respond to Christianity? A Comparison of Rashi with Rashbam and Bekhor Shor," in *The Idea of Biblical Interpretation*, ed. Hindy Najman and Judith H. Newman (Leiden: Brill, 2004), pp. 449–72.

[73] *Toledot Yeshu*, ed. and trans. Michael Meerson and Peter Schäfer (Tübingen: Mohr Siebeck, 2014). For its origins: John Gager, "Simon Peter, Founder of Christianity or Saviour of Israel?" in *Toledot Yeshu (The Life Story of Jesus) Revisited*, ed. Peter Schäfer, Michael Meerson, and Yaacov Deutsch (Tübingen: Mohr Siebeck, 2011), pp. 221–45.

prophecies of consolation to Israel, they say 'we are Jacob's descen-
dants,'" complained Joseph Kimḥi.[74] His *Sefer ha-Berit* (Book of the
Covenant, c. 1170) represented the first generation of open medieval
Jewish polemics.

In literature and iconography alike, Jewish polemics contested
Christian appropriations of Jacob.[75] Scholars are divided on whether
Jewish polemics reflected actual disputation or registered anxieties
about potential Christian challenges.[76] The scurrilous attacks on
Christian dogma and practice, encoded in Hebrew, suggest that the
polemics were intended for Jews.[77] Still, Jacob & Esau polemics
recorded both real and fictive Christian arguments. Jews rebutted
potential Christian claims that "because Jacob obtained the blessings
through trickery, they were fulfilled for the Gentiles [descendants of
Esau] and not the Jews," and that "the birthright remained with
Esau."[78] Was this an argument they heard from Christians? Probably
not. It is not impossible that views conjured in Jewish polemics of a
deceptive Jacob, a stereotypical money-lending Jew, circulated among
the populace and militated against the church's hegemonic Christian
Jacob. *Sefer Yosef ha-Meqane* responds to the claim that "your ancestor,
Jacob, was a thief and an unsurpassed usurer: For one bowl worth but

---

[74] *Sefer ha-Berit u-vikuḥei Radak im ha-Naẓrut*, ed. Frank Talmage (Jerusalem: Bialik
Institute, 1974), pp. 55–56. *Sefer ha-Berit* and Jacob ben Reuben, *Sefer
Milḥamot Hashem* (Book of wars of the Lord), ed. Yehudah Rozental (Jerusalem:
Mosad Ha-Rav Kook, 1963), are the first-known medieval European Jewish
polemical works.

[75] Katrin Kogman-Appel, "Coping with Christian Pictorial Sources: What Did Jewish
Miniaturists *Not* Paint?" *Speculum* 75:4 (2000): 816–58.

[76] For a bibliography of Jewish polemics, see Yehudah Rozental, "Anti-Christian
Polemical Literature Until the End of the Eighteenth-Century" (in Hebrew),
Aresheth 2 (1960): 130–79 and 3 (1961): 433–39. For an overview: David
Berger, "The Jewish-Christian Debate in the High Middle Ages," in *Essential
Papers on Judaism and Christianity in Conflict*, ed. Jeremy Cohen (New York: New
York University Press, 1991). Simon Schwarzfuchs, "Religion populaire et
polémique savante: Le tournant de la polémique judéo-chrétienne au 12ᵉ siècle,"
in *Medieval Studies in Honor of Avrom Saltman*, pp. 189–206, argues against the
idea that Jewish polemics reflect actual disputes, and Elazar Touitou, "Rashi and
His School," in *Medieval Studies in Honor of Avrom Saltman*, pp. 231–51 argues for
it. David Berger had supported the first position in *The Jewish-Christian Debate in
the High Middle Ages: A Critical Edition of the Nizzahon Vetus* (Philadelphia: Jewish
Publication Society of America, 1979), but appears to have moved toward the
latter in "The Jewish-Christian Debate" (1991).

[77] The hostility to Christianity that medieval Jewish polemics reveal was one reason why
Wissenschaft des Judentums, child of Jewish emancipation, turned away from it. Intensive
study of polemics began in the postwar years. See Hanne Trautner-Kromann, *Shield and
Sword*, pp. 16–25.

[78] David Berger, *Nizzahon Vetus*, pp. 56, 58; Yehudah Rozental, "Chapters of Polemics"
(in Hebrew), in *Salo Wittmayer Baron Jubilee Volume*, 3 vols. (Jerusalem: American
Academy for Jewish Research, 1974): 3: 353–95, esp. 365–67.

half a coin he bought the birthright worth a thousand fold."[79] More likely, however, Jewish anxieties summoned these Christian arguments. They reveal how authentic the view of the Christian neighbors as Esau's descendants had become.

Usury emerged as the one major theological issue implicating Jacob & Esau. Christians argued that usury was universally prohibited: "[He] who does not put out his money at interest … he shall never be shaken" (Psalms 15:5).[80] Deuteronomy 23:21, however, prohibits taking interest only from "your brother" and permits it from foreigners: "To a foreigner you may lend upon interest, but to your brother you shall not lend upon interest; לנוכרי תשיך ולאחיך לא תשיך." Christians and Jews alike had little difficulty inventing business arrangements that circumvented the prohibition, but in thirteenth-century Christian theology, usury became an excoriated "Jewish" activity. The Jew as a usurer was a salient feature of late medieval antisemitism, and Jewish moneylending was a frequently used rationale for expelling the Jews.[81] Medieval rabbinic discourse revealed anxieties similar to those of Christians about usury and developed a business ethic in response, but Jews still felt compelled to defend their own interpretation of Scripture, which permitted interest from Christians.[82] As brotherhood (אחוה) was the grounds for prohibiting interest, usury involved Jacob & Esau.

---

[79] Joseph ben Nathan Official, *Sefer Yosef ha-Meqane* (Book of Joseph the zealot), ed. Yehudah Rozental (Jerusalem: Meqiẓe Nirdamim, 1970), p. 41. The Patriarchs came under high medieval Christian criticism: Ofir Mintz-Manor, "Why Are You Giving an Opening to the *Minim*?" (in Hebrew) *Tarbiz* 70:3/4 (2001): 637–44. Berger traces in Jewish polemics the Christian critiques of the Patriarchs and discusses the possibility that Christians conceived of themselves as Esau & Edom in *Nizzahon Vetus*, pp. 246, 291. See also his "The Morality of the Patriarchs in Jewish Polemics and Exegesis," in his *Cultures in Collision and Conversation* (Boston: Academic Studies Press, 2011), pp. 236–41.

[80] Jerome used the verse to universalize the prohibition against usury. See David Berger, *Nizzahon Vetus*, p. 133, and cross-references, p. 291.

[81] Theology, more than Jewish economic practice, created the myth of the Jewish moneylender. See Giacomo Todeschini, "Franciscan Economics and the Jews in the Middle Ages," in *Friars and Jews in the Middle Ages and Renaissance*, ed. Susan Myers and Steven McMichael (Leiden: Brill, 2004), pp. 99–118; Julie Mell, *The Myth of the Medieval Jewish Moneylender*, 2 vols. (New York: Palgrave Macmillan, 2017).

[82] For medieval rabbinic anxieties about usury: Yehudah ben Shmuel, *Sefer Ḥasidim* (Book of the pious), ed. Yehudah Hakohen Vistineẓqi (Berlin: Mekiẓe Nirdamim, 1891): 808, pp. 203–4; 1233, pp. 305–6. In contrast, anti-Christian polemics vindicate the practice. Meir ben Shimeon of Narbonne, *Milḥemet Miẓvah* (Holy war, c. 1270), suggests to Christians that just as they had "spiritualized" other biblical prohibitions, they may lift the usury prohibition. *Yosef ha-Meqane* protests that Christians themselves take interest and charge higher rates. (This was historically true.) See Hanne Trautner-Kromann, *Shield and Sword*, p. 77. *Nizzahon Vetus* (pp. 133–34) argued that interest was legitimate gain.

It is not clear that Christians used Edom's brotherhood to argue the impropriety of Jewish lending practices, but the prospect of such an argument preoccupied Jewish halakhic rulings. Most medieval and early modern European rabbis permitted interest from Christians, and the rational was that "Obadiah annulled (הסיר removed) the [stipulation of] fraternity (אחוה brotherhood)" in response to Edom's unbrotherly actions toward the Jews.[83] *Nizzahon Vetus* suggested further that "brother" is "brother in faith": "[Christians] consider themselves foreigners, for they are not circumcised," and the Torah says specifically: "'You may take interest from the foreigner,' i.e., the uncircumcised."[84] Finally, while Europeans were religiously Idumaean, says *Nizzahon Vetus*, ethnically they represented a mix; hence the prohibition of brotherhood did not apply.[85] Diminishing Edom's brotherhood, Jewish polemics highlighted Edom's Christian character and marginalized its ethnic one, attenuating the genealogy of Edom-Rome upon which it insisted elsewhere.

Brothers became estranged. Christians were strangers. Ancient Edom's persecution of Jacob's descendants presaged Christian ones, releasing Jews from any fraternal obligation, any recognition of a special relationship between Judaism and Christianity. *Halakhah* and polemics endeavored to escape the impossible situation in which Jewish typology put them. Abravanel and the Italian polemicist Abraham Farissol (1451–1525) reiterated the arguments about the limits of Christian brotherhood, as did several early modern writers, and the arguments survived all the way to Jewish emancipation. Napoleon's challenge to the Sanhedrin, a Jewish assembly he set up in 1808 – Do Jews consider their fellow citizens, French Christians, to be brothers? – forced a Jewish declaration that Christians were, indeed, brothers. Their declaration reflected the radical character of the modern nation-state's endeavor to transform Jewish–Christian relations and break with the past.[86]

---

[83] Joseph ben Nathan Official, *Sefer Yosef ha-Meqaneh*, pp. 49, 61; David Berger, *Nizzahon Vetus*, p. 123. *Sefer Ḥasidim* (paragraph 808 Parma MS; not in the Bologna MS) has a sweeping prohibition on interest, a notable exception. For an elaborate discussion and additional sources: Yehudah Rozental, "Ribit min ha-Nokhri III," in his *Meḥqarim u-Meqorot*, 2 vols. (Jerusalem: Reuven Mas, 1967): 1: 299–311.

[84] David Berger, *Nizzahon Vetus*, pp. 133–34, and cross-references to the polemical literature, pp. 291–92.

[85] Yehudah Rozental, "Ribit min ha-Nokhri II," *Talpiyot* 6:2 (1953): 152.

[86] Abravanel, commentary on Deuteronomy 23:21, and Farissol, *Magen Avraham* (Abraham's shield), quoted in Yehudah Rozental, "Ribit min ha-Nokhri III," pp. 308–10. Rozental discusses early modern sources in detail: pp. 311–23.

Edom from *Midrash* to *Kabbalah*: The *Zohar* and the Late Middle Ages

Rabbinic Edom remained virtually a closed book to Christians until the mid-thirteenth century. High medieval Christians still viewed the Jews as a biblical people, and such a view was conducive to Augustinian tolerance of the Jews as witnesses to biblical prophecies. The Victorine commentators upheld the *Hebraica veritas*, the Hebrew Bible, as the definitive version. But as Christian knowledge of Hebrew and rabbinic literature increased, the homiletic dimension of rabbinic commentary, and its anti-Christian disposition, became obvious. The Jews, Christians found, were no literalists. The rabbis claimed privileged access to revelation through an Oral Law given on Mt. Sinai and passed on to them. To Christians, Midrash departed radically from the Bible, was typological in character, and sacrilegious.[87] The idea of a "second Torah" was heretical. Christians were startled, as if discovering the diabolic character of the neighbors they had long thought they knew. The medieval Christian encounter with Jewish culture began with a sense of familiarity with the biblical people and their legitimacy, and it ended with recognition of their Talmudic otherness and their delegitimization. Late medieval Christians judged the Jews unfit for tolerance.

From the mid-thirteenth century on, Christians sought to convert the Jews, or expel them. A triumphant church, armed with a new theology that charged the Jews with deicide and using the mendicant orders and the Inquisition to detect and persecute heresy, competed with centralizing states in efforts to impose religious conformity. The terrain of Jewish–Christian debate shifted from the Bible to rabbinic literature. Jewish converts to Christianity first introduced Christians to the Talmud, and continued to be crucial in navigating rabbinic literature throughout the late Middle Ages, but in time, Christians acquired a measure of independence.[88] Dominican Raymond de Peñaforte (c. 1185–1275) opened schools for Hebrew, Aramaic, and Arabic as part of missionary work, and Franciscan friars taught Hebrew at universities. Peñaforte's students Raymond Martini and Pablo Christiani (formerly Shaul of Montpellier) employed the Talmud in efforts to convert the Jews.

---

[87] Blasphemy was an issue in the Paris Trial of the Talmud in 1239. For a record of the accusations, supported by Talmudic quotations, see Chen Merchavia, *Ha-Talmud Biryi Ha-Naẓrut* (The church vs. Talmudic and midrashic literature [500–1248]) (Jerusalem: Bialik Institute, 1970), and Judah Rosenthal, "The Talmud on Trial I–II," *Jewish Quarterly Review* 47 (1956–57): 58–76, 145–69.

[88] Chen Merchavia, *Ha-Talmud Biryi Ha-Naẓrut*, tracks Christian knowledge of rabbinic literature to 1240 and concludes that Christian convert Nicholas Donin and his colleagues made the first translations from the Talmud in the mid-1230s.

Ironically, while the Talmud was prosecuted and burned – only one complete fourteenth-century manuscript has survived – the 1263 Barcelona Disputation and the 1272 second Paris Disputation focused on Christiani's claims to have found evidence for Christ in the Talmud. As this chapter will later show, Christian polemics now confronted newly rabbinic Edom, emerging with surprising Christian–Jewish hybrids.

Jewish responses to the attack on the Talmud reflected dismay. Future German rabbinic leader Meir of Rothenburg wrote a lamentation about the 1242 Paris burning of the Talmud, evoking the burning of Jerusalem: "Ask, she who was burnt by fire, for your mourners' welfare."[89] The Oral Tradition, rabbinic Judaism's essence, was on trial under conditions not permitting full-fledged defense. Seeking to deflect the attack, some Jewish leaders claimed that Judaism did not command belief in Midrash. Naḥmanides, aware of the Christological uses to which Christian polemics put Talmudic tales, such as about the Messiah sitting at Rome's gates, professed not to believe in them. No proof can be brought from Midrash, said Avraham ben Shmuel of Rouen in the second Paris Disputation. In vain: Aquinas, in Paris at the time, concluded that the Jews knew that Jesus was the Messiah and killed him all the same.[90] Jewish responsibility for knowingly crucifying Christ was becoming a major charge in disputations, and French Jews dreaded them. The tone of the Provençal polemics, *Milḥemet Miẓvah*, written over a quarter of a century from the early 1240s to 1270, changes markedly from triumphalism to cautious defense.[91]

Heightened persecution and Jewish powerlessness converged with new intellectual currents to trigger a shift in the Jacob & Esau typology, reflected in Jewish mysticism's foundational work, *Sefer ha-Zohar* (Book of splendor).[92] The *Zohar*, a highly allegorized Midrash on the Pentateuch, elucidating its cosmogonic significance, and delving into

---

[89] *The Koren Mesorat HaRav Kinot* (in Hebrew and English), 2d ed. (Jerusalem: Koren Publishers, 2011), p. 591. The Spanish Jewish poet Yehudah Halevi (1085–1141) provided the model in "Zion, will you not ask for your prisoners' welfare?" after Psalms 122:6: "Ask for the peace of Jerusalem": Ibid., p. 555.

[90] Joseph Shatzmiller, *Le deuxième controverse de Paris: Un chapitre dans la polémique entre Chrétiens et Juifs au Moyen Age* (Paris: E. Peeters, 1994); Jeremy Cohen, "The Second Paris Disputation and Thirteenth-Century Jewish–Christian Polemics" (in Hebrew), *Tarbiẓ* 68:4 (1999): 557–78.

[91] Hanne Trautner-Kromann, *Shield and Sword*, p. 73. Yet a generation later, *Nizzahon Vetus* (p. 207) madly imagines Gentiles serving Jews: They are allowed to exist because the elder shall serve the younger. Such bravado was rare.

[92] Daniel 12:3: "The enlightened (*maskilim*) will shine like the splendor (*zohar*) of the sky." *The Zohar*, trans. and with commentary by Daniel C. Matt, 11 vols. (Stanford, CA: Stanford University Press, 2004–16). *Zohar* references are to the first printed edition, uniformly used in scholarship and marked in Matt's translation. For *Zohar Ḥadash* (a misnomer: older layers of *Zohar* literature that did not find their way into the first printed

the creation's secrets and into Divinity's design and machination, was composed by a circle of Castilian Kabbalists (Jewish mystics) around Moses de Léon (1250–1305), who attributed it to the second-century Tanna Shimeon bar Yoḥai.[93] The *Zohar* literature spread among Spanish and Italian Kabbalists in the first half of the fourteenth century, and following the expulsion from Spain, throughout the Spanish Jewish Diaspora. The *Zohar* was first printed in 1558–60 in Cremona and Mantua, and with the rise of the sixteenth-century Safed Kabbalah, the book became virtually canonical throughout the Jewish world.[94]

The *Zohar* presented a novel cosmic vision of Jacob & Esau's struggle, with Jacob representing divine and Esau demonic forces. Jacob had already appeared as Divinity's human face in pseudepigrapha and early rabbinic literature, especially in the mystical ascent literature, *hekhalot* (palaces) and *merkavah* (chariot). One midrash called Jacob "God" (El אל), and his image (*iqonin*) was said to be engraved on God's throne, symbolizing Adam and humanity, the people of Israel, and, alternately, the *logos* and *Meṭaṭron*, the angel creating the universe.[95] *Genesis Rabbah* (82:6) spoke of the Patriarchs as God's chariot, and the animal (חיה) in Ezekiel's chariot vision had, at least in one source, Jacob's image.[96] *Hekhalot Rabbati* told that when the people of Israel recited the *Kedusha* (*Trisagion*; sanctification), "God descends from His throne to embrace, fondle and kiss the countenance of Jacob."[97] Jacob was said not to have

edition): *Sefer ha-Zohar im perush ha-Sulam* (in Aramaic and Hebrew), trans. and with commentary by Yehudah Ashlag (London: Shlomoh Dazyeleẏski, 1970–71), vols. 9–10.

[93] Yehudah Liebes, "How the *Zohar* Was Written," *Studies in the Zohar* (Albany: State University of New York Press, 1993), pp. 85–138, revised Gershom Scholem's view of Moses de Léon's single authorship: *Major Trends in Jewish Mysticism* [1941] (New York: Schocken Books, 1995), pp. 156–204.

[94] Boaz Huss, *Like the Radiance of the Sky: Chapters in the Reception History of the Zohar and the Construction of Its Symbolic Value* (in Hebrew) (Jerusalem: Bialik Institute and Ben-Zvi Institute, 2008). The *Zohar* literature advanced the idea of an ancient Zohar book already in the fourteenth century, but only the printed edition gave the compilation its final shape.

[95] *Babylonian Talmud*, Megilah 18a: "And the God of Israel called him [Jacob] 'El' [God]" (Genesis 33:20; the conventional reading is that Jacob was the one who named an altar for the God of Israel), *Bereshit Rabba* 79:8; Ḥulin 91b, *Bereshit Rabba* 68:12, 78:3, *Pseudo-Jonathan* on Genesis 28:12: "You [Jacob] are the righteous one whose image is engraved on God's throne"; *Bereshit Rabba* 98:3 and *Va-yiqra Rabbah* 36:4 for homilies (Genesis 49:2 and Isaiah 43:1, respectively) on Jacob as creator of the world; Jonathan Z. Smith, "The Prayer of Joseph," in *Religions in Antiquity*, ed. J. Neusner (Leiden: Brill, 1968), pp. 253–94, for the *Meṭaṭron* tradition; Elliot R. Wolfson, "The Image of Jacob Engraved Upon the Throne: Further Reflections on the Esoteric Doctrine of the German Pietists," in his *Along the Path* (Albany: State University of New York Press, 1995), pp. 1–62.

[96] David Halperin, *The Faces of the Chariot* (Tübingen: J.C.B. Mohr [Paul Siebeck], 1988), p. 121.

[97] Peter Schäfer, ed., *Synopse zur Hekhalot-Literatur* (Tübingen: J. C. B. Mohr [Paul Siebeck], 1981), pp. 72–73 §164.

died: "Just as his descendants are alive, so he too is alive."[98] He could be assumed to have ascended to the heavens.

The mystical, divine Jacob seems to have emerged independently of Jacob & Esau's struggle. The *Hekhalot* literature makes virtually no mention of Esau and has no room for the Edom eschatology. Several Amoraic midrashim suggest, however, that Jacob & Esau's struggle extended to the world to come and hints at its cosmic significance. *Genesis Rabbah* (2:3) likens Esau to darkness and Jacob to the moon (6:8). The moon shines both day and night, in this world and the world to come, and once Esau's sun sets, Jacob's light will shine. *Genesis Rabbah* (78:14) and *Deuteronomy Rabbah* (1:20) present Jacob's refusal to join Esau on his way back to Seir, after their reconciliation, as conceding worldly dominion to Esau until messianic times. Until the *Zohar*, however, Jacob & Esau's cosmic struggle remains an underdeveloped idea.

In their biblical commentary (Genesis 49:33), Rashi and Naḥmanides recite the tradition that "Jacob our ancestor did not die." Naḥmanides interprets it in the context of the belief that the righteous souls are "bound in the bundle of the living (צרור החיים)" under God's throne.[99] Struggling to avoid Christological parallels, neither commentator (nor the *Zohar*) asserts Jacob's ascent to divinity, but medieval German Jewish Pietists, especially Eleazar of Worms (1176–1238), were much preoccupied with mystical ascent. They associated Jacob's ladder with the divine chariot, and his engraved image on God's throne with the *Meṭaṭron*.[100] Their ideas resonated among contemporary Kabbalists in Provence and Catalonia, the centers of the emergent Kabbalah.

Midrash *Bereshit Rabbati*, a twelfth-century compendium drawing on the *Yesod* (foundation) of Rabbi Moshe ha-Darshan of Narbonne (c. first half of the eleventh century), contains an Adam-Jacob homily especially close to the *Zohar*. God's blessing to Adam and Eve (Genesis 1:28–30), it says, prefigured Isaac's blessing to Jacob, and presaged Israel's dominion over the nations, the earth, and the heavens.[101] For Moshe ha-Darshan, Adam became a figurehead for Jacob and Israel. The turn to literal-historical exegesis two generations after Moshe ha-Darshan marginalized this

[98] Babylonian Talmud, Taanit 5b.
[99] Rami Reiner, "From the 'Garden of Eden' to the 'Bundle of the Living': The Blessing for the Dead on Medieval Ashkenazi Grave Stones" (in Hebrew), *Ẕiyon* 76 (2011): 5–28.
[100] *Sefer Gematriot of R. Judah the Pious*, introduced by Daniel Abrams and Israel Ta-Shema (Los Angeles: Cherub Press, 1998), 10a–b, 16a, 20b, 23 b, 56b; Elliot Wolfson, "The Image of Jacob Engraved Upon the Throne," pp. 1–29.
[101] *Midrash Bereshit Rabbati*, ed. Chanoch Albeck (Jerusalem: Meqiẓe Nirdamim, 1940), pp. 55, 18–19. Jeremy Cohen, *Be Fertile and Increase, Fill the Earth and Master It* (Ithaca, NY: Cornell University Press, 1989), p. 120, drew my attention to this source.

typology, but similar ideas circulated among Kabbalists. All the same, the *Zohar*'s Jacob & Esau cosmogony comes as a surprise.

The *Zohar* deploys ten spheres (*sefirot*) to portray the structure of Divinity and the universe. The spheres first appeared as the basic cosmic elements in the late antique Palestinian *Sefer Yeẓira* (Book of creation).[102] They resurfaced in the twelfth-century Provençal *Sefer ha-Bahir* (Book of clarity), which set the kabbalistic genre: a midrash attributed to a Tanna reputed for his mystical interests.[103] The *Zohar* saw the spheres as the Divine's progressive emanation and identified the cosmic elements with God's attributes as enumerated in I Chronicles 29:11: "Yours, O Lord, is the greatness, the power, the glory, the majesty and the splendor; yours is the kingdom." Man having been created in God's image, the *Zohar* organized the spheres as a profile of the divine body, with head, arms, torso, legs, and genitals. Jewish tradition has insisted that this was symbolic and not material representation of God and that Divinity was One.

The lowest sphere, Kingdom (*Malkhut*), was humanity's gate to Divinity, the abode of the feminine *Shekhinah*. The Shekhinah, the rabbinic "Divine Presence" accompanying Israel in exile, now became the feminine aspect of God. The divine order depended on the spheres' orderly interaction, above all, on the union of the Blessed Holy One and his Shekhinah, Glory (*Tiferet*) and Malkhut, masculine and feminine Divinity. Adam's sins, then those of Israel, created cosmic disruptions; human behavior had direct impact on the spheres. The Shekhinah went into exile and no longer united with the masculine God. Redemption depended on repair (*tiqun*) of the Blessed Holy One's relationship with his Shekhinah.

The Patriarchs were pillars of the divine order and restored a measure of orderliness after Adam's sins. They represented three spheres: Abraham embodied grace (*Hesed*), Isaac justice (but also courage, *Gevurah*), and Jacob glory (*Tiferet*). "Jacob, whom I have chosen" (Isaiah 41:8) was the superior patriarch, as his mediation between Abraham's mercy and Isaac's judgment (*din*) assured the flow of grace (1: 96a). Judgment unmitigated by mercy brought a breach in the creation, with the forces of evil, represented by Esau, Samael (the devil), and the demons, separating and creating a duplicate universe, the cosmic "other side" (*sitra aḥra*). Jacob sustained Divinity, the Tree of Life,

---

[102] *Sefer Yeẓira*, edited and translated with text-critical commentary by A. Peter Hayman (Tübingen: Mohr Siebeck, 2004).
[103] *The Book Bahir*, ed. Daniel Abrams with an introduction by Moshe Idel (Los Angeles: Cherub Press, 1994).

against them.[104] Residing in *Tiferet*, the divine torso, he constituted the universe's central column, channeling the flows between Divinity's upper and lower, right and left, reaches. His union with Rachel, representing the Shekhinah, produced perfect progeny, the people of Israel (1: 135a–136a). "Jacob did not die" because the people of Israel were alive (*Zohar* 2: 48b; 1: 235b).

In contrast, Esau was the Serpent, cosmic embodiment of evil (2: 111a). By seducing Eve, the Serpent upset not only Adam and Eve's union but also the heavenly spheres. The Holy Blessed One and his Shekhinah, the sun (*Tiferet*) and the moon (Malkhut, Shekhinah), could not unite. For earthly and heavenly peace to be restored, Jacob's cunning had to surpass that of the Serpent (1: 138ab–139a; 143a).[105] Already in Rebecca's womb, and later during birth, Jacob struggled with Esau, endeavoring to toss him back to his demon hole (138a). By offering Esau red lentil potage, Jacob disempowered him and bought his servitude: Esau's loss of birthright meant that Satan could no longer intercede with God to punish Israel for its transgressions (139b). With the two goats, which Jacob brought Isaac for his meal, he received Adam's blessings, shattered with the Fall, and rejuvenated the union of masculine and feminine Divinity. But the Serpent constantly threatens to cling to the moon (Shekhinah), obscure its light, and prevent it from joining the sun. The two goats prefigured the monthly offering at the Temple on the occasion of the new moon, designed to protect the moon against demonic powers. The Hebrew for goat is *seir*, Esau's nickname, and the expiating goat lured Satan away from the moon, back to his realm (138b–139a).[106] The Temple sacrifices, like all of the Torah's commandments, were designed to sustain the universe. By observing the Torah, Jacob-Israel protected the Shekhinah and heavenly union against Esau.

[104] On Jacob as a second Adam, see Elliot Wolfson, *Venturing Beyond: Law and Morality in Kabbalistic Mysticism* (New York: Oxford University Press, 2006), pp. 145–48. Wolfson discerns here anti-Christian polemics, a counterargument to the Pauline view of Jesus as the second Adam and the Tree of Life, redeeming the creation from the Original Sin.

[105] Jacob's cunning was justified: He restored a universe usurped by Esau the Serpent. Elliot Wolfson, *Venturing Beyond*, pp. 142–51, rewrites Jacob's struggle with Esau as an anti-Christian sexual drama: Upholding circumcision (removal of the foreskin, the feminine *atarah*), Jacob restores the universe to its original holy androgyny and to masculine hegemony: The Shekhinah is integrated into the masculine God (via the ninth sphere, *Yesod*, the phallus). He overcomes the Serpent's impure androgyny – Samael rides the Serpent, but the Serpent threatens to penetrate the Shekhinah – that unleashed demonic femininity. ודו״ק.

[106] The moon's diminution in the creation and its monthly waning reflected, to the more Gnostic among the Kabbalists, the *sitra aḥra*'s work. They conceived of the Temple's sacrifices, especially the monthly goat, as amending cosmic defects by expiating the *sitra aḥra* (rather than the Holy Blessed One or Israel's sins). See also 1: 45b.

Recounting Jacob's reconciliation with Esau, the *Zohar* married its theogony to the traditional messianic narrative (1: 143b; 146b). On the eve of the reconciliation, Jacob struggled with an archdemon. The *Zohar* was not clear about his identity, but tradition had him as Esau's guardian angel.[107] Jacob won, but not completely, as fulfillment of the blessings for Israel was deferred to the end of days (169b–170b). When Jacob and Esau met, Esau offered Jacob to "let us share together this world," but Jacob declined: "You have first your dominion of this world, and [I shall] reserve myself for the world to come and for the latter days" (172a). "Not one of Jacob's blessings has so far been fulfilled," says the *Zohar* emphatically, against Christian views (172a). "Jacob gazed into the distant future ... when his descendants should need the blessings in the struggle against the nations of the world ... and therefore deferred the[ir] fulfillment" (145a, 172a). At the end of days, Esau will be deprived of his worldly dominion, and Jacob will inherit both this and the next world.

Why has Esau retained his power and Israel languished in the "long and dark exile"? The *Zohar* elaborated a range of traditional and new answers: "Israel has suffered on account of the tears that Esau shed before his father, in his desire to be blessed by him, out of the great regard he had for his father's words" (1: 145a). God was disciplining Israel as a father did his son, and Esau thrived precisely because God no longer cared for him (3: 114a–115b). Exile did not reflect a loss of election. Israel was atoning for the world's sins to bring healing to it (3: 218a). Jacob-Israel remained God's only son – "My firstborn son, Israel" (Exodus 4:22) – dispenser of judgment and mercy, subject of all blessings, and the Tree of Life (2: 105a; 3: 149a, 191b).[108] Esau and Jacob had divided dominion in this and the world to come, and Jacob let Esau temporarily rule the earth (1: 143b). The answers' traditionalism concealed the *Zohar*'s novel framework. Esau's power was no longer vested in political dominion; rather, it reflected cosmic disorder. The messianic events ending Esau's rule would signal restoration of the creation.

Edom remained subdued in most of the *Zohar*, but it showed up, in a highly original fashion, in the *Zohar*'s most esoteric parts, the ones deliberating on the cosmic creation: *Sifra de-Zeniuta* (Book of concealment, 2:

---

[107] *Tanhuma* va-yishlah 8: "And a man wrestled with him (Genesis 32:24): This was Samael, Esau's guardian angel."

[108] This is anti-Christian polemic: The Jewish people and not Christ is God's only son, the Servant of the Lord (Isaiah 53), and the Tree of Life. *Zohar: The Book of Enlightenment*, trans., with introduction by Daniel Matt (New York: Paulist Press, 1983), pp. 18–20. Elliott Wolfson, *Venturing Beyond*, pp. 155–65, notes how much more subdued the *Zohar*'s polemics against Islam are.

176b–179a), *Idra Rabbah* (Great convocation, 3: 127b–145a), and *Idra Zuta* (Smaller convocation, 3: 287b–296b). In the *Idrot*, Shimeon bar Yoḥai revealed deep theogonic secrets about the creation to two convocations of mystics. Departing from the midrash that God created and destroyed several worlds prior to this one (*Genesis Rabbah* 3:7), the *Zohar* unexpectedly associated the biblical genealogy of Edomite kings (Genesis 36:31–39) with a stillborn primordial universe, which had gone through *tiqun* (repair). The Kings of Edom were central to the *Zohar*'s cosmogony and would become a prominent kabbalistic theme that coexisted in tension with Edom of Midrash and with the *Zohar*'s vision of Jacob & Esau.

Genesis 36 speaks of eight kings who had ruled in Edom before the Israelites established kingship. About the first seven, Genesis says that they had died; for the eighth, named Hadar, Genesis cites no death but mentions his wife's name, Mehetavel. Modifying a pre-Zoharic kabbalistic tradition, the *Zohar* conceived of the Edomite kings as primal supernal entities that died away, as Divinity was seeking the proper mode of revealing itself, but reemerged as constituents of a newly reshaped universe.[109] The primal universe's deficiency appears to have been the inability to balance judgment and mercy, as well as the absence of sexual union. Ancient divinity, called *Atiqa*, was all mercy, whereas the kings represented judgment untempered by compassion: Edom's red color signaled harsh judgment. Sexual unions could not take place because the female divinity, *Nuqvah*, had not yet been created, and the kings remained celibate (2: 176a; 3: 135a–b, 142a, 292a–b, 296a).[110] The reshaping of Divinity's three countenances, Atiqa (Ancient One), *Zeir Anpin* (short faced; the Irascible) and Nuqvah (Female) – the last two in Adam's image – rectified the imbalances (3: 128a, 135a, 142a, 292a). Zeir, sometimes identified with the eighth king, Hadar, coupled with Nuqvah (Mehetavel), and turned to face Atiqa with a loving look, the orderly flow of divine bounty secure, male and female assuring cosmic sustainability. Edom vanished in a reconstituted universe.[111]

---

[109] Avishar Har-Shefi, *The Myth of the Edomite Kings in Zoharic Literature: Creation and Revelation in the Idrot Texts of the Zohar* (in Hebrew) (Los Angeles: Cherub Press, 2014), provides a careful and lucid account of the Kings of Edom in the Zoharic literature.

[110] Pinchas Giller, *Reading the Zohar* (New York: Oxford University Press, 2001), pp. 95–98.

[111] Avishar Har-Shefi insists that "Edom did not vanish," and especially Atiqa's tiqun (3: 128a) makes its survival possible (emails to author September 12 and 19, 2011). He wonders whether the *Zohar* may not hint at a radically new cosmic conception of Christianity. If the *Idrot* move in this direction, they articulate an alternative view to Elliot Wolfson's misogynist, anti-Christian, and antiuniversalist Kabbalah (*Venturing Beyond*, esp. pp. 73–80, 90–107). The *Zohar* becomes multivocal. צריך למוד.

The *Zohar* spoke of the Kings of Edom cursorily and obscurely, as if apprehensive about revealing a deep mystery. The reticence may well have been due to the incompatibility of a stillborn Edom with the Edom eschatology, that is, with Edom as Christian Rome and the anticipation of messianic triumph over it.[112] The *Zohar* did away with Edom – "the primordial kings died and their armaments vanished, and the land came to naught" (2: 176b) – but Christianity could not be so easily dismissed, and traditional eschatology, which postponed Edom's elimination to the end of days, required historical Edom. Pre-Zoharic Kabbalah reconciled primordial and historical Edom by making the destroyed Edomites the origin of the demonic universe, identified with Esau, and there were traces of this view in the *Zohar* (1: 167b; 2: 111a, 168b).[113] But at least in the *Idrot,* the *Zohar* Kabbalists, apprehensive about the Gnostic implications, rejected this solution: The *sitra aḥra* (the demonic forces) originated, with Esau, in Isaac's sphere, *Gevurah,* in excessive judgment and not in evil. Esau, too, originated in holiness, and this prepared the grounds for future kabbalistic innovations. But the Kings of Edom remained out of place in the *Zohar*'s Jacob & Esau narrative. Cosmogonic Edom, the kings, had vanished before Esau entered the picture.

The *Zohar* represented a shift from historical to cosmogonic messianism, but both visions – cosmic restoration and vengeance visited upon Edom – remained part of it.[114] Shimeon bar Yoḥai's *devequt* (mystical union) in the Shekhinah in the *Idrot* revealed theurgic *tiqunim,* measures of cosmic healing, that coexisted in tension with the messianic triumph over Edom. The Kings of Edom accentuated the tension: They represented a tiqun and had vanished before history began. Kabbalah and Midrash represented alternative Edoms that stood in stark contrast in the biblical commentary of Baḥya ben Asher, who was close to the *Zohar* circle. Typology and eschatology, shaped by Naḥmanides, envisioned Roman kings and messianic triumph over Edom, and kabbalistic

---

[112] Yehudah Liebes, "The Messiah of the Zohar," *Studies in the Zohar,* pp. 1–84, sees the fall of the kings as alluding to messianic times, but he has to explain "why the author of the *Zohar* did not explicitly mention the historical implications of his discourses at the *Idra*" (67). Liebes uses *Zohar* 1: 177a–b, 2: 108b, 111a–b, where the kings presage messianic triumph, as evidence for the convergence of primordial and historical Edom, but the two visions of Edom seem to me to provide competing eschatologies. צריך עיון.

[113] Yiẓḥak Hakohen, "Al ha-Aẓilut ha-semalit (On the emanation of the left universe)," in *Kabbalot Rabbi Yaakov ve-Rabbi Yiẓḥak benei Rabbi Yaakov Hakohen,* ed. Gershom Scholem (Jerusalem: Ha-Madpis, 1926), pp. 31–35, 82–102; Moshe Idel, "Ha-Maḥashavah ha-raah shel ha-El (God's Evil Thought)," *Tarbiẓ* 49:304 (1980): 356–64; Avishar Har-Shefi, *The Myth of the Edomite Kings,* pp. 218–40. Har-Shefi illustrates the *Zohar*'s break with pre-Zoharic literature.

[114] *Zohar* 3: 212b and *Zohar Ḥadash* 68b on Numbers 24:17 (Balaam's oracle) depict the messianic triumph over Edom, but the *Zohar* does not dwell on it for long.

cosmogony, shaped by the *Zohar*, envisioned a restored universe.[115] Midrash predominated in Baḥya and late medieval Judaism, but to the *Zohar* Kabbalists, eschatology proved inadequate. Cosmogonic Edom represented a move to transcend it.

Yehudah Liebes observes that "the Zohar was written in a setting of wealth and security" and projected intellectual excitement.[116] But the *Zohar* also reflected anxiety about Jewry's future, frustration with traditional Midrash, and impatience with Naḥmanides' students, who refused to spread the Kabbalah. In late medieval Europe, history was closing down on the Jews, and the possibilities for Jewish life were diminishing. Castile was one of the last to turn for the worse, but in 1281, Alfonso X ordered the arrest of Jewish tax farmers. A decade later, his successor put an exorbitant levy on the Jews, and popular anti-Jewish sentiments mounted. The *Zohar* Kabbalists anticipated redemption, but hope for messianic intervention was wearing thin. They shifted their gaze away from a hopeless history to cosmic restoration, shaping redemptive tools out of Jewish life, out of love of God and Torah. The enlightened elite of the Kabbalists, who had unlocked divine secrets, could advance cosmic healing through tiqunim, and liberation from Edom would come as a by-product. "Fear not my servant Jacob," reaffirmed the *Zohar*, grounding its confidence in the cosmic order, rather than in a history that was turning hopeless (145b).

Late Medieval Edom: A "Judeo-Christian" Culture?

The Jewish turn to the Kabbalah came as Christians progressively appropriated Jewish biblical commentary and Midrash. The *Zohar*'s popularity in late medieval Jewish life remained limited, however, and polemics over Bible and Talmud dominated Christian–Jewish exchange until the Spanish expulsion. Dominican Raymond Martini's *Pugio Fidei* (Dagger of faith, 1278), a polemic against Jews and Muslims, and Franciscan Nicholas of Lyra's *Postillae*, the most popular biblical commentary of the late Middle Ages and early modern period, represent the two faces of Christian deployment of Jewish sources.[117] Both reworked the Jewish

---

[115] *Perush Rabbenu Baḥya al ha-Torah*, 1: 186–88 (on Genesis 36:31; 36:39).

[116] *Studies in Jewish Myth and Jewish Messianism*, trans. Batya Stein (Albany: State University of New York Press, 1993), p. 4.

[117] Raymond Martini, Joseph de Voisin, and Johann Benedict Carpzov, *Pugio Fidei adversus Mauros et Judaeos, Raymundi Martini* [1687] (reprint: Farnborough, UK: Gregg Press, 1967), http://judaica-frankfurt.de/urn/urn:nbn:de:hebis:30-180010008006; *Biblia Sacra cum glossis, interlineari et ordinaria: Nicolai Lyrani postilla, ac moralitatibus, Burgensis additationibus & Thoringi replicis*, 6 vols. (Venice: n.p., 1588). This Lyra edition has the

concept of Edom and showed rabbinic literature leaving its mark on European culture.

In the aftermath of the 1263 Barcelona disputation, Martini (c. 1220–1285), a graduate of Peñaforte's language school for missionaries, was appointed a member of Aragon's royal commission, and charged with inspecting Jewish literature for errors and blasphemies. Yet Martini was persuaded that behind Jewish errors lie Christian truths: The Talmud contained hidden Christian tenets that could be effectively used to missionize the Jews. He intended his *Pugio Fidei* to serve as a teaching manual for Dominican missionary schools. The book was the richest compendium of Midrash and Jewish biblical commentary that medieval Christians had: Babylonian Talmud, *Genesis Rabbah*, Moses ha-Darshan, Rashi, Maimonides, and Radak (David Kimḥi).[118] Reading Christ into the rabbinic vision of redemption, Martini daringly accepted the Edom-Rome typology. His Edom showed Christian Midrash at its best. There is nothing like it for sophistication and intellectual agility among medieval Christian readings of rabbinic literature.

A homily from *Bereshit Rabbati* on Zechariah 2:12 (2:8) – "thus spoke the Lord of Hosts: He sent me after glory to the nations" – suggests that the Messiah will come only after Esau has received his due, worldly glory, for honoring his father. To Martini, "He sent me" meant that Zechariah's God was speaking of sending the Messiah, his Son, and yet being sent Himself. Zechariah's messiah was Christ.[119] The glory bestowed on Esau prior to the Messiah's coming was the Roman emperor's throne: "Following the opinion of Jewish sources, I say that the Romans were Esau's sons. In numerous places in the *Talmud*, the Romans are called Esau, Edom, Seir" (399). "The[y] are [so] called not only after the flesh," but, as the Talmud suggests, "all of those who persecuted and are persecuting the people of God are called Esau by way of imitation" (400).[120]

---

clearest print. (The 1971 reprint of the 1492 Strasbourg edition, 4 vols., Frankfurt: Minerva, is unclear.)

[118] Contemporary scholars turn to *Pugio Fidei* to recover lost Jewish writings: Chen Merchavia, "On the Hebrew Citations of *Pugio Fidei* in the Saint Genevieve MS" (in Hebrew), *Qiryat Sefer* 51 (1976): 283–88; Saul Lieberman, *Shkiin: A Few Words on Some Jewish Legends, Customs and Literary Sources Found in Karaite and Christian Works* [1940], 2d ed. (Jerusalem: Wahrmann Books, 1970). Martini's knowledge of rabbinic literature was unparalleled, but Lieberman observes that mistakes in *Pugio Fidei* suggest that Martini needed a team of converts: He could read and use material pulled out for him but could not survey rabbinic literature on his own.

[119] The homily from *Bereshit Rabbati* is now lost, but it expands on the early medieval *Pesikta Rabbati* 23, ed. Meir Ish-Shalom (Vienna: Kaiser, 1880), p. 124. Lieberman argued persuasively for the authenticity of Martini's quotes.

[120] *BT* Avodah Zara 10b: "'There will be no remnant to the house of Esau' – to those whose evil deeds are like those of Esau."

Martini offered a sweeping legitimation for the rabbinic typology. To him, Jews no longer needed to search for Roman genealogy or religious affinity to Edom – all enemies of Israel were Edom.

Of course, Martini's Israel, the people of God, was not the Jews, and his messiah was not the rabbis' messiah. Using Jewish sources, he read Christ and Rome into biblical prophecy, emulating Augustine and the Gloss. He cited Rashi and the *Pseudo-Jonathan Targum* to show that Obadiah's prophecy (1:21) – "saviors shall climb Mt. Zion to judge Mt. Esau, and the Kingdom shall be the Lord's" – was directed at Rome, and he added a Talmudic story (*BT* Pesaḥim 118b) about Rome paying homage to the Messiah. Using another Talmudic homily suggesting that the Persians, the youth of the sheep, would bring about Rome's downfall, Martini opined that the Jews misunderstood: The youth of the sheep (*minores ovium*) were the Apostles.[121] The conversion of Edom-Rome to Christianity, accomplished by the Apostles and Pope Sylvester I (in Constantine's time), fulfilled biblical prophecies: "The Romans were destroyed [by] having been made Christians" (400–401). Martini made rabbinic literature tell a story of Christian redemption. Europe's leading missionary Christianized the rabbinic typology. Missionaries now told rabbinic stories to Jews to press them into conversion. Edom-Rome became, in persecution, a Jewish European story.

Nicholas of Lyra (1270–1349), too, composed two polemics against the Jews, but he upheld a tradition of Franciscan Hebrew biblical scholarship reflecting older Victorine views of Jewish testimony, and a belief that the Jews would eventually convert (when they see through the anti-Christ).[122] Born in Lyre, Normandy, he joined the Franciscan order in 1300 and was sent to study theology in Paris. He climbed up the Franciscan echelons, cultivating both royal and papal connections, and became the chief Franciscan administrator for France and Burgundy. He was involved in his age's major theological controversies but somehow

---

[121] *BT* Yoma 10a: "Rome is destined to succumb to Persia, as it is written (Jeremiah 49:20): 'Therefore hear the plan that the Lord has made against Edom. . . . Surely the least of the flocks [Martini's Apostles; the rabbis' Persians] shall drag them away.'"

[122] English Franciscans were the foremost Hebrew and biblical scholars, and Augustinian in their theology: Deeana Copeland Klepper, "Nicholas of Lyra and Franciscan Interest in Hebrew Scholarship," in *Nicholas of Lyra: The Senses of Scripture*, ed. Philip D. W. Krey and Lesley Smith (Leiden: Brill, 2000), pp. 287–311. In explaining why the Jews do not accept the Trinity, Lyra suggested that a people not growing up Christian and suffering from exile could not grasp such a difficult notion: Deeana Copeland Klepper, *The Insight of Unbelievers: Nicholas of Lyra and Christian Reading of Jewish Text in the Later Middle Ages* (Philadelphia: University of Pennsylvania Press, 2007), p. 106. Lyra's 1334 anti-Jewish polemics was a response to Jacob ben Reuben's *The Wars of the Lord* (c. 1170), which used the Matthew Gospel to argue against Christians. Luther later used Lyra's polemics in his diatribe against the Jews.

emerged unscathed from the struggles between the French monarchy and the pope and between the pope and the Franciscans. Scholars debate the extent and sources of his knowledge of Hebrew and rabbinic literature, but as Deeana Klepper suggests, it became his academic trademark and facilitated his rise to prominence.[123]

Lyra distinguished between the Hebrews as biblical exegetes and the Jews as a community, consulted the first extensively, and treated the latter mostly, but not invariably, negatively. Setting out to compose the first literal-historical Christian commentary on the entire Bible, he had little choice but to consult Rashi: No significant Christian resources existed.[124] His literal *Postilla*, composed between 1322 and 1331, and aimed at lectors and preachers, was exceptional for its clarity. It was the first Christian biblical commentary to be printed (1471–72), surrounding the biblical text, opposite the Gloss. His moral *Postilla* (composed 1333–1339) appeared, with other additions, below the literal *Postilla*. Lyra exercised great influence on Reformation commentaries and was the major Christian source for Jewish traditions until the early modern Christian Hebraists.

Lyra treated Rashi, who came to dominate fourteenth-century Jewish biblical commentary, as a *Glossa Ordinaria*, a summary of Jewish traditions.[125] He also had access to selections from other Jewish commentators, such as Joseph Kara and Rashbam.[126] Like the Jewish *peshat* exegetes, he preferred to interpret Hebrew prophecies as having been fulfilled in biblical times, but again like them, at crucial junctures, as in Genesis 49:10 "until Shilo comes," the Hebrew Bible pointed toward the distant future, for Lyra to Christ. In those places, he was scathing of Jewish "obstinacy," and insisted that when biblical commentary touched on Christology, the Jews could not be trusted. Elsewhere, he often preferred Jewish to Christian interpretation: "Rashi seems to have

---

[123] Deeana Copeland Klepper, *The Insight of Unbelievers*, p. 8. Ari Geiger, "Ha-Perush shel Nicholas de Lyra al Vayikra, Bamidbar u-Devarim" (Nicholas of Lyra's commentary on Leviticus, Numbers, and Deuteronomy), (Ph.D. diss., Bar-Ilan University, Ramat-Gan, 2006), chap. 3, emphasizes the limits of Lyra's understanding of Hebrew texts. Geiger doubts that Lyra worked with Hebrew manuscripts and read Rashi independently. When quoting Rashi, Lyra, on occasion, skips parts essential to his argument in a way that makes no sense for someone who had read the text. Lyra must have had helpers, probably converts.

[124] Ari Geiger, *Ha-Perush shel Nicholas de Lyra*, chap. 1. See also his "Nicholas of Lyra's Literal Commentary on Lamentations and Jewish Exegesis: A Comparative Study," *Medieval Encounters* 16 (2010): 1–22.

[125] Deeana Copeland Klepper, *The Insight of Unbelievers*, p. 51.

[126] Lyra's access to Kara and Rashbam remains mysterious, as Rashi's domination made other Ashkenazi commentaries rare. Michael A. Signer, "Nicholas of Lyra on the Prophet Ezekiel," in *The Senses of Scripture*, suggests that Lyra's Rashi manuscripts may have included other commentaries, such as Kara's.

become Nicholas' guide. . . . Once the problem of Messiah/Christus was resolved . . . Rashi [simply] believed in the wrong Messiah."[127]

Lyra entertained Rashi's view of Roman-Idumaean genealogy, suggesting that Esau's descendant "chief Magdiel" (Genesis 36:43) was founder of the Roman dynasty.[128] Like Martini, he accepted the rabbinic Edom-Rome typology but claimed that Edom-Rome prophecies had been fulfilled when Christ converted the Romans.[129] Having consigned much of Obadiah's prophecy to the time of the Maccabees, Lyra suggested that the concluding prophecies referred to the conversion of France and Spain (Zarefat and Sepharad) to Christianity and to the Apostles Paul and Peter going to Rome (Mt. Esau) to upbraid Constantine on the Roman treatment of Christians and impel him to found churches. Through Christ's conversion of the remnants of Jews and Gentiles, both the churches of Jews and of Gentiles – Mt. Zion and Mt. Esau – emerged (as in the *Glossa Ordinaria*). When the emperor gave Rome to the pope (the Donation of Constantine), "the Kingdom shall be the Lord's" was fulfilled.[130] The horizons of Jewish and Christian interpretations converged.

To be sure, Lyra retained the Christian ambiguity on the Jewish legacy. Christian typology still lurked in the background, potentially undermining the Jews as Jacob's descendants. Unconverted Jews were not the remnant saved on Mt. Zion but, at the same time, it was difficult to see them inhabiting Mt. Esau. Theology had long left the Jews suspended between Israel and Edom, but Lyra highlighted their Jacob lineage at a time when Christian policy was moving in the opposite direction, progressively expelling the Jews from France. Where Christology seemed at issue, Lyra did not hesitate to reject Edom-Rome, by using the conventional arguments about Rome's Japethian origins.[131] Yet seeing Jewish exegesis powerfully present in late medieval Europe's most popular Christian commentary, as Western Europe was being emptied of its Jews, is remarkable.

---

[127] Michael A. Signer, "Nicholas of Lyra on the Prophet Ezekiel," in *The Senses of Scripture*, p. 170.

[128] This originates in *Pirqe de-Rabbi Eliezer* 38 and *Targum Pseudo-Jonathan*.

[129] "The elder shall serve the younger" was partially fulfilled in King David's time, "but more perfectly when Christ subjected the Roman Empire, which the Jews say is signified by Esau": Et perfectius impletum est in Christo cui colla gentium, & principum terre subdita sunt & maxime imperium Romanum quod Iudæi dicunt significari per Esau.

[130] A document forged in the papal chancellery in the 750s of Constantine's award of jurisdiction over the Western Roman Empire to Pope Sylvester I.

[131] Isaiah 52:11; 63:1; Psalms 80; Lamentation 4:21. See Herman Hailperin, *Rashi and the Christian Scholars* (Pittsburg, PA: University of Pittsburgh Press, 1963), pp. 128–132, 174–80; Yehudah Rozental, "Ribit min ha-Nokhri II," 151; Ari Geiger, "Jewish Sources of Nicholas of Lyra's Literal Commentary on Lamentations" (in Hebrew) (Master's thesis, Bar-Ilan University, Ramat-Gan, 2002). Thanks to Ari Geiger for the references.

This was too much for Jewish converts to Christianity. They were the avant-garde educating Christians about Judaism and, at the same time, leading the polemical charge against the Jews. They could not overlook Edom-Rome's anti-Christian polemical character or share in Martini's and Lyra's adept neutralization of the typology. Edom prophecies appeared to challenge the momentous step they had undertaken in converting to Christianity and evoked their emotional response. Two vociferous rejections of Edom-Rome came from Avner of Burgos (Alfonso da Valladolid, 1270–1350) and Paul, Archbishop of Burgos (Shlomo ha-Levi; Pablo de Santa Maria, 1351–1435).

Avner's *Moreh Ẓedeq* (Teacher of righteousness), an imagined dialogue between Avner and a Jew, drew on sources as rich as those of *Pugio Fidei* in formulating a philosophical critique of Judaism.[132] Exchanges with his former compatriots followed, and Avner used Ibn Ezra to expound, in razor-sharp arguments, that Edom had nothing to do with Rome, neither in ethnicity nor in religion:

Romans cannot be called Idumaeans just because … a person of Idumaean origins [Zepho or Constantine] reigned over them [any more than] Israel [can be called] Idumaean or Roman [just because] Herod reigned over them.… Names should reflect substance.… Just as the Kingdom of Edom vanished when [the Idumaeans] converted to Judaism, and they were called Jews … so the [Roman Empire vanished and] Romans were called Christian after converting to Christianity [under Constantine].[133]

Greece, not Rome, was Daniel's Fourth Kingdom, and all prophecies on Edom were fulfilled when the Hasmonaeans subdued their territory, opening the road to the messiah under Rome. Most contemporary Jewish authorities declined to respond to Avner, but his exchanges with philosopher Isaac Pollegar and mathematician Joseph Shalom exhibited a learned Christian–Jewish dialogue.[134] The polemics' intellectual élan could not conceal its grave political import. Repeated Jewish rebuttals

---

[132] Only a Castilian translation has survived: *Mostrador de Justicia*, ed. Walter Mettmann, 2 vols. (Opladen: Westdeutscher Verlag, 1994–96). The main Jewish response was Yiẓhak Pulqar (Isaac Pollegar), *Sepher Ezer ha-Dat*, ed. George S. Belasco (London: J. Jacobs, 1906).

[133] Yehudah Rozental, "Mi-Tokh 'Sefer Alfonso' (selections from the book of Alfonso)," in *Studies and Essays in Honor of Abraham A. Neuman*, ed. Meir Ben-Horin, Bernard D. Weinryb, and Solomon Zeitlin (Leiden: Brill, 1962), p. 613, and " Sefer Teshuvot ha-Meshuvot: Mi-Tokh Ketavav ha-Ivriyim shel ha-Mumar Avner mi-Burgos (Book of responses to errors: Selections from the Hebrew writings of Avner of Burgos)," in his *Meḥqarim u-meqorot*, 2 vols. (Jerusalem: Reuven Mas, 1967): 1: 339. I modified the order in which I quoted from the two sources in this extract. For Ibn Ezra's rendering of Edom-Rome, see this chapter's first section.

[134] Jonathan Hecht, "The Polemical Exchange Between Isaac Pollegar and Abner of Burgos/Alfonso of Valladolid according to Parma MS 2440: Iggeret Teshuvat

of Avner over the next century suggest that his role in undermining the Jewish case and propelling the conversion movement among Spanish Jews was regarded as crucial.[135]

Paul of Burgos made no pretension of dialogue: His anti-Jewish polemics were violent. A rich and learned Castilian tax farmer, Paul converted with most of his family at the height of the 1391 anti-Jewish pogroms, went to study theology in Paris, and returned to lead the missionary charge to convert the Jews.[136] A highly placed royal administrator and, from 1415 on, the Archbishop of Burgos, he drafted anti-Jewish legislation. His "Additions" (*Additiones*) to the *Postillae* upheld Aquinas – who (he said) had inspired his conversion – against Lyra. They elicited a vitriolic Franciscan response (Matthias Döring, 1390s–1469). Both the *Additiones* and *Replicae* were published in the *Postillae*'s many printed editions.[137]

Paul merged biblical exegesis with an attack on the Talmud to create the first full-blown Christian typology of Jewish Edom. Martini and Lyra treated Edom-Rome as if the typology was still anti-imperial. Paul directed his fire at the medieval Jewish view of the Roman Church as Edom. The Jews, he complained in his commentary on Isaiah 34, "feign that the kingship [regnum] of the Romans, [and the fourth] beast of the revelation of Daniel, is one and the same with the Church [and that it] descended from Esau.... [I]n the nefarious Talmudic teaching, ... they call [it] Idumaean ... Rashi and all the Hebrew expositors explain" Isaiah's prophecy of vengeance against the nations (34:1) "as referring to ... the Roman Church ... which they say is to be destroyed by the Messiah." *Pace* Lyra, "to say that the Roman kingship descended from chief Mabdihel [*sic*], Esau's descendant, is manifestly false": The Romans descended from Kittim. "Christians ... descend by faith ... principally from Christ, ... who descended from David, [hence] from Jacob, not from Esau. According to the flesh, they descend from all nations."

Rewriting at length the Jacob & Esau story as a struggle of Synagogue and Church from Rebecca's womb to eternity, Paul deployed "the nefarious Talmud" to demonstrate that "those 'who say that they are Jews and are not, but are a synagogue of Satan (Revelations 2:9),' [those are] the

Apikoros (Epistle to the Apostate) and Teshuvot la-Meharef (Response to the Blasphemer)" (Ph.D. diss., New York University, 1993), esp. pp. 333–34, 420–22.

[135] Yehuda Shamir, *Rabbi Moses ha-Cohen of Tordesillas and His Book "Ezer ha-Emunah" – A Chapter in the History of the Judeo-Christian Controversy* (Coconut Grove, FL: Field Research Projects, 1972).

[136] His student Joshua ha-Lorki (Jerome de Santa Fide) led the Tortosa Disputation 1413–14, which proved most damaging to Spanish Jewry.

[137] *Biblia Sacra cum glossis, interlineari et ordinaria: Nicolai Lyrani postilla, ac moralitatibus, Burgensis additationibus & Thoringi replicis*, 6 vols. (Venice: n.p., 1588).

enemy of the house of Jacob, namely, the true Church, [and they] ought to be called Idumaea" (Isaiah 34). Using the Talmudic tale that the Tanna Rabbi Meir was an Idumaean proselyte, Paul suggested that he authorized the Pharisaic doctrine of an Oral Torah, and Rabbi Judah the Patriarch, the *Mishnah*'s redactor, received it from him.[138] The Talmud was an Idumaean work. The Church carried on the Jewish Apostles' legacy, and the Synagogue carried the Idumaean Talmud's legacy. Contemporary Jews were Idumaeans. Biblical prophecies on Edom were directed at the Synagogue. They were bloody because the punishment of Jews was proportionate to deicide, and the spilled blood of the righteous from Abel to Christ was to be avenged. Paul described the horror of unburied Jewish cadavers raising a stench. Roman massacres in Jerusalem and Bethar, and the pogroms against Jews in France, England, and Spain, all fulfilled Isaiah's prophecy against Edom.

Paul of Burgos's Jewish Edom was a feat that Christianity had dared not imagine for fifteen centuries. Even Tertullian and the early Church Fathers, who had likened Jewish hounding of Christians to Esau's persecution of Jacob, had not developed a concept of Jewish Edom. Paul ended Christian ambiguity, which left the Jews suspended between Mt. Zion and Mt. Esau, placing the Jews squarely into the Edom space, making them the church's enemy par excellence. Jewish Edom, *Idumaea = synagoga iudeorum*, reflected the growing savagery of Spanish and European anti-Jewish feelings, and made anti-Jewish edicts and expulsions seem almost graceful when the ignoble death that Edom prophecies presaged for the Jews was envisioned.

Isaac Abravanel, a wandering leader of Iberian Jewry in exile, responded to Paul. A statesman and financier, on the run from a succession of alternately persecuting and collapsing regimes, from Portugal to Castile (1483) to Naples (1492) to Corfu (1495) to Venice (1496), he repeatedly gained and lost the confidence and favor of royalties, as well as his fortune. He is reputed to have made valiant efforts to revoke the Edict of Expulsion from Spain – in vain. A scion to an Iberian Jewish aristocracy tracing its origins to King David, he made it his mission to secure the Jewish redemptive vision vouched for in Edom prophecies. He repeatedly returned to the subject in his biblical commentaries and in his *Mashmia*

---

[138] Paul does not distinguish between *Mishnah* and Talmud. His Talmudic examples were taken from *Pugio Fidei* and previous anti-Talmudic collections; he did not consult the original. Chen Merchaviah, "The Talmud in the *Additiones* of Paul of Burgos," *Journal of Jewish Studies* 16:3/4 (1965): 115–34. *BT*, Sanhedrin 86a, Eruvin 96b suggest that unattributed statements of the law represent Rabbi Meir's views, intimating his key role in forming the *Mishnah*. Gittin 56a and Maimonides' introduction to *Mishneh Torah* (the foremost medieval halakhic code) have Rabbi Meir as a proselyte. In the Talmud, he is the Emperor Nero's descendant, hence Idumaean.

Yeshuah (Proclaiming redemption, 1498), mobilizing all Jewish and Christian authorities to reaffirm the Jewish typology, taking on at length not only Paul of Burgos but also Ibn Ezra.[139] Unlike his predecessors, he anchored Edom in a historical vision of Europe's place in the world.

Abravanel discounted medieval challenges to Edom. *Josippon*, he said, traced Rome's genealogy; Lyra affirmed Esau's descendant, chief Magdiel, as founder of Rome; and the Patriarch Isaac blessed Esau with "Greece of Italy."[140] Rome was the first to advance Christianity, the Idumaeans were the first Christians, and they converted Constantine. Besides, metaphorically, all enemies of Israel were called Edom. Christian Rome fancied itself the messianic Fifth Empire, a global power, but it was not. Christian triumphalism was vacuous: "Africa and much of Asia had reverted from Christianity to Islam, and the Muslims constitute a global majority.... . Christian Europeans are but a small minority." With the Ottoman Empire offering refuge to the Sephardi remnant, Abravanel emphasized the brotherhood of Isaac and Ishmael and envisioned the Muslims taking part in the destruction of Rome.[141]

Abravanel joined messianic eschatology and political realism, prophecy on Christian Rome's destruction with discourse on the virtues of Roman and Venetian republicanism, and rabbinic Judaism with European acculturation. His Christian Edom represented a crescendo: The typology would never again possess the power it had in the immediate aftermath of the Spanish expulsion. His vision came apart quickly. He emphasized Christian Europe's geopolitical limits on the eve of Europe's greatest global expansion. Hope for Ottoman Ishmael's help against European Esau did not last long: Safed Kabbalists would soon be complaining about Muslim oppression. With the Jewish population's rapid sixteenth-century growth in Eastern Europe, world Jewry's majority no longer lived, as Ibn Ezra noted for his time (Daniel 12:11), under Muslim rule. Christian Rome would not fall to the Turks: Christendom would implode from within, with the Reformation. Within a generation, nothing would remain from Abravanel's medieval Jewish European synthesis.

Yet Abravanel's Christian Edom conveyed a message to Europe. Medieval Christianity shaped Europe in confrontation with Judaism and Islam. Late medieval Edom embodied Judeo-Christian European

---

[139] Part III, *Migdal Yeshuot* (Tower of redemption) (Koenigsberg: Albert Rosbach, 1860), pp. 17b–19a.

[140] Commentary on Isaiah 35:10 and Obadiah 1:10, *Perush al Neviim u-Ketuvim*, 3: 169–73 and 4: 114–16, respectively.

[141] Commentary on Genesis 25 (ḥaye Sarah), *Perush al ha-Torah* (Jerusalem: Bnei Arabel, 1964): 1: 292; commentary on Jeremiah 49:7, *Perush al Neviim Aḥaronim*, 3: 421; *Maayane ha-Yeshuah*, pp. 17a–b (quote on p. 17b; maayan 6, tamar b); and *Mashmia Yeshuah*, 17b, respectively.

culture, emergent precisely as Spanish Jews and Muslims were forcibly converted and expelled. Jacob & Esau – but also Isaac & Ishmael – were hopelessly entangled. Expulsion did not undo their ties. The Sephardi Diaspora's nostalgia for Spain, their sense that they were expelled from civilization and were upholding Spanish culture in exile, would gain partial recognition centuries later when, in 1924, Spain would extend citizenship to them, and in World War II when Franco would allow Jews escaping from Nazi Europe to go through Spain and his emissaries in Athens, Bucharest, and Budapest to intervene on behalf of Sephardi Jews.[142] A rethinking of the meaning of "European," so that the ties that bind over centuries, borders, and religion count most and anxieties about the otherness of minorities diminish, could be helped by perspectives such as Abravanel's, chastening Christian European triumphalism and displaying the Europeanness of minority cultures.

Converts and the Writing of Jewish European History

The Jews entered European history, and the Middle Ages, confronting a Roman Empire that was Christian and exited medieval Europe confronting Christendom, the foremost imperial manifestation of which was the Roman Church. Edom would diminish in early modern Europe not only because Christendom shattered but also because it proved a Jewish failure. The destruction of the First and Second Temples had each given rise to an Edom typology, and the 1096 pogroms solidified medieval Christian Edom. Abravanel's affirmation after 1492 was habitual but futile. What hope could a paradigm formed in anticipation of redemption provide when catastrophe revisited? What guidelines could messianic Edom provide for Jewish life in the aftermath of the expulsion? Kabbalistic Edom, theurgic in character, focusing on cosmic healing (tiqun), would prove a popular early modern alternative. But the real future lay in early signs of Jewish rehabilitation of empire and, equally, in Abravanel's republican models, in short, in efforts to imagine Christian–Jewish coexistence, shared polity and culture, rather than in messianic Edom.

Power disparity and polemics between Christians and Jews characterized medieval and modern European culture alike, but medieval and modern polemics were starkly different. "'But the Israelites had marched through the sea on dry ground (Exodus 14:29),'" says *Sefer Yosef ha-Meqane* (Book of Joseph the zealot); "that is a sign that we must live

---

[142] Haim Avni, *Spain, the Jews, and Franco* (Philadelphia: The Jewish Publication Society of America, 1974). Thanks to Gena Olan for the reference.

among you [Christians], but we must not be polluted by the water [baptism]." Modern Jewish acculturation into European culture would assume the opposite – fertilization rather than pollution, exchange rather than closure. The two periods present the Jewish European historian with different challenges. Narrating medieval culture, the challenge is to track Jewish–Christian exchange; narrating the modern European intelligentsia, the challenge is to track the Jewish. In both medieval and modern Europe, the outliers, Jewish converts and highly acculturated intellectuals, respectively, provide opportunities for telling a Jewish European story. But the medieval historian is, strangely, in an easier position. In the tale of assimilated Jewish intellectuals, rabbinic Judaism is dead. In the converts' Edom, both rabbinic Judaism and Christian culture are alive.

Jewish converts, members of Christian and Jewish cultures in conflict, and neither tell best Edom's medieval Jewish European history. The ultimate irony is that in a Western Europe almost free of its Jews, the Christian Bible reflected, more than ever, Jewish commentary, and ex-Jews criticized the Jewish facets of Christian culture in debate with Jews. The authentically Jewish, too, emerges through as obnoxious a figure as Paul of Burgos. His Isaiah commentary used the Christian compendium of Talmudic blasphemies, prepared for the 1240 Talmud Trial. Paul ridiculed the Talmudic account of God's daily schedule. Even Paul did not dare challenge one divine assignment, however: God teaching the Torah to little children who died before reaching school age. Paul could not possibly appreciate the tale, but he left it alone. "Fear not my servant Jacob!"

4 Waning Edom? Early Modern Christian–Jewish Hybridities

Shattering Christendom, the Reformation commenced a quiet transformation of Jacob & Esau in Jewish life that created modest room for Christian–Jewish coexistence and religious innovation. The typology survived in Jewish and Christian discourses all the way through the Enlightenment, but in its traditional forms, it ceased to provide orientation for ever-growing spheres of life. Alternatives emerged. The Lurianic Kabbalah reshaped a cosmological vision of redemption, in which Edom played a positive role, and Sabbatean discourses – so-called after the would-be messiah Shabbetai Zevi (1626–1676) – offered hybrid visions of Jacob & Esau. The modern nation-state and Jewish emancipation would put an end to such experimentation by expanding opportunities for Jewish European integration and changing its rules. Early modern European models of limited Christian–Jewish coexistence remain edifying, nonetheless, as they represent a divergent mode for engaging tradition.

Jewish responses to early modern catastrophes did not echo with Edom. The 1648–49 pogroms in Poland, known as the Chmielnicki *Gezerot* (persecution), provide the prime example.[1] Edom was so firmly identified with the Roman Church that the Cossacks attacking the Poles and Jews, members of the Greek Orthodox Church descended from Byzantium, were identified as Greek. Jews viewed the rebellion as a war between Edom and Greece, Catholic Poles, and Greek Orthodox Ukrainians.[2] Curiously, the Jews found themselves on

---

[1] After Bohdan Khmelnytsky (c. 1595–1657), leader of the Ukrainian Cossacks who rebelled against the Polish-Lithuanian Commonwealth,

[2] The pogroms chronicle, *Yeven Mezulah*, repeatedly refers to the Ukrainian Cossacks as Greek, and uses "Kings of Edom" as an appellate for Catholic kings (pp. 34, 41) and "Alufe Edom" for the Polish generals (p. 50). The titles of both chronicles narrating the pogroms identify the catastrophe as brought on by Greece, and the martyrology of the Jews who refused Greek Orthodox conversion is modeled on stories of ancient Jewish refusal of idol worshipping, ordered by Greek rulers. Natan Neta Hanover, *Sefer Yeven Mezulah* (1653; Book of deep mire) (Tel Aviv: Ha-Qibutz Ha-Meuḥad, 1945); Shmuel Fayvush ben Natan Faydl, "Sefer Tit ha-Yaven" (1649; Book of the pit of destruction), in *Le-Qorot*

Edom's side.[3] Catholic persecution of Jews increased in eighteenth-century Poland, and the Roman Church and the Inquisition remained fearsome, especially to crypto-Jews in the Iberian Peninsula and Latin America, but multiple churches now represented Christendom, undermining typological Edom. Medieval Christian Rome withered away as the major target of Jewish hatred.

With the departure of Emperor Karl V in 1556, the fragmented Holy Roman Empire no longer projected imperial might. The 1512 Cologne Diet changed its name to the "Holy Roman Empire of the German Nation." The Roman feature became attenuated. Voltaire's witticism "neither Roman, nor holy, nor an empire" applied throughout the early modern era.[4] At the same time, Jewish endorsement of royal and imperial power became consistent and clear. Postexpulsion Spanish-Jewish historiography, exemplified in Solomon ibn Verga (1460–1554), reflected the conversion of *Josippon*'s benevolent view of Rome into a political strategy: a vertical alliance between ruler and Jews.[5] The 1648 chronicle *Yeven Meẓulah* spoke of German emperors and Polish kings as righteous. Rulers past and present, from Emperor Titus (who destroyed the Temple) to Portuguese King Emmanuel I (who forcibly converted the Jews) to Polish Prince Jeremi Wiśniowiecki (who tried but failed to protect the Jews in 1649), became friends of the Jews.[6] Prague historian and cosmographer David Gans (1541–1613) wondered how to reconcile the demonic Titus emerging from the Talmud with the Josipponian picture, but loyalty and closeness to the ruler became the touchstone of Jewish politics.[7] Even

---

ha-Gezerot al Yisrael, ed. Hayim Yonah Gurland, 5 vols. (Odessa: Aba Dukhno, 1892), 4: 17–28. *Yeven* and *Yaven* evoke the Hebrew for Greece – Yavan. (Originally in Psalms 40:2: "He brought me up out of the pit of destruction [*Yeven Meẓulah*].")

[3] But not completely: Polish protection of the Jews in 1648–49 proved inadequate, and occasionally treacherous. The pogroms did give rise to a Sabbatean concept of Poland as Edom. With the eighteenth-century deterioration in Catholic–Jewish relations, Poland became "Edom" for a brief period, at least for some Jews. See the discussion later in this chapter.

[4] *Essai sur les mœurs et l'esprit des nations, Oeuvres complètes de Voltaire*, 35 vols. (Paris: Hachette, 1859), 7: 416: "Ce corps qui s'appelait et qui s'appelle encore le saint empire romain n'était en aucune manière ni saint, ni romain, ni empire."

[5] Shmuel ibn Virgah, *Sefer Shevet Yehudah* (Judah's scepter), ed. Azriel Shoḥet and Yiẓhak Baer (Jerusalem: Bialik Institute, 1946); Yosef Hayim Yerushalmi, *The Lisbon Massacre of 1506 and the Royal Image in the Shebet Yehudah* (Cincinnati, OH: Hebrew Union College, 1976).

[6] For Titus, see my discussion of *Josippon* in chap. 2 and of Abrahan ibn Daud in chap. 3; for Emmanuel I, Shmuel ibn Virgah, *Sefer Shevet Yehudah*, p. 126: "The King of Portugal was a benevolent king, מלך חסיד היה"; for Prince Wiśniowiecki, Natan Neta Hanover, *Sefer Yeven Meẓulah*, p. 30: "Prince Wiśniowiecki, may his memory be a blessing, was a great lover of Israel and a war hero without equal."

[7] David ben Shlomo Ganẓ, *Sefer Ẓemaḥ David*, ed. Mordechai Breuer (Jerusalem: Magnes, 1982), p. 85 (paragraph 829).

more than Christian Edom, imperial Edom withered away in early modern Europe.

In the aftermath of the Spanish exile, the failure of the Edom-Rome eschatology seemed obvious. Pious Jacob continued to accompany Jews in their exile travails, and popular Yiddish and Ladino (Judeo-Spanish) biblical compendia vouchsafed his traditional role, but the Edom eschatology declined. Overall improvement in Jewish–Christian relations in seventeenth- and eighteenth-century Western and Central Europe contributed to medieval Edom's waning. The terms of Jewish–Christian coexistence made tolerance contingent on the Jews not giving offense to Christianity. This entailed censorship, both politically imposed and self-administered.[8] It impinged even on Jewish liturgy: The malediction against the apostates (*Birkat ha-Minim*) was modified. The version recited today is an early modern product.[9] As print culture widened Christian access to Jewish writings, coexistence and censorship silenced traditional Edom discourse.

Edom now required redefinition. As the Kabbalah triumphed throughout the early modern Jewish world, historical redemption became subsidiary to cosmic restoration, and the traditional Edom eschatology played a diminished role. Isaac Luria (1534–1572) developed the Zohar's conception of the Kings of Edom and turned them into martyrs for cosmic salvation. Other kabbalistic works retained the typology of Jacob & Esau but turned Jacob into an ascetic mystic and Esau into a glutton. Cosmological mystical *tiqun* and patient and peaceful waiting for redemption became the leitmotifs of early modern Jewish culture. Innovation went even further. In the aftermath of Shabbetai Zevi's apostasy to Islam in 1666, Jacob & Esau played a major role in syncretic Sabbatean theologies that broke with Jewish and Christian traditions alike. To be sure, the space that the Enlightenment opened for them was limited, and heretical hybridity was confined to the margins. A mute midrashic Jacob, cosmogonic kabbalistic Edom, and a Sabbatean Jacob donning Esau's clothes competed among eighteenth-century European Jews as portrayals of Jewish–Christian relations. Jewish emancipation would challenge all

---

[8] Amnon Raz-Krakotzkin, *The Censor, the Editor, and the Text: The Catholic Church and the Shaping of the Jewish Canon in the Sixteenth Century*, trans. Jackie Feldman (Philadelphia: University of Pennsylvania Press, 2007).

[9] As recited today by Orthodox and Conservative Jews, the malediction substitutes the "informers" (*malshinim*) and "insolent" (*zedim*) for the medieval "apostates" (*meshumadim*) and Christians (*minim*): Ruth Langer, *Cursing the Christians? A History of Birkat HaMinim* (New York: Oxford University Press, 2012). Compare versions on pp. 212 and 226.

three. Typological Jacob & Esau outlines a distinct early modern period in Jewish European history.[10]

Protestant Jacob & Esau

Luther's vision of Jacob was strangely familiar to Jews. The Protestant endeavor to recover the primitive church and rescue biblical meaning from medieval Christian exegesis returned the Reformers to the Old Testament and the *Hebraica Veritas*, and led to their engagement with rabbinic exegesis, which was made accessible by both Lyra and emergent Christian Hebraism.[11] Protestant rejection of the cult of the saints resurrected the Patriarchs as role models. Luther's *Commentary on Genesis*, composed over a decade between 1535 and 1545, shaped the Protestant image of Jacob and Esau for centuries.[12] Searching for the literal sense, his commentary engaged Lyra's *Postilla* critically, and, through Lyra, rabbinic exegesis.[13] Luther's portrayal of Jacob on the eve of his final meeting with Esau, preparing for war, praying for salvation, and offering gifts, bore remarkable similarities to the rabbinic picture, even if the tribulations that Jacob faced were those of Christian calling rather than Jewish exile.

Luther's Jacob is perfect, chaste, and pious, but unlike saints, he is not celibate, and he suffers while fulfilling his vocation in life. His household provides a model of Christian marriage: He marries late, not out of sexual desire but the wish to build up the church. Luther rationalizes evidence of discord in Isaac's household and rejects suggestions of sexual impropriety so consistently that he exempts even Esau from rabbinic allegations of incest (Genesis 36:18). Jacob and Rebecca knew of divine will; hence, buying the birthright and tricking Isaac – who mistakenly preferred natural to divine law (birthright to spirit) – were just. The "two nations" prophecy was fulfilled first in David, then, spiritually, in Christ. Jacob became the father of the church.[14]

---

[10] David Ruderman, *Early Modern Jewry: A New Cultural History* (Princeton, NJ: Princeton University Press, 2010), forcefully argues the case for a distinct early modern period in Jewish history.

[11] M. H. Goshen-Goldstein, "Christianity, Judaism and Modern Bible Study," *Vetus Testamentum Supplements* 28 (1975): 69–88.

[12] *Luther's Commentary on Genesis*, trans. J. Theodore Mueller, 2 vols. (Grand Rapids, MI: Zondervan, 1958).

[13] Thomas Kalita, "The Influence of Nicholas of Lyra on Martin Luther's *Commentary on Genesis*" (Th.D. diss., Catholic University of America, 1985). Goshen-Goldstein, however, shows Luther's anxieties about prospective rabbinic influence on Christian exegesis: "Christianity, Judaism and Modern Bible Study," 73–75.

[14] Marilyn McGuire, "The Mature Luther's Revision of Marriage Theology: Preference for Patriarchs over Saints in his Commentary on Genesis" (Ph.D. diss., St. Louis University, 1999).

Luther's portrayal of Esau became just as predominant among Protestants. He drew it with the Catholic Church, rather than the Jews, in mind: "Esau is a type, a figure of the false church, which boasts the name and Word of God yet despises its birthright, namely the Gospel of Jesus Christ, and seeks only the glory, power and enjoyment of this earthly life. The false church makes the belly its God" (*Commentary on Genesis*, 2: 69). Still, Luther surmised that Esau was saved and that many of his descendants became church members. The trope of Esau's belly lived on among the seventeenth-century Puritans, but not Luther's promise of his salvation. "Esau did sell his Birth-right indeed, and so do many besides; and by so doing, exclude themselves from the chief blessing," said John Bunyan in *The Pilgrim's Progress* (1678).[15] "Esau will part with the heavenly birthright for . . . god belly," echoed Roger Williams, "and Jacob will part with porridge for an eternal inheritance."[16]

Hans Sachs (1494 – 1576), a prolific Protestant *Meistersinger* (popular poet) who lived in the German national imagination as a folk hero, dutifully carried on the Lutheran picture in his "Comedy: Jacob and His Brother Esau" (1550).[17] He kept close to the biblical story but invented a happy ending, a family scene of Jacob uniting with his parents. Sachs uses the happy ending to didactically tell the story's moral, tying it to Christ. More interesting was his carnival play "The Devil Tries Marriage," where Esau appears as a Jewish usurer duped by the devil.[18] Shakespeare, a few decades later, would have Shylock associate himself with Jacob, but Sachs associated the Jewish usurer with Esau.[19] He vindicated Luther's image of Esau as a "craving belly," yet ignored his theology: His Esau was Jewish, and not one who denied Christ but a petty criminal. Sachs affirmed Christian communal boundaries with no reference to theology.[20] Luther had no need for a Jewish Esau in his violent attack on the Jews, but in Sachs, old and new Christian typology dovetailed with popular antisemitism.

---

[15] *The Pilgrim's Progress from This World to That Which Is to Come* (Chapel Hill, NC: Yesterday's Classics, 2007), p. 145.

[16] "A Letter from Roger Williams to Major Mason, 22 June 1670," *Collections of the Massachusetts Historical Society* 1 (1792): 280.

[17] "Comedia: Jacob mit seinem Bruder Esaw," in *Hans Sachs*, ed. Adelbert von Keller, 26 vols. (Stuttgart: Literarischer Verein, 1870), 1: 88–110.

[18] "Der Teuffel nam ein Weib" [1557], in *Hans Sachs: Eine Auswahl für Freunde der älteren vaterländischen Dichtungkunst*, ed. Johann Adam Göz, 4 vols. (Nuernburg: Bauer und Raspe, 1829), 1: 197–219.

[19] *The Merchant of Venice* (London: Oxford University Press, 1914): Act I, Scene III, lines 70–96.

[20] John D. Martin, "The Depiction of Jews in the Carnival Plays and Comedies of Hans Folz and Hans Sachs in Early Modern Nuremberg," *Baylor Journal of Theatre and Performance* 3:2 (2006): 43–65.

Lutheran schoolmaster Johann Hübner (1668–1731) in Hamburg redrew Luther's Jacob & Esau in the most influential Bible instruction book in eighteenth- and early nineteenth-century Germany. *Selected Biblical Stories, fifty-two each from the Old and New Testament, redacted for the youth* (1714) came out in thirty editions, sold two hundred thousand copies in the first hundred years, and was translated into fifteen languages, having also Catholic and Calvinist versions.[21] Using shortened biblical verses, Hübner recited Old and New Testament stories, one of each to be read per week. The stories were followed by simple questions, moral instruction, and uplifting Christian appeal. Jacob is a Christian model, Esau godless: Hübner unusually adds the words pious (*fromm*) and *gottlos* to the biblical text. He tells of the unedifying birthright sale only indirectly, as he explains that Esau suffered no injustice by Jacob's taking over the blessing. Rebecca acted on God's oracle. The stories lose much of their typological significance; only Jacob's struggle with the angel, interpreted, following Luther, as an encounter with God the Son, resonates with eschatology. The moral instruction is that parents' blessings count for much; the pious are rewarded; whatever God has decided – the older shall serve the younger – must take place; and the power of faith is great (Jacob winning against the angel). The Christian appeal is for confidence in God and his judgment. The Jews no longer appear as part of the story. Neither in struggle nor in reconciliation do Jacob and Esau tell a story about Christians and Jews.

Early Modern Jewish Bibles

Similar relaxation of eschatology occurred on the Jewish side. Edom polemics were rare in early modern Judaism.[22] Jews knew Jacob & Esau primarily through three popular works: *Sefer ha-Yashar*, an early sixteenth-century Italian biblical history, and two biblical compilations, the Yiddish "women's bible," *Ẓenah u-Renah* (*Tsenerene*; Go forth and gaze, c. 1616), and the expansive Ladino anthology *Me-Am Loez* (From a people of foreign tongue, 1730–1777). These works give a firmer sense of the Jacob & Esau stories circulating among the populace than we have for

---

[21] *Zweymal zwey und funffzig Auserlesene Biblische Historien, der Jugend zum Besten abgefasset*, 1st U.S. ed. (Harrisburg, PA: Wm. Wheit and Wm. Boyer, 1826). For a history of the book and its impact: Christine Reents, *Die Bibel als Schul- und Hausbuch für Kinder* (Göttingen: Vandenhoeck & Ruprecht, 1984).

[22] A notable exception: Issac Lopez (Lupis), *Kur mezaref ha-Emunot u-mareh ha-Emet* (Crucible of the faiths and mirror of truth) [1695] (Metz: J. Mayer Samuel, 1847), pp. 36a–b. The polemics came from Aleppo, echoing Abravanel, and Edom was not a central concern.

medieval Jewry. Remarkably, they pay little attention to Christian Edom or Rome.

The anonymous *Sefer ha-Yashar* was published in 1625 and soon rivaled in fame medieval Jewry's foremost history book, *The Josippon*.[23] It told the biblical story from the creation to Joshua's conquest of Israel, but it could not provide access to rabbinic commentary. This remained the biblical compendia's task. Early modern rabbis complained profusely about a decline in biblical study. Schools de-emphasized the Bible, considering it inferior to the Talmud and irrelevant to observance. Most Jews did not have sufficient Hebrew (and Aramaic) to approach biblical or rabbinic literature. Both *Zenah u-Renah* and *Me-Am Loez* were written in simple language to assure the widest access. The authors expressly intended the compendia for an audience with limited literacy: Only knowledge of the Hebrew alphabet and basic reading was assumed, and the titles designated women as the major audience.[24] The compendia took advantage of the opportunities opened up by print culture to address the educational needs of a mass market.

Zenah u-Renah was the most popular work in the Ashkenazi Diaspora: a homiletic-exegetical rendering of the Pentateuch, *Megilot* (the five scrolls read on Jewish holidays), and *Haftarot* (portions from the Prophets read on the *shabbat* in the synagogue after the Torah reading).[25] An itinerant preacher, Jacob ben Isaac Ashkenazi of Janów (Poland, 1550–1625), composed it, using select *midrashim* and Ashkenazi and Sephardi commentators, most frequently Rashi and Baḥya. *Zenah u-Renah* came out in more than a hundred and fifty editions, some illustrated (with pictures often taken from Christian bibles).[26] It shaped the informal education of women and preschool children for centuries.[27]

Jacob Culi (Yaakov Khuli, c. 1689–1732), a leading rabbi in Jerusalem and Constantinople, used a much broader array of *Midrash* and biblical

---

[23] *Sefer ha-Yashar*, ed. and introduction by Joseph Dan (Jerusalem: Bialik Institute, 1986).

[24] *Zenah u-Renah* (Go forth and gaze) rehearses Song of Solomon 3:11: "Go forth, O daughters of Zion, and gaze on King Solomon with the crown." The Torah is the crown. *Me-Am Loez* (From a people of foreign tongue) follows Psalms 114:1: "When Israel came out of Egypt, the house of Jacob from a people of foreign tongue." "The house of Jacob" is traditionally interpreted as the women; *loez* connotes *la'az*, a foreign language, the Ladino spoken in exile.

[25] Jacob ben Isaac Ashkenazi, *Tz'enah Ur'enah*, trans. from the Yiddish by Miriam Stark Zakon, 3 vols. (New York: Masorah Publications, 1983). The 1798 Yiddish edition, published in Sulzbach (Germany), is available at http://www.hebrewbooks.org/42459

[26] Chone Shmeruk, *The Illustrations in Yiddish Books of the Sixteenth and Seventeenth Centuries* (in Hebrew) (Jerusalem: Akademon Press, 1986).

[27] The *maskilim* (Jewish enlightenment intellectuals), aware of *Zenah u-Renah*'s influence, tried an enlightenment version: Chava Turniansky, "A *Haskalah* Version of *Zenah u-Renah*" (in Hebrew), *Ha-Sifrut* 2 (1971): 835–41.

commentary to begin *Me-Am Loez*: a synthetic compendium of Midrash, *Targum*, and biblical commentaries on the Pentateuch, *mishnah* Avot, and the Passover *Haggadah*, accompanied by moral instruction and con-cise halakhic rulings.[28] Culi's successors completed the commentary on the Pentateuch in 1777, with nineteenth-century additions on the Prophets and the Writings bringing the collection up to twenty-three folio volumes. *Me-Am Loez* came out in eleven editions and was the most popular work in the Sephardi Diaspora, especially in Mediterranean communities where families often read it around the shabbat table.[29] *Zenah u-Renah* and *Me-Am Loez* became the foremost examples of Yiddish and Ladino cultures.

Both works seem to tell traditional rabbinic stories of Jacob and Esau. In *Zenah u-Renah*, wicked Esau loses the birthright because he cannot possibly assume the priesthood role. Rebecca, having received the oracle "the elder shall serve the younger," forces Jacob into tricking Isaac to get the blessing of the firstborn, and Isaac, when finding out that he mista-kenly blessed Jacob, confirms the blessing. Jacob goes into exile to live with the wicked Laban but faithfully keeps the Torah in exile. The struggle with the angel confirms his merits, and he returns to the Land of Israel perfect (*shalem*) in his body, wealth, and morals. *Me-Am Loez* expounds in greater detail on Esau's vices, yet also emphasizes his honor-ing of Isaac. It intersperses the biblical narrative with stories showing the power of prayer (Isaac and Rebecca's prayer for children and Jacob's prayer to be saved from Esau); instructions on mourning rituals (Jacob cooks lentils on the day Abraham dies); blessings over fragrances (Isaac commends the scent of Jacob's clothes) and *kashrut* (the sciatic nerve in cattle is prohibited to commemorate the injury Jacob incurred from the angel); and advice on business practices (minding, like Jacob, small things). It puts Esau's design to kill Jacob in the worst light (combined fratricide and parricide), and casts doubt on his reconciliation with Jacob. In both *Zenah u-Renah* and *Me-Am Loez*, Jacob refuses any collaboration with Esau, and concedes to him domination of this world.

The narratives' traditionalism is misleading. Posed against medieval accounts, the absence of the Edom-Rome eschatology is striking. *Zenah u-Renah* makes no mention of Rome and Edom. *Me-Am Loez* recognizes the Romans as Esau's descendants on several occasions, and even

---

[28] Jacob Culi, *The Torah Anthology: MeAm Lo'ez*, trans. Aryeh Kaplan, 19 vols. (New York: Moznayim, 1977). The 1864 Ladino edition of Genesis, published in Izmir (Turkey) is available at http://www.hebrewbooks.org/22704.

[29] Esther Benbassa and Aron Rodrigue, *Sephardi Jewry: A History of the Judeo-Spanish Community, 14th-20th Centuries* (Berkeley: University of California Press, 2000), pp. 60–64.

suggests that Israel's rule will succeed Rome, but the narrative lacks any urgency. It is free of hostility toward Rome, as if Esau's wickedness is dissociated from his descendants: Esau is an idol worshipper more than a Christian. Both *Zenah u-Renah* and *Me-Am Loez* recount the friendship between Rabbi Yehudah the Prince and the Emperor Antoninus, and *Me-Am Loez* suggests that Italy was created especially for Esau. Neither works identifies any contemporary empire or church with Esau or Edom. *Sefer ha-Yashar* provides an expanded *Josippon* Zepho story, detailing how Esau's descendants came to inhabit Rome. In its author's discursive universe – that of Abravanel – the story had polemical significance. For early modern readers it became just a good story. The Edom-Rome typology lost its specificity and urgency. Early modern narratives were centuries away from medieval anti-Christian polemics.

To be sure, neither *Zenah u-Renah* nor *Me-Am Loez* envisions genuine reconciliation between Jacob and Esau. *Zenah u-Renah* is deafeningly silent about the brothers' kiss, and *Me-Am Loez* is skeptical. Both interpret the final encounter as a division of the world: Jacob refuses collaboration with Esau and concedes this world, in the hope of winning the next: "I will bear the yoke of exile. I will speak gently to my persecutors . . . so they will not harm me. I will hide from them. . . . Thus, I will survive."[30] The tribulations of exile continue and the traditional eschatology remains intact, if marginalized. Jacob Katz's view, no longer popular today, that early modern Europe experienced increased closure of the Jewish community and improved Jewish–Christian relations simultaneously could derive some support from early modern biblical narratives.[31]

Zenah u-Renah and *Me-Am Loez* show limited exposure to the Kabbalah: *Zenah u-Renah* barely touches on it, via Baḥya, and *Me-Am Loez* uses the *Zohar* but does not meddle in its theogony. Neither treats Esau as a cosmic force. Both reflected what rabbinic elites thought common Jews should know and, especially in the aftermath of Shabbetai Ẓevi, this did not include the Kabbalah. Neither the Sabbatean outbreak nor Frankism is explicable in the discursive universe of "I will bear the yoke of exile." One wonders whether the biblical compendia's mellow traditionalism was not contingent on redemptive hopes shifting to the Kabbalah, less exposed to the public eye.

---

[30] *Me-Am Loez* on Genesis 33:14, III: 150.
[31] Jacob Katz, *Tradition and Crisis: Jewish Society at the End of the Middle Ages* (New York: New York University Press, 1993), and *Between Jews and Gentiles* (in Hebrew) (Jerusalem: Bialik Institute, 1960), esp. pp. 131–56. Of course, the multifarious Jewish–Christian exchanges recounted here are just as much a part of the early modern story.

From Eschatology to Cosmogony: Edom in the Lurianic *Kabbalah*

The Kabbalah's spread throughout the early modern Jewish Diaspora owed much to the *Zohar*'s publication, but the Safed Kabbalah mediated the *Zohar*'s reception, reshaping Jewish liturgy and devotional practices. Safed, a town in the mountainous Upper Galilee, arose mercurially in the sixteenth century into a Jewish intellectual center. A textile-manufacturing hub under the newly established Ottoman rule, the city drew Jewish traders, among them Spanish exiles and *conversos*, and grew to about eighteen hundred Jewish households in 1568–69. Many exiles wandered through Mediterranean Kabbalah centers on their way out of Spain. The proximity of Tannaitic rabbis' alleged burial places – above all, the burial place of the *Zohar*'s putative author, Shimeon bar Yoḥai – served as a draw to Safed. Safed rabbinic scholars and Kabbalists were permeated with messianic anticipation, with the sense that they were living the gathering of the exiled and taking part in an oncoming redemption. They generated authoritative *halakhah* books, masterpieces of liturgical poetry, and kabbalistic teachings that, over the next two centuries, reshaped the intellectual and emotional life of early modern European Jewry.[32]

Emulating the *Zohar*'s ancient rabbis, Safed kabbalistic circles organized around eminent teachers. Moses Cordovero (1522–1570), a prodigious writer who systematized the *Zohar* into theosophy, was such a master. Shortly before his death in June 1570, Isaac Luria (Yizḥak ben Shlomo Ashkenazi), known as the ARI (literally, the lion, an acronym for the Ashkenazi, or the divine [אלוהי], Rabbi Isaac), joined his group. The charismatic Luria had only recently arrived from Egypt (possibly via Jerusalem), but he quickly emerged as the group's indisputable leader. He established a reputation for moral perfection and for healing damaged souls through penitential rites. Luria expounded on the kabbalistic vision of the Torah's commandments (*mizvot*) as measures for spiritual perfection and cosmic healing, and instituted mystical rituals, known as the *yiḥudim* (unifications), to commune with the souls of the pious, living and dead alike. Claiming spiritual descent from a line of prophets and martyrs going back to Moses, Luria appeared to his disciples a saintly mystical messiah, a potential cosmic redeemer. He died eighteen months after Cordovero, passing on a rich body of oral teaching but few writings,

---

[32] Moshe Idel, "On Mobility, Individuals, and Groups: Prolegomenon for a Sociological Approach to Sixteenth-Century Kabbalah," *Kabbalah* 3 (1998): 145–73; Lawrence Fine, *Physician of the Soul, Healer of the Cosmos: Isaac Luria and His Kabbalistic Fellowship* (Stanford, CA: Stanford University Press, 2003), pp. 41–77.

leaving his disciples to record his legacy, struggle over its authoritative interpretation, and ponder the vanished mystical giant.[33]

In contrast with Cordovero, who synthesized diverse kabbalistic traditions emerging from the *Zohar* into a rational systematic theology, Luria parted with tradition and offered new cosmogony and theurgy, tying together cosmic and spiritual regeneration. He reshaped the *Zohar*'s universe of ten spheres into one of *parzufim* (countenances), divine configurations with distinct identities.[34] Reading the *Zohar*, he focused on the *Idrot*, the esoteric convocations contemplating the creation and mystical ascent, and made biblical homiletics subservient to theogony. The *Zohar* still endeavored to make rabbinic Edom part of cosmic restoration. Luria marginalized the Edom eschatology and focused on messianic redemption through cosmic healing alone. Edom came to play an unexpected role in it.

Luria depicted an unstable cosmic order that called for human engagement to perfect the world.[35] For the creation to occur, Divinity (the *Ein*

---

[33] Lawrence Fine, *Physician of the Soul, Healer of the Cosmos*; Menachem Kallus, "Pneumatic Mystical Possession and the Eschatology of the Soul in Lurianic Kabbalah," in *Spirit Possession in Judaism: Cases and Contexts from the Middle Ages to the Present*, ed. Matt Goldfish (Detroit: Wayne State University Press, 2003), pp. 159–85; Jonathan Garb, "The Cult of the Saints in Lurianic Kabbalah," *Jewish Quarterly Review* 98:2 (2008): 203–29.

[34] The *parzufim* are at the center of the *Zohar*'s *Idrot* (without the term being used), but they remain undeveloped and marginal to the rest of the *Zohar*. Luria shifted the Kabbalah's focus from the spheres to the *parzufim*.

[35] Scholars have traced the contours of Luria's account of the creation, but it remains convoluted due to divergent posthumous recitations. My outline reflects Luria's views toward the end of his short life, in Safed and, of necessity, simplifies. Yosef Avivi provides taxonomy of the Lurianic corpus of manuscripts in *Binyan Ariel* (Jerusalem: Misgav Yerushalayim, 1987) and *Kabbalat ha-Ari (Kabbala Luriana)*, 3 vols. (Jerusalem: Ben-Zvi Institute, 2008), and, in the last volume, traces Luria's argument on emanation from writings ascribed directly to him, especially the commentary on *Sifra de-Zeniuta* (Book of concealment, *Zohar* 2: 176b–179a). Ronit Meroz tracks biographically the intellectual formation of Lurianic Kabbalah in "Geula be-Torat ha-ARI" (Redemption in the Lurianic teaching) (Ph.D. diss., Hebrew University of Jerusalem, 1988). (For a dissent from Meroz, inspired by Yehudah Liebes: Yosi Yarhi, "Maamar 'Aseret Haruge Malkhut u-Mot ha-Melakhim' she-mi-Ketivat Yad ha-ARI: Hebetim shel Torat ha-Gilgul ba-Meot ha-13-16" (A discourse on "the Ten Martyrs and the kings' death" in Luria's handwriting: Aspects of the incarnation doctrine in the 13th–16th centuries), Master's thesis, Hebrew University of Jerusalem, 1995.)

Luria's student Hayim Vital transcribed and edited his teachings several times, and his manuscripts were further redacted by seventeenth-century Kabbalists. I used the Ashlag-Brandwein edition, *Kol Kitve ha-ARI* (Collected works), 15 vols. (Jerusalem: n.p., 1988), including *Shemonah Shearim* (Eight gates), the version edited by Shmuel Vital (vols. 5–11); *Ez Hayim* (Tree of life, vols. 1–2), the version edited by Meir Poppers; *Sefer ha-Liqutim* (Collected homilies, vol. 15), ed. Poppers; and *Sefer Mevo Shearim* (The gates' entry, vol. 4), ed. Yaakov Zemah and Natan Shapira. *Ez Hayim* is subdivided into sections according to palace, gate, and chapter, and *Mevo Shearim* according to gate, part, and chapter.

Sof, one without end) had to contract to make empty space available. Once contraction (*zimzum*) had occurred, Primal Man (*Adam ha-Qadmon*) emerged, a divine *anthropos*, the *logos*, projecting light from his eyes, emanating ten spheres, divine vessels. But standing alone and isolated, the vessels were too fragile to contain the light, the three upper spheres became damaged, and the lower ones shattered and fell below, to the world of creation. This "shattering of vessels" (*shevirat ha-kelim*) created the "shells," or "peels" (*qelipot*), forces of evil, prevailing in the universe's lower reaches, or on its left side. Sparks (*nizozot*) of light remained entrapped among the peels. Humanity's task was to release and gather them to accomplish cosmic healing (*tiqun*). The *shevirah* was a cosmic disaster, but it made human free will possible. Humanity could now choose between good and evil and improve the creation.

The first tiqun was not, however, human. *Adam ha-Qadmon* repaired the broken vessels by shaping the isolated spheres into five *parzufim*. The three upper spheres required only minor alteration and became *Arikh Anpin* (the Patient One) and *Abba* and *Imma* (father and mother), but the seven lower spheres were radically reconfigured as *Zeir Anpin* (the Irascible) and his *Nuqvah* (female), also known as the Blessed Holy One and His *Shekhinah* (*Ez Hayim, Kol Kitve ha-ARI*, 2: 184–94, 6:36:1–40). Cosmic harmony was only temporary, however. Adam's sins and, later, Israel's transgressions repeatedly disrupted the divine order. The Shekhinah was the *parzuf* most vulnerable to human transgression, and Luria tracked Her rise and fall through Israel's history. Obedience to the Torah and performance of the *mizvot* (commandments) enhanced the Shekhinah, and transgressions, such as worshipping the idol (the Golden Calf), diminished Her.

With the Second Temple's destruction, the Shekhinah fell as low as the *qelipot*, went into exile, and no longer coupled with the Blessed Holy One. Raising the fallen Shekhinah, and encouraging Her union with the Blessed Holy One, was the task of the *tiqunim* that the Lurianic Kabbalah devised, such as midnight prayer and study (*tiqun hazot*), or the Friday evening welcoming of the shabbat (*kabalat shabbat*). The tiqunim made it possible for the Shekhinah to collect sparks entrapped among the shells, and the sparks, in turn, facilitated divine unions. Israel's mission in exile was to facilitate the Shekhinah's task: They "became subject to the seventy nations to release the sparks from amongst them."[36]

I reference all of these sources in my discussion of Luria on the following pages. I list the section after the page.

[36] *Sefer ha-Liqutim* (on Psalms 80), *Kol Kitve ha-ARI*, 15: 440. See also Gershom Scholem, *Major Trends in Jewish Mysticism*, p. 284.

When enough sparks have been gathered, the Shekhinah will be restored, united with the Holy Blessed One, and redemption will come forth.

The *Zohar*'s obscure Kings of Edom became Luria's major parable in telling the creation story. In most Lurianic accounts, the kings appear as the seven spheres that shattered because they could not contain the bounty of divine light, or as sparks that came to inhabit the spheres, causing them to shatter, then drop and die.[37] As in the *Zohar*, they embody the primordial universe's instability, and Luria attributed the instability to the spheres' inability to form *parzufim*.[38] The kings' deficiencies vary in different Lurianic narratives, but in most accounts, their purge, separating their sparks from their peels – scholars speak of catharsis – contributed, in one fashion or another, to shaping the *parzufim* and facilitating their unions.[39] In late Lurianic narratives, the kings become virtual martyrs for healing the world (*Rashbi* 167–68; *Eẓ Ḥayim* 2: 221–30, 6:40:1–3; *Mevo Shearim* 19, 2:1:5). Israel's chief oppressor and the *Zohar*'s moribund Edom became, for Luria, martyr and healer of the universe.

The *Zohar* (2: 254a–b) associated the four rabbis who pursued mystical ascent ("entered Pardes": *BT* Ḥagigah 14b) with the Ten Martyrs (*Aseret Haruge Malkhut*) who fell victim to the Romans.[40] Rabbi Aqiva belonged in both groups. He was the only one to come out unharmed from the mystical ascent, hence granted martyrology. The martyrs' bodies, the *Zohar* explained, were sacrificed to appease the *sitra aḥra*, the Romans, so as to release their souls for ascent, as sparks, to perfect the upper spheres. The Safed halakhists and Kabbalists, from Joseph Karo to Cordovero to Luria, dwelled on martyrology. Cordovero first used the *Zohar*'s expression for Aqiva's mystical ascent – עלה במחשבה – in connection with the Edomite kings' partaking in cosmic improvement.[41] But it

---

[37] *Sefer Shaar Maamarei Rashbi, Kol Kitve ha-ARI*, 6: 188–90, 203–14 (henceforth *Rashbi*); *Eẓ Ḥayim*, 1: 113–17, 2:8:4–6, 144–65, 2:11:1–10. The eighth king (Genesis 36:39), Hadar, who had a wife, Mehetabel, did not die. He represented the tiqun: *Eẓ Ḥayim* 1: 140, 2:10:3.

[38] In *Eẓ Ḥayim* 1: 135–36, 2:9:8, the kings represented only the feminine *Malkhut* sphere; hence they were called *melakhim* (kings). The tiqun will add the other nine spheres to each *parzuf*.

[39] The spheres that dropped to the lower worlds served as *malbushim* (garments) for their spheres so that they could better contain the divine light and avoid shattering (*Rashbi* 203–14); the kings' remains served to build all four worlds (*Eẓ Ḥayim* 1: 36, 1:1:4); their holy sparks repaired the spheres and enhanced divine unions (*Rashbi* 163–66, 305–10; *Eẓ Ḥayim* 1: 118–37, 9:1–8, 2: 221–30, 6:40:1–3).

[40] *Midrash Ele Eskerá*, ed. Adolph Jellinek (Leipzig: A. M. Colditz, 1853); *Eichah Rabbah* 2:4; *Eichah Rabbah*, ed. Buber 2:8; *Midrash Tehilim*, ed. Buber 9:13. The legend of the Ten Martyrs is recited in prayers on Yom Kippur and the Ninth of Av.

[41] *Sefer Shiur Qomah* (Warsaw: Yiẓḥak Goldmann, 1882), p. 65d; *Or Yaqar, Sefer ha-Zohar im Perush Or Yaqar*, 23 vols. (Jerusalem: "Or Yakor" Organization: 1989): 11: 292, 22:

was Luria who made the daring move of identifying the Kings of Edom with the Ten Martyrs.[42] The Kings of Edom's purge released their sparks (*Eẓ Ḥayim* 1: 118–37, 9:1–8, 2: 221–30, 6:40:1–3). They engraved Adam's *parẓuf* on the *qelipot*, and from Adam's image sparks emerged to create human souls (*Rashbi* 163–66). The Edomite kings began the creation's healing.

The kings' tiqun proved insufficient. Adam's tiqun came next, and had he not sinned, the world would have lingered in messianic bliss, as the Blessed Holy One and His Shekhinah would have remained in constant embrace. History – the Flood, the Patriarchs, and Israel – represented cosmic ups and downs. The Second Temple's destruction threatened a cosmic catastrophe. All divine unions ceased. Only the souls of the Ten Martyrs, whose bodies turned into spirits, restored a measure of cosmic normalcy, making occasional union of the exiled Shekhinah and the Holy Blessed One possible (*Eẓ Ḥayim* 2: 221–30, 6:40:1–3). Thus, the kings and martyrs were the righteous whose souls made cosmic procreation possible (*Mevo Shearim* 19, 2:1:5). Lurianic Kabbalah instructed that prayers on the graves of the righteous had special power to restore divine unions (*zivugim*) and generate new souls. Those who prostrated themselves on the graves joined their souls with the righteous to advance messianic healing. Kabbalists, it would appear, communed with the Kings of Edom as part of tiqun.

Luria's Edom martyrology is the intellectual development that the historian least expects. Edom was irrevocably Christian, and Edom eschatology prevailed in Luria's biblical homilies (*Sefer ha-Liqutim* 76–78, 89–108). The homilies offer an alternative myth of the Kings of Edom, merging eschatology and cosmogony, Edom of Midrash and Kabbalah. According to the alternative, the kings' purge represented cosmic separation of sparks properly belonging to Israel from Edom's peels, and the purged peels constituted the "field of Edom," the *sitra aḥra*.[43] The sparks that made divine unions possible were not of the kings

---

89. Esther Liebes expounds on Cordovero's martyrology, based on unpublished chapters of his *Sefer Elimah*: "Cordovero and Luria: A Reexamination of the Myth of the Kings of Edom's Death," in *Maayan Eyn Yaaqov*, ed. Bracha Sack (Beer-Sheva: Ben-Gurion University in the Negev Press, 2009), pp. 32–60. *Pace* Liebes, Cordovero stopped short of identification of the kings and martyrs.

[42] The idea was revolutionary, and Luria moved tentatively as he had difficulty reconciling the kings as martyrs and as reflecting harsh judgments. *Mevo Shearim* (19, 2:1:5) is the single place where "Luria" declares the kings and martyrs one group and removes any ambiguity. Could the explicit association be the redactors' work, rather than Luria's own?

[43] See also *Mevo Shearim* 150–52, 3:2:14. Isaiah Tishbi, *Torat ha-Ra ve-ha-Qelippah be-Kabbalat ha-ARI* (The doctrine of evil and the peel in the Lurianic Kabbalah) (Jerusalem: Aqademon, 1965), pp. 41–42, highlights this vision. Luria may betray here a debt to pre-Zoharic kabbalistic tradition: *Kabbalot Rabbi Yaakov ve-Rabbi Yizḥak benei Rabbi Yaakov*

but of Jewish martyrs, and the martyrs appear on the Day of Judgment with garments soiled with blood to exact vengeance upon Edom. Lurianic Kabbalah provided alternative visions of the Kings of Edom, and Luria made no effort to reconcile them. Cosmic healing, and the kings as martyrs, seemed to be more pronounced than messianic vengeance, but as Luria left the Edom eschatology intact, messianic vengeance was incomprehensibly visited upon an Edom whose kings were martyrs advancing cosmic redemption.

Independently of the Edomite kings, Jacob went through a major transformation in the Lurianic Kabbalah. The historical patriarch vanished together with the biblical narrative recounting his travails, and reemerged as a divinity identified with Zeir Anpin. Jacob, Leah, and Rachel were personal countenances of the primary *parzufim*, Zeir and Nuqvah. All three emerged as divinities in the aftermath of the Edomite kings' downfall, part of the first tiqun. Luria recounted their creation in minute detail, changing countenances and cosmic location, as well as manifold coupling (*Ez Hayim* 2: 109–18, 5:31:1–5; 184–221, 6:38:1–9). Rachel represented the Shekhinah, the divinity closest to the people of Israel, merciful carrier of their hopes but vulnerable to the peels. Jacob coupled with her in the lower spheres, and in the upper spheres, assuming his Israel countenance, with Leah. Weekday prayers encouraged the multiple unions among Jacob-Israel, Leah, and Rachel: The morning prayer enhanced Jacob and Rachel's union, the afternoon prayer that of Israel and Leah, and the evening prayer that of Jacob and Leah.[44] Luria transformed the meaning of Jewish ritual and biblical and midrash stories.

Esau made only a fleeting appearance in Luria. His proximity to Isaac on the universe's left side explained his father's love for him, but he never became part of Jewish genealogy (2: 122–24, 5:32:2, 377, 7:48:3). He competed with Jacob for divine illumination, the blessings, and, standing by Jacob, left no room for Zeir's coupling. He was lured away from his position to wander in the peel field; Jacob moved over and took his place, thereby making room for Rachel to couple with Zeir face to face, generating divine bounty that descended on Jacob. Coming back, Esau, to his chagrin, recognized what had just happened, to no avail (2: 123–24). Luria's play with incestuous, interchanging, divine identities aside, he reduced Jacob & Esau's historical struggle to a single cosmological event

Hakohen, ed. Gershom Scholem, pp. 82–102; Ronit Meroz, "Geula be-Torat ha-ARI," pp. 141–42; Yosi Yarḥi, "Maamar 'Aseret Haruge Malkhut,'" 87–90, 98–101.
[44] *Sefer Shaar ha-Kavanot, Kol Kitve ha-ARI*, 8: 125–28 (qeriat shema), 9: 9–14 (shinui ha-tefilot).

of limited significance.[45] The *Zohar* had already severed the Edomite kings from the Jacob & Esau narrative. In *Eẓ Ḥayim*, Jacob & Esau's struggle rarely surfaces, and Midrash's central motif appears to have vanished.

Luria made biblical history tell theogonic stories, but his theogony lost much of the Jacob story, the travails of the nation's wandering father (*Eẓ Ḥayim* 2: 121–36, 5:32:2–9). Whereas Rachel as the Shekhinah amplified her role as the mother crying for her lost children, cosmogonic Jacob became irrelevant to Christian–Jewish relations. Reenchanting the world by making Jewish daily life into a work of redemption, an ongoing tiqun, Luria disenchanted Jacob. Zeir's heavenly coupling could not elicit sympathy as the wandering ancestor. But for all its popularity, Lurianic Kabbalah did not undermine midrashic Jacob. In an age of expanding print culture, it uniquely made its impact through manuscripts, copied by the thousands but guarded by Kabbalists. It enjoyed a reputation as the most advanced Kabbalah, but it shaped Jewish culture in conjunction with the *Zohar* and other kabbalistic works that retained the Edom eschatology. Moreover, midrashic Jacob continued to dominate biblical commentary. Luria's own commentary, and that of his disciple Ḥayim Vital, reflected eschatology at variance with Lurianic cosmogony.[46] Kabbalistic Edom and Jacob cohabited with midrashic ones in early modern Jewish culture.

Isaiah Halevi Horowitz's (c. 1558–1630) *Shenei Luḥot ha-Berit* (Two tables of the covenant של"ה), a synthetic kabbalistic work of ethics, homiletics, and halakhah, did much to spread the Kabbalah in Central and Eastern Europe, and provided an alternative kabbalistic vision of Jacob & Esau.[47] Jacob & Esau were polar opposites, morally, physiologically, and cosmologically. Jacob embodied the world to come – which, for Horowitz and other Kabbbalists, was identical with the messianic age – and Esau this world. They were part of Horowitz's ascetic discourse on consumption, particularly eating (1: 390–98). Worldly Esau resembled the Protestant hunter and a glutton, but he was also an archdemon, dweller of the *sitra aḥra*. Jacob, in contrast, was an ascetic mystic and divine. Jacob was carrying out the Patriarchs' unified project. Esau embodied the threat – halakhic, moral, and physical, internal and external – to Jacob-Israel.

---

[45] For a different Lurianic account of the blessings: *Shaar ha-Pesuqim* 67–68, section 27.

[46] Ḥayim Vital, *Sefer Eẓ ha-Daat Tov*, 2 vols. (Jerusalem: Ahavat Shalom, 2000), 1: 6a–23b.

[47] *Sefer Shenei Luḥot ha-Berit ha-Shalem*, 4 vols. (Haifa: Mekhon Yad Ramah, 1992). Horowitz wrote the book as an ethical will to his family after his arrival in Jerusalem in 1620. His son, Shabbetai Sheftel Horowitz, published it in 1648 in Amsterdam. I reference the volume and section numbers in my discussion on the following pages.

Horowitz depicted the Patriarchs as martyrs, and found the meaning of Israel's exile in suffering that prepared the people, and the world, for redemption (3: 84–104). The Patriarchs healed the creation by offering their lives to sanctify God's name (3: 87, 101).[48] Their lives were spared so that they could give birth to the nation of Israel. Whether in practice or thought, the Patriarchs all experienced *Galut* (exile, 3: 91). Jacob's suffering at Esau's and Laban's hands purged the impurity passed on from the Serpent and assured that he would become Israel and that his descendants would release themselves from the impure peels. Jacob was Israel in the heavens and Jacob on earth, and Esau was Samael (Satan) in the heavens and Esau on earth (3: 88, 111). The struggle between them went on in both realms, and focused on the world to come. Isaac knew that Esau could not inherit the world to come, but recognizing his holy roots, wished to sanctify his worldly dominion. Jacob had to cunningly present himself in Esau's garments, marking this world, in order to win the blessing and complete the creation's healing (3: 94–97). The triumph was complete when King David issued from Jacob, red like Esau, marking the conquest of bad inclination (3: 89–90).

Jacob and Esau's final meeting represented a crescendo (3: 109–18). The person with whom Jacob struggled on the eve of his meeting with Esau was Samael, heavenly Esau, the fallen archangel who libels Israel before God. Samael complained that against the Torah's injunction, Jacob married two sisters (3: 110).[49] He injured Jacob's thigh to mark the transgression. Jacob still triumphed, becoming El (a god) and Israel, one who struggled with gods and men and overcame them (3: 117). Horowitz took pains, however, to depict Jacob's struggle as spiritual and not physical, so that he could convert Jacob's conduct into a contemporary guide for action, a "pillar of the Diaspora":

Just as Jacob prepared with gifts, prayer and arms, so do we with Esau's descendants, but our power is only to pray to God in time of trouble, and fighting against the nations is not our mission. "War" means [today] that the *shetadlanim* (interceders, pleading for Jews) dare to show their faces in front of kings and ministers, and, when rejected, return, all the same.... [Jacob guides] our worship: [His] "gifts" are charity, his "prayer" is still prayer, and his "war" is repentance, the conquest of the evil inclination.... All three bring forth redemption.... This is the foundation sustaining the Diaspora for all generations to come until our righteous Messiah arrives (3: 118).

---

[48] Abraham was thrown into a fire oven for testifying to the Lord (*Bereshit Rabba* 38:13); Isaac consented to be sacrificed to God (Genesis 32).

[49] The *Mishnah* (Kidushin 4:14) maintained that the Patriarchs observed the Torah. Naḥmanides (on Genesis 26:5) explained that they did so without obligation but only in the Land of Israel. Jacob could marry sisters abroad.

Shenei Luḥot ha-Berit retained the Edom eschatology, but its vision of redemption was nonviolent. Interpreting Balaam's oracle, Horowitz maintained that "there is something like redemption every day: [Israel is] like a lamb among seventy wolves, and the Blessed Holy One saves us. [We], recipients of the miracle, just do not recognize it" (3: 359). Complete redemption will come in due time – the date is set – but it could come earlier if Israel repented. Exile purified and softened; its curse was also a blessing. The Diaspora assured Israel's survival: "If Esau comes to the one camp and attacks it, then the camp that is left will escape" (Genesis 32:9) (3: 118, following *Genesis Rabbah* 76:3 and Naḥmanides' commentary). Horowitz channeled messianism away from history and toward mystical tiqun. He emphasized self-sacrifice and moral regeneration and left historical intervention to God. He found redemption in the everyday, ensured that his eschatology did not provoke the *goyim* (non-Jews), and believed that Jewish life under foreign rule was viable. Horowitz exemplified early modern messianism.

Lurianic Kabbalah, with its emphasis on martyrology and tiqun, shared important aspects of Horowitz's messianism, but, theurgic rather than just mystical, it manifested deeper tension between patient restoration and messianic expectation. The Safed Kabbalists anticipated imminent redemption and designed a permanent framework for redemptive work. A look at the *siddur* of German Rabbi Jacob Emden (1697–1776), a compendium of prayer, ritual, and halakhah composed by a scholar not uncritical of kabbalistic traditions, would corroborate the Kabbalah's profound influence on daily Jewish life.[50] Luria entrusted the messianic task, collecting sparks through devotional practice, to collective Israel, but a kabbalistic elite was to lead the effort, and a personal messiah was by no means ruled out.[51] Marginalizing the Edom eschatology and centering on tiqun, Luria redrew the portrait of the Messiah as a Kabbalist, remote from the traditional Messiah leading the military charge against Edom. Without Edom's diminution in the early modern Kabbalah, a pathetic messiah like Shabbetai Ẓevi would be inconceivable. The waning of Edom was a precondition to both the modus vivendi that Christians and Jews increasingly imagined and the greatest messianic explosion in early modern Judaism.

---

[50] *Siddur ha-Yaavaẓ: Amudei Shamayim, Beit Yaaqov*, 2 vols. (Jerusalem: Eshkol, 1993).
[51] Ronit Meroz, "Geula be-Torat ha-ARI," pp. 328–59.

Christian Hebraism and Edom

The sacralization of kabbalistic works, such as the *Zohar*, presented a stark contrast to Christian Hebraist scholarship, which began historicizing rabbinic texts. Paradoxically, interest in Kabbalah gave rise to Renaissance Hebraism in Pico della Mirandola and his student, Johannes Reuchlin (1455–1522). Reuchlin was a humanist jurist versed in Hebrew and rabbinic commentary. He successfully defended the Talmud against a coalition of Jewish converts, the Inquisition, the Dominicans, and the universities who were trying to launch a Spanish-style conversion bid in Germany.[52] Reuchlin asserted that the offenses in Jewish books were minor, they contained Christian wisdom, and they were necessary for Jewish practice. These views became common tenets of Protestant Hebraism.

The Protestant search for the *Hebraica veritas* reflected, among others, hopes of settling biblical scores with both the Catholics and the Jews. Expanding Hebrew presses facilitated access to Hebrew writings. Beginning in the second half of the sixteenth century, universities such as Altdorf, Basel, Heidelberg, Leiden, and Leipzig established chairs of Oriental languages. In Basel, Johannes Buxtorf the Elder (1564–1629) composed a bibliography and dictionaries of rabbinic literature and wrote an ethnographic study of the synagogue.[53] Buxtorf was involved as business agent, editor, and censor with the Jewish press.[54] Over the next century, Hebraists wrote numerous theologico-ethnographic studies of Jewish life, and printed Hebrew biblical commentaries, *Targumim*, the *Zohar*, and medieval Jewish and Christian polemics. They established massive Hebrew libraries in universities, royal courts, and the Vatican.[55] Christian knowledge of Jewish culture increased exponentially.

The Hebraists' encounter with the European Other, and especially with the wrath that Jews had poured on Christians for a millennium through Esau and Edom, evoked ambivalent responses. In their works, the Hebraists can be seen struggling with their feelings, revealing, intermittently, respect and contempt, anger and pity. They created both the largest compendium of Jewish anti-Christian polemics, Eisenmenger's

---

[52] David Price, *Johannes Reuchlin and the Campaign to Destroy Jewish Books* (Oxford: Oxford University Press, 2011), pp. 95–192.

[53] Yaacov Deutsch, *Judaism in Christian Eyes: Ethnographic Descriptions of Jews and Judaism in Early Modern Europe* (Oxford: Oxford University Press, 2012).

[54] Stephen Burnett, *From Christian Hebraism to Jewish Studies: Johannes Buxtorf (1564-1629) and Hebrew Learning in the Seventeenth Century* (Leiden: Brill, 1996).

[55] Stephen Burnett, *Christian Hebraism in the Reformation Era (1500-1660): Authors, Books, and Jewish Learning* (Leiden: Brill, 2012). Thanks to Yaacov Deutsch for the reference.

Entdecktes Judenthum (Judaism exposed), a mine for future antisemites, and the first society, founded in 1730 in Halle, for cross-cultural understanding among Christians, Jews, and Muslims as a precondition for missionary work.[56] Nineteenth-century *Wissenschaft des Judentums* used the Christian Hebraists, and some regard them as founders of Jewish Studies.

Unlike medieval Hebraists, the Protestant professors were usually not active missionaries, but for many, converting the Jews remained a goal, and some engaged in polemics or advised on how best to advance them. Most came out against the desecration of the host and blood libels, and a good number protested the attack on the Talmud, insisting that the Jews had the right to worship as long as they did not insult Christianity. They highlighted Jewish mistrust and hatred of non-Jews and condemned it as inhuman, but they sometimes explained it as a result of Christian mistreatment, and they endeavored to ground, philologically and historically, the charges they still levied against the Jews. They could not envision a Christian commonwealth accepting the Jews as members: Theirs was not Unitarian or Deist politics, which sought to expand the religious parameters of citizenship.[57] Rather, they viewed the Jews as an ethno-religious culture, the existence of which amidst Christian society should be tolerated and regulated. Theology and ethnography were mixed in their understanding of Jewish life.

Amnon Raz-Krakotzkin suggests that the paradigm of censorship set the parameters of modus vivendi between Jews and Christians in early modern Europe, and the Hebraists exemplified it.[58] Jews were recognized as a minority culture on condition that they suspend anti-Christian polemics. Christians were free to continue noncoercive missionizing, but when the Jews claimed – as they did with Eisenmenger – that a book put their community at risk, political authorities could intervene to suppress publication.[59] Protestants, Catholics, and Jews alike shared the censorship paradigm. The apologetics of Solomon ibn Verga, Leon (Yehudah Aryeh) Modena (1571–1648), and Menasseh ben Israel

---

[56] Johann Andreas Eisenmenger, *Entdecktes Judenthum* (Königsberg, 1711); Christoph Rymatzki, *Hallischer Pietismus und Judenmission: Johann Heinrich Callenbergs Institutum Judaicum und dessen Freundenkreis (1728–1736)* (Tübingen: Max Niemeyer, 2004).

[57] Shmuel Ettinger, "The Beginnings of the Change in the Attitude of European Society towards the Jews," *Scripta Hierosolymitana* 7 (1961): 193–219.

[58] *The Censor, the Editor, and the Text*, esp. the Conclusion.

[59] The Frankfurt Jewish community obtained an imperial injunction against the book's distribution, but the book was published posthumously in Prussia, outside the imperial jurisdiction, with Frederick I's support: Jacob Katz, *From Prejudice to Destruction: Anti-Semitism, 1700-1933* (Cambridge, MA: Harvard University Press, 1980), p. 14.

skirted theology and highlighted Jewish ethnic virtues. Early modern Jewish silence on Christian Edom abided by the modus vivendi.

Johann Christoph Wagenseil's (1633–1705) confrontation with Edom embodied the Christian Hebraist's ambivalence. Wagenseil was a professor of Oriental languages and theology at Altdorf, who, early in his career, had had friends among the Jewish community of Vienna. His *Tela ignea Satanae* (The fiery darts of Satan), a major collection of medieval and early modern Jewish polemics, showed him trying, and failing, to contain his rage and arbitrate Jewish claims.[60] Publishing anti-Christian polemics was controversial, and Wagenseil constructed a Christian Hebraist tradition to legitimize his project. He opened with a prayer to Christ to convert the "wretched Jewish race," and promised that his tireless exposition of anti-Christian polemics would assist missionary efforts. His rhetoric about secret Judaism was malevolent, but it aimed mostly to establish his scholarly authority. He provided a preliminary account of the formation of the *Mishnah* and Talmud and came out forcefully against prohibiting them. For all their nonsense, "there are many useful things in [them], and they advance learning" (pp. 63–64). Beginning with "the wretched Jews," he ended up with a plea for the preservation of Jewish culture. Were his emotional turmoil not evident, one would suspect esoteric writing.[61]

Wagenseil proposed instruction of the Jews. Those who pray for vengeance against Christian Edom should be shown "in word and deed . . . that we are not their enemies and the name 'Edomite' is not appropriate for us. . . . For a long time now the [Holy] Roman Empire has been different from [the one] deservedly labeled in the Talmud 'wicked empire' (*Regni impii*)" (p. 216). But then Wagenseil turned the tables and used Edom to argue that Jewish–Christian brotherhood, as

---

[60] *Tela ignea Satanae: hoc est arcani, & horribiles Judaeorum adversus Christum Deum, & Christianam religionem libri Aneklotoi* (Fiery darts of Satan, that is, the secret and horrible books of the Jews against Christ, God, and the Christian religion) (Altdorf: J. H. Schönnerstaedt, 1681), http://books.google.com/books?id=0xMtAAAAYAAJ&printse c=frontcover&dq=Tela+ignea+Satanae&hl=en&ei=7B64TdC9KMLTgAfpw-Rz&sa= X&oi=bookresult&ct=result&resnum=2&sqi=2&ved=0CC0Q6AEwAQ#v=onepage& q&f=false. Peter Blastenbrei, *Johann Christoph Wagenseil und seine Stellung zum Judenthum* (Erlangen: Harald Fischer Verlag, 2004), views Wagenseil as decidedly philosemitic.

[61] No esoteric writing would be suspected in Jesuit Hebraist, theologian, and censor Franz Haselbauer (1677–1756). Like Wagenseil, he endeavored to gain Jewish confidence by presenting Christianity anew. His *Gründlicher Bericht von dem Christenthum* (in German and Judendeutsch), 2 vols. (Prague: Colleg. S.I., 1719–22): 1: 1–8, conducts more traditional polemics against Edom but opens with: "The Jews have been living among Christians for sixteen centuries, and they still do not know the truth about basic Christian beliefs." To counter the Idumaean origins of Christianity, Haselbauer underlines Jesus' Jewishness. Thanks to Michael Miller of CEU for the reference.

articulated by Abravanel, should have prohibited Jews from taking interest from Christians (or Muslims) (pp. 599–608). He cited the Talmudic story (Rosh-Hashanah 19a) of the Jews protesting to the Romans: "Are we not your brothers, children of one father and one mother? Why do you discriminate against us among the nations with your harsh decrees?" Jacob & Esau betrayed a common humanity prohibiting usury.

Wagenseil was scathing of halakhic opinions that suggested that the Prophets had abolished Edom's brotherhood, Christians were not brothers, and taking interest from them was permissible. The authorities, or the Jews themselves, Wagenseil fumed, should have censored these opinions (p. 604). He called upon magistrates to take firm action to restore illegitimate Jewish profits to Christians so that they would not be reduced to poverty. Scholarly arbitration of Jewish claims ended up with a call for Christian control of Jewish life, the effort to draw brotherhood from Jewish sources with calls for repression. This was a warning sign for the Enlightenment. Dormant typologies and withering eschatologies created an early modern modus vivendi that universal humanity, the move to reconcile Jacob and Esau, could endanger.

The Reconciliation in Thirty Years' War Painting

Universal humanity emerged most transparently in paintings of Jacob & Esau's reconciliation. Until the Thirty Years' War (1618–48), a succession of civil and religious conflicts that devastated Central Europe, the reconciliation did not figure prominently in discourse or art. In popular medieval and early modern comedies, the reconciliation served as a happy ending (often followed by a typological explanation of Jacob's election), but the scene seldom appeared in churches or illustrated Bibles, and biblical commentaries marginalized it.[62] Seventeenth-century painting, especially Flemish and Dutch, revealed increased interest in Jacob & Esau. Portrayals of the birthright sale and of Isaac's blessing remained prominent, but there was unprecedented attention to the reconciliation. The search for European peace between Catholics and Protestants recalled the peace that the biblical brothers made to end their lifelong conflict.

---

[62] "Jacob," in *The Towneley Mysteries* (London: J. B. Nichols; William Pickering, 1836), pp. 45–48; "The Historie of Jacob and Esau" [1568], *The Cambridge History of English and American Literature*, 18 vols., ed. A. W. Ward, A. R. Waller, W. P. Trent, J. Erskine, S. P. Sherman, and C. Van Doren (New York: G.P. Putnam's Sons, 1907–21), 5: 125–26. The oldest English Bible, the illustrated Anglo-Saxon Hexateuch (Pentateuch and Joshua) of the second quarter of the eleventh century, shows Jacob & Esau embracing, with Esau's retinue of armed men in the background. (Library of the British Museum, Cotton Claudius B. IV, 10570.tif, f. 51.)

Figure 5: Sir Peter Paul Rubens, *The Reconciliation of Jacob and Esau*, about 1625–1628. Courtesy of the National Galleries of Scotland (NG 2397).

Peter Paul Rubens' (1577–1640) oil sketch model (c. 1624) of the reconciliation may have set the pattern for Flemish painting (see Figure 5).[63] Rubens foregrounded Jacob dressed in blue, heading a family camp of women, children, servants, camels, and cattle. His left hand on his heart, as if asking forgiveness, Jacob prostrates himself, stretching his right arm to a

---

[63] National Galleries of Scotland: http://www.nationalgalleries.org/art-and-artists/5656/reconciliation-Jacob-and-Esau.

robust Esau, who is dressed in red, heading an armored camp, a horse and soldiers behind him. Full of emotion, Esau opens his arms to embrace Jacob, while Jacob's right arm holds on tentatively to Esau's arm, his eyes querying, begging, and his expression ambiguous. Rubens's understanding of Genesis is literal: The typology of Jew and Christian is gone. The protagonists retain their biblical characters, but they channel the helpless civilian population's hope for an end to military violence, the reconciliation posing a stark contrast to contemporary Europe.[64]

Rembrandt's reconciliation pen drawing (c. 1655) had motifs similar to the Rubens painting, but he portrayed Jacob & Esau in a firm embrace, an armed Esau bending over a partially hidden, prostrating Jacob, almost overwhelming him with the embrace, and a woman, possibly Rachel, seated on a camel, watching.[65] The reconfiguration of biblical characters in light of Amsterdam's multicultural tapestry was most evident, however, in Rembrandt's painting of Jacob on his deathbed, blessing Joseph's children (c. 1656): An elderly bearded Jacob reclines on a pillowed bed, and by his bedside stands Joseph (possibly Rembrandt's Dutch patron), wearing an Oriental hat, his Egyptian wife by his side, and crouching on the bed are the two European-looking grandchildren.[66] The dispute of Jacob and Joseph over which of the two grandchildren should get the elder's blessing vanishes, and the characters project generational and ethno-religious harmony.[67] The Netherlands escaped the ravages of the Thirty Years' War, but memories of the civil and religious conflicts that had torn Spanish Flanders apart from the predominantly Protestant North two generations earlier were alive, and the fragility of the new arrangements was evident. Dutch and Flemish painting parted with Christian typology to present Jacob & Esau as protagonists of European reconciliation.

---

[64] Several painters, notably Flemish Abraham Willemsens (1627–1672), drew the reconciliation after Rubens. Dutch painter Jan Victor (1619–1677), who had Portuguese Jews for patrons, provided an altogether different framing. He depicted a black-bearded Jacob prostrating himself, asking for forgiveness, his family at his side, his left hand on his heart, a staff in his right hand, Esau and his camp nowhere to be seen – reconciliation as a prayer for mercy. (*Jacob Seeking Forgiveness of Esau*, Indianapolis Museum of Art.)

[65] Rembrandt Harmensz. van Rijn, *The Reconciliation of Jacob and Esau*, Kupferstichkabinett – Museum of Prints and Drawings, Berlin: http://www.artbible.info/art/large/87.html. Rembrandt's Jacob & Esau paintings included also a pen-drawing of the birthright sale and a painting of Jacob wrestling with the angel (c. 1660, *Gemäldegalerie*, Berlin): A red clad, reddish haired Jacob, looking almost like Esau, struggles – or does he embrace? – an effeminate angel, as if foreshadowing tomorrow's reconciliation, characters reversed.

[66] *Jacob Blessing the Children of Joseph*, *Gemäldegalerie Alte Meister*, Kassel (Germany): http://www.artbible.info/art/large/421.html.

[67] But the new types do not lose their grounding in biblical narrative, or in recent biblical commentary. The sale of the birthright to Jacob commonly highlights the Protestant hunter-glutton Esau.

The break with theology in favor of universal humanity was most pronounced in two reconciliation paintings of German baroque painter Johann Heinrich Schönfeld (1609–1684). Schönfeld's life and work represented a struggle to overcome the rifts of the Thirty Years' Wars.[68] He was born to a Protestant family of goldsmiths in Biberach on the Riss, a Swabian town with a mixed Protestant and Catholic population. Blind in one eye and with a disabled right hand, he trained in painting in southwestern German towns, such as Memmingen and Stuttgart. The area was devastated in the early 1630s by the fights between imperial and Swedish troops, and Schönfeld left. In 1633 he arrived in Rome, joining a German colony of Netherlandish painters. Training in Italy was customary, even for Protestant painters, and Schönfeld found a powerful patron in the Orsini family. In 1637–38 he moved to Naples and stayed there until 1650. His first reconciliation painting dates to his time in Rome (1634–35) and the second to Naples (1640–42). He returned to Germany in 1651, married in Ulm, and in 1652 became a burger and master in Augsburg. Augsburg, celebrating the 1648 restoration of joint Protestant-Catholic rule (*paritätische Reichsstadt*), became his home. He had both Catholic and Protestant patrons, among them the Archbishop of Salzburg (where his paintings stand in the cathedral and the archbishop's residence). A 2011 Salzburg exhibition celebrated him as the international German baroque painter par excellence.

Schönfeld's Jacob and Esau do not display strong individual characters, their red and blue clothing the only sure way of marking them apart. In the first reconciliation painting, they march toward the horizon, away from the viewer, with their backs turned. The landscape is rocky, a camp of nomads, camel riders, herders, and sheep on one side, a single sitting classical figure on the other (see Figure 6). The second painting (see this book's cover) adds Roman ruins to the landscape, a sitting Roman soldier replaces the lonely classical figure, and a group of soldiers stand behind the seated Roman.[69] Jacob and Esau embrace, sideways to the viewer,

---

[68] Christoph Bellot, "Schönfeld, Johann Heinrich," *Neue deutsche Biographie* 25 vols. (Berlin: Schinzel-Schwarz, 2007), 23: 408–9. Hermann Voss, *Johann Heinrich Schönfeld: Ein Schwäbischer Maler des 17. Jahrhunderts* (Biberach an der Riß: Biberacher Verlagsdruckerei, 1964), has a biography and 79 paintings.

[69] Conservator Mag. Verena Graf of the *Kunsthistorisches Museum*, Vienna, introduced me in June 2001 to Schönfeld's reconciliation paintings, at the time in restoration, and conservator Mag. Ina Slama in 2015 provided details on the completed restoration and comments on this section. Lee Sorensen of Lilly Library at Duke University called my attention to Protestant German painters who got their training in Rome. Herbert Pée, *Johann Heinrich Schönfeld: Die Gemälde* (Berlin: Deutscher Verlag für Kunstwissenschaft, 1971).

Figure 6: *Reconciliation of Jacob with Esau*, painting by Johann Heinrich Schönfeld, c. 1634–35. Courtesy of Kunsthistorisches Museum, Vienna (GG 1139).

who sees their profile, Jacob turning his head a bit toward the viewer. The troops behind Esau contrast with the pastoral nomads behind Jacob, but the Jacob and Esau figures are similar. Schönfeld dissociated the reconciliation from the biblical narrative. Jacob & Esau become universal types, and the reconciliation gains significance when posed against such paintings as *Battle Image* (*Schlachtenbild* 1640; also called *Pyrrhic Battle*), depicting a bloody battlefield. The classical setting cannot mislead: Protestants and Catholics in the Thirty Years' War are signified. Conscious dehistoricization and detypologization of the biblical story suggest that shared humanity must overcome historical and religious conflict. Jacob & Esau reconcile a confessionally fractured Europe.

Haskalah Traditionalism: Jacob & Esau in Mendelssohn's Bible

If Schönfeld dehistoricized Jacob & Esau so that he could see them as contemporaries, Enlightenment biblical scholarship acquired critical distance toward Christian typology precisely by historicizing the Bible as a document of an ancient culture. Historians traditionally track the modern crisis of biblical authority to seventeenth-century French rationalism or to English Deism or to eighteenth-century German historical theology and biblical scholarship.[70] They regard the gradual transformation of the Bible from sacred text to cultural document as reflecting secularization's inevitable march in the wake of Enlightenment. Recent scholarship has attenuated this view by insisting that the Enlightenment expressed itself as much in exploration of new forms of religiosity as in attacks on established churches and orthodoxy. Secularization consisted as much in proliferation of religious movements and in reconfiguration of biblical attachments as in desacralization of polity, community, and religious text.[71] The Jewish enlightenment, the *Haskalah*, sustains this view, as does Jacob & Esau's fate in the age of Enlightenment. The Haskalah's Bible, the *Biur* (commentary, 1780–83) – a German translation of the Pentateuch, printed in Hebrew letters and accompanied by Rashi, the Aramaic *Targum*, and a Hebrew commentary by Moses Mendelssohn (1729–1786) and his colleagues – retains the traditional Jacob & Esau typology.[72]

The Jewish *maskilim*, advocates of educational reform and acculturation, began coalescing in midcentury into a "Jewish Republic of Letters" in urban centers, from Königsberg to Breslau to Berlin to Hamburg-Altona to Amsterdam and London. They constituted an alternative intellectual elite to the rabbis, and, like the rabbinic network, they tied Europe together across borders. Their number was small – writers numbered in the tens, the reading audience in the hundreds – but they set intellectual trends that in the aftermath of the French Revolution and Jewish emancipation appear to historians as the first Jewish encounter with modernity. By the late 1770s, they had established a school in Berlin and launched the *Biur*; by the mid-1780s, they had a press and a Hebrew journal, *Ha-Measef* (The gatherer; המאסף). In the Berlin salons, Jewish and non-Jewish intellectuals regularly met. Christian Wilhelm von Dohm's 1781 proposal

---

[70] Hans Frei, *The Eclipse of Biblical Narrative: A Study in Eighteenth and Nineteenth Century Hermeneutics* (New Haven, CT: Yale University Press, 1974); Klaus Scholder, *The Birth of Modern Critical Theology* [1966], trans. John Bowden (London: SCM Press, 1990); Henning Graf Reventlow, *The Authority of the Bible and the Rise of the Modern World*, trans. John Bowden (Philadelphia: Fortress Press, 1985); Henning Graf Reventlow, Walter Sparn and John Woodbridge, eds., *Historische Kritik und biblischer Kanon in der deutschen Aufklärung* (Wiesbaden: Otto Harrassowitz, 1988).

[71] Jonathan Sheehan, *The Enlightenment Bible: Translation, Scholarship, Culture* (Princeton, NJ: Princeton University Press, 2005); David Sorkin, *The Berlin Haskalah and German Religious Thought* (London: Vallentine Mitchell, 2000); Dale Van Kley, *The Religious Origins of the French Revolution: From Calvin to the Civil Constitution, 1560-1791* (New Haven, CT: Yale University Press, 1996); Eric Wilhelm Carlsson, "Johann Salomo Semler, the German Enlightenment, and Protestant Theology's Historical Turn" (Ph. D. diss., University of Wisconsin–Madison, 2006).

[72] Moses Mendelssohn, *Sefer Netivot ha-Shalom*, 9 vols. (Vienna: Anton Schmid, 1818). A reprint edition in Jerusalem in 1974 includes an additional commentary, "ha-Korem" (the winegrower), by Mendelssohn's student, Herz Homberg.

for extension of economic and civil rights to the Jews – a first such German proposal ever – was a major topic of debate. Dohm set the context for Haskalah reform in the 1780s, just as French emancipation would set it for the 1790s.

Naphtali Herz Wessely's "Words of Peace and Wisdom," the maskilim's 1782 manifesto, argued for the compatibility of education in the arts and sciences with rabbinic visions.[73] But in the 1780s, the maskilim's relationship with the rabbinic elite became confrontational – a "culture war," says Shmuel Feiner.[74] Campaign rhetoric concealed the codependence of Haskalah and rabbinic culture. The early reform urge came from within rabbinic ranks, and traditional eighteenth-century rabbis, such as Jacob Emden of Altona-Hamburg, manifested growing acculturation. Parallel Catholic, Protestant, and Jewish theological enlightenments served as a context for educational reform, and David Sorkin emphasizes their traditionalism.[75] There was no unified rabbinic opposition to the Haskalah: The *Biur*, Moshe Samet shows, became part of traditional rabbinic libraries.[76] Andreas Gotzmann further insists that the rabbinic establishment was never as anxious about the Haskalah as its rhetoric may suggest: Communal structure never came under stress.[77] Only emancipation would bring modernity's pressures to bear on the *Kehillah*.

Two very different figures may display the rabbinic *Haskalah*.[78] Prague Rabbi Ezekiel Landau (1713–1793), perhaps the leading halakhic authority of his generation, led a quiet revolution, endeavoring to return to the Talmud text, purged of Kabbalah and early modern exegesis. He urged the use of scientific and scholarly aids, for example, for determining historical changes in measurement units, in deriving Halakhah from the

[73] *Divre Shalom ve-Emet* (Berlin: Ḥinukh Naarim/Jüdische Freyschule, 1782); Naphtali Herz Wessely and David Friedländer, *Worte der Wahrheit und des Friedens an die gesamte jüdische Nation* (Vienna: J. F. Edlen von Schönfeld, 1782).

[74] *The Jewish Enlightenment* (Philadelphia: University of Pennsylvania Press, 2002), pp. 87–183.

[75] *The Religious Enlightenment: Protestants, Jews, and Catholics from London to Vienna* (Princeton, NJ: Princeton University Press, 2008).

[76] "Moses Mendelssohn, Naphtali Herz Wessely and Their Generation's Rabbis" (in Hebrew), in Moshe Samet's *He-Ḥadash Asur min ha-Torah: Chapters in the History of Orthodoxy* (Jerusalem: Merkaz Dinur, 2005), pp. 67–92.

[77] Andreas Gotzmann, *Jüdisches Recht im kulturellen Prozeß* (Tübingen: Mohr Siebeck, 1997), pp. 70–106, and "On the Confrontation of Maskilim and Rabbis at the End of the Eighteenth-Century" (in Hebrew), in *"The German-Jewish History We Have Inherited": Young Germans Write Jewish History*, ed. Henry Wassermann (Jerusalem: Magness, 2004), pp. 11–35.

[78] The term "rabbinic *Haskalah*" belongs to Michael K. Silber, "The Historical Experience of German Jewry and Its Impact on Haskalah and Reform in Hungary," in *Toward Modernity*, ed. Jacob Katz (New Brunswick, NJ: Transactions Books, 1987), pp. 107–57.

reconfigured text.[79] A generation later, the young *maskil* Rabbi Saul Berlin (1740–1794) showed hyperbolically how vested the Jewish enlightenment was in rabbinic culture. His 1793 *Besamim Rosh* (Finest fragrance; also: fragrance of Rabbi Asher) feigned to be a medieval halakhic *responsa* collection, to which the editor, Berlin, only added a commentary. The work pushed halakhic logic to its unreasonable limits. In a carnivalesque fashion, Berlin parodied the perversity of the contemporary halakhic regime and, at the same time, offered possibilities for reforming it from within. Berlin articulated the Haskalah in rabbinic idiom.[80]

The Haskalah's course was shaped as much by political developments as by internal Jewish debates, however. In October 1781, Emperor Joseph II issued the first *Toleranzpatent* (Edict of Toleration) for Jews, a series of Austrian decrees, beginning in Bohemia and extending later to the other Austrian provinces, removing economic and educational restrictions on the Jews. The edicts reinforced the urgency of Dohm's proposals. Dohm argued that education and economic opportunities, and the prospect of citizenship, would transform the Jews. Joseph II's *Toleranzpatent* was a halfway measure, he thought; he, Dohm, would do better, by envisioning citizenship.[81] He conceded that contemporary Jews showed a range of liabilities, but insisted that political oppression had shaped them the way they were, and that they had no inherent national vices; others would respond to oppression the same way. Christians should be educated to accept the Jews.[82] Dohm gave eloquent expression to enlightenment universalism – to empathy with the downtrodden, a rethinking of religious prejudice, and belief in the malleability and improvement of human character.

---

[79] Maoz Kahana, *From the Noda BeYehuda to the Chatam Sofer: Halakha and Thought in Their Historical Moment* (in Hebrew) (Jerusalem: Zalman Shazar Center, 2015). Mendelssohn endeavored to return to medieval rationalist philosophy with Maimonides, Landau to return to the medieval Talmud. I am aware that Landau placed himself in opposition to the Berlin Haskalah, but if we pluralize the Haskalah in the same way as the Enlightenment, Landau fits.

[80] Shaul ben Ẓevi Hirsch Berlin, *Sefer Shelot u-Teshuvot Besamim Rosh* (Berlin: Verlag der Jüdischen Freyschule, 1793); Shmuel Feiner, *The Jewish Enlightenment*, pp. 335–41; Talya Fishman, "Forging Jewish Memory: *Besamim Rosh* and the Invention of Pre-Emancipation Jewish Culture," in *Jewish History and Jewish Memory: Essays in Honor of Yosef Ḥayim Yerushalmi*, ed. Elisheva Carlebach, John Efron, and David Myers (Hanover, NH: University Press of New England, 1998), pp. 70–88; Moshe Samet, "*Besamim Rosh* by Rabbi Saul Berlin" (in Hebrew), in his *He-Ḥadash Asur min ha-Torah*, pp. 45–66.

[81] Robert Liberles, "Dohm's Treatise on the Jews: A Defense of the Enlightenment," *Leo Baeck Institute Year Book* 33 (1988): 29–42.

[82] Christian Wilhelm von Dohm, *Über die bürgerliche Verbesserung der Juden*, 2 vols. (Berlin: Friedrich Nicolai, 1781–83), esp. 1: 26–39, 142–44.

Mendelssohn first drew Dohm's attention to the "Jewish Question" by asking him to help defend the Alsatian Jews against a wave of popular antisemitism.[83] His engagement in the debate on Dohm's proposals shaped his mature philosophy. Such scholars as Alexander Altmann and Jacob Katz regarded Mendelssohn as the first modern Jew, maker of the "image of the future," but Mendelssohn's hopes for historical progress in Christian–Jewish relations remained modest to the end.[84] He intervened in the Dohm debate by publishing a German translation of Menasseh ben Israel's 1654 *Vindicae Judaica*, with an introduction, supporting Dohm but criticizing the view that Jews were especially in need of "improvement."[85] He confronted Dohm's enlightenment civic virtue with preenlightenment defense of Jewish virtue. Dohm's proposals and Joseph II's *Toleranzpatent* exceeded his expectations and pushed him to imagine Jews as citizens. He did so in his magnificent *Jerusalem* (1783).[86] He redrew the boundaries between natural religion and Judaism, state and religion, so that neither Christianity nor citizenship could encroach on the Torah. Natural religion and politics were made sufficiently capacious to allow for Jewish citizenship but sufficiently narrow to leave room for Jewish law. Judaism emerged as the rational religion par excellence, the one most compatible with the civic order.

The *Biur* shows Mendelssohn as an enlightened traditionalist, a culmination of early modern Christian–Jewish coexistence, rather than an emancipation philosopher. His translation and commentary alike put a premium on philological precision. To combat kabbalistic homiletics, he recalled medieval commentators, above all the literalists Ibn Ezra and Rashbam, but also Rashi and Ramban. Mendelssohn, and his colleague Solomon Dubno who wrote most of the Genesis commentary, omitted well-known homilies about Jacob & Esau. At crucial moments, however, the typology resurged: "[S]ometimes the elder serves the younger," said

---

[83] Dohm's memo on the Alsatian Jews was printed as an appendix to *Verbesserung der Juden*, I: 151–200.

[84] Alexander Altmann, *Moses Mendelssohn: A Biographical Study* (Philadelphia: Jewish Publication Society of America, 1973); Jacob Katz, *Out of the Ghetto: The Social Background of Jewish Emancipation, 1770-1870* (Cambridge, MA: Harvard University Press, 1973), esp. pp. 47–79.

[85] *Menasseh ben Israel Rettung der Juden*, with an introduction by Moses Mendelssohn, "as an appendix to military counselor Dohm's essay *Über die bürgerliche Verbesserung der Juden*." Mendelssohn also responded to the Orientalist Johann David Michaelis, Dohm's critic, who disqualified Jews from citizenship on account of their unsuitability for military service (as well as their racial difference and Mosaic political constitution): *Verbesserung der Juden*, 2: 72–77.

[86] Moses Mendelssohn, *Jerusalem, or: On Religious Power and Judaism*, trans. Allan Arkush, introduction and commentary by Alexander Altmann (Hanover, NH: University Press of New England, 1983).

Dubno, "as will be after our restoration, and sometimes the younger serves the elder, in our time, in our sins" (Genesis 25:23). There were occasional echoes of critical scholarship – Esau & Jacob served also as hunter and shepherd types – but theology still reigned supreme: Rebecca loved Jacob because "she recognized his perfection (תומתו) and knew also God's will" (Genesis 25:28). In interpreting Esau's blessing (Genesis 27:40), Midrash was allowed in: Esau triumphed when Israel sinned and transgressed the Torah. Nahmanides was cited to the effect that God urged Israel not to provoke the Edomites, a hint to Jewish–Christian relations. The *Biur* abided by the rules of the early modern modus vivendi: The typology withdrew into the background to avoid giving offense to Christians, but it remained intact.

Mendelssohn's limited expectations for Jewish–Christian relations may explain the *Biur*'s silence on Jacob & Esau's reconciliation. The peculiar orthography of "and he [Esau] kissed him [Jacob]" – the points above the word *va-yishakehu* in the Masoretic text – cried out for clarification, but it never came, and Rashi, relating the controversy over the genuineness of Esau's reconciliation, guided the commentary, and remained unqueried (Genesis 33:4). In his supplementary commentary to the 1818 edition, Herz Homberg (1749–1841), Mendelssohn's student and colleague and the leading Austrian-Jewish reformer, intervened: Esau, a hunter, he said, could not possibly have behaved like disingenuous courtiers (החצרנים הזייפנים) – he cried with all his heart. Homberg had already witnessed emancipation in Western Europe; Mendelssohn still thought within early modern limits. Cautiously, in the name of "our rabbis," the *Biur* suggested (Genesis 32:8) that Esau's anger was great but Jacob's prostration turned his heart toward the good. Esau imagined that Jacob was surrendering the birthright, and, hence, his feelings of mercy welled up. Early modern modus vivendi was founded on the concealment of Jewish expectations for the end of days.

What did Mendelssohn envision for messianic times? Commentary on the oracle on the nations in Numbers 24, the *locus classicus* for messianic Edom prophecies, gave a measure of his thoughts in the early 1780s. Like Ibn Ezra and the medieval literalists, Mendelssohn (and Aaron Friedenthal, who wrote the Numbers commentary) insisted that most of the prophecies – including "a star shall come out of Jacob" – referred to biblical and not to messianic times: Why would we imagine fighting all the nations, asked the *Biur*? But in settling controversies on the Four Empires, the *Biur* left no doubt: Rome was the last one. Toward the oracle's end (v. 24) – "ships shall come from Kittim and shall afflict Asshur and Ever, but they too shall come to ruin" – the *Biur*, hastily and shyly, concluded: "Rome will torture the Hebrew exiles in Assyria, but their day will come, too." A year later, in *Jerusalem*, Mendelssohn would propound a Jewish vision of universal redemption. In the *Biur*, he envisaged a peaceful messianic age, but Edom-Rome had to meet its end. Well into the 1780s, the Haskalah tweaked early modern parameters but could not imagine emancipation.

Mendelssohn professed disinterest in history, yet the *Biur* spent great efforts in trying to reconcile biblical Edom (Genesis 36) with the Idumaean origins of Rome, as recounted in *Sefer ha-Yashar*. Sixteenth-century rabbis, such as Leon Modena, had questioned *Sefer ha-Yashar's* authenticity, but the *Biur* showed no hint of critical historical conscious-ness and treated the book as authoritative. Its reconciliation of the Bible and *Sefer ha-Yashar* was sensitive to narrative, but lacked rudimentary source criticism. Concluding the discussion, the *Biur* noted that Rashi's view that "Chief Magdiel" (v. 43) referred to "Rome" was problematic but proposed that names could still provide hints for the future, after Naḥmanides, "that which happened to our ancestors will happen to us." Edom-Rome highlights the limits of Mendelssohn's enlightenment.

Rapidly moving political events and a radicalizing Berlin Haskalah quickly overtook Mendelsohn's enlightenment. French emancipation (1790–91) made Dohm's and Joseph II's idea of gradual integration look timid and presented a stark contrast to Prussian resistance to repeated Jewish appeals for equal rights between 1787 and 1793. Mendelssohn's vision of a traditional Judaism compatible with the mod-ern civic order reached a crisis. Younger Berlin reformers, like Saul Ascher and David Friedländer, concluded that only radical reform of Judaism would make Jews acceptable to German society.[87] In 1799, David Friedländer proposed, in an open letter to Wilhelm Teller, head of the Berlin Consistory, that leading Berlin Jewish families would convert to Lutheranism, provided they were exempt from affirming Jesus' divinity and participating in ceremonies attesting to it.[88] They, in return, would renounce most Jewish ceremonial laws. Friedländer expressed the senti-ments of only a fraction of the Berlin patriarchate, but his desperate attempt to create a Judeo-Christian religion suggested that the Berlin Haskalah had reached a dead end. In 1797, *Ha-Measef* closed down. Neither separation of religion and state nor a Hebrew Jewish culture

---

[87] Steven Lowenstein, *The Berlin Jewish Community: Enlightenment, Family, and Crisis, 1770-1830* (New York: Oxford University Press, 1994), pp. 75–103; Jonathan Hess, *Germans, Jews and the Claims of Modernity* (New Haven, CT: Yale University Press, 2002), pp. 137–203.

[88] *Sendschreiben an Seine hochwürden, herrn Oberconsistorialrath und Probst Teller zu Berlin von einigen hausvätern jüdischer Religion* (Berlin: August Mylius, 1799).

seemed compatible with German acculturation. One could not hope to be integrated as a Jew in absolutist Prussia.

Patrician Jewish Berlin of the late eighteenth century transgressed early modern parameters of Christian–Jewish relations, but the forms of modern Jewish culture negotiating emancipation, such as Reform and Orthodox Judaism, had not yet emerged to sustain German-Jewish life. The Berlin Haskalah would later inspire educational reform elsewhere: in Galicia, where it would be soundly defeated by popular pietism; in Westphalia, where Israel Jacobson (1768–1828) would establish, in Seesen, the first Reform school and temple (in 1801 and 1810, respectively); and in Prague, where moderate curricular and liturgical reforms would set the pattern for the Austrian Empire.[89] For nineteenth-century German Jews, and even for Eastern Europeans, Mendelssohn and the Berlin Haskalah became, for good or bad, the fountainhead of Jewish modernity. Jewish historians from Isaak Markus Jost to Heinrich Graetz formed this vision, and many hold on to it today. For Shmuel Feiner, the Haskalah was an enlightenment revolution, a Jewish equivalent to the French Revolution.[90]

Yet, a chasm opened between Haskalah and emancipation, the corporate absolutist order and the democratic nation-state.[91] Dohm spoke of "improving" the Jews and "making them equal" (*gleichstellen*) and not of a right to citizenship. "The early discussions of the civic improvement of the Jews," which sought to make them "useful to the state," noted Jonathan Hess, "rarely made reference to conceptions of a 'German nation.'"[92] Dohm's model for Jewish integration was the Roman Empire, which exemplified, he thought, religious and national pluralism. Precisely because his model was imperial and not national, he was content to let the Jewish Kehillah retain its legal autonomy. Mendelssohn responded by counterposing Jerusalem to Rome, and suggesting that Jerusalem (and the Kehillah) did not require the political sanction Dohm offered them. But no more than Dohm could he foresee Jewish citizenship in the nation-state, the quid pro quo of complete equality for

---

[89] Dirk Sadowski, "Maskilisches Bildungsideal und josephinische Erziehungspolitik – Herz Homberg und die jüdisch-deutschen Schulen in Galizien 1787-1806," *Leipziger Beiträge fuer Jüdischen Geschichte und Kultur* 1 (2003): 145–68; Louise Hecht, *Ein jüdischer Aufklärer in Böhmen: Peter Beer* (Vienna: Böhlau, 2008); Hillel Kieval, *Languages of Community: The Jewish Experience in the Czech Lands* (Berkeley: University of California Press, 2000), chap. 2.

[90] Shmuel Feiner, *The Jewish Enlightenment*, pp. 366–74.

[91] See also the discussion in chapter 5.

[92] *Germans, Jews and the Claims of Modernity*, p. 5. Indeed, it was the Jews who were frequently defined as a nation (of foreign origin), whose social integration presented a challenge.

complete integration. Dohm aimed to modernize the well-ordered absolutist state. He lived to witness emancipation in Westphalia (1807) and Prussia (1812) and felt ill at ease. In the *Aufklärung* (German enlightenment) and Haskalah debates, enlightenment universalism, author of Jewish emancipation, had not yet settled on the nation as the political site par excellence.

All the same, there was a crucial continuity between the enlightened absolutist and national projects: Resolution of the "Jewish Question" became an ultimate test of their political viability. Joseph II's Jewish *Toleranzpatente* followed the 1781 edict removing Protestant disabilities, and British discussions of Jewish naturalization dovetailed with removal of the Dissenters' disabilities and Catholic emancipation. But Jewish integration seemed the most difficult – the case limit, a test for Enlightenment theories, statecraft, and nation building. This recentering on the Jews – the first since late medieval expulsions – regenerated the Jacob & Esau typology. The rabbinic fantasy of imperial Edom confronting Israel was waning with the early modern modus vivendi, but the Jewish Question brought the typology back.

Sabbatean Enlightenment? Edom in Eibeschütz and Frank

The best evidence for the Edom typology's vitality in the Enlightenment came not from the Haskalah but from hybrid Jewish–Christian Sabbatean movements. In figures like Rabbi Jonathan Eibeschütz (1690–1764), a prominent halakhist, head of the Prague *yeshivah* and then rabbi in Metz and Altona-Hamburg-Wandbsbek, Sabbateanism revealed a divergent enlightenment universalism, one that sought to bring Jews and Christians together through kabbalistic theosophy, rather than through natural religion and politics. In Jacob Frank (1726–1791) and his followers, Sabbateanism displayed a mass movement of Jewish converts to Catholicism, with a syncretic theology claiming to synthesize Jacob & Esau. Among the Moravian Sabbateans, there were founders of a Christian-Jewish Masonic lodge, the Asiatic Brothers of St. John the Evangelist, with a syncretic rite.[93] Sabbateanism exemplifies the pluralist Enlightenment emerging from recent scholarship. It confronts the common narrative of Haskalah to emancipation with an equally compelling closing scene for early modern Europe.

---

[93] Jacob Katz, *Jews and Freemasons in Europe, 1723–1939*, trans. Leonard Oschry (Cambridge, MA: Harvard University Press, 1970), chaps. 3–4.

The apostate messiah Shabbetai Zevi haunted eighteenth-century Jewry. The shock at his conversion to Islam tore apart Jewish communities. Among the minority continuing to uphold Zevi as a messiah were groups, disparagingly called *Dönmeh* (apostates), who converted to Islam, establishing Islamic-Jewish communities in Turkey and Greece. Openly Sabbatean Jewish communities grew in eighteenth-century Podolia (contemporary southwest Ukraine), and a network of crypto-Sabbatean circles existed throughout Europe.[94] Kabbalistic Sabbatean works fed into major eighteenth-century Jewish currents, such as *Hasidism*. Sabbatean hybridity soon extended from Islam to Christianity. With Eibeschütz, it reached into the heart of traditional Judaism, transgressing Christian–Jewish borders more radically than the Haskalah.

Sabbateanism forced the Jewish community to move, however reluctantly, toward drawing boundaries of orthodoxy. Several bans of excommunication (*haramot*) were declared against the Sabbateans, with Jacob Emden, Eibeschütz's nemesis, taking the lead. To Emden, monotheistic religions each had a role in God's design, and hybridity confounded it: He urged the church to burn the Frankists as Christian heretics. Trying to preserve an early modern status quo, Emden reverted to a medieval practice, still current in the Iberian Peninsula. The Enlightenment made it possible for Sabbateanism to turn into syncretic universalism, but the old corporate order set limits to transgression: Sabbateans had to keep their heads low, and the Frankists were induced to convert to Catholicism, to the mutual joy of Jews and Catholics. Sabbatean hybridity would dissipate with emancipation precisely because the boundaries of Jewish self-definition would expand well beyond Emden's allowance.[95]

The early 1750s controversy over Sabbatean formulae that Emden discovered in Eibeschütz's amulets divided the European Jewish world and spilled over to the non-Jewish press. It overshadowed an earlier episode of interest here. In 1725, a Sabbatean emissary (Frank's uncle)

---

[94] Pawel Maciejko, *The Mixed Multitude: Jacob Frank and the Frankist Movement, 1755-1816* (Philadelphia: University of Pennsylvania Press, 2011).

[95] Gershom Scholem, critical of emancipation, saw the Sabbatean and *maskilic* challenges to tradition as congruent: Sabbateanism prepared the grounds for the Haskalah. I view them as incongruent: Emancipation rendered Sabbateanism irrelevant by opening up new possibilities for acculturation. Scholem, "Redemption through Sin," in his *The Messianic Idea in Judaism* (New York: Schocken Books, 1971), p. 141. Jacob Katz scrutinized Scholem's view: "The Suggested Relationship between Sabbatianism, Haskalah, and Reform," in his *Divine Law in Human Hands* (Jerusalem: Magnes, 1998), p. 510. My thanks to Michael Miller of CEU for conversation and the references.

was caught in Mannheim distributing literature to the underground Sabbatean network during a European trip. Among his books was a manuscript that originated in the young Eibeschütz's Prague yeshivah, "Va-avo ha-Yom el ha-Ayin" (I came this day to the spring [of wisdom]).[96] "Va-avo ha-Yom" appeared radically antinomian, "a *summa* of Sabbatean Kabbalah," says David Halperin.[97] Its portrayals of sexual rites – including homoerotic relationships among the gods – were explicit. It became a foundational work for eighteenth-century Sabbateanism.[98] A scandal erupted, leading, a year later, to the Prague anti-Sabbatean ban, which Eibeschütz, typically for crypto-Sabbateans, signed.

In *Va-avo ha-Yom*, as in other Sabbatean works, the God of Israel and his Shekhinah are inferior to *Atiqa Qadisha* (Holy Ancient One), an older divinity identified with Arikh Anpin, in whose realm the Torah is not binding.[99] All three divinities emerge from the Root (*shoresh*) in Ein Sof (one without end), Divinity before the creation. Atiqa is the cosmic Head (*rosh*), and the God of Israel & his *Shekhinah*, as well as the primal Adam & Eve, had all been part of the Head in their latent state, before they expanded away from Atiqa (*hitpashtut*) (7a–8a). Eibeschütz surprisingly identifies the Root with Esau and Seir, and Atiqa and the primal Adam and God of Israel with Edom. Esau's name (עשו), he conjectures, meant "to do," hinting at the creative role of the Ein Sof. Esau was "father of Edom" (Genesis 36:9), as the Ein Sof generated Atiqa. Edom and Adam both implied silence (דום *dom* in Hebrew), as one had no right to

---

[96] Five MSS are extant. David Halperin made two – Oxford 955, Bodleian Library MS Mich. 157, and National and University Library, Jerusalem, Heb. 8o 2491 – available to me, as well as his 2009 AJS paper: "The Hole in the Sheet, and Other Topics in Sabbatian Kabbalah." Pagination here follows Oxford 955. Meanwhile, a critical edition came out: Jonathan Eibeschütz, *And I Came this Day unto the Fountain* (in Hebrew), ed. and introduction by Pawel Maciejko, with additional studies by Noam Lefler, Jonatan Benarroch, and Shai Alleson Gerberg, 2d ed. (Los Angeles: Cherub Press, 2016). David Halperin is at work on an English translation.

[97] "Sabbatianism and Kabbalistic Heresy," unpublished MS written for *The Cambridge Companion to the Kabbalah*, ed. Elliot Wolfson (Cambridge: Cambridge University Press, 2012).

[98] Yehudah Liebes, "New Writings in Sabbatean Kabbalah Originating in Rabbi Jonathan Eibeschütz's Circle" (in Hebrew), *Meḥqerei Yerushalayim be-Maḥshevet Yisrael* 5 (1986): 191–348. Liebes thinks that young Eibeschütz and a leading Sabbatean teacher, Judah Leib (Leibele; Löbele) Prossnitz, jointly wrote "Va-Avo ha-Yom," but most scholars recognize Eibeschütz as the sole author.

[99] These divinities were all as old as the *Zohar*, and Lurianic Kabbalah associated Zeir Anpin with the Blessed Holy One and the Israelites' God. But tradition insisted that all were aspects of One Divinity. The Sabbateans, notably Abraham Miguel Cardozo (1626–1706), coined the term "the God of Israel" and restricted him, and the Torah, to the lower spheres.

speak of esoteric Atiqa and primal Adam (11b).[100] Genesis states that kingship in Edom began earlier than in Israel, implying, says Eibeschütz, that the God of Israel was initially under Atiqa-Edom's rule and only later became King of Israel, ruler in His own sphere (13b). For the Kabbalah's view of primordial Edom as shattered spheres of unremitting judgment, purged of their impure peels, Eibeschütz substitutes an eternal benevolent Edom hosting the God of Israel.

Atiqa is an abode of tranquility, mercy, and holiness in the universe of *Aẓilut* (emanation). Atiqa "loves the nations (*ḥovev amim*, Deuteronomy 33:3)," and makes no distinction between righteous and sinful, Jew and Gentile (35a–b). But the creation requires distinction and balance between grace (*ḥesed*) and judgment (*din*), and Atiqa's overflowing mercy (*rahamim*) proved catastrophic, triggering the shattering of vessels (11b).[101] Esau embodied the creation's problem: Like Luria's Kings of Edom, he was an unstable mix of grace and judgment (7b). His head (*rosh*) was holy, but his hairy body signified judgment. Isaac, who sensed the holiness in Esau, wished to bless him so that mercy might overcome judgment, but as Isaac himself represented judgment (the sphere of *Gevurah*), he could not empower grace (7b). Hence Jacob, smooth and holy in his body, had to resort to trickery to receive the blessings. Jacob is identical with the God of Israel who resides in the sphere of Glory (*Tiferet*) and mediates grace and judgment. While Israel was on its land, the Torah provided a blueprint for the cosmic order.

Israel's exile signaled a cosmic crisis. The God of Israel left the sphere of Glory. He no longer coupled with the Shekhinah, and the Torah could not retain a cosmic balance (35a). Shabbetai Ẓevi rectified the situation. Eibeschütz never mentions him by name, but he assumed the role of Jacob and the God of Israel as a cosmic mediator (34b). Sabbateans understood Ẓevi's apostasy as a descent into the abyss to gather sparks and perform the great cosmic Tiqun (29a). They focused on the sinfulness that Ẓevi had taken upon himself in order to initiate redemption.

---

[100] *Zohar* III: 22a (interpreting Isaiah 21:11, "oracle on Dumah") speaks of Edom's exile as "the burden of silence" (as its end time is not known), and Moses Cordovero speaks of Edom as "the land of silence" (ארץ הדממה), where divine thought alone performs deeds: *Sefer Shiur Qomah*, p. 65d; *Maayan Eyn Yaaqov*, p. 21. (In *Eyn Yaaqov*, however, דממה signals both silence and bleeding.) Neither the *Zohar* nor Cordovero identified Edom with a beneficent god.

[101] An additional distinction, originating in Ẓevi's prophet, Nathan of Gaza, between "mindless light," the aspect of the Ein Sof that is indifferent to the creation, hence destructive, and "mindful light" is central to "Va-avo ha-Yom." Atiqa's overflowing mercy is destructive "mindless light," and rechanneling it so that it becomes mindful, i.e., benevolent to the creation, is the messianic tiqun.

Eibeschütz focuses instead on the ascent. Having collected sparks of mercy, Zevi ascended all the way to Atiqa, coupled with it (as the Shekhinah does with the God of Israel), and thereby established a reliable alternative channel for mercy to flow between the universe's upper and lower echelons (34b–35a). The true messiah's (משיח האמתי, in *gimatria* [alphabetical numerology], Shabbetai Zevi) relationship with Edom-Christianity overcame – or, at least, provided a model for overcoming – the cosmic crisis.

Zevi is the new Jacob (associated with Zeir and the God of Israel), but Eibeschütz intimates that he is also Esau. Esau had long been identified with the Serpent, and Zevi's followers called him a "holy serpent." Eibeschütz notes that Esau is, in gimatria, "serpent lives" (נחש חי) – a thinly veiled reference to Zevi (11b). The *Zohar* had stressed that Jacob's cunning had to surpass that of the Serpent Esau, and Sabbateans had Zevi take over Samael and the *sitra ahra*'s demonic qualities to overcome them. But Eibeschütz went beyond such a Jacob & Esau convergence: He intimated Jewish–Christian reconciliation.

For Eibeschütz, Jacob and Esau were, in essence, holy brothers. Esau's holy head was buried with Jacob.[102] The Torah commands, "You shall not detest an Edomite for he is your brother (אחיך הוא) (Deuteronomy 23:8)." "He" (הוא), says Eibeschütz, is a different name for Atiqa (*rosh*, head), where holy brotherhood between Edom and Israel prevails (7b). Esau's confusion of kindness and judgment made him a source of cosmic instability (and may explain his troubled relationship with Jacob, i.e., the Jewish people), but possessing his body made it possible for Zevi to reach the lower universe, where Jacob and the Torah's hold had always been shaky. Esau was vital to the cosmic order. He was the Root, part of the Head, Atiqa, and the messiah. Zevi-Jacob-Esau coupled with Edom-Atiqa, restoring the primal unity of the *Azilut* universe, and the intimacy between Edom and the God of Israel.

Coupling with Atiqa, the messiah followed a venerable model for courting a foreign religion. King David worshipped Atiqa (35a): "David arrived at the head (*ha-rosh*, the mountain's summit), where he [*sic*] worshipped God (II Samuel 15:32)."[103] It was inappropriate for David to do so while Israel was on its land, but "Va-avo ha-Yom" implies that, in

---

[102] Eibeschütz quotes Luria, following Midrash: *Sefer ha-Liqutim* (on Genesis 25:28), p. 78; *Pirqe de-Rabbi Eliezer* 39, ed. C. M. Horowitz (Jerusalem: Maqor, 1972); *Targum Pseudo-Jonathan* on Genesis 50:13.

[103] This follows a Talmudic homily (Sanhedrin 107a), suggesting that David contemplated worshipping an idol, so that the blame for Absalom's rebellion will fall upon his, the King's, head rather than profane God's name.

exile, and certainly with the onset of the redemption, the Torah is no longer binding on Israel. One should not pray *to* the God of Israel but, rather, *for* the God of Israel and the Shekhinah to join again and bring forth Israel's redemption. This is best done, following Ẓevi's example, through "enclothement" (*hitlabshut*), donning the host religion's garments – Christianity or Islam (34b–35a). But the meaning of "enclothement" remains unclear. Eibeschütz specifically rejects praying to Atiqa – which may be tantamount to Christian conversion – because, without the Jewish messiah's mediation, Atiqa's flow of pure mercy remained destructive, "wasted seed" (זרע לבטלה) that created no cosmic union (34b–35b). Ẓevi's mediation seems crucial to any Jewish relationship with Atiqa-Christianity. The ritual implications remain mysterious – the mystery of crypto-Sabbateanism.

Eibeschütz had close relations with Christian theologians, and rumors circulated that he was a crypto-Christian.[104] His biography would suggest that he was content to live as a traditional Jew, and remain a member of a Sabbatean elite of – dare I say – *maskilim*, aware of the alternative. His halakhic works function in the Torah's realm and not in the Sabbatean world, and he is hypernomian – a strict halakhist and moralist.[105] In his homiletic *Yaarot Devash* (Honeycombs), Edom appears as a historical rather than a cosmic agent: as Jerusalem's destroyer, Israel's powerful ruler in exile, and the enemy to defeat before Israel is restored.[106] Using similar homilies to "Va-avo ha-Yom," Eibeschütz mentions that Esau's head contained sparks of holiness, but the context is not Jacob & Esau's shared holiness; rather, Jacob-Israel in exile collects sparks from other nations (45a).[107] "Va-avo ha-Yom" and *Yaarot Devash* represent

[104] Pawel Maciejko, "Controverse sur la crypto-chrétienté de Rabbi Jonathan Eibeschütz," *Les cahiers du judaïsme* 29 (2010): 130–34. Like Scholem, Moshe Arie Perlmuter thinks of Eibeschütz's Sabbateanism as distinctly Jewish: *Rabbi Jonathan Eibeschuetz and His Attitude Toward Sabbatianism* (in Hebrew) (Jerusalem: Schocken, 1947), pp. 146–70, 270–71, 337–38.

[105] Perlmuter, *Rabbi Jonathan Eibeschuetz*, finds Sabbatean hints throughout Eibeschütz's halakhic corpus and treats the works as esoteric writing.

[106] Jonathan Eibeschütz, *Yaarot Devash*, 2 vols. (Józefów: Setzer and Reiner, 1866), 1: 10a–b, 20a, 24b, 33b, 61a. The title alludes to I Samuel 14:27: Jonathan tastes the honeycomb (literally, forest honey), and his eyes brighten.

[107] There is, however, no call for vengeance against Edom: The vengeful God's bloodied clothes in Isaiah's prophecy (63:1–6) become the royal red of Edom's governors, a mark of their affluence (10a–b). Edom's exile appears tolerable. Edom will be punished not for inflicting violence on Israel but for Israel's own transgressions in exile: Their meager share in Edom's wealth evokes their evil inclination. Ironically, Eibeschütz offers this commentary as a homily on *Birkat ha-Minim*, the blessing (invective) against the apostates.

alternative engagements in the world, and Eibeschütz never reconciled them. They are testimony to a double life.[108]

Sabbatean theosophy was, however, superior to the Torah, wider in scope and time: It encompassed the world of Aẓilut, both prior to the creation and after the messianic restoration. If the Torah remained valuable, it was because the messianic advent had not progressed enough for the Sabbatean *torah de-Aẓilut* to take over, and it remained inaccessible to most Jews. There were radical antinomian dimensions to Eibeschütz. His theogony highlighted incestuous relationships – the Shekinah was, at one and the same time, the God of Israel's daughter, wife, and mother – and he said explicitly that cosmic survival demanded incest and only the Torah prohibited it.[109] Yet Eibeschütz never drew a picture of the future religion, never clarified the current stage of messianic advent, and never hinted at what it meant to live as both a Sabbatean and a great halakhic authority. This explains the ongoing scholarly debate on his message.[110]

Eibeschütz's student Carl Anton, a convert to Christianity, defended Eibeschütz in the amulets controversy as a Jew who loved Christians. The association of Edom with Atiqa suggests that Christian universalism appealed to Eibeschütz, and Esau's association with the Root suggests that he considered Christianity's cosmic role as crucial. But the God of Israel and the Torah, not Esau and Christianity, held the cosmos together – at least for a while – and redemption still meant restoration of the union of the God of Israel with his Shekhinah: "The Lord shall be One and His name One (Zechariah 14:9)." Eibeschütz may have been, at one and the same time, *ḥovev Torah* and *ḥovev amim*, lover of the Torah and of "the nations": Both exist as moments, however incompatible, in his life.

This much is clear: Ẓevi provided a model for how Atiqa-Christianity's mercy may flow to all and rectify the cosmic catastrophe that caused history's misfortunes, chief among them the struggle of Christians and Jews. Eibeschütz transcended Jacob & Esau's traditional hostility. Edom turned from a malevolent destructive force into a benevolent dispenser of mercy. Jacob & Esau both had a role in cosmic regeneration. The *Zohar* had established Esau as the cosmic destroyer and Jacob as the healer. For

---

[108] Eibeschütz's son, Wolf, an aspiring Sabbatean leader, no longer observed Jewish law and fraternized with the Christian nobility. He declined, however, to convert, even for ennoblement. See: Pawel Maciejko, *Mixed Multitude*, chap. 8.

[109] *Tiferet Yehonatan* (Jonathan's glory) (Yozifov, 1873), p. 170.

[110] David Halperin, who notes Eibeschütz's promise of future erotic pleasure (in contrast with his halakhic asceticism), sees "*Va-avo ha-Yom*" as "a charter for the world religion of the future, rooted in Kabbalistic Judaism but universal in its scope and distinct from any religious system previously known": "Some Themes in the Book *Va-Avo Ha-Yom el Ha-ʿAyin*," paper presented at the Duke-UNC Jewish Studies Seminar (November 24, 2013).

Eibeschütz, Christians and Jews were holy brothers, victims of the cosmic catastrophe, partners in healing: "The third generation [of Edomites] shall enter into the congregation of the Lord (Deuteronomy 23:9)" ("Va-Avo ha-Yom" 7b).

"Va-avo ha-Yom" circulated widely in the Sabbatean network. The Asian Brothers of St. John incorporated part of it into their Masonic rite.[111] But it remained a short work addressed to a cultivated crypto-Sabbatean elite. Jacob Frank's "Collection of the Words of the Lord" likewise formed an original vision of Jacob & Esau's reconciliation, but in contrast, it expressed the ideas of a mass-movement leader. The book – if it deserves the name – is a vast disorderly compilation of Frank's dicta on his life and mission. His disciples took minute notes of his every speech, beginning in the mid-1770s. The challenge that "Va-avo ha-Yom" presents is esoteric writing and elusive Sabbatean discourse. "Words of the Lord" is an incoherent, barely edited text, generated by an eclectic charismatic leader who claimed divinity.[112]

Frank was born in 1726 in Podolia as Yaakov Leib to a Sabbatean family but grew up in Ottoman urban centers, becoming known as Frank, a nickname for "European." Marrying into a family of the Salonika Dönmeh, he was initiated in 1752 into their most radical sect, the *Koniosos*, whose former leader, Berukhiah Russo (Osman Baba, 1677–1720), claimed to reincarnate Zevi and the God of Israel. Frank first struck a claim to the Dönmeh's leadership as Berukhiah's reincarnation, then in 1755 returned to Podolia, presenting himself as a Dönmeh emissary. Frank was organizing the Podolian Sabbateans when he and his disciples were caught in January 1756 in an antinomian ritual (sexual orgy) and arrested. Released as a Turkish subject, he returned to Turkey and converted to Islam.[113]

A Brody rabbinic assembly proclaimed a ban against the Sabbateans, and appealed to the church to prosecute the offenders. This was a gross

---

[111] Pawel Maciejko, *Mixed Multitude*, p. 312, n. 170.

[112] *Zbiór Słów Pańskich* is extant in three divergent Polish MSS. I used the English translation: "The Words of the Lord [Jacob Frank]," ed., trans., and annotated by Harris Lenowitz, https://archive.org/stream/TheCollectionOfTheWordsOfTheLordJacobFrank/TheCollectionOfTheWordsOfTheLordJacobFrank_djvu.txt. For the composition and dating of the MSS, see Pawel Maciejko, "The Literary Character and Doctrine of Jacob Frank's *The Words of the Lord*," *Kabbalah* 9 (2003): 175–210.

[113] Pawel Maciejko, *Mixed Multitudes*, provides a contextual biography of Frank up to his conversion, and beyond. My account is indebted to his groundbreaking work. Scholarly study of Frankism began with Alexander Kraushar, whose two-volume *Frank i frankisci polscy, 1726–1816* [1895] is now available in English: *Jacob Frank: The End to the Sabbataian Heresy*, trans. from Polish by Herbert Levy (Lanham, MD: University Press of America, 2001). Majer Bałaban's and A. Y. Brawer's works cited in subsequent notes both provide additional documents.

miscalculation. The Frankists' answer to the threat of church persecution was predictable: They claimed to represent anti-Talmudic kabbalistic Judaism, close to Catholicism. With artistry they reformulated kabbalistic-Sabbatean doctrines on the triune Godhead and the messiah so that they appeared to be Christian.[114] The local bishop declared them victorious in the 1757 Kamieniec Podolski disputation with rabbis, extended to them protection as a Jewish group, and ordered a burning of the Talmud.[115] He died shortly thereafter, but another bishop, Kajetan Sołtyk, known for having orchestrated a ritual murder trial, stepped in and arranged for a summer 1759 disputation in Lwów. Frank urged Sabbateans from across the Turkish border to flock to Poland in anticipation of revelation. The Frankists were advancing pronouncedly Christian theses, and in a petition for baptism, they appealed to Christian expectation of Jewish conversion by using the rubric of "Jacob's Return": "We fulfill the prophecy that the remnants of the house of Jacob will return at the end of days."[116]

Biblical prophecy envisioned Jacob's return as collective redemption: "A remnant will return, the remnant of Jacob, to the mighty God" (Isaiah 10:21). The return was associated with the Jewish people's national restoration (Ezekiel 39:25; Micha 5:6–7; Naḥum 2:2). Christians, too, conceived of Jacob's return as collective: the Jews' conversion. Jacob Frank had a different idea: *He* was the returning Jacob, and *his* house, the "House of Jacob," was to accept Christianity, Edom's religion.

The Lwów disputation focused on the blood libel, and it severed the Frankists' relations to Judaism. During and after the disputation, some three thousand people in Lwów, Lublin, and Warsaw converted to

---

[114] The Catholic clergy may have helped them formulate their theses. Judith Kalik, "Christian Kabbalah and Polish Jews: Attitudes of the Church to Jewish Conversion and the Idea of 'Jacob's Return' in the Polish-Lithuanian Commonwealth in the 18th Century," *Jewish History Quarterly* (2004): 492–501; Pawel Maciejko, *Mixed Multitudes*, pp. 75–85.

[115] Majer Bałaban, *Le-Toldot ha-Tenuah ha-Frankit*, 2 vols. in 1 (Tel Aviv: Dvir, 1934–35), surveys the documentary sources for the Frankists to 1760 and quotes extensively from the disputations and exchanges between the rabbis and bishops. A. Y. Brawer, *Studies in Galician Jewry* (in Hebrew) (Jerusalem: Bialik Institute, 1956), pp. 210–75, covers similar territory, quoting extensively from the major Hebrew source, Ber Birkenthal of Bolechów, "Sefer Divre Binah" (MS Hebrew 8° 7507, Jewish National Library).

[116] As quoted in Judith Kalik, "'Jacob's Return,'" 500. Sources leave it unclear whether Christ was mentioned by name in the theses (compare Majer Bałaban, *Le-Toldot ha-Tenuah ha-Frankit*, 2: 209, and A. Y. Brawer, *Studies in Galician Jewry*, p. 227), but the petition left no doubt: "Jesus Christ . . . was the true messiah." The Jews' conversion prior to the Second Coming was central to the Jansenites and German Pietists, and scholars have tracked their influence in Poland. Kalik includes references. See especially David Bankier, "The 'Return of the Jews' in French Jansenism," in *Israel and the Nations* (Jerusalem: Historical Society of Israel and Zalman Shazar Center, 1987), pp. 71–86.

Catholicism with great fanfare. Shortly thereafter, an ecclesiastical court put Frank under house arrest to limit his influence on the new converts. For twelve years he lived comfortably with his entourage at the fortress monastery of Jasna Góra in Częstochowa, Poland's foremost pilgrimage site, shrine to the Black Madonna, patron of the Polish kingdom. Attending Catholic services, the Frankists also continued their own rituals, observed, but undisturbed, by monks and pilgrims. The local Marian cult inspired Frank to transform preconversion Sabbateanism into a syncretic Christian-Jewish cult. No longer did he reincarnate Berukhiah, Zevi, and the God of Israel, but his own advent announced the messianic epoch that would culminate with the revelation of the Maiden, his daughter Eve-Rachel-Esther.

Russian troops, putting down the Polish nobility's uprising and enforcing the First Partition of Poland, freed Frank in May 1772. He moved with his entourage to Moravia, where relatives lived. He made a smooth transition from his low-class Polish followers to the cultivated upper-class crypto-Sabbateans in Brünn (Brno). He now styled himself first a rich merchant then Count Frank, befriended aristocrats curious about Sabbateanism, and had audiences with Emperor Joseph II and Empress Maria Theresa, suggesting, at one point, the drafting of troops to support a war against Turkey. The "Words of the Lord" were noted mostly in Brünn. His mounting debts and a breach with the emperor forced him to move in 1786 to Offenbach am Main near Frankfurt. When he died in 1791, most of his Polish followers left, but support from the Prague Sabbateans sustained the community under Eve's leadership until her death in 1816.

Frank saw himself as the new Jacob, leading the people to Edom and fulfilling the promise Jacob made to Esau, at their reconciliation, to come to his place. Rabbinic and kabbalistic exegesis had already envisioned Jacob's return to Edom as messianic. Reading the prophecies on the restoration of Israel's remnant, the House of Jacob, back into Genesis was unexceptional. Frank, however, read into Genesis the Christian view of the remnant, and Jacob's return to Edom entailed embracing Christianity, conversion to Edom's religion, *Das* (דת) Edom, Roman Catholicism.

Edom connoted Christianity but geopolitically, it no longer meant the Holy Roman Empire; rather, it was contemporary Poland, the *field* of Edom (Genesis 32:3, *sede Edom, Polska*). A popular tradition associated with the Lithuanian Sabbatean Heschel Zoref (1633–1700) spoke of Poland as the metropolis of Edom, and of the 1648 pogroms as the redemption's birth pangs.[117] Frank carried on the tradition of Polish Edom. He understood Jacob the Patriarch's donning of Esau's attire to receive Isaac's blessings as a Sabbatean enclothement, putting on Esau's religion to heal the world.[118] In bringing the Jews to Edom, he was following in Jacob the Patriarch's footsteps, completing his mission. He reshaped the traditional Edom eschatology to deliver a message of imminent redemption in contemporary Poland.

Christianity was but a stage in the redemptive process, but it went beyond the Torah. The cross, Frank decided, exemplified the first letter in the Hebrew alphabet, *Alef* (א). Contemporary Ḥasidic rabbis spoke of God's revelation on Mount Sinai as a voice silently uttering the Alef for *Anokhi* (I am [the Lord your God]), and a kabbalistic tradition had it that Genesis begins with the second letter, *Bet* (ב), because the creation comes after the world of *Aẓilut* (emanation), of which one cannot speak.[119] Whether marking revelation or Aẓilut, Frank opined that the chiefs of Edom (*Alufe Edom*, אלופי אדום, Genesis 36:43), the Polish nobility, took possession of the Alef, and he, Frank, shall repossess it. Ber Birkenthal of Bolechów reports a dramatic speech, in which Frank adjured his followers not to fear going through baptism because salvation will come through both the cross and the Alef.[120] In the Red Letters he sent from Jasna Góra in 1767–68, Frank urged Jews to take on "Edom's holy religion" and save

---

[117] Zevi Hirsh Koidanover, *Kav ha-Yashar* [1709] (Jerusalem: Haktav Institute, 1982), pp. 333–35, quoting Zoref. Zoref was aware of his Edom's novelty and used multiple gimatria to explain it. Zefo (Zepho; צפו), Esau's descendant (founder of the Roman dynasty), had a gimatria equivalent to Poland (פולין). He was the demonic parallel of *Zuf* (nectar) who founded Poland. Redemption and destruction struggled against each other in Poland. Jeremiah 1:14 suggests that "out of the north (*Zafon*, צפון) disaster will break forth" (the 1648 pogroms). *Zafon*'s gimatria is equivalent to Poland-Lithuania. But redemption, too, will start from Poland: "Awake, O north wind" (Song of Solomon 4:16).

[118] "Words of the Lord," sections 93, 123, 183, 373, 404, 516, and 869. Esau's robe, said to have belonged initially to an ancestor, Nimrod, has elaborate mystical meanings in Midrash and Kabbalah. On Frank's fascination with Jacob donning masks: Rachel Elior, "'Sefer Divre ha-Adon' le-Yaakov Frank," in *Meḥqerei Yerushalayim be-Maḥshevet Yisrael* 16/17 (2001): 471–548.

[119] Naftali Zevi Horowitz (Ropshitser), *Zera Qodesh*, 2 vols. (Jerusalem: Y. T. Horowitz, 1970): 2: 40a, relates the Alef teaching of Menaḥem Mendel of Rymanov (1745–1815). See Benjamin Sommer, "Revelation at Sinai in the Hebrew Bible and in Jewish Theology," *Journal of Religion* 79:3 (1999): 439–40. Thanks to Shaul Magid for this reference. On the *Alef* as *Aẓilut* and as a motif in Frank, my thanks to Pawel Maciejko for his unpublished "The Dangers (and Pleasures) of Religious Syncretism."

[120] "Words of the Lord," sections 85, 531, 598, 658, 2158, and 2163; Ber Birkenthal of Bolechów, "Sefer Divre Binah," quoted in A. Y. Brawer, *Studies in Galician Jewry*, p. 224. Brawer provides a brief biography and context for "Sefer Divre Binah" (pp. 197–209).

themselves from the approaching apocalypse.[121] He led his group outside Judaism by joining historical and cosmic, Christian and kabbalistic, redemption, articulating them in the familiar Edom vocabulary, promising fulfillment of familiar Edom prophecies, and using a familiar Sabbatean stratagem.

There was, however, a radically new element in Frank's messianism – the redemptive Maiden, a female messiah.[122] The *Zohar* had Jacob take over Adam's role by overwhelming, with Rebecca's aid, the Serpent Esau's cunning, and making it possible for the Holy Blessed One and His Shekhinah to be joined. Lurianic Kabbalah had supernal Jacob-Zeir coupling with Rachel and Leah, and Sabbatean traditions had Zevi reenact Jacob by coupling with supernal entities.[123] Frank thought that this was all insufficient. From Jacob to Jesus to Zevi, messiahs had failed to see that just as the redemptive union of masculine and feminine divinities required a new Adam-Jacob, it also required a new Eve-Rachel. Zevi (and Berukhiah) made a mistake by remaining wedded to Islam, which lacked a female divinity. The Maiden, the Virgin Mary, exemplified in the Black Madonna, became Frank's messianic figurehead. He, Frank, was the new Adam-Jacob, and his daughter Ewa was the Maiden, the new Eve-Rachel.

The death of Frank's wife in 1770 launched Ewa as the messianic Maiden. Frank joined the Virgin Mary to the Sabbatean Queen Esther (who "apostatized" in order to save the Jews) to configure a female messiah, incarnated in his daughter (and partner?) Rachel-Eve, whose advent he, Jacob, was announcing. The relationship of the messianic father-daughter couple remained ambiguous: Rachel-Eve was a Maiden, but her revelation would announce a sexual union, and with the exception of Mary, the prototypes – Eve, Rachel, and Esther – were not chaste. Frank presented himself as the Maiden's agent, but their revelation would be joint. Jacob & Rachel, human but also divine, would reveal themselves, exemplifying the heavenly reunion of Adam &

---

[121] The letters were included in the Frankists' missives to European Jewry after Frank's death. (A. Y. Brawer, *Galician Jewry*, pp. 270–72 provides the text; Pawel Maciejko, *Mixed Multitudes*, pp. 184–85 and p. 302, nn. 22–23, discusses the extant MSS). The letters were written in red ink, Frank wore red clothes, and he chose red furnishings, all to allude to Edom-Christianity but also to Shabbetai Zevi, who had chosen red as the *sitra aḥra*'s color.

[122] I am indebted here to Ada Rapoport-Albert, *Women and the Messianic Heresy of Sabbatai Zevi: 1666-1816* (Oxford: Littman Library of Jewish Civilization, 2011), pp. 175–236, and Pawel Maciejko's unpublished "Sabbatian Jesus: Nathan of Gaza and Jacob Frank."

[123] Zevi's gender remained ambiguous in Sabbatean traditions. (See Ada Rapoport-Albert, *Women and the Messianic Heresy of Sabbatai Zevi*, pp. 189–90, and references there.) Eibeschütz, for example, had him couple with masculine Atiqa. But Frank wanted a female and not a transsexual messiah.

Eve, the masculine and feminine god. Their advent will overcome the Fall and bring forth eternal life, spiritual as well as physical.

Frank recast the biblical Jacob & Esau narrative in a highly original way so that it could support his theological innovation. He was no scholar, but he masterfully manipulated Midrash and Kabbalah to create a story of missed opportunities that pointed toward the future and paved the way for him. Jacob was the choice patriarch, but he was timid and deceptive, and not up to the messianic task. He provided the road's signposts but committed a series of blunders. His journey abroad to Laban was a religious pilgrimage equivalent to Frank's going to Edom, and he should have completed it instead of returning home after twenty years. Had he stayed for another three, the true Rachel would have revealed herself. Staying with Laban was tantamount to a Sabbatean apostasy. Genesis 31 recounts how, on the family's escape from Laban, Rachel stole and hid her father's idols. Laban chased the family and demanded the return of his gods. Jacob, unaware of Rachel's misdeed, unwittingly pronounced death on whoever possessed the idols. Midrash says that Rachel died in childbirth on the road back home on account of Jacob's curse.[124] For Frank, Rachel-Eve was an emergent divinity in Laban's household and cult. Jacob became scared about the new religious exploration and departed, and Rachel died, delaying redemption.[125]

Jacob had another opportunity to bring forth redemption when he reconciled with Esau. Once again he missed it. On the eve of meeting Esau, as he was struggling with the angel, he was told of the future revelation in Poland and what it entailed (acceptance of Christianity). He was shocked and became disabled. He would no longer be Jacob – another Jacob would come to fulfill his mission – and he received the name Israel instead. He could no longer remain a cosmic mediator and became the vulnerable God of Israel. (Frank reverses the common understanding of the name Israel.) The next day, when the family was meeting Esau, Joseph stood in front of Rachel to protect her, preventing an encounter between Rachel and Esau that could have led to revelation. Jacob promised Esau to follow him to Edom but reneged, leaving the mission to the second Jacob, Frank.[126]

The failure of reconciliation opened a tragic Jewish history. Joseph was punished when his brothers sold him into slavery in Egypt, the people of Israel followed him into exile, and on Mount Sinai, they accepted a hideous legal code, detrimental to life. Several messiahs tried to

---

[124] *Bereshit Rabba* 74:4, 9.
[125] "Words of the Lord," sections 63, 67, 84, 92, 93, 107, and 123.
[126] "Words of the Lord," sections 63, 84, 149, and 185. Joseph protecting Rachel from Esau follows *Bereshit Rabba* 78:10 or *Zohar* III: 202b.

overthrow the Torah's yoke and explore a "way to life." Early in his career, Frank had seen Zevi and Berukhiah as predecessors who lacked understanding of Christianity (Zevi) or, like Jacob, lacked the courage to take it on (Berukhiah). Later, he saw himself as superseding Jesus, advocating the transgression of taboos in order to transform the creation's laws and gain physical immortality. He returned to Edom, put on Esau's robe, and had it not been for his disciples' little faith – they failed him, for example, by not joining him quickly enough in Częstochowa – he would have repossessed the Alef and revealed himself, possibly with Rachel.[127] Now he was nurturing Rachel in the Laban-Edom cult, preparing for their joint revelation in Edom-Poland.

Frank may have been a psychopathic charlatan, but his tragic sensibility of the reconciliation as a missed opportunity remains unmatched, even during the age of emancipation when we would expect it most. Jacob & Esau's convergence in Jewish–Christian syncretism was an eighteenth-century moment. Sabbateanism and Enlightenment loosened religious identity and Jewish communal boundaries just enough to make Jewish interest in Christian universalism and non-Jewish interest in Sabbateanism possible, but not enough to make either of them mainstream. In 1790, Romantic poet William Blake announced in London the coming "dominion of Edom," and his friend Richard Cosway styled himself Esau, revealing Frankist and Asian Brethren influences.[128] The French Revolution would quickly dissipate this Edom discourse. The nation-state would undermine Jewish communal authority, emancipation expand Jewish exploration, churches reform confessional identities, and historicization and natural science put distance between intellectuals and Kabbalah. A vibrant debate on the Jewish participation in national culture would supersede Jewish–Christian hybridity. The terms of Christian–Jewish endearment would change and never be such as to invite wishful thinking about Jacob & Esau's reconciliation. Modernity cavalierly dismissed the opportunities opened in early modern Europe for creative engagement with tradition. This chapter has sought to call attention to them.

---

[127] "Words of the Lord," sections 67, 72, 85, 263, 373, 397, 404, 516, 531, and 877.
[128] "On the Marriage of Heaven and Hell," in *Complete Writings* (Oxford: Oxford University Press, 1966), p. 149; Marsha Keith Schuchard, "From Poland to London: Sabbatean Influences on the Mystical Underworld of Zinzendorf, Swedenborg, and Blake," in *Holy Dissent: Jewish and Christian Mystics in Eastern Europe*, ed. Glenn Dynner (Detroit: Wayne State University Press, 2011), pp. 270–72.

The End of Imperial Edom

Poland did not survive as Edom (or as an independent state) into the nineteenth century, and its early modern Idumaean identity remained tentative. In the 1790s, Ber of Bolechów, recounting the Frankist saga, spoke of the events leading to the First Partition as fulfilling Ezekiel's prophecy on Edom (25:14): "'And I will lay my vengeance upon Edom,' that is, upon the Polish nation (Gentiles being called Edom), 'by the hand of my people Israel': As they dealt with Israel, so were they dealt with."[129] The century-old identification of Poland with Edom was sufficiently recognizable to be used, but not without a clarifying gloss. This was the first time since the biblical period that a nonimperial government was designated Edom, and it reflected the demise of empire as an Edom topos. For Frank, the Holy Roman Empire no longer registered as Edom. Having moved from Poland to Moravia, he told his disciples simply that he needed to see the emperor (Joseph II). Empire was now normalized in Jewish discourse.

Poland had world Jewry's largest population, it was devoutly Catholic, and Polish–Jewish tensions were mounting after 1648. Jewish hostility toward the Holy Roman Empire, meanwhile, was on the decline. Poland-Edom signaled an end to imperial Edom, but also reaffirmed Edom's association with Western Christianity, particularly Roman Catholicism. The modern evil empire par excellence, Russia, which inherited most of Polish Jewry, did not qualify on account of its Greek Orthodoxy. When Poland-Edom vanished, together with Polish independence, no modern state proved formidable and hateful enough to Jews to carry the label – until Nazi Germany. Rather than be associated with a specific geopolitical entity, modern Edom would become a marker for ethno-religious and national hatred of Jews.

On the eve of its dissolution, the Holy Roman Empire was a subject of Jewish approbation the way it had never been in its history. Marc Saperstein discerns Jewish imperial sympathies, even a burgeoning feeling of belongingness, in Ezekiel Landau's 1782 eulogy for Maria Theresa.[130] Under her successor, Joseph II, Landau endorsed Jewish military service.[131] The

---

[129] *The Memoirs of Ber of Bolechow (1723-1805)*, trans. M. Vishnitzer (Humphrey Milford, UK: Oxford University Press, 1922), pp. 149–50.

[130] Ezekiel Landau, "Derush Hesped al Mitat ha-Qesarit Maria Theresa," in Marc Saperstein, *"Your Voice Like a Ram's Horn": Themes and Texts in Traditional Jewish Preaching* (Cincinnati, OH: Hebrew Union College, 1996), pp. 147–61, 445–68.

[131] Landau's sermon to the departing Jewish conscripts (*Ha-Measef* 5 [1789]: 252–55, reprinted in Abraham Stein, *Die Geschichte der Juden in Böhmen* [Brünn: Jüdischer Buch- und Kunstverlag, 1904], pp. 121–22) recognized, as Marc Saperstein suggests, that "conscription was an obstacle to observance but also an opportunity to demonstrate loyalty": *"Your Voice Like a Ram's Horn,"* p. 157. Traditional Jews viewed conscription

Jewish–imperial partnership should not be exaggerated: Maria Theresa was notoriously contemptuous of Jews and reinforced residential restrictions on them. Joseph II's reforms, welcomed in Bohemia, were received as *Gzeyres* (evil decrees) in Galicia. But the waning of imperial Edom and the disbanding of the Holy Roman Empire in 1806 under Napoleonic pressure opened space for a new modern relationship between Jews and empire.

The Jewish elites' excited response to Dohm and his French counterpart, the Abbé Gregoire, presaged the Jewish response to emancipation everywhere for the next hundred and twenty years: enthusiastic makeover of Jewish identity and culture to suit the national culture, so that Jews could enjoy full membership in the nation. Until Napoleon's troops exported French emancipation to Germany, however, Central European Jews did not fully grasp its revolutionary implications. Throughout the 1790s, they assumed that imperial corporatism, rather than the nation-state, would continue to stipulate the terms of Jewish membership in the commonwealth. In the Red Letters that the Frankists circulated from their Offenbach headquarters between 1798 and 1800, they assured European Jewry that "Jacob our father did not die," and adjured the "House of Israel" to join Edom and bring forth redemption.[132] On the Enlightenment's opposite side, Friedlander's 1799 open letter to Teller proposed a rationalist convergence of Judaism and Christianity. Neither the Frankists nor the maskilim imagined that emancipation would render religious convergence both unnecessary and insufficient for Jewish acceptance.

Jacob & Esau's powerful resurgence in Eibeschütz and Frank demonstrated that any major renegotiation of Jewish–Christian relations would recall the typology from its dormancy. Sabbatean syncretism disappeared with emancipation, but the urgency of Jewish–Christian negotiations would only increase and keep the Jacob & Esau typology alive. Viewing the Napoleonic Wars through the lens of traditional Edom eschatology, Ḥatam Sofer gave an inkling of what was to come. He recalled the biblical oracle "Edom shall be dispossessed, Seir shall also be dispossessed by his enemies; and Israel shall do valiantly (Numbers 24:18)." "The sign for

with alarm, and Landau's son petitioned against it, and so not all historians view Landau's sermon, delivered in front of officers, as an endorsement. For conscription's significance and the Jewish debate: Michael K. Silber, "From Tolerated Aliens to Citizen-Soldiers: Jewish Military Service in the Era of Joseph II," in *Constructing Nationalities in East Central Europe*, ed. Pieter Judson and Marsha Rozenblit (New York: Berghahn Books, 2005), pp. 19–36.

[132] A. Y. Brawer, *Galician Jewry*, pp. 270–74. ("Jacob did not die": *Zohar* I:235b, II:48b, II:141b.) Austrian, Russian, and Prussian agents tracking the letters described the "sect of Edom" as a "state within a state" – a phrase that would become central to modern antisemitism – and put it under investigation: Pawel Maciejko, *Mixed Multitudes*, pp. 240–42.

the rising star of Jacob is that Edom shall be disinherited," he said, "but by whom? Not by another nation but by Seir, his enemies who are themselves [part of] Edom, exemplifying [the verse] 'I will stir up [brother against brother ... kingdom against kingdom, Isaiah 19:2].' One part of Edom will take over another. Then Israel, too, will mobilize for war, and afterwards, 'a ruler will come out of Jacob (Numbers 20:19).' But the wise (*maskil*) must keep silent in witness of the Lord ('ידום דום לה) ... and we shall see what will come of it."[133]

---

[133] *Hatam Sofer al ha-Torah*, ed. Yosef Naftali Shtern, 5 vols. (Jerusalem: Ḥatam Sofer Institute, 1987), 4: 125–26.

5   Jacob & Esau and Jewish Emancipation, I: 1789–1839

"We should refuse everything to the Jews as a nation and accord everything to the Jews as individuals.... . They must become citizens individually.... . It is objectionable that there will be an association of noncitizens in the state, a nation within the nation," declared Count Stanislas de Clermont-Tonnere on December 23, 1789, in the French National Assembly.[1] Clermont-Tonnere was expressing his support for extending citizenship to the entire French-Jewish population. He advanced the most radical change in Jewish–Christian relations in millennia. Jewishness would no longer constitute civic disability, and Jews would enjoy equal rights as citizens. However, the traditional Jewish community, the *Kehillah*, could no longer be an autonomous corporation, or fulfill any function the state deemed juridical or political. Clermont-Tonnere opened the age of Jewish emancipation in European history. He encapsulated nationalism's liberating potential, on the one hand, and the nation-state's dilemmas on the other: Jews were acceptable as individuals, but a Jewish community was problematic. The dilemmas would end up undermining the great modern experiment in solving the Jewish Question.

Historians have recently attenuated the divide between premodern and modern management of Jewish–Christian relations by discerning continuity of policy and rhetoric. Kenneth Stow tracked rights granted to early modern Italian-Jewish communities in exchange for adaptation to Christian norms.[2] Lois Dubin found Old Regime "privileges and

---

[1] *Archives parlementaires* 10 (1878): 756, as quoted in David Sorkin, *The Count Stanislas de Clermont-Tonnerre's "To the Jews as a Nation ... "*: *The Career of a Quotation* (Jerusalem: Leo Baeck Institute, 2012), pp. 8–9: "Il faut refuser tout aux juifs comme nation, et accorder tout aux juifs comme individus.... . [I]l faut qu'ils soient individuellement citoyens. Il répugne qu'il y ait dans l'État une Société de non-citoyens, & une Nation dans la Nation."

[2] "Jewish Pre-emancipation: 'ius commune,' the Roman 'comunità,' and Marriage in the Early Modern Papal State," in *Tov Elem: Memory, Community and Gender in Medieval and Early Modern Jewish Societies: Essays in Honor of Robert Bonfil*, ed. Elisheva Baumgarten, Amnon Raz-Krakotzkin, and Roni Weinstein (Jerusalem: The Bialik Institute, 2011), pp. 79–102.

equalities" continuous with modern equality among the Jews of Habsburg Trieste.[3] Analyzing French emancipation debates in the 1790s, Ronald Schechter insisted that the Jews gained civic rights by showing special aptness for citizenship – as Menasse ben Israel had done – and not by promising to relinquish their particularity.[4] Ari Joskowicz likewise finds that in nineteenth-century German parliamentary debates, Jewish delegates avowed Jewish particularity and universalist rhetoric directed against them.[5] Yet, against a two-millennia history, these appear as caveats, and Jewish emancipation looks as revolutionary today as it had appeared to Jacob Katz in the previous generation.[6] Nationalism's universalizing and homogenizing principles drove emancipation. The idea that Jacob & Esau could live as brothers without regard to their Jewish and Christian identities was unprecedented, revolutionary, and, to Katz, hopelessly utopian.

From the French Revolution to the Congress of Berlin (1878), Jewish citizenship remained constantly on the European agenda. In France, the Constitution of 1791 extended citizenship to all Jews. Over the next fifteen years, French troops marched into the Netherlands, Italy, and Germany, reorganized their political structures, and emancipated the Jews. In 1812, Prussia granted the Jews civic rights as part of the reforms in the aftermath of the Prussian defeat by Napoleon. Notwithstanding the joint efforts of Wilhelm von Humboldt and Klemens von Metternich at the Congress of Vienna (1815), the Restoration retracted many emancipation gains in Germany and Italy, and the Jews had to fight to rewin them. For three decades, even German liberals balked at extending political rights to the Jews, but they shifted their position in the 1840s. In the 1848 "Spring of Nations," Jewish emancipation became part of the German and Italian unification programs. The 1848 revolutions met with defeat, but Italian unification between 1859 and 1870, German unification between 1866 and 1871, and the 1867 compromise that created Austria-Hungary enshrined Jewish civic and political rights in the new

---

[3] "Between Toleration and 'Equalities': Jewish Status and Community in Pre-Revolutionary Europe," *Jahrbuch des Simon-Dubnow-Instituts* 1 (2002): 219–34.

[4] Ronald Schechter, *Obstinate Hebrews: Representations of Jews in France, 1715–1815* (Berkeley: University of California Press, 2003), pp. 150–93.

[5] *The Modernity of Others: Jewish Anti-Catholicism in Germany and France* (Stanford, CA: Stanford University Press, 2014).

[6] *Emancipation and Assimilation: Studies in Modern Jewish History* (Westmead, UK: Gregg International, 1972). David Sorkin is presently at work on *Interminable Emancipation: European Jewry and the Quest for Equality, 1550–2000*, which seeks to expand emancipation to early modern improvements in Jewish conditions, and to show that they shaped modern legislation as well. He confronts head-on the polarity of nation-state and empire proposed by this book. I look forward to the engagement.

constitutions. Jewish emancipation appeared to be an essential component of nationalization, and a marker of the European nation-state.

Antisemitism testified to nationalism's liberating power – and its dangers. In his 1793 defense of the French Revolution, German philosopher Johann Gottlieb Fichte popularized a new rubric against the Jews: They cannot become citizens, he said, because they constituted a "state within a state."[7] This became the foremost antisemitic argument, and it was repeated in virtually every nineteenth-century emancipation debate. In its original use against the Huguenots, the Jesuits and the Freemasons, the rubric implied that they breached the king's sovereignty. Now the focus shifted to the nation. The Declaration of the Rights of Man and of the Citizen of August 1789 stated: "The principle of any sovereignty resides essentially in the Nation. No body, no individual can exert authority which does not emanate expressly from it." By remaining a community, the Jews risked offense against the nation's sovereignty. There could be no "nation within a nation," warned Clermont-Tonnere: The Jews could not become citizens as a collective. He thought that the Jews could become individual citizens, whereas Fichte thought that they could not. The alternative was obvious to both – the philosemite and antisemite alike: "If the [Jews] do not want to be individual citizens . . . we should banish them."[8]

The nation-state had little choice but to extend citizenship to the Jews. The alternative was declaring them foreigners, subject to expulsion. Gone was pluralist, multilayered, premodern governance, and also gone were the protections, however unreliable, of Christianity, of traditions delimiting a subservient Jewish community. Romantic Prussian King Friedrich Wilhelm IV, upon assuming the throne in 1840, contemplated relegating the Jews to a corporation. Friedrich Julius Stahl, a conservative thinker and Jewish convert, imagined a Christian nation-state retaining a

---

[7] *Beiträge zur Berechtigung der Urteile des Publikums über die Französische Revolution: Zur Beurteilung ihrer Rechtmäßigkeit* (Danzig: Verlag Ferdinand Troschel, 1793), pp. 54–56. First to apply "state within a state" to the Jews was the Protestant pastor, later defrocked, Johann Heinrich Schulz, in 1784, and next, in a nonhostile fashion, was the Abbé Gregoire, but only Fichte popularized it: Jacob Katz, "A State Within a State: The History of an Anti-Semitic Slogan," in his *Emancipation and Assimilation*, pp. 56–64. The rubric caught on quickly. A 1795 Jewish appeal to the Prussian government for citizenship received the response, three years later, that the Jews constituted not mere religion but a nation and a state within a state: Renate Best, "Juden und Judenbilder in der gesellschaftlichen Konstruktion der deutsche Nation (1781–1804)," in *Nation und Religion in der deutschen Geschichte*, ed. Heinz-Gerhard Haupt and Dieter Langewiesche (Frankfurt: Campus Verlag, 2001), pp. 196–99.
[8] *Archives parlementaires* 10 (1878): 756: "Eh bien! S'ils veulent ne l'être pas, qu'ils le disent, et alors, qu'on les bannisse."

protected Jewish community of noncitizens. The idea never caught on: It was citizenship or exclusion.

In Central Europe, admission to citizenship remained difficult. Liberals expected Jewish self-improvement in return for citizenship: The Jews were expected to modify their religious and socioeconomic profile to appear mainstream. In the 1840s, liberals agreed that citizenship would come first but their expectation for improvement remained, and fighting Jewish stereotypes proved difficult. German liberals envisioned the state as religiously neutral, but did not accept liberal Jews' claim to be Germans of the Mosaic persuasion. They freely admitted that the Christian legacy shaped the national culture. How could the Jews join qua Jews? In an 1831 emancipation debate with Gabriel Riesser, Heinrich Paulus, a liberal Protestant theologian, rehearsed J. D. Michaelis's argument that the Jewish religion was a national marker, concluding that the Jews constituted a state within a state.[9] The Jews were repeatedly faced with the demand that they cease being a community. In response, they formulated pluralist visions of a multiethnic Germany, a nation-state united by a humanist political culture.[10] These visions, much admired today, had no traction among non-Jews. Nationalism liberated the Jews; the threat of banishment, should they fail to become part of the nation, always hung in the balance.

Becoming part of the nation turned out to be elusive. Jews and anti-semites alike jumped at the opportunity that the nation afforded. Saul Ascher, the Kantian *maskil* and early reformer, ridiculed the sacralization of the German nation, but jurist Gabriel Riesser (1806–1863), an emancipation activist, took advantage of it: The blood shed by Jews and Germans on the battlefield during the wars of liberation against Napoleon created one nation, regardless of confession or ethnicity, he claimed.[11] Over the century and a half between the French Revolution and the Holocaust, liberal Jews experimented with collective identities that would make them bona fide members of the nation and leave them as Jews. In Germany, *Bildung* (culture) and *Sittlichkeit* (propriety) became central to Jewish education, reflecting the conviction that the legacy of

---

[9] Gabriel Riesser, *Über die Stellung der Bekenner des mosaischen Glaubens in Deutschland*, 2d ed. (Altona: Hammerich, 1831); H. E. G. Paulus, *Die jüdische Nationalabsonderung nach Ursprung, Folgen und Besserungsmitteln* (Heidelberg: Winter, 1831).

[10] Till van Rahden, "Germans of the Jewish *Stamm*: Visions of Community Between Nationalism and Particularism, 1850–1933," in *German History from the Margins*, ed. Nils Roemer and Neil Gregor (Blomington: Indiana University Press, 2005), pp. 27–48.

[11] Saul Ascher, *Die Germanomanie: Skizze zu einem Zeitgemälde* (Berlin: Achenwall, 1815); Gabriel Riesser, *Vertheidigung der Bürgerlichen Gleichstellung der Juden Gegen die Einwürfe des Herrn Dr. Paulus* (Altona: Hammerich, 1831).

German humanism united the nation.[12] As for Jewishness, German Jews defined it, alternatively, as religious, ethnic, or cultural. The diversity of Jewish responses to emancipation created the plurality of modern Judaism. Yet a majority of Europeans remained skeptical about all of them and the viability of Jewish integration.

Worst was progressive and populist antisemitism. Kantian philosopher Jakob Friedrich Fries, as well as the students reveling at the Wartburg Festival in 1817, gave one of its early public displays.[13] The festival commemorated the Reformation's three hundredth anniversary, and protested the Restoration's repression of democracy and nationalism, among others, by burning "antinationalist" books – French, Jewish, and reactionary. Against the old imperial order – the aristocracy and the Catholic Church – and the Jews, Fries defined nation, religion, and culture as expressions of the German people (*Volk*). German national culture was nondenominationally Christian. The Jews were inherently incapable of sharing its legacy or joining the *Volk*. Modern antisemitism emerged vested in a nation that remained closed to the Jews and left them nowhere to turn.

Nationalism arose with lightning speed, but throughout the age of emancipation, the old imperial order fought back, especially in Central Europe. Both the Restoration and the Dictate of Olmütz in 1850, asserting Austria's primacy in Germany, reaffirmed imperial solidarity against nationalism. The 1834 Customs Union (*Zollverein*) and the 1855 Concordat between Austria and the papacy were viewed as federalist alternatives to German unification. Goethe could make light of the Holy Roman Empire's dissolution in 1806, but the vision of a multi-confessional Christian European federation, headed by the Habsburg emperor, continued to inspire German Catholics and also appealed to conservative Protestants outside Prussia. The imperial legacy remained imprinted in the Second Reich's federalist structure after German unification, and it shaped ideals and institutions in the Austrian half of the "imperial and royal Monarchy (*kaiserliche und königliche Monarchie*)," Austria-Hungary.

---

[12] George Mosse, "Jewish Emancipation," in *The Jewish Response to German Culture*, ed. Jehudah Reinhartz and Walter Schatzberg (Hanover, NH: University Press of New England, 1985), pp. 1–16.

[13] Jakob Fries, "Über die Gefährdung des Wohlstandes und Charakteres der Deutschen durch die Juden," *Heidelberger Jahrbücher*, 16/17 (1816): 241–64, and *Von deutschem Bund und deutscher Staatsverfassung* (Heidelberg: Mohr und Winter, 1816); Joerg Echternkamp, "'Religioeses Nationalgefuehl' oder 'Froemmelei der Deutschtümler'?" in *Nation und Religion*, ed. Heinz-Gerhard Haupt and Dieter Langewiesche (Frankfurt: Campus Verlag, 2001), pp. 142–69. Ascher's book was among those burned.

The Catholics never recovered from the 1803 Imperial Diet (*Reichsdeputationshauptschluss*) that dispossessed the Catholic Church of its political authority, territories, and much of its property throughout French-controlled Germany. In a stark contrast with German Jews, Catholics turned overwhelmingly against nationalism. German national identity emerged as a liberal Protestant project forged in a struggle against Catholic internationalism and evoking the Reformation in defense of "freedom." The Prussian Historical School envisioned German unification as a triumph of liberal Protestantism and the nation-state over Catholic internationalism and the imperial legacy. In the Austrian Empire (1804–67), however, German nationalism ran up against formidable resistance from imperial and ecclesiastic institutions, an overwhelmingly Catholic population, and ethnic pluralism. The Catholic Church retained its authority, wealth, and schools, and a rapprochement took place between empire and papacy. Austro-German nationalism became vehemently anticlerical, but it could not overcome the odds. Austria retained the imperial legacy and remained the Catholics' best hope.

Catholics viewed the Germans as a European imperial people (*Kaiservolk*), and not as a nation in search of popular sovereignty. They spoke of a German empire of seventy million people in Central Europe that included many nations, with Austria representing Germany beyond national borders, in Italy and the Netherlands.[14] The Church was the unifier of the German tribes (*Staemme*). Catholic cosmopolitanism, imperial federalism, and religious pluralism represented peaceful governance against bellicose nationalism. The French and the Jews were instigators of atheism, liberalism, and nationalism, and the benefactors of a revolutionary modernity that shattered the empire.

The Catholic Church rejected Jewish emancipation consistent with its opposition to the nation-state. Liberal Jews, seeking to legitimize their national membership, responded by joining the liberal Protestant anti-Catholic crusade.[15] Traditional Jews, in contrast, were partial to Catholic imperial visions, but the nationalist rift undermined Catholic tolerance of a Jewish minority. In Austria, especially, liberal Jews joined the German nationalist movement, and redirected their traditional hostility to Edom-Rome to anticlericalism. They were rewarded with emancipation by the liberal constitution of 1867, but within fifteen years, they faced nationalism's other side, populist Pan-German antisemitism, and found themselves in need of imperial protection. German nationalism liberated the

---

[14] Heinz-Gerhard Haupt and Dieter Langewiesche, "Nation und Religion zur Einfuehrung," in *Nation und Religion*, pp. 11–29; Nikolaus Buschmann, "Auferstehung der Nation," in *Nation und Religion*, pp. 333–88.
[15] Ari Joskowicz, *The Modernity of Others*.

Jews, which the Austrian Empire would not do, but the Jews would require imperial protection to prevent Janus-faced nationalism from taking away what it had given.

A prospective return of imperial arrangements – Friedrich Wilhelm IV's plan to reestablish the Jewish community as an autonomous corporation in Christian society – triggered the emancipation debate among German intellectuals that gave rise to the term "Jewish Question" (*Judenfrage*).[16] German-speaking Central Europe was the site of the most intensive emancipation debates anywhere and the birthplace of modern Jewish pluralism, from Reform to Orthodoxy. The protracted nature of Jewish emancipation in Germany, as opposed to its immediacy in France and its gradual evolution in England; Germany's fragmented political structure – thirty-nine states, each with its own Jewish policy; and the competition of nation and empire: All of these peculiarities of German history resulted in multifarious efforts to reshape Jewish identity to meet emancipation's prospects and demands. "In no other country," said Jacob Katz, "did [assimilation] assume the character of a social program, hailed by the supporters of emancipation, Gentiles and Jews alike, as in Germany."[17] German Jews, quips Todd Endelman, were thinking the acculturation that other Jews were acting.[18] The eighty-year political struggle for emancipation made the modern Jew's emergence a transparent and conscious process.

No wonder it was in Central Europe that we find the Jacob & Esau typology revitalized, repressed, transformed, rechanneled, and deflected, all in an effort to make it possible for Jacob to become a modern European Jew. The early modern pact of Christian tolerance and pacific missionizing in return for not giving Jewish offense to Christianity, a pact that sent Jacob & Esau into dormancy, was undone on both sides: Jews claimed

---

[16] Young Hegelian philosopher Bruno Bauer and an unknown journalist, Karl Marx, responded by offering visions of universal emancipation, which was to be accomplished by dissolving religion and the state, respectively, and freeing humanity from Judaism. Reform Jewish leader Ludwig Philippson defended Judaism as humanitarian monotheism, and Gabriel Riesser and other Jewish intellectuals responded to the anti-emancipationists. Bruno Bauer, *Die Judenfrage* (Braunschweig: Friedrich Otto, 1843); Karl Marx, "Zur Judenfrage" (1844), in Karl Marx/Friedrich Engels, *Werke*, 41 vols. (Berlin: Dietz Verlag, 1959–68): 1 (1976): 347–77; Gabriel Riesser, "Die Judenfrage: Gegen Bruno Bauer," *Konstitutionelle Jahrbücher* 2 (1843), 3 (1843), 2 (1844): 1–42, 14–57, 172–236, respectively; Ludwig Philippson, "Antibaueriana: Noch ein Artikel," *Allgemeine Zeitung des Judenthums* 32 (5 August 1844): 445–49. For context: Jacob Toury, "The Jewish Question – A Semantic Approach," *Leo Baeck Institute Yearbook* 11 (1966): 92–104.

[17] "Introduction" to his *Emancipation and Assimilation*, p. x.

[18] "The Englishness of Jewish Modernity in England," in *Towards Modernity: The European Jewish Model*, ed. Jacob Katz (New Brunswick, NJ: Rutgers University Press, 1987), pp. 225–26. This paraphrases Marx: "In politics, Germans have thought what other nations have done": "Zur Kritik der Hegelschen Rechtsphilosophie: Einleitung," *Werke*, 1: 385.

citizenship and were pushed to convert to the nation and cease being Jews.[19] Michael Meyer characterizes the age of emancipation as one of exploration and a "feeling of duality," of a passion for German culture and *Bildung* conflicting with a commitment to remain Jewish.[20] Jacob & Esau, now putatively brother-citizens, reflected the struggle to shape the modern European Jew.

Jewish discourse on Jacob & Esau during the age of emancipation was graceful. Edom eschatology was repressed across the Jewish spectrum, and Edom virtually vanished. Heinrich Heine's 1824 poem, addressed "To Edom," bitter about past persecution and ironic about current friendship, turned out to be not so much an opening to the age of emancipation as a closure on the past.[21] Repressing Edom was a political survival strategy. From Fichte to Bruno Bauer, enemies of emancipation made use of J. A. Eisenmenger's *Entdecktes Judenthum* to demonstrate that Jews hated Christians, wished them ill, and could not be trusted. Broaching Edom-Rome would have been suicidal. But it is also true that for all emancipation's polemics, Western and Central European Jews recognized that they were living in a time of graceful Christian rule, when opportunities they could only dream about were opening for them, and they were flourishing and expecting an even brighter future. Curiously, the age's spirit may have been captured best across the Russian border, when Naphtali Ẓevi Yehudah Berlin wrote in 1879 that "whenever the seed of Esau is prompted by sincere motives to acknowledge and respect the seed of Israel, then we, too, are moved to acknowledge Esau: For he is our brother."[22]

If Edom had vanished, Jacob was ever present. To be sure, Reform Jews felt ill at ease with rabbinic Jacob, an embodiment of exilic survival strategy, all too reminiscent a figure of the "national character" that their enemies imputed to Jews. They redefined Judaism as a progressive monotheistic creed, with a universal humanitarian ethics articulated by the Prophets, and with traditional Jacob and Esau stories diminished. Whether the stories dealt with theft or bloody enmity, they represented the traumatic history of Christian–Jewish relations, which liberal Jews

---

[19] Dan Diner speaks of "secondary conversion." See the editorial by Dan Driner and discussion in *Jahrbuch des Simon-Dubnow-Instituts* 3 (2004).

[20] Michael A. Meyer, "Jewish Identity in the Decades After 1848," in Michael Brenner, Stefi Jersch-Wenzel, and Michael A. Meyer, *Emancipation and Acculturation, 1780–1871, German-Jewish History in Modern Times*, ed. Michael A. Meyer, 4 vols. (New York: Columbia University Press, 1997): 2: 319–47. The "duality" was typical of the 1850s and 1860s. By the 1880s and 1890s, scholarly recovery and invention of historical traditions permitted a convergence of German culture and Jewish commitment, and gave rise to a new Jewish identity.

[21] "An Edom," *Werke und Briefe*, 10 vols. (Berlin: Aufbau Verlag, 1972): 8: 166–72.

[22] *Ḥumash Haameq Davar, Sefer Bereshit* [1879] (Jerusalem: Yeshivat Volozhin, 1999) on Genesis 33:4.

wanted to leave behind. Abraham, father of three monotheistic religions, and Moses, monotheistic lawgiver, became Reform heroes. Yet as Vienna's Chief Rabbi Adolf Jellinek noted, Jacob and not Abraham was father of the Jewish people.[23] Jacob emerged from Reform sermons remarkably transformed: a high-minded German Jew, personification of *Bildung* and *Sittlichkeit*, the embodiment of Judaism's cosmopolitan mission.

For Jacob to become a cultivated bourgeois and a cosmopolitan, Reform Jews needed to override the biblical text and rabbinic interpretive traditions. The didactic sermon, the center of Reform liturgy, facilitated their task. A Protestant rite commonly adapted to Jewish liturgy even in Orthodox synagogues, the sermon used moments in the biblical narrative to abstract a homiletic principle, creating its own discursive universe.[24] In contrast with the traditional *derashah*, it could have only limited engagement with the text. Liberal preachers used Jacob's vow to found a house of worship (*Beit Elohim*), his prayer to be saved from his brother, and his new name, Israel, to expound moral principles. They diagnosed Isaac's family as disorderly, and in high rhetoric, enjoined their congregants to put their own houses in order. They remained silent on Jacob's treachery, and he emerged as a model only after he had escaped abroad. Esau remained a negative type, but he came to embody Jewish apostasy and pagan hedonism, rather than Christian malevolence. Reform Jews sustained the typology but reconfigured the protagonists to suit the needs of Jewish integration into German society.

Liberal revisionism paled in comparison with that of the Orthodox. Orthodoxy emerged in response to Reform Judaism.[25] Led in the first generation by Rabbi Moses Sofer (1762–1839), Orthodox Judaism rejected liturgical reform, relaxation of the *halakhah*, the historicization of Judaism, and the struggle for emancipation. Sofer sanctioned

---

[23] Adolf Jellinek, "Esau," in his *Predigten*, 3 vols. in 1 (Vienna: Carl Gerold's Sohn, 1862–66): 2: 203–14.

[24] Alexander Altmann, "Zur Frühgeschichte der Jüdischen Predigt in Deutschland: Leopold Zunz als Prediger," *Leo Baeck Institute Yearbook* 6 (1961): 3–59; Sigmund Maybaum, *Jüdische Homiletik* (Berlin: Ferd. Dümmlers Verlagsbuchhandlung, 1890).

[25] "Orthodoxy" emerged when tradition came into question. The term was originally Christian: Enlightenment proponents used it to describe conservative Lutherans. The orientalist Michaelis applied the term to Mendelssohn's observance of Jewish law. Saul Ascher attacked adherence to *halakhah* as "orthodoxy" in his *Leviathan oder über Religion in Rücksicht des Judentums* (Berlin: Franck, 1792). See Christoph Schulte, "Saul Ascher's *Leviathan*, or: The Invention of Jewish Orthodoxy in 1792," *Leo Baeck Institute Yearbook* 33 (1988): 27–34. In the nineteenth century, "Orthodoxy" came to describe the organized opposition to Reform Judaism. Jacob Katz, "Orthodoxy in Historical Perspective," *Studies in Contemporary Jewry* 2 (1986): 3–17; Michael K. Silber, "Orthodoxy," in *The YIVO Encyclopedia of Jews in Eastern Europe* (New Haven, CT: Yale University Press, 2008), pp. 1292–97; Moshe Samet, *He-Hadash asur min ha-Torah: Chapters in the History of Orthodoxy* (in Hebrew) (Jerusalem: Carmel, 2005). All emphasize Orthodoxy's novel modern character.

traditionally nonbinding customs and invented a history of halakhic consensus to justify his militant stance. He did not oppose emancipation as much as he did Jews fighting for it, which, he thought, put Jews and Judaism at risk and betrayed the hope for a return to Zion. He supported the imperially sanctioned autonomous Kehillah, endorsed royal protection of the Jews without civic rights, and rejected the idea of joining the German nation. Instead, he formed a unified European identity of Ashkenazi Jewry, staged against Esau's otherness. As Reform Jews rather than Christians began appearing as the greater danger, Esau reacquired a Jewish profile as an apostate and a Christian convert (*mumar* מומר). Yet whether he was a wayward brother or a Christian, Esau was a non-Jew. In a revolutionary strike against the Enlightenment, national brotherhood, and Reform Jews, Sofer declared in one of his responsa that once Esau had ceased to observe the law, Jacob and Esau were no longer brothers.[26]

Unlike Sofer, Christians felt no pressing need to reconfigure Jacob & Esau for the modern age, let alone imagine a different future for Jewish–Christian relations. Among Catholics, Christian Jacob still reigned supreme, consistent with their rejection of the nation-state and emancipation, and the fencing off of tradition. Among liberal Protestants, a growing historical consciousness of the distance between the early biblical world and Christianity and the reconceptualization of Jewish otherness as primarily ethnic and national, rather than religious, undermined the typology of a Christian Jacob and began his re-Judaization through a series of stereotypes, such as Jewish cunning and treachery. Neither biblical criticism nor antisemitism had yet advanced enough, however, for Johann Gottfried Herder, Goethe, or the next generation of theologians to declare a break from the Old Testament and Jacob.

Herder's portrayal of Hebrew civilization did much to dissociate biblical Jacob from Christianity, but he still declared himself a Hebrew. Goethe followed suit. In his *Autobiography*, he recounted the biblical tale of the Patriarchs:

For the first time . . . appears a member [Jacob] who has no scruple in attaining by prudence and cunning the advantages which nature and circumstances have denied him. It has often enough been remarked . . . that the Sacred Scriptures by no means intend to set up any of the patriarchs . . . as models of virtue. . . . But there is one leading trait, in which none of these men after God's own heart can be wanting: that is, unshaken faith that God has them and their families in his special keeping.[27]

---

[26] *Teshuvot Ḥatam Sofer* (Ḥatam Sofer responsa), 8 vols., Nussenzweig ed. (Jerusalem: Hatam Sofer Institute, 2000–2008): 4: *Even Ha-Ezer*, part 2, sections 74, 88–9.

[27] Johann Wolfgang von Goethe, *Autobiography: Truth and Fiction Relating to My Life*, trans. John Oxenford (Boston: S. E. Cassino, 1882), pp. 113-114.

Goethe concluded with a declaration of intimacy with the Patriarchs: "When the medley of fable and history, mythology and religion, threatened to bewilder me, I liked to … plunge into the first books of Moses, and to find myself there, in the greatest solitude and the greatest society."[28]

The first four decades of emancipation left the Central European Jewish struggle for equal rights unresolved. To the end of his life, Moses Sofer believed, like most Christians, that emancipation could be contained. Reform Jews had already advanced reforms, but like their Jacob, the reforms had not yet taken hold on German-Jewish life. Containment did not entail conservatism: Herder, Jewish Orthodoxy, and Reformers all advanced radically new visions of Jacob & Esau, and their visions are at the center of this first emancipation chapter. In the early 1840s, the "Jewish Question" became the rubric framing the debate about emancipation, and shortly thereafter, emancipation expanded in several German states. The great syntheses of Reform and Neo-Orthodoxy followed suit, and they will be the subject of the next chapter. First, however, to emancipation's opponents.

Wrestling Forever: Herder on Jacob & Esau's Embrace

In the cacophony of voices debating Jewish emancipation, the voice of Johann Gottfried Herder (1744–1803), one of Germany's foremost intellectuals, was notably missing throughout the 1790s. Prussian only by birth, and immersed in the Weimar milieu, Herder was remote from Berlin high society (and any Jewish community), and could keep his distance for a while. Emancipation and the new antisemitism alike were alien to him, and his cultural conception of humanity could not speak to the nation-state. Yet after the turn of the nineteenth century, when the debate reached a new high pitch in Prussia, Herder could no longer avoid it. He was editor and publisher of a literary journal, *Adrastea*, seeking to nurture the new century in justice, truth, and humanity. He had to enter the debate, and he endeavored to arbitrate and civilize it.

Throughout the 1790s, the Prussian government had rejected Jewish appeals for civic equality. In response to German-Jewish acculturation and French expansion of emancipation into Germany, opponents of Jewish citizenship fashioned a new antisemitic discouse that represented a convergence of old and new antisemitic vocabularies and addressed the nation-state. The works of jurists Christian Ludwig Paalzow and Karl Grattenauer, both high-ranking civil servants, were especially

---

[28] Ibid., p. 141.

popular.[29] Both appeared as enlightened figures, but suggested that the state and its citizenry embodied Christianity's universal ethos, alien to the Jewish religion. The Jew as a social parasite, unproductive and immoral, incapable of citizenship, became the paramount antisemitic stereotype, and Paalzow and Grattenauer threatened that emancipation would render Christians the Jews' slaves. Radical proposals flourished, from ghettoization to deportation to Palestine. The debate became so heated – no less than sixty publications in 1803 alone – that the government ordered the censor, in October 1803, to stop it.[30] Remarkably, opponents and advocates of emancipation alike, including some Jews, agreed about German Jewry's deplorable state and differed only on the prospects for its cultural improvement.

Echoes of this debate, and its antisemitism, can be heard in Herder's 1803 essay "Converting the Jews" (*Bekehrung der Juden*), but the shrill tone is absent. Ambivalent though Herder was about the Jews, he was too gentle, and too much of a cosmopolitan and a pluralist, to indulge in crude antisemitism.[31] His view of the nation was vested in eighteenth-century concepts of culture, and he was no devotee of modern national-ism (to the development of which he had made a major contribution). He endeavored to put a historical perspective on the emancipation debate by showing the recent transition from pursuit of the Jews' conversion to queries concerning their suitability for citizenship, but he was himself unable to negotiate this transition. He had no concept of citizenship or the nation-state, and he held no hope for Jewish emancipation. His imagined Europe – a mosaic of indigenous national communities – had no place for a Diaspora or for a "foreign Asiatic people." He could not arbitrate the Jewish Question, but he drew an inimitable picture of Jacob & Esau's struggle and made the typology into a symbol of his Judeo–Christian history. Moreover, the Jewish Question pushed him to break through

---

[29] Christian Ludwig Paalzow, *Tractatus historico-politicus de civitate judaeorum* (Berolini: C. G. Schoene, 1803); Anon. [Karl Wilhelm Friedrich Grattenauer], *Wider die Juden: Ein Wort der Warnung an alle unsere christliche Mitbürger*, 4th ed. (Berlin: Schmidt, 1803).

[30] Renate Best, "Juden und Judenbilder," p. 210. Grattenauer was dismissed in February 1804 (p. 205). A review in a distinguished German literary journal, *Allgemeine Literatur-Zeitung* 2: 108 (9 April 1804): 57–64, two months later showed that the profile of the Jew as naturally (rather than theologically) incapable of citizenship was becoming hegemonic.

[31] "Bekehrung der Juden" [1803], in *Sämmtliche Werke*, ed. Bernhard Suphan, 33 vols. (Berlin: Weidmann, 1877–1913): 24: 61–74; *Adrastea*, ed. Günter Arnold, Vol. 10 of *Johann Gottfried Herder: Werke*, 10 vols. (Frankfurt: Deutscher Klassiker Verlag, 2000): 10: 629–42. "Adrastea" was launched in 1799 as "Aurora," pronouncing the dawn of a new century, but quickly reconceptualized under the new name, recalling the protective Greek nymph. Liliane Weissberg, "Juden oder Hebräer? Religiöse und politische Bekehrung bei Herder," in *Johann Gottfried Herder: Geschichte und Kultur*, ed. Martin Bollacher (Würzburg: Königshausen & Neumann, 1994), pp. 191–212.

the limits of his "illiberal multiculturalism" and imagine, if only for a moment, German Jews. Toward the end of his life, Herder had already lived past his time, but he still had missives for the Jewish European future.

Herder was born in 1744 in a small town in Eastern Prussia, Mohrungen, to a poor Pietist family of a church cantor and custodian. He remembered the town's provincial Lutheran culture as stifling. In 1760, a newly appointed enlightened pastor with a library provided him with housing, and a refuge. Two years later, owing to the generosity of a stranger, Herder went to study in Königsberg, where he encountered both Johann Georg Hamann and Kant and formed lifelong intellectual relationships with them. In 1764 he was appointed to the Cathedral School of Riga, a former Hanseatic city enjoying autonomy under Russian rule, and he was ordained a preacher there three years later. A year-long journey to France in 1769–70 proved life changing and shaped his critical engagement with the Enlightenment. He tutored the Prince of Holstein's son for a year, traveling through Germany, and in 1771 became the chief pastor of the small principality of Schaumburg-Lippe, in the capital, Bückeburg. His growing literary fame and friendship with leading intellectuals, Christoph Martin Wieland and Goethe, led to his appointment as chief pastor, court preacher, and educational superintendent in Weimar. He remained there until his death in 1803, becoming, with Goethe, Schiller, and Wieland, a central figure in the efflorescent courtly culture known as Weimar classicism and humanism.[32]

Herder has been enjoying an outstanding reputation among scholars over the past half century. Earlier he had been considered a fountainhead of German nationalism. Karl Popper denounced him for his Romantic organic concept of the nation, and in the aftermath of World War II, few disagreed.[33] But Herder's foremost English interpreter, F. M. Barnard, and philosopher Isaiah Berlin led a postwar reconfiguration of Herder as a philosemitic pluralist and made him within three decades a founding father of multiculturalism.[34] Berlin regarded Herder as the liberal

---

[32] The standard biography remains Rudolf Haym, *Herder nach seinem Leben und seinen Werken dargestellt*, 2 vols. (Berlin: R. Gaertner, 1880–85).

[33] Karl Popper, *The Open Society and Its Enemies*, 2 vols. (London: Routledge & Sons, 1945): 2: 52–53. Hans Kohn made a valiant effort to rescue Herder in *The Idea of Nationalism* (New York: Macmillan, 1944), chap. 7, but his book became famous precisely for the dichotomy between Western civic nationalism and Central European ethnic nationalism, which doomed Herder.

[34] Isaiah Berlin, "Herder and the Enlightenment" [1965], in his *Three Critics of the Enlightenment: Vico, Hamann, Herder*, ed. Henry Hardy (Princeton, NJ: Princeton University Press, 2000), pp. 168–242; F. M. Barnard, *Herder's Social and Political Thought: From Enlightenment to Nationalism* (Oxford: Clarendon, 1965), and

pluralist par excellence. Herder's insistence on the primacy of communal belonging, his critique of Enlightenment cosmopolitanism in the name of individuality (*Individualität*), and his empathy for diverse national cultures expressed Berlin's sentiments. He found in Herder's *Humanität* the balance that he sought between nationalism and cosmopolitanism, plurality and universal humanity.[35] Berlin's view of Herder as a Counter-Enlightenment thinker has recently come under criticism, but the critics have only completed Herder's reintegration into the Enlightenment by expanding the concept and dissociating him from ethno-nationalism.[36] Herder's reputation today is as high as it has ever been.

This is surprising in light of Herder's ambiguous position on the Jewish Question. His pronouncements on the Jews were ridden with ambivalence. His admiration for the ancient Jews as God's people and his recognition of the continuity between ancient and contemporary Jews were mixed with negative portrayals of postbiblical Jews, using such notorious antisemitic metaphors as the parasite.[37] He rejected efforts to convert the Jews and called for their humane treatment, but he said not a word in support of emancipation, and the meaning of his "good wishes to them in Palestine" remains

---

"Introduction," in his *J. G. Herder on Social and Political Culture* (Cambridge: Cambridge University Press, 1969), pp. 3–60.

[35] Malachi Hacohen, "Berlin and Popper Between Nation and Empire: Diaspora, Cosmopolitanism, and Jewish Life," *Jewish Historical Studies* 44 (2012): 51–74.

[36] Counter-Enlightenment was Isaiah Berlin's term for Enlightenment-age thinkers Giambattista Vico, Hamann, and Herder, who had questioned universalism and emphasized the unique richness of each culture: Isaiah Berlin, "The Counter-Enlightenment" [1973], in his *Against the Current: Essays in the History of Ideas*, ed. Henry Hardy (New York: Viking, 1980), pp. 1–24. H. B. Nisbet suggested Herder's indebtedness to the Enlightenment in " Zur Revision des Herder-Bildes im Lichte der neuen Forschung," in *Bückeburger Gespräche über Johann Gottfried Herder 1971*, ed. J. G. Maltusch (Bückeburg: Grimme Bückeburg, 1973), pp. 101–17. John H. Zammito, Karl Menges, and Ernest A. Menze show how recent diversification of the Enlightenment allows for Herder's reintegration: "Johann Gottfried Herder Revisited: The Revolution in Scholarship in the Last Quarter Century," *Journal of the History of Ideas* 71:4 (2010): 661–84. Steven Lestition argued eloquently for the viability of Berlin's Counter-Enlightenment in an exchange with Robert Norton: *Journal of the History of Ideas* 68:4 (2007): 635–81, and 69:2 (2008): 339–47.

[37] Johann Gottfried Herder, *Ideen zur Philosophie der Geschichte der Menschheit* (book 12: chap. 3: "The Hebrews"), *Sämmtliche Werke*, 14: 67; *Werke*, 6: 492: "eine parasitische Pflanze auf den Stammen andrer Nationen"; (book 16: chap. 5: "Foreign People in Europe"), *Sämmtliche Werke*, 14: 283; *Werke*, 6: 702: "Die Juden betrachten wir hier nur als die parasitische Pflanze, die sich beinah allen Europäischen Nationen angehängt." Herder may have been the first (1787) to use the biological image in reference to the Jews. Traditionally it meant people, usually poor, eating at the tables of rich people, obtaining hospitality, patronage, and favor through obsequiousness and flattery, and difficult to get rid of. The traditional use may have been more in line with Herder's view of Jewish fate. Alex Bein, "The Jewish Parasite," *Leo Baeck Institute Yearbook* (1964): 3–40, esp. 10.

ambiguous.[38] Yet Barnard and Berlin viewed Herder's emphasis on the Jews' non-Europeanness as resistance to forced assimilation. Herder became a crypto-Zionist.[39] He putatively offered the Jews both emancipation and a state in Palestine. Kant's cosmopolitanism left no room for the Jews. Herder's multicultural world accommodated them. The Counter-Enlightenment did not contravene universality but expanded it.

Barnard and Berlin were not alone. Herder's biographer, Rudolf Haym, had already shown the path by assimilating Herder into a Dohm-like emancipation through a *Bildung* program.[40] German-Jewish intellectual historian Ludwig Geiger followed suit at the turn of the twentieth century, and in the interwar years, Hannah Arendt recommended Herder as a friend of the Jews, cognizant of Jewish nationality.[41] In the postwar years, Emil Adler, a careful and judicious student of Herder's archives, explained Herder's description of Jews as parasitical as an effort to get his heterodox *Ideen* past the watchdogs of Protestant orthodoxy.[42] More recently, leading political theorist Charles Taylor and literary historian Karl Menges declared Herder, respectively, a prophet of multiculturalism and a poststructuralist critic of the Enlightenment.[43] Menges argued that Herder's use of Jewish stereotypes did not so much criticize the Jews as analyze the cross-cultural interaction between Jews and Christians, recognizing Jewish "difference." Herder exposed the futility of Enlightenment universalism and liberal emancipation.

Dissenting voices have been few recently. Paul Rose correctly discerned Herder's opposition to emancipation but absorbed him into a

---

[38] "Bekehrung der Juden," *Sämmtliche Werke*, 24: 67; *Werke*, 10: 633: "Glück also, wenn ein Messias-Bonaparte sieghaft sie dahin führt, Glück zu nach Palästina!"

[39] F. M. Barnard, "The Hebrews and Herder's Political Creed," *Modern Language Review* 54 (1959): 533–46, and "Herder and Israel," *Jewish Social Studies* 28 (1966): 25–33.

[40] Rudolf Haym, *Herder*, 2: 793–94. Martin Bollacher agrees. Like Dohm, Herder viewed the Jews' negative traits as a result of Christian persecution. Acculturation would transform Jewish character, and the Jews would be integrated in German culture while retaining their religion: "'Feines, scharfsinniges Volk, ein Wunder der Zeiten!' – Herders Verhältnis zum Judentum und zur jüdischen Welt," in *Hebräische Poesie und Jüdischer Volkgeist*, ed. Christoph Schulte (Hildesheim: Georg Olms, 2003), pp. 17–33.

[41] Ludwig Geiger, "Herder und das Judentum," in his *Deutsche Literatur und die Juden* (Berlin: Georg Reimer, 1910), pp. 63–80; Liliane Weissberg, "Ortswechsel: Hannah Arendts Suche nach dem "asiatischen Volk," in *Hebräische Poesie*, ed. Christoph Schulte (Hildesheim: Georg Olms, 2003), pp. 245–56.

[42] "Herder und das Judentum," in *Herder Today: Contributions from the International Herder Conference*, ed. Kurt Mueller-Vollmer (Berlin: Walter de Gruyter, 1990), pp. 382–401.

[43] Charles Taylor, "The Importance of Herder," in his *Philosophical Arguments* (Cambridge, MA: Harvard University Press, 1995), pp. 79–99; Karl Menges, "Integration oder Assimilation? Herders Äußerungen über die Juden im Kontext der klassischen Emanzipationsdebatte," *Euphorion* 90 (1996): 394–415. "Poststructuralism" is my term for Menges's Herder, not his, but it fits the bill.

German tradition of revolutionary antisemitism.[44] Truly, Herder's refusal to become a modern nationalist made him reject emancipation. Liliane Weissberg brilliantly exposed the tensions between Herder's idealized ancient Hebrews and depraved modern Jews, and, in his "Converting the Jews," between Jewish authenticity and German acculturation.[45] Yet precisely when Herder, in a fleeting recognition of hybridity and Jewish Europeanness, imagines German Jews, Weissberg charges him with German nationalism. Rather, in a momentary transgression against his own indigenous view of nationality, Herder made good on *Humanität* by imagining German Jews. He could not join the nation-state project.

Postwar scholars have found Herder's conflicting statements on the Jews so challenging because they did not appreciate that he remained first and foremost an enlightened Protestant theologian. Earlier generations of German scholars had thought of Herder as "the theologian among classic writers" who responded to the challenges of Deism and biblical criticism.[46] Klaus Scholder showed how Herder's turn to history, his concepts of individuality and nation, and his understanding of the historical formation of national culture laid the foundations of modern biblical scholarship.[47] Yet Herder sought to contain the theological damage that historicization threatened. He would not engage in source criticism or in heavy-duty contextual study that might break down biblical unity. Rather, having affirmed that the Bible speaks human language and ought to be considered

---

[44] *Revolutionary Antisemitism in Germany: From Kant to Wagner* (Princeton, NJ: Princeton University Press, 1990), pp. 97–109.

[45] "Juden oder Hebräer?" pp. 191–212.

[46] Karl Barth called Herder "Der Theologe unter den Klassikern": Daniel Weidner, "Secularization, Scripture and the Theory of Reading: J. G. Herder and the Old Testament," *New German Critique* 94 (2005): 169. Herbert Schöffler, "Johann Gottfried Herder aus Mohrungen," in his *Deutscher Geist im 18. Jahrhundert*, ed. Götz von Selle (Göttingen: Vandenhoeck und Ruprecht, 1956), pp. 61–85, noted that many Enlightenment intellectuals in Herder's generation began as theologians or their children. In Mohrungen, young Herder encountered different exemplars of German religious life, but the Lutheran tradition was strongest, and his life represented a continuous struggle with it.

[47] "Herder und die Anfänge der historischen Theologie," *Evangelische Theologie* 22 (1962): 425–40. In a 1769 draft to *Älteste Urkunde des Menschengeschlechts* (Oldest document of humankind, published 1774), Herder already observed, in Genesis 1–2, two creation stories, using different names for God. He spoke of the Bible as a Hebrew national document, about its canonization, and the Christian heritage: "Über die ersten Urkunden des menschlichen Geschlechts: Einige Anmerkungen," in *Schriften zum Alten Testament*, ed. Rudolf Smend, *Werke*, 5: 9–178. On Herder as a biblical scholar, see Hans Joachim Kraus, "Herders Alttestamentliche Forschungen," in *Bückeburger Gespräche über Johann Gottfried Herder*, ed. Johann Gottfried Maltusch (Bückeburg: Verlag Grimme Bückeburger, 1973), pp. 59–75; Thomas Willi, "Die Metamorphose der Bibelwissenschaft in Herders Umgang mit dem Alten Testament," in *Johann Gottfried Herder*, ed. Martin Bollacher (Würzburg: Königshausen & Neumann, 1994), pp. 239–56.

as literature, he rushed to close the historical context for its composition, regarding it as an expression of the spirit of the Jewish people.[48] The Jewish people thus served as the great unifier – it was one throughout history, a guarantor of the integrity of the canon and God's message. This was also a defensive move against Deistic natural religion. To circumvent the issue of miracles, Herder turned the focus from nature to history, suggesting that the Jewish people's miraculous survival over three millennia was sufficient testimony to Scripture's truth and God's guidance of history.[49]

To the ancient Hebrews, Herder, in *Vom Geist der ebräischen Poesie* (On the spirit of Hebrew poetry, 1781–83), showed unbound admiration. He imagined the Hebrews in all their glory and, seeking to legitimate biblical poetry in a literary world that cared little for it, explained their otherness as appropriate to their time and place. He rejected typology, which Christianized the Hebrews, yet the Hebrews remained strangely familiar because they were God's people, and Christians had inherited their heritage. The Bible was a Hebrew national document, a work of art, history, and culture, but it was also divine, as God's voice was heard in Hebrew. Moses' constitution formed the Jews as a nation, a free people subject to the rule of law, a bridge between nation and humanity. Defending the Hebrews and the Bible against Deists and biblical scholars, Herder defended Christianity as well and affirmed European civilization's Judeo-Christian origins.

Herder staged an all-out defense of the Patriarchs, especially Jacob, against Enlightenment criticism. Isaac bestowed on Jacob his predestined blessing, as Jacob was chosen to carry out the divine mission. Jacob's cunning had its uses, and the mature Jacob showed that like Odysseus, he had learned his lesson. The name Israel, which Jacob received after his struggle with God, testified to his faith, prayer, and divine power.

---

[48] *Briefe, das Studium der Theologie betreffend* [1780–81], in *Theologische Schrifte*n, ed. Christof Bultmann and Thomas Zippert, vol. 9 part 1 of *Johann Gottfried Herder: Werke*, 10 vols. (Frankfurt: Deutscher Klassiker Verlag, 2000), esp. first letter, pp. 145–49: "Menschlich muß man die Bibel lesen: denn sie ist ein Buch durch Menschen für Menschen geschrieben: menschlich ist die Sprache, menschlich die äußern Hülfsmittel, mit denen sie geschrieben und aufbehalten ist; menschlich endlich ist ja der Sinn, mit dem sie gefaßt werden kann" (p. 145). Hans Frei, *The Eclipse of Biblical Narrative: A Study in Eighteenth and Nineteenth Century Hermeneutics* (New Haven, CT: Yale University Press, 1974), pp. 186–89, showed how Herder arbitrated the relationship between the Bible's literal and historical meanings and rescued its unity by deferring the question of literal truth to the spirit of the Jewish people.

[49] *Briefe, Werke*, 9:1, twelfth letter, 252–266. In a posthumously published appendix to *Vom Geist der ebräischen Poesie*, *Sämmtliche Werke*, 12: 311–13, "on the miracles during the Mosaic giving of the law and journey [in the desert]," Herder suggested that biblical testimony to certain miracles, which could not be explained naturally, such as the manna God provided for the Israelites, was incontrovertible, but in other cases, he urged consideration of alternative accounts.

Ishmael's and Esau's exclusion did not reflect national hatred: Both remained blessed and ended up rich princes. The violent Israelite conquest of Canaan and the prophecies about Jewish return to Israel reflected the people's attachment to the Land: Their culture – legends, laws, and poetry – all depend on it, and in exile, they are like a tree suspended in midair. The Hebrews' poetry, ideals, and faith compensated for their lack of political and military talent. They were a superior people, God's appropriate choice for his universal plan.[50]

Herder defended a supersessionist Judeo-Christian history, which left Jacob carrying the divine mission, but he provided a historical and cultural portrait of Hebrew civilization that made its otherness to Christianity obvious. Jacob emerged as a non-Christian Hebrew.[51] Herder also gathered the anti-Jewish stereotypes associated with Jacob and the Hebrews, defending them as expressions of the national spirit, continuous with contemporary Jews. His defense of the Bible's integrity and the Jews' divine mission would soon collapse, but the organic view of a nation full of vice would remain. Hebrew otherness attenuated religious supersessionism, but Jewish national character provided continuity. The Prophets had already protested against Jewish vices, and postbiblical Jews manifested spiritual decline. Herder reinvented the Jewish nation to save his Christian faith and ended up undermining the Jews' position in Christian civilization. Against his every intention, the Counter-Enlightenment humanist thus made a major contribution to modern antisemitism.

To Herder, postbiblical Jews had played out their role in history. His autochthonous view of national culture reinforced the theological conviction that Christianity superseded Judaism: The exile ended the Hebrews' poetic period, as their poetry was bound to the homeland.[52] Herder's accounts of postbiblical Jews alternated between anger and admiration for their devotion to obsolete traditions, contempt and respect for their culture, sympathy for their suffering, and hostility toward their putative socioeconomic practices. His historical explanation of Christian–Jewish relations deployed the stereotype of the Jews as a commercial people, taking advantage of barbaric medieval Europe and Christian vices to develop a parasitical existence. He was deeply puzzled by the Jewish Diaspora, by a people that was, and yet was not, a nation, foreigners everywhere, having no territory, no state, and no definite

---

[50] Discussion 9, "Accusations made against the Israelites: ... On the shortcomings of the Patriarchs, especially Jacob," *Vom Geist der ebräischen Poesie, Werke*, 5: 875–94.

[51] This agrees with Hans Frei, *The Eclipse of Biblical Narrative*, pp. 1–7, 183–201.

[52] Thomas Willi, *Herders Beitrag zum Verstehen des Alten Testament* (Tübingen: J. C. B. Moher, 1971), p. 84. Herder spoke of Mosaic borrowing from Egypt as "nationalization," but of postbiblical ones as "Judaization" (pp. 75–76).

historical time. National abnormality reinforced the theological Ahasuerus, the eternally wandering Jew, banished from society because of his sin.

Facing the modern Jewish Question in "Converting the Jews," Herder virtually threw his hands into the air. The essay's style reflected his struggle with the Jewish Question. Martin Bollacher noticed a multiplicity of voices, attitudes, and approaches, some discordant.[53] The essay's first part, "Conversion," positions historically the recent emancipation debate; the second, "Montesquieu," explains the Jews as a commercial people and the tragic history of Christian–Jewish relations; the third envisions a future Jewish acculturation and Christian–Jewish coexistence. Yet it is the picture of Jacob & Esau's eternal wrestling that dominates the essay and presciently conveys Herder's vision of Christian–Jewish relations.

Herder opens by parodying the efforts of the Callenberg institute in Halle to convert the Jews. He urges suspension of theological debates. The Jews are a dignified foreign nation, and Christians and Jews should await the end of days to resolve their theological dispute. This profound futuristic tolerance is vitiated, however, by a flat rejection of emancipation. The Jews are foreigners in Europe, fulfilling a dubious commercial role: "Rather than discuss human rights abstractly, the question is simply: How many of these foreigners may practice their trade in a European state without detriment to the natives?"[54] Each state must answer this question for itself. Herder solicits the help of two seventeenth-century Jewish apologists, Menasseh Ben-Israel and Shlomo Luzzato, to prove that the Jews' economic usefulness to the state is the criterion deciding their admission. In any case, the Jews may return one day to Palestine, their native land. If Napoleon takes them there – good luck!

Herder then plays Montesquieu, endeavoring to explain historically the Jews' corrupted mores by their commercial character. Montesquieu spoke of the civilizing effects of commerce and had no objections to Jewish economic practices: We hear Herder's voice.[55] In ways evocative of Bernard of Clairvaux, Herder suggests that Christian vices were the root of Jewish depravity, as Jews took economic advantage of Christians in order to survive. Abuse led to Christian persecution, and persecution in

---

[53] "Herders Verhältnis zum Judentum," pp. 29–30.

[54] "[W]ozu jene entfernteren Diskussionen z. B. über Rechte der Menschheit, wenn bloß die Frage ist: 'wie viele von diesem fremden Volk dürfen in diesem Europäischen Staat dies ihr Geschäft ohne Nachteil der Eingebornen treiben'"? ... Nicht allgemeine Menschenfreundliche Grundsätze, sondern die Verfassung der Nation, in welcher Juden ihr Gewerbe treiben, gibt hierüber Auskunft": *Werke*, 10: 630, 631, respectively.

[55] Arnold Ages, "Montesquieu and the Jews," *Romanische Forschungen* 81:1/2 (1969): 214–19.

turn exacerbated abuse. Christians must reform themselves, then reeducate the Jews. Opening new business opportunities to Jews – emancipation – is wrong. On the contrary: Penalties on economic abuse should become stiffer, and, simultaneously, opportunities should be open for Jewish cultural improvement. Jews should go through national reeducation for the sake of humanity, and their contributions to the arts and sciences should be recognized, so that they learn self-respect. Philosophers from Spinoza to Mendelssohn testify to the viability of such reform. In the future, Christians and Jews will live together, mutually respectful of each other.

There is a silver lining in this depressing Herderian story. When Herder imagines postreform Jews, he parts momentarily with his essentialist view of nationality, and envisions Jews sharing in the national culture. He articulates the liberal cosmopolitan assumptions that could have made him an emancipator:

A shared culture of the soul unites people of all times, places and nations. . . . The Jews' way of life no longer constitutes an obstacle, as boundaries between the three continents have been loosened over the millennia. . . . Their spiritual temple will emerge from the ruins not [in] Palestine . . . but everywhere they live.[56]

This remains, however, Herder's end-of-days vision. It exists in tension with his essentialist view of Jewish national character and with his immediate policy recommendations, which include restricting Jewish economic opportunity. Opposition to humiliating laws, such as the cattle tax, is as far as Herder carried *Humanität* politically. He had no operational concepts of state or civil society: "Culture" had to bridge *Humanität* and nation, and community and nation. He would neither entrust the state with reform nor, like Humboldt, recognize that emancipation would remove Jewish disabilities, and Jews become German.[57] By nationalizing the Hebrews and Jews, Herder problematized early modern coexistence without providing modern solutions. His suggestion of the acculturated Jews eventually finding their Palestine in Europe may

---

[56] "Gemeinschaftliche Kultur der Seele vereinigt die Menschen aller Zeiten, Gegenden und Völker. . . . Übrigens zu welcher Lebensart die Jüden geneigt sein, ist kein Problem mehr; die drei alten Weltteile haben es Jahrtausende hindurch längst aufgelöset. . . . Nicht auf den nackten Bergen Palästina's, des engen, verheerten Landes, allenthalben stünde da geistig ihr Tempel aus seinen Trümmern empor": *Werke*, 10: 640–41.

[57] Wilhelm von Humboldt, "Über den Entwurf zu einer neuen Konstitution für die Juden [1809]," *Werke*, 5 vols. (Darmstadt: Wissenschaftliche Buchgesellschaft, 1964), 4: 95–112; trans. as "Wilhelm von Humboldt on the Principles of Jewish Emancipation Legislation and His Relations to the Jews," in Max J. Kohler, *Jewish Rights at the Congresses of Vienna (1814–1815) and Aix-la-Chapelle (1818)* (New York: The American Jewish Committee, 1918), pp.71–83.

intimate that he had no intention of deporting them and was resigned to seeing Jews and Christians continue to coexist in tension, as they had for centuries.[58]

Concluding his emancipation discussion, Herder recovers the scene of Jacob & Esau's reconciliation, which Jews and Christians had laid away for centuries. "According to the ingenious commentary of one of their rabbis," says Herder, "Esau and Israel embrace each other crying. The kiss is painful to both, but they cannot draw themselves apart."[59] This is Herder's *midrash*, and not the rabbis'.[60] The midrash is remarkable. Christians had ignored the reconciliation because typology knew not what to make of it. Herder, having undermined Christian typology, sees Jewish Jacob and Christian Esau historically intertwined, struggling painfully trying to reconcile. Both elicit sympathy, a testimony to Herder's humanity. But his vision is dark. Jews and Christians are tragically entangled, reconciliation is painful, and there is no resolution in sight. There is no possibility for change, no crossing over, no synthesis. God loves both Jacob and Esau, but they are forever Others. Humboldt envisioned a nation of Jewish and Christian citizens, and opened up space, however conscripted, for plurality within unity, for a diversity of life in between – for German Jews. The vision is foreign to Herder. Jews are Jewish, and Germans German.

Herder's impasse is symptomatic of the promise and limits of the Counter-Enlightenment imagination, of cultural diversity not underwritten by universal politics and cross-cultural dialogue. Resistant to the universalist imagination that expressed itself in the nation-state, Herder skirted equally Fichte's and Fries's nationalist antisemitism and Humboldt's emancipation. His *Humanität* struggled against his own anti-Jewish prejudices, shared by emancipators and antisemites alike, and contained them – for a time. A philosopher of "difference," he would not cross over to the nation-state. For good and bad, illiberal multiculturalism held him from entering modernity. Those who know how emancipation ended may not judge him too harshly.

---

[58] "Ihr Palästina ist sodann da wo sie leben und edel wirken, allenthalben": *Werke*, 10: 641.

[59] "Nach der genialischen Gloße eines seiner Rabbinen liegen Esau und Israel einander weinend am Halse; beide schmerzt der Kuß, aber sie können nicht auseinander": Ibid., 634.

[60] The rabbis were divided on whether Esau's reconciliation was genuine (see Chapter 2, and discussion of *Bereshit Rabba* 78:9 there). Two millennia of Christian–Jewish enmity assured that the brothers' reconciliation would be viewed, for the most part, as a continuous battle by other means. Contrary to Herder, the rabbis all assumed that Jacob and Esau separated – forever.

"There is No Brotherhood Anymore": Moses Sofer and the Orthodox Counterrevolution

Moses Sofer shared Herder's illiberal multicultural vision of Jewish–Christian coexistence. He never doubted that the Jews, albeit a Diaspora, were a nation in Herder's sense, or that they were foreigners in Europe. Herder's "dream" of Jewish cultural conversion was, to Sofer, the major threat facing Jewry. He was hostile to emancipation and the nation-state and felt comfortable with imperial management of Jewish–Christian relations. He lived his entire life under the Habsburg dynasty, considered it benevolent, and in the struggle with the Jewish Reformers, elaborated a divine-right theory of imperial rule. A native of Frankfurt, Sofer ended up leading the Pressburg (Bratislava) Jewish community, one of Austria's (and Hungary's) largest, and shaped the course of traditional Hungarian and European Jewry.

Sofer supported Restoration visions of the Christian state, and like other conservatives, he responded to emergent nationalism by forming a European, or, more precisely, counter-European, Jewish identity: Ashkenazi Jewry, unified by a halakhic cultural tradition. Facing a rising tide of Jewish Reform in Germany, Sofer found his early "Herderian" reliance on local custom inadequate, and appealed to an invented tradition, leading from ancient authorities to early modern halakhists and shared by northern European Jewry. Orthodoxy proved a resilient opponent to nationalization, and Sofer's rabbinic network, reflected in his *responsa*, extended throughout Europe. Yet Orthodoxy, too, was not immune to nationalization: Sofer's generation was the last one in which traditional rabbis could comfortably fill positions interchangeably across the German and Russian borders.[61] Sofer's imperial alliance did not defend Jewish tradition the way he had hoped, and like the Restoration order, the strategy collapsed in the decade after his death, when emancipation and Reform Judaism made major strides. Still, molding a counter-European Jewish identity and fortifying, especially in Hungary, anti-modern Orthodox Jewry, Sofer staged a formidable resistance to nationalization and shaped an enduring Jewish alternative to modernity.

A comparison of two succeeding Jewish halakhic authorities, Ezekiel Landau (1720–1793) and Moses Sofer (1762–1839) – both said to have been sent from heaven to set the Law – provides a measure of the transition from traditional to Orthodox Judaism. Landau co-opted modernity. He sought to produce a "scholarly" version of the Talmud so as to determine Jewish law with precision. To facilitate commercial engagement, he permitted

---

[61] Yaakov Ariel of UNC–Chapel Hill pointed out to me that later in the nineteenth century, financially strapped German-Jewish communities, unable to afford a German rabbi with a doctorate, hired traditional Eastern European Jewish rabbis in the hundreds, but the latter felt themselves outsiders, and tensions mounted.

beards to be shaved on the intermediate festival days. The Prague court regulated coffeehouses open on the *shabbat*. In Sofer's universe, *Haskalah* and rabbinic culture parted ways. Prospective emancipation and Reform Judaism presented a revolutionary situation to which the *halakhah* could no longer respond traditionally, or offer guidance, and he built bulwarks against modernity. He had no confidence in halakhic deliberation producing inconvertible results, and he opposed reduction of the Bible or the Talmud to single meanings. Text was multilayered, and tradition encompassed the totality of interpretations. Interpretation represented continued revelation, and only divinely inspired scholars could be entrusted with it. Against Landau's traditionalist modernism, Sofer sought to preserve premodernity by proposing a postmodern vision of text and tradition.[62]

There was little of the traditional rabbi in Moses Sofer. His hagiographers tell of a precocious child who publically challenged his teacher and father in halakhic debate, a youth who was a member of a controversial mystical pietistic group and, at age twenty, left town with his mentor, without bidding farewell to his mother. As a young rabbi he married a widow, older than he was and poorer than he could afford, and did not divorce her though she was barren; indeed, he did not even pray for a child lest he harm her. When she died after a twenty-four-year marriage, he married another widow, this time one distinguished for her lineage and half his age, but devoid of a reputation for beauty. She was the daughter of another halakhic giant, Aqiva Eger (1762–1835).[63] Through Sorel Eger, Sofer established a new rabbinic dynasty.

Aqiva Eger's hagiographers nicely illustrate Sofer's break with tradition. They depict Eger as scion to a distinguished rabbinic family, a frail and abstemious child prodigy, respectful of his parents and teachers, a student of noted authorities who rises in the rabbinic echelons and marries into affluent families, an ailing and ascetic scholar who cries that he is

---

[62] Maoz Kahana, *From the Noda BeYehudah to the Chatam Sofer: Halakha and Thought in Their Historical Moment* (in Hebrew) (Jerusalem: Zalman Shazar Center, 2015). Working under Jacob Katz, Moshe Samet first elaborated the new vision of Orthodoxy as modern in his 1967 Hebrew University dissertation, revised and published in his *He-Hadash asur min ha-Torah*. The epithet "Ḥatam Sofer" represents the acronym for his work: *Ḥidushei Torat Moshe* (Novelties of Moses' Torah) – ḤaTaM. Unless otherwise noted, I used the recent Nussenzweig edition: *Teshuvot Ḥatam Sofer* (Ḥatam Sofer *responsa*), 8 vols. (Jerusalem: Ḥatam Sofer Institute, 2000–2008). Henceforth *Responsa*; numbers refer to volume and response (and not to page).

[63] Biographies by relatives: Shlomo Sofer, *Ḥut ha-Meshulash* (Book of the threefold cord: Bios of Moses Sofer, Aqiva Eger, and Avraham Shmuel Benyamin Sofer) (Beregszász: S. Schreiber, 1894); Yiẓḥaq Weiss, *Avnei Beit ha-Yoẓer* (Jerusalem: Hatam Sofer Institute, 1970). Scholarly: Jacob Katz, "Towards a Biography of the Hatam Sofer," in *Profiles in Diversity*, ed. Frances Malino and David Sorkin (Detroit: Wayne State University Press, 1998), pp. 223–66, and previous note.

lost when his first wife dies. He dies venerated but poor because he used private funds to support public projects.[64] Eger contrasts with Sofer, ever confident in his conduct and rulings, a capable administrator, a politically astute and indefatigable fighter, an innovator who sanctions tradition, regards Torah study as continuous revelation, and regularly communes with heaven on matters public and private. Sofer's portrait, in an oil painting and a lithographic print, shows an expressive face with glaring eyes and an ironic smile, a person self-possessed and at peace with himself (see Figure 7 and Figure 8).[65] The founder of Jewish Orthodoxy, who viewed himself as the prophet of his generation and potentially a messiah, was at home in the world.[66]

Figure 7: Oil painting of Ḥatam Sofer, courtesy of the Hungarian Jewish Museum and Archives.

Figure 8: *Ḥatam Sofer*, lithograph by J. Kriehuber (Ö.K. Kriehuber 12, bl.Nr. 1672), Wurzbach 2016. Courtesy of The Albertina, Vienna.

---

[64] Avraham Moshe Bleichrode, *Toldot Rabenu Aqiva Eger* (Berlin: n.p., 1862); Shlomo Sofer, *Ḥut ha-Meshulash.*

[65] The painting is based on a contemporary drawing by Ber Frank Halevi (c. 1777–1845). A photo of the lithograph by the painter Josef Kriehuber (1800–1876) appears in Wolfgang von Wurzbach, *Katalog der Porträtlithographien Josef Kriehubers*, 2d ed. (Vienna: Walter Krieg Verlag, 1955), nr. 2016.

[66] Maoz Kahana, "The Chatam Sofer: A Decisor in his Own Eyes" (in Hebrew), *Tarbits* 76:3 (2007): 519–56.

Born to a respectable but not prominent Frankfurt family, Sofer left home at ten to live with his mentor, the charismatic Rabbi Nathan Adler (1741–1800). Adler's group (*minyan*) adopted Lurianic liturgy and practiced kabbalistic asceticism. Members would disturb the community by sharing frightening visions, and in 1779, the court defrocked Adler and tried to close down the minyan. Meanwhile, Sofer also studied in a traditional *yeshivah*, that of eminent halakhist Pinḥas Horowitz, and in 1776–78 in Mainz, where he became familiar with secular learning. In 1782, Sofer accompanied Adler to Boskowitz in Moravia and never returned to Frankfurt. He seemed to have almost fled the city of his youth but would uphold its traditions and customs throughout his life, as well as inscribe its name at the end of each and every one of his responsa: "The humble Moses Sofer [Schreiber; scribe] from Frankfurt am Main."

Adler returned to Frankfurt in 1785, but Sofer settled in Prossnitz, Moravia, a rabbinic, Sabbatean, and, later, maskilic center. He probably taught there for a couple of years, then married in 1788. When his father-in-law could no longer support him, he became the rabbi of a smaller Moravian city, Dressnitz, in 1794, and four years later moved on to a respectable position in Mattersdorf (today's Mattersburg in Austria, then in western Hungary), one of the Burgenland's seven Jewish communities. His reputation was growing, but still mostly regional, until he moved to Pressburg in 1806. Pressburg, one of Hungary's major cities and the seat of its Diet, straddled the boundary between the still traditional Hungarian-Jewish world and the quickly changing German-Jewish one. There, Sofer established a yeshivah that grew to become Europe's largest, with four hundred students. The yeshivah became a model for Hungary, and the place of training for its next generation of rabbis.

Sofer shaped a new rabbinic model. He was active in communal affairs, especially in education, and delivered ten *derashot* (traditional homiletic sermons) annually, rather than the customary two. He faced major challenges from the community's affluent and acculturated leaders. He fought them, compromised, and much of the time overcame their resistance. Having failed to prevent the opening of a state school (*Normalschule*), he participated, from 1830 on, in directing its Jewish Studies curriculum. Among traditionalists, his charisma and mysticism made him the community's holy protector in times of crisis, especially during the 1809 French siege. He never published a book but had his extensive responsa, midrashim, and derashot diligently transcribed and copied. They produced a massive corpus, posthumously published, unparalleled in its influence, making him his generation's foremost decisor. After his death, Orthodox rabbis in Austria and Hungary were given lifetime appointments. He is perhaps the most venerated figure among Ultra-Orthodox Jews.

Sofer's opposition to the Haskalah and Reform was evident early on, but in traditional Moravia and the Burgenland, Sabbateanism was more of a concern than Hasklalah. Sofer was not hostile to professional training or scientific learning but insisted that they take second place to rabbinic education and, crucially, that they leave no trace on it: Traditional rabbinic approaches were superior and the only legitimate ones in Jewish Studies. He offered an annual sermon on the eighth of Tevet, the date on which the Septuagint translation of the Bible into Greek was said to have been completed. The commemoration was a sad event: Translation could not capture the richness of the holy language and stripped the Torah of meaning. (This explains Sofer's lifelong animosity to Mendelssohn and his *Biur*, which seemed unusual and disproportionate.) Still, Sofer's defense of Frankfurt traditions against local decisors almost made him appear, on occasion, to be a representative of Western acculturation, grounded in Rhineland customs, against Polish-inspired halakhic fundamentalism.[67]

The advent of educational and liturgical reform in German-speaking Europe caught up with Sofer in Pressburg, a big city with an acculturated Jewish elite. German reformer Israel Jacobson used the Westphalian Consistory, established under Napoleonic auspices in 1810, to open a temple, and the Consistory suspended the prohibition against the consumption of legumes (*qitniyot*) during Passover, a custom that originated in medieval times. Sofer thought it best to squelch reform initiatives locally by delegitimizing the opponents and declined the request of German rabbis to intervene lest he publicize the reformers. He did, however, offer a new formula for curtailing local reform by deferring any proposed change to a "gathering of sages," a European assembly of Ashkenazi rabbis. Only a rabbinic consensus could change a custom, even when the original rationale for it no longer obtained. The struggle against reform became a European affair.

Shortly thereafter, Sofer faced a reform initiative at home: In January 1811, community leaders proposed opening a Normalschule. Sofer mobilized the community in an emotional sermon, decrying the reformers as shamans poisoning God's children.[68] He proposed an appeal to the government: The reformers were irreligious, he said, neither Jews nor

---

[67] Maoz Kahana, *From the Noda BeYehudah*, pp. 242–89, and *Shut* [שו״ת] *Ḥatam Sofer ha-ḥadashot* (New Ḥatam Sofer *responsa*), ed. S. E. Shtern (Jerusalem: Ḥatam Sofer Institute, 1989): 10.

[68] *Sefer Ḥatam Sofer. Derashot* (Ḥatam Sofer's book of sermons), ed. Yosef Naftali Shtern, 3 vols. in 2 (Jerusalem: Ḥatam Sofer Institute, 1989): 1: 112a–115b. Henceforth, *Derashot*.

Christians, and the authorities would look askance at their undermining of tradition. The heresy charge was old – Jews had used it to undermine medieval converts – and so was also the view that the authorities would oppose any confusion of religious boundaries. But the anxiety about religious hybridity acquired a new meaning in the context of acculturation: German Jews were not really Jews.

Sofer's imperial allegiance, too, represented old and new. The Frankfurt Jewish ghetto's gate carried the inscription "under the protection of His Majesty the Roman Emperor and the Holy Roman Empire," commemorating the Habsburg restoration of the Jewish community after the 1614 expulsion. Sofer observed the holiday all his life, celebrating the restoration far away from Frankfurt, as Jews celebrated all holidays in exile. Yet only a decade earlier, he had bemoaned the emperor's consorting with the Prague Sabbateans, and intimated that he represented a convergence of Ahasuerus and Haman, royal folly and malign design.[69] Now Sofer began laying the Orthodox counterrevolution's foundations. Restoration rulers, he was convinced, did not want Jewish citizens, but they would protect a loyal traditional Jewish community. He pursued an antiliberal alliance with the Austrian Empire and sought to shape a European Jewish identity hostile to reform.

Prussia's grant of civil rights to the Jews in 1812 reinforced Jewish reform efforts throughout German-speaking Europe. In 1815, Jacobson and leading Berlin families opened a Reform minyan, but the authorities, responding to the community's appeal, closed it down. The minyan restarted in 1817, and the organizers solicited rabbinic opinions to legitimize liturgical reform. They found several Italian and Hungarian rabbis, most notably the reform-minded Aaron Chorin of Arad (1766–1844), willing to accept the changes. They added their own reflections and published both in 1818.[70] Later that year, Hamburg Reformers opened their own temple. They limited service to weekends and holidays, prayed in German rather than Hebrew, shortened the prayers, dropped references to the return to Zion, and introduced the harp (played by a non-Jew so as not to violate the shabbat). The Hamburg rabbinical court objected, and, in defense, the Reformers forwarded the rabbinic endorsements to the City Senate. The Hamburg court now beseeched rabbis throughout Europe to rebut the Reformers. Central Europe's leading halakhic authorities responded, and their opinions were published in

---

[69] *Derashot* 1: 126b–130b.
[70] Eliezer Liberman, *Or Nogah* (Light of splendor) (Dessau: Schlieder, 1818); *Sefer Nogah ha-Ẓedeq* (Splendor of justice) by Shem Tov, Yaakov Ḥai Reqanaṭi, Aaron Chorin, and Mosheh Kunits (Dessau: Schliede, 1818).

Eleh Divre ha-Berit (These are the words of the Covenant), Jewish Orthodoxy's founding document.[71]

The Hamburg Temple controversy catapulted Sofer to the leadership of Orthodoxy. His three letters to the Hamburg court elaborated a historical vision of the Jews as a people living in anticipation of redemption, and of the antiquity of Jewish prayer, transmitted through the generations from the Second Temple period. He could find no firm halakhic rationale to reject most of the reforms, but he insisted that Jews must keep away from non-Jewish customs, such as harp use in churches, and that "little foxes" like the Reformers could not overturn a millennia-old tradition. A general assembly – a rabbinic court greater in number and stature than the court establishing the custom – was required for any reform. Dissenters were not permitted to withdraw from the community. Sofer bemoaned the destabilizing effects of recent challenges to rabbinic authority but assured his audience, including the Hamburg Senate, that the overwhelming majority of Jews were still loyal to the Torah, and that the Reformers were but a negligible minority.

Taking the opportunity of the Restoration struggle against liberalism and nationalism, Sofer elaborated a political theory that presented traditional Jews as government allies and the liberal Reformers as rebels. He felt that the Reformers had put traditional Jews' loyalty in question by urging Jews to pray for their nations' welfare and drop all mention of Zion. Indeed, *Or Nogah* intimated that the tragedies of Jewish history, such as Roman persecution, resulted in part from lack of Jewish civic engagement. Sofer retorted that a Jew was commanded to love the king as his soul and hate the king's enemies. God appointed every king, and each minister represented an angel in the heavenly retinue (הפמליא של מעלה). One was prohibited from challenging them, and should not join those who questioned their authority.[72] Even bad rulers, like the Pharaoh and Aḥab, were due respect and praise, let alone the gracious Habsburg emperor (קיסר חסיד), the Jews' protector and their haven in the Diaspora, the King of all earthly Kings who maintained peace and security throughout Europe and allowed Jews to observe the Torah and increase learning.[73] Rebels (liberals?) were not

---

[71] *Eleh Divre ha-Berit* (Farnborough, UK: Gregg International, 1969). On the Hamburg Temple controversy: Jacob Katz, *Halacha in Straits* (in Hebrew) (Jerusalem: Magnes Presss, 1992), pp. 43–72; Michael A. Meyer, *Response to Modernity: A History of the Reform Movement in Judaism* (New York: Oxford University Press, 1988), pp. 53–61; Moshe Samet, *He-Ḥadash asur min ha-Torah*, pp. 228–305.

[72] *Eleh Divre ha-Berit*, pp. 41–44.

[73] *Dershot* 2: 395a–399a, sermons under "Honoring the King," 1821–35, on the occasions of Napoleon's death (1821), the emperor's sixtieth birthday (1828), and a eulogy (1835); *Responsa* 5: 190 (previous omissions השמטות). "King of the Kings of all Kings" (מלך מלכי המלכים) is an epithet reserved for the Lord. Sofer was backing the

Jewish. Jews also prayed for peace among the nations, which mirrored harmony in the heavenly entourage. Messianic expectation for a return to Zion intimated no dual loyalty. Christians, too, shared those messianic prophecies. Israel's redemption would benefit the nations, and God would surely reward benevolent rulers. Not the longing for Zion but the liberal Reformers' undermining of distinctions between religious communities threatened the public order.

Sofer's 1819 Purim sermon posited that the conspiracy to annihilate the Jews of Ancient Persia in the Book of Esther was a result of Jewish assimilation.[74] Imitation of non-Jews, that is, acculturation, was the major source of antisemitism and the cause of the expulsion from Spain: The more Jews forgot Jerusalem and became integrated, the more they were hated. The Pressburg City Council's hostility to Jewish emancipation reinforced Sofer's conclusion that the *goyim* did not want Jews to be part of them and that the separation between Christians and Jews was conducive to peaceful relations. The French Revolution, the nation-state, and emancipation brought threats of assimilation and anti-semitism: They undid the Kehillah's authority, encouraged sectarianism (i.e., pluralism), and blurred Christian–Jewish boundaries. God dispersed His people in the Diaspora as a punishment, and promised eventual redemption (which Sofer expected in his own lifetime). Emancipation would delay redemption.

Sofer now headed a war of containment against Reform across Europe. He wrote to the leading Hungarian rabbi, Moses Münz, to lean on Chorin to withdraw his endorsement of liturgical reform. Chorin did, but in 1820, Vienna Reformers endeavored to draft him in order to introduce the Hamburg rite in the new Stadttempel, which they were negotiating with the authorities.[75] On January 22, 1820, Franz II issued ordinances for university training of rabbis throughout Austria and for the use of German as the language of prayer, "provided no issues of propriety prevailed against it."[76] Sofer consorted with the Trieste rabbi on approaching the emperor, and traditional rabbis in Bohemia and Moravia joined in protest.[77] In many cities, however, the Reformers

---

Habsburg dynasty's imperial claims and recognizing Austria as inheritor of the Holy Roman Empire.

[74] *Derashot* 1: 179a–182b.

[75] A. F. Pribram, ed., *Urkunden und Akten zur Geschichte der Juden in Wien* (Vienna: Wilhem Bräumüller, 1918), includes official documents that reflect the Viennese community's negotiations with the government and resistance to the plans. Thanks to Michael K. Silber for the reference.

[76] Ibid., p. 306: "falls keine Anstände, die Mir anzuzeigen wären, dagegen obwalten."

[77] Michael Miller, *Rabbis and Revolutionaries* (Stanford, CA: Stanford University Press, 2011), p. 81. Michael Silber writes that "the state demand for university education was

belonged to the community leadership, and the imperial bureaucracy was sympathetic to the Haskalah and to moderate reform.[78] Eager to avoid controversy, the government usually opted for a compromise. When the Stadttempel opened in 1825, the appointed rabbi was Reformer Isaac Noah Mannheimer, but he introduced the Vienna rite that retained traditional Hebrew liturgy. Sofer's "imperial alliance" did not always produce the results he expected, but he had nowhere else to turn.

Instead, Sofer poured his wrath on the Reformers. He told the Trieste rabbi that if it were up to him, he would declare them non-Jews and let them go their separate way like previous sects that had split from Judaism – the Christians, Sadducees, and Karaites.[79] He could not excommunicate them, he said, because the authorities would not allow him to do so. Truly, he had never moved to split Jewry, and in 1820 he still hoped to win the war. Yet he saw a greater danger in allowing the Reformers "to build themselves a *bamah* (idolatrous altar)" than in losing them as Jews.

Sofer now conjoined a history of halakhah to his history of liturgy and political theory. In all three, he turned scattered legends, midrashim, and halakhic opinions that provided fragments of history and had never before been taken as binding into a coherent tradition, anchoring contemporary practice and legitimizing his new rulings. Only a generation earlier, Landau had sought to diminish the halakhic authority of sixteenth-century Polish Rabbi Moses Isserles. Now Sofer declared that "the people of Israel fulfill the commandments through RaMA" (Rabbi Moses Isserles רמ"א, a pun on Exodus 14:8).[80] Recognizing that halakhic debates were open-ended and rarely produced an unequivocal result, Sofer declared that in times such as this, custom must be sanctioned and any innovation is prohibited by the Torah: חדש אסור מן התורה.[81]

Yet in German-speaking Europe, Sofer seemed to be fighting a losing battle. German acculturation progressed apace, and the emergent

---

filled spottily in Hungary and Galicia, while in Bohemia and Moravia, by midcentury almost all of the younger rabbis were Dr. Rabbiner," albeit still a minority (email to author, April 7, 2014).

[78] Michael K. Silber, "Roots of the Schism in Hungarian Jewry" (Ph.D. diss., The Hebrew University of Jerusalem, 1985), pp. 125–29.

[79] *Responsa*, 6: 89.

[80] *Responsa*, 3: 98 (Even ha-Ezer I): Isserles wrote an extensive commentary, the *Mapa* (Tablecloth), on the foremost early modern Jewish halakhic work, Joseph Caro's *Shulḥan Arukh* (Set table). It was widely but not universally accepted among Ashkenazi Jews until Sofer.

[81] *Responsa*, 1: 28 (Oraḥ Ḥayim), 2: 19 (Yoreh Deah), 4: 29 (Even ha-Ezer II). Yet Sofer was himself a great innovator. To the Reformers, Sofer said that innovation was prohibited, but to his students that studying was a continuous expansion of the Torah, a discovery of new meanings in a multidimensional text: Maoz Kahana, "How Did the Hatam-Sofer Wish to Trump Spinoza? Text, Hermeneutics, and Romanticism in the Writings of R. Moses Sofer" (in Hebrew), *Tarbits* 79:3 (2011): 557–85.

generation of university-educated rabbis contrasted with the graduates of Sofer's yeshivah. In the big cities, Reform was gaining the upper hand. It made no difference to Sofer that Prague and Vienna represented moderate Haskalah and Reform as opposed to radical Berlin and Hamburg. In his own community, powerful leaders endeavored to close down his yeshivah in 1826. Sofer prevailed but was shaken. In 1830, Crown Prince Ferdinand visited the Jewish Normalschule, showing support for reform. Maoz Kahana notes in Sofer a desperate change of strategy in the 1830s. Neither government nor rabbis could be trusted any longer to resist reform: "Let people listen to their fathers rather than to rabbis."[82] The still-traditional, mostly poor, people, led by charismatic rabbis, were to present a last-ditch effort to block reform-oriented leaders.

As the aging Sofer set the boundaries of Jewishness against acculturation, his anxieties focused on Jacob & Esau's brotherhood. His benevolent view of Christian rulers made no dent in his hostility toward Esau or in his anticipation of redemption from Edom. To be sure, his homilies, more open to Kabbalah than his halakhic rulings were, highlighted the struggle between Jacob and Esau for the world to come, implicitly conceding history to Christian rulers. He emphasized that Israel's restoration would not involve Jacob spilling blood. Still, Israel remained the king's children in exile, Esau's descendants were servants, and the biblical narrative culminated in Jacob's winning of the blessings from Esau's angel. The reconciliation was a charade. Having temporarily attained this world, Esau endeavored to gain the future Temple as well. He failed, and both brothers cried, recognizing that they could not overcome each other and that their struggle would be eternal.[83]

Throughout the 1830s, Sofer was preoccupied with Esau as an apostate and eager to establish his non-Jewishness. Esau was thought to have been born in a Jewish household and to have become an idolater. Already the Talmud referred to him as an apostate (מומר), and used his territorial heritage to argue that idolaters (עכו״ם) have the right of inheritance.[84] In medieval times, the apostate and Christian convert tended to merge, and Esau's Christian identity was not in doubt. As emancipation and religious reform raised the prospects of German Jewishness, and of a life in between Judaism and Christianity, the question of Esau's identity reemerged. In 1800, the early Sofer had implicated Esau as an evil sorcerer (ידעוני), a Sabbatean.[85] A decade later, Esau became a Reformer,

---

[82] Maoz Kahana, *From the Nuda BeYehuda*, pp. 382–411.
[83] *Ḥatam Sofer al ha-Torah*, ed. Yosef Naftali Shtern, 5 vols. (Jerusalem: Ḥatam Sofer Institute, 1987): 1: 166–67, 174–78; *Sefer Torat Moshe* (1881), ed. Shimeon Sofer (Jerusalem: Ḥatam Sofer Institute, 1967) 1: 16b.
[84] *BT* Nazir 61a; Qidushin 18a.   [85] *Ḥatam Sofer al ha-Torah*, 1: 106.

threatening to dissuade Jacob's children from the right path.[86] Deploying a medieval tradition that Esau had never been circumcised, the later Sofer argued in 1834 that Esau had never been a Jew and was never subject to the Torah.[87] Restoring Esau as an apostate and then arguing that he was never Jewish may make no interpretive sense, but it does make sense as an expression of anxiety about hybridity and as a strategy against acculturation. Sofer endeavored to establish clear boundaries between Jews and Christians, and between Orthodox and Reform Jews.

It required no stretch of imagination to see Jacob & Esau's brotherhood in acculturation and citizenship: Rabbis around Sofer were pondering the command to love one's neighbor in relation to Christians.[88] Medieval sages had debated whether Talmudic rulings on relations with idolaters (עכו"ם, literally worshippers of stars and the Zodiac) applied to Christians (and Muslims). Menaḥem ha-Meiri of Provence (1249–1315) ruled not only that Christians were not idolaters but also that in business transactions, they were considered "brothers."[89] Early modern prayer books often carried an inscription that pronouncements against the nations were not directed at the present gracious hosts of Jews but at ancient culprits. Sofer's beloved *Sefer ha-Berit* (Book of the Covenant, 1797), a popular Jewish scientific encyclopedia written by Pinḥas Eliahu Horowitz of Vilnius, stated that "the essence of loving a neighbor is to love the human species, regardless of ethnic or linguistic origin, just because your neighbor is a person, like you, made in God's image."[90] Landau's student, Eliezer Flekles of Prague, endeavored to educate the Jews to citizenship and elaborated a rabbinic vision of universal humanity. Christians observed the Noaḥide commandments, and Jews must strictly observe all laws of contemporary nations and rulers.[91]   Finally, Sofer's nemesis, Aaron Chorin, ruled, in the

---

[86] *Derashot* 1:113a: Jacob was pleased to witness Esau's demise (see the midrash in *Sifre Devarim*, ve-zot ha-berakhah 7 and *BT* Sotah 13a, discussed in Chapter 2) because he could rest assured that his children would not be subject to Esau's incitement.

[87] *Hatam Sofer al ha-Torah*, 1: 105; *Sefer Tosafot ha-Shalem*, ed. Yaakov Gelis, 10 vols. (Jerusalem: Mifal Tosafot ha-Shalem, 1984): 3: 19.

[88] Jacob Katz, "The Vicissitudes of Three Apologetic Statements" (in Hebrew), *Ẓiyon* 23/24 (1958–59): 174–93.

[89] *Beit ha-Beḥirah al Baba Matẓia*, ed. Kalman Schlesinger (Jerusalem: Meqitẓe Nirdamim, 1972), p. 219 (on Baba Matẓia 59b). Ha-Meiri's view was an outlier. "Brotherhood" meant that prohibitions on taking advantage of business partners applied equally to Jews and Christians. It did not extend to matrimonial law. See also the discussion on taking interest from Christians under "Brothers Estranged" in Chapter 3.

[90] *Sefer ha-Berit* (Brünn: J. K. Neumanns, 1797), part II: 13: 1, p. 43a.

[91] "Kesut Einayim," an introduction to part I of *Teshuvah me-Ahavah* [1809] (New York: Yisrael Zeev, 1966), n.p.

pamphlet promoting Viennese liturgical reform, that Christians were also considered "brothers."[92]

Sofer understood the universalist urge and dreaded it. He never spoke ill of Christians, only of Jewish Reformers, and he, too, had a vision of human nature. Yet he was anxious to protect Jewish life against universalist incursions, and he set strict and far-reaching limits to "nature." Even Jewish physiognomy, he thought, may be different due to dietary restrictions. Reading Ha-Meiri's ruling, extending "brotherhood" to Christians, he reacted in disbelief: "This could not have come out from his holy mouth, and must be deleted."[93] In 1839, Sofer restored Christians to the status of "idolaters."[94]

A series of three responsa in the fall and winter of 1833–34 brought Jacob & Esau's brotherhood under Sofer's scrutiny, and he reshaped "brotherhood" to reflect his understanding of membership in the Jewish community and relations with non-Jews.[95] The case, sent by Rabbi Yosef Yoel Deutsch of Ternopol in easternmost Galicia, involved a levirate (yevamah יבמה), a widow without children who requires dispensation (חליצה) from her brother-in-law (yabam יבם) to remarry because, in principle, he is to marry her in order to continue the family's lineage. The levirate in this case required a dispensation from a convert to Christianity (מומר). He was said, with insufficient reliability, to be dead, and if the court accepted the testimony, the woman would be permitted to remarry.

For a testimony to provide sufficient grounds for a ruling, Jewish law normally requires two male witnesses with no vested interest. In this case, the witnesses' identity shifted from one response to another: Initially, there was none, only a rumor that had reached the woman of her brother-in-law's demise; then Sofer assumed that there was one witness, the convert's son (who was a Jew); but the case ended with two unqualified witnesses, the convert's daughter and the woman herself, who had heard of his death from his son. Sofer resolved the case quickly, permitting the woman to remarry, remaining firm throughout: "In case of [a levirate and] a convert, with one acceptable witness [to his death], she is permitted to remarry without any doubt.... In such a case of a deserted wife (agunah), leniency could do no damage. Let the court even accept

---

[92] Davar Be-Ito; Ein Wort zu seiner Zeit über die Nächstenliebe und den Gottesdienst (in Hebrew and German) (Vienna: Anton Strauß, 1820), p. 20.

[93] Qovez Teshuvot (Responsa collection) (Jerusalem: Ḥatam Sofer Institute, 1973): 90. Sofer assumed that Ha-Meiri ruled this way (in his commentary on Baba Qama 113a) to appease detractors. However, as the aforementioned reference suggests, Ha-Meiri applied "brotherhood" similarly in several places.

[94] Responsa, 2: 131 (Yoreh Deah). Yet he tried to minimize the human cost: He permitted Jewish doctors to help Christian women give birth on the shabbat.

[95] Responsa, 4: 74, 88, 89 (Even ha-Ezer II).

testimony of one witness [a man] from another [the daughter] and permit her [to remarry]."[96]

Like many premodern halakhists, Sofer could be lenient when issues did not seem foundational.[97] He seemed chagrined about the protracted situation. His own inclination would have been to follow an older tradition, from the Geonic period, that did not require a convert's dispensation at all.[98] Unlike Rashi, who had affirmed that "a Jew, although he has sinned, remains a Jew," and required a convert's dispensation, Sofer wished to remove apostates from communal life and not to attract them back, let alone permit them to determine Jews' lives.[99] Sofer was aware, however, that on Rashi's authority, late medieval rulings had run against leniency, and early modern halakhists made an exception only if one witness created doubt that the *yabam* was alive.[100] Sofer respected these limits: "We are not permitted to add or detract from medieval rabbinic rulings (דברי הראשונים)."[101]

Sofer's first letter sorted out the conflicting medieval halakhic rationales, the second reconsidered their applicability, as it now appeared that there was no reliable witness, and the third focused on acceptance of questionable witnesses, especially of relatives, as the daughter's testimony became crucial. One rationale for exempting a levirate from a convert's dispensation was that neither she nor her husband could have intended to marry to this end, as even a woman eager for marriage – "it is better to be together than alone" – could not possibly wish to marry a convert. Moreover, levirate marriage was grounded in brotherhood. Could a convert be considered a brother? One of Sofer's sources, *Trumat ha-Deshen*, exposed the absurdity of requiring dispensation from the convert, who

---

[96] Ibid., beginning of 74 and end of 89, respectively.

[97] He was known for leniency with *agunot*. Moshe Samet, *He-Ḥadash asur min ha-Torah*, pp. 11, 309–18.

[98] *Responsa*, 4: 88, beginning; *Oẓar ha-Geonim*, ed. B. M. Levin, 13 vols. (Jerusalem, 1928–43): 7: 84 (on Yevamot 22), p. 37. The *Geonim* were Babylonian Jewry's spiritual leaders and highest decisors from the eighth to the eleventh centuries.

[99] *Teshuvot Rashi*, ed. Israel Elfenbein (New York: Schulsinger Bros., 1943): 173, pp. 193–94; Jacob Katz, "Even Though He Has Sinned, He Is Still a Jew" (in Hebrew), *Tarbiz* 27:2/3 (1958): 203–17. The original phrase is in *BT*, Sanhedrin 44a.

[100] *Shut Maharam be-rabi Barukh* (Meir of Rothenburg's responsa), ed. Moshe Aryeh Bloch (Budapest: Sternberg & Comp, 1895): 456, 564 (Prague print); Mordekhai ben Hillel (1250–1298), *Sefer rav Mordekhai* (Trent, 1558) on Yevamot 89, 44–46; Yisrael Isserlein (1390–1460), *Trumat ha-Deshen* (Benei Beraq: n.p., 1971), part I: 223, pp. 73–74. The *Mordekhai* and *Trumat ha-Deshen* summarize the debate and quote additional medieval sources. Both note that Meir of Rothenburg endorsed the lenient Geonic position in principle and yet ruled according to Rashi in practice. The one-witness exemption: Yosef Qolon (1420–1480), *Shut u-Fisqe Mahariq he-ḥadashim*, ed. Eliahu Dov Pines (Jerusalem: Or ha-Mizraḥ, 1984), pp. 90–97; Shmuel Fayyush (1640–1698), *Beit Shmuel* (Fürth, 1689): 158b on *Shulḥan Arukh*, Even ha-Ezer 158c.

[101] *Responsa*, 4: 74, first paragraph.

would be prohibited from marrying the levirate (or any Jew).[102] Still, apostates might contemplate returning to the fold at any time, thereby making themselves eligible as yabam. Rashi's "apostates remain Jews" retained its sway.

The apostate's liminality became Sofer's quandary – and his great opportunity. Medieval rabbis had remained divided on whether a particular set of commandments, such as the prohibition of usury and the obligations of charity and levirate marriage, applied to apostates. The Bible specifies brotherhood (אחוה) as grounds for these commandments. The rabbis understood brotherhood as partaking in the observation of the Law. Apostates excluded themselves from such brotherhood. As Esau was considered an apostate, the rabbis' "brotherhood" seemed to exclude him and his descendants. Yet *Trumat ha-Deshen* noted that the Bible speaks of Jacob and Esau's brotherhood as grounded in genealogy, that is, in their siblinghood, and not in observance of the Law. The Israelites approaching Edom on their way out of Egypt address the Edomites with "Thus spake your brother Israel" (Numbers 20:14), and Obadiah (1:10) chastises the Edomites: "Because of the violence done to your brother Jacob, shame shall cover you." They seem to call upon the Edomites to recognize obligations grounded in common descent. *Trumat ha-Deshen* used this conception of brotherhood to buttress Rashi's position against the *Geonim*.[103] Some obligations of brotherhood, such as levirate marriage, might be extended beyond the religious divide.

Sofer, in contrast, declared the obligations of brotherhood between Edom and Israel to be a huge problem. The problem, he said, requires an expert craftsman in order to be resolved. His rhetoric suggested that more was at stake in Esau's brotherhood than the halakhic case: The prospective brotherhood of Christians and Jews and the Reformers' Jewishness were at stake. Sofer could not let Esau's brotherhood stand.

The Edomites, decided Sofer, were never really brothers. Esau's apostasy and marriage with non-Jewish women excluded him from brotherhood. Biblical prophecies expressing dismay that the Edomites forgot their brotherhood and took part in destroying Jerusalem were meant to chastise the Edomites for violating human obligations – sympathy and avoidance of cruelty – and not for violating familial or legal obligations:

---

[102] Yisrael Isserlein, *Trumat ha-Deshen*, p. 74. Isserlein quotes Meir of Rothenburg as having raised the question. The halakhic consideration for requiring dispensation may be that although the marriage is prohibited, if the convert did go ahead and become betrothed to her, his marriage would be valid.

[103] Aryeh Leib Hacohen-Heller (1745–1812), *Avnei Miluim* (New York: Yisrael Zeev, 1966): 157: 4, wondered how the *Geonim* could have ruled the way they did. The issue remains for him halakhic, and not ideological, as it is for Sofer.

"Because of the violence done to your brother Jacob" surely does not convey a legal principle, or [an obligation grounded in] siblinghood, but rather [a principle of] human nature: Since [Edom and Israel] both descend from the same parents, [the Edomites] should be ashamed for having stood aside when foreigners took Jacob's army hostage. (88)

Brother could mean a "fellow human being" or it could mean a "fellow Jew." Siblinghood entailed the former but not the latter. Esau's descendants, Edomites and Christians, were fellow human beings, but no legal obligations were generated on account of their genealogical proximity to Jews.

The verse "Was not Esau Jacob's brother?" [Malachi 1:2] shows that this is indeed the meaning of brotherhood. Was not Esau by birth, womb, and pregnancy Jacob's brother? "Yet I loved Jacob" because his good deeds drew him close to me "but Esau I hated" because his deeds distanced him as he became an apostate. Love toward the one and hatred toward the other disrupt the brotherhood (אחוה) and there is none of it anymore. (88)

Anxious about Enlightenment universalism and the brotherhood of Christians and Jews, Sofer translated Edom's brotherhood into universal humanity, and then rendered it virtually meaningless: Jewish law, and not brotherhood, mattered. Ezekiel Landau had used "human nature" (האנושי טבע) to designate biophysical nature.[104] Sofer extended it to include psychology and emotions but declared that "the natural course of things" had no legal ramifications. He was aware that this was revolutionary: He called Naḥmanides' view of the Edomites as brothers "incomprehensible." Departing from the long-accepted, and plain, meaning of Scripture and revising a millennia-old typology, Sofer declared that Esau's brotherhood did not matter: Obedience to Jewish Law defined membership in the community.

Sofer likened Reform Jews to Esau and placed them outside the community. He never seriously contemplated modifying the rulings on Christian converts, or actually splitting Jewry, but his rhetoric made it possible for a few of his Hungarian disciples to withdraw from the community a generation later and launch Ultra-Orthodoxy. Claiming exclusive legitimacy for Orthodoxy, Sofer set the tone for its future relations with the majority of the Jewish people. A leader of his caliber could have paved a more accommodating path to modernity and Europeanness for traditional Jews. Instead, he reset the markers of Jewish identity and communal boundaries to maintain closure against the Enlightenment, emancipation, and the nation-state.

---

[104] *Noda bi-Yehudah* (New York: Halakhah Berurah, 1960): 94, 102, 107 on *Yoreh Deah*.

Despite himself, Sofer was a great innovator. He did not so much preserve tradition as transform it to meet the nation-state's challenge. His political theory was revolutionary: There was no Jewish precedent for such close identification of Jewish and imperial interests, of earthly and divine rule. Allying Orthodoxy with the Restoration, Sofer banked Jewry's future on containment of liberalism and the nation-state. To the Reformers' vision of Jewish citizenship, he counterposed an illiberal multicultural vision: a benevolent Christian emperor overseeing Christian and Jewish communities that coexist in harmony but remain closed one to the other. He glamorized the Holy Roman Empire, deepened Jewish attachment to Austria, and created the illusion of imperial continuity into the modern age. He represented European counterrevolutionary discourse: support for corporatism against national uniformity, international peace against revolutionary warfare, and religious against civic culture. He was the Jewish European Restoration thinker par excellence.

Emancipation Jacob: "Our Pious Patriarch" and His "House of Prayer for All Nations"

Rejection of emancipation rather than religious issues divided Moses Sofer from the wide consensus of German Jewry, stretching from Reform to Neo-Orthodoxy. Reformers and Neo-Orthodox Jews struggled over the meaning of Judaism and the observance of Jewish Law, but all pursued German acculturation and national integration. In Germany proper, Sofer lost the war. Acculturation was rapid and thorough. By the middle of the nineteenth century, half the population of Jewish children were attending German schools and receiving no Jewish education; all German yeshivot had closed down; young rabbis had academic degrees and regarded themselves as preachers and spiritual guides, rather than decisors; communities experimented with liturgical reforms, the sermon became the religious service's centerpiece, and "Confirmation" marked the transition to adulthood; observation of the halakhah waned, and the Orthodox communities diminished to several hundred families. German Jews methodically converted Judaism into a bourgeois confession, compatible with national integration. Whereas contemporary Catholics made confession an integrative force, closing themselves off from non-Catholic Germans, Jews crossed religious lines to collaborate with non-Jews in civil associations.[105]

---

[105] Till van Rahden, "Situational Ethnic Affiliation vs. Milieu Based Identity: The Making of the Jewish Public and Catholic Public in the German Empire" (in Hebrew), in *"The German-Jewish History We Have Inherited": Young Germans Write Jewish History*, ed. Henry Wassermann (Jerusalem: Magness, 2004), pp. 214–41, and "Jews and the

In Austria, the pace of change was slower and reform more moderate. Religious education remained a state requirement in German-speaking schools, and all reforms were state authorized. Even in the major cities of Vienna and Prague, Jewish life retained a more traditional character. The Vienna Rite introduced by Rabbi Isaac Noah Mannheimer (1793–1865) in 1826 kept Hebrew as the language of liturgy, preserved the traditional prayers for the Return to Zion, avoided the organ, and put the emphasis on decorum, exquisite cantorial music with a choir, and edifying German sermons that conveyed Jewish universalism and bourgeois respectability.[106] The Haskalah's investment in both rabbinic culture and synagogue reform was clearer in Austria than in Germany: Maskilic rabbis led the change. From the 1850s on, Vienna also had a continuous influx of traditional Jews, first from Hungary and then from Galicia. They sustained traditional urban communities right beside militantly secular Jewish groups. Sofer's son-in-law, Salomon Spitzer (1811–1893), was the rabbi of the Schiffschul in Vienna's Leopoldstadt for forty years. No one would imagine him a rabbi in contemporary Berlin, or confuse the services in Vienna's Stadttempel with the Reform rite at the Hamburg Temple.

As German Jews pursued acculturation, they reshaped Jacob to display the emancipation worldview, and made him the embodiment of the emancipation social contract. "Our Patriarch Jacob" emerged from Reform sermons more pious than he had been for the rabbis, conveying perfect belief and trust in God, founding prayer houses, courageously fighting for universal recognition of the God of Israel, and demonstrating the bourgeois values of hard work, frugality, abstemiousness, and wise household management. Reform Jacob was the Jew whom Reformers imagined that Germans would find irresistible

Jacob became a prime Reform site for negotiating Jewish ethnicity and cosmopolitanism. As late as the mid-1840s, Reform leader Ludwig Philippson (1811–1889) was speaking of a "Jewish nation."[107] But a national minority vitiated integration, and the Jewish intelligentsia were searching for a collective identity between religion and nation. In 1834, Mannheimer referred to Jacob as our "Stammesvater," our ethnic ances-tor, and a generation later, Adolf Jellinek, Vienna's next chief rabbi, developed the idea of a Jewish tribe (*Stamm*), constituting one of the

---

Ambivalences of German Civil Society: Assessment and Reassessment," *Journal of Modern History* 77 (2005): 1024–47.

[106] Marsha Rozenblit, "Jewish Assimilation in Habsburg Vienna," in *Assimilation and Community: The Jews in Nineteenth-Century Europe*, ed. Jonathan Frankel and Steven Zipperstein (Cambridge: Cambridge University Press, 1992), pp. 225–45.

[107] Ludwig Philippson, *Die Entwickelung der religiösen Idee im Judenthume, Christenthume und Islam* (Leipzig: Baumgärtner, 1847).

many ethnicities composing the German nation.[108] As a Diaspora, the Jews had a unique mission, however: the spread of monotheism and its concomitant humanistic ideals. Reformers made Jacob's struggle with the angel, and his second name, Israel (Yisrah-El: God shall rule), into a new typology: His struggle prefigured Israel's travails among the nations, carrying the Lord's name. Religion, ethnicity, and cosmopolitanism merged in emancipation Jacob.

It was no coincidence that Austrian rabbis, keenly aware of the German nation's diversity, were the ones to develop the idea of Jewish ethnicity. Yet the idea caught on in Germany, too: With the racialization of national discourse in the second half of the nineteenth century, Jewish ethnicity provided a resolution to the conundrum of national integration. Ethnicity historicized and diversified race and nation, posited the ideal of multi-ethnic nationality and state, and vindicated the Jews as German. It was the Jewish response to the threat of racial exclusion from the nation.

Heinrich Heine's 1824 poem "To Edom" encapsulated the dead end of the Edom topos in the emancipation era and the indispensability of Reform negotiation of ethnicity and cosmopolitanism. The young Harry Heine (1797–1856) was, at the time, at the height of his "Jewish period." Having grown up in urban commercial households in Düsseldorf and Hamburg, receiving minimal Jewish education, he wandered among several German universities, studying law and repeatedly encountering nationalist antisemitism in student fraternities. He was a radical liberal, thankful to the French for emancipating German Jews, and contemptuous of the Restoration and of the Prussian government. In 1821 in Berlin, he joined the Association for the Culture and Science of the Jews. Among the famous members were Edward Gans, Isaak Markus Jost, and Leopold Zunz. They were looking for ways to make Jewish history and literature speak to German culture so that they could address the needs of modern Jewry. This entailed the scholarly study of Jewish history and literature and the writing of new ones. The restless Heine, frustrated in his efforts to bond with Germans, took direction from the association in his search for identity as a German-Jewish intellectual.

In 1824, Heine was writing a historical novel, *The Rabbi of Bacherach*, recounting the escape of a medieval Jewish rabbi and his wife from blood libel persecution, their sojourn in the Frankfurt ghetto, and their wandering and travails. He read Jacques Basnage's *History of the Jews*, the first modern Christian account of Jewish history, and it affected him

---

[108] Isaak Noah Mannheimer, "Warnung an Väter in Israel" [December 6, 1834], in *Gottesdienstliche Vorträge*, 2 vols. (Vienna: Winter, 1876), 2: 1–19; Adolf Jellinek, *Studien und Skizzen: Erster Theil: Der jüdische Stamm: Ethnographische Studien* (Vienna: Herzfeld & Bauer, 1869).

deeply.[109] He showed an interest in medieval Spanish Jewry, taken as a model of "assimilation," and corresponded with Zunz, asking for sources on the Abravanel family. Still enchanted with Romantic poetry, and wandering, in the fall of 1824, in the Harz Mountains in search of love and home, he was greatly preoccupied with the novel. It was to be his great œuvre, one that would bring the history of Jewish suffering to German consciousness, and reflect, at one and the same time, Jewish glory and misery. He thought Jewish life to be in need of major repair, and his criticism came out in the novel's unappealing depiction of the Frankfurt Jews. A scion of the Abravanel family, a noble Sephardi Jew, a crypto-Jew or an apostate, was to provide a countermodel to the traditional Ashkenazi Jew. Through *The Rabbi of Bacherach*, Heine was exploring a range of real and imagined possibilities for being Jewish in 1820s Germany.

In October 1824, as part of a lengthy letter to his friend from the association, Moses Moser, Heine enclosed "To Edom," a poem in three stanzas, written, he said, in September to express the state of his feelings after having read Basnage.[110] He added a second poem, in four stanzas, to describe the novel's significance for him. These addenda were intended just for Moser's eyes, he said. He never published them.

"To Edom" commented with irony on the historical relations between Christians and Jews, brothers whose actions were to reflect forbearance but truly expressed violence and rage. The poet, standing for Israel, addresses Edom, unmistakably Christianity, and reflects on the ramifications of Christian persecution for the age of emancipation. Basnage found ritual murder charges and pogroms an outrage and a violation of Christianity, but in the manner of early modern Christian Hebraists, also apportioned blame to the Jews. Heine vindicates Basnage's foregrounding of Christian violence but undermines his judgment by pointing to the power difference and asymmetry in Christian–Jewish relations: "You [Edom] tolerated that I breathed, and I tolerated your rages." He likewise affirms and undermines the emancipation age's historical narrative, contrasting the dark Middle Ages, when "you colored your religiously loving little paws with my blood," with modernity, when German–Jewish friendship has putatively been steadily growing. Having

---

[109] *The History of the Jews, from Jesus Christ to the Present Time* (London: n.p., 1708). Basnage (1653–1723) was a leading French Protestant preacher and scholar, who went into exile in the Netherlands with the revocation of the Edict of Nantes in 1685.

[110] October 24, 1824, in *Briefe 1815–1831*, ed. Fritz Eisner, *Säkularausgabe*, 27 vols. (Berlin: Akademie Verlag, 1970–1986): 20: 177–180. My thanks to my former student, Seth Rogoff, writer and teacher in the Maine College of Art, for directing me to Heine and Else Lasker-Schüler at an early stage of this study.

experienced this "friendship" in student fraternities, Heine concludes: "I myself have started to rage, and I have become almost like you." Recognition of Edom's violence and of the duplicity of friendship fills Heine with rage, which is invested in *The Rabbi of Bacherach*.

The second poem signals a change of protagonists, scenery, and mood: The poet is now alone and calls upon his long-silenced martyr song to break out and touch the presumably non-Jewish audience, so that they may become aware of his prolonged mourning for the losses of Jewry. The audience's tears, he hopes, will flow in streams, merging into the Jordan River, possibly marking the future path of German–Jewish relations. Literary evocation of Jewish suffering and Christian recognition thereof would pave the way for Heine to be recognized as a German-Jewish poet. Little did Heine know that German, and European, recognition of Jewish loss would indeed pave his way to recognition as a German-Jewish and European poet, but that the final triumph would take well over a century to come, and arrive only in the aftermath of the Holocaust.

In Heine's time, the German-Jewish path remained obstructed. His letters inquiring about Jewish historical material are interspersed with reflections on baptism, considered "an admission ticket to European culture," or, more prosaically, the path to an academic position. His family had nothing against conversion, but when Gans became a Christian in December 1824, Heine still wished he had not done so. In June 1825, Heine himself was baptized Lutheran. *The Rabbi of Bacherach* was never completed: It reflected an unsuccessful search for German-Jewish identity, or at least a search that took a different turn with the conversion. The novel (and Heine) remained part of Jewish history. On hearing of the 1840 blood libel in Damascus, Heine returned to the novel, added a chapter, and published the fragments. The Jewish publishing house Schocken brought the book fragments out in 1937 as a comment on Nazi policy, and published the English translation in 1947 in New York.[111]

The decision to convert was excruciating, but the choice of Christian denomination was not: Evangelism, or Lutheranism, was the religion of liberal nationalism, enlightenment, and putatively Jewish emancipation as well. Baptism did not open the gates to the academy, however. In 1831, after the July Revolution in France, Heine moved to Paris where he served as the French correspondent of the *Allgemeine Zeitung* and became a

---

[111] *Der rabbi von Bacherach: Ein Fragment*, with a selection from Heine's letters and an epilogue, ed. Erich Loewenthal (Berlin: Schocken Verlag, 1937); *The Rabbi of Bacherach: A Fragment*, trans. E. B. Ashton (New York: Schocken, 1947). An earlier English translation by C. G. Leland appeared in a Heine collection: *Florentine Nights* (New York: John W. Lovell Company, 1891).

popular poet. In later years, Prime Minister François Guizot provided support for him in the form of a stipend. Heine wrote several works to introduce German culture to the French and saw himself as a mediator between the two cultures, an ambassador of one to the other. He is admired today as a German-Jewish cosmopolitan, a European intellectual in the age of nationalism.

Heine's story is sobering about the prospects for Jews to be recognized as German in the age of emancipation, but Reform Jews remained sanguine about integration and worked diligently toward it. Among the association's members, Gans and Heine converted, yet others, like Jost and Zunz, went on to lay the foundations of modern Jewish Studies. Conversion and reconfiguration of Jewish identity were proximate options for contemporaries. Conversion will remain a distinct option even after Reform Judaism's rise, but there is little doubt that the reconciliation of cosmopolitanism and ethnicity, reflected in the emergence of the new Jacob, opened up possibilities for modern German-Jewish life, which traditional Judaism and the Edom discourse could not do. "To Edom" turned out to be an obituary to medieval Jacob & Esau, rather than the birth announcement of a modern typology. Reform Jews had first to transform Jacob before he could become usable for emancipation.

Transforming Jacob into a cosmopolitan was a complex intellectual operation difficult to accomplish in school. The biblical narrative did not easily lend itself to such an interpretation, yet Bible or religious instruction, either in the modern German-Jewish schools established by the maskilim or state schools in Austria, was most likely the site of their first encounter with Jacob for many Jewish children. Reform Judaism shaped the curricula and textbooks for both. In Austria, the state hired Reform pedagogue Peter Beer (1758–1838) to supervise schools in Bohemia, and he wrote history and religion textbooks that inculcated Reform Judaism's religious and moral vision. Hebrew instruction continued to be part of religious education, and in contrast with the Talmudic focus of traditional Jewish education, the Bible was the center of the modern curriculum.

German-Jewish schools grew rapidly in the age of emancipation, rising from one in Berlin, on the eve of the French Revolution, to more than a dozen in 1812. The schools were far from an unqualified success. Most Jewish parents who could afford to do so sent their children to German schools, and the Jewish schools, which offered free instruction, drew mostly from poor families. Less than 20 percent of Jewish children attended them, a total of two thousand at their height. Still, these were the first schools to have a modern Jewish curriculum, drawing on Jewish sources but emulating German pedagogy, with textbooks in both Hebrew and German. The curricula and textbooks provided models for future Jewish schools.[112]

Reform textbooks, from elementary school to high school, always made mention of Abraham and his discovery of monotheism, and did not hesitate to draw on Midrash to tell the story.[113] Occasionally, they stated explicitly that this showed the Jews as having been the first to believe in One God. Many books mentioned Israel's choice as Abraham's descendants, and the *Aqedah* (the binding of Isaac), but only about half mentioned the covenant of circumcision. Jacob received a cursory treatment. Mention was made of the brotherhood of Jacob & Esau: Jacob was pious and did well in God's eyes, and Esau was unruly and did evil. The stories of Jacob's purchase of the birthright and theft of the blessings were usually omitted, and Jacob's adventures in Laban's household were told, at best, synoptically. Jacob often reappeared with the prayer to God to save him on his return from Ḥaran, but the event was quickly left behind for meditations on the nature and virtues of prayer. Rabbinic Jacob vanished.

Andreas Gotzmann noted that a state requirement for the teaching of catechism made even Orthodox textbooks convert Jewish law, history, and literature into theology and ethics.[114] Beliefs and morals were recognized as superior to the "ceremonial laws," and Christian-inspired pedagogy undermined the halakhah. Reform pedagogy may have been inclined this way in the first place, but one result was that it left the

---

[112] Zohar Shavit, "From Friedländer's Lesebuch to the Jewish Campe: The Beginnings of Children's Literature in Germany," *Leo Baeck Institute Yearbook* 33 (1988): 385–415; David Sorkin, "The Impact of Emancipation on German Jewry," in *Assimilation and Community: The Jews in Nineteenth-Century Europe*, ed. Jonathan Frankel and Steven Zipperstein (Cambridge: Cambridge University Press, 1992), pp.177–98.

[113] Aaron Wolfsohn, *Abtalion* [1790], 3d ed. (Vienna: Anton Schmid, 1814), Hebrew instruction for beginning students; Peter Beer, *Dat Yisrael oder Das Judenthum: Das ist einer Versuch einder Darstellung aller wesentlichen Glaubens- Sitten- und Ceremoniallehren heutiger Juden zum Gebrauche bey den Elementarreligionsunterrichte ihrer Jugend nebst einem Anhange fuer Lehrer* (Prague: Karl Barth, 1810), a religius instruction book for elementary school; Beer, *Die Mosaischen Schriften* (Prague: n.p., 1815), German Bible with extensive commentary; Beer, *Handbuch der Mosaischen Religion* (Vienna: Karl Haas, 1821), religious instruction; David Zamosc, *Nahar me-Eden* (Breslau: H. Zultsbakh, 1836), German and Hebrew Bible instruction; Jacob H. Jacobson, ed., *Abtalion, Deutscher Theil* [1842 German part], 3d ed. (Breslau: Leuckart, 1862), religious instruction for advanced students; Jacobson, ed., *Rimonim: Ein deutsches Lesebuch fuer Israeliten in Schule und Haus* (Leipzig: Friedrich Brandstetter, 1859), also called Abtalion III, German readings and religious instruction for the upper levels of elementary school. Ran Hacohen, "Die Bibel kehrt Heim: Biblische Gedichte für jüdische Kinder," in *Kinder- und Jugendliteraturforschung 1996/7*, ed. Hans Eino-Ewers, Ulrich Nassen, Karin Richter, and Rüdiger Steinlein (Stuttgart: Metzler, 1997), pp. 9–21. I am thankful to Hacohen for directing me also to his "Bible Stories for Jewish Children in the German Haskalah" (in Hebrew), Master's thesis, Tel Aviv University, 1994.

[114] "The Dissociation of Religion and Law in Nineteenth-Century German-Jewish Education," *Leo Baeck Institute Yearbook* 43 (1998): 103–26.

Jacob & Esau typology empty of content: It did not manage to read the beliefs and morals it taught into "our pious Patriarch." The textbooks must have left the students wondering why Jacob was virtuous and Esau wicked, that is, if the students cared at all. The books acknowledged Jacob as an ancestor, but they left him an amorphous, marginal figure.

David Zamosc's *Nahar me-Eden* (1837; A river flowing from Eden) was an exception: It provided a fairly complete version of the Jacob & Esau stories. The reason was remarkable: The textbook was a reworking of the foremost Protestant Bible instruction book, that of Johann Hübner (discussed in chapter 4). Jacob was declared pious using Christian reasoning: His snatching of the blessings "was not rebellion or treachery because Esau had already sold the right of the firstborn, and God had already told Rebecca: The elder shall server the younger."[115] The proximity of Protestant and Reform Jacob is suggestive, but its significance should not be exaggerated. Reform Jews left the intellectual work of tracing Reform principles to "our pious ancestor" to Reform sermons. There, we find Jacob demonstrating loyalty to family and community, trust in God and courage in the struggle for justice, and heading Israel's mission. Reform Judaism was an emergent project: Pedagogy had not caught up with homiletics.

Emancipation-age sermons varied in style and content, but they were similar in the picture they drew of Jacob because their Jacob was an answer to a universal question: the acculturation and integration of German Jewry. In his history of Jewish homiletics, Zunz intended to demonstrate to the Prussian authorities that sermons had their roots in Midrash, but even Orthodox preachers acknowledged that liberal Protestant theologians provided their model.[116] The traditional *derashah*, delivered in Yiddish or Hebrew, called for repentance before the Day of Atonement or gave instructions on the laws of Passover before the holiday. It drew on diverse texts and referred back to them repeatedly. The modern sermon, delivered in German, systematically developed a theme in the weekly readings, referred back to the text only infrequently, and aimed at moral edification rather than legal instruction. Yet from the early sermons at the Hamburg Temple, almost Christian in their style and motifs, to Hermann Jonas's sermons there in the 1860s, or to Jellinek's Stadttempel sermons, there emerges a trend toward the convergence of sermon and derashah. This trend permitted Orthodox preachers like

---

[115] Chap. 12, verse 38.
[116] Leopold Zunz, *Gottesdienstliche Vorträge der Juden* [1832] (Frankfurt am Main: J. Kauffmann, 1892). The Prussian government prohibited German sermons in response to Orthodox demand. Later, the German sermon became a state requirement in many places.

Salomon Plessner and Samson Raphael Hirsch to share with Reformers the universe of preaching and emancipation Jacob.[117]

Already in their early sermons, Hamburg Reform preachers Eduard Kley and Gotthold Salomon were setting paradigmatic features of emancipation Jacob. They established Jacob's plea "I am unworthy of all the kindness and faithfulness you have shown your servant" (Genesis 32:10) as the model for all prayer, as the plea reflected the universal human condition: It expressed humility in recognition of human weakness and divine omnipotence, gratitude for divine grace, and sympathy for humanity in need of help, for fellow citizens of whatever creed. Jacob embodied the cosmopolitan citizen.[118] His journey abroad exemplified the pilgrim's journey on earth, and the vows in Bethel were a model of piety: Jacob asked God only for meager sustenance and clothing, anticipated hard work to earn a living, and looked forward to an eventual return, at the end of life, to the House of the Lord; hence he lay down the foundation stone.[119] Future Reformers would balk at this Christian pilgrimage and restore the House of the Lord for departed souls as a House of Prayer for the living, but they would, like Kley, view Jacob's vows as a model of piety and ignore the promise of the Land of Israel to Jacob in the Bethel covenant.[120] They would likewise relieve Jacob of the burden of the Christian–Jewish past by ignoring the rabbinic Jacob & Esau story. Paradoxically, Jacob was never as Christian in Jewish discourse as when early Reformers excluded Christianity from exegesis.

If religious difference did not goad the Jacob & Esau conflict, what did? Kley and Salomon focused on Isaac's disorderly household. Isaac and Rebecca failed to educate their children: They did not devote proper

---

[117] Alexander Altmann, "Zur Frühgeschichte der jüdischen Predigt in Deutschland," and "The New Style of Preaching in Nineteenth-Century German Jewry," in *Studies in Nineteenth-Century Jewish Intellectual History*, ed. Alexander Altmann (Cambridge, MA: Harvard University Press, 1964), pp. 65–116.

[118] Eduard Kley, "On Honoring God," in *Predigten* (Hamburg: Hoffmann und Campe, 1819), pp. 99–114; Gotthold Salomon, "Jakobs Sterne und Israels Scepter," in *Predigten in dem neuen Israelitischen Tempel*, 3 vols. (Hamburg: I. Ahrons, 1826): 1: 223–38. Reform variations: Moses Präger, *Gebet- und Erbauungsbuch für Israeliten*, 2d rev. ed. (Brilon: M. Friedländer, 1860), pp. 19–21; Leopold Stein, "Homiletische Beilage," *Der Israelitische Volkslehrer* 5 (1855): 127–28. For a more traditional rendering, emphasizing the hostile world from which prayer saves Jacob: Abraham Treuenfels, "Die Stimme Jakobs," *Predigt Magazin: Homiletische Monatsschrift* 1 (1874–75): 95–102.

[119] Kley, "The Wishes of the Pious," in *Predigten in dem neuen Israelitischen Tempel gehalten von Eduard Kley* (Hamburg: I. Ahrons, 1827), pp. 169–82.

[120] Salomon Formstecher, "Wie können Wir Gott verehren?" in *Zwölf Predigten* (Würzburg: Etlinger'schen Buchhandlung, 1833), pp. 176–92; Hermann Jonas, "Die Gelübde," in his *Nib Sefataim: Dreissig Predigten* (Hamburg: Frederking & Graf, 1870), pp. 149–56; Moses Präger, *Gebet- und Erbauungsbuch*, pp. 16–18; Leopold Stein, "Homiletische Beilage," 127–28.

attention to them, they were divided in their love for them, and they failed to see Esau's delinquency when it could still be corrected.[121] Bad parenting was not the only problem: The Jewish Matriarchs exceeded their proper roles as mothers. Kley launched a vicious attack on Rachel, for her jealousy of her sister's fecundity, her persistent pleas to God for sons, and her introduction of idol worship into Jacob's household. Leah, having competed with her sister for Jacob's love, came off only a little better. Her loveless marriage to Jacob, originating in treachery, was the epitome of a failed bourgeois marriage. Jacob's household violated every rule of monogamic bourgeois marriage.[122] Disruption of gender roles led to tragedy: Rebecca's manipulations ended in Jacob having to leave home, and Rachel's relentless pursuit of sons ended in her death. Parents, know your children! Young men and women, rationally plan your marriage! Fathers, put your house in order!

Jacob still emerged from his household troubles unscathed, a noble paterfamilias. While his wives were scuffling and conspiring at home, he was working day and night to increase the family's wealth, and reaping divine rewards. There is nothing wrong in property honestly gained, said Kley: Our Patriarchs were all rich.[123] Having arrived in the Land of Israel, Jacob resolutely put an end to superstition in his household, eliminating idol worship. Superstition, the obsession with magic, ghosts, dreams, and spirits of the dead, is the plague of religion. Kley beseeched his community to fight against superstition, never mentioning traditional Judaism or Catholicism by name.[124] He was offering a Jewish-inflected liberal Protestantism as authentic Judaism, and preaching misogyny and intolerance under the guise of enlightened liberalism.[125]

---

[121] Gotthold Salomon, "Das väterliche Segen," in *Predigten*, 3: 167–80; Eduard Kley, *Predigt-Skizzen: Beiträge zu einer künftige Homiletik* (Grünberg and Leipzig: Levysohn, 1844), pp. 247–74. Reform variation: Moses Präger, *Gebet- und Erbauungsbuch*, pp. 13–15. For an Orthodox dissent: Salomon Plessner, "The Silent Observer," in *Sabbath-Predigten für allen Wochenabschnitte*, ed. Elias Plessner (Frankfurt am Main: I. Kaufmann, 1888), pp. 51–60: The household conflicts are at work in a divine drama, the meaning of which for the future of the people of Israel is not clear even to participants.

[122] Eduard Kley, *Predigt-Skizzen*, pp. 294–304, 312–25.   [123] Ibid., pp. 304–12.

[124] Ibid., pp. 312–25. Salomon Plessner instead emphasized loyalty to the Torah, in the context of Ḥanukkah and the Hasmonaean opposition to Hellenization: "The Strict Responsibility," in *Sabbath-Predigten*, pp. 73–81.

[125] Yaakov Ariel of UNC suggests that this critical note on the early Hamburg Reformers is discordant with my otherwise sympathetic account of Reform Judaism. He is right: Kley and Salomon represented a unique type. In two millennia of Jewish and Christian exegesis, no one has attacked a matriarch as a petty and avaricious idol worshipper the way Kley attacked Rachel. Dying young in childbirth, buried on the roadside away from her husband and the family burial ground, Rachel became a tragic figure. She was the matriarch crying over the children of Israel, murdered or exiled from the Land, consoled

Moving to Mannheimer's Vienna, one encounters a different sermon culture. The rhetoric and didactic style seem similar, the bourgeois morals certainly are, and so is the choice of Jacob *topoi*: disorder in Isaac's household, God's majestically governed universe in Jacob's dream, and good citizenship.[126] Yet quietly, almost covertly, Mannheimer engages with the biblical narrative and overhauls the conventional view of Jacob and Esau in ways both more profound and more traditional than those of the Hamburg preachers. To Mannheimer, the struggle of Jacob and Esau was a story of missed opportunities, one of a futile and tragic struggle. Modernity would rectify biblical errors by choosing differently than Jacob & Esau did. Polished in his rhetoric, measured in tone, and politically savvy, the preacher who for four decades kept the notoriously contentious Viennese community together was an intellectual subversive.

Esau's cry to his father, upon hearing of Jacob's theft of the blessings, "Have you only one blessing, my father," represented, to Mannheimer, the key question that Jacob & Esau answered wrongly, with deadly consequences. God's blessing is multifarious: There was more than adequate space, goods, and tasks in God's bountiful universe for both Jacob and Esau. They vied in vain for worldly goods and ended up receiving, each precisely, the land that God had foretold for them.[127] Unusual for Reform sermons, Jacob himself played only a secondary role in Mannheimer's sermons, and he viewed Esau as a well-disposed but misguided fellow, a loss to Judaism. Like many Vienna youth growing up in homes devoid of Jewish education, said Mannheimer, Esau proceeded in a bad way. Just as young men in Vienna await their father's death to convert to Christianity, so was Esau waiting for his father's death to kill his brother. Mannheimer beseeched fathers to create a Jewish religious environment at home. For Mannheimer, as for Sofer, Esau became a rebellious son, an apostate, but he cared more about keeping him in the Jewish fold.[128]

Mannheimer highlighted the deceitful offer of Jacob's sons to the people of Shekhem "to live with you and become one people" (Genesis 34:16) and the Shekhemites' view that "these men [Jacob's tribe] are at peace with us" (34:21). The biblical episode ended tragically with the destruction of Shekhem by Jacob's sons, but the vision of

only by God's promise of their return (Jeremiah 31:15–17; Matthew 2:17). In the Kabbalah, she embodied the *Shekhinah*. Kley was using hate speech.

[126] Isaak Noah Mannheimer, "Warnung an Väter in Israel," in *Gottesdienstliche Vorträge*, 2: 1–19, and "Die Vorsehung" and "Die Pflichten der Fremden und Geduldeten," in *Gottesdienstliche Vorträge* (Vienna: Carl Gerold, 1835), pp. 117–36, 137–56, respectively.

[127] "Der Vatersegen," in *Gottesdienstliche Vorträge* [1835], pp. 99–116.

[128] "Warnung an Väter in Israel," 1–19. Reform variation: Salomon Formstecher, "Der Werth des elterlichen Segens," in *Zwölf Predigten*, pp. 162–75.

coexistence they articulated, and then violated, said Mannheimer, may come true with emancipation. He insisted that Jews were neither a *Volk* nor a *Nation* or society, and that they do not have a constitution of their own but abide by their homelands' laws and morals. He used "foreigners" and "natives" to describe the relationship between Jews and non-Jews, but he was clearly looking for a new vocabulary to articulate Jews' relationships with their homelands. In a few years, he would discover Jewish "ethnicity."

Jews were dispersed by God to spread His name among the nations, said Mannheimer. They were the Patriarchs' and the Prophets' descendants but also citizens and subjects, born and raised on German soil, and they strove to "become one people" with the nations among which they lived. To justify their claims for tolerance and human rights, Jews should reciprocate with brotherly love. Each advanced nation has its own mores and manners, and Jews should acculturate and acquire professions and crafts. They should uphold Judaism but recognize other religions, as the laws concerning idol worship did not apply to the advanced nations of the day, which abided by their ancestors' religions. Emancipation would realize a vision of brotherhood that had been shattered in biblical times.[129]

Mannheimer's sermon was entitled "The Duties of the Aliens and the Tolerated." He was calling on Austro-German Jewry to acculturate before emancipation: They were still "aliens" and "tolerated" and not citizens. Historians concur that German-speaking Jewry acculturated rapidly, and well before emancipation was complete, but they diverge on the extent of Jewish integration, that is, German Jews' ability to cross over into non-Jewish society. David Sorkin, focusing on the pre-1850 period, defines German Jews as an invisible community with its own subculture, and Marion Kaplan sees the formation of a Jewish bourgeoisie, separate in social contacts from non-Jewish ones. In contrast, Till van Rahden, focusing on post-1850 Breslau, finds Jews heavily involved in non-Jewish associational life.[130] He suggests that Jewish integration was more successful than that of the Catholics: German Jews crossed over and became national, whereas Catholics built their own institutions and cultivated a confessional identity. Emancipation presented a complex

---

[129] "Die Pflichten der Fremden und Geduldeten," 137–56.
[130] David Sorkin, "The Impact of Emancipation on German Jewry: A Reconsideration," pp. 177–98; Marion A. Kaplan, *The Making of the Jewish Middle Class: Women, Family, and Identity in Imperial Germany* (Oxford: Oxford University Press, 1991); Till van Rahden, "Jews and the Ambivalences of German Civil Society," 1024–47.

picture, and Jacob & Esau's changing identity hints at tensions and anxieties.

Jacob Katz thought that emancipation was grounded in misunderstanding: Its non-Jewish advocates expected the Jews to assimilate either by renouncing Judaism or by changing their socioeconomic profile, and often both. The Jews, for their part, had an unrealistic expectation of being accorded equal status with the majority. Both sides envisioned a utopian reality, and emancipation was doomed from the start.[131] This book takes a different perspective. The different expectations of Jews and Christians for emancipation reflected less misunderstandings and more permanent dilemmas of the European nation-state. Nationalism was emancipatory but sought uniformity, threatened pluralism, focused national anxieties on minorities, and demanded impossible assimilation. Throughout the age of emancipation, it was not obvious whether German Jews or Catholics were the major targets for nationalist anxieties. In today's Europe, Muslim and Roma communities meet with demands similar to those presented to the emancipated Jews. What gave the Jewish Question its special poignancy was the European scope of the Jewish Diaspora, its historical span, and the Jewish–Christian background. *Pace* Katz, Jewish emancipation tells a European story, one of utmost significance for Europe's future.

---

[131] Jacob Katz, "The German Jewish Utopia of Social Emancipation," in his *Emancipation and Assimilation*, pp. 91–110.

6   Jacob & Esau and Jewish Emancipation, II: 1840–1878

The 1840s and 1850s were decades of confessional realignment among German Jews. In the previous two decades, traditional Judaism had been losing its hold on German-Jewish communities, but neither the Orthodox nor the Reformers contemplated establishing alternative national organizations. Three Reform national conventions in 1844–46, where Reform rabbis failed to reach a consensus on confessional and liturgical reform, and the Geiger-Tiktin affair, 1838–40, when Breslau's traditional Jews, led by Rabbi Solomon Tiktin, failed to block the appointment of Abraham Geiger as a community rabbi, gave rise to major Orthodox and Reform institutional initiatives.[1] The Orthodox began to organize separate congregations, and in later years, to withdraw from the Jewish community altogether. Radical Reformers, frustrated with mainstream resistance to a clean break with rabbinic Judaism, established the Berlin *Reformgemeinde* in 1845. Arguing for autonomy, Reform and Orthodox Jews both used the idiom of religious freedom, which they shared with liberal Catholics and Protestants, all imagining a multiconfessional nation.

Most scholars designate as "Orthodox" only traditional communities that organize, nationally and internationally, to thwart the combined threat of nationalization and nontraditional Judaism. In the Russian Pale of Settlement and in Congress Poland, traditional Judaism remained hegemonic until the rise of Zionism. To be sure, nineteenth-century Jewish intellectual currents, including the Lithuanian *yeshivot*, reflected responses to the *Haskalah*, but the bulk of Jewry remained traditional, and the Haskalah did not undermine the leadership. In the nineteenth century, former Polish territories experienced the spread of *Ḥasidism*. In Galicia, Ḥasidism overwhelmed an early Haskalah, and nascent Polish nationalization proved no match for the Jewish traditionalists. The

---

[1] Meyer, Michael A., *Response to Modernity: A History of the Reform Movement in Judaism* (New York: Oxford University Press, 1988), pp. 100–142; Andreas Gotzmann, "Der Geiger-Tiktin Streit: Trennungskrise und Publizität," in *In Breslau zuhause? Juden in einer mitteleuropäischen Metropole der Neuzeit*, ed. Manfred Hettling, Andreas Reinke, and Norberg Conrads (Hamburg: Dölling und Galitz 2003), pp. 81–98.

contrast with German-speaking Central Europe was stark and was reflected in divergent visions of Jacob & Esau. Ḥasidic Judaism developed a vision of Jacob & Esau as complete Others, yet capable of peaceful coexistence in an illiberal multicultural society. Esau remained Christian, but he was not murderous.

Jewish confessional patterns in the Austrian Empire (and, from 1867 on, in Austria-Hungary) represented hybrids between those in Germany and Eastern Europe. Austria proper and the Czech Crown Lands replicated German divisions, but Vienna and Moravia retained a significant traditional Jewry, Reform was moderate, and the authorities permitted no withdrawal from the community. Hungary, in contrast, saw the first national split in the Jewish community and the genesis of Ultra-Orthodox (*Ḥaredi*) Jewry. When the Neologs, representing moderate Reform, reached a majority in the 1860s, the Orthodox withdrew and in 1867 established an alternative national organization.[2] This proved insufficient for the Ultra-Orthodox, who rejected acculturation outright. "And Jacob arrived safely [*shalem*] in the city" (Genesis 33:18), they interpreted, following *Midrash*, "perfect in his faith." Using the acronym of *shalem* (שלם) to designate "name" (שם), "language" (לשון) and "clothing" (מלבוש), they pleaded for retaining traditional Jewish names, language, and dress. They viewed modern Jews as a "mixed multitude," and demanded to be recognized as a different nation.[3]

Christian German communities likewise went through confessional realignment in the 1840s and 1850s. In 1845, when internal feuds broke out between Prussian Protestantism's liberal and conservative wings, Berlin preacher Ernst Orth recalled Jacob & Esau in Paul to redraw confessional boundaries against the fundamentalists.[4] The traditional asymmetry between Jewish and Christian typology, between Jacob & Esau's centrality in Jewish discourse and its relative marginality in the Christian one, remained unchanged in the age of emancipation. Yet the Christian typology remained alive and well among Catholics and

---

[2] Jacob Katz, *A House Divided: Orthodoxy and Schism in Nineteenth-Century Central European Jewry*, trans. Ziporah Brody (Hanover, NH: New England University Press, 1998).

[3] Michael K. Silber, "The Emergence of Ultra-Orthodoxy: The Invention of a Tradition," in *The Uses of Tradition: Jewish Continuity in the Modern Era*, ed. Jack Wertheimer (New York: JTS, 1992), pp. 23–84; Aqiva Yosef Schlesinger, "Letter to Montefiore in August and September 1874," quoted in Michael K. Silber, "Alliance of the Hebrews, 1863–1875: The Diaspora Roots of an Ultra-Orthodox Proto-Zionist Utopia in Palestine," *Journal of Israeli History* 27:2 (2008): 146.

[4] Ernst Orth, *Jakob und Esau: Drei Predigten nebst einem offnen Schreiben an Herrn Prediger Kuntze, als Antwort auf dessen am 15. Sonntage nach Trinitatis gehaltene Predigt* (Berlin: Oehmigke's Buchhandlung, 1845). The Evangelical State Church in Prussia represented a Protestant union of the Lutheran and Calvinist communities, ordered in 1817 under one roof by Friederich Wilhelm III.

Protestants alike, and entrenched in school textbooks. Its stability across both the Christian and Jewish spectra suggests that Christians and Jews accomplished no breakthrough in their relations. No vision of Christian–Jewish brotherliness emerged to accompany Jewish emancipation.

Indeed, the dearth of the scene of Jacob & Esau's reconciliation in Christian and Jewish discourse is striking. The reconciliation represented a potential model of national brotherhood, and its absence is a testimony to emancipation's limits: The nation was not capacious enough to allow Jacob & Esau to function as a national signifier. Reform Jews could not use Jacob and Esau to reconcile Jewish particularity and the nation's universality, only to silence Edom and reconfigure Jacob as a cosmopolitan, as Samuel Holdheim (1806–1860) did. The one notable exception to this generalization was Rabbi Samson Raphael Hirsch (1808–1888), the foremost representative of Jewish Neo-Orthodoxy, a marriage of Torah and *Bildung*. Having retained, unlike the Reformers, the Edom eschatology, he could reinterpret biblical reconciliation as presaging emancipation, and use Jacob & Esau in his commentary on Genesis (1867) to imagine an alternative messianism. Almost alone, he presented Jewish emancipation as fulfilling Jacob & Esau's reconciliation.[5]

The Edom eschatology did resurge, however, in Reform discourse in moments of crisis, violent as ever. At the height of the emancipation struggle in Austria in December 1862, none other than German integration's chief Jewish exponent, Viennese Rabbi Adolf Jellinek (1821–1893), burst out during an anxious sermon against emancipation's opponents: "Deliver me, I pray Thee, from the hand of my brother, from the hand of Esau; for I fear him, lest he come and smite me, the mother with the children" (Genesis 32:11).[6] Little did he know! ‏ניבא ולא ידע מה ניבא‏!

Christian Jacob & Esau: Catholicism to Liberal Protestantism

Ismar Schorsch has shown how modern Jewish Studies, *Wissenschaft des Judentums*, transformed Jewish consciousness by historicizing the rabbinic tradition and presenting its documents as embedded in historical cultures.[7] Yet Jewish Jacob did not fully reflect Reform Judaism's historical outlook: Preachers had no difficulty forming Jacob as a national

---

[5] *Der Pentateuch*, trans. and interpreted by Samson Raphael Hirsch, Part I: *Die Genesis* (1867), 3d ed. (Frankfurt am Main: J. Kaufmann, 1899), on Genesis 33:4. The Reform Jews' vision of a cosmopolitan messianic age emerged from the Prophets.

[6] *Predigten*, 3 vols. in 1 (Vienna: Carl Gerold's Sohn, 1862–66): 2: 203–14.

[7] *From Text to Context: The Turn to History in Modern Judaism* (Hanover, NH: University Press of New England, 1994).

type. Christian Jacob, however, was about to go through a radical transformation, and, among liberal Protestants, would lose his Christian identity. Historical criticism opened a gap between the Old and New Testaments, undermining Christian typology. But not quite yet: Remarkably, until the late nineteenth century, the turmoil created by higher biblical criticism, that is, the inquiry into the Pentateuch's sources and composition, did not register in an exegetical transformation of Christian Jacob.

Reform Judaism and liberal Protestantism shared the historical viewpoint, but historicization triggered no Jewish *crise de conscience* comparable to the Christian one. Liberal Jews accepted with virtual equanimity the results of biblical criticism.[8] For Christians, the historicization of the Old Testament had bearings on the character and mission of Christ and triggered the quest for the historical Jesus.[9] As Jacob was not only a patriarch but also a prefiguration of Christ and the church, Christology was at stake in maintaining typology. Only the limited audience of historical theology and the success of Restoration politics, which blocked the academic appointment of liberal theologians, explain how Christian Jacob could reign supreme long into the nineteenth century. Until the fin-de-siècle years, Jewish and Christian Jacob alike escaped historicization.

Hermann Samuel Reimarus (1694–1768), the German enlightenment Deist, opined in a posthumously published work that the Old Testament could not be a divinely inspired work. He protested the educational effects that stories about the Jewish ancestors from Abraham to Moses had on youth. Cunning Jacob committed fraud and Moses murdered, yet young people were told that God had chosen them to lead His people. Only the Jewish and Christian churches held books such as the Bible as

---

[8] This calls for caveats. Geiger joyfully historicized rabbinic literature and recognized biblical criticism's importance, but showed little inclination to engage in it; Ludwig Philippson had first declared biblical criticism unimportant, then, when the academic winds shifted, recognized it, feared lest it shatter the biblical text, but found a palliative in the unity of biblical message; Heinrich Graetz and Leopold Zunz (1794–1886), founder of *Wissenschaft des Judentums*, were supportive, and convinced that Julius Wellhausen's source criticism, with its antisemitic implications, was just wrong and could be overcome. Things changed around the turn of the twentieth century, when liberal Protestant scholars, discussed in chapter 9, began questioning the Old Testament's originality and moral stature. But early on, with the exception of Jewish Neo-Orthodoxy (discussed later in this chapter), there was little Jewish anxiety. See Ran HaCohen, *Reclaiming the Hebrew Bible: German-Jewish Reception of Biblical Criticism* (Berlin: Walter de Gruyter, 2010).

[9] D. F. Strauss, *The Life of Jesus Critically Examined* [1835], trans. George Eliot (Cambridge: Cambridge University Press, 2010); Albert Schweitzer, *The Quest for the Historical Jesus: A Critical Study of Its Progress from Reimarus to Wrede* (London: A. and C. Black, 1910).

divine.[10] God could not have spoken through the morally dubious Patriarchs. As to Jesus, he delivered a universal message compatible with natural religion, and his disciples distorted his message by claiming his resurrection and turning him into Christ. Reimarus proved too radical to be accepted by anyone, but he outlined future facets of biblical criticism and liberal theology.

W. M. L. de Wette (1780–1849), considered a founder of academic biblical criticism, questioned the historicity of biblical tales and figures, denied the Mosaic authorship of the Pentateuch, and pointed to two documentary sources, distinguished by their use of different names for God, *Jehovah* and *Elohim*, as composing the biblical narrative. De Wette distinguished between the biblical Hebrews and post-exilic Jews, thought that the Prophets represented the apex of the Israelite religion, and viewed Judaism as degenerated, petrified Hebraism. Jesus had recovered Hebraism's vitality. He struggled against rabbinic Jews, the Pharisees, who obeyed dead laws. De Wette grounded Christianity's theological claim to supersede the Jews in history and predated it to the Second Temple. Biblical criticism supported liberal theology. Judaism became a particularist religion averse to Christian universalism. Liberal Protestantism displayed Christian universalism, compatible with enlightenment natural religion.[11]

Liberal Protestantism was hostile to Jacob. De Wette regarded the Pentateuch as a literary document propounding national myths. Jacob & Esau's competition over Isaac's blessing reflected Hebrew myths on the origins of the conflict with the Edomites and advanced Israelite claims. Jacob's wandering and place naming reflected local myths on towns' origins. De Wette's rhetoric was not as strident as that of Reimarus, but his judgment on the Patriarchs, and the Hebrews, was similar: "It was very characteristic of the Hebrews that they did not shy away from the means Jacob deployed and that they made Jacob into an embodiment of craftiness. The Greeks, too, had their Odysseus, but how much nobler and more dignified he was in comparison with

---

[10] Hermann Samuel Reimarus, *Fragmente des Wolfenbüttelschen Ungenannten*, ed. Gotthold Ephraim Lessing, 4th ed. (Berlin: C.M. Eichhoff, 1835), pp. 288–90. Lessing had originally published the fragments, anonymously, in the 1770s.

[11] Thomas Albert Howard, *Religion and the Rise of Historicism: W. M. L. de Wette, Jacob Burckhardt and the Theological Origins of Nineteenth-Century Historical Consciousness* (Cambridge: Cambridge University Press, 2000); John Rogerson, *Old Testament Criticism in the Nineteenth-Century: England and Germany* (Philadelphia: Fortress, 1985); James Pasto, "W. M. L. De Wette and the Invention of Post-Exilic Judaism," in *Jews, Antiquity and the Nineteenth-Century Imagination*, ed. Hayim Lapin and Dale Martin (Bethesda: University Press of Maryland, 2003), pp. 33–52.

Jacob!"[12] Ancient Hebrews and modern Jews converged in the liberal nationalist imagination. Those who rejected Jacob found it difficult to welcome Jews into Germany.

Recognizing the distance that historical criticism had opened between the Old and New Testament, Friedrich Schleiermacher (1768–1834), the foremost German theologian of his generation, drew radical conclusions: Christology and typology were insupportable. The Old Testament expressed Jewish, and not Christian, religion, and should be declared noncanonical: "One has to abandon the whole theory . . . of revelation of God in the Jewish people."[13] This mattered little: "Living Christianity . . . does not need a stronghold in Judaism," as belief in Scriptures was superfluous to the religion of feeling and contemplation of the universe. Within a generation, biblical criticism and liberal theology had reconfigured Christian–Jewish relations in ways that would require a century to take hold. So radical was the change that Schleiermacher himself found it impossible to part with the Old Testament. His Jacob shows that he even retained loose typology: On his deathbed, Jacob, "seeing in his sons . . . all the generations that were to follow, pronounced on each of them, by the spirit of prophecy, a blessing specially adapted to the peculiar characteristics of he who received it."[14]

Liberal theologians from F. C. Bauer and the Tübingen school to Albrecht Ritschl kept historical theology alive in mid-nineteenth-century Germany, but biblical criticism, especially of the Old Testament, was stalled by the academic hegemony of de Wette's replacement in Berlin, Ernst Wilhelm Hengstenberg (1802–1869). Founder and editor of the *Evangelische Kirchenzeitung* for more than forty years, Hengstenberg campaigned against "unbelief" and indifference in the Evangelical State Church, which was the union of Lutheran and Reform churches established by royal decree in the early Restoration years in Prussia. An admirer of Calvin's biblical exegesis, Hengstenberg rejected historical criticism and inveighed against rational theology. Facing mounting national liberal currents, he managed to promote his protégés for academic appointments and to block liberals, thus containing biblical criticism until the 1860s.

---

[12] W. M. L. de Wette, *Beiträge zur Einleitung in das Alte Testament: Kritik der Israelitischen Geschichte* (Halle: Schimmelpfenning und Compagnie, 1807), pp. 117–41; quotation on p. 123.

[13] Henning Graf Reventlow, "The Role of the Old Testament in Liberal Protestant Theology of the Nineteenth-Century," in *Biblical Studies and the Shifting of Paradigms, 1850–1914*, ed. Henning Graf Reventlow and William Farmer (Sheffield: Sheffield Academic Press, 1995), pp. 132–48; quotation on p. 135.

[14] Friedrich Schleiermacher, "The Christian Training of Children," in *Selected Sermons of Schleiermacher*, trans. Mary F. Wilson (London: Hodder and Stoughton, 1890), pp. 146–67. Quotation is on pp. 159–60.

As Hengstenberg reaffirmed Christology and typology against de Wette and other critics, he moved in a biblical world that had already been historicized. He himself spoke of Jacob's family move to Egypt as a transition from nomadic life to settlement, including the acquisition of literacy. He dwelled on etymologies. Rather than view them, like de Wette, as originating in local myths, he underlined their symbolism. Esau and Edom conveyed heathen roughness and sensuousness. Jacob connoted artifice and overreaching, supplemented by Israel, God's fighter. *Elohim* and Jehovah were not two gods, and they did not indicate two documentary sources; they were aspects of one God: *Elohim* as he appeared universally, and Jehovah as the God of the Patriarchs, Israel, and the Church. The books of the Prophets referred to the Jacob story in Genesis, suggesting the Pentateuch's historicity and integrity. Isaac's blessings to Jacob & Esau foreshadowed Edom's and Judah's conflicts under King David; Jacob's blessing to Judah, "the scepter shall not depart from Judah … until Shiloh comes" (Genesis 49:10), presaged Christ, as did Balaam's oracle, "a star shall rise from Jacob" (Numbers 24:17); and Obadiah's prophecy (1:18), "the house of Jacob shall be a fire … and there shall be no survivor for the house of Esau," predicted the Church's universal triumph.[15] Rearticulating Christology, Hengstenberg ensured that Christian Jacob would hold its sway in the public sphere throughout the age of emancipation.

Schoolchildren continued to encounter Jacob in religious instruction. School textbooks are commonly conservative, and Christian biblical instruction was exceptionally so.[16] Until midcentury, Johann Hübner's *Biblische Erzählungen aus dem Alten und Neuen Testamente*, discussed in the previous chapter and more than a century old, was still the most popular Protestant textbook. Apprehensive about heterodox influences in education, the Prussian authorities in 1814 prohibited the use of anything but the complete Bible in catechism but still left Hübner intact. S. C. G. Küster "modernized" the book by introducing open-ended questions, encouraging reflection rather than recitation.[17] He also ensured that the

---

[15] Ernst Wilhelm Hengstenberg, *Dissertations on the Genuineness of the Pentateuch*, trans. J. E. Ryland, 2 vols. (Edinburgh: John D. Lowe, 1847), esp. vol. 1, and *Christology of the Old Testament*, trans. Theod. Meyer, 2 vols. (Edinburgh: T&T Clark, 1854), esp. vol. 1.

[16] Even progressive Jews revealed pedagogical conservatism: The 1869 Reform Jewish synod was sympathetic to biblical criticism, but encouraged teachers to exercise caution in rationally explaining miracles, lest they "confuse" the students. Ran HaCohen, *Reclaiming the Hebrew Bible*, p. 198.

[17] Samuel Christian Gottfried Küster, *Zweimal zwei und fünfzig auserlesene Biblische Erzählungen aus dem Alten und Neuen Testamente [nach Johann Hübner mit Fragen zum Nachdenken, nüzlichen Lehren, gottseligen Gedanken und Bibelsprüchen]* (Berlin: Enslin, 1819).

book conformed to current bourgeois morals: Nakedness disappeared from the Garden of Eden. Editions of Hübner-Küster were tweaked for different denominations, the Catholics included. After 1847, however, many Catholic schools used a current Jesuit catechism. It told the traditional Patriarch stories about monotheist Abraham and pious Jacob. Jacob was father of the tribes of Israel. His vows at Bethel were a model of piety, and his blessing to his son Judah presaged Christ.[18] Pious Christian Jacob was not a central catechist figure, but he showed up in all biblical instruction textbooks.

Jacob also appeared in Johann Matthias Schröckh's popular history book. A Lutheran Church historian of Pietistic origins, Schröckh (1733–1808) composed a universal history, adapted in infinite editions for the different German states. The last edition was used in Catholic schools as well.[19] Schröckh used the traditional Christian periodization, but wove ecclesiastical and sacred history into secular and natural history. In telling the history of the Hebrews, he presented the Patriarchs as emerging from nomadic society. Abraham was a loyal shepherd who recognized God in the midst of idolatry. God chose Abraham as the father of his nation, preparing the world for Jesus. At about 2000 BC, God ordered Abraham to go to Canaan and promised him the Land of Israel. God renewed the Covenant with his descendants, Isaac and Jacob, who, like him, were pious nomads. Jacob, whom God called Israel (the strong one), had twelve children, one of whom, Joseph, emerged from slavery in Egypt to save the empire from hunger. Schröckh's history left room for Christology, loosely tying Old and New Testament.

For the Catholic Church, the Scriptures' integrity became a battle cry against liberal Protestantism during the Restoration. Catholic sermons insisted on Christological interpretation of the Old Testament and revealed the traditional ambivalence toward Jews, occasionally expressing appreciation for the Jewish legacy. These were contentious years in Jewish–Catholic relations. The Catholic Church opposed emancipation, and liberal Jews used anti-Catholicism to forge a national alliance with liberal Protestants and promote secularization.[20] Not unexpectedly, Catholic sermons displayed, on the side of traditional theological stereo-

---

[18] Joseph Deharbe, *Katholischer Katechismus, oder, Lehrbegriff, nebst einem kurzen Abrisse der religions-Geschichte von Anbeginn der Welt bis auf unsere Zeit* (Cincinnati, OH: Verlag bei Kreuzburg und Nurre, 1850), pp. 7, 111, 62, respectively. Notably, Joseph rather than Jacob prefigured Christ.

[19] Johann Matthias Schröckh, *Lehrbuch der allgemeinen Weltgeschichte für katholische Schulen* (Stuttgart: Stoppani, 1845).

[20] Ari Joskowicz, "Jewish Anticlericalism and the Making of Modern Jewish Politics in Late Enlightenment Prussia and France," *Jewish Social Studies* 17:3 (2011): 40–77.

types, a host of new ones, deploring the Jews as ungodly capitalists. It is interesting to note that together with liberal Protestants, the Catholics also advanced the new charge of Jewish "legalism," blind obedience to laws with no regard for their spirit. Yet in later decades, Catholics presented Reform Jews as devoid of any religion on account of their break with the rabbinic tradition.[21]

All the same, Jacob's Christian identity continued to shield him from Catholic anti-Judaism. All of the Patriarchs prayed with humility, faith, and trust, said the Augsburg Cathedral's pastor, using Jacob as an example. In a eulogy to the Duchess of Saxony who had died in childbirth, he mentioned the Rachel exemplar, depicting her perfect marriage with Jacob, the "pious Patriarch."[22] Jacob remained a Christ prefiguration: Christmas sermons repeatedly suggested that Balaam's oracle "a star shall rise from Jacob" was fulfilled in Jesus.[23] Jacob's Bethel vision, of the heavens opening with angels descending and rising, was a vision of the church. Jacob was startled as he woke up because only Jesus would reassure Christians that they no longer needed to dread God's presence and show them the way to heaven.[24] The unity and hierarchy between the New and Old Testament were both reaffirmed.

The typology retained its hold on the Evangelical State Church in Prussia, too, and the church's leadership deployed Jacob & Esau to respond to liberal and conservative challenges. The liberal challenge came from the Association of Protestant Friends, the *Lichtfreunde* (Light lovers), established in 1841. They promoted a liberal theology that endeavored to conform to enlightenment universalism, keep pace with historical biblical studies, and respond to nationalist aspirations for an ecumenical German church. Their "rationalist" creed included a universal God, moral life and progress, an afterlife, and Jesus as the model of and means to an exemplary life. Lichtfreunde meetings grew to several thousand strong by 1845 and drew conservative fire. The *Evangelische Kirchenzeitung* used the Lichtfreunde as a lightning rod in its criticism of

---

[21] Walter Zvi Bacharach, *Anti-Jewish Prejudices in German-Catholic Sermons*, trans. Chaya Galai (Lewiston, NY: Edwin Mellen, 1993).

[22] Franz-Anton Heim, "Wie und um was wir beten sollen," *Predigt-Magazin in Verbindung mit mehreren Katholischen Gelehrten, predigern und Seelsorgern* 6 (1841): 128–29, and "Trauer-Rede," *Predigt-Magazin* 6 (1841): 172.

[23] Joseph Fuhlrott, "Das heute geborne Kind ist der Sohn Gottes," in *Predigten auf alle Sonn-und Festtage des Kirchenjahres* (Regensburg: Georg Joseph Maus, 1869), p. 52; Georg Rienecker, "Am Feste der Heiligen Drei Koenige," in *Predigten auf die Sonn- und Festtage des katholischen Kirchenjahres*, ed. Franz Keller (Nuremberg: Fried. Korn'schen Buchhandlung, 1868), pp. 87–88.

[24] Anton Lechner, "Die Kirche – Vorbild des Himmels und Thüres zum Himmel" [1828], *Predigt-Magazin in Verbindung mit mehreren Katholischen Gelehrten, predigern und Seelsorgern* 10 (1843): 304.

the State Church. The paper called on the Prussian king to intervene against the Lichtfreunde, and suggested that their demands for academic freedom and lay engagement in the church amounted to liberal constitutionalism. Unexpectedly, the Lichtfreunde became a movement for religious and national freedom.[25]

Throughout the summer of 1845, antigovernment protests using Lichtfreunde rubrics grew strong, arriving, on August 1, 1845, in Berlin. The Prussian government outlawed the gatherings. The church leadership in Berlin, long under pressure from the conservatives, grew alarmed. On August 15, eighty-seven noted ecclesiastical and civic figures signed a declaration chastising both the *Kirchenzeitung* and Lichtfreunde for endangering the church's unity. There could hardly have been a more distinguished group: two Lutheran bishops, sixteen pastors of leading churches, and high-ranking civil servants responsible for finance, school, and church administration. Most were academically trained, a few mildly liberal and nationally conscious, but none were radical. They criticized the conservatives for curbing religious freedom and vying for clerical hegemony. They affirmed the creed of "Jesus Christ as the sole and eternal source of our bliss," but expressed their support for pluralism in the church and called for inclusion of all parties in a discussion of its future.[26]

The declaration resulted in religious turmoil. Old confessional disputes had already been pulling the State Church apart. In July 1845, Friedrich Wilhelm IV recognized a confessional Lutheran Church, representing those who dissented from the state union of Lutheran and Reform Churches. Both liberals and conservatives now began to establish alternative communities. The 1847 Prussian Edict of Tolerance permitted Lichtfreunde and liberal Catholic congregations. In 1859, the Lichtfreunde united with liberal Catholics to establish an ecumenical national church, the Union of Free Religious Congregations (*Bund freier religiöser Gemeinden*). In the late 1840s, the conservatives began an international collaboration with Methodists and Baptists, and in 1851, they established the North German Evangelical Union. Friedrich Wilhelm IV supported their 1857 Berlin convention, distancing himself from his own State Church. Nationalism and religious reform were triggering a major church realignment in Germany.

---

[25] Todd H. Weir, *Secularism and Religion in Nineteenth-Century Germany: The Rise of the Fourth Confession* (New York: Cambridge University Press, 2014), pp. 47–53.

[26] The declaration was printed in Berlin papers on August 26 and, again, as part of Friedrich Julius Stahl's critique: *Zwei Sendschreiben an die Unterzeichner der Erklärung vom 15., beziehungsweise 26 Aug. 1845* (Berlin: E. H. Schroeder, 1845), pp. 3–4.

The Berlin church leaders were losers in this realignment. In the August 1845 Declaration, they sought to reassert their leadership as peacemakers of the Protestant camp. Yet the declaration backfired. Eduard W. T. Kuntze, pastor of St. Elisabeth Church, the Evangelical Union's future headquarters, led the charge, questioning, in a published sermon, the signers' creed and calling on their congregants to leave their churches.[27] Other attacks followed. The leadership's responses, in open letters and sermons, generated a minor literature.[28] In three artfully crafted sermons on Jacob & Esau, Pastor Ernst Orth (1803–1892) of the prominent Friedrichs-Werdersche Kirche endeavored to reestablish the leadership's credentials. He wished to show their conformity with the Lutheran confession, justify their politics as emulating Jacob, and explain the current church tribulations as Christian in character and not a crisis of faith.

Just as Luther had used Jacob as a countermodel to the Catholic saint, Orth used him to define the State Church's position against the Lichtfreunde and the fundamentalists. The world was divided into two spheres, the Christian spiritual one of Jacob and the heathen natural one of Esau. Their biblical story showed how Christians ought to live with wayward brothers. Orth's first lecture reclaimed the Pauline-Lutheran use of Jacob & Esau to describe the working of grace through faith, and hinted that both the Lichtfreunde and the fundamentalists endeavored, like Esau, to triumph via worldly deeds, through works. The second lecture presented Jacob's travails as punishment for his trickery in obtaining the blessings, and used his travails as a paradigm for the contemporary church. The third lecture made Jacob's struggle with the angel, God himself, the model for the Christian believer and the church's struggle for the blessing.[29] It also showed Jacob reconciling with Esau. Like Jacob, the State Church extended itself to non-Christians but never united with them.

Each of Orth's sermons focused on one of the three episodes at the center of Reform Jewish preaching: the blessing, the Bethel vision, and the struggle with the angel. Both Reform Jews and Protestants observed Isaac's dysfunctional household, criticized Jacob's polygamy and the matriarchs' envy and contention, and celebrated Jacob's wealth. Orth

---

[27] *Predigt [on Rom. xvi. 17, 18] über die Pflichten des Christen in dieser so bewegten Zeit, gehalten am 15. Sonntage nach Trinitatis 1845*, 2d ed. (Berlin: Bethge, 1845), pp. 11–15.

[28] O. W. Dietlein, *Die Berliner Erklärung vom 15. August 1845 und deren Literatur* (Berlin: F. A. Herbig, 1846).

[29] Orth reworked Luther's view that the angel was Christ and the struggle was spiritual: Jacob had to recognize that he could inherit the blessing only by submitting to God's grace. See David Steinmetz, "Luther und Calvin am Jabbokufer," *Evangelische Theologie* 57:6 (1997): 522–36.

also saw Jacob's exile in Haran as retribution for his trickery and training for perfection. Yet for Orth, the discipline and punishment of exile were part of the working of grace; hence he dwelled on Jacob's deficiencies, overlooked by most Jewish preachers. Orth reaffirmed the Christian typology: The Bethel vision presaged Christ's revelation to the youth in John (1:49–51), and the struggle with the angel foretold of Christ's tribulations at Gethsemane the night before the Crucifixion. Having triumphed in his struggle with the angel by submitting to divine grace, Jacob was endowed with the blessing, and with the church's universal mission. To Reform Rabbi Holdheim, the new Jacob-Israel would embody the chosen nation and receive a cosmopolitan mission. Protestant pastors and Reform Jewish rabbis shared a liberal bourgeois world, and their respective Christian and Jewish typologies developed in parallel, yet church and nation divided them as of old.

The audience for Orth's sermons was, however, exclusively Christian. Orth aimed to distance the State Church from the Lichtfreunde and rebut the fundamentalists. When speaking of the pride and blindness of Esau's descendants, he may have had the Jews in mind, too, but he kept his eyes on the Lichtfreunde. As to the fundamentalists, they erred in highlighting piety (*Gläubigkeit*) so that it became a channel for faith (*Glaube*), a value of its own, a Catholic work. They emulated Esau, who repeatedly tried to correct his ways, but instead of joining the church and serving Jacob, endeavored to inherit the blessing through worldly deeds and ended up conspiring to murder Jacob. The *Kirchenzeitung* should take note and cease its hate speech. The State Church emulated Jacob. Jacob could have assembled a coalition of princes to fight Esau, as the *Kirchenzeitung* did when it called on the king to intervene, but instead, Jacob fought spiritually – painful though the experience was – and sought to reconcile with Esau. Why were the fundamentalists refusing reconciliation?

Orth's Esau was a fallen Christian. Just as internal Jewish struggles in the wake of reform triggered re-Judaization of Esau as an apostate, so did the internal Christian struggles in the wake of liberal Protestantism complete the early modern transformation of Esau from a Jew into a secular Christian. Jacob, in contrast, remained Christian until the late nineteenth century. Only the triumph of liberal nationalism and the rise of racial antisemitism made liberal theology's turn against the Old Testament into mainstream and re-Judaized Jacob. Orth's use of the traditional typology to address a major church upheaval showed its vitality into the modern age across a wide spectrum of Protestantism. Christian Jacob signified obstacles to Jewish emancipation, however. Orth never imagined that Jacob & Esau's reconciliation could be relevant to the emancipation debate, and mainstream Protestantism appeared devoid of theological resources for accommodating the Jews as citizens. Christians who retained Jacob and the Old Testament could not easily support emancipation.

Even more worrisome was the anti-Judaism of those who were expected to support emancipation – the liberal Protestants. Their instinctive hostility to Jacob and the Old Testament paralleled their efforts to de-Judaize Jesus. Biblical criticism did not always produce the results they anticipated. They were happy to exclude the Hebrews from Christian culture but were distressed to discover Jesus' Jewishness, and chagrined when the leading Reform rabbi and Jewish Studies scholar, Abraham Geiger (1810–1874), showed him to have been a rabbinic Jew.[30] Ancient Hebrews and modern Jews were presumably millennia apart, but liberal theologians seemed inclined to deny the Jews any major contribution to European civilization. This was an ominous sign for Jewish emancipation. Jews wagered that liberal nationalism would overcome anti-Judaism, but the wager was implausible. Those who loved Jacob rejected emancipation on religious grounds, and those who hated him would not support it for racial reasons. Jacob & Esau show emancipation to have been in trouble before it ever took off.

Jacob's Diaspora Mission: Samuel Holdheim and Rabbinic Cosmopolitanism

Samuel Holdheim, rabbi of Berlin's small *Reformgemeinde*, and the most radical German Reform leader, made Jacob the founder of the Jewish diasporic mission. Holdheim received both *yeshivah* and academic education and led the campaign to release Judaism from its national associations and from the rabbinic tradition. With the destruction of the Jewish state and the people's dispersion, said Holdheim, the Jews had ceased being a nation. The preponderance of *halakhah* consisted of ceremonial laws intended to preserve a political community. To become German, Jews needed to shed any national pretension, anything that might identify them as a political community. Jewish marriage law should be annulled, and state laws permitting interreligious unions should take its place. Holdheim constructed a counterhalakhic Reform legal system by providing Talmudic-like rationales for remaking Judaism.[31]

---

[30] Susannah Heschel, *Abraham Geiger and the Jewish Jesus* (Chicago: University of Chicago Press, 1998).

[31] Andreas Gotzmann, "From Nationality to Religion: Samuel Holdheim's Path to the Extreme Side of Religious Judaism," in *Redefining Judaism in an Age of Emancipation*, ed. Christian Wiese (Leiden: Brill, 2007), pp. 23–62.

To Holdheim, Jewish monotheism represented the first and most authentic religion of humanity. Mosaic revelation was at the core of Judaism, and the protection of monotheism was the original aim of Jewish law. With monotheism's global progress, the value of these laws had diminished. In the Reform conventions of 1844–46, Holdheim pushed for radical liturgical reforms. He retained circumcision, but as working Jews could not show up in the synagogue on Saturday, he held services on Sunday and extended the shabbat's observance. Modernity represented the culmination of the Jewish messianic vision. As Jews become part of the nations among which they lived, Judaism would gradually be recognized as a universal religion. Holdheim made Jacob the original missionary for Jewish cosmopolitanism. His Jacob sermons advanced sustained criticism of rabbinic Judaism and affirmed the Reform mission, and yet they were invested in Midrash, displaying the conflicted world of a Reform Talmudist.

Waking up from his Bethel dream, Jacob expresses surprise at having found God in the place (Genesis 28:16). Holdheim took this as a cue for each generation's rediscovery of the Torah, and suggested three basic orientations toward Jewish Antiquity. The first, which he associated with Orthodoxy and took to be the rabbinic approach, regarded revelation and law as a one-time event and sanctioned ancient institutions and rites. The second regarded them as products of their time and no longer relevant. The third historicized them, and continuously renegotiated their meaning for today. This midway position was his, but he further insisted that scientific or national interest, as demonstrated by *Wissenschaft des Judentums*, was insufficient: Historicization must be religiously motivated by the wish to "find God in this place," by the study of Torah for its own sake (תורה לשמה). Past and present had to interact, as the angels going up and down on Jacob's ladder did. Holdheim called upon traditional Jews to rediscover God in this place today. "The Land on which you lie" (28:13), Zion and Jerusalem, were now wherever the House of God, founded by Jacob, was, wherever Jews encountered God. Holdheim's wonderful sermon was rabbinic in method and message alike: Jacob, once again, became the forefather of the rabbinic approach. But Holdheim did not see it this way. Like his Orthodox counterpart, he confused contemporary Orthodoxy with the rabbinic tradition. He did not realize that his approach was, despite himself, rabbinic.[32]

---

[32] Samuel Holdheim, "Die verschiedenen Auffassungsweisens des jüdischen Alterthums und unsere Stellung zu demselben," *Predigten über die jüdische Religion*, 3 vols. (Berlin: Julius Springer, 1855): 3: 1–10, and "Gotteshaus," *Predigten*, 3: 56–65. Yaakov Ariel opines: Both Orthodox Jews and Reformers were aware that identifying Orthodox

Holdheim made Jacob's struggle with the angel, ending with his being renamed Israel, the center of his Reform Jewish vision. The name change was emblematic of an identity transformation. The struggle with the angel was one between the old letter of the text (*Schrift*), now dead, and the human spirit. The spirit expressed itself in an exegetical tradition that continuously revealed new facets in the text and adjusted Judaism to changes. Like the mother of the tribe, Rebecca, contemporary Jewry did not know how to reconcile the twins fighting within it, old letter and new spirit, but the oracle revealed: "The elder (letter) shall serve the younger (spirit)"; text and letter must serve the innovative interpreter so that Judaism remains forever young.[33] Holdheim tweaked the Christian Jacob & Esau typology, which posed the dead letter of Jewish Law against the young Christian Spirit so that he could legitimate Reform Jacob (who was, *pace* Holdheim, a rabbinic exegete) as spirit against Orthodox Esau, decried as dead letter.[34] The exercise was as hilarious as it was irresponsible. It exemplified less the complex identity of Reform Judaism than it did the struggles of a yeshivah renegade who became a Reform preacher.

Once Holdheim turned his eye, and Jacob's struggle against the angel, from internal Jewish squabbles to Israel and the nations, Reform's identity emerged as unmistakably, and traditionally, Jewish. The Bible was emphatic, said Holdheim, that natural preference for first birth mattered less than individual merit. "Jacob" referred to contingency at birth; Israel, in contrast, meant God's fighter. It reflected the new mission that Jacob received to fight, spiritually, against darkness and superstition. Jacob, said Midrash, faced the angel after he had crossed back to retrieve jars of oil so that he could spread light and truth among the nations (the sermon occurred around Ḥanukkah) and eventually turn them from enemies to

---

Judaism with the rabbinic tradition and Reform with its overhaul was a charade; but it was one that suited them both well.

[33] "Der Kampf der jüngern mit der ältern Richtung im Judenthum," in *Neue Sammlung jüdischer Predigten*, 3 vols. in 1 (Berlin: Carl David, 1852), 1: 290–300. Holdheim was drawing בעו״ה on a familiar Reform trope. The *Reformgemeinde*'s 1845 manifesto stated: "We want to interpret Scriptures according to their divine spirit; we can no longer sacrifice our divine freedom to the tyranny of the dead letter." "Aufruf an unsere deutschen Glaubensbrüder," quoted in Samuel Holdheim, *Geschichte der Entstehung und Entwickelung der Jüdischen Reformgemeinde in Berlin* (Berlin: Julius Springer, 1857), p. 51.

[34] Abraham Geiger had it right: "The principle of tradition, to which Talmudic and rabbinic literature owed its rise, is one of constant progress and historical development, [so as] not to be enslaved by the letter of the Bible, but to interpret it, again and again, according to the spirit and cognizance of belief": "Der Kampf christlicher Theologen gegen die bürgerliche Gleichstellung der Juden," *Wissenschaftliche Zeitschrift für jüdische Theologie* 1:3 (1835): 349. Holdheim and the *Reformgemeinde* claimed for Reform Judaism the mantle that Geiger designed for the rabbis, and endorsed the Christian critique of rabbinic Judaism.

friends. The great empires of the past disappeared without a trace, said Holdheim, but Israel had survived and will survive, protected by God, until such day as it is recognized that the Jews were God's people, the ones who carried the divine mission to spread light, and that they alone may carry the name Israel, as the single carriers of God's mission.[35]

Holdheim made Reform Jacob once again the embodiment of the Jewish people. Without as much as mentioning Edom and Rome, he vindicated rabbinic eschatology but gave it a cosmopolitan character and a peaceful ending. Israel was in the Diaspora not just for its sins: God entrusted Israel with enlightening the nations. Adventurously deploying Christian tropes in his crusade against Orthodoxy, Holdheim remained grounded in rabbinic Judaism, and an ingenious exegete thereof. He spoke out for the exclusive Jewish inheritance of Israel, against Christianity, in ways that Moses Sofer would not dare (and think ill-advised). An anecdote, true or not, reveals Holdheim's ambivalent attachment to Jewish tradition. On the Day of Atonement, he would retire alone, between the morning and early evening services, to a Berlin neighborhood café. Malefactors slandered him for breaking the fast there. In fact, he went there so that he could quietly read all the prayers and liturgical poems that he had so valiantly fought to exclude from the service.[36]

Holdheim's cosmopolitan eschatology was contingent on silencing the rabbinic typology: Israel's struggle had to be singly spiritual, and the ending peaceful. Edom could not show up. Lest one suspect that Reform preachers were oblivious to rabbinic Jacob & Esau, Hermann Jonas's 1869 sermon, "The Purchased Birthright," removes any doubt.[37] Representative of the third generation of the Hamburg Temple preachers, Jonas provided a scholarly history of the typology, and suggested that emancipation transcended it.

---

[35] "Der Name Israel," in *Predigten über die jüdische Religion*, 3 vols. (Berlin: Carl David, 1853), 2: 1–12, and "Höre Israel, der Ewige unser Gott ist einzig!" *Predigten*, 2: 13–21. See also Holdheim's earlier *Jakob und Israel: Predigt* (Schwerin: Kürschner'schen Buchhandlung, 1841). Reform variations: Salomon Friedländer, "Das Bewußsein unsres Werthes, II: als Israeliten," in *Predigten: gehalten im Tempel der Genossenschaft für Reform im Judenthume zu Berlin* (Leipzig: Wigand, 1847), pp. 105–16; Jacob H. Jacobson, "Die Nennung Jisrael," in *Eine Auswahl Jisraelitischen Kanzlervorträge* (Leipzig: Fritzsche, 1854), pp. 41–53; Moses Präger, *Gebet- und Erbauungsbuch für Israeliten*, 2d rev. ed. (Brilon: M. Friedländer, 1860), pp. 13–21.

[36] Shmuel Yosef Agnon, "Samuel Holdheim," in his *A Shroud of Stories* (in Hebrew) (Jerusalem: Schocken, 1984), p. 160. Michael A. Meyer concludes his "'Most of My Brethren Find Me Unacceptable': The Controversial Career of Rabbi Samuel Holdheim," in *Redefining Judaism*, ed. Christian Wiese, pp. 21–22, with the anecdote.

[37] "Die erkaufte Erstgeburt," in his: *Nib Sefataim: Dreissig Predigten* (Hamburg: Frederking & Graf, 1870), pp. 141–49.

Esau's sale of his birthright to Jacob, said Jonas, was symbolic of a transfer from physical to spiritual power.[38] Among all of humanity, all of God's children, Israel was the first to reach consciousness of the divine, and received, in Sinai, the mission of serving as God's priests. Historically, Esau's physical power became identified with the Roman Empire, against which the Jews led a desperate struggle. Christianity, springing from Judaism, created yet a new Rome, which embodied intolerance and led a religious war against the Jews, using the sword to force its dogmas upon them and other people. The Jews displayed courage and martyrdom in the face of overwhelming power, and remained convinced of their mission and the eventual triumph of peace. Esau's statement "I am about to die" should serve as any empire's rubric: Its fate is to decline and fall, and all of humanity, all family members, will regather in one household, presumably the emancipatory nation-state.

(Catholic) Rome continues today to oppress the Jews, but elsewhere – one assumes in Germany and the newly emerging nation-states – a new brotherly relationship has emerged between Jacob's descendants and non-Jews. Israel holds no anti-Esau feelings toward its neighbors and claims no priority on account of being God's first nation. Just as the Hellenistic legacy – no longer the property of Greeks alone – has shaped civilization, so, too, has the legacy of Israel. Hellenes and Jews have created a new tolerant enlightenment culture, and society has become a "house of prayer for all nations." This is the fulfillment of the brotherly reconciliation and family peace that Genesis envisioned.

It was no coincidence that Jonas's vision of reconciliation came out in 1869, at the height of emancipation. For a brief moment, Jews believed that their dream of national integration would be fulfilled. Anti-Catholicism and a Jewish Protestant national alliance facilitated Jonas's recovery of Esau as Rome, but the nation-state as a heroic liberator was the core of his vision. There were limits to his reconciliation: Jonas bedeviled Esau, and so he could not claim him for his vision. In contrast with Hirsch's exegesis of Genesis, published two years earlier, the Hellenes, and not Esau, were Jonas's non-Jewish partners. Germans and Jews recognized themselves as inheritors of a shared Judeo-Hellenic culture, but it was not clear that Christians and Jews were reconciled. All

---

[38] Worldly Esau and spiritual Jacob represented "Judaization" of the Christian typology. They had appeared first in Ludwig Philippson's early 1840s sermons: "Die beiden Menschenklassen," *Shiloah: Eine Auswahl von Predigten*, 2 vols. 2d ed. (Leipzig: Baumgärtner's Buchhandlung, 1843–45): 1: 204–13. Remarkably, Philippson suggested that both were necessary: Inwardly looking Jacob went to Ḥaran to learn to respond to the challenges of daily life, for knowledge and virtue must find their application in worldly action.

the same, Jonas outlined an emancipation master narrative: a millennial reconciliation of Jews and non-Jews.

The question is why this narrative, full of grandeur and pedagogical potential, remained marginal. Jonas's exemplar appears unique among hundreds of sermons, and emancipation as reconciliation never became a trope. This suggests that Reform Jews were well aware of the limits and fragility of emancipation. In an 1855 homily on Isaac's conflict with the Philistines over wells, Frankfurt Reform Rabbi Leopold Stein suggested that the three wells were tracking historical relations between Jews and non-Jews. The first well reflected medieval conflicts, and the third well future universal freedom. His own generation was still in the second period, modernity, characterized by a well called "hostility" (שׂטנה; Genesis 26:21), reflecting obstructions to freedom.[39] Only for a very short period, in their elation over recent emancipation, did Jonas and Hirsch feel confident enough about its prospects to depict it as a millennial reconciliation.

Reform rabbis demanded redress from Christianity for past persecution. Imagining an acculturated medieval Spanish Jewry as their predecessors, they remembered well how the Spanish golden age had ended, and, from Heine to Graetz, constructed histories reflecting Jewish martyrology that called Christians to account and demanded that the present and future be different.[40] Edom eschatology, presaging bloody vengeance upon Christians, vanished from the Reform universe because it would undermine the demands for redress. Reform Jews also considered it undignified. They stated repeatedly that all of humanity were God's children, and that Jews were the first to recognize it. The only way for Edom to return was through Jacob & Esau's reconciliation. Reform rabbis were too hardheaded to believe that it would be accomplished anytime soon.

In his famous attack on *Wissenschaft des Judentums*, Gershom Scholem charged that apologetic preachers turned Jacob, "the prince of the nation," into a "municipal civil servant."[41] Nothing could be further

---

[39] "Homiletische Beilage," *Der Israelitische Volkslehrer* 5 (1855): 126.

[40] Ismar Schorsch,"The Myth of Sephardic Supremacy," in his *From Text to Context: The Turn to History in Modern Judaism* (Hanover, NH: University Press of New England, 1994), pp. 71–92; Heinrich Graetz, *Geschichte der Juden von den ältesten Zeiten bis auf die Gegenwart*, 11 vols. (Leipzig: Oskar Leiner, 1853–74), esp. 6–8; for medieval Spain and Askenazi martyrology in urban commemoration: Nils Roemer, *German City, Jewish Memory: The Story of Worms* (Hanover, NH: University Press of New England, 2010), pp. 71–90.

[41] "Reflections on Modern Jewish Studies" [1944], in *On the Possibility of Jewish Mysticism in our Time & Other Essays*, ed. Avraham Shapira, trans. Jonathan Chipman (Philadelphia: Jewish Publication Society, 1997), pp. 51–71.

from the truth for Reform rabbis. They reconfigured Jacob as a bourgeois paterfamilias but also as a cosmopolitan citizen, and he emerged more sublime than he had ever been, an embodiment of the highest ideals that enlightened Germans and Jews could fathom. Neo-Orthodox Hirsch and radical Reformer Holdheim were at one: Their emancipation Jacob advanced Jewish claims for dignified German citizenship.

In the 1850s, Holdheim assailed conservative Prussian philosopher Friedrich Julius Stahl, a converted Jew, who proposed a Christian nation-state that would deny Jews citizenship but protect an autonomous Jewish community.[42] A rabbi and a converted Jew circumscribed the possibilities for the nation-state, and debated the future of Germany and Europe. Jewish European history was never as vital as in the age of emancipation. Moses Sofer would have welcomed Stahl's proposal. He, and traditional Eastern European Jews, put their trust in imperial multi-culturalism in the hope of realizing Stahl's, as opposed to Holdheim's, vision. Yet imperialism could not always secure the result: In Hungary, where nationalization proceeded with a vengeance, Ultra-Orthodoxy defined itself as a Jewish national minority. Scholem was right that the nation-state ended up disappointing Holdheim's hopes for Jewish integration, but it was Reform and not Orthodox Jews, Holdheim and not Sofer, who provided the model of a proud fighting Jew to the Zionist youth of Scholem's generation. Scholem did not know his fathers.

Ḥasidic Jacob & Esau: The *Kabbalah* and Illiberal Multiculturalism

While non-German-speaking Eastern Europe is outside the focus of this book, a look at Jacob & Esau in nineteenth-century Ḥasidic literature may accentuate the typology's transformation in response to the convergent challenges of emancipation and acculturation. *Ḥasidism* spread in the early nineteenth century throughout the Pale of Settlement in Poland and Russia, and, across the Austrian border, into Galicia and northeastern Hungary. The majority of Eastern European Jewry, residing in Russia, had no immediate prospect of civic equality, but Hungarian and Galician Jewry did, and emancipation arrived in Hungary in 1867 and in Galicia in 1868. Acculturation and integration were vital, controversial, and divisive questions for traditional Jewry across the Russian–Austrian border. Ultra-Orthodoxy fought Magyarization in Hungary, the German

---

[42] Samuel Holdheim, *Stahl's Christliche Toleranz beleuchtet* (Berlin: Julius Abelsdorff, 1856); Avraham Doron, "Nationalism and Judaism in the Conservative Thought of Friedrich Julius Stahl" (in Hebrew), *Ẓiyon* 77 (2012): 67–94.

Haskalah and Ḥasidism struggled in Galicia, and the Russian Jewish Haskalah presented the establishment with ever-growing challenges. The matrix of Jacob & Esau, acculturation, and integration was Jewish European.

East and West diverged, however, not only in the greater prospects of emancipation in the West but, more crucially, in the imperial and pluralist context for Jewish politics in the East. Jacob & Esau's transmutation among traditional Jews had affinities throughout Europe: Esau became a Jewish *maskil* without quite losing his Christian character. But national and cosmopolitan Jacob, product of the nation-state and German acculturation, was virtually absent in the East. Moses Sofer's illiberal multiculturalism and his preference for empire over nation-state became Ḥasidic mantra.

The 1772 ban issued by the Gaon, Rabbi Elijah of Vilna (Vilnius), turned the diverse Pietistic mystical groups proliferating in Poland and the Ukraine, known as *Hasidim*, into a movement.[43] The groups were led by charismatic leaders who claimed mystical powers, the most famous of whom was Rabbi Yisrael Baal Shem Tov (Master of the Good Name, 1698–1760). After his death, the *Magid* (popular preacher), Dov Ber of Mezeritch (d. 1772), molded the movement's ideology, emphasizing simple people's access to God, joy and certitude in divine beneficence and gratitude for it, and the role of the *Zadiq*, the holy leader, as intercessor for the community with God. Discounting the value of wealth, erudition, and yeshivah study, Ḥasidism appeared to be a counterestablishment movement. Around the turn of the nineteenth century, Ḥasidic leaders began forming "courts" and passing leadership to their sons, rather than to disciples, establishing dynasties. By the mid-nineteenth century, the bitter fights between Ḥasidim and their opponents, the *Mitnagdim*, were over, and both sides united to repel the Haskalah challenge.

Ḥasidic commentaries retained rabbinic Jacob & Esau faithfully, but they, too, show the age of emancipation as a grace period in Jewish–Christian relations. Apocalyptic eschatologies are absent in Ḥasidism, and the rejection of Esau is tempered by recognition of his potential merit. Ḥasidic mildness is due in part to the Kabbalah's pervasive influence in Ḥasidism: The cosmogenic view of Jacob, exile, and redemption occupied the space of historical eschatology.[44] Ḥasidic emphasis on the

---

[43] Moshe Rosman, *Founder of Hasidism: A Quest for the Historical Ba'al Shem Tov* (Berkeley: University of California Press, 1996).
[44] See the discussions of the *Zohar* and Lurianic Kabbalah in chapters 3–4.

individual's access to God and the possibility of immediate deliverance reinforced the Kabbalah's pacifist import.

The Jacob & Esau struggle is virtually absent in the *Tanya*, the work of Rabbi Schneur Zalman of Liadi (1745–1812), Ḥabad Ḥasidism's founder. There is a hint to it, when Schneur Zalman adduces "one people [nation] will be stronger than the other" (Genesis 25:23) to buttress his image of the animal soul fighting the spiritual one over the governance of the human body, but, significantly, Esau is not mentioned.[45] Edom is solely the "exile of Edom," where the *Shekhinah* accompanies Israel. Schneur Zalman ruminates on the theogenic rearrangements enabling access to divinity in exile.[46] His Jacob is the Kabbalist one, the universe's central column. Jacob's kiss to Rachel is God's kiss to Israel, and the divine attributes of truth, love, mercy, and humility associated with Jacob emerge from the biblical narrative to the Kabbalist universe.[47] The *Tanya* retains the traditional identifications of Jacob, Esau, and Edom but the apocalypse is gone.

In contrast, the Jacob & Esau struggle is central to Ẓadoq Hacohen of Lublin (1823–1900), one of the most prolific and creative Ḥasidic rabbis.[48] Israel and Amaleq, the people recognizing God's universal rule and the people aspiring to terminate it, lead a cosmic struggle. Hacohen commonly folds Esau into Amaleq, suggesting that Amaleq was the essence of Esau, and that Haman, who conspired to destroy the Persian Jews, was the essence of Amaleq.[49] At other times, he underlines the difference between Esau, a Jewish apostate who fulfilled a constructive cosmic role, and Amaleq, whose role was singularly destructive.[50] Yet Amaleq appears less as a historical people than as a cosmic principle: Amaleq is the evil inclination. Israel's struggle with Amaleq is internal more than historical, a fight to overcome the evil instinct. Amaleq's elimination, associated with Jewish redemption, means eradication of the evil instinct and not genocide.[51] Ḥasidic reworking of the Kabbalah thus shows marks of modernity and the Enlightenment.

---

[45] *Liqute Amarim: Tanya* (New York: Qehot Publication Society, 1956), pp. 13b–14a.

[46] "Igeret ha-Qodesh," in: *Tanya*, pp. 133b, 140a, 152b.

[47] *Tanya*, pp. 19a, 41b, 64a–b; "Igeret ha-Qodesh" and " Quntras Aḥaron," in *Tanya*, pp. 103b, 109b, 110b, 111a, 147a, 161b.

[48] My thanks to Yitzhak Melamed, Hilda Nissimi, and Elchanan Reiner for directing me to Ẓadoq Hacohen, and to Zohar Maor of Bar-Ilan University for providing me with the relevant references. יבואו על הברכה.

[49] *Ẓidqat ha-Ẓadiq* (The righteousness of the righteous) (Lublin: n.p., 1913): 250; *Divre Sofrim* (Words of scribes) (Lublin: n.p., 1939): 38.

[50] *Resisei Layla* (Drops of the night) (Lublin: n.p., 1926): 37.

[51] Ibid.: "The complete victory, the sacrificing of the bad instinct, is the eradication of all idol worshipping; hence you find [Amaleq's] destiny is to be destroyed." In *Resisei Layla* 15 and 18, Hacohen suggests that Esau and Amaleq have no real existence. Amaleq

Hacohen's Jacob & Esau responded to maskilic pleas for acculturation. Israel and the nations lead separate but codependent existences. The nations descend from Esau, and each has a virtue moving it, and a role in the divine plan. The virtues represent extremes, and the Torah mediates all of them, as conveyed by the Midrash about God offering the Torah first to the nations, which rejected it. Like Jacob, the Torah is the center pillar of the universe, deviating neither right nor left. The danger of exile is that Jews would absorb national virtues rather than adhere to the Torah. The Jews' redemption would come when the nations realize that they would not swerve from the Torah. Truly, the nations exist for Israel, so that converts like Rabbis Aqiva and Meir could join Israel, and, eventually, at the end of days, all recognize the God of Israel and serve Israel. Amaleq alone has no such prospect, and it must disappear.[52] Hacohen essentializes differences between Jews and non-Jews and stresses cultural separation, while at the same time affirming their common origins, border crossing possibilities (converts), and peaceful coexistence. Rabbinic Judaism emerges triumphant from a traditional narrative tweaked to accommodate nineteenth-century views of a multinational world and to render maskilic acculturation unnecessary.

Emancipation age re-Judaization of Esau reaches a high point in Ẓadoq Hacohen. Esau was born in holiness, made of the same drop (טיפה) as Jacob, and – Hacohen insists – was circumcised. Jacob held onto his heel in order to draw his holiness and, in buying the birthright, took over Esau's righteous descendants, the converts to Judaism. Esau was conscious of the Torah commandments but rejected them because, born "completely made" (עשוי), he saw no point in striving (השתדלות) for improvement. Full of desire and appreciation of material goods, he, like the *maskilim*, obeyed only the dictates of reason and nature, such as honoring parents. He pretended to his father, however, that he observed the entire Torah, and hypocrisy was his epithet. Isaac was aware of his worldliness but hoped that his prowess and courage would serve Jacob, as the Torah required material sustenance. But Esau maligned Jacob to Isaac, and used his power to bad ends. He received his due: Isaac blessed

---

represents contingency, the idea of the lack of necessity in the order of creation, which is patently false. Likewise, Esau represents the imagination of a self-contained material world, which is nothing but an illusion because the creation is full of divinity. Esau being "hated" by God (Malachi 1:2) is just the opposite image of reality, full of divine love. Esau's and Amaleq's vanishing is merely the end of an illusion.

[52] Ibid., 37, 42, 52; *Poqed Aqarim* (Visitor to the barren ones) (Lublin: n.p., 1922): 7. Amaleq had no virtue, but as a mirror image of Israel, he was able to change capacities at will and to incite everywhere against the divine plan. But in *Ẓidqat ha-Ẓadiq* 250, it appears that Amaleq (identified with Esau) does have merit: converts to Judaism. It is prohibited to receive Amaleqites as converts, but those who did convert become Jews.

Jacob, "your curser will be cursed." Esau became father of the nations, yet he is for Hacohen a model of the Jewish apostate. Whether a Jewish offender or a Christian convert, Esau remains, *pace* Sofer, Jacob's brother.[53]

Hacohen's Jacob is molded in the *Zohar*'s image, without blemish, a perfect mediation of Abraham and Isaac's virtues, as well as those of the nations. In contrast with Esau, Jacob was perfect in his faith in God, independent of reason, and free of any improper desire, especially sexual. All his deeds reflected devotion to God and aimed at the fulfillment of his mission as the Jewish people's ancestor. The purchase of the birthright drew Esau's holy parts into Judaism and expunged desires (the boiling potage) impeding its advent. As the world is full of lies and but an illusion, Jacob had to deploy deception to accomplish his mission, hence the "enclothing" in Esau's garments, those of Adam. The declaration to his father "I am Esau your firstborn" laid claim to future converts to Judaism and to the Jewish offenders, insisting that they who seem to belong to Esau actually belong to Jacob. Esau had the power to separate himself from Israel, but Reform Jews, Jacob's descendants, do not. Against Sofer and the Ultra-Orthodox, Hacohen affirms that even Jewish offenders (פושעי ישראל) are full of *miẓvot*, and no matter how sinful, they remain Israel.[54]

Ẓadoq Hacohen's reworking of Kabbalist Jacob & Esau extended across Ḥasidism. The Sefat Emet, Rabbi Yehudah Leib Alter (1847–1905), leader of Gerrer Ḥasidism, affirmed similar rationales for Jacob's trickery: In a world of lies, the pious aiming at the truth must be cunning, and God so wished. Through Isaac's blessing to Jacob, the world's bounty increased, and Esau and the nations benefited as well. Esau still received the worldly blessing – this was not Jacob's blessing but the one of Abraham, that he become father of Israel – but he had to receive it through Jacob. It could not have been otherwise. Esau contemplated repentance, and Isaac's blessing was to help him, but kabbalistically, Isaac represented judgment, and correction could come only when mercy and judgment converged. Esau's willpower to become a good Jew failed, yet his head was buried with the Patriarchs in acknowledgment of his partial holiness.[55]

The Sefat Emet continued the conversion of Jacob & Esau's struggle from a politico-historical to a cosmic spiritual one. Righteous biblical

---

[53] Ibid. 47; *Divre Sofrim*, 28, 38; *Ẓidqat ha-Ẓadiq*, 228; *Yisrael Qedoshim* (Holy Israel) (Lublin: n.p., 1928): 7.

[54] *Divre Sofrim*, 28, 38; *Ẓidqat ha-Ẓadiq*, 250, 245; *Resisei Layla*, 34, 47.

[55] *Sefer Sefat Emet* (Book of the language of truth), 5 vols. (Piotrków: n.p., 1905), 1: Toledot 1873, 1877, and 1884, respectively.

figures until Jacob represented a contingency, and only with Jacob, Israel's ancestor, was the world's continuous improvement assured. Esau represented the principle opposing improvement, but as such, he was coterminous with Jacob's project, his opposition serving to increase its holiness. Jacob & Esau's struggle reflected the soul's struggle to control the body. When Jacob triumphed over Esau's angel, his name changed from Jacob, alluding to the body (heel), to Israel, signifying the soul's mastery. Such spiritual triumphs were possible independent of who governed the world. Those subject to the Torah were free of political rule and protected from evil powers (סטרא אחרא). "One nation will be stronger than the other": When the heavenly kingdom rises, the human one vanishes. For bloody medieval eschatologies, Ḥasidism substituted spiritual pacifist odysseys, matching its calculated political reticence and its loyalty to the government.[56]

Ḥasidic political docility contrasted with maskilic calls for engagement. The de-historicization of Jacob & Esau reflected Ḥasidism's benevolent view of Jewish–Christian relations, but at the same time, it also avowed Jewish superiority and hostility to acculturation. If Ẓadoq Hacohen found in converts to Judaism the main rationale for non-Jews' existence, the Sefat Emet declared that converts' souls never ascended to heaven as did those of ethnic Israel, and the interiors of Jewish souls were superior to any among the nations.[57] Notwithstanding the emphasis on Esau's holy origins, he had an animal-like soul, in contrast with Jacob's divine soul, and the nations inherited the one, Israel the others. Ẓadoq Hacohen never tired of mentioning that the miẓvot were intended for Israel alone. The Sefat Emet opined that the conditional tense of Jacob's blessing, and the unconditional one of Esau's blessing, suggested that the nations, too, depended on Israel's observance of the Torah, as the bounty descending on earth would cease should Jewish observance fail.[58] Ḥasidism drew an illiberal multicultural vision of the peaceful coexistence of closed Jewish and Christian communities.

The Sefat Emet captured inimitably the Ḥasidic spirit in his rendering of Esau's kiss. *Genesis Rabbah*'s (78:9) play on "and he kissed him" (וישקהו) and "and he bit him" (וישכהו) should not be explained, he suggested, by the disingenuousness of Esau's kiss but by its effect: The kiss was worse than a bite. Recognizing that he could not overcome Jacob in war, Esau decided to undermine him by intimacy. Foreigners' friendship was worse than their violence, and acculturation was more dangerous than persecution.[59] Unchallenged by emancipation, and confident in its

---

[56] Ibid., Toledot, 1880, 1876, and 1885, respectively.   [57] Ibid., Toledot, 1901.
[58] Ibid., Toledot, 1884.   [59] Ibid.

mastery over a preponderantly traditional Jewry, Hasidic leadership turned Jacob & Esau polemics away from Christianity and against the maskilim. Just as Esau and the Reform Jew converged in Sofer's imagination, so did Esau and the maskil in Hasidic discourse. Across Central and Eastern Europe, Esau, for traditional, Orthodox, and Reform Jews alike, became a liminal figure between Christianity and Judaism.

Esau's Kiss: Samson Raphael Hirsch and Jacob & Esau's Reconciliation

German Jews could not avail themselves of Kabbalist cosmic struggles or ethnic superiority in responding to emancipation. Kabbalah undercurrents may have survived in nineteenth-century Germany, but Neo-Orthodox and Reform rabbis were united in their rejection of it, and critical of Hasidism.[60] German Jews endeavored to overcome antisemitic racialization of character and argued that *Bildung* shaped personality. They could not respond to antisemitism with counterracialization but needed to deploy Enlightenment universalism. The Neo-Orthodox challenge was to reconcile the Jacob & Esau eschatology with the Enlightenment. It was a tall order.

Jewish Neo-Orthodoxy sought to bridge Bildung and rabbinic Judaism. It combined strict religious observance and affirmation of traditional belief with German education and civic engagement. A generation of university-educated Orthodox rabbis, a rabbinic seminary in Berlin, several journals, and an expansive literature, including Hirsch's programmatic and pedagogical writings and his Torah commentary, Rabbi Jacob Ettlinger's (1798–1871) responsa, Rabbi Azriel Hildesheimer's (1820–1899) scholarly research and children's literature – all shaped the life of observant German Jews. In the 1850s, the movement made strides in Moravia and Hungary, regions of the Austrian Empire undergoing modernization but with a traditional Jewry. The rise of Hungarian Ultra-Orthodoxy in the 1860s curtailed Neo-Orthodox influence there. Like Reform Judaism, Neo-Orthodoxy never got a foothold in Eastern Europe. A German phenomenon, it provided a blueprint for future modern Orthodoxy.[61]

---

[60] Werner Cahnman, "Friedrich Wilhelm Schelling and the New Thinking of Judaism," in his *German Jewry: Its History and Sociology* (New Brunswick, NJ: Transactions Books, 1989), pp. 209–48; Mordechai Breuer, "Orthodoxy and Change" (in Hebrew), in *Torah im Derekh Eretz Movement*, ed. Mordechai Breuer (Ramat-Gan: Bar-Ilan University, 1987), pp. 85–86.

[61] Michael K. Silber, "Orthodoxy," *The YIVO Encyclopedia of Jews in Eastern Europe* (New Haven, CT: Yale University Press, 2008), pp. 1292–97; Mordechai Breuer, ed., *Torah im Derekh Eretz Movement*; Andreas Gotzmann, *Jüdisches Recht im kulturellen Prozess: Die*

Emancipation guided Neo-Orthodoxy's pursuit of German culture. Hirsch's writings radiated German Jewry's hopes, and his Genesis commentary drew a majestic vision of emancipation as Jacob & Esau's mutual recognition. Hirsch uniquely joined Reform and rabbinic views of Esau, and redrew the biblical narrative in original and sophisticated ways, accepting rabbinic Jacob & Esau and the Edom eschatology, yet inventing a peaceful cosmopolitan end. His vision explains why modern Orthodox congregations around the globe still find Hirsch's commentary appealing today (in an English translation), and why traditional Eastern European Jewry, with limited emancipation prospects, never did.[62]

Hirsch was an imposing person, self-possessed and distant in manner, full of opposites. Bourgeois in his bearing and stylish in his dress, he had a family of ten children, yet instituted women's education and inveighed against their diminution. He accepted the Haskalah's program and, like the Reformers, insisted on the compatibility of Judaism and the Enlightenment, but his Judaism included full observance of the Torah. A brilliant intellectual and an eloquent preacher, he aspired to interpretive simplicity and clarity, spent only one year each in a yeshivah and at a university, questioned traditional Talmudic study, opposed Wissenschaft des Judentums, and offered his own symbolic interpretation of the Torah, the product of a systematic philosophical mind, instead. He exempted students from covering their heads unless during Torah study, and tried to expunge the hallowed "Qol Nidrei" from the Yom Kippur service, but turned belief in a heavenly Torah into a dogma, and inveighed against the historical view of the oral tradition. An articulate spokesperson for *Torah im Derekh Erez* (Torah with worldly engagement), and teacher of historian Heinrich Graetz and radical Reform leader Kaufmann Kohler, he opposed the Orthodox Berlin seminary for rabbis and declined to establish a yeshivah in Frankfurt. He began his career by opening traditional Judaism to German Bildung and ended it with a withdrawal of his Orthodox Frankfurt congregation from the Jewish community.

Born to a merchant family in Hamburg, Hirsch studied with Isaac Bernays (1792–1849), the traditional but German-acculturated spiritual leader of the Hamburg community, appointed as a compromise candidate in the aftermath of the Temple controversy. He spent a year

---

Wahrnehmung der Halacha im Deutschland des 19. Jahrhunderts (Tübingen: Mohr Siebeck, 1997).

[62] Samuel Raphael Hirsch, *Der Pentateuch 1*: Genesis 33:4; *The Pentateuch*, trans. Isaac Levy, 2d rev. ed. (London: I. Levy, 1963); *Ḥamishah Ḥumshe Torah* (in Hebrew), trans. Mordechai Breuer (Jerusalem: Mosad Yiẓḥak Breuer, 1966). The popular English edition, *The Hirsch Chumash*, trans. Daniel Haberman (New York: Feldheim, 2000), represents an abridgment.

(1828–29) in Ettlinger's yeshivah in Mannheim, followed by a year at the University of Bonn, with Abraham Geiger as a classmate. A student of the first notable modern Orthodox rabbis, Hirsch recognized by the 1830s that German sermons and cosmetic liturgical changes would not save traditional Judaism. His *Nineteen Letters on Judaism* (1836) and *Ḥorev* (1837) outlined an agenda for Jewish renewal by reading Enlightenment values into Jewish law, sketching Jewish civic engagement and a cosmopolitan mission, and, conceding the woeful inadequacy of traditional Jewish education, offering a pedagogical program combining Torah and German Bildung.[63] Overnight he became a spokesman for traditional German Jews, and by 1839, he was heading the opposition to Geiger's reform proposals.

Appointed rabbi in Oldenburg in 1830, Hirsch moved on to Emden in 1841, and in 1846 was appointed to the prestigious rabbinate in Nikolsburg, Moravia, a position that made him the chief rabbi of Moravia and Austrian Silesia a year later. He headed the Nikolsburg yeshivah and served in the *Landtag*, where in 1848 he tried to advance Jewish emancipation. In the yeshivah, he modified the Talmudic curriculum to include study of the Psalms. But he felt resistance from both traditionalists and Reformers, and in 1851 left the coveted position to build up the small Orthodox congregation, Adat Jeschurun, recently established in Frankfurt. An indefatigable publicist and organizer, burning with the mission to construct an acculturated faithful Judaism, Hirsch was a spiritual leader not content with yeshivah learning or adept at negotiating compromise.

He shaped Adat Jeschurun as an ideal modern Orthodox community, affluent, acculturated, and devout. Under his leadership, it quadrupled in size to two thousand. He was intimately involved in running its institutions, from the new synagogue to the *Realschule*, fashioning ritual, designing school curricula (for both boys and girls), and writing teaching manuals. In 1854, he founded *Jeschurun*, a scholarly monthly. His Torah and Psalms commentaries, written in German, his *siddur* and *Haggadah*, all aimed at building Orthodox community life. He had little appreciation for Talmudic erudition or for learning for its own sake, and opened neither a yeshivah nor a gymnasium or seminary, which could have sustained a future rabbinic leadership. His ideal *Mensch-Israel*, a modern observant Jew, conscious of Israel's divine mission while socially engaged, the embodiment of Enlightenment and Torah universalism, was not shaped in the image of a rabbi.

---

[63] Ben Usiel (pseud.), *Neunzehn Briefe über Judentum* (Frankfurt am Main: J. Kaufmann, 1911); Samson Raphael Hirsch, *Horev: Versuche über Jissroels Pflichten in der Zerstreuung, zunächst für Jissroels denkende Jünglinge und Jungfrauen* (Frankfurt am Main: J. Kaufmann, 1909).

Hirsch's impatience with academic learning converged with his theological dogmatism into a rejection of modern Jewish Studies that was unique in its force, but indicative of the difficulties faced by Orthodoxy in accommodating a historical understanding of Judaism. Orthodox and Reform Judaism's divergence on historicizing the rabbinic tradition polarized them even more than their disagreements on observance. Liberal Jews joyfully engaged in historical scholarship, recovered rabbinic literature in its historical context, and used scholarship to advance emancipation and reform. They vindicated Jewish culture against Christian charges of fossilization, and refashioned Judaism to meet citizenship. In contrast, Orthodox scholars' ability to take part in Wissenschaft des Judentums remained constrained.[64] Neo-Orthodoxy asserted the uninterrupted transmission of an Oral Torah revealed at Sinai, and became the sole Jewish branch to reveal anxieties about history reminiscent of the crisis history occasioned among Christians.

To be sure, Hirsch's opposition to modern Jewish Studies represented an exception.[65] Hildesheimer and David Zevi Hoffmann did academic scholarship at the Berlin rabbinic seminary, although they stopped well short of biblical criticism, which remained the butt of Hoffmann's disparagement. When Hirsch, in consecutive issues of *Jeschurun*, conducted a book-length attack on Graetz for his handling of the oral tradition, he must have raised eyebrows.[66] Yet Neo-Orthodoxy defined itself against the Reformers as defender of an authentic single revelation at Sinai, containing both the written and oral Torah. Ettlinger's 1845 manifesto against the Braunschweig Reform rabbinic conference, signed by 116 rabbis from Central and Western Europe, came under the title: "Perfect in the Faith of Israel" (שלומי אמוני ישראל).[67] Hildesheimer declared an observant Jew, Rabbi Zacharias Fraenkel (1801–1874), founder of the

---

[64] Admittedly, liberal scholars, too, showed limited appetite for high biblical criticism: Rabbinic and not biblical Judaism required rescue from Christian attacks and historicization to legitimize reform, and, hence, it received greater attention: Leopold Zunz, "Etwas über die rabbinische Literatur," in his *Gesammelte Schriften*, 3 vols. (Berlin: Gerschel, 1875), 1: 1–31; M. H. Goshen-Goldstein, "Christianity, Judaism and Modern Bible Study," *Vetus Testamentum Supplements* 28 (1975): 69–88. There was also residual apprehension about tampering with revelation: Max Wiener, *Jüdische Religion im Zeitalter der Emanzipation* (Berlin: Philo, 1933), pp. 228–30. Yet Geiger and his compatriots easily managed the transition from biblical to rabbinic Judaism.

[65] David Ellenson, *Rabbi Esriel Hildesheimer and the Creation of a Modern Jewish Orthodoxy* (Tuscaloosa: University of Alabama Press, 1990).

[66] "Geschichte der Juden: Vom Untergang des jüdischen Staats bis zum Abschluß des Thalmuds," *Jeschurun* 2 (1855–56): 47–69, 89–103, 156–76,198–214, 315–25, 424–42, 529–49; 3 (1856–57): 63–78, 229–54, 396–413, 557–71; 4 (1857–58): 289–307, respectively. Trans. as *The Origin of the Oral Law*, vol. 5 of *Collected Writings of Rabbi Samson Raphael Hirsch*, 8 vols. (New York, Feldheim, 1997).

[67] *Shelome Emune Yisrael = Treue Gläubige in Israel! Erklärung gegen die Beschlüsse der Braunschweiger Rabbiner-Versammlung 1844* (n.p.: n.p., 1845).

Breslau rabbinic seminary, an apostate on account of his statement on the oral tradition's historicity.[68] Hirsch merely accentuated the Orthodox trend.

The trend was new. Tacit beliefs had remained background knowledge for much of Jewish history; now they were formulated as dogmas. Brief Talmudic excursions into theology suggest that in defining itself against a diversity of *minim*, rabbinic polemics may have indulged, on occasion, in a similar exercise. Maimonides (and a few others) formulated principles of Jewish belief in response to medieval Christian theology. These were exceptions. For the most part, traditional Judaism was indifferent to dogma: The Sabbateans, and not mainstream Jews, declared before performing a *mizvah*, "I believe in perfect faith." Rejecting the historical vision, Neo-Orthodoxy defined Judaism in a nontraditional fashion.[69] Most Orthodox leaders did so with a certain unease. Ettlinger and Hildesheimer disliked the Christian label "Orthodox" and preferred *Traditions-* or *Torahtreu* instead. Hirsch alone carried the tag "Orthodox" proudly, and by the 1880s, it became conventional.

Hirsch's Jacob & Esau represented a convergence of daring originality and traditionalism. His originality can be measured against two contemporary Reform Torah commentaries. Philippson's work was surprisingly traditional and used the old commentators.[70] Few Reform themes appeared. He emphasized Jacob's inheritance of the promise, endorsed his trickery (in light of destiny), and cited the Sages on the reconciliation. Only the Edom eschatology was missing. Salomon Herxheimer's commentary had more of an edge, offering Reform sermons' familiar lessons, but he focused on philological explanation rather than on portraying Jacob & Esau.[71] He suggested that Jacob's reconciliation with Esau taught humanity to live peacefully, but there was nothing in the commentary on emancipation. For Hirsch, in contrast, Jacob & Esau told a history both universal and Jewish, reaching a crescendo in his own time when the two were drawing together. Jacob's cosmopolitan mission, the universal recognition of the God of Israel, had been repressed throughout history

---

[68] David Ellenson, "The Orthodox Rabbinate and Apostasy in Nineteenth-Century Germany and Hungary," in *Jewish Apostasy in the Modern World*, ed. Todd M. Endelman (London: Holmes & Meier, 1987), pp. 172–73.

[69] Fraenkel's view of continuous revelation of the Torah was more in line with Sofer's than Neo-Orthodox insistence on a single "closed" revelation, with every generation standing again at Sinai.

[70] *Die israelitische Bibel – Der Pentateuch*, ed. Ludwig Philippson (Leipzig: Baumgärtner, 1844). The traditionalism is surprising in light of Philippson's innovative *Shiloah* sermons, discussed in my notes to Holdheim and Hirsch. Reform innovation, it appears, can be found in sermons, rather than in catechism or biblical commentaries.

[71] *Der Pentateuch*, ed. Salomon Herxheimer, 2d ed. (Bernburg: Gröning, 1854). Herxheimer (1801–1884) was a radical Reform rabbi and educator.

by Rome's overwhelming political power. With the Enlightenment and emancipation, oppression was about to end, and Europeans would soon recognize the Jews as cosmopolitanism's messengers and work together with them for human rights. Hirsch was profoundly original.

Hirsch's Jacob & Esau is a *Bildungsroman*, a story of humanity's spiritual growth. History began with a series of educational failures, extending from Adam & Eve to the Patriarchs. "Train a child in the way appropriate for him" (Proverbs 22:6): Esau, the adventurous hunter, and Jacob, the pious tent dweller, required different education, each according to his character, directing them both to the Abrahamic mission. Had the voice of Jacob, moral and intellectual, been brought together with Esau's hands, so adept at managing this world, the history of humanity would have looked different. Instead, Isaac and Rebecca made all possible mistakes. They imposed bookish education on both sons, and they showed preferential love for one over the other. Isaac, brought up in the moral perfection of Abraham's household, admired Esau's worldly talents, and Rebecca, a convert brought up among treacherous idol worshippers, revered Jacob's intellectualism and moral perfection. Having no appreciation for domestic life or for scholarly accomplishment, Esau grew to loathe the Abrahamic tradition and wished to escape it. He coped the best he could by bringing venison to his father or pretending to fulfill the miẓvot. To call Isaac's attention to Esau's failings, Rebecca and Jacob needed trickery. The rest was history.[72]

No Reform preacher was radical enough to fault the Patriarchs with humanity's tragic history. None drew as lively a picture of the dysfunctional patriarchal household, which explained Esau's exclusion and yet preserved his and the Patriarchs' dignity, and the Jewish mission's integrity. For Hirsch, the Patriarchs were the apogees of moral perfection, the embodiment of *Mensch-Israel*: Perfect humanity had preceded perfect Judaism.[73] But the Patriarchs were not ideal fathers or educators, and their moral rigor and intellectualism, as well as their fortification of the family as a private sphere against a hostile superstitious world, made them disregard Esau's aptitude for political power. Contemporary Judaism risked emulating the Patriarchs by imposing yeshivah study on youth with little aptitude for it, and alienating them from Judaism. Farmers and merchants were no less necessary for Judaism than sages. Emancipation and the Enlightenment could mend human history, but

---

[72] Samuel Raphael Hirsch, "Pädagogische Plaudereien," *Jeschurun* 8:4 (January 1862): 153–65, trans. as "Lessons from Jacob and Esau," in his *Collected Writings*, 7: 319–32.

[73] Mordechai Breuer, "The Torah with *Derekh Ereẓ* Principle in Samson Raphael Hirsch's Teaching" (in Hebrew), in his *Asif* (Jerusalem: Rimonim, 1999), pp. 328–29, and references there.

only if Jews recognize that Esau's hands are as essential as Jacob's voice, for "great is study that leads into action" (*BT*, Qidushin 40:2).

Hirsch retained Esau as worldly and political and Jacob as domestic and moral throughout his commentary, but as Esau's historical identity as Roman and Christian increasingly overshadowed his origins as a Jewish rebel, Hirsch's sympathy for him diminished and his appreciation for Jacob's spirituality increased. "One nation shall be stronger than the other, and the elder shall serve the younger": Jacob & Esau would represent different national principles, one based on spirit, the other on power, Jerusalem versus Caesarea. Unlike European nations, which resembled one another, Israel would be unique, serving universal ideals. At the end of days, the stronger and larger people would put itself at the service of the universal ideals, and Israel and the nations would work together to realize the Abrahamic mission. Emancipation opened the gate to collaboration. The Jews had emerged from slavery and now anticipated the day when they would be honored, not despite being Jewish but because they were Jewish.

Hirsch worked out the transition from Jewish to non-Jewish Esau through Isaac's blessing. He stated in no uncertain terms that Rebecca and Jacob had performed trickery to obtain Esau's blessing, and Esau's tears would haunt Jacob throughout history. Yet, effectively, no blessing was ever stolen, and none was forfeited. Esau's blessing, of material bounty and political power, was of no value to Jacob, and Isaac ended up bestowing such a blessing on Esau anyway. Jacob's blessing was the Abrahamic inheritance, and he received it from Isaac upon his departure to Ḥaran. Isaac had intended this blessing for him from the start. Isaac was blind, but he knew his children well enough to recognize Esau's worldliness and Jacob's moral perfection. He had hoped that Esau could participate in the Abrahamic mission by supporting Jacob: Political power would be put at the service of moral ideals. Rebecca recognized the futility of such hopes, and knowing well that her trick would be exposed, decided to waken Isaac to Esau's failings. She succeeded: Isaac's blessing to Esau made him the world's master by the sword, but indicated that all his conquests would eventually serve Jacob's ideals. Until such time at the end of days that Esau should lay down his sword and recognize Jacob's ideals, he would have no share in the Abrahamic mission.[74]

---

[74] Hirsch gives an unconventional interpretation to "when you grow restless [תריד] you shall break his yoke from your neck" (Genesis 27:40): When you finally submit to his ideals (תריד meaning "take yourself down"), you will break the yoke of always having to conquer for goals that are not yours. Jacob's ideals will then be also those of Esau, and no conquest will be necessary any longer.

Neither the birthright's purchase – youth's game, said Hirsch – nor Esau's blessing did Jacob any good: He had to go penniless into exile, leaving everything for Esau.[75] Abraham had gone wandering as a rich man, universally recognized as a prince, whereas Jacob had to depend on his spiritual gifts alone and worked most of his life like a slave. He, and not Abraham, was the first Jew. He went to Ḥaran to mature into a Jewish patriarch. Already at the start of his journey, in Bethel, he discovered that the home was the center of Jewish civilization, *Beit Elohim*. His night vision revealed the future covenant of Sinai: The ladder symbolized the altar's ramp, and the altar was stationed on the ground, where the Lord's house, the Jewish home, was destined to stand. There, Jacob became the first Jew, vowing to establish a home that would be a center for spreading spirituality, for humanity. This was the mission he would carry in Ḥaran.

In contrast with Reform preachers who looked askance at Jacob's household, Hirsch gave a lofty description of the growing Jewish family in exile. Jacob married the servants only at the matriarchs' request. Hirsch found textual hints that Jacob loved both Leah and Rachel, and the names Leah gave her sons, the future tribes of Israel, suggested how much she appreciated them as enhancing her relationship with Jacob. Rachel, too, craved children so that she would have a share in building the Jewish people. The competition of Leah and Rachel over Jacob was sisterly, sometimes a joke. Jacob held it against neither of them that they acquiesced in Laban's trickery of marrying Leah to him first. All were dedicated to building a Jewish home in a hostile environment. The sisters were aware that their father had repeatedly cheated Jacob and treated them like foreigners. After two decades, they all recognized that there was no way of continuing to build up a family in exile. They had to leave. On their departure, Rachel stole the idols so that her father would cease worshipping them. Even the angels were impressed with Jacob's family when they encountered them on his return to the Land.

The sad bride (Leah) had a happy family, observed Hirsch, and the happy and loved bride (Rachel) a tragic one. He found irony in human love and fortune's fragility and reassurance in the Jewish family, whereas Reform preachers found in both didactic lessons about mismanaged polygamy. Hamburg Reform pastors and Hirsch shared similar liberal values, and both commented on Jacob's family from nineteenth-century perspectives. But Edward Kley's and Gotthold Salomon's reductive

---

[75] The idea that Jacob derived benefit neither from the birthright purchase nor from Esau's blessing but had to go as a slave to Ḥaran to mature as a patriarch can already be found in Philippson's 1840s sermons: "Die Bestimmung Israel's," *Shiloah*, 2: 3–13.

readings turned the matriarchs into petty quarrelsome conspirators, whereas Hirsch's mediation of tradition made them the makers of Jewish destiny. Rebecca, especially, emerged as a caring mother, a discerning reader of character, and a sagacious architect of history. The modern family arose out of the biblical household instead of out of its rejection. Matthias Morgenstern also observes that in centering Jewish life on the family and in underlining Esau's aptitude for public affairs and Israel's renunciation of political power, Hirsch used idioms for Judaism that, in bourgeois discourse, could not but be understood as feminine.[76] Effeminizing Judaism meant losing Esau, however. Hirsch's initial plea to find room for Esau in Judaism became all the more difficult as he pleaded the matriarchs' virtues.

For Hirsch, Jacob's struggle with the angel represented the saga of Jewish exile and emancipation. He acknowledged that there was no historical connection between Edom and Rome, but empire and expansive political domination represented the very opposite of Jewish ideals. In the struggle between Esau's sword and Jacob's spiritual strength was written the history of humanity. Throughout the long night of the exile, Esau's angel tried to fell Jacob, yet bloody persecution failed to subject and assimilate the Jews; it only weakened them physically. Jacob limped but remained standing. With the Enlightenment dawn, humanity's blurry consciousness became clearer, and the angel blessed Jacob, acknowledging his universal mission. The angel's own mission of singing God's praise would only be accomplished when he acknowledged Jacob's ideals. The angel would not disclose his name, since soon "the Lord shall be One, and his name One." Jacob would limp for a while longer in order to call attention to his mission by showing that he did not depend on physical power but on spiritual strength and God's protection.

The angel's blessing set the stage for Jacob & Esau's reconciliation. For millennia, said Hirsch, imperial Rome had been unwittingly preparing the world for Jacob's cosmopolitanism, unifying it by force and guile. The Enlightenment and the nation-state advanced freedom and self-determination against aristocracy and empire. The rule of Laban and Esau, of estate owners cheating their workers out of their earnings and of military aristocrats brandishing their swords and subduing the meek, was over. Jewish emancipation pronounced universal liberation, mutual recognition between Jews and Christians, and the beginning of universal collaboration. When Jacob and Esau met, Jacob conceded to him the

---

[76] "Between the Noahide Laws and Israelite Edomite Brotherhood: Paradigms of Humanity in Modern Jewish Orthodoxy," in *The Quest for a Common Humanity; Human Dignity and Otherness in the Religious Traditions of the Mediterranean*, ed. Katell Berthelot and Matthias Morgenstern (Leiden: Brill, 2011): pp. 101–21.

birthright and the blessing: He acknowledged Esau's nobility and priority and relinquished to him political power. Esau recognized Jacob's rights and spiritual gifts, "embraced him, and fell on his neck and kissed him, and they wept" (Genesis 33:4):

[A] genuine human feeling overcame Esau. . . . These kisses and tears permit us to see in Esau, too, Abraham's descendant. . . . Esau relinquishes the sword and allows ever-growing space for humanity. Indeed, it is precisely through Jacob that Esau has the opportunity to show the principle of humanity burgeoning in him. . . . Only when the strong, as Esau is here, embraces the weak and casts the sword of violence away, only then does it become clear that justice and humanity have triumphed in him.[77]

Post-Holocaust commentators commented acerbically on Hirsch's vision of Esau laying down his sword and recognizing Jacob.[78] It was an exceptional vision even for the age of emancipation, too good to be even an ideal. It was also full of tensions. Hirsch retained the polarity of worldly Esau and spiritual Israel. In his educational vision, he seemed eager for Jews to acquire some of Esau's talents, but after his lofty account of Jacob and the bitterness he expressed about Christian persecution, Jacob's acknowledgment of Esau's nobility seemed empty. Reconciliation was a prelude to Esau's wholesale acceptance of Israel's mission, and to putting his political power at the service of Jacob's ideals. Esau's hands would ensure Jacob's voice being heard. What could Jacob possibly learn from Esau? Hamburg preacher Jonas acknowledged the Hellenic contribution to the religion of humanity. Hirsch's Esau made no such contribution. Hirsch was explicit that Israel would not imitate Esau. Jacob renounced politics and, limping, trusted in God. Jews would be German acculturated, but, truly, the Enlightenment was embedded in Judaism. There was no mutual learning, no in-between, not even an acknowledgment of Jewish or Christian pluralism. The typology expressed Hirsch's emancipation dream, but it constrained his vision of German Jews.

Illiberalism was not, however, Hirsch's main liability: Utopianism was. He observed insightfully that "the behavior of the people and of any

---

[77] *Der Pentateuch*, I: Genesis 33:4: "[E]in reines menschliches Gefühl in Esau zum Ausbruch gekommen. . . . Dieser Kuß und dieser Thränen lassen uns auch in Esau den Nachkommen Abrahams erkennen. . . . Esau legt . . . das Schwert aus der Hand, giebt immer mehr und mehr der Humanität Raum und zwar ist es gerade Jakob, an dem Esau zumeist Gelegenheit hat zu zeigen, daß und wie das Prinzip der Humanität bei ihm zum Durchbruch zu kommen anfängt. . . . Erst wenn der Starke, wie hier Esau, dem Schwachen um den Hals fällt und das Schwert der Gewalt weithin von sich wirft, erst dann zeigt sich, daß Recht und Menschlichkeit in ihm zum Siege kommen."

[78] Nehama Leibowitz, *Studies in the Book of Genesis in the Context of Ancient and Modern Jewish Bible Commentary*, trans. and adapted from the Hebrew by Aryeh Newman (Jerusalem: World Zionist Organization, 1972), pp. 372–78, commentary on Va-yishlaḥ.

government toward the scattered children of the House of Jacob abiding in their midst forms a yardstick of the degree of their own civilization."[79] Jewish emancipation was the European nation-state's ultimate test. It was also the way in which Christians might release themselves from the moral burden of millennial persecution of the Jews, especially as they recognize the beauty of enlightened Judaism. In the aftermath of the Holocaust, this is what a remorseful German academic elite would do. For its time, Hirsch's dazzling vision was detached from reality. The nation-state granted emancipation grudgingly and conditionally, anticipating that the Jews would disappear as a community. Hirsch was a visionary. Conviction and dogmatism were joined with brilliance and insight to create his emancipation utopia.

Hirsch's utopia makes for the single emancipation-age Jacob & Esau story that one may tell children today to their benefit. For intellectual virtuosity and grandeur, for range and detail, and for the ability to make the rabbinic tradition speak to modern life – Hirsch had no match among contemporaries. Historian Mordechai Breuer argued that, unlike the Reformers, Hirsch did not wish for Jews to join the German nation but to live as a nation with them.[80] It would be more correct to say that Hirsch envisioned both Germans and Jews as European, in the manner that liberal Germans think of both today, and hence he saw no difficulty in a nation united by the Torah and, decidedly nonpolitical, being German. His vision carried other messages ahead of their time. From among the protagonists of the Jacob & Esau saga, Hirsch identified most with the Matriarch Leah. During the reconciliation, Jacob told Esau, said Hirsch, that his wives were to thank for his fortune, which Esau so admired. As Jacob's wives, children, and serfs approached Esau, one after the other bowing, Leah, said Hirsch (using a textual hint), stood tall: The Jewish matriarch remained composed and dignified when others prostrated themselves in fear.

Visionary dogmatism had its costs, however. Hirsch found ever fewer partners for his project, even among his fellow modern Orthodox. Unlike Hildesheimer, he would not collaborate with any Reform-oriented Jewish organization.[81] He began a campaign to allow the Orthodox minority in Frankfurt to withdraw from the Jewish community: It was a matter of democracy and religious liberty, he said. Traditional Würzburg Rabbi

---

[79] Mendel Hirsch, *Seder ha-Haftarot* (1896), trans. Isaac Levi (New York: Judaica Press, 1966): Obadiah 1:16. The text emerged from classes in Hirsch's school. Hirsch also expresses the idea in his commentary on the reconciliation (Genesis 33:4), quoted in this section.

[80] "Emancipation and the Rabbis" (in Hebrew), in his *Asif*, pp. 166–71.

[81] David Ellenson, "The Orthodox Rabbinate and Apostasy," pp. 173–74.

Dov Baer Bamberger warned him that it was impermissible to split the Jewish community as long as an Orthodox congregation was allowed to retain its own institutions. Hirsch would not listen. He cited, in response, Moses Sofer, and insisted that one should not finance breach of the Torah. Following the law of 1876 permitting withdrawal, he took *Adat Jeschurun* out of the Frankfurt Jewish community. What had begun as a hopeful embrace of modernity ended in a withdrawal to medieval autonomy. Increasingly beleaguered and isolated, Hirsch in his later years echoed the prophet Elijah, "I have been left all alone" (I Kings 19:10, 14).

In the biblical scene marking the end of his prophecy, Elijah was back at Ḥorev, where the Torah had first been given. God's response to Elijah's "I have been jealous for the Lord of Hosts ... and I have been left all alone" was the instruction for him to anoint Elisha as his successor (I Kings 19:16). The rabbis, as apprehensive about Elijah's zealotry as they were about the priest Pinḥas' vigilantism against intermarriage in Numbers (25:7–8), created a prototype zealot: Pinḥas and Elijah were the same person, they said.[82] Hirsch must have been aware of rabbinic unease about Elijah when he adopted his mantle, but the affinity was too strong: He chose to join the zealots. This limited his historical achievement. The constraints of a small German minority may have limited the impact of German Neo-Orthodoxy anyway, but greater acceptance of Jewish pluralism, and openness to history and to rabbinic intellectualism, could have built bridges to wider traditional groups and sustained a modern rabbinic leadership. This may have preempted Neo-Orthodoxy's absorption into Agudat Yisrael in the twentieth century, and the radical nationalist takeover of modern Orthodoxy. Neither Ḥaredi nor national Orthodoxy ever shared the stunning cosmopolitan vision that Hirsch had drawn with Jacob & Esau.

Adolf Jellinek's Esau: The Anxieties of Emancipation

Christian Esau and Amaleq made brief return visits to Jewish preaching at the height of emancipation in Jellinek's sermons. Known for his flourishing and forceful oratory, Jellinek was considered one of his age's leading preachers and a major Jewish Studies scholar. His sermons displayed erudition, with richly cited rabbinic sources, especially Midrash. The sermons were historical in their conception of Judaism and in their use of the sources. History led the Reform sermon back to tradition. Just as

---

[82] *Pirqe de-Rabbi Eliezer* 29, ed. C. M. Horowitz (Jerusalem: Maqor, 1972). *Shir Hashirim Rabbah* 1:38 is critical of Elijah's zealotry. *Va-yiqra Rabbah* 37:4 holds Pinḥas responsible for failing to prevent the sacrifice of Jephthah's daughter "and accountable for her blood."

Jellinek reintegrated, through historical study, the Kabbalah and Talmudic commentators into Reform Judaism, so too did his preaching return the sermon to the traditional *derashah*: He paid careful attention to text and used midrashim serially to build his arguments. The resurrection of rabbinic Jacob & Esau in the sermons of a leading advocate of the German-Jewish partnership reflected the maturation of Reform discourse, but also its anxieties. Hirsch dwelled on emancipation as an ideal and expressed its hopes. Jellinek's sermons expressed both anxiety and hope and reflected emancipation's sober reality.

Jellinek grew up in Ungarisch Brod, a major Jewish community in eastern Moravia, and attended the yeshivah at Prossnitz, then, at the age of seventeen, moved on to Prague where he prepared on his own for the *Matura*, the end-of-Gymnasium exam that allowed university registration.[83] In 1842, he began studies at the University of Leipzig, focusing on Orientalism, and acquired several Semitic languages, including Arabic. At the same time, he edited Jewish Studies journals, translated Adolphe Franck's formative study of the Kabbalah, and in the early 1850s, began collecting and publishing little-known medieval Midrashim. In 1845, he became preacher of a newly established Leipzig congregation, under the auspices of Zacharias Fraenkel. He identified with Fraenkel's historical view of Judaism, which advocated cautious reform in light of tradition. As Fraenkel, a decade later, trained Moritz Güdemann, Jellinek's future successor in Vienna, his approach shaped two generations of Viennese rabbis, providing Vienna's moderate reform with a theoretical foundation.

During the 1848 revolution, Jellinek established a Christian–Jewish alliance for religious understanding and emancipation and supported the German cultural claims in Eastern Europe. Liberalism and *Deutschtum* (Germanness) were one and the same to him, but he dissociated the German nation and culture from ethnicity and the state. His Deutschtum entailed a German cultural sphere in Central Europe and was Austrian in character: German culture was to liberate retrograde Jews and Slavs in the context of a pluralist empire, not a German nation-state. His Austrian patriotism grew with the years. The emperor had executed his younger brother Hermann for his involvement in the 1848 revolution in Vienna, but in 1867, after the Austrian emperor's own brother, Maximilian, Emperor of Mexico, was executed, Jellinek delivered an emotional eulogy in which he evoked Hermann's memory and pleaded

---

[83] Moses Rosenmann, *Dr. Adolf Jellinek: Sein Leben und Schaffen* (Vienna: Schlesinger, 1931); Klaus Kempter, *Die Jellineks 1820-1955: Eine familienbiographische Studie zum deutschjüdischen Bildungsbürgertum* (Düsseldorf: Droste Verlag, 1998).

for abolition of the death penalty.[84] The fate of the two families, imperial and Jewish, had converged.

In 1856, Jellinek went to Vienna to serve as *Prediger* (preacher) of the new Leopoldstädter Temple. When Isaak Noah Mannheimer died in 1865, he moved to the Stadttempel and became Vienna's leading preacher. His arrival in Vienna coincided with communal upheaval due to the Orthodox congregations' wish to withdraw from the Jewish community. The Orthodox Jews were, for the most part, recently arrived Hungarian and Galician immigrants, while the old-time liberal elite controlled the community. Jellinek made it his goal to prevent a split: He appealed to the authorities (as the Orthodox did), delivered impassioned sermons, and, importantly, gave up on his own plans to introduce the organ and liturgical reforms. He was less observant than either his predecessor or successor, and decidedly anti-Orthodox in his sentiments, but his inclusive Judaism made room for pluralism. His conception of Judaism was grounded in the rabbinic tradition and accorded respect to every expression of Jewish life, and he was on the alert to defend all Judaism against antisemitism. After years of unrest, the Orthodox grudgingly gave up their efforts to secede in the early 1870s. Jellinek became the public face of Viennese Jewry.

Jellinek saw himself as Viennese Jewry's intellectual leader, a preacher and not a rabbi. He relegated halakhic decisions, pastoral duties, and political negotiations to others, and he refused the title of chief rabbi until it was imposed on him in the early 1890s. In 1861, he established the weekly *Die Neuzeit*, liberal Jewry's organ for four decades, and, in 1863, "Beit ha-Midrash," a Jewish Studies institute, converted against his wishes into a seminary in the early 1890s. He devoted himself to his weekly sermons, which responded to Jewish life's ongoing challenges. In the controversy over messianism in the early 1860s, he defended, against both Catholics and Orthodox Jews, Mannheimer's vision that the Jewish messiah was the people and not a person, but he also insisted that the messianic prayers for return to Zion were central to Jewish liturgy, and that the redemption they envisioned was universal in character.[85] In the mid-1860s, he was quick to note antisemitism's changing nature, the growing essentialization of Jewish character. He responded with popular scholarly studies on the Jewish *Stamm* (ethnos), drawing an anthropological-psychological portrait of Jewish culture, intended to make it

---

[84] Adolf Jellinek, "Gedächtnisrede auf Se. Majestät Ferdinand Maximilian Josef, Kaiser von Mexico (14. Juli 1867)," in his *Reden bei verschiedenen Gelegenheiten* (Vienna: Brüder Winter, 1874), pp. 67–71.
[85] "Zion (erste Rede)"; "Zion (zweite Rede)," *Predigten*, 2: 155–66, 167–78.

possible for Jews to be Jewish, German, and Austrian, all at the same time.[86]

Jellinek's sermons had a political urgency that did not allow for the intricate elaboration of a multifaceted vision, typical of the great Reform preachers. The sermons were part of the ongoing struggle for emancipation and against antisemitism. At the height of emancipation in Austria, 1859–67, the sermons portrayed Judaism as a cosmopolitan religion, a foundation for good citizenship and fraternal relations with non-Jews, but also inveighed against opponents with the rhetoric of Amaleq and Esau, resurrecting the eschatology of darker times. A quick interchange of the two modes and moods can be tracked in the sermons within a few months. Jellinek's 1861 Passover sermon on the Song of Solomon celebrated the liberals' recent ascent to power and beamed with redemptive hopes.[87] Only three months later, the "Balaam" sermon forewarned against leaders who, like the Moabite king Balaq and the Midyanite prophet Baalam, failed to understand the divine plan and conspired against the Jews.[88] Emancipation's hopes and anxieties alternated.

The Israelite religion was the first to recognize humanity's common origin, said Jellinek in his sermon on the post-Noaḥide dispersion of peoples. All of humanity, regardless of skin color, culture, or social organization, descended from one father. Yet providence designed the world so that unity and diversity alike serve progress. God wished to be worshipped universally, but by each people according to its way. Ethnicity, language, the land, and folklore accounted for the diversity of nations, and each nation had the right to its own development. National constituents were constantly in shift. No one group had the right to arrest the nation's development, or exclude people from it because they did not conform. No nation had the right to impose its culture over another. Jews living among the nations shared in their cultures, and blessed were modern times that recognized pluralism and permitted the Jewish Diaspora to participate in national life while carrying on the idea of a universal religion.[89]

Jellinek was considered a leading apologist. In an 1859 sermon, he assailed the prejudice against "Jewish particularism." Not acculturation but Judaism made the Jews good citizens, he said. From Abraham to Solomon to Isaiah, Jewish patriarchs, kings, and prophets recognized God as the universal ruler and not as a tribal god. Abraham was exemplary in his love of humanity, and his endeavor to prevent Sodom's

---

[86] Adolf Jellinek, *Studien und Skizzen: Erster Theil: Der jüdische Stamm: Ethnographische Studien* (Vienna: Herzfeld & Bauer, 1869), and *Der jüdische Stamm in nichtjüdischen Sprichwörtern* (Vienna: Löwn Buchhandlung, 1881).
[87] "Schir ha-Schirim," *Predigten*, 1: 13–30.   [88] "Balaam," *Predigten*, 1: 47–62.
[89] "Die Einheit und die Mannigfaltigkeit des Völkerslebens," *Predigten*, 2: 73–84.

destruction was but one example. Rabbinic Judaism developed the bib-lical universalist legacy. "A non-Jew who keeps the Torah is like the High Priest," Jellinek quoted Midrash.[90] The Talmud's derogatory expressions against the "nations of the world" were directed at debauched pagans and not applicable to people observing the Noaḥide commandments, identi-fied with natural religion. The monotheistic religions, Christianity and Islam, were preparing for the messianic days. Had Christians treated Jews according to the Gospel, he quoted Jacob Emden, the great tragedies of Jewish–Christian relations would have been spared. Tendentiously inter-preting rabbinic sources, Jellinek created a portrayal of Judaism as a universalist religion par excellence.[91]

Yet at the same time, Jellinek recalled Amaleq in order to fight eman-cipation's opponents. Sometime in the late fall of 1860, between the liberal triumphs of the October Diploma and the February 1861 Patent, he may have gotten wind of people in the imperial court or cabinet endeavoring to delay Jewish relief as part of the constitutional reform. They became Amaleq. This was a dicey move: The biblical command to exterminate Amaleq – "you shall erase the memory of Amaleq from under heaven" (Deuteronomy 25:19) – weighed heavily on Judaism and could undermine Jellinek's efforts to present it as a universal religion. Reform preachers assiduously avoided Amaleq. Hirsch and his students con-verted the genocidal command to "erase the memory of Amaleq" into "erase the memory of evil," as if the Bible spoke of the evil inclination and not of a people.[92] Jellinek walked casually where others treaded lightly. Amaleq appeared thrice in Jewish history, he said, during the Exodus from Egypt, the foundation of kingship, and the Persian Diaspora, each time with a genocidal design, the last by King Ahasuerus's minister, Haman. Malicious advisors to the prince had incited against the Jews and undermined Jewish–Christian relations in the past. Now they were threatening to do it again with Emperor Franz Joseph. Fight them![93]

Notwithstanding Jellinek's anxieties, emancipation in Austria moved onward, but his apprehensions never died out. In the summer of 1861, he recalled rabbinic Balaam, the prophet of the nations, to fight the opposi-tion to emancipation. King Balaq and the prophet Balaam could not grasp the grandeur of the people of Israel, dedicated to truth, freedom,

---

[90] "Israel's Lehre über die Beziehungen von Juden zu Nichtjuden," *Predigten*, 2: 139; *Sifra*, aḥarei mot 13; *BT* Baba Qama 38a; Avodah Zarah 3a. (Jellinek uses the first.)

[91] Ibid., 2: 121–39. Jacob Katz described (and censored) the procedure in " The Vicissitudes of Three Apologetic Statements" (in Hebrew), *Ẓiyon* 23/24 (1958–59): 174–93.

[92] *Der Pentateuch*, Exodus 17:14–16; Deuteronomy 25:17–19; *Seder ha-Haftarot*, Zakhor, I Samuel 15:1–34.

[93] "Amalek," *Predigten*, 1: 63–74.

and justice, newly emerging on the horizon after their Exodus from Egypt. Balaq, a convergence of brute force and magic, called upon Balaam, inspired by divine revelation but shifty in character, to curse Israel. Together they embodied contemporary antisemites, statesmen, and intellectuals who were deploying force and deceit to obstruct the Jews' rise. God disrupted Balaam's plan and forced him to recognize Israel's grandeur. Force and deceit would not prevent the triumph of Jewish universalism.[94]

A year later, Esau returned to haunt emancipation. In December 1862, Jellinek delivered a seething attack on Esau's evil designs, alluding to Christian persecution. Meditating on Jacob's prayer "Deliver me, I pray Thee, from the hand of my brother, from the hand of Esau; for I fear him, lest he come and smite me, the mother with the children" (Genesis 32:11), Jellinek reaffirmed the rabbinic typology. Jacob, and not Abraham, he noted, had given his name to the Jewish people because his life foreshadowed Jewish life in the Diaspora. He was a wandering Hebrew, using his acumen to defeat a wicked, powerful brother, and survived persecution by dividing his camp (becoming a Diaspora) and offering prayer and gifts. "Esau's character," emphasized Jellinek, "is that of Israel's enemies; Esau's struggle is that of Israel's enemies." Jellinek's Esau was unmistakenly Christian: Having perused the Hebrew books, Esau pretended to speak in God's name, but persecuted the Jews and threatened to decimate them, mother with children, leaving the Jews no choice but to offer him gifts to save themselves. But "Jacob's salvation [too] is a picture of the future salvation of Israel." In a manner that would have pleased Zionists, Jellinek called upon Jews to rise up and fight Esau, just as Jacob had struggled with Esau's angel and prevailed.[95]

Against the background of emancipation, and the pictures of cosmopolitan Jacob and Jewish Esau in Reform sermons, Jellinek's Christian Esau comes as a surprise. The precise occasion that evoked his sermon may be less important than the pattern: Esau was the culmination of Jellinek's restoration of traditional rabbinic portrayals of Israel's enemies. He used Amaleq prolifically to mark opponents. His 1864 call for unity in the Jewish community was accompanied by the warning that Amaleq was lurking behind, ready to take advantage of a Jewish split.[96] He sensed emancipation's fragility and fretted about it. The rabbinic typology's resurrection at the height of emancipation suggests that for all the age's silence on Edom, the typology remained a site of bitter historical

---

[94] "Balaam," *Predigten*, 1: 47–62.   [95] "Esau," *Predigten*, 2: 203–14.
[96] "Wajehi ha-mischkan echad, oder die Einheit und Einigkeit Israel's"; "Lo tischkach, oder: Israelit, vergiß nicht!" in *Aus der Wiener israelitischen Cultusgemeinde, 5624: 7 Zeit-Predigten* (Vienna: Herzfeld & Bauer, 1864), pp. 1–11, 12–24.

memories. A nation, observed Ernest Renan, requires that its citizens forget the past as much as that they remember it.[97] Jellinek's Esau showed that liberal Jews had forgotten nothing, and emancipation did not assuage their fears of the past's return. Jewish citizenship remained problematic, and Jewish membership in the nation elusive.

Conclusion

The tenacity of Jacob & Esau in the age of emancipation was remarkable. As German-acculturated Jews were negotiating their identities, they reshaped the patriarch who had embodied Jewish exile and made him into a citizen. Ultra-Orthodox Jews reinvented Jacob as an antiemancipatory traditionalist. Yet emancipation remained an age of grace. Jews – all Jews – fell silent about Edom, as if the eschatology had vanished, and transformed Esau from a Christian persecutor into a Jewish apostate (or, in Hasidism, into the evil inclination). A reduction in hostility to Christianity was reflected across Judaism, yet the marginalization of Jacob & Esau's reconciliation also reflected Jewish realism about emancipation's limits: Esau never became a brother. Jellinek's anxieties were just as authentic as were the hopes of Hirsch's cosmopolitan vision. Neither vision may claim privilege in elucidating the significance of emancipation.

If Jacob & Esau remained a major discourse for Jewish and Christian self-definition, the typology ceased being a major idiom of Christian–Jewish polemics. As nation and citizenship putatively became religiously neutral fields, Jacob & Esau was relegated to internal Jewish and Christian discourses, and emancipation was negotiated using universal Enlightenment idioms. To be sure, emancipation debates hinged on the Jewish religion's national character, and Christian theology and Jewish tradition were reintroduced through the back door, but palpably messianic Jacob & Esau no longer suited a purportedly secular debate. Heinrich Paulus and Gabriel Riesser, Stahl and Holdheim, August Röhling and Jellinek argued about anything but Jacob & Esau. All the same, discursive fields where Jews felt free to let tradition address emancipation best reveal the polemics' significance: Holdheim's cosmopolitan Jacob and Jellinek's Christian Esau bespeak emancipation's tensions in a way that open polemics cannot.

Emancipation's discursive transformations should be projected against Jacob & Esau's resilient traditionalism. Among Christians, the distance

---

[97] *Qu'est-ce qu'une nation?* (Paris: Calmann Lévy, 1882), pp. 3–32.

that biblical criticism opened between the Hebrew Bible and the New Testament failed to undermine Christian Jacob – yet. Among Jews, the rabbinic typology's resurgence in Hirsch and Jellinek reflected the maturation of Reform and Orthodox responses to emancipation. The rabbinic tradition converged with Jewish citizenship, and Jacob remained as central as he had ever been to Jewish life. With the secularization of political debate, the typology's discursive range may have diminished, but its intensity increased. All modern forms of Jewish life emerged in the first fifty years of the age of emancipation. When the age drew to a close in 1878, Judaism was facing modern life with confidence.

"Deliver me . . . from the hand . . . of Esau; for I fear him, lest he come and smite me, the mother with the children": One cannot read Jellinek's evocation of mother and children without thinking of the Holocaust. He would live to see Jewish emancipation challenged by Pan-German nationalists who were willing to bring down Austria-Hungary to realize a racial German empire, but even he could imagine only that the Christians would endeavor to relock the Jews in ghettos. In a universe ruled by Christian Jacob, this was indeed the worst he could expect. The urge to read the murder of the Jews into the age of emancipation ought to be resisted. It should not obscure Holdheim's and Hirsch's cosmopolitan visions, which can still speak to Europeans today. The empire in which Moses Sofer had put his trust has fallen, but in yeshivot across the globe, thousands of students peruse his responsa. The nation for which Hirsch, Holdheim, and Jellinek had held such high hopes collapsed, and turned murderous, too, but Jellinek's Beit Midrash has now expanded, with Jewish Studies, across the academy. Hermann Jonas spoke of emancipation as a time when, following Isaiah (11:9), "the earth shall be full of the knowledge of the Lord as the waters cover the sea." That has happened before our own eyes. Fear not my servant Jacob!

Few historical transitions were as stark as the one between the ages of
emancipation and antisemitism. At the Congress of Berlin in 1878,
a European Jewish coalition, led by German Jews and the Alliance
Israélite Universelle, collaborated with the European powers to extend
emancipation to the newly established states in the Balkans, Serbia,
Bulgaria, and Rumania (the last defied the treaty). Emancipation seemed
in triumphal progress, and the Jewish Question on its way to resolution:
Jewish citizenship was becoming a test of a state's modernity. Even
Russia, initially reluctant, ended up supporting the Balkan treaties, and
its own unemancipated Jewry, Europe's largest, was universally regarded
as a mark of Russian backwardness. Within a few years, racial antisemitism in Central Europe and the pogroms in Russia were putting emancipation in jeopardy. To be sure, acculturation and integration continued
apace, and when the February 1917 Revolution finally did arrive in
Russia, it promptly extended citizenship to the Jews. Prior to the 1930s,
emancipation was nowhere reversed, but the Jewish Question no longer
appeared as resolvable as before.

Remarkably, the attacks on the Jews by German journalist Wilhelm
Marr, Prussian Court Preacher Adolf Stoecker, and National Liberal
historian Heinrich von Treitschke all came in one year, 1879, a year
that also signaled the end of Otto von Bismarck's war on the Catholics,
the *Kulturkampf* (culture war), and his break with the National Liberals.[1]
The attacks represented the convergence into modern antisemitism of old
and new discourses, liberal and confessional, nationalist and racial. With
Marr, racial antisemitism was already articulating an apocalyptic vision:

---

[1] Wilhelm Marr, *Wählet keinen Juden! Der Weg zum Siege des Germanenthums über das
Judenthum: Ein Mahnwort an die Wähler nichtjüdischen Stammes aller Confessionen* (Berlin:
Hentze, 1879); Adolf Stoecker, "Unsere Forderungen an das moderne Judenthum"
[1879], in his *Das moderne Judenthum in Deutschland, besonders in Berlin: Zwei Reden in
der christl-socialen Arbeiterpartei gehalten* (Berlin: Wiegandt und Grieben, 1880), pp. 3–19;
*Ein Wort über unser Judenthum: Seperatabdruck aus der 44. und 45. Bande der Preußischen
Jahrbücher (1879–1880)* (Berlin: G. Reimer, 1880). Marr founded the Antisemitenliga
(League of the Antisemites) in 1879, Stoecker the Christian Social Party the year before.

German survival was at stake, and it was either us or them, the Germans or the Jews. By the early 1880s, petitions to reverse emancipation became frequent, and single-issue antisemitic political parties emerged. The Kulturkampf was turned against the Jews: The formation of German national identity and culture would be accomplished, among other things, in confrontation with the Jewish Other.

In Austria, the Vienna student fraternities began excluding Jews in 1878, and the early 1880s saw antisemitic reform associations giving rise to Georg von Schönerer's Pan-German Party and, later, to Karl Lueger's Christian Social Party. Schönerer opted for dissolving Austria-Hungary, breaking with Rome, unifying with Germany, and founding a racial German imperial nation in Central Europe; Lueger sought to redefine imperial Austria as exclusively Christian and diminish Jewish participation in politics and culture. Both signaled the Jews' rapid exclusion from the German liberal camp. Across the Hungarian border, the 1882 Tiszaeszlár ritual murder trial evoked widespread antisemitic agitation, reaching parliament. Farther east, across the Russian border, a wave of pogroms in the aftermath of Tsar Alexander II's assassination in 1881 swept the Pale, inducing massive Jewish emigration west, primarily to the United States. Jewish response was immediate. On the side of philanthropy and international mobilization for Russian Jewry, Zionist movements, from the Russian *Ḥibat Ẓiyon* to the Viennese *Kadimah* fraternity, sprang up, highlighting emancipation's limitations and seeking a Palestine-centered national revival.

Historians have recently downplayed the transition between the ages of emancipation and antisemitism. They have shown that confessionalism and racialism had always been intertwined in nineteenth-century antisemitism, and they discerned emergent Jewish nationalism in the Russian *Haskalah*, opining that Diaspora nationalists and even Zionists regarded their project as completing emancipation by different means.[2] They also pointed out that antisemitism failed to stem Jewish integration, which reached its height in many countries in the interwar years. Yet these remain caveats. The contemporary shock at the pogroms and ritual murder charges was evident and widespread: A regression to medieval times, thought many, who could not imagine modern genocide. However divergent across Europe, the racialization of liberalism and nationalism in the 1880s set permanent features of the postemancipatory Jewish

---

[2] Helmut Walser Smith, *The Continuities of German History: Nation, Religion, and Race across the Long Nineteenth Century* (Cambridge: Cambridge University Press, 2008); Dimitri Shumsky, "Leon Pinsker and 'Autoemancipation!': A Reevaluation," *Jewish Social Studies* 18:1 (2011): 33–62; Joshua Shanes, *Diaspora Nationalism and Jewish Identity in Habsburg Galicia* (Cambridge: Cambridge University Press, 2012).

European landscape all the way to the Holocaust: racial and populist antisemitism, reinforced by confessional movements seeking emancipation's reversal; Jewish defense organizations and coalitions against antisemitism; Jewish nationalism; and an emergent North American Diaspora appearing as a refuge.

Jacob & Esau's transformation under the impact of racial antisemitism will be discussed later, in chapter 9. Here, I begin by exploring the interaction of nation and empire in Central Europe, the opportunities for Jewish self-definition opened by pluralist Austria, and the richness of the Jewish imperial imagination. Germany and Austria were both nationalizing empires, but unlike Germany, Austria was nationalizing against its will. The contrast between the two provides a key to understanding the divergence of fin-de-siècle Jewish politics.

The German *Reich* was a federalist compromise, which made it possible for the king of Bavaria and his fellow princes to retain their titles and a measure of autonomy. But a rapidly nationalizing political culture eroded the political and cultural restraints of imperial federalism. The Kulturkampf, antisemitism, and anti-Polish policies reflected German national anxieties, and revealed an intolerance of minorities – Catholics, Poles and Jews. Yet if empire was nationalized, nation also became imperial. Unification under a Reich triggered shifts in liberal anti-imperialism. Liberals who had earlier resisted drawing on medieval imperial glory as part of the national ethos now reconceptualized empire as democratic, modern, and national. They shaped an expansive imperial national culture that repressed federalism and claimed European prominence. In less than two decades, the imperial nation would pursue overseas expansion and develop a modern concept of a *Weltreich*, a global empire that would render imperial federalism secondary in significance.[3]

Imperial realities diverged radically in Austria-Hungary. After the *Ausgleich* (compromise) of 1867, the Hungarians turned their half of the monarchy into a nationalizing state. The liberal Hungarian elite retained hegemony over diverse minorities through manipulation of the electoral process and an arrangement allowing for Croatian autonomy. In Austria, the Germans proved incapable of retaining a similar hegemony but responded aggressively to the Slavic minorities' demands for political and cultural autonomy and for a share in imperial governance. Language wars between Czechs and Germans in the Czech Crown Lands brought the Reichsrat to a standstill in the late 1890s.

[3] Peter Moraw, Karl Otmar Freiherr von Aretin, Notker Hammerstein, Werner Conze, and Elisabeth Fehrenbach, "Reich," in *Geschichtliche Grundbegriffe*, 8 vols. (Stuttgart: Klett-Cotta, 1972–97): 5: 488–508.

The imperial administration negotiated the different nationalities' conflicting demands the best it could, and the court cultivated an imperial ethos, presenting the monarchy as embodying a supranational ideal. Competing visions of imperial reform circulated, and their common denominator, in contrast with Germany, was their genuine federalism. Nationalization was taking place all over Europe, but, in Austria, empire did not nationalize; it federalized. Instituting universal male suffrage in 1907, Austria became a democratic federalist hybrid between nation-state and empire, constitutional monarchy and autocracy.

Ironically, Austria-Hungary ceased to be an empire by name after 1867: The Austrian Empire (*Kaisertum Österreich*) ended with the *Ausgleich*. "The Kingdoms and Lands Represented in the Imperial Council and the Lands of the Hungarian Holy Crown of St. Stephen" were known, from 1868 on, as the Austro-Hungarian Monarchy (*Österreichisch-Ungarische Monarchie*), and designated as both imperial and royal (K. u. K., *kaiserliche und königliche*). Franz Joseph was Emperor of Austria and King of Hungary. To his Jewish subjects, however, Franz Joseph remained indisputably "His Highness the Emperor" (הקיסר ירום הודו). In the Hebrew prayer for the country's welfare, "empire," too, is designated "kingdom," and so "imperial and royal," confusing terms elsewhere, made perfect sense: Franz Joseph was both. To traditional Jews, the imperial tradition carried on seamlessly with the Holy Roman Empire, the Austrian Empire, and Austria-Hungary: The Habsburgs remained the emperors, kings above other kings. Hyperbolically stated, in Jewish tradition, the Roman Empire did not fall until after World War I.

Late imperial Austria was the most beloved empire in Jewish history. The distance between Austria-Hungary and the Holy Roman Empire did not disrupt the Austrian imperial tradition but was sufficient to put to rest any reminiscent hostility to Rome and to facilitate the unprecedented emotional attachment of Austrian Jews to Franz Joseph. The emperor's popularity extended even across the Russian border: "Froyim Yossels Yidden" (Franz Joseph's Jews) was what envious Russian Jews called their Austrian brethren, Judaizing the Austrian emperor's name. (They would not contemplate doing so for the Russian tsar.) Moses Sofer had already established Austria as inheritor of the Holy Roman Empire and Franz I as the foremost European emperor. In his history of the Habsburgs from the eleventh century to his own time, as well as in his "Eulogy on the Austrian Emperor Franz," Yeḥezqel Penet, a rabbi in the German-speaking region of Transylvania, affirmed the continuity of imperial dynastic rule. Penet made no mention of the 1806 dissolution of the Holy Roman Empire.[4] After emancipation, the image of Franz Joseph as a Roman emperor granting his lands a constitution also spread among liberal Jews. Joachim Jacob Unger (1826–1912), rabbi of Iglau on the Bohemian-Moravian border, reconfigured Franz Joseph as an enlightened emperor.[5] With the rise of national tensions, the traditional appellation *Pater Patriae*, the caring and loving father of all his peoples, acquired a special meaning.

Liberal Jews, committed to German nationalism, may have been the least susceptible to the imperial appeal. Throughout German-speaking Central Europe, liberal Jews had assumed, until 1848, the affinity between Jewish emancipation and German liberal nationalism. Ignaz Kuranda (1812–1884), a Czech Jew, and Adolf Fischhof (1816–1893), a Hungarian Jew, were among the leaders of the 1848 liberal revolution in Vienna. As a delegate to the Frankfurt Parliament, Kuranda envisioned a Greater Germany, including all Habsburg territories. Fischhof, in contrast, was a Vienna delegate to the Austrian Reichstag that wrote the federalist Kremsier Constitution, which never took hold but would guide imperial reform efforts all the way to World War I.

The Czech and Hungarian 1848 uprisings made it clear that Austria faced a different nationality problem from that in most German states. Fischhof emerged from the experience chastened, Kuranda, who in 1861 became a leader of the Liberal Party, the *Verfassungspartei*, not at all. Austria's expulsion from the German Confederation in 1866, however, forced all German Austrians to redefine their relationship to German nationalism. Fischhof parted with the nationalists and advocated recognition of Austrian multinationalism and federalization. Kuranda and the majority of Austro-German liberals refocused on Austria, but opted to promote the German cause through centralization and the expansion of German culture. The liberal Jewish intelligentsia still viewed the imperial project through *Deutschtum* (Germanness). To the end of his life, Adolf Jellinek remained committed to bringing German *Bildung* to Eastern European Jews.

Only German nationalism's racialization and the rise of antisemitism in the 1880s disrupted the Jewish liberal project and triggered a generational shift. The Austrian Jewish Union (*Österreichisch-Israelitische Union*), the Jewish defense organization against antisemitism established in 1886, reassessed the Jewish allegiance to German nationalism. In a February 1897 meeting, its leader Gustav Kohn called for a "return to the program of

---

[4] *Sefer Mareh Yeḥezqel* (שאלות ותשובות, יחזקאל מראה ספר; Book of Ezekiel's vision: *responsa*) (Benei Beraq: Benei Shileshim, 2003).

[5] *Patriotische Casual-Reden*, 2d ed. (Prague: Jakob B. Brandeis, 1899).

reconciliation of peoples (*Völker*) and nationalities (*Stämme*)," a move back to Fischhof.[6] Finding the liberals insufficiently responsive on antisemitism, Viennese Jews began voting for small progressive parties, mostly Jewish, and the Socialists. Empire, socialism, and Jews coalesced as centripetal forces protective of imperial bonds against ethno-nationalism.[7] The interwar alliance between the Jews and the Socialists was already beginning to emerge in the mid-1890s: Traditional and middle-class Jews voted for the avowedly secular *Sozialreformer* and the Socialists. Those whose German liberal allegiance persisted soon learned better. When Camillo Kuranda, son of Ignaz, was elected to the Reichsrat in 1907 as a representative of the German Progressives (*Deutsche Fortschrittspartei*), he faced exclusion from the parliamentary German Club (*Deutschnationaler Verband*) on racial grounds.

In the German Reich, liberalism went through less radical racialization, but antisemitism became, to use Shulamit Volkov's term, a cultural code for "good Germans" in all major parties.[8] German national culture restricted the repertoire of responses to antisemitism. Liberal historian Theodor Mommsen was an indefatigable fighter against antisemitism. He ridiculed myths of an Aryan Germany: German nationality, he told antisemites, was an ethnic amalgamation. Still, he insisted that ethnocultural fusion must now occur, and its product must be one national culture.[9] He was puzzled by liberal Jews' refusal of Protestant conversion. In response, Moritz Lazarus developed a "multicultural" definition of the German nation. Deploying Ernest Renan's model of the nation as a daily referendum, he established collective consciousness as constitutive of the nation, and conceived of the Jews as one of the ethnicities and subcultures contributing to it.[10] His liberal multicultural vision pluralized the nation-state, and provided the only tangible definition of a national culture. Yet

---

[6] Gustav Kohn, addressing a meeting concerning the coming parliamentary elections, February 20, 1897: *Mittheilungen der Österreichisch-Israelitischen Union* 9: 92 (March 1897): 3. See also Werner Cahnman, "Adolf Fischhof and his Jewish Followers," *Leo Baeck Institute Year Book IV* (1959): 111–40.

[7] This strange coalition suggests that we rethink recent dismissals of Oscar Jászi's distinction between centripetal and centrifugal forces: *The Dissolution of the Habsburg Monarchy* [1929] (Chicago: University of Chicago Press, 1961). See the discussion later in this section.

[8] "Antisemitism as a Cultural Code: Reflections on the History and Historiography of Antisemitism in Imperial Germany," *Leo Baeck Institute Yearbook* 23:1 (1978): 25–46.

[9] Theodor Mommsen, *Auch ein Wort über unser Judenthum* (Berlin: Weidmannsche Buchhandlung, 1880).

[10] Moritz Lazarus, *Was heißt National?* (Berlin: Ferd. Dümmlers Verlagsbuchhandlung, 1880); Till van Rahden, "Germans of the Jewish *Stamm*: Visions of Community Between Nationalism and Particularism, 1850–1933," in *German History from the Margins*, ed. Nils Roemer and Neil Gregor (Blomington: Indiana University Press, 2005), pp. 27–48; Marcel Stoetzler, *The State, the Nation, and the Jews: Liberalism and the Antisemitism Dispute in Bismarck's Germany* (Lincoln: University of Nebraska Press, 2008).

an ethnicized national culture made multiculturalism seem hopeless. Jews could redefine German culture against the ethno-nationalist grain as pluralist and cosmopolitan; they still needed to belong in it, and fin-de-siècle German liberalism had no place for a Jewish culture.

Austrian Jews were in a more comfortable situation. Jews could declare themselves a separate culture, an ethnicity, or even a nation and yet remain Austrian. They could oppose German nationalism and be loyal to the emperor. Racial antisemitism made it impossible for German-acculturated Jews, like the liberal Jellinek or the socialist Otto Bauer, to be accepted as Germans, but imperial pluralism left them room to maneuver. Like Lazarus, they dissociated state and nation from ethnicity, defining membership in the nation as cultural and the Jews as an ethnicity. But in Austria, the state was a pluralist empire, the German nation was not hegemonic, Deutschtum was ambiguous and contentious, the Jews were one ethnicity among many, and the Jews' Austrian identity did not depend on their Germanness.[11] The Jewish intelligentsia, itself of multicultural origins, experimented with a broader spectrum of political options than did its German counterpart.

Imperial pluralism gave rise to diverse Jewish politics. In Hungary, liberal Jews became Hungarian nationalists, and in opposition to Magyarization, leading Ultra-Orthodox rabbis declared the Jews a separate nation.[12] In Galicia, where two-thirds of Habsburg Jewry lived, Polonization had made headway among the Jewish intelligentsia, but after 1863 they faced increasing hostility from Polish nationalists. The majority of Galician Jews remained traditional and *Kaisertreue* (imperial patriots), but in the fin-de-siècle years, Zionism, Diaspora nationalism, and Jewish socialism emerged. In 1907, Jewish nationalists elected four representatives to the Reichsrat. Multicultural Bukovina became a center of Jewish Diaspora nationalism at the turn of the century. Czech Jews found themselves pressed by the competing national demands of Germans and Czechs. In Bohemia in the 1890s, they seemed to be moving from German to Czech as the daily language, language serving also as a political marker. Kafka famously spoke about the "linguistic impossibilities" of German-acculturated Jewish writers, but the recent debate on the Prague Zionists – were they German- or Czech-

---

[11] Marsha Rozenblit speaks of German-acculturated Austrian Jews as having a tripartite identity: politically Austrian, culturally German, and ethnically Jewish: *Reconstructing a National Identity: The Jews of Habsburg Austria during World War I* (New York: Oxford University Press, 2001).

[12] Michael K. Silber, "The Emergence of Ultra-Orthodoxy: The Invention of a Tradition," in *The Uses of Tradition: Jewish Continuity in the Modern Era*, ed. Jack Wertheimer (New York: JTS, 1992), pp. 23–84.

oriented or both? – suggests that national identity in imperial settings was highly complex and that empire opened possibilities whereas nationalism closed them.[13] Late imperial Austria was inimitable for the opportunities it offered Jewish self-definition.

Interwar Jewish émigrés were wistful about these opportunities but also convinced that in a Europe of nationalizing states, they represented a doomed imperial order living on borrowed time. Historians concurred. "The national principle, once launched, had to work itself out to its conclusion," stated British historian A. J. P. Taylor, radicalizing a view first formed by Hungarian émigré historian Oscar Jászi and Austrian statesman Joseph Redlich (both of Jewish origin).[14] Recent studies depict Austria-Hungary, in contrast, as a modernizing society and economy, guided, on the Austrian side, by an enlightened bureaucracy, effecting on the eve of World War I a series of political compromises, mini *Ausgleiche*, that advanced equal rights for the nationalities (*Gleichberechtigung der Nationalitäten*).[15] They suggest also that the nationalities were far from solid, natural, or self-evident but were being formed, even invented, as the mini Ausgleiche were taking place. National protest and demonstrations were not anti-imperial but intended to effect alternative arrangements that would change the balance of power within the monarchy. The emperor was popular.[16] Nineteenth-century Europe represented nationalizing empires and not nation-states, and Austria-Hungary was not so much of an anomaly.[17] But for the war, the imperial order could well have survived.

---

[13] Hillel Kieval, *The Making of Czech Jewry* (New York: Oxford University Press, 1988), but see Michael Miller, *Rabbis and Revolutionaries* (Stanford, CA: Stanford University Press, 2011), on Moravian Jews for a modification; Scott Spector, *Prague Territories: National Conflict and Cultural Innovation in Kafka's Fin de Siècle* (Berkeley: University of California Press, 2000). Franz Kafka to Max Brod, June 1921, *Briefe 1902–1924* (Frankfurt am Main: S. Fischer, 1966), p. 337: "That in which their despair found an outlet could not be German literature, [although] outwardly it seemed to be. They existed among ... linguistic impossibilities (sprachliche Unmöglichkeiten)." For literature on the Prague Zionists, see the next section.

[14] A. J. P. Taylor, *The Habsburg Monarchy, 1809–1918* [1941] (Chicago: University of Chicago Press, 1976), p. 7; Oscar Jászi, *The Dissolution of the Habsburg Monarchy* (Chicago: University of Chicago Press, 1929); Joseph Redlich, *Emperor Francis Joseph of Austria* (New York: The Macmillan Company, 1929).

[15] James Shedel provides a historiographical overview in *"Fin de Siècle or Jahrhundertwende: The Question of an Austrian Sonderweg,"* in *Rethinking Vienna 1900*, ed. Steven Beller (New York: Berghahn, 2001), pp. 80–104.

[16] Laurence Cole and Daniel Unowsky, eds., *The Limits of Loyalty: Imperial Symbolism, Popular Allegiances, and State Patriotism in the Late Habsburg Monarchy* (New York: Berghahn Books, 2007).

[17] Stefan Berger and Alexei Miller, eds., *Nationalizing Empires* (Budapest: CEU Press, 2014).

Revisionist historiography may have gone too far in dismantling the teleology of nationalism, but among its virtues, it diminishes the anomaly of the Jews as the "state-people."[18] Just like other Austrians, Jews used emergent nationalization to claim rights as a culture, an ethnos, or a nation, while remaining loyal to the monarchy. They were not the only Austrians, only the case limit for Austrianness, the best Austrians because, to paraphrase Joseph Bloch, they never even pretended to put conditions on remaining Austrian.[19] They are also the best Austrians to tell the imperial story because they were part of virtually every region's nationalization, and display the full spectrum of imperial politics. For the Pan-Germans, there is historian Heinrich Friedjung; for the liberals, Ignaz Kuranda and Fischhof; for the progressives, *Sozialreformer* Julius Ofner; for the Socialists, Victor Adler and Bauer; for the Iron Ring, Graf Taaffe's antinationalist conservative coalition, Bloch (and traditional Galician Jews); for the Zionists, Diaspora nationalists, and Orthodox Jews, Nathan Birnbaum (1864–1937) in each of his political metamorphoses – and this represents just the German-Jewish spectrum. Imperial history is at its most diverse when told through the Jews.

The Austrian story has ramifications beyond its context, for one, for Jewish history in Russian Eastern Europe and in Palestine. Carrying Fischhof's federalization proposals one step further, Socialist Karl Renner invented nonterritorial nationality, enabling Germans and other minorities in a reorganized monarchy to affiliate with their nationality across district borders. Renner's proposals shaped Galician Jewish nationalists' claims for autonomy. Marcos Silber suggests that, across the Russian border, they also informed Jewish historian Simon Dubnow's Diaspora nationalism, as well as World War I schemes for an Austrian Poland, and Jewish interpretations of the post–World War I Minority Treaties.[20] In Palestine, interwar Zionist visions of a future Jewish commonwealth took shape with proposed federalist solutions to

---

[18] Hannah Arendt presents the Jews as the state-people par excellence in *The Origins of Totalitarianism* (New York: Harcourt, Brace & Co, 1951).

[19] Joseph Bloch, *Der nationale Zwist und die Juden in Österreich* (Vienna: M. Gottlieb, 1886), p. 41: "Wenn eine specifisch österreichische Nationalität construirt werden könnte, so würden die Juden ihren Grundstock bilden."

[20] Marcos Silber, *Different Nationality, Equal Citizenship: Efforts to Achieve Autonomy for Polish Jewry during the First World War* (in Hebrew) (Tel Aviv: Tel Aviv University, 2014); "The Metamorphosis of Pre–Dubnovian Autonomism," in *Homelands and Diasporas: Greeks, Jews and Their Migrations*, ed. Minna Rozen (London: I. B. Tauris, 2008), pp. 235–55, 391–400; and "Lithuania? But Which? The Changing Political Attitude of the Jewish Political Elite in East Central Europe toward Emerging Lithuania, 1915–1919," in *A Pragmatic Alliance: Jewish-Lithuanian Political Cooperation at the Beginning of the 20th Century*, ed. Vladas Sirutavičius and Darius Staliūnas (Budapest: Central European University Press, 2011), pp. 119–57.

the nationality conflicts in Central and Eastern Europe in mind, especially to the German–Czech conflict in Prague.[21] Leading Zionists consciously contrasted imperial solutions to the Arab–Jewish conflict with the current ethno-nationalizing practices of the interwar European states. Ironically, until the Holocaust, Israel's founders had pre–World War I imperial solutions in mind for Palestine.

Not Jewish history alone is at stake, of course, in the imperial Austrian story. Socialist conceptions of nonterritorial nationality reflect a convergence of imperial and postnational conceptions. Progressive Austrians nowadays are reluctant to take advantage of such opportunities to bridge the imperial Austrian past and contemporary Europe.[22] Living among vestiges of the imperial past, they insist on a civic republican vision of the European Union and relegate the monarchy to oblivion. The result is an Austrian national history that begins at the earliest in 1918 (and preferably in 1945). The incongruence between daily reminders of the past and the inability to tell a national narrative about it is stark.

This chapter and the next are an attempt to persuade my Austrian friends to rethink the monarchy so that they can find new ways to belong in Europe. This chapter surveys the diversity of imperial Jewish politics to 1918, and the next examines Austrian and Jewish politics in the First Republic, with a focus on the imperial legacy in the Austrian political imagination. Both chapters discuss imperial pluralist ideals, as well as cosmopolitan internationalist ones. Traditional Jews were devotees of the first, German-acculturated Jews the leading proponents of the second. I conclude this chapter with Karl Popper, who represents the cosmopolitan internationalist pole. Popper rediscovered the empire during World War II in exile. His intellectual world had been shaped first by fin-de-siècle progressive Vienna, then by interwar Red Vienna. Neither was especially kind to the monarchy. The fate of the predominantly Jewish progressive intelligentsia was intertwined with that of the empire, but most did not recognize it any more than contemporary Viennese do: Internationalism and imperialism coexisted among pre–World War I socialists, but they did not mesh among the majority of fin-de-siècle progressives and interwar socialists.

---

[21] Adi Gordon, "The Ideological Convert and the 'Mythology of Coherence': The Contradictory Hans Kohn and His Multiple Metamorphoses," *Leo Baeck Institute Year Book* 55 (2010): 273–93; Dimitry Shumsky, "Brith Shalom's Uniqueness Reconsidered: Hans Kohn and Autonomist Zionism," *Jewish History* 25 (2011): 339–53; Yfaat Weiss, "Central European Ethnonationalism and Zionist Binationalism," *Jewish Social Studies* 11 (Fall 2004): 93–117.

[22] For a well-reasoned objection: Mathias Weber, "Ein Modell fuer Europa? Die Nationalitätenpolitik in der Habsburger Monarchie Österreich und Ungarn 1867–1914 im Vergleich," *Geschichte in Wissenschaft und Kultur* 47 (1996): 651–72.

Most post–World War I Austrians considered Austria-Hungary a dismal failure. Socialist imperial politics appeared opportunistic and imperial federalism seemed disingenuous, the final verdict being passed by Renner's and Bauer's endorsements of the *Anschluss*: They, too, were German nationalists. As a result, contemporary socialists have no past to which they can return to imagine Europe. Yet if we remove the nation-state teleology, and assume instead that socialist imperial federalism in the 1900s was just as authentic as the 1938 pro-Anschluss stance, we may recover a socialist past that can speak to postnationalism. Popper did so in his New Zealand exile. A non-Marxist socialist, he protested that the nation-state was a charade and reinvented the cosmopolitan democratic empire as an antidote to ethno-nationalism. Contemporary Austrians should follow his lead. One *can* write an imperial history from a progressive perspective and endow the "Republic of Vienna" with a deeper and richer past.[23]

Jewish Imperial Politics: The Court, the Jews, and Catholic Antisemitism

In the flagship Hebrew historical journal *Ziyon* (Zion; also *Tsiyon*), young Israeli academics conducted a debate a few years ago on the cultural identity of the Prague Zionists, a group of intellectuals, among them Hugo Bergmann, Max Brod, Hans Kohn, and Felix Weltsch, who, under the inspiration of Martin Buber, undertook a reconstruction of Judaism as a national culture and were later supporters of a binational state in Palestine. Zohar Maor modified Dimitry Shumsky's observations on their hybrid Czech-German identity: The conceptual world of Prague Jewish nationalism, he showed, was formed in a conscious working through of German concepts and aimed at reconfiguring the German–Jewish relationship.[24] The exchange was remarkable for its setting – Zionist historiography's citadel – for deploying Hebraized postcolonial terms, and for illuminating the paradoxes of nationalization and multiculturalism in fin-de-siècle Central Europe. Seeking to rescue an

---

[23] I use the "Republic of Vienna" to describe contemporary progressive Viennese who promote a civic republican vision of Vienna, Austria, and Europe. I set out the imperial alternative in "Das Kaiserreich, die Sozialdemokratie und die Juden: Ein Versuch, die k. und k. Monarchie wieder in die österreichische Geschichte einzuschreiben," in "1914–2014 – Monarchie als Integrationsmodell?" *Wiener Journal Beilage* (March 12, 2014): 12–13.

[24] Zohar Maor, "Identity and Confusion: One More Glance at the Whirlpool of Identities in Prague," *Ziyon* 71 (2006): 457–72; Dimitry Shumsky, "Historiography, Nationalism and Bi-Nationalism: Czech-German Jewry, the Prague Zionism and the Origins of the Bi-National Approach of Hugo Bergmann," *Ziyon* 69 (2004): 45–80.

authentic modern Judaism from the jaws of German assimilation, the Prague Zionists staged a Jewish nationalist protest against the liberal fathers, yet their nationalism represented a Czech-German-Jewish hybrid. Nationalization across the monarchy entailed increased cross-cultural interaction and assimilation of "foreign" discourses. All "national" communities transgressed cultural boundaries. The Prague Zionists were exceptional only in doing so openly.

The Prague Zionists' negotiation of Jewish identity emulated that of their fathers. Jews' relationship to the national culture(s) was an open and contested question across Europe, and the different responses produced modern Judaism's diversity: Traditional Galician Jews rejected acculturation but manifested it in practice, while Western liberal Jews openly debated strategies for national and imperial integration. The Jews provide such a precious opportunity to display the paradoxes of imperial nationalization and multiculturalism because negotiation of identity across cultures, elsewhere covert, was overt with the Jews. The historian need not track discursive subterfuges. The Jews often tell us what they do.[25]

Imperial Patriotism as Supranationalism: The Court and the Jews

Nowhere were the Jews more open than in their imperial patriotism. They were the one people who enthusiastically adopted the official *Staatsgedanke* (imperial idea). Poor Galician traditionalists and refined Viennese assimilationists, Orthodox rabbis and liberal scholars, Zionists and socialists all declared their loyalty to the monarchy. "Jews are the standard-bearers of the Austrian idea of unity," stated Jellinek.[26] "If one could construct a specifically Austrian nationality," said Bloch, "Jews would form its foundation."[27] They were the only minority whose "golden age of security" depended wholly on Austria-Hungary's survival.[28] Other minorities, too, preferred the monarchy but had a fallback position: They threatened, on occasion, that they would opt for national independence, whereas the Jews did not and could not. Well into the final days of World War I, when the empire already lay in ruins, Viennese Jewish papers insisted that, federally reorganized, the

---

[25] A classic statement: Aḥad Ha-Am, "Imitation and Assimilation," *Selected Essays of Ahad Ha'Am*, trans. and ed. Leon Simon (Philadelphia: Jewish Publication Society, 1912), pp. 107–22.

[26] Adolf Jellinek, "Jüdisch-österreichisch," *Die Neuzeit* (15 June 1883): 225: "Die Juden … sind die Träger des österreichischen Einheitsgedankens."

[27] Joseph Bloch, *Der nationale Zwist und die Juden in Österreich* (Vienna: M. Gottlieb, 1886), p. 41: "Wenn eine specifisch österreichische Nationalität construirt werden könnte, so würden die Juden ihren Grundstock bilden."

[28] Stefan Zweig, *The World of Yesterday* (New York: Viking, 1943).

multinational empire was viable.[29] The Austrian imperial ideal offered a patriotism whose rationale was pluralist rather than nationalist, making Jewish participation unproblematic. Jews took advantage of it. With exceedingly few exceptions, Austrian-Jewish imperial patriotism trumped any nationalism. Imperial patriotism was the politics of nationalization's prospective losers.

Without intending it, Franz Joseph put together a Jewish coalition that no politician has ever succeeded in accomplishing. The emperor had multiple options for building imperial support among his subjects, and, half wittingly, ended up using all of them with the Jews: dynastic legitimacy, religion, constitutionalism, popular consent, economic growth, and protection of minorities.[30] In the aftermath of 1848, Franz Joseph first chose the dynastic and religious options. This endeared him to traditional Jews but not to liberal ones. The constitutional reforms of 1860–61 and the 1867 Constitution (*Grundgesetz*), however, made him the emancipating emperor and an embodiment of the Enlightenment and the rule of law. Forty years later, he added universal suffrage, enacted in a silent pact with Socialist leader Victor Adler against Parliament. This provided him with a measure of democratic legitimacy. The Austro-Slavist view of Austria as protector of minority nations, articulated in 1848 by the Czech leader František Palacký, did not survive the *Ausgleich* and Hungarian vetoes of federal reform, but with the rise of antisemitism in the 1880s, and Karl Lueger's election as mayor of Vienna in 1895, the ideal reemerged in force among the Jews.[31] Jews were patriots across Europe, but no ruler matched Franz Joseph in popularity.

The deeper nationalization progressed, the greater the emperor's popularity among Jews. Frustration mounted about Austria-Hungary's inability to reform its political structure at the turn of the twentieth century, but so did also Jewish recognition, even among liberals and progressives, that the alternative to the monarchy could only be worse. Imperial ideals, too, went through a measure of modernization and appeared to be more appealing. The imperial cognizance (*Gesamtstaatbewusstsein*) of the court, the bureaucracy (*Verwaltung*), and the military began manifesting

---

[29] David Rechter, *The Jews of Vienna and the First World War* (London: Littman Library of Jewish Civilization, 2001).

[30] James Shedel, "The Problem of Being Austrian: Religion, Law, and Nation from Empire to *Anschluß*," in *Pluralitäten, Religionen und kulturelle Codes*, ed. Moritz Csáky and Klaus Zeyringer (Innsbruck: Studien Verlag, 2001), pp. 117–29.

[31] The idea of a federalist empire enabling the Slavs to organize as a third major imperial constituent to the Germans and Hungarians remained alive among Slavic peoples until World War I, but the Czechs opted for national autonomy. Andreas Moritsch, ed., *Der Austroslavismus* (Vienna: Böhlau, 1996).

supranationalism. Indeed, nationalization itself made premodern imperial ideals look modern and multinational. The Austrian emperor became a supranational figure almost by default.

The instruments of imperial rule, the Verwaltung and officer corps, were multiethnic and multilingual. They provided a measure of administrative uniformity throughout Austria, integrated diverse troops into a loyal imperial force, enjoyed a reputation for relative impartiality, and made efforts to settle provincial conflicts fairly. István Deák noted that the military frame of mind was traditional, looking backward to prenationalism, but nationalization made it supranational.[32] Liberal court circles and modernizing administrators were clearer in their visions of imperial pluralism. Crown Prince Rudolph's monumental ethnography of the imperial peoples, "The Austro-Hungarian Monarchy in Words and Images," a twenty-four volume illustrated guidebook published in German and Hungarian between 1886 and 1902, gave expression to a multicultural view of the empire.[33] When populist nationalism seemed to have taken over Vienna, city and parliament alike, the press introduced peaceful, multinational Bukovina, above all its capital, Czernowitz, as an imperial model, a perfect showcase of pluralism.[34] "Habsburg multinationalism" may have been a product of émigré nostalgia, but it had a grounding in reality.

The Failure of the Jewish–Catholic Alliance: Joseph Bloch and Christian Social Antisemitism

James Shedel has shown how Catholicism, *Rechtstaat* (rule of law), and dynasty merged to define Austrian imperial identity from the Enlightenment to World War I.[35] The vision of the Habsburgs as the most devoted Catholic dynasty, *Pietas Austriaca*, became subdued after Joseph II, but it was still robust enough for Friedrich Schlegel

---

[32] István Deák, *Beyond Nationalism: The Social and Political History of the Habsburg Officer Corps, 1848–1918* (New York: Oxford University Press, 1990). The officer corps did not succumb to national tensions because they depended on dynastic "feudal" traditions. Refusing ideological modernization, they remained beyond the reach of nationalism.

[33] James Shedel, "The Elusive Fatherland: Dynasty, State, Identity and the Kronprinzenwerk," *Inszenierungen des kollektiven Gedächtnises: Eigenbilder, Fremdbilder*, ed. Moritz Csáky and Klaus Zeyringer (Innsbruck: StudienVerlag, 2002), pp. 70–82.

[34] H. F. van Drunen, "'A Sanguine Bunch': Regional Identification in Habsburg Bukovina, 1774–1919" (Ph.D. diss., University of Amsterdam, 2013); David Rechter, *Becoming Habsburg: The Jews of Austrian Bukovina, 1774–1918* (Oxford: The Littman Library of Jewish Civilization, 2013), explains how Bukovina's unique social, ethnic, and geographic landscape created a supranational society.

[35] James Shedel, "The Problem of Being Austrian," pp. 117–29.

(1772–1829) to envision Austria as a universal Catholic monarchy.[36] The Roman Church considered Austria's defeat to Prussia in 1866 a disaster, and Prussian historians celebrated German unification as a Protestant triumph. All the same, Austria remained the bulwark of the pre–World War I European imperial order, and the church recognized Franz Joseph as emperor by divine right. Catholic efforts to preserve the monarchy continued to the very end. During World War I, poet Hugo von Hofmannsthal presented Austria as heir to a cosmopolitan Catholic legacy, contrasting it with Prussian nationalism, and a future Austrian chancellor, Msgr. Ignaz Seipel, proposed a federalist reform to hold the Catholic empire together.[37] Like Jews, Catholics were vested in the monarchy.

Yet a Jewish–Catholic imperial coalition was inconceivable. Emancipation deepened the religious breach between Catholics and Jews. Jewish emancipation was accomplished in the face of church hostility, and Catholic leaders endeavored to diminish the Jewish public role even after emancipation. In turn, postemancipation liberal governments in Germany and Austria were militantly anti-Catholic, and liberal Jews vigorously supported them. During the *Kulturkampf*, liberals compared German–Jewish integration with Catholic separatism in a favorable manner. The Jew became for Catholics an archetype of a threatening modernity. Then, precisely at the moment when Pope Leo XIII sought accommodation with modernity and the nation-state, antisemitic Catholic movements emerged, insistent on the Christian character of state and culture. In Austria, the Christian Social Party, established in 1891, appeared initially as antiestablishment, but by the early twentieth century, high and low Catholicism and traditional and populist antisemitism had converged. The pro-imperial Christian Socials counterbalanced the Pan-Germans' anti-imperialism, but their antisemitism ruled out Jewish–Catholic collaboration and completed the racialization of Austrian politics.

The most prescient advocate of a Jewish–Catholic imperial alliance against German nationalism was Rabbi Joseph Bloch (1850–1923), editor of the Viennese weekly *Oestereichichsche Wochenschrift*. Educated in

---

[36] See his Cologne lectures, 1804–6, in *Kritische Friedrich-Schlegel-Ausgabe*, 36 vols. (Munich: Schöningh, 1964), 13, esp. p. 165. If the lectures still left the identity of the Christian empire in doubt, Schlegel's conversion to Catholicism and move to Vienna in 1808 established it firmly. For the Austrian Empire as embodying German Catholics' hopes prior to 1866, see the introduction to chapter 5.

[37] Ignaz Seipel, *Nation und Staat* (Vienna: Wilhelm Braumüller, 1916). On this episode: Klemens von Klemperer, *Ignaz Seipel: Christian Statesman in a Time of Crisis* (Princeton, NJ: Princeton University Press, 1972), pp. 54–73. David Luft, *Hugo von Hofmannsthal and the Austrian Idea: Selected Essays and Addresses, 1906–1927* (West Lafayette, IN: Purdue University Press, 2011).

a Lemberg *yeshivah*, and then at the universities of Munich and Zurich, Bloch ended up a rabbi of the Florisdorf Jewish community on the outskirts of Vienna. His journalistic attack on the antisemitic theology professor August Röhling, who lent his support to the Tiszaeszlár ritual murder charges, resulted in an 1883 libel trial that catapulted Bloch to prominence. Röhling's popular *Der Talmudjude* (The Talmudic Jew, 1871) had rehashed Eisenmenger's allegations about the Talmud, but Röhling, apprehensive that he would be put to the test of reading the Talmud, failed to show up in court and lost his Prague chair. Bloch became a celebrity. In 1885, he was elected Reichsrat representative from heavily Jewish Kolomea in eastern Galicia. He was reelected twice, with growing Jewish support, but failed in his third run in 1896, when the Polish nationalists withdrew their support. His Reichsrat tenure draws the time limits of the viability of the interconfessional alliance against nationalism. By the mid-1890s, his strategy had reached an impasse. Nationalism and popular antisemitism superseded imperial guards.

Bloch gave a theoretically grounded expression to traditionalist politics. Orthodox Viennese and Galician Jews opposed the German commitments of liberal Jewry: They rejected German acculturation, and they sought collaboration with the Polish leadership and with the Graf Taaffe's conservative Catholic government. Bloch gave them a voice because he thought that nationalist tensions would undermine the monarchy. He was present at the 1882 founding of Adolf Fischhof's abortive *Deutsche Volkspartei* (German People's Party), a progressive federalist party that aimed for national reconciliation, and he witnessed Georg von Schönerer and Heinrich Friedjung disrupting the proceedings. He brought Fischhof's anxiety about German nationalism and his commitment to imperial reconciliation to bear on the Jewish Question. Growing national tensions conflicted with Jewish interest in imperial pacification, he said. Liberal Germanophilia effaced authentic Jewish identity, exacerbated nationalism, reinforced antisemitism, and undermined the imperial project. Taaffe's motley coalition, product of negotiated deals with multiple constituencies, including the Czech and Polish leaderships, was conducive to peace and deserved Jewish support.[38]

Like no one else, Bloch grasped the unique opportunity that Austria offered Jews in the ethno-nationalist age – and its fragility. Austrian state patriotism made it possible for diverse people to be Austrian, and Jews should lead the effort to construct an Austrian nationality.

---

[38] Joseph Bloch, *Der national Zwist und die Juden in Österreich*, and *Israel and the Nations* (Berlin: B. Harz, 1927); Ian Reifowitz, *Imagining an Austrian Nation: J.S. Bloch and the Search for a Multiethnic Austrian Identity, 1846–1919* (New York: Columbia University Press, 2003).

Multilingualism and ethnic pluralism were the monarchy's foundations, and federalization and democratization along Fischhof's ideas should facilitate them. Bloch searched for a democratic Austrian national culture that would emulate the United States, yet remain vested in a constitutional dynastic imperial order. He somehow hoped to contain nationalization by cultivating ethnicity. While benefiting from Galician Jewish Diaspora nationalism in the 1890s, he remained wedded to Austrian nationality and opposed a Jewish one. He saw his statements that Catholics and Poles were averse to antisemitism brusquely refuted. A Jewish alliance with Taaffe and collaboration with the Polish Club were conceivable in the 1880s, but not with the Christian Socials and Polish nationalism in the 1890s. Progressive nationalization rendered Bloch's Catholic alliance and multiethnic Austrian identity utopian.

Bloch ended up turning increasingly to the Socialists. This was not surprising. They were the single Austrian party to offer a measure of protection against antisemitism. Far-sighted Austrian statesmen, like Ernst von Koerber, repeatedly told the emperor that the Socialists were invested in holding the monarchy together. The emperor listened: In 1907, he opted to undermine the nationalist elites with universal suffrage, even at the risk of Socialist growth. As the largest party from 1911 on, the Socialists were *Rechtstaat* devotees, and notwithstanding their Marxist erudition, as Trotsky observed, "not revolutionaries."[39] "K. u. k. Sozialdemokratie" (royal and imperial social democracy) ran the playful appellation.

Unlike Trotsky, the Austrian Socialists did not expect to rely primarily on state power to initiate social transformation, and turned instead to secular education, guided by German humanist ideals, as their instrument. Socialist Jews, like Otto Bauer, were especially vested in secular education, which also served to ground their German identity. This conflicted head-on with the Catholics. Traditional Jews had no choice but to forgive the Socialists their atheism, but the Catholics did not. John Boyer has shown how the Catholic–Socialist culture war undermined first a potential imperial coalition and then, in the interwar years, a republican one.[40] Likewise, progressive Jews and Catholics fought each other, as if German nationalism did not threaten them both. Populist antisemitism rendered impossible the bridges that Bloch and Orthodox Jewry endeavored to build to Catholics, and Catholic anxieties about secularism made Catholic–Socialist collaboration difficult. Socialist and progressive Jews

---

[39] Leon Trotsky, *My Life: An Attempt at an Autobiography* (New York: Pathfinder, 1970), p. 207. My thanks to Wolfgang Maderthaner for the reference.

[40] *Culture and Political Crisis in Vienna: Christian Socialism in Power, 1897–1918* (Chicago: University of Chicago Press, 1995), chap. 4.

underestimated the German nationalist threat and exaggerated the Catholic one, but in the end, it was Catholic mismanagement of nationalization that undermined the Catholic empire, an empire supported by the Socialists and beloved by the Jewish and Muslim minorities.[41]

Socialist Federalism and Multinationalism

Neither historians nor the Socialists themselves have recognized, any time since 1918, just how embedded the Socialists were in the empire. Of the Austrian political parties, their federalist structure replicated most closely the imperial one, their constituency was multinational, and they alone developed a federalist plan for Austria-Hungary and a modern rationale for its existence as a multinational state. Their 1899 Brünn program proposed turning the monarchy into a democratic multinational federation (*Nationalitäten-Bundesstaat*). The historical Crown Lands would be dismantled, and national entities would be set in their place, to be governed by assemblies elected by universal suffrage. Recognizing the difficulty of territorial division along national lines, Karl Renner in the same year suggested a modification that would make the administrative districts, legacy of the Theresian-Josephine period, the governing units. He assumed that the majority of districts would be national in character, but for the minority of "mixed" districts, he fashioned the concept of extraterritorial nationality. As a cultural community (*Kulturgemeinschaft*) and an autonomous association of people (*autonomer Personenverband*), nationality should not be territorially delimited. Czechs and Germans, Hungarians and Slovaks, Poles and Ukrainians inhabiting the same district could have uniform political rights, yet claim allegiance to different nationalities and enjoy cultural autonomy.[42] "Personal national autonomy" became the Austrian Socialists' solution to the monarchy's nationalities' problem.

In *The Question of Nationalities and Social Democracy*, Otto Bauer provided the Marxist underpinnings for Renner's scheme.[43] As a socialist, Bauer confronted a nationality problem for which no serious Marxist

---

[41] Peter Urbanitsch, "Pluralist Myth and Nationalist Realities: The Dynastic Myth of the Habsburg Monarchy – a Futile Exercise in the Creation of Identity?" *Austrian History Yearbook* 35 (2004): 101–41.

[42] Synopticus [Karl Renner], *Staat und Nation* (Vienna: Josef Dietl, 1899); Rudolf Springer [Karl Renner], *Der Kampf der Österreichischen Nationen um den Staat* (Leipzig: Franz Deuticke, 1902).

[43] Bauer, *The Question of Nationalities and Social Democracy*, ed. Ephraim J. Nimni, trans. Joseph O'Donnell (Minneapolis: University of Minnesota Press, 2000); *Die Nationalitätenfrage und die Sozialdemokratie* (Vienna: Wiener Volksbuchhandlung Ignaz Brani, 1907).

explanation existed. A theoretician in every bone, he developed a Marxist theory of nationality. Nationality was not a figment of the bourgeois imagination, he said, but had objective historical determinants. It developed from a "community of fate" (*Schicksalsgemeinschaft*) to a cultural association whose members displayed a collective identity, "a community of character" (*Characktergemeinschaft*).[44] Contrary to Marx, capitalism brought not the dissolution of nations but a reawakening of even those nations that Marx considered "historyless," the Czechs and South Slavs. Modern capitalism and urbanization increased economic and cultural interaction, solidified collective identities, and facilitated national cultural development. The nation-state was superior to the monarchy in allowing nationality a democratic expression, but the nation-state constrained minorities whereas multinational Austria-Hungary (*Nationalitäten-Staat*) opened cultural opportunities for them.

A German-acculturated Jew of Galician and Moravian origins, Bauer had to address, at one and the same time, the German and Jewish Questions. They had uncanny similarities: Germans and Jews alike represented East-Central European diasporas anxious about the surrounding peoples' nationalization. Federalism and personal national autonomy were to sustain imperial integrity and reassure the Germans of protection and cultural autonomy, perhaps even of hegemony, while being inviting and protective of other nationalities. To the Jews, however, Bauer offered nothing more than citizenship and cultural assimilation among the surrounding nations. If the Jews were recognized as a nationality, Bauer's own German identity would be at risk, and so he had to negotiate skillfully between ethnicity and culture. He needed the nation to be solid and "objective" enough to explain the current political conflicts and justify socialist nationality policy, and yet remain loose and contingent enough to allow him, a Jew, to become German. Culture had to trump race, character to beat fate.

The Socialists were forced to confront the Jewish Question when the Polish section denied the Galician Jewish socialists' demand for national recognition. The party endorsed the Polish position, leading to the withdrawal of most Galician Jews and an independent Galician Jewish Workers Party. Bauer devoted a chapter in his book to the question, and it remains an embarrassment. The Jews, insisted Bauer, were once a nation but are no longer so. Following Marx in "On the Jewish Question," he stereotyped the Jew as *homo economicus*. Jewish collective identity was grounded in the Jews' mercantile role in the precapitalist economy. Their special economic function permitted their anomalous

[44] Ibid., esp. p.135 (in German), p. 117 (in English).

existence as a people without territory. Wherever capitalism arrived, the Jews lost this function and assimilated. The modern world was turning entirely Jewish, as "Christians themselves have become Jews."[45] In Western urban centers, Jewish merchants interacted with other groups, and their communal identity dissolved; in Eastern rural areas, peddlers were transformed into an industrial proletariat. Socialist Yiddish culture was admirable, but it was temporary. The Galician Jewish proletariat would have to find national expression among the (increasingly unsympathetic) Poles.

A proponent of the idea that the autonomy of the *Kulturnation* did not depend on territory, Bauer became autochthonous when it came to the Jews: What future, he asked, could a people without territory, common history, or culture have? Jewish identity was ethnic; the modern nation was cultural. The Jews were losing the former to join the latter. The assimilation of Western and Central European Jews – his own first and foremost – demonstrated the proposition: He exchanged German humanism and a vision of universal emancipation for ethnic communal identity, character for fate.[46] The Jewish Socialist who encouraged emergent nationalities to seek cultural autonomy denied it to the one people who, even postnational historians concede, displayed authentic national characteristics, the Jews.[47]

The Galician Jewish problem was minor compared with the Czech problem. In 1911, the Czech socialists left the Socialist Party, dealing a major blow to its supranational aspirations. The Socialists structured their organization – the most extensive of all parties – to emulate imperial federalism and reflect their internationalism: The "little international" is what they called the party. The Czech withdrawal signaled federalism's limits, and evoked Victor Adler's gloomy reflections on class solidarity retreating before nationalism.[48] Yet the Socialists' imperial commitment never wavered. Marx and Engels had already viewed Austria-Hungary as antiquated, yet preferable to Russian despotism.[49] Renner and Bauer thought that the monarchy badly needed modernization – Renner looked

[45] Ibid., p. 374 (in German), p. 294 (in English).
[46] Bauer confused German acculturation with assimilation: Unlike the Adlers and many socialists, he himself remained, in defiance of the antisemites, a member of the Jewish Viennese *Kultusgemeinde*.
[47] Otto Bauer, *Nationalitätenfrage*, pp. 366–81, *The Question of Nationalities*, pp. 291–308; Robert Wistrich, *Socialism and the Jews: The Dilemmas of Assimilation in Germany and Austria-Hungary* (London: Associated University Presses, 1982), chap. 8.
[48] Hans Mommsen, *Die Sozialdemokratie und die Nationalitätenfrage im habsburgischen Vielvölkerstaat* (Vienna: Europa-Verlag, 1963).
[49] Ernst Hanisch, *Der kranke Mann an der Donau: Marx und Engels über Österreich* (Vienna: Europaverlag, 1978), esp. pp. 339–42.

up to Britain as a democratic nationalizing empire – but they rejected any suggestion of dissolving it into its national constituents. They had no love for Franz Joseph, but they were emphatic that Austria-Hungary was viable: It created an integrated economic market, and most nationalities feared Russia and held no prospect of independence. Indeed, the monarchy presaged the universal order of humankind.[50] The Czech comrades, too, would come back.

As the Central Powers scored their successes against Russia and Serbia in the first two years of World War I, Renner rushed to reap imperial benefits. Nation-states, he declared in 1916, have become obsolete. Austria-Hungary showed its viability by withstanding Russian attacks, and the newly acquired territories represented an opportunity to reorganize the monarchy by applying national autonomy. Austria should annex Russian Poland and create an autonomous Greater Poland; and Croatia should absorb Serbia and Montenegro. Poland and Croatia would complete a new Austrian-Hungarian-Slavic imperial triangle, overseeing an integrated Central European economy. A powerful imperial administration would protect the Germans, autonomy would reduce Slavic anxieties, and the Slavs and Germans would join in containing the Hungarians. Renner now identified socialist internationalism and imperial multinationalism. War economy advanced socialization, and proletariat and state, socialism and empire have become one.[51]

It is tempting to view Renner's wartime imperial program as German nationalist: German military victories brought together the programs of the 1848 Frankfurt and Kremsier Parliaments, creating a (no longer democratic) Greater Germany, an Austrian counterpart to German *Mitteleuropa*, and a preamble to the Third Reich. Like every anachronism, this one contains a grain of truth: As a Moravian-born statesman, Renner grasped at any opportunity to consolidate imperial power and assure the German Diaspora national autonomy, and possibly even hegemony. But dissolving socialist imperial federalism into German ethno-nationalism misses the mark. Socialist federalism was, for the most part, democratic and pluralist. It offered to a nationalizing Central Europe a program that respected cultural diversity and made peaceful coexistence possible. At its best, it represented what historian Terry Martin calls "affirmative action imperialism": Endowing emergent Slavic nationalities with autonomy, it

---

[50] Karl Renner, *Die Nation als Rechtsidee und die Internationale* (Vienna: Verlag des Vereines in Kommisssion bei Ignaz Brand, 1914).

[51] Karl Renner, *Österreichs Erneuerung: Politisch-programmatische Aufsätze*, 3 vols. (Vienna: Ignaz Brand & Co., 1916), and *Marxismus, Krieg und Internationale* (Stuttgart: J. H. W. Dietz, 1918), p. 378.

empowered them to become partners in an imperial federation.[52] Socialist federalism was a democratic alternative to imperial authoritarianism and a pluralist alternative to ethno-nationalism.

Bauer shared neither Renner's indulgence of imperial power nor his wartime schemes: He was opposed to World War I and became a Russian prisoner of war. He spoke of the German cultural mission in Eastern Europe, one embodied in his own German acculturation: *Deutschtum* was German humanism and Enlightenment universalism, decidedly nonethnic and nonterritorial, open to Jews and all others. If personal national autonomy was intended to support the German Diaspora, membership was based on individual cultural choice, a postnational concept of Germanness. Contemporary Europe has emerged as a federalist project, and nowadays Europe imagines national identifications as cultural and exterritorial, European-wide. If Austrians could see the image of this Europe in their old empire, they, too, would find a home in Europe.

Liberal Jews Between Nation and Empire

Many German-acculturated liberal Jews felt apprehensive about imperial pluralism and ambivalent toward imperial policies that seemed in conflict with German nationalism. They credited liberal nationalism with emancipation, and endorsed Josephine centralism. They found it difficult to change course when Austria's German role ended in 1866 and, again, when antisemitism terminated the German–Jewish partnership in the 1880s. From Viennese Jewish leader Joseph Ritter von Werthheimer's proud statement, "We shall not approach the Graf Taaffe" (to ask for government protection against antisemitism), to Freud's Count Thun dream (where Freud whistled the Marseillaise to protest Thun's imperious indifference to lawfulness and Deutschtum), liberal Jews appeared reluctant to recognize that the rules of the game had changed: German nationalism was no longer liberal, and Taaffe and Thun were fighting the Jews' own fight.[53] Liberal Jews also resented imperial Catholicism: Freud

---

[52] *The Affirmative Action Empire: Nations and Nationalism in the Soviet Union, 1923–1939* (Ithaca, NY: Cornell University Press, 2001). The Soviets put a premium on fashioning new nations, the Austrians on winning over emergent ones, but both sought to make them federal partners. As Dimitry Shumsky notes in "Brith Shalom's Uniqueness Reconsidered," the Soviets delimited national territories, whereas the Austrians defined the nation culturally and proposed personal autonomy. The Russians imputed national culture; the Austrians offered autonomy. The possible influence of Austrian socialist federalism on the Russian multinational experiment deserves further investigation.

[53] "Zum Grafen Taffe gehen wir nicht!" Joseph Bloch, *Erinnerungen aus meinem Leben* (Vienna: Löwit, 1922), p. 167. For Freud's Count Thun dream, as well as his identification with Hannibal's hatred of Rome, see *The Interpretation of Dreams*, trans. James Strachey (New York: Avon Books, 1965), pp. 241–47, 228–30, respectively. For the

saw himself as taking over Hannibal's mission of visiting vengeance on Rome, and rechanneled traditional Jewish hostility to Edom-Rome into anticlericalism. His German nationalist *Los von Rom* (away from Rome) rubric aside, Catholic antisemitism made it difficult for liberal Jews to see that between an aristocratic Catholic empire and a racialized German nation, they were better-off with empire than with nation.

Yet historians have exaggerated liberal Jewish ambivalence about the monarchy.[54] The focus on the Viennese leadership and intelligentsia and on the *Neue Freie Presse* has created a lopsided view of liberal Jewish politics. Provincial intellectuals and rabbis articulated unabashedly pro-imperial liberal politics, virtually indistinguishable from that of traditional Jews. Moreover, a close reading of Jellinek's essays in the 1880s suggests that he, too, was rethinking liberal politics, distancing himself from German nationalism and imagining an Austrian nation. He sounded increasingly like Bloch. His endorsement of Bloch's 1891 parliamentary campaign was in line with the new liberal Jewish politics.

The recently published fragment of Benjamin Kewall's (1806–1880) "Diary of the 1848 Revolution," written in *Judendeutsch*, suggests that already in 1848, some liberal intellectuals preferred the Austrian Empire to German unification. Kewall was a Czech Jew who found himself in Vienna as the tutor to an aristocratic family. During the revolutionary years, he was heavily engaged in journalism. Hopeful about the March 1848 Revolution, which advanced Jewish emancipation, Kewall was startled by the Czech and Hungarian rebellions, and feared for the empire's integrity. Unlike Ignaz Kuranda, he saw himself first as Austrian and not as German. He followed the debate on emancipation in Germany but was indifferent to the nationalist cause, and relieved when imperial authority was restored. Disappointed that Austrian emancipation was partially rescinded, he still put his trust in imperial reform and prized above all imperial order.[55]

Joachim Jacob Unger (1826–1912), the longtime liberal rabbi of the new religious community of German-speaking Iglau (Jihlava) on the Bohemian-Moravian border, manifested Austrian imperial patriotism

---

classical analysis: Carl Schorske, *Fin-de-siècle Vienna: Politics and Culture* (New York: Knopf, 1980), pp. 181–207.

[54] Steven Beller, "Patriotism and the National Identity of Habsburg Jewry, 1860–1914," *Leo Baeck Institute Yearbook* 41 (1996): 215–38; Robert Wistrich, *The Jews of Vienna in the Age of Franz Joseph* (Oxford: Oxford University Press, 1988). Both represent outstanding work.

[55] *Erlebte Revolution 1848/49: Das Wiener Tagebuch des jüdischen Journalisten Benjamin Kewall*, ed. Wolfgang Gasser in collaboration with Gottfried Glassner (Vienna: Böhlau, 2010), esp. pp. 137, 165–75 (August 27–September 5, 1848), and 331 (September 1, 1850). My thanks to Wolfgang Gasser and the late Siegi Mattl for exchanges on Kewall.

without any of the German nationalist trappings. The Hungarian-born Unger was educated at the University of Berlin and published works in Jewish Studies and Orientalist scholarship, as well as collections of sermons and articles, among others, in honor of the European heroes of liberal Jewish culture, the German Moritz Lazarus, the French Adolphe Crémieux, and the British Moses Montefiore.[56] His 1874 essay in Jellinek's *Die neue Zeit* attacked the German Catholics for their postemancipation effort to exclude Jews from the public sphere, specifically from academic appointments.[57] He was attacking the Prussians and thinking of the Austrians. Like most liberals, he viewed Catholicism as an enemy. But his sermons idolized the emperor and the monarchy in ways similar to those of the *kaisertreu* Orthodox Jews. The cult of the emperor extended into the heart of liberal Judaism.

Unger's imperial patriotism represented a convergence of liberal and traditional Jewish motifs. He transformed Franz Joseph into a liberal monarch, an emperor abiding by the law, respectful of the freedom of conscience, and cognizant of the people's will. Franz Joseph was also a reformer who rejuvenated the monarchy by extending equal citizenship and political representation to all. Unger also cast Franz Joseph as a Roman emperor granting a constitution, and a *Pater Patriae*, a father caring for his peoples. Simultaneously, he used models of biblical kingship. Like Moses Sofer, he portrayed imperial government as a heavenly chorus: Franz Joseph was a liberal emperor by divine right. The imperial family's celebrations and tragedies were frequent subjects of Unger's sermons. In his later years, he thanked the emperor for his service and for sustaining the public spirit against the parties. Franz Joseph reconciled liberal and traditional Jewish political discourses.[58]

There was no Deutschtum in Unger's sermons. Even basic nationalist concepts were absent. Imperial discourse prevailed: *Kaiser, Vaterland* (fatherland), *Völker* (nations) and *Verfassung* (constitution) combined to portray the monarchy as a mosaic of peoples, bonded by law and imperial affection. In their struggle with the Czechs, German nationalists turned

---

[56] *Gesammelte Aufsätze* (Prague: Jakob Brandeis, 1908).

[57] Joachim Jacob Unger, "Mallinckrodt und die Judenfrage in Preußen," *Die neue Zeit* 14:30 (24 July 1874): 254–55. My thanks to Tracey Beck of the Leo Baeck Institute (NY) for tracking down the essay.

[58] "Die Grundsäulen einer wahrhaft freisinnigen Verfassung: Festrede zur Jahresfeier der österreichischen Staatsverfassung, gehalten am 26. Februar 1862," in *Patriotische Casual-Reden*, pp. 3–17; "Die Merkmale der gottberufenen Herrschermacht: Festrede zur Jubelfeier der 25 jährigen Regierung Seiner Majestät, des Kaisers Franz Joseph I, gehalten am 2. December 1873," in ibid. pp. 27–36; "Zwei strahlende Vorbilder: Festpredigt zur Jubelfeier der silbernen Hochzeit Ihrer Majestäten, des kaiserpaares Franz Josef 1. und Elisabeth, gehalten am 24. April 1879," in ibid., pp. 51–58. My thanks to Rachel Ariel of Duke University for first drawing my attention to Unger.

Joseph II into a hero, in veiled criticism of Franz Joseph.[59] In contrast, Unger celebrated Joseph II as a human rights activist and an advocate of religious tolerance. Joseph II had wished to emancipate the Jews, but his shortsighted contemporaries failed him. Like biblical Joseph, he was a visionary: He "knew his brothers but they did not recognize him" (Genesis 42:8). The seeds that the righteous Joseph (יוסף הצדיק) had sown bore fruits three generations later, when Franz Joseph brought his work to completion. Unger created a seamless history of philosemitic Austrian imperialism and directed his arrows against "local patriotism": Josephine reforms had advanced the state's welfare, he said, and not the German nation's interests alone. German nationalism was particular; Austrian imperial patriotism was universal.[60]

Lest Kewall and Unger appear as liberal outliers, Jellinek's politics began looking similar to theirs in the 1880s. In 1866, Jellinek had been the first to warn that racial antisemitism was new and revolutionary, and like many Austrian Jews, he blamed it on the Prussians. In the 1879 electoral campaign, he campaigned for the Liberals by underlining Jewish support for the constitution, a strong central government, and, for one last time, German nationalism.[61] Four years later, he beat a strategic retreat. Jewish support for the Josephine state remained intact: Austrian Jews "cannot forget that it was the central parliament ... which voted for the *Grundrechte*," and not the provincial diets, the Slav nations, or the federalists. Yet choosing the rising Catholic theologian Karl von Vogelsang as his target for attack, Jellinek now redefined liberal Jews' allegiances away from German nationalism.

In 1883, Vogelsang's *Vaterland*, the journal that spearheaded the Christian Socials, charged that the Liberal Era (1861–1879) had turned Austria into "Jewish German." Jellinek responded that Austria was neither Jewish nor German and ridiculed Vogelsang's notion of "Jewish power." He ascribed to liberalism universal ideals – equal citizenship, religious freedom, popular education (*Volksbildung*), and the general draft – and omitted any mention of Deutschtum. The Germans in Austria, he said, were first and foremost Austrians and claimed no allegiance to the Reich. They were not a political nation. To define the nation racially would threaten the monarchy. The Austrian political nation was

---

[59] Joseph II had made German the uniform language of imperial administration. Nancy Wingfield, "Statutes of Emperor Joseph II as Sites of German Identity," in *Staging the Past*, ed. Nancy Wingfield and Maria Bucur (West Lafayette, IN: Purdue University Press, 2001), pp. 178–204.

[60] "Der verkannte Joseph: Rede zur Gedenkfeier der hundertjährigen Thronbesteigung des hochseligen Kaisers Joseph II, gehalten am 30. November 1880," *Patriotische Casual-Reden*, pp. 66–73. Against "local patriotism": "Vorwort," p. iii.

[61] Adolf Jellinek, "Zur Wahlkampagne," *Die Neuzeit* (6 June 1879).

imperial and multiethnic, and the Jews were its standard-bearers. Jellinek sang the praises of Franz Joseph, the emancipating emperor.[62]

Jellinek's strategic retreat did not placate a younger generation, who were enraged by antisemitism. In 1886, they founded the *Österreichisch-Israelitische Union*, the first major Jewish defense organization against antisemitism, and ousted the old *Kultusgemeinde* leadership. Contrary to a common misperception, the response of liberal Jews to racial antisemitism was quick and vigorous. The following years saw the Vienna leadership returning to a more traditional Judaism. The title "Rabbi" was imposed on Jellinek in 1891, and his Jewish Studies school (*Beit ha-Midrash*) was converted into a rabbinic seminary two years later. His successor was Moritz Güdemann (1835–1918), like Jellinek educated in Breslau but more traditional. To be sure, Jewish liberalism remained vigorous. In his medieval Jewish history, Güdemann described the Middle Ages as a period of Jewish–Christian cultural exchange.[63] Responding to Theodor Herzl's *Der Judenstaat*, he reaffirmed the cosmopolitan Jewish mission, rejecting both Zionism and German nationalism as backward.[64] But from then on, liberal innovation reflected more of a conscious effort to rework Jewish traditions than a carefree adaptation of non-Jewish models. Emancipation was under siege. Its accomplishments were defended while its great hopes were gone.

Liberal Judaism and German nationalism parted ways in turn-of-the-century Austria. Deutschtum in its Jewish uses had always meant *Aufklärung* and *Haskalah*. German-acculturated Jews were perplexed that other nationalities did not see Deutschtum's blessings, but they aimed to enlighten the Eastern Jews and not to Germanize the Slavic communities. Now Jewish Deutschtum was purged of German nationalism. In 1894, the Union presented the *Verfassungspartei* with an ultimatum: Dissociate from the antisemites or risk losing the Jewish vote. The Liberals chose to risk losing the Jewish vote. Jewish politics turned elsewhere: to the Socialists, the progressives, and Jewish nationalism.

---

[62] Jellinek, "Jüdisch-Österreichisch," *Die Neuzeit* (15 June 1883), and "Jüdisch-Deutsch," *Die Neuzeit* (15 July 1883).

[63] Moritz Güdemann, *Geschichte des Erziehungswesens und der Cultur der abendländischen Juden, während des Mittelalters und der neueren Zeit*, 3 vols. (Vienna: Hölder, 1880–88).

[64] Moritz Güdemann, *Nationaljudentum* (Leipzig: Breitenstein, 1897); *Nationaljudentum* (Leipzig: Breitenstein, 1897); and *Jüdische Apologetik* (Glogau: C. Flemming, 1906), esp. chaps. 3 and 7.

Imperial Federalism and Jewish Nationalism: Fischhof to Birnbaum

To renegotiate Enlightenment and nationality, Jews of different political persuasions – liberal, socialist, or nationalist – turned to the "Sage of Emmersdorf," Adolf Fischhof. After 1848, the German-educated, Hungarian-Jewish doctor withdrew to a village in Carinthia, but continued to influence politics through his publications and disciples. In 1869, he broke openly with the *Verfassungspartei* by outlining a federalist solution to the monarchy's multinational problem. Austria, he said, was not a nation-state *(Nationalstaat)* but a multinational one *(Nationalitätenstaat)*. If the constitution guaranteed only individual rights and no collective cultural and linguistic ones, then national minorities would remain oppressed. Germans must cease their efforts to exercise hegemony through a centralized administration and abandon hope of arresting emergent nationalities. Instead, Austria must be decentralized along the Swiss model, national minorities must be granted cultural autonomy, and minority rights must be legally protected. National curiae in parliament should be given veto rights on legislation pertaining to their culture. Fischhof's federalism was multicultural and postnational in character. He provided the original blueprint for an affirmative-action empire, empowering emergent nationalities, which would inspire socialists and Zionists in the future.[65]

The ethno-national tensions that gave rise to Fischhof's postnationalism also doomed it. His effort in 1882 to launch the *Deutsche Volkspartei* on a platform combining social reform, universal suffrage, federalism, and national reconciliation, failed miserably. The voice of German national moderation was feeble. Fischhof himself was not impervious to nationalism.[66] His federalism reflected Realpolitik: If the Slavic nationalities turned to Moscow, the monarchy would be lost. Racial feeling, he said perceptively (presaging Arendt on the Pan movements), reflected national loss. He sought to cultivate nationality to contain racism. Affirmative-action imperialism would retain the emergent nationalities' allegiance to Vienna by assuring them cultural autonomy. German culture would flourish and, possibly, remain hegemonic. At moments, Fischhof seemed wistful about Western nation-states and dejected

---

[65] Adolf Fischhof, *Österreich und die Bürgschaften seines Bestandes* (Vienna: Wallishausser, 1869); Fischhof to Franz Rieger, September 29, 1871, concerning the Bohemian language laws, in Richard Charmatz, *Adolf Fischhof* (Vienna: J.G. Cotta, 1910), pp. 270–73; Fischhof, *Die Sprachenrechte in den Staaten gemischter Nationalität* (Vienna: Manz, 1885).

[66] Ian Reifowitz underlines Fischhof's Social Darwinistic view of the German predicament in "Threads Intertwined: German National Egoism and Liberalism in Adolf Fischhof's Vision for Austria," *Nationalities Papers* 29:3 (2001): 441–58.

about the German prospects in a multinational setting. At others, he recognized that Austria represented a unique opportunity for the multiculturalism he was struggling to develop. Responding to the quandary of an empire nationalizing against its will, Fischhof's federalism would become applicable to the European polity only when both imperialism and nationalization were spent.

On the Jewish Question, Fischhof retained the typical biases of a German-acculturated Jew: He saw himself as German and never contemplated a Jewish nationality. The closest he got to linking federalism and the Jewish Question was in 1882 when he suggested to the Viennese Jewish leaders that unless the nationalities were pacified, they would turn antisemitic. His disciples were split: Socialists and progressives retained his German orientation, and Bloch cultivated Jewish ethnicity (*Stamm*) but regarded himself an Austrian, refusing Jewish nationality. In contrast, Jakob Kohn, Isidore Schalit, and other young Jewish nationalists, founders of *Kadimah* in 1882, thought of themselves as applying Fischhof's principles to the Jewish Question. Fischhof's name resurfaced in Jewish nationalist conferences throughout Austria into the twentieth century. Renner's nonterritorial nationality, which reflected the development of Fischhof's principles, shaped the thinking of Galician Jewish nationalists.[67] Diaspora nationalists and Zionists alike became proponents of imperial federalism.

Nationalization in Galicia and Bukovina, the Eastern centers of the Austrian-Jewish population, raised the prospect of Austrian-Jewish nationality. Galicia, known as the "Piedmont of Jewish, Polish, and Ukrainian nationalism," had at the turn of the century a Jewish population of about nine hundred thousand, and Bukovina about ninety thousand. In Galicia, the Poles were a majority in the West and the Ukrainians in the East. The Jews were a major urban element, negotiating between the politically dominant Poles and burgeoning Ukrainian nationalism. Bukovina had the most diverse population imaginable, with Germans, Poles, Ukrainians, Jews, Rumanians, Hungarians, and Old Russians. Germans and Jews collaborated in Czernowitz, but in 1905, Bukovina also witnessed the singular imperial proposal to recognize the Jews as a nationality. In contrast with Russia, Western Europe, and even Vienna, neither violence nor exclusion played a major role in shaping Jewish national consciousness. To be sure, difficulties encountered in integration into the local German and Polish elites reinforced Jewish

---

[67] Werner Cahnman, "Adolf Fischhof and his Jewish Followers," 111–40; Marcos Silber, "The Metamorphosis of Pre-Dubnovian Autonomism into Diaspora Jewish-Nationalism," esp. p. 316; Joshua Shanes, *Diaspora Nationalism and Jewish Identity in Habsburg Galicia*.

nationalism, but the setting of a nationalizing, pluralist, and constitutional empire itself encouraged Jewish nationalist efforts.

Among the German-acculturated Galician Jewish intelligentsia, a major segment went through Polonization after 1867. From the 1880s on, a plurality of Jewish representatives to the Reichsrat belonged to the Polish Club. With the ethnicization of Polish nationalism, they encountered increasing difficulty, from antisemitism to outright demands for Jewish assimilation. The majority of Galician Jews remained traditionally and imperially patriotic, but emergent industrialization created a proletariat, open to socialist and nationalist appeals. A majority of Jewish nationalists believed that the Zionist call for territorialization in Palestine was unrealistic, and Zionists and Diaspora nationalists alike promoted political, cultural, and economic rights for the Jews in Galicia and Bukovina. Even after Herzl launched Palestinocentric political Zionism, says Joshua Shanes, the boundary between Diaspora nationalism and Zionism remained blurred, and the Zionists, too, focused on cultural and political work and not on emigration.[68]

Within the Polish Socialist Party, a Jewish group sought recognition of national cultural claims, and when refused, established their own small party that sought recognition for Yiddish as a national language. In elections, the Jewish socialists continued to support socialist candidates, but they had to compete with a robust Jewish nationalist movement, which made inroads among traditional Jews in ways the socialists never had. The 1907 parliamentary elections saw Jewish nationalists winning, in a pact with the Ukrainians, three representatives in Galicia and one in Bukovina. The Austrian Reichsrat was now unique in having a Jewish Club, promoting nonterritorial Jewish nationality grounded in an imperial vision.

The imperial administrators negotiating the mini-*Ausgleiche* among nationalities in Moravia, Bukovina, and Galicia in the decade preceding World War I were not unreceptive to Jewish national claims. In Galicia, the Poles vetoed them, but in a compromise worked out in Bukovina in 1905, a national Jewish curia was recognized for the first time. Leading Viennese Jewish liberals rushed to the emperor to protest that the new "electoral ghetto" denied Jews their Germanness, and the administration had to rework representation for the Jews as part of the German curia. Waning German-Jewish liberalism was still potent enough to sway the monarchy away from viewing Jewish nationality as part of the imperial mosaic.

[68] Joshua Shanes, *Diaspora Nationalism*, esp. p. 198 f.

The counterpoint to Diaspora nationalism was not liberalism or Zionism, however, but, as Ḥanan Ḥarif suggests in his pioneering study of the Austrian-Jewish-Orientalist imagination, Pan-Asian visions of Jewish integration in a supranational East as an Oriental people. The Oriental vision of the Jews rejected Europe and opted for Semitic solidarity and Jewish regeneration in Asia, but it could not but be imprinted with imperial, national, autonomist ideals. Imperial Austria shaped the Orientalist imagination, and the rejection of Jews as European, which was also part of mainstream Zionism, was of necessity European in character.[69] Ḥarif also questions our understanding of Zionism as nation-state oriented. The imagination of the Jewish future in the East is Pan-Jewish, the gathering of the exiles, and, at the margins, also Pan-Semitic and Pan-Asian. The nation-state is nowhere in sight; the framework is traditional imperial, progressive imperial, or pan-imperial in character.

The potency of the Austrian imperial imagination was also evident among Zionists, whose federalist designs remained vested in Europe. Eugenicist and social scientist Alfred Nossig (1864–1943), who tirelessly sought recognition for Jewish nationality, viewed the nation-state as a threat and thought that Austria-Hungary provided a model for negotiating national diversity. He proposed a continental federalist union, grounded in a French–German reconciliation that would countervail British maritime hegemony. The union would protect Austria-Hungary, make recognition of Jewish nationality possible, and, extending to global imperial collaboration, oversee Jewish settlement and national autonomy in Palestine. As Katherine Sorrels observes, the Zionist Nossig thereby joined progressive antinationalists in imagining an Austrian pluralism that would give rise to European and global federalism.[70]

Yet nobody exemplifies better than Nathan Birnbaum the convergence of Jewish nation and Austrian Empire. Having rejected his Orthodox upbringing in his youth, Birnbaum was a founder of the Viennese student fraternity *Kadimah* in 1882, the first Zionist organization outside of Eastern Europe. For a decade he edited *Selbst-Emancipation*, the sole Western Zionist journal, and was Austrian Zionism's undisputed leader until Herzl. Just as he had coined the term "Zionism" in 1882, he also

---

[69] Ḥanan Ḥarif, "'Revival of the East,' Pan-Semitism and Pan-Asianism in Zionist Discourse" (in Hebrew) (Ph.D. diss., Hebrew University of Jerusalem, 2013).

[70] Alfred Nossig, *Die Politik des Weltfriedens: Die deutsch-französische Annäherung und die Kontinentalunion* (Berlin: Hermann Walther, 1900); Katherine Sorrels, *Cosmopolitan Outsiders: Imperial Inclusion, National Exclusion, and the Pan-European Idea, 1900–1930* (New York: Palgrave Macmillan, 2016), pp. 80–91.

coined, about 1890, the term *Ostjudentum* (Eastern Jewry). In his tour through Galicia in 1892–93, he encountered firsthand the Eastern Jews, and in 1893, participated in founding in Cracow the "Organization of Austrian Zionists," the platform of which combined national regeneration in Palestine with welfare and cultural rights for Austrian Jews. His break with Herzl led him, around 1900, first to cultural Zionism and then to Diaspora nationalism and autonomism. In 1905, he recognized Yiddish as central to Jewish national culture, and in 1908, organized the first Yiddish Language Conference in Czernowitz. Early in World War I, he turned to Ultra-Orthodoxy, and in 1919, became the First Secretary of Agudat Yisrael World Organization. There, too, he remained an oddity, a towering figure who found no permanent home. Notwithstanding the changes in his political stance on the Jewish Question, he always called for resettling Palestine, affirmed the Jewish people's uniqueness, inveighed against "Hellenization" (assimilation), and, until Austria-Hungary fell, underlined the monarchy's integrity as crucial to solving the Jewish Question.[71]

Birnbaum thought that Austria offered Jewish nationalism unique opportunities. Vienna was "a capital of a multinational state, and hence incomparably more suitable for our movement than, for example, Berlin."[72] Located between West and East, Vienna gave rise to a secular Zionist leadership, yet retained connections to Galicia's authentic Jewishness. Zionism shared the ethno-national premises of the antisemitic Pan-Germans, and, like them, it insisted on the unity of state and nation. But whereas they turned against the monarchy, Zionism, paradoxically, could only thrive in an imperial framework. Affirming Jewish identity, suggested Birnbaum, Zionism would help the monarchy dispel antisemitism, which was nothing but expression of natural racial dislike for assimilated Jews. The Jews were an Oriental people, yet they could become a civilizing, European avant-garde in the East. Reterritorializing and productivizing them, Zionism would normalize them and alleviate antisemitism in Europe. Birnbaum's own antisemitism and romantic belief in the Land's redeeming power dissipated over the years, but his conviction that the multinational empire was crucial to Zionism, and that Zionists

---

[71] Biographies: Jess Olson, *Nathan Birnbaum and Jewish Modernity: Architect of Zionism, Yiddishism, and Orthodoxy* (Stanford, CA: Stanford University Press, 2013); Rober Wistrich, "The Strange Odyssey of Nathan Birnbaum," in his *Laboratory for World Destruction: Germans and Jews in Central Europe* (Lincoln: University of Nebraska Press, 2007), pp. 118–53.

[72] Nathan Birnbaum, "Die Zionistische Partei," *Selbst-Emancipation* 5:4 (1892): 40.

must place the interest of the Habsburg state before those of any party, remained firm.[73]

In the early years of the twentieth century, Birnbaum broke with Zionism and became the chief proponent of "*Golus* (or Diaspora) Nationalism." He opined that Jews must be recognized internationally as a nationality, having rights for political and cultural autonomy wherever they resided. In the "Nationalities Congress" in June 1905 in Vienna, he tried to ride the Socialist national autonomy program to promote a Jewish curia. He endorsed extraterritorial nationality, with the Yiddish language as Jewish nationality's main cultural marker, and predicted that nationalization would drive assimilated Jewish cosmopolitans back into Jewish nationalism.[74] Friedrich Hertz delivered the Jewish Socialist response: The curia, like the ghetto, was a corporate imperial relic, whereas Socialist multinationalism was democratic, federalist, and modern. Social Democracy could lead the fight against antisemitism, whereas a Jewish curia would forgo emancipation's hard-won rights. Imperial federalism and extraterritorial nationality framed the debate on the Jewish Question among Jewish nationalists and socialists alike.

Birnbaum's Diaspora nationalism idealized the Eastern Jews as carriers of Jewish *Kultur* against their Western brethren's European *Zivilisation*, and as guardians of the national culture in modern Hebrew and Yiddish. They, and not Herzl's Western Jews, were the people's future. Eastern European emancipation was coming, unlike its Western predecessor, in an era of nationalism, and the Eastern European Diaspora would remain Jewish and unified even after emigrating across the ocean. Hebrew might become once again a spoken language in Palestine, but the rising Jewish proletariat was asking for its spoken language, Yiddish, to be recognized as national. The Russian Bund's role, in the wake of the Revolution of 1905, and emergent industrialization in Galicia suggested that new political and economic opportunities were opening up for Jews everywhere, and the Russian pogroms should not be a deterrent.[75] Birnbaum testified to the pre–World War I optimism, which the

---

[73] Birnbaum, "Zu den Reichsrathwahlen," *Selbst-Emancipation* 4:4 (1891): 2–3; "Die Principien des Zionismus," *Selbst-Emancipation* 5:3, 5:5, 5:6/7 (1892): 27–28, 52–54, and 57–58, respectively.

[74] Solomon A. Birnbaum, "Nathan Birnbaum and National Autonomy," in *The Jews of Austria*, ed. Joseph Fraenkel (London: Vallentine, Mitchell, 1967), pp. 131–46. Birnbaum was perceptive in diagnosing Jewish cosmopolitanism as the product of a rejection by the host nations.

[75] Nathan Birnbaum, *Ausgewälte Schriften zur jüdischen Frage* (Czernowitz: Verlag der Buchhandlung Dr. Birnbaum & Dr. Kohut, 1910); "The Task of Eastern European Jews," trans. Joshua Fishman, *International Journal of the Sociology of Language* 226 (2014): 83–99 (originally: "Ostjüdische Aufgaben," *Bukowinär Post*, July 1905, repr. in *Ausgewälte Schriften*, pp. 260–75).

Austrian monarchy sustained among Jewish nationalists, a spirit so foreign to us who know how things turned out.

Birnbaum's "conversion" to Ultra-Orthodoxy in the early years of World War I reflected a generational pattern of rebellion against modernity, familiar first from the Prague Zionists, then from Franz Rosenzweig and Weimar Jewish intellectuals.[76] The Jews, Birnbaum decided, were not a nation in the modern sense. They were God's people (עם השם), whose mission was to shape history without national power.[77] The Jews gave the nations religious monotheism, but their own idol instincts rebelled against it, issuing in *Haskalah* and emancipation, modern-day Hellenization, and idol worship. Modern Jews, Zionists included, were pagan Europeans (*Heidenjuden*, עכו"ם). Traditionally, the return to Zion fulfilled the commandment to settle the Land, and not just to provide a refuge. Becoming a nation like others in Palestine was denying traditional Zion, and meant exile in the Land, *Golus bei Juden*.[78] Eastern European Jewry, too, "sinned" in not dedicating themselves to a messianic regeneration, which was needed to prevent Zionism from taking over. He was critical of the *Agudah*, too: Passive waiting would not do. Into the 1930s he pleaded for a Jewish turn to agriculture and the crafts, and for support of emigration to Palestine.[79] Austria-Hungary disappeared from Birnbaum's discourse after its disintegration, but his war on Europeanization and his protest against universal Western norms still reflected the old pleading for Jewish uniqueness on the basis of now-bygone imperial diversity.

The monarchy's disintegration in the aftermath of World War I dealt a debilitating blow to Jewish hopes for national autonomy. Signs that nationalization could run its most extreme course and undermine the monarchy had been in the air much earlier.[80] When in 1897 the Badeni Cabinet advanced official bilingualism for Bohemia, even progressive German Jews opposed it, and the Reichsrat became ungovernable. A series of provincial compromises in the decade preceding World War I in Moravia (1905–6), Bukovina (1909–10), and Galicia (1914) gave hope that the monarchy might yet be able to negotiate the equal rights of nationalities (*Gleichberechtigung der Nationalitäten*). But the exit of the Czechs from the Socialist Party in 1911 was a bad omen: The party was

---

[76] Of course, Birnbaum was older, had passed through earlier rebellions, and was unique in adopting Ultra-Orthodoxy.

[77] *Gottes Volk* (Vienna: R. Löwit, 1918).

[78] *Selected Works* (in Hebrew), trans. M. Shonfeld (Tel Aviv: Neẓaḥ, 1942), esp. pp. 10–16.

[79] *Der Aufstieg: Eine jüdische Monatsschrift* 1–12 (1930–32).

[80] Gerald Stourzh, *Die Gleichberechtigung der Nationalitäten in der Verfassung und Verwaltung Österreichs 1848–1918* (Vienna: Verlag der österreichischen Akademie der Wissenschaft, 1985).

a mirror image of the empire. Then came the war and all tables were turned.

World War I brought about the collapse of the continental European imperial order: Gone were the Russian, German, and Ottoman Empires, and gone was Austria-Hungary. Russia imploded first, and the Bolshevik Revolution put pressure on the Austrian Socialists to withhold their support of the Austrian war effort. But the multinational imperial army, which suffered massive losses and major defeats on the Russian front, held on to the end. The population, suffering unimaginable hardship, became restive in the winter of 1917–18, a wave of spontaneous strikes broke out in January 1918, and the sailors at Cattaro mutinied in February.[81] Compared with the French (or British) strikes and mutinies, which were brutally suppressed and brought Georges Clemenceau to power in November 1917, the Austrian uprisings were quelled with a limited use of force, and the Socialist leadership helped negotiate the agreements. In and of itself, World War I did not bring down the monarchy.

The end came almost unexpectedly. Thomas Masaryk, Czechoslovakia's founder, may have determined as early as 1914 that national independence was the course to follow, but his national committee in exile had only limited influence. President Woodrow Wilson's Fourteen Points, which outlined the principles of the prospective postwar European order upon entry of the United States into the war in March 1917, included national self-determination, but until well into 1918, few imagined that this meant the dissolution of Austria-Hungary. The collapse came quickly with the disintegration of central authority in the aftermath of the German military defeat. In the power vacuum created in the fall of 1918, authority devolved into the new self-proclaimed national leaderships. Viewed from the perspective of the interwar order of nationalizing states, Austria-Hungary's writ seemed to have been issued long before the war. Historians nowadays view it as far more contingent.

Empire, socialism, and Jews remained interdependent to the end. As the young Emperor Karl offered a last-minute federal reorganization plan, Socialist leader Victor Adler and the new national leaders were exploring the prospect of a Danubian federation. The antiwar Socialist Left, led by Otto Bauer, had opted to dissolve the monarchy into its national constituents as early as January 1918, but this became a party

---

[81] Hans Hautmann, *Die verlorene Räterepublik: Am Beispiel der Kommunistischen Partei Deutschösterreichs* (Vienna: Europa Verlag, 1971), pp. 19–61; Alfred Pfoser and Andreas Weigl, eds., *Im Epizentrum des Zusammenbruchs Wien im Ersten Weltkrieg* (Vienna: Metroverlag, 2013), pp. 558–77.

consensus only in October. For the Socialists, too, German unification was a last resort. As for the Jews, well into the final days of World War I when the monarchy already lay in ruins, Viennese Jewish papers were insisting that, if it were federally reorganized, it would be viable. The Galician Jewish refugees, amassing in Vienna's dilapidated Second District, blamed their suffering on the war and the Russians, and never on the emperor. When Friedrich Adler, son of Socialist leader Victor, murdered Prime Minister Karl von Stürgkh in October 1916 to protest the war, Galician Jews in Vienna bemoaned the tragedies of both the first socialist and the royal families.[82]

By offering Jews the prospect of national autonomy, late imperial Austria extinguished the ghosts of Edom, lying dormant at its own foundation. Ancient Rome had put an end to Jewish autonomy and devastated the Jewish homeland; the monarchy, which traditional Jews saw as Rome's successor, had been recreating a homeland for them. Without it, the Jews sensed that the golem of national autonomy might yet arise against its maker. In 1879, the administrative high court *(Verwaltungsgerichtshof)* in Vienna privileged "subjective" factors in defining nationality: "Belonging *(Zugehörigkeit)* to a certain nationality [is] essentially a matter of consciousness and feeling."[83] But nationalist efforts to exclude dissenting representatives from one's own curia, or place Trojan horses in the enemy's camp, led the courts to rely increasingly on "tangible evidence" in determining nationality. This all ended, during the interwar period, with Austrian courts excluding Galician Jews from citizenship on racial grounds.[84] Ethno-nationalism turned national autonomy on its head by reifying national identity into race. Responding to the wave of pogroms in Galicia and Ukraine in the aftermath of World War I, Birnbaum published a volume of Jewish testimonies on the Crusades under the title: "Edom."[85] Once Austria-Hungary had fallen apart, the ghosts of Edom returned.

---

[82] Manès Sperber, *All das Vergangene . . .* (Vienna: Europaverlag, 1983), p. 187. I owe the reference to Wolfgang Maderthaner.

[83] Gerald Stourzh, *Die Gleichberechtigung der Nationalitäten in der Verfassung und Verwaltung Österreichs, 1848–1918*, p. 205.

[84] Gerald Stourzh, "Ethnic Attribution in Late Imperial Austria: Good Intentions, Evil Consequences," *Austrian Studies* 5 (1994): 67–83.

[85] *Edom: Berichte jüdischer Zeugen und Zeitgenossen über die Judenverfolgungen während der Kreuzzüge*, trans. Nathan Birnbaum and Hugo Herrmann (Berlin: Jüdischer Verlag, 1919).

Karl Popper, the Open Society, and the Cosmopolitan Democratic Empire

Ernest Gellner spoke of nostalgia for the Austrian Empire as the product of pariah liberalism.[86] Truly, in its time, the empire was least beloved by liberals, even if Jewish. Karl Popper, Gellner's mentor and lifelong nemesis, provided his model for pariah liberalism, yet Popper, a pro-imperial Austrian progressive, was more of an exception than the rule. He represented an *acte final* in the coalescence of empire, socialism, and Jews.[87] His rediscovery of empire during World War II was momentous for progressive and socialist discourse. Holding Austria-Hungary's dissolution to be a major tragedy, and nationalism and the nation-state to be the scourge of modernity, and thus responsible for the catastrophe that had sent him fleeing from Europe, Popper envisioned a cosmopolitan democratic empire. No Austrian Socialist ever dared dream of such an empire because few had made as clean a break with German nationalism or had as critical an outlook on Marxism as he did. Popper called his empire the Open Society, and it shaped the post–World War II, Cold War liberal imagination. The coalescence of empire, socialism, and Jews helped form the postwar world even after all three had vanished from World War II Europe.

A stranger in his homeland even before he emigrated in 1937, Popper has become something of an Austrian national philosopher in recent decades. Born, raised, and buried in Vienna, he is still known primarily as a Western intellectual, an anticommunist prophet of Cold War liberalism. Yet he was the foremost philosopher to refashion the progressive Viennese legacy into postwar transatlantic liberalism. His cosmopolitan empire emerged from the Austrian-Jewish experience of national exclusion, yet provided the opposite response to that of the Jewish nationalists. Whereas they were looking for a pluralist empire to create national autonomy, Popper delighted in empire's ability to break down national boundaries, initiate a cross-cultural dialogue, and give rise to cosmopolitanism. His cosmopolitan democratic empire offered opportunities and represented problems not encountered in earlier discourses. Having emerged

---

[86] *Language and Solitude: Wittgenstein, Malinowski and the Habsburg Dilemma* (Cambridge: Cambridge University Press, 1998), pp. 30–36. Gellner himself was a pariah liberal, but, unlike Popper, he had warm feelings for Czech nationalism and never felt quite as much a homeless cosmopolitan. John A. Hall, *Ernest Gellner: An Intellectual Biography* (London: Verso, 2010).

[87] But perhaps not really the *acte final*? Could Chancellor Bruno Kreisky, who reconfigured Austria's role in postwar Central Europe, be considered the last emperor? A May 2017 conference in Vienna, "Empire, Socialism and Jews V," discussed this possibility. Proceedings have been coming out in *Religions*: http://www.mdpi.com/journal/religions/special_issues/empire_socialism_jews.

during World War II, when the path of Austrian socialism seemed blocked, it disappeared in postwar culture. It is time to recover it.

Viennese Progressivism and Cosmopolitanism

The fortunes of the Popper family tell the story of the mercurial rise and decline of late imperial Habsburg Jewry. Karl's father came from Bohemia, and his maternal grandparents from Silesia and Hungary. In Vienna, they adopted German culture, sent their children to German schools, and became part of Vienna's professional and commercial elite.[88] Simon Popper became the legal partner of Vienna's last liberal mayor, Raimund Grübl, took over the firm in 1896, and moved the family into a huge apartment with adjoining offices across from St. Stephen's Cathedral.[89] He married "up": Popper's mother, Jenny Schiff, was daughter to a family of the Viennese high bourgeoisie. Entrepreneur Max Schiff had come from Breslau, made a small fortune, and had an apartment in the ninth district and a villa on the outskirts of Vienna. He also became a benefactor of the arts. The Popper household embodied the ideals of *Besitz* (property), *Recht* (law) and *Kultur* (culture).[90]

In 1900, Simon and Jenny Popper renounced their membership in the Jewish community and converted to Lutheranism.[91] Simon Popper espoused liberal anticlericalism and preferred the *Aufklärung*'s religion. He was not alone. Vienna had the highest conversion rate of any European urban center, and Lutheranism was the religion of choice for upper-class Jewish converts. Assimilated Jews remained a small minority, however, and neither acculturation nor religious conversion broke the barriers of ethnicity. Upper-middle-class assimilated and nonassimilated Jews belonged to the same social networks. Simon Popper had close non-Jewish friends, but the family's social circle remained primarily Jewish. The progressive Jewish intelligentsia built bridges to nonantisemitic,

---

[88] Marsha Rozenblit, *The Jews of Vienna: Identity and Assimilation, 1867–1914* (Albany: State University of New York Press, 1983); Steven Beller, *Vienna and the Jews: A Cultural History, 1867–1938* (New York: Cambridge University Press, 1989).

[89] Karl Popper, *Unended Quest: An Intellectual Autobiography* (La Salle, IL: Open Court, 1976), pp. 8–10 (henceforth, *Autobiography*), and "Autobiography: Draft," Hoover Institute Archives, Popper Papers (134, 4, 9), (henceforth, Popper Archives).

[90] *Verlassenschaftsakt* of Max Schiff, *Meldearchiv, Wiener Stadt- und Landesarchiv,* Vienna; Popper, *Autobiography*, pp. 53, 82, and "Autobiography: Draft," Popper Archives (134, 4); photos, Popper Archives (86039–10, A and BB). On *Besitz* and *Kultur*: Carl Schorske, *Fin-de-siècle Vienna.*

[91] Tax record for Simon Popper, IKG Archives, Central Archives for the History of the Jewish People, Hebrew University, Jerusalem (A/W 805, 23); *Verlassenschaftsakten* of Simon Popper and Max Schiff, *Meldearchiv,* Vienna; photo negatives, Popper Archives (86039–10, BB). For intermarriage in Vienna: Marsha Rozenblit, *Jews of Vienna,* chap. 6.

secular Austrians, but both groups remained marginal within their own cultures, dissociated from the Jewish community and Catholic and nationalist Vienna. Contrary to their aspirations, assimilated Jews did not become German Austrians. The Poppers spent much of their life in the company of other Jews.

Progressive intellectuals who rebelled against the social conservatism of mainstream liberalism, and sought a dialogue with socialists, surrounded the young Popper. They organized a political party, the *Sozialpolitische Partei*, but it ran against the twin obstacles of Catholicism and antisemitism, and so remained small. The progressives increasingly channeled their efforts into a large network of associations for educational reform, social welfare, and economic planning.[92] The young Popper's social and intellectual milieu was secular and politically radical, trusting in social reform, popular education, and technological progress. It reflected a late-enlightenment spirit (*Spätaufklärung*).[93]

Ethno-nationalism was *Spätaufklärung*'s greatest enemy, but the progressives failed to understand it, underestimated its danger, and responded ambivalently to it. Their ranks included pacifists and federalists, but also German nationalists. They fought antisemitism that offended their humanity and excluded their Jewish members from the German nation, but they could see no harm in expanding the German cultural sphere in Central Europe and regarded Slavic nationalism as reactionary. The *Sozialpolitiker* declined to endorse federalism, or the Badeni language ordinances. Like the Socialists, they piously suggested instead that a democratic electoral reform would facilitate agreement among the nationalities. Analyzing the Czech-German conflict, they found it rooted in divergent socioeconomic development among the monarchy's provinces, hence a transitional problem. Ethno-politics was a passing frenzy. An enlightened administration, encouraging economic development in German areas, could resolve the conflict.[94] Most of them refused to implicate German nationalism with antisemitism. They

[92] Eva Holleis, *Die Sozialpolitische Partei: Sozialliberale Bestrebungen in Wien um 1900* (Munich: Oldenbourg, 1978); Ingrid Belke, *Die sozialreformerischen Ideen von Joseph Popper-Lynkeus (1838–1921)* in *Zusammenhang mit allgemeinen Reformbestrebungen des Wiener Bürgertums um die Jahrhundertwende* (Tübingen: Mohr, 1978), esp. pp. 5–56; Albert Fuchs, *Geistige Strömungen in Österreich, 1867–1918* (Vienna: Löcker, 1949), pp. 133–62; John Boyer, "Freud, Marriage, and Late Viennese Liberalism: A Commentary from 1905," *Journal of Modern History* 50 (March 1978): 72–102.
[93] Friedrich Stadler, "Spätaufklärung und Sozialdemokratie in Wien, 1918–1938," in *Aufbruch und Untergang: Österreichische Kultur zwischen 1918 und 1938*, ed. Franz Kadrnoska (Vienna: Europaverlag, 1981), pp. 441–73.
[94] Michael Hainisch, *Die Zukunft der Deutsch-Österreicher* (Vienna: F. Deuticke, 1892); Otto Wittelshöfer, *Politische und wirtschaftliche Gesichtspunkte in der österreichischen Nationalitätenfrage*, Preußische Jahrbücher 76: 3 (Berlin: Walther, 1894).

believed that antisemitism was rooted in religious prejudice – amply demonstrated by the Christian Social Party – and that secular education was its proper antidote. Clericalism, not nationalism, was their major enemy.[95] They contested antisemitic rhetoric with German *Aufklärung*, rather than with imperial pluralism.

Indeed, the silence of progressives on imperial questions was staggering. Several Fischhof students were prominent among them, but only Ferdinand Kronawetter carried on the Vienna Democratic Party tradition of combining social reform with national reconciliation. Julius Ofner had no interest in the nationality question and regarded himself a moderate German, and Theodor Hertzka leaped into utopianism, imagining an African commonwealth. Paradoxically, among Fischhof's disciples, advocates of Jewish particularity like Rabbi Joseph Bloch and Zionist Isidor Schalit were the ones to promote his vision of imperial pluralism. Most of the progressive Viennese intelligentsia displayed a curious detachment from the empire they helped govern. In Robert Musil's interwar novel, *The Man Without Qualities*, the prominent progressive activist and philanthropist Eugenie Schwarzwald, and her husband Hermann, play leading roles as Diotima, the moving spirit of the imperial campaign, and Tuzzi, the cautious diplomat.[96] Diotima views Austria as bearer of the world spirit and endeavors to grasp its meaning. This must have reflected a measure of nostalgia already. Truly, the Schwarzwald social circle demonstrated complete indifference to the empire.[97] The monarchy appeared too outmoded to deserve progressive attention, and Western states seemed better governed. Musil expressed an attachment that had not existed among the Viennese progressives in imperial times.

The Popper family represented the cosmopolitan pacifist pole on the progressive spectrum. Simon Popper was master of the leading Freemason's lodge Humanitas, and relatives and friends were identified with the Austrian Peace Movement.[98] Unlike the Socialists, neither the Freemasons nor the pacifists drew plans for imperial reform, but the Peace Movement gave rise to the foremost fin-de-siècle imperial cosmopolitan project, Alfred Fried's (1864–1921) proposal for a federalist Europe. Entertaining a materialist-evolutionist view of human

---

[95] John Boyer, *Culture and Political Crisis in Vienna: Christian Socialism in Power, 1897–1918* (Chicago: University of Chicago Press, 1995), chap. 4.

[96] *The Man Without Qualities*, trans. Sophie Wilkins, 2 vols. (New York: Knopf, 1995).

[97] Deborah Holmes, *Langweile ist Gift: Das Leben der Eugenie Schwarzwald* (Vienna: Residenz Verlag, 2013). Holmes confirmed in a conversation with this author March 22, 2013, that she could not remember the subject of the empire emerging in the couple's extensive correspondence.

[98] Popper, *Autobiography*, pp. 11, 13–14; *Offene Geswellschaft – offenes Universum: Franz Kreuzer im Gespräch mit Karl R. Popper* (Vienna: F. Deuticke, 1982), p. 23.

development, Fried regarded the nation-state as a mere stage in the growth of international government, and he expected it to encompass the entire globe eventually. Global government's growth would be gradual, a matter of scientific necessity. To advance it, he proposed a federalist European union, extending to imperial collaboration overseas. As Katherine Sorrels aptly observes, all pre–World War II Pan-European projects were vested in continued European global domination, but in contrast with racial supremacist schemes, Fried envisioned progress toward universal egalitarian humanity.[99] Fried also cherished Austrian pluralism, but if he expected his federalist Europe to protect it, as it would all European states, it is also true that in his evolutionary scheme, the monarchy appeared a vestige of the past and not the blueprint for the future. All the same, as the 1911 Nobel Peace Prize winner, he represented the prime example of progressive Viennese imperial cosmopolitanism prior to Popper.

For the rest, the progressives' grand designs for a future society had little use for Austria-Hungary and instead tended toward utopia. Imagined progressive communities were modern, technologically advanced, and socially engineered, but they seemed contextless. Neither Theodor Hertzka's *Freiland* (free land) nor Anton Menger's *Arbeitsstaat* (labor-state) nor Josef Popper-Lynkeus's *Nährarmee* (nutrition army) was tailored to the monarchy.[100] They may have surreptitiously expressed supranationalism, but they also reflected the progressives' inability to negotiate imperial problems: They divested their utopias of any national attribute. It would make little sense to regard their utopias as German. The requirements of a good social order, in their opinion, were a matter of scientific management, not cultural difference. They may have confounded Aufklärung and Deutschtum, but for most, it seems, Deutschtum was an instrument for realizing Aufklärung, rather than the opposite. They were less nationalists in a cosmopolitan guise than cosmopolitans in a German guise, and in despair.[101]

Like the Socialists, the progressives denied that Jews were a nationality. Striving for recognition as German Austrians, they sought to strip religion and ethnicity of significance – their own first and foremost. Their utopias

---

[99] Katherine Sorrels, *Cosmopolitan Outsiders*, pp. 65–100.

[100] Theodor Hertzka, *Freiland: Ein soziales Zukunftsbild* (Leipzig: Duncker & Humblot, 1890); Anton Menger, *Neue Staatslehre* (Jena: G. Fischer, 1904); Joseph Popper-Lynkeus, *Die allgemeine Nährpflicht als Lösung der sozialen Frage* (Dresden: Carl Reissner, 1912). Ulrich Bach, *Tropics of Vienna: Colonial Utopias of the Habsburg Empire* (New York: Berghahn, 2016), however, emphasizes the way the colonial imagination opened the door to Austrian utopian thinking.

[101] Steven Beller, "Patriotism and the National Identity of Habsburg Jewry, 1860–1914," 215–38.

were commonwealths free of religious superstition and ethnic prejudice, where they would finally find a home: No one would probe their ethnic origins, or challenge their claims to be German. The progressive Jewish intelligentsia could gain nothing from ethno-nationalism: They were "a class ... which claims no particular [national] right ... but can evoke only a human title [and] cannot emancipate itself without ... the complete redemption of humanity."[102] To overcome the burden of their own ethnicity, they needed to dissolve all ethnicity and recover universal humanity. Cosmopolitanism represented the response of ethno-politics' losers.

The progressives' denial of ethno-nationalism flew in the face of historical reality. Progressive culture remained marginal. It conflicted with the religious beliefs, nationalist values, and ethnic identity of most Germans. There was nothing *essentially* Jewish about it, but they remained a narrow segment of the German intelligentsia allied with a subgroup of an ethnic minority who posed for a short time as a social and cultural elite: Vienna's "non-Jewish Jews."

Popper would spend much of his life refashioning progressive philosophy and politics. He purged Viennese progressivism of its ambiguity about German nationalism, relieved Austrian socialism of its German commitments, and highlighted the cosmopolitanism of both. Nowhere was this more evident than in his reintroduction of empire into progressive discourse. Responding to the predicament of German-Jewish identity, he rejected both German and Jewish identities in favor of cosmopolitanism, and made the democratic empire cosmopolitanism's agent. No one else, progressive or socialist, went this far. Popper remained a permanent exile, a citizen only in an imaginary Open Society.

Rejecting Deutschtum and dissociating the Aufklärung from Germany, Popper vindicated the Enlightenment, but also inherited its dilemmas. He was almost as impatient as the progressives had been with imperial pluralism. Discounting all national, ethnic, and religious identity, he posited universal visions of the Open Society and the democratic empire where none of them counted.[103] His hostility toward Zionism, his rejection of any political role for religion (for Judaism even more than Christianity), and his defense of liberalism and the Enlightenment were

---

[102] Karl Marx, "Zur Kritik der Hegelschen Rechtsphilosophie. Einleitung," In *Werke*, 41 vols. (Berlin: Dietz, 1959–68): 1 (1976): 390.

[103] *The Open Society and Its Enemies*, 2 vols. (London: Routledge & Sons, 1945). Michael Polanyi, another cosmopolitan fugitive from Central Europe and, like Popper, an assimilated Jew, popularized the term "Republic of Science" in the postwar years: "The Republic of Science" [1962], in his *Knowing and Being* (Chicago: University of Chicago Press, 1969), pp. 49–72.

metamorphoses of Viennese progressivism. He remained an assimilated progressive Jew to the end of his life. Through his migration and exile, the democratic empire, a product of marginal Viennese milieux, made cosmopolitan dreams and dilemmas a part of mainstream Western culture.

Socialism and the Democratic Empire

"The breakdown of the Austrian Empire and the aftermath of the First World War ... destroyed the world in which I had grown up," wrote Popper in his *Autobiography*.[104] Following the dissolution of the empire in the fall of 1918, he left the *Realgymnasium* to participate in the Austrian Revolution. He first joined the Socialist students, then switched to the Communists. But he was not one to accept party discipline and dogma. After the failed Communist *Putsch* of June 1919, he dissociated himself from the party. His rejection of communism was a prolonged process, stretching over years, not months, as his *Autobiography* might suggest. He continued to spend his time with communist youth. In the early 1920s, he was involved in socialist educational programs, and for a year (1924–25), he became a full-time social worker at a day-care center (*Hort*) for proletarian youth. But he always seemed the odd person out, and, having been sued by the city for a youth's injury, and acquitted, he withdrew from social engagements and focused on his academic career.[105] Still, he remained a Socialist and left Vienna in January 1937, considering himself a member of the now-banned party.

Popper was a socialist dissenter, however, and he was developing a critique of Marxism and the Austrian Socialists. Already in 1924, he was suggesting that Eduard Bernstein's revisionism and Carl Menger's marginalism provided an alternative to Austro-Marxism.[106] In his 1927 essay "Toward a Philosophy of the Homeland Idea," Kant, and not Marx, showed the way to socialism and internationalism.[107] Noting the amorphous character of homeland (*Heimat*), he expressed anxiety lest it foreclose new experiences as "foreign," and purged the concept of Romantic nationalist meanings. *Heimat* established a "naturally given primitive cultural community," but the nation was a legal association, and law, not cultural heritage, set national boundaries. A universal ethic must shape national legal codes, making good citizenship compatible with internationalism. Education should cultivate respect for law, a sense of justice, and a critical awareness of social inequities. It should not foster

---

[104] Popper, *Autobiography*, p. 32.
[105] Ibid., pp. 7–8, 10, 31–41, 53–55, 71, and 197 n. 2.
[106] My interview with Peter Milford (Hilferding), January 30, 1999.
[107] "Zur Philosophie des Heimatgedankens," *Die Quelle* 77 (1927): 899–908.

patriotism, or love of Heimat. "From good Germans to good cosmopolitans," he quoted Eduard Burger, a noted socialist school reformer. He offered the Socialists no help in appropriating Heimat from the Right. On the contrary: He sought to free Socialism from the German nationalist *Heimat* and return them to internationalism.

Popper and his future wife were among the crowd in front of the Justizpalast on Bloody Friday, July 15, 1927. They watched incredulously as the police opened fire on "peaceful and unarmed social democratic workers and bystanders. We were lucky to escape."[108] He thought that the police attack was unprovoked, but, all the same, blamed the Socialist leaders for the "massacre." Their "suicidal" policies gave the government an opportunity to use violence. He understood well the event's historical significance. His call in *The Open Society* for a steadfast defense of democracy encapsulated his policy proposals to the Austrian Socialists. He thought that the government's commitment to democracy was shaky and the fascist threat real. The Socialists needed to contain their rhetoric so as not to provoke a coup, but failing that, they had to defend democracy by force. The two goals may have been in conflict, but already as a young man, Popper saw the situation clearly, and his socialism was sui generis.

In the scientific philosophy of the Vienna Circle, Popper found – for all his lifelong confrontation with it – the legacy of the Enlightenment and of fin-de-siècle progressivism. The Circle was the fountainhead of the logical positivist movement that, during the interwar period, developed an organizational network in Central Europe's urban centers: Vienna, Berlin, Prague, Warsaw, Budapest, Lvov, and Bratislava. It had disciples throughout Europe and North America. The Circle sought to apply recent advances in logic, mathematics, and scientific theory to philosophy. Many members were deeply influenced by Ludwig Wittgenstein's *Tractatus Logico-Philosophicus* (1922) and declared war on traditional philosophy, especially metaphysics. Among the more famous were Moritz Schlick, Otto Neurath, and Rudolf Carnap. Popper's relationship to the Circle was problematic. He developed his philosophy of science in critical dialogue with theirs, but within a framework foreign to positivism, that of the marginal Kantian tradition leading from Jakob Fries to Leonard Nelson. Recognizing his originality, the Circle provided him with opportunities

---

[108] "Autobiography: Draft," Popper Archives (135, 1).

that eventually made him famous, but the disjunctions between their positivism and his Kantianism remained a source of constant tension.[109] All the same, having completed *Logik der Forschung* in 1934, Popper became an active member of the Circle's network, a "Central European intellectual."[110]

By 1934, however, the Circle's network was living on borrowed time. In Germany, it could no longer operate openly. Most members lost their academic positions and emigrated when they could. In Austria, they were under attack in the academy and considered suspect by the *Ständestaat*. Proto-fascist regimes were harassing them in other East-Central European countries, too. Beginning in 1935, none of the Circle's annual congresses for scientific philosophy could take place in Central Europe. Instead, they were held in Paris, Copenhagen, Cambridge (England), and Cambridge (Massachusetts). They solidified British and American interest in scientific philosophy and facilitated the members' migration. Within a few years, most of them had left Central Europe for England and the United States.

After the failed Nazi coup of July 25, 1934, Popper thought that a Nazi takeover and a German invasion of Austria were merely a matter of time. In a letter from 1942, a close friend remembered his foreboding of the impending disaster: "[We] often recall your remarkable predictions of the catastrophe in its totality as well as in more detailed features."[111] He had no chance of an academic appointment and was searching desperately for a way out of Austria. After much travail, he accepted an offer from Canterbury College in Christchurch, New Zealand. In January 1937, he left Austria forever, leaving behind friends and relatives, including his sick mother and a sister.[112] Most of them he would never see again. But he was determined not to revisit his past, and would spend the postwar years in

---

[109] Popper, *Autobiography*, pp. 72–90 and "Autobiography: Draft," Popper Archives (134, 12); Herbert Feigl, "The 'Wiener Kreis' in America," in *The Intellectual Migration: Europe and America, 1930–1960*, ed. Donald Fleming and Bernard Bailyn (Cambridge, MA: Harvard University Press, 1969, pp. 630–73); Malachi Hacohen, *Karl Popper – The Formative Years, 1902–1945* (New York: Cambridge University Press, 2000), chaps. 5–6; Friedrich Stadler, *Studien zum Wiener Kreis* (Frankfurt am Main: Suhrkamp, 1997).

[110] Karl Popper, *Logik der Forschung: Zur Erkenntnistheorie der modernen Naturwissenschaft* (Vienna: Springer, 1935). Translation: *The Logic of Scientific Discovery*, trans. Karl Popper (London: Hutchinson, 1959).

[111] Frederick Dorian (Fritz Deutsch) to Popper, April 10, 1942, Popper Archives (28:6, under Hellin). The "we" are Dorian and Fritz Hellin, Viennese friends from Popper's youth.

[112] On Popper's emigration, see my "Karl Popper in Exile: The Viennese Progressive Imagination and the Making of The Open Society," *Philosophy of the Social Sciences* 26 (1996): esp. 455–57.

England. In 1945, Carnap inquired whether he might consider going back to Austria. "Never," answered Popper.[113]

As German troops overran Europe and the Japanese advanced down the Pacific Ocean, Popper worked feverishly to complete *The Open Society*, thinking at times that he might be writing civilization's testament.[114] The book was his contribution to the war effort, and he invested it with a fighting soldier's zeal. *The Open Society* explained the triumph of fascism, the surrender of Central European democracies, the issues at stake in the war, and the principles for social reconstruction afterward. Completed in February 1943, the work consisted of three controversial critiques of Plato, Hegel, and Marx that traced modern totalitarianism to the "intellectual leaders of humankind."[115] Popper opined that the fascist drive to return to "tribal" society fed on anxieties arising from rapid changes in open societies. Plato conspired to halt the economic development of Athens and substitute an authoritarian regime for democracy. Hegel twisted progressive philosophy and politics so that they served Prussian "tribal nationalism." Marx was essentially a progressive democrat, but his scientific pretensions concerning historical inevitability weakened the socialists' resolve to confront fascism. To socialists, fascism's rise and socialism's eventual triumph were historically predetermined. They fought fascism halfheartedly, leaving liberal democracy defenseless. The fascists were quick to destroy democracy.

Postwar reconstruction of an open Europe was Popper's project. His Open Society was the assimilated Jewish philosopher's cosmopolitan homeland, an imagined community that would end his national exclusion and cultural marginalization. It was a society that paid no attention to one's ethnic origins or religious and national affiliation. It was democratic, but it resembled an empire and not a nation-state. Empires, opined Popper, provided a necessary transition between tribal nationalism and cosmopolitanism. They were the only effective remedy to nationalism. Imperialism lowered barriers among ethnic groups, permitted enlightenment to penetrate into ghettos, and forced closed communities open. Popper was willing to see an imperial metropolis temporarily gain at the expense of the peripheries for the sake of an eventual dissolution of the boundaries between center and margins. He willingly took the risk of

[113] Popper to Carnap, June 23, 1945, Carnap Collection, Archives for Scientific Philosophy, University of Pittsburgh.
[114] Colin Simkin, "The Birth of *The Open Society*," in his *Popper's Views on Natural and Social Science* (Leiden: Brill, 1993), pp. 183–90, and email communication to author, May 23, 1997.
[115] *The Open Society*, 1: 1.

imperial hegemony of a (German or Hungarian) *Staatsnation* in the hope that it would promote Aufklärung rather than racial Deutschtum.

The Austrian legacy explains Popper's imperial idealism. He thought that German nationalism and Austrian imperialism were at odds and that Aufklärung and empire were concordant. His charitable view of the British Empire reinforced his imperialist bias. He considered the British Commonwealth to be the largest free community on earth. He was little aware, if at all, of the British vogue of progressive imperialism, but the Commonwealth first extended hospitality to him in its metropolis, England, then provided him with a refuge in New Zealand during the war.[116] German totalitarianism and British democracy were at war. If the democratic cosmopolitan empire could be saved, nationalism would subside and enlightenment would spread. The Open Society represented the last metamorphosis of late imperial Austria, projected onto the British Empire.

The democratic cosmopolitan empire dominated *The Open Society* from beginning to end. The history of humanity was a struggle between progressive imperialism and reactionary nationalism. Classical Athens was the first open society, the first to break "tribalism's" chains, to overcome myth, magic, and custom, and to found politics on *logos* and law. Secular, commercial, democratic, and cosmopolitan, it embodied the progressive imperial ideal, but eventually succumbed to totalitarian Sparta.[117] Later, Alexander the Great and the Roman Empire advanced universalism. "From Alexander onward, all the civilized states of Europe and Asia were empires, embracing populations of infinitely mixed origin. European civilization [has] remained international or, more precisely, inter-tribal ever since."[118] In the nineteenth century, tribal nationalism reared its ugly head once again. Hegel and German intellectuals promoted Prussian nationalism, and within a century, Central Europe succumbed to German barbarism. Nationalism must be reined in if postwar Europe is to be an Open Society. An international legal order would best accomplish such a task.[119]

---

[116] Alfred Zimmern, *The Third British Empire*, 3d ed. (London: Oxford University Press, 1934).

[117] In *The Greek Commonwealth: Politics and Economics in Fifth Century Athens* (London: Oxford University Press, 1911), Alfred Zimmern developed a similar vision of the Athenian Empire as anticipatory of the British Commonwealth, but there is no sign that the book was available to Popper in New Zealand. Popper's view of Athenian democracy was anachronistic. I discuss it in detail in *Karl Popper*, pp. 410–16, and "La città celeste di Popper: Platone, Atene e la società aperta," in *Karl R. Popper, 1902–2002: Ripensando il razionalismo critico (Nuova Civiltà delle Macchine* 20: 2), ed. and trans. Stefano Gattei, 2 vols. (Bologna: Analisi-Trend, 2002), 2: 12–33, 160.

[118] Popper, *The Open Society*, 2: 48.   [119] Ibid., 1: chap. 10, 2: chap. 12.

Central European conceptions of nationality and imperialism shaped Popper's account. Imperial Austria made *Volksstamm* (ethnicity) the basis of claims for *Nationalität* and cultural autonomy. Popper spoke, therefore, of "tribal nationalism" (ethno-nationalism).[120] But there were no good and bad nationalisms: He would not second a cultural Deutschtum any more than an ethnic one. The only nation he recognized was a political one, founded on the French Revolution's concept of citizenship, and he subjected it, too, to international law.

Almost alone among progressives and socialists of his generation, Popper challenged national self-determination and the nation-state. Nationalities did not really exist. German thinkers from Herder to Fichte to Hegel invented them to serve the interests of reactionary states.

The idea that there exist natural units like nations or linguistic or racial groups is entirely fictitious.... The principle of the national state ... owes its popularity solely to the fact that it appeals to tribal instincts.[121] ... None of the theories, which maintain that a nation is united by common origin, or a common language, or a common history, is acceptable, or applicable in practice. The principle of the national state ... is a myth. It is an irrational, a romantic and Utopian dream.[122]

Wilson's and Masaryk's "well meant" effort to apply national self-determination consistently throughout Central Europe – "one of the most mixed of all the thoroughly mixed regions of Europe" – was an incredible folly that brought about the failure of the Treaty of Versailles: "An international federation in the Danube basin might have prevented much."[123] National Socialism represented the nation-state's culmination. So did the tragedy of Bosnia, he said in his 1994 Prague speech. If national self-determination did not lose its authority, postcommunist Central Europe could also fall prey to ethnic terrorism. The only remedy was abandoning self-determination, recognizing state boundaries as conventional, sanctioning the status quo, and establishing an armed international organization to guarantee peace. National identities were false, reactionary, and utopian. Individual, imperial, and cosmopolitan identities were true, progressive, and possible.[124]

---

[120] Auriel Kolnai's use of "tribal egotism" in *The War Against the West* (New York: Viking Press, 1938), may have suggested the term "tribal nationalism" to Popper, but it seemed so fitting because it both connoted primitivism and conformed to official terminology.
[121] *The Open Society*, 1: chap. 9, n. 7(1).   [122] Ibid., 2: 49.   [123] Ibid., 2: chap. 12, n. 53.
[124] Ibid., 1: chap. 5, n. 13(2); chap. 6, n. 44 (in later editions, Popper expanded this note to rebut Hans Morgenthau's dismissal of an international legal order); chap. 9, n. 7; 2: 238; chap. 12, nn. 19, 53; chap. 13, n. 2(1); Popper, "Kant's Critique and Cosmology," in *Conjectures and Refutations* (New York: Basic Books, 1963), esp. p. 182; "Epistemology and Industrialization," in *The Myth of the Framework* (London: Routledge, 1994), pp. 185–87; "On Culture Clash," in *In Search of a Better World* (London: Routledge, 1992), pp. 118–21; and "Prague Lecture," https://www.lf3.cuni.cz/3LFEN-255.html.

To his contemporaries, Popper's view of nationalism as a curiously successful intelligentsia's fraud, a catastrophe brought upon Central Europe by treacherous intellectuals – *la trahison de clercs par excellence* – seemed incredible.[125] Recent decades have seen postnational U.S. historians of Central Europe developing a historiography that sustains precisely such a view.[126] Popper ingeniously deconstructed nationality, pointing out its complex historical formation and diffused character. He never extended the same mode of inquiry to imperialism, however. The nation-state was historicized and delegitimized; empires went unexamined and were vindicated. His recollection of historical episodes of imperialism was selective. He recalled Alexander's cosmopolitanism, the Napoleonic Code, and Austrian pluralism, not Spanish colonialism, the Middle Passage, and Nazi *Lebensraum*. Imperialism represented cosmopolitanism's possibility: This was enough. The historicity of imperial identities – past or future – never became an issue. They were divested of historical specificity. They did not emerge from historical identities but overcame them.

Popper emphasized that if we deconstruct false collectives and get to the individual, we will reach the truly universal. Yet unlike Austrian imperial identities, his cosmopolitan identity seemed abstract and unreal. Popper himself conceded that "concrete groups" – families, churches, voluntary associations, possibly even ethnic communities – would remain even in the Open Society. They would continue to fulfill some of the functions that kinship groups had in the "closed society," and so an absolutely open society was sheer utopia. Indeed, closed groups were essential: People, Popper said unsympathetically, will "try to satisfy their emotional social needs as well as they can."[127] But "emotional social needs" remained foreign to him, implicated with fascism. He never negotiated between the closed society and Open Society, ethnicity and cosmopolitanism, nation and empire, or showed their possible convergence in his future cosmopolitan federation.

There was no room for negotiation with fascism. Popper's categorical rejection of the claims of closed communities against the cosmopolitan empire ought to be understood in the context of Central European

---

[125] I would make mention today of my own offenses (Genesis 41:9): In my earlier work, I, too, was incredulous about Popper's theory of nationalism. He had seen deeper than I did.

[126] Rogers Brubaker, *Nationalism Reframed* (New York: Cambridge University Press, 1996); Pieter Judson, *Guardians of the Nation* (Cambridge, MA: Harvard University Press, 2007); Jeremy King, *Budweisers into Germans and Czechs* (Princeton, NJ: Princeton University Press, 2002).

[127] *The Open Society and Its Enemies*, 2d ed. (London: Routledge & Kegan Paul, 1952), 1: 175; p. 171 of the American ed. (Princeton, NJ: Princeton University Press, 1950).

fascism. He acknowledged "diversity" and assailed efforts to suppress difference. In one of his last public appearances, he acerbically suggested that the "homogenous populations" of Germany and France were due to nationalizing states using "political and educational means [to] suppress minorities or dialects."[128] Still, he thought that ethnic and religious differences were insignificant. Imperial pluralism existed, but unlike universal humanity, it was no cause for celebration and must not infringe on cosmopolitanism. The first response to the racist argument that those who are different are inferior and cannot be members of the nation is *not* that we ought to respect difference; it is that we are all equally human and entitled to equal rights as citizens.

The Open Society defended this universal vision eloquently. Central Europe ensured that it remained utopian. Ethno-nationalism first gave rise to cosmopolitan dreams, and then made them impossible. But Popper would not give up. He searched throughout Western history for cosmopolitan moments to provide instruction and encouragement for those fighting fascism. He found Socrates, Pericles, and classical Athens. They became the origin of the Open Society. It mattered little that it happened two millennia ago, far from Central Europe. Where the Austrian Empire failed, Athens succeeded. Progressive imperialism triumphed over nationalism and ethno-politics. Where he found success once, the exile could hope, amid global ruins, for another.

Cosmopolitanism Without Jews?

Popper presented his views on the Jewish Question as flowing from his cosmopolitanism. Jewish religion and nationality were impediments to cosmopolitanism; hence, assimilation was a moral imperative. In fact, he got the relationship between cosmopolitanism and assimilation wrong. It was precisely the difficulties of assimilation that gave rise to cosmopolitanism. Finding themselves excluded from the nation, Jewish intellectuals imagined cosmopolitan communities that would accept them. Cosmopolitanism became a precondition to assimilation, not, as Popper surmised, vice versa.

An unbridgeable gap separated cosmopolitan dreams from reality, the Open Society from nationalizing Central Europe. The gap haunted Popper with a vengeance as he tackled the Jewish Question. In stark contrast with his constructionist view of the nation, Popper held an essentialist racial view of the Jews and Jewish history. The Hebrew Bible was, he said, the fountainhead of tribal nationalism, and the doctrine of

---

[128] Popper, "Prague Lecture."

the Chosen People presaged modern racism.[129] Rabbinic Judaism shut the Jews off from the world for two millennia, and the ghetto was the ultimate closed society, a "petrified form of Jewish tribalism."[130] Its inhabitants lived in misery, ignorance, and superstition, their separate existence evoking the suspicion and hatred of non-Jews and fueling antisemitism. It was imperative that the ghetto be opened and that enlightenment should follow. Integration was the only solution to the Jewish problem.[131]

For Popper, Jewish nationalism reaffirmed tribal bonds, and was a colossal mistake.[132] He made no distinction between Diaspora nationalism and cultural or political Zionism: All were misguided. Reviving the ancient language (Hebrew) in Europe was no more legitimate than colonization in Palestine. As an ethno-national response to antisemitism, Jewish nationalism was bound to increase hatred of the Jews in Europe, and Zionism was sure to incite a new conflict with the Arabs in Palestine. Israel was a tragic error: "The status quo is the only possible policy in that maze of nations which peoples Europe and the Near East."[133] Once Israel was founded, there was no way to undo the mistake, and he "strongly opposed all those who sympathize with the Arab attempts to expel the [Jews]."[134] But he remained highly critical of the Jewish state, insisting that its "racial" character give way to equal citizenship.[135]

A viable Jewish diaspora could have solved Popper's quandary, but in a world threatened by the National Socialists or dominated by their memory, a secure diaspora appeared just as much a dream as cosmopolitanism.[136]   A   separate   Jewish   community,   however

---

[129] Karl Popper, "Toleration and Intellectual Responsibility," in his *In Search of a Better World*, pp. 188–90; Popper, *The Open Society*, 1: 6–8, chap. 2, n. 3; 2: 21–22.

[130] Popper, *The Open Society*, 2: chap. 11, n. 56.

[131] Such views of Jewish history and culture were not uncommon among assimilationist intellectuals in Austria and Germany who internalized the liberal Protestant critique (Adolf von Harnack et al.) of postbiblical Judaism. (See chapter 9.) Occasionally, even intellectuals who remained Jewish, like philologist and literary historian Erich Auerbach, shared them. (See chapter 11.)

[132] Until the last decade of his life, Popper rarely expressed himself in public about Zionism or the Jewish Question, but he poured out his wrath on Israel in private. His single major treatment of the Jewish Question is in his *Autobiography*, sec. 21. It proved highly controversial.

[133] Popper, "Autobiography: Draft."   [134] Ibid.

[135] My interview with Popper, January 26, 1984. He began with: "Of all the countries benefiting from European civilization, only South Africa and Israel have racial laws that distinguish between rights of different groups of citizens. The Jews were against Hitler's racism, but theirs goes one step further. They determine Jewishness by mother alone."

[136] Even George Steiner, who more than any postwar intellectual conceived of the cosmopolitan diaspora as the Jewish contribution to humanity, could not foresee a secure future for it, and he wondered whether its burden, for Jews and the rest of humanity alike, was justified. See George Steiner, *The Portage to San Cristóbal of A.H.* (New York:

acculturated, thought Popper, endangered the Jews. Antisemitism was to be feared in all places and times, and assimilation was the only viable response: "[A]ll people of Jewish origin [had] to do their best not to provoke [antisemitism]." The Jews did the opposite. They "insisted that they were proud of their [racial origins]" and triggered a racial war that brought their own destruction.[137] They "invaded politics and journalism," drawing attention to their wealth and success, and, assuming leadership positions among the Socialists, they contributed to fascism's triumph.[138] In his critique of Austrian Jews, Popper descended from cosmopolitanism to a position dangerously close to the antisemitism he feared. The increasing nationalization of Central European politics overwhelmed his cosmopolitanism. Jews were not to expect the fulfillment of cosmopolitanism but to accommodate themselves to ethno-nationalism. They had to disappear as Jews. They could only become cosmopolitan citizens in a Kantian Kingdom of Ends.

The antinomies of cosmopolitanism meant that Popper did not leave much more room for the assimilated Jew than he did for the Zionist. Jews were citizens of the cosmopolitan empire but advised to keep a low profile in politics. He gave up on imperial pluralism's promise to the Jews to be recognized as a nationality, and yet he could not make good on his cosmopolitan empire, which turned out to be utopian. His difficulties, however, were historically contingent due to fascism, and not essential to his cosmopolitanism. Contemporary Europeans negotiate more easily between pluralism and cosmopolitanism, and recognize the Jews as European. Popper's cosmopolitanism can appeal to them in ways more immediate than Habsburg imperial pluralism. His democratic cosmopolitan empire provides a historical link between late imperial Austria and contemporary Europe. Presaging empire's rehabilitation in contemporary academic discourse, Popper made a progressive Austrian national narrative leading from the monarchy through the First and Second Republic to a European Austria seem attractive.[139] We have not yet heard the last of his cosmopolitanism.

Simon and Schuster, 1981), as well as "Our Homeland, the Text" [1985] and "Through That Glass Darkly" [1991], both in his *No Passion Spent: Essays 1978–1995* (New Haven, CT: Yale University Press, 1996), pp. 304–27, 328–47.

[137] Popper, "Autobiography: Draft": "It was most understandable that [the Jews] who were despised for their racial origin should insist that they were proud of it. But the logic of this racial pride was, obviously, mutual contempt, and ultimately racial war."

[138] Ibid.

[139] Michael Hardt and Antonio Negri, *Empire* (Cambridge, MA: Harvard University Press, 2000); Jane Burbank and Frederick Cooper, *Empires in World History: Power and the Politics of Difference* (Princeton, NJ: Princeton University Press, 2010).

Conclusion

Empire, socialism, and Jews: The Austro-Hungarian Monarchy opened exceptional opportunities for diverse Jewish identities and politics, and offered a measure of protection against antisemitism. Jews responded with vibrant imperial patriotism, and this chapter tracked it across the Jewish spectrum, often visiting less familiar Jewish quarters. Imperial patriotism represented an alternative to German national patriotism, and was at least as powerful. In the Austrian capital, imperial patriotism did not inhibit the early growth of a Jewish–Socialist alliance from the 1890s on. (The alliance existed in Galicia as well but was limited there to the working class, whereas the Jewish nationalists were more successful.) The Socialists, who seemed antagonistic to the monarchy, were actually invested in the empire, indeed, the one political party that replicated the imperial pluralist structure and supported the empire the most.

An anecdote from the first Socialist family's private life may illuminate Socialist investment in the imperial Jewish world. Victor Adler had begun his political career as a German nationalist and a "strict antisemite." In 1884, he and his young children converted to Lutheranism out of a conviction that in order to assimilate into European civilization, Jews ought to be nominally Christian, and contribute to the "self-extermination (*Selbstvernichtung*) of Judaism."[140] His wife, Emma Braun-Adler, remained Jewish, "the only Jew in the family and a poor one at that."[141] His first son, Friedrich, declared himself an atheist (*konfessionslos*) in his youth. Studying physics in Zurich, Fritz met Katja Germaničkaja of a traditional Jewish family in the Russian Pale. Her father insisted that she could only marry him in a traditional Jewish wedding in Russia. Fritz protested the charade but Victor calmed him down: "A Jewish heart is after all also a heart," he said.[142] Fritz crossed the Russian border as a Protestant to be welcomed as a Jewish bridegroom by Kathia's family, and they were married in an Orthodox Jewish ceremony in Lithuania. Returning to Zurich, the couple contemplated a civil marriage in Zurich and a Reform Jewish wedding in Geneva in order to validate their marriage in Switzerland and marriage certification in

---

[140] Victor and Emma Adler to Victor's parents, April 30, 1884, VGA, Vienna, Adler collection, 80:2. My thanks to the VGA Director, Michaela Maier, for the transcript of this and other letters cited in this section.

[141] "Nun bin ich die einzige und noch dazu arme jüdin in dieser familie": Michaela Maier, "Jew, Madonna and Socialist: Emma Braun-Adler (1858–1935)," *Religions* (forthcoming).

[142] "Ein jüdisches Herz ist schließlich auch ein Herz": April 1902, VGA, Adler collection, 71:4. Letters from Fritz to his parents, beginning with February 17, 1902, 76:2 and ending with February 27, 1903, 76:4, tell the story.

Vienna (where they could marry as *konfessionslos* and Jew). Kathia's family helped them financially; they were used to a bourgeois lifestyle but had only limited means. A traditional Russian Jewish family thus subsidized the first family of Austrian Socialism.

Kathia and Fritz Adler's story is international and European, Austrian, Socialist, and Jewish, all at the same time. It demonstrates that, notwithstanding their German nationalist conviction, Austrian Socialist leaders were embedded, like the empire, in international European networks and in Jewish life. However much Austro-Marxism and socialist practices subdued traditionalism and Jewishness, imperial cultural diversity and a broad range of Jewish identities found their way into Austrian Socialism. As identities and institutions shifted in late imperial Austria, becoming "modern," Socialist leaders remained vested in family, religious, and cultural affiliations across national boundaries. The pre–World War I Austrian Socialist leadership was imperial in character.

Victor Adler died on November 11, 1918, the day before the First Austrian Republic was declared, and with him also died Jewish imperial Socialism. Franz Theodor Csokor's play *3. November 1918* depicts a disintegrating imperial Austrian regiment, with the soldiers going home to fight against one another in national battles. The soldiers gather to bury their commander who, like the empire, committed suicide.[143] One after the other, each throws a clod of soil, representing their homeland, on the grave. The Jewish physician, Dr. Grün (nicknamed "Dr. Jod" by the troops), is the single remaining Austrian in uniform. He hesitates, and then resolves his quandary by throwing "soil out of Austria." He has no country to which he can return. The empire was his homeland. It is now gone.

---

[143] *3. November 1918* (Vienna: Paul Zsolnay, 1936).

8   Imperial Peoples in an Ethno-national Age? Jews and Other Austrians in the First Republic, 1918–1938

"L'Autriche, c'est ce qui reste," quipped French Premier Georges Clemenceau in Versailles: "Austria is what remains" after the monarchy is partitioned among the newly created and territorially enlarged "nation-states." The Allies disbanded the empire in the name of national self-determination. However much the Treaty of St. Germain diverged from the national principle in practice, the nation(alizing) state became the European norm, and national sovereignty seemed sacrosanct. Yet bringing Europe's ethno-cultural mosaic into conformity with the ethno-national principle proved a gargantuan (and eventually genocidal) task. The nationalizing states were almost as ethnically diverse as the disbanded empire. The Minority Treaties tried to confront the challenge of defending "national" minorities in sovereign states. Their failure, and the inability to manage ethnic and cultural diversity in the European nation-state, precipitated World War II.[1]

During the interwar years, the European mosaic still resisted the new political boundaries. Imperial commercial and intellectual networks persisted in the Danube basin in defiance of national economy and culture. Continuous efforts were made to find new European international frameworks to mediate among the nation-states, highlight their shared economy and culture, and, above all, settle minority issues so as to protect citizenship rights and assuage homeland nationalism. In the Danube region, such efforts necessarily invoked the imperial legacy and consisted of reconfiguration of imperial patterns. By the 1930s, the efforts had reached a stalemate almost universally. The onset of the global economic Depression brought to power National Socialism in Germany and clerical fascist dictatorships in Austria and East-Central Europe, and accelerated everywhere the ethno-nationalization of economy and culture. The European crisis, it became clear, would only be resolved through conflict, exclusion, deportation, and, when World War II broke out, mass murder.

---

[1] Carole Fink, *Defending the Rights of Others: The Great Powers, the Jews, and International Minority Protection* (New York: Cambridge University Press, 2004).

Of continental Europe's two largest Diasporas, the Germans and the Jews, the Germans, like most European minorities, had a European homeland and, in their dream, could imagine it expanding into an empire incorporating much of the Diaspora. In contrast, the Jews could not call on a homeland for protection, and depended on divergent strategies for national integration and autonomy. The smaller and less acculturated, integrated, and organized Roma Diaspora faced similar dilemmas. With growing antiminority sentiments in the 1930s, Jews were progressively pushed out of civil society throughout Central and East-Central Europe. The Roma, who remained on the fringe of the region's civil societies, lost whatever modest gains they had made during the early interwar years. Both became victims of the German Diaspora's homeland nationalism, which served as a major impetus and rationale for Nazi expansion. The Nazi European order postulated the two diasporas' elimination.[2] The largely successful genocide was one reason that with the collapse of Nazi Germany, the Soviets and the neighboring people moved swiftly to eliminate the German Diaspora by means of ethnic cleansing. Murder and ethnic cleansing ended centuries-old diasporas and irreparably damaged European pluralism.

Uniquely in Austria, perhaps, the Jews' dual life as Austrian nationals and a diasporic people mimicked the national pattern. German Austrians, too, were losers of the ethno-national age. They were Austrian nationals, yet felt homeless members of a diaspora. The First Republic was a nation-state no one wanted, and throughout the interwar period, conflicting visions for Austrian integration into a broader international framework – from the German *Anschluss* to a Danubian federation to *Paneuropa* – competed. Austrian nationality's peculiar dilemmas ensured that Jews would not remain the only ones to negotiate between national and transnational identity. To be sure, their dilemmas of integration were unique, and the stakes they had in each of the competing international visions differed from those of non-Jewish Austrians. But by tracking their concomitant engagement in Austrian national and international politics along those of German Austrians, this chapter will highlight the First Republic's fundamental dilemma: its inability to accommodate ethnic,

---

[2] The similarities to the Jews in the exclusion and murder of assimilated Roma in Germany and Austria were striking: Andrea Härle et al., eds., *Romane Thana: Orte der Roma und Sinti* (Vienna: Czernin Verlag, 2015), esp. pp. 86–97; Anton Weiss-Wendt, ed., *The Nazi Genocide of the Roma: Reassessment and Commemoration* (New York: Berghah Books, 2013). Many Roma living in the Axis-allied states survived, and postwar ethnic cleansing ("population transfers") left them the largest postwar diaspora in Europe. My thanks to David Crowe of Elon College for his help.

cultural, and political diversity. Jews and other Austrians tell the European story of the nationalizing state's failure.[3]

The chapter concludes with the return of empire in the forms of anti-republican politics among the Austro-Romantics and nostalgia and utopia among the Jewish writers. The Austro-Romantics, who refused to reconcile with the nation-state, and dreamed about a Greater Austria, first created the "Habsburg Myth," and, in their hands, it often had a German national, and even racial, character. The Jews joined later, in the 1930s, in response to the Central European crisis, and their nostalgia highlighted old Central European pluralism. Zionist writers, too, shared in the imperial myth. Only the socialists and communists remained hostile to the memory of the monarchy, but socialist mavericks like Friedrich Hertz, Karl Polanyi, and Karl Popper took a major reassessment of empire's prospects. The imperial past also reemerged surreptitiously in utopias, such as Otto Neurath's Republic of Scholars (*Gelehrterrepublik*).

Outside of Austria, in the monarchy's successor states, the memory of the empire was mostly negative. Hungarian nationalists remembered it as oppressive, and viewed the liberal imperial elites as collaborators. Even in Poland, where national memory of the Austrian Empire was more positive, Galician writers of Jewish origins, like Józef Wittlin, were the monarchy's leading admirers. In Austria itself, historians were divided on whether the monarchy hindered German nationality or advanced German culture. They blamed the Hungarians and the other nationalities for the empire's dissolution, and insisted that it defended Europe against Russian barbarism and represented progress for the Slavic nationalities, but they were also critical of the emperor, the government, and the constitution.[4] The Jews turned out to be the monarchy's most loyal subjects even after its demise.

Even before Jewish and Austro-Romantic nostalgia waxed, two historians had shaped the Western vision of Austria-Hungary: Oscar Jászi and Joseph Redlich.[5] Both were sympathetic to the monarchy but regarded its decline as programmed by emergent nationalism. Jászi, a Hungarian liberal democrat of Jewish origins, minister of national minorities in the first Hungarian national government, thought that obstructed

---

[3] For a brilliant analysis of the interdependence of interwar Austrian and Jewish identities, see Lisa Silverman, *Becoming Austrians: Jews and Culture Between the World Wars* (Oxford: Oxford University Press, 2012).

[4] Adam Kożuchowski, *The Afterlife of Austria-Hungary* (Pittsburgh, PA: University of Pittsburgh Press, 2013).

[5] Oscar Jászi, *The Dissolution of the Habsburg Monarchy* [1929] (Chicago: University of Chicago Press, 1961); Joseph Redlich, *Emperor Francis Joseph of Austria* (New York: Macmillan, 1929).

democratization and federalization, as well as continued feudal economic exploitation, had doomed the monarchy. He was critical of Franz Joseph, imperial dualism, and Hungarian intransigence, and established the distinction between centripetal forces that acted to preserve the empire, such as the *Verwaltung* (bureaucracy) and the Socialists, and nationalist centrifugal ones that tore it apart. Redlich, a jurist of Jewish origin in a liberal constitutionalist mold, a Reichsrat member and an imperial advisor on federal reform, was likewise critical of Franz Joseph and admiring of the Verwaltung, but he blamed German nationalism the most for subverting the constitution and pushing the emperor toward autocracy. A younger Austrian émigré, Robert A. Kann, reworked Jászi's and Redlich's narratives into an influential synthesis in the early postwar years, and set the parameters of imperial historiography to the end of the twentieth century.[6] This chapter revisits the historiography by perusing the interwar Austrian confrontation with the imperial past in all its diversity.

The Socialists: Red Vienna and Democratic Greater Germany

The disintegration of Austria-Hungary was a disaster for the Jews. They did not give up easily on the empire. Marcos Silber has tracked the persistent efforts made by Polish and Lithuanian Jews during World War I to facilitate autonomous Austrian Poland and German Lithuania. They hoped that an imperial federalist structure would contain nationalist excesses, secure state protection for the Jews, and make possible Jewish autonomy. Many Jewish leaders feared the newly forming nationalizing states in East-Central Europe, and, in the Minority Treaties, they tried in vain to turn a multiethnic Poland, for example, into a mini empire by replicating federalism.[7] In predominantly German Austria, however, Jews had trust in the robustness of emancipation. For German-acculturated Jews, the nation-state was a harbinger of modernity and political rights, and in the aftermath of a bloody war that had brought out the old

---

[6] *The Multinational Empire: Nationalism and National Reform in the Habsburg Empire* (New York: Columbia University Press, 1950); C. A. MacArtney, *The Habsburg Empire 1790–1918* (London: Weidenfeld & Nicholson, 1968).

[7] Marcos Silber, "The Development of a Joint Political Program for the Jews of Poland During World War I – Success and Failure," *Jewish History* 19 (2005): 211–26; "Lithuania? But Which? The Changing Political Attitude of the Jewish Political Elite in East Central Europe toward Emerging Lithuania, 1915–1919," in *A Pragmatic Alliance: Jewish-Lithuanian Political Cooperation at the beginning of the 20th Century*, ed. Vladas Sirutavičius and Darius Staliūnas (Budapest: Central European University Press, 2011), pp. 119–57; and *Different Nationality, Equal Citizenship: The Efforts to Achieve Autonomy for Polish Jewry during the First World War* (in Hebrew) (Tel Aviv: Tel Aviv University, 2014).

order's worst aspects, the monarchy seemed a colossal failure, an obsolete state that had outlived its term. So socialists and liberals alike looked forward to the completion of modernization and Jewish integration by the democratic Austrian Republic. It took National Socialism for Stefan Zweig to dream of the blissful *World of Yesterday*.[8]

If Austrian Jews were united in demanding equal citizenship, they remained divided about the Jews' relationship to the nation-state. The Zionists, weakened by the loss of their Galician constituency, yet emboldened by the even greater loss of the Diaspora nationalists who had lost their natural habitat, were the only ones to demand autonomy as a national minority. Traditional "Eastern" Jews, as of old, still regarded themselves a separate community, united by observance of Jewish law, the Yiddish language, and a common ancestry, and loyal to the state even if the emperor was gone. The traditional Vienna community was reinforced by the wartime migration of Galician Jews, but acculturation pressures progressively diminished it. For "Western" acculturated Jews, in contrast, the republic's removal of the remaining legal barriers to Jewish advancement and integration fulfilled emancipation's promise – in theory: Interwar barriers in the academy and state institutions were higher, and informally enforced. The Jews thus had a major stake in the debate that non-Jewish Austrians were having on Austrian identity. It could, and did, determine their fate.

The leading Jewish role in Austrian socialism continued unabated in the interwar years: Otto Bauer replaced Victor Adler at the helm of the Socialist Party (and, unlike him, remained a member of the Jewish community), and major party functionaries, from Julius Braunthal to Julius Deutsch to Julius Tandler, and theoreticians Max and Friedrich Adler were likewise of Jewish origins. Whereas the Socialists commanded the allegiance of only a minority of the imperial Jewish electorate, they had the support of an overwhelming majority of Austrian Jews under the republic, at least until the mid-1930s. The changes in the political landscape, Jewish electorate, and Austrian identity from the monarchy to the republic explain this shift. Traditional Galician Jews, who had been voting increasingly for Jewish nationalist candidates, no longer constituted the Jewish majority. The overwhelming majority of Austrian Jews lived in Vienna, where the Jewish–Socialist alliance had been growing since the 1890s. In the interwar years, the Socialists became a major political player and, from May 1919 to February 1934, controlled Vienna. An imperial

---

[8] *The World of Yesterday* (New York: Viking, 1943). The transition from empire to republic is admirably described in Marsha Rozenblit, *Reconstructing a National Identity: The Jews of Habsburg Austria during World War I* (New York: Oxford University Press, 2001).

supranational Austrian identity was no longer possible, only a national one, and the national options were limited. The Catholics and Pan-Germans – the Socialists' major competitors – were virtually closed to Jews. For Austrian Jews not vying for Zionism – and even for a good many who were – this left only one option open: national integration in a socialist community that professed an internationalist commitment – Red Vienna.

The Soviet Revolution, the collapse of three continental empires, and the new nationalizing states in East-Central Europe transformed the socialist international outlook. No longer would any Socialist identify imperial multinationalism with internationalism. The lost war discredited the monarchy, and the Socialists did their best to erase from memory their investment in it. When they recalled the monarchy, resentfully and in passing, they remembered it as oppressive, a colossal failure. They directed their hostility at the surviving imperial family and aristocracy. They had always considered nation-states modern and democratic and monarchies obsolete and oppressive; World War I seemed to prove them right. Like Marx and Engels, Victor Adler and Bauer had supported Austria-Hungary in order to contain reactionary Russia; now Russia was Bolshevik and the monarchy was gone. The Socialists repressed their earlier recognition of the affinity of imperial pluralism and internationalism and forgot about imperial federalism.

The break with the monarchy was abrupt. Throughout the war, Karl Renner had been busy developing schemes for an imperial *Mitteleuropa*, and Victor Adler endeavored to save a Danubian federation until the last minute. But responding to the revolutionary strikes in January 1918, the Bauer-led antiwar Socialist Left passed a resolution calling for national self-determination and statehood for the monarchy's peoples. On October 1, 1918, the entire party endorsed it.[9] The 1848 dream of a democratic Greater Germany resurged, and Socialist support for German unification became axiomatic. The Socialists suspended their call for unification only in October 1933 after the Nazis had come to power. When the Anschluss came in March 1938, they accepted it unhappily as a fait accompli.

In 1923, Bauer stated that the Socialists could resist the Right's imperial concept of a hegemonic German *Mitteleuropa*, promoted under the *alldeutsch* rubric, only by counterposing a Greater German Republic, reflecting the principle of self-determination, under the *grossdeutsch*

---

[9] Wolfgang Maderthaner, "Das revolutionäre Prinzip: Arbeiterbewegung und Krieg (2)," In *Im Epizentrum des Zusammenbruchs Wien im Ersten Weltkrieg*, ed. Alfred Pfoser and Andreas Weigl (Vienna: Metroverlag, 2013), pp. 566–71.

rubric.[10] The monarchy's rationale in its time was that it facilitated the spread of German culture.[11] This suggested less that Bauer was becoming a militant Pan-German nationalist and more that, with the disintegration of the pluralist empire, he was groping for new ways of realizing a convergence of German humanism and socialist internationalism and not finding them. Greater Germany was less a nationalist maneuver and more a social democratic effort to imagine a German republic as a solution to what Bauer viewed as an unsustainable and probably reactionary Austria. The Socialists, who had previously no choice but to be multinational, now had no choice but to opt for German nationalism.

The change was epochal: The monarchy disappeared forever from the Austrian Socialist universe. Renner continued probing Danubian frameworks in the interwar years, Central European commercial networks survived nationalization (and played a more crucial role in the Austrian economy than German ones), and Red Vienna's urban architecture carried the marks of Otto Wagner's "imperial metropolis," but imperial vestiges all remained surreptitious.[12] Without even believing they had a nation-state in Austria, the Socialists became the nation-state party par excellence. In the interwar years, they envisioned the nation-state as a democratic Greater Germany, in the postwar years as a democratic Austria. The welfare state would become vested in the nation-state, so that prospective European unity would seem almost like a threat.

The death of Socialist imperialism also meant the waning of Socialist internationalism. Bauer and his colleagues were genuine democrats, and clear-eyed about Soviet Bolshevism's dictatorial character: "The Jacobin superstition of the guillotine's omnipotence has reemerged in St. Petersburg as the machine gun's omnipotence," Bauer reported to Karl Kautsky in 1917.[13] The Socialists kept their distance from the Comintern, but no effective socialist internationalism emerged to compete with it. For two years, Friedrich Adler led the 2½ International, or the Vienna International, which endeavored to pave a third way between reform socialism and communism, but in 1923, the Austrians ended up joining the Labour and Socialist International (*Sozialistische Arbeiter-Internationale*), which continued the Second International. Unlike the

[10] *Die österreichische Revolution* (Vienna: Volksbuchhandlung, 1923), p. 69.
[11] Ibid., p. 101.
[12] Eve Blau, "Supranational Principle as Urban Model: Otto Wagner's *Großstadt* and City Making in Central Europe," in *Histoire de l'art du XIXe siècle (1848–1918)*, ed. Claire Barbillon, Catherine Chevillot, and François-René Martin (Paris: Collections des Rencontre de l'Ecole de Louvre, 2011), pp.501–14.
[13] Quoted in Wolfgang Maderthaner, "Das revolutionäre Prinzip," p. 567.

Comintern, it was a loose federation of national parties. Austrian Socialist internationalism culminated in displaying Red Vienna as a city embodying the socialist future, that is, in imagining Vienna as a cosmopolis. The combination of nationalizing states and the Comintern stultified Social Democratic internationalism.

Unlike other Socialist parties, the Austrians did not think they had a nation-state, and yet party policy was focused less on resolving the German Question and more on protecting Red Vienna. Austro-German relations remained relatively loose, and there was no policy coordination. The Austro-Marxists had some intense theoretical exchanges with their German compatriots, but they remained a distinct school.[14] There was an ethereal quality to the democratic Greater Germany of 1848. Socialist support for the Anschluss was as much a consequence of paralyzed Austrian nationalization and stultified internationalism as it was an expression of German nationalism. To be sure, there was an alternative that the Socialists declined to explore: their own imperial federalist legacy, which could have inspired transnational bridge building, as it had done under the monarchy. The Socialists gave up on the legacy, and so do their successors nowadays, depriving the Socialists of federalist concepts and exposing them to the charge of nationalism. Truly, once they had rejected the imperial legacy, the Socialists had nowhere to go but Germany.

The Soviets represented the new internationalism, and the Austrian Socialists confronted it from the moment they came to power, in a coalition government, in October 1918. The wave of Central European socialist revolutions, from Berlin to Munich to Budapest, raised the prospect of a Central European socialist order, inspired by the Soviet example. Segments of the Jewish intelligentsia, above all the Viennese students who had gone through rapid politicization during the late war years, were enthralled, and constituted the nucleus of the tiny Austrian Communist Party. Otto Neurath was perhaps the most noted progressive Viennese intellectual who joined the Bavarian Revolution. But Bauer steadfastly refused the calls to establish a socialist dictatorship at home or assist the Hungarian Communists militarily. He used the revolution to pressure the conservatives for socialist legislation and hoped that unification with a more heavily industrialized socialist Germany would create the conditions for democratic socialism. This tied Austrian socialism's

---

[14] Rudolf Hilferding, who moved to Germany in 1906 but continued editing *Marx-Studien* with Max Adler until 1923, and served in the Austrian army in World War I but later became the German finance minister in Weimar, was the exception rather than the rule.

fortunes to the German Question and left the international arena to the Soviets on the Left and to Catholics and liberals on the Right.[15]

By the summer of 1919, the revolutionary wave had subsided, and by the fall, the Treaty of St. Germain had prohibited political or economic union with Germany. Both the international and German national paths to socialism were obstructed. Bauer, skeptical about Austria's economic *Lebensfähigkeit* (survivability) and aware of his diminishing bargaining power with the conservatives, had doubts that an Austrian national path existed. The Socialists left the government in June 1920, and the October 1920 elections made the Christian Social Party the largest. Paul Lazarsfeld and Otto Neurath represented the majority of revolutionary students and intellectuals who gradually returned to the socialist fold to help build up municipal socialism – Red Vienna.

In the May 1919 municipal elections, the Socialists won an absolute majority in the capital (and other industrial centers). The constitution gave Vienna a provincial status, and so the Socialists were now free to focus their reform effort on the capital, inhabited by about a third of Austria's population, including 200,000 Jews (about a tenth of the capital's population). The progressive and socialist Jewish intelligentsia mobilized for Red Vienna. The Viennese progressives had already collaborated with the socialists before the war, and since the turn of the century, the two had constituted a united anticlerical front. Unlike the socialists, they were not Marxist, but occupied the space on the political map that democratic, reform-oriented, social liberalism filled in Britain and the United States, an exceedingly narrow space in Austria. They hoped that a bourgeois–proletarian alliance under the auspices of an enlightened bureaucracy applying scientific management would transform society without a violent revolution. The building of municipal socialism in the interwar years proved a solid terrain for socialist–progressive collaboration.

Red Vienna inherited the progressive network. In 1919, the progressives established an umbrella organization, the *Freier Bund kultureller Vereine*, including the Ethical Society and the Monists, who focused increasingly on socialization and economic planning; *Die Bereitschaft*, dedicated to *Volksbildung* (popular education); the Austrian feminists; and organizations for anticlerical causes, such as marriage law reform.

---

[15] Helmut Konrad and Wolfgang Maderthaner, eds., *Das Werden der Ersten Republik: ... der Rest ist Österreich*, 2 vols. (Vienna: Gerold, 2008), esp. 1: 65–82, 187–206; Norbert Leser, *Zwischen Reformismus und Bolschewismus: Der Austromarxismus als Theorie und Praxis*, 2d ed. (Vienna: Böhlau, 1985), pp. 181–244; Anson Rabinbach, *The Crisis of Austrian Socialism: From Red Vienna to Civil War, 1927–1934* (Chicago: University of Chicago Press, 1983).

Another umbrella organization, the *Freidenkerbund*, included three hundred and ten organizations with forty-five thousand members and advocated separation of church and state and school reform. Their organ, the Freemasons' *Pionier*, had a circulation of about fifty thousand. Devoid of political power, Viennese progressives remained a well-organized activist community, embedded in Red Vienna.[16]

Why was Austrian socialism so successful in mobilizing a politically diverse Jewish intelligentsia behind Red Vienna? Why did famous apolitical liberals like Freud, Arthur Schnitzler, and Zweig remain the exception rather than the norm? Patronage and employment opportunities are inadequate explanations: They solidified support for the socialists but somehow proved less successful with the non-Jewish intelligentsia. During the Cold War, it became common to explain the socialist appeal as secular messianism, a promise of a revolutionary breakthrough into a perfect new world – a search for the millennium – attractive especially to Jewish intellectuals reared in religious messianic suspense. Red Vienna did promise a new society, but municipal socialism was hardly messianic, and the Jewish intelligentsia was not revolutionary for the most part (nor did most of them have a religious upbringing). Revolutionary promise and material rewards combined are still insufficient to explain the breadth of Jewish support for the socialists.

The Jews simply had nowhere else to go. Interwar Austria lacked a liberal public sphere, political culture, or party that could appeal to the Jewish intelligentsia. Viennese progressivism's last electoral showing in February 1919 was dismal. Julius Ofner lost his seat, and the *bürgerliche Demokraten* elected one representative, Michael Hainisch, to the constituent assembly. Hainisch became a consensus candidate of the Socialists and Catholics for president precisely because he had no political base. Where were Jewish intellectuals to turn? In the midst of antisemitic Austria and ethno-national Central Europe, the Socialists offered them integration into the community along the democratic ideals of 1848 and leadership in a socialist project creating a model for humanity. Is it any surprise they flocked in?

As long as Austrian socialism seemed capable of protecting parliamentary democracy and Red Vienna, it could count on wide Jewish support, including the majority of the liberal and part of the Zionist intelligentsia. Socialist hegemony in Viennese cultural life was such that even Hans Kelsen, liberal framer of the constitution, an avowed neutralist in

---

[16] Friedrich Stadler, "Spätaufklärung und Sozialdemokratie in Wien 1918–1938," in *Aufbruch und Untergang: Österreichische Kultur zwischen 1918 und 1938*, ed. Franz Kadrnoska (Vienna: Europaverlag, 1981), pp. 441–74, and *Vom Positivismus zur "Wissenschaftliche Weltauffassung"* (Vienna: Löcker, 1982), pp. 151–66.

domestic affairs and anti-Marxist, found himself participating in the socialist-oriented *Soziologische Gesellschaft*. Support for the Socialists reached its peak in the contentious 1927 elections, when pronounced bourgeois liberals like Freud and *Neue Freie Presse* writer Felix Salten were among a long list of Viennese cultural luminaries to endorse the Socialists.

The *Justizpalastbrand* of July 15, 1927, as in everything else, was a turning point, but the Jewish intelligentsia's support wavered seriously only in 1933 when the Nazi threat became imminent and Engelbert Dollfuss encountered no adequate Socialist response to his coup against parliament. Many concluded that Dollfuss remained the only bulwark against Nazism. The failure of the Socialist uprising in February 1934 and the declaration of the *Ständestaat* the following May brought a sea change among the Jewish intelligentsia. Karl Kraus, Salten, and Franz Werfel, who had earlier expressed support for the Socialists, came out for the Ständestaat. Sigmund Freud, too, put his trust in "the Catholics." Meeting in London in 1935, Ernst Gombrich and Karl Popper – the latter a heterodox Socialist and a party member – criticized the Socialists for trying to undermine Kurt von Schuschnigg. "No one liked Schuschnigg's dictatorship," recalled Gombrich, "but Schuschnigg was not the problem. Hitler was."[17]

Most Jewish Socialists could not face the loss of their dream with such equanimity. They were personae non grata in the Ständestaat; some went underground and others fell silent. In the aftermath of the February uprising, the Jewish doctors, suspected of having aided the rebellion, became subject to legislation prohibiting political activity and were dismissed en masse. Jewish socialists in other professions suffered harassment. The leadership of the (illegal) Revolutionary Socialists of Austria, the successor to the defunct party, included Jews, from Manfred Ackermann to Otto Leichter to young Bruno Kreisky (all of whom were arrested in 1935). But their situation was difficult; the rank and file blamed the old Jewish leadership for the disaster and for having fled abroad. Militant youth sought collaboration with the Communists, thinking that they might offer more effective resistance to fascism. Political economist Walter Schiff, the "red professor," former Socialist deputy minister and future leader of the "Free Austrian Movement" in Britain, crossed over to the Communists. Many intellectuals were looking for a way out of Austria via academic appointments abroad. The emigration story of philosophers, sociologists, and psychologists has been told many times over. Red Vienna would end up shaping foreign academies in ways it never did in Austrian academia.

---

[17] My interview with Gombrich, December 7, 1983.

Recent criticism of Red Vienna has highlighted the tensions between the Socialists' heavily Jewish bourgeois leadership and the party's rank and file, between the Jewish intelligentsia and working-class culture, between the cultivated inner city and the "wild" suburbs, between Jewish Vienna and Socialists in the provinces.[18] It has also illuminated the Socialist equivocation on antisemitism and their penchant for antisemitic caricaturization of capitalism. Most significantly, it has highlighted their German nationalism. When the Anschluss arrived in March 1938, Renner, taking exception with the method, welcomed the result. From his Paris exile, Bauer opined that while the Nazi Anschluss itself was indefensible, unification was an accomplished fact, the end of a historical process. Socialist émigrés refused collaboration with other Austrian organizations in exile lest they vindicate Austrian nationality, which they regarded as reactionary, a Catholic and communist invention. Only after the Moscow declaration of 1943 had made it clear that the Allies would not allow a postwar Greater Germany did the Socialists change their policy. A few held onto the dream even afterward: Friedrich Adler declined to return to "reactionary" postwar Austria and settled in Switzerland. They, too, succumbed to the age of ethno-nationalism.

There were dissenting voices. The socialist historian Friedrich Hertz (1878–1964), educated broadly as a sociologist and economist, articulated a critique of nationalism similar to that of Karl Popper. A German-acculturated Jew, Hertz considered the identification of culture with race or nation a myth. Nationalist movements, led by demagogues who dissuaded the masses from attending to real economic problems, constituted a destructive force. The most dangerous of them all was German nationalism, which promoted racism and antisemitism. The Austro-Hungarian Monarchy endeavored to contain and arbitrate national conflicts, and its collapse resulted in a plethora of states conducting nationalist economic policy and destroying the Danube region's shared economy.[19] Socialists like Hertz and Popper represented an option that interwar Austrian socialism failed to grasp: an internationalism anchored in Austrian history, translating imperial federalism into a Europe of the nations. In the age of ethno-nationalism, this alternative had only remote

---

[18] Helmut Gruber, *Red Vienna: Experiments in Working Class Culture, 1919–1934* (New York: Oxford University Press, 1991); Wolfgang Maderthaner and Lutz Musner, *Unruly Masses: The Other Side of Fin-de-siècle Vienna* (New York: Berghahn Books, 2008).

[19] Friedrich Otto Hertz, *Rasse und Kultur: Eine kritische Untersuchung der Rassentheorien* (Leipzig: A. Kröner, 1915); *Nationalgeist und Politik: Beiträge zur Erforschung der tieferen Ursachen des Weltkrieges* (Zurich: Europa-verlag, 1937); and Frederick Hertz, *The Economic Problem of the Danubian States: A Study in Economic Nationalism* (London: V. Gollancz, 1947).

chances, but it would have energized Austrian socialist internationalism, which has remained stultified ever since the fall of the empire.

To break with German nationalism in the mid-1930s, one needed to be inspired by a messianic internationalism promising universal redemption. The Soviet Union, at the time the foremost antifascist force, provided those Communist intellectuals who could overlook the horrific costs of Soviet collectivization and the Great Purges with such inspiration. In 1937, an Austrian Communist of Jewish origin, Alfred Klahr (1904–1944), published two brief essays that may be credited with the first concept of Austria as a modern nation-state.[20]

Klahr couched his proposal theoretically as a Stalinist critique of Bauer's "unhistorical" concept of the nation. Nations were not ethno-cultural but economic and political entities; they did not constitute a "community of character," as bourgeois ideologists surmised. Austria had never been politically part of Germany. The Holy Roman Empire was fragmented and the democratic national project failed in 1848. The Austrian bourgeoisie turned away from Germany, allied itself with the Habsburg nobility, and invested in the Danubian region. The year 1866 sealed a developing economic reality: State and capitalism divided Germany. Only the intelligentsia and the petite bourgeoisie, unhappy with their position in the monarchy, cultivated Pan-Germanism. The working class (as opposed to its Socialist leadership) was Austrian minded. Bourgeois and Socialist betrayal of the 1918 Revolution in both Germany and Austria confirmed their separation and permitted the Junkers' continued domination of Germany. The failure of the 1934 Austrian Nazi *Putsch* showed the unpopularity of the German nationalist project in Austria, and the Ständestaat's reactionary elites took advantage of it to assert their leadership. Socialist commitment to German unification damaged the working class's antifascist struggle, and permitted the reactionary elites to lead. The antifascist struggle should become a national battle for Austria's self-determination, in solidarity with the antifascist fights in Germany and the rest of Central Europe.

Klahr was adamant that the Austrian nation-state constituted a break with the imperial past. Unlike the Catholics and monarchists, the Communists were not staging a claim to the Habsburgs' supranational heritage, which was equally foreign and oppressive to all the nations, but an Austrian nationalist claim. Still, what were Austria's cultural markers? Klahr perused the imperial past while discounting it, inventing the now-

---

[20] Rudolf (pseud.), "Zur nationalen Frage in Österreich," *Weg und Ziel* 2: 3/4 (1937): 126–33, 173–81. See also "Zur Entwicklung der deutschen Nation" (1944), all collected in *Zum 100. Geburtstag und zum 60. Todestag: Der theoretische Begründer der "österreichischen Nation", Dr. Alfred Klahr, 1904–1944*, http://www.antifa-info.at/archiv/KLAHR.PDF.

familiar procedure of salvaging moments from the imperial past to construct an Austrian national narrative. He overlooked the imperial economic networks that he had earlier used to explain Austria's turn away from Germany, and instead availed himself of literature and music, providing the first rendition of a Central European Austrian culture. Unlike the émigrés, he ignored his writers' imperial background: Many of them had been born outside Austrian national boundaries. Soviet foreign policy carved a space for the Communists to create an Austrian nation as part of the struggle against the Anschluss, but their concept of Austrian nationality was so abstract that neither contemporaries nor historians, only post–World War II progressives, could find it attractive.

Klahr's utopian nation could only appear after Red Vienna had already vanished, as Red Vienna, a utopia in the making, was tangible in ways that Klahr's Austrian nation was not. Yet Red Vienna, too, could exist only as long as the national question remained in suspense and German nationalism did not triumph. Red Vienna promised the Jews the integration that Austria and Central Europe denied them, but the promise was impossible to keep: Vienna turned out to be an Austrian island, "die Judenregierung in Wien" (Jewish government in Vienna), as provincial papers had it. The democratic Greater Germany was just as much a phantom. If the history of Austrian Pan-Germanism from Georg von Schönerer on gave insufficient warning, National Socialism should have provided decisive evidence that the endeavor to gather ethnic Germans, or to turn the *deutsche Kulturbereich* into a nation-state, ran the risk of racial imperialism. The Socialists' endeavor to counter *alldeutsch* reactionary nationalism with a *grossdeutsch* democratic one was fraught with danger and ultimately futile. Whether their Marxism or nationalism was at fault, they despaired of reconciliation with provincial, rural, Catholic Austria. An Austrian nation was impossible. A democratic Greater Germany remained their sole hope.

The fascination that Red Vienna continues to hold for the Austrian intelligentsia today is understandable. In the midst of a continent swamped by antisemitism and national hatred, German and Jewish Socialists collaborated in building a model community. Why should a democratic socialist Greater Germany, which seemed within reach in 1918, a nation-state that would be defined politically and not ethnically, have been impossible? The ideal seemed not a betrayal of internationalism but its fulfillment. For generations, German-acculturated Jewish intellectuals had endeavored to square their German patriotism with cosmopolitanism. Socialist ambiguity about internationalism suited them admirably. The only difference between Jewish and non-Jewish Socialists on German unification was the Jewish stress on the imperative of democracy – the guarantor of integration. The Socialists provided such a unique example of German–Jewish collaboration in the ethno-national age that however hopeless their situation was, contemporaries still linger over the moment, imagining that which could have been. Doing so, however, they miss the imperial Socialist past. Like the interwar Socialists, today's "Republic of Vienna" remains a victim of the age of ethno-nationalism, which it has so strenuously fought to overcome.

The Catholics and the Imperial Legacy: European Greater Austria

If late imperial and interwar Austria lacked a liberal public sphere, the Austrian liberals were largely at fault: They behaved first and foremost like German nationalists. After the war, the *Deutschliberale* shed any liberal pretension and joined with other German nationalists to form the antisemitic *Grossdeutsche Volkspartei*. In prewar years, anticlericalism had united most socialists and nationalists. The hardening of ideological and ethnic barriers in the aftermath of the Soviet Revolution, which was reflected in Pan-German anti-Marxism and antisemitism, made anything beyond ad hoc collaboration – Chancellor Ignaz Seipel's nightmare – impossible in the interwar years. An earlier generation of Jewish-German patriots, exemplified by the assimilated historian Heinrich Friedjung, had knocked on the door of the Pan-Germans begging for admission and been rebuffed: From the late 1880s onward, race had come to define membership in the nation for the Pan-German community, and the standard was gradually extended across the "liberal" camp. In the interwar years, the Jews stopped knocking. Philosopher Heinrich Gomperz, a quixotic polymath, was one of the few diehards. The Ständestaat (corporative state, the proto-fascist dictatorship instituted in 1934) dismissed him from his Vienna professorship in 1934 for refusing to join the *Vaterländische Front* (Fatherland Front, the corporative alternative to political parties) on account of its opposition to German unification. From his U.S. exile, Gomperz cheered the Anschluss.

   In their resentment toward the Treaty of Versailles, the Pan-Germans transformed World War I from a war for the monarchy, which they despised, into a German national war, lost because of (Jewish) traitors. Visions of Central Europe's future became ever more aggressive. In time, the Pan-Germans found that they had sacrificed not only liberalism but also, paradoxically, nationalism. In the 1932 regional elections, they were virtually wiped out by the National Socialists. Pan-Germanism converted Habsburg pluralism into a racial imperialism that undermined the German nation-state.

The Christian Social Party and Catholic camp present a more complex picture. If the Socialists were sure that they wanted a German nation-state and confused to find it bound by Austria, the Catholics were sure that they wanted Austria but confused to find it bound by the nation-state. Catholic allegiances were regional and international, tied to provincial and occupational identities, to a clerical organization and hierarchy, to imperial and church traditions. They were local and cosmopolitan in character – anything but national. At least until the rise of National Socialism, the Republic of Austria as a nation-state made no more sense to the Catholics than it did to the Socialists. No wonder Seipel and his colleagues were groping throughout the interwar years for some transnational framework that would lend meaning – and offer economic viability – to Austria. It is no coincidence that Christian Social chancellors from Seipel to Dollfuss and Schuschnigg found themselves presidents of the Austrian Paneuropa league.

German nationalism easily frustrated the Catholic exploration of transnational allegiances. The Catholic leadership did not wish to find Austrians a minority within a predominantly Protestant Germany, but they were aware that their constituents in the provinces had voted overwhelmingly for the Anschluss in elections and plebiscites, 1919–21, and that in later years, provincials regarded unification as a way of ridding themselves of Red Vienna. In the church, young prelates organized in the Catholic youth movement *Bund Neuland* were *Gesamtdeutsch* (all-German) minded, and they challenged the hierarchy. Seipel insisted that the German nation and state need not overlap – the nation-state was a French and Western invention, incompatible with German and Catholic traditions – but he could only keep the two apart by emphasizing Austria's German character. If he dreamed of Austria spearheading a counterreformation in Central Europe, interwar Europe offered him no opportunity, and he had to bide his time. He excelled at obstructing undesirable paths, such as the Anschluss or a French-inspired Danubian federation, rather than at breaking new ones. Protestations of German solidarity were essential to his obstructionism. German nationalism diminished Austria's international options.

The Ständestaat broke German solidarity by demarcating Austria from Germany, but it could still do so only by claiming Austria as the better Germany. Austria's avowed German character reduced its ability to draw on the pluralist imperial legacy and complicated any bridge building among the Danubian states. Austrian multinationalism appeared to the neighbors to be a nationalist ploy. They had no intention of submitting to Austrian leadership, of which they had just been liberated, and Austria would not join the pack as just another small nation-state. Wavering among multiple international options, Catholic German Austria ended up with none.

Catholic German Austria also emptied the imperial legacy of its domestic pluralist potential. It had an exceedingly narrow space for Jews. Antisemitism was a defining plank of the Christian Social Party, and openly espoused by its platform. Interwar Catholic antisemitism represented an amalgam of traditions, reflecting clerical anxieties about the Jews as the religious Other, Lueger-style popular resentment of Jewish socioeconomic preeminence, Seipel's high-minded indictment of "Judaism's corrosive influence" (secular culture and socialism), and the racially inflected antisemitism of Leopold Kunschak and the Catholic trade unions. The net effect was to poison the political culture of the First Republic, to close the way to Jewish integration, and to inhibit bourgeois collaboration to save the republic. The Jewish bourgeoisie and the liberal antisocialist intelligentsia, potential allies of the governing party, were left stranded and virtually shut out of politics. Jewish industrialists could still channel funds to the party and Jewish professionals still serve in the ministries, but with very few exceptions, they could not assume a public role. Catholic antisemitism, mimicking ethno-nationalism throughout East-Central Europe, underlined the limits of Catholic internationalism in the ethno-national age.[21]

Both Ludwig von Mises and Joseph Redlich, two liberals of Jewish origin who managed to negotiate their way into influential governmental positions as economists (Redlich even becoming finance minister in 1931), remained alienated from Catholic political culture. Mises held a private seminar whose participants were fugitives from fascist sociologist Othmar Spann's university courses. In 1934, after the Ständestaat (which Mises supported) had taken over, he left for Geneva. The anglophile Redlich spent most of the interwar years teaching at Harvard. Rockefeller Foundation funds supported the *Institut für Konjunkturforschung* (institute for trade-cycle research) that Mises founded in 1927 (with Friedrich Hayek and then Oskar Morgenstern as heads). As the Rockefeller Foundation was debating in 1934 how it might encourage an internationally oriented, open-market Austrian economy, it took note of the need to work around antisemitism.[22]

---

[21] Klemens von Klemperer, *Ignaz Seipel: Christian Statesman in a Time of Crisis* (Princeton, NJ: Princeton University Press, 1972); Helmut Konrad and Wolfgang Maderthaner, eds., *Das Werden der Ersten Republik*, esp. 1: 241–61, 381–92; Klaus Taschwer, *Hochburg des Antisemitismus: Der Niedergang der Universität Wien im 20. Jahrhundert* (Vienna: Czernin Verlag, 2015).

[22] Robert Leonard, *Von Neumann, Morgenstern, and the Creation of Game Theory: From Chess to Social Science, 1900–1960* (New York: Cambridge University Press, 2012), pp. 140–81.

From the crossroads of Europe, Catholic German Austria became a recipient of foreign aid to encourage its internationalization.

This was especially unfortunate as Austria had a Catholic-Jewish minority and intelligentsia, with a distinct subculture. Hermann Broch, Friedrich Engel-Janosi, Karl Kraus, Gustav Mahler, and Bruno Walter are just a few famous representatives of the Catholic-Jewish intelligentsia.[23] Conversion rates in the Viennese Jewish community were the highest in Europe for a generation. Many converts remained only nominally Christian, and a good number chose Protestantism (the *Aufklärung*'s religion), but a majority became Catholic.[24] The ghetto of mostly assimilated and intermarried Jews, established by the Nazis in Leopoldstadt during World War II, was a dark reflection of this group's otherwise little-noticed existence.[25] The Catholic Jews included noble and grand bourgeois families, from the Hofmannsthals to the Moldens, who counted Jews among their multiethnic ancestors. They were the vanguard of Catholic cosmopolitanism.

In the midst of World War I, Hugo von Hofmannsthal reconfigured the "Austrian Idea," envisioning the monarchy as inheritor of the Holy Roman Empire, a state dwelling "on the banks of the great stream that unites Europe with the Orient." Multicultural Austria mediated between Europe and Asia, nationalities and cultures. It was "a point of departure for [cultural] colonization ... but also receiv[ed] ... the counterwave striving westward," reconciling old Latin-German and new Slavic Europe.[26] It provided the foundation for a new European identity that broke with essentialist nationality and with Prussian power politics, and facilitated the merging of German and European. "Europe" had no geographical boundaries or racial unity. Rather, it represented a

---

Deliberating over Austrian antisemitism, the Rockefeller guarantors subtly disclosed their own American anti-Jewish prejudices.

[23] Kraus left the church in 1923. Assimilated Jews constituted a subculture. In interwar Austria, they were identified as Jews, and this had serious consequences, but their choice of Christian identity and their intellectual endeavors created unique Jewish-Christian cultures.

[24] In the interwar years, those who declared themselves *konfessionslos* were probably a majority. Among the intellectuals mentioned in this chapter, Victor Adler, Gombrich, Kelsen, Popper, Redlich, and Schönberg were Protestant. (Schönberg later returned to Judaism.) I focus here on the Catholic Jews. The previous chapter's discussion of Karl Popper provides a good example of the Protestant-Jewish subculture.

[25] Philomena Leiter, "Assimilation, Antisemitismus und NS-Verfolgung: Austritte aus der Jüdischen Gemeinde in Wien 1900–1944" (Ph.D. diss., University of Vienna, 2003). Partners of "nonprivileged mixed marriages" – husband Jewish, wife non-Jewish, and no children – were required to move to the ghetto.

[26] "Die österreichische Idee," in *Reden und Aufsätze II*, vol. 9 of *Gesammelte Werke*, ed. Bernd Schoeller and Rudolf Hirsch, 10 vols. (Frankfurt am Main: Fischer Taschenbuch, 1979): 9: 454–58.

convergence of the *civitas dei* (city of god) with *res publica litterria* (republic of literature), which was embodied intellectually in German humanism and politically in Austria. Austrian Europe called for "the common citizenship of civilized people, . . . cutting through every national ideology." It could claim to be universal precisely because it acknowledged itself to be a mediation of divergent cultures and was open to all.[27]

Hofmannsthal reinvented the Austrian Idea to help preserve the monarchy, and, through a "self-overcoming" of the "immeasurable suffering" of the war, give birth to a new Europe. With the monarchy's downfall, the Austrian Idea became the groundwork for different platforms that sought to revitalize its legacy. It was a leitmotiv for Austrian Romantics and monarchists, for the Ständestaat, and for Jewish exiles of all political shades – the foundation of the Habsburg myth. The Salzburg Festival expressed it in cultural performances. As the boundaries of the "Austrian Space" were now less clear than ever, cultural more than political, Hofmannsthal hoped that an Austro-German culture would unify Central Europe. The festival's repertoire represented his collaboration with director Max Reinhardt and stage actor Alexander Moissi, both of Jewish origin. Salzburg's resident poet, Hermann Bahr, who had known Hofmannsthal since turn-of-the-century *Jung Wien* (young Vienna) days, helped launch it by securing the backing of the city and church officials. The festival articulated a vision of a Catholic Austro-German culture, drawing on Baroque traditions. Its international cast, audience, and financing, its performance of Italian, English, and French works, in addition to German ones, as well as Hofmannsthal's rhetoric about German–Slavic exchange, projected cosmopolitanism.

Recent critics view the festival as a nationalist strategy for retaining German hegemony, a Greater Austria alternative to Pan-Germanism.[28] The critique suits mainstream interwar Austrian Romanticism, typically represented by the antisemitic Catholic journal *Das neue Reich*, quite well.[29] Richard von Kralik, Josef Eberle, and their compatriots articulated a *Gesamtdeutsch* imperial vision of Central Europe that progressively nationalized and racialized the empire. In their vision, German hegemony substituted for old imperial pluralism: Germans were to dominate Central Europe but under Austrian Catholic rather than Prussian

---

[27] "Die Idee Europa: Notizen zu einer Rede," in *Reden und Aufsätze II*, pp. 43–54: Sketch for a lecture in Bern, Switzerland, held on March 31, 1917.

[28] Michael Steinberg, *The Meaning of the Salzburg Festival* (Ithaca, NY: Cornell University Press, 1990).

[29] Janek Wasserman, *Black Vienna: The Radical Right in the Red City, 1918–1938* (Ithaca, NY: Cornell University Press, 2014).

Protestant (or socialist) leadership. The Salzburg Festival seemed different. In the context of Central European ethno-nationalism, its internationalism was almost provocative, affirming the hybridity of Austro-German culture. The strident Salzburg antisemites who attacked the festival as Jewish may have sensed that such hybridity would open up space for the Catholic Jews in Austria. The space was, to be sure, limited and insecure. An imagined Austrian Central Europe was multicultural, but it was also consciously Catholic and illiberal: Its pluralism seemed shaky, its cross-cultural dialogue halting, its hybridity restricted. It had a place for Catholic Jews – but not for Jewish Jews.

These proved to be the limits of all interwar Austrian Romantic visions. The *Österreichische Aktion* (Austrian action), a group of Catholic monarchists, including, among others, August Maria Knoll, Alfred Missong, and Ernst Karl Winter, pushed the Austrian Idea in a European direction, away from Mitteleuropa. Their 1927 manifesto opined that the Habsburg Empire was Europe's grand mediator, inheritor of a millennium-old Latin-Christian reich, disrupted first by the Reformation and then by Prussian nationalism – revolutionary, violent, Protestant. As the successor of a pluralist empire, Austria offered the new Europe a mode for reconciling national and cultural differences that was antithetical to the nation-state and essential for European survival. Winter contemplated a Catholic Central European federation (Austria, Bohemia, Hungary, Croatia, and Poland), but Missong declared that Austria's future depended on *Gesamteuropa*, Europe as a whole. He urged acceptance of both the League of Nations and Pan-Europa – liberal, modern, and vulnerable to Jews and Freemasons though they might be – as the surrogates for old Austria and the kernel of a new Europe. To think of Europe was to be Austrian; to think of Austria was to be European.[30]

Some historians find in the Österreichische Aktion a "modernization" of the Austrian Idea.[31] Yet the new Catholic politics was grounded precisely in a rejection of the nation-state, and an endeavor to rebuild society around traditional institutions – family, church, and estate – that were putatively under socialist attack. They called for a popular monarchy (*Volksmonarchie*) that would reconcile elites and workers and dissolve the proletariat (*Entproletarisierung*) into the new social order. Their apprehension about nationalism and state invasion of the family and religious

---

[30] August M. Knoll et al., *Die Österreichische Aktion* (Vienna: Selbstverlag der Verfasser [Ernst Karl Winter], 1927), esp. p. 6 for Winter and pp. 53–54 for Missong.

[31] Thomas Angerer, "De l'‘Autriche germanique’ à l'‘Autriche européenne’? Identités nationales et internationales de l'Autriche depuis 1918," in *Le rôle et la place des petits pays en Europe au XXe siècle*, ed. Gilbert Trausch (Brussels: Bruylant, 2005), pp. 407–64.

sphere may strike a chord with contemporary historians, but if socialist federalism was postnational, interwar Catholic Europeanism was prenational.[32] The Österreichische Aktion's indebtedness to Karl von Vogelsang and affinities with Spann were significant. Missong and Winter would come out in the 1930s against racial antisemitism, lead the Catholic opposition to National Socialism, and in 1938 go into exile, but in the 1920s, both remained steeped in antisemitic culture. Missong stayed on as editor of the antisemitic *Schönere Zukunft* until 1938 (while publishing under a pseudonym in the pro-government *Christliche Ständestaat*). Knoll received his Habilitation degree under Spann in 1943. What place could Jews or Protestants have in their antidemocratic and illiberal European Austria?

The Österreichische Aktion disbanded in 1931. Responding to the threat of National Socialism, Winter moved further than any Catholic intellectual to rethink the Austrian nation. He now endorsed democracy and called for reconciliation with the Socialists and for an Austrian nationality that would reflect the monarchy's pluralist legacy.[33] He assailed German racism and declared that the two-millennia-old confrontation between Christians and Jews was over, now that both faced a common mortal enemy – National Socialist paganism. These were courageous ideas, innovatively drawing on the imperial legacy to frame an Austrian nation. Still, Winter remained committed to a social monarchy (*soziale Monarchie*) and to a Catholic–Socialist alliance against capitalism and liberalism. His critique of racism and antisemitism was anchored in a *Heilgeschichte* (salvation history) that made the Jew part of the West but only as Christianity's Other.[34] The Jews acquired their significance first as Christianity's Old Testament predecessors, later as its opponents. The nation-state emancipated them; they embodied anti-Catholic modernity; modernity now came back to haunt them. Pluralism and Augustinianism assured Winter's Jews a measure of protection, but his Austria was not one capable of integrating them.

---

[32] This, James Chappel shows, would begin changing in the 1930s and, more decisively, in the postwar years: *Catholic Modern: The Challenge of Totalitarianism and the Remaking of the Church* (Cambridge, MA: Harvard University Press, 2018). On the *Österreichische Aktion*, see also Janek Wasserman, *Black Vienna*.

[33] Ernst Karl Winter, "Die Staatskrise in Österreich," *Wiener Politische Blätter* (16 April 1933), esp. 35–38, and "Die Österreichische Idee," *Wiener Politische Blätter* (27 August 1933), reprinted in K. H. Heinz, ed., *E.K. Winter: Ein Katholik zwischen Österreichs Fronten, 1933–1938* (Vienna: Hermann Böhlau, 1984), pp. 88–111.

[34] Winter, "Deutschtum und Judentum," *Wiener Politische Blätter* (3 December 1933), reprinted in Heinz, *Ein Katholik*, pp. 122–27, and "Die Judenfrage," *Wiener Politische Blätter*, 4 (24 May 1936), reprinted (in part) in *Ernst Karl Winter: Bahnbrecher des Dialogs*, ed. with an introduction by Alfred Missong (Vienna: Europa Verlag, 1969), pp. 178–85.

Deeper ambiguities still ran through the Ständestaat, established in the aftermath of the Socialist defeat in the civil war of February 1934. Just as it wavered among the varieties of authoritarianism (including fascism) and vacillated among German national, Austrian imperial, and European international identity, so too did it assure Jews of equal rights while doing little to contain rampant antisemitism. It displayed Jews prominently in public culture, while excluding most of them from public service, and cultivated both Catholic-Jewish modernism and *Vaterländische Blut-und-Boden* (blood and soil) ideology. The Ständestaat claimed to be both German and European. Nazi Germany – pagan and violent – betrayed its European mission. Catholic-German Austria, however small, inherited the monarchy's historical role in protecting the Christian West against the barbarians – the Bolsheviks and the Nazis. Ambiguity about the Jews conveyed the confusion of identity. As German Catholic, Austria was antisemitic, yet as the imperial successor, it was open to the Jews. As German Catholic, it was backward looking, antimodern, and illiberal. Seeking recognition as a better Germany, it identified with Paneuropa, allowed the Freemasons to operate (though supervised), and offered refuge to German-Jewish intellectuals escaping National Socialism.[35]

The Jewish community did not need to have a fine understanding of the nuances of Ständestaat identity. It knew only that if the Ständestaat went down, they could well face the Nazis. Social Democrats and Jews were the most reliable constituencies of parliamentary democracy in interwar Central Europe. When democracy collapsed, non-Jewish Socialists could join the racially redefined nation, as many Carinthian Socialists did by switching over to the Nazis throughout the 1930s. The Jews did not have this option. In 1934, Jewish integration was no longer a prospect: The Socialists were out, antisemitism was triumphant throughout Central Europe (Czechoslovakia excepted), and the Jews were being ousted from civil society everywhere. Dollfuss and his successor, Schuschnigg – not antisemitic personally, cognizant of their mutual interest with the Jews in containing the Nazis and eager for Jewish financial support, and concerned about Austria's international image – offered the Jewish community a measure of protection. Protection was a paltry substitute for integration, but it was preferable to exclusion from civil society, not to mention violent persecution. The official Jewish community – Orthodox, liberals, and Zionists, all but the Socialists – switched their allegiance to the government. One *Israelitische Kultusgemeinde*'s official after another expressed support for the regime.

[35] Paneuropa and anti-Germanism became subdued after the 1936 *Juliabkommen* (July agreement) with Germany.

Wishing to make good on its claim for Austria as a European cultural power, counterpose Catholic modernism to Socialist "*Kulturbolschewismus*," and distance itself from German racism by displaying a selective integration of Jews, the Ständestaat cultivated a Catholic-Jewish elite comprised of converts and Jews who made the Catholic legacy central to their work. It supported the Salzburg Festival, enabled Bruno Walter to continue as head of the Vienna State Opera and conduct concerts by the Vienna Philharmonic Orchestra, allowed the Vienna Theater in der Josefstadt to remain a center for Jewish actors, playwrights, and directors, and in 1937, turned Franz Werfel into Austria's poet laureate by awarding him the *Österreichische Verdienstkreuz für Kunst und Wissenschaft*. The majority of the Jewish intelligentsia played no role in the Ständestaat, but like other Jews, they compared it with the Nuremberg Laws. On the eve of the German invasion of March 12, 1938, the entire community mobilized behind the Ständestaat in a last-ditch effort to retain Austrian independence. They failed.

Werfel was lucky enough to be ill at the time in Capri. A year earlier he had published "An Essay on the Meaning of Imperial Austria," recounting the passing of the monarchy and the irreparable loss of a peaceful, pluralist Central Europe, wisely governed by Franz Joseph.[36] Werfel marked the transition of the Austrian Idea from state ideology to exile literature, from political deployment for changing the world to literary nostalgia for the world of yesterday. He was emblematic of the Catholic failure to negotiate the pluralist legacy and accommodate the Jews. One of Austria's two most widely read authors (the other was Zweig), Werfel personified the Jewish-Catholic symbiosis. He felt attached to the Apostle Paul and saw Christianity as part of his Jewish heritage. He held the Augustinian view of the Jews as witnesses to Christian truth and did not convert out of solidarity with his people – he would not endeavor to escape their fate. He seemed the very Jew to vindicate Catholic-German Austria's openness. Yet the poet laureate, whose salon served as a meeting place for the Ständestaat's cultural elite, felt homeless.[37] Catholic-German Austria could offer overnight shelter but not a home. These were the limits of Jewish partnership with the Ständestaat.

Two millennia of Jewish-Christian relations, for which Jacob & Esau may serve as the best rubric, set the almost transhistorical limits. In a 1937 speech at Pauluswerk – the mission house of a Catholic Jew, Fr. Johannes Österreicher – Dietrich von Hildebrand, editor of the *Christliche Ständestaat* and an eminent anti-Nazi theologian, himself a German refugee (partly of Jewish ancestry), offered the Catholic view on "The

---

[36] Franz Werfel, *Twilight of a World* (New York: Viking Press, 1937), pp. 3–40.
[37] Friedrich Buchmayr, "Stufen der Entfremdung: Franz Werfels letzte Jahre in Österreich," *Chilufim: Zeitschrift für Jüdische Kulturgeschichte* 2 (2007): 51–97.

Jews and the Christian West."[38] He criticized antisemitism and the race idea and brilliantly commented on the ambiguity of Jewish emancipation in the nation-state. Yet the Jews' historical existence, their belongingness in the West, remained determined, in his account, by their position vis-à-vis Christianity. They had been living for millennia in suspense, their return to the Lord eagerly awaited. This was 1930s Catholic philosemitism at its best, and it could neither serve as an opening to genuine Catholic–Jewish dialogue nor create a secure place for Jews in the Catholic state. In the aftermath of the Holocaust, Vatican II would recognize the coexistence of Christianity and Judaism as normative and move the expectation of Jewish conversion to the end of days, thereby opening up a new period in Christian–Jewish relations.[39] In the 1930s, the old limits were stricter than ever. Christian Social Austria could present no viable alternative for Jewish life.

The Zionists: An Imperial Multinational Dream in German Austria

The Jewish nationalists felt deeply the monarchy's loss. Interwar Austria, unlike imperial Galicia, was not a natural habitat for Jewish autonomy. Yet the Zionists also benefited from the nation-state's failure. The vanishing prospects for Jewish integration triggered a radical change in the Jewish community's leadership, with the Zionists, in 1932, obtaining a majority in the *Kultusgemeinde*, the last bastion of Austrian liberalism. The electoral maps of Jewish and national politics differed significantly. Whereas more than 80 percent of Viennese Jews voted Socialist in the municipal elections of 1932, the Socialists comprised only a small minority in the Kultusgemeinde: Most liberals and Zionists voted Socialist in municipal and national elections, and the great majority of Jewish Socialists did not participate in communal affairs. In the republic's first decade, both the liberals and the Zionists tried running their own candidates in municipal and national elections. In 1919, the Zionists elected one representative, Robert Stricker, to the Constituent Assembly – the single vote against the symbolic resolution on unification with Germany – and three to the Vienna City Council. They were never able to repeat this performance and by 1930, with few exceptions, stopped running

---

[38] "Die Juden und das Christliche Abendland," in *Die Menschheit am Scheideweg* (Regensburg: Verlag Josef Habbel, 1955), pp. 312–40.

[39] In postwar years, Hildebrand and Österreicher would be instrumental in moving the Catholic Church toward changing its policy and doctrines on the Jews: John Connelly, *From Enemy to Brother: The Revolution in Catholic Teaching on the Jews, 1933–1965* (Cambridge, MA: Harvard University Press, 2012).

candidates. The liberals failed outright, desisted earlier, and endorsed the Socialists. The Ständestaat, suspicious of the liberal leadership and disposed to accentuate Jewish difference, recognized the Zionists as the community's sole representatives.[40]

The electoral maps suggest that whereas the Jewish community was involved in Socialist politics, the Socialists had little interest in Jewish politics. Their disposition toward the organized Jewish community ranged from indifferent to hostile. The Socialists regarded the Kultusgemeinde as a strictly religious organization – not cultural, ethnic, or national. Anticlerical advocates of the separation of church and state, and often assimilated Jews themselves, they declined to support Jewish institutions, schools included. Their own Jewish integration was at issue. Zionist Socialists, who were staunchly loyal to the party, beseeched the Socialists to reconsider their position on Palestine but were met with a closed door. No Socialist representative attended the opening of the World Zionist Congress, held in Vienna in 1925. No Socialist was a member of the Pro-Palestine Committee, established in 1927. The Jewish Socialist leaders, above all Bauer, were more adamant in their opposition to Zionism than their non-Jewish colleagues. Bauer was determined in his belief that German Socialism was the sole solution to the Central European Jewish Question, and he was not going to open up questions about the Austrian Jews' German national identity.

Socialist hostility was unfortunate because Viennese Zionism was predominantly integrationist and had a wide reach. The Zionists adopted most of the Diaspora nationalist platform and added Palestine. With the single European Zionist daily and a legendary athletic club, *Hakoah*, interwar Vienna retained its distinguished place in the history of Zionism. Renowned Jewish intellectuals across the political spectrum were engaged with Zionism at some juncture in their lives, and they commonly retained the Zionist moment as a dimension of their thought: poet Richard Beer-Hofmann, socialist psychologists Siegfried Bernfeld and Manès Sperber, liberal writer Felix Salten, composer Arnold Schoenberg, and novelist Franz Werfel. Zionists of all shades were immersed in Austrian culture and politics, and even the most Palestinocentric ended up focusing on Austrian-Jewish concerns. Their demand for recognition as a national minority was decidedly not a rejection of integration but a call for the possibility of a Jewish culture in Austria, for a pluralized nation-state; in short, the Zionists wished for Austria to become a mini empire.

---

[40] Harriet Pass Freidenreich, *Jewish Politics in Vienna, 1918–1938* (Bloomington: Indiana University Press, 1991).

A unique understanding of Jewish nationality emerged from the Vienna and Prague Zionists: Beer-Hofmann, Samuel Hugo Bergmann, Max Brod, Martin Buber, Hans Kohn, Manès Sperber, Friedrich Torberg, and Felix Weltsch. Both groups were shaped by the pre–World War I nationalizing empire, and sought to carve a space for Jewish nationalism in a multicultural setting. They were often in touch: Torberg lived in both cities and had Max Brod for a mentor. Formed at the heart of the Central European ethno-national struggles, the Vienna and Prague Zionists cultivated Jewish ethnicity – blood kinship, religion, and cultural inheritance – as the core of nationality, but also recognized its hybridity and gave ethnicity a universal ethical twist. The Prague members' troubling pre–World War I romance with race and blood dissipated in the interwar years, and they all ended up maintaining that Jewish suffering and the biblical heritage had sensitized Jews to the national claims of others, and that Jewish nationality would be different. Jews would remain humanity's ethical teachers, possibly as an Oriental people in Palestine.[41]

Leading Prague Zionists emigrated to Palestine in the interwar years, where they joined with like-minded immigrants like Galician Yehoshua Radler-Feldman, alias Rabi Binyamin, and American Judah Leib Magnes to found *Berit Shalom* (Peace Covenant), a group critical of mainstream Zionist politics that rejected Jewish statehood and advocated a binationalist and federalist Palestine. Their focus on Jewish ethnicity meant acceptance that the Jews were not European but Oriental, and they sought a rapprochement with the Palestinian Arabs that would be grounded in a common racial culture. Some mimicked the European Pan movements, particularly Pan-Germanism, by extending Jewish racial solidarity into Pan-Semitism or Pan-Asianism, and expressing the hope for a joint anti-imperialist uprising against the Western powers. They turned antisemitism on its head by conceptualizing Zionism as a Pan movement, imperial and racial in character, and creating anti-Aryan counterpolitics. They redefined ethnicity and nationality away from the nation-state and integrated them into

---

[41] Matti Bunzl, "The Poetics of Politics and the Politics of Poetics: Richard Beer-Hofmann and Theodor Herzl Reconsidered," *German Quarterly* 69 (Summer 1996): 277–304; Adi Gordon, *Toward Nationalism's End: An Intellectual Biography of Hans Kohn* (Waltham, MA: Brandeis University Press, 2017); Zohar Maor, *New Secret Doctrine: Spirituality, Creativity and Nationalism in the Prague Circle* (in Hebrew) (Jerusalem: Shazar Center, 2010); Paul Mendes-Flohr, "Martin Buber as a Habsburg Intellectual," in *Jüdische Geschichte als Allgemeine Geschichte: Festschrift für Dan Diner zum 60. Geburtstag*, ed. Raphael Gross and Yfaat Weiss (Gottingen: Vandenhoeck & Ruprecht, 2006), pp. 13–29; Dimitry Shumsky, "On Ethno-Centrism and Its Limits – Czecho-German Jewry in Fin-de-Siècle Prague and the Origins of Zionist Bi-Nationalism," *Jahrbuch des Simon-Dubnow-Instituts* 5 (2006): 173–88.

federalist, imperial structures, providing a sui generis Zionist nonterritorial nationality, paralleling that of Renner.[42]

Mainstream Zionism was more conventionally ethno-national, but unlike other nationalisms, it had to address the problems of a Diaspora without a European homeland. The Zionists actively participated in the European Congress of Nationalities, established in 1925, to protect the political rights and interests of minorities in the newly established and territorially expanded nationalizing states. Until 1933, the Zionists colla- borated with the Baltic Germans. The National Socialist *Gleichschaltung* ended the collaboration: The Germans insisted that a country was entitled to dissimilate ethnic groups, that is, declare the Jews non- Germans and undo emancipation.[43] Ethno-nationalism became a golem rising up against its creator, and the Zionists appeared as a major negotiator of the Austrian imperial legacy, trying to contain it.

The Socialists remained closed to the new Jewish cultural currents, and their closure highlighted both their hostility to the imperial legacy and the limits of the integration they offered the Jews. The socialist commonwealth was to include Jews, and those wishing to practice were (almost) welcome to do so (at their own expense), but Jews who wished to become part of socialist culture needed to relegate their Judaism to inconsequential marginality. (Bauer did so but continued dutifully to pay his Kultusgemeinde tax.) Jews could in no way, how- ever, be part of *another* national culture. They could only be Austrian Germans. Opting for German nationalism, socialist integration set lim- its to being Jewish. The Zionist nostalgia for the pluralist empire was understandable.

Liberal Internationalism and the Imperial Legacy: The Freemasons and *Paneuropa*

Interwar Austria did have vestiges of liberal internationalism. The Freemasons epitomized them. Active participants in the progressive

---

[42] Adi Gordon, ed., *Brith Shalom and Bi-National Zionism* (in Hebrew) (Jerusalem: Carmel, 2008); Zohar Maor, "Between Anti-Colonialism and Postcolonialism: *Berit Shalom*'s Critique of Nationalism and Secularization" (in Hebrew), *Theory and Criticism* 10 (Summer 2007): 12–28; Ḥanan Ḥarif, "'Revival of the East,' Pan-Semitism and Pan- Asianism in Zionist Discourse" (in Hebrew) (Ph.D. diss., Hebrew University of Jerusalem, 2013).

[43] Gil Rubin, "From Minority Protection to 'National Dissimilation': German and Jewish Minority Politicians and the Rise of National Socialism, April–September 1933," B.A. thesis, School of History, Hebrew University of Jerusalem, 2010; Frank Nesemann, "Leo Motzkin (1867–1933): Zionist Engagement and Minority Diplomacy," *Central and Eastern European Review* 1 (2007): 1–24.

Viennese network, they represented its cosmopolitan and pacifist wing. Viennese lodges, which reached a membership of close to two thousand in the late 1920s, predominated. They had a bourgeois profile – affluent merchants, well-to-do professionals, and academics – and Jews were heavily represented, giving Austrian lodges a different countenance from their German counterpart.[44] The Freemasons regarded the monarchy's dissolution as unfortunate: It represented an advance over the nation-state in humanity's march toward cosmopolitanism, and they saw themselves "as guardians of liberal values and as the intellectual elite of a huge state whose composition gave it the appearance of the international order of humankind in miniature."[45] But they had hopes for the republic. Until 1918, they had been illegal in Austria, and had to organize in *Grenzlogen* (border lodges) across the Hungarian border, and as charitable and educational societies in Vienna. They could now organize normally. On December 9, 1918, they established the *Grossloge von Wien* (great lodge of Vienna), their choice of name skirting the treacherous issue of national identity.[46]

The Freemasons had been collaborating with the Socialists since the turn of the century in promoting educational and social reform. A few Socialist leaders were Masons, and, in an uncommon bourgeois–proletarian collaboration, two Lessing Lodge brothers, industrialist Josef Trebitsch and Socialist minister Ferdinand Hanusch, helped put together the 1919 social welfare legislation. Adjusting to the transition from a European imperial order to a Europe of the nations, the Freemasons retooled quickly. Efforts at European reconciliation and at building a durable international *Völkerbund* (league of nations) assumed center stage in the interwar years. Membership in the lodges and in the pacifist Austrian Peace Society tended to overlap, and the Freemasons collaborated with lodges throughout Europe – especially France – to counteract *revanchisme*. Alfred Fried, who died in 1921, saw World War I as vindication of his prewar European federalism, and advocated for an international organization to arbitrate disputes according to international law

---

[44] Rainer Hubert, "Freimaurerei in Österreich 1871 bis 1938," in *Zirkel und Winkelmass* (Vienna: Eigenverlag der Museen der Stadt Wien, 1984), pp. 31–46. On German lodges: Jacob Katz, *Jews and Freemasons in Europe, 1723–1939* (Cambridge, MA: Harvard University Press, 1970), esp. pp. 163–70.

[45] Paul Silverman, "Law and Economics in Interwar Vienna: Kelsen, Mises and the Regeneration of Austrian Liberalism" (Ph.D. diss., University of Chicago, 1984), p. 26.

[46] Rainer Hubert and Ferdinand Zörrer, "Die österreichischen Grenzlogen," *Quator Coronati Jahrbuch* (1983): 153; Gustav Kuéss and Bernhard Scheichelbauer, *200 Jahre Freimaurerei in Österreich* (Vienna: O. Kerry, 1959), pp. 137–222; Marcus Patka, *Freimaurerei und Sozialreform: Der Kampf für Menschenrechte, Pazifismus und Zivilgesellschaft in Österreich 1869–1938* (Vienna: Löcker, 2011).

and prevent a tragic reoccurrence.[47] Fried was a major inspiration to Richard Coudenhove-Kalergi, who, in 1922, joined the Freemasons' oldest Austrian lodge, Humanitas. The next year, published *Paneuropa*, launching the largest interwar movement for European unification. The Freemasons became staunch supporters.

"If Austria had had no Freemasons," argued Carlos von Gagern in 1878, "the government should have called on them to come from abroad . . . and supported their expansion with all its powers – in the Monarchy's obvious interest!"[48] The Freemasons' universal humanity, he suggested, was a prescription against divisive nationalism. The prescription remained valid for the First Republic. The Freemasons considered the Anschluss superfluous because national boundaries were obsolete, and even in a union with Germany, Austria would become part of Pan-Europe. With the triumph of German Nazism, they thought of an anti-Nazi Europe as the guarantor of Austria's survival. As a small state, Austria needed Europe. If one searches for imperial antecedents of Austria's European identity, Fried and the Freemasons may have been their best arbitrators. The Socialists, who addressed the domestic problems of imperial pluralism, were more original in their postnationalism, but they were hostile to the monarchy and silent on Europe in the interwar years. The Catholics staged a European Austria, but it was not a modern nation-state. The Freemasons first deployed the imperial legacy for a Europe of nation-states.

Prophets of a postnational Europe, the Freemasons seemed odd in ethno-national times and, to German nationalists, outright treacherous. "The Austrian Freemasons are avowed pacifists and have undertaken exchanges with the Great Lodges of France, Italy, the U.S. and other World War I winner-states," complained the *altpreussische Loge* (old Prussian lodge) in 1924.[49] From 1926 on, the major German lodges broke relations with the Austrians one after the other. The Ständestaat, suspicious of the Freemasons' secular liberalism and socialist affinities but solicitous of their anti-German Pan-Europeanism, allowed them to operate but put them under surveillance. Lodge membership dropped. The Freemasons offered Schuschnigg their support in March 1938. The Nazis plundered the *Grossloge*, closed it down, and arrested the longtime *Grossmeister*, Richard Schlesinger, who died shortly thereafter. Only seventy members convened in 1945 to reopen the lodge.[50]

---

[47] Alfred H. Fried, *The Restoration of Europe* (New York: Macmillan, 1916), and *Der Völkerbund: Ein Sammelbuch* (Leipzig: E. P. Tal & Co., 1919).

[48] *Zirkel*, no. 11 (1878), quoted in Hubert and Zörrer, "Die österreichischen Grenzlogen," 153.

[49] Kuéss and Scheichelbauer, *200 Jahre Freimaurerei*, p. 203.

[50] Marcus Patka, *Österreichische Freimaurer im Nationalsozialismus: Treue und Verrat* (Vienna: Böhlau, 2010).

Freemason lodges gave the founder of the *Paneuropa* movement, Richard Nikolaus Eijiro, Count of Coudenhove-Kalergi (1894–1972), his first organizational base. However, Paneuropa represented an amalgam of old imperial supranationalism and new Austrian internationalism, and not Masonic ideas exclusively. If Coudenhove-Kalergi had not existed, he would need to have been invented to illuminate the complexity of Austrian identity and the ambiguity of the imperial legacy in the interwar period. An aristocrat descended from multiracial origins, the son of an Austrian diplomat and a Japanese mother (who descended from the samurai), he married a Viennese theater actress of Jewish and Slavic origins, Ida Roland, née Klausner. (He is himself a Pan-European organization, quipped an observer.) Having passed his adolescence on the Bohemian family estates in Ronsperg, attended the Viennese Theresianum (a gymnasium with a military aristocratic tradition), and obtained a philosophy Ph.D. from the University of Vienna in 1917, Coudenhove-Kalergi became a Czech citizen after World War I but spent most of the interwar years in Vienna promoting Paneuropa. Recognizing the "liberal Jewish" burden that a Masonic association carried, and wishing to expand his influence to Catholics and conservatives, he left his lodge in 1926. In 1938 he escaped first to Czechoslovakia, then to France (where he became a citizen), and then in 1940 to the United States, via Switzerland and Portugal. He is widely viewed as the leader of the first major movement for European unity.[51]

In 1922–23, Coudenhove-Kalergi sketched out a "United States of Europe," excluding Britain and Russia, a federal state with a single currency, customs union, two-house parliament, and a unified judiciary that would protect the plurality of national cultures and languages. The old European balance of power died with the imperial order, he said, and was replaced by global powers: Pan-America, the British Empire, Soviet Russia, and emergent East Asia. To pursue national self-determination and collective security through the League of Nations was to risk European subservience to the global powers. Without regional security, Europe's nation-states would not survive renewed internal fighting, Soviet military aggression, or British and American economic imperialism. Nationalism undermined European collaboration, but Wilsonian-style internationalism would not overcome it. Economic collaboration and a shared culture were prerequisites for European unity. Paneuropa was to begin as an economic and cultural project.[52]

---

[51] Anita Ziegerhofer, *Botschafter Europas: Richard Nikolaus Coudenhove-Kalergi und die Paneuropa-Bewegung in den zwanziger und dreißiger Jahren* (Vienna: Böhlau, 2004).

[52] Richard N. Coudenhove-Kalergi, *Paneuropa* (Vienna: Paneuropa Verlag, 1923).

Austria epitomized the small European nation-state, and Coudenhove-Kalergi, Czech citizen of the German minority, the national minority in ethno-nationalizing Europe. To Coudenhove-Kalergi, Austria was *lebensunfähig* (incapable of survival). It belonged economically in the Danube basin, but national feeling directed it toward Germany. The only way around the dilemma was Paneuropa: rendering political borders insignificant, vindicating national cultures, and facilitating economic collaboration. Separating nation from state, Paneuropa would also alleviate the national minority problem. To Coudenhove-Kalergi, the Ständestaat's conception of Austria as German European seemed exemplary of a European national culture. He envisioned Vienna, a *Welthauptstadt* (metropolis) aspirant, as the European capital. It served as host to the movement's headquarters and founding congress. Paneuropa almost seemed an Austrian project.

Paneuropa became a broad international movement because it conveyed the anxieties that Europeans had about the new European order and the divergent hopes for their resolution. Coudenhove-Kalergi managed to expand the reach of the European idea from a narrow Masonic, liberal–bourgeois, primarily Jewish constituency to a wide range of groups, including conservative Catholics. Intellectuals, artists, and politicians across the political spectrum joined the movement, from Albert Einstein to Thomas Mann to Pablo Picasso. The three-day congress in Vienna in October 1926 had two thousand participants, attracted a few heads of state (albeit none from a major European power), and elected Aristide Briand as its honorary president. A series of congresses and economic conferences followed, the last in 1936. The movement had between six and eight thousand members. Hamburg banker Max Warburg and major German and Austrian banks helped financially. Coudenhove-Kalergi engaged European statesmen right and left, from National Liberal Chancellor Gustav Stresemann to Socialist Reichstag President Paul Löbe in Germany, and from Pan-German leader Franz Dinghofer to Chancellors Johann Schober and Seipel to Renner in Austria. Paneuropa was able to keep Pan-Germans and pacifists, Catholics and Socialists together as long as European unity remained a distant prospect. Their visions conflicted, but each could keep his intact – for a time.

Most Austrian Socialists remained suspicious of Paneuropa, and when Coudenhove-Kalergi sharpened his anti-Bolshevik rhetoric in the early 1930s, even Renner walked out. This made it easier for Coudenhove-Kalergi to pronounce his support for the Ständestaat and promote Dollfuss as founder of a new Austrian nation. Yet Catholic support for Paneuropa was shaky, too. International Catholic networks, suspicious of the democratic nation-state and fearful of communism, flourished in interwar Europe, and overcame national borders in ways that socialists did not, bringing together German humanists and the French *Action Française*. Seipel's first commitment was to one such network, Karl Anton Rohan's *Europäisches Kulturbund* (European cultural association), which was comprised of about three hundred European intellectuals and also associated with the Catholic journal *Abendland*, which Seipel coedited.[53] Like Coudenhove-Kalergi, Rohan was an Austrian Bohemian aristocrat, but his *Europäische Revue* advocated a conservative revolution and criticized Paneuropa as liberal. He initially supported a Greater Austria and opposed Pan-Germanism but eventually turned to the Nazis. Fragments of the collapsed imperial order thus continued to have a life in interwar Europe, trying to reshape the new order, and it was unfortunate that the Socialists never entered the fray. Seipel, in contrast, was keeping one foot in Paneuropa to maintain his options for revising Versailles.

The reality check for Paneuropa came in 1930, and it failed miserably. Aristide Briand proposed a European federation to the League of Nations. The German and Austrian governments countered in 1931 by proposing a German–Austrian *Zollverein*, an Anschluss-inspired alternative to Paneuropa. Both plans came to naught. Paneuropa's success was a symptom of a disease that it could not possibly cure. Any proposed unification would encounter the objections of those who joined, expecting to see a different Europe emerging.

Coudenhove-Kalergi managed to hold divergent camps together for such a long time because his own worldview, full of tensions, represented their convergence. A Freemason, pacifist, and critic of racism and antisemitism, he was also vehemently anticommunist, anti-American, skeptical of democracy, enamored of Mussolini, and in search of a new European aristocracy. He could be insightful and daring: The racial nation was a fantasy; all nations represented a racial *Mischung*; and the Nuremberg laws were a travesty.[54] Nations were cultural constructions, formed by geniuses who endowed them with spiritual principles. They did not need to be coupled with states and ought to be protected against liberalism's leveling effects. As European consciousness had to be an outgrowth of a European culture, a new creative elite – a Nietzschean "aristocracy of the spirit," – had to emerge to shape the new culture. Jews

---

[53] Guido Müller, *Europäische Gesellschaftsbeziehungen nach dem Ersten Weltkrieg: Das Deutsch-Französische Studienkomitee und der Europäische Kulturbund* (Munich: R. Oldenbourg, 2005).

[54] *Judenhass von Heute: Das Wesen des Antisemitismus*, introd. and ed. R. N. Coudenhove-Kalergi (Vienna: Europa Verlag, 1935).

would play a prominent role. Coudenhove-Kalergi modernized the Austrian idea, turning imperial pluralism into liberal multiculturalism, but his modernity remained ambiguous. Nietzsche served as the bridge between the old and new world. European culture was to be a convergence of his Old Europeans and *Übermensch*.

The political ambiguity of Paneuropa went deeper. It represented a transition between the old imperial order and the new nation-states, a convergence of nation and empire. Coudenhove-Kalergi called his principles "strictly aristocratic," stated that Paneuropa did not take sides in the struggle between democracy and fascism, pleaded with Mussolini for collaboration, and warmly supported the Ständestaat against the Nazis and the Anschluss. Still, at a time when few believed in liberal democracy, the Paneuropa scheme was liberal and was denounced as such by most conservatives. The huge portraits of Kant, Nietzsche, and Napoleon hanging at the founding congress reflected the quixotic mixture of ideas and traditions informing Paneuropa. Like the Freemasons, it envisioned a postnational Europe solving the Austrian (and Jewish) question. Unlike the Freemasons, the solution was not unequivocally modern and liberal. This allowed Paneuropa to attract a broader and more variegated constituency, but in the end, it made no difference. The constituents sought to use the postnational vision to ethno-national ends, and Europe was back at point zero. Postnational Europe was impossible at the height of ethno-nationalism.

Imperial Nostalgia and Jewish Cosmopolitanism

The collapse of the Versailles order and of Central European democracies in the 1930s set off a major rethinking on the part of the Jewish intelligentsia of its relationship to Austria. The pluralist monarchy, irretrievably lost, now appeared so much more hospitable to Jews than the nation-state, and the old order seemed to embody values and aspirations that the First Republic failed to realize. Jewish writers expressed irrepressible nostalgia for the world of Franz Joseph and, in memorable works, remade the *habsburgische Mythos* (Habsburg myth).[55] Their nostalgia reflected helplessness and marked the end of politics, but, inadvertently, they began shaping a usable past for the Second Republic.

Nostalgia for the monarchy had begun even before it collapsed. For writers like Ferdinand von Saar, Franz Joseph's final decades were marked by a sense of loss and doom, a world passing away. When the

---

[55] Claudio Magris, *Der habsburgische Mythos in der modernen österreichische Literatur* [1963] (Vienna: Paul Zsolnay Verlag, 2000).

empire finally came apart, the Habsburg Myth served monarchists and Austro-Romantics – Leopold von Andrian, Josef Eberle, Richard von Kralik, Richard von Schaukal, Friedrich Schreyvogl – as a political ideology. They called for a Habsburg restoration or for a new Greater Austria, and often for both. Many promoted a *Gesamtdeutsch* Catholic alternative to secular *Grossdeutsch* (Pan-German) nationalism. Most Jewish writers, notably Joseph Roth, Werfel, and Zweig, joined the wave of imperial nostalgia only in the 1930s, after their hopes for the republic had already been dashed. Their nostalgia expressed despair.

Both the Jews and the Romantics – commonly former nobility or civil servants – lost their place in the imperial order and felt homeless in the republic. For the Romantics, imperial pluralism reflected the human condition, and the new nation-states, like modernity itself, were unidimensional and reduced politics to a mechanical operation. They remained ambivalent about German nationalism, and envisioned a conservative utopia in the form of an antimodern Catholic German Austria. They had more options open, however, than did the Jews. In 1932, their organ, *Das neue Reich*, joined *Schönere Zukunft*, and the unified journal provided a platform for Catholic bridge building to National Socialism. Fear of socialism and hostility toward democracy could lead non-Jewish conservatives from the Habsburg Myth to the National Socialist one. Nationalized and racialized, Austrian imperial visions paved the way for the Third Reich. Even outside Austro-Romantic circles, imperial nostalgia did not prevent the future famous writer Heimito von Doderer from joining the Nazi Party, and Alexander Lernet-Holenia from becoming the German army's chief playwright. The Jews did not have this luxury. In their own homeland – or outside of it – they became exiles.

The Catholic Jews, Hofmannsthal and Felix Braun, were among the Austro-Romantic avant-garde. Braun's 1927 work *Herbst des Reiches* (Imperial autumn) described in detail the empire's fall, a mild, peaceable, traditional Austria crushed under modernity's blows.[56] Roth joined a few years later. Until 1932, his works dissected the outcome of the monarchy's fall but revealed no sentiment for it. He still considered himself a socialist of sorts. From *The Wandering Jews* (1927) to *Job* (1930), Roth bemoaned the fate of the Eastern Jews, destitute in their homeland, alienated anywhere else they wandered, and finding no home, not even in affluent America.[57] By the early 1930s, he had become a monarchist, and the empire became the foremost subject of his work. Likewise, in his 1936 prologue to *Twilight*

---

[56] *Herbst des Reiches* (Olten: Walter-Verlag, 1957); the book was first published as *Agnes Altkirchner* (Leipzig: Insel-verlag, 1927).

[57] Joseph Roth, *Juden auf Wanderschaft* (Berlin: Die Schmiede, 1927), and *Hiob: Roman eines einfachen Mannes* (Frankfurt am Main: Suhrkamp, 2011).

of a World (1937), Werfel wrote that "he has not . . . until very late recognized . . . the imperial idea."[58] His book endeavored to reshape scenes from Prague life, which had been published earlier and were now translated into English, into portrayals of imperial Austria. And until 1933, Zweig had been busy building up his European networks. He was among the last to despair of Versailles Europe because he had nowhere else to turn. *The World of Yesterday* reflected his late recognition that German successes in World War II meant that his Europe was gone forever. Nostalgia was no substitute for politics. For Zweig, it meant suicide.

Imperial Austria emerged among the Jewish writers as the golden age, and they were unanimous in cherishing its pluralism. Yet they imagined it differently, each after his own background and ideology. They set up several models of pluralism, bequeathing a divergent imperial legacy. Roth, himself the quintessential Western European urban nomad, spoke for his homeland's Galician Jews (as well as the provincial Slavs). He turned the *shtetl* – which he escaped as soon as he could, never contemplating a return – into an idealized community, an embodiment of authentic relations with God and humans. In *The Radetsky March* (1932), he cherished the imperial authorities' benevolence and piety, the multinational army and administration's loyalty and rectitude, provincial autonomy, and, above all, the ethno-cultural communities' peaceful coexistence in rural provinces untouched by nationalism and modernity.[59] Peasants, shtetl dwellers, and aristocracy were loyal to a gentle emperor, who mysteriously maintained a personal relationship even with lowly "Caftan Jews." Nationalism and socialism appeared as destructive intrusions of modernity, inventions of an urban Westernized intelligentsia, bound to put an end to the natural idyll. Roth represented illiberal multiculturalism, and not cosmopolitanism: The supranational empire made a mosaic of indigenous ethno-cultural communities possible. He himself never imagined a homecoming to any of them. Rather, he turned exile into a parable of modern humanity and nostalgia for home into an exemplum of contemporary Europe, and thereby made the fate of late imperial Austria that of humanity, creating the Roth myth we love.[60]

Werfel gave a refined expression to the Austro-Romantic vision of a universal Christian empire. Multinational empires represented ideals of

---

[58] *Twilight*, p. 39.   [59] *Radetskymarsch* (Berlin: Kiepenheuer, 1932).
[60] In her brilliant *The Grace of Misery: Joseph Roth and the Politics of Exile, 1919–1939* (Leiden: Brill, 2013), Ilse Lazarom shows how Roth, by narrating the loss of family, home, community, country, and civilization, transformed his personal misery into political exile. Inventing a series of authorial identities – the suffering writer, Job (the single Jewish figure he ever cherished), the imperial army officer linking people without striking roots, the hotel patriot living German culture, presaging its collapse – he turned the monarchy's loss into instantiation of the writer's existential homelessness.

humanity the way that nation-states never could. Austria provided a home to people of diverse confessions and nationalities. It was not a melting pot, but the hegemonic German culture gently prodded different nationalities to relax their egoism and recognize broader claims. Becoming Austrian was becoming human, and Austria was preceptor to the East. The gallery of types in Werfel's Prague stories – aristocrats, military officers, civil servants, lawyers, professors, students, bourgeois parents and youth, a poor governess, prostitutes – did not cast heroic or virtuous figures. Most negotiated life and desire with a mixture of decency and human failings. Even Franz Joseph, who embodied Charlemagne's legacy, was not heroic. Extraordinarily dedicated to his post, he conciliated the workers and deferred nationalist crises until the war (which he did not want) brought down his empire. Werfel contrasted imperial traditionalism, mediation, and equivocation with modern nationalism and capitalism – efficient, militant, and ruthless. The Prague Jewish intellectuals, the Austro-Romantics, and Werfel's own Jewish Catholicism joined to produce this classical formulation of the Habsburg Myth. Werfel represented an urban and humane convergence of multiculturalism and cosmopolitanism, but one that remained anti-modern and mildly authoritarian.

Zweig spoke for the German-acculturated Viennese Jewish intelligentsia. He recalled the empire's order, security, and predictability but marveled most at Viennese culture. Multiculturalism was the secret of Vienna's efflorescence. Stationed at the crossroads of Europe in an age of ethnic migrations, the capital benefited from ethno-cultural cross-traffic. The Jews played a prominent role and experienced a golden age, such as they had not known since medieval Spain. Without discounting Zionism, Zweig spoke of the cosmopolitan Diaspora as the Jewish mission and of European culture as the Jewish *Heimat*. His heroes were the suffering Prophet Jeremiah and the beleaguered scholar Erasmus, who had defended the European Republic of Letters against religious and political fanaticism.[61] He endeavored to expand the cosmopolitan spirit in Europe. A mediator between French and German cultures, he hoped that European cultural understanding would give rise to a political one. Nationalism was his principal enemy; he envisioned a pacifist European federation and supported Pan-Europa and Romain Rolland's *L'Europe*. Of all imperial legacies, Zweig's liberal cosmopolitanism speaks most easily to contemporary Europeans.

---

[61] Stefan Zweig, *Jeremias* (Leipzig: Insel-verlag, 1917); *Triumph und Tragik des Erasmus von Rotterdam* (Vienna: Reichner, 1934), and *The World of Yesterday*.

Robert Musil's *The Man Without Qualities* revealed neither Austro-Romantic nor Jewish imperial nostalgia, but it did develop a commemorative model for the empire: a laboratory of modernity. Musil's life took him first through the monarchy's provinces, then to Berlin and Vienna, and ending in World War II Switzerland. Married to a Jew, Musil belonged to circles where acculturated Jews were prominent and non-Jewish intellectuals spent much of their lives with them.[62] There was no love for the empire in his literary circles, and, with pity and sarcasm, *The Man Without Qualities* exposed Kakania as contradictory and absurd, "absolutism moderated by sloppiness."[63] Yet Kakania represented a universal condition. There was no alternative: Nationalism was disruptive, a dangerous substitute for religion, the invention of a self-serving intelligentsia. Conscious of the monarchy's waning traditionalism, Musil used Kakania to stage the problem of modernity and the writer, and inquired after the possibility of literary creativity, genuine ethics, and authentic philosophy. Precisely the absence (in contrast with Germany) of a cohesive legal system and political ideology, precisely the absurdity, had created the modern condition, a reality of loss and confusion. Austria-Hungary, a traditional continental empire, not quite a modern state, became the paradigm of modernity, a laboratory for the future, and a global experiment. Carl Schorske would redeploy Musil's model in *Fin-de-siècle Vienna*: Late imperial Austria and its capital became modernism's birthplace.

Roth, Werfel, Zweig, and Musil are famous. Almost unknown is the Hebrew Zionist writers' imperial nostalgia. To Zionists, the destruction that World War I brought on Eastern European Jewry made Zionism an imperative but also promoted an idealized picture of life under Franz Joseph. From Rabi Binyamin to Shmuel Yosef Agnon to Haim Be'er, late imperial Austria had a continuous presence in Hebrew literature, well into the State of Israel.[64] The foremost Austro-Romantic was Asher Barash, a native of East Galicia, a major author whose writings have not yet seen translation into German. Barash's novels include precious

---

[62] David Hollinger, "Communalist and Dispersionist Approaches to American Jewish History in an Increasingly Post-Jewish Era," *American Jewish History*, 95:1 (2009): 1–32, argues persuasively for their inclusion in Jewish history, and Daniel Bessner, *Democracy in Exile: Hans Speier and the Rise of the Defense Intellectual* (Ithaca, NY: Cornell University Press, 2018), does so splendidly.

[63] "Absolotismus, gemildert durch Schlamperei." The phrase belonged to Victor Adler. Robert Musil, *The Man Without Qualities*, trans. Sophie Wilkins, 2 vols. (New York: Knopf, 1995). For Carl Schorske's deployment of Musil: *Fin-de-siècle Vienna: Politics and Culture* (New York: Knopf, 1980), esp. p. 116.

[64] Rabi Binyamin, *From Zborov to Kineret* (in Hebrew) (Tel Aviv: Devir, 1950); Shmuel Yosef Agnon, *Temol Shilshom* (Heretofore) (Tel Aviv: Schocken, 1968); Haim Be'er, *Feathers*, trans. Hillel Halkin (Lebanon, NH: University Press of New England, 2004).

pictures of Galician Jewish life: traditional and Zionist cultures competing among the intelligentsia, love and hatred in the Jewish community, trust and betrayal between Jews and non-Jews, and the urban landscape of oil and salt towns that have recently become the subject of historical scholarship.[65]

Jewish attachment to the monarchy and the imperial family is a major motif in Barash's novels. Jews follow with concern and sympathy the imperial family's tragedies. A poor, religious, crippled Jewish seamstress in a small Galician town carefully collects newspaper reports about the beautiful Empress Elisabeth, whose picture hangs in her room, and claims to have a spiritual relationship with her: They are sisters. The empress is described as a Heine admirer, and hence clearly a friend of the Jews. (Heine's apostasy seems not to disturb the traditional seamstress.) All imperial class, ethnic, and confessional divisions are overcome in the seamstress' world. She dies shortly after the empress is murdered.[66] In several Barash stories, Jews serve in the military, sometimes as officers, and expect justice in court. The emperor's portrait in court assures a Jewish defendant that all will be well: "I know you were a good soldier in my army. If I see those who wish you ill get their way, I will step down from the picture and save you."[67] Arrested under suspicion of Russian espionage, two Jewish intellectuals, gently handled by the police throughout, are released with an apology.[68] A fair-trade violator gets his way because his name corresponds to that of the emperor and the rabbi declines to put a spell on it.[69] Jewish sentiment about World War I Austrian military actions against putatively pro-Russian Ukrainians – veritable war atrocities – is never in question: Austria is a Kingdom of Grace.[70]

Austro-Romantic nostalgia in Hebrew literature never cohered as an ideology – there was no need for one: Zionism emerged from the 1930s as the only open venue for European Jews, however narrow the opening was. Roth, Werfel, and Zweig were forced into exile, desperate; Barash had voluntarily emigrated to Palestine in 1914 at age twenty-five to build a new culture. Yet even in the Land, the world of his youth remained the center of his literary work, and he used it to comment on contemporary

---

[65] *Kitve Asher Barash* (Collected works; in Hebrew), 3 vols. (Tel Aviv: Massada, 1952).

[66] *Riqmah* (Embroidery) [1949], ibid., 1: 167–89.

[67] *Ahavah Zarah* (Foreign love) [1938], ibid., 1: 352.

[68] *Min ha-Maasar* (From the prison) [1927], ibid., 1:140–64.

[69] *Temunot mi-Bet Mivshal ha-Shekha*r [1928], ibid., 1: 73; *Pictures from a Brewery*, trans. Katie Kaplan (New York: Bobbs-Merrill, 1971).

[70] *Azmot Rabi Shimshon Shapira* [1928], *Kitve Asher Barash*, 1: 505–22; " The Bones of Reb Shimshon Shapiro," in *Though He Slay Me*, trans. M. Reston (Tel Aviv: Massadah, 1963), pp. 218–85.

events. Jewish life in Barash's empire had been dominated by a sense of doom, but the same doom also prevailed in Barash's stories about the *Yishuv* (Zionist settlement).[71] Late imperial Austria shaped Zionist destiny in more than one way.

Jewish socialist intellectuals, deprived even of nostalgia, were in the most difficult position of all after the collapse of Red Vienna. The most original among them, like Hertz, Polanyi, and Popper, were rethinking socialism. Could the imperial legacy help? Friedrich Hertz's reassessment of nation and empire was discussed earlier. More radical was Karl Polanyi's shift from the Hungarian nationalism of his youth to "tame empire" in the late 1930s. An assimilated Jewish refugee from the 1919 Hungarian Revolution, Polanyi (1886–1964) spent the interwar years ias the editor of *Der österreichische Volkswirt* (The Austrian economist) in Vienna, where he formed an increasing attachment to Protestant guild socialism and joined an international network of Christian socialists. He left for London in 1933 and, on a 1935 U.S. college lecture tour, addressed the question of national minorities in Europe. "A timely change to a federal form of government with full cultural autonomy for the minorities could well have rescued [the Danubian Empire] from destruction," he said. "It offered a kind of home to numerous people and its dissolution resulted in serious danger of new wars."[72]

Once empire reentered Polanyi's universe it never left. His postwar work would focus on early empires' trade economies.[73] At the center of his classic *The Great Transformation* (1944) was the interwar crisis, however.[74] Research for it had begun in 1938 with a project on "tame empire."[75] With Central Europe's collapse, Polanyi concluded that the Versailles order of nationalizing states had failed, and the emerging global division into autarchic imperial blocs provided the best arrangement for containing economic crisis and war – provided empire remained

---

[71] *Ish u-Veto nimḥu* (Man and his home were wiped out) [1934], *Kitve Asher Barash*, 2: 99–137.

[72] " Extramural Lectures: Report No. 1," in *Institute of International Education: Seventeenth Annual Report of the Director* (New York: Institute of International Education, 1936), pp. 11–12.

[73] Karl Polanyi, Conrad M. Arensberg, and Harry W. Pearson, eds., *Trade and Market in the Early Empires: Economies in History and Theory* (Glencoe, IL: Free Press, 1957).

[74] *The Great Transformation: The Political and Economic Origins of Our Time* (New York: Rinehart, 1944).

[75] The record at the Karl Polanyi digital archives at Concordia University, Montreal, Con_20_Fol_02, suggests that "Tame Empires," a book outline and introduction, dates to 1938–39. The introduction must, however, be 1941 or later, as Polanyi mentions the Atlantic Charter, and the treatment of Germany after a prospective victory by the Allies is a central concern. http://kpolanyi.scoolaid.net:8080/xmlui/handle/10694/718. My thanks to Gareth Dale of Brunel University London for calling my attention to Polanyi's "tame empire."

tame: free, federal, stable, and peaceful. A reformed Austria-Hungary that neutralized German and Hungarian hegemony was the model, and the predatory Nazi Reich, practicing *Grossraumpolitik* (expansionary politics), the countermodel. Unlike nineteenth-century naval empires, tame empires would not aim to become universal but remain regional and particular, collaborate, and create a pluralist world. Central control of economic life would contain the havoc caused by free trade and national competition, which had destroyed interwar Europe, and reduce wars to local skirmishes. *The Great Transformation*'s concern with collective economic management was already evident in this early project, but the road still passed through international reorganization and imperial management. By 1944, empire had all but vanished and communal management of the embedded economy was becoming the focus, with little attention to the international framework.

Polanyi's recovery of imperial traditions was deliberate. In Otto Neurath's Republic of Scholars, they reemerged surreptitiously. Neurath and his Vienna Circle colleagues had been involved in Red Vienna's cultural experiments. In 1935, as he was organizing the first Congress for Scientific Philosophy, he began speaking of the Circle's network as a *Gelehrterrepublik*. It mattered not that Red Vienna had collapsed, and he and most of his colleagues already lived in exile or were scrambling to leave Central Europe. The 1935 Paris Congress showed that their "republic" was spreading across the globe, becoming American, British, French, Polish, and Scandinavian. They were starting a new Enlightenment. Launching the "International Encyclopedia of Unified Science," Neurath concluded his address to the Paris Congress with "Vive les nouveaux encylopédistes!" (Long live the new encyclopedists)[76] His bravado was a counsel of despair. Trying to snatch victory from the jaws of defeat, he imagined exile as a cosmopolitan triumph. The encyclopedists staged their republic against a European imperial order. Neurath's new internationalism deployed prenational traditions to conjure up an imperial republic.

Karl Popper was less sanguine about cosmopolitanism's immediate prospect, but equally committed to its future. Fascism had destroyed cosmopolitan science and democratic politics in Austria. Popper responded in exile by shaping science and politics in the image of the lost culture: free cosmopolitan communities, engaged in critical debates. Imagining the Central European Jewish intelligentsia's international

---

[76] Otto Neurath, "Une encyclopédie internationale de la science unitaire," in *Actes du congrès international de philosophie scientifique*, 8 vols. (Paris: Hermann, 1936), 2:54–59, and "L'encyclopédie comme 'modèle,'" *Revue de Synthèse* 12 (1936): 187–201.

networks as a commonwealth, he created a surrogate for the Austrian Empire in the cosmopolitan Open Society. The Open Society, an ideal-type Austria – imperial, liberal, pluralist – now set the universal standard for liberal socialism and democratic politics. With the Cold War, the Open Society became the Western credo and a battle cry against communism. In a roundabout way, which conservative promoters of a German European Austria could never have imagined, "Austria" – liberalized, democratized, socialized – did become the Western defense against the "East" and the image of the free world.[77]

Conclusion: Austrians and Jews – Imperial Peoples?

"The only unconditional Austrians in this state union," said Joseph Bloch of the Jews under the monarchy.[78] This remained true for the First Republic. The Socialist and Pan-German commitment to Austria depended on German unification and, for the Socialists, also on Austria remaining democratic; the Catholic commitment depended on Austria remaining Catholic and resistant to socialism. Only the Jews were unconditionally Austrian, willing to settle for any Austria that would accept them. Until the early 1930s, Red Vienna seemed to offer integration. The Jews overwhelmingly supported the Socialists. In the mid-1930s, the Ständestaat seemed to offer protection. The Kultusgemeinde's support shifted to the Catholics. Neither helped. The logic of nationalization was driven to racial imperialism, and the Jews were excised from Austria and Central Europe. The Second Republic would have to do without the archetypal Austrians.

The Jews were quintessentially Austrian in the way they negotiated their identity. Curiously, Jewish and Catholic negotiations of Austrian identity resembled each other more than either resembled the Socialist. Both Jews and Catholics were acutely conscious of having lost their place in the old imperial order. The Socialists were cognizant of having won a place in the new one. Both Jews and Catholics had an attachment to the pluralist imperial legacy; the Socialists were more welcoming of nationalization. Both were insecure about their national identity, negotiating across ethnic and cultural lines. The Socialists confidently proclaimed German nationality. No wonder Jewish writers who felt an imperial attachment, like Roth and Werfel, developed Catholic affinities. But nationalization

---

[77] *The Open Society and Its Enemies*, 2 vols. (London: Routledge, 1945).
[78] "[D]ie einzige bedingungslosen Oesterreicher in diesem Staatsverband": Joseph Bloch, "Nichts gelernt und nichts vergessen," *Österreichische Wochenschrift* (22 June 1917): 390.

only exacerbated the divide between Jews and Catholics, racializing religious and cultural differences. The secular Socialists offered the Jews integration; the Catholics did not.

The Socialists represented a (partial) exception to the rule obtaining for liberals and Catholics in Central Europe – that the more socially progressive a movement is, the more antisemitic it is, owing to its popular support base. The strange affinities between the Jews and conservative Catholics and their limited alliance during the Ständestaat suggest that the prevailing stereotype of the Jew as modern is questionable. Since the nation-state emancipated the Jews, critics and admirers alike have regarded them as modernizers of European life. Austrian history suggests the opposite. The Jews flourished under the late empire; the nationalizing state, the heart of modernity, was their death writ.[79] In most of the monarchy's successor states, its memory was that of an oppressor; the Jews were full of imperial nostalgia. The postwar Western popularity of the "multinational empire" owed much to Jewish émigré scholarship. Postnational Europe has proved more welcoming of the Jews than the nationalizing one. The Jews may be anything but modern, or they are modern in an altogether different way.

Inheritors of a pluralist imperial legacy, Austrian Germans and Jews were strangers in a nationalizing Europe. Their searches for a new home across borders were uncharacteristic of other nationalities and often overlapped. They were imperial peoples in an ethno-national age, and notwithstanding their power difference, they resembled each other more than either could see. Their imperial worlds had vanished. The year 1942, which represented the apex of Austro-Nazi plans for *Grossraumpolitik* in Southeastern Europe, was also the last year in which thinkers like Polanyi and Popper or, for that matter, Hannah Arendt could imagine a postwar empire reshaping global politics.[80] The Moscow Declaration of April 1943, which stipulated the restoration of a small independent Austria, made it clear that the Allies had

---

[79] Like other readers, Hilda Nissimi of Bar-Ilan University objected that imperial Russia and nationalist France suggested the opposite: persecution in a premodern pluralist empire and integration into a modern nationalizing state. She is right, but I seek more to destabilize the old model than to establish a new one.

[80] Gabriel Trop, "Politik der Vertriebenen: Hannah Arendt im Schatten des Zweiten Weltkriegs," paper presented at the conference *Atempause: Intellektuelle Nachkriegskonzeptionen 1943-1947* (April 24, 2014) at the Ludwig Boltzmann Institut, Vienna. Arendt retained a vital interest in empire during the Cold War but reconfigured the Roman Empire as prelude to the American Republic, an image far removed from her 1942 pluralist British Commonwealth: Dirk Moses, *"Das römische Gespräch* in a New Key: Hannah Arendt, Genocide, and the Defense of Republican Civilization," *Journal of Modern History* 85:4 (2013), 867–913.

decided to restore the discredited nation-state system in Europe, and would consider no Central European federalist state that would build on the imperial legacy.[81]

Federalism and empire now parted ways, at least in continental Europe, with federalism joining the nation-state system (as it had done in Paneuropa) to form new European projects. The final war years witnessed the emergence of the United States and Soviet Union as world powers and the decline of the traditional European powers. The new superpowers represented nontraditional empires, sympathetic to decolonization of the old ones. They were not partial to imperial federalist projects.[82] In the postwar era, empire quickly became a pejorative term, associated with humanity's darkest chapters. The idea that empire could be the historical norm and have something to recommend itself remained a taboo until the twenty-first century. The imperial world of Jews and other Austrians survived only in the literary imagination. This book has set out to reclaim it.

---

[81] Gil Shalom Rubin of Columbia University writes (email to author, July 14, 2015): "The resurgence of the nationalizing state system in Eastern Europe and population transfers were, initially at least, a Soviet design. As the Soviet Union entered the war, it broke off the Polish-Czech discussions in London on a confederation, fearing it could entrench British-American interests in the region."

[82] Mark Mazower, *No Enchanted Palace: The End of Empire and the Ideological Origins of the United Nations* (Princeton, NJ: Princeton University Press, 2008).

9   Jacob the Jew: Antisemitism and the End of Emancipation, 1879–1935

The surge of ethno-nationalism and racial antisemitism in 1880s Central Europe, and the Zionist response, once again transformed the Jacob & Esau typology. For almost two millennia, Christian theology had retained a measure of ambiguity about Jacob's identity: The Christian claim to have inherited Jacob's legacy and become true Israel (*Verus Israel*) conflicted with the recognition of continuity between biblical Israel and contemporary Jews (as well as with popular perceptions of Jacob as a trickster). Now racial thinkers sought to Aryanize Jesus and were happy to let biblical Jacob become a Jew again. Liberal Protestant biblical criticism assailed traditional views of a pious Jacob and distanced Christianity from the Hebrew Bible. Catholicism offered only feeble theological resistance to racialization, and race overwhelmed theology. "Jacob the thief and liar," a leitmotif of liberal Protestant historian Hermann Gunkel (1862–1932), became an emblem of the Jew in German culture.

Racialized Jacob was not, however, the work of antisemites alone. In Jewish discourse, too, Jacob became an ethnic Jew. To be sure, until World War I, Reform sermons, exemplified by those of Berlin Rabbi Dr. Sigmund Maybaum (1844–1919), resisted the Jews' racialization, but they, too, showed the strains that racial antisemitism put on emancipation ideals. In a silent admission of Jacob's racialization, liberal Judaism sidelined him, the father of the people, and looked to other figures to advance its agenda. A backlash came from two generations of younger rabbis who became active in the fin-de-siècle and Weimar years. They showed a growing consciousness of Jewish ethnicity and an overwhelming concern with antisemitism and assimilation. Orthodox Rabbi Hirsch Perez Chajes (1876–1927) and Reform Rabbi Joachim Prinz (1902–1988), both Zionist, represented the outermost cases but they reflected a trend. For them, Jacob had always been an ethnic Jew.

Between racial antisemitism's rise in the 1880s and fascism's triumph in Central and East-Central Europe in the 1930s, antisemitism and Jewish integration grew in tandem and vied against each other. As many as a hundred thousand Jews, or 15 percent of German Jewry, converted by World War I, and a majority kept their distance from traditional Jewish life. In Breslau, a sizable Jewish middle class actively participated in civic life and helped shape a left-liberal administration for a pluralist city. Jews intermarried into the lower middle class and crossed over to non-Jewish civic and professional associations more easily than did Catholics. Yet, precisely in Breslau, the Nazis scored an impressive success, polling 43 percent of the vote in 1932.[1] As Jews rose to unprecedented levels of cultural and political prominence, antisemitic parties formed, antisemitism became a cultural code for the "good German," allegations of ritual murder and attacks on Jewish ritual slaughter mounted, and mainstream German liberals questioned the Jews' German character. The Jews, opined journalist Moritz Goldstein in "The German-Jewish Parnassus" (1912), were administering "the spiritual property of a nation that denies their right and ability to do so."[2]

All the same, where hopes of emancipation and integration remained alive, Jewish nationalism failed to capture the mainstream.[3] British and French Jewry remained committed to integration. Together with other religious minorities, French Jews supported the Third Republic's struggle against the alliance of church, court and army, and in the Dreyfus Affair, the secular state and the Jews scored an impressive victory over the antisemites.[4] In Germany, the old elites remained hegemonic and colluded in making antisemitism a cultural code, but the Jewish response to antisemitism was immediate and vigorous, and was aided by a liberal association of leading non-Jewish public intellectuals. The early 1890s saw the foundation of both the *Centralverein deutscher Staatsbürger jüdischen Glauben* (1893; Central association of German citizens of Jewish faith) and the *Verein zur Abwehr des Antisemitismus* (1890; Association for defense against antisemitism).[5] Emancipation came under stress but remained alive. Only in the 1930s was the contest between Jewish nationalism and integration swayed in favor of the nationalists, and only in Central and East-Central Europe, in countries where emancipation was already dying.

[1] Till van Rahden, *Jews and Other Germans: Civil Society, Religious Diversity, and Urban Politics in Breslau, 1860–1925*, trans. Marcus Brainard (Madison: University of Wisconsin Press, 2008).

[2] "Deutsch-jüdischer Parnass," *Der Kunstwart* 25:11 (1 March 1912): 281–94, as quoted in Paul Mendes-Flohr, *German Jews: A Dual Identity* (New Haven, CT: Yale University Press, 1999), p. 55.

[3] This holds true for Russia and Poland, too, but their traditional Jewry represents a different profile, discussed, together with Jewish national literature, in the next chapter.

[4] Philip Nord, *The Republican Moment: Struggles for Democracy in Nineteenth-Century France* (Cambridge, MA: Harvard University Press, 1995).

[5] Jehuda Reinharz, *Fatherland or Promised Land? The Dilemma of the German Jew, 1893–1914* (Ann Arbor: University of Michigan Press, 1975).

That said, a consciousness of Jewish ethnicity was forming throughout the period and reaching its culmination in the 1930s. German-Jewish thinkers from Adolf Jellinek to Moritz Lazarus found in ethnicity a category between religion and nation that would allow Jews to become German, yet permit their continued existence as a cultural community. They endeavored to pluralize the nation-state and sustain emancipation against racialized conceptions of the nation. From the 1880s on, a wide spectrum of German-speaking rabbis, in both Germany and Austria, spoke of the Jews as a people (*Volk*), and in ever more pronounced terms. During the Weimar years, younger Jewish intellectuals despaired of liberal hopes for the German nation and rebelled against their fathers by affirming Jewish ethnic difference. The struggle of fathers and sons alike to be recognized as both Jews and Germans continued until National Socialism triumphed in 1933.

Racialization was only one reason for Jacob's marginalization in Jewish discourse. Just as crucial was the joint refusal of rabbinic traditions by cosmopolitan fathers and ethnic sons, and their retreat from history. In Hermann Cohen's philosophy and Leo Baeck's theology, Jewish cosmopolitanism reached new heights by recentering Judaism on the Hebrew Prophets. Martin Buber and Franz Rosenzweig's Bible claimed Jewish authenticity by facilitating individual encounters with divinity, seeking revelation and dialogue unmediated by tradition. Both appear nowadays as the apex of German-Jewish culture, but the historian must also note that they represented a retreat from history and followed a familiar pattern in Jewish history: When history turned against the Jews, Jewish thinkers looked for salvation elsewhere. Disaffection with the rabbinic Jacob & Esau typology was symptomatic of moments of anxiety. Notwithstanding their cultural resourcefulness, German Jews may have sensed, like their medieval predecessors who were exploring the Kabbalah, that European history was once again closing down on them.

Benno Jacob's Genesis commentary, published in 1934, reflected emancipation's twilight. Jacob gave an unmatched performance of modern *Midrash* and drew a captivating picture of Jacob's universal mission. However, he lost any hope that non-Jews would ever recognize the mission. Not unexpectedly, while returning to rabbinic Midrash, he refused the Jacob & Esau typology. Moreover, while drawing insight from historical scholarship, he sought to close the Bible to history and declare its exegesis a hermeneutical task to be carried out by Jews alone. Emancipation was reaching its end.

Liberal Protestantism, Nationalism, and Jewish Difference

Apart from Austrian ethnic pluralism, liberal Protestantism may represent the most striking divergence of the German and Austrian cultural landscapes as they relate to Jewish emancipation. Liberal Protestantism, virtually absent in Austria, was a major force propelling German unification and the *Kulturkampf*. It dominated German academic culture until World War I, and beyond, with intellectual leaders who have become cultural icons. They ranged from Cultural Protestants like theologian Adolph Harnack and sociologist Ernst Troeltsch, who saw in the growth of liberal Protestantism a national mission, to skeptics like historian Theodor Mommsen and sociologist Max Weber, who recognized secularized Protestantism as formative for German culture.[6]

Postunification liberal Protestants had an ambivalent relationship toward German Jews: They supported emancipation but demanded assimilation, and opposed antisemitism but distanced Christianity from Judaism. Initially enthusiastic about modernity and the nation-state, liberal Protestants became more somber about their prospects toward the end of the nineteenth century, and the new consciousness was reflected in historicism and cultural pessimism. Yet in Germany, unlike in Catholic Austria, Jews could imagine that they had found an ally in a progressive religion, which had affinities with Reform Judaism and offered Jews acceptance as citizens. The contours of the relationship, which began with an anti-Catholic alliance and ended with liberals opening the gate to racialization, tell an edifying story about nationalism. They are registered in the Jewish and non-Jewish responses to the re-Judaization of Jacob. This section peruses the liberal Protestant stance on Jewish citizenship, and the next one will highlight Protestant biblical scholarship's new racialized Jewish Jacob. It will conclude with the German churches' collusion in Nazi legislation.

✳✳✳

The period of intense conflict between German nationalism and the German Catholics, 1858 to the end of the Kulturkampf in 1879, was also the one during which Jews seemed most welcome as political allies of the liberal Protestants. Jewish anti-Catholicism was part of the emancipation struggle, and the anti-Catholic alliance was grounded in the nation-state's promise of citizenship. Liberal Protestants appeared to be proponents of the Enlightenment and German unification, and the Catholic Church opposed both. Traditional Jewish animosity toward Christian Esau, represented

---

[6] Gangolf Hübinger, *Kulturprotestantismus und Politik: Zum Verhältnis von Liberalismus und Protestantismus in wilhelmischen Deutschland* (Tübingen: Mohr, 1994).

primarily by the Roman Church, seemed rechanneled into anti-Catholicism in the Jewish emancipation struggle. Whatever reservations Protestant and Jewish liberals may have held about each other, they became both ideological and strategic allies. National Liberal publicists, including those notoriously prone to the use of antisemitic stereotypes, like Gustav Freytag, upheld the Jews as a model for national integration against the Catholics: "*Bildung* raised the Jews, their fanaticism had disappeared.... . The grandchildren of this Asiatic wandering tribe are our compatriots.... . The clerical society of Jesus on the other hand ... is until today ... alien to German life."[7]

Flirting with Protestants and the nationalizing state in "othering" Catholics was foolhardy for liberal Jews. Once Bismarck recognized anticlericalism's failure, he ended the Kulturkampf and facilitated Catholic reconciliation with the German state. The political alliance between liberal Jews and Protestants collapsed, and, almost overnight, antisemitism surged. Heinrich von Treitschke's 1879 attack on Jewish difference signaled a change of heart among German liberals. While retaining in principle the invitation to Jews to join the German nation, liberals now insisted that the national culture must remain Christian, and highlighted the Jews as aliens. They advanced German culture's emancipation from Christian ambiguity about the Jews and, unwittingly, helped racialize them. The Catholics happily joined in. Protestants de-Judaized Jesus and re-Judaized Jacob; then Nazi-inspired Germanic Christians counterposed them as Aryan and Jew. Recognition that Jacob was incapable of becoming German or European was growing everywhere.

Paradoxically, the absence of a denominational marker to German nationality advanced the racialization of culture. A comparison of German and French antisemitism highlights the paradox. Both Germany and France displayed a convergence of religious and racial antisemitism, but the transition to race in Germany was sharper.[8] Édouard Drumont, founder of the Antisemitic League of France (1889) and editor of the popular *La Libre Parole*, joined Catholicism with racism to define French identity. In the aftermath of the Dreyfus Affair, the *Action Française* completed the nationalist integration of religion, race,

---

[7] Quoted in Ari Joskowicz, *The Modernity of Others: Jewish Anti-Catholicism in Germany and France* (Stanford, CA: Stanford University Press, 2014), p. 55.

[8] Christian Wiese, "Modern Antisemitism and Jewish Responses in Germany and France, 1880–1914," in *Jewish Emancipation Reconsidered: The French and German Models*, ed. Michael Brenner, Vicki Caron, and Uri R. Kaufmann (Tübingen: Mohr Siebeck, 2003), pp. 129–47. Wiese concurs on this issue with Jacob Katz, *From Prejudice to Destruction: Anti-Semitism, 1700–1933* (Cambridge, MA: Harvard University Press, 1970), pp. 292–300. Vicki Caron, "Comment," in *Jewish Emancipation Reconsidered*, pp. 147–53, takes exception.

and hostility to the ideas of 1789, and led the antisemites throughout the interwar years and into Vichy. French antisemitism was both Catholic and ethnic. The Left's response to the Dreyfus Affair delegitimated earlier socialist antisemitism, and there was no French equivalent to Wilhelm Marr and Eugen Dühring's racial scientific antisemitism. In Germany, in contrast, secular racism was alive. Adolf Stoecker's Christian Social Party and Treitschke's Christian national culture may have had greater resonance than anti-Christian antisemitism, but the latter ended up leading the charge in the Weimar years, and culminated in National Socialism.

Crucially, Christianity, stripped of denominational affiliation, and of much of its ritual and intellectual legacy, became a marker of German identity and character, associated with ethnic stereotypes, and defined, culturally, against the Jews. The antisemitism debate, occasioned by Treitschke's denunciation of Jewish particularism, revealed German national anxieties about cultural difference and exposed the dilemmas, which liberals desperately tried to negotiate until the National Socialist triumph. Treitschke had no intention of reversing emancipation, he said, and honored both baptized and unbaptized Jews who truly became German. But he castigated Jewish historian Heinrich Graetz, who had just completed a history highlighting Christian persecution of Jews and the latter's inspirational role in German culture: Graetz embodied Jewish outrageousness. Treitschke resented what he regarded as emancipation-era political correctness preventing criticism of Jewish economic practices, press domination, and cultural prominence, and, above all, the Eastern European Jewish invasion: Sephardic Jews had assimilated in western and southern Europe, but traditional Eastern European Jews were inassimilable and constituted a national threat similar to that of the Poles: "What we . . . demand from our Jewish fellow-citizens is simple: That they become German . . . for we do not want thousands of years of Germanic civilization to be followed by an era of German-Jewish mixed culture."[9]

Treitschke articulated the demands of a nationalism undergoing ethnicization for cultural unity. The sense that Germany was a "delayed nation" (*verspätete Nation*), in acute need of such unity, exacerbated the anxieties. He did not so much reconfessionalize the nation as claim Christianity as the national culture and a prerequisite to citizenship:

---

[9] Heinrich von Treitschke, "Unser Aussichten," *Preussische Jahrbücher* (15 November 1879), trans. Helen Lederer and reprinted in part in Marcel Stoetzler, *The State, the Nation, & the Jews: Liberalism and the Antisemitism Dispute in Bismarck's Germany* (Lincoln: University of Nebraska Press, 2008), p. 312.

National unity required Christianity.[10] Jewish difference was not merely religious but cultural, and it needed to be erased. This was a move toward racialization, as Christianity became an aspect of German national character, and the Jews needed to go through a character change to become German. Any hope for pluralism, for a German-Jewish culture, was gone. The Liberal Nationalist joined earlier antisemites, like Jakob Friedrich Fries, in declaring the German nation Christian.

Alarmingly, most of the liberals who rose up to defend the Jews in the next half century shared Treitschke's nationalist logic and upheld the desirability of Jewish assimilation. The Association for Defense against Antisemitism, founded in 1890 and led by Mommsen, Rudolf von Gneist, and Heinrich Rickert, rejected racism and ethno-nationalism, protested against ritual murder charges and the scapegoating of Jewish entrepreneurs, but advocated Jewish assimilation. The Union of Free Religious Congregations, whose Berlin leaders were among the first to respond to Treitschke, regarded their Jewish members' communal affiliation as the main obstacle to an interconfessional national church.[11] Mommsen's puzzlement about liberal Jews' refusal of conversion told it all. Nationalism made negotiation of community, nation-state, and humanity difficult. The unity of national culture seemed an imperative, and any ethnic and cultural difference, any ethno-religious community or subculture, became problematic. Jews who wished to remain Jewish had only narrow room to maneuver.

The Cultural Protestants narrowed this room even further. Unlike their more secular colleagues, they promoted progressive Protestantism as the foundation of German liberalism and national culture. A free church in a free state meant for them ideally a democratic national church (*Volkskirche im Volksstaat*).[12] They recognized acculturated Jews as sharing in Protestant culture, and insisted that they be accepted as German, but they were also emphatic that Jewish difference must be erased. They considered antisemitism poisonous, but supported the defense association only lukewarmly. Progressive theologians themselves, they rejected attacks on the Jews as modernizers, but they did not dismiss negative Jewish stereotypes outright, instead discussing them "scientifically." Their historical theology and biblical criticism reformulated the traditional boundary between Christianity and Judaism, relegated Judaism to ancient ethnic particularism, and elevated liberal Protestantism to

---

[10] Explicitly so, in his response to Lazarus: Stoetzler, *The State, the Nation, & the Jews*, p. 108.

[11] Todd Weir, "The Specter of 'Godless Jewry': Secularism and the 'Jewish Questions' in Late Nineteenth-Century Germany," *Central European History* 46 (2014): 815–49.

[12] Gangolf Hübinger, *Kulturprotestantismus und Politik*, pp. 263–75.

modern universalism compatible with the nation-state. They provided religious grounding for their secular colleagues' discomfort with Jewish difference.

Diminishing the Old Testament's role in Christianity, and claiming the latter to be a radical departure from Judaism, the Cultural Protestants highlighted the Jews' alterity. This made defending Jewish emancipation all the more difficult. Their wishes to uphold religious freedom and civic equality and find a place for the Jews in Germany conflicted with their support for a Protestant national culture, in which the Jews appeared as foreign. Not surprisingly, they also refused Jewish Studies a place in the academy and discounted the Jews' remaining political disabilities in Wilhelmine Germany. Like Treitschke, they unwittingly racialized German culture by contrasting Christian and Jewish essences and viewing Jewish difference as their expression. During Weimar, leading liberal Protestants denounced Nazi racism and defended Jewish citizenship, yet they also formulated a liberal version of the antisemitic code.[13]

No one more than Troeltsch sensed the tensions among the claims of religious tolerance, national inclusion, and universal humanity, on the one hand, and those of a Protestant national culture on the other. Weber, his close colleague, confronted the incompatibility of modern value spheres with resignation, but Troeltsch struggled, in the post–World War I years, to reconcile them. His political stance was conventional, but he made an interesting use of sociology to resist racialization and strove to make his history of the West, and German culture, more inclusive. The Jewish Question, said Troeltsch, was neither religious nor racial but sociological: The Jews were a minority with distinct history and national characteristics, and yet they needed to become German. The Jewish community was diverse, and the *Ostjuden*, resistant to assimilation, were the real problem. He resented the Jewish revolutionaries and the Jews' leading role in Weimar politics, especially in his own German Democratic Party (DDP), but he opined that one could not restrict political access to Jews. The Jews did need to modify their economic practices, as some had profited unethically from the war, but antisemitism was the wrong response: It impeded the German-acculturated Jews who were leading the way to assimilation.[14]

In his World War I debate with Hermann Cohen, Troeltsch testily challenged Cohen's view of the Hebrew Prophets as Western

---

[13] Kurt Nowak, *Kulturprotestantismus und Judentum in der Weimarer Republik* (Göttingen: Wallstein, 1993), agrees with the first statement and disagrees with the second.
[14] "Vorherrschaft des Judentums?" [1920], in *Spectator-Briefe und Berliner Briefe (1919–1922)*, ed. Gangolf Hübinger, *Ernst Troeltsch kritische Gesamtausgabe*, 20 vols. (Berlin: Walter de Gruyter, 2015): 14: 209–17.

universalism's source, but in his post–World War I conciliatory mood, he endeavored to find a place for Catholics and Jews in Protestant national culture and to develop the notion of the German European.[15] Christianity incorporated the Hebrews' personal ethical God and their Prophets' universalism, he said, and Protestantism sought to return to the Hebraic Jesus. Hebraism also influenced European culture independently, as exemplified in Spinoza. At his most ecumenical, then, Troeltsch reaffirmed Christianity's Jewish origins against the Aryan Jesus, and yet he integrated the Jews into Western culture primarily as Hebrew predecessors of Christianity. He endeavored to find aspects of postbiblical Judaism that could be part of a Protestant national culture, and to soften Christian supersessionism, but they had to be palatable enough for Protestant intellectuals, hence Spinoza. Rabbinic Judaism was beyond the pale.

In liberal Protestantism, nationalism and Christian supersessionism converged into a single problem – a national culture inhospitable to the Jews, undermining their citizenship. Among their close friends, the progressive nationalists, Jews could find support only for assimilation into a Christian culture that recognized their earlier contribution as Hebrews. Liberal Protestantism still seemed inviting enough to some: Erich Auerbach would construct his Judeo-Christian history in *Mimesis* on the model of his teacher, Troeltsch, and would present the Jews as Hebrew makers of the West, whose legacy Christianity carried on. But the liberal Protestants' dilemmas caught up with them in the 1930s, and with the National Socialist triumph, some reconciled themselves to racial legislation. In response, Auerbach adopted a more robust Catholic supersessionism that offered a modicum of resistance to racialization. However, he was still seeking the same protection that liberal Protestantism had afforded the Jews as ethnic Hebrews who ought to assimilate into Christian civilization.

Max Weber's work inadvertently showed the loss that liberal Protestantism suffered by shutting out the Jews. Weber ended "Science as a Vocation" with a plea for a heroic confrontation with modern challenges that would pay no heed to the Hebrew Prophets' call for life in expectation of redemption. That call, he said, had left the Jews languishing in exile for millennia, ever the "Pariah people." Shutting modernity

---

[15] Editing Troeltsch's *Gesammelte Schriften*, 4 vols. (Tübingen: J.C.B. Mohr, 1925), Hans Baron added to the anti-Cohen article, "Glaube und Ethos der Habräischen Propheten" [1916], an appendix reflecting Troeltsch's later, more generous thoughts: "Schlußabschnitt über der Fortwirkung des Haebraismus auf dem Abendland": 4: 34–65, 818–21, respectively. See the section on "Leo Baeck, Hermann Cohen, and Liberal Jewish Apologetics" later in this chapter for further details on the Troeltsch–Cohen exchange in the press.

off to traditional Jewish (and Christian) expectation so as to complete the nationalist project, Weber and the liberal Protestants deprived modernity of a home and turned Christians and Jews alike into pariahs.

Hermann Gunkel: Old Testament Critique and the Jewish Jacob

The reconfiguration of Jacob as a Jew in liberal Protestant scholarship registered the Jews' increasing racialization. Christian typology of the Patriarchs was losing ground: It is difficult to imagine a Prussian State Church pastor using Jacob & Esau in 1900 to draw the boundaries of proper Christian conduct as Pastor Ernst Orth had done in 1845. Christian exegesis had always found it difficult to constrain popular images of Jacob as a Jew. Now it was discordant with the racial imagination. Two generations earlier, Coleridge had viewed Jacob as a conniving Jew, yet a peaceable character. He pleaded for him as a Romantic lover: No one who loved Rachel as Jacob had could be truly bad.[16] Antisemites thought otherwise. Endeavoring to wean Christians from the Hebrew Bible, they could find support in an expanding body of biblical scholarship. As the academic barriers to historical criticism went down in the 1870s, the liberal Protestants advanced in the academy. By the late nineteenth century, they were closing the gap that historical theology had opened earlier between the Hebrew and Christian Jacobs: Typology gave in, and Jacob became a Jew.

In 1878, Julius Wellhausen formulated his influential documentary hypothesis.[17] The Pentateuch, he conjectured, had been composed in the fifth century BCE, the early Second Temple period, after the return of Jewish leaders from Babylonia to Jerusalem, later than had earlier been assumed. The Pentateuch was an edited composition of four major sources, or documents, redacted by the postexilic priestly elite. The "Priestly" source, traditionally marked P (RQ in Wellhausen), contained the Temple ritual and holiness code in Leviticus and Numbers, but also left its mark on the narratives by editing the earlier sources. J had originated in the tenth century BCE in the Southern Kingdom of Judea; E originated in the ninth century BCE in the Northern Kingdom of Israel; and D, Deuteronomy (and the Early Prophets), originated in Judea during King Josiah's monotheistic reforms in the late sixth century BCE. J and E, sometimes treated as one source, JE, each used a different name,

---

[16] Samuel Taylor Coleridge, *Specimens of the Table Talk*, 2d ed. (London: John Murray, 1836), p. 70.

[17] *Geschichte Israels*, 2 vols. (Berlin: G. Reimer, 1878).

Jehovah (Yahweh) and Elohim, respectively, for the Hebrew God, but both assumed multiple cultic centers and showed traces of polytheism. D insisted on monotheism and on the Jerusalem Temple as the sole site of worship. The Priestly source revealed growing ritualization and legalization of Judaism, reflecting the loss of Jewish sovereignty and the degeneration of national life. Wellhausen and his students read the Pauline critique of Pharisaic Judaism into the early Second Temple period, and made it possible for contemporaries to trace rabbinic Judaism in the Pentateuch, all the way back to Genesis and Jacob.

Hermann Gunkel, a professor in Göttingen, Halle, Berlin, and Giessen, represented the next generation of Old Testament scholars, who established the History of Religions school. They moved biblical studies from text to culture, and viewed the Bible ethnologically as displaying the evolution of Israelite religion from local tribal cults to a rational moral religion that culminated in Christianity. Gunkel advanced form criticism (*Formgeschichte*): Rather than focus on the documents composing the Bible, he perused the literary forms inhabiting the documents – poetry and myths, cultic legends, oracles, taunt and love songs, hymns of praise, and historical narratives. He searched for the culture of the precompositional stage, for oral traditions and folklore embedded in biblical narratives redacted in later times, and explored fragments of divergent legends that appeared in transmuted forms in advanced national and religious narratives. Comparative studies of Ancient Greek and Near Eastern myth and poetry guided his hypotheses about the ancient Israelites. He expanded the field of Old Testament studies, opening it up, for good and bad, to the German ethnological and Orientalist imagination.

Jacob & Esau served Gunkel as a major site for demonstrating his method's agility. In what he called the "Jacob legends cycle" (*Sagenkranz*), Gunkel discerned a broad range of literary forms and the Israelite religion's different historical stages. The cycle's core was the story of Jacob & Esau's rivalry. It began as a story of the cunning shepherd cheating the rash hunter of his inheritance (Genesis 25 and 27), with a sequel added later about the shepherd saving his household from a gang headed by the hunter (Genesis 32–33, Jacob & Esau's reconciliation). Another cycle of stories on a young cunning shepherd tricking his wily uncle became associated with the first (Genesis 29–31, Jacob & Laban). When Jacob, known first as a Near Eastern god, *Jaqob-el*, became the ancestor of Israel, the folk story became a national one: The shepherd was identified as Jacob, and the hunter and uncle became Israel's enemies, Esau as the ancestor of Edom and Laban of Aram. Local legends associated with holy places, such as Bethel and Penuel, joined the narrative as accounts of God's revelation to Jacob during his journey, and the stories about Jacob's children, ancestors of the tribes of Israel, were added last.[18]

Centuries of cultural development separated the short stories of the cunning shepherd from the long polished novella about Joseph and his brothers. Just as long a period of time passed from the cultic legend of a river god attacking a passerby, still traceable in the story of Jacob's struggle with the angel, to Jacob's humble prayers for deliverance from Esau, the product of a moral religion. The Israelites advanced from local cults to a national religion, centered in Jerusalem, from crass mythology to a moral religion, and from polytheism to monotheism with a universal potential. The different narratives composing Genesis, J, E, and P, were themselves edited collections, the development of which could be tracked in the Jacob cycle. Gunkel dated J and E to the early ninth century BCE at the latest, and thought that they were unified in one Jacob & Esau story no later than the late sixth century.[19] Early legends were first converted into national narratives; then, with the Hebrew Prophets' exalted heavenly God, local cultic legends were transformed into stories of Jacob's consecration of sites of divine revelation. Later generations could not endure unjust crafty ancestors either. The postexilic Priests rounded out the picture of pious patriarchs by adding Jacob's prayers and ending the saga with the brothers jointly burying their father Isaac.

Yet Jacob was also the biblical figure chosen by Gunkel to arbitrate the Hebrew legacy to contemporary civilization. He underscored Jacob's difference from Christianity, expressing a historian's joy in subverting religious pieties but also racial prejudice. His *Genesis* reflected a liberal Protestant effort to outline the Jews' proper place in Germany. "Older and recent theologians have felt obligated to justify religiously and ethically the biblical standpoint," he said, and "in equally unhistorical fashion, modern 'antisemites' deploy [Jacob's] stories to illustrate the true character of the Jewish people (*Volk Israel*), indeed of the Bible itself. In this battle, in which false piety and mean impiety vie against each other, the voice of the truth-loving historian ... has ... gone unheard."[20] He, Gunkel, a "truth-loving historian," was going to arbitrate between

---

[18] Hermann Gunkel, *The Legends of Genesis*, trans. W. H. Carruth (Chicago: Open Court, 1901). This is the translated introduction to Gunkel, *Genesis: Übersetzt und erklärt* (Göttingen: Vandenhoeck & Ruprecht, 1901). References are to the first German edition unless otherwise noted.

[19] Gunkel accepted the historicity of the biblical account in Samuel and Kings of David's conquest of Edom, and Edom's rebellion under his grandson. This required his early dating of JE's Jacob & Esau stories.

[20] *Genesis* (1901), p. 281; 3d ed. (1910), trans. Mark E. Biddle (Macon, GA: Mercer University Press, 1997), p. 300.

Christian theologians and antisemites, and outline a vision for the Old Testament's place in modern society.

The Jacob & Esau story, said Gunkel, was no *Bildungsroman*. Ancient Hebrew storytelling was incapable of describing character development or inward change. At its early stages, protagonists were simple characters, each displaying one distinctive trait: Jacob was crafty, Esau rash. Genesis had no depth psychology: Rarely do we even learn of a protagonist's thoughts. Action unambiguously revealed intention. Jacob never changed: From beginning to end, he staged a repertoire of deceit. At no point did he show regret, feel guilty, or experience personal growth, and he was never punished: "All that modern interpreters claim to have found in *Genesis* along these lines is imported into the sources."[21] The ancient Israelites identified with Jacob, enjoyed his trickery, and saw him as exemplifying their national character. Religion and morality had not yet come together. "Later times … could not endure the thought that the Patriarchs have done wrong."[22] When the Priests moralized the Patriarchs, they created dissonance: Could the *Aqedah* turn Abraham, who had offered his wife repeatedly to host kings, into a model of faith? Could prayer turn sly Jacob, sleek as an eel, into an example of humility? Genesis spoke in multiple voices, coming from different periods. There was no way of reconciling Jacob and Christian morality.

"The correct position is to view these things historically," said Gunkel, and offered his commentary as a counterpart to traditional exegesis.[23] For each biblical episode he provided an analysis of sources and composition, followed by a precis, and ending with a commentary verse by verse. He searched for etymologies in the broad culture but could occasionally resort to Midrash-style commentary, as when suggesting that the site Penuel may be called so because Jacob told Esau that his countenance looked like that of God.[24] Indeed, Gunkel showed rabbinic-like sensitivity to textual tensions, one reflecting shared reading practices. If his commentary, the apex of liberal historical criticism, remained the polar opposite of rabbinic exegesis, it was for his refusal to see the text as a unit and, even more, for his insistence on the historicization of each moment in a way that made rendering a moral principle impossible. Multiple Jacobs emerged, reflecting successive periods in Israelite history: The giant struggling with God in Penuel could not be the fainthearted crafty shepherd ingratiating Esau or the righteous patriarch receiving revelation in Bethel. As Benno Jacob would later complain, Gunkel disregarded the redactor's viewpoint, and privileged the voices he thought were older over "the prophets" and "priests."

---

[21] *Genesis* (1901), p. xxvi; (1910), p. xxxiii.   [22] *Genesis* (1901), p. lii; (1910), p. lxiii.
[23] *Genesis* (1901), p. 282; (1910), p. 301.   [24] *Genesis* (1901), p. 344; (1910), p. 321.

Gunkel escaped historical relativism by upholding an evolutionist view of moral development, in which one progressed from Hebrew tribalism to Israelite nationalism to Christian universalism. This historical outlook was joined with the fin-de-siècle ethnological imagination, replete with national, racial, and liberal Protestant prejudices, to guide his project. The Hebrew Bible was made to conform to modern expectations: Hebrew legends kowtowed to tribalism, biblical narratives abided by Israelite nationalism, and legal codes and morality reflected priestly particularism. From among Gunkel's multiple Jacobs, he highlighted the cunning shepherd. Contemporary Jewish stereotypes shaped his imagination of the ancient Israelite. Racial prejudice subverted Gunkel's historicization and belied his historical standpoint.

Assailing the antisemites for identifying Jacob with contemporary Jews, Gunkel observed, only a few lines down, the Hebrew shepherd's legacy in Jewish business practices: "One may see in the ancient Hebrew's delight in cunning and deceit, which sometimes permitted him even treachery and lies, a feature of character transmitted, as everyone knows, as a highly questionable legacy to his latest descendants."[25] To the 1910 edition of *Genesis*, Gunkel added an observation on racial smells, the *foetor iudaicus* or Negro smell, and a suggestion that Jacob's unjust preference for Rachel, demonstrated first by his marital neglect of Leah and then by protecting Rachel's family against Esau at Leah's family's expense, can still be discerned in contemporary Jewish families.[26] First Gunkel denied cultural continuity between ancient Hebrews and modern Jews, then reaffirmed it, using antisemitic observations on Jews "as everyone knows" them.

Gunkel's mischievous delight at the ancient Israelites' healthy national instincts was mixed with his moral revulsion, and his joy at unveiling Hebrew primitivism joined with recognition that the Hebrews had no Homer. This put him in a difficult position both scholarly and political. He emerged as a leading Old Testament scholar at a time when recognition of the role of Near Eastern cultures in the Bible's formation was reaching its apex. The *Bibel oder Babel?* (Bible or Babylonia) controversy was raging, and both the Bible's originality and the Hebrew contribution to Western culture were being questioned.[27] Concomitantly, antisemites dismissed the Hebrew Bible as a Jewish document. Babylonia and

---

[25] *Genesis* (1901), p. 282; (1910), p. 301.
[26] *Genesis* (1910), pp. 304, 354, respectively. Gunkel already spoke about the disordered state of Jewish family life in 1901, p. 300, but his references were to biblical Israel; hence, his "Israel" was ambiguous. The antisemitism becomes more pronounced with the years.
[27] Friedrich Delitzsch, *Babel und Bibel* (Leipzig: J.C. Hinrichs, 1902); *Zweiter Vortrag über Babel und Bibel* (Stuttgart: Deutsche Verlags-Anstalt, 1904); and *Babel und Bibel Dritter (Schluß-) Vortrag* (Stuttgart: Deutsche Verlags-Anstalt, 1905).

antisemitism both threatened to devalue Gunkel's work and undermine his position as a cultural arbitrator.

In response, Gunkel negotiated a liberal Protestant midway position between the Old Testament's adherents and detractors, distancing Christianity from its Jewish origins and yet affirming them. He discussed Near Eastern influences on Genesis and criticized Wellhausen for ignoring them, but he also defended the Hebrews' contribution to Western culture. The Old Testament might no longer provide a sure guide to religion and morality: Jacob did not provide an educational model. Much of the Old Testament could only be read as a cultural document, displaying artistic and literary creativity, and as the Ancient East's greatest history. But the Decalogue, monotheism, and eschatology became inalienable features of Christianity, and "let us not forget that the emphasis on morality in religion is ... a legacy we owe to ancient Israel and its Prophets."[28] The Israelite religion was inferior to Christianity but remained its foundation. Jesus and Paul rejected priestly legalism and ritualism, and liberated the Israelite religion from its nationalist constraints, but they were still its descendants, and one could not understand the New Testament without the Old. Jesus was born and grew up as a Judean: "It was within ... the synagogues that Christianity spent its early days.... . This position of the Old Testament in the Christian Church is a historical fact, against which it would be foolish to grumble."[29]

Jacob and the Patriarchs, however, became religiously irrelevant. Gunkel's injunction not to ask more of Jacob than of Odysseus was dissembling. Putting them on a par was revolutionary: Jacob had been a prefiguration of Christ, whereas Odysseus never was. Now both became wily folk heroes without sanctity, each of their tales an adventure without a moral. There was no grandeur to Jacob & Esau's reconciliation. Sly Jacob, an unarmed shepherd, saved his household from an armed gang leader, a good-natured buffoon, Esau, and, refusing any collaboration, sent him on his way placated. The story had no significance for Jewish–Christian relations. Gunkel inveighed at once against "Christian Orthodoxy" and "Jewish interests" for ill-advised efforts to render Jacob & Esau an educational story. Liberal Protestant scholarship denuded the Old Testament of millennia of Christian and Jewish exegesis.

---

[28] *Genesis* (1901), p. 282; (1910), p. 301.
[29] Gunkel, "What Is Left of the Old Testament" [1914], in *What Remains of the Old Testament and Other Essays*, trans. A. K. Dallas (London: Macmillan, 1928), pp. 34–35. Christian Wiese, "'The Best Antidote to Anti-Semitism'? *Wissenschaft des Judentums*, Protestant Biblical Scholarship, and Anti-Semitism in Germany before 1933," in *Modern Judaism and Historical Consciousness*, ed. Andreas Gotzmann and Christian Wiese (Leiden: Brill, 2007), pp. 177–80, similarly works out Gunkel's position from his direct responses to Delitzsch.

Such radicalism destabilized Gunkel's efforts to retain the Old Testament and required frequent reformulation. The leading liberal Protestant theologian, Adolf von Harnack, to whom Gunkel dedicated his *Genesis*, called for decanonizing the Old Testament in the spirit of Marcion, the second-century Christian theologian. Yet Harnack, too, admired the Hebrew Prophets, and so Gunkel defined parts of Isaiah and Psalms as New Testament units in the Old, presaging the Gospel. When it came to Jewish interlocutors, however, the Prophets were deflated. Against Hermann Cohen, who argued for their cosmopolitanism, Troeltsch underlined their particularism: Theirs was still the national God. Gunkel and Troeltsch were at one in pitting the Gospel against Jewish particularism, and this remained the one permanent feature of successive liberal Protestant reformulations. All began with restoring Jesus to his origins and undermining the typology of Christian Jacob, and ended up distancing Jesus from his Jewish background and reifying types: Jewish Jacob versus Protestant Isaiah, the Psalms and Prophets as Christian *avant la lettre*, so long as Jews did not claim them as theirs.

Gunkel's message was that Christianity and Western culture had left Judaism behind. The Priests' theocracy meant national degeneration, issuing in the Pharisees whom Jesus had confronted, and in the rabbis, whose descendants Gunkel encountered. Jews had to face it: The Jewish Question's solution was the Jews' disappearance qua Jews. There was no room for Jewish Studies in the academy any more than there was for a Jewish voice in public affairs: Only liberal Protestants were capable of objective scholarship on religion and the Bible; rabbinic sources were not appropriate scholarly material; and an antiquated cultural identity would thwart Jewish assimilation.[30] Gunkel's Hebrew Jacob showed liberal Protestantism advancing biblical scholarship and, at the same time, allowing racist prejudice to shape it; confronting the antisemites by ridiculing their Aryan Jesus, yet making Jesus a Christian alien to the Jews; and trying hopelessly to retain the Hebrew Bible while rejecting the Jews. Ambivalent as the liberal Protestants remained about Jewish emancipation and susceptible as they were to racialization – viewing liberal Jews as competitors rather than allies, and regarding ethno-religious pluralism as incompatible with a national culture – it was no surprise that their resistance to

---

[30] Gunkel to Martin Rade, March 26, 1912, and June 3, 1913, quoted in Christian Wiese, "'The Best Antidote to Anti-Semitism?'" pp. 153–54. Joseph Eschelbacher, *Das Judentum und das Wesen des Christentums* (Berlin: M. Poppelauer, 1908), bitterly documented liberal Protestant resistance to Jewish Studies.

antisemitism was never resolute enough to present a serious challenge.[31]

Liberal scholarship enjoyed academic prestige, but populist antisemitism had greater popularity. Traditional antisemites of Stoecker's ilk, who attacked the Jew as an agent of secular culture and capitalism and as a threat to the Christian state, had neither the motivation nor the intellectual ability to query the Old Testament. But the initially less influential racial antisemites extended the Old Testament's Judaization to the New. Already Marr signaled a departure from religious anti-Judaism, and Houston Stuart Chamberlain popularized the Aryan Jesus, whose message the Jewish Paul and New Testament had distorted. Parts of the New Testament had to go the way of the Old. Gunkel still treated such ideas as quixotic, but under the Nazis, they culminated in German Christianity, with its 1937 Godesberg Manifesto calling for a new order in the Lutheran Church that would recognize God-created nationality (*Volkstum*), and with theologian Walter Grundmann and his institute attempting a thorough de-Judaization (*Entjudung*) of Christianity.[32] Liberal distancing of Old and New Testaments appears to have been, in hindsight, a step toward cutting the umbilical cord of Christianity and European culture.

More pernicious yet was the racialization of the mainstream churches. Jacob's Judaization signaled increasing difficulty for Jews to be accepted as converts to Christianity, and, under the Nazis, the removal of virtually any protection for them. The Jews were no longer wayward brothers who could return. A Christian Jacob did not exist. The Lutheran Church largely complied with the Nazi Aryan clause, excluding its members of Jewish origin, and this was a major reason that dissenters split from it in 1934 and founded the Confessing Church (*Bekennende Kirche*). But even the Confessing Church recognized racial concerns as legitimate for national policy as long as they did not encroach on Christian freedom. Theologian Karl Barth, who inspired the Confessing Church, made it clear that while the Old Testament remained part of the canon, it could not stand on its own: The two testaments represented a unity whence the Old derived its meaning from the New.[33] The idea that Jews and Judaism

---

[31] Christian Wiese, "'The Best Antidote to Anti-Semitism?'" pp. 180–83, shows prominent theologian Rudolf Kittel arguing, in a libel suit brought by the Jewish community in 1913, for acquitting notorious antisemite Theodor Fritsch, who claimed that the Hebrew God was nefarious and that rabbinic literature gave evidence of a Jewish world conspiracy.

[32] Grundmann's story is admirably told in Susannah Heschel, *The Aryan Jesus: Christian Theologians and the Bible in Nazi Germany* (Princeton, NJ: Princeton University Press, 2008).

[33] Christian Wiese, "'The Best Antidote to Anti-Semitism?'" pp. 183–91, speaks of Protestant theologians' dual strategy in the interwar years: "taking over" the Old

were integral to Europe was beyond the horizons of even Nazism's opponents.

Unlike the national Protestant churches, the Catholic Church represented a formidable international institution. Immutable to biblical criticism, it appeared as guardian of traditional exegesis, and showed little anxiety about Jacob's Jewishness. While German Catholics underwent nationalization in Wilhelmine Germany and experienced, like others, the racialization of culture, the church remained jealous of its autonomy and on guard against state encroachment. Munich's Cardinal Faulhaber was a linchpin of opposition to National Socialism. Yet his famous 1933 Advent sermon on the Old Testament and the Jews was disappointing. His defense of the Old Testament was tenuous, and he made sure that it did not interfere with racial policy toward the Jews.

The Old Testament's holiness and stature were lesser than those of the New, said Faulhaber, and Christ rendered parts of it, including genealogies, Temple rituals, and practical commandments, irrelevant. Yet it remained the Word of God, and offered models of Christian belief. (Jacob was not one.) Together with biblical history, it would continue to be part of the Christian curriculum, and "antagonism to the Jews of today must not be extended to the books of pre-Christian Judaism."[34] Reaffirmed within the context of Nazi racial policy, Faulhaber's distinction between pre- and post-Christian Jews was momentous: He underlined rabbinic Jews' exclusion from the Covenant and excluded unconverted Jews from Christian protection. Using the specter of the Wandering Jew, Ahasuerus, he also intimated Israel's guilt in the crucifixion. Furthermore, he stated, the church had no objection to national racial policy; it only insisted that the orders of nature and revelation not be confounded: Christians were not redeemed by German blood but by that of Christ. Faulhaber retained the Old Testament only by restating an emphatically anti-Jewish version of Christian supersessionism, which attenuated Christianity's Jewish origins. He tenuously protected Christian Jacob but, gesturing with anti-Jewish images, left German Jews vulnerable to Nazi racial policy.

The Christian churches' near acquiescence in Nazi racial policy was still deemed insufficient by the Nazis. As inadequate as the protection Christianity extended to the Jews was, the Nazis aimed to put an end to

---

Testament and disinheriting the Jews by claiming the Prophets' fulfillment in Christ, and "distancing," underlining Jesus' break with the Hebrew Bible.

[34] Michael von Faulhaber, "Judaism, Christianity and Germany," in *Germany: Advent Sermons Preached in St. Michael's, Munich, in 1933*, trans. George D. Smith (New York: Macmillan, 1934), p. 15; http://archive.org/stream/judaismchristian009622mbp/judais mchristian009622mbp_djvu.txt.

the brotherhood of Jacob & Esau, relieve Western civilization of its foundational ambivalence toward Jews, and undo once and for all the Jewish making of Europe. In 1942, Hitler's private secretary and head of the party Chancellery, Martin Bormann, sent a letter to the Nazi district leaders (*Gauleiters*) outlining the pernicious influence that Christianity had had on European life, with a plan for weakening all the organized churches. At the time, the Germans still expected to win the war and imagined a reordering of populations in the Eurasian space, to which the Final Solution, reaching its height, was only an introduction. Nazi leaders sensed that Christianity was incompatible with such a project. In re-Judaizing Jacob, liberal Protestantism helped free Christianity from ambiguity about Judaism, turning ambivalence into animosity. It continued the Enlightenment project, which opened up opportunities for Jews that they could not have dreamed about before modern times, and, at the same time, removed the protection signified by Christian Jacob that made a premodern Holocaust unthinkable.

Jewish Generational Change: From Cosmopolitan to Ethnic Jacob

Bernard Lazarus's 1880 response to Treitschke's antisemitic attack "What Is National?" constituted a head-on Jewish liberal confrontation with the liberal Protestant vision of a uniform German nation. Lazarus (1824–1903) outlined a daring proposal for a multiethnic and multicultural Germany. Its failure set the stage for the ensuing four decades of incessant Jewish efforts to renegotiate German and Jewish identity against the backdrop of mounting antisemitism. These efforts resulted in a generational shift in Jewish politics and in a transformation of Jacob & Esau that encompasses the rest of this chapter.

Lazarus staged a Jewish liberal claim for German recognition of Jewish ethnicity. An empiricist philosopher and psychologist, he suggested that the nation was constituted by individuals' expression of will to become a community. Germany was a recent nation, an intellectual (*geistige*) construct: Consciousness of a common German destiny was molded historically, through shared experiences, such as fighting for unification. Germany was not a naturally developing organism and could not be racially defined: "Race and ethnicity (*Stamm*) define humans objectively [but] humans define themselves as a people (*Volk*) subjectively; they attribute themselves to a people."[35] The nation-state was capacious

---

[35] Moritz Lazarus, *Was heißt National? Ein Vortrag* (Berlin: Ferd. Dümmlers Verlagsbuchhandlung, 1880), trans. in Marcel Stoetzler, *The State, the Nation, & the*

enough for diverse linguistic, religious, and ethnic groups. Judaism was just as German as Christianity, and both were Semitic in origin. As Europe's longest surviving *Stamm*, one that had witnessed many nations' demise, the Jews had a mission to humankind and must offer their vision of universal justice as a unique contribution to Germany.

Lazarus offered a brilliant concept of a pluralist nation-state, identical to Ernst Renan's theory of the nation as a continuous plebiscite.[36] Drafting social science to his project, Lazarus mobilized demographic evidence that neither nation and state nor nation and race corresponded: Some states were multinational and almost all nations were multiracial. He offered numerous examples. Austria-Hungary was not one. Was the monarchy too antiquated for this multicultural visionary? Did he not recognize that the Austrian imperial model was more applicable to his project than Switzerland or Belgium? His theory represented the high point in Jewish endeavors to pluralize the nation-state, but coming in response to ethno-nationalism, it suggested the project's hopelessness. Consciousness of Jewish difference would increase in the coming decades, but racialization of the Jews assured that Lazarus's theory would leave only faint tracks. Even among Jews, racial vocabulary would be increasingly used to describe difference, *Rasse* rather than *Stamm*. The endeavor to make Jews one among many German ethnicities never caught on.

Emancipation-era Jacob, the Jewish cosmopolitan, did not weather racialization. He gradually vanished from Reform sermons after 1880, and to promote Jewish cosmopolitanism, philosophers and rabbis highlighted the Hebrew Prophets instead. Antisemitism and Jewish assimilation became the paramount sources of rabbinic anxiety. Until the 1930s, fear for Jewry's future had not quite transformed conceptions of Jewish citizenship, but it did result in a growing recognition of Jewish difference and an increasing willingness to confront non-Jewish Germans with the demand that the nation-state accommodate pluralism. This may have been best reflected in Ḥanukkah and Purim, which increasingly became holidays of Jewish national commemoration in circles well beyond those of the Zionists.

To be sure, not everyone joined the trend. Sigmund Maybaum, Leo Baeck, and Hermann Cohen insisted on Jewish cosmopolitanism. The last two accepted the liberal Protestant premise that Germany

---

Jews, pp. 1–40. Quotation is on p. 13. Lazarus used *Nation, Nationalität*, and *Volk* interchangeably.

[36] *Qu'est-ce qu'une nation?* (Paris: Calmann Lévy, 1882). Renan was seeking to explain, two years later, why German-speaking Alsace appropriately belonged in France: The Alsatians so willed. He may have borrowed from Lazarus.

needed a cohesive political culture and a religion to support it, but insisted that Judaism provided superior support and that the state must allow religious pluralism. A wide range of liberal and conservative rabbis, as well as younger Weimar Jewish intellectuals, went further: They rearticulated Lazarus's open demand for ethno-cultural pluralism in national life. German nationalism was moving in the opposite direction. World War I solidified the generational transition between cosmopolitan and ethnic Jacob, setting Jewish identity and German nationalism on a collision course.

The generational transition from the liberal fathers' cosmopolitan Jacob to the children's ethnic Jacob is this section's subject. It peruses representative pre–World War I rabbis across German-speaking Europe from Maybaum in Berlin to Felix Kanter in Moravia to Chajes in Trieste and Vienna. The next section will focus on Baeck and Cohen's wartime liberal apologetics, and the one after on Buber, Rosenzweig, and Prinz's Weimar rebellion against rabbinic Jacob. This chapter concludes with Benno Jacob's racialized Jacob & Esau in Nazi Germany. All of the protagonists display incessant efforts to negotiate between German and Jewish identities, which resulted in brilliant intellectual accomplishments in what proved to be a losing political battle.

$$***$$

Seeking to ridicule German-Jewish patriotism, Gershom Scholem, in his "Reflections on Modern Jewish Studies," cited a pamphlet "famous among resourceful researchers," *Unser Erzvater Jacob – das Vorbild einer Stadtverordeneten* (Our Patriarch Jacob, the model of a city-councilor).[37] He castigated the "uninspiring" author for turning the patriarch into a municipal German civil servant. He provided no reference, and scholars have repeatedly cited the pamphlet without one, but it was not a figment of Scholem's imagination. *Bischlômâh schel malkhûth* (For the kingdom's welfare), a collection of lectures by Moses Jacobson (1853–1930), at that time rabbi in Gnesen (near Posen), included the same Jacob sermon, delivered on the occasion of the 1895 municipal elections.[38] Jacobson nicely recaptured the rabbinic practical Jacob, laying down the foundations of urban civic life on his arrival in the city of Shekhem: coinage, markets, public baths, and later, on the way down to Egypt, a *yeshivah*, which he sent his son to found.[39] Civic engagement and municipal

---

[37] *On the Possibility of Jewish Mysticism in our Time & Other Essays*, ed. Avraham Shapira, trans. Jonathan Chipman (Philadelphia: Jewish Publication Society, 1997), pp. 51–71.

[38] *Bischlômâh schel malkhûth: Reden über des Staates, Führer Dinge und Fragen: Gehalten in der Synagoge* (Breslau: W. Jacobsohn, 1900), pp. 95–102.

[39] *BT*, Shabbat 33:2 on Genesis 33:18: "Rav said: He instituted coinage for them. Shmuel said: He instituted markets for them; Rabbi Joḥanan said: He instituted baths for them."

service, however prosaic, were essential to the public welfare, intimated Jacobson. There were other lectures in the collection celebrating the emperor and German accomplishments in ways that may strike us today as odd. It is doubtful, however, that Scholem would have taken exception to Jacob's municipal labors if they were dedicated to building the Land of Israel.

Significantly, Jacobson's sermons were untypical in their unreflective nationalism and cheerful optimism and do not provide an accurate portrayal of the fin-de-siècle rabbinic mood. It is important to recall that optimism and chauvinism were part of Jewish life in Wilhelmine Germany because the picture emerging from the homiletic literature of a wide range of rabbis is very different: Anxieties about the German-Jewish future surface everywhere. German rabbinic leader Sigmund Maybaum, a Jewish cosmopolitan, the last classical Reform preacher and the erudite head of the *Lehranstalt für die Wissenschaft des Judentums* in Berlin, the seminary that trained Reform rabbis, embodies the conundrums of fin-de-siècle German-Jewish liberalism.

Accepting much of Protestant biblical criticism, Maybaum saw the Prophets as the origin of monotheism and himself as promoting their legacy (against the Priests). He thought of Jewish exile as intellectually formative and of Diaspora as an ethical mission, and he opposed Zionism. Now that emancipation was a fact, he struggled with both the antisemites and the liberal Protestants over the terms of Jewish engagement in German national life. Above all, he led a relentless fight against assimilation and, in its course, proved as zealous as any Orthodox rabbi. He struck new, unfamiliar chords in the Reform symphony, ones expressing anxiety about Israel's enemies seeking to destroy it, and about waning Jewish commitment to Judaism. At the same time, he had to defend the dwindling ranks of Reform Judaism against the newly emergent, and more committed, Jewish nationalists. Maybaum had a lot of conflicting commitments to arbitrate, and the stress was apparent, not least in his negotiation of the Jacob & Esau legacy.

Jacob was not one of Maybaum's chief heroes. He preserved aspects of Reform Jacob, but Abraham emerged as the paragon of Jewish virtue. Abraham was the Jewish people's father, a model for ethical conduct, dignified behavior, and pious belief. The people of Israel inherited his ethos, were defined by it, and exemplified it.[40] His blessing was appropriately conferred on Jacob, and the blessing of wealth, for which Jacob & Esau vied, was superfluous. Jacob's pursuit of wealth and worldly power,

---

[40] Sigmund Maybaum, *Predigten*, 6 vols. (Berlin: [imprint varies], 1892–1910): 2: 14–36 (sermons 1889–92).

like that of his descendants in the First and Second Temple periods, was in vain. His grandeur emerged only when he became thankful to God for his lot in life – "God has been gracious to me and I have all I need (Genesis 33:11)" – and assumed the prophetic mission of universal spirituality, abandoning his search for political power. His new name Israel marked his universal ethical mission. All the same, Maybaum's Jacob remained a blurred figure, remarkable only for Maybaum's emphatic abnegation of Jacob's political pursuits. Maybaum contrasted Abraham, respected by all, sitting at the entrance to his tent to welcome guests, with Lot sitting at the gate of the city, resented by his compatriots for trying to become a judge. In the wake of German and Jewish nationalism, was Maybaum sounding a liberal Jewish retreat from politics, strangely reminiscent of Ultra-Orthodoxy?[41]

Esau remained a subdued figure in Maybaum's sermons, a hedonist in pursuit of wealth and fame, and decidedly pagan, but Maybaum saw him as honoring his father, and this virtue served as grounds for the brothers' reconciliation: Jacob and Esau buried their father together. Esau's paganism was befitting of the Jews' new enemies, the racial antisemites. The anxiety they evoked in Maybaum came out in his rendering of Balaam's messianic oracle. He omitted all historical reference to Edom, Rome, and the Jewish–Christian struggle, but reaffirmed the typology of Israel and its enemies. "A star shall rise from Jacob" (Numbers 24:17), he said, prophesied Israel's universal mission as an exemplary people spreading belief in God and justice, which would eventually be acknowledged by all.[42] Balaq and Balaam exemplified contemporary antisemites who were suspicious of the Jews just because they were "dwelling next to me" (Numbers 22:5). The antisemites did not recognize Jews as citizens, and sought first to turn them into strangers, then to destroy them.[43] But Balaam also portrayed the exemplary people that Israel was, "a people dwelling alone, and not counting itself among the nations" (Numbers 23:9). The Jews were a people with a distinct identity, but they neither lived in isolation nor constituted a nation, said Maybaum, overturning traditional interpretation. They guarded their unique mission but remained members of the nations among which they dwelled (and hence did not count as one among them).[44] To Maybaum, Jacob's descendants were good German cosmopolitans, and they were threatened by pagan antisemites.

---

[41] *Predigten*, 2: 70–123 (sermons 1885–92), pp. 57–62 (sermon 1892), respectively.
[42] *Predigten* 4: 52–53 (sermon 1886).   [43] Ibid., pp. 38–40 (sermon 1900).
[44] Ibid., pp. 60–62 (sermon 1899).

The antisemites' ghosts came out to haunt Maybaum on the Purim festival. He imagined the Ancient Persian Empire as contemporary Germany (curiously overlooking the more fitting example of Austria). Purim reaffirmed the *Gleichberechtigung* (equal rights) of all peoples in the multicultural empire, he said. Haman sought to eliminate the Jews in order to establish national religious unity (Esther 3:8), but nations required no religious uniformity. If the state adopted a national religion (*Volksreligion*), humanity would be the loser, as it would arrest progress toward a cosmopolitan world religion (*Weltreligion*) that would permit pluralistic expression. Jews must be allowed to maintain their religious community – for humanity's sake.[45] Maybaum presciently sensed that the search for national religious unity could potentially threaten not only Jewish spiritual survival but physical survival as well. He responded by reaffirming Jewish identity against the antisemites and the liberal Protestants alike.

Maybaum's balancing of cosmopolitan, national, and Jewish identities got ever more tenuous with the years, and his room for maneuvering in a racializing culture diminished. He resisted the ethnicization of Judaism by Germans or Jews (hence, Jacob became less useful), but reaffirmed a strong religious identity in an age when religious commitment was waning. Among liberal Jews, the more secular were gravitating toward the Society of Ethical Culture, and Zionism appealed to others. Against both, and the antisemites, too, Maybaum denied vehemently that Judaism represented national particularism. The Hebrews may have begun as a nation with a vision of a fighting God, but the Prophets' universal message of peace, justice, and spiritual strength was their everlasting legacy. He turned the Maccabees, the Zionist national heroes, into liberal Jews. He disavowed their military victories, and presented their triumph as one of spirit over imperial power, *Geist* over *Macht*. By wielding the sword, the Greeks had arrested the symbiosis of Hellenism and Judaism that would nourish Western civilization. As Jewish monotheists, the Maccabees resisted political oppression and, like German Jews, they struggled for religious tolerance and pluralism. German nationalism's drive for a unified Christian culture recapitulated Greek imperial oppression, and contemporary Jews were resisting spiritually; nothing had changed over millennia![46]

Unfortunately, Maybaum found too few Jews resisting, and commented bitterly that in Balaam's days, too, the Jews had remained unaware of the danger from which God saved them. Whence was salvation to come?

---

[45] *Predigten* 3: 62–69, 54–61 (sermons 1895–97, respectively).
[46] *Predigten*, 2: 124–50 (sermons 1884–92).

He put his hopes in the Jewish woman. He turned secondary biblical figures, Zelofḥads's five daughters, who married their cousins to assure the tribe's survival, into heroes (Numbers 27:1–11, 36:1–12). Israel's daughters, he said, who cared for the home and were responsible for the children's education, took charge of the tribal legacy when the men failed to do so.[47] He also availed himself of the Matriarchs' help. Abraham and Sarah provided a model Jewish home, with Abraham sitting at the entry to his tent, guardian of the house's relationship with the world, and Sarah inside the tent, governess of the domestic sphere.[48] Rebecca and Isaac's marriage was exemplary for joining love and heritage: The romance did not transgress tribal boundaries (as intermarriages do), for Isaac married within the family.[49] Leah and Rachel astutely managed their household and educated their children, and Rachel, especially, courageously removed the idols from her father's house. The disorderly household and petty Matriarchs of early Hamburg Reform preachers disappeared. It all depended on the mother, emphasized Maybaum.[50]

This was a desperate move. Historians do suggest that among German acculturated Jews, women were better positioned to assure the continuity of Jewish traditions by virtue of their management of the house and of children's early education.[51] Anecdotal evidence may also suggest their greater loyalty to Judaism. Maybaum, welcoming the bourgeois family as protective of the Jewish future, was testy in rebuffing progressive criticism of patriarchalism. Defense of patriarchalism (or liberal masculinity) was not his issue, however. Jewish liberals sensed that the public sphere was becoming hostile to them. They withdrew into the private sphere in order to protect Judaism. They were similarly positioned vis-à-vis politics, as were the women to whom they appealed as saviors. To be sure, they remained bourgeois patriarchs within the family, but their feminine position in politics was more telling of the present and future fortunes of Judaism.

Maybaum's political despair showed in two daring interpretive moves. One made him appear to be an Orthodox zealot, the other a Christian. Delivering a sermon on Pinḥas, the zealot priest who executed an Israelite tribal leader and his Moabite mistress (Numbers 25:7–8), Maybaum acknowledged the rabbis' apprehension about Pinḥas's vigilantism and, similarly, their criticism of the Prophet Elijah's zealotry.[52] Surprisingly, he endorsed the actions of both Pinḥas and Elijah as expressing

---

[47] *Predigten*, 4: 69–74 (sermon 1901).   [48] *Predigten*, 2: 37–56 (sermons 1884–86).
[49] Ibid., pp. 57–62 (sermon 1892).   [50] Ibid., pp. 70–123 (sermons 1885–92).
[51] Marion Kaplan, *The Making of the Jewish Middle Class: Women, Family, and Identity in Imperial Germany* (New York: Oxford University Press, 1991).
[52] *BT*, Sanhedrin 82a–b for Pinḥas; *Shir Hashirim Rabbah* **1:38** for Elijah.

appropriate concern for the collective. Elijah, he noted, was celebrated as a benevolent protector around the Seder table: There was time for zealotry, and time for benevolence.[53] Germany's leading liberal rabbi, anxious about rising intermarriage, fantasized about vigilantism!

Maybaum felt equally helpless in the face of Jewish and German nationalism. Abraham's plea "I am a stranger and a sojourner among you; give me a burial site" (Genesis 23:4) suggested, he said, that ancestors' burial places were the Jews' primary attachment to the land, and, *pace* antisemitic stereotypes of Mr. Moneybags and Zionist demands for the Land, the Jews advanced no other claim of ownership. They were sojourners everywhere, the grave their only attachment.[54] Jewish liberalism began emancipation with hopes for a new *Heimat* and nation. By the turn of the twentieth century, its leaders could be caught articulating Hugh of St. Victor's unearthly Christian cosmopolitanism, which future émigrés, like Auerbach, would carry into exile.

Unlike Maybaum, younger rabbis were responding to assimilation and antisemitism with a return to traditional Judaism and an acknowledgment of Jewish ethnicity. The change seemed generational rather than denominational. An increasing number of German rabbis came from East-Central Europe, some even from Russia. They were a joint product of traditional Jewish learning and German academic education. While Austria-Hungary offered Jews more capacious political options than did Germany, antisemitism confronted the Jews throughout Central Europe, and growing traditionalism and ethnic consciousness became typical of Jewish communities across the Austrian border, too. Abraham, founder of monotheism, was the patriarch of choice for all rabbis, but with Ḥanukkah celebrated as a triumph of Jewish monotheism, and Purim viewed as a miraculous salvation from antisemitism, Abraham appeared more Jewish than ever.

An earlier chapter described the rebellion against the Viennese Jewish establishment, which led in 1892 to the appointment of a traditionalist chief rabbi, Moritz Güdemann, to replace Jellinek. His successor in 1918 was the Zionist Chajes. In Moravian Zwittau, a German nationalist town, Felix Kanter (c.1870–c.1935), known from Schindler's biography as a liberal-minded rabbi whose children played with Oskar, was truly a liturgical conservative, who upheld the rabbis as the ultimate ethical ideal, was deeply concerned about assimilation and antisemitism, and expressed ethnic pride and Zionist sympathies.[55] Jacob & Esau would

---

[53] *Predigten*, 4: 63–68 (sermon 1889).   [54] *Predigten*, 2: 63–69 (sermon 1891).
[55] Thomas Keneally, *Schindler's Ark* (London: Hodder and Stoughton, 1982). Keneally misspells the name as Kantor. Felix Kanter, *Gleichniße für Reden über jüdische Angelegenheiten* (Frankfurt am Main: J. Kauffmann, 1911), pp. 93–102.

only reconcile in messianic times, opined Kanter. He thought of Balaq and Balaam as antisemites who libeled the Jews with a design to own the world. In a way evocative of Moses Sofer, he lamented the waning Jewish commitment to Judaism. He interpreted Jacob's struggle with the angel in pitch darkness to show that when the sun went down and the people of Israel were persecuted, they fought for Judaism, but when the sun came up and they attended to their own, they found themselves, like Jacob, covered with dust and limping.[56] Unlike his older colleague in Iglau on the Bohemian border, Joachim Unger, Kanter no longer seemed to trust the emperor to defend the Jews and felt that they were on their own. The generational mood shift was remarkable.

Back in Germany, Abraham the Hebrew appeared as the Jewish nation's father to Max Beermann (1873–1935), a rabbi first in Insterburg, East Prussia, then in Heilbronn in Württemberg. If Kanter spoke of Abraham as the embodiment of Jewish ethics, Beermann saw him as the sublime messenger of universal monotheism. Both rabbis still constructed tenuous bridges between Jewish ethnicity and cosmopolitanism. But to Beermann, the Purim story seemed the most essential in Jewish history: Its "memory . . . should never die out among the [Jews]" (Esther 9:28). Haman assailed Jewish religious and ethnic identity. He met with inadequate Jewish response, not unlike antisemitism in contemporary Germany. His charge that the Jews "do not obey the King's laws" (Esther 3:8) best applied to God's laws, said Beermann, homiletically mimicking Sofer: In a pluralist environment, the Jews were abandoning Judaism.[57] Beermann was personally inclined to Orthodoxy but served as the leader of the whole Heilbronn community. The spread of Sofer-like lamentation among mainstream rabbis was an ominous sign of emancipation's declining fortunes.

Traditionalism and nationalism culminated in Hirsch Perez Chajes. Born in Brody, Galicia, he had been a rabbi in Florence and Trieste before coming to Vienna at the end of World War I. An Orthodox and Zionist rabbi in a community still led by liberal Jews, he quietly reintroduced traditional elements into the Viennese rite and reinforced Jewish education, including the gymnasium and rabbinic seminary. Judaism was a national marker, he thought. It embodied the shared memories and hopes that shaped the Jews as a nation. If until 1789 Jews had been religiously defined, with modern nationalism they became entitled to national rights. He supported the emperor and the monarchy to the end

---

[56] Felix Kanter, *Homiletische Essays* (Frankfurt am Main: J. Kauffmann, 1910), pp. 193–200, 29–41, respectively.
[57] Max Beermann, *Festpredigten* (Frankfurt am Main: J. Kauffmann, 1909), pp. 330–34.

but saw national self-determination and republicanism (perhaps on the Italian model?) as ideals.[58] Jewish citizenship, however, could not be dependent on membership in the German nation. The Jews should be accorded national minority rights in every country, and the Land of Israel become both a Jewish cultural center and a refuge.[59]

Chajes developed a Jewish national cosmopolitanism, joining the fighting Maccabees, his favorite motif, with a Jewish universal mission, highlighting Ancient Israel's putative concern for the nations and the Ten Commandments' role in the making of European culture.[60] Both Abraham and Jacob played roles. Abraham appeared as the Zionist lover of the Land, the immigrant who took risks and suffered for them, and as a courageous and generous warrior. Jacob, in contrast, was the traditional Jew, guardian of the name of Israel.[61] Chajes was aware that Jacob's liabilities made contemporaries shy away from him – "they blame us that Jacob is the most like us among the Patriarchs" – yet Jacob consistently appeared in his speeches from Trieste to his last address in Vienna.[62] That which happened to Jacob is happening to his children, too, said Chajes: Like Jacob in Laban's house, the Jewish people were paying the price of emancipation. Responding to the antisemites' perceptions of Jews as sly, he continued, the originally honest Jews became crafty in their business practices and only Zionism would reform their character. Let Jews not fear carrying Israel's name but fight to receive the angel's blessing, while pursuing, as Jacob did, peace and alliances.[63]

Yet, having engaged in indefatigable fights against antisemitism, especially in higher education, and witnessed the post–World War I pogroms in the Ukraine, Chajes had little confidence in alliances with non-Jews. Like the Philistines who hated Isaac yet needed him, and asked to make an alliance, so too are Europeans with Jews: They need Jewish genius and commerce yet resent the Jews. There was no room for trust, as Haman always lurked behind. Intermarriage was a national disaster. Maybaum endorsed Pinḥas vigilantism against intermarriage, but Chajes surpassed him. Overruling Jacob's censure of Simon and Levi, he sanctioned their murder of the population of Shekhem to avenge their sister's violation.[64] If, as Chajes opined, Jewish blood was "strong" enough to assimilate all

---

[58] Hirsch Pereẓ Chajes, *Reden und Vorträge* (Vienna: Moritz Rosenfeld, 1933), pp. 133–35.

[59] Ibid., pp. 234–38. See also *Speeches and Lectures* (in Hebrew) (Boston: Beit ha-Midrash le-Morim, 1953), pp. 391–92, for his 1927 celebration of the republic.

[60] *Reden und Vorträge*, pp. 41–45, 149–50 (speeches in 1914 and 1919, respectively).

[61] *Speeches and Lectures*, pp. 209–11, 375–76; *Reden und Vorträge*, pp. 37–40. But Jacob, too, asked to be buried in Israel: *Speeches and Lectures*, p. 378.

[62] *Speeches and Lectures*, p. 377.   [63] Ibid.; *Reden und Vorträge*, pp. 206–9.

[64] *Speeches and Lectures*, pp. 392–94 (Isaac and the Philistines), pp. 379–80 (Haman), pp. 385–86 (avenging Dinah).

others, from Canaanite to Khuzarite, whence the worry?[65] From the liberal cosmopolitan Maybaum to the liberal nationalist Chajes, the strains of antisemitism and assimilation were evident in Jewish liberalism. The weak adopted the oppressors' weapons, creating an Israel tainted by their enemies' vision.

Sidelining Jacob: Leo Baeck, Hermann Cohen, and Liberal Jewish Apologetics

Historian Uriel Tal pointed out the similarities between the liberal Jewish and Protestant worldviews.[66] Their competition and enmity, he said, were born out of similarity, both laying claim to Western monotheism and universalism, both preaching historically aware and morally centered rational religion, both, he might have added, uncomfortable with the Hebrew Bible's ethno-centricity, if for different reasons. But, of course, the power of liberal Protestants and Jews diverged. By the turn of the twentieth century, the first represented the academic establishment and national avant-garde, whereas the latter were a minority seeking legitimacy for continued integration as Jews. Unlike Christian theology and history, Jewish Studies were not – and would not be until the Nazis – an academic field. Liberal Jews were fierce in defending Judaism: Abraham and the Prophets were earlier and better representatives of universalism than Jesus and the early Christians; Second Temple Judaism was formative for Christianity; and the Trinity belied Christian monotheism. Yet, as critics noted, the liberal Jewish view was reactive in character, and the Judaism emerging from the great age of liberal apologetics looked suspiciously Protestant.[67] In the writings of leading liberal Rabbi Leo Baeck (1873–1956) and prominent neo-Kantian philosopher Hermann Cohen (1844–1918), rabbinic Jacob vanished.

Judaism and Protestantism developed confrontational liberal cultures. Liberal Jews sought to counter Protestant supersessionism by showing Judaism to represent Enlightenment values, which, both camps claimed, underlaid German civic culture. Appropriating the Protestant Romantic view of prophecy as original, creative, and ethically monotheist, Baeck and Cohen recentered Judaism around the Prophets. They argued that

---

[65] Ibid., p. 211.

[66] *Religion, Politics, and Ideology in the Second Reich, 1870–1914*, trans. Noah Jonathan Jacobs (Ithaca, NY: Cornell University Press, 1975).

[67] Christian Wiese observes that liberal Jewish apologetics were founded on the liberal Protestant view of the Prophets and on the Rabbis' marginalization: "The Best Antidote to Anti-Semitism?" pp. 145–92. See also David Myers, "Hermann Cohen and the Quest for Protestant Judaism," *Leo Baeck Institute Yearbook* 46 (2001): 195–214.

ethical monotheism – a term capitalizing on monotheism's civic potential in a secularizing culture – was formative both for the Jewish cosmopolitan mission and for early Christianity. Harnack distilled the "essence of Christianity" so that it corresponded to liberal Protestantism, which he thought best served the needs of German national culture, in a world increasingly skeptical of Christ's divinity and church traditions. He retained the traditional anti-Judaic prejudice about the obsolete Jewish Law.[68] In response, liberal Jews reaffirmed a Jewish essence that looked similar to the Protestant, shed biblical layers and rabbinic traditions, and presented Judaism as an edifying philosophy.[69] To Cohen, Kant and the Prophets delivered the same message.[70] Judaism, the better ethical monotheism, could serve as an alternative German civic religion, yet one close enough to liberal Protestantism to stake a claim for a share in *Deutschtum*.

Liberal Jews went even further, however. Following Abraham Geiger's earlier lead, they sought to re-Judaize Jesus and show Judaism to have been formative of Christianity. Contestation over the historical Jesus became a boundary marker. Baeck suggested that in going back to Jesus and giving up on dogmas, liberal Protestants were actually returning to Judaism. The daring maneuver moved the struggle into the enemy's territory, asserting Jewish legitimacy and partnership in German culture by writing early Christianity into Jewish history.[71] Alas, it also played havoc with Judaism's historic base camp, the rabbinic tradition. Neither focused on the rabbis, but Baeck discussed Tannaitic traditions to demonstrate Harnack's misleading view of the Pharisees, and Cohen elaborated on the Talmudic teaching of "love thy neighbor."[72] He saw the next scholarly task as showing "the unity of the Talmud and Midrash ... and of the religious-philosophical literature of the Middle

---

[68] Adolf von Harnack, *Das Wesen des Christentums: Sechzehn Vorlesungen vor Studierenden aller Fakultäten im Wintersemester 1899/1900 an der Universität Berlin*, ed. Claus-Dieter Osthövener (Tübingen: Mohr Siebeck, 2005).

[69] Leo Baeck, *The Essence of Judaism* [1905], rev. ed. (New York: Schocken Books, 1948), and *Judaism and Christianity*, trans. and introduction by Walter Kaufmann (Philadelphia: Jewish Publication Society, 1964); Hermann Cohen, *Der Begriff der Religion im System der Philosophie* (Giessen: A. Töpelmann, 1915).

[70] "Innere Beziehungen der Kantischen Philosophie zum Judentum" [1910], in *Hermann Cohens Jüdische Schriften*, ed. Bruno Strauss, 3 vols. (Berlin: C. A. Schwetschke, 1924): 1: 284–305.

[71] Christian Wiese, "Struggling for Normality: The Apologetics of *Wissenschaft des Judentums* in Wilhelmine Germany as an Anti-Colonial Intellectual Revolt against the Protestant Construction of Judaism," in *"Towards Normality?" Acculturation of Modern German Jewry*, ed. Rainer Liedtke and David Rechter (Tübingen: Mohr Siebeck, 2003), pp. 80–89.

[72] Leo Baeck, *Die Pharisäer: Ein Kapitel Jüdischer Geschichte* (Berlin: Schocken, 1934); Hermann Cohen, "Die Nächstenliebe in Talmud" [1888], in *Jüdische Schriften*, 1: 145–74.

Ages" with biblical Judaism, that is, the unity of Judaism as ethical monotheism.[73] This meant reconfiguring the rabbis so that they drew the opposite portrait from rabbinic Jacob and resembled Kant. The edifying task, inspiring in its humanity and creativity, had never been completed, but in the contest between liberal Protestants and Jews, Jacob was cast away, by the former explicitly and by the latter implicitly.

Liberal Jews and Protestants alike defined themselves against traditionalists and secularists (*freireligion*). Baeck and Cohen concurred that ethical monotheism was the foundation of German national culture. Having conceded most nationalist assumptions, they faced a difficult time in arguing for pluralism. Argue they did, but atheists and traditional Jews and Christians alike would be ill at ease in their liberal Jewish Germany. The challenges from both within and outside the Jewish community only grew with the years. Responding in his World War I writings to rising antisemitism, on the one hand, and to the Zionists and socialist internationalists, on the other, Cohen redefined the meaning of the "German-Jewish." He underlined his antiassimilatory position and conceded that the Jews were a nationality. Taking note of neighboring Austria's multinational character, he distinguished between the German nation, defined by the state, and the many nationalities constituting it. Germany was a multiethnic state and the Jews were one of its nationalities. This was a bold move that could have opened the gates for pluralism. But Cohen also insisted that Jews remained Jews primarily to carry out Judaism's cosmopolitan mission, which had great affinities with German humanism. Jewish nationality and religion manifested Deutschtum.[74] The idea that liberal Judaism provided a firmer foundation for a German civic culture than did Christianity (or traditional Judaism) was as ingenious as it was far-fetched, and it was not pluralist.

Baeck and Cohen also opened the gates to a German patriotism that cast doubt on their cosmopolitanism. Both viewed the German state and culture as major achievements of humanity and supported World War I as their necessary defense. Baeck would chafe at Deutschtum in 1926, but desperately trying to establish a working relationship with the Nazi leadership after 1933, he expressed a willingness, as head of the Jewish community, to participate in the remaking of Germany (*Erneuerung*). In his

---

[73] *Der Begriff der Religion*, p. 113.

[74] Cohen, "Deutschtum und Judentum I & II," "Religion und Zionismus," and "Antwort auf das offene Schreiben des Herrn Dr. Martin Buber," in *Jüdische Schriften*, 2: 237–301, 302–18, 319–27, 328–40, respectively. Paul Mendes-Flohr, *German Jews: A Dual Identity*, pp. 59–63, 112–13, called my attention to Cohen's World War I redefinition of the German-Jewish symbiosis.

1934 Hindenburg obituary, he waxed nostalgically about the deceased president as a modern Abraham.[75] He would speak sympathetically of a Jewish national home only after the Holocaust, when his references to Jews as a "people" would also become easier and more frequent.[76] Rabbinic Jacob seemed to have remained persona non grata to the end.

For the liberal Protestants, the Jewish alternative was a nonstarter. The reaction ranged from dismay and dismissal to outright hostility.[77] Harnack ignored Baeck, but Troeltsch could not ignore Cohen, who was a leading philosopher and a Berlin professor. Toward the end of World War I, the two carried on a sharp journalistic exchange. Troeltsch denied the Jewish Prophets' universalism, rejected the proximity of Jewish and Protestant religious histories, and intimated that Cohen's narrative was not authentically German.[78] During the same years, his colleague Weber was developing his view of the Prophets as representatives of a "Pariah People." Both reaffirmed Jewish particularity and difference. This was the type of exchange that the young Georg Scholem found alienating and, fifty years later, decried as a charade of a dialogue.[79] German-Jewish cosmopolitanism was a cry in the desert.

Scholem and the Weimar generation defined themselves against Cohen and Baeck, but in strange ways, the fathers paved the road for the children. They had begun the turn against history, for which Weimar became known, and redefined philosophically and theologically the German–Jewish relationship. To be sure, they advanced historical arguments to deny the Protestants exclusive ownership of Jesus, but they contained biblical history, and so ethical monotheism remained not just a moment but became Judaism's "essence." For Baeck in *This People Israel*, which he began in the Theresienstadt concentration camp,

---

[75] *Briefe, Reden, Aufsätze*, ed. Michael Meyer, Vol. 6 of *Leo Baeck Werke*, ed. Albert H. Friedlander et al., 6 vols. (Gütersloh: Gütersloh Verlagshaus, 2006): 6: 204–6, 210–13, respectively.

[76] *Briefe, Reden, Aufsätze*, pp. 477–83; Baeck, *This People Israel: The Meaning of Jewish Existence* [1955], trans. and introduction by Albert Friedlander (New York: Holt, Rinehart and Winston, 1964).

[77] Christian Wiese, *Challenging Colonial Discourse: Jewish Studies and Protestant Theology in Wilhelmine Germany* (Leiden: Brill, 2005).

[78] Troeltsch, "Glaube und Ethos der Habräischen Propheten" [1916]; Cohen, "Der Prophetismus und die Soziologie," in *Jüdische Schriften*, 2: 398–401; Steven Schwarzschild, "The Theologico-Political Basis of Liberal Christian–Jewish Relations in Modernity," in *Das deutsche Judentum und der Liberalismus*, ed. Friedrich–Naumann–Stiftung and Leo Baeck Institute (Sankt Augustin: COMDOK, 1986), pp. 70–95, esp. pp. 79–80.

[79] Gershom Scholem, "Against the Myth of the German-Jewish Dialogue," in *On Jews and Judaism in Crisis*, ed. Werner J. Dannhauser (New York: Schocken, 1976), pp. 61–64. Yet Cohen's view engendered sympathy among his neo-Kantian Marburg colleagues, to whom his 1915 study was dedicated, and this infuriated Troeltsch.

Covenant and Exodus framed the Jewish people and its history. In his 1944 historiography essay, the Prophets, in Hegelian fashion, articulated the national spirit and life, the essence of Judaism as a community of faith.[80] Around the turn of the twentieth century, such containment of historicization was not unique to liberal Jews. David Zevi Hoffmann (1843–1921), leader of the Orthodox seminary in Berlin, closed the Bible to history even more radically. He defended Torah's integrity against Julius Wellhausen by showing the textual incompatibility of late Priestly origins. Rabbi Benno Jacob, the biblical exegete, moved similarly to demonstrate the impossibility of a historical reconstruction of the biblical text. The flight from history reflected declining Jewish confidence in the ability to master it against liberal Protestantism and anxieties about the future of Judaism that belied any celebratory pronouncement of German–Jewish patriotism.

Nineteenth-century *Wissenschaft des Judentums* had highlighted rabbinic texts and ranged over Jewish history, historicizing diverse moments and documents. Baeck and Cohen rechanneled all historical interests toward ethical monotheism. The very disciplines they chose in order to confront liberal Protestantism, theology and philosophy, were prejudicial to both historicity and rabbinic Judaism. They defined many of the questions that their Weimar successors would endeavor to resolve.[81] Weimar Jewish intellectuals would reject the fathers' liberal Judaism but would retain their mistrust of history and predilection for theology. Between liberal fathers and ethnic children, rabbinic Jacob vanished, a victim to the loss of history.

Beyond the Rabbis? Weimar and Its Bible

A new understanding of the German–Jewish relationship and brilliant articulations of Jewish difference have become the Weimar generation's trademark. Martin Buber's cultural literary journal, *Der Jude* (1916–28), and the Buber-Rosenzweig translation of the Bible (1925–36) set the tone. The Zionist journal served as a platform for Weimar Jewish intellectuals to renegotiate German-Jewish identity and display their cultural creativity. The translation highlighted the Bible's Oriental otherness, and endeavored to capture its divine voice, as well as engage it in a dialogue.

---

[80] Baeck, "The Writing of History" [June 15, 1944], *The Synagogue Review* (November 1962): 51–59.

[81] Focusing on the Hermann Cohen–Franz Rosenzweig nexus, Peter Eli Gordon, *Rosenzweig and Heidegger: Between Judaism and German Philosophy* (Berkeley: University of California Press, 2003), pp. 39–81, shows, lucidly and intelligently, that this is true for an even broader set of questions.

Recent scholarship concurs with the Weimar Jewish activists that they launched a Jewish cultural renaissance and highlights it as a moment of Jewish authenticity.[82] To a historian of the two-millennia Jacob & Esau typology, however, it is the dearth of Weimar's ties to rabbinic traditions and the reinvention of Jewish identities that is striking. The diminution of rabbinic Jacob in Weimar Jewish discourse was a measure of its nontraditionalism. The most innovative reconfiguration of Jacob during Weimar belonged to a non-Jewish writer, Thomas Mann.

Weimar Jewish authenticity seems problematic. The quest for individual religious experience and access to revelation, independently of tradition, characterized Romantic Christianity from Friedrich Schleiermacher on. The Weimar return to the Bible in the search for truth that would countervail liberal historical theology is commonly associated with Karl Barth's "theology of the Word"; that is, it was Christian. Most Weimar Jewish intellectuals – Buber was the notable exception – lacked traditional Jewish learning. Their efforts to break with history, grasp the Jewish essence, and acquire the liberty to innovate ironically produced a Judaism that looked no less Protestant than that of their liberal fathers. In *The Star of Redemption*, Franz Rosenzweig made revelation the touchstone of Judaism.[83] Revelation had always been rabbinic tacit knowledge, but theological questions had never before been central in mainstream Judaism. The Oral Tradition made it possible for successive generations to work out the Torah's meaning. Nineteenth-century Neo-Orthodoxy first made belief in the Oral Law's divinity a defining Jewish tenet; then Weimar intellectuals made direct human engagement with the divine the central question for the modern Jew. Atheism and Gnosticism suddenly appeared heroic rather than nebulous. The Weimar rebellion against the liberal fathers was not a return to Jewish tradition but a daring effort to reinvent Judaism.

The new Judaism took ethnicity for granted, and cultivated it. Utopian socialist Gustav Landauer (1870–1919) had already articulated the new configuration of German and Jewish nationality before World War I. He was so convinced of Jewish nationality that he despised nationalist efforts to promote it and argued that its best expression was the socialist drive to redeem humanity. The Jewish national mystical force had so far been contained by the patient awaiting of the Messiah. Now it was exploding in socialist internationalism, in collective work to redeem the world. There was no need for a German or a Jewish state to carry out the socialist

---

[82] Michael Brenner, *The Renaissance of Jewish Culture in Weimar Germany* (New Haven, CT: Yale University Press, 1996): Paul Mendes-Flohr, *German Jews: A Dual Identity*.

[83] *The Star of Redemption* [1921], trans. William W. Hallo (New York: Holt, Rinehart and Winston, 1971).

project: It was precisely the Jewish exile that made Jews the messianic socialist people. Landauer rejected hyphenated German-Jewish identity: Yes, he was a German and a Jew at the same time, and equally so, but each identity was distinct.[84] Rosenzweig would later express a similar sensibility in speaking of Germany as a New Babylon, a land of two rivers. Paul Mendes-Flohr captures the generational mood in his notion of a bifurcated dual identity, German and Jewish, with an emphasis on the conjunction *and*. There was no German-Jewish hybrid.[85]

Paradoxically, an open rejection of history accompanied the rediscovery of Jewish messianism. The turn against history represented a sea change. From emancipation's onset, German Jews had deployed history to recover forgotten culture, thwart Christian supersessionism, and counter German nationalist narratives. Jacques Ehrenfreund suggests that grand Jewish narratives, such as Graetz's, became common only after German unification, but *Wissenschaft des Judentums*, in all its guises, had been historically engaged for decades.[86] Responses to Wellhausen's biblical reconstruction likewise centered on historical scholarship. Now history was judged the wrong path: Historiography ignored religious experience, and disputes against the liberal Protestants produced a Protestant Judaism. Philosopher and Reform Rabbi Max Wiener (1882–1950) mercilessly exposed the subterfuge of nineteenth-century Jewish discourse. To enable a phantom integration, Jewish scholars had concealed both the centrality of revelation and mounting doubts about it, and suppressed national consciousness.[87] Isaac Breuer (1883–1946), Samson Raphael Hirsch's grandchild, rediscovered the messianic nation and rebelled against his Orthodox bourgeois mileu. He argued for Zionism among the Ultra-Orthodox *Agudah*, advocated a compromise with Reform Jews, and declared history immaterial to the Jewish essence now unfolding in messianic redemption.[88] Resistance to history, as David Myers shows, cut across Weimar Jewish intellectual life.

---

[84] "Sind das Ketzergedanken?" in *Gustav Landauer: Dichter, Ketzer, Außenseiter: Essays und Reden zur Literatur, Philosophie, Judentum*, ed. Hannah Delf (Berlin: Akademie Verlag, 1997), pp. 170–74.

[85] Franz Rosenzweig, *Zweistromland: Kleinere Schriften zur Religion und Philosophie* (Berlin: Philo Verlag, 1926). Paul Mendes-Flohr, *German Jews: A Dual Identity*, pp. 93–94, 139–40, sees Landauer's vision as conceding German priority and as syncretist, while Rosenzweig was endeavoring to establish symmetry and balance between German and Jewish. צריך עיון.

[86] *Mémoire Juive et Nationalité Allemande: Les Juifs Berlinois à la Belle Epoque* (Paris: Presses Universitaires de France, 2000), pp. 133–48, 169–71.

[87] Max Wiener, *Jüdische Religion im Zeitalter der Emanzipation* (Berlin: Philo, 1933).

[88] David Myers, *Resisting History* (Princeton, NJ: Princeton University Press, 2002), pp. 130–56.

The Buber-Rosenzweig Bible encapsulated the Weimar Jewish agenda. It imagined the Ancient East and the Patriarchs in their otherness and presented them as an authentic Jewish alternative to the Christian and modern. It consciously dehistoricized, breaking away from rabbinic or Haskalah domestication of the biblical text, seeking direct access to the Bible's voice beyond the rabbinic tradition, and beyond history.[89] Paradoxically, the translation had to reinvent the Other in contemporary German to make it accessible and usable. Buber and Rosenzweig rejected Moses Mendelssohn's scholarly *Biur* as deferential to German culture. Among Protestants, a call for a return to Luther's Bible signaled resistance to liberal theology. Buber and Rosenzweig provided the Jewish counterpart. Using Luther as their point of departure, they set their Bible against his. *Verdeutschung*, making the Bible German (rather than translating), is what they called their enterprise, mimicking Luther, but with a Jewish difference, reclaiming the Bible as Jewish.[90]

Rosenzweig believed that Judaism's absolute reality was beyond history and nature and could be grasped only through revelation. Buber thought of revelation as a dialogue between humanity and God. The Bible's translation endeavored to capture the divine voice and facilitate the dialogue, that is, create Buber's famous I–Thou relationship with Scripture. Like the rabbis, Buber and Rosenzweig insisted that the Torah was not beyond human reach – "it is not in the heavens" (Deuteronomy 30:12) – but, against them, they sought direct access to the divine, unmediated by tradition. The possibility of ongoing revelation, the hearing of God's voice, was crucial, they thought, to Jewish life. Only through living religious experience could Jews sustain Judaism and renegotiate their relationship with Germans. Their Bible set out to make it possible.

The Jacob & Esau story is exemplary of their translation. Buber and Rosenzweig tell the story in simple language and short sentences. The form is poetic rather than prosaic, the style is rhythmical, complicated biblical constructions are made fluent, and rough transitions are smoothened. They ignore German punctuation rules and the Hebrew

---

[89] Abigail Gillman, "Between Religion and Culture: Mendelssohn, Buber, Rosenzweig and the Enterprise of Biblical Translation," in *Biblical Translation in Context*, ed. Frederick Knobloch (Bethesda: University Press of Maryland, 2002), pp. 93–114; Mara Benjamin, *Rosenzweig's Bible: Reinventing Scripture for Jewish Modernity* (Cambridge: Cambridge University Press, 2009).

[90] *Die Schrift und ihre Verdeutschung* (Berlin: Schocken, 1936), a collection of articles by Buber and Rosenzweig expounding the project. For passages from Genesis in the following paragraphs: *Genesis: Die fünf Bücher der Weisung: Fünf Bücher des Moses*, trans. (*verdeutscht*) by Martin Buber together with Franz Rosenzweig (Berlin: Lambert Schneider, 1930).

tropes to produce phrases resembling speech more than writing. Verse numbers are noted only at the page top (or bottom), and biblical terms are elucidated as part of the text so that the flow is not interrupted: "Let me gobble from that red, that red there, as I am weak. Hence, his name is called Edom, the Red" (Genesis 25:30). The authors considered terms and turns of phrase carefully, but literary or scholarly accuracy was not their goal; rather, it was the recovery of biblical voices, making them accessible. Jacob and Esau emerge as more familiar and understandable than they seem in the Hebrew text, yet the authors wished also to effect estrangement (*Verfremdung*). They did so, among others things, by using Hebrew names: Jizchak, Ribka, Jaakob, and Eßaw (rather than the German Isaak, Rebekka, Jakob, and Esau). With Luther (and modern translations), and against the rabbinic tradition (and the King James Bible), they translated Isaac's blessing to Esau as meager and mean: "Away from [rather than "Of"] the fatness of the earth shall your dwelling be" (Genesis 27:39). Their Bible sought to affirm Jewish difference against Christian culture. Whether or not they thought of Jacob and Esau as Christian and Jew, they highlighted their conflict. The authorial stance was confrontational, and the mood ungenerous.

Buber thought initially of the Bible's target audience as primarily Christian, wishing to confront them with Jewish difference and begin the German–Jewish dialogue anew.[91] As the translation progressed – Buber was doing the bulk of the work but consulting regularly with the ailing Rosenzweig – the authors became increasingly concerned that in underlining the Bible's alterity, they would provoke Christian wrath. But as Peter Gordon shows, the new Bible received a fairly warm reception as a German modernist work, albeit mostly among the Weimar avantgarde.[92] Buber brought the project to completion on his own in 1936. The Buber-Rosenzweig Bible did not reset the German–Jewish dialogue, but it remains a monument to the Weimar Jewish renaissance.

Cultural critic Siegfried Kracauer's 1927 response to the translation's first volume, *Das Buch im Anfang* (*Genesis* translated as "The Book in the Beginning"), highlighted the Weimar generation's rejection of history.[93] Every translation was a political act and rooted in a particular lifeworld, he said. Buber and Rosenzweig had misdiagnosed their own time. Scholarly

---

[91] Zohar Maor, *Martin Buber* (in Hebrew) (Jerusalem: Zalman Shazar Center, 2016).
[92] Peter Eli Gordon, *Rosenzweig and Heidegger*, pp. 237–74.
[93] "The Bible in German," in Kracauer's *The Mass Ornament: Weimar Essays*, trans. and ed. Thomas Levin (Cambridge, MA: Harvard University Press, 1995), pp. 189–201. Martin Jay, "The Politics of Translation: Siegfried Kracauer and Walter Benjamin on the Buber-Rosenzweig Bible," *Leo Baeck Institute Yearbook* 21 (1976): 3–24, first drew attention to the debate.

mediation was necessary in order to render a text of an ancient sacral culture comprehensible in modern German. A traditional commentary, such as Mendelssohn's *Biur*, provided it. The attempt to dispense with commentary and, instead, retrieve religious truth through stylistic devices produced an archaic translation that substituted Neo-Romantic fiction – not the ancient Hebrews – for contemporary reality. Kracauer was right, but like Walter Benjamin, he sought religiosity in modern profanity, not in religious tradition. He would have been equally unsympathetic to a mediation of contemporary Jewish identity via the rabbinic tradition. Rabbinic Jacob remained without advocates in Weimar.

Weimar Jewish intellectuals' creativity was so striking that one may forget that most Jews were not associated with Rosenzweig's House of Jewish Learning (*Freie Jüdische Lehrhaus*) in Frankfurt but with communities where more traditional Judaism prevailed. For all the anxieties and generational changes noted earlier, Reform Judaism held sway all the way to 1933. As late as 1930, the Berlin *Reformgemeinde* rabbi, Julius Jelski (1865–1937), could uphold the cosmopolitan Jewish mission and the old hopes for a Jewish home in Germany. His Purim sermon addressed the new Amaleq, the antisemites who had not internalized the lessons of the old. Nationalist scapegoating of Jews mimicked Haman's allegations about Jewish disobedience to the law. Yet Jews were famously obedient, and the Prophets remonstrated with them for not keeping the laws strictly. Currently, Israel was no longer a people or a nation as it was in the Persian Empire, and modern Christians were not ancient pagans. Since Mendelssohn, Jews had sought integration by emulating him. Racists could count the Jewish names among Europe's cultural leaders to recognize the success of integration. Jewish memory of the old home in Zion did not intimate a wish to restore the old community or Temple rituals. It was the spiritual, cosmopolitan Jerusalem that Jews were seeking. Evoking emancipation fighter Gabriel Riesser, Jelski concluded: "We are Germans or we are homeless!"[94]

The 1933 triumph of National Socialism constituted a caesura. Jelski's sermon, reflecting Jewish anxieties but holding onto the liberal vision, could not have been delivered three years later. Guy Meron has documented the radical shift in Jewish views of emancipation after 1933, and the calls for Jewish national renewal (*Erneuerung*).[95] Historian Jacob Katz, rushing to complete his Ph.D. dissertation on Jewish assimilation under

---

[94] Julius Jelski, "Judenhaß" and "Alte und neue Heimat," in his *Im Wandel der Zeiten: Predigten*, 2 vols. (Berlin: Philo-Verlag, 1930): 2: 88–95, 96–100, respectively.

[95] *The Waning of the Emancipation: Jewish History, Memory, and the Rise of Fascism in Germany, France, and Hungary* (Detroit: Wayne State University Press, 2011), esp. pp. 165–82.

Karl Mannheim in Frankfurt, provided a bitter assessment of emancipation as an impossible paradox.[96] This view would inform his lifework and become the prevailing Zionist narrative. During the spiritual mobilization of the Jewish community in the 1930s, however, even mainstream Reform rabbis could sound like Zionists. In 1938, after *Kristallnacht*, young Manfred Swarsensky told Jewish youth the Hanukkah story, highlighting the Maccabees' resistance and martyrology.[97] The evaluation of Mendelssohn and of *Wissenschaft des Judentums* still divided liberal and Zionist Jews: The liberals cast them as antiassimilatory models, whereas the Zionists denounced them as assimilatory. (Read in this context, Scholem's 1944 "Reflections" come as no surprise.) All recognized that the German–Jewish symbiosis was reaching a crisis.

The most striking example of liberal Judaism's transformation was Zionist Reform Rabbi Joachim Prinz. A popular young Berlin rabbi, cultivating an informal antiestablishment style, he launched an attack on liberal Judaism from within in his 1934 *Wir Juden* (We Jews).[98] He criticized the Haskalah, emancipation, and current Jewish leadership for stymieing Jewish ethnic identity, and he upheld the ghetto as a space of inner freedom. Responders objected to his reghettoization of Judaism, but his populist appeal was evident: History itself seemed to have spoken. In his Jewish history, Prinz used German Orientalist scholarship to draw a picture of the Hebrew Near East. Jacob became a tribe, Israel a tribal alliance, and both were stages in national development.[99] He composed biblical stories for children.[100] As they were to mimic national folk tales, and children were to take pride in their ancestors, no patriarch appeared a hero. Moses was the earliest figure, and Prinz highlighted kings, military leaders, and powerful women. Deborah alone, who led military action, was chosen from among the Prophets. There were, of course, no priests or rabbis. Jewish history was nationalized, and the nation racialized.

Unlike many Weimar Jewish intellectuals, Prinz did not break with history but, rather, used the enemy's tools to construct a Jewish nation.

---

[96] "Die Entstehung der Judenassimilation in Deutschland und derren Ideologie" [1935], in Jacob Katz, *Emancipation and Assimilation: Studies in Modern Jewish History* (Farnborough: Gregg, 1972), pp. 195–276.

[97] *Die Chanukah-Geschichte* (Berlin: Jüdischer Buchverlag Erwin Löwe, 1938). The pamphlet was part of an effort to raise donations for the Jewish Community's *Winterhilfe*.

[98] *Wir Juden* (Berlin: Erich Reiss, 1934). In place of a biography, see *Joachim Prinz, Rebellious Rabbi: An Autobiography: The German and Early American Years*, ed. and with an introduction by Michael A. Meyer (Bloomington: Indiana University Press, 2008).

[99] Prinz, *Jüdische Geschichte* (Berlin: Verlag für Kulturpolitik, 1931), pp. 11–15; *Illustrierte Jüdische Geschichte*, 2d ed. (Berlin: Brandussche Verlagsbuchhandlung, 1933), pp.13–17.

[100] *Helden und Abenteurer der Bibel: Ein Kinderbuch* (Berlin: Paul Baumann-Verlag, 1930).

He was playing a dangerous game, and it came back to haunt him later in life. As an activist rabbi in the Civil Rights movement in the United States, he argued that Zionism provided no countervailing force to assimilation, and that there was a need for an ethical revival, for a cosmopolitan mission for the Jews.[101] In a valedictory to Weimar, he returned to the liberal fathers whom he had cavalierly dismissed in his youth. The Weimar experience suggests, however, that Jews and Judaism have nothing to win by forging an ethnic defense and everything to lose by trying to leap beyond history. The attempt to go back beyond two and a half millennia of rabbinic and Second Temple Judaism, beyond rabbis, priests, and prophets, to the ancient Hebrews and rescue an authentic Jewish experience from the Bible cut across intellectual camps. Weimar invented Jewish differences and mythologized Judaism. It lost Jacob along the way. לא זה הדרך.

Benno Jacob: Rabbinic Jacob and the End of Emancipation

Rabbinic Jacob staged a single powerful performance at the end of Weimar. In Benno Jacob's massive biblical commentary on Genesis (1934), rabbinic Jacob returned to announce the impasse reached by emancipation.[102] Benno Jacob (1862–1945) was a Reform rabbi, academically trained in both Breslau's university and its rabbinic seminary, serving until 1906 in Göttingen, then, until his retirement in 1929, in Dortmund. Versed in Jewish Studies and classical philology, he was a frequent polemicist against Protestant biblical scholars, an activist against antisemitism, and a board member of German Jewry's major organization, the *Centralverein*. He emigrated to England in 1939 and died there in January 1945. His life spanned Wilhelmine, Weimar, and Nazi Germany, and he witnessed emancipation at its apex and nadir.

Jacob's commentary was a brilliant synthesis of rabbinic and nineteenth-century liberal exegetical traditions. It displayed a modern hermeneutics shaped in light of biblical criticism. Israel's foremost biblical commentator, Neḥamah Leibowitz, declared her preference for Jacob

---

[101] Joachim Prinz and Louis Pincus, *Israel and the Diaspora: Two Points of View* (Geneva: World Jewish Congress, 1973), pp. 7–19.

[102] *Das erste Buch der Tora: Genesis*, trans. and interpreted by B. Jacob (Berlin: Schocken Verlag, 1934), henceforth, *Genesis; The First Book of the Bible: Genesis*, interpreted by Benno Jacob, his commentary abridged, ed. and trans. Ernst Jacob and Walter Jacob (New York: Ktav, 1974). I used the German edition, as the English omits most scholarly references.

over Samson Raphael Hirsch.[103] The comparison was fitting. Both of their commentaries advanced syntheses of rabbinic and liberal Jacob. Hirsch was more original, Jacob the more insightful reader. Hirsch was didactic and Jacob scholarly: Consulting every rabbinic and academic commentary, he combated Gunkel and his ilk every step of the way. Hirsch reflected emancipation's high hopes, and Jacob their demise.

The Babel–Bible controversy was the political crucifix of Jacob's scholarship. He was dismayed by the antisemitic endeavor to disinherit the Hebrew Bible of monotheism and by Protestant scholars' timid response, which rescued the Old Testament for Christianity but left the Jews on their own. He recognized the importance of Near Eastern archaeological findings for biblical interpretation but insisted that biblical monotheism was unique and that the Jews had a special relationship with the Bible. Biblical meaning was available only to scholars who read the Hebrew Bible from the perspective of the people for whom it was intended: A Christian could not grasp it.[104] In the 1907 *Wissenschaft des Judentums* congress, Jacob came out with a bold statement, urging the development of academic Jewish biblical scholarship.[105] He reviewed the historic mission of Jewish Studies in advancing emancipation, and suggested that in light of antisemitism and Christian theological prejudice, the project would remain political for the foreseeable future. He warned that unless Jews gave up religious dogmatism and developed biblical scholarship, Jewish Studies would remain an untenable enterprise, a tower built up in the air without foundation. A heated debate followed Jacob's speech, marking his entry into biblical studies as a recognized scholar.

Jacob's "multicultural" politics, peculiar for his age, and the ethnocentric claim of ownership over the Bible, were actually directed toward promoting liberal Judaism. He upheld ethical monotheism, and, a vehement anti-Zionist, remained committed to emancipation and hopeful about it. German Jews felt religious and ethnic solidarity with Jews around the world, he said, but they were part of the German nation.[106] His Jacob & Esau commentary made no effort to recapture the messianic expectation of national redemption but, on the contrary, vindicated Israel's universal mission. Like his younger Weimar colleagues, however,

---

[103] Neḥama Leibowitz, *Studies in the Book of Genesis in the Context of Ancient and Modern Jewish Bible Commentary*, trans. and adapted from the Hebrew by Aryeh Newman (Jerusalem: World Zionist Organization, 1972), commentary on Va-yishlach.

[104] Christian Wiese, "The Best Antidote to Anti-Semitism?" pp. 173–81.

[105] Benno Jacob, *Die Wissenschaft des Judentums: Ihr Einfluß auf die Emanzipation* (Berlin: Poppelhauer, 1907).

[106] *Krieg, Revolution und Judentum* (Dortmund: n.p., 1919).

Jacob thought that Protestant theology and biblical scholarship required a firm Jewish response, and, like them, he went to the Bible to draft his response (albeit with the rabbis as his methodological guide). His commentary highlighting the ethnic impurity of Esau's family reflected the age's growing racialization of culture. German-Jewish liberalism showed marks of racialization just like its non-Jewish counterpart.

Above all, however, Jacob's commentary was a hermeneutical project. The Torah, he said, expressed the Jewish people's essence, its worldview and spirit. As a literary composition, it melded diverse traditions and sources. He understood Moses' authorship and the Torah's divinity, spiritually rather than historically. His Patriarchs were literary figures, and their historicity was of no interest. He occasionally called biblical stories "legends." Unlike the Orthodox Hoffmann, he did not seek to refute Wellhausen but, rather, to show that the historical project of dating layers of the text and tracking Israel's religious development was nebulous and untenable. The Torah's editor(s) intervened so decisively that they created a unifying text with new themes. The J & E sources were interwoven beyond recognition in the Jacob & Esau narrative. It made more sense to ask for any P addition's meaning in the context of the story, rather than speculate on what it might have originally looked like. Indeed, the Torah showed such cogency and artfulness of design that it was more proper to speak of its author (*Verfasser*) than its redactor, and inquire first and foremost about its meaning as a unified work.[107] Two millennia of Jewish exegesis had undertaken such an exegetical task, and Jewish culture emerged from them. Benno Jacob was bringing the project up to date. Midrash had elucidated meanings as they emerged from textual tensions, and modern biblical criticism pointed to textual fissures that called for similar elucidation. "Exegesis has the first word": The proper approach to the Torah was hermeneutical, and the method literary and philological.[108]

To Benno Jacob, the Jacob & Esau story constituted the final episode in the transmission of God's blessing among the Patriarchs. He noted that Isaac, the least developed patriarchal figure, was also the one most often called "blessed"; hence, his major role was as a transmitter: The blessed Isaac blessed Jacob (rather than Esau). To critics who viewed the

---

[107] Jacob, *Die Thora Moses* (Frankfurt am Main: Kauffmann, 1912/13).
[108] Quoted in Almuth Jürgensen, "Die Exegese hat das erste Wort: Zu Benno Jacobs Bibelauslegung," in *Die Exegese hat das erste Wort: Beiträge zu Leben und Werk Benno Jacobs*, ed. Almuth Jürgensen (Stuttgart: Calwer, 2002), p. 124. See also Walter Jacob, "The Life and Work of Benno Jacob," and Maren Ruth Niehoff, "Benno Jacob's Concept of a *Wissenschaft des Judentums*," in the same volume, pp. 11–31, 85–97, respectively.

Avimelekh story (Genesis 26) as interrupting the Jacob & Esau flow, and a mere repetition of the Abraham story (Genesis 20), which was due to a competing tradition, Jacob suggested that the Avimelekh story was essential in establishing Isaac as the transmitter.[109] He also noted that the Jacob & Esau narrative was composed of a series of encounters, each between two figures, and only two. After the sale of the right of the firstborn, Jacob and Esau would never meet until they reconciled. The absences and dialogues allowed for plot development: Misunderstandings, schemes, and tensions mounted, but the end showed them all to have been part of the divine plan for Israel.[110]

Like nineteenth-century liberal commentators, and unlike the rabbis, Benno Jacob viewed critically Jacob's birthright purchase and his trickery in obtaining the blessing. In contrast, he regarded Jacob's struggle with the angel, and his new name Israel, as transformative and triumphal. The Jacob & Esau story represented for him less a *Bildungsroman* and more a tragedy. All protagonists misinterpreted God's oracle, "the elder shall serve the younger," assuming that it referred to Jacob and Esau themselves, rather than to their descendants. Jacob's travail was in vain. Abraham's blessing, the one given by Isaac to Jacob before he went abroad, bestowing fatherhood of the nation and the Land of Israel, was going to Jacob anyway. The blessing of political dominion, stolen at Rebecca's behest, never materialized. Earning his brother's enmity, Jacob had to endure twenty years of drudgery in exile, returned trembling for his life, conceded the blessing to Esau in humiliation, and ended up limping. The high value that all parties set on the father's blessing, said Jacob, was the story's only redeeming dimension.[111]

That said, Benno Jacob consistently defended Jacob and the patriarchs against Gunkel's stereotyping of them as conniving Jews acting in a primitive tribal culture. In tricking Isaac to receive the blessing, the biblical narrative showed Jacob to be a passive agent of Rebecca's scheme, and not a conniver, said Jacob.[112] While mistaken, Rebecca, for her part, was not unreasonable in wishing for her beloved worthy son to get the blessing. Gunkel's suggestion that Isaac asked to touch Jacob in order to identify a peculiar Jewish smell was ridiculous: If racial smell were at stake, Isaac, Jacob, and Esau would surely have all had the same one![113]

The blessing trickery had been Jacob's low point, and he was improving as time went on. His Bethel vow should not be understood, said Benno Jacob, as making his service to God conditional upon God's protection: It meant that if he survived, he would be able to serve God, and he noted

---

[109] *Genesis*, pp. 555–60. Abimelech is the common English spelling.
[110] Ibid., pp. 574–77.   [111] Ibid.   [112] Ibid., pp. 562–63.   [113] Ibid., p. 566.

survival's minimal conditions.[114] Abroad, at his uncle's place, Jacob dealt squarely with Laban, an avaricious peasant who took advantage of his love for Rachel and cheated him. This was, indeed, a tit for tat for his trickery in obtaining the blessing.[115] Gunkel's sniping criticism of Jewish family life received equally sniping responses. For the mandrakes, which Leah gave Rachel in return for a night with Jacob, Benno Jacob conjectured a lovely romantic exchange between the sisters. For Jacob's partiality toward loved ones in placing Rachel and Joseph in the rear before meeting Esau, Benno Jacob opined that it was a matter of orderly presentation of nobility and not of protection.[116] Besides, he scoffed, what did all this have to do with modern Jewish family life?

When Jacob prostrated himself before Esau in their final encounter, he underwent great humiliation to gain Esau's forgiveness. How could Gunkel see him scheming, asked Benno Jacob?[117] Gunkel's suggestion that, in the original primitive story, it was actually Jacob who dislocated the river divinity's hip, and not the angel who dislocated Jacob's, met with Benno Jacob's incredulity. "Jacob, the tribal ancestor of the 'Jews,'" he said acerbically, "is especially unsympathetic to the [Religious Historical] School, so they do not shy away from impossible tricks to make him into one."[118] Always taking the Torah author's perspective, and discounting possible earlier voices, Benno Jacob relentlessly exposed Gunkel's use of cultural anthropology and history as masquerading racial prejudices.

Yet Benno Jacob had his own racial prejudices. Why was Esau excluded from the blessing? Benno Jacob followed the rabbinic philology of Edom and Seir, drawing on "red" as signaling Esau's bloody savagery and on "hair" as intimating his coarse and intemperate passion, but, insistent on viewing the Torah as reflecting Moses' universe, he stopped short of the rabbis' imputation of Roman and Christian mores to Esau. Providing on occasion a hint to the rabbinic typology, he always hastened back to his own hermeneutics, set in the imagined Mosaic author's time. This meant that Benno Jacob lacked the rabbis' cultural resources to vindicate Jacob's choice over Esau. Instead, he underlined Esau's racial impurity. Intermarriage was Esau's major inadequacy. First marrying Canaanite women, then undiscerningly opting for Ishmael's ethnically impure daughter (Genesis 29:9), Esau renounced Abraham's blessing.[119] Genesis 36 outlined Esau's genealogy (*toledot*) to explain why he did not become the third patriarch.[120] Both Midrash and liberal commentators elicited multiple biblical voices to explain Esau's moral depravity.

---

[114] Ibid., pp. 584–85.   [115] Ibid., pp. 588–91.
[116] Ibid., pp. 597–98 and 644–45, respectively.   [117] Ibid., p. 645.   [118] Ibid., p. 641.
[119] Ibid., p. 574.   [120] Ibid., p. 692.

In Benno Jacob, morality itself became racial. Esau's incestuous Edomite genealogy was a caricature, he said: "Not their different religious belief but their immorality is the foremost abomination to Israel."[121] A racializing German culture sensitized Jacob to the Priestly redactor's concern with ethnic purity, and his imagined Mosaic author and denial of the Torah's multivocality came to haunt his liberalism with a vengeance. Jacob was morally superior because racially pure.

Benno Jacob's imagined author and Gunkel's taunting were also responsible, however, for Jacob's greatest insight. The struggle with the angel, he said, was the response to Jacob's earlier prayer to be saved from Esau. A midrash suggested that the stranger struggling with Jacob in the midst of night was Esau's guardian angel.[122] By enduring the struggle with his Satan, the obstacle in his life path, Jacob withstood a test comparable to the *Aqedah*, and showed himself ready for the divine mission. He went through an internal transformation, casting off his reprehensible ambition – symbolized by the sinew removed by Jews from slaughtered animals – and became Israel, God's fighter, the Torah's messenger to humanity. His reward was not only the blessing and new name but also, unbeknownst to Jacob, the injury itself. By causing Jacob's limp, the angel undid, symbolically and physically, his earlier life, and removed the cause of Esau's enmity: Jacob's endeavor to supplant Esau that had earned him his name, Yaakov.[123] The injury saved him from Esau. Seeing the limping Jacob prostrate himself, Esau, a sentimental savage, quick to anger and reconcile, no longer saw the young Jacob who had outmaneuvered him. The rabbis' suspicion of Esau's reconciliation was justified in view of the future history of Edom–Israel relations, and Jacob and Esau did have to separate as they had different missions, but Jacob made peace with both God and Man, and was now forgiven by both.

There are few, if any, moments in modern exegesis comparable to Benno Jacob's Jacob & the angel for their insight into the redactor, for weaving Midrash and liberal exegesis, and for sheer beauty. "He opened our eyes to see things which we had not seen before," said the Orthodox Neḥamah Leibowitz, explaining her affinity for Jacob, "an extreme Reformer [and] anti-Zionist."[124] Rosenzweig and Buber appreciated Jacob, as did a few European and Israeli commentators. A leading German biblical scholar, Gerhard von Rad, would discover him in the postwar years. But in Weimar, let alone in Nazi Germany, there was only limited audience for his commentary, and no prospect for the

---

[121] Ibid.   [122] *Bereshit Rabba*, 73:8, 74:8; *Genesis*, p. 643.   [123] *Genesis*, p. 642.

[124] Neḥamah Leibowitz, "Accept the Truth from Wherever It Comes," letter to Rabbi Yehudah Ansbacher, http://www.library.yctorah.org/files/2016/09/Accept-the-Truth-from-wherever-it-Comes.pdf. Original in *Alon Shvut-Bogrim* 13 (1999): 71–92.

multicultural politics that gave rise to it. To appreciate his commentary, uncommon skills were needed. Christian scholars ignored him, and his Jewish audience vanished with his immigration. In England, with limited library and financial means at his disposal, he labored, almost alone, over an Exodus commentary that would be published only decades later.[125] In today's academy, biblical scholars could have accommodated his effort to turn Midrash into an academic discipline, and his Jewish ethnocentrism would have been no obstacle. In Weimar Germany, neither stood a chance.

Unlike Samson Raphael Hirsch's celebration of Jacob & Esau's reconciliation, Benno Jacob's exegesis was free of eschatology and references to Jewish–Christian relations, but it was equally instructive about the fortunes of emancipation. In Jacob, gone are Hirsch's joy and hopes, his Bildungsroman, and his majestic Matriarchs. Instead, racialized Jacob and Esau step in, each going his separate way, with Jacob limping and his universal mission remaining unrecognized by non-Jews. Yet Jacob's limping still evokes Esau's sympathy. Emancipation's hopes are dimmed, but an injured, submissive Jacob could still affect Esau. Hitler and the Nazis do not figure in this picture. Amaleq is not an imminent danger, and genocide is beyond Jacob's horizons. Jacob's *Genesis* commentary marks the twilight of emancipation but not of the Holocaust.

Unlike most of his Wilhelmine and Weimar contemporaries, Benno Jacob staged a loving return to rabbinic Jacob, and showed the vitality of the rabbinic tradition and its potential for innovation. Like Baeck, Buber, Cohen, and Rosenzweig, however, he endeavored to close the Bible to history, a protective measure against Protestant biblical criticism that became antisemitic. The retreat of exegesis from history in the age of antisemitism contrasted with its joyous deployment of history at the height of emancipation. The retreat was an alarming sign of emancipation's diminishing prospects, and it did not protect Jewish culture against its own racialization. Rabbinic and scholarly constructions of Jacob & Esau track the damage that racialization inflicted on the Jews. Today's reader of Benno Jacob's *Genesis* may experience a combination of wonder and disquiet, marveling at his insight while being unnerved by his ethnocentrism. Only a short time ago, academic celebration of postcolonial "reversal of the gaze" was common. Jacob was presumably using the masters' tools to undermine their domination. One would only wish! Reversal is double-edged, and racism corrupts the oppressed minorities, too. German Jews did not remain immune.

---

[125] Benno Jacob, *Das Buch Exodus*, ed. Shlomo Mayer in collaboration with Joachim Hahn and Almuth Jürgensen (Stuttgart: Calwer, 1997).

10 Esau the *Goy*: Jewish and German Ethnic Myths, 1891–1945

"Only the memory of Jewish nationality has survived . . . truly, it is dead," the Jewish emancipation warrior and future vice president of the 1848 Frankfurt parliament, Gabriel Riesser, reassured his Prussian compatriots in 1832.[1] He spoke too soon: Jewish nationality was about to be reinvented. To the eighteenth-century encyclopedist, the Jews were "the most ancient of nations," but, like other Europeans, Jews were developing a modern consciousness of ethnicity and nationhood in the second half of the nineteenth century.[2]

A powerful sense of belongingness to the majority nation stymied Jewish national consciousness in Western Europe and Germany proper. Only a single delegate, Oskar Cohn, wished for the Weimar Constitution to extend minority language rights, given to the Poles and the Danes, to the Jews as well. Things looked different, however, across Germany's eastern and southern borders. Pre–World War I nationalization in pluralist empires, the lack of emancipation in Russia, and, in the interwar years, the new ethno-nationalizing states encouraged Jewish nationalization. In the 1921 national census, 53.6 percent of Czechoslovakian Jews declared Jewish nationality, ranging from 14.5 percent of Bohemian Jews to 87 percent of Subcarpathian Ruthenian Jews.[3] In Bohemia, the percentage increased to about twenty by 1930. In intensely antisemitic Poland, a consciousness of separation from the Polish nation grew rapidly among Jews in the 1930s.[4] Across Europe, sometimes obliquely and always unevenly, the Jews were becoming a nationality.

---

[1] *Gesammelte Schriften*, 4 vols. (Frankfurt am Main: Riesser-Stiftung, 1867), 3: 366–67.

[2] "Juif," in *Encyclopédie ou dictionnaire raisonné des sciences, des arts et des métiers* [1772], ed. Denis Diderot, 9:25, http://encyclopedie.uchicago.edu: "Nous ne connaissons point de nation plus ancienne que la juive." My thanks to Michael Silber for the reference.

[3] Michael Brenner, "Religion, Nation oder Stamm: Zum Wandel der Selbstdefinition unter deutschen Juden," in *Nation und Religion in der deutschen Geschichte*, ed. Heinz-Gerhard Haupt and Dieter Langewiesche (Frankfurt: Campus Verlag, 2001), p. 592.

[4] Kenneth Moss, "Negotiating Jewish Nationalism in Interwar Warsaw," in *Warsaw: The Jewish Metropolis*, ed. Glenn Dynner and Francois Guesnet (Leiden: Brill, 2015).

In Russian Eastern Europe, nationalization often appeared to be the road to emancipation rather than an alternative to it. Jewish Diaspora nationalism sought emancipation premised on imperial multinationalism, securing the Jews cultural and political autonomy. That said, Zionism's differential regional spread showed an intimate relationship between emancipation's dimming prospects and Zionism's rise: Pogrom-ridden Ukraine became the center of Zionist Ḥibat Ẓiyon – "Come, descendants of Jacob, let us go" (Isaiah 2:5) – whereas the less violent Russian North became the center of the socialist *Bund*.

Traditional Jewry, still a majority in Russia, sought neither Eastern- nor Western-style emancipation but retained an older religious understanding of the Jews' separateness. Its leaders responded testily to the Russian-acculturated Jewish intelligentsia and, later on, to the Zionists, but showed creativity in responding to other cultural challenges. The Volozhin Yeshivah, with its highly intellectualized study method, was a prime example. Its closure, in 1891, for refusing to open up a general studies program was an alarming signal that Jewish Orthodoxy found the room for intellectual maneuvering narrowing. The Bolshevik Revolution upset all schemes. The militantly secular acculturation, enforced from above, was not the one that most Russian Jews dreamed about. It threw traditional Jewry into despair. Well before the Nazis, Amaleq, the mythical perpetrator of genocide, staged a return in Ultra-Orthodox discourse, designating Jewish communists and others who challenged rabbinic Judaism as such.

A rising national literature provides one sign of a nationality's formation. Not surprisingly, modern Yiddish and Hebrew literatures were preponderantly Eastern rather than Western European in origin. In Congress Poland (Russian Poland, as created by the Congress of Vienna) and Russia alike, the Jewish intelligentsia operated in divergent settings from those in Germany or Austria: Russian imperial administration was hostile, constitutional protections were limited, as were professional opportunities, and the inspiration offered by Russian populism and the Russian revolutionary intelligentsia was unique. In Poland, Romantic nationalism closed avenues of integration to the Polish-Jewish intellectual, which the German-Jewish intellectual imagined having, and the landed gentry provided a motif unique to Polish-Jewish literature, the haughty estate owner, the פּריץ. All the same, the boundaries of East and West, and especially of German-speaking Europe, were permeable. Not only did Galician Austrian-Jewish writers play a major role in Jewish national literature, but many Eastern European Jewish writers lived for a while in Germany proper, and German literature left a deep mark on

Hebrew literature. Jewish nationalist networks crossed borders, and the Zionists represented the quintessential international network. Yiddish and Hebrew literatures were formed in conversation with German culture.

Esau returned as a major literary *topos* in Jewish national literature. He cast divergent figures. In their Yiddish works, Russian- and Polish-acculturated Jewish writers, from Mendele Moykher Sforim to Sholem Aleichem to Y. L. Peretz, adopted popular conceptions of Esau from the rabbinic idiom and turned them into ethnic ones. Esau emerged as the *Goy*, the non-Jew, the quintessential Other. Zionist writer Ḥayim Naḥman Bialik provided the equivalent in Hebrew, as did other authors. This remained by far the most common view of Esau. Yet as racialization was running amok throughout Europe in the 1930s, Esau's ethnicity began to overwhelm his typological otherness. In Itẓik Manger's Yiddish poetry, Asher Barash's Hebrew novels, and Soma Morgenstern's German novels, Esau appears as a Jewish youth gone astray. In the novels of Barash and Morgenstern's, Esau comes back home.

Homecoming brought out Esau's traditional Jewish qualities, precisely those that right-wing Zionist poet Uri Ẓvi Greenberg (1896–1981) rejected. Elucidating the rabbinic vision of Rome as Jewish history's great trauma, Greenberg renounced rabbinic Jacob & Esau and explored a fascist politics vested in a Roman Esau. The Roman legionnaire and Zionist settler became one. Returning as multiple figures – the Goy, the Jew, or the Zionist – the new Esau displayed racialization's potency but also revealed contesting Jewish visions of relations with non-Jews, in Europe and Palestine alike.

Esau's return signaled Jacob's demotion in Jewish national discourse. For many Zionists, rabbinic Jacob cast an unheroic figure, unsuitable for the national struggle. They objected to rabbinic idealization of Jacob's piety and peacefulness and, seeking to reshape Jewish national character, rejected his "exilic" personality. In contrast with Zionism, in German-Jewish literature, Jacob & Esau continued to convey cosmopolitan messages of reconciliation and peace. Unlike nineteenth-century visions of reconciliation, which projected a better world coming with emancipation, twentieth-century portrayals of Jacob & Esau represented dreams of peace that were staged against a reality of national conflicts and world war. This was as true for Zionist Richard Beer-Hofmann as it was for the expressionist poet Else Lasker-Schüler, or for the assimilated Russian-Jewish émigré dramatist Waldemar Jollos. Their Jacob & Esau were utopias dreamed in a world turned awry, and they were no match for mounting antisemitism.

The racial antisemites themselves made a cursory effort to deploy Jacob & Esau – folkish German nationalist writer Wilhelm Schäfer was one example – but largely desisted. Nazi racial myths made only sparing use of traditional antisemitic stereotypes of Jacob. The silence was more ominous than the stereotypes: It indicated that the Nazis were seeking a break with Europe's biblical heritage.

How was one to answer the Nazi racial myth? Orthodox Jewish playwright Sammy Gronemann tried satirical subversion. Thomas Mann, in contrast, constructed a countermyth: He turned the Jewish Patriarchs into Oriental demigods. In a two-decade-long project that stretched from Weimar into World War II, Mann delved into the Ancient East, remythologized the Bible, and made both Jacob and Joseph emblems of European culture. Like his Weimar Jewish compatriots, Mann, too, endeavored to retrieve the biblical world without the mediation of tradition and disposed of two millennia of Christian and Jewish typology. His Jacob & Esau story used *Midrash* extensively but purged any meaning that appeared to go beyond the biblical world. Such a project involved grave risks, and by the time Mann was done, he recognized as much. In purging the Jewish and Christian legacy, he appeared on many occasions to be toying with myths as gruesome as those of his Nazi enemies.

Mann's myth was no more a match for the Nazis than were German-Jewish dreams. Antisemites searched for ways to exorcise the Jews from European life. They found no way of doing so: The Jews, after all, had always been a part of Europe and the foundation of its Christian heritage. Jewish nationalism represented no solution: For most Jews, emigration to Palestine was not an option, and the nationalizing states of East-Central Europe were not going to recognize Jewish autonomy. Jewish nationality emerged in a world that had no room for it. The more radical antisemites, persuaded that either Europe or the Jews had to go, began imagining Europe without them.[5] The political and intellectual groundwork that would make the mythical Amaleq into a reality began forming. The Holocaust signaled the collapse of the two-millennia paradigm and the triumph of secular racism, an illegitimate child of nationalism, over the belligerent brotherhood of Christians and Jews.

Among traditional Jews, especially the Ultra-Orthodox rabbis, the Holocaust brought a powerful return of Amaleq in Jewish discourse. As Europe moved from exclusion to murder, Amaleq absorbed Edom and Esau. Just prior to the Holocaust, a Galician Jewish writer, Soma Morgenstern (1890–1976), provided an alternative model to both

---

[5] Alon Confino, *A World without Jews: The Nazi Imagination from Persecution to Genocide* (New Haven, CT: Yale University Press, 2014).

Mann and Jewish Orthodoxy in negotiating modernity's challenges. He sought a loving rapprochement between Jewish Orthodoxy and modern culture. During the 1930s and the early years of World War II, he wrote a trilogy, *Sparks in the Abyss*, that evoked Jacob & Esau by telling of the return home of lost sons.[6] He may be instructive as to how one might begin a post-Holocaust *tiqun*, collecting sparks in the abyss by reconfiguring Jacob & Esau to tell a story different from the ones that Christians and Jews had told for millennia, and yet one grounded in history and tradition.

Yiddish Literature Between Nationalism and Internationalism

The Jewish national intelligentsia transformed rabbinic Jacob and Esau into ethnic types. They became folk heroes and national models, and Jewish–Christian relations emerged as a prolonged ethno-cultural conflict rooted in the trauma of Jewish homelessness. At the same time, by subverting rabbinic models, Jewish nationalism also opened up opportunities for new Jacob and Esau types, even universal ones: Jacob the lover and Esau the fighter and man of nature. The innovation generated by nationalism was as extensive as the one that had been triggered earlier by emancipation. Jewish writers recognized themselves as Jacob's descendants, and for most, Esau was a Goy and a hostile non-Jew. Yet as they wished to overcome exilic life and reconstitute nationhood, the nationalists sought also to transcend rabbinic Jacob. Nationalist discourses either reconfigured Jacob or searched for alternative protagonists who would better convey the national message. As nationalist visions diverged, so did Jacob & Esau, who embodied Jewish nationality's competing visions.

Yiddish, Hebrew, and German-Jewish literatures reconfigured Jacob & Esau against the backdrop of growing antisemitism and World War I. Not surprisingly, in Jewish national literature, the brothers' reconciliation virtually disappeared. It did persist, however, in German-Jewish literature. This section focuses on Jacob & Esau in Yiddish literature, using Mendele Moykher-Sforim, Sholem Aleichem, Y. L. Peretz, and Itzik Manger to track Esau's image from late imperial Russia to interwar Poland. The next section moves on to Hebrew literature and the new Zionist Esau, highlighting Ḥayim Naḥman Bialik, Uri Zvi Greenberg, Anda Amir-Pinkerfeld, and Asher Barash. Three German-Jewish utopias are the subject of a third section, concluding the discussion of Jewish literature. On the eve of World

---

[6] Soma Morgenstern, *Der Sohn des verlorenen Sohnes: Erster Roman der Trilogie Funken im Abgrund; Idyll im Exil: Zweiter Roman der Trilogie Funken im Abgrund; Das Vermächtnis des verlorenen Sohnes: Dritter Roman der Trilogie Funken im Abgrund*, ed. with a postscript by Ingolf Schulte (Lüneburg: Zu Klampen, 1996).

War I, expressionist poet Else Lasker-Schüller imagined peaceful romantic togetherness between Jacob and Esau, and in World-War I Switzerland, Waldemar Jollos, a German-educated Russian-Jewish exile, wrote an expressionist drama, *Esau und Jakob*, that ended with reconciliation, resignation, and hope for divine revelation.[7] Likewise, in Richard Beer-Hofmann, a saintly Jacob, embodying the Jewish ethical mission, carried on a pacifist struggle against a violent Esau, ending in their reconciliation and Jacob's acceptance of his mission as the world's suffering servant.[8] Expressionist visions of peace and war stretched from German-Jewish to Zionist Hebrew literature, reflecting the shared intellectual universe of divergent and competitive Jewish European cultures.

***

"Woe to Esau, the Goy! His wineglass is his life, drink he must ... strike he must, for he is a Goy." But "behold how good Jacob's portion is! The Rock of God his life is, thanks [to God] he must give, for Jacob is his name."[9] Bialik's 1922 poem, purportedly a folk song transcribed by the author, captured Jacob and Esau's prototypes in Yiddish literature. The learned, pious Jew, loyal to his family, contrasted with the violent drunken Goy. Bialik's portraits drew on the rabbinic original but also reflected Jewish and antisemitic racial stereotypes: the frail but clever Jew contrasted with the dim masculine Goy. Literary motifs associated with the Goy could be tracked in earlier Rabbinic literature, for example, in the *Zenah u-Renah*, but the Jewish national writers did not merely record folk tales, and their Goy was not the rabbinic Other.[10] Rather, the national writers refashioned popular discourse to construct Esau as a model Goy. Esau remained unmistakably Christian, but his ethnicity overwhelmed his religious character. Early modern distinctions between Greek Orthodoxy and Roman Catholicism collapsed, and Esau expanded his reach east into Russia as the national Other.

Israel Bartal pointed out the simultaneous growth of acculturation and ethnicization, internationalism and tropes of the non-Jewish Other, the Goy, among Russian-Jewish intellectuals. In the Jacob & Esau portrayals in Yiddish literature, one can track the changing fortunes of Jewish–non-Jewish relations, as early hopes for acculturation and reform dissipate and antagonism toward the Russian authorities and suspicion of non-Jews grow.[11] Sholem Yankev Abramovich

---

[7] *Esau und Jakob* (Berlin: S. Fischer, 1919).
[8] *Jaákobs Traum: Ein Vorspiel* (Berlin: S. Fischer, 1919).
[9] Chaim Nachman Bialik, *Collected Poems – Critical Edition* (in Hebrew), ed. Dan Miron et al., 3 vols. (Tel Aviv: Devir, 1983–90): 2 (1899–1934): 359–60.
[10] Israel Bartal, "Non-Jews and Gentile Society in East European Hebrew and Yiddish Literature, 1856–1914" (in Hebrew) (Ph.D. diss., The Hebrew University, 1980), p. 5.
[11] Ibid., pp. 10, 269.

(1836–1917), better known under his literary name, Mendele Moykher-Sforim (Mendele the book peddler), exemplified the *Haskalah*'s criticism of traditional Jewish life and initial hopes for political reform. His Jacob was lame, and his Esau was benevolent. In Solomon Rabinovich (1859–1916), known as Sholem Aleichem, and Isaac Leib Peretz (1852–1915), Esau reassumed his traditional role as a "pogromist." By the 1930s, Itzik Manger (1901–1969) had to resort to a midrashic mode to envision the biblical rivalry playing out in contemporary Poland. Deteriorating ethnic relations made deployment of a realistic literary mode difficult.

Mendele Moykher-Sforim's *Sefer ha-Qabzanim* (1869; Book of beggars), a novel about Jews on the margins of the *shtetl*, showed the Jewish poor strategizing about getting food and charity, rather than educating themselves and working to improve their lot. Jacob's voice conveyed Jewish impotence and intimated a dissimulating Jewish character, however harmless, whereas Esau's hands did the good work. As the carriage of two traditional Jews gets stuck in the mud, the *goyim*, "Esau's folkskins," push it out, "and it was obvious from their ability that the hands were Esau's hands. Our power, in contrast, was only our voice: 'The voice is Jacob's.' As the [*goyim*] were pushing, we exclaimed repeatedly, 'push well,' as if voice could help pushing. We sighed, and our bodies jerked, as if we were really pushing."[12] The goyim may be unrefined, and they taunt the Jews for their religious dressing, but, physically strong, they accomplish the task. As farmers, they can be models for Jews. Later in Mendele's life, the Goy's image became less positive: When Jews collect berries on his land, "Esau," the owner, may fall upon them, rob and beat them.[13] Yet Mendele remained an optimist. The goyim's violence was generally not directed against Jews. Encounters between Jews and non-Jews in the pub created parodic scenes of Jacob & Esau friendship.[14]

The change of mood was evident in Sholem Aleichem. The pogrom waves and government repression transformed Esau into a surrogate for antisemitic officials and violent mobs. *Tevye the Milkman* described the goyim initiating a 1905 pogrom, and the policeman bringing Tevye an

---

[12] *Sefer Ha-Qabzanim*, with an essay by Dan Miron (Tel Aviv: Devir, 1988), p. 11; *Kol Kitve Mendele Mocher Sefarim* (Tel Aviv: Devir, 1947), p. 92. Mendele wrote the novel, titled *Fishke der Kramer* (Fishke the lame), first in Yiddish, then, together with Bialik, translated the novel into Hebrew.

[13] *Kol Kitve Mendele*, p. 278.

[14] Israel Bartal, "Non-Jews and Gentile Society," pp. 128–29. As Bartal points out (pp. 122–23), Mendele's benevolent view of the Goy drew the ire of Hebrew literary critics. One such critic, Avraham Qariv, thought that the picture of non-Jews drawing a Jewish carriage out of the mud reversed historical reality.

order of expulsion from his village in 1912, as Esau.[15] Tevye had lived in peace with the villagers, and thought that the help he had rendered them protected him. Not so. Even his appeal to the villagers' God did not help. In the end, Esau came back to avenge himself on Jacob, as he always would. Suspicion and hostility appeared to be the norm of Jewish–non-Jewish relations, and religious difference now marked a heritage of national hatred. Ukrainians and Russians, Uniate and Orthodox, all merged into one collectivity of non-Jews, configured as Esau, the Jews' archenemy.

Even more telling than Esau the pogromist was Esau the Christian convert. In a touching scene in *Haye Adam* (A man's life), the protagonist, the boy Shalom, is curious about a river barge's driver, a boy, like him, pulling the barge's rope.[16] He pities the boy for doing Esau's hard work and feels fortunate to be among Jacob's descendants, and not condemned, like Esau, to servitude. He is then surprised to discover, under the boy's heavy professional clothing and smutty face, a familiar look – Jacob's eyes. The driver turns out to be Beryl, a widow's son who had converted to Christianity. Their looks meet, and they recognize each other. Shalom wishes first to query him how a Jew can replace his soul with an alien spirit, but soon enough a feeling of revulsion toward the stranger rises up in him. He feels separated from Beryl forever, yet he still pities him: What good has becoming a non-Jew done for his childhood playmate, who now wears weird clothing and, working exposed to the elements, seems condemned to eternal drudgery? Shalom expresses Sholem Aleichem's conflicting sentiments: The author's universalism is at war with his growing sense of Jewish separateness. Crossing the lines, the assimilated Jew became Esau. Yet precisely because ethnicity, so sharply delineated, turns out to be ephemeral – Beryl started out as Jacob – Esau, too, has a claim to humanity. The author mourns the loss of Beryl in a dual fashion: Like traditional Jews, he mourns a Jew lost, and like the intelligentsia, he bemoans humanity's loss.

Contemporaneously in Congress Poland, Y. L. Peretz made a similar trip from Polish–Jewish collaboration to neoromantic cultivation of Jewish difference. Peretz rewrote the rabbinic vision of exile and of

---

[15] *The Complete Tevye the Dairyman* (in Hebrew), trans. Dan Miron from the Yiddish (Jerusalem: Keter, 2005), pp. 161–67, 175–76. These Tevye episodes were first published in 1914 and 1916. See also Armin Eidherr, *Sonnenuntergang auf eisig-blauen Wegen: Zur Thematisierung von Diaspora und Sprache in der jiddischen Literatur des 20. Jahrhunderts* (Vienna: Vienna University Press, 2012), pp. 248–56. Eidherr's "Ejssev – das Gegenüber im Goleß," ibid., pp. 242–63, also discusses the Yiddish poets mentioned later in this section.

[16] *Haye Adam*, trans. Y. D. Berkowitz from Yiddish into Hebrew, 3 vols. (New York: Shtibel, 1920), 2: 47–48.

Esau's tutelage as a saga of the Jewish people's torment, first at God's hands, then at those of Esau. The Jews were God's piano, created to play His praise. God and Esau both played cruelly on the piano. Displeased with the piano's performance, Israel's vengeful God smashed it to pieces. The dispersed keys were the tormented Jews who had fallen silent, until rough hands, Esau's hands, pressed on them. Then they cried out in pain and expressed a lament on their loss and longing for redemption. "Esau plays," and his cruelty brought the Jewish people back to life.[17]

The shared universe of Yiddish and Hebrew national writers became evident in another Peretz short piece, "Esau's Hands."[18] Jacob, opined Peretz, became deformed in exile. He was now but a huge walking head, with big eyes and pale cheeks, mounted over a tiny body. The Jewish head, representing intellect and imagination, ascended to the highest spheres, dreaming of freedom and justice. The Jewish legs, wandering around the earth, were well enough developed, but the hands were degenerated and withered as they had not been accustomed to labor. Among non-Jews, with their tiny heads and hands like tree trunks, the Jewish head aroused fright. When non-Jews encountered it, they smacked its visage – "the hands are Esau's hands." The Jewish head, with tearful eyes and bitten lips, remained silent, and only a sigh emerged. Zionists expressed anger and a determination to fight, and dreamed of the body's regeneration – hands, fists, and nails. Not the nicest dream, said Peretz, but superior to the fantasy that Polish nationalism would combat anti-semitism: If one placed a Jewish head on a Polish nationalist's body, the body would never obey it. Peretz had arrived at a frightening view of the deformity of life in exile and the prospect of Jewish–non-Jewish relations. Jewish and antisemitic visions of the body converged, and Jacob and Esau became racial types.

For Jewish communists, the Bolshevik Revolution represented hope for fundamental change in Jewish–non-Jewish relations. Leib Kvitko (1890–1952), a member of the Kiev group of Yiddish poets, sojourned in Germany from 1921 to 1925, where he joined the Communist Party. In 1922, he published an expressionist poem, "Esau," exceptional for its beauty, offering an alternative vision of Jacob and Esau's relations.[19] Kvitko turned his attention to the fragrance of Esau's body and garments,

---

[17] *Kol Kitve Y. L. Peretz* (in Hebrew), trans. Shimshon Meltzer from the Yiddish, 10 vols. (Tel Aviv: Devir, 1961), 8: 374. The dispersed keys were a dark and dispiriting counterpart to the kabbalistic sparks.

[18] Ibid., 8: 265–66.

[19] Leib Kvitko, "Esau," (in Yiddish and English), trans. Allen Mandelbaum and Harold Rabinowitz, in *The Penguin Book of Modern Yiddish Verse*, ed. Irving Howe, Ruth R. Wisse, and Khone Shmeruk (New York: Viking, 1987), pp. 296–99.

a fragrance ignored for millennia, as rabbinic interpretations etherealized it: "The smell of my son is like the smell of a field that the LORD has blessed" (Genesis 27:27). To Kvitko, a remorseful and disenchanted Jacob (never mentioned by name) was envious of handsome Esau, the blessed man of nature. Jacob recognized that he had been living out Esau's legacy, of the "robust draft of your fragrant fields ... lying deep inside me, buried in my hidden treasures." He begged Esau to overlook his debt, as his own life's path over the ages had turned disastrous. Esau now inhabited his deepest dreams. The fields' fragrance, the good fortune Jacob had coveted in ancient times, gradually seeped into his miserable life. Merging with his guilt and pain, it spun his "great dreams [and] dark glaring stare. Look there," he urged Esau; leave me alone and return to tending your sheep. Esau's appeal was as obvious as Jacob's need for forgiveness. Esau's coveted fragrant fields still remained beyond Jacob's reach, but the revolutionary prospect alone brought to life an Esau never before seen.

In contrast with Kvitko, some noncommunist poets were thrown into despair by the wave of pogroms in the Ukraine in the aftermath of World War I. Across the Atlantic in the United States, young expressionist poet Jacob Gladstein (1896–1971), a recent émigré, sweatshop worker, and City College graduate, saw himself as "Yankl [Jacob], Reb Isaac's son," diminishing into a "tiny round dot (קײלעבדיקע פינטעלע), swirling in the eternities of ether, swathed in red veils."[20] Not only the blood spilled in the pogroms, "red, red, red," but also the waning of their Jewish heritage among the acculturated Jewish intelligentsia, "leaving behind a little heap of dirty ash," gave rise to Gladstein's anguish. In "1919," it appeared to him that Jewish life was approaching its end. In Eastern Europe, the pogroms were devastating, and in America, the attraction of non-Jewish culture was irresistible: "The great lord ringed the whole earth with sky blue. And no escape."

Not everyone was as morose, but in interwar East-Central Europe, too, hopes for the Jewish future were dying out in the 1930s. Itzik Manger (1901–1969), born in Czernowitz, Bukovina, and receiving both a traditional Jewish and a German education, was a leading figure of the Warsaw literary scene in the interwar years. In 1935, he brought out his *Khumesh-lider* (*Ḥumash* poems), republished in the postwar years as part of his *Medresh Itsik* (Itzik's *Midrash*).[21] The poems relocated biblical stories to interwar Poland, weaving together biblical, midrashic, and folkloristic

[20] Jacob Gladstein, "1919" (in Yiddish and English), trans. Cynthia Ozick, in *Modern Yiddish Verse*, pp. 425–27.

[21] *Medresh Itsik*, introduction by Dov Sadan, ed. Chone Shemruk, 2d ed. (Jerusalem: Hebrew University, 1969).

motifs to retell the Patriarchs' stories so that they spoke to contemporary life. Three poems dealt with Jacob and Esau: "The Patriarch Isaac Examines His Sons on *Shabbat* after the Meal," "Jacob Purchases the Firstborn Right from Esau," and "Jacob Snitches the Blessing from Isaac." The three poems reflected the diverse modes deployed by Manger in rewriting the biblical story, but also the burden that antisemitism imposed on the literary imagination. Like Midrash, Manger made the biblical story speak to a future age and to the conflicts of Jews and non-Jews. Unlike traditional Midrash, he made valiant efforts to relieve the stories of the conflicts' burden, to make the Patriarchs speak to domestic Jewish issues, and to portray reconciliation. With Jacob & Esau, he was only partially successful.

The scene at Isaac's shabbat table was typical of Manger's Midrash. He deployed ethnic stereotypes of Jacob and Esau, but ignored Christian–Jewish hostility and portrayed a peaceful familial scene. On a shabbat afternoon, after the meal, Isaac was humming a Ḥasidic melody that he had first heard as a baby, when Abraham rocked his cradle as Sarah was milking the goats. Isaac asked Rebecca to call the children in from the street and proceeded to ask them to recite the Torah's weekly portion. Esau, confounded, stood silent, holding in his hand a red button. Rebecca recognized that he was dumb (פארשטאפטן קאפ). Jacob, in contrast, recited the portion flawlessly, and Rebecca, proud of her wonder child (עלוי), looked at him tenderly, rejoicing. Esau had a *goyische Kopf* (non-Jewish head), but he was a Jew, and utterly harmless. Ethnic stereotypes were alive, but, ironically, Esau's genealogy undermined them: He was a family member.[22]

The birthright's purchase represented a radically different scene.[23] The topos was so heavily invested in ethnic stereotypes that interwar antisemitism made a peaceful scene impossible. Jacob was an innkeeper, a crafty traditional Jew, and Esau a dull Goy, a glutton and a drunkard. Jacob enticed Esau to the inn with the promise of free wine. Esau was at first suspicious of the "little sly Zhid" (pejorative for a Jew), but came over to him all the same. Drunk, he was hungry and asked for a dessert. The food is not free, said Jacob; let me have your birthright for the evening meal. You would not get a better price anywhere! Once again, Esau hesitated, but the stew's aroma persuaded him and he relented. Jacob hastened to put the birthright certificate in his silverware box. As Esau was eating, a rage welled up within him, and in a fit of anger, he smashed his glass and threw away the empty bowl. The atmosphere at the poem's end intimates a pogrom to come. Esau the pogromist, creation of the

[22] Ibid., pp. 47–48.   [23] Ibid., pp. 49–50.

earlier "folklorists" – Bialik, Aleichem, and Peretz – had returned. *Medresh Itsik* could not do its usual work of dissociating biblical stories from ethnic conflict. Historical reality overwhelmed peaceful familial life.

"Jacob Snitches the Blessing from Isaac" represented a median between Manger's peaceful and conflictual *midrashim*, and showed him using the Bible interchangeably to domesticate conflict and to reaffirm the national narrative.[24] The poem focused on Isaac's gluttony, Rebecca's scheme, and Jacob's wavering. It ended before Jacob would receive the blessing, and Esau was nowhere to be seen. Isaac appeared as a blind old man sleeping much of the time, and complaining, once he woke up, that "he had to fast the entire night." He loved Esau dearly for the meat he brought home. Jacob appeared to be a hapless fellow, whose mother was pushing him to take advantage of Isaac's gluttony and beat Esau to the blessing. Jacob hesitated, but he then had a vision of the future – of the ladder going up to heaven, the well with the heavy stone on it (that he would roll away to water Rachel's flock), and the two sisters waiting for him. He understood what was expected of him and proceeded to bring Isaac the food. Welcoming him joyfully and tenderly as "Esau, my golden child," Isaac inquired what he brought from the hunt. Responding, Jacob stuttered, then fell silent, and the poem ends with the oven and the grill whispering in the background, simultaneously mocking the spectacle and portending the future, an uneven combination of irony and pathos.

Manger often had his protagonists, biblical figures masquerading as Polish Jewish characters, consult the biblical narrative and fulfill their roles accordingly. When Rachel went to the well to meet Jacob, the biblical narrative reminded her that a guest would be waiting there, and she had to rush.[25] The encounter with the Bible was often humorous, and modern typology – Jacob and Rachel reenacting their biblical meeting – created parodic romantic scenes. But with Jacob as a national ancestor, things were different. The ladder and well reaffirmed his mission. The patriarchs could be pathetic but the mission, and the national narrative, remained intact. Irony and playfulness had their limits, and Manger's repression of ethno-national conflict was tenuous. In *The Interpretation of Dreams*, Freud insisted that all dreams were wish fulfillment, and that even nightmares concealed greater fears. Critics of Freud may chafe, but in *Medresh Itzik*, Manger's desperate endeavor to imagine a peaceful familial world amidst ethnic strife suggests that even his angry Esau, breaking the dishes, concealed deeper anxiety about Jewry's future.

[24] Ibid., pp. 51–52.   [25] Ibid., pp. 53–56.

The Zionists' New Esau

Jacob & Esau show the intellectual worlds of Yiddish and Hebrew literatures converging. Leading Zionist poet Ḥayim Naḥman Bialik (1873–1934) wrote mostly in Hebrew, but his portrayal of Esau as a Goy mirrored Yiddish literature. Hebrew and Yiddish patterns, however, also diverged. Jacob was not a Zionist hero: He embodied the diasporic Jew whom Zionists wished to reform. They shared Gladstein's anxiety that Yankl, Reb Isaac's son, was becoming "a tiny round dot," and they were determined to arrest the Jewish Diaspora's purported decline, but they were not about to protect rabbinic Jacob. Instead, they both transformed his character and marginalized him. Zionist poets imagined Jacob as a romantic lover, and schoolbooks pictured him, along with the other Patriarchs, as representatives of the Jewish people's life in the Land before the exile.[26] Moreover, they invented military heroes, from Judas Maccabeus to Bar-Kokhba, who sidelined pious Jacob. The military heroes reflected collective national goals, whereas the romantic lover expressed Zionism's individualist dimension. Jacob remained present in the Zionist imagination, but as a shadowy ancestor he faded into the background.

Remarkably, the overthrow of rabbinic authority also made previously unimaginable Esau portrayals possible. Right-wing Zionist poet Uri Żvi Greenberg represented the most radical version: He envisioned Zionist youth as Roman legionnaires. But there were also gentle portrayals of Esau. Anda Amir-Pinkerfeld (1902–1981) portrayed him as a kind, loving man of nature. Asher Barash's protagonist in *Ahavah Zarah* (Foreign love; אהבה זרה), Pereż, was a gentle Jewish Esau. Released from the Austrian army, Pereż returned to his traditional Galician Jewish family, and, ending an unconsummated love affair with a Polish girl, he, as well as his brother Kovke (Jacob), married their step-sisters.[27] Responding to the impassable ethnic boundaries of the 1930s, Manger and Barash both brought Esau back home. Ironically, nationalism re-Judaized Esau. Ethnicization and secularization opened up new avenues as they closed older ones.

This may seem outlandish to readers tracking Jacob & Esau in Zionist authors, and some backtracking may help. Jacob the wandering Jew and Esau his violent persecutor did remain a leitmotif in Bialik's work. An early poem from Bialik's time in the Volozhin Yeshivah, "Jacob & Esau:

---

[26] J. Schoneveld, *The Bible in Israeli Education* (Amsterdam: Van Gorcum, 1976).

[27] *Kitve Asher Barash* (Collected works; in Hebrew), 3 vols. (Tel Aviv: Massada, 1952), 1: 253–353. I owe the discovery of Jacob & Esau in Barash to Shai Ginsburg of Duke University.

A Folk Legend," deployed the stereotypes of Jacob the innkeeper and Esau the raging robber.[28] Losing his way in the snow, the hunter Esau, hungry and desperate, notices a light in the distance – Jacob's inn. Jacob had fled his home penniless fourteen years earlier, fearful of his brother's persecution, and left his dying old father and a loving mother behind. He was armed only with their blessing, but the ladder vision reassured him, and in a lonesome place, he built the inn. Now Esau knocks on the door and, coming in, demands wine, warning Jacob not to cheat him. Envious of Jacob's warm abode and imagining the inn but another ruse to cheat him out of money, Esau, in a mounting rage, threatens Jacob and throws him out. Once again, Jacob sets out on foot to wander. "But where will I go? O, my blessed God! Shall I be persecuted forever?"[29]

Bialik's message was that the Diaspora was untenable: Esau would always hate Jacob and persecute him, and Jacob would find no respite. As with the Yiddish writers, Zionism took over the rabbinic typology, ethnicizing and modernizing it. Unlike them, it deployed the typology to advance the return to the Land. This holds true for numerous writers. In his masterpiece *A Guest for the Night*, Shmuel Yosef Agnon suggested that there was, and would be, no respite for the Jews from the pogroms, for "Esau's hands are hot, and when he is enraged he takes an axe and kills."[30] Agnon's hometown was in decline, and the Land was the only hope. Significantly, he needed only a brief reference to Esau to summon a cultural tradition shared by his audience.

Bialik and Agnon showed the Diaspora's ultimate impossibility, but their Jacob and Esau could not be the protagonists leading the return to the Land. Rabbinic Jacob was not a Zionist hero. The Zionists accepted critiques of the Jews as an unhealthy people and were committed to transforming them from merchants and intellectuals into workers and farmers. Jacob, the arch wheeler-dealer who cheated his brother and father, tricked his host, and, fearing an oncoming confrontation with Esau, prepared an escape for his dearest ones, appeasing Esau by gifts and prostration, embodied the Diaspora Jew the Zionists wished to reform. Publicist Elḥanan Leib Levinsky, writing in Aḥad Ha-Am's Odessa Hebrew periodical *Ha-Shiloaḥ*, cited Jacob's self-humiliating efforts to appease Esau as exemplary of the futile endeavors to establish relationships with non-Jews: "Esau went on his way, and Jacob went on his way.... Other than 'gift' and prostration – there is nothing between

---

[28] Bialik, *Collected Poems*, 1: 172–77.   [29] Ibid., p. 177.
[30] *A Guest for the Night*, trans. Misha Louvish (New York: Schocken Books, 1968), p. 13. See also pp. 27 and 391.

them."[31] The Zionists' ancient heroes were military leaders who refuted the antisemites' stereotype of the effeminate Jew and served as a blueprint for the muscular Jew.[32] Bialik elucidated rabbinic Jacob's tragedy. The Zionists thought they could help him, but he had to go through an identity transformation.

Jacob could not be made a military hero but he could become a romantic lover. Like Coleridge and Thomas Mann, Yakov Shteynberg (1887–1947) saw the biblical story of Jacob and Rachel as the quintessential tale of romantic love. On his deathbed, Jacob evoked his early loss of Rachel (Genesis 48:7). Shteynberg's poem "Jacob" describes his life as a prolonged, glowing sunset, as extended mourning over the loss of Rachel while the family was growing and Jacob was getting old and weary. In "Jacob at the Wellhead," Avraham Shlonsky (1900–1973) focused on Jacob and Rachel's meeting at the well, perhaps the most celebrated scene in their love story. Jacob rolled the stone away and watered Rachel's flock. Shlonsky used richly archaic biblical language to convey modern romantic love. Shteynberg's glorious sunset was "appealing to the eye and a signpost for the people among the numerous sunsets in the book of the history of humanity."[33] Beauty and love became national symbols and a source of pride precisely because of their universal appeal.

More fundamentally, Zionism in the interwar years began a revolutionary transformation of Esau that would be completed only in our own time. Uri Ẓvi Greenberg poignantly demonstrated Zionism's ambivalence about rabbinic Jacob & Esau. At both ends of his poetic life, Greenberg, who had been traditionally educated in Austrian Galicia, upheld the rabbinic worldview of Christian Rome. His 1923 Yiddish poem "In the Kingdom of the Cross" (אין מלכות פון צלם), responding to the pogroms he had witnessed in Lemberg in the aftermath of World War I, indicted Christian Europe and portrayed the Arabs and the East as agents of Jewish liberation.[34] The dark imagery of body parts hanging from trees was expressionist, but the hatred of Christianity was

---

[31] *Kitve E. L. Levinsky*, 3 vols. (Odessa: Yavneh, 1911), 1: 104–5. Matya Kam, *Israel and the Nations via the Jacob and Esau Story* (in Hebrew) (Tel Aviv: Center for Educational Technology, 1996), p. 150, directed me to Levinsky.

[32] Mitchell Hart, *Social Science and the Politics of Modern Jewish Identity* (Stanford CA: Stanford University Press, 2000).

[33] Malkah Shaked, *I'll Play You Forever: The Bible in Modern Hebrew Poetry*, 2 vols. (Tel Aviv: Yediot Aḥaronot, 2005), 1: 161–64, 2: 220 (Shteynberg), 222 (Shlonsky).

[34] *In the Kingdom of the Cross* (in Hebrew and Yiddish), trans. Benjamin Harshav from the Yiddish (Tel Aviv: Beit Moereshet Uri Ẓvi Greenberg, 2007); *Collected Yiddish Works* (in Yiddish), 2 vols. (Jerusalem: Magnes Press, 1979), 2: 457–72, with reference to the Arabs on p. 472.

traditional. Similarly, in *Streets of the River* (רחובות הנהר), written in the shadow of the Holocaust, Greenberg rearticulated the split between the bloody goyim, Christians and Muslims alike, and the Jews.[35] He began and ended his poetic life expressing hatred for Christian Rome.

Yet in the interim from 1924, when he moved to Palestine, all the way to World War II, Greenberg disrupted rabbinic and Zionist paradigms. In his late 1920s confrontation with Labor Zionism and in his 1930s Polish sojourn as the leading revisionist poet, Greenberg portrayed Zionism as a messianic movement violently forcing its way to redemption, and cultivated the myths of blood, nation, and race. His 1928 "Vision of a Legionnaire" (חזון אחד הלגיונות) envisioned Zionist youth as a conquering Roman legion.[36] "To realize the revolution," says Dan Miron, "the 'I' needed to internalize the Other: Jerusalem had to become also Rome, and the conqueror had also to be the conquered."[37] Greenberg's interwar poetry broke with mainstream Zionism and represented the polar opposite of rabbinic Judaism.

Greenberg expressed a fervent hope for a messianic breakthrough to a Jewish kingdom and, at the same time, a deep anxiety that the Zionist leadership, and the Hebrew writers, were betraying the legions of youth who had come to conquer the Land. Zionism was about to miss a one-time opportunity and could end up with an autonomous Jewish Pale in Palestine and a return to exilic life. Individual and national traumas converged in Greenberg's poetry: wounded masculinity, the experience of World War I battles in the Austrian ranks, the postwar pogroms, the 1929 Arab riots in Palestine, the 1936 national Arab rebellion, and the Holocaust. Contemporary ordeals converged with Jewish historical ones: Jerusalem's destruction, the exile from the Land, medieval pogroms, and the Spanish expulsion all came together in a prolonged Jewish trauma. Greenberg depicted a besieged Jewish community in Palestine awaiting the Messiah, surrounded by Muslim and Christian troops. Would the Kingdom of David come or would an Arab Kingdom arise? The Messiah was sitting in Rome, under the Titus Arch, but the generation was not ready for him (a rabbinic motif), and another two thousand years of exile could be in store. Greenberg's nightmare, as Shai Ginsberg says, was "that Jerusalem is caught in another vicious cycle of destruction and desolation."[38]

---

[35] Greenberg, *Kol Ketavav* (Collected works), 19 vols. (Jerusalem: Bialik Institute, 1990), vols. 5–6.

[36] *Kol Ketavav*, 2: 7–31.

[37] Dan Miron, *Ha-Adam Eno Ela* ... (Man is nothing but) (Tel Aviv: Zemorah-Bitan, 1999), p. 220.

[38] Shai Ginsberg, "The City and the Body: Jerusalem in Uri Tsvi Greenberg's *Vision of One of the Legions*," in *Jerusalem: Conflict and Cooperation in a Contested City*, ed. Madelaine

Greenberg reshaped the rabbis' Christian Rome into the prisms of Jewish history, then turned the prisms upside down. The British Empire, Daughter of Edom, reduced the Sons of David into subjects and humiliated them. It put obstacles in the way of Jewish defense against the Arabs and rejoiced, like old Rome, in seeing Jewish blood streaming down the streets. As in ancient times, Flavian traitors emerged from among the Zionists, seeking to weaken the national resolve. Like the mythical Serpent, the archseducer who had triggered the Fall, the traitors could prevent the Messiah's return and Jerusalem's rise. Greenberg positioned himself as both a Jewish martyr and an ancient Zealot (סיקריקין) or gangster (בריון), fighting the Romans to the end. Even if Arabia and India should bow to Britain, he, the author, armed with only David's broken shield, would not: His Jewish soul was ready for martyrdom. He would be an insurgent against the empire, aiming to force the Messiah to move back from Rome to Jerusalem.[39]

For a moment, however, Greenberg imagined himself not as a Zealot but as a Roman legionnaire. Drawn by the messianic vision of the Kingdom of Judah, Zionist youth, young legionnaires, returned from a two-millennia Roman exile to Palestine to build up the nation and conquer the Land. The Zionist leadership betrayed them, ignored the Messiah's call, abandoned the hungry legions, and reduced Zionism to petty economics. Like Judas and Josephus Flavius before them, the debauched leaders did the Serpent's work, allowing the Land to display a multiconfessional mosaic. At times, it appears that their treachery was successful. Mimicking traditional lamentation over Jerusalem, the legionnaire bemoans "the coffin of the kingdom that failed to come" and imagines the apocalypse: The legions collapse, Roman and Jewish rule in Jerusalem ends, leaving an eerily beautiful city with blood streaming in its streets and human bodies displayed everywhere.[40] Up the Jerusalem mountains race "bald leprous camels, carrying on their heads crowns of the House of David and laurels of the House of Rome."[41] Eternal primeval fear returns to rule the dead city. In the final nightmare, the legionnaire, who fled Jerusalem, sets his bed on the shores of the Dead Sea across from dark Masada, and the Jewish and personal pasts return to haunt him. The spirit of ancient zealotry is gone, and the legionnaire imagines himself back in exile, oppressed by the

Adelman and Miriam Fendius Elma (Syracuse NY: Syracuse University Press, 2014), p. 166; Uri Zvi Greenberg, *Kol Ketavav*, 2: 9–31, 49, 52; 3: 13, 45; 16: 164, 166, 217.
[39] *Kol Ketavav*, 2: 50–52, 140; 3: 75–77, 86–89, 109, 184–89.
[40] Ibid., 2: 22, 28 (respectively).   [41] Ibid., 2: 28.

cross.[42] Betraying its legions, Zionism has collapsed. Jerusalem failed to become Rome.[43]

Greenberg's 1936 "One Truth and Not Two" (אמת אחת ולא שתים) collapsed the rabbinic and mainstream Zionist ethos together, and assailed them together, encapsulating a revolution he futilely sought to launch:[44] "Your rabbis taught: The Messiah will arrive in future generations, and Judah will be founded without fire and blood. It will arise with every tree, with yet another house. And I say: If your generation delays and does not force the end with its hands … with fire … and blood … – the Messiah will not come even in a faraway generation, and Judah shall not rise."[45] Your rabbis taught that land is acquired by buying and cultivating it. No, one only buries the dead this way.[46] Land is truly acquired by blood and in war. "Your rabbis taught: There is one truth for the Nations – blood for blood – but it is not a Jewish truth. And I say: one truth and not two, … the truth written in Moses and Joshua's *Torah* of conquest, … a truth eaten away by exile and traitors." A day will come when Jewish youth will summon Israel's enemies for the final battle, "and blood shall decide: Who the single ruler here is." Greenberg drew an idealized vision of peaceful rabbinic and Zionist redemption, and then smeared it with blood. History took its vengeance. The Jews' enemies summoned Jewish youth for a final battle, and blood decided: Greenberg lost his family in the Holocaust.

Curiously, Greenberg kept Esau at a distance from his Roman drama. He appropriated the rabbinic typology but virtually ignored the ancestor at its fountainhead. His references to Edom were numerous, but those to Esau were rare. A 1934 poem castigating the *Yishuv* for being unprepared to combat an Arab Esau, about to yield his sword again, was an

---

[42] Ibid., 29–31. Ḥanan Ḥever, *Poets and Zealots* (in Hebrew) (Jerusalem: Bialik Institute, 1994), pp. 139–84, suggests that on the contrary, "neither Yodfat in the Galilee, nor Beitar in Judah, nor Masada" (2: 17, 29) were a response to Yizḥak Lamdan's "Masada" (1927), and negated Zionist martyrology by posing the Roman legion rather than besieged martyrs as the motif for Judah's messianic regeneration.

[43] Shai Ginsburg, "The City and the Body," insists that Zionism, and messianic history, were doomed to failure from the start, as the legionnaire's vision replicated individual as much as collective trauma, and the first (articulated in "The Rising Manhood" [הגברות העולה], 1: esp. 78–79), was primary. Zionism was an epiphenomenon. In my view, however, neither Greenberg's politics nor his deep sense of betrayal can be adequately explained without some hope for a messianic breakthrough remaining. תיקון

[44] *Kol Ketavav*, 3: 179–80.

[45] Greenberg refers to *BT*, Ketuvot 111a: God adjured Israel that they should not rebel against the nations, climb the walls [and conquer the Land], and force the end [another version: delay the end]: שבועה שלא ידחקו את הקץ.

[46] Greenberg refers to Genesis 23: Abraham bought the burial site in Hebron for Sarah.

exception.[47] As a rule, the Roman Empire remained Greenberg's focus, and Esau was left in the shadow. This freed Esau from the typology to become, in the poetry of Greenberg's admirer Anda Amir-Pinkerfeld, the Zionist New Man.[48]

Pinkerfeld's "Esau" draws four Genesis scenes that contrast Esau, the man of nature, with the exilic Jew, Jacob. Strong and athletic, Esau invites the pale and anxious tent dweller, Jacob, to play with him in the fields. Esau views nature as safe and welcoming, and is perturbed by the lonesome Jacob, whose shifty eyes seem always to be conspiratorial. Esau next asks Jacob to let him enjoy the soup, and he, Jacob, can have the birthright: What use is the birthright for Esau in the fields? When Jacob next steals the blessing, cheating Isaac, their blind and tearful father, Esau is furious. Lazy Jacob deprived him of the reward for his laborious hunting. Esau does not need the blessing – he takes his own blessing from the earth – but Jacob is contemptible, low beyond belief. Run away, Jacob, or I shall kill you with my two hands! Upon Jacob's return from abroad, an elderly but still virile Esau, content with life, invites him to see his large family. "You are fearful of me, and I no longer resent you," he tells Jacob. "The bountiful water has washed away the insult I suffered. I have only contempt for you." Nazi ideology deployed rabbinic Jacob only marginally in racial stereotyping and never adopted Esau as an ideal. But the lovely poetry of a lovable Zionist children's poet sustained the antisemitic portrait of Jewish Jacob and Aryan Esau in ways that Nazi ideology never did.

There were happier returns of Esau to the Jewish fold in Zionist literature. In his 1938 *Ahavah Zarah*, Asher Barash lovingly explored the opportunities for identity shifts that Zionism opened for Jacob & Esau. Jacob, as Kovke, was a *maskil* and a Zionist intellectual, an apostate rather than a rabbinic Jew. His brother Pereẓ (literally "breach") was, in contrast, a Jewish Esau: athletic and blond, decidedly nonintellectual, but, like rabbinic Jacob, perfect in his Jewish faith. Pereẓ remained a practicing Jew while serving in the Austrian army, and, unlike fellow soldiers, avoided flings with (non-Jewish) girls. Upon his return home, however, he fell in love – delicate, tortuous, and pure – with Frania, a Polish girl from a devoutly Catholic family, a neighbor whom he had

---

[47] *Kol Ketavav*, 3: 118. Neta Stahl, "'Man's Red Soup': Blood and the Art of Esau in the Poetry of Uri Zvi Greenberg," in *Jewish Blood*, ed. Mitchell Hart (London: Routledge, 2009), might add the allusion to Esau in Greenberg's castigation of Hebrew writers ("Against Nine Nine": *Kol Ketavav*, 16: 203) for their refusal to taste from "man's red soup."

[48] "Esau," in Anda Amir-Pinkerfeld's *Gitit: Poems* (Tel Aviv: Ha-Qibuẓ ha-Meuḥad, 1937), pp. 18–24.

known from childhood. The relationship was not to be. Barash was open to friendships with non-Jews, but a successful intermarriage was unimaginable.[49] Christian and Jew remained a binary in *Ahavah Zarah*, and antisemitism lurked in every corner, above all in Frania's family. The arrival in town of an antisemitic police chief – the Jews called him Haman – who won Frania's love resolved the plot. In the biblical story, Esau marries outside the tribe, sealing his exclusion from the people. In Barash, the story ends happily with Perez marrying his stepsister Elki.[50] Order is restored. In the antisemitic 1930s, Amaleq (Haman) drove Esau back home. The specter of racial genocide re-Judaized Esau, the Christian Jew.

Utopias of German-Jewish Literature

National literature was constrained in exploring genuine border-crossing and religious hybridity in ways that German-Jewish modernism was not. Else Lasker-Schüler and Soma Morgenstern refused a Barash-like restoration of the ethno-religious order, and explored interreligious togetherness. Like Richard Beer-Hoffman and Waldemar Jollos, they endeavored to transcend historical experience, and their Jacob & Esau narratives represented utopian experiments that pushed against reality, defying racialization. Yet utopia, too, registered a new Jewish consciousness. Lasker-Schüler's and Beer-Hofmann's avowal of Jewish identity and their respective multicultural and ethical visions accommodated Jacob's nationalization. Jollos alone remained impervious to nationalization: He no longer identified himself as a Jew.

To her admirers, expressionist poet Lasker-Schüler, was the "Black Swan of Israel" and "the greatest woman poet that Germany ever had."[51] A social misfit and cultural transgressor all her life, she lived, until her flight from the Nazis, among Berlin's literary and artistic cafes, migrating destitute from one hotel and temporary residence to another. Her *Hebrew Ballads* appeared in 1913, concluding a decade of cultural creativity that saw her ending two marriages, inventing the multicultural Orient, and forming a unique relationship to "my people" and the

---

[49] On the friendship of an eccentric rabbi and a Catholic priest, see "Me-Ḥaye Barukh Vilder" (Of the life of Barukh Vilder), in *Kitve Asher Barash* (Collected works), 1: 393–409.

[50] *Ahavah Zarah*, in *Kitve Asher Barash*, 1: 253–353. Esau was to marry Leah: *BT, Bava Batra* 123a. (Shai Ginsburg insists that Elki is evocative of Leah, and possibly a hybrid of Leah and Rachel. אפשר) The happy ending of *Ahavah Zarah* was uncharacteristic for love stories between Jews and non-Jews in Zionist literature, and for Barash's novels, too.

[51] Poets Peter Hille and Gottfried Benn, respectively. Both were Lasker-Schüler's friends and lovers: *Your Diamond Dreams Cut Open My Arteries: Poems by Else Lasker-Schüler*, trans. with an introduction by Robert P. Newton (Chapel Hill: University of North Carolina, 1982), pp. 3, 51.

Land.[52] She collapsed the biblical and modern worlds together and assembled, into her "ancient East," biblical figures, friends, and herself. Her Orient, drawn in pictures and poems alike, was multiconfessional – Jewish, Muslim, and Christian: The star of David, the crescent, and the cross interplayed; Jesus and Mary, child and mother, were Jewish and Christian, divine and human at the same time. The Hellenic, Hebrew, and Arab worlds merged in the figure of Yussuf, Prince of Thebes, whose transgender identity Lasker-Schüler herself assumed. The German reader would unmistakably identify her figures and symbols as belonging to familiar religions and ancient civilizations, but her Orient was a counterpoint to German Orientalism and ethnonationalism, a hybrid that mainstream Germans could find quixotic at best.

Lasker-Schüler dedicated the poem "Jacob and Esau" to her two "dearest playfellows." Rewriting the biblical story, she introduced the figure of Rebecca's maid, probably drawn in her own self-image: "a heavenly stranger, an angel," wearing "a frock of rose petals," and "looking upward to the light," a star (of David) on her face. The angelic maid (and not Jacob) sorts golden lentils into a meal, and "Jacob and Esau blossom in her presence and do not quarrel" over the sweet meal in her lap, the erotic allusion evident. To gain her favor, "the brother," putatively Esau, lets "the younger" have his hunt and his birthright, and wildly cloaks himself with the thicket.[53] Lovers and brothers live in peace, undisturbed by competition over the maid's love, and Esau's wildness is unthreatening.[54] Gently and effortlessly, the heavenly maid resolves all potentially divisive issues.

In Lasker-Schüler's poems, friends populate the Bible, transform the text, and overturn interpretive traditions. She herself appears as Tino of Baghdad and Prince Yussuf of Thebes, who is sometimes also the biblical Joseph. She upsets historicity, disrupts ethnic and religious boundaries, and reshapes gender identities. Crescent and (Jewish) star alternate, Mary of Nazareth holding Jesus – the beloved little God – also wears a

---

[52] Lasker-Schüler, "Hebräische Balladen," in *Gedichte 1902–1943*, ed. Friedhelm Kemp, Vol. 1 of *Gesammelte Werke*, 3 vols. (Munich: Kösel Verlag, 1961): 1: 289ff.; *Hebrew Ballads and Other Poems*, trans. and ed. Audri Durchslag and Jeanette Litman-Demeestère (Philadelphia: The Jewish Publication Society, 1980).

[53] "Der Bruder läßt dem jüngeren die Jagd/Und all sein Erbe für den Dienst der magd;/Um seine Schultern schlägt er wild das Dickicht": *Gesammelte Werke*, 1: 296; *Hebrew Ballads*, pp. 60–61; *Poems by Else Lasker-Schüler*, pp. 252–53.

[54] In Lasker-Schüler's "Jakob," *Gesammelte Werke*, 1: 297; *Hebrew Ballads*, p. 63, Jacob assumes the powerful image of a raging bull, leaving his brother for the wild forest and river to heal his injury, collapsing exhausted, yet with an everlasting smile. The social and literary context that made it possible for Jacob to assume, in this poem, a benevolent Esau-like character remains mysterious but לא עלי המלאכה לגמור.

Jewish star on her face, like Rebecca's maid, and Lasker-Schüler declares herself a fervent Hebrew. Autobiography, love, and play convey cosmic and religious meanings, and personal, collective, and natural histories merge. Her peculiar relationship to "my people," and her idiosyncratic Jewish identity, allowed her to transform religious types and offered an alternative vision of German–Jewish relations.

The beauty and appeal of Lasker-Schüler's heavenly vision were contingent on its radical dissociation from history. Her secret in telling of togetherness under worsening ethno-national tensions is in substituting archaic types for religious and national ones and, even more, in keeping religious and national identities amorphous and unstable. Jacob and Esau are brothers, playmates, and lovers, and they have no religious identity. Her imagined Orient is interchangeably Greek, Hebrew, and Arab, and Christian and Jew overlap. Just enough traces of the Jacob & Esau typology remain to enable the brothers to convey a message of peaceful coexistence, but Jacob & Esau's freedom from history and religion allowed Lasker-Schüler to escape the typological quagmire and ethno-national tensions and envision moments of grace.

Poetic overcoming of history has its limits, however. Lasker-Schüler's "Jacob and Esau" could not speak to German–Jewish relations as effectively as national writers, rabbis, and antisemites did. Her admirers were distinguished – St. Peter (poet Peter Hille, Catholic), Giselheer the Barbarian (poet Gottfried Benn, lover, Protestant), and the Cardinal (Karl Kraus, converted Jew) – but few German Jews could find in her Orientalism a palliative for worsening ethnic relations. An exile in her homeland and homesick for the Land of the Hebrews, Lasker-Schüler spent her final years, and World War II, in Jerusalem, where, alas, she found no home either. "She is here, on the brink of insanity," reported Scholem to Benjamin, and he added: "She would do better in any other place in the world than in the real Orient."[55] Her dreamlike Land of the Hebrews (*Das Hebräerland*, 1937) showed no awareness of the difficulties of life in Palestine, or of the ongoing national conflict. The Land was governed magically, she said, "and the return of the sons and daughters of Isaac caused the descendants of Ishmael no harm. . . . Arabs and Hebrews speak in the same voice."[56] Reality eventually sank in: "The same

---

[55] Letter dated July 11, 1934, in *The Correspondence of Walter Benjamin and Gershom Scholem, 1932–1940* (Cambridge, MA: Harvard University Press, 1980), p. 104. Elsewhere, Scholem spoke of *Hebrew Ballads* as formative for his youth.

[56] *Das Hebräerland* (Zurich: Verlag Oprecht, 1937), p. 136. The book came out after her first visit to Palestine. She dedicated it to the memory of her parents and beloved son. The motto folded Jewish religion and nationality into her oriental dream: "You will be for me a kingdom of priests and a holy nation (Exodus 19:6)."

Jerusalem that I so glorified in my poems offers me no home," she complained in her final years. Still, to the prominent Hebrew poet who offered to translate her poems, she responded, "Oh, but they *are* written in Hebrew."[57] Few contemporaries grasped her poetical grammar. Only in recent decades has Lasker-Schüler become an iconic German expressionist poet.

Viennese modernist Beer-Hofmann does not enjoy comparable recognition today, but in his time, his popularity exceeded that of Lasker-Schüler. *Jacob's Dream*, a theater drama he had completed in 1915, was staged in Vienna in 1918, in Tel Aviv in 1925, and later in New York. It was performed repeatedly before Jewish audiences in 1930s Berlin.[58] Beer-Hofmann intended *Jacob's Dream* to be the prologue to a three-part drama on King David, of which he completed only the first part in 1936, prior to his emigration to the United States.[59] Both his Jacob and King David represented a curious synthesis of Viennese modernism, Jewish nationality, and Christian motifs. Beer-Hofmann renounced violence and found national grandeur in sacrifice, loss, struggle, and doubt. In contrast to Lasker-Schüler, he drew sharp ethnic boundaries between Jacob and Esau, and so it was all the more surprising when Jewish Jacob ended up looking Christian.

Jacob's Dream consisted of two scenes, the first taking place in Isaac's household in Beer-Sheba, just after Jacob departed on his way abroad, and the second in Bethel, where Jacob confronts first Esau, then God, and receives his mission. The first scene is the author's invention: Esau's return from the hunt interrupts a conversation between his foreign wives and Rebecca, and a confrontation between Rebecca and Esau ensues. In the second scene, Beer-Hofmann collapses together two biblical narratives, Jacob's ladder dream and his fight with the angel, and turns a third one, the reconciliation of Jacob & Esau, into a confrontation. Throughout, Esau is called Edom: Beer-Hofmann imposes on him the typology's historical weight and deprives him of his redeeming features in the biblical narrative. Jacob retains his name until the last line, when he becomes Israel, but he is likewise remote from the worldly character of Genesis, and becomes a godlike figure, permeated with Beer-Hofmann's vision of Israel's mission.

---

[57] Yehuda Amichai, "Preface" to *Hebrew Ballads*, p. ix. Amichai was recounting the story of Lasker-Schüler's friend, Rachel Katinka. Avraham Kariv was the Hebrew writer who offered to translate Lasker-Schüler's poetry. In the 1960s, Amichai translated her ballads into Hebrew.

[58] Richard Beer-Hofmann, *Jacob's Dream*, trans. Ida Bension Wynn (Philadelphia: Jewish Publication Society, 1946).

[59] *Vorspiel auf dem Theater zu König David* (Vienna: Johannes-Presse, 1936).

The conversation between Rebecca and Edom's two wives highlights their alienation from each other. Edom then enters the house, furious and dismayed. He was called back from hunting by the news that Jacob had stolen his blessing. He finds that the blessing is irretrievable. Isaac, old and ailing, is nowhere to be seen: He remains out of sight and serves merely as the vehicle for God's blessing. Rebecca tells Edom that Jacob was chosen, predestined to be blessed, and that the blessing, inspired by God, poured out of Isaac as if the patriarch had no control over it. Rebecca's hostility is painful to Edom, and he asks how she could be so cruel toward her own son. She tells him that his way of life and foreign wives created the distance between them. Edom vows to kill Jacob. Rebecca tries to convince him not to pursue Jacob, as the household, and all material possessions, remain his. In vain: Edom leaves on the chase.

At the top of the Bethel mountain, Jacob frees his slave and sends him back to the camp. He remains alone, with a lamb that he rescued. The night is falling, and Edom emerges from the shadows. He calls on Jacob to fight, and his arrow strikes the lamb. Jacob declares the lamb a sacrifice to God in his stead and refuses Edom's persistent calls to fight, intentionally leaving himself exposed. Edom cannot bring himself to strike a defenseless Jacob, and the two reconcile. Jacob assures Edom that his blessing extends to all of humanity, that he loves him as a brother, and that he has no joy in his own fate. They are different, he says, and have different destinies. Unlike Edom, he, Jacob, has no home to which he can return. Edom leaves for home, resigned.

Jacob retires to sleep and the night vision, veritably a revelation, begins. The angels descend, rejoicing in Jacob's prospective mission, promising him glory and beseeching him to join them in praising God. Jacob declines to sing God's praises and rejects the promise of worldly power. Samael (Satan) prophesies instead that Jacob's future lot would be eternal suffering and enjoins him not to accept his mission. A divine voice declares Samael to be true. Jacob struggles with his destiny and decides to accept the mission, recognizing that his universal ideals, pacifism, and battle with divinity will inspire simultaneous admiration and rejection in the nations of the world. He will become a model for the nations, and yet be hated by them all. Jacob has now become Israel, fulfilling Isaiah's vision of the Servant of the Lord, despised and mocked for the nations' sins. Having vied with God and prevailed, Israel is a Christ-like figure, god and man at the same time.

Racialization accentuated some religious differences between Christians and Jews but erased others. For German-acculturated intellectuals like Beer-Hofmann, who were no longer versed in Jewish traditions, the divergence of Judaism and Christianity had lost some of its historical significance and retreated into the background, with a culture suffused with shared Christian and Jewish motifs taking its place. They identified the shared motifs and symbols as Jewish. The sacrifice of Isaac was central to both Judaism and Christianity. Medieval Jewish iconography emphasized that Abraham sacrificed a ram and not a lamb in lieu of Isaac in order to accentuate the *Aqedah*'s divergent interpretation in the two religions.[60] In Beer-Hofmann, the lamb took over, making Jacob look like St. Francis, an *imitatio Christi*. The chosen people and the Lord's Servant were biblical ideas, but their Christian character in *Jacob's Dream* is overwhelming. Rebecca speaks about Jacob as chosen by grace, and of Edom as outcast. Unlike Jesus, Jacob and the people of Israel survive their travail, but they might as well have not, as they derive no joy or benefit from it. The rationale for their suffering is provided by the Aqedah, viewed, in turn, through the prism of the crucifixion. Nothing remains of biblical and rabbinic Jacob, of the wily shepherd or devoted Jew. Ironically, it took a Viennese Jewish modernist to produce a modern Christian Jacob.

Beer-Hofmann's Jacob was modern because his heroism, while Christian, was nontraditional. The God with whom Jacob vies occupies a marginal space in the drama: The focus is on Jacob's struggle, on a godlike man defying the angels. Beer-Hofmann avowed the doubt, conflict, and indeterminacy that modernity introduced, and, like Max Weber, made the open-eyed struggle with destiny the emblem of modern heroism. Unlike Weber, however, he did not situate heroism in science or politics but in religion, and found the meaning of modern struggle not in war but in pacifist cosmopolitanism, which he identified with the Christ-like Jews. In Beer-Hofmann, Viennese modernism reenchanted the world through religion and the Jews.

Waldemar Jollos's *Esau und Jakob*, a psychological drama in verse written in the shadow of World War I, likewise deployed Jacob's struggle with God to query the modern pursuit of divinity. Unlike Lasker-Schüller and Beer-Hofmann, Jollos is not a household name among literary scholars, but his fascinating biography charts the European Jewish intelligentsia's networks, and shows him traversing ethnic lines and initiating cultural exchange across national borders. Jollos was born in Moscow to a high-bourgeois Jewish family: His father, the journalist and constitutional lawyer Gregori Jollos, was a leader of the (liberal democratic) Cadet Party, and was murdered in 1907 by the reactionary Black

---

[60] Eva Frojmovic, "Blood as a Symbol Between Jews and Christians: The Case of the Laud Maḥzor," paper presented at the Oxford Seminar in Jewish Studies, November 30, 2016.

Hundreds. Like his two brothers, Waldemar grew up and received his education in Germany, earning a Ph.D. in Berlin in 1910 with a dissertation on workers in the metallurgy industry.[61] Supervised by the leading historical economist, Gustav von Schmoller, the dissertation exhibited the Historical School's *enquête* into the workers' social and economic life, but intimated, at the same time, Jollos's radical socialist politics. At the beginning of World War I he found himself in Switzerland, where he remained for the rest of his life, becoming an intermediary of Russian culture and Soviet politics to Central Europe and Italy, a Swiss midpoint for the interaction of French, German, and Italian cultures, and an exemplum of the vital émigré communities in Switzerland that still await their historian.

Dismayed by the senseless slaughter of World War I, Jollos became involved with radical artistic movements, searching for an alternative European future.[62] A friend of Tristan Tzara and Hans Arp who founded the Dada movement in Zurich in 1916, Jollos was the lively spirit behind a series of German expressionist exhibitions in the Dada Gallery in Zurich in 1917. The Dadaist critique of capitalist rationalism appealed to him, as did emergent forms of socialist collectivism, but neither left him satisfied. His hero was Munich artist Paul Klee, whose work he promoted in lectures and reviews.[63] In Klee and expressionism, he found the craving for a new individuality, compatible with communal life, and, more crucially, the exploration of a new religiosity, grounded in Europe's Christian past. He thought that modernity's renunciation of God exemplified its deadening impact. In 1916, he told his future wife, Lavinia Mazzucchetti (1889–1965), that Friedrich Gundolf's books on Shakespeare and Goethe, heroic individuals who overcame alienation by bridging past and present and embodying the *Zeitgeist*, reflected "my entire art theory and ... *Weltanschauung*."[64] In Jollos' *Esau und Jakob*, the protagonists struggle with the existential despair that Klee and Gundolf sought to overcome.

Before they married and settled in 1946 in Melide (Tessin), Switzerland, on the Italian border, Jollos and Mazzucchetti had conducted a three-decade-long relationship constrained by distance, border

[61] "Untersuchungen über die wirtschaftliche und soziale Lage der Berliner Metallarbeiter" (Ph.D. diss., Friedrich-Wilhelms-Universität, Berlin, 1910).

[62] Waldemar Jollos, *Arte tedesca fra le due guerre*, ed. with an introduction by Luigi Rognoni (Milan: Mondadori, 1955).

[63] Ibid., pp. 49–92; O. K. Werckmeister, *The Making of Paul Klee's Career, 1914–1920* (Chicago: University of Chicago, 1984), pp. 95–97.

[64] Letter dated October 15, 1916, in Lavinia Mazzucchetti Collection, Fondazione Arnoldo e Alberto Mondadori, Milan. My thanks to Michela Scanavacca of Udine, Italy, for researching the archives.

closures (and racial threat) during World War II, economic exigencies, family obligations, and two professional careers, respectively, in Switzerland (and Germany) and Italy. Mazzucchetti was a leading translator of German literature into Italian, and introduced German-Jewish authors, like Stefan Zweig, to Italian audiences, earning the title of "the Trieste Jewess" in a Nazi cultural attaché's report.[65] Jollos was a partner and a mentor. His family had lost its property in the Bolshevik Revolution, and together with his brother, a professor of genetics in Berlin, he had to take care of his mother, living in Germany, and a younger sister, completing her degree in Zurich. He became a correspondent on Russian affairs, and a commentator on German literature and art, for the *Neue Zürcher Zeitung*. To make ends meet, he also wrote for a range of German cultural magazines and became a major translator of Russian literature into German. His *Das Vergessens Gottes* (Forgetfulness of God, 1929) and *Die Vergeltung* (Retribution, 1937) testified to an abiding concern with the themes of *Esau und Jakob*, the "poetic greatness" of which, testified Stefan Zweig, "moved me deeply"[66]

Esau und Jakob's five acts rewrite the biblical reconciliation of Jacob and Esau by making Jacob's struggle with the angel part of it, and by introducing several unexpected turns in the brothers' encounter. Rachel plays the role of intermediary between the brothers, and Esau's family – his wife, Ada, their boy, and her brother, Ahab (not biblical characters) – appears at the beginning and the end. All action takes place in Esau's tents. The drama opens with the spreading news of Jacob's camp approaching. In a reversal of Genesis, whereby Jacob fears the advent of Esau's camp, the land's princes ask Esau for protection from the invaders. Ada fears a war, but to her surprise, Jacob sends gifts to placate Esau, and Esau has forgotten and forgiven Jacob. The first act ends well enough with a reunion feast.

The brothers emerge from the first act, however, as divergent characters. Jacob is at home in the world: He is rich and successful, wily, and, flashing blond curls, looks young. In contrast, Esau has aged, his land is poor, he is straight in speech and spontaneous in action, and he has become an eternal outsider. A hunter and a wayward fighter all his life, he nurses bitter memories of his parents' home: Already as a boy he was regarded as inept. He thinks of Jacob as a crafty merchant and envies his

<hr />

[65] Anna Antonello, *La rivista come agente letterario tra Italia e Germania (1921–1944)* (Pisa: Pacini Editore, 2012), pp. 267–68. See also her *"Tra l'agro e il dolce: Note biografiche su Lavinia Mazzucchetti,"* in *"Come il cavaliere sul lago di Costanza": Lavinia Mazzucchetti e la cultura tedesca in Italia*, ed. Anna Antonello (Milan: Fondazione Arnoldo e Alberto Mondadori, 2015), pp. 7–28.

[66] Stefan Zweig to Waldemar Jollos, quoted in Waldemar Jollos, *Arte tedesca*, p. 42.

success. When Jacob endeavors, in the second act, to convince Esau that all his deeds, including the blessing's theft, were guided by God, and implies that his success is a mark of God's blessing, Esau explodes. Engaging God in petty material affairs seems to him to diminish divinity, and offends his pride, which is vested in his refusal of an easy life and his ongoing search for deep answers. He throws a knife at Jacob, and it appears that peace between the two is impossible.

In the third act, "Earth," Rachel visits Esau and prevails over his pride, envy, and temptation to ravish her, his enemy's beautiful wife. She startles Esau by disclosing that Jacob himself is a seeker, like him, and is in no way sure of God's proximity. Baring Esau's own heart, she redirects his desperate search for earthly answers toward the forgotten God. All creatures thrown into this incomprehensible and hostile world seek meaning in God, she says. Esau recognizes in his own life the human condition, and reconciles himself to living without the blessing. He goes to Jacob's tent, and in the fourth act, "Solitude" (*Einsamkeit*), they share in a mystical search for God. Shaken by the recognition that he could have lost Rachel to Esau, Jacob reveals the fragility of worldly success, the loneliness of existence, and his despair of finding God. The two brothers' shared despair means that their struggle over the blessing has become insignificant. Jacob asks Esau, who has experienced solitude, for help in finding God. Does God exist at all? Esau says that God is far, and alien, and yet may also be so very close. When the time comes, "a heart knows: You are it, my dear brother God."[67] Jacob cries to God: "I wrestle with you, and will not let you go! Bless me!"[68]

The morning after, as Jacob and his family take leave of Esau, Jacob tells him that God appeared to him in the form of their father and blessed him. He asks Esau to bless him, too, and Esau does. Jacob and his family now go on to the promised land to become the people of Israel, Esau and his family leave to continue their wandering, and Esau's brother-in-law, Ahab, stays to rule as king over the locals. He alone craves worldly power. The two brothers, one blessed and the other not, will continue striving for God.

Reconciling Jacob & Esau, Jollos tenuously brought together the polarities that modernity opened up and expressionism aimed to bridge. He deployed existential despair to save a semblance of individuality in the age of collectivism, and projected hope for humanity by finding glimmers of the divine in the human, of the transcendent in the immanent, of heaven on earth. Striving with God was the primary facet of the biblical story that Jollos rescued. His God was vested in

[67] Waldemar Jollos, *Esau und Jakob*, p. 86.   [68] Ibid., p. 87.

Protestant existential despair. Revealing himself in divergent humans, in father and brother, God appeared more Christian than Jewish, but the break with tradition was radical, and He was no longer Christian either. Jacob and Esau's traditional identities were disrupted, too. Esau became a seeker, and Jacob appeared, at least initially, worldly. The gender difference seemed to be the most stable one. Rachel plays an extraordinary role in the reconciliation, understanding Jacob and Esau better than they themselves do, but she remains a facilitator of the search for God and not a seeker herself. She emerges as the protagonist possessing the greatest wisdom and insight, but women are not seekers. Ada and Rachel provide (motherly) care and are at peace in the world. Men are anxious and strive for God.

The reconciliation also offers a social vision. Jollos's Jacob appears disturbingly close to the antisemitic stereotype of the Jewish merchant, and Esau's disparagement of Jacob's crafty materialism is a picture of the antisemitic litany about the Jews' economic role. This is so much the case that Jacob's blond curls seem odd, a conscious authorial effort to free the social question from the antisemitic burden and define it as the problem of the bourgeoisie rather than the Jews. Truly, the two problems converged in Jollos's life: His family fell victim first to anti-semitism, then to the Bolshevik Revolution. In the midst of the revolutionary wave sweeping Europe, from Russia to Germany and beyond, Jollos, sympathetic to socialism but never a Bolshevik, offered a reconciliation of social tensions that relegated class and status differences to destiny. Envy and vengeance dissipate, and Jacob and Esau find human brotherhood in shared existential despair and the search for God.

War looms large in both Jollos and Beer-Hofmann. *Esau und Jakob* opens with Esau's son questioning whether, like his father, he will have to fight when he grows up. His mother responds affirmatively. Rumors of an invasion then spread, and the threat of violence is ever present in Jacob and Esau's intercourse. Beer-Hofmann offers pacifism as a radical alternative to violence. Contrasting pacifist Jacob and violent Edom, he highlights Jewish suffering as the paradigmatic endurance. Lasker-Schüller lets a maiden's love dissolve tensions among the brothers and avoid conflict. Emerging as they did from World War I, one is struck by the gap separating these German-Jewish works from the Holocaust. In the aftermath of World War II, Jacob could not have triumphed over Edom by exposing his vulnerability, the alien God would not have been found through shared human despair, and Aryans and Jews would not have played for a maiden's favors. Jollos's dispassionate analyses of the great purges in the Soviet Union similarly fail to capture the otherness of totalitarianism.[69] World War I German-Jewish utopias reflect the crisis of a two-millennia paradigm of Jewish–Christian relations but have not quite fathomed the depth of the abyss awaiting humanity.

Jollos survived World War II in Switzerland, as did his mother and sister. Exploration of his possible emigration to the United States came to nothing: He had no academic credentials beyond the doctorate degree, and his partner, Mazzucchetti, was across the Italian border. He died suddenly in 1953 while conversing with her in the garden of their Melide house. She later issued, in Italian, a selection of his interwar writings on art and culture, and, in German, a collection of his Soviet commentaries and Russian literary essays.[70] Otherwise, Jollos was quickly forgotten. His brother's family faced some tough times in the United States, and in the 1990s, his niece looked to German reparations to supplement her meager New York City existence.[71] Numerous eulogies for the Jewish European intelligentsia have been delivered in recent decades, enshrining its legacy. Let this precis of Lasker-Schüller, Beer-Hofmann, and Jollos be another *petit mémorial*.

German Racial Myths

If German-Jewish literature represented veiled responses to Jacob & Esau's racialization, the veil is removed in the works discussed in this section. Wilhelm Schäfer's antisemitic stereotyping of Jewish Jacob and German Esau is as open as Sammy Gronemann's parodying of racial stereotyping. In the next section, Mann's Hebrew myth counters German racial myth. Schäfer presaged Nazi antisemitism, and Gronemann and Mann responded directly to it. National Socialism brought the debate on race and the Bible into the open.

Given the rich antisemitic discourse available to the Nazis, it would seem surprising how sparingly they used Jacob & Esau in their propaganda. To be sure, they did. Leading Nazi racial theorist Alfred Rosenberg (1893–1946) used Jacob as an emblem for Jewish deceit and thievery.[72] Likewise, Nazi Minister of Propaganda Joseph Goebbels designated the Jews, in an educational manual for the SS, as "the

---

[69] Jollos, *Russische Gestalten und Ereignisse* (Zurich: Neue Zürcher Zeitung, 1953), pp. 35–41.

[70] *Arte tedesca fra le due guerre* and *Russische Gestalten und Ereignisse*, respectively.

[71] Peter Bölke, "Erbschein aus dem KZ," *Der Spiegel* (19 May 1997): 64–67.

[72] *Race and Race History and Other Essays*, ed. Robert Pois (New York: Harper and Row, 1971), p. 180. Rosenberg cites the conversation of Jacob and Rachel, as imagined in *BT* Megilah 12a, where Jacob assures Rachel that he will outmaneuver Laban and get her hand. "I am his brother in deceit," he says, and cites Psalms 18:27 to show that one must be "trustless to the false" (that is, to non-Jews, says Rosenberg).

descendants of Jacob, the Shylocks with the red potage."[73] Still, Jacob the liar and thief never assumed center stage in Nazi propaganda, and the Nazis did not turn him into a major racial archetype. Why?

Schäfer's theater drama *Jakob und Esau* provides an answer.[74] Wilhelm Schäfer (1868–1952) was a populist nationalist writer and the editor of *Die Rheinlande*, a magazine for the German arts. He was best known for his prodigious stories exemplifying "the German soul." In the late Weimar years, he led the efforts to purge the Prussian Academy of Arts of non-nationalist poets. Never a proper member of the Nazi Party, he collaborated in advancing the Nazi cultural agenda, became a poster writer for the Nazi regime, and was rewarded with multiple prizes, notably, in 1941, the Goethe Prize. *Jakob und Esau* was Schäfer's first published composition, and the drama was staged in Berlin in 1897. He made full use of the antisemitic repertoire to Judaize Jacob and Germanize Esau, and expressed anxieties about the Jews and modern life. At the same time, the drama made clear the difficulty of Aryanizing Esau. While critical of traditional religion, Schäfer found himself referring repeatedly to the biblical narrative. He could neither obscure Esau's Jewish origins nor define a new ethno-religious identity for him. Ironically, racialization made it impossible for Schäfer to Aryanize Esau. The Nazis wished to uproot the Old Testament. An ethnic Jew who became a good German was their nightmare and not their ideal. Schäfer's populist nationalism, however antisemitic, did not cross over the line that separated Nazi ideology and policy from two millennia of Jacob & Esau.

In five acts and a prologue, *Jakob und Esau* tells the story of the demise of two neighboring families, the Jewish Baumann and the German Rauch families, whose fates are intertwined by love and money. The prologue is a parodic portrayal of the launching of a wayward pilgrimage for "the source" (*Quelle*) with a hapless wagon. It introduces the drama's protagonists colorfully dressed as pilgrims, and they express, alternatively, lofty wishes for the holy and a craving for wine. The five scenes that follow take place on consecutive days, Thursday to Monday, at the Rauches' small apartment and, alternately, the Baumanns' stately abode. The first act reveals the Rauches' resentment of the Baumanns, who inherited their stately house. The Rauch mother, who is descended from the nobility, and her drunkard and violent son Paul blame the Baumanns for the suicide of their husband and father, as he was allegedly driven to despair by his financial debts. In contrast, the long-suffering Rauch daughter,

---

[73] Quoted in Uriel Tal, *Political Theology and the Third Reich* (in Hebrew) (Tel Aviv: Sifriat Poalim, 1989), p. 89.

[74] Wilhelm Schäfer, *Jakob und Esau* (Berlin: Schuster & Loeffler, 1896).

Ada, refuses to hate and accepts her fate. The two Baumann sons, the elder, Johannes, and younger, Nathaniel, both love Ada, and Johannes tries to convince her to begin dreaming about life and love. The first act is dark and forbidding, but it also raises hope, embodied in Johannes.

From the following two acts, the Baumanns emerge as despicable Jews. The father, aging and blind like Isaac, appears to have amassed a fortune, and is eager for Johannes to assume his role as a Jewish community leader. He has little sense of reality, speaks in pompous rhetoric of God and his blessings, despises Christians as idol worshippers, and prohibits his servants from attending church. His wife is yet uglier. Busy with money lending, she speaks of God and divine judgment, dislikes Johannes, and pleads for Nathaniel, who labors in the family business. She mistreats the servants and would expel Becher, the clever servant who lost his arm in the thresher (an emblem of the mechanized agriculture introduced by Jews). Johannes alone emerges as virtuous, and he wants to leave the Jewish community behind and wander elsewhere with Ada. Schäfer endows him with virtues associated traditionally with both Esau and Jacob: good looks, sociability, a commanding authority, and culture.[75] Nathaniel, his younger brother, is envious of him and feels inferior. Schäfer portrays Nathaniel with stereotypical antisemitic features: He is weak in body and mind and a coward, his voice is coarse and his speech halting, and his learning is narrow and bookish. Schäfer delights in showing Nathaniel losing the competition over Ada to Johannes. "I know how happy you are," he wrote to his mentor, poet Richard Dehmel, "that now Jacob is finally going away and Esau is coming, as you love life as much as I do" (p. 5). In Johannes's character, Esau has come to embody the German hope for overcoming modernity's deadening impact on life.

At the end of the second act, Paul Rauch attempts to set the estate house ablaze and is later apprehended and jailed. The Baumann father, shaken by the incident and having a sense of foreboding about his own demise, wishes to make his will. He calls for a witness and plans to designate Johannes, his first son, as the sole inheritor of his estate. Mrs. Baumann urges Nathaniel to intervene: It is now or never. "I am your first son," he tells his father. "Your voice is Nathaniel's voice," responds his father. "I am Nathaniel, your only son," he answers (p. 89). Johannes, he relates, is no longer a Jew and cannot represent the Jewish community.

---

[75] Nathaniel complains (ibid., p. 46) that Ada is taken with Johannes's *glatten Gesicht* (smooth look) and speech. Genesis describes Esau as hairy and Jacob as smooth. Andreas Freinschlag and Amandine Schneebichler, "Esau in der deutschsprachigen Literatur," in *Esau: Bruder und Feind*, ed. Gerhard Langer (Göttingen: Vandenhoeck & Ruprecht, 2009), pp. 277–79, note Johannes's hybridity.

The incredulous father confronts Johannes, who says that he remains true to God and morality but not to the Jewish god. Baumann declares Johannes dead and Nathaniel his only son.

It turns out that Nathaniel wanted the inheritance primarily to win Ada. But Ada declares her love for Johannes, who, disinherited of the estate, persuades her to leave home with him. They plan to break away from their families, leave behind the Jewish–Christian past, and wander in search of a better future. The Baumann servants, Emma and Becher, likewise decide to leave the estate and get married; theirs will be the only happy escape. Hearing of her daughter's plan to marry Johannes, the Rauch mother, sizzling with hatred for the Baumanns, threatens her with suicide. Finding no way out of her conflicting commitments to Johannes and her mother, Ada commits suicide; her mother follows suit the next day. Nathaniel, shaken by the loss of Ada, recognizes that his scheme was futile and his sentiments were base. "I wanted to be master but one must be born to it," he tells Johannes (p. 117). "We shall always remain slaves to you. . . . We each carry within us the gods who annihilate us. We should not have other gods." Seeking to reconcile Johannes with his father, he tells him that Johannes has truly kept the holy faith whereas he, Nathaniel, made a mockery of it. The world collapses on Baumann, who feels that his life and mission have been in vain. He reconciles with Johannes, asks for God's forgiveness, and, in his last moment, blesses Johannes in what seems an acknowledgment of Christianity.

If the final scene of *Jakob und Esau* looks like the Last Judgment, there is neither victory nor hope in it. The two families, Jewish and German, are destroyed. The German people may survive through the lower classes, the servants who got away, but the commercial and agricultural elites collapse. Ada and Johannes represented the hope for German–Jewish relations. Johannes-Esau, the Jew who had become German, embodied it. He fails. Schäfer's message is that assimilation is impossible because of deep hatreds on both sides. Yet Schäfer is no Nazi, at least not yet. German hatred is an obstacle to Jewish integration, too, and Paul, the arsonist, is a criminal. He parodies Christian ideals with pagan conviviality, and plays havoc with Christian Jacob, but Christianity remains the marker of German nationality, and the Bible remains its frame of reference; only Esau, rather than Jacob, wears the mantle of the heroic ancient Hebrew (p. 74). Schäfer searches for language that will articulate new racial gods, German and Jewish, sever Esau from his Jewish origin, and decouple Jacob & Esau, but he does not find it. *Jakob und Esau* pushed conservative nationalist antisemitism to its limits – and it still fell short of Nazi requirements.

In Schäfer's drama, antisemitic politics was still emergent. Forty years later, in Sammy Gronemann's (1875–1952) comedy *Jakob und Christian* (1937), antisemitic politics is in full bloom: Protagonists freely utter Nazi slogans, such as "Kauf nicht bei Juden" (Don't buy from Jews) and "Juden unerwünscht" (Jews unwelcome).[76] Zionists commonly responded to Nazi racialization by counterposing a new Jewish racial type, but, unexpectedly, Gronemann, an Orthodox Zionist lawyer and playwright, parodied Nazi and Jewish stereotypes alike by driving "Jew" and "Aryan" *ad absurdum*. Using a comedy of errors in its Jewish variation, the *Purimspiel* (Purim play), with cross-references to Shakespeare's *The Merchant of Venice* – "Who is here the Jew and who is the merchant?" – Gronemann had Aryan and Jewish identities shifting between the two protagonists, Jakob and Christian. He subverted Nazi racial stereotypes and the Jacob & Esau typology as well, and yet he also showed their power: Identities shifted, but the stereotypes remained intact, and racialization proved overwhelming. Working around race was the best that the protagonists (and Enlightenment universalism) could hope to do.

Gronemann received legal academic and Orthodox Jewish education in Berlin, but responded enthusiastically to Theodor Herzl and became a lifelong Zionist activist, serving on the court of the World Zionist Congress. His memoirs reflect mainstream Zionist views on Jewish–non-Jewish relations.[77] The stereotypes of the drunkard and dull Goy and the business-savvy Jew remain intact throughout *Jakob und Christian*. The rabbinic imperative inspiring the Purimspiel – "One must get drunk on Purim until unable to distinguish between accursed Haman and blessed Mordekhai" (*BT* Megilah 7b) – does not assume a change of characters, only the inability to distinguish between them. The literary medium, however, overcomes these limits: Racialization collapses when uncertainty emerges as to the identity of Aryan and Jew, and Jakob and Christian alike articulate antisemitism.

Gronemann wrote *Jakob und Christian* during his Paris exile (1933–36), just before he moved to Palestine. The play was performed in Vienna in 1936, in the Ha-Matateh Satirical Theater in Tel Aviv in 1937 (under the title *Yaakov or Christian*), and in the same year, in Warsaw (under

---

[76] Jan Kühne of the Hebrew University drew my attention to Gronemann and kindly provided me with typescripts of both the German original and the 1937 Hebrew translation by Avigdor Hameiri. Both are available at the Israeli Center for the Documentation of Performing Arts, Tel Aviv, 15.2.6 and 2.4.7, respectively.

[77] Sammy Gronemann, *Reminiscences of a Yeqe* (in Hebrew), trans. Dov Stock (Sadan) from the German (Tel Aviv: Am Oved, 1946).

Jakob und Esau). Jewish comedy laughed at Nazi antisemitism, the last time Jews could so do.[78]

The play is set in a small pre–World War I German town. It opens after the funeral of Emerentia, the mother of Christian and wet nurse of Jakob. Christian was an illegitimate child, whose father, it turns out later in the play, was the drunkard Dr. Wendel. Poor Emerentia, who was thrown into the street and taken in by the town's single Jew, Saul Paradies, the only one to show her "Christian mercy." Jakob was born a few days after Christian as his family was traveling through town. His mother died at birth, and his father hired Emerentia to nurse him. The Jewish father provided for Christian's upkeep, and Emerentia accompanied the rich Jewish family to Bucharest, leaving Christian behind and returning three years later. Christian grew up splendidly, turning the money she earned from the Jews into a fortune. He has become a firm director and an outspoken German nationalist and antisemite. He is about to marry the Baroness Aurora. Her brother, the local governor, aware of Christian's inheritance, approves of the marriage and encourages Christian to run for the Reichstag.

The great surprise comes after the funeral: The priest reveals to Christian that Emerentia, in her last confession, told him that she exchanged the babies before going to Bucharest so that she would not be separated from her child and he would grow up in an affluent family. Christian is Jakob, and his world has now collapsed: Racial antisemite that he is, he refuses to take comfort in his baptism. His German duty, he tells Aurora, is to tell her that he is a Jew. Aurora, who is Gronemann's equivalent of Shakespeare's Portia, is full of acumen and good sense, and tells Christian that as an aristocrat, she has never taken to populist anti-semitism, and that he, Christian, demonstrates the vitality of the Jewish race. Let his origins remain a secret. As a candidate for parliament, Christian now delivers a fiery antisemitic speech, calling for a boycott of Jewish businesses. The papers portray Christian as a candidate of peasant origins, a thorn in the Socialists' side, and celebrate his engagement to Aurora as the making of an ideal German family.

At the opening of the second scene, Jakob Jacubowitz, called to present himself by the notary of Emerentia's will, arrives from Bucharest. All anticipate a rich Jew, but instead, Jakob arrives as a peddler who was arrested by the police. It turns out that he squandered his parents' fortune. The will is then read: Emerentia has given all her money to Jakob. Christian now reveals his recently acquired identity: He is truly

---

[78] Jan Kühne, "'Wer ist wer?!' Sammy Gronemanns *Jakob und Christian*," *Pardes* 19 (2013): 191–206, provides a history of the reception.

Jakob. Those present begin adjusting to the forthcoming public scandal, and Jakob begins advancing claims as an Aryan German, when Dr. Wendel throws a second bomb. Unbeknownst to Emerentia, he, too, may have switched the babies so that his son could go with Emerentia to Bucharest, but he cannot remember whether he actually did so or not. However, he did record a birthmark on one of the boys. Before he reveals what is recorded, both Aurora and Paradies suggest that no winner would emerge from the disclosure of true racial identity, as both lives would be destroyed by public scandal, legal trouble, and difficulty in assuming a new identity. They propose a compromise: The inheritance would be equally divided, and none of the mix-up would be made public. Christian would remain an Aryan German and run for parliament and Jakob would remain a Rumanian Jew, but his poverty would be alleviated. All agree, but the governor still wishes to know the identity of the real Jew. Wendel is about to reveal it – when the curtain falls.

Initially, it is not difficult to guess that Christian is the real Jakob. Gronemann counterposes the savvy Jewish businessman to the hapless Goy, and even Christian's antisemitism is construed as Jewish self-hatred. Destabilization first occurs when, confronting Jakob, Christian imagines himself as this "Jew," and the governor recognizes that his future brother-in-law may be Jewish; so Jacob "the Jew," appearing as Christian, has once again outwitted the Germans. The uncertainty that comes with the prospect of a double switch then undermines not only "ancient German blood" but also the notion of Jewish race, as Jakob, now again truly a Jew, continues to channel German antisemitism. Who is the Jew here? Aurora's wisdom is to accept life in a racialized world without succumbing to racial essentialism: Whatever their race, Christian cannot be Jewish and Jacob cannot be German. She can see through the matter of race because, like the Jew Paradies, she upholds the ideals of humanity, empathy, and love. But her ideals are not powerful enough to shape reality. Race is undermined but racialization vindicated.

Aurora's compromise constitutes an unusual ending to a Purimspiel or a Shakespearian comedy and is just as utopian as the *convivencia* envisioned by German-Jewish literature. Gronemann still viewed German antisemitism as largely instrumental: Like Esau, the Germans would sell their morals for lentil soup: They enjoy Jewish food and crave Jewish money. But Nazi slogans make it clear that race relations have advanced beyond Gronemann's cheerful disposition, and with Haman's presence intimated in any Purimspiel, there is even a hint of an extermination threat. Amaleq lurks in the background.

Thomas Mann's Hebrew Jacob

Schäfer and Gronemann wrote their theater plays quickly. Thomas Mann devoted nearly two decades, from the mid-Weimar years to the middle of World War II, to *Joseph and His Brothers*. The mammoth novel, a tetralogy, reflected the rapidly changing context of its production. *The Tales of Jacob* and *The Young Joseph*, the tetralogy's first and second books, carried the story from Jacob & Esau to the brothers' sale of Joseph into slavery. They reflected Mann's engagement with myth in Weimar and had been completed before the Nazis arrived in power; they were published in Berlin, in 1933 and 1934, respectively.[79] *Joseph in Egypt* developed the story of Joseph's Egyptian master's wife's obsessive love for him. It was written, in part, during Mann's Swiss exile, when he was still keeping his anti-Nazi politics subdued, and was published in Vienna in 1936.[80] *Joseph the Provider*, the fourth and final book, recounting Joseph's rise to Viceroy of Egypt and his reunification with his family, was written in the United States between 1940 and 1942. It celebrated the New Deal and American global leadership and was published in 1943 in Stockholm.[81]

In his 1948 introduction to the complete novel, Mann underlined its political character.[82] His commitment to the Enlightenment increased over the two decades as did his disenchantment with irrationalism, but *Joseph and His Brothers* still carried a unified message. Against the backdrop of violent antisemitism, Mann cultivated the Hebrew Patriarchs Jacob and Joseph as mythological figures that answered modernity's queries. His daring, grandiose, and revolutionary project constituted a reaffirmation of the Jews' role in the making of European civilization and made them, via their Hebrew ancestors, the prime agents articulating modernity's response to the crisis of National Socialism.

In *Joseph and His Brothers*, Mann turned to religious myth for an answer to the existential challenge posed in *The Magic Mountain* (*Der Zauberberg*, 1924).[83] The latter book left the struggle of life and death, and the conflicting appeals of reason and decadence (illness), unresolved. Mann was now exploring whether myth could bring the two together and still

---

[79] *Die Geschichten Jaakobs* (Berlin: S. Fischer, 1933); *Der Junge Joseph* (Berlin: S. Fischer, 1934); *Joseph and His Brothers*, trans. H. T. Lowe-Porter (New York: A. Knopf, 1934); *Young Joseph*, trans. H. T. Lowe-Porter (New York: A. Knopf, 1935).

[80] *Joseph in Ägypten* (Vienna: Bermann-Fischer, 1936); *Joseph in Egypt*, trans. H. T. Lowe-Porter, 2 vols. (New York: A. Knopf, 1938).

[81] *Joseph, der Ernährer* (Stockholm: Bermann-Fischer, 1943); *Joseph the Provider*, trans. H. T. Lowe-Porter (New York: A. Knopf, 1944).

[82] *Joseph and His Brothers*, trans. H. T. Lowe-Porter (New York: A. Knopf, 1948). I have used this edition. A new Everyman's Library translation by John E. Wood was published by Knopf in 2005.

[83] *The Magic Mountain*, trans. H. T. Lowe-Porter (New York: A. Knopf, 1927).

affirm life and reason. He went down "the well of history" to the Ancient East in search of a truth beyond history, a pattern against which historical development, above all of modernity and the West, could be measured. Myth appeared as a timeless presence, and the ever-changing seasons reflected in ancient symbols and rituals seemed like a natural pattern underlying history. Myth was cyclical: Ancient gods – the Babylonian Tammuz, the Egyptian Osiris, the Greek Adonis – died annually and went down to the underworld, only to reemerge and come back to life with the change of seasons. Mann thought that the Hebrew Patriarchs were modeled on the ancient eastern gods, that they replicated the pattern by going down to Egypt and returning to the Land. Yet against cyclical myth, they, especially Joseph, represented progress: monotheism, orderly government, and social welfare. Could biblical myth vindicate modernity's quest for rationality and progress?

Nietzsche enthusiasts were the leading proponents of myth in Weimar culture, and members of the George Circle – a literary group centered on the poet Stefan George – romanticized it. The conflicting roles in civilization of Apollo and Dionysius, rationality and irrationality, provided their major theme. In his romantic exposition of Swiss anthropologist Johann Jakob Bachofen, future Nazi intellectual Alfred Bäumler amplified the contrast of father, sun, and *Geist* with mother, earth, emotion, fertility, sexuality, and death.[84] These became motifs in Mann's reworking of myth. Myth was not, however, an exclusively right-wing affair: Psychologists from Freud to Jung showed a keen interest in it. Mann felt enraptured, fascinated, and repelled at the same time. He expressed his aversion to the "dark romantic celebration (Nachtschwärmerei) . . . of earth, folk, nature, past, and death," and affirmed that "a return to [myth] can happen only as a result of self-delusion, [of] ultraromantic . . . exorcizing of the mind."[85] Yet he, too, was seeking "the transformation of Tradition into Present as a timeless mystery, or the experiencing of the self as myth."[86] In 1934, he told philologist Károly Kerényi that he wanted to move from bourgeois individuality to the universally human via the mythical archetype, and thereby humanize myth.[87] He would

---

[84] Alfred Bäumler, "Einleitung: Bachofen der Mythologue der Romantik," in *J. J. Bachofen: Der Mythus von Orient und Occident*, ed. Manfred Schroeter (Munich: Beck, 1926), pp. xxiii–ccxciv.

[85] Thomas Mann, "Pariser Rechenschaft" [1926], in *Gesammelte Werke*, 13 vols. (Frankfurt am Main: S. Fischer, 1960), 11: 48; *A Sketch of My Life*, trans. H. T. Lowe-Porter (New York: A. Knopf, 1960), p. 67.

[86] Mann to Ernst Bertram (of the George Circle), December 28, 1926, in *Letters of Thomas Mann, 1889–1955*, selected by and trans. Richard and Clara Winston (Berkeley: University of California Press, 1990), pp. 141–42; henceforth *Letters*.

[87] February 10, 1934, in *Letters*, pp. 182–84.

construct, "by means of a mythical psychology, a psychology of the myth," reorienting myth (*Umfunktionierung*) so as to create a new humanism.[88]

The new humanism needed a new god. The biblical story of Joseph, Mann told Frankfurt Rabbi Jakob Horovitz, was one of god making: Joseph was a "Tammuz-Osiris-Adonis-Dionysius figure. . . . The realization of the essentially timeless (Tammuz) myth would have been a major psychological trait in all the people of that world."[89] Joseph identified with the Oriental gods, and the Egyptians must have treated him as one. The George Circle was in search of a god-man. A series of biographies, from Friedrich Gundolf on Goethe and Shakespeare to Ernst Kantorowicz on Emperor Friedrich II, sought to portray heroic individuals, Nietzschean supermen who embodied the spirit of the age and overcame value relativism.[90] Max Weber ridiculed such efforts and acquiesced in modern life's fragmentation, and in unresolvable ideological conflicts, which he likened to demons competing.[91] Unlike the George Circle's historical individuals, Weber's ideal types were conceptual structures that ordered reality and made understanding and explanation possible, neither ideals nor reality itself. Mann deployed the mythical archetype, Joseph as god-man, to close the gap between Weber's ideal type and the George Circle's heroic individuals. This was a dangerous exercise. Mann foreswore history and Christianity and descended to the underworld, hoping to reemerge with a biblical myth, a god-man, that would ground humanism and countervail National Socialism.

Mann was unique in deploying Oriental myth to support the Enlightenment. Against the romanticism of the George Circle and the Nazis, he asserted, with increasing aggressiveness, the Apollonian ideal and shaped Joseph-el as a perfect balance of desire and control. Yet more radical, he turned to the Bible for myth instead of to the classical world or the Orient. He folded Greece into the Orient, and showed biblical myth emerging from, and yet transcending, Babylonian and Egyptian myths. Most revolutionary was his recognition of the Old Testament as Hebrew,

---

[88] *A Sketch of My Life*, pp. 67–68; "The Theme of the Joseph Novels" [1942], in *Thomas Mann's Addresses Delivered at the Library of Congress, 1942–1949* (Washington DC: Library of Congress, 1963), pp. 1–19. *Umfunktionierung* appears only in the German version: "Joseph und seine Brüder: Ein Vortrag," in *Gesammelte Werke*, 11: 658. I am aware that Mann's 1942 statement defines the project in a way that was not available to him earlier.

[89] Dated June 11, 1927, in *Letters*, pp. 143–45.

[90] Friedrich Gundolf, *Shakespeare und der deutsche Geist* (Berlin: G. Bondi, 1914), and *Goethe* (Berlin: G. Bondi, 1916); Ernst Kantorowicz, *Kaiser Friedrich der Zweite* (Berlin: G. Bondi, 1927).

[91] Max Weber, "Science as a Vocation," in *The Vocation Lectures*, ed. David S. Owen and Tracy B. Strong, trans. Rodney Livingstone (Indianapolis, IN: Hackett, 2004), pp. 1–31.

which was tantamount to its re-Judaization, and his positing of the Jews, qua Hebrews, as the Western ideal and the answer to the modern predicament. He considered the Jewish Question European, indeed, pivotal for civilization. The Jewish people (qua Hebrews) were the carriers of Western culture.[92] Joseph exemplified masterful management of modernity's ills. Having gone through hell, he reemerged triumphant from the educational (*Bildung*) process, able to pacify Weber's raging demons, men and gods alike. Joseph married into the Egyptian priestly nobility and became integrated in Egyptian society, while retaining his Jewish identity. A master of context and of accommodating change, he answered, at one and the same time, modernity's quest and the Jewish Question.

Recent scholarship has tended to view the Hebrew Bible, and specifically the Genesis stories, as a late literary invention, embedding, to be sure, earlier narratives but reshaping them beyond historical recognition. Even adherents of more traditional source criticism, dating the narratives to the First Temple period, no longer believe in the Genesis stories' historicity. Bluntly stated, there was no "Patriarchal Age." Mann and his contemporaries thought otherwise: Biblical stories reflected a historical reality. Mann moved between myth and history to tell the biblical story, and created a colorful picture of the biblical Orient. The Patriarchs appeared to be conversant with a plurality of gods and myths around them – Joseph and Akhenaten had a theological exchange on monotheism – but Israel's religion emerged as unique and dignified. Mann had no interest in source criticism, that is, in the Bible's historical formation. Encountering biblical discrepancies and repetitions, he did not assume divergent sources but availed himself of Midrash or myth to explain them. His rare challenges to the biblical narrative, as with the story of Dinah, were grounded in his psychology – he thought the protagonists must have acted otherwise – and not in history, and were used as opportunities to expand the biblical story. History provided material for Mann's psychology of myth, but his interest in it was centered on grounding his psychology. Precisely because he remythologized texts, which historians treat as literature, the historicity of myth was of secondary importance.

All the same, Mann did significant research on the biblical Orient. He could not survey the biblical literature tracked in this book, but his diaries suggest that several works on the Ancient East and a compendium of Midrash provided him with shortcuts. Alfred Jeremias's book on the Old

---

[92] "The Dangers Facing Democracy" [1940], in *Gesammelte Werke* 11: 491–98. During the war years, Mann showed an increasingly positive attitude toward Christianity, which *Joseph and His Brothers* marginalized. In attacking the Jews, he thought, the antisemites sought to undermine Christian civilization.

Testament and the Ancient East, which, written from a Pan-Babylonian perspective, saw biblical myth as derivative, provided his main source for Babylonia.[93] Arthur Weigall's *Akhnaton, Pharaoh of Egypt* (1910), which tracked the breakthrough to monotheism, was crucial for Egypt.[94] A bit later, a book by the wandering Sephardi Jewish scholar Abraham Shalom Yahuda, *The Language of the Pentateuch*, became a major source for Egyptian civilization.[95] Yahuda envisioned the Patriarchs retaining their Hebrew identity in Egypt but shaped by Egyptian civilization, in ways more crucial to Israel's formation than their Babylonian origins. Mann's correspondence, beginning in 1934, with Hungarian classical philologist and cultural anthropologist Károly Kerényi (1897–1973), who was developing his interpretation of Greek myth against mainstream German philology, contributed to the project's later parts.[96] Influenced by psychologist Carl Jung, Kerényi viewed the Greek gods as archetypes of the human soul and, like Mann, interpreted Greek myths in an Oriental context and sought to humanize myth against National Socialism. Finally, Max Scheler's *The Human Place in the Cosmos* (1928), an attempted anthropologico-philosophical synthesis of Greek rationality, biblical theism, and biological evolution, served Mann as a model inquiry.[97] Scheler viewed myth, religion, and metaphysics as developmental stages but, for Mann, opened up possibilities for thinking about myth as working its way into the present.

Myth provided Mann's leitmotif, but Midrash enriched his biblical story. He used Midrash extensively, if selectively, weaving it so seamlessly with myth that readers unfamiliar with rabbinic literature could easily miss it. Where the rabbis struggled with discrepancies in the biblical text and told stories to make the biblical narrative cohere, Mann embellished them further. The sale of Joseph into slavery was a case in point: Did the brothers or the Midianites do it first? Following late Jewish sources, Mann

---

[93] Alfred Jeremias, *Das Alte Testament im Lichte des Alten Orients*, 3d ed. (Leipzig: J.C. Hinrichsche Buchhandlung, 1916).

[94] Arthur Weigall, *The Life and Time of Akhnaton, Pharaoh of Egypt* (Edinburgh: W. Blackwood and Sons, 1910); *Echnaton, König von Ägypten und seine Zeit*, trans. Hermann Kees (Basel: B. Schwabe, 1923). The 1922 discovery of the tomb of Akhenaton's son, Tutankhamun, made waves and overhauled perceptions of the period.

[95] Abraham Shalom Yahuda, *Die Sprache des Pentateuch in ihren Beziehungen zum Aegyptischen* (Berlin: Walter de Gruyter, 1929); *The Language of the Pentateuch in Its Relations to Egyptian* (Oxford: Oxford University Press, 1932). Mann visited Egypt twice, in 1926 and 1930.

[96] Károly Kerényi, *Romandichtung und Mythologie: Ein Briefwechsel mit Thomas Mann* (Zurich: Rhein-Verlag, 1945).

[97] Max Scheler, *Die Stellung des Menschen im Kosmos* (Darmstadt: Reichl, 1928); *The Human Place in the Cosmos*, trans. Manfred S. Frings (Evanston, IL: Northwestern University Press, 2009).

arranged for the Midianites to pull Joseph out of the pit, and for the brothers to sell him to them.[98] Where the rabbis sought to diminish the Patriarchs' transgressions (Genesis 35:22), suggesting that Reuben did not have intercourse with his father's mistress but merely upset the couple's bed to protest Jacob's neglect of his mother, Leah, Mann joined the stories of incest and the son's jealousy, and had Joseph report the transgressions to Jacob in order to establish the grounds for the brothers' hatred.[99] Mann could show homiletic ingenuity of his own: Attentive to Jacob's blessing of Reuben as "my firstborn, my strength, and the first fruit of my vitality" (Genesis 49:3), he colorfully portrayed Jacob's prowess on the marriage night, when he thought that he was making love to Rachel.[100] *Joseph and His Brothers* represents a foremost example of the use of Midrash in nonrabbinic literature.

Mann needed only limited erudition to become a master of the rabbinic tale: He used Micha Josef Bin Gorion (Berdyczewski's) compendium *Die Sagen der Juden* (Legends of the Jews) and supplemented it by correspondence with scholarly rabbis, like Jakob Horovitz of Frankfurt.[101] Yet myth remained closer to his heart than Midrash. The ruminations of Oskar Goldberg (1885–1952), the maverick Jewish religious philosopher and Weimar socialite, on the interdependence of the Mosaic God and his people shaped the novel conceptually in ways that Midrash did not. To Goldberg, the tribal God offered the Hebrews protection in exchange for their war service. Their triumph in the fight against foreign gods was his. Religious myth was about biological survival. The Prophets' universal God represented a decline.[102] Mann wove myth and history in ways that softened Goldberg's racial conceptions, but they still colored his Hebrews. Varieties of Judaism, some divergent, found their way into the novel, and each enabled the project in a different fashion. When Mann stated that *Joseph and His Brothers* was not a Jewish novel, he meant only

---

[98] *Joseph and His Brothers*, pp. 392–407. For the rabbinic quandary, see the exchanges of medieval commentators on Genesis 37:28, in *Miqraot Gedolot ha-Keter*, ed. Menaḥem Kohen (Ramat-Gan: Bar-Ilan University, 1992–2013). For Mann's sources: *Die Sagen der Juden*, ed. Micha Josef Bin Gorion, 5 vols. (Frankfurt am Main: Rütten und Loening, 1913–1927): 3: 66–68; *Joseph und seine Brüder*, ed. Micha Josef Bin Gorion (Berlin: Schocken, 1933), pp. 11–13. Bin Gorion's main source was *Sefer ha-Yashar*, ed. and introduction by Joseph Dan (Jerusalem: Bialik Institute, 1986), 81b–82a.

[99] *Joseph and His Brothers*, pp. 48–54. For the rabbis: *BT*, Shabbat 55:22. Mann also knew Jubilees' recitation of the incest: *Die Sagen der Juden*, 3: 230–31.

[100] *Joseph and His Brothers*, pp. 199–202.

[101] Jakob Horovitz, *Die Josephserzählung* (Frankfurt am Main: Kauffmann, 1921); *Letters*, pp. 158–60.

[102] Oskar Goldberg, *Die Wirklichkeit der Hebraer* [1925] (Wiesbaden: Harrassowitz, 2005); Christian Hülshörster, *Thomas Mann und Oskar Goldbergs "Wirklichkeit der Hebräer"* (Frankfurt am Main: V. Klostermann, 1999). Richard Wolin of the CUNY Graduate Center first directed me to Goldberg.

that he deployed the Hebrews to answer a European and not a Jewish question.[103] The Jewish story became the story of civilization.

***

Joseph and His Brothers begins slowly with a prelude entitled "Descent into Hell." Mann describes going down the well of history in search of human life's mythical pattern, and likens it to the descent into the underground world that his protagonists, the Oriental gods and the Hebrew Patriarchs, will go through in the novel. A meeting between Jacob and Joseph by a well on a moonlit night follows. Jacob, at 66, is an old man, thin, bearded and tall, an imposing figure, walking with a cane, always concerned about losing his favorite son, the seventeen-year-old Joseph, child of his beloved wife Rachel, "so incomprehensibly taken away" by a jealous God seven years earlier. The sternly monotheistic father has caught the handsome youth half naked, performing a dance to display his beauty to the moon and the Eastern goddess Ishtar. A deep conversation follows, in which Jacob, introspective and musing, reveals his anxious search for God, and Joseph shows his rhetorical and social skills, as well as his comfort with religious innovation in a polytheistic universe. Joseph assures his father that God will never again ask for the sacrifice of the firstborn, and opines that what Jacob describes as a superstitious and corrupt Egyptian culture may manifest traits not incomparable to their own religion. To Mann, Joseph, versed in several languages and cuneiform writing, manages both religious diversity and the "Jewish Question" more aptly than his father.

Jacob & Esau become central in the second chapter. Introducing the two as archetypes, Mann defines their identity and relationship as the accursed firstborn versus the younger blessed child. Yet mythical archetypes are not without irony, which opens up room for change, history and storytelling: The name that Jacob receives after struggling with the angel, Israel, is incongruent with his personality. He has a deep aversion to violence, and his struggles are spiritual. This becomes evident as Mann, using a late rabbinic midrash, introduces Jacob at his nadir: On his flight abroad, Jacob is robbed by Esau's son Elifaz and begs for his life.[104] The event "touched Jacob's pride and honor more sorely than anything else all his life; it would have undermined forever the dignity and self-confidence

---

[103] For an exhaustive bibliographical consideration of Mann's use of Jewish sources and the novel's Jewish character, see Heike Breitenbach, "Thomas Mann und die jüdische Tradition: Untersuchungen zu Joseph und seine Brüder unter besonderer Berücksichtigung der Schriftauslegung des Midrasch" (Ph.D. diss., Rheinisch-Westfälischen Technischen Hochschule Aachen, 2009).

[104] Rashi on Genesis 29:11 and *Midrash Agadah*, ed. S. Buber (Vienna: A. Fanto,1894), p. 74 (Genesis 28:20). Both probably had an earlier source, now lost. Mann found the story in *Sagen der Juden*, ed. Bin Gorion, 2: 397–99.

of another man.... He wanted to live not out of common cowardice ... but because he was consecrated, because the promise and the blessing handed down from Abram lay on him" (pp. 87–88). Against this song of praise for the Jewish archetype, Mann depicts Esau as a weeping, dejected loser, an accursed man destined for bondage, a hunter who will cast his fate with the desert people against civilization. Not surprisingly, the reconciliation of Jacob & Esau has none of the grandeur others see in it. Esau appears as a pathetic brute, and Jacob is contemptuous of him and eager to send him on his way. Esau, who is no longer Christian, as Mann returned him to the Orient, has no role to play in Jewish history.

In the third chapter, Mann follows with a colorful description of the rape of Dinah and the sack of Sichem (Shekhem) by Jacob's sons, which makes it possible for him to describe the religious, cultural, and political relationships obtaining between the Hebrew Patriarchs and the peoples of the Land, and to display the range of characters among Joseph's brothers who will play crucial roles later in the novel. He then settles on retelling the story of Jacob from the theft of the blessing to the death of Rachel. Rebecca appears as the moving spirit behind his trickery, with Jacob reluctantly obeying, but to Mann, Rebecca was fulfilling mythical destiny. Esau's claim that his father loved him most, and that he was robbed, ignored nature: Esau could not be blessed as he represented the accursed Cain type and his intermarriages to idol worshippers demonstrated as much. Isaac's blindness alone prevented him from recognizing this truth. All the same, God's ways are such that Jacob has to pay for Esau's tears, go into exile, be cheated by Laban in a tit for tat, and never know rest.[105]

Jacob brings blessings to Laban's bleak home. He discovers underground water and demonstrates business acumen that benefits both him and his host. "There must be more: if a man is easily content, so is God for him and withdraws the hand of blessing," he tells Laban upon arrival (p. 154). Beginning as Laban's servant, he moves on to contract work and is promised Rachel. He labors a long seven years for her and dreamily awaits the time when they will join together, only to be misled on the wedding night and find himself with Leah. Mann is unkind to Leah, as he is to most biblical women, and portrays Jacob as equally ungenerous toward her, as she reinforced his disappointment in life. Having expended his love on Leah on the wedding night, Jacob finds that his marriage to Rachel is not quite the fulfillment of a lover's dream. God's jealousy of his boundless

---

[105] Mann used Midrash as the source for both Isaac's blindness and Esau' tears: *Midrash Tanḥuma*, ed. Solomon Buber (Vilnius: Romm, 1913): toledot 8, 24, respectively. The source for the Cain archetype is also the rabbinic genealogy: *Va-yiqra Rabbah* 27:11 (*Midrash Va-yiqra Rabbah*, ed. Mordechai Margaliot, 5 vols. [Jerusalem: Ministry of Education, 1953–60]).

love for Rachel and for Joseph results in the heartbreaking loss of both, the first forever, the second for long decades. Only Joseph's adept management of gods and men, and his better navigation of love, breaks the cycle of Jacob's defeats.

Joseph and His Brothers parted with two millennia of Christian and rabbinic typology and substituted the mythical archetype for it, cyclical repetition for linear progression. The novel makes a few allusions to Christ, but they are nonstarters.[106] Contrary to some views, Joseph is less a prefiguration of Christ and more a new variation of the Tammuz. At certain points, Mann seems bent on folding Christ, too, into the Tammuz myth, and the crucifixion and the Eucharist into ancient Eastern totemism.[107] His focus is on the Hebrews in ancient culture. He uses Midrash to elucidate the text but adamantly refuses any rabbinic typology that points beyond the ancient world. He reads modernity, and the Jewish Question, into Antiquity, but surreptitiously. Joseph represents a departure from tradition, and may exemplify the ideal bourgeois individual with his perfect balance of passion and control, but he can only emerge from the mythical archetype as a god-man, Joseph-el. Individual identities remain blurred: Abraham is typically but not biologically Isaac's father, and Eliezer is the typical head servant for all of the Patriarchs. The mythical archetype is the bridge across the ages, the principle of the social order, and the foundation for communal and familial ties. Myth serves the Enlightenment via the archetype, rescued from an imagined Orient by cutting through millennia of Christian and Jewish history.

Precisely because Mann's Jacob does not emerge as Isra-el, he appears more individual than does Joseph, a struggling modern man who has not quite found his way. Jacob casts an impressive figure. Seeker of divinity and wonderer of myth, he suffers for his uncompromising monotheism, and is repeatedly chastened by God for his passions. He shows dignity in poverty and humiliation, responds to violence by pondering the divine design, and is reassured by revelation that, for all his travails, he remains the man of the blessing. Like Weber's Calvinist, he sees a calling in economic engagement and labors incessantly, is cunning in trade, and witnesses the marks of divine blessing in his business success. A stern moralist and an imposing figure in his family, he is also a lover of nature

---

[106] On their deathbeds, Isaac prophesied a future Aqedah, "there shall be slain the man and the son instead of the beast [the ram] and in the place of God and ye shall eat" (p. 122), and in his blessing to Judah, Jacob prophesied Shilo's coming (traditionally Christ).

[107] Hermann Kurzke, *Thomas Mann: Epoche, Werk, Wirkung* (Munich: C. H. Beck, 1985), pp. 242–46, discusses a range of authors who see Joseph as a Christ figure. Todd Kontje, *The Cambridge Introduction to Thomas Mann* (Cambridge: Cambridge University Press, 2011), p. 80, sees in the Joseph *Bildungsroman* the beginning of salvific history. Notably, Judah's and not Joseph's genealogy leads to Christ.

and the open fields, and, apprehensive about urban life, a nomad by choice. Mann insists on Jacob's dignity, shows solidarity with him in defeat and oppression, and explains away his cunning as part of his calling. Jacob, the blessed, must exercise a measure of cunning so that Esau, an accursed primitive hunter, would not disrupt the universal order. Mann adopts the rabbinic view of Jacob but redefines his piety as biblical Oriental so as to bridge ancient and modern. Jacob embodies the dignity of the modern struggle, and renders meaningful Weber's hopeless wrestling with the demons, reenchanting his disenchanted world.

For all that Mann insisted on Jacob as an ancient Hebrew, he stands in defeat and suffering, in dignity and cunning, for the Jews. Mann crafted Jacob in the Jew's image and redefined negative Jewish stereotypes as positive Protestant ones. His philosemitism represented an unusual working out of liberal Protestant culture, a counterpart to its antisemitic pole. In Mann's secularized Protestantism, *sola scriptura* (by Scripture alone) no longer means direct access to the Word of God, but it still means disposing of two millennia of Christian and Jewish readings of the Bible and going down the well to the Ancient East to recover the Bible's original meaning. Rabbinic and Christian typologies of Cain and Jacob may be reconceptualized as Oriental archetypes, so that they do not lead to Gog u-Magog and Christ, but it is difficult not to see *sola gratia* (by Grace alone) and predestination behind the archetypes of Jacob the blessed and Esau the damned. If Weber bemoaned the irony of capitalism undermining the religious calling that gave rise to it, Mann again found the early modern Calvinist in the Oriental Jew, Jacob. Triumphant Joseph, redeemer of Egypt, may have solved the "Jewish Question" better than Jacob through successful assimilation, but it is Jacob who stands the most for the historical Jews whom Mann made an emblem for modern culture.

In contrast, Mann's Esau shows the loss incurred by his turn to myth. Mann works laboriously to mythologize Esau and render him meaningful. "Esau the Red" is associated with the planet Mars and the foreign gods, with the underworld and the "dark moon of the South," and at other times with the desert people and the sun (pp. 123–27). He is not, as the Bible tenuously suggests, the Edomites' ancestor, but he is associated with them, as they are deemed a goat people and he is considered a friend of the satyrs. Everyone around him, and he himself, recognizes that he, an emotional, shallow, and brutish hunter, is the accursed first son, the Cain type. The rabbinic Cain genealogy does not lead beyond Genesis in Mann, and he finds the transformation of Esau into a Roman puzzling: Why would "teachers and seers rail at Esau the red skinned ... more violently than his commonplace earthly person really merits" (p. 127)?

Mann is happy, however, to use late Midrash to expand his mythology. Ishmael and Esau, representatives of the underworld, join in a conspiracy to murder Isaac and Jacob.[108] Parricide exceeds Esau's depravity, and even the fratricide he leaves to his son Elifaz, and so the conspiracy comes to naught, but Mann has meanwhile filled in a gap in the biblical story: Elifaz's robbery of Jacob's gifts explains why he arrived penniless at Laban's house. Mann enriched the biblical story but, unlike Jacob, Esau has no message for modern life.

Mann accepted as unproblematic biblical consciousness of the Jews' ethnic difference, but insisted that religious calling, and not race, made Jacob and the Jews into a people. "Not even in a dream could the people of El Elyon assert that their community possessed racial purity. Godly was the bond of continuity; and in all the admixture of blood, it united the spiritual community" (pp. 82–83). The Hebrews were unique for their monotheism. They were chosen, that is, blessed, for their care in transmitting the religious mission across generations. Yet the Hebrews also learned foreign languages, followed foreign fashions, absorbed external cultural influences, and intermarried. Joseph's Egyptian acculturation, leadership, and intermarriage provided the ultimate response to antisemitism and the Jewish Question. Egypt was, like the contemporary West, an advanced civilization, but a sick one. The Egyptian Pharaoh, the tolerant, cosmopolitan, and monotheist Akhenaton, was, like the appeaser Neville Chamberlain, incapable of action. Joseph, who was acculturated in Egypt but retained the Hebrew nomads' sense of mission, became Egypt's savior by offering the Egyptians a "New Deal." Modern Jews, carriers of the biblical legacy, might become the West's saviors.

Mann's philosemitism deepened over time, but throughout his life, he paid homage to the cultural contribution that Jews had made to Europe.[109] He could disparage Jewish critics in antisemitic terms, but his wife was of Jewish origins, and Jews constituted a significant part of his audience. Unlike other liberal Protestants, he wished to retain a Jewish profile of European culture and was denounced as Jewish himself. His antiassimilationist stance became pronounced in *Joseph and His Brothers*: Joseph's Egyptian sons, Menashe and Ephraim, were to remain Jews. In interwar Germany, Mann was out of season, and the fate of Walther

---

[108] *Midrash Ha-Gadol* on Genesis 27:41, 28:8–9, ed. S. Schechter (Cambridge: Cambridge University Press, 1902). Note that while Midrash made Esau the leading conspirator, Mann reversed the order. His portrait of Ishmael is a prime example of anti-Arab Orientalism.

[109] Jacques Darmaun, *Thomas Mann et les juifs* (Basel: Peter Lang, 1995); Hermann Kurzke, *Thomas Mann: Life as a Work of Art: A Biography*, trans. Leslie Willson (Princeton, NJ: Princeton University Press, 2002), pp. 188–214, 264–66.

Rathenau, the German-Jewish counterpart to *Joseph the Provider*, is well known. In the United States, in contrast, Franklin Delano Roosevelt's New Deal team included Jews, and an American Jewish culture appeared to prevail over antisemitism. Cast in Roosevelt's image, *Joseph the Provider* appeared as a remote, but not quite utopian, prospect.

Utopian prospects aside, Mann increasingly realized, as he was nearing the novel's completion, that he was playing with fire. He took an enormous risk by driving humanity underground in the hope that, like Joseph, it would spring up again, revitalized by myth. Already in 1934, he was expressing concern about the anti-intellectualism and irrationalism involved in the "return of the European mind to ... the mythic realities."[110] His aversion to Romanticism grew with the years. In the last book, the Joseph myth is Apollonian, and free of the goriest portrayals of myths in the earlier books. For all of his apologetics, there is little doubt that Mann himself was fascinated by the decadent and toyed with death and racial myth. Oskar Goldberg denounced Mann in 1945 as an Enlightenment buff who failed to acknowledge his debt to him.[111] He was right, but so was Mann who, in *Dr. Faustus*, returned the favor by portraying Goldberg as a reckless and obnoxious Jewish intellectual who represented a decadent German culture that had prepared the way for National Socialism.[112]

There were also signs that the late turn to the Enlightenment did not produce altogether satisfactory results. Comparing Jacob's love for Rachel with Joseph's affection for Asenath, it is evident that Apollonian control and balance brought Joseph only limited joy. His adept management of the passions may have been the way that Mann came to terms with both his own homoerotic desires and the Jewish Question, but at the end of a long Bildung process, the author and the protagonist alike appear to have emerged as contented but joyless gods. The pacification of Weber's demons, it appears, was a story of civilization and its discontents. These were hardly the hopes for modernity with which the myth project began.

More crucially, by breaking with two millennia of Christian and rabbinic interpretive traditions, Mann gave up on resources for cultural healing that they had put at his disposal. Noticing the rabbis' discomfort with Joseph's intermarriage, he dismissed as "a pious fraud" their suggestion

---

[110] Letter to Károly Kerényi, February 10, 1934, in *Letters*, p. 183.
[111] Letter to a reader of the *Atlantic Monthly* who had previously criticized Mann in his letter to the editor, c. 1945, in *Thomas Mann und Oskar Goldberg*, pp. 277–79.
[112] *Doctor Faustus: The Life of the German Composer Adrian Leverkühn as Told by a Friend*, trans. H. T. Lowe-Porter (New York: A. Knopf, 1948), p. 279.

that Asenath was none other than Dinah's daughter, whom Jacob had saved from the brothers' wrath by delivering her to Egypt, where she grew up as Potifar's daughter (p. 1003).[113] Mann insisted that Dinah's child died of exposure to the elements at Jacob's command. There is no biblical evidence for infant exposure among the Hebrews, just as there is no source for Mann's account of Laban burying his infant son alive as a sacrifice to the gods. These were horrendous figments of Mann's imagination, part of his remythologization of the Bible. His cruel myths evinced his attraction to decadence, jettisoned Jewish and Christian consecration of human life, and stained the image of the Patriarchs whom he otherwise idealized. He missed the opportunity to put a bearable closure on the Shekhem massacre, as the rabbis had tried to do. Like Mann, they suspected that the brothers' primitive notion of honor might have put Dinah's issue at risk. Unlike him, they had Jacob save the child. Out of Shekhem's ruins, they built an Egyptian–Jewish marriage, בנין עדי עד. Jews would not have survived throughout the ages without such continual healing. Sadly, Mann's heroic modern effort to circumvent history and reach a mythical essence left humanity and the Jews ill-equipped for what was to come. לֹא זֶה הַדֶּרֶךְ.

Amaleq's Return: Orthodoxy in the Shadow of the Holocaust

The Soviet Revolution and the ethno-nationalizing states in Central and Eastern Europe confronted traditional Jewry with a major crisis in the interwar years. The Soviet Revolution brought emancipation but also a rapid dissolution of the traditional Jewish community, encouraged, indeed forced, from above by the Communist Party's Jewish section, the *Yevsektsiya*. Until its own dissolution in 1929, the Yevsektsiya conducted a militant campaign for atheism and Jewish assimilation, closed down communal Jewish institutions, disrupted Jewish education, and harassed the traditional leadership. In Eastern Europe, Jews encountered heightened national hostility and economic hardship, and traditional Jewish communities experienced the increasing pressures of secularization and nationalization. Traditional Jewry saw its constituency diminishing, as more and more Jews sought economic opportunity and pursued

---

[113] *Pirqe de-Rabbi Eliezer* 38, ed. C. M. Horowitz (Jerusalem: Maqor, 1972); *Targum Pseudo-Jonathan* on Genesis 41:45, 46:20, 48:9 (*Targum Pseudo-Jonathan of the Pentateuch*, ed. E. G. Clarke [Hoboken, NJ: Ktav Pub. House, 1984]). Mann says that the rabbis accomplished nothing: Asenath remained the issue of a foreigner, Shekhem. As Dinah was Jewish, the rabbis could not care less. Moreover, the rabbis were concerned at least as much about Asenath and Joseph's religious culture as they were about her ethnicity. And they badly wanted a happy ending to the Shekhem affair that filled them with horror.

secular culture. Zionism and the *Bund* offered alternatives to both Jewish Orthodoxy and Polish nationalism. The effort of the Ultra-Orthodox Party, the *Agudah*, to negotiate a special deal with the Polish government that would guarantee Jewish interests, in exchange for their withdrawal from the minorities' bloc, failed. Emigration to the United States, difficult after the Immigration Law of 1924, was not considered a viable option for Orthodox Jews: America was *treifidike* (impure; nonkosher), a country where Jews assimilated and lost their soul. Orthodox Jewry felt under siege. Edom and Amaleq were returning in force to haunt Jews in ways not seen since medieval times.

Two discursive changes marked Orthodox Jewry's siege mentality: The first was the Ḥasidic reaffirmation of Jacob's estrangement from Esau, and the second, a novelty, was the reincarnation of Amaleq in non-Orthodox Jews. The charitable nineteenth-century conceptions of Amaleq as the evil inclination in humanity became marginalized. The enemy was not an inclination but living humans, Jews and non-Jews. *Die Torah Quelle*, a compilation of biblical homilies published in interwar Warsaw by the leading Agudah ideologist, Alexander Zysha Friedman, rearticulated the *Sefat Emet*: "When Esau kisses Jacob, this is to Jacob a most painful bite."[114] Secular education and cross-cultural exchange cause harm. Those who promoted them now became Amaleq.

Until World War II, Ultra-Orthodox leaders viewed non-Orthodox Jews, whether liberal, Zionist, Bundist, or Polish nationalist, as the main threat to the future of the Jewish people and, disturbingly, blamed them for anti-semitism. Later on, as the Holocaust began, they held non-Orthodox Jews at least partially responsible for it. Ultra-Orthodoxy's indisputable leader, the aging Ḥafeẓ Ḥayim (Yisrael Meir Hakohen, 1838–1933), designated the Yevsektsiya as Amaleq.[115] One did not need to be a communist bent on destroying Judaism to be called Amaleq, however. Elḥanan Wasserman (1875–1941), Ḥafeẓ Ḥayim's student and the leader of Lithuanian Jewry, affirmed that Jews who had cast away the Torah were Amaleqites: "Since the rule of the Torah was overthrown, the seed of Amaleq has swarmed among us, like the *Yevsektsiya* . . . who spread throughout the Diaspora . . . including the Holy Land, and there is no difference between the two, only the first write in Yiddish and the latter in Hebrew . . . and God has vowed that his name is not perfect and his throne is not perfect until both are blotted out of the world."[116] Amaleq was Jewish.

---

[114] *Maayana shel Torah*, 5 vols., trans. M. Ẓevi (Tel Aviv: Peer, 1956), 1: 153.

[115] Elliott Horowitz, *Reckless Rites* (Princeton, NJ: Princeton University Press, 2006), p. 141.

[116] Elḥanan Wasserman, *Omer Ani Maasai la-Melekh* (I address my verses to the King) (Vilnius: n.p., 1936), p. 5. The author of this exterminationist statement, directed against Jews, went nobly to his death in the fall of 1941.

Ultra-Orthodox leaders seriously underestimated the Nazi danger. The halakhically innovative German rabbi, Jeḥiel Jacob Weinberg, who had been traditionally educated in Lithuania but came to admire modern German Orthodoxy, saw in National Socialism an understandable reaction to communism and the excesses of modern culture.[117] The Nazis were violently antisemitic and Amaleq, to be sure, but as Gershon Greenberg has shown, well into World War II Ultra-Orthodox leaders were seeing them as God's instrument for punishing Israel, and a messenger who might return the Jews to their roots.[118] In racial theory and in the 1930s anti-Jewish legislation, which reversed emancipation, Friedman and Wasserman found a tit for tat for the Jews' breaking of the commandments and for their efforts to "behave like non-Jews." Judaism's internal destruction had preceded the external one. Amaleq had always been there, they reasoned, and had always been bent on destroying Israel and the Torah. Until modern times, however, the walls separating Jacob from Esau had afforded Jews protection. Emancipation and assimilation removed the barriers and made it possible for Amaleq to unleash destruction. Amaleq was unwittingly doing God's work. Ironically, nationalism and socialism, which had so appealed to the Jews and destroyed the Torah world for millions, now became National Socialism, which excluded them. The Jews who wished to write themselves into the history of the nations, said Wasserman, were getting kicked out of it. Their sole escape was repentance and a return to Torah observance.

A call for a return to Judaism came in February 1939 from Shlomo Zalman Ehrenreich (1863–1944), rabbi in Şimleu-Silvaniei, Transylvania, and a former graduate of the Pressburg yeshivah. Following mounting reports of Nazi persecution in Germany and Austria, and witnessing battered refugees passing through a nearby city, the Jewish community declared a day of fasting. Ehrenreich's sermon elucidated a homily from *Genesis Rabba* on the verse "The voice is Jacob's voice but the hands are Esau's hands" (Genesis 27:22).[119] Balaam advised Israel's enemies that as

---

[117] Marc B. Shapiro, *Between the Yeshiva World and Modern Orthodoxy: The Life and Works of Rabbi Jehiel Jacob Weinberg, 1884-1966* (London: Littman Library. 1999), pp. 110–37.

[118] Gershon Greenberg, "Amaleq in the Holocaust Period" (in Hebrew), in *Derekh ha-Ruaḥ: Festschrift for Eliezer Schweid*, ed. Yehoyada Amir, 2 vols. (Jerusalem: Van Leer Institute, 2005): 2: 891–913, and "Introduction: Ultra-Orthodox Responses during and following the War," in *Wrestling with God: Jewish Theological Responses during and after the Holocaust*, ed. Steven T. Katz with Shlomo Biderman and Gershon Greenberg (Oxford: Oxford University Press, 2007), pp. 11–26.

[119] *Bereshit Rabbah* 65:20; Shlomo Zalman Ehrenreich, *Derashot leḥem Shlomo* (Brooklyn NY: Joshua Katz, 1976), p. 285 f. The same idea is repeated on p. 184 in the fall of 1943. English translation: *Wrestling with God*, pp. 62–65. See also the discussion by Barbara

long as the voice of Jewish children was heard in synagogues and study halls, they would not prevail against Israel, but if the voice stopped, Esau's hands might prevail. Ehrenreich suggested a different reading. He noted that the first "voice" is spelled without the vowel (קל) while the second has it (קול). The ו addition, equal to the number six, was for the *Mishnah*'s six orders, the Oral Torah. When Jacob's voice was the Torah's voice, when קל was קול, the hands remained only his, and Israel prevailed. But when the Torah's voice stopped, Esau's hands became God's agent against the Jews, and Israel's enemies prevailed. This was happening around them. In response to Zionist and Reform Jews' transgressions, and in retribution for the sinfulness of urban life, God had turned the Germans, a civilized people, into beasts of prey who persecuted Israel. Let the Jews repent and turn persecution, as in Haman's day, into a renewal of the Covenant between God and his people. As late as 1943, Ehrenreich was still promoting the idea of Esau's hands being God's hands. God would surely not permit the destruction of a faithful Jewish people.

Yet God did just that. As the catastrophe unfolded, the concept of Amaleq as God's agent lost much of its power, and apocalyptic expectation for the coming of the Messiah and for Amaleq's destruction surged. Ehrenreich and Shlomo Zalman Unsdorfer, the last rabbinic leader of the Bratislava ghetto (and, like Ehrenreich, a graduate of the Sofers' Pressburg yeshivah), encouraged their congregants to ready themselves for redemption. Both were murdered in 1944.

In the aftermath of the war, the Agudah leader, Yiẓḥak Meir Levin, who survived in Palestine, and Simḥa Ellberg, who survived in Shanghai, spoke of the Holocaust as an incomparable Aqedah, *Olah* (sacrificial offering), and *Qidush Ha-Shem* (sanctification of God's name), all of which, they said, signaled Israel's forthcoming redemption and the end of history.[120] Ultra-Orthodoxy found itself where Jews had been after the First Crusade and the Expulsion from Spain: unable to confront history, resorting to messianic redemption. The topos of the Kingdom of Esau and Amaleq, which had vanished since medieval times, reemerged, and Esau and Amaleq, the exterminator, converged. Not unexpectedly, Galician-born and Czernowitz Rabbi Meshulam Rath, a member of the Israeli Chief Rabbinate in 1948, ruled that the command to blot out Amaleq applied to Esau as well; indeed, it extended to the Germans who were Canaanite by origin, no less.[121] Modernity and emancipation

---

Krawcowicz, "Paradigmatic Thinking and Holocaust Theology," *Journal of Jewish Thought & Philosophy* 22 (2014): 164–89.

[120] Gershon Greenberg, "Amaleq in the Holocaust Period."

[121] *Responsa Mevaser Qol* (Jerusalem: Mosad Ha-Rav Kook, 1956): 42. Meshulam Rath was a Ḥasidic rabbi sympathetic to Zionism but respected by the Ultra-Orthodox.

once triggered Orthodoxy's rise, and it thrived as a protest against them. Now that they had both collapsed, Ultra-Orthodoxy knew not what to do.

Virtually the entire Ultra-Orthodox leadership that was wiped out in the Holocaust remained hostile to Zionism to the end. On the train to Auschwitz, Ehrenreich is said to have blamed the Zionists for the misfortune that had befallen him and his community.[122] The notable exception was Hungarian Ḥasidic Rabbi Yissakhar Shlomo Teichthal (1885–1945), whose book, *Em ha-Banim Semeḥa* (A mother of sons is happy), came out in Budapest in 1943.[123] Teichthal argued for a shift in the traditional hostility to Zionism. The Holocaust, he said, signaled a divine call to the Jews to end their exile, and together with non-Orthodox Jews, resettle the Land of Israel and begin the redemption process. Copies of the book circulated in the postwar years in the Merkaz Ha-Rav Yeshivah in Jerusalem, founded by the first Ashkenazi Chief Rabbi, Abraham Isaac Kook (1865–1935), an Orthodox Kabbalist and halakhist invested in the Zionist project. The book served as a conceptual bridge between Orthodox Zionism and Ultra-Orthodoxy, and the yeshivah played a major role in the formation of religious Zionism in the State of Israel.

Orthodox Zionism, known also as the *Mizraḥi* movement, was in a better shape than Ultra-Orthodoxy to respond to the Holocaust, as it could, at the very least, redirect Jewish hopes and energy toward Palestine. Yiẓhak Nisanbaum, its leader in interwar Poland, saw Amaleq as enjoining Jews to return to the Land. In Palestine, Mizraḥi leaders were quick to identify the Holocaust as the tribulations marking the messianic time and, after the Holocaust, to regard it as the prelude to redemption, for which the State of Israel represented the beginning and the disappearance of Amaleq and the descent of God's kingdom the end.[124] Among the Ultra-Orthodox, Teichthal remained controversial, but Rabbi Reuven Katz of Petaḥ Tiqvah, a Mir Yeshivah graduate, pleaded with Holocaust survivors not to go back to Egypt, that is, not to return to their European homelands, as the command to blot out Amaleq entailed abandoning all hope that Europeans would change. Rather, the refugees should erase their former countries' memory and head for the Land of Israel, to ensure that it was full of Torah and that the terrible sacrifice, the *Olah* and *Aqedah* that expatiated Jewish sins for transgressions, was not in vain.[125]

[122] Shlomo Zalman Ehrenreich, *Derashot*, pp. 33–35, 282.
[123] Yissakhar Shlomo Teichthal, *Em ha-Banim Semeḥa* (Budapest: S. Katzburg, 1943); *Em Habanim Semeha: Restoration of Zion as a Response during the Holocaust*, ed. and trans. Pesach Schindler (Hoboken, NJ: Ktav Pub. House, 1999).
[124] Gershon Greenberg, "Amaleq in the Holocaust Period," 903–13.
[125] Reuven Katz, "Amaleq Transmigration through the Generations," in *Wrestling with God: Jewish Theological Responses during and after the Holocaust*, ed. Steven T. Katz

The dismay at what God had permitted Amaleq to do to His people, which Orthodox Jews experienced but dared not express, was captured by the Galician-born American Yiddish poet Jeremiah Hescheles. His 1943 poem, "Esau on a Visit," was composed of three sonnets.[126] In the first, Esau fell upon the town and zealously demolished all Jewish houses, robbing the holy places. God came, witnessed the ruins and the ashes, and left. In the second sonnet, Hescheles describes his God-fearing and observant grandparents, whose grandchildren were "rewarded" with the total destruction of the family and town, so that not even a wall was left in the synagogue for a memorial candle. In the third sonnet, the God of Israel looks through His tears at his people, the bleeding pious lamb that became a sacrifice, and sees "the ax ready to fall on Jacob's head [and] Israel drinking the cup of poison to the bottom." God wonders: "Is this my people whom I chose and spread, endowed with mercy, amidst pain, so that their body may become a target for the enemy's arrow? ... And *Arikh Anpin* [the ancient kabbalistic universal God who preceded the God of Israel] whimpers in silence." The God of Hescheles is helpless, the Jewish people have done no wrong, and the Holocaust is inexplicable. Jewish Orthodoxy's troubling theodicies are mercifully absent, and author and reader alike are left in dismay. The dismay has never gone away. Ultra-Orthodoxy's failure to express it meant that however successful it has proved to be in rebuilding after the Holocaust, it has never come to terms with it.

Soma Morgenstern's Two Homelands

The dismay put an end to Soma Morgenstern's exploration of a possible convergence between rabbinic and modern European culture. Morgenstern completed his trilogy *Sparks in the Abyss* in 1943 and, "six months later, the horrible news about the destruction of Eastern European Jewry began to arrive [and] a contemporary work became a historical novel."[127] Truly, his story was utopian from the start: An assimilated Viennese Jewish youth, Alfred Mohilevski, returns in 1928

---

with Shlomo Biderman and Gershon Greenberg (Oxford: Oxford University Press, 2007) pp. 101–4.

[126] Jeremiah Hescheles, "עשׂו צו-גאסט" (Esau on a visit), in *Soneten fun Tohu Vavohu: Poems* (New York: Eigenweg, 1957), pp. 84–86. Armin Eidherr discusses the poem in *Sonnenuntergang auf eisig-blauen Wegen*, pp. 261–62.

[127] Ingolf Schulte, "Nachwort des Herausgebers," in *Die Blutsäule* (Lüneburg: Zu Klampen, 1997), p. 175, quoting an unpublished typescript: "Genesis of the Works and Curriculum Vitae." (I owe the reference to Kata Gellen of Duke University.) *Sparks in the Abyss* (*Funken im Abgrund*) may have been the post-Holocaust title given the trilogy. In the interwar years, the abyss had not quite yet opened up, and the anticipated tiqun was less kabbalistic and more historical.

to the Galician village that his father, Joseph, left before World War I, and explores agricultural life and Orthodox Judaism. Antisemitism and ethnic tensions generate the novel's major crisis – the death of the gifted child, Lipusj, whom Alfred loves – and the ever-present imperial legacy cannot overcome nationalism. Yet Morgenstern envisaged a conjunction, an alignment of the stars that would make possible a synthesis of rural Jewish life and urban modern culture, and a love relationship between a Viennese Jewish boy and a Ukrainian rural girl, who learn each other's language. Until the Holocaust, Morgenstern could imagine such a conjunction, but utopia died with the Holocaust.

Born in eastern Galicia to a well-to-do Ḥasidic farm bailiff who was migrating between villages for his work, Salomo Morgenstern received both a traditional Jewish and a German education.[128] He grew up speaking Yiddish and Ukrainian, and learned Hebrew in Ḥeder, German in tutorials at home, and Polish in a Tarnopol gymnasium. His youthful rebellion against religion ended with his father's untimely death about 1909. While never an observant Jew, he began a lifelong negotiation between traditional Judaism and modern culture.

He started his university studies in Vienna in 1912 and moved to Lemberg in 1913. With the advance of Russian troops into Galicia in 1914, he escaped with his family to Vienna. He enlisted in the army and served for four years. He completed a law degree in 1921, but found Vienna's theater, literary, and musical scenes more appealing than practicing law, and tried his hand at script writing. Success was slow in coming, and he was slow to write, but a network of close friends, among them composer Alban Berg and author Joseph Roth, provided him with intellectual and emotional support. In 1924, he met his future wife, Ingeborg von Klenau, daughter of a Danish musician (who later collaborated with the Nazis) and the niece of the *Frankfurter Allgemeine Zeitung*'s assimilated Jewish editor. Inge left the Lutheran Church so that they could marry in a civil ceremony in 1928, but their single child, Daniel, was not raised Jewish and the marriage was rocky. That same year, Morgenstern became the FAZ's Vienna cultural correspondent, a position he retained until the Nazis dismissed Jewish journalists.

In 1929, Morgenstern attended the World Congress of Agudat Yisrael in Vienna, and the mass meeting of Ultra-Orthodox Jews left a deep impression on him, leading to his launching of *The Son of the Lost Son*, the trilogy's first volume. In the novel, the Congress provides the occasion for the protagonist, Alfred, to encounter his devout uncle, Velvel (Wolf),

---

[128] The Soma Morgenstern website, authored by George B. Deutsch, is the most updated source for his biography: http://www.soma-morgenstern.at/lebenslauf.php. See also *Soma Morgenstern – Von Galizien ins amerikanische Exil*, ed. Jacques Lajarrige (Berlin: Frank & Timme, 2015).

and for his decision to part with his family's assimilated Viennese milieu and go to Dobropolia (Dobropolje) in rural Galicia. Morgenstern transposed figures, events, and relationships from his youth into the novel. Alfred revisits the past and renegotiates the dilemmas of his father, Joseph, so as to explore alternatives to his father's conversion and assimilation. The book was printed in 1935 by a Berlin Jewish press, and only Jews could legally buy it in Germany. Notwithstanding the limited audience, *The Son of the Lost Son* struck a chord, as Central European Jews were rethinking assimilation in the 1930s.[129] As cosmopolitan an author as Stefan Zweig upheld it as "a great epic novel, a masterpiece, the classic novel of the Jewish nation." Zweig later found an English translator for the book.[130]

When Morgenstern escaped to Paris on the day of the *Anschluss*, the second volume, *Idyll im Exil* (Idyll in exile), was largely complete.[131] The title *Idyll* could be misleading. Alfred becomes an observant Jew in Dobropolia, but like his father before him, he transgresses the rural Jewish world's limits and begins a relationship with a Ukrainian girl, Donja. He endeavors to quell tensions between the Poles and the Ukrainians, incited by an antisemitic Polish agitator, through a "festival of brotherhood." Tragically, a brawl results in the death of Alfred's protégé, Lipusj, whose image now guides Alfred toward melancholic mystical worship. At the second volume's conclusion, life in Dobropolia is hellish and Alfred must carve a new path, as Orthodoxy can no longer provide direction.

As Morgenstern was completing *Idyll im Exil*, he was facing major challenges himself. Living in the same Paris hotel as Joseph Roth, he was surviving on a small stipend arranged by the American Guild for German Cultural Freedom (on Thomas Mann's recommendation). His wife and son moved from Vienna to Denmark, as they would be stateless in France, and he was unable to get a Danish visa. Except for their visit to Paris in the spring of 1939, he would not see them again until they arrived in New York City in 1947. He began in Paris the trilogy's third volume,

---

[129] *Der Sohn des verlorenen Sohnes* (Berlin: Erich Reiss, 1935). About 4,000 copies were sold. *The Son of the Lost Son*, trans. Joseph Leftwich and Peter Gross (Philadelphia: Jewish Publication Society, 1946).

[130] Morgenstern's paraphrase of Zweig's statement: "A Conversation with Dr. Soma Morgenstern" (radio interview, September 30, 1973), in *Kritiken, Berichte, Tagebücher*, ed. Ingolf Schulte (Lüneburg: Zu Klampen, 2001), p. 707, http://soma-morgenstern.at/userfiles/file/Materialien/The%20Eternal%20Light.pdf.

[131] The manuscript apparently needed reconstruction as parts of it were lost: *Idyll im Exil* (Lüneburg: Zu Klampen, 1996); Soma Morgenstern, *In My Father's Pastures*, trans. Ludwig Lewisohn (Philadelphia: Jewish Publication Society, 1947).

The Testament of the Lost Son, probably not sure himself about the path that Alfred would forge.[132]

At the beginning of World War II, Morgenstern was incarcerated in France as an enemy alien and was in and out of camps for nine months. After France's collapse, he staged a harrowing escape from a camp already staffed by Nazi guards, crossed over to Vichy France, and reached Marseilles.[133] He was rearrested. After another eight months of desperate waiting for a U.S. visa, he left for Lisbon by way of Casablanca, and from there, in April 1941, to the United States. He checked into the Plaza Park single-residency hotel in New York, where other émigrés were staying, and, except for a two-year sojourn in California during World War II, this would remain his abode for the next quarter of a century. He formed friendships among the German and Austrian exile communities in Los Angeles and New York, but they were no substitute for the intellectual milieus of Vienna or Galicia. He completed his novel worlds away from its Central European origins.

The relationship between Vienna and Dobropolia provides the axis for the novel's third volume. Alfred's father's closest friend, Dr. Stefan Frankl, an acculturated Jew whom Alfred knew as Uncle Stefan, comes from Vienna to Dobropolia with the father's testament. Written shortly before his death as an Austrian officer in World War I, Joseph's testament is autobiographical, and explains his conversion to Greek Catholicism. Like Esau & Jacob, he, the firstborn, competed with Velvel, the younger son, and responded violently when losing out to Velvel. Velvel was pious, whereas Joseph pushed boundaries.[134] To punish him for an affair with a Ukrainian girl, his father beat him with the stick of their great-granduncle Rabbi Abba. In school, Joseph became a close friend of Partyka, the future cleric who would convert him. Christian friendship and Orthodox severity led Joseph to break with his parents and renounce Judaism.

Antisemitism also contributed to Joseph's decision to convert. He remembered vividly the attack by neighboring youths on Koppel, the Jewish cloth printer. Joseph's friend, the future Zionist Katz, sought to intervene in the scuffle, but Koppel waved him away, telling him: "May it be as easy for you to breathe air as it is for me to be a Jew." "The question

---

[132] *The Testament of the Lost Son*, trans. Jacob Sloan in collaboration with Maurice Samuel (Philadelphia: Jewish Publication Society, 1950).

[133] Morgenstern recounted the story in *Flucht in Frankreich: Ein Romanbericht*, ed. with a postscript by Ingolf Schulte (Lüneburg: Zu Klampen, 1998).

[134] Gerhard Langer, "Wer ein lebendiges Wesen tötet, der tötet die ganze Welt: Soma Morgensterns Bezüge zur jüdischen Tradition, zu Judentum und Christentum," *Chilufim* 9 (2010): 19–35, tracks midrashic Jacob & Esau motifs in the novel.

is," responded Katz, "must it all continue this way to eternity?"[135] Joseph thought that it should not. By converting, he endeavored to solve the Jewish Question so that he could live in as much "serenity *with* the world" as the traditional Jew lived *against* it.

Morgenstern interrupts the reading of the testament by having the estate manager, Yankel (Jacob), arrested for public incitement in connection with the nationalist agitation that led to Lipusj's death. Alfred helps release him, calling on an imperial countess, a Zionist lawyer, and his father's old friends in the bureaucracy for help. The literary ploy of two narratives, conversion and arrest, a generation apart, allows Alfred to explore the Galician towns and countryside that the testament describes as the landscape for Joseph's conversion. The testament reveals that the conversion made Joseph miserable for the rest of his short life, and he concludes his testament with *Shema Yisrael*. The novel itself ends with Alfred's plan to travel to Vienna for a vacation but to return to Dobropolia, renovate an abandoned house, and open an agricultural training school for youth emigrating to Palestine. Donja will await his return. In a final dream, a stork relates Lipusj's message to him: One should have two homelands, and the voyage between them provides the meaning of life.[136]

Sparks in the Abyss is often read as a *Bildungsroman* charting a return to traditional Judaism (*teshuvah*) and reflecting nostalgia for the past, especially for the Austrian Empire. Nostalgia and exploration of Jewish Orthodoxy are, indeed, part of Morgenstern's great novel, but highlighting them risks missing its message: Neither Jewish tradition nor the Habsburg legacy can stand on their own or stay as they are. If the traumas that brought about their decline and collapse are to be overcome, both require renegotiation and integration into a new modern synthesis.

To be sure, the novel displays the Jews' loyalty to Austria, and critics correctly note that in the Jewish imagination, interwar Central European geography refuses to adjust to the new nation-states. Vienna and Dobropolia still appear part of an imperial cultural space, as if Galicia were still a Crown Land and Vienna the imperial capital.[137] Yet Morgenstern noted change and continuity in now-Polish Galicia, and staged old friendships and political ties against the newly forming and threatening nationalist forces. Yankel's incarceration is the result of the

---

[135] *The Testament of the Lost Son*, pp. 138–39.

[136] Kata Gellen, "'One Should Have Two Homelands': Discord and Hope in Soma Morgenstern's Sparks in the Abyss," *Religions* 8:2 (2017), http://www.mdpi.com/2077-1444/8/2/26.

[137] Andrew Barker, *Fictions from an Orphan State: Literary Reflections of Austria between Habsburg and Hitler* (Rochester, NY: Camden House, 2012), pp. 95–112, esp. p. 106.

machinations of a nationalist intellectual and state official, and his release comes about through an alliance of the old aristocracy, a friendly cleric, Zionist activists, and a local administrative official, whom Alfred contacts via an old prison guard resembling Franz Joseph. Nationalism and anti-semitism have undermined multicultural coexistence, and the imperial legacy is not strong enough to overcome them: Yankel and Dr. Frankl declare the age of liberalism gone, the friendly countess's letter fails to register its anticipated impact, and Alfred declares his Zionist sympathies. Yet the young Viennese can still master sufficient forces of decency to score a local victory and restore, at least temporarily, the old imperial idyll to Dobropolia.

Jewish Orthodoxy's liabilities are more obvious. Joseph's testament makes it clear that the harsh punishment meted out by Orthodoxy to those who dared explore beyond tradition pushed him out of Judaism. Rabbi Abba mistook Joseph's school uniform for a soldier's uniform, and, upholding Jewish ethics, declared that causing the death of even one soul was like destroying the world. In the dream preceding Joseph's conversion, the prosecutor, channeling Rabbi Abba, confronts him with the choice: Either be a student of (Jewish) law or a soldier dishonoring your parents, an Esau and an outcast. Joseph is declared guilty as a soldier. He would still rather go home and be reconciled with his family, but "it was a stick that weakened me."[138] A Hasidic rabbi's magical stick walked him to the trial, and the very same stick was used by the red-haired *gabbai* (deacon) to beat him, "the rabbi's stick and my father's stick in one." As Joseph departs the town after his conversion, the Jews raise a forest of sticks against him, and he imagines Velvel with Rabbi Abba's stick leading them. Rabbinic Judaism stands for high moral principles, but it knows not how to apply them. The stick can point the way, but all too often it inflicts a trauma. Morgenstern needed little familiarity with Ultra-Orthodox polemics against Jewish Amaleqites to know that Orthodoxy was on the wrong path. There was no future for Judaism in the stick.

Alfred, Esau's son, returns home to reshape a viable Jewish alternative to both assimilation and Orthodoxy. Velvel, who lost his family in World War I, depends on him to continue the tradition. Like his father, Alfred crosses boundaries, but he has more room to maneuver, and he negotiates more aptly between Jewish and non-Jewish culture. To quell nationalist agitation and contain antisemitism, he first tries "universal brotherhood." When it backfires, he opts for Diaspora Zionism, sustaining Dobropolia's rural life by engagement with Jewish national renewal. Learning from Lipusj the religious heart's purity, he invests Orthodox ritual with

---

[138] *The Testament of the Lost Son*, p. 261.

mystical belief. Revisiting the problems that drove his father out, he learns and changes as he grows, and opens up prospects for Jewish reconstruction.

Dobropolia's old-timers have no sense of his grand design. Discovering his affair with Donja, Yankel and Pessa, the pious house manager, try to arrange an advantageous peasant marriage for Donja, lest they see a replay of Joseph's apostasy. The stick is nowhere in sight, but their gentle and wily response exposes tradition's limits. Donja, who is also Pessa's assistant, may actually become a solution to assimilation. She represents a fusion of Alfred's refined and beautiful mother, Fritzi Peschek, who embodies the tantalizing prospect of Viennese assimilation, and pious, capable, but less attractive Pessa, who sustains Orthodox Judaism. Negotiating with Alfred her prospective long wait to marry him, Donja begins speaking Yiddish and shows the marks of a Jewish "woman of valor" (אשת חיל). Working through his father's dilemma, Alfred has begun the healing process. Esau's son has come back home bringing a closure to two millennia of Jacob & Esau.

The challenges of shaping Jewish life between Orthodoxy and European culture still lie ahead for Alfred. Before going to sleep, he is warned to put out Pessa's oil lamp. The lamp's warmth induces his dream but also wakes him up, with a painful burn, his mission incomplete – a parable for the role that Orthodox Judaism has come to play in his life, and in modernity in general. In the dream itself, a stork, who says that he is Lipusj's friend, tells him that Lipusj was appointed a narrating judge, a judge whose gentle voice Alfred can still recall from his father's dreams. He reassures Alfred (as God assured Jacob before going into exile) that he need not worry about leaving for Vienna: Storks, like Jews, have two homelands, both rather swampy and uninhabitable, but the voyage between them is the story of their life. Vienna and Dobropolia, Galicia and Palestine, European culture and Jewish Orthodoxy – one should love both at the same time. Moving between them is Jewish history.

Spreading its wings, black and white, the stork – *ḥasidah* in Hebrew – tells Alfred that he is so called because he looks like a *ḥasid*, wrapped in a prayer shawl (*tallit*). The reader remembers that, earlier, the author related that the stork showed charity (*ḥesed*) only to its kind – Orthodoxy's vice. The stork complains that its Dobropolia owner cut its wings, and so it could not fly. New feathers have since grown, but a few dead ones need to be plucked if he is to fly. Lipusj wants him, Alfred, to help. Alfred stretches his hand to pluck out Orthodoxy's dead flight-obstructing feathers, but the stork responds by pecking his hand, and flames shoot from its beak. Alfred wakes up with an oil lamp burn. The stork is not quite able to fly; the risky project of reforming Orthodoxy has been charted but is still incomplete. Yet now that Lipusj, the narrating judge, is at one with the project, Alfred is at peace. Going to sleep, he recalls Lipusj's beautiful recitation of *shema al ha-mitah*, the prayer said in bed before sleep: "Lay me to sleep in peace and ... perfect be my bed before You." How Alfred may bring Donja to this bed and yet keep it perfect before God remains a mystery. It is his great challenge – and ours.

Morgenstern gave up the challenge after the Holocaust. As he was imagining a Ukrainian-Jewish marriage and a new Galician Zionism, Galicia already lay in ruins and most of its Jews were dead, murdered by the Germans and their Ukrainian accomplices. He lost almost his entire family in the Holocaust. When the news arrived, he sank into a depression, contemplated suicide, and stopped writing for several years. He now hated the German language, blamed the Poles, too, for the Holocaust, and felt antagonistic toward Europe in general. The three books of the trilogy came out successively in English from 1946 to 1950 but enjoyed only a limited readership. He made little effort to see his works published in German, and most of them, including an unfinished autobiography and recollections of Alban Berg and Joseph Roth, would be published only in the 1990s.[139]

The founding of the state of Israel provided a ray of hope, and Morgenstern returned to writing. *The Third Pillar*, one of the first Holocaust novels, recounts the destruction of the Galician landscape he so lovingly preserved in his trilogy.[140] A German edition came out in 1964, and this was the last book he would see published.[141] He lived a meager existence in New York City, supported after 1959 by a German allowance. Having suffered a heart attack in 1967, he reunited with his wife for his final years. A prayer from *The Third Pillar*, which some U.S. congregations had already been using in their Yom Kippur liturgy for years, was formally adopted for the Conservative *Maḥazor* (High Holidays prayer book) in 1972.[142] This was, said Morgenstern, a greater honor for him than if he had won the Nobel Prize.[143] Little notice was taken when he passed away in 1976, and he is not yet a household name today. He deserves to be.

---

[139] Soma Morgenstern, *Werke in Einzelbänden*, ed. Ingolf Schulte, 11 vols. (Lüneburg: Zu Klampen, 1994–2001).

[140] *The Third Pillar*, trans. Ludwig Lewisohn (New York: Farrar, Straus and Cudahy, 1955).

[141] *Die Blutsäule: Zeichen und Wunder am Sereth* (Vienna: Hans Deutsch Verlag, 1964). *FORVM*'s editor, Friedrich Torberg, an Austrian remigré who shaped the canon of "Austrian literature," was instrumental in publishing the book.

[142] *The Third Pillar*, pp. 137–38; *Prayer Book for the Days of Awe*, ed. Jules Harlow (New York: Rabbinic Assembly, 1972).

[143] "Soma Morgenstern Dies at 85," *New York Times* (19 April 1976).

Morgenstern's hope that the return home of Esau's son could heal Jacob, too, vanished in the postwar years. It is easy to see why the idea of the two homelands and of revisiting the trauma of assimilation and working it out differently the second time no longer held the prospect of healing: The Holocaust left nowhere to return and nothing to revisit. "I started to realize," said Morgenstern, "that I belong to Judaism, not to European culture."[144] (Of course, he belonged to both.) He still believed that "a book that does not end in hope ... is not a Jewish book," but the redemptive kabbalistic vision emerging from *The Third Pillar* resembled the Orthodox one and was foreign to the project of reconciling traditional Judaism and European culture in his great novel.[145]

In his final years, Morgenstern became hopeful again about American Jewish life, but as an outsider, he was too old and broken to restart negotiations. He left the challenge to us. As this book's final chapters show, postwar European culture has opened unprecedented opportunities for Jewish cosmopolitanism and lionized Jewish writers. Esau's return home has recently become a leitmotif in Israeli culture. No other author, however, exemplifies as profoundly as Morgenstern the convergence of rabbinic Judaism and European history that this book has set out to accomplish.

---

[144] "A Conversation with Dr. Soma Morgenstern," p. 712.   [145] Ibid.

11   Typology and the Holocaust: Erich Auerbach and Judeo-Christian Europe

Among the Jewish émigrés who sought sanctuary in World War II on the outskirts of the old continent, in Istanbul University, was literary historian and philologist Erich Auerbach (1892–1957), author of the monumental *Mimesis*.[1] In 1947 he emigrated to the United States and sent *Mimesis* to an admired German author, Thomas Mann, who was commuting between his U.S. war refuge in Pacific Palisades and his postwar European one in Ascona, Switzerland. "The central theme of *Mimesis*, European realism, has the greatest attraction for me," responded Mann in 1949. "Your approach, treating [realism] historically and tracking the everlasting artistic disposition for it through the centuries carries a pedagogical message."[2] Neither of them spoke openly about the Holocaust. Ironically, Mann resurrected biblical myth to respond to the Nazi racial one, whereas Auerbach saw Mann's realism, and biblical insistence on truth as opposed to classical myth, as the only proper response. But both questioned the German humanist focus on the classical and the claim to ownership over it, and both resurrected the Hebrew Bible to challenge classical heritage's hegemony in German culture and to thwart Nazi efforts to cut off European civilization from its Jewish roots. Well beyond Jewish-Catholic circles, secular German and Jewish intellectuals responded to National Socialism by reaffirming a Judeo-Christian Western tradition.[3]

---

[1] *Mimesis: Dargestellte Wirklichkeit in der abendländischen Literatur* [1946], 2d ed. (Bern: Francke, 1959); *Mimesis: The Representation of Reality in Western Literature*, trans. Willard R. Trask (Princeton, NJ: Princeton University Press, 1953).

[2] Mann to Auerbach, September 23, 1949, in *Süddeutsche Zeitung* (27–28 May 2006), with a discussion by Martin Vialon, "Passion und Prophetie: Eine Entdeckung: Thomas Manns Dankesbrief an Erich Auerbach für das Buch 'Mimesis.'"

[3] American Jews and Protestants who wished to repel late 1930s antisemitic populism and had urged U.S. anti-Nazi intervention in Europe were the first to use "Judeo-Christian" to describe a shared Western legacy. (Mark Silk, "Notes on the Judeo-Christian Tradition in America," *American Quarterly* 36:1 [1984]: 65–85.) The term became common in Europe only in the postwar years. Auerbach may have been among the first to use it. In *Mimesis*, "Judaeo-Christian" (jüdisch-christlich) expands from early Jewish–Christian culture (*Mimesis*, pp. 72, 320 [English]; pp. 73–74, 305 [German]) to a European Western

Auerbach occupies a unique place in recent scholarship on German-Jewish intellectuals. With Hannah Arendt and Walter Benjamin, he is among the most revered. Like them, he remained Jewish, but, unlike them, he showed deep interest in Christian traditions and their role in shaping Western civilization. *Mimesis* offered a blueprint for a Judeo-Christian European culture. Christian typology or, as Auerbach called it, *figura*, was the pivot of this European culture, the predominant trope that wove together life and discourse until modern times, and provided the connecting thread of Western history. Auerbach had no traditional Jewish learning and was ignorant of Jewish typology, yet recent scholarship has insisted on regarding him as Jewish and on turning "Figura" and *Mimesis* into quintessential Jewish documents.[4] The procedure requires overriding textual and historical resistance, and the invention of terms of Jewish affinity unavailable to Auerbach himself. This contrasts with scholars' usual reluctance to define the works of German-Jewish intellectuals as Jewish against their cognizance.

The racialization of European identity in the 1930s excluded traditional Jews, assimilated Jews, and cultural Christians who remained Jewish, all alike. Their intellectual creativity addressed their predicament. Benno Jacob's *Genesis*, Karl Popper's Open Society, and Auerbach's *figura* were all products of the Jewish predicament, but Jacob's biblical exegesis was Jewish, Popper's cosmopolitanism secular, and Auerbach's Europeanism Christian. Auerbach was a cultural Christian. "Judaizing" him risks essentializing Jewishness and drives *ad absurdum* the current trend to crown German-acculturated Jews as Jewish European and to marginalize traditionalist Jews. Focusing on Jewish typology, this book is a rejoinder to Auerbach and his disciples. The short Auerbach biography offered here disentangles the Jewish and Christian dimensions in his life. It shows Auerbach's German-Jewish identity reaching a crisis under National Socialism, his desperate effort to carve out a space for German Jews as cultural Christians and make all Europeans inheritors of the Hebrews, and, in the aftermath of the Holocaust, his exile and despair. Auerbach ended with Hugh of St. Victor and Christian cosmopolitanism. This book journeys with Jacob and Jewish hope.

---

mode of representing reality (pp. 119, 201 [English]; pp. 116, 192 [German]). (Thanks to Avihu Zakai of the Hebrew University for the references.)

[4] *Locus classicus*: James Porter, "Erich Auerbach and the Judaizing of Philology," *Critical Inquiry* 35:1 (2008): 115–47. See also Avihu Zakai, *Erich Auerbach and the Crisis of German Philology* (Cham, CH: Springer, 2017).

Vico and Dante: A Jewish Cultural Protestant in Weimar Germany

Born to an affluent and German-acculturated Berlin Jewish family, Auerbach grew up in a predominantly Jewish neighborhood in Charlottenburg and attended the French gymnasium (*französisches Gymnasium*), first established by Huguenot exiles and now carrying on French cultural traditions. Auerbach was by no means an accomplished student, but republican France became his second *Heimat*, and his future pursuit of Romance languages owed much to this early French exposure. Son of a jurist, he pursued law, earning a doctoral degree from Heidelberg in 1913. In Heidelberg, he apparently made the acquaintance of several members of the Max Weber circle, including Georg Lukàcs, Walter Benjamin, and Karl Jaspers.[5] French sympathies made no dent in his German patriotism: He served on the western front in World War I, and was wounded and decorated. The loss of friends was traumatic, but, like the Holocaust later, he consigned it to silence. Auerbach's literary concerns alone alluded to the pain, loss, and injustice of a cruel and unpredictable world.

Returning to civil life, Auerbach sought a change of profession. In 1921, he earned a second doctorate in Romance philology with a dissertation on French and Italian early Renaissance novellas. The rise of the novella, he suggested, reflected the historical transition from the medieval to the Renaissance world, with the rise of Renaissance man, conscious of his individuality, seeing himself in the midst of earthly life (*irdischen Dasein*).[6] His early publications, dedicated to Dante, launched into arguments that he would pursue throughout his life. Dante's characters in *The Divine Comedy*, though they inhabited Hell, Purgatory, and Paradise, forever retained their earthly nature. Auerbach celebrated Dante as a German poet, an Italian who joined, as Shakespeare did,

---

[5] Martin Vialon, "The Scars of Exile: Paralipomena concerning the Relationship between History, Literature and Politics – Demonstrated in the Examples of Erich Auerbach, Traugott Fuchs and Their Circle in Istanbul," *Yeditepe'de felsefe* 2 (2003): 198. The Heidelberg information is based on a letter from Marie Auerbach to Traugott Fuchs, April 11, 1973; Martin Vialon, *Erich Auerbachs Briefe an Martin Hellweg (1939–1950): Edition und historisch-philologischer Kommentar* (Tübingen: Francke, 1997), pp. 82–83, n. 7. It is not altogether clear when Jaspers and Auerbach met, and if and when Jaspers read Auerbach's work. But in 1929, Jaspers and Friedrich Gundolf (1880–1931), a leading member of the Stefan George Circle, unsuccessfully pushed to appoint Auerbach in Heidelberg.

[6] "The novella is situated in the midst of time and place; it is a piece of history.... It must be realistic inasmuch as it takes for granted empirical reality.... [Its] Ethos must be not metaphysical but grounded in the laws of social community": *Zur Technik der Frührenaissancenovelle in Italien und Frankreich* (Heidelberg: C. Winter, 1921), p. 1.

a German European pantheon.[7] Dante spoke to Germany's spiritual crisis because he conveyed confidence in the viability of a Christian community and a providentially guided universe, where rewards and punishments were justly meted and the protagonists' character was their destiny. This confidence, Auerbach recognized, was now woefully lost. He was groping for a literary sensibility appropriate to a secularized Christian culture, for a dignified attention to the social world, to everydayness (*täglichen Dasein*).

"A Prussian of the Mosaic faith," Auerbach described himself in the dissertation's bio.[8] In 1923, he married Marie Mankiewitz, daughter to an affluent Jewish family (the largest private shareholder of Deutsche Bank).[9] He gave his son, born later that year, the distinctly Christian name of Clemens, and did not have him circumcised (until a doctor recommended the procedure for medical reasons fourteen years later).[10] There was nothing traditionally Jewish in Auerbach's education or culture. He accepted the liberal Protestant view, articulated by Adolph Harnack, that postbiblical Judaism no longer retained its intellectual vitality and had become obsolete, a particularist religion in a universal Christian world. Yet the liberal Protestant call to Jews to convert and become part of the German nation never seemed to tempt him, and he remained a member of the Jewish community. Unlike Franz Werfel, he did not think of the Jews, in an Augustinian fashion, as witnesses to Christian truth. A cultural Christian of Jewish origins, he could not believe in Jesus as Christ, and accepted his Jewish fate with composure.

Cultural Protestantism shaped Auerbach's view of contemporary life. He thought that secularization and historicism had created a cultural crisis that left the world disenchanted, devoid of firm cultural norms. A student of philosopher and theologian Ernst Troeltsch (1865–1923) – he attended Troeltsch's seminar and belonged to his circle in the Weimar

---

[7] "Zur Dante-Feier," *Neue Rundschau* 23 (1921): 1005–6. This short article commemorated the six-hundredth anniversary of Dante's death. "Stefan Georges Danteübertragung," *Cultura Italiana e Tedesca* 2:1 (1924): 17–20, was a laudation for George's rendering of (parts of) *The Divine Comedy*. Both are reprinted in: *Erich Auerbach: Geschichte und Aktualität eines europäischen Philologen*, ed. Martin Treml and Karlheinz Barck (Berlin: Kulturverlag Kadmos, 2007), pp. 407–13.

[8] "Ich bin Prüßn, jüdischer Konfession": Karlheinz Barck, "Erich Auerbach in Berlin: Spurensicherung und ein Porträt," in *Erich Auerbach*, ed. Treml and Barck, p. 197.

[9] Earl Jeffrey Richards, "Erich Auerbach's *Mimesis* as a Meditation on the Shoah," *German Politics and Society* 19:59 (2001): 64.

[10] Clemens Auerbach, "Summer 1937," in *Erich Auerbach an Martin Hellweg*, ed. Treml and Barck, p. 497. Yet, somehow, Clemens must have retained, or acquired, a dim awareness of things Jewish. He noted that his parents arrived in the United States "on September 23, 1947, which happened to be Erev Yom Kippur!" Martin Vialon, *Erich Auerbachs Briefe*, p. 95, n. 1.

Republic's early years – Auerbach searched for the secular equivalent of Christian religious ideals.[11] Harnack and Weber, too, inspired his historical mode of inquiry, but all three – Harnack, Troeltsch, and Weber – left him without answers. Like them, he was willing to see modern cultural values as vouched in the nation, but they lacked his social sensitivity. He viewed the Christian concern for the poor as exemplary of attentiveness to daily life, and upheld St. Francis as the embodiment of authenticity.[12] His fascination with the sacred and his affinity for the downtrodden were reminiscent of the expressionists around Waldemar Jollos. Weber made light of such sensibilities, but they became the overriding theme of Auerbach's lifelong work.[13]

Troeltsch represented liberal historical theology pushed to its limits. His history denuded Christianity of supernatural claims, the incarnation included. Jesus became a world-historical figure, embodying humanity's aspirations, founder of a Christian culture that evolved into Europe's legacy. Troeltsch's comparative study of world religions progressively disrupted his sense of Christian and European superiority. The cultural relativism that historicism occasioned was palpable and painful to him, a Protestant theologian, and he looked back longingly to medieval Europe as an integral civilization free of doubt. Yet even in the aftermath of World War I, Troeltsch was still hoping against hope that history would reveal a transcendental pattern.[14]

Troeltsch's Jesus, a world-historical figure, became a point of departure for Auerbach's lifelong work. Like Troeltsch, Auerbach secretly believed that history displayed divine intentions and searched his entire life for patterns rendering its meaning. Like him, he longed for past communities where God and man cohabited peacefully. National Socialism constituted a caesura because it became impossible for Auerbach to reconcile

---

[11] Ernst Troeltsch, *The Social Teaching of the Christian Churches*, trans. Olive Wyon, 2 vols. (Chicago: University of Chicago Press, 1976). Matthias Bormuth, "Menschenkunde zwischen Meistern – Auerbach und Löwith," in *Erich Auerbach*, ed. Treml and Barck, pp. 85–87, tracks Harnack's influence on Auerbach, especially on his view of Augustine.

[12] "Über das Persönliche in der Wirkung des hl. Franz von Assisi" [1927], in Erich Auerbach, *Gesammelte Aufsätze zur romanischen Philologie*, ed. Fritz Schalk (Bern: Francke, 1967), pp. 33–42.

[13] Max Weber, "Science as a Vocation," in *The Vocation Lectures*, ed. David S. Owen and Tracy B. Strong, trans. Rodney Livingstone (Indianapolis, IN: Hackett, 2004), pp. 29–30.

[14] Ernst Troeltsch, *Der Historismus und seine Probleme* [1922], ed. Friedrich Wilhelm Graf and Matthias Schlossberger, 2 vols. (Berlin: Walter de Gruyter, 2008), esp. the editor's account of Troeltsch's seminar and the Auerbach-Troeltsch relationship in 1: 26–30, 46, 283–84; *Historismus und seine Überwindung* [1924] ed. Gangolf Hübinger and Andreas Terwey (Berlin: Walter de Gruyter, 2006).

"all the evil that is happening" with "God and the eternal world."[15] He never ceased searching for meaning in history, but in the post-Holocaust years, hope was gone.

Much as Troeltsch and Auerbach craved meaningful patterns, they rebuffed the Hegelian confidence in a universal history, and refused a unifying narrative integrating the plurality of cultures. In Oswald Spengler's *The Decline of the West*, Troeltsch saw a monistic history, hostile to liberal culture.[16] Seeking countermodels, Troeltsch encouraged Auerbach to study Giambattista Vico (1668–1744), the Italian philosopher of history who was not well known in Germany at the time. To Vico, culture was a human creation, and history a succession of epochs represented in a plurality of nations, each an aspect of the divine. His "world of nations" consisted of civil societies at divergent stages of development spread around the globe, which followed a pattern, leading from aristocratic polities, imagining gods and heroes governing, to rational organization in monarchies and republics. Troeltsch and Auerbach found in Vico a history accentuating cultural pluralism, divinely inspired but human made. Vico's history became the site for the interplay of tensions between universalism and pluralism, divine and human, which Auerbach never wished to resolve or think through to their end, allowing them to coexist and motivate his work.

After Auerbach became a librarian at the Prussian National Library in 1923, he had the leisure to translate Vico's *Scienza Nuova* and engage his views on language, culture, and history.[17] "Vico's conception of philology and of the 'world of nations,'" he said in the postwar years (when he thought the world of nations was approaching its end), "complemented and molded, in my thinking and in my work, the ideas deriving from German historicism."[18] Auerbach's distaste for Cartesian rationalism

---

[15] Auerbach to Traugott Fuchs, October 22, 1938, in "Scholarship in Times of Extremes: Letters of Erich Auerbach (1933–46), on the Fiftieth Anniversary of His Death," trans., with an introduction by Martin Elsky, Martin Vialon, and Robert Stein, *Proceedings of the Modern Language Association* (henceforth PMLA) 122:3 (2007): 752 and 755, respectively.

[16] Oswald Spengler, *Der Untergang des Abendlandes: Umrisse einer Morphologie der Weltgeschichte* [1918–23], 2 vols. (Munich: C. H. Beck'sche Verlagsbuchhandlung, 1927).

[17] Giambattista Vico, *Die neue Wissenschaft über die gemeinschaftliche Natur der Völker* [*Principi di una scienza nuova*, 3d ed., 1744], trans. Erich Auerbach (Munich: Allgemeine Verlagsanstalt, 1924); *New Science: Principles of the New Science Concerning the Common Nature of Nations*, trans. David Marsh (London: Penguin, 1999). In his editor's introduction (p. 39), Auerbach acknowledged Troeltsch's inspiration.

[18] "Introduction: Purpose and Method," in Erich Auerbach, *Literary Language and Its Public in Late Latin Antiquity and in the Middle Ages* [1958], trans. Ralph Manheim (Princeton, NJ: Princeton University Press, 1993), p. 7.

and French classicism, his consciousness of the multiple perspectives available into a historical period, his historical philology and contextual approach to literature, and his interpretive reenactment of historical agents all reflected an adaptation of German historicism via Vico. He rejected only Vico's cyclical historical determinism, which was too reminiscent of Spengler. In "Vico und Herder" (1932), he suggested that Vico parted with Christian transcendentalism by having providence work its way immanently through history, a move toward secularization.[19] Yet Vico did not question the individual's relationship to God, and, like Vico, Auerbach was content to live with the tension between an immanent history and a transcendently oriented individual. He declined to move toward an emphatically secular historicism.

Vico made it easier for Auerbach to escape, if only barely, the traps of Heidegger and the "Conservative Revolution." Auerbach admired Stefan George – his Dante book was, at various points, reminiscent of the hero-worshipping biographies of the George Circle – and he thought Heidegger a profound thinker. "An awful fellow," he said after World War II. "I am glad I did not fall into his hands when I was young." "But," he added, "he had substance."[20] In the Weimar years, young academic Germany turned against formal and idealist philosophy in search of authenticity. The poet embodied authenticity, whether in the aristocratic heroic fashion of the George Circle or in Heideggerian overcoming of the "everydayness of existence" (*Alltäglichkeit des Daseins*). One sought to explore the "life-world" as it revealed itself, uncorrupted by the traditional philosophical pursuit of objectivity.[21] "Everydayness" became a central motif for Auerbach but with a "progressive" twist, one affirming the grandeur of the daily struggles of the downtrodden.[22] He made literary concern for the everyday tragic the acid test of modern literature,

[19] "Vico und Herder," *Deutsche Vierteljahrsschrift für Literaturwissenschaft und Geistesgeschichte* 10:4 (1932): 671–86.

[20] "Heidegger ist ein furchtbarer Kerl, aber er hat wenigstens Substanz": Auerbach to Martin Hellweg, May 16, 1947, in Martin Vialon, *Erich Auerbachs Briefe an Martin Hellweg*, p. 84, n. 8. "Was für ein grossartiger Mann! Aber ich bin doch froh, dass ich ihm nicht in die Hände gefallen bin, als ich jung war": Auerbach to Karl Löwith, May 26, 1953, quoted in Matthias Bormuth, "Menschenkunde zwischen Meistern – Auerbach und Löwith," in *Erich Auerbach*, ed. Treml and Barck, p. 85, n. 12.

[21] Hans-Ulrich Gumbrecht, "Everyday-World and Life-World as Philosophical Concepts: A Genealogical Approach," *New Literary History* 24:4 (1993), esp. 753–56. Gumbrecht's "'Pathos of Earthly Progress': Erich Auerbach's Everydays," in *Literary History and the Challenge of Philology: The Legacy of Erich Auerbach*, ed. Seth Lerer (Stanford, CA: Stanford University Press, 1996), pp. 13–35, is also helpful in understanding Auerbach in the 1920s.

[22] Auerbach may well have found the *alltäglich* (everyday) in German translations and literary criticism of Horace's doctrine of styles in *Ars Poetica*, which designated everyday language as appropriate for comedy or satire but not for tragedy: *Ars Poetica des Horaz*,

and he judged the success of literary realism by its grasp of concrete social life. He found the seventeenth-century French classical tragedian Racine empty because his characters did not emerge from daily life, and he lauded Proust for having captured the earthly world.[23] Auerbach "democratized" George's search for the hero via the "everyday tragic" and rechanneled Heideggerian everydayness via Vico, rendering it more sociocultural, less existential.

If Vico made a democratic redirection of everydayness possible, Auerbach's politics remained unclear until National Socialism forced him to clarify it. Marxist literary critic Walter Benjamin (1892–1940) and philosopher Ernst Bloch (1885–1977) were his houseguests in the early 1920s, but his politics were not leftist. His student, literary historian Werner Krauss (1900–1975), remembered him as a liberal nationalist. "You know me sufficiently . . . to realize that I can understand the motives of your political views," Auerbach wrote to historian Erich Rothacker when the latter joined the National Socialist Party.[24] "It would pain me much . . . if you wanted to deny me the right to be a German." Until the Nazi triumph, however, the temptations of George's "secret Germany" (which included intellectuals of Jewish origin) and of Heidegger's call for the authentic were great. Only when the political order collapsed, and Auerbach faced exclusion as a Jew, did he affirm, elliptically via Christianity, the socially progressive bent of "everydayness" – and his own inclusion.

In 1929, Auerbach published *Dante: Poet of the Secular World*.[25] His book portrayed Dante as a transformative realist poet who broke with allegory and revealed human character – concrete and historical. In *The Divine Comedy*, disembodied spirits in Hell emerge as tragic personalities, as if still alive. Cato, a pagan and a suicide, guards Purgatory's gates (and not a Christian saint, as the secular empire was the fount of justice). To Auerbach, Dante captured and transformed

---

trans. and interp. Th. Kayser (Stuttgart: Liebioh, 1888). Line 90, "indignatur item privates ac prope socco" is translated as "ebensowenig als je die gemeinalltägliche Sprache," and line 235, "non ego inornata et dominantia nomina solum" as "immer nur schmockloss schlichte, alltägliche Worte zu wählen." But the "everyday" became significant for Auerbach because of *Alltäglichkeit*'s resonance in Weimar discourse.

[23] "Racine und die Leidenschaften" [1926] and "Marcel Proust: Der Roman von der verlorenen Zeit" [1927], in *Gesammelte Aufsätze zur romanischen Philologie*, ed. Fritz Schalk (Bern: Francke, 1967), pp. 196–203 and 296–300, respectively.

[24] Dated January 29, 1933, PMLA 122:3 (2007): 745.

[25] *Dante als Poet der irdischen Welt* (Berlin: Walter de Gruyter, 1929); *Dante: Poet of the Secular World*, trans. Ralph Manheim (New York: New York Review of Books, 2007). Auerbach used the term *irdisch*, meaning earthly, or worldly, and not secular. Ironically, Dante's earthliness became the fountain of secularization, but neither Dante's nor, arguably, Auerbach's worldliness was secular. The English title could be misleading.

classical and Christian literary genres and created new possibilities for literary realism.[26]

Plato was notoriously suspicious of mimetic reality, poetic or artistic, and Aristotle, considering tragedy the noblest genre, "states very clearly that [it] must not represent [reality] as it comes to us, in its apparent disorder and disunity [but as] a correction of actual events, a happening superior to actual happening."[27] Classical tragedy depicts "the hero's final struggle with his destiny, [and it] so divides and consumes him that nothing remains of his personality but his age, race, class and the most general traits of his temperament."[28] But with Christ and the crucifixion – that "problematic and desperate injustice of an earthly happening" – "the drama of earthly life took on a painful, immoderate, and utterly unclassical intensity."[29] Gospel narratives, focusing on Jesus' life and leading to the Passion, captured this historical drama. Christianity opened up new mimetic possibilities, enabling new forms of literary representation.

To be sure, Christianity relegitimized the earthly world only within the framework of eschatology and otherworldly justice. Neoplatonic efforts to allegorize biblical narratives repeatedly tested Christianity's earthly character. But with the earthly world, realism persevered, and Dante repossessed, reshaped, and pushed it further. Envisioning a "happy end" to his otherworldly tour, and using the "vulgar" vernacular, Dante, misunderstanding Aristotelian criteria, felt compelled to call his masterpiece a comedy. Truly, *The Divine Comedy* endowed the earthly world with a tragic vision of humanity that would not vanish even when secularization did away with Christian eschatology.

Dante served as Auerbach's Habilitation subject under philologist, medievalist, and Romanist Leo Spitzer (1887–1960). With Spitzer's endorsement, and the support of Germany's most eminent medievalist, Karl Vossler, Auerbach was appointed in 1929 to the Marburg chair in Romance languages vacated by Spitzer (who had moved to Cologne). Auerbach arrived in Marburg the year after Heidegger had left. Philosophers Hans-Georg Gadamer and Karl Löwith and theologian Rudolf Bultmann were on the faculty – the latter two were close colleagues – and Marburg was thought to have a fairly liberal mandarin culture. The Auerbachs would remember their Marburg years as a golden age – the time when Erich was a full professor (*ordinarius*) surrounded by gifted students and colleagues and they lived in a congenial German milieu.

---

[26] Auerbach uses the term "realism" only rarely in *Dante*. In the introduction, he notes the term's vagueness, and moves on to speak of the mimetic problem. All the same, rudiments of "everyday tragic realism" are already in *Dante*.
[27] Auerbach, *Dante* (English edition), p. 8.   [28] Ibid., p. 90.   [29] Ibid., pp. 13–14.

These were also the turbulent years of the Nazis' rise to power. The Marburg student associations were, as elsewhere, the Nazi avant-garde. Auerbach did his best to distance himself from politics and, in 1932, enjoyed a summer vacation with a convertible in Italy. Historian Matthias Bormuth observes that Auerbach's 1932 "The Writer Montaigne" drew the contrast between Christian martyrdom and Montaigne's inner solitude (*Einsamkeit*), and diverged from *Mimesis* by sympathizing with Montaigne's withdrawal from public life to his home.[30] Feelings of vulnerability as an intellectual of Jewish origin seemed only to have reinforced Auerbach's mandarin proclivity to opt for inner freedom when politics were becoming oppressive. Personal martyrdom was never an option for him, but in 1932, the ideal itself, which would become a subject of contemplation and admiration with the advent of World War II, still seemed remote, intangible.

Other German humanists, in contrast, took an open political stance. They constitute an important context for understanding Auerbach's work and politics. In 1932, leading Romance philologist Ernst Robert Curtius (1886–1956) published a call for reconstituting a new Christian humanism against National Socialism and communism.[31] Curtius was both a literary critic and a medievalist, a Protestant fascinated with medieval Catholicism. He introduced T. S. Elliot to Germany, and familiarized the Germans with English, French, and Italian literature. He regarded himself a German cosmopolitan and a European: "My conviction is cosmopolitan (not inter-nationalist)," he said, to distance himself from socialist internationalism, "European on the basis of impartial . . . national (not nationalist) feelings."[32]

As a leading conservative proponent of German–French reconciliation and a member of international Catholic networks, such as the *Europäischen Kulturbund*, Curtius inveighed against nationalism and secu-larism, and called for an intellectual elite to lead a cultural revival grounded in a shared European Christian culture: "Limiting the French message to Enlightenment and Revolution overlooks that France has long been the most Christianized European nation [and] ignores the best . . . in the French spirit [and] tradition."[33] He attacked sociologist Karl

---

[30] Auerbach, "Der Schriftsteller Montaigne" [1932], in *Gesammelte Aufsätze*, pp. 184–95; Matthias Bormuth, "Menschenkunde zwischen Meistern – Auerbach und Löwith," in *Erich Auerbach*, ed. Treml amd Barck, pp. 99–101.

[31] *Deutscher Geist in Gefahr* (Stuttgart: Deutsche verlags-anstalt, 1932).

[32] Ernst Robert Curtius to André Gide, July 12, 1921, as quoted in Guido Müller, *Europäische Gesellschaftsbeziehungen nach dem Ersten Weltkrieg: Das Deutsch-Französische Studienkomitee und der Europäische Kulturbund* (Munich: R. Oldenbourg, 2005), p. 68, n. 121.

[33] Curtius, "Die geistige Bewegung in Deutschland und der französische Geist," *Westdeutsche Wochenschrift* (31 October 1919), as quoted in Guido Müller, *Europäische Gesellschaftsbeziehungen*, p. 102.

Mannheim and secular Jews for their historicism, relativism, and skepticism, and for their refusal to adopt Christianity, humanism, and *Deutschtum*.[34] The Jew became the signifier for hated modernity, but this was not simple antisemitism. Curtius's model for cultural renovation was identical to that of Hugo von Hofmannsthal, the icon of European Catholic cosmopolitanism.

Auerbach and Curtius had much in common. Both represented a younger generation of Romance philologists who expanded into literary criticism, ranging from classical to medieval to modern. Both were German humanists drawn to Dante, French literature, and high modernism – Joyce and Proust. Both were German cosmopolitans, committed to a Christian European culture and averse to the German nationalist denunciation of France as a *Negernation*. Both were rooted in a "Europe of nations," now threatened by ethno-nationalism. But Auerbach did not share Curtius's deep hostility to modernity and could not but sense that drawing Christian culture's boundaries threatened Jews like him. His response to Nazism was demure and more oblique than Curtius's but also more progressive. If Curtius turned to Catholic France, to contemporary poets Paul Claudel and Charles Péguy, Auerbach turned to republican France and nineteenth-century French social realism. He folded German romanticism into French realism, and declared the French the most authentic realists, European culture's peak achievement. Like other humanists, he sought to build a European culture on French–German affinities, a bulwark against Nazism, but his culture was more democratic and liberal.

Auerbach's 1929 inaugural lecture at Marburg on Dante and the Romantics reclaimed his past work for his new interest in modern realism: He recounted the discovery of Dante by Hegel, Friedrich Wilhelm Schelling, and Vico, and argued that it reinforced the realistic bent of romanticism.[35] As he was teaching French literature in Marburg, he noticed that the French realists followed a pattern he had observed in Dante, a pattern he now called *Stilmischung*, the "mixing" or merging of styles through the everyday tragic. Realism ended the classical *Stiltrennung* (separation of styles) by breaking the decorum rules designating the appropriateness of style (and genre) to subject, separating noble tragedy from lowly comedy. In his 1933 "Romanticism and

---

[34] *Deutscher Geist in Gefahr*, p. 85. Curtius spoke of secular Jews as *abgefallene Juden*, literally "apostates," or better, "heterodox Jews." For Curtius in Weimar, see Hans Manfred Bock, *Kulturelle Wegbereiter politischer Konfliktlösung* (Tübingen: Gunter Narr Verlag, 2005), p. 61 ff.

[35] Auerbach, "Die Entdeckung Dantes in der Romantik" [1930], in *Gesammelte Aufsätze*, pp. 176–83.

Realism," Auerbach claimed Stendhal and Balzac, the great French realists, as inheritors of the Romantic tradition of *Innerlichkeit* (inwardness). Everydayness emerged as central for the Romantics and realists alike, and both rejected French classicism and formalism, with their elitist presumptions. Tragic realism reflected egalitarianism in the aftermath of the French Revolution. The French may have led the trend, but they built on German romanticism.[36]

If *The Divine Comedy* represented a perfect fusion of styles, French classicism, a child of French absolutism, was its opposite, a combination of laicism and hierarchy. Auerbach's 1933 essay on the emergence of the seventeenth-century French literary public reflected his hostility toward classicism.[37] The essay dovetailed with contemporary scholarly interest in court culture and the French bourgeoisie, such as that expressed in the works of Bernard Groethuysen and Norbert Elias.[38] Throughout the seventeenth century, a powerless aristocracy and an alienated bourgeoisie competed for cultural leadership, the former acquiring empty manners, the latter counterposing salon to court, and claiming that *honnêteté* (integrity) could be had by all (but the common people). But to Auerbach, the emergent urban public and aristocratic court alike were superficial. Absolutism had a stifling effect on public life and culture.

In contrast, nineteenth-century social realism was the secular equivalent of Christian universalism. In "On the Serious Imitation of the Everyday" (1937), Auerbach presented Flaubert's *Madame Bovary* as an ultimate expression of "existential realism" that probed the depth of being-in-the-world. The imitation of everydayness transcended the classical separation between tragic and comic, between Racine and Molière, and for the first time, applied a sophisticated psychology to daily life.[39] Rousseau was a central figure in the development of the new literary sensibilities, which reflected the democratization of French society in the aftermath of 1789 and 1848.

In constructing French absolutism, court and classical tragedy as a countermodel to historical Christianity, democracy, and mixed literary

---

[36] "Romantik und Realismus," in *Erich Auerbach*, ed. Treml and Barck, pp. 426–38.

[37] Auerbach, *Das französische Publikum des 17. Jahrhunderts*, Münchener romanistische Arbeiten 3 (Munich: Hueber, 1933); "La Cour et la Ville" [1951], in *Scenes from the Drama of European Literature*, trans. Ralph Manheim (Minneapolis: University of Minnesota Press, 1984), pp. 133–79.

[38] Bernard Groethuysen, *Origines de l'esprit bourgeois en France: 1, L' Eglise et la bourgeoisie* [1927] (Paris: Gallimard, 1977); Norbert Elias, *Die höfische Gesellschaft: Untersuchungen zur Soziologie des Königtums und der höfischen Aristokratie* [1933] (Neuwied: Luchterhand, 1969). Groethuysen's and Elias's fame arrived even later than Auerbach's.

[39] "Über die ernste Nachahmung des Alltäglichen" [1937], in *Erich Auerbach*, ed. Treml and Barck, pp. 437–65.

genres, was Auerbach thinking of 1930s Germany? He was too sensitive a historian not to recognize the gap separating racist populism and nationalism from aristocratic hierarchy and royal authoritarianism. Yet in the aftermath of 1933, he developed a deep suspicion of abstract norms and heroic ideals, of myth and legend, and of hierarchies, and his suspicion toward them converged with his contempt toward "the dreadful inauthenticity of 'blood and soil' propaganda" and Nazi racial hierarchy that made exclusion of the Jews from European culture possible.[40] Against classicism and racism alike he posed Christian authenticity: historical truth (contrasted with myth), daily life, egalitarianism, and the dignity of the oppressed. Racism was inauthentic. There were nations, they could be ethnic, and they each had a unique cultural character. But German Jews, however different racially, were German because they shared in a German European culture that inherited the Judeo-Christian legacy.

"Figura" and Exile: Christian Typology and Jewish Emancipation

This culture had now to go into exile. As a decorated soldier who had served at the front, Auerbach escaped the first wave of academic dismissals of Jews in the spring of 1933. To the very end, he attempted to keep a low profile and ride out the storm, and advised others to do the same. He told the *Romanische Forschungen* editor, Fritz Schalk, who was under attack by Nazi students at Rostock, to keep his nerves in check and not provoke the students, and he added: "Something of what the youth want is right. We should take the wind out of their sails by accomplishing it better and in a different fashion."[41] What Auerbach found acceptable in Nazi demands is unclear, but Leo Spitzer, who had lost his Cologne position in April 1933 and went to Istanbul University, thought that Auerbach was betraying the tribal "feeling of solidarity in times of sudden misery."[42]

Auerbach self-identified as a Jew, but Jewishness was for him a matter of fact and not a commitment. He occasionally qualified an

---

[40] Auerbach to Benjamin, January 3, 1937, in Karlheinz Barck and Anthony Reynolds, "Walter Benjamin and Erich Auerbach: Fragments of a Correspondence," *Diacritic* 22: 3/4 (1992): 81–83.

[41] Dated May 19, 1936, in "Erich Auerbach: Briefe an Paul Binswanger und Fritz Schalk, Teil I (1930–1937)," ed. Isolde Burr and Hans Rothe, *Romanistiches Jahrbuch* 59 (2009): 178. Auerbach wrote from Geneva and was already bound for Istanbul.

[42] Spitzer to Karl Löwith, April 21, 1933, Karl Löwith papers, *Deutsches Literaturarchiv*, Marbach, as quoted in Matthias Bormuth, "Menschenkunde zwischen Meistern – Auerbach und Löwith," p. 98.

acknowledgment of his Jewish origin by declaring his German and Christian affinities, and he cared and spoke about these affinities a great deal more than about Jewishness. To Auerbach, their descent marked German Jews from non-Jews, but he offered no insight as to what the community of fate might mean to him. The closest he got was the startling statement (in a 1941 letter to Alexander Rüstow discussed at the end of this section) on the "uncanny existence" of postbiblical Jews in the aftermath of their rejection of Christianity. His terms were Christian and theological, and he eliminated postbiblical Jews from his narratives. Spitzer, who was no longer a Jew himself, felt that common ethnic origins entailed solidarity. Auerbach's solidarities lay elsewhere – they were German national and cosmopolitan and not Jewish.

Auerbach postponed the mandatory pledge of allegiance to Hitler as long as he could, but on September 19, 1934, he took the oath in order to retain his job. Aware that his position was becoming untenable, he shifted his teaching duties to his assistant, Werner Krauss. On leave in Italy in September 1935, he immediately grasped the implications of the Nuremberg Laws and began looking for a position abroad. His suspension came in mid-October. Marburg was determined not to begin the new academic year with Jews on the teaching faculty. Auerbach contacted the Warburg Institute in London but they could offer no help. Preferring Europe to the United States – Palestine was never considered – Auerbach competed with another German-Jewish cosmopolite, Victor Klemperer (1880–1960), for a professorship in "Western European philology" at Istanbul University.

Klemperer was, like Auerbach, a decorated war veteran and a Romance philologist who had just been dismissed from his Dresden position. With a letter from Italian philosopher Benedetto Croce (who had collaborated with Auerbach on the Vico translation), and with support from the previous chair holder, once again Spitzer (who was now going to the United States), Auerbach prevailed. He requested, and received, a leave from Marburg and permission to take up residence abroad. He went to Switzerland to brush up on his French before showing up for his new job in Istanbul in September 1936; the family followed him in November. The assimilated Klemperer, married to a non-Jew, survived the Holocaust in Germany by a thread. His Diary, published half a century later, *Ich will Zeugnis ablegen bis zum letzten* (I will bear witness to the last), would rivet Europeans.[43] He, a cosmopolitan German European, was the

---

[43] Victor Klemperer, *Ich will Zeugnis ablegen bis zum letzten*, 2 vols. (Berlin: Aufbau-Verlag, 1995).

true German, not the Nazis, he said. "How did you manage to survive in Germany?" wondered Auerbach in a postwar letter to Klemperer.[44]

Auerbach was one of about a hundred and thirty German exiles to whom Turkey provided refuge from Nazism. Istanbul Üniversitesi was a traditional Islamic school, reorganized in 1933 as a university, as part of Mostafa Kemal Atatürk's Westernization and secularization effort. The education ministry dismissed many teachers and looked for Europeans to head newly established departments. For obvious reasons, Nazi Germany provided the largest pool of applicants. At one time or another in the 1930s, Istanbul University had on its staff such future luminaries as economists Fritz Neumark, Wilhelm Röpke, and Alexander Rüstow; mathematician Richard von Mises and philosopher Hans Reichenbach (both connected with the Vienna Circle network); and philologists Leo Spitzer and Auerbach.[45] Most were of Jewish origin, but they brought with them non-Jewish German assistants, and together they constituted a German exile community on the Bosporus. They turned German humanistic education into a model for Turkish higher learning. Almost all left eventually, some before the war, for the United States and Switzerland; others returned to Germany after the war. In the interim, they shaped a generation of Turkish scholars and participated in Europeanizing the Turkish university.[46]

Auerbach felt ambivalent about Turkey's Westernization. As department head, he was responsible for the curriculum of European language instruction, wrote a French textbook, and helped set up a library catalogue. He needed to lay the groundwork for all fundamentals of university education and constantly negotiated with a recalcitrant

---

[44] Martin Vialon, "Wie haben Sie es geschafft, in Deutschland zu überleben? Zum fünfzigsten Todestag des großen Romanisten erstmals publiziert: Erich Auerbachs Brief an Victor Klemperer vom 7. Mai 1949," *Süddeutsche Zeitung* (13 October 2007).

[45] Surgeon Rudolf Nissen headed the Bosporus medical school; sculptor Rudolf Belling taught at the Academy of Fine Arts; urban planner Ernst Reuter, mayor of postwar Berlin, taught in Ankara, where classicist Georg Rohde established a classical library; and German musicians contributed to the state opera and conservatory. See Azade Sehan, "German Academic Exiles in Istanbul: Translation as the *Bildung* of the Other," in *Nation, Language, and the Ethics of Translation*, ed. Sandra Bermann and Michael Wood (Princeton, NJ: Princeton University Press, 2005), pp. 274–88.

[46] Kader Konuk, "Jewish-German Philologists in Turkish Exile: Leo Spitzer and Erich Auerbach," in *Exile and Otherness: New Approaches to the Experience of the Nazi Refugees*, ed. Alexander Stephan (Bern: Peter Lang, 2005), pp. 31–47. Emily Apter, "Global *Translatio*: The 'Invention' of Comparative Literature, Istanbul, 1933," *Critical Inquiry* 29:2 (2003): 269–70, suggests that Spitzer, Auerbach, and the journal *Romanoloji Semineri Dergisi* (Journal of the Romance Studies Seminar) were instrumental in developing the comparative literature discipline.

bureaucracy.[47] He was not an administrator by nature, and unlike Spitzer and some of his friends, he attempted no Turkish immersion. As a German-Jewish professor teaching French to Turks, he felt alienated. He despised Turkish nationalism and considered the nation-building project destructive: an assault on multiple old cultures, an invented barbarous language, and a fictitious secular identity.[48] In addition, he was aware that the refugees took over the positions of Islamic scholars, who, like them, were deposed by secular nationalists, and that the refugees were resented by large Turkish constituencies. Vico's world of nations was running amok. Auerbach held copycat modernization and nationalization from above to be responsible for this turmoil.

Istanbul was a war haven but it was exile, and "the bread of exile," Auerbach quoted Dante, "tastes salty."[49] Like other German émigrés, he lived in the picturesque suburb of Bebek, riding the tram to the university in the Beyazit district. He admired the city's cultural legacy, especially the old architecture (and despised modernized quarters), and he enjoyed the colorful scenery and gastronomy. He sent his son Clemens to an international school. The low cost of living made a decent, if modest, life possible, even as his resources were dwindling during the war. But he felt uprooted. He never applied for Turkish citizenship. Once his German travel documents expired in 1941, he had no clear legal status.

The German government was watchful over Germans living in Turkey. Upon arrival in Istanbul, Auerbach had signed that he would not engage in political activity (so as to protect Turkish neutrality), but the German government regarded the émigrés as potential cultural ambassadors for the Third Reich. Nazis infiltrated émigré clubs and took them over. A 1939 German report bemoaned the fact that Istanbul University had been Judaized (*verjudet*) and the director of European languages was a non-Aryan, a former Marburg professor who could not be trusted. The report urged the expatriation of all non-Aryan émigrés. Then, in 1943, over émigré objections, Istanbul

---

[47] Auerbach to Karl Vossler, June 8, 1938; October 10, 1938; April 28, 1939, in Martin Vialon, *Und wirst erfahren wie das Brot der Fremde so salzig schmeckt: Erich Auerbachs Briefe an Karl Vossler, 1926–1938* (Warmbronn: Keicher, 2007), pp. 22–27.

[48] Auerbach to Johannes Oeschger, May 27, 1938, in *Süddeutsche Zeitung* (14 October 2008), with a discussion by Martin Vialon, "Wie das Brot der Fremde so salzig schmeckt: Hellsichtiges über die Widersprüche der Türkei: Erich Auerbachs Istanbuler Humanismusbrief"; Auerbach to Walter Benjamin, January 3, 1937, in "Scholarship in Times of Extremes," *PMLA* 122:3 (2007): 750–51.

[49] Auerbach to Karl Vossler, October 10, 1938, in Martin Vialon, *Erich Auerbachs Briefe an Karl Vossler*, p. 25.

University established a German department under a Nazi. Auerbach was not completely safe.[50]

Exile came as a shock. Auerbach found himself excluded from the German European culture in which his scholarship was grounded and of which he was an exponent. German journals were closed to him, and in Romance philology there was really no non-German equivalent. His pathbreaking essays during his Turkish sojourn – two of them in French and English, languages in which he had never written – were published in Finnish, Italian, and U.S. journals and in new Turkish series. A Swiss publisher brought out *Mimesis* in 1946. Istanbul University had no academic library. However, Angelo Roncalli, future Pope John XXIII and at the time the papal delegate in Greece and Turkey, opened for Auerbach the library at the Dominican monastery in San Pietro di Galata, which had the complete *Patrologia Latina*.[51] But the sparse and occasionally incorrect scholarly references in his essays made his isolation evident. He was homesick before his first year in Istanbul was over.

The family took its 1937 summer vacation in Germany. While in Berlin, Clemens was summoned by the Gestapo to check on his residence, yet Marie still dared to return the next summer to finish family business. On the way back to Istanbul, the Auerbachs traveled via Salzburg, Trieste, and Athens, clinging to the German European culture they inhabited, refusing to accept their exile.[52]

Nevertheless, experiencing humiliation and exclusion, observing the collapse of the European order from the margins of the continent, and witnessing Turkey's modernization, Auerbach acquired a measure of distance from European culture and a more global perspective on it. He sensed that he was witnessing Europe's dissolution, and the experience was painful and sobering. Already in the fall of 1935, upon reading a section of Benjamin's reminiscences of his Berlin childhood around 1900 in the *Neue Zürcher Zeitung*, Auerbach spoke of "memories of a home that vanished so long ago!"[53] His renewed correspondence with Benjamin was tinged with nostalgia, mourning, and redemptive hope for

---

[50] Kader Konuk, *East West Mimesis: Auerbach in Turkey* (Stanford, CA: Stanford University Press, 2010), pp. 102–32. Auerbach knew he was not safe: "That we would be exiled from here, if one had the power to do so, is certain; and, then again, we lack no enemies here either." "Dass 'man' uns von hier vertreiben wird, wenn man die Macht dazu hat, steht fest, und dann werden auch hier die Feinde nicht fehlen." Auerbach to Johannes Oeschger, May 27, 1938, p. 16.

[51] Auerbach, "Epilegomena zu Mimesis" [1954], in *Erich Auerbach*, ed. Treml and Barck, p. 473, n. 12.

[52] Clemens Auerbach, "Summer 1937," in *Erich Auerbach*, ed. Treml and Barck, pp. 495–500.

[53] Auerbach to Benjamin, September 23, 1935, and October 6, 1935, in "Scholarship in Times of Extreme," PMLA 122:3 (2007): 747–52, 759–60; Walter Benjamin, *Berlin*

European culture, all mixed together. He retained just enough providen-tialism – or was it after all Hegelian historicism? – to assume a moral pattern to history, from which one could derive instruction for action. The triumph of National Socialism and the end of Jewish emancipation upset this pattern, and he was at a loss, searching for sources of spiritual renewal for European civilization:

> The challenge is not to grasp and digest all the evil that's happening – that's not too difficult – but much more to find a point of departure for those historical forces that can be set against it. To seek for them in myself, to track them down in the world, completely absorbs me. The old forces of resistance – churches, democ-racies, education, economic laws – are useful and effective only if they are renewed and activated through a new force not yet visible to me.[54]

Where was he to turn in exile, searching for this new force? He went back to an earlier crisis of Western civilization, to the waning of Second Temple Judaism (as he saw it) and the Christian breakthrough, hoping to learn what direction "a new force" might take in the present. He was searching for language that could bring together refined elites and uncul-tivated people, like the Nazi youth he witnessed craving inspiration. Correspondence with Benjamin, says Martin Elsky, may have directed him toward *figura*. In *The Origin of German Tragic Drama*, published in 1928, Benjamin examined the workings of allegory in Baroque tragedy, and noted the emblem of the ruin, which reflected both the destruction and preservation of civilization.[55] Auerbach had helped Benjamin with his failed Habilitation work, and reminiscences of old Berlin, now lost, may have brought back the ruin. *Figura*, the predominant Christian trope, captured Benjamin's ruin allegory, and "provided Auerbach with a way of conceiving both the destruction and preservation of Jewish civilization, a sense of mourning and consolation" for the culture that had once made him, and German Jews, feel at home, and was now vanishing before his eyes.[56]

In their predicament, traditional Jews could turn to Jacob, their wan-dering ancestor, and seek comfort and instruction in his travails. In 1940 in a British detention camp, sociologist Norbert Elias, a secular Jewish

---

Childhood Around 1900, trans. Howard Eiland (Cambridge, MA: Belknap Press of Harvard University Press, 2006).

[54] Auerbach to Traugott Fuchs (Spitzer's assistant who became a close friend in Istanbul), October 22, 1938, *PMLA* 122:3 (2007): 752–55 (German and English).

[55] Walter Benjamin, *The Origin of German Tragic Drama*, trans. John Osborne (London: NLR, 1977).

[56] Martin Elsky, "Erich Auerbach and Walter Benjamin in Flight: *Figura* and Allegory," paper presented at the Exile and Interpretation Conference, Wake Forest University (November 16–18, 2012), p. 5.

intellectual, composed "The Ballad of Poor Jacob," which retold the story of the wandering Jew as a parable for the universal refugee: "And once again he walked without money a little further into the wide world."[57] Exile, as experience and motif, still tied Auerbach to his Jewish heritage: In *Mimesis*, he noted in passing that "Jacob really [was] a refugee." He apparently lectured to the Istanbul Jewish community on educational issues (something he was unlikely to do in Germany).[58] But Jewish sources and traditions were a closed book to him. One wonders what Auerbach could say to the Jewish community.

Instead, Auerbach turned to Augustine and Dante, whom he considered the great spiritual and literary innovators of the West. The topoi of his exile essays were the Passion, *sermo humilis*, and figura: the Passion's shaping of Western emotions, Augustine's refashioning of *sermo humilis* – Scriptures' lowly style when speaking of the sublime – and Dante's deployment of figura, typology, as a bridge between the historical and the transcendent.[59] All provided models for Christian engagement in the world. All were grounded in the incarnation and the Passion – in Christ human and divine. Werfel believed as a Catholic in the cross and remained Jewish as an act of solidarity with his people. Auerbach was just secular enough not to believe in the miracle of the cross and remain Jewish by default, but more than cultural Christian enough to uphold the event and the biblical narrative recounting it as world transformative – conveying symbols and ideals that nourished Western civilization. He sought the guidance of Augustine and Dante as to how to translate these ideals into a renovation of the West.

Auerbach thought that, like him, Augustine lived through the dissolution of a civilization – that of the Western Roman Empire. He remolded

---

[57] "Und dann zog er wieder ohne Geld ein Stueck weiter in die weite Welt": "Die Ballade von armen Jakob," in Norbert Elias, *Los der Menschen* (Frankfurt am Main: Suhrkamp, 1987), pp. 87–98.

[58] *Mimesis*, p. 18 (in English). Jacob is one of several biblical figures used by Auerbach to argue that biblical characters are intended as real and not mere symbols. Martin Vialon, "Wie das Brot der Fremde so salzig schmeckt," quotes a 2007 report of the former head of the Rome Jewish community, Giacomo Saban, who had known the Auerbachs in Istanbul as a young student. Vialon ventures the opinion that exile may have been a motif of Auerbach's talks.

[59] "Figura," *Archivum Romanicum* 22 (1938): 436–89; rev. edition: Erich Auerbach, *Neue Dantestudien* (Istanbul: I. Horoz basimevi, 1944), pp. 11–71, trans. Ralph Manheim [1959], in Erich Auerbach, *Scenes from the Drama of European Literature*, pp. 11–76. "Sacrae scripturae sermo humilis" [1941], in *Neue Dantestudien*, pp. 1–10; rev. and expanded edition: "Sermo humilis," in Erich Auerbach, *Literary Language and Its Public*, pp. 25–67. "'Passio' as Passion," PMLA 56 (1941): 1179–96. Auerbach uses "figura" rather than typology, but the latter term has been universally used for the figurative thinking he outlined. He later acknowledged the identity of the two: "Epilegomena zu Mimesis," p. 474.

Latin to make culture accessible to the common people, "fill[ing] this language with new content and giv[ing] it a special style ... *sermo humilis.*"[60] The transformation of rhetoric, accompanied by Augustine's new psychology and ethics, shaped the Western understanding of the individual and the literary possibilities for expressing it. Still, Augustine was of limited use to Auerbach. His view of history as an inconsequential interim between Christ's first and second coming, of earthly life as a sojourn, a pilgrimage, and an exile from the Lord, and of the Roman Empire as a pact of criminals, ran contrary to Auerbach's earthly Christian world and to his experience of exile.[61] Augustine would never have recognized Auerbach's "everyday tragic."

Dante presented a stark contrast to Augustine. The Florentine exile's views on Christian and civic life, like Auerbach's own, left no place for permanent homelessness. Auerbach's October 1938 letter to medievalist Karl Vossler suggested that he began viewing his own exile via Dante's protagonist in *The Divine Comedy.*[62] He found in Dante two models for engaging the world: The first, exemplified in "Figura," drew on the Christian legacy to transform literary style and culture; the second, exemplified in *Mimesis*, shaped a cosmopolitan literary public to become its spokesperson. Dante showed how the predicament of exile and the crisis of European culture could be overcome through cultural innovation. Standing at the apex of medieval culture and presaging the Renaissance, he sustained Auerbach's hope, prior to World War II, of cultural restoration.

Whence, Auerbach wondered, *The Divine Comedy*'s transformative power? How did Dante manage, historically, to break with both Christian allegory and the classical *decorum* and create the everyday tragic? The recovery by Dante and medieval literature of a patristic mode of biblical exegesis, *figura*, or typology, which entailed an omni-temporal conception of history that superseded cyclical and linear ones, was Auerbach's answer:

Figural interpretation establishes a connection between two events or persons, the first of which signifies not only itself but also the second, while the second

---

[60] *Literary Language and Its Public*, p. 335. More on sermo humilis later.

[61] *Locus classicus*: Augustine, *De civitate Dei: The City of God Against the Pagans* (in English and Latin), 7 vols. (Cambridge, MA: Harvard University Press, 1957–72): I:15, V:17, XIX:18.

[62] Auerbach to Karl Vossler, October 10, 1938, in Martin Vialon, *Erich Auerbachs Briefe an Karl Vossler*, p. 25: "Si sa di sale la pane altrui; und mich ängsten die Gedanken an weitere fremde Treppen (How salty the bread of others is; and thoughts of more foreign steps make me anxious)." Auerbach quoted to Vossler *Paradiso* XVII: 58–60: "You shall leave everything you love most. ... You are to know the bitter taste of others' bread, how salty it is, and how arduous and bitter the walk is, climbing and descending another's stairs."

encompasses and fulfills the first. The two poles . . . are separate in time, but both, being real events or figures, are within time, within the stream of historical life.[63] Moses and Christ . . . are related as figure and fulfillment [but] Moses is no less historically real because he is a . . . *figura* of Christ, and Christ, the fulfillment, is no abstract idea but also a historical reality.[64]

Dante could so skillfully make historical figures express transcendental meaning because medieval literature capitalized on a millennium-old typological understanding of history and text, paving the way for *The Divine Comedy*.

Auerbach had not known figura's universe very well prior to his exile. He was neither a classicist nor a patristic scholar by training but a Romance philologist, a Dante and Vico scholar who expanded his interests to French literature. His study of Dante required that he reconstruct historically the mimetic problem and its Christian transformation, but he had no detailed knowledge of classical and patristic sources beyond the education of a humanistic scholar. In exile, he studied patristic literature intensively and felt moved. He found in it consolation and encouragement, and that experience would shape *Mimesis*. In the postwar years, he would still be enraptured by the survival of Christian culture through the early Middle Ages, but the focus would no longer be patristic. Figura constituted the intellectual and emotional world of Auerbach's Turkish exile.

Figura also signaled Auerbach's turn to Catholicism. In 1921 he had declared himself a Prussian Jew (rather than a German Jew), intimating his preference for Protestant culture.[65] But with the Nazi triumph, cultural Protestantism, wholly invested in the nation-state, appeared bankrupt, and many of its protagonists were rushing to reconcile with the new regime. Auerbach's method continued to reflect his Protestant training, but his vision, from the mid-1930s on, showed significant marks of the Catholic understanding of modernity and secularization, and he expressed admiration for medieval Christendom.[66] Already in his 1933 essay on the seventeenth-century French public, Auerbach offered a rudimentary theory of secularization, inspired by Catholic philosopher Étienne Gilson (1884–1978). The emergent public, designed to distance

---

[63] "Figura," 468 (I use the original 1938 German edition unless otherwise noted), p. 53 (in English), Manheim's translation.

[64] "Figura," 454 (German), p. 34 (English).

[65] Martin Elsky writes (email to author, January 6, 2013): "The religious education textbook at the *französisches Gymnasium* [which Auerbach attended] centered around the Bible but, although deeply anti-Jewish, did not mention typology. I suspect the school was under liberal Protestant influence, and this made it popular with Jews."

[66] *Das französische Publikum des 17. Jahrhunderts*, pp. 45–53. Auerbach cut this section from the postwar German and English editions of "La Cour et la Ville."

the bourgeoisie from "everyday life," was the moral agent behind classical tragedy's revival. Like Descartes' epistemological subject, the public reflected de-Christianization, a disavowal of the divine in the mundane. National Socialism's anti-Christian turn mimicked early modern absolutism.

"I belong to the Jewish community," said Auerbach in 1935, "but my work has been engaged for many years with Christian theology, especially of Catholic circles (Guardini, Gilson)."[67] Romano Guardini (1885–1968) was a leading German Catholic scholar and an anti-Nazi public intellectual. Auerbach's protagonists for the next decade would resemble Guardini's: Augustine, Dante, and Pascal. Luther was nowhere to be seen. Typology was primarily a Catholic affair, first of Gilson and then of Jesuit theologian Henri de Lubac (1896–1991), who assailed antisemitism as anti-Christian and would inspire Vatican II.[68] For a cultural Christian and a German Jew, it was not unreasonable to sense in the 1930s that Catholic culture offered greater protection for Christian Jews than did the Protestant. Moving between cultural Protestantism and Catholicism, Auerbach made typology address the Jewish predicament.

"Figura," Auerbach's most famous essay, provides a history of typology as a literary and artistic form, from the Roman poets to patristic literature to Dante. Auerbach began "Figura" with the Hellenization of Roman education in the first century BCE and the transmission of Greek literary and philosophical concepts, such as $sch\check{e}ma$, into Roman culture. He moved from republican-era poets Lucretius and Cicero to imperial-era poets Virgil, Catullus, and Ovid, and from them to architecture, jurisprudence, and, above all, to Quintilian's rhetoric. The poets were fascinated by "the play between model and copy, the changing form, the deceptive likeness of dream figures."[69] The architects contemplated models to emulate, and Quintilian designated by $figura$ multiple literary tropes, product of the metaphoric imagination, which enriched rhetoric. Figura remained primarily literary, of interest to limited intellectual circles.

---

[67] Emergency Committee in Aid of Displaced Foreign Scholars, Box 38, Folder 55, Manuscripts and Archives Division, New York Public Library (henceforth, Emergency Committee, NYPL; my thanks to Matthias Bormuth for the document). Auerbach was responding to a questionnaire, querying whether the Academic Assistance Council might approach religious communities on his behalf.

[68] The German academic authority on typology in medieval poetry was Julius Schwietering: "Typologisches in mittelalterlicher Dichtung," in *Vom Werden des deutschen Geistes*, ed. Paul Merker and Wolfgang Stammler (Berlin: De Gruyter, 1925), pp. 40–55. Auerbach does not cite him and, instead, engages Gilson ("Figura," 60–61, 235–36, n. 41 [English] and 474–75, n. 37 [German]). Notwithstanding the poor library in Istanbul, this is puzzling.

[69] "Figura," 444 (German), p. 21 (English).

The advent of Christ, the crucifixion, and Christian sacraments radically changed figura's meaning and significance.[70] Jesus' disciples naturally looked to the Hebrew Bible for prophecies figuring his advent. The Greek *typos*, used in early accounts to designate prefiguration of events and persons connected with Christ, devolved into the Latin *figura*, now combining biblical "prophecy" with classical "representation." "Figure" turned into "prefigure" (of the New Testament by the Old); the literary notion became historical, designating real events and persons.[71] For Paul, on his mission to the Gentiles, the Hebrew Bible turned "from a book of the law and history of Israel into one of a unique great promise and a prehistory of Christ.... What the Old Testament thereby lost in the efficacy of its law and in the autonomy of its national history, it gained in concrete dramatic actuality."[72] "[T]o the newly converted peoples, [it gave] a basic conception of world history," "its integral teleological view ..., the providential order ... captur[ing] the[ir] imagination and innermost feeling ... with its living historicity."[73] *Figura* became constitutive of the Christian conception of reality and history. It represented "a fresh beginning and rebirth of creative powers."[74]

Christian typology combined historical depth with popular reach. The future was concealed yet embodied in persons who were not historically contingent but signified universal and eternal meaning; God himself was incarnated in figures and sacraments. Allegorical, ethical, and spiritual interpretations, rendering biblical persons and events symbolic, provided an alternative to typology. From Jewish philosopher Philo to Church Father Origen and the Alexandrian school to medieval times, allegory coexisted with figura. But allegorization, insisted Auerbach, remained an elite project, whereas Christian typology, phenomenal and historical, expanded the reach of figural thinking to the socially downtrodden, bringing together high and low. Beginning its triumphant march in patristic literature in the third century with Tertullian, typology became hegemonic with Augustine in the fourth century. Both Tertullian and Augustine were staunch realists who rejected allegorical spiritualism. "When you hear an exposition of the mystery of Scriptures

---

[70] The Last Supper, said Auerbach, was "the purest picture of the concretely present, the veiled and tentative, the eternal and supratemporal elements contained in the figures": "Figura," 474 (German), p. 60 (English), Manheim's translation.
[71] "Figura," 461–62 (German), pp. 44–45 (English).
[72] "Figura," 466 (German), p. 51 (English).
[73] "Figura," 468, 470–71 (German), pp. 53, 56 (English), respectively.
[74] "Figura," 471 (German), p. 56 (English).

telling of things that took place," admonished Augustine, "believe what is read to have actually taken place . . . lest . . . you seek to build in the air."[75]

Medieval allegory was doctrinally included in the fourfold sense of Scriptures, but figura predominated, insisted Auerbach.[76] Separating typology from allegory, Auerbach rebutted the common view of *The Divine Comedy* as allegorical. Virgil, who guided Dante through Hell, and Beatrice, who welcomed him in Paradise, were figures, not allegories – real historical persons, not theological principles. An embodiment of poetic eloquence and worldly virtues – liberty, wisdom, justice, and piety – Virgil, the fullness of earthly perfection, had the capacity to guide Dante to the threshold of insight into the divine. Beatrice, sent by divine grace to guide Dante (and humanity) to salvation, incarnated revelation, but her relationship to Dante could not fully be explained by dogmatic considerations. She *was* also his beloved Florentine, and their lives did intersect. Every mythical or historical figure in the *Comedy* had a meaning connected with what Dante knew about his or her life. Virgil was not "virtue" or "reason"; rather, the literal meaning figured the theological, and the theological confirmed and fulfilled it, both meanings having a place in a providential history.[77]

"Figura" ended on a rather minor note that seemed to diminish the brunt of Auerbach's tour de force. To his earlier call to revisit allegory and figura in medieval literature, he now added the observation that figura's history showed how a word could develop into a world-historical situation. Paul's mission to the Gentiles endowed the classical concept with structures that would shape the late antique and medieval intellectual worlds.[78] The view of Paul's move from national to world religion (Judaism to Christianity) as the crucial turning point in history was in line with the common Christian view, but it did not elucidate the implications of figura for Europe. How did Christian realism shape modern culture? Auerbach hinted that medieval literature already contained the origin of secular realism, but he shunned any suggestion as to how secularization had taken place. His caution reflected his genuine bewilderment about the origins of the European crisis – he sensed that secularization prepared the way but he just did not know how.

---

[75] "Figura," 458 (German), p. 39 (English). Dante spoke of *The Divine Comedy* as "allegorical" but he meant "typological": " Dante's Letter to Can Grande," trans. Nancy Howe, in *Essays on Dante*, ed. Mark Musa (Bloomington: Indiana University Press, 1964), pp. 32–47.
[76] "Figura," 478 (German), p. 63 (English).
[77] "Figura," 477–89 (German), pp. 64–76 (English).
[78] "Figura," 489 (German), p. 76 (English).

All the same, "Figura" did have a political agenda, if not as open as the academic one. Academically, Auerbach intervened in medieval studies, urging scholars to distinguish between allegory and typology, between the diversity of literary metaphors and figura. Typology, he insisted, was the quintessential Christian mode, and Christian realism was mainstream. But his professional intervention was politically loaded. He discovered figura just as the exclusionary power of race made him painfully conscious of his Jewishness. "Figura" took a position in German debates on the "Jewish" character of the Old Testament. Auerbach sought to renegotiate Jewish membership in German European culture, that is, Jewish emancipation, by highlighting the Jewish origins of European culture.

As the earlier discussion of Hermann Gunkel showed, thinkers ranging from liberal Protestant to Nazi dissociated the New Testament from the Old. The liberals aimed to rescue a Christian mission – universal or national – from "Jewish particularism," the German Christians to establish Aryan Christianity. Even Karl Barth (1886–1968), a leader of the anti-Nazi Confessing Church, affirmed that the Old Testament had no value as a book about Ancient Israel: "For us the Old Testament is valid only in relation to the New. If the Church has declared itself to be the lawful successor to the Synagogue, this means that the Old Testament is witness to Christ before Christ but not without Christ."[79]

Against this chorus, Auerbach underlined the historical continuity between the Old and New Testaments by using typology. He reargued the case for the Old Testament against the likes of Adolf von Harnack who wished to decanonize it. "It was not until very late," he said acerbically, "that Europeans began to regard the Old Testament as Jewish History and Jewish Law."[80] He uncovered a patristic and medieval interpretive mode that superseded the progressive conception of history. Still, precisely because he wished to sustain Jewish integration, and in 1938 still held out hope for Germany, he never took the Barthian turn of Jewish rebels of his cohort, who radically separated reason and revelation, challenged their parents' optimistic historical theology, and affirmed authentic Jewish identity. He would not commit himself to the Catholic critique of Enlightenment and the nation-state either. Barth, the Catholics, and Auerbach agreed that the Old and New Testaments were of a piece, but Barth's antinationalist, antihistorical, unearthly Christianity left the Jews forever as the Other, and the Catholics were profoundly antimodern.

---

[79] Karl Barth, *Homiletics*, trans. Geoffrey W. Bromiley and Donald E. Daniels (Louisville, KY: Westminster/J. Knox Press, 1991), p. 80 (Bonn seminar lectures, 1932–33), and *Church Dogmatics I. 2* [1938], trans. G. T. Thomson (London: T&T Clark International, 2004), pp. 70–101.

[80] "Figura," 468 (German), p. 53 (English).

Liberal histories brought Jews and Christians so close to each other that Auerbach would not give them up for Barth's Christocentric history or forgo modernity. He preferred to work through history rather than through theology, negotiate with Harnack rather than with Barth, argue with prejudice rather than concede incommensurable truth and otherness, and heal rather than reject modern life.

"Figura" was a desperate attempt to salvage emancipation and German-Jewish cosmopolitanism through a shared Judeo-Christian tradition. It allowed only for a diminished space for Jews, and indeed, it was not clear that they could any longer be recognized as Jews. In the debate between Judaism and Christianity, Auerbach accepted the Christian argument: Christianity superseded Judaism. A December 1941 letter to an Istanbul colleague, Alexander Rüstow, made his view about Judaism's obsolescence clear: Jewish life had long been reified, and Jews were leading a ghostly existence:[81]

The uncanny feeling Judaism evokes, the sense that it is laden with a curse, grew, and became concrete, through the role the Jews played in the rise of Christianity. Christianity originated with the Jews but they rejected it, so that the mission reverted to the Gentiles, forming a contrast between Jewish Law (now but a shadow and a ghost) and the fulfillment of Christian Grace (which disempowered the Law).[82]

The Jews had had no authentic spiritual life since the time of the Prophets, but they still presented the spectacle of a people living apart in exile, attached to their ancestry. Throughout the ages, they survived as a minority, subject to hatred and persecution, while other nations, with viable political life, vanished. The Enlightenment constituted a break, removing the taboo against the Jews – forever. Modern antisemitism was a by-product of nationalist struggles, an opportunistic endeavor to use atavistic relics to reinforce exclusion, historically hopeless and meaningless. The Jews were part of European culture, and antisemitism had no object, purpose, or prospect. It was "a side issue." In time, it would

---

[81] Dated December 12, 1941, *Nachlass Alexander Rüstow*, Bundesarchiv Koblenz, quoted in Martin Vialon, "Helle und Trost für eine 'neue Menschlichkeit' – Erich Auerbachs türkisches Exilbriefwerk," *Deutsche Akademie für Sprache und Dichtung: Jahrbuch 2010* (Göttingen: Wallstein Verlag, 2011), pp. 38–40. I am grateful to Vialon for a prepublished version of his essay.

[82] Ibid., p. 38: "Ihr eigenes geistiges Leben, das eigentlich Jüdische im Geistigen ist längst erstarrt und wirkt gespenstisch. . . . Das Gefühl des Unheimlichen, Fluchbeladenen wurde gesteigert und konkretisiert durch die Rolle, die sie bei der Entstehung des Christentums gespielt haben. Das Christentum ging von ihnen aus, aber sie haben es verworfen, so dass die Mission sich an die Heiden wandte und der Gegensatz zwischen dem jüdischen Gesetz (das nur noch Schatten und Gespenst sei) und christlicher Gnadenerfüllung (die das Gesetz entkräftete), konstruierte."

disappear.[83] The Jews might meanwhile suffer, but they should be thankful for the role of martyrs for humanity – a role they did not deserve – that fell to their lot.

This extraordinary statement, made at a time when, unbeknownst to Auerbach, Soviet Jews were already being shot in the tens of thousands, and Hitler was completing plans for destroying all of European Jewry, provides precious insight into Auerbach's worldview. It reflects crude Christian supersessionism, incredible optimism about Jewish emancipation, a profound misreading of antisemitism, and an avowal of the Christian martyr role for the Jews. Auerbach's disregard for Jewish typology reflected his conviction that postbiblical Jewish life was not part of European history. The Jews became part of Europe only when the Enlightenment made their integration possible – and no longer as Jews: "Anything significant that came out of the Jews was absorbed by the host nations."[84] Jewish history – if such existed – was not part of European history.

Jewish ethnic survival was for Auerbach, as for Herder, a source of puzzlement – of wonder (and perhaps hidden pride) mixed with apprehension about their "uncanny" existence. Like Herder, he believed in the ethnicity of nations, but wanted to be recognized as German.[85] He could break through ethnicity only via Christianity, that is, by arguing for Jewish cultural inclusion in Germany and Europe as Christian founders. Like Popper, he had no doubt that it was high time for Jewish life to end – for the Jews to become part of Christian Europe. Popper imagined the culture integrating the Jews as secular, and its relationship to Christianity was tenuous; for Auerbach, European culture was secularized Christianity. The National Socialist attack on the Jews was significant for its denial of Christianity and humanity, and the Jews acquired their role as Christian martyrs. Christian martyrology became paradigmatic of the Jewish experience, and Auerbach, captivated, devoted to it increasing attention during and after World War II. The murdered Jews

---

[83] Ibid, p. 40: "Der Antisemitismus seit etwa 1820 ist nichts mehr als eine Ausnützung solcher Atavismen im Dienste ganz anderer Ziele, er ist nur noch ein Anhängsel von sozialen und nationalistischen Kämpfen. Im Rahmen der uns erwartenden Probleme wird der Antisemitismus gegenstandslos werden, davon bin ich fest überzeugt, er ist nur noch ein Randproblem, das nie gehört werden, aber verschwinden wird."

[84] Ibid., p. 38: "Alles was seither Bedeutendes von ihnen ausging, ist an die Kulturen der Wirtsvölker angerankt": This would suggest that Jews did actually make postbiblical contributions to European culture, but Auerbach insists that when a contribution was made, it would no longer be defined as Jewish but as European.

[85] "Die Entstehung der Nationalsprachen im Europa des 16. Jahrhunderts" [1939], in Erich Auerbach, *Kultur als Politik: Aufsätze aus dem Exil zur Geschichte und Zukunft Europas (1938–1947)*, ed. Christian Rivoletti (Konstanz: Konstanz University Press, 2014), esp. pp. 53–54.

were integrated into European civilization – as (undeserving) Christian martyrs.

"Figura" was emblematic of European histories that integrated the Jews as Christians. Auerbach's turn to Catholicism facilitated a transformation of cultural Protestant narratives, but he retained them, however altered, because he did not wish to give up on modernity or emancipation. He modified Harnack by skipping over Marcion (who rejected the Hebrew Bible), highlighting Tertullian and Augustine, and ending with Dante rather than with Luther or modern Protestantism. Dante became a starting point of modernity, of secularization that would de-eschatologize Christian history but absorb Dante's vision of humanity, leaving a universal history to be shared by Christians, Jews, and all. This universal history, however, still bore its Christian marks – it did not permit Jews to remain Jews. A Christian humanist who remained Jewish, Auerbach constructed a narrative of Western civilization that appealed to the highly acculturated German-Jewish intelligentsia – and today's Europeans.

Mimesis and the Holocaust: The Jewish Origins of European Civilization

European restoration, German-Jewish cosmopolitanism, and emancipation all depended on the survival of Vico's world of nations. With the collapse of Europe in World War II, Auerbach lost hope for them. *Mimesis*, written (according to Auerbach) between May 1942 and April 1945, at the height of the war and the Holocaust, reflected a change of orientation. As a refugee without national identity on the outskirts of a devastated continent, Auerbach no longer wrote as a German European. His previous audience was gone, at least for the duration of the war (and he suspected forever), and he did not know who his prospective audience might be, or what shape postwar Europe might take, indeed, if it, and he, survived at all. He had to refashion his authorial identity and imagine a new audience. "The Jewish refugee in Istanbul," says Carl Landauer, "very much the outsider, reestablished himself as an insider" by reconfiguring both the European audience and himself as members of the Western tradition.[86]

---

[86] "'Mimesis' and Erich Auerbach's Self-Mythologizing," *German Studies Review* 11:1 (1988): 88. Landauer emphasizes the intersubjectivity of Auerbach's Western tradition. This evokes a comparison with Popper. It would appear that for Auerbach, the intersubjectivity of the Western classics relied on the community of readers' shared background, on the similarity of ideals and sentiments among benefactors of the classico-Christian tradition. For Popper, the intersubjectivity of philosophy, science, and democracy required only

Deploying a style suggested by high modernist novels, Auerbach began writing as a cosmopolitan spokesperson for a "European classico-Christian literary culture."[87] He appeared as a Pan-European, at once a Christian humanist and a modernist, drawing the boundaries and charting the legacy of Europe for a cosmopolitan audience. In exile from Florence, Dante had proclaimed "the world is my fatherland," and the Swiss historian Jacob Burckhardt echoed him: "My country is the whole world."[88] Auerbach joined this lineage of aspiring cosmopolitans, imagining "a European world in which he was at home."[89]

Mimesis charted the history of Western literary styles and their representation of reality in nineteen (and, in later editions, twenty) exquisitely crafted essays on the classics of Western literature. Auerbach began with the Odyssey and the Hebrew Bible, continued with the classical Roman poet Petronius and the New Testament, moved on to the fourth-century historian Marcellinus Ammianus and Augustine, and captured the transition from the late antique to the medieval with Gregory of Tours's *History of the Franks*. He skipped half a millennium to the medieval epic of Roland, the romance of Yvain, and "Adam and Eve" Christmas plays, paid homage to Dante in the unforgettable "Farinata and Calvacante," and showed Boccaccio and the fifteenth-century chivalrous chronicler Antoine de la Salle negotiating the Renaissance and the waning Middle Ages. The sixteenth-century giants, Rabelais, Montaigne, and Shakespeare (and, in later editions, Cervantes), gave a measure of secularization; Molière and his critics displayed seventeenth-century French classicism; an Abbé Prévost 1731 sentimental novel, paired with Voltaire's *Candide* and Saint Simon's *Memoirs* of Louis XIV's court,

---

an open critical public, an exchange of arguments. All the same, the wartime appeal of intersubjectivity to both Jewish exiles, reared on a liberal Protestant view of the West, is thought provoking.

[87] *Mimesis*, pp. 547–48: In Joyce, Proust, and Wolfe, "there is greater confidence in syntheses gained through full exploitation of everyday occurrence than in chronologically well-ordered total treatment.... [T]his technique of modern writers [compares] with that of certain modern philologists who hold that the interpretation of a few passages from *Hamlet*, *Phèdre*, or *Faust* can be made to yield more ... decisive information about Shakespeare, Racine, or Goethe and their times than would systematic [biographies]. The present book may be cited as an illustration." The expression "European classico-Christian literary culture" belongs to J. B. Trapp, quoted in Carl Landauer, "'Mimesis' and Erich Auerbach's Self-Mythologizing," 95, n. 24.

[88] Dante, *De Vulgari Eloquentia* (I, vi, paragraphs 11–12, in Latin and English), ed. Warman Welliver (Ravenna: Longo, 1981), pp. 52–53; Jacob Burckhardt, *Die Kultur der Renaissance in Italien*, 2d ed. (Leipzig: Seemann, 1869), p. 108. Burckhardt transformed the tormented Florentine patriot into an avowed cosmopolitan. Dante wrote: "nos autem, cui mundus est patria," translated as "I, however, to whom the world is fatherland." Burckhardt rendered it: "meine Heimath ist die Welt überhaupt!"

[89] Carl Landauer, "'Mimesis' and Erich Auerbach's Self-Mythologizing," 88.

marked an emergent Enlightenment; and Schiller and Goethe drew the German enlightenment's limits and their import for German realism. *Mimesis* concluded with three essays on modern realism, beginning, respectively, with Stendhal, the brothers Goncourt, and Wolfe, but comparing their works with other exemplars of French, English, German, and Russian realism.

The format for the essays in *Mimesis* was uniform: Auerbach opened with a long quotation from the work, which provided the focus for his analysis. He tracked the uniqueness of the literary style and placed it in its life-world, accentuating comparable or competing literary modes. The book had no footnotes. The limits of the Istanbul library, Auerbach suggested, made writing a book covering three millennia possible but also dictated his textual focus and his daring construction of context. *Mimesis* had no introduction or conclusion to provide an overarching argument or context. Only a brief epilogue lent the book a measure of coherence, offering a historical outline of the doctrine of styles. Critics complained that Auerbach's realism was impossible to pin down, as the meaning of reality kept shifting from epistemological (empirical and sensational) to sociological (class structure) to psychological (emotional state). *Mimesis* remained elusive.

As if to increase the mystery surrounding *Mimesis*, Auerbach made very few allusions, mostly oblique, to his own world – to National Socialism, exile, and the war. The book's opacity, together with its aesthetic appeal and daunting reach and erudition, gave rise to a lively debate on Auerbach's narrative of Western civilization. Commentators have viewed *Mimesis* alternatively as literary Christology, Jewish philology, secular criticism, minority literature, and literary modernism.[90] This much is clear: Postwar U.S. and European critics alike have found Auerbach enthralling, and his fame has been on the increase. He told a story that postwar Europeans loved to hear. *Mimesis* did end up shaping the new cosmopolitan audience imagined by Auerbach and became a charter for a new Europe.

The focus of *Mimesis*, however, remained on the current European crisis. Auerbach offered clues to its origins by putting forward an ironic vision of secularization and a rudimentary theory of the failure of German literary culture. His leitmotif was the emergence of modern literary

---

[90] Helmut Kuhn, "Literaturgeschichte als Geschichtsphilosophie," *Philosophische Rundschau* 11 (1963): 222–48; James Porter, "Erich Auerbach and the Judaizing of Philology," 115–47; Edward Said, "Erich Auerbach, Critic of the Earthly World," *Boundary 2* 31:2 (2004): 11–34; Amir Mufti, "Auerbach in Istanbul: Edward Said, Secular Criticism, and the Question of Minority Culture," *Critical Inquiry* 25:1 (1998): 95–125; Carl Landauer, "'Mimesis' and Erich Auerbach's Self-Mythologizing," 83–96.

realism in the secularization of Christian realism.[91] Like Weber's story of capitalist rationality, Auerbach's secularization narrative was ironic.[92] Christian realism legitimated the earthly world, and the earthly world, in turn, diminished the divine. Dante never intended to dispel the enchanted life depicted in his *Comedy*, but "Dante's work made man's Christian-figural being a reality, and destroyed it in the very process of realizing it."[93] Auerbach could not fully explain the secularization process, but the vanishing of typology and the rise of historicism gave a measure of it. He located several literary sites, notably among sixteenth-century authors, to show secularization happening. For Montaigne, "life on earth is no longer the figure of the life beyond. . . . To live here is his purpose and his art."[94] Modernity confronted an eclipse of the divine, loss of providential history, and an irreparable breach between the earthly and transcendental.

Auerbach found all secular substitutes for Christian realism falling short, unable to make up for transcendental loss. Neither historical progress nor aesthetic perfection or self-cultivation (*Bildung*) could make up for the dissolution of the bond between human and divine. But the French realists' social criticism and their grasp of the everyday tragic reflected a dignified literary sensibility, one appropriate to a secular culture undergoing democratization. In *The Red and the Black*, Stendhal's narration of his protagonist's progressive disillusion with the Parisian elite gave realism its most authentic expression. Both the Flaubert generation's turn to aestheticism, to art for art's sake, and the realists' indifference, especially Zola's, to the transcendental were inadequate responses to bourgeois materialism, but they could not diminish the grandeur of their cultural and social critiques. The French realists gave a glimpse of lost Christian realism. The Christian humanist found in secular democratic realism the closest approximation to the original.

Humanism itself, however, came under scrutiny and revision. This emerged most clearly in Auerbach's critique of Goethe. Goethe confronted Germany's political fragmentation and conservative social order with equanimity. Historicism opened possibilities for literary realism by highlighting process and change, but Germans could not look beyond their regional cultures. When the French Revolution raised the prospect of a democratic national culture, Goethe recoiled, reaffirmed his

---

[91] Matthias Bormuth is helpful here: *Mimesis und der christliche Gentleman: Erich Auerbach schreibt an Karl Löwith* (Warmbronn: Verlag Ulrich Keicher, 2006). Bormuth kindly provided me with an English translation of this hard-to-obtain book.

[92] But his sense of the irreparable modern loss of the divine was profound: A Catholic sensibility of modernity's inadequacy complemented the ironic Protestant vision.

[93] *Mimesis*, p. 202 (English).   [94] *Mimesis*, p. 310 (English).

preference for the nobility, and posed Bildung and the integrated personality as ideals. But a national culture required social engagement, not self-cultivation. Germany developed no realist literary tradition. When unification came from above, Germany found itself without a culture adequate to modernity's challenges. Thomas Mann, in the fin-de-siècle years, was the first serious German realist, and shortly thereafter, World War I threw European realism into turmoil, from which it emerged with a fragmentary modernist style, unable to sustain a national culture. Nazism encountered no cultural barrier on its way to power. German humanism was implicated in the German catastrophe.

Goethe was the George Circle's hero, their model for fashioning the "self as character." Auerbach's critique of German culture represented a reevaluation of the Circle, philological humanism, and his own past.[95] Human perfectibility and aesthetic integrity were incompatible with a secular democratic age. They reflected refusals to pay heed to social deprivation and to come to terms with transcendental loss – harmonious personality was forever gone, along with the divine. Self-cultivation displayed overappreciation of classicism and the aesthetic and a failure at Christian humility. To make philological humanism more socially responsive, "Figura" and *Mimesis* underlined the limits of classicism, and *Mimesis* parted with scholarly style and emulated high modernism. Just as French realism responded to democracy, Auerbach's modernism responded to European turmoil and globalization. He held German culture responsible for democracy's failure, but the challenge was global. The European nation-state was approaching its end. Philological humanism had now to address a cosmopolitan public.

French authors predominated in *Mimesis*, reflecting Auerbach's move from German to European cosmopolitanism. Not one German work provided the title or focus for any of its chapters. "Romance literatures are more representative of Europe than ... the German," insisted Auerbach.[96] German humanists, like Curtius, shared his French and modernist sympathies, not to mention his Christian appreciation, but he parted with the national tradition in ways they never did. He was unique in his democratic vision of Christianity, in aligning realism and democracy, in rooting them in Christian realism, and in criticizing Bildung, humanism's fountain. His critique presaged postwar liberal theories of a German *Sonderweg*, a unique German path, divergent from Western liberal democracy. Postwar liberals, too, traced the roots of the

---

[95] Esp. *Mimesis*, p. 550, speaking obliquely of sects "crystallizing around poets, philosophers, and scholars."
[96] "Epilegomena zu Mimesis," p. 476.

German catastrophe in cultural authoritarianism and elitism and focused on German intellectuals' political irresponsibility. But Auerbach did not think he was exploring a Sonderweg. No national culture, he said, reached the height of French realism. The German failure had the most serious consequences, but the crisis was European, indeed global, and it went to the heart of secular modernity.

Mimesis could offer no solution to the European crisis. Re-Christianizing the secular world was no more possible than escaping Weber's iron cage of capitalism. Works such as Georg Lukàcs's *Theory of the Novel*, emerging from Weber's Heidelberg circle and pre–World War I mandarin sociology, showed an understanding of modern literary genres as reflective of the breakdown of a holistic premodern world, the dissolution of *Gemeinschaft* (community).[97] *Mimesis* updated them with a consciousness of the end of Europe. Lukàcs and Auerbach upheld realism for its social consciousness, admired Mann, and censured German *Kultur* for the Nazi disaster.[98] But Lukàcs strove to break out of the iron cage through communism; Auerbach, a mild liberal, remained entrapped. To Auerbach, secularization, not capitalism, was the root of modernity's travails. Concern for the poor was at the heart of Christianity, but atheistic socialism could not undo transcendental loss, only reinforce it. Auerbach was permeated with Weber's tragic vision, reinforced by a Catholic sensibility of modern loss. His disposition toward European culture was a combination of nostalgia and criticism, detachment and engagement, depression and exhilaration.

One wonders how Auerbach could maintain this interplay of proximity and distance in view of the Holocaust. But the murder of the European Jews is not mentioned even once in *Mimesis* and appears not to figure in Auerbach's European crisis. Postbiblical Jews vanish from Auerbach's narrative of Western literature. He made a special effort to ignore them: In discussing Shylock as a (non)tragic figure, he overlooked his Jewishness. Contemporary readers find his silence so baffling that they strive to find clues to the Holocaust in *Mimesis*.[99] Is Auerbach's

---

[97] Georg Lukàcs, *Die Theorie des Romans: Ein geschichts-philosophischer Versuch über die Formen der grossen Epik* [1916] (Neuwied am Rhein: Luchterhand, 1963). Shai Ginsburg of Duke University has tracked in *Mimesis* strong traces of Lukàcs's 1930s *Essays on Realism*, ed. and introduction by Rodney Livingstone, trans. David Fernbach [Cambridge, MA: MIT Press, 1981]). He insists that these essays, and not the early *Theory of the Novel*, shaped Auerbach's intellectual horizons in *Mimesis*.

[98] Georg Lukàcs, *Die Zerstörung der Vernunft: Der Weg des Irrationalismus von Schelling zu Hitler* (Berlin: Aufbau-Verlag, 1954).

[99] Earl Jeffrey Richards, "Erich Auerbach's *Mimesis* as a Meditation on the Shoah," 62–91, and, more subtly, James Porter, "Erich Auerbach and the Judaizing of Philology," esp. 119. Both begin with Auerbach's statement on the rise of National Socialism as a history unsuitable for legend: *Mimesis*, pp. 19–20 (English), pp. 22–23 (German).

discussion of the binding of Isaac, the *Aqedah* – a Jewish martyrology topos emerging repeatedly in Holocaust discourse – not a gesture toward the Holocaust?[100] Is the vindication of the Hebrew Bible against classical epic, of bound Isaac against Odysseus, destroyer of Troy, not a claim to Jewish spiritual superiority – and survival – over German might? Was the Jewish exile surreptitiously imparting "fear not my servant Jacob"?

One could only wish! To be sure, *Mimesis* did respond to the Jews' exclusion from European culture, and showed them to have been its founders. The binding of Isaac, and the crucifixion, could indeed be oblique references to contemporary Jewish martyrology. But Auerbach was ignorant of Jewish Aqedah typologies and chose the binding of Isaac with an eye to the real world-making event, the "scandal of the cross," that is, with an eye to Christian typology.[101] However much he defended the dignity and independence of the Old Testament, and sought to remain neutral on the Christian interpretation of the Aqedah as prefiguration of the crucifixion, he absorbed the binding of Isaac into a Christian narrative of Western literature. Moreover, he thought of World War II as a European and German catastrophe, not as a Jewish one. He was writing *Mimesis* as representative of "European classico-Christian culture," and not as a Jew. He had every apprehension that were he to appear a Jew, he would not be recognized as an authentic representative. His strategy for Jewish integration via Christian culture remained the same even as his projected audience expanded from the nation to the cosmopolis (and even as the Jews were being murdered). He insisted on calling biblical authors (of the Gospels, too) "Jewish," and on using the appellation "Judeo-Christian" for the emergent Western tradition, but postbiblical Jews became part of Western history only insofar as they were part of Christian civilization. The Pan-European space of *Mimesis*, and its cosmopolitan audience, had no room for Jews qua Jews.

This was less than evident because Auerbach did not openly pursue the agenda of *Mimesis*. Even his thrust against classical hegemony and the promotion of the Judeo-Christian heritage remained camouflaged. The contents, or essay titles, would suggest a classical transmission line from Homer's *Odyssey* to Petronius's poetry to Ammianus's history. Not

---

[100] Isaac was bound (ne-ekad, נֶעֱקַד) to be offered as "olah," or a "burnt offering," the Hebrew term for sacrifice, rendered in Greek as "holokau(s)ton." The term Holocaust did not become common, however, until the late 1950s.

[101] Shalom Spiegel, *The Last Trial: On the Legends and Lore of the Command to Abraham to Offer Isaac as a Sacrifice: The Akedah*, trans. (from the Hebrew) with an introduction by Judah Goldin (New York: Pantheon Books, 1967). James Porter, "Erich Auerbach and the Judaizing of Philology," 122–23, suggests that the German Christians' use of the binding of Isaac to demonstrate the Old Testament's perversity also made the Aqedah Auerbach's topic of choice for his first essay.

until medieval Christian drama did Auerbach place a religious text at the center of an essay, and this was the single essay in *Mimesis* where he did so. There was no biblical transmission line. The major works that Auerbach used to control the classical – the Hebrew Bible, the New Testament, Augustine's *Confessions* – appeared as comparisons in essays dedicated to classical works. Christian typology, *figura*, did its work behind the scenes. Not surprisingly, critics push Auerbach just a bit further – beyond what his intentions or intellectual resources would allow – by suggesting that he camouflaged a Jewish agenda under Christian rubrics.

The Old Testament became in *Mimesis* the central conduit for Jewish membership in the West. Auerbach's comparison of the Odyssey and the Hebrew Bible in the magnificent opening chapter, "Odysseus' Scar," reads as a response to liberal Protestantism's diminution of the Hebrew Bible. He contrasted the two models of realism informing Western literature: Greek epic and the Hebrew Bible. Gunkel had noted that the Hebrews had no Homer, and highlighted the Bible's use of lyric poetry, poor descriptions, and Jacob's trickery, to suggest that the Hebrews were incapable of epic and had no depth psychology, and that Genesis imparted no moral truths. Auerbach countered by contrasting Greek myth with biblical truth, and Homer's ornate, superficial portrayals with spare, but deep, biblical description. The Hebrews were more profound than the Greeks and equally formative of Europe.

The Homeric poem's elevated style, its rich and intricate description of worldly scenes, which were uniformly, completely, and unmistakably explained, contrasted with the Bible's economical use of language and its rough narrative accentuating aspects of characters and scenes, leaving much unexpressed in the background, calling for interpretation. Biblical protagonists had inner psychological intensity and grappled with multi-layered consciousness, while Homer's heroes never changed, their emotions laid bare in the foreground. Claiming absolute truth, biblical narrative constructed a universal history, however disjointed, to impart ethical and pedagogical messages, and events found their meaning in temporal connections. For Homeric legend, historical time, and truth, were inconsequential, and horizontal connections – a tightly and beautifully woven web – provided the meaning. The Homeric epic displayed everyday realism, but "everyday" was confined to the idyllic home, in contrast with biblical struggles, which, pregnant with transcendental significance, took place in the domestic and public sphere alike. The epic reflected a static "feudal" society, and its heroes were aristocrats; the Old Testament reflected a nomadic society, its protagonists were often humble in origin, and the entire social ladder was immersed in everyday life: "In the Old Testament stories, the sublime, tragic, and problematic take shape precisely in the ... everyday."[102] The Hebrew Bible was the fountainhead of Western realism.

The fragmentary character of biblical narrative reflected the difficulty of complete representation of any historical situation. Classical Greece discovered historical complexity and psychological intricacy and, with them, the mimetic problem – Homer's horizontal connections could no longer be easily, let alone fully, established. The classical response, from Aristotle to Horace, was the doctrine of styles, separating among high (epic), middle (didactic; historical), and low (pastoral) style. Everyday life, appropriate as a popular comic subject, was proscribed for noble tragedy. Judeo-Christian writings, argued Auerbach, presaged modern realism by overcoming the separation. In the Gospel of Mark, Peter's denial of Jesus showed a lowly human undergoing psychological and emotional turmoil, "trembling for his miserable life," and acquiring through the "despair and remorse following his desperate failure" the consciousness of sin, revealing to him, and us, "the significance of Christ's coming and Passion."[103] That a fisherman would emerge as a tragic hero through an all-too-human failure, and that this failure would embody sublime universal meaning, was unthinkable to classical literature:

A scene like Peter's denial fits into no antique genre. It is too serious for comedy, too contemporary and everyday for tragedy, politically too insignificant for history.... . It portrays something which neither the poets nor the historians of antiquity ever set out to portray: the birth of a spiritual movement in the depths of the common people, from within the everyday occurrences of contemporary life, which thus assumes an importance it could never have assumed in antique literature.[104]

Christ's dual character as Son of God and son of a carpenter, his "humiliation and elevation" on the cross, broke through class barriers and literary styles, joining the humble and the sublime. The Passion forced a confrontation with reality, made aristocratic distance and disdain impossible, and reshaped Western emotional life. It created a new universal message:

[M]issionary work to the Gentiles characteristically began with a member of the Jewish diaspora, the Apostle Paul [who] adapted the message to ... a far wider audience, detach[ing it] from special preconceptions of the Jewish world ... by a method rooted in Jewish tradition but now applied with incomparable greater boldness, the method of revisional interpretation.[105]

---

[102] *Mimesis*, p. 22 (English), p. 25 (German).   [103] *Mimesis*, p. 42 (English).
[104] Ibid., pp. 45, 42–43, respectively.   [105] Ibid., p. 48.

Interpreting the Old Testament figuratively, the new method, typology, detached meaning from sensory perception, and deepened the antagonism between sensory appearance and meaning, emergent in the Hebrew Bible and permeating Christian reality. The great challenge, and attraction, of Christian realism consisted in this tension – in finding the transcendental represented in the mundane, in projecting an earthly world infused with transcendental meaning. Jewish Christians introduced typology as they launched universalism. Restoring early Christianity to its Jewish context, Auerbach made the Jews the shapers of Western destiny.[106]

Christians still lacked a literary language. Throughout Late Antiquity, the Church Fathers progressively took over classical rhetoric, even as they remained suspicious and ambivalent toward it. By Augustine's time, they could speak eloquently to the educated. Yet witnessing the waning of classical culture, Augustine, a master of rhetoric himself, recognized the need to shape a Christian style. More than anyone before him, he sensed that the Passion "engendered a new elevated style," "a new kind of sublimity," "which was ready to absorb ... the ugly, the undignified, and the physically based." The result was "a new *sermo humilis*, a low style [that] encroaches on the sublime and the eternal," of which Augustine gave splendid examples in his writings.[107] But sermo humilis still had no capacity to represent concrete historical events. Typology had annihilated classical history, and Augustine's concern was to bring the Roman Empire's trajectory, not everyday life, into conformity with Christian universal history. For Christian realism to emerge, concluded Auerbach in a historicist fashion, time and "the sensuality of new peoples" were necessary.[108]

Auerbach found the apex of Christian realism in the high Middle Ages – in twelfth-century liturgical dramas about the Fall, thirteenth-century popular religious poetry about Mary at the cross, the letters of St. Bernard and St. Francis, and, of course, in Dante. They managed to bring the incarnation and the Passion, the convergence of humility and sublimity, to bear on the common people's daily lives in ways never accomplished before. St. Francis drew the *imitatio Christi* out of rhetoric and into his own life and became an inimitable model. Auerbach credited him – "a great poet, an instinctive master of the art of acting out his own being" – with "awakening the dramatic powers ... of the Italian

---

[106] Contemporary scholarship would prefer "the Jesus movement" to "early Christianity" and "Jewish followers of Jesus" to "Jewish Christians." Christianity was not a religion separate from Judaism prior to the second century, if then.
[107] *Mimesis*, pp. 72, 154, 72 (English), respectively.   [108] *Mimesis*, p. 76 (English).

language."[109] St. Francis prepared the way to Christian realism's greatest work, *The Divine Comedy*. Mastering the typological art of transcendental significance in earthly events, Dante fulfilled the potential created by Augustine with sermo humilis and, in the very act, began its destruction. The height of Christian realism was also the beginning of secularization.

The Christ of *Mimesis* – the Christ of sermo humilis – was the one nailed to the cross, not the triumphantly rising Christ, certainly not the judge at the end of days. He was Christ who walked among and cared for the downtrodden, was himself an outcast, and bespoke the equality and dignity of humankind. He was the Christ of Auerbach's exile and the Holocaust. A poor, humiliated outcast in Istanbul, Auerbach found solace in the convergence of sublimity and humility, in sermo humilis, aptly translated as "subaltern" style.[110] That Auerbach saw his own condition in literary depictions of Christ is likely; that he saw the fate of his persecuted and murdered brethren in Europe in the cross is possible. Christ was Jesus of Nazareth, a Galilean Jew, son of a Jewish carpenter, but, equally crucial, he was also the Christian God.

It would be no use pretending that the ways of Christianity and Judaism never parted, and that Auerbach was pursuing a Jewish agenda. In response to the Holocaust, traditional Jews turned to the Aqedah and Jewish martyrology and, in anger, evoked the memory of the ancient perpetrator of genocide, *Amaleq* (Esau's descendant).[111] Auerbach turned to Jesus on the cross, Mary at the cross, Augustine's sermo humilis, and, in the postwar years, to Christian martyrology as well. Christian realism may have had its origin in the Hebrew Bible, but the world in which Auerbach found it fulfilled, that of St. Bernard, St. Francis, and Dante, was as closed to Jews as any has been. That the cosmopolitan European public envisioned by *Mimesis* would be more

---

[109] *Mimesis*, p. 173 (English). The laudation of St. Francis, reminiscent of the George Circle, was all the more remarkable for Auerbach's acknowledgment that his style was poor. But St. Francis vividly conveyed emotional reality, and this counted for Auerbach more than aesthetics. This was also evident in Auerbach's sympathetic treatment of Gregory of Tours, and in his elevating St. Perpetua into a model of sublime humility in the postwar years: "Sermo humilis," in *Literary Language and Its Public*, pp. 60–65.

[110] "Sermo humilis," p. 39; "subaltern" is also used in the German original: *Romanische Forschungen* 64:3/4 (1952): 316.

[111] Shalom Spiegel, *The Last Trial*; Gershon Greenberg, "Introduction: Ultra-Orthodox Responses during and following the War," in *Wrestling with God: Jewish Theological Responses during and after the Holocaust*, ed. Steven T. Katz with Shlomo Biderman and Gershon Greenberg (Oxford: Oxford University Press, 2007), pp. 11–26. The Jewish homiletic tradition that Isaac was actually sacrificed and burned to ashes, but rose from the dead, and his ashes protect the Jewish people as *zekhut* (merit, זכות) against transgression and persecution makes Auerbach's turn to Christ especially poignant.

open to Jews was a desperate Auerbach wager (for once, a successful one). Auerbach's "stylistic analysis [was] so Christ-centered that it seem[ed] on the verge of . . . a Christological literary history."[112] The Judeo-Christian project for Jewish integration was a cultural Christian's work.

A German-Jewish Cosmopolitan in Despair: Globalization, Postwar Germany, and the United States

"May my study reach its readers – both my friends of past years who have survived and all others for whom it is intended," concluded Auerbach in *Mimesis*, "and may it contribute to bringing together again those who clearly kept their love for our Western history."[113] His call for a survivors' meeting to learn what could be salvaged of Europe was sad and uncertain, but not hopeless: The cosmopolitan literary public that *Mimesis* envisioned might yet be constituted. He still had no sense of the magnitude of the destruction, and his feelings about his own future were similar: uncertain but not hopeless. He did not wish to remain in Turkey, where the enthusiasm for humanist educational reform was waning, and was considering a return to Germany. Having sent his son Clemens to Harvard for a graduate education in the fall of 1945, he was contemplating a move to the United States. The success of *Mimesis*, his 1947 immigration to the U.S., his 1950 appointment at Yale, and his growing reputation on both sides of the Atlantic represented a great personal accomplishment. But his postwar reflections on the future of Europe became increasingly gloomy. In the bipolar Cold War world, the progressive German mandarin thought his Europe was gone. The Jews were gone. The emancipation project to which he had still clung in 1941 proved a phantasm; that "side issue," as he had called antisemitism, rendering it irrelevant. He would no longer entertain any projects for a Judeo-Christian civilization. His studies now focused on early medieval Europe, trying to decipher how late antique culture survived through the Dark Ages once the Western Roman Empire had collapsed. His cosmopolitanism was not a happy one.

Auerbach still felt German and European. In the immediate postwar years, he was trying to reestablish connections with friends left behind and

---

[112] Helmut Kuhn, "Literaturgeschichte als Geschichtsphilosophie," *Philosophische Rundschau* 11 (1963): 248.

[113] *Mimesis*, p. 518 (German); *Mimesis*, p. 557 (English): "Möge meine Untersuchung ihre Leser erreichen; sowohl meine überlebenden Freunde von einst wie auch alle anderen, für die sie bestimmt ist; und dazu beitragen, diejenigen wieder zusammenzuführen, die die Liebe zu unserer abendländischen Geschichte ohne Trübung bewahrt haben." I modified Trask's translation. James Porter, "Erich Auerbach and the Judaizing of Philology," 118–19, called my attention to the translation difficulties.

to explore the possibility of a Marburg reappointment. Just as he feared, more than a few of his friends had not survived. He heard of students of draft age sent to the Russian front who did not come back.[114] For the survivors – German colleagues undergoing postwar hardship – Auerbach cared deeply. He sold furniture and books to send Clemens to Harvard, but he still went out of his way to mail Care packages to Germany, especially to his former (non-Jewish) assistant, Werner Krauss, who was in poor health after prolonged incarceration.[115] Emotionally and intellectually, he remained vested in Germany and, in many ways, would remain so all of his life. Untenable as his situation in Turkey was, he still felt he needed to explain to German colleagues why a German European would send his son to study in the United States and explore emigrating there.[116] Until 1947, his preference was a return to Marburg. Had the call from Marburg arrived, Auerbach would probably have accepted it.

War and exile did transform the German European Auerbach, however. They impressed upon him that he was not, and could never hope to be, a German insider. Krauss, now a communist professor in Marburg, and later in Leipzig, did everything he could to attract him back, repeatedly broaching a Berlin appointment with the Soviet Zone's education administration. In the summer of 1946, he assured Auerbach that nothing more than goodwill toward socialism would be required of him. Longing for Berlin but apprehensive about its geopolitics and the ideological burden, Auerbach hesitated. "I am very liberal.... . Here [in exile] I could free myself like nowhere else of any commitment; precisely my position as someone who is nowhere an insider, fundamentally and inassimilably a foreigner, is what one wishes and expects of me; where you want me back, one expects 'basic favourable disposition (*Grundbereitschaft*).'"[117] His alienation, his sense of himself as a permanent outsider, incapable of commitment, was new. He would not have spoken of himself as a foreigner in Germany prior to the war, and even *Mimesis* underlined social commitment. His newly discovered

---

[114] Auerbach to Martin Hellweg, June 22, 1946, in Marin Vialon, *Erich Auerbachs Briefe an Martin Hellweg*, pp. 69–76. Auerbach to Werner Krauss, January 30, 1946; June 22, 1946; October 27, 1946; and Krauss to Auerbach, March 26, 1946, in Karlheinz Barck, "Eine unveröffentliche Korrespondenz: Erich Auerbach/Werner Krauss," *Beiträge zur Romanischen Philologie* 26:2 (1987): 310–16, 319–20.

[115] Auerbach to Martin Hellweg, June 22, 1946, 69. Auerbach to Werner Krauss, June 22, 1946; August 27, 1946; October 27, 1946; December 18, 1946; February 22, 1947, 314–17, 319, 323. Krauss to Auerbach, March 15, 1947, 326.

[116] Auerbach to Martin Hellweg, June 22, 1946, 69; Auerbach to Victor Klemperer, May 7, 1949, *Süddeutsche Zeitung* (13 October 2007).

[117] Auerbach to Krauss, August 27, 1946, 317.

marginality reinforced his move away from the nation and toward an ephemeral European cosmopolis.

Family and scholarship joined alienation in challenging the nation's call for his return. His son was in the United States, and a flood of reports about the hardship of life in Germany was reaching Turkey. In Istanbul, he was getting poorer, unable to afford support for Clemens at Harvard, feeling ever more dejected about the bureaucracy and with no career prospect. Germany had to address some of these needs for him to return. Krauss urged upon him the importance of his repatriation for the build-up of a new Germany: "Reintegration in the *Heimat* [is] an inner need that one cannot resist with impunity. . . . Germany is only bearable and worth affirming as a project, not in its present state."[118] In vain: Early in 1947, Auerbach got three offers from German universities – Greifswald, Halle, and Münster – the first two in the Soviet Zone, Münster in ruins. It was evident that working conditions would be inadequate, and he declined. He admired his former assistant's dedication, but, Krauss's communism aside, he could not share his commitment to Germany.

Auerbach was still waiting for Marburg – the hub of university life in the U.S. Zone, with a glorious tradition and old colleagues on the faculty, site of his fondest memories of Germany. One wonders whether he did not also think of a Marburg invitation as restitution, an apology to rectify the injustice done to him. In April 1947, he received a letter from Marburg's reform-oriented philosophy dean, former Vienna Circle associate Kurt Reidemeister, suggesting that if Krauss left for Leipzig, and the ministry approved a full professorship, a position would open up for him. Auerbach gave rare expression to his frustration, saying that he was tired of building his career on a house of cards that repeatedly collapsed.[119] He now opted for the United States, but only as a breathing spell, he assured Krauss: "I want to be back in Germany." Krauss contacted him again, from Leipzig in the summer of 1949, offering Humboldt University in Berlin for him to try for a year. "We must have you among us," he pleaded.[120] Auerbach, his reputation in the United States growing, accepted a position in Yale's French Department shortly thereafter. The two would never see each other again.

Disappointed as he was at having to bid farewell to Europe, perhaps even bitter, Auerbach did not project any bitterness toward Germany. He acknowledged no Jewish dimension to the tragedy that had befallen

---

[118] Krauss to Auerbach, September 29, 1946, 318.
[119] Auerbach to Krauss, April 16, 1947, in Karlheinz Barck, "Eine unveröffentliche Korrespondenz: Erich Auerbach/Werner Krauss," *Beiträge zur Romanischen Philologie* 27:1 (1988): 161–63.
[120] Krauss to Auerbach, October 25, 1949, 183.

Europe, and if he now recognized his own liminality in German culture, he never thought of it as ethnic in origin – his liberalism, he suggested, was implicated, or his own character. The "survivors" note in *Mimesis* – "my surviving friends of past years" – was not a veiled allusion to the Jews: The friends after whose fate Auerbach inquired were for the most part non-Jews. He was critical of people counseling the émigrés, "especially Jews," not to return to Germany, of "prominent and otherwise quite sensible people who try to exercise a kind of moral pressure."[121] He assured Rudolf Bultmann that he neither held the Germans collectively responsible for the tragedy nor thought it right to single them out for blame.[122] Like other Europeans, Germans had fallen victim to the contradictions of modernity. Like the Jews, they were survivors, too.

Both Bultmann and Krauss served on Marburg's "planning committee," and both warned Auerbach of creeping renazification.[123] Frustrated with the failure of university reform, Krauss left for Leipzig.[124] Auerbach, in contrast, was skeptical about university reform and defensive about charges of nazification in the German academy.[125] He showed sympathy for German efforts to return to normalcy: "Bourgeois orderliness is ... a human need," he told former student Martin Hellweg. "After three decades of such horrible experiments ... the Germans can be nothing other than terribly tired and in need of rest."[126] The closest he came to implicating Germans in the Holocaust was in his letter to Klemperer, that is, in internal Jewish assimilationist discourse: "It is strange for someone in my situation to find out increasingly that the Germans, except perhaps the Jews, are really the most efficient and, insofar as work is concerned, the most reliable people (*Volk*)," but, he added, "this in itself is quite insufficient."[127] Just as obliquely, he advised Germans to begin thinking globally again, but in a new fashion, with greater awareness of cultural

---

[121] Auerbach to Krauss, June 22, 1946, *Beiträge zur Romanischen Philologie* 26: 2 (1987): 312.

[122] Martin Vialon, "Erich Auerbach und Rudolf Bultmann: Probleme abendländischer Geschichtsdeutung," in *Marburger Hermeneutik zwischen Tradition und Krise*, ed. Matthias Bormuth and Ulrich von Bülow (Göttingen: Wallstein Verlag, 2008), esp. pp. 178–79.

[123] Bultmann to Auerbach, June 18, 1948, in Martin Vialon, "Erich Auerbach und Rudolf Bultmann," p. 184; Krauss to Auerbach, July 23, 1947, *Beiträge zur Romanischen Philologie* 27:1 (1988): 166–68.

[124] For the failure of postwar German university reform, with a focus on Marburg, see Craig K. Pepin, "The Holy Grail of Pure Wissenschaft: University Ideal and University Reform in Post World War II Germany" (Ph.D. diss., Duke University, 2001).

[125] Auerbach to Martin Hellweg, Easter Sunday 1948 and December 25, 1948, in Martin Vialon, *Erich Auerbachs Briefe an Martin Hellweg*, pp. 102, 116.

[126] June 22, 1946, p. 69.

[127] May 7, 1949, *Süddeutsche Zeitung* (13 October 2007). He would never dare write this way to a non-Jewish German or a traditional Jew.

difference and global needs.[128] What his innermost thoughts about the murder of the Jews were, we may never know. Like many of his generation, he said not a word about the Holocaust.

Auerbach's 1946 essay, "The Triumph of Evil in Pascal," provides, however, further hints about his view of culpability in the Holocaust. The Christian confronting evil political power was at the center. For Pascal (1623–1662), might was evil, but it made right. Earthly laws were arbitrary, but obedience to them was divinely sanctioned as punishment for corrupt human nature. Evil laws were just, and "one must obey unquestioningly ... without devotion, or rather from devotion to God."[129] The Passion provided the model for suffering injustice, and liberation from it was only in the life beyond. Resistance was only permitted as an expression of God's will, and a good measure of its legitimacy was its hopelessness. Striving for victory was impermissible, as those seeking to suppress the resistance were also doing God's will.

Combining Augustinianism and *raison d'état*, Pascal's wretched earthly world was a far cry from Dante's, and his hateful endorsement of murderous absolutism was a long way from realist social criticism. Yet Auerbach found his ethical theory cogent and moving, and, ironically, a starting point for secular political criticism. Members of Auerbach's October 1949 Princeton seminar on Pascal sensed that they were hearing the quiet protest of a German-Jewish émigré against totalitarianism. "Auerbach," said one, "had faced with his flesh and blood the reality of evil force; the extremity of Pascal's thought answered, for him, an extremity of experience. Pascal, too, had lived in a totalitarian state."[130] True enough, but they were also hearing a vindication of good Germans (and Jews) who obeyed Hitler. Those who offered hopeless resistance were admirable, but one could not incriminate even perpetrators who "obeyed unquestioningly, without regard for any possible benefit, but also without devotion." By the mid-1950s, Auerbach was expressing his wish that Germans, and Europeans in general, rid themselves of the guilt complex that was obstructing their intellectual recovery.[131]

---

[128] Auerbach to Martin Hellweg, June 20, 1950.

[129] Auerbach, "On the Political Theory of Pascal," in *Scenes from the Drama of European Literature*, p. 129, a slightly expanded version of the translation of the German original, published in *The Hudson Review* 4:1 (1951): 79.

[130] Robert Fitzgerald, *Enlarging the Change: The Princeton Seminars in Literary Criticism, 1949–1951* (Boston: Northeastern University Press, 1985), p. 15.

[131] Henri Peyre, "Erich Auerbach (1892–1957)/Romanist" (in French), in *Marburger Gelehrte in der ersten Hälfte des 20. Jahrhunderts*, ed. Ingeborg Schnack (Marburg: N. G. Elwert Verlag, 1977), pp. 10–11: "His dream would have been ... to contribute to the reconstruction of universities like Marburg, Heidelberg, or Bonn, of which he

Auerbach was never a decisive person, let alone a risk taker. He had to be forced to go to the United States, without a promised job, in his mid-fifties, and start a fourth career. Departing from Istanbul in July 1947, the Auerbachs left behind "furniture and porcelain, ... the residues of our bourgeois past," material vestiges of Germany and Europe.[132] Emotionally and spiritually, however, they never left Europe. Auerbach held the typical German mandarin's prejudices against "America" and never rid himself of them. Western literature remained European literature for him, *abendländische* in the interwar sense, not *westliche* in the postwar transatlantic sense. *Mimesis* made no mention of American authors. When Auerbach contemplated a new global literary public, the making of early medieval Europe provided the model, and contemporary Europe the focus.[133] He wrote in German to the end of his life, saw his major audience and interlocutors as European, repeatedly visited Europe, and, in response to German job offers, periodically reconsidered a return to the Heimat. Marie Auerbach never spoke English fluently and harkened back to the blissful Marburg years.[134] The United States would never become the Auerbachs' cultural home.

The Auerbachs landed on the East Coast in September 1947, "falling into [Erich's former colleague Leo] Spitzer's arms for the third time."[135] Auerbach had approached former Istanbul colleagues and German émigrés at Harvard, Johns Hopkins, and Princeton in a desperate search for a job.[136] The United States was kind to him. At the Modern Language Association convention in December, he got a job for the spring of 1948 at Penn State College. For eighteen months, this urbane German mandarin found himself at a state university, predominantly an engineering and natural science school, in the heart of rural America.

---

expected much, once Germany and the rest of Western Europe freed themselves from their guilt complex."

[132] Another emigration, another loss, and another new start – "a somewhat late start," Auerbach told Krauss self-mockingly on July 9, 1947, "but better late than never." *Beiträge zur Romanischen Philologie* 27:1 (1988): 166.

[133] Carl Landauer, "'Mimesis' and Erich Auerbach's Self-Mythologizing," 95, n. 24.

[134] Stephen G. Nichols, "Philology on Auerbach's Drama of (Literary) History," in *Literary History and the Challenge of Philology*, ed. Seth Lerer, pp. 63–65.

[135] Auerbach to Krauss, October 1, 1947, as quoted in Martin Vialon, "Die Stimme Dantes und ihre Resonanz," in *Erich Auerbach*, ed. Treml and Barck, p. 46, n. 1.

[136] In 1940, when Auerbach was concerned about the approaching expiration of his German permission to reside in Turkey, his U.S. friends searched for a position for him in the United States and collected money to support a potential first-year salary: letter of the Association of Immigrant Scholars (*Notgemeinschaft*) to the Committee in Aid of Displaced Foreign Scholars, December 30, 1940, Emergency Committee, 38:5, NYPL.

Writing to German colleagues, Auerbach shared his impressions of rural America: from the standpoint of human relations – delightful, intellectually – beneath criticism.[137] The United States, he said, must be the world's happiest and easiest country to live in. Americans were sympathetic and ready to help; their optimism, naïveté, and trust in the future "strike a European who has experienced the last thirty years" as incredible. Daily interaction was relaxed, warm, and free of hierarchy, inhibition, or complexity. But he found the intellectual level at Penn State unacceptably low, and he was pleased to have a fellow German émigré philologist around with whom he could "speak European."[138] He was aware that intellectual life was different at elite universities, but he projected this opinion from his state university to American culture. Moving to Yale in 1950 would not change his view. At Yale he had a superior library, and colleagues and graduate students the likes of whom he had not known since Marburg. He appreciated them, but he was still dismayed by the informal relations between undergraduates and professors and reflected unfavorably on academic sports culture. America embodied rampant modernization, the standardization and leveling process threatening European and global culture with dreary uniformity.

Auerbach's U.S. reflections reinforced his apprehensions about proposed university reforms in Germany. He was critical of American involvement and warned his friends that the U.S. academy could provide no model for Germany. The German system, on the whole, was "incomparably better," and U.S.-style democratization would lower the intellectual level. He acknowledged that, "after all that happened," German universities might require change, but it should be grounded in German conceptions.[139] *Mimesis* probed the limits of Bildung and humanist ideals and offered an egalitarian Christian vision as an alternative. Now that humanist education faced a serious democratic challenge, Auerbach recoiled. Contemporary critics view the anxiety he expressed about the loss of diversity (*Mannigfaltigkeit*) in "Philology and *Weltliteratur*" as an appeal for cultural pluralism, or, in contemporary parlance, multiculturalism.[140] They are not wrong, but Auerbach's pluralism was

---

[137] Auerbach to Krauss, March 3, 1948, in Vialon, "Die Stimme Dantes," p. 47: "menschliches sehr gut, sachliches indiskutabel." See also his letters to Martin Hellweg, October 5, 1947, Easter Sunday 1948, pp. 94, 102–3, and to Klemperer, May 7, 1949.

[138] Auerbach to Karl Vossler, June 5, 1948, in Martin Vialon, *Erich Auerbachs Briefe an Karl Vossler*, p. 29.

[139] Auerbach to Martin Hellweg, December 25.1948, and June 20, 1950, pp. 116, 136.

[140] "Philology and *Weltliteratur*" [1952], trans. Maire and Edward Said, *Centennial Review* 13:1 (1969): 1–17.

a product of German mandarin discourse and reflected ambivalence about modernity and democracy, cultural pessimism (*Kulturpessimismus*), and anti-Americanism.[141]

Auerbach remained a captive of the Bildung discourse he criticized, and this raises questions about his progressivism and cosmopolitanism. His intellectual profile defies a sharp outline. As a young man in Weimar – a George admirer and a German patriot – he was fairly conservative, but he also kept the company of Marxists, like Benjamin and Bloch. He deployed historicist categories as the national spirit, but they were attenuated by contextual analysis – historical, even sociological. His disposition toward the nation was ambivalent: He liked it in its premodern phase, thought well enough of nineteenth-century democratic nationalism, but regarded ethnic and populist nationalism as destructive of the nation. He trusted German state officials and adhered to bureaucratic procedure ad absurdum (submitting, in early 1941 from Istanbul, a request to extend his permission to reside abroad), but his ideal state was always part of a cosmopolitan Europe of nations.

The colleagues Auerbach retained were, for the most part, the more liberal mandarins, like Bultmann and Vossler. Among the humanists, his response to Nazism was distinctive for affirming a democratic vision of Christianity. He considered the history of the last thousand years that of mankind's achievement of self-expression, but he also thought that it ended in stultifying uniformity and leveling. A product of Protestant academic culture, his affinities were with Catholic cosmopolitanism. The epitome of upper-bourgeois Jewish urbanity, he remained an advocate of Christian sermo humilis, critical of Castiglione and Montaigne for cultivating a courtly style. His class prejudice came out mostly in contempt for American culture and fellow Jews (and, in both cases, prejudice also reflected his resentment of their accomplishments). "Son of a Viennese Jew and an opera singer," he said of Spitzer, a colleague to whom he would owe his life, "he is full of activity and tactlessness, and has very lively ideas but not even a shadow of culture and true critical spirit."[142] So much for Christian clemency for Jews lacking proper composure, and yet clemency and humility remained Auerbach's cherished ideals.

---

[141] Fritz Ringer, *The Decline of the German Mandarins: The German Academic Community, 1890–1933* (Cambridge, MA: Harvard University Press, 1969).

[142] Auerbach to Paul Binswanger, March 3, 1930, *Romanistisches Jahrbuch* 59 (2009): 164. Auerbach knew that this was unfair: Letter to Karl Vossler, October 10, 1938, in Martin Vialon, *Erich Auerbachs Briefe an Karl Vossler*, pp. 25–26: "He is my friend, he has done for me more than anyone, he is a generous man, full of life, and a major scholar. All the same, everything he says, does and writes irritates me."

Auerbach's students suggest how unconventional a mandarin he was. He was surrounded by dissenters (partly, no doubt, because he was Jewish). Hellweg and Krauss were Marxist socialists who were let off by the Nazis, while other students could not make a career in Nazi or postwar Germany. Krauss joined the *Rote Kapelle* (Red Orchestra) resistance group in Berlin, was arrested in November 1942, sentenced to death in January 1943, and saved only through the intervention of the Marburg faculty, which had his sentence commuted to a prison term by declaring him psychologically deranged. In the postwar years, both Helwegg and Krauss were involved in programs for the democratic reeducation of Germans. Krauss helped lay the foundations of East Germany's academic culture by developing Marxist literary studies and drafting the services of Bloch and Klemperer. Auerbach helped Krauss get the Bloch appointment through but refused to join, repeatedly making his liberal stance explicit.[143] He admired Krauss for acting on his convictions but also feared what awaited him in the Soviet Zone.

Auerbach's anticommunism never translated into Cold War politics. He was equally apprehensive about capitalist and communist modernization and resentful of what he regarded as a bipolar world squelching European diversity. More conservative intellectuals were content to use U.S. military power against communism while inveighing against the Americanization of European culture, but Auerbach declined political engagement in the postwar years, just as he had done in interwar Germany. If he did not advocate resistance to Nazism, he would not second anti-Soviet mobilization. Against totalitarianism, he consistently turned to Christian martyrology, first to Christ himself, then, in the postwar years, to St. Perpetua, whose triumphal vision was to Auerbach a source of consolation and unbounded admiration.[144] Auerbach was by no means a conventional cultural critic, but it was to disabuse intellectuals like him of their anti-American prejudices and coax them toward a warmer acceptance of modernity and an unwavering commitment to Western liberal democracy that the Congress for Cultural Freedom was established. Postwar transatlantic liberalism represented hopeful cosmopolitanism, Popper's Open Society, not Auerbach's pessimistic Christian humanism.

"European civilization is approaching the term of its existence," wrote Auerbach in his last, posthumously published, book. "[A]lready it is

---

[143] Krauss to Auerbach, November 25, 1947, and January 8, 1950, *Beiträge zur Romanischen Philologie* 27:1 (1988): 170, 184.
[144] "Sermo humilis" (English), pp. 60–65.

beginning to be engulfed in another, more comprehensive unity."[145] He was unable to describe the emergent "unity," but he was not looking forward to it. Already in the 1930s, he found behind fascism and nationalism – German, Italian, and Turkish – "a ruse of providence, designed to lead us along a bloody and tortuous path to an Internationale of triviality and a culture of Esperanto."[146] Technologies of modernization and nationalization undermined European pluralism. The European nation, and its state, Germany in particular, could not be saved. One had now to turn from nation to humanity, and think globally. But how was global culture possible when uniformity and leveling made humanistic education ever more problematic? Goethe's cosmopolitanism, the search for *Weltliteratur*, did not turn out as expected. Globalization served as an opening not to Weltliteratur but to morbid uniformity and a "European crisis."

What could the humanist philologist do to address the European crisis? Unable to outline a new cosmopolitanism, Auerbach sought instead to form a coherent picture of European civilization and its legacy. Just as he had looked back in the 1930s to the rise of Christianity, he looked back now to the making of Europe to learn how the decline of the West (*Abendland*) could be not averted but weathered. Ironically, he was perusing the history he was living in reverse – looking at the dissolution of imperial Rome and Europe's formation, while living Europe's dissolution and the formation of a new universal culture. Still, the cultural transmission from Late Antiquity to the Middle Ages was to yield the essence of the European legacy.

Empire was never Auerbach's ideal: He loved the late Roman Empire about as much as Augustine did. He described imperial Roman culture as living on borrowed time. Having undermined the ancient city-states' civic cultures, the empire was incapable of cultural innovation and became lifeless, its aristocratic literary public progressively diminishing. Empire meant stagnation. In contrast, Auerbach loved the plurality of medieval Europe, the authenticity, however primitive, of the new peoples' cultures, and the interplay between national life and "a European society," between "vulgar" culture and "a European ... *Hochsprache* (language of high culture)."[147] The medieval moment metamorphosized later, it

---

[145] "Introduction: Purpose and Method," in *Literary Language and Its Public in Late Antiquity and in the Middle Ages*, p. 6.

[146] Auerbach to Benjamin, January 3, 1937, PMLA 122:3 (2007): 750–51. See also his letter to Benjamin, December 12, 1936, 749, on Turkish ur-nationalism, and to Johannes Oeschger, May 27, 1938, *Süddeutsche Zeitung* (14 October 2008), on nationalization and modernization as "barbarization" (*Barbarisierung*).

[147] Auerbach, "The Western Public and Its Language," in *Literary Language and Its Public*, p. 338.

seems, in the Viconian world of nations, extending into the nineteenth century in Europe prior to the triumph of ethno-nationalism. These were the high points of European culture, moments long gone, which he was trying to recapture as the European essence.

The flowering of European culture, Auerbach decided, was dependent on Christian reworking of the classical heritage. As the literary public, always a narrow elite, was progressively diminishing in Late Antiquity, Christianity became, against its will, the custodian of classical culture. Through sermo humilis, Christianity made the sublime "accessible to all, descending to all men in loving-kindness ... at one with the entire Christian congregation."[148] Here was a model of cultural transmission appropriate for a democratic global age – Christianity helping shape a new universal culture:

What unites [European nations] is their common root in antiquity and Christianity. For this combination contains the dialectical force which – even if Europe, like Rome before it, should now lose its power and even cease to exist as such – has prefigured the forms of a common social and cultural life on our planet.[149]

Christianity tied together the divergent metamorphoses of Auerbach's cosmopolitanism, from the Weimar Dante, a German European cosmopolitan, to the wartime Pan-European modernist public of *Mimesis*, to the hopeless globalism of postwar years. But the variety of Auerbach's cosmopolitanism was also grounded in the German nation. He was unable to imagine a vital imperial culture, as Austrian intellectuals did. Hugo von Hofmannsthal, Karl Popper, Joseph Roth, Friedrich Torberg, and Franz Werfel had each negotiated between imperial and national identities, and their cosmopolitanism reflected negotiation's results. Auerbach's cosmopolitan public remained ephemeral, and the new global culture an intangible nightmare, because he could never see beyond the Europe of nations. Once the German nation was gone, he faced the void.

The Europe of nations first emancipated the Jews, then, at its moment of collapse, murdered them. As if acknowledging the fait accompli, Auerbach's classico-Christian literary public had no place for the Jews in his last book. They vanished from Europe, losing even the role they had had in *Mimesis*, as makers of European civilization. Their disappearance reshaped Auerbach's cosmopolitanism. The German cosmopolitan who had begun his way hopefully with Dante and Christian engagement in the earthly world, and went into exile with Dante, bemoaning having to eat foreign bread and imagining a cosmopolitan literary public, ended up in

---

[148] Ibid., p. 65.   [149] Ibid., p. 338.

despair with Pascal's hatred of the world and Hugh of St. Victor's espousal of permanent exile as the grounds for cosmopolitanism: "The man who finds his homeland (*patria; Heimat*) sweet is still a tender beginner; he to whom every soil is as his homeland is already strong; but he is perfect to whom the entire world is a foreign land (*exsilium*)."[150] Auerbach finally brought his cosmopolitanism in conformity with Jewish exile – through Christian sources and with no hope for the future. A cultural Christian of Jewish origin, lamenting and yet succumbing to humanity's fate in the secular age, he could no longer live in a state of expectation, as traditional Jews and Christians have for millennia.

German-Jewish Cosmopolitanism Triumphant: Auerbach in Contemporary Europe

The despair and alienation characterizing Auerbach's postwar writings contrasted remarkably with their spectacular success. In the spring of 1949, just as Auerbach found out that his heart condition would make it impossible for him to continue at Penn State (he lost his university health insurance), he received an invitation to the Institute of Advanced Studies at Princeton for 1949–50. Princeton literary critic and Dante scholar Francis Fergusson, who had met Auerbach in Vermont in late 1947, urged the institute director, Robert Oppenheimer, to invite the still-unknown visitor so as to facilitate the launching of a (soon to become famous) literary seminar. The émigrés' network, above all Princeton's art historian, Erwin Panofsky, joined in lending their support. Fergusson and most U.S. critics read no German, and so Auerbach's reputation was initially based on émigré reports and personal encounters. But not for long: As different *Mimesis* essays began showing up in 1950 in U.S. literary journals, the enchantment was immediate. The sophisticated, beautifully crafted essays were a pleasure to read. Scholarly encounters with the quietly erudite Auerbach left the impression of a rare exemplar of old-world urbanity. "All around you hear nothing but *Mimesis*," complained a jealous Curtius, on a visit to Princeton in 1949.[151]

In the spring of 1950, Auerbach received a "very good offer" from Yale, which would become the final station in his tumultuous life: "The good

---

[150] "Philology and *Weltliteratur*," 17. Auerbach quotes Hugh of St. Victor, *Didascalicon* III: 19: *The Didascalicon of Hugh of St. Victor*, trans. Jerome Taylor (New York: Columbia University Press, 1961), p. 101.
[151] Konrad Bieber to Carl Landauer, February 2, 1986, reporting on Curtius in Princeton in 1949, quoted in "*Mimesis* and Erich Auerbach's Self-Mythologizing," 83.

traveler arrived at his destination and rested."[152] He and Marie received U.S. citizenship, a security they had not known since the Nuremberg Laws.[153] A Marburg chair offer arrived, all too late, in March 1953. It found the Auerbachs staying in the United States, not altogether happily but with pride that they no longer had to depend on the Heimat that had cast them out. In 1956, Auerbach became the first Sterling Professor of Romance Languages at Yale. The next fall he died, just short of his sixty-fifth birthday.

Already in the last years of his life, Auerbach was becoming a mythical figure in the United States, a model of the émigré scholar, survivor of a superior culture, who was propelling the American academy to new heights. Henri Peyre, a leading French Studies scholar and the chair of Auerbach's department at Yale, testified to the emerging legend: "Jew by birth (*Israélite de naissance*), agnostic by formation and cast of mind, painter of Greco-Roman culture and reader of the Church Fathers and Dante, [Auerbach] seemed to us to embody the precious qualities of the European humanist of the time of Lessing, Herder and Goethe."[154] *Mimesis* appealed to wide and diverse audiences. Selected essays were first published in the New Critics' literary magazines. Auerbach's German historical philology challenged the New Critics' formalism, yet his agile stylistic analysis appealed to them. Reviews of *Mimesis* were admiring: "hailed as 'the most important and brilliant ... literary history that had been published in the last fifty years,'" wrote René Wellek.[155] Wellek himself remained critical, and Auerbach's reviews of American works on Dante were a rejoinder, creating an exemplary dialogue between divergent interpretive traditions. *Mimesis* also contributed to the emergent comparative literature field and was popular among medievalists. No consensus has ever emerged on its arguments, but there was no denial of Auerbach's achievement.[156]

---

[152] Dante, *The Banquet (Il Convivio)* (IV: xii, par. 19), trans. Katherine Hillard (London: Kegan Paul, 1889), p. 290; *Opere* (Florence: Bemporad & Figlio, 1921), pp. 273–74.

[153] Stephen Nichols, "Philology on Auerbach's Drama of (Literary) History," 65.

[154] "Erich Auerbach (1892–1957)/Romanist," 10.

[155] Wellek, "Auerbach's Special Realism," *Kenyon Review* 16 (1954): 299; for a list of early reviews of *Mimesis*, see Herbert Lindenberger, "On the Reception of *Mimesis*," in *Literary History and the Challenge of Philology*, pp. 212–13; for a bibliography of Auerbach's reviews, and text of his reviews of Fergusson's and Charles Singleton's works on Dante, see *Gesammelte Aufsätze*, pp. 368–69, 317–19, 313–14, respectively.

[156] For the U.S. reception of *Mimesis*, see also Carl Landauer, "Auerbach's Performance and the American Academy," in *Literary History and the Challenge of Philology*, pp. 179–94, and William Calin, *The Twentieth-Century Humanist Critics: From Spitzer to Frye* (Toronto: University of Toronto Press, 2007), pp. 43–56. Among Auerbach's students at Yale were two future leading literary critics, Geoffrey Hartmann and Frederic Jameson. *Mimesis* also inspired the linguistic turn in intellectual history, as

New York intellectuals Alfred Kazin and Delmore Schwartz wrote the first two blurbs for the cover of the paperback edition of *Mimesis*.[157] This was no coincidence. The post-Marxist Jewish intelligentsia sought integration into the Western literary tradition via high modernism. *Mimesis* provided a blueprint. Historian David Hollinger has shown how a secular cosmopolitan worldview, emphasizing scientific universalism, served Jewish entry into the U.S. academy in the postwar years.[158] The Congress for Cultural Freedom, representing a collaboration of European remigrés and New York intellectuals, made this worldview central to an emergent liberal transatlantic culture. The secular Jews usually left it to their non-Jewish colleagues to think through the possibilities of Christian cosmopolitanism for a religiously tolerant Europe. But in Auerbach, they found a Christianity-inspired Jew who provided an unmatched narrative for Jewish integration into a secularized Christian West. To be sure, Auerbach left no room for ethnic Jewish consciousness, but the majority of U.S. Jewish intellectuals never sought it in the postwar years. With relish they taught college students the grand narrative of Western civilization, from Homer and the Bible via the medieval Christian West to the scientific revolution and the Enlightenment to twentieth-century modernism. Auerbach provided the ultimate vindication for the postwar Jewish secular, liberal, cosmopolitan worldview.

Mimesis had appeared in German in the fall of 1946, seven years earlier than the U.S. edition. European responses were a bit slower to appear and were more muted. Germans were more familiar with the book's distinctive blend of historical philology, stylistic analysis, and modernism, which had been introduced by the interwar generation of humanist philologists. Europe also had no equivalent of the U.S. progressive Jewish intelligentsia that could turn Auerbach's *abendländische* narrative into a liberal *westliche* one, no comparable secular Cold War liberalism. Still, numerous positive reviews established Auerbach securely as a leading German philologist. The polemics with Curtius over the history of *Stiltrennung*, which elicited Auerbach's reaffirmation of the German identity of

represented by Hayden White, *Metahistory* (Baltimore: Johns Hopkins University Press, 1973), esp. pp. 2–3, n. 4.

[157] The Princeton, 1968, edition. The blurbs represented selections from their laudatory essay (Kazin) and review (Schwartz) in *American Scholar* 34:3 (1965): 474–98 (quotation on 484) and the *New York Times Book Review* (29 November 1953): 40, respectively.

[158] David Hollinger, *Science, Jews, and Secular Culture: Studies in Mid-Twentieth-Century American Intellectual History* (Princeton, NJ: Princeton University Press, 1996).

Mimesis – and his own – highlighted Auerbach's prominence.[159] The 1953 Marburg chair offer reflected his new status.

By the late 1960s, however, the Western civilization narrative of the Cold War years was coming under siege. The U.S. Jewish intelligentsia was exploring its ethno-religious identity; the 68ers on both sides of the Atlantic challenged the Western narrative on grounds of class, gender, and race and highlighted its imperialist implications; and the German 68ers, in particular, attacked the interwar philological humanists as anticommunists and fascists. Auerbach never drew as much fire as did Curtius, but the critique spilled over to him, too.[160] The liberal grand narrative had not quite emerged from under the 68ers' attack when the poststructuralists demolished whatever remained of it. *Mimesis* seemed to have lost its luster, and Auerbach was in danger of becoming obsolete.

Just at this moment, help came from the least expected quarter – from Edward Said and postcolonial studies. Said was not known for forgiveness toward Eurocenteric Western narratives, but Auerbach was an exception. From early in his career, when he and Maire Said translated "Philology and *Weltliteratur*" (1969), to his 1983 essay collection *The World, the Text, and the Critic*, to one of his last essays – an introduction to a new edition of *Mimesis* – Said was engaged with Auerbach.[161] Their parallel use of Vico as an *Ansatzpunkt* (starting point) for their work may have first triggered Said's interest, but his emotional attachment to Auerbach was mostly due to a feeling of shared liminality as cosmopolitan intellectuals in exile. Both Said and Auerbach shared secularized Christian inspiration and humanist training, and yet, living on the East–West boundary, were liminal to the traditions that formed them. Better than anyone, Said captured Auerbach's peculiar position as "a non-Christian explaining Christianity's achievement [and] in so doing, travel[ing] from his roots still further."[162]

To be sure, as representatives of their respective "minority cultures," Auerbach and Said displayed opposite attitudes.[163] Auerbach assumed

---

[159] Ernst Robert Curtius, "Die Lehre von den drei Stilen in Altertum und Mittelalter (zu Auerbachs *Mimesis*)," *Romanische Forschungen* 64 (1952): 57–70; Erich Auerbach, "Epilegomena zu Mimesis," *Romanische Forschungen* 65 (1954): 1–18 (reprinted in *Erich Auerbach*, ed. Treml and Barck, pp. 466–79).

[160] Michael Nehrlich, "Romanistik und Anti-Kommunismus," *Das Argument* 4:3/4 (1972): 276–313.

[161] Auerbach, "Philology and *Weltliteratur*," trans. Maire and Edward Said, *Centennial Review* 13:1 (1969): 1–17; Edward Said, *The World, the Text, and the Critic* (Cambridge, MA: Harvard University Press, 1983), and "Erich Auerbach,"*Boundary 2*, 31:2 (2004), 11–34, respectively.

[162] "Erich Auerbach," 20.

[163] Amir Mufti, "Auerbach in Istanbul: Edward Said, Secular Criticism, and the Question of Minority Culture," *Critical Inquiry*, 25:1 (1998): 95–125.

a distance toward his Jewishness and sought nothing more than integration in the Western mainstream. When Martin Buber requested that
Auerbach write an introduction to the Hebrew edition of *Mimesis* in
1956, Auerbach declined, mentioning that he had refused a similar
Italian request and was unfamiliar with Israel.[164] He made it clear that
he had no special relationship to modern Hebrew culture. In contrast,
Said imaginatively espoused Palestine and the Arab world, and sought to
vindicate them against the West. But Said recognized that he, too, "tra-
velled further from his roots," and, precisely because Auerbach's
Jewishness was nonthreatening, exile's affinities could count the most.
Said was kind to Auerbach. Where I see Auerbach as a German mandarin,
lamenting modernization and Bildung's decline, Said saw him protesting
nationalist uniformity, presaging the rise of other civilizations, and rescu-
ing sense and meaning from fragments of modernity, from exile, by
reconstructing an alternative European history from the margins.[165]
To Said, Auerbach had become a postcolonial prophet.

Since the 1980s, there has been a global explosion of interest in
Auerbach. The Jewish German émigré, who skirted the cultural and
geographic boundaries of three continents, has become a prime site for
the search for cosmopolitan concepts of global culture and transnational
European history. East German scholars may have led the way, in the late
1980s, with the publication of Auerbach's correspondence with Benjamin
and Krauss.[166] Since then, Auerbach's centenary, the fiftieth anniversary
of his death, and the fiftieth anniversary of *Mimesis* have been celebrated
with major conferences and publications. Auerbach's sparse archives and
surviving correspondence have been painstakingly collected and studied
in detail.[167] Literary and historical studies of every aspect of his biography, work, and global reception have continuously appeared, and the
stream is growing. In Great Books courses, "Odysseus' Scar" and
"Farinata and Calvacante" are read in conjunction with Homer and
Dante. No German-Jewish émigré, other than Arendt and Benjamin,

---

[164] Buber to Auerbach, December 31, 1956; Auerbach to Buber, January 12, 1957, in *Erich Auerbach*, ed. Treml and Barck, pp. 488–89; *Mimesis* (in Hebrew), trans. Barukh Karo, introduction by Dov Sadan (Jerusalem: Bialik Institute, 1958).
[165] "Erich Auerbach," 33.
[166] Karlheinz Barck, "5 Briefe Erich Auerbachs an Walter Benjamin in Paris," *Zeitschrift für Germanistik* 6 (1988): 688–94, and "Eine unveröffentliche Korrespondenz: Erich Auerbach/Werner Krauss," *Beiträge zur Romanischen Philologie* 26:2 (1987): 301–26 and 27:1 (1988): 161–86.
[167] Auerbach's papers are in the *Deutsches Literaturarchiv* in Marbach. Much of his corre-
spondence has been published, and Martin Vialon has been preparing a comprehensive
scholarly edition.

has attracted similar attention in recent decades. Auerbach has become a European and global intellectual par excellence.

It is not difficult to see Auerbach's attraction for contemporary Europeans. *Mimesis* constructed a cosmopolitan literary public and a Pan-European space, inclusive of Jews, and, due to its Istanbul production site – "a non-European, albeit Europeanizing space" – gesturing toward the East and Muslim inclusion.[168] The cosmopolitan culture (*weltliche Kultur*) into which Auerbach, the exile, performing as a modernist writer versed in Europe's traditions, wished to be integrated is the world that Europeans would like to see themselves creating today.[169] *Mimesis* seems to allude to the Holocaust, but recollects cherished literary moments, highlights Europe's Christian past, and seems to open it up universally. Auerbach projects Europe as it could have been, if only National Socialism had not triumphed: cosmopolitan and multicultural, accepting of Jews and Muslims (on condition they became secular Christians). The German-Jewish émigré wrote a cultural history that Europeans love, offering a triumph over Europe's past (*Vergangenheitbewältigung*) in which all wish to take part.

Auerbach made no demands as a Jew. He negotiated his way into European culture via Dante. He confronted Europe and the Holocaust with Christian martyrology – with Christ on the cross, St. Perpetua, St. Augustine, St. Bernard, and Pascal – not with the Aqedah, Amaleq, or Jacob & Esau. The dark past of Jewish–Christian relations was not part of his history. His humanism articulated a society living on its Christian heritage, open to nonbelievers who were willing, like him, to become part of that heritage. Burckhardt had created the figure of Dante as a cosmopolitan exile, and Auerbach inhabited it. The German-Jewish émigré became the great mediator of European culture, the best of Europeans, a culturally Christian Jew, and the better for it.

The traditional Jewish historian cannot but feel irate about Auerbach becoming for contemporaries the paradigmatic European Jew. His life and work show Jewish assimilation at the limits of its success. His friends and associates were mostly non-Jewish, tied by genuine solidarity, friendship and love, and a shared German European culture. Most of them opposed the Nazis, and some risked their lives resisting. They do give a measure of what Germany could have been like if the disastrous turn that nationalism took in the 1880s had not culminated with National Socialism. But they also show the limits of Jewish life permitted by

---

[168] "The book owed its existence to the very fact of Oriental, non-Occidental exile and homelessness": Edward Said, *The World, the Text, and the Critic*, pp. 7–8.
[169] Carl Landauer, "'Mimesis' and Erich Auerbach's Self-Mythologizing," 89.

assimilation, and suggest that we resist both the cultural history that Auerbach offers and histories of the European Jewish intelligentsia that make him, a cultural Christian, the paradigmatic German-Jewish intellectual.

To be sure, the Jewish European histories foregrounding Auerbach, and the definition of Europeanness they form, are among the most benevolent that Jews have been offered in more than two millennia. Jewish life will continue, perhaps even thrive, in Auerbach's Europe, even if traditional Jews are relegated to the margins. But contemporary Europe, where progressive Germans are easing even Gershom Scholem's way back into German culture, and where appreciation of Jewish culture and acceptance of Jewish difference are not uncommon, can do better. There must be other ways of writing Jewish European history. This book pursues them, offering a traditional Jewish rejoinder to the assimilated Jew's vision of Europe.

An alternative Jewish European history cannot return to nationalist narratives, and it must include Auerbach: a Jewish intellectual, working through European, and specifically Christian, materials, to express universal ideals. He was a German-acculturated Jew, a cultural Christian, and a German intellectual – all at the same time. Primo Levi recounts the elevation of feeling he experienced in Auschwitz when reciting the Ulysses Canto from Dante's *Inferno* – "you were made men, to follow after knowledge and excellence" – while walking to a paltry lunch.[170] Lodz (Litzmannstadt) Ghetto diaries describe the elevation experienced at the Jewish Orchestra's performance of German composers – the Jews seen in photos wearing the yellow star armbands.[171] Spitzer, who rebuked Auerbach for his lack of ethnic solidarity, confessed in his April 1933 letter to Löwith: "I have recently heard the Passion of St. Matthew, its meaning is very timely when describing the loneliness of the persecuted."[172] No one can deny the authenticity of these experiences or suggest that Dante, Beethoven, and Bach – and even the St. Matthew Passion – did not become part of Jewish European culture. But they cannot stand alone as signifiers for the European Jew and European

---

[170] *Survival in Auschwitz* (New York: Touchstone, 1996), pp. 112–15, quoting *Inferno* XXVI: 116–17: "fatti non foste a viver come bruti, ma per seguir virtute e canoscenza."

[171] Alan Adelson, producer, *Łódź Ghetto* (videorecording), directed by Kathryn Taverna and Alan Adelson (Westport, CT: Jewish Heritage Project, 1992).

[172] Leo Spitzer to Karl Löwith, April 21, 1933, as quoted in "Menschenkunde zwischen Meistern – Auerbach und Löwith," in *Erich Auerbach*, ed. Treml and Barck, p. 98. The Jewish–Christian nexus is even deeper: Composer Felix Mendelssohn-Bartholdy, a Protestant grandson of the Haskalah leader, recovered Bach's forgotten St. Matthew Passion: Celia Appelgate, *Bach in Berlin: Nation and Culture in Mendelssohn's Revival of the St. Matthew Passion* (Ithaca, NY: Cornell University Press, 2005), chap. 1.

Jewish culture. Their Europeanness entailed a loss of traditional Jewish culture, a culture that must remain part of Jewish European history.

Visiting his *Habilitationsvater* in Cologne shortly after he had been appointed in Marburg, Auerbach wrote in Spitzer's guestbook: "Our subject is ... *that* Rome whence Christ is Roman," echoing *Purgatorio* XXXII: 102: "Quella Roma onde Cristo e romano."[173] The Jewish historian, aware of Christian Rome's significance in Jewish history, can barely restrain himself from responding to Auerbach with Christian Rome's own wrathful cry at the Muslim reconquest of Jerusalem from the Crusaders: "Deus venerunt gentes" (Psalm 79:1) – "O God, the nations have invaded your inheritance." Instead, and more productively, the historian may confront Auerbach and Spitzer with the history of Jacob's struggle against Esau-Rome – and "fear not my servant Jacob"!

---

[173] As quoted in Hans Ulrich Gumbrecht, "Pathos of the Earthly Progress," pp. 25, 253 n. 46. Auerbach used the phrase again in "Figura," 482, n. 43 (German), p. 236, n. 47 (English) to denote the convergence of earthly and heavenly Rome in Dante.

12 Postwar Europe: Austria, the Jewish Remigrés, and the Internationalization of Culture

"Your parents . . . would be very pleased with you, if they were alive now," wrote Hannah Arendt to Daniel Cohn-Bendit in June 1968.[1] Cohn-Bendit had just been expelled from France to Germany as an "undesirable alien" for his role in the May 1968 Paris student revolution. His parents had been members of a close-knit circle of radical German-Jewish exiles in France in the 1930s that also included Walter Benjamin and Arendt. They shared the experience of French internment and the escape for their lives from the advancing German troops.[2] The parents, the elder refugees, now declared their solidarity with the deported children: "Both we [Arendt and her husband, Heinrich Blücher] and Channan Klenbort stand ready to help as much as we can."

Arendt's solidarity with the 68ers was as ill-founded as other émigrés' hostility. It is doubtful that Erich Cohn-Bendit, a Trotskyist attorney, would have found the Movement of March 22, led by his son to launch the Paris May 1968 events, appealing. The movement drew its greatest popularity from the demand for free access to the women's dormitories at the University of Nanterre, and sexual liberty even for men was not high on the Old Left agenda. Yet watching slogans familiar from the Dreyfus Affair and the Popular Front reappear on Paris streets, Arendt sensed, with her typical mixture of insight and error, that she was witnessing epochal events.

---

[1] June 27, 1968: Hannah Arendt Papers, Box 9, Library of Congress, Washington DC: "My dear boy, I have been long thinking how one may reach you without the police intercepting. . . . I wish to tell you only two things: First, that I am absolutely sure that your parents, especially your father, would be very pleased with you, if they were still alive. Second, that if you find yourself in need, perhaps of money, both Channan Klenbort and we stand ready to help as much as we can." Quoted in Sebastian Voigt, "'Nous sommes tous des Juifs allemands': Daniel Cohn-Bendit, Pierre Goldman und der Pariser Mai 1968," *Medaon – Magazin für jüdisches Leben in Forschung und Bildung*, 4:7 (2010): 1–18, http://medaon.de/pdf/AVoigt-7–2010.pdf.

[2] Elisabeth Young-Bruehl, *Hannah Arendt: For the Love of the World* (New Haven, CT: Yale University Press, 2004), pp. 122, 150–57, 412–13.

"Nous sommes tous des Juifs allemands" (We are all German Jews), chanted the Parisian students, hopelessly seeking to defend Cohn-Bendit against deportation.[3] This evocation of the Holocaust in May 68 was momentary, and it elicited no comment from Arendt. The 1968 events did not end what Dan Diner calls the postwar "latency" of the Holocaust in European culture.[4] But the rubric "We are all German Jews" resurfaced three decades later on a popular T-shirt, under the European Union emblem, during Cohn-Bendit's campaign for the European Parliament: The son of German-Jewish Holocaust survivors, born in 1945, became the symbol of the New Europe. However imaginative and unhistorical the associations between 1968 and the past and future were, the Europeanness of the Jews was at stake in 1968.

Symptom and catalyst of the internationalization of European culture, 1968 was a signpost, rarely noticed, for a fundamental shift in the Jews' place in Europe. The 1968 events signaled the emergence of a new Jewish European intelligentsia that would be transformed within two decades from largely cosmopolitan and anti-Zionist to predominantly Jewish and Zionist. The new Jewish intelligentsia arose in an international display of generational conflict with the old Jewish émigrés, and the display concealed a complex, symbiotic, and paradoxical relationship between the two. Arendt's solidarity with 1968 provides a hint of the confusion and misconception that characterized the relationship of émigrés and 68ers, of a generation gap and also of affinities and collusion. The public conflict between the two catapulted the old Jewish émigrés to the center of European culture and made the 68ers agents of internationalization, completing, albeit unwittingly, the elders' cosmopolitan project.

The émigrés were the victims, symbolic and real, of the European past against which the 68ers rebelled, the remnant of a thriving Central European Jewish intelligentsia largely destroyed by the Holocaust. Wishing to set the past aright, the 68ers focused social and academic attention on the émigrés, sought their approval, and developed a new field, *Exilforschung*, to research their biographies. They drew theoretical inspiration from them, and made Frankfurt School philosopher Herbert Marcuse (1898–1980) an icon of 1968. A significant number of 68ers, albeit a minority, were of Jewish origins, but neither the émigrés' Jewishness nor the non-Jewishness of the 68ers ever came into the limelight in 1968. Both generations were dedicated prima facie to cosmopolitan

---

[3] For the origin and context of the rubric, see note 4 to the Introduction.

[4] Dan Diner, "Vom Stau zur Zeit: Neutralisierung und Latenz zwischen Nachkrieg und Achtundsechzig," in *Latenz: Blinde Passagiere in den Geisteswissenschaften*, ed. Hans Ulrich Gumbrecht and Florian Klinger (Göttingen: Vandenhoeck & Ruprecht, 2011), pp. 165–72.

projects, and cosmopolitanism, rather than *Vergangenheitsbewältigung* (mastery of the past) or Jewish Europeanness, served as the grounds for collaboration and confrontation alike.

More often than not, the émigrés came to represent the cultural and political order that the 68ers wished to undermine. The students' radical activism and revolutionary utopianism alarmed many émigrés, reminding them, ironically, of the interwar Nazi youth. "We shall not allow the destruction of democracy by a bunch of people who have no idea what they could be doing," warned the Austrian Socialist Party (SPÖ) chair and future prime minister, Bruno Kreisky (1911–1990).[5] Kreisky, a Jewish remigré and a legendary figure in Austria today, embodied the establishment in 1968, and the rebelling socialist students (VSStÖ) included his own son, Peter.[6] The bare-breasted young women occupying Theodor Adorno's podium in Frankfurt in 1969 seemed emblematic of the conflict of cultures between the old and new intelligentsia, the émigrés and their children.

Pictures of confrontation and adulation can likewise be misleading. There was no uniform pattern to the relationship of émigrés and 68ers. Antinuclear activists and theorists Günther Anders, Robert Jungk, and Marcuse inspired the 68ers all the way through, just as Cold War political scientist Richard Löwenthal and two novelists and journalists, Manès Sperber and Friedrich Torberg, opposed them from the start. Many, such as Arendt and Austrian writer Hilde Spiel, were sympathetic yet critical. Whatever their stance, none fully understood how intimately the two generations were bound together, and how their bitter confrontation represented collusion in Europeanization and internationalization.

In between the 68ers and the émigrés were the 58ers (or the 45ers, as historians call them today): Almost all non-Jewish, they were the generation that experienced Hitler as youth, went through military or paramilitary service during the war, received their academic education in the postwar years, often from the remigrés, and, in the aftermath of 1968 and German university reform, rose to academic leadership.[7] In the late

---

[5] "Kreisky: Keine Politik des Terrors!" *Arbeiter-Zeitung* (20 April 1968): "Wir werden uns die Vernichtung der Demokratie durch eine Handvoll Menschen, die nicht wissen, was aus all dem werden kann, nicht gefallen lassen."

[6] The students responded: "We shall not allow the destruction of democracy through a bunch of functionaries and journalists who know all too well what they are doing": *Kurier* (25 April 1968), as quoted in Paulus Ebner and Karl Vocelka, *Die Zahme Revolution: '68 und was davon blieb* (Vienna: Ueberreuter, 1998), p. 152.

[7] Matthew Specter, *Jürgen Habermas: An Intellectual Biography* (New York: Cambridge University Press, 2010); A. Dirk Moses, *German Intellectuals and the Nazi Past* (New York: Cambridge University Press, 2007), pp. 55–73, 186–218. Specter speaks of the 58ers, Moses of the 45ers, but they refer to the same generation. For a 1970s generational

1950s and 1960s, they endeavored to Westernize and liberalize the German academy and public life. Many were initially sympathetic to the students and shared their criticism of the Bonn Republic for failing to confront the Nazi past. But student calls to substitute direct for parliamentary democracy, and a turn to violence among certain groups, triggered a conservative shift among the 58ers, reinforced by their anxiety that university reforms could limit academic autonomy. They split down the middle, with former liberals like political theorist Karl-Dietrich Bracher growing progressively wary of the students and of reform, and with leftists like Habermas trying to maintain the bridges between the students and the émigrés, and shape an agenda for social transformation.

The tensions between émigrés and students reflected divergent generational experiences. Founders of the postwar transatlantic networks, the Western émigrés savored European elite culture and remained hostile to American popular culture that spread across the Atlantic during the Cold War years and became part of growing up European. Émigré cosmopolitanism, born out of hypernationalist but also multiethnic interwar Europe, exile, and totalitarianism, jarred with student internationalism, born out of a divided Central Europe, stable nation-states, and a search for revolutionary solidarity. Having lived through Stalin, Hitler, and the Holocaust, most émigrés were immune to utopian projects, and many viewed the United States as Europe's savior, while the 68ers saw continuity between the Nazi and postwar regimes, regarded anticommunism as a *Feindbild* (imaginary enemy) designed to fend off domestic reform, and viewed the United States through the lenses of Vietnam and the Civil Rights movement. The fight against imperialism underscored the 68ers' international solidarity, promising a new global society (and, for some, surreptitiously, national liberation from the United States). More than a few 68ers saw Auschwitz and Hiroshima as of a piece. Anticommunist émigrés, such as Arthur Koestler, Sperber, Arendt, and even critics of capitalism like the Frankfurt School, became, for the 68ers, establishment ideologues against whom one pitted Marcuse and Anders.

Still, the émigrés were, directly and indirectly, the 68ers' teachers, the intelligentsia that helped shape postwar European culture, internationalize and liberalize it, and, paradoxically, make 1968 possible. Without the émigrés – without the opening of the Central European academies and public cultures to Western liberal democracy and to critiques of

profile of the progressive and leftist 58ers, see Jürgen Habermas, ed., *Stichworte zur geistigen Situation der Zeit*, 2 vols. (Frankfurt: Suhrkamp, 1979). For the 58ers' consciousness of themselves as a generation, see Jürgen Habermas, "Interview mit Angelo Bolaffi" [1988], in *Die Nachholende Revolution*, Kleine politische Schriften 7 (Frankfurt am Main: Suhrkamp, 1990), p. 23.

authoritarianism, without the transatlantic culture that enabled a maligned "Americanization" – 1968 would have been impossible in Central Europe. The 68ers, in turn, made the émigrés major spokespersons for European culture. Unwittingly, they advanced the long-sought integration of the old Jewish intelligentsia, and spelled out the beginning of a new young one.

In this chapter, I use the foremost international organization of émigré intellectuals during the Cold War, the Congress for Cultural Freedom (henceforth CCF), to scrutinize the convoluted relationship between the émigrés and the 68ers. Consistent with the book's Austrian focus, the chapter centers on the Second Austrian Republic and, specifically, on the CCF's Austrian organ *Forvm* (1954–65), which in 1966 became Austria's foremost New Left magazine, *Neues Forvm*.[8] I show the émigré networks contributing to the creation of an Austrian public sphere, however limited, and to opening up, liberalizing, and internationalizing postwar Austrian culture.[9] Contrary to the accepted maxims, Cold War clashes between pro-Western and procommunist intellectuals often contributed to, rather than hindered, the formation of an Austrian public sphere.

Moreover, I argue that 1968 and its aftermath advanced the liberalization and internationalization that the émigrés had begun.[10] While many émigrés and most 68ers were decidedly illiberal in thought and action, they both, whether in conflict with each other or in collaboration, created a more open European culture, in which the émigrés, too, could feel at home. To be sure, the reevaluation of the Holocaust and Jewish history as part of the European experience had not yet begun in 1968,

---

[8] *Forvm: Österreichische Monatsblätter für kulturelle Freiheit*, 1954–65; *Neues Forvm: Österreichische Monatsblätter für kulturelle Freiheit* (alternative subtitle: *Internationale Zeitschrift links von der Mitte*), 1966–79; *Forvm: Internationale Zeitschrift für kulturelle Freiheit, politische Gleichheit und solidarische Arbeit*, 1980–95. Reprinted as *Forvm*, 28 vols. + index vol. (Vienna: Ueberreuter, 2002–4). Alternative titles: *Forum* and *Neues Forum*. The alternative conventional spelling will henceforth be used.

[9] This is in line with recent work on émigré culture, the "long 1960s," "Americanization," youth culture, and the politics of memory in postwar Europe: Heinz Bude and Bernd Greiner, eds., *Westbindungen: Amerika in der Bundesrepublik* (Hamburg: Hamburger Edition, 1999); Heidi Fehrenbach and Uta G. Poiger, eds., *Transactions, Transgressions, Transformations: American Culture in Western Europe and Japan* (New York: Berghahn, 2000); Gerd-Rainer Horn and Padraic Kenney, eds., *Transnational Moments of Change: Europe 1945, 1968, 1989* (Lanham, MD: Rowman & Littlefield, 2004), esp. pp. 81–94; Richard Ned Lebow, Wulf Kansteiner, and Claudio Fogu, eds., *The Politics of Memory in Postwar Europe* (Durham, NC: Duke University Press, 2006); Axel Schildt and Detlef Sigfried, eds., *Between Marx and Coca-Cola: Youth Cultures in Changing European Societies, 1960–1980* (New York: Berghahn Books, 2006); *Culture and International History*, ed. Jessica Gienow-Hecht and Frank Schumacher (New York: Berghahn Books, 2003).

[10] On 1968 and internationalization, see Martin Klimke, *The Other Alliance: Student Protest in West Germany and the United States in the Global Sixties* (Princeton, NJ: Princeton University Press, 2010).

inasmuch as "Europe" itself was not yet central to the 68ers' discourse. Yet the 68ers' radical reevaluation of the past challenged national narratives, and their pronounced internationalism relaxed the boundaries of national cultures, thereby advancing Europeanization and confrontation with the Holocaust, opening up space for the Jews, and making the long-sought integration of the Jewish intelligentsia possible. Integration meant, however, that the preconditions for the old intelligentsia – partial exclusion of the Jews from the national culture – no longer existed. The Jewish intelligentsia of the European Union inhabits the legacy of the émigrés, but it is radically new. Even before their last vestiges vanished from the world, the old intelligentsia had been gone. Having educated the generation that arose for and against it, the old intelligentsia retired, greatly celebrated, in favor of a younger intelligentsia seeking to build a new Europe.

Austria may not seem a clear choice for tracking the old intelligentsia's influence on the 68ers, and it has certainly received less attention than Germany or France (not to mention the United States). Austria had no remigré circle equivalent in influence to the Frankfurt School. The remigrés dominated important sectors of public culture, such as the theaters and cabarets, and had a major presence in journalism and in socialist and communist politics, but they had a lesser impact on postwar academic culture.[11] *Forum* could not compete with the congress's German organ, *Der Monat*, which had at least three times as large an audience and, unlike *Forum*, was liberal, secular, and progressive. Austria also went through a less severe crisis than did Germany or France in 1968. The corporate order held firm, the Socialists controlled student unrest, and the universities resisted a major reform. For all of *Neues Forum*'s cultural experimentation and its support of new political movements, the New Left in Austria never matched in political action or in influence the German and French students. Not surprisingly, recent surveys of 1968 simply omit Austria.[12]

---

[11] Their absence was felt especially in the social sciences. In a report to the Ford Foundation in 1963, Paul Lazarsfeld and Oskar Morgenstern attributed the sorry state of Austrian social science to the brain drain due to Nazi-era emigration and, nowadays, the pull of German affluence. See Anton Pelinka, "The Impact of American Scholarship on Austrian Political Science: The Making of a Discipline," in *The Americanization/ Westernization of Austria*, ed. Günter Bischof and Anton Pelinka (New Brunswick, NJ: Transaction Publishers, 2003), pp. 226–34. On the natural sciences: Wolfgang Reiter, "Naturwissenschaften und Remigration," in *Vom Weggehen: Zum Exil von Kunst und Wissenschaft*, ed. Sandra Wiesinger-Stock, Erika Weinzierl, and Konstantin Kaiser (Vienna: Mandelbaum, 2006), pp. 177–218.

[12] E.g., Carole Fink, Philipp Gassert, and Detlef Junker, eds., *1968: The World Transformed* (Cambridge: Cambridge University Press, 1998); Gerd-Rainer Horn, *The Spirit of '68* (Oxford: Oxford University Press, 2007); Martin Klimke and Joachim Scharloth, "1968

Nevertheless, Austria does present the single case of an old intelligentsia journal turning from anticommunism to the New Left, from *Forum* to *Neues Forum*, and still remaining culturally bound to the remigrés. This journal was at the center of Austria's political and cultural life. In its nuanced nostalgia for old Central Europe, it negotiated the imperial legacy for postwar Austria and helped shape a national identity compatible with a postnational Europe. It took a leading role in forming the canons of "Austrian literature" and Viennese modernism still holding in our own time and made them emblems of a Central European culture, the foremost representatives of which were Austrian Jewish writers. Like no other journal, it reflected the cosmopolitanism of the old Central European Jewish intelligentsia. It was the longest-surviving CCF magazine, weathering a series of political transformations, ownership and editorial board changes, and even a name change, closing down only in 1995, the year after the foundation of the European Union. *Forum* shows the legacies of the Austrian Empire and of Jewish European culture working their way, in dreams and in reality, toward contemporary Europe, and doing so in ways not always obvious to contemporary devotees of Europe in the "Republic of Vienna" and in the progressive academy. This chapter tracks them.

Forum, the Congress for Cultural Freedom, and Postwar Austrian Culture

The Holocaust and postwar "ethnic cleansing" – the expulsion of Germans and other minorities "back to their homelands" – turned Central Europe into a conglomerate of ethno-national states as it had never before been in history. The Cold War divided Europe and made a Central European culture impossible. Surviving members of the interwar Jewish intelligentsia were mostly émigrés who had escaped the Nazis – to the West, to Sweden and Switzerland, to Soviet Russia, and to Palestine. In exile, they endeavored to keep their old European networks and created new ones. Many had participated in the war effort against Germany, and a few continued their U.S. government service into the postwar period, playing crucial roles in shaping Cold War strategy.[13]

in Europe," in *1968 in Europe: A History of Protest and Activism, 1956–1977*, ed. Martin Klimke and Joachim Scharloth (New York: Palgrave Macmillan, 2008), pp. 1–9. The "Bibliographic Essay" in Gerd-Rainer Horn and Padraic Kenney, eds., *Transnational Moments of Change*, pp. 229–33, includes literature on "small countries" – but not on Austria.

[13] Daniel Bessner, *Democracy in Exile: Hans Speier and the Rise of the Defense Intellectual* (Ithaca, NY: Cornell University Press, 2018); Udi Greenberg, *The Weimar Century:*

Most émigrés did not return to Europe after the war.[14] Their Central Europe vanished; an Iron Curtain came down in its midst, splitting it between the Soviet and Western camps. It also lost its multicultural vitality. In communist East-Central Europe, cosmopolitanism became synonymous with treason. The economic infrastructure lay in ruin. Neither Germany nor Austria welcomed Jewish remigrés. Those émigrés who either returned to Central Europe or chose to settle in Western Europe were best positioned to rebuild international cultural relations. Their international network integrated intellectual refugees from Eastern Europe and contributed to the formation of a new Western European and transatlantic culture.

Western European remigrés were split among pro-Western, neutralist, and communist camps. The pro-Westerners, or the "Atlanticists," regarded the Soviet domination of Eastern Europe as a tragedy and feared further Soviet expansion west that would put an end to liberal democracy. They sought U.S. protection against Soviet expansion through the North Atlantic Treaty Organization (NATO). A fair number of émigrés had returned initially to East Germany, hoping to build a new socialist society, but in later years, many left for West Germany, disappointed. For a while, academic exchange continued among the occupation zones in Germany, but communication between East and West was getting difficult: "I am in touch with [Werner] Krauss and [Ernst] Bloch [in East Germany] but the letters are infrequent and not easy to interpret," wrote Erich Auerbach in 1950.[15] The correspondence soon died out, and Auerbach never saw his old colleagues again.

Communist intellectuals, who were often party members, returned to their home countries, too. They typically came back from Moscow, where they had weathered war and purges, but also from the West, notably from England. They retained the single international network that was capable of breaking through the Iron Curtain. Yet their colleagues in Eastern Europe were subject to tight state control that loosened in Czechoslovakia, Hungary, and Poland only about 1964, when dialogue with Western noncommunists began again in earnest. Neutralist intellectuals, the third major Western European group, generally wanted to prevent military confrontation in Europe between the two blocs at all costs. They opposed NATO and endeavored to build bridges to the East.

German Émigrés and the Ideological Foundations of the Cold War, (Princeton, NJ: Princeton University Press, 2015).

[14] Marita Krauss, "Jewish Remigration: An Overview of an Emerging Discipline," *Leo Baeck Institute Yearbook* 49:1 (2004): 107–20.

[15] Auerbach to Martin Hellweg, June 20, 1950, in *Erich Auerbachs Briefe an Martin Hellweg (1939–1950)*, ed. Martin Vialon (Tübingen: Grancke, 1997).

The Germans among them hoped that such bridges would make German reunification possible, and that Central Europe would regain its political and cultural vitality. They were major targets for Western and communist propaganda, each of which sought to draw neutralist intellectuals to its camp.

In the Western camp, many found their way to the Congress for Cultural Freedom.[16] Founded at a major international conference in June 1950 in Berlin, and headquartered in Paris, the CCF was the major international organization of the anticommunist intelligentsia during the height of the Cold War, 1950–67. It sought to counter postwar Soviet propaganda, expose communism as totalitarian, and shape a pro-American democratic consensus. Members were mostly liberal and socialist intellectuals, many of Jewish origin. They included Central European émigrés, a remnant of transnational interwar networks who had escaped National Socialism and resettled in Western Europe. The émigrés collaborated with the (predominantly Jewish) New York intellectuals across the Atlantic in launching and running the CCF. The organization had branches in most Western European countries, the United States, Australia, and several African, Asian, and Latin American countries, thirty-five in all.

The CCF became the major hub of Cold War liberal culture. It supported an international seminar program, established sophisticated politico-cultural magazines in several languages, and built up a transatlantic intellectual network that contributed to the internationalization of European and American cultures. Clandestine funding came from the U.S. Central Intelligence Agency, as well as from private U.S. foundations (especially the Ford Foundation). Rumors of CIA support circulated almost from the beginning, but most members made little effort to inquire about the sources of their funding and remained unaware of CIA involvement. When the CIA's role became public in 1966, a scandal erupted, discrediting the CCF. For the Left, and for many liberals in Europe and the United States alike, the CCF has become an emblem of Cold War liberal duplicity, CIA conspiracy, and the U.S. menace. This view has weathered the fall of communism and remains widely shared in the academic community.[17]

---

[16] Malachi Hacohen, "Kongress für kulturelle Freiheit," *Enzyklopädie jüdischer Geschichte und Kultur*, ed. Dan Diner, 7 vols. (Stuttgart: J. B. Metzler'sche Verlagsbuchhandlung, 2012): 2: 22–28.

[17] Christopher Lasch, "The Cultural Cold War: A Short History of the Congress for Cultural Freedom," in *The Agony of the American Left* (New York: Vintage, 1968), pp. 61–112; Frances Stonor Saunders's best-seller: *Who Paid the Piper? The CIA and the Cultural Cold War* (London: Granata, 1999).

Recent historiography has produced a more balanced view of the CCF and underscores the agency of its intellectuals.[18] The initiative for the CCF came from ex-communist intellectuals outside of the CIA; there were serious policy rifts and ideological disagreements at every level, and the CIA repeatedly lost control over the organization. The CCF (and the CIA) depended on the initiative of preexisting émigré networks. The CIA had to accommodate itself to what the intellectuals, allegedly under its control, wanted and were willing to do. Where a network of solidarity, hardened by exile and international experience, did not exist, the CCF had difficulty making progress, and no amount of CIA resources could help. The CCF's difficulties in rebuilding its West German chapter in the mid-1950s and its failure in the Third World corroborate its dependency on local networks and its inability to generate new ones.[19] Shared experience – cosmopolitan background, immigration, and exile – were crucial.

Central European Jewish émigrés and remigrés were prominent among the CCF activists, editors, and magazine contributors.[20] Many had childhood memories of pre–World War I Central Europe, especially of cultural pluralism in the Austro-Hungarian Monarchy, and most were active in interwar German-speaking international networks. Many had had a brush with communism, but by 1939, virtually all were critics of Soviet "totalitarianism" – a concept they developed comparing the Nazi and Stalinist dictatorships. In the postwar years, most were close to social democracy, supportive of the emergent Western welfare state.

Across the Atlantic, the émigrés found collaborators in the first generation of college-educated children of Jewish immigrants, who entered journalism and the academy in New York, in the shadow of the Great

---

[18] Peter Coleman, *The Liberal Conspiracy: The Congress for Cultural Freedom and the Struggle for the Mind of Postwar Europe* (New York: Free Press, 1989); Pierre Grémion, *Intelligence de l'anticommunisme: Le Congrès pour la liberté de la culture à Paris (1950–1975)* (Paris: Fayard, 1995); Michael Hochgeschwender, *Freiheit in der Offensive? Der Kongress für Kulturelle Freiheit und die Deutschen* (Munich: Oldenbourg, 1998); Giles Scott-Smith, *The Politics of Apolitical Culture: The Congress for Cultural Freedom, the CIA, and Post-War American Hegemony* (London: Routledge, 2002); Michael Warner, "Origins of the Congress for Cultural Freedom, 1949–50," *Studies in Intelligence* 38:5 (1995): 89–98; Hugh Wilford, *The Mighty Wurlitzer: How the CIA Played America* (Cambridge, MA: Harvard University Press, 2008), esp. chaps. 4–5.

[19] Michael Hochgeschwender, *Freiheit in der Offensive?* esp. pp. 390–411, 480–95.

[20] Among the statesmen closest to the congress, future German and Austrian Chancellors Willy Brandt and Bruno Kreisky were both exiles, one in Norway and the other in Sweden. James Chappel drew my attention to the engagement of Catholic remigrés in the congress: Waldemar Gurian and Eugen Kogon (both of Jewish origins) in Germany, and the Personalist circle around Jacques Maritain in France. Of the latter circle, Denis de Rougemont, a leading advocate of European federalism (and a Swiss Protestant), had the highest activity profile. As a rule, the congress was a sideshow to the Catholic networks.

Depression and the Cold War. The New York intellectuals transitioned, like the European émigrés, from anti-Stalinist socialism in the 1930s to Cold War liberalism and social democracy. Their magazines, especially *Partisan Review*, *Politics*, and *Commentary*, presaged the CCF magazines. They combined literary modernism with heterodox Marxism, and American pragmatism with European culture and anticommunism. The cultural affinities and memories of the New York intellectuals often extended to the Eastern European Jewish culture of their parents, however remote it was in time, context, and lifestyle from their current American urban environment. Together with the European émigrés, they were poised to reconstitute international culture in a shattered Europe. Pouring resources into Cold War culture, the CIA rekindled the dying embers of the old cosmopolitan European intelligentsia, helped it build bridges to America, and gave it a final lease on life in Europe.

Nowhere was this more obvious than in postwar Austria. Surrounded on three sides by communist countries, with Vienna a mere fifty miles from the Hungarian border, postwar Austria, previously the crossroads of Central Europe, was now on the outskirts of the West. The two super-powers viewed the country as an open battleground, and Vienna as a gate to the enemy's world. U.S. cultural diplomacy made Austria a major target. Yet in the early 1950s, all efforts of the Congress for Cultural Freedom to open a branch failed. The CCF required a supraparty orga-nization for its activities, and the Austrian Socialists and Catholics, thor-oughly anticommunist though they were, saw no reason to collaborate on a CCF project.[21] Only the marginal free-floating Jewish remigrés were willing to engage in bridge building. Historically identified with the Socialists but with only limited standing in the postwar party, the remigrés found kindred spirits among conservative Catholic cosmo-polites and other mourners from old Central Europe.[22] The remigrés proved the only ones capable of pulling together the CCF coalition.

Unable to attract mainstream Austrian figures, the CCF's executive secretary and CIA coordinator, Michael Josselson (1908–79), reluctantly turned to remigré writer and journalist Friedrich Torberg (1908–1979). Warm and effusive but also irascible and belligerent, Torberg touched every raw nerve of the CCF leadership. They were, like him, Eastern and

---

[21] International Association for Cultural Freedom papers, Joseph Regenstein Library (Special Collections), the University of Chicago, II, 40:7–9, 110:1 (henceforth IACF); *Nachlaß Friedrich Torberg*, Wienbibliothek im Rathaus (MA 9), 18:3 (henceforth *Nachlaß Torberg*).

[22] Those who had a standing in the Socialist Party, like Oscar Pollak, the powerful editor of the *Arbeiter-Zeitung*, were the first approached by the congress. But Pollak was not interested. Kreisky kept close relations with *Forum*'s editors, but was not involved.

Central European émigrés, but they became quintessential Western liberals, anxious about McCarthyism and thoughtfully anticommunist. Many of them were refined, assimilated Jews. Torberg remained a Central European cosmopolitan, openly Jewish and pro-Zionist, and fiercely anticommunist. He led the Brecht boycott in Austria: "McTorberg," some émigrés called him (after U.S. Senator Joseph McCarthy). Josselson had worked hard to shift CCF strategy from political warfare to cultural diplomacy. He emphasized the shared cultural community of Americans and Europeans, and marginalized the hardline ex-communists. He would now have to watch as Torberg undermined the dialogue that the CCF had opened with neutralist intellectuals: As *Forum*'s editor, Torberg would repeatedly collide with the CCF by attacking the German neutralists.[23] All the same, Josselson had little choice: No one else stepped in to head an Austrian chapter. In 1954, Torberg became the editor of the CCF's Austrian organ, the new Viennese monthly *Forum*.

Forum quickly became Austria's premier politico-cultural magazine. With a circulation of three thousand by 1958, and up to five thousand in 1965, *Forum* was the third-largest monthly of its kind in German-speaking Europe. (*Der Monat*, the CCF's German organ, was first, with an edition of twenty-five thousand.) *Forum* was a magazine of the intelligentsia, and the readers included politicians, professionals, academics, and the Viennese Diaspora around the globe: Israel provided the third-largest market (after Austria and Germany). Subscriptions in communist Europe, however, remained few, mostly official ones. More copies got through the Iron Curtain than subscription figures indicate, but *Forum* was not widely read. This was a major disappointment, as engagement of East European intellectuals was a major CCF goal. In Austria, in contrast, *Forum* was the constant talk of Vienna. Within a couple of months, Austria's leading politicians were standing in line to write political pieces. There was no other publication like it in Austria for cultural and political discussion, and for diversity of interests and intellectual resources.

The sight of an international magazine occupying elegant editorial offices in a still war-ravaged Vienna, and, against the background of provincialism and antisemitism, edited by a Jewish remigré carrying a U.S. passport, may seem surreal. Yet among the CCF publications, *Forum* was the one to strike the deepest roots into the local culture. The editorial board represented a political and ethnic spectrum seemingly

---

[23] I recount the conflicts between Torberg and the congress's Paris headquarters in "The Congress for Cultural Freedom in Austria: *Forum*, the Rémigrés and Postwar Culture," *Storiografia* 11 (2007): 135–45.

drawn from late imperial Austria: Austria's leading poet, progeny of the military aristocracy, Alexander Lernet-Holenia (1897–1976); Catholic journalist Friedrich Hansen-Löve (1919–1997), replaced in 1955 by Friedrich Abendroth; *Arbeiter-Zeitung* literary editor Felix Hubalek (1908–1958), replaced in 1959 by socialist journalist Günther Nenning (1921–2006); and Torberg, scion to the vanishing Central European Jewish intelligentsia, rendered "homeless" (his expression) by World War II. Commitment to anticommunism and to Austrian nationality united the editors, and most of them also showed unrepressed nostalgia for "The World of Yesterday," for multicultural Central Europe. Under Torberg, these lost souls set out to redefine the political culture of postwar Austria, a land in which most of them felt ill at ease.[24]

Forum provided a stage for the exchange of divergent perspectives on controversial, and painful, issues in Austrian and Central European history, such as the Austrian Civil War of 1934, neo-Nazism, the *Anschluss*, Austrian-German relations, Marxism, democracy, and the welfare state. The debates on Austrian identity – Is Austria a nation? – and on Austria's place in Europe were most acute. *Forum* broke no radically new ground: On issues such as Austria's culpability in Nazi crimes, it pushed the boundaries of the national consensus but never crossed them. The Second Republic's foundation myth – Austria as a victim of Nazism – remained virtually untouched. None of the contributors drew on Austria's multicultural past to envision a future cosmopolitan Europe. Still, by providing a prime site for interparty debate and bringing it to an uncommonly high level, the magazine bolstered a fledgling public sphere. Austrian corporatism bought industrial peace by limiting public debate. The postwar "social partnership" of Catholics and Socialists, determined not to repeat interwar mistakes, negotiated differences in closed quarters in order to avoid political strife. However illiberal *Forum*'s anticommunist rhetoric was, it became an agent of liberalization in a country sorely lacking a liberal political culture.[25]

---

[24] On the Habsburg nostalgia among *Forum*'s editors: Anne-Marie Corbin, "Die österreichische Identität in Friedrich Torbergs *Forum*," *Österreich in Geschichte und Literatur* 46:1 (2002): 2–16; Robert von Dassanowsky, "'Mon Cousin de Liernut': France as a Code for Idealized Personal Political Identity in the 'Austrian' Novels of Alexander Lernet-Holenia," *Austrian Studies* 13 (2005): 173–90; Felix W. Tweraser, "Paris Calling Vienna: The Congress for Cultural Freedom and Friedrich Torberg's Editorship of Forum," ibid., 158–72. For the background: Claudio Magris, *Der habsburgische Mythos in der modernen österreichische Literatur* [1963] (Vienna: Paul Zsolnay Verlag, 2000).

[25] For a resume of *Forum* themes, see Anne-Marie Corbin-Schuffels, *L'image de l'Europe à l'ombre de la guerre froide: La revue Forum de Friedrich Torberg à Vienne (1954–1961)* (Paris: Harmattan, 2001). For *Forum* selections (focusing on the post-Torberg era) with authors' indexes and short biographies, see Günther Nenning, ed., *FORVM: Die*

Forum also opened a Western cultural window onto a society that had lost its intellectual vitality and had been relegated to the margins of the Atlantic world. Mainstream Austrian culture in the 1950s was conservative. Authors and motifs associated with the *Ständestaat*, the clerical authoritarian regime of 1934–38, were hegemonic.[26] *Forum* was different. The culture section – about equal in size to the political one – included literature, theater, music, film, and pictorial arts. If Austrian authors predominated, there were also translations of foreign writers – W. H. Auden, Albert Camus, Eugène Ionesco, and Boris Pasternak, among others. Philosophers as diverse as Adorno, Arendt, and Karl Popper published essays on music, political theory, and philosophy, complementing commentaries by leading intellectuals of the Congress for Cultural Freedom, like Ignazio Silone, Stephen Spender, and Manès Sperber. Historian Gerald Stourzh, on his visits to Vienna from the University of Chicago in the mid-1950s, found *Forum* a breath of fresh air.[27]

There were limits to the magazine's innovation. Viennese theater, opera, and music provided much material, but not the city's rich "underground culture" – the experimental cabarets and arts, or the literary *Wiener Gruppe* around Friedrich Achleitner, H. C. Artmann, Gerhard Rühm, and Oswald Wiener.[28] Emphatically Austrian in character, *Forum* marginalized German topics, and virtually ignored the legendary *Gruppe 47*, although Austrian authors (Ilse Aichinger, Ingeborg Bachmann, and Erich Fried) took part in their meetings.[29] At least until the early 1960s, *Forum*'s culture remained backward looking. Torberg, conservative in his cultural tastes, his eyes set on the dying world of his youth, and his anxieties fixed on communism, could not dream of a new Austrian or European future.

---

[26] *berühmsten Beiträge zur Zukunft von einst von Arrabal bis Zuckmayer* (Vienna: Amalthea, 1998).

Friedbert Aspetsberger, Norbert Frei, and Huber Lengauer, eds., *Literatur der Nachkriegszeit und der fünfiger Jahren in Österreich* (Vienna: ÖBV, 1984), esp. pp. 46–58; Katrin Kohl and Ritchie Robertson, eds., *A History of Austrian Literature 1918–2000* (Rochester, NY: Camden House, 2006), esp. pp. 107–26, 163–80.

[27] Gerald Stourzh in a conversation with Malachi Hacohen, spring 2001, Vienna. See his "Unterrichtsfach 'Gesellschaft,'" *Forum* 1 (September 1954): 12–13, reporting on his Chicago experience, and "Deutsche Geschichtsschreibung über Österreich," *Forum* 2 (October 1955): 358–60, a contribution to *Forum*'s discussion of Austrian identity.

[28] Lutz Musner, "Ist Wien Anders? Zur Kulturgeschichte der Stadt nach 1945," in *Wien: Geschichte einer Stadt*, ed. Peter Csendes and Ferdinand Opll, 3 vols. (Vienna: Böhlau, 2006), 3: 739–819.

[29] Michael Hochgeschwender notes (email to author October 28, 2009): "Yet, one should not forget that the *Gruppe 47* did not have the almost canonical appreciation it enjoys today prior to its famous [1966] U.S. trip."

Forum's bête-noir, the communist *Tagebuch*, could not facilitate intellectual exchange among Austria's political parties, but by giving voice to communist remigrés, it likewise opened up Austrian culture to international perspectives. Ernst Fischer, Bruno Frei, and Viktor Matejka were the editors, the first two remigrés from Moscow and Mexico, respectively, and Matejka having returned from German concentration camps. *Tagebuch* introduced Austrian readers to international authors who would otherwise rarely appear in the Austrian press. Its gallery of authors was, naturally, somewhat different from *Forum*'s: Right beside classical Austrian and Western authors it featured such communist writers as Pablo Neruda and Anna Seghers, as well as such philosophers and historians as Georg Lukàcs and Eric Hobsbawm. *Tagebuch*, too, displayed conservative literary and artistic tastes and ignored the avant-garde. It sold only a few hundred copies in Austria, but it was influential among leftist youth. Even more significantly, thousands more copies were distributed across the countries behind the Iron Curtain. *Tagebuch* preserved a communist intellectual network and a semblance of an international European culture.

Forum and *Tagebuch*, the competing pro-Western and pro-Soviet magazines, looked more like each other than like other Austrian magazines. Both were far more international, and remigrés played a major role on their respective editorial boards. Their competition had beneficial effects for Austria. Ideological warfare can be stultifying: The closing down of the communist-affiliated *Neue Theater in der Scala* in 1956, and the migration of its team (including musician Hanns Eisler) to East Berlin, symbolized the tragic constraints of Cold War culture. But ideological rivalry also had the opposite effect: It enhanced the Austrian public sphere. The Brecht boycott provoked a major debate in *Forum*: Should a democracy finding itself in an emergency (*Notstand*) permit politically subversive performances? The balance of *Forum* opinion was against Torberg: Brecht should be performed. The boycott kept Brecht's work out of major Austrian theaters until the early 1960s, but the debate reinforced his stature. Neither *Forum* nor *Tagebuch* displayed political tolerance or liberal openness, and *Tagebuch* was monitored by the Austrian Communist Party, but they opened Austrian culture to the world. Contrary to conventional views, Cold War culture also meant liberalization and internationalization.[30]

---

[30] Christina Zoppel, "Linientreue und Liberalität: Die Rezeption der zeitgenössischen österreichischen Literatur im kommunistischen 'Tagebuch,' 1950–1960," Master's thesis, University of Vienna, 1995; Norbert Griesmayer, "Die Zeitschrift 'Tagebuch': Ergänzende Beobachtungen zur kulturpolitischen Situation in den fünfiger Jahren," in *Literatur der Nachkriegszeit und der fünfiger Jahren in Österreich*, pp. 75–111; Günther

In Austria and Germany alike, the CCF magazines, conferences, and seminars brought the émigrés' scholarship back to the societies that had previously expelled them. Liberal German émigrés in the United States, formerly Weimar dissenters, launched a fundamental critical examination of Germany's past, and they were joined by the remigrés in Germany. Both groups trained a generation of intellectual and social historians who explored the roots of National Socialism and highlighted the burden of the German past.[31] To be sure, conservative historians continued to play a major role in Germany, and the remigrés themselves were by no means exclusively liberal: The names of Arnold Bergstraesser, René König, Karl Löwith, Hans Rothfels, and Erich Voegelin figure prominently among the conservative remigrés who internationalized postwar German political science, sociology, philosophy, and history.[32] But the CCF magazine, *Der Monat*, reflected an emergent transatlantic liberal consensus on the German *Sonderweg*: The origins of National Socialism were in illiberal German traditions and in unique antidemocratic social structures. The émigrés and the CCF contributed together, if often in diverse ways, to the emergence of a transatlantic scholarly community.[33]

The CCF encountered hostility on the European Right, among conservative critics of "Americanization." Postwar Europe witnessed a resurgence of conservative international networks, often Catholic, groping for an alternative to both communism and Western liberalism. Most of their members were chastened by the Nazi experience, and the Christian Democratic vision of Europe accommodated itself to democracy and to

Nenning, *FORVM*, pp. 15–53, ten *Forum* essays on Brecht, 1954–64. For a summary of Torberg's involvement in the Brecht boycott, see Heidrun Ultes-Nitsche, *"Ich bin eine feine Monarchiemischung": Identitätskonstruktionen in Friedrich Torbergs nichtfiktionalen Texten* (Hamburg: Verlag Dr. Kovač, 2005), pp. 108–31.Torberg had more freedom to maneuver politically than his *Tagebuch* counterpart. The congress tried persistently to moderate *Forum*'s anticommunist politics but failed. See Malachi Haim Hacohen, "The Congress for Cultural Freedom in Austria," 135–45.

[31] Steven Aschheim, *Beyond the Border: The German-Jewish Legacy Abroad* (Princeton, NJ: Princeton University Press, 2007), pp. 45–80.

[32] Arnd Bauerkämper, "Americanisation as Globalization? Remigrés to West Germany After 1945 and Conceptions of Democracy: The Cases of Hans Rothfels, Ernst Fraenkel and Hans Rosenberg," *Leo Baeck Institute Yearbook* 49:1 (2004): 153–70; Alfons Söllner, "Normative Westernization? – The Impact of Remigres on the Foundation of Political Thought in Post-War Germany," in *German Ideologies Since 1945*, ed. Jan-Werner Müller (New York: Palgrave Macmillan, 2003), pp. 40–60.

[33] Michael Hochgeschwender, "The Intellectual as Propagandist: *Der Monat*, the Congress for Cultural Freedom and the Process of Westernization in Germany," conference paper presented at the German Historical Institute, Washington, DC, March 1999, http://web .archive.org/web/20000917091401/www.ghi-dc.org/conpotweb/westernpapers/hoch geschwender.pdf; Axel Schildt, "Reise zurück aus der Zukunft: Beiträge von intellektuellen USA-Remigranten zur atlantischen Allianz, zum westdeutschen Amerikabild und zur 'Amerikanisierung' in den fünfziger Jahren," *Exilforschung* 9 (1991): 25–45.

transatlantic collaboration. Deeply anticommunist, conservatives reconciled themselves to U.S. military protection, but they resented the loss of national autonomy and were anxious about "threats" to religion, family, community, and mandarin culture. Many continued to identify Americanization with popular culture and liberalism, feared it, and were contemptuous of it. They counterposed a conservative "West" against the liberal one: *Das Abendland* was their battle cry *gegen den Westen*. They shaped a vision of "Europe" as an alternative to both the Soviet Union and the United States.[34] *Der Monat* was subject to their trenchant critiques.

The CCF combated conservative anti-American prejudices as much as leftist ones, but *Der Monat* and *Forum* developed different political styles. Edited until 1958 by an American, Melvin Lasky, *Der Monat* hammered unabashed liberal democratic politics – militantly secular, critical, and progressive, all Western. It created dissonance in German public culture. *Forum* – Viennese, Austrian, and Central European – was more accommodating of postwar culture, and conciliatory toward conservative Catholics. Torberg himself was no Western liberal. Like other CCF intellectuals, only more so, he shared the conservative cultural prejudices that the CCF entrusted him to combat. He considered the United States devoid of charm and culture, obsessed with accumulation.[35] The best thing he could say about the American way of life was that nobody forced him to accept it. Like European conservatives, Torberg, too, wanted U.S. power to protect an old vanishing Central Europe, but not to promote what one historian calls "Coca colonization."[36]

Among Torberg's close friends were Catholic remigrés – former anti-Nazi supporters of the *Ständestaat* like journalist Klaus Dohrn and theater director Ernst Lothar (the latter of Jewish origins). Conservative intellectuals and politicians who had U.S. exposure, like the editor and publisher of *Die Presse*, Fritz Molden, were engaged in *Forum* from the beginning. *Forum* drew less internationally oriented Catholics into collaboration, opening Austrian public culture to the Western influences. Each in its

---

[34] Vanessa Conze, *Das Europa der Deutschen: Ideen von Europa in Deutschland zwischen Reichstradition und Westorientierung (1920–1970)* (Munich: Oldenbourg 2005); Wolfram Kaiser, *Christian Democracy and the Origins of European Union* (Cambridge: Cambridge University Press, 2007); Axel Schildt, *Zwischen Abendland und Amerika: Studien zur westdeutschen Ideenlandschaft der 50er Jahre* (Munich: Oldenbourg, 1999).

[35] Torberg (from his U.S. exile) to Viennese literary critic and historian Heinz Politzer (in Jerusalem), as quoted in David Axmann, *Friedrich Torberg: Die Biographie* (Munich: Langen Müller, 2008), pp. 173–74.

[36] Reinhold Wagnleitner, *Coca-Colonization and the Cold War*, trans. Diana M. Wolf (Chapel Hill: University of North Carolina Press, 1994). For a different view of "Americanization": Heidi Fehrenbach and Uta G. Poiger, eds., *Transactions, Transgressions, Transformations* (New York: Berghahn, 2000).

own way, *Der Monat* and *Forum* contributed toward the development of liberal public spheres in postwar Central Europe.

Friedrich Torberg, Austrian Literature, and Central European Culture

Forum was closely identified with it chief editor, Torberg, in its first twelve years. Torberg regarded himself as the literary executor of old Central Europe. Born in Vienna and educated in Prague, he frequented, as a young author, the literary cafés of both capitals, where one could pretend throughout the interwar period that the Austro-Hungarian Monarchy never fell apart and Central Europe was alive and well.[37] There he met, loved, and fought the mentors and peers who would accompany him into exile and into the postwar years. His first novel, describing a youth's last year in gymnasium, ending with his suicide, won him recognition in literary circles in Vienna and Prague at age 22.[38] He was close to the Prague German-Jewish writers: Max Brod was his mentor, and Franz Werfel was an acquaintance and closer friend later in exile. He was active in Zionist sports, regarded himself a socialist, and sympathized with socialist Zionism.[39] Initially critical of the *Ständestaat*, he supported its struggle to retain Austrian independence. The Anschluss in March 1938, not the failed socialist uprising in February 1934, constituted for Torberg the major catastrophe, the end of the Austria he loved, and the *caesura* from old Europe.[40]

Sensing what was in store for Czechoslovakia in the aftermath of the Munich Agreement, Torberg left Prague for Zurich in the fall of 1938. He continued on to Paris in 1939, joined the expatriate Czech army, and ended up fleeing the German advance into France in June 1940. He crossed over the border to Spain and went on to Lisbon. His friend William S. Schlamm, former editor of *Die Weltbühne*, an ex-communist

---

[37] For Torberg's biography, see Marcel Atze and Marcus G. Patka, eds., *Die "Gefahren der Vielseitigkeit": Friedrich Torberg 1908–1979* (Vienna: Holzhausen, 2008); David Axmann, *Friedrich Torberg: Die Biographie*; Josef Strelka, ed., *Der Weg war schon das Ziel: Festschrift für Friedrich Torberg zum 70. Geburtstag* (Munich: Langen Müller, 1978); Frank Tichy, *Friedrich Torberg: Ein Leben in Widersprüchen* (Vienna: O. Müller, 1995).

[38] Friedrich Torberg, *Der Schüler Gerber hat absolviert: Roman* (Berlin: P. Zsolnay, 1930).

[39] "Ich halte mich nach wie vor für einen Sozialisten, wenngleich nicht marxistischer Prägun": Torberg to Max Brod, August 17, 1947, in his *In diesem Sinne … Briefe an Freunde und Zeitgenossen* (Munich: Langen-Müller, 1981), p. 72.

[40] Friedrich Torberg, "Wien oder Der Unterschied" [1934], in his *Wien oder Der Unterschied: Ein Lesebuch*, ed. David Axmann and Marietta Torberg (Munich: Langen Müller, 1998), pp. 53–59, and "Was ist des Dichters Vaterland?" [1948], in his *Voreingenommen wie ich bin*, ed. David Axmann and Marietta Torberg (Munich: Langen Müller, 1991), pp. 187–96.

who became a conservative anticommunist, got him on the American PEN list of the "Ten Outstanding German Anti-Nazi Writers." Torberg was lucky and got a U.S. visa quickly.

Arriving in the United States, Torberg worked initially as a Hollywood screenwriter. He wrote the script for a successful 1943 United Artists film, *Voice in the Wind*, and received offers from several film studios. He declined them all: He felt ill at ease in Hollywood and disliked the leftist German émigrés there, including Brecht, Lion Feuchtwanger, and Heinrich Mann. Instead, he deepened his friendship with Catholic Jews, such as Hermann Broch, Bruno Walter, and Werfel. Like most literary exiles, Torberg could not switch to writing solely in English. All three novels written in America – *Mein ist die Rache* (Vengeance is mine), *Hier bin ich, mein Vater* (Here I am, my father), and *Die zweite Begegnung* (The second encounter) – were in German.[41] Expressing his yearning for Austria in a series of poems, "Hebräische Melodien" (Hebrew melodies) – "Longing for Alt Aussee . . . to the gently sloped pastures, . . . the sky, after heavy rain, clear all the way to the Dachstein Glacier" – Torberg was already looking in 1944 for the possibility of returning to Central Europe.[42]

Before having left Europe, Torberg had completed a novel (posthumously published and made into a film) that portrayed an assimilated Viennese Jewish writer and his non-Jewish lover, a theater actress, facing the new realities of racially defined Jewishness in 1937–38 Central Europe, culminating in the Anschluss.[43] In his novels of the 1940s, the Jewish heroes confront the limits of permissible collaboration and resistance to the Nazis. The psychological dramas had what Torberg regarded as an undercurrent of Jewish ethics: May one kill a Nazi camp commander to exact revenge, or escape to save oneself, while putting fellow inmates at risk? May one spy for the Gestapo to save one's father from a concentration camp?[44] The understanding Torberg showed in his novels

---

[41] Friedrich Torberg, *Mein ist die Rache* (Los Angeles: Pazifische Presse, 1943); *Hier bin ich, mein Vater: Roman* (Stockholm: Bermann-Fischer, 1948); and *Die zweite Begegnung: Roman* [1950] (Munich: Langen Müller, 1963).

[42] Friedrich Torberg, *Wien oder Der Unterschied*, pp. 71–87: "Sehnsucht nach Alt Aussee (1942)": "Wo die Triften sanft sich neigten . . . Himmel war nach manchem Regen bis zum Dachsteingletscher klar" (ibid., pp. 72, 71).

[43] *Auch das war Wien* (Munich: Langen Müller, 1984). The film "38 – Auch das war Wien" was nominated for an Oscar (best foreign film) in 1987.

[44] The title *Mein ist die Rache* renders the biblical phrase לי נקם ושלם (Vengeance is mine: Deuteronomy 32:35): God claims the authority and power to extract revenge. Can humans, too, claim this power? asks Torberg. *Hier bin ich, mein Vater* reverses Abraham's response to Isaac הנני בני (Here I am, my son) as the two walk to the mountain where Isaac is about to be sacrificed.

for ethical dilemmas and psychological ambiguity would be wholly absent from his future anticommunist crusade.

Schlamm came to Torberg's rescue again by hiring him to work on a German edition of *Time* (that never came to fruition). Torberg moved to New York in 1944, and his modest Manhattan rooftop apartment, the "penthouse," became a social center for Austrian exiles. A year later, he married Marietta Bellak, a Viennese Jew of slightly greater means than his own.[45] He was turning into a fervent cold warrior during those years. Growing American anxieties about the Soviets reinforced his own fears for the future of Jewish culture under communism. His mother and older sister had died in Auschwitz, but he blamed the Soviets for putting the last nail in Central Europe's coffin, and he was persuaded that they would not stop there. "Mit Prag ist es vorbei" (It's all over with Prague), he wrote his sister Ilse, the single survivor of his close family, in Palestine in January 1946.[46] His Central Europe was dead.

He wanted badly to go back to Vienna all the same. Refusing to return to Central Europe because his family was murdered there, he reasoned, would only mean that Hitler had achieved his goal of eliminating the European Jews.[47] To friends who opposed a Jewish return to Central Europe, he said that he could not live elsewhere. "I neither can nor wish to imagine my life without Austrian theater and newspapers," he wrote to literary historian Fritz Thorn in London.[48] Another friend, Alexander Inngraf of the interwar Café Herrenhof circle, warned him in 1946 that "There is no way back to our Vienna! ... 'Reservations' such as [Café] Herrenhof, Europa, or any other will in all likelihood no longer exist."[49] Torberg would not listen. He completed an anticommunist novel, *Die zweite Begegnung* – a story of love rediscovered, intellectual deception, and political betrayal set in postwar Prague, with the 1948 Communist coup as its climax – and returned to Vienna in 1951, as part of a European lecture tour to promote the book.[50]

He found employment in Vienna as a correspondent with the U.S. Office of Public Affairs and brought back his wife, Marietta. His family and most of his friends were now gone – murdered, in exile, or in Israel – but he could not make a home elsewhere and lived in Vienna to the end of his days. He clung to vestiges of reality that assured him that his "home" was still in Central Europe. He was elated to walk again in the familiar

---

[45] Friedrich Torberg, *Wien oder Der Unterschied*, pp. 71–87.
[46] David Axmann, *Friedrich Torberg*, p. 165.
[47] Torberg to Fritz Thorn, in *Kaffehaus war überall*, ed. David Axmann and Marietta Torberg (Munich: Langen Müller, 1982) p. 165.
[48] *Kaffehaus war überall*, p. 166.   [49] Ibid., p. 130.
[50] Friedrich Torberg, *Die zweite Begegnung*.

sites, visit the cabarets, opera, and theater, and, above all, sit at the Cafe Herrenhof "with the same people as of last time, at the same table, called to the same phone by the same waiter."[51] This illusion of continuity, sustained by a maddening and desperate sense that "only the small pleasures of life remain," was the tenuous link, the hazardous bridge between the Central European past and the Austrian future that made the postwar legend of Central Europe possible.[52]

As "the last of the Mohicans" living among the ruins of a culture, Torberg did not push for reckoning with the past. His reticence was in no way a reflection of Jewish subservience; on the contrary, he was a proud Jew. His generation of Central European Jewish youth had rebelled against their liberal parents, rejecting German assimilation in the name of Jewish ethnicity.[53] Like the Prague and Vienna Zionists, he gave Jewish ethnic difference ethical meaning: Judaism taught a universal ethic. Relationships with non-Jews, he insisted, could only be built on the basis of respect for Jewish difference and recognition of a unique Jewish destiny. But the idea that German and Austrian youth would one day grieve and be outraged at what their parents and grandparents had done to the Jews was beyond his – and his contemporaries' – wildest dreams.

Antisemitism, Torberg thought, was endemic in Central Europe, "a vital course of Austrian life: It belongs to Austria just as naturally as the Jews."[54] Like contemporary Orthodox Jews, he absorbed the Holocaust into Jewish history as a monumental but not unprecedented destruction: "Hitler invented nothing new, especially in regard to the Jews, he only multiplied older innovations and, taking advantage of contemporary racial preconditions, proved more thorough than any predecessor."[55] Torberg had no illusion about his welcome in Vienna: He was, he said, postwar Austria's Jew on Duty (*Jud vom Dienst*), fulfilling a required token presence.[56] Zionism was "the only way Jews could find their place in the world . . . and, without Palestine, we cannot survive. This does not mean that every Jew should go there," and he could not. "One must not

---

[51] Friedrich Torberg to William S. Schlamm, January 18, 1952, Wienbibliothek im Rathaus, *Nachlaß Schlamm*, 235888: "mit denselben Menschen wie zuletzt am selben Tisch und von selben Kellner zum selben Telephon gerufen."

[52] Torberg to Fritz Thorn, July 7, 1947: *Kaffehaus war überall*, p. 169.

[53] "[Wir sind] seinerzeit hauptsächlich deshalb Zionisten geworden, weil die Anweisung unsrer Eltern und verantwortlichen Aufseher, uns auf 'Religionbekenntnis: mosaisch' zu beschränken, uns falsch und feig und unappetitlich und gefährlich vorkam." Torberg to Heinz Politzer, February 12, 1946, in *In diesem Sinne*, p. 295.

[54] Torberg to Weigel, May 12, 1946, in *In diesem Sinne*, p. 413.

[55] Torberg to Fritz Thorn, in *Kaffehaus war überall*, p. 166.

[56] Evelyn Adunka, "Der deutschen Sprache letzter 'Jud vom Dienst,'" p. 143. For Torberg's apprehensions about returning to Vienna, see also his correspondence with *Die Presse* journalist and future editor Milan Dubrovic, in *Kaffehaus war überall*.

be in Palestine but one must be for it."[57] As for life elsewhere, one fought antisemitism but reconciled oneself to living with it.[58]

Outside of the émigrés circle, Torberg's friends, allies, and even protégés often had a checkered past: Some came to admire old Central Europe only after they had become disenchanted with the one the Nazis promised to bring. Torberg had a profound understanding of the subterfuges and rationalization of collaboration, and he judged it contemptible but all too human.[59] Forcing a confrontation with the past would not bring back lost relatives or years in exile, but it could make life as a remigré in Vienna impossible and worse, he reasoned, it could play into the communists' hands and undermine democracy. The acquittal in 1963 of a notorious Nazi war criminal, Franz Murer, commander of the Vilnius ghetto, occasioned a savage critique by Torberg in *Forum*. In it he unmasked with supreme irony Austria's postwar self-image of innocence and *Gemütlichkeit*.[60] But it also confirmed to him that a genuine *Vergangenheitsbewältigung* was beyond the capacity of contemporary Austria. One adjusted to the limits of the new Europe and struggled to avoid new catastrophes, rather than right old ones.

Forum pushed the boundaries of permissible debate about the past, but it was careful not to cross them. Helmut Qualtinger's *Der Herr Karl* – a 1961 theatrical satire, a one-man television performance that created a scandal and heralded a change in the political culture of the republic – received only a brief note in *Forum*.[61] Qualtinger portrayed the average Viennese as an opportunist and a hedonist who collaborated with every occupation force and benefited from every regime, while presenting himself as a victim. An admiring Torberg, a touch envious and perplexed, defended Qualtinger against the charge of historical distortion by

---

[57] Torberg to Heinz Politzer, in *In diesem Sinne*, p. 302.

[58] Evelyn Adunka, "Friedrich Torberg und Hans Weigel – Zwei jüdische Schriftsteller im Nachkriegsösterreich," *Modern Austrian Literature* 27 (1994): 213–37, and "Der deutschen Sprache letzter 'Jud vom Dienst': Friedrich Torberg und sein Judentum," in *Die "Gefahren der Vielseitigkeit,"* pp. 143–62; David Axmann, *Friedrich Torberg*, pp. 185–89; Marcus G. Patka, "'Ich möchte am liebsten in Jerusalem begraben sein': Der Zionist Friedrich Torberg," in *Die "Gefahren der Vielseitigkeit,"* pp. 163–79.

[59] "One of the unwritten human rights is the right to cowardice and conformism." Torberg, "Internal and External Emigration: An Imaginary Dialogue" [1947], trans. Scott Denham, *New England Review* 20:4 (1999): 38–56. Quotation is on p. 53. *Hier bin ich, mein Vater* likewise shows subtle understanding of the psychology of collaboration.

[60] Friedrich Torberg, "Motivenbericht zu einem Freispruch," *Forum* 10 (June 1963): 321.

[61] Helmut Qualtinger, *Der Herr Karl und andere Texte fürs Theater* (Vienna: Deuticke, 1995), pp. 163–87. (Carl Merz coauthored the televised satire, *Der Herr Karl*.) Friedrich Torberg, "Der Herr Qualtinger," *Forum* 8 (December 1961): 456. Torberg's critique of Qualtinger's rendering of Karl Kraus nicely captures their generational differences: "Ist Karl Kraus vorlesbar? Helmut Qualtinger und 'Die letzten Tage der Menschheit,'" *Forum* 10 (May 1963): 301.

reminding readers, disingenuously, I think, that satires do not draw realistic pictures: Herr Karl, Torberg assured readers, tongue in cheek, had never existed. *Forum* thrived on periodically attacking Freedom Party activists as Nazis and getting its edition seized by the court. In the early 1960s, it became progressively bolder in querying Austria's past, calling for a review of the records of currently serving judges under the Nazis, but it trailed, not led, the young in demanding that the past be revisited.[62]

Indeed, Torberg, *Forum*, and the remigrés may have contributed to the founding myth of the Second Republic by inventing "Austrian literature."[63] They circumscribed an Austrian cultural sphere in Central Europe, distinguished from that of Germany, and made it possible for the small nation-state to claim the legacy of the multinational empire. Austria's postwar leaders were determined to detach Austria from Germany, and they contrasted nationalist Prussia with cosmopolitan Austria, but they did not quite know how to make the empire's legacy have a bearing on the Second Republic. Postwar school textbooks, literary histories, museum exhibitions, and debates on "Austrian culture" all suggest that Austrians encountered major difficulties in forming a national historical narrative.[64] Austrians remembered both the Dual Monarchy and the First Republic as failures, and considered Austro-German nationalism the chief culprit. The First Republic failed to negotiate the transition from empire to nation-state, and Austrians now lived with this failure's result – a disgraced nation-state, purged of its Jews. An Iron Curtain now divided the space previously occupied by Austria-Hungary. What were Austrians to do with the imperial past?

The Socialists made short shrift of the monarchy and reaffirmed their hostility to the "reactionary" Habsburgs. In 1945, communist Viktor Matejka stated the need for a new Austria, for which no model existed in the past.[65] The Socialists took this statement literally and remained with an impoverished past, divested of any national narrative going back

---

[62] Marcel Atze, "'Einen, der Unfaßbares verübt, kann man nicht fassen': Friedrich Torberg und die justizielle Aufarbeitung nationalsozialistischer Gewaltbrechen," in *Die "Gefahren der Vielseitigkeit,"* pp. 181–99; Sigurd Paul Scheichl, "Why and How Friedrich Torberg's *Forum* Did Not Confront the Past," *New German Critique* 93 (2004): 87–102.

[63] For a brief overview of the debate on "Austrian literature," see Katrin Kohl and Ritchie Robertson, "Introduction," in *A History of Austrian Literature 1918–2000*, pp. 1–20. For a recent synthesis: Herbert Zeman, ed., *Literaturgeschichte Österreichs von den Anfängen im Mittelalter bis zur Gegenwart* (Graz: Akademische Druck- u. Verlaganstalt, 1996), pp. 377–563.

[64] Douglas Patrick Campbell, "The Shadow of the Habsburgs: Memory and National Identity in Austrian Politics and Education, 1918–1955" (Ph.D. diss., University of Maryland, 2006); Wolfgang Kos, *Eigenheim Österreich: Zu Politik, Kultur und Alltag nach 1945* (Vienna: Sonderzahl, 1994).

[65] Viktor Matejka, *Was ist österreichische Kultur?* (Vienna: Selbstverlag des Verfassers, 1945).

past 1918. They referred obliquely to 1848 and to a Europe of democratic nations, occasionally also to the Socialist International (now denuded of Marxism), but unless they were telling the history of Austrian socialism, their Austria began with the republic and Red Vienna. Their postwar motifs, reconstruction (*Wiederaufbau*), modernization, and a democratic constitution, provided for a flimsy Austrian identity. World War II thoroughly discredited the idea of a socialist German Central Europe, the only option that the Socialists had seriously entertained once the monarchy had collapsed. Short on historical resources, the Socialists had nowhere to go in their search for Austrian identity.

The conservatives, in contrast, repeatedly referred to Austria's imperial past, but their rhetoric was vacuous, incapable of forging a relationship between past and present. In conservative discourse, supranationalism and Catholic cosmopolitanism somehow formed a benevolent Austrian national character, but the references to the baroque and, less frequently, to imperial pluralism remained oblique. Austrians' relationship to the empire in the 1950s was superficial: Films like *Sissi*, on Empress Elizabeth, and music festivals were emblematic. Asked about the monarchy's significance in his intellectual formation as a youth, future Vice Chancellor Erhard Busek (b. 1941), who in the mid-1980s revived the idea of *Mitteleuropa*, responded: "None."[66]

More tangibly, conservative discourse reflected the Ständestaat vision of Catholic German Austria. In the interwar years, both German-Catholic nationalists and Jewish-Catholic modernists, such as Hugo von Hofmannsthal, Max Reinhardt, and Franz Werfel, articulated this vision. The modernists merged imperial baroque and pluralist traditions. In the postwar years, most Catholic Jews were gone and with them much of the experimentation. Ernst Lothar (1890–1974), former director of the Josefstadt Theater, did direct the Burg Theater and Salzburg Festival, and, assisted by a younger remigré, Ernst Hauesserman (1916–1984), he sought to amplify Hofmannsthal's vision. But this vision was now implicated in the Ständestaat and could provide no guide for a modern nation-state. The Ständestaat's leading intellectuals, including those blemished with National Socialism, reemerged in the 1950s, speaking the language of German humanism and Austrian cosmopolitanism. Their difficulties in speaking to contemporary Austrian identity were palpable.[67]

---

[66] Busek spoke in a seminar on postwar Europe and Austrian memory at Duke University, February 2009.

[67] Friedbert Aspetsberger, Norbert Frei, and Huber Lengauer, eds., *Literatur der Nachkriegszeit*; Katrin Kohl and Ritchie Robertson, *A History of Austrian Literature 1918–2000*, pp. 107–26, 163–80; Hanni Mittelmann and Armin A. Wallas, eds.,

Pietas Austriaca, a landmark historical work on baroque Catholic piety as a mode of Habsburg political legitimation, published in 1959, captured the drift of postwar conservative imperial attachment.[68] Author Anna Coreth highlighted public piety as the Habsburg dynasty's foremost attribute and depicted its loss in the *Aufklärung*, under Joseph II and his successors. Many conservatives wished to skip over the multinational past to prenational, preenlightenment, Counter-Reformation Austria, when the Habsburgs faced the Ottomans to the east and looked west and south, to Spain and Rome, for political support and intellectual inspiration. The early modern empire dovetailed with postwar Austria. The Hungarians and the Slavic nationalities having all been lost to the communists, Austria was again the bulwark of the "Christian West," *das Abendland*, against the heathens. This Austria had affinities with visions of Europe common among reactionary Catholic intellectuals elsewhere, rather than with mainstream Christian Democracy.

There was very limited space for Jews, or the émigrés, in the Christian West. *Forum* and the émigrés' reshaping of the Austrian imperial heritage must be understood against this background. They shifted the focus on the empire from the baroque to multinational Central Europe, and they foregrounded the German-Jewish writers as quintessentially Austrian. Already in their wartime exile, Austrian émigrés began conceptualizing a literary tradition setting Austria apart from National Socialism. *Forum* expanded their vision in the postwar years, joining Hermann Broch, Franz Kafka, Karl Kraus, Joseph Roth, Arthur Schnitzler, Franz Werfel, and Stefan Zweig to Hofmannsthal, Robert Musil, Rainer Maria Rilke, and Georg Trakl in shaping an Austrian literary sphere in Central Europe, the centers of which were Vienna and Prague but extending all the way to Galicia. The émigrés anchored the twentieth-century Jewish writers in classical nineteenth-century Austrian authors, including Franz Grillparzer, Johann Nestroy, and Adalbert Stifter, and *Forum* joined them to twentieth-century ethno-cultural hybrids, like Fritz von Herzmanovsky-Orlando and Lernet-Holenia, who embodied the old cosmopolitan aristocracy. Their Austrian Central Europe was German speaking yet multiethnic; its foremost representatives were cosmopolitan Jewish writers. As visions of the Christian West declined in the early 1960s, the émigrés' Central Europe remained

---

Österreich-Konzeptionen und jüdisches Selbstverständnis: Identitäts-Transfigurationen im 19. und 20. Jahrhundert (Tübingen: Max Niemeyer Verlag, 2001), esp. pp. 263–72.

[68] Anna Coreth, *Pietas Austriaca: Ursprung und Entwicklung barocker Frömmigkeit in Österreich* (Vienna: Verlag für Geschichte und Politick, 1959).

the single imagined past that could successfully claim the imperial legacy for the Second Republic.[69]

Forum also wove fin-de-siècle Viennese modernism into Central European culture. This was a progressive move for an aesthetically conservative magazine. Mainstream postwar culture treated Freud and modernism with suspicion, and they remained marginal.[70] By contrast, *Forum* highlighted them. The Vienna of Carl Schorske and "Traum und Wiklichkeit," featuring modernist architecture (Adolf Loos), music (Arnold Schönberg), and painting (Gustav Klimt, Oskar Kokoschka, and Egon Schiele), made its first appearance on *Forum*'s pages.[71] As *Forum*'s editors, a remnant of the old Central European intelligentsia, were looking backward, they forged a bond between the golden past, now irretrievably lost, and the uncanny reality of postwar Austria: That bond was the melancholic memories of a benevolent empire, multiethnic Central Europe, and a vibrant Viennese culture. Paradoxically, they created a blueprint for Austrian national identity that was most compatible with a postnational Europe.

Initially marginal, *Forum*'s view of Austria's Central European past became hegemonic in the 1980s. Along the way, it integrated a number of competing narratives. In 1946, Franz Theodor Csokor completed his European trilogy, outlining the shattering of the empire and the old European world but finding hope for the future in the antifascist resistance he witnessed as an exile in Yugoslavia.[72] The novels of Heimito von Doderer and Lernet-Holenia built a bridge to imperial Austria and interwar Vienna, elliptically addressing the issue of Austrian culpability in

---

[69] Anne-Marie Corbin, "Die österreichische Identität in Friedrich Torbergs *Forum*," *Österreich in Geschichte und Literatur* 46:1 (2002): 2–16; Wolfgang Muchitsch, "The Cultural Policy of Austrian Refugee Organizations in Great Britain," *Austrian Studies 7* (1995): 22–40; Hilde Spiel, ed., *Die zeitgenössische Literatur Österreichs* (Zurich/Munich: Kindler, 1976), and *Vienna's Golden Autumn 1866–1938* (New York: Weidenfeld and Nicolson, 1987); Friedrich Torberg, "Austrian Literature Since 1927," *Books Abroad* 28 (1954): 15–20, and *Wien oder Der Unterschied*, pp. 127–75; Hans Weigel, *Flucht vor der Grösse: Beiträge zur Erkenntnis und Selbsterkenntnis Österreichs* (Vienna: Wollzeilen Verlag, 1960).

[70] Lutz Musner, "Ist Wien anders?" esp. pp. 743–45. Sculptor Fritz Wotruba's Galerie Würthle was the single art gallery to consistently exhibit modernist works in the 1950s: *Gustav Klimt bis Paul Klee: Wotruba und die Moderne*, ed. Klaus Albrecht Schröder and Antonia Hoerschelmann (Vienna: Edition Minerva, 2003).

[71] Carl Schorske, *Fin-de-Siècle Vienna: Politics and Culture* (New York: Vintage, 1980); *Traum und Wirklichkeit: Wien 1870–1930*, Kataloggestaltung und Plakatserie Tino Erben, preface by Robert Waissenberger (Vienna: Eigenverlag der Museen der Stadt Wien, 1985), exhibition catalog, Historisches Museum der Stadt Wien.

[72] Franz Theodor Csokor, *Europäische Trilogie: Erstes Stück, 3. November 1918; zweites Stück, Besetztes Gebiet; drittes Stück, Der verlorene Sohn* (Vienna: P. Zsolnay, 1952).

National Socialism.[73] Speaking of "Anschluss an die Tiefe der Zeiten" (Joining in the depth of time), Doderer tied together baroque and multinationalism and argued that Austrian culture and national identity were cosmopolitan because they had absorbed multicultural influences.[74] Younger writers, influenced by both Doderer and the émigrés, proposed their own versions.[75] Austria's leading communist intellectual, Ernst Fischer, an early proponent of Austrian nationality, formed a view of Austrian literature similar to that of *Forum*.[76] The émigrés' version was singularly successful in that it tied together Austria and Central Europe through living individuals. Contemporaries could still witness the survivors of interwar transnational networks among them.

The émigrés' "Central Europe" was a permeable and expandable *Literaturraum*, enabling Austrians to belong without violating national borders. It reached wherever Austrians found their legacy – to Brody with Joseph Roth, or to Czernowitz with Paul Celan. Even the Jewish *shtetl* and Holocaust poetry became "Austrian." The new Austrian identity emulated the old proposals of extraterritorial nationality advanced by

[73] Heimito von Doderer, *Die Strudlhofstiege; oder, Melzer und die Tiefe der Jahre: Roman* (Vienna: Luckmann, 1951), and *Die Dämonen: Roman* (Munich: Biederstein, 1956); Alexander Lernet-Holenia, *Der Graf von Saint-Germain* (Zurich: Morgarten Verlag [Conzett & Huber], 1948), and *Der Graf Luna: Roman* (Vienna: P. Zsolnay, 1955); Robert Dassanowsky, *Phantom Empires: The Novels of Alexander Lernet-Holenia and the Question of Postimperial Austrian Identity* (Riverside, CA: Ariadne Press, 1996). Lernet-Holenia confronted Austrian guilt with greater forthrightness; Doderer assiduously avoided the Nazi period, never going in *Die Dämonen* past 1927. Hélène Barrière, Thomas Eicher, Manfred Müller, eds., *Schuld-Komplexe: Das Werk Alexander Lernet-Holenias im Nachkriegskontext* (Oberhausen: Athena, 2004); Wolfgang Fleischer, *Das verleugnete Leben: Die Biographie des Heimito von Doderer* (Vienna: Kremayr & Scheriau, 1996).

[74] Heimito von Doderer, "Österreichs national Bewußtsein ist übernational," *Die kleine Zeitung* (20 June 1964); reprinted as " Athenerrede: Von der Wiederkehr Österreichs," in his *Die Wiederkehr der Drachen*, ed. Wendelin Schmidt-Dengler (Munich: Biderstein Verlag, 1970), pp. 239–47. The 1954 unpublished lecture's title was "Der Anschluß ist vollzogen" (The Anschluss is completed, Doderer substituting an attachment to Austrian history for German unification). To Doderer, with the empire's downfall, German Austrian culture, which had absorbed multinational influences, was fortunately permitted national development, or else it would have dissolved. For the émigrés, Austrian identity and culture remained multinational and multicultural. See Andrew Barker, "Tiefe der Zeit, Untiefen der Jahre: Heimito von Doderers 'österreichische Idee' und die 'Athener Rede,'" in *"Excentrische Einsätze,"* ed. Kai Luehrs (Berlin: Walter de Gruyter, 1998), pp. 263–72.

[75] Otto Basil, Herbert Eisenrech, and Ivar Ivask, *Die Grosse Erbe: Aufsätze zur österreichischen Literatur* (Graz: Stiasny-Verlag, 1962). These and other writers are discussed in David Luft, "Cultural Memory and Intellectual History: Locating Austrian Culture," *Studies in Twentieth and Twenty-First Century Literature* 31:1 (2007): 30–51.

[76] Ernst Fischer, *Von Grillparzer zu Kafka* (Vienna: Globus Verlag, 1962); Jürgen Egyptien, "Die unvollendete Symphonie: Das Konzept einer *österreichischen* Identität und nationalen Souveränität in den Schriften von Ernst Fischer," in *Österreich-Konzeptionen und jüdisches Selbstverständnis*, pp. 249–62.

Adolf Fischhof and Otto Bauer to solve the Habsburg Empire's nationality problem (only now, Jewish ethnicity became a surrogate for Austrian nationality). It reflected less Austrian cultural imperialism, or, to use Robert Menasse's terms, *Verösterreicherung der Welt* (turning the world Austrian), and more a postnational search for cultural heritage. Without ever intending such a feat, the émigrés brought together Central Europe's imperial past and its future. Constructing an Austrian national narrative, the émigrés turned the eternal outsiders, the Jewish intelligentsia, into the embodiment of Europe's postnational future.[77]

Neues Forum, 1968, and the Central European Jewish Intelligentsia

In December 1964, when *Forum* ran into financial difficulties, the City of Vienna stepped in to save it.[78] *Forum* had become a cultural asset that Vienna, aspiring to be once again a cultural metropolis (*Weltstadt*), did not wish to give up. The Socialists, who controlled the city administration, were beginning to make their peace with the Habsburg legacy, but only halfheartedly. The imperial past crept into *Weltstadt Wien*: Tourism drew on Vienna's imperial legacy, and the city cultivated its image as a *Musikhauptstadt* (capital of music) in the annual *Wiener Festwochen*. Still, the Socialists' heart was in projects of modern architecture and mass transportation, casting the image of a young, masculine, progressive city, modern to the tooth – *neue Menschen* without Marxism. Red Vienna, a mecca to the socialist world, and not imperial Vienna, inspired

---

[77] My account of Austrian literature offers an alternative to Robert Menasse's "Die sozialpartnerschaftliche Ästhetik: Das Österreichische an der österreichischen Literatur der Zweiten Republik," in his *Die sozialpartnerschaftliche Ästhetik* (Vienna: Sonderzahl, 1996), pp. 13–124. We agree on the centrality of Austrian literature to national identity, but we diverge on its significance. I see the émigrés as contesting alternative visions and opening up Austria to Europe; Menasse sees them as reifying the domestic order. He overlooks the postwar order's fragility, fissures, and international setting and exaggerates its integrative force. This reflects generational experience. Menasse (b. 1954) came of age as the postwar order thwarted the 68ers and celebrated Austria as an "island of the blessed." Marcuse's "repressive tolerance" and Hans-Ulrich Wehler's "negative integration" explained consensus formation in capitalist democracies and shaped his analysis. Yet the *Sozialpartnerschaft* was never as secure as Menasse assumes; Austrian identity was fragile, and the theories are no longer accepted. All the same, Menasse remains a crucial reading.

[78] Deputy Mayor Hans Mandl (1899–1970), a Revolutionary Socialist in the 1930s, and Vienna's cultural tsar in the postwar years, made the decision to take over *Forum*. Torberg to Josselson, December 4, 1964, *Nachlaß Torberg* 1:1. Beginning in 1962, the Hans Deutsch Verlag, privately owned, was the publisher of *Forum*, but the congress continued to support the magazine financially for two years. When the Deutsch Verlag collapsed at the end of 1964, the city took over. The congress continued to pay Torberg a small subsidy until he retired at the end of 1965.

socialist efforts to make the capital a metropolis. Not until the 1980s, under Mayor Helmut Zilk, did the Socialists come to view Vienna as a *Kulturhauptstadt Mitteleuropas*, inheritor of the imperial legacy. Many Socialists remained skeptical even after that. The Habsburg's legacy has never become a socialist thing.

Two mid-1960s book portrayals of Vienna capture the cultural gap between *Forum*'s old editors and new owners.[79] *Wien: Vorstadt Europas* (Vienna: Europe's suburb) was a beautifully photographed coffee-table book that featured pictorial essays accompanied by narratives, authored by Doderer, Herbert Eisenreich, Lernet-Holenia, Qualtinger, Torberg, and Hans Weigl. The essays highlighted Vienna's imperial past, the Wurstelprater, the café, public pomp and fashion, theater, opera and concerts, and the suburbs. The book was replete with satire, irony, and melancholy, with loving attentiveness to Vienna's provincialism and nostalgia for its past; the Nazi period was passed over in silence. The authors were conscious of the ways in which the past lives in Vienna, but also of its distance. In contrast, *Wiedergeburt einer Weltstadt: Wien, 1945–1965* (Rebirth of a metropolis: Vienna, 1945–1965) was a socialist celebration of two decades of postwar achievement. It consisted of twenty-five articles by socialist academics and politicians on the welfare system, education and youth, public housing, transportation, parks and sports, science and the humanities, theater, film, literature, music and art, and radio and television. There were few references to pre-1945 Vienna; the *Jahre Null* (year zero) and *Wiederaufbau* clichés prevailed; and optimism, pride, and confidence in the future abounded. *Vorstadt Europas* versus *Weltstadt*, old resigned cosmopolitanism, rich in history (however selective) but without hope for the future, confronted new socialist internationalism, poor in history but projecting a modern social-democratic metropolis.

Yet the two cultures – émigré and socialist – coexisted peacefully in postwar Austria and even coalesced. *Forum* was the proof. In the mid-1960s, the two cultures were getting closer: Kreisky, who belonged in both, emerged as the Socialist leader, and Nenning, a mediator between the two, as the editor of *Neues Forum*. Socialists of Mandl's ilk – an all-Austrian 1930s Revolutionary Socialist turned pragmatist in the postwar years – had little interest in Central European cosmopolitanism, but *Forum* represented a resolution of their ambivalence about the imperial past: a classy Western international magazine, anchored in Habsburg

---

[79] *Wien: Vorstadt Europas*, photos by Franz Hubmann, texts by Alexander Lernet-Holenia et al. (Zurich: Artemis, 1963); *Wiedergeburt einer Weltstadt: Wien, 1945–1965*, ed. Karl Ziak (Vienna: Verlag für Jugend und Volk, 1965).

Central Europe. They were pleased to make *Forum* part of their Weltstadt.

For all of its growing cachet, émigré culture still had a limited reach in the 1960s. The Austrian remigrés cultivated younger writers, like Ingeborg Bachmann (Weigl) and Herbert Eisenreich (Torberg), but they were few. Authors associated with the *Wiener Gruppe* wrote in conscious opposition to the old intelligentsia. The younger writers of Graz's *Forum Stadtpark* (Wolfgang Bauer, Peter Handke, Elfriede Jelinek, and Alfred Kolleritsch) established an avant-garde journal, *manuskripte*, that advanced an alternative Austrian literature. They found intellectual support, and a publisher, in Germany. There, too, however, and throughout Europe, no way was found to bridge the divergent experiences and cultural styles of the émigrés and the postwar generation. Émigré culture was becoming mainstream European, and the CCF magazines were its agents. But Austrian literature and Viennese modernism had barely begun to leave their mark on the mainstream when they became, for the 68ers, "establishment culture."

Revelations about the CIA funding of the CCF contributed to the appearance of the émigrés as "the establishment." Torberg dismissed the scandal as a joke.[80] He may have guessed for a long time that *Forum* was U.S. government funded, but he could not have cared less. The CCF enabled him to put together the magazine he wanted. Yet Torberg exemplified the CCF's problems in the 1960s. Having won the cultural Cold War, Congress officials were aware that they had to reinvent themselves by addressing Third World problems. But Torberg had no interest in a new agenda. He withdrew into his literary work, which he regarded as a testament of Jewish Central Europe, and left *Forum*'s editorial board to Nenning and younger writers who had joined in the early 1960s. Recent trends in Viennese culture began showing up in *Forum*, and the magazine followed new European political movements with sympathy.[81] *Forum* was now more popular than ever, but Torberg did not care for it: "[T]he

---

[80] Torberg to Josselson, November 17, 1966, *Nachlaß Torberg* 17:13: "[T]he New York Times discovered that we all have been spying for the CIA." Nenning was just as dismissive. *Neues Forum* 14 (March 1967): 256 included a mocking telegram, ostensibly sent to the *Die Presse* correspondent, who had reported that *Forum* received CIA funds until 1961: "CIA money has never arrived here. Please expedite at the CIA." Gerald Stourzh drew my attention to this "telegram."

[81] *Forum*'s horizons were still limited: The magazine reacted with silence to the U.S. Civil Rights movement, which was formative for the 68ers. Even Torberg complained that Nenning was emphasizing Austrian at the expense of international politics: Torberg to François Bondy, November 22, 1965, *Nachlaß Torberg* 37:F; Torberg to Josselson, December 2, 1965, IACF II, 111:1.

direction [of] the magazine," he said, "is not my own."[82] He retired at the end of 1965.

Apprehensive about what was coming, Torberg insisted that the magazine change its name. *Neues Forum* was the result, and it quickly acquired a new identity. Nenning began by focusing on the Christian–Marxist dialogue, and expanding the editorial committee and writer pool to both the right and the left. He established an international consultation board that included such well-known leftist émigrés as Ernst Bloch, Erich Fromm, Lucien Goldmann, and Eric Hobsbawm.[83] The events of 1968 caught Nenning by surprise, like everyone else, but he was quick to adjust, siding with the socialist students against the party leadership and turning *Neues Forum* into the Austrian New Left's organ. Lernet-Holenia walked out, together with the conservatives whom Nenning had brought in for the Christian–Marxist dialogue, including the ÖVP youth leader and future vice chancellor, Erhard Busek. *Neues Forum* acquired a distinctly leftist profile, but its range of writers still extended from the Catholic Left – historians Friedrich Heer, Kurt Skalnik, and Erika Weinzierl – to the former communist elder, turned dissident, Ernst Fischer. *Neues Forum* became a site for collaboration between the leftist émigrés and the 68ers.

Such collaboration was difficult, even in Austria, where political unrest remained contained. Youth protests began in Austria with the antinuclear Easter marches and the 1965 demonstrations against a Nazi-sympathizer professor, Taras Borodajkewicz. The demonstrations claimed the life of a participant, Ernst Kirchweger, who was struck by a neo-Nazi, the single death in the protest movement's history. Eighteen thousand came to his burial on April 6, 1965, by far the largest event of the protest years. Demonstrations against the U.S. war in Vietnam began in March 1966, and demonstrations against the Greek and Iranian dictatorships followed over the next two years. The students made increasing efforts to radicalize the Socialist Party and held teach-ins on Vietnam, Marxism, and capitalism. The *Kommune Wien*, a student group advocating social revolution and sexual liberation, began staging public protests in October 1967. Most demonstrations drew hundreds, not thousands. The challenge mounted by the Austrian New Left was modest: This much was evident from the start.[84]

---

[82] Torberg to François Bondy, November 22, 1965, *Nachlaß Torberg* 37:F. Nenning's 1979 obituary for Torberg put the best face on the split: *FORVM*, p. 206. But the transition was tense: Torberg to Nenning, July 4, 1965, *Nachlaß Torberg* 18:2.

[83] Paulus Ebner and Karl Vocelka, *Die Zahme Revolution*, pp. 100–103.

[84] Fritz Keller, *Wien, Mai 68: Eine heiße Viertelstunde* [1983] (Vienna: Mandelbaum Verlag, 2008), pp. 50–108; Paulus Ebner and Karl Vocelka, *Die Zahme Revolution*, pp. 59–74.

All the same, 1968 in Austria was part of a broader European scene, and CCF intellectuals found the students alarmingly utopian. The presumption that seemed to underlie student solidarity with Vietnam, and with the anticolonial and Civil Rights struggles, was that but for American imperialism, a decent global society was at hand. Military defense against communism seemed dispensable, and the U.S. influence in Europe appeared pernicious. The antiwar demonstration of February 13, 1968, took place in front of the Vienna Amerika Haus, symbol of the transatlantic exchange that CCF had built. The students' resort to direct action, dispensing with institutional channels, seemed especially unnerving. At Vienna University, academic disruptions became frequent. Germany provided examples of just how violent demonstrations could turn. To many émigrés, the student action recalled interwar communist subversion and Nazi student conduct, which had undermined the Weimar Republic. Romantic regression, charged Richard Löwenthal.[85] Reliving their youthful traumas, anticommunist émigrés feared that they were witnessing an interwar replay, the past returning to haunt the postwar order that they had helped shape.

Leftist émigrés viewed Weimar and the Cold War's problems as rooted more in capitalism than in illiberalism, and this sometimes made it easier to talk to the 68ers. Anders and Marcuse discovered in the students the radical agents whom they had almost despaired of finding in late capitalism. The 68ers' exploration of heterodox Marxism, which seemed a misguided déjà vu to liberals, was for the leftist émigrés a continuation of their own lifework. Critical theorists Adorno, Ossip Flechtheim, Fromm, Leo Kofler, and Marcuse, as well as antinuclear activists Anders and Jungk, participated in the Vienna teach-ins on Vietnam, Marxism, and sexual liberation. Such 58ers as Iring Fetscher and Hans Mommsen led teach-ins on Max Adler, Bauer, and the Austro-Marxists.[86] Intergenerational dialogue did take place on the left.

The dialogue was sometimes tense, full of misunderstandings, and did not include everyone. The cold warriors, no matter how strong their socialist credentials, were out. Adorno and Max Horkheimer, of the older Frankfurt School, were occasionally subject to student parody. Marcuse permitted love-ins and communes to invoke his vision of erotic liberation, but was not familiar with student life. Arendt's initial declaration of solidarity with Cohn-Bendit gave way to a more critical analysis in *On Violence*.[87] Conversely, the distance between the émigrés and the

---

[85] Richard Lowenthal, *Der romantische Rückfall* (Stuttgart: W. Kohlhammer, 1970). He was responding primarily to the German students.
[86] Fritz Keller, *Wien, Mai 68*, pp. 110–12, 227–38.
[87] Hannah Arendt, *On Violence* (New York: Harcourt, Brace, Jovanovich, 1970).

68ers became clear when the 68ers began writing émigré biographies in the 1970s, as part of *Exilforschung*. Hilde Spiel felt that the 68ers featured the émigrés to complete a political project in which she had no part, her own exile experience failing to come through.[88] The political horizons of the émigrés and 68ers never converged.

Neues Forum's success in building bridges between the émigrés and the 68ers was largely due to Nenning's political acumen. To his critics, Nenning was the Second Republic's great chameleon, or, more charitably, he was postwar culture's bellwether. Quickly grasping rising trends, he would periodically reposition himself on the political scene with fanfare, wit, insight – and blindness. Son of a Lower Austrian Pan-German politician, Nenning served in the German *Wehrmacht* during World War II. In the 1950s, having earned two doctorates, he rose quickly in socialist journalism to become, in 1960, the head of the Austrian journalists' union. A Protestant at birth, he converted to Catholicism in 1965. As *Neues Forum*'s editor, he turned into a colorful New Left intellectual, declaring himself a feminist, fighting censorship laws by publishing the Marquis de Sade, founding an Austrian–Cuban friendship society, leading antiwar demonstrations, and advocating abolition of the Austrian military. Beginning in the early 1970s, he had a regular column in the popular magazine *Profil*, and from the early 1980s on, he was a talk-show host on Austrian TV. In the late 1970s, he took an ecological turn, fighting the nuclear plant in Zwentendorf (1978) and the Danube power plant in Hainburg (1984). He was a founding father of the Austrian Greens. In the early 1990s, he opposed Austria's joining the European Union. In his final years, he became a *Kronen-Zeitung* journalist, a populist monarchist singing the church's praises.[89] "Red-Green-light Black," Nenning described his politics late in life, encompassing a life trajectory that covered almost the entire political spectrum.

Nenning's capacity to identify with conflicting positions and hold the rope on both sides was valuable to *Neues Forum* and the Austrian New Left.[90] The magazine represented every political cause and cultural trend on the left in the late 1960s and 1970s, from neo-Marxism to anticolonialism to feminism to sexual liberation to disarmament and ecology. The surprise was that it represented them all. The Austrian

---

[88] Birgit Lang, "Ein Aufenthalt der Dauer: Walter A. Berendsohn und Exilforschung," *Leipziger Beiträge zur jüdischen Geschichte und Kultur* 3 (2005): 61–79.

[89] Nenning regarded a multivolume anthology of postwar Austrian literature, which he edited, as his major testament. It became, like everything he did, controversial: Günther Nenning and Milo Dor, eds., *Landvermessung*, 21 vols. (St. Pölten: Residenz, 2005).

[90] In 1970, Nenning turned *Neues Forum* into an editorial cooperative, but he retained actual control.

New Left was just as fragmented as its counterpart elsewhere, a small Marxist-Leninist student group splintering into Trotskyites and Maoists, the feminists establishing in 1972 their own organization (AUF), and diverse cultural trends represented by competing organizations. But no group or magazine matched *Neues Forum*'s resources, audience – at its height an edition of thirty thousand – and prestige. Print culture gave the Austrian New Left a semblance of unity. Uniquely, the Austrian New Left is primarily identified with a magazine: *Neues Forum*.

The impressive gallery of authors included both Austrian artists and writers and international intellectuals, from H. C. Artmann, Bachmann, Thomas Bernhard, Fischer, Handke, Alfred Hrdlička, Jelinek, and Qualtinger, to Adorno, Karl Barth, Simone de Beauvoir, Bloch, Elias Canetti, Celan, Rudi Dutschke, Eisler, Antonio Gramsci, Habermas, Václav Havel, Horkheimer, Leszek Kolakowski, Karl Korsch, Norman Mailer, Marcuse, Claude Levi-Strauss and Jean-Paul Sartre. Curiously, while it shifted the focus from the anticommunist émigrés of the old *Forum* to the leftist émigrés, it continued to open up Austrian culture to new domestic and international perspectives. And just as the old communist *Tagebuch* paralleled *Forum* on the left, so did the new *Wiener Tagebuch*, edited beginning in 1969 by communist dissenter Franz Marek, parallel *Neues Forum*. Only now, *Wiener Tagebuch* authors were also writing for *Neues Forum*, signaling the end of Cold War culture in Austria.

The limits of the Austrian 1968 – *eine heisse Viertelstunde* (a hot quarter of an hour), Fritz Keller calls it – made it easier for *Neues Forum* to establish its preeminence. Events in Berlin, Paris, and Milan reverberated in Vienna, but the radical students were no match for the establishment: a powerful and unsympathetic Socialist Party, a conservative university, hostile government and police, and a conservative culture still enjoying a broad national consensus. In the spring of 1968, the socialist students tried to forge a front with the workers at the Elin locomotive factory near Vienna, who faced plant closure. Their effort met with Socialist Party opposition, firm police action, and indifferent workers, and it came to naught. Disruptions of the May 1 celebration triggered a harsh police and Socialist Party response. The collaboration between the socialist students and the Viennese avant-garde was shattered by the scandalous *Aktionist* performance (which included defecating on the lectern) at the "Art and Revolution" teach-in of June 7 at the university. The authorities used an anti-Nazi censorship law to send several performers to prison. The event undermined the efforts to persuade the socialist student organization (VSStÖ) to split with the party and move toward extraparliamentary opposition, on the German APO model. Austria was not ready for a French, German, or Italian 1968.[91]

In the January 1969 student elections, the Left – the VSStÖ, the Aktion group (lodged in the Vienna Philosophy Faculty) and the communists – polled just about a fifth of the votes. The brutal end of the Prague Spring in August 1968 had exhausted attractive European models of communism, and the Chinese Cultural Revolution took center stage at the 1969 teach-ins. The Maoist turn reflected growing dogmatism and detachment from reality across the radical Left, and deepened the chasm with the émigrés. The U.S. invasion of Cambodia in 1970 triggered, over the next two years, larger demonstrations (five thousand strong) than those against the Vietnam War previously. But the hard-core radicals despaired of political action and withdrew into small and doctrinaire *Basis Gruppe* to prepare for a future revolutionary conjuncture.

The VSStÖ was under Socialist Party pressure to coordinate its policy. Kreisky had been trying repeatedly, but unsuccessfully, to lure the radicals into the party. In the spring of 1971, with the Socialists already heading a minority government, the party engineered a change of guard in the VSStÖ Viennese leadership. The April VSStÖ meeting, boycotted by the radicals, returned a majority friendly to the party. In the October 1971 elections, the Socialists won a majority. Kreisky, a former Revolutionary Socialist and Jewish remigré, was now the unchallenged head of a Socialist government. As for the 68ers, they began the long march through the institutions, on the party's terms.

The postwar Austrian order was waning, but no one took notice: Austria settled down for a long, prosperous thirteen years of Socialist hegemony. While Germany was beset by terrorism, ideological warfare, and economic difficulties, Austria was acclaimed as "the island of the blessed."[92] In the early 1970s, Kreisky passed limited educational and military reforms, but nothing on the order of German university reform. The New Left no longer had political clout, but the 68ers' culture was expanding, dovetailing with postindustrial values and styles. Experiments

---

[91] Siegfried Mattl, "Art & Revolution in the Austrian 1968," paper presented in a panel on "1968: Student Revolutions in America and Europe," March 7, 2005, Duke University; Paulus Ebner and Karl Vocelka, *Die Zahme Revolution*, pp. 145–84; Fritz Keller, *Wien, Mai 68*, pp. 108–51; Anton Pelinka, "Die Studentenbewegung der 60er Jahre in Österreich: 8 Thesen aus politikwissenschaftlicher Sicht," in *Wendepunkte und Kontinuitäten*, ed. Forum Politische Bildung (Innsbruck: Studien Verlag, 1998), pp. 148–57.

[92] Pope Paul VI called Austria an "island of the fortunate" in November 1971. Journalist Hellmut Andics popularized the phrase as "island of the blessed," alluding to Elysium, in his *Insel der Seligen: Österreich von der Moskauer Deklaration bis zur Gegenwart* (Vienna: Molden-Taschenbuch-Verlag, 1976). It has become an appellation for the Austrian welfare state under Kreisky.

with communal living, production cooperatives, nonprofit bookstores, feminist journalism, and artistic, literary, and musical protest proliferated.[93] They could not provide societal blueprints, but they stimulated and reflected broader changes in social mores and lifestyle that sustained new social movements, above all, the Greens.[94] Alternative political engagements and cultural affiliations began eroding the integrative party cultures of the postwar years, and pluralizing and liberalizing Austrian society.[95] The Austrian New Left did not trigger these changes, which reflected generational patterns throughout Europe, but it presaged them and, especially in Austria, was part of them. It became primarily a cultural phenomenon. *Neues Forum* was its emblem.

Equally unnoticeable was the transformation in the émigrés' place in European culture in the aftermath of 1968. The postwar era was a period of rare silence on the Jewish Question in European discourse. Both the Holocaust and the State of Israel showed Jewish difference to be irreducible and dispelled demands for and dreams of assimilation. Openly denying Jewish citizenship became unacceptable, and the political vision of a racially blind nation-state was upheld against Nazi antisemitism. But this vision conflicted with the reality of ethno-national states and the public memory of World War II, which had no place for the Jews, multiethnicity, or multiculturalism. There was no public conversation on the Jewish Question because it was so obviously insoluble in the ethno-national state, yet other than Zionists, no one could suggest that it was so without being suspected, correctly, of antisemitism. The émigrés helped rebuild postwar European cultures without these cultures ever coming to grips with the émigrés' place in them.

The events of 1968 initiated a transformation in this unfavorable postwar configuration. It exposed the march of internationalization and accelerated its pace. By forging political solidarity, cultural affinities, and sociability across borders, the 68ers mimicked the émigré networks and formed transnational communities. Their protests had an international character, and the émigrés and the 68ers were often in dramatic conflict for long months. Government responses to the protests, such as efforts to deport "foreign agitators" (Cohn-Bendit in France, Günter

---

[93] Bärbel Danneberg, Fritz Keller, Aly Machalicky, and Julius Mende, eds., *Die 68ers: Eine Generation und ihre Erbe* (Vienna: Döcker, 1998), pp. 127–383.

[94] Ronald Inglehart, *The Silent Revolution: Changing Values and Political Styles among Western Publics* (Princeton, NJ: Princeton University Press, 1977), and *Culture Shift in Advanced Industrial Society* (Princeton, NJ: Princeton University Press, 1990).

[95] Anton Pelinka, "Die Studentenbewegung der 60er Jahre in Österreich." Pelinka also argues for the student movement's democratic character and its transformative political impact. In my argument, the existence of alternative communities, of whatever character, had a liberalizing effect.

Maschke and Fritz Teufel in Austria), revealed the challenge facing the nation-state and the futility of border policing. Ongoing Europeanization, reflected in an expanding European Economic Community (1974) and a directly elected European Parliament (1979), dovetailed with the internationalization of culture, easing national closure and relaxing ethnic boundaries. Public perception of the prerequisites for membership in the nation and in Europe began shifting. In the newly emergent Europe, national boundaries were to become looser, and transnational communities were to cut across national territory; 1968 was at once symbol and stimulant of internationalization.

The 68ers also mounted a challenge to national histories. To be sure, the Marxist narrative of uninterrupted authoritarianism from fascism to postwar was unpersuasive, but it constituted a decisive step toward opening up national narratives, and facilitated the reception of revisionist histories offered by the emergent academic leaders, mostly 58ers. The new histories, highlighting authoritarian social structures and intellectual traditions, delegitimized ethno-nationalism and were more conducive to Jewish membership in Europe and the nation. Indeed, they made progressive émigré cosmopolitanism appear the preferable vision for the nation and Europe. As the search for new forms of national and European identities intensified, the émigrés, for the first time in history, became bona fide members of national and European culture.

The 68ers unwittingly advanced the prospects of "Central Europe" as well. They intended no such thing: They were suspicious of "Austrian literature," and had no wish to legitimate another national narrative. Yet by highlighting the émigrés, advancing internationalization, and undercutting conservative histories, they left Central Europe as optimal for Austrian national identity. Émigré cosmopolitanism represented a past morally unencumbered by the Holocaust, which could be deployed to envision a new Austria and Europe. Seeking cultural renewal, international recognition, and closure to a painful past, Kreisky issued a call for the émigrés to return home in 1980, recognizing them as "the tenth Austrian province." Austria was to be identified with cosmopolitan culture. A few years later, Busek envisioned a resurgent Mitteleuropa, and Zilk contemplated Vienna as its cultural metropolis, with Viennese modernism its foremost expression. Busek and Zilk were responding to early 1980s opportunities, but cultural transformation in the aftermath of 1968 had opened up the space for their projects. The émigrés were becoming icons of a newly imagined Central Europe.

The rise of émigré culture had preceded Austria's confrontation with the National Socialist past. The Holocaust lurked in the background of the 68ers' discourse, surfacing for moments, only to be reabsorbed in the

National Socialist past, the omnipresence of which the 68ers combated.[96] Europe's coming to terms with the Holocaust was a prolonged process, starting before 1968 and ending well after, but it is interesting to note that the more severe the 1968 crisis was, the quicker was also the confrontation with the Holocaust. By the late 1970s, West Germany, France, and Italy were more advanced in their reassessment of the fascist past than was Austria. Vienna's mild May '68 and Kreisky's "island of the blessed" meant a two-decade delay in revisiting Austria's foundation myth.

By the early 1980s, however, the struggle for recognition of Austria's culpability in the Holocaust became central to the Jewish 68ers who sought to renegotiate their place in Austria and Europe. Intellectuals of Jewish origin were prominent among the 68ers in Austria, as they were elsewhere. Bernhard Frankfurter headed the *Wiener Aktion* and Robert Schindel the *Kummune Wien*. Commune members were often children of communist activists and émigrés. The Jewish 68ers were vaguely aware of their ethnic origins, but until after 1968, they had dissociated themselves from the mainstream Jewish community and Zionism. They sought integration in Austria and Europe through the universal maxims of socialism and humanity, not as Jews.

Greater openness to ethnic and cultural diversity in the aftermath of 1968, reflected in the 68ers' growing attention to foreign worker communities in Central Europe, allowed the Jewish 68ers, too, to explore the Jewish dimensions of their lives. The Holocaust became central to their exploration, the experience that redefined their relationship to Austria. The Waldheim Affair – the international controversy in the wake of the 1985–86 revelations of the incriminating World War II military service of the former United Nations Secretary-General and current candidate for the Austrian presidency, Kurt Waldheim (1918–2007) – was formative for Jewish intellectuals. They represented several generations, from *Neues Forum*'s editor Ilse Maria Aschner (b. 1918) and Aichinger (b. 1921) to Schindel (b. 1943), Frankfurter (b. 1946), and Jelinek (b. 1946) to Ruth Beckermann (b. 1952), Peter Stephan Jungk (b. 1952), and Robert Menasse (b. 1954) to Doron Rabinovici (b. 1961).[97] All participated in

---

[96] Explanations for the Holocaust's marginality in 1968 are legion. As the rebellion was generational, most explanations are psychological, and some view the 68ers' politics as displacement.

[97] Eleonore Lappin, ed., *Jewish Voices, German Words: Growing Up Jewish in Postwar Germany and Austria*, trans. Krishna Winston (North Haven, CT: Catbird Press, 1994); Dagmar C. G. Lorenz, ed., *Contemporary Jewish Writing in Austria: An Anthology*, trans. Dagmar C. G. Lorenz (Lincoln: University of Nebraska Press, 1999). Aichinger wrote on the Holocaust earlier than the other authors. This list does not include émigrés abroad, like Jean Améry, Erich Fried, and Ruth Klüger.

reconfiguring Jewish identity in Austrian and European culture and signaled the emergence of a new Central European Jewish intelligentsia.

The émigrés could not grasp the radical change they were witnessing but took pleasure in their new celebrity. With their students at the helm of academies on both sides of the Atlantic, and interwar culture (especially Weimar) becoming a household name in the United States, the émigrés enjoyed unprecedented popularity in both Europe and the United States during the 1970s and 1980s. Torberg's revival of the old Jewish humor in *Die Tante Jolesch* proved a great success, and, shortly before his death in 1979, he received the Great Austrian State Prize for Literature.[98] Manès Sperber, a Jewish writer who was born in Galicia, had grown up in Vienna, and lived during the postwar years in Paris, became a familiar figure on the Austrian literary scene in the 1970s. When he returned to Vienna for a visit in 1947, he became depressed at the *Stadt ohne Juden* (City without Jews), and did not come back for fifteen years. Now he was finding his Heimat in Vienna again, he said.[99] A new Europe was emerging, one where openly Jewish émigrés, like Sperber and Torberg, could feel more comfortable.

Still, the confrontation with the 68ers convinced Sperber and Torberg more than ever that they represented a dying civilization. "I am one of the last, one of the wandering coffins of an exterminated world," wrote Sperber, seeking to give testimony to the lost shtetl of his youth: "I must speak of it."[100] Torberg echoed: "I am a German-Jewish writer, ... probably the last one.... My Jewish function ... is ... to make as many non-Jews as possible perceive the death of the last German-Jewish writer as a loss, ... the end of something for which they have no substitute."[101] He left *Forum* so that he could complete *Süsskind von Trimberg*, a novel about a thirteenth-century German minnesinger who, in one of his songs, professed to be Jewish.[102] At the end of his life, Süsskind-Torberg, who

---

[98] Friedrich Torberg, *Die Tante Jolesch oder Der Untergang des Abendlandes in Anekdoten* (Munich: Langen-Müller, 1975).

[99] Hugo Bettauer's satire became a nightmare: *Die Stadt ohne Juden* (Vienna: Gloriette, 1922); Manès Sperber, *Alles das Vergangene* ... (Vienna: Europaverlag, 1983), pp. 917–23; Manès Sperber to Rudolf Henz, no date, in *Die Analyse der Tyrannis: Manès Sperber, 1905–1984*, ed. Marcus G. Patka and Mirjana Stančić (Vienna: Holzhausen Verlag, 2005), p. 167: "nun habe ich das 78. Lebensjahr erreicht und empfinde wie ein Kind Heimweh nach der Stadt meiner Jugend."

[100] Manès Sperber, "Petit mémorial" [1952], in his *Être Juif* (Paris: Éditions Odile Jacob, 1994), p. 118: "Cependant, il faut que j'en parle comme si j'étais le dernier à l'avoir connu. Et, en effet, je suis un des derniers, un de ces cercueils ambulants d'un monde exterminé." The occasion for the memorial was Stalin's execution of the Soviet Yiddish poets and the suppression of Yiddish culture in the Soviet Union.

[101] Torberg to Max Brod, March 15, 1955, *Nachlaß Torberg* 25:5.

[102] Friedrich Torberg, *Süsskind von Trimberg: Roman* (Frankfurt: S. Fischer, 1972).

taught Jewish universal ethics to Christians, goes back to his people. In Torberg's multicultural world, the ethnic community remained primary, transgression of its boundaries creative but provisional, and intercommunal dialogue magnificent but fragile. Torberg could not see that his own new place in European culture permitted greater hope for the future of German-Jewish culture and Jewish–non-Jewish relations.

Yet Sperber and Torberg were not altogether wrong. The generational gap between the émigrés and the 68ers did expose the old intelligentsia's fragility. However significant the imprint it left on the academic and public cultures throughout Western Europe and the United States, the émigrés had no successors. The Holocaust had destroyed the cultures of their youth, and intergenerational continuity became impossible. As if this were necessary, 1968 confirmed that the Holocaust could not be undone. But the émigrés did not see that a young Jewish intelligentsia was emerging, and it was forging a new relationship with Europe. In time, this intelligentsia would build on their legacy and, together with the non-Jewish intelligentsia, celebrate it. They could not see the new intelligentsia because it seemed so different from their own, and they could not see the new Europe because the change from the old one was subtle, and yet it was momentous.

The pre-Holocaust Jewish intelligentsia existed by default, a result of the nation-state's failure to integrate the Jews fully. The premise for its existence was partial inclusion of the Jews in the nation, making good on emancipation's promise of citizenship, and partial exclusion. German-Jewish thinkers made valiant efforts to circumscribe a space for a Jewish intelligentsia, but the national culture remained hostile to Jewish difference. The easing of the nation-state's political and cultural boundaries, and the growing acceptance of a measure of ethnic and cultural diversity accompanying Europeanization, attenuated, though by no means resolved, the problem of Jewish difference. Crucial above all was the growing European confrontation with the Holocaust and the definition of a new Europe, in the 1990s, against the Holocaust experience. Even today, when xenophobic nationalism has returned, vivid memory of the European past, and the determination not to repeat it, still offer Jews a measure of protection from the hostility directed toward Muslim and Roma communities. The Jews have become European.

At the turn of the twenty-first century, the European Jewish intelligentsia could expect, for the first time, to be accepted qua Jewish, as part of the national and European cultures. This meant that the preconditions for the existence of a Jewish intelligentsia changed. The old intelligentsia could not see that and could not be expected to participate in the building up of a German-Jewish culture on new premises. As late as 1969, Marcel Reich-Ranicki (1919–2012), Germany's most influential literary critic in recent decades, spoke of Aichinger, Wolf Biermann, and Günter Kunert as "the very last generation of Jews writing in German."[103] A younger, more innocent generation, having greater confidence in humanity and the future than did Ranicki, Sperber, or Torberg, have meanwhile shaped new German-Jewish and European cultures.

Toward Contemporary Europe: Jews as Europeans

"NEUES FORVM," quipped Torberg, "is the very magazine against which I founded the old FORVM."[104] We need not accept Torberg's view of a breach between *Forum* and *Neues Forum*. Their politics were different, but the Jewish remigrés played an important role in both, giving the magazine its international character, opening new perspectives to Austrian youth, and displaying vigorous political debate, the likes of which was not available elsewhere in Austria. Never liberal, the magazine contributed, all the same, to a more open political culture and to the formation of an Austrian public sphere.

Nenning called Torberg the most gifted of cold warriors, and insisted that *Forum* was vital and open. Once Torberg had passed away, Nenning returned *Neues Forum* to its old name, *Forum*, in 1980, suggesting continuity with the CIA-funded magazine. "The CIA has already had more idiotic ideas than supporting good magazines financially," he wrote.[105] No other New Left leader professed such tolerance of Cold War culture in the 1970s. Nenning understood better than Torberg the bond tying the émigrés and the 68ers: Each group in its own way was trying to overcome the Central European past, and both were vested in opening up Austria and Europe to political, cultural, and ethnic diversity.

In his 1998 commemoration of Brecht and Torberg, Nenning observed that the Cold War hindered both of them from developing their creative potential.[106] Like Nenning, I have noted the parallels between communist and anticommunist Cold War culture, *Forum* and *Tagebuch*, but I suggest that Cold War ideological struggles could also be intellectually productive and enhance internationalization. *Forum* and the remigrés

---

[103] Marcel Reich-Ranicki, "Außenseiter und Provokateure," in his *Über Ruhestörer: Juden in der deutschen Literatur*, rev. ed. (Stuttgart: DVA, 1989), p. 36.

[104] "NEUES FORVM ist das Blatt, gegen welches ich das alte FORVM gegründet habe." This is Nenning's rendering: *FORVM*, p. 7. The original quip may belong to Hellmut Jaeserich, *Der Monat*'s editor. Torberg rehearsed it to Manès Sperber (November 20, 1968, Österreichisches Literaturarchiv, Sperber Collection, 2/B 1220/32).

[105] "Lieber kalter Krieger: Zum Tod Friedrich Torbergs, Begründer des FORVM," in *FORVM*, p. 206.

[106] Günther Nenning, "Die Ballade von armen F. T. Gesungen zu Friedrich Torbergs 90. und Bertolt Brechts 100.," in *Wien oder Der Unterschied*, pp. 269–76.

contributed less remarkably to liberalizing and Westernizing Austria than their counterpart in Germany did. But precisely because they drew on the imperial past, on pluralism rather than on cosmopolitanism, their visions of "Central Europe" and "Austrian literature" provided a blueprint for a national culture in a European setting. Their conception of Austria left room for Jewish culture in ways that German-Jewish cosmopolitanism could not.

If 1968 signaled the end of the old Jewish intelligentsia, it was an end in triumph, a comic, if also ironic, closure to the émigrés' saga. The prestige bought first by CIA money ended up serving an anti-American counter-culture, but this culture, in turn, facilitated the rise of a Europe that the anticommunist émigrés would have gladly accepted. To be sure, the new social movements that sorted out the 68ers' antiestablishment ideology were not free of anti-Americanism, and the early Greens, especially in Austria, were suspicious of the emergent European Union. But the alter-native Europe they counterposed to the EU sealed the death of Pan-German nationalism.[107] When waves of immigrants to Central Europe gave rise in the late 1980s and 1990s to new xenophobic German and Austrian nationalism, the Greens were in the forefront of multicultural Central Europe, and have been there since. This was a Europe that the émigrés would have enjoyed. In roundabout ways, the émigrés and the 68ers both created a home for the Jewish intelligentsia in European culture.

This became clear in the 1990s when, in the aftermath of the Soviet Union's collapse and the European Union's formation, Europe made the Holocaust definitive of its identity, the shared past against which the new Europe defined itself. If, on occasion, the Jews of today are still considered outsiders against whom Europeans committed crimes, they have also become, in the image of the cosmopolitan émigrés, the Europeans par excellence, the embodiment of the culture that Europe would like to claim as its own. Few episodes in twentieth-century European history ended as well as the story of the émigrés. The "look back in anger" that is typical of writing on the CCF and Cold War liberalism, on the one hand, and on 1968 and the 68ers, on the other, is misplaced.

---

[107] Of course, not all 68ers ended up internationalists: Critics of 1968 highlight German New Left activists Horst Mahler (of Baader-Meinhof reputation) and Maschke, who became radical German nationalists.

Recent political developments suggest that I was too quick to envision a comic end to the émigrés' saga: There is no end. But there were two decades of great hope for a new Europe, when the émigrés became icons of European culture, as they remain for many Europeans today.

Two major protagonists of 1968 (and this chapter), Nenning and Cohn-Bendit, played divergent roles in the final emergence of Europe. As a leader of the Austrian Greens, Nenning headed the 1990s opposition to what he termed Austria's annexation to the EU, EU-Anschluss.[108] During the first decade of the twenty-first century, he repeatedly inveighed, in the name of "the people of Europe" and "our Austria," against Brussels "bureaucrats and brutal capitalists," who were violating human rights, among others, by sending an avalanche of trucks emitting carbon dioxide across Austria. He suggested setting up roadblocks against them, 1968 redivivus, national and European resistance convergent.[109]

Daniel Cohn-Bendit, in contrast, has been an eloquent spokesperson for the new Europe. A member of the German Greens since 1984, and EU Parliament delegate since 1994, he ran for the EU Parliament in 1999 at the helm of the French Greens, and has been the leader of the European Greens since 2002. Together with Joschka Fischer, a close friend from the 1970s Frankfurt street protests who emerged through the Greens to become the foreign minister and vice chancellor of Germany, Cohn-Bendit has marched through the institutions, translating the politics of protest into that of reform. He has constantly used the émigrés to reassess the legacy of 1968. "That the 68ers read Marcuse rather than Koestler, Manès Sperber and Hannah Arendt," he said in 2005, with Fischer at his side, "that was bad, just as bad as the Red Army Faction."[110]

Cohn-Bendit's rehabilitation of the theorists of totalitarianism – Arendt, Koestler, and Sperber – appropriately closed the circle he had

---

[108] Günther Witzany, ed., *Verraten und verkauft* (Salzburg: Unipress-Verlag, 1993), and, *Zukunft Österreich: EU-Anschluss und die Folgen* (Salzburg: Unipress-Verlag, 1998).

[109] "Blockade!!!" *Kronen Zeitung* (3 November 2003), and "Unser Wasser," *Kronen Zeitung* (29 January 2003), respectively, as quoted in Christian Kamer, *Negotiating National Identities: Between Globalization, the Past and 'the Other'* (Farnham, UK: Ashgate, 2011), pp. 75–76. It is interesting that Alpine nature, and not multiculturalism, defined Austrian national identity, the imperial legacy sidelined. So the dissonance between the two *Forum* editors, the remigré and the Austrian 58er, remained to the end.

[110] "Ein Abend mit Joschka Fischer," *Frankfurter Allgemeine Sonntagszeitung* (20 February 2005). Cohn-Bendit has since repeated the statement on many occasions. His reformulation of the émigré–68ers relationship is not, of course, the only possible one. For Gerhard Oberschlick, *Forum*'s editor in its final ten years, 1986–95, Anders served as inspiration. Either way, the 68ers were never released from the émigrés' spell: It had formed them and made it possible for them to become who they were.

   This chapter was completed before recent waves of populist nationalism threw the postwar order, the EU, and the transatlantic world into a crisis. The Jews and the Jewish intelligentsia are mercifully not, at this time, in the eye of the storm, but the culture that has welcomed them is under attack and is being eroded. The anomaly of the postwar moment in Jewish European history may be approaching its end more quickly than I anticipated, and this chapter already reflects a measure of nostalgia.

opened in 1968, bringing the anticommunist émigrés and the 68ers together, recognizing both as makers of contemporary Europe. Running for the EU Parliament, Cohn-Bendit invoked 1968, his Jewishness, and internationalism, all together, articulating the new European identity: "We are all German Jews now."

Figure 9: Daniel Cohn-Bendit's portrait with the European Union's emblem and the 1968 rubric: "We are all German Jews now."

13   A Post-Holocaust Breakthrough? Jacob & Esau Today

Jacob's Voice

The tears.
The tears in the brother's eye.
One has remained hanging, and growing.
We live in it.
Breathe, so it may be released.[1]

Paul Celan's 1959 poem created a convergence of Jacob's voice and Esau's tears. Celan saw Jews and Christians living in one big, growing tear, and envisioned a breath that may release it. The poem provides both the motto and the motif for this chapter. Only European accountability for the Holocaust made this vision of togetherness possible: Jacob's voice and Esau's tears – or are they Jacob's? – cohabit in one space, and healing appears to be a prospect. Celan reversed the midrashim that intimated that Esau's cry and his tears over the injustice of the stolen blessing were the source of Jewish suffering throughout history, and that redemption would tarry until the well of tears has dried up.[2] In the aftermath of the Holocaust, Jacob's voice, originally beguiling and the cause of Esau's cry and tears, cries out itself, and the tears appear in either brother's eye; indeed, both live in Esau's growing tear. Yet a breath signaling a stop to the crying can be envisioned, even if it remains unclear that there is life once the tear has dropped. However one interprets Celan, the two-millennia typology of Jacob & Esau has collapsed in the aftermath of the Holocaust and the State of Israel.

Not immediately, however: Celan was a harbinger of future paradigmatic changes, but they occurred, for the most part, only after the Six-Day War (1967). Israel's War of Independence (1948–49) did not

---

[1] "Jakobsstimme," in *Sprachgitter* (Frankfurt am Main: S. Fischer Verlag, 1959), http://www.lyrikline.org/de/gedichte/stimmen-162#.VaEB4Ovt5t4: "Die Tränen. Die Tränen im Bruderaug. Eine blieb hängen, wuchs. Wir wohnen darin. Atme, daß sie sich löse." My thanks to Moshe Lavi of the University of Haifa for introducing me to the poem.
[2] *Bereshit Rabba*: 67:4; *Midrash Tanhuma*, ed. Buber (Vilnius: Romm, 1913): toledot 24; *Zohar*. 1: 145a: "Israel has suffered on account of the tears which Esau shed before his father, in his desire to be blessed by him, out of the great regard he had for his father's words"; 2: 12b: "Those [Esau's] tears brought Israel down into his exile."

overcome the sense of powerlessness generated and reaffirmed by the Holocaust. Yael Feldman showed "the *aqedah* becom[ing] a key figure in Zionist thought and Hebrew letters" during the 1940s and 1950s.[3] Displays of Masada as a countermyth to the Holocaust – "Never again shall Masada fall!" – only highlighted the self-sacrificial moment in the Israeli national ethos but provided no comfort.[4] The painting commemorating the 1948 war at the entranceway to Israel's leading Art School, the Beẓalel Academy in Jerusalem, depicts mourning over a fallen soldier. At the moment of Israel's foundation, and for the next fifteen years, images of Jewish victimhood predominated in Beẓalel and overwhelmed the "New Jew," the venerated icon of Labor Zionism.[5] Only the 1967 war, which confirmed Israel as a regional power but also made its national problem unresolvable, engendered Jewish empowerment and triggered the millennia-old paradigm's dissolution.

Latent Loss and Empowerment: Jacob & Esau, 1945–1967

In mainstream Zionist poetry, Jacob remains a symbol of the national project until the late 1960s. From Yiẓḥak Lamdan's "You!" (1953) to Amir Gilboa's "We were like Returnees" (1953) and "Israel" (1963) to Abba Kovner's "All My Bell" (1970), Jacob was called upon to ascend the ladder and struggle against the angel to realize the dream of national return. He was promised a glorious future, and assured, on Mount Sinai, of his ladder's strength.[6] Less celebratory about the national

---

[3] *Glory and Agony: Isaac's Sacrifice and National Narrative* (Stanford, CA: Stanford University Press, 2010), p. 20: "Janus-like, [the *Aqedah*] came to represent both the slaughter of the Holocaust and the national warrior's death in the oldnew homeland." In fairness, Feldman does not see the post-1967 "Israeli psycho-political assault on the *aqedah*" as issuing from victory but as solidifying the Israeli "Isaac syndrome." Ari Dubnov of George Washington University and Shai Ginsburg of Duke University pointed out to me that the transformations of the Aqedah and the Jacob & Esau typologies dovetailed in Israel.

[4] Yael Zerubavel, *Recovered Roots: Collective Memory and the Making of Israeli National Tradition* (Chicago: University of Chicago Press, 1995). Yiẓḥak Lamdan, *Masadah* (Tel Aviv: Hedim, 1927), was crucial in formatting the myth.

[5] Lisa Bonnifield, "Modern Jewish Art and Zionism" (B.A. thesis, Duke University, 2008); Dalia Manor, *Art in Zion: The Genesis of Modern National Art in Jewish Palestine* (London: Routledge, 2005); Gideon Ofrat, *One Hundred Years of Art in Israel*, trans. Peretz Kidron (Boulder, CO: Westview Press, 1998).

[6] Malkah Shaked, *I'll Play You Forever: The Bible in Modern Hebrew Poetry*, 2 vols. (Tel Aviv: Yediot Aḥaronot, 2005), 1: 120–21, 1: 122–23, 1: 125–26, respectively. It is interesting to note that in 1943, Gilboa also published "Isaac" (1: 96), which Yael Feldman considers subversive of earlier Zionist portrayals of Isaac as a self-sacrificing military hero: *Glory and Agony*, pp. 134–36. Mourning over relatives who perished in the Holocaust may have subverted native martyrology of fallen soldiers, but it preserved life-loving Jacob for the national project.

Figure 10: *Jacob and Esau* by Jakob Steinhardt. Courtesy of the Israel Museum, Jerusalem.

prospect, Israeli painter Jacob Steinhardt's 1950 woodcut of Jacob and Esau embracing expressed hopes for Jewish–Arab reconciliation (see Figure 10): The sentiments may have been new but the typology's use was traditional.[7] Far Right poet Uri Zvi Greenberg, who in the late 1920s toyed with Esau as a Zionist New Man, returned in the aftermath of the Holocaust to the typology's traditional use: Esau became again the murderer of Jews.[8]

The pattern of continuity and change transcended political camps. Diaspora nationalist philosopher and historian Simon Rawidowicz

---

[7] Steinhardt (1887–1968) belonged to the Berlin Secession, then, having immigrated to Palestine in 1933, to the new Bezalel Group. He became head of the Bezalel Academy (1954–57). Ziva Amishai-Maisels, "Steinhardt in the Land of Israel," *Jacob and Israel: Homeland and Identity in the Work of Jakob Steinhardt* (in Hebrew and English), ed. Gabriel Ma'anit, Ruthi Ofek, and Avraham Hai (Tefen: Open Museum, 1998), pp. 70–126 (Hebrew), 197–230 (English). I learned of Steinhardt's Jacob and Esau woodcut from Ezra Mendelsohn, *Painting a People: Maurycy Gottlieb and Jewish Art* (Lebanon, NH: Brandeis University Press, 2002), p. 215.

[8] See my earlier discussion of Greenberg's poetry in chap. 10.

(1897–1957), founder of the Jewish and Near Eastern Studies Program at Brandeis, protested that in uprooting hundreds of thousands of Arabs from their homeland and turning them into refugees, Jacob had for the first time since the Hasmoneans spilled blood, committing violence that cried out to God, a moral transgression inviting criticism:

> Esau has been defiling Jacob; the two have become alike. The twins are no longer struggling with each other. . . . Jacob is a brother to Esau, who always made of the credo "live by the sword" a positive commandment. Perhaps one day Esau and Ishmael will join forces . . . to repay Jacob for the act that he committed in 1948. When the avengers are given the authority to avenge, will they know any limit?[9]

Rawidowicz's critique of Jewish power and statehood reflected new political realities, indeed, unprecedented ones, but it articulated the traditional Eastern European Jewish apprehension about identifying the nation – even the Jewish one – with the state. Predictably, his typology also remained traditional: He merely bemoaned Jacob behaving like Esau.

Similarly, on the Christian side, the soul-searching among Christian churches occasioned by the Holocaust came fully into the open only in the mid-1960s with Vatican II and Protestant initiatives for Christian–Jewish dialogue. The immediate postwar period remained one of Holocaust latency, as historian Dan Diner suggests: A reevaluation was taking place but was not apparent.[10] In the 1950s, missionary evangelist books on the Patriarchs could still use old Christian typology mixed with antisemitic stereotypes. If Abraham was the man of perfect faith, Jacob was a questionable youth. Encountering God at Penuel, Israel became God's soldier, and yet, meeting with Esau the next day, he was a master of guile all over again.[11] The contrast with future ecumenical Abraham, the main figure for interreligious dialogue among Christians, Muslims, and Jews, was great.[12]

---

[9] Simon Rawidowicz, "Between Jew and Arab," in *Between Jew and Arab: The Lost Voice of Simon Rawidowicz*, ed. David N. Myers (Hanover, NH: Brandeis University Press, 2008), pp. 150–51.

[10] Dan Diner, "Vom Stau zur Zeit: Neutralisierung und Latenz zwischen Nachkrieg und Achtundsechzig," in *Latenz: Blinde Passagiere in den Geisteswissenschaften*, ed. Hans Ulrich Gumbrecht and Florian Klinger (Göttingen: Vandenhoeck & Ruprecht, 2011), pp. 165–72.

[11] G. R. Brinke, *Abraham: der Freund Gottes* (Bern: Ährenlese-Verlag, 1957), and *Der Erzvater Jabob: Ein Lebensbild in Skizzen* (Bern: Ährenlese-Verlag, 1959).

[12] Matthias Morgenstern, "Vom 'Götzenzerstörer' zum Protagonisten des Dialogs – Der Erzvater Abraham in 1800 Jahren jüdischer Tradition," in *Interreligiöser Dialog: Chancen abrahamischer Initiativen*, ed. Reinhard Möller and Hanns Christoph Goßmann (Berlin: Lit, 2006), pp. 101–26. Yaakov Ariel of UNC, Chapel Hill, points out that Abraham did not become a central figure until the Christian–Muslim dialogue took off at the turn of the twenty-first century, by which time the Christian–Jewish dialogue had already become secondary.

The turnaround in the 1960s was surprising, and the surprise contributed to Orthodox Jews' suspicion of the Vatican II call for dialogue. The leader of U.S. modern Orthodoxy, Rabbi Yosef Dov Soloveitchik (1903–1993), advised against theological exchange. He regarded Jacob & Esau's separation after their reconciliation as marking destiny: Non-Jews could not truly accept Jewish difference, and "it is easier and better for Esau to live on Mt. Seir, and for Jacob and his Sons to be in the Land of Israel."[13] The great Ultra-Orthodox halakhist, Rabbi Moshe Feinstein (1895–1986), rejected Paul VI's call for a Christian–Jewish dialogue as a new conversion ploy. In a 1967 *responsum* advising British Jewish leaders not to appeal their government's refusal to support Jewish schools to international organizations lest they evoke British wrath, he opined that "hatred of the Jews by all nations is great, even in states that treat Jews well.... 'It is a well-known *halakha* (maxim) that Esau hates Jacob.' ... Just as *halakha* never changes, so also Esau's hatred of Jacob never changes."[14] His son, David Feinstein, suggested that Jacob could not keep his promise to come to Esau (Genesis 33:14) because he was concerned about his impressionable family. The time had not yet come for Jacob & Esau to become brothers or for Jews to conduct dialogue with Christians.[15]

Indeed, Ultra-Orthodox Jews have endeavored to retain the traditional typology all the way through. Most Ultra-Orthodox Jews believe that the Holocaust came for assimilation's sins, and vindicated Moses Sofer's warning that mimicry of the Gentiles would provoke their (and God's) wrath and end up disastrously. With the exception of the radically anti-Zionist Satmar Ḥasidim, they have desisted from calling the Zionists (and assimilated Jews) Amaleq, as they had done before the Holocaust, and Amaleq is now reserved for the Nazis. In his *Megilat Polin* (1966), Gur leader Yehudah Leib Levin, founder of the Ultra-Orthodox Daily *Ha-Modia*, suggested that remembering the antisemitic Nazi design to obliterate the entire Jewish people, and commemorating the saints who perished in the Holocaust, was fulfillment of the Torah's command to remember Amaleq.[16] Christians were charged for withholding help

---

[13] "Jacob and Esau" (in Hebrew), in *Divre Hashqafa*, trans. (from the Yiddish) by Moshe Crone (Jerusalem: World Zionist Organization, 1992), p. 27.

[14] *Igrot Moshe* (Benei Beraq: Moshe Feinstein, 1985): *Ḥoshen u-Mishpat*: 2:77 (p. 319).

[15] *Kol Dodi on the Torah* (Brooklyn, NY: Masorah Publications, 1992), pp. 55–56.

[16] Michal Shaul, *Beauty for Ashes: Holocaust Memory and the Rehabilitation of Ashkenazi Haredi Society in Israel, 1945–1961* (in Hebrew) (Jerusalem: Yad Vamhem; Yad Izhak ben-Zvi, 2014), pp. 307–16. Levin was a harbinger more than a trendsetter: Until the 1990s, the Ultra-Orthodox leadership downplayed Holocaust commemoration, fearing it might hinder the reconstruction of Jewish life. See Dan Michman, "The Impact of the Holocaust on Religious Jewry," in *Major Changes within the Jewish People in the Wake of the*

from Jews, but they were not the Holocaust's perpetrator. Pagan Amaleq was. However, this did not amount to an Ultra-Orthodox Holocaust theology, and the lacuna suggests that the Holocaust's legacy has not yet been fully fathomed.

Ultra-Orthodoxy is even less able to account for the Jewish State. A minority, the Satmar Ḥasidim, flatly reject Israel, and regard the State as yet another trial for Jews "to find out whether you love the Lord your God with all your heart" (Deuteronomy 13:3). Most of the Ultra-Orthodox have developed an ambivalent attitude toward Israel: God has mercifully provided a refuge to the Jews in Israel in the aftermath of the Holocaust, but they remain outrageously obdurate. Why God has so chosen remains a mystery.[17] The reluctance to think through the Holocaust and Israel is exemplified by their traditional use of Jacob & Esau. "It is a maxim that Esau hates Jacob," said Eliezer Shakh, the venerated leader of Israeli Ultra-Orthodoxy's Lithuanian wing. He had no confidence in U.S. benevolence: Non-Jewish governments should never be trusted but also never provoked. Jews have weathered hostile governments for millennia by keeping loyal to the Torah, and Jewish politics ought to be limited to maneuvering among existing political options. Jews were not to declare war or make peace. All the same, just as no traditional option existed at the time of the birth of Orthodoxy in a postrevolutionary Europe undergoing emancipation, none truly exists after the Holocaust, and in the face of Jewish statehood. Reluctant to acknowledge the new national and diasporic options, Ultra-Orthodoxy has found itself inadvertently transforming the typology by applying it to the Mideast conflict. Esau has come to stand for Arab leaders, now perceived as the foremost threat to the Jewish population.

If Ultra-Orthodoxy has endeavored to buck post-Holocaust typological changes, the national religious camp has led them. This was no coincidence. Secular Zionists had limited interest in the rabbinic typology, whereas religious Zionists sought to use it to address politics. The prayer for the Jewish State's welfare, recited in modern Orthodox synagogues weekly on the shabbat, speaks of Israel as "the beginning of the growth of our redemption" (ראשית צמיחת גאולתנו), thereby integrating the Zionist project into the Jewish messianic vision. National religious

---

Holocaust (Jerusalem: Yad Vashem, 1996), pp. 659–707. Ultra-Orthodoxy's revival has since given rise to a bountiful literature.

[17] Aviezer Ravitzky, *Messianism, Zionism, and Jewish Religious Radicalism*, trans. Michael Swirsky and Jonathan Chipman (Chicago: University of Chicago Press, 1996); Barbara Krawcowicz, "Covenantal Theodicy Among Haredi and Modern Jewish Thinkers During and After the Holocaust" (Ph.D. diss., University of Indiana, Bloomington, 2013). My thanks to Krawcowicz and to Moshe Hellinger of Bar-Ilan University (email to author, May 29, 2014) for their help.

circles around the Merkaz Ha-Rav Yeshivah were the first to see the Holocaust as messianic tribulations, and the yeshivah head and founder's son, Zevi Yehudah Kook, spoke of the divine liquidation of exile as preparation for redemption. Unlike Ultra-Orthodoxy, religious Zionism offers a compelling theological explanation for the Jewish State and an outrageous one for the Holocaust, but one that ties it intimately with the Jewish State. No wonder religious Zionists have been at the forefront of typological innovation: Modern Jewish messianism required the Jacob & Esau paradigm to be reworked.

The beginning of the paradigmatic change in the 1950s was modest. In her legendary textbook for training teachers in Bible instruction, Nehamah Leibowitz (1905–1997) crafted traditional commentaries on the weekly portions of the Torah. Born to an Orthodox Jewish Riga family that immigrated to Berlin in 1919, Leibowitz graduated from the University of Marburg in 1930 and moved to Palestine. A self-effacing erudite scholar, she rekindled interest in school teaching of the Bible with the medieval Jewish commentators. In her Genesis commentary, she compared Samson Raphael Hirsch's view of Jacob and Esau's reconciliation as presaging emancipation with that of Benno Jacob, who, she said, found Esau's conduct suspicious. She suggested that the Holocaust exposed Hirsch's view that Esau was laying down his sword and reconciling as wishful thinking.[18]

A scandalized Samuel Hugo Bergmann, carrying the Prague Zionist and *Berit Shalom*'s legacy, protested that she ignored the reconciliation's grandeur, which recalled to him Schiller's "Ode to Joy" (An die Freude), as embedded in Beethoven's Ninth Symphony: "Embrace, millions!" (Seid umschlungen, Millionen!)[19] In response, Leibowitz faulted Hirsch for deriving his love for humanity from German humanism and not from Jewish sources. She preferred, she said, Naphtali Zevi Yehudah Berlin's view of the reconciliation: When Esau's descendants genuinely respect Israel, "then we, too, are moved to acknowledge [him as] our brother." She reaffirmed the traditional typology, listing the atrocities that Israel's enemies had perpetrated, from medieval pogroms to forced draft and conversion in the tsarist Russian army to the Holocaust. Israel is still a lamb among the wolves, she told Bergmann.

Surprisingly, those wolves now became Arab, and Leibowitz projected onto them two millennia of mostly Christian persecution. Unwittingly

---

[18] Nehama Leibowitz, *Studies in the Book of Genesis in the Context of Ancient and Modern Jewish Bible Commentary*, trans. and adapted from the Hebrew by Aryeh Newman (Jerusalem: World Zionist Organization, 1972), commentary on Va-yishlach.

[19] The December 1957 exchange of letters between the two was published in Aviad Hacohen, "Does Esau Hate Jacob" (in Hebrew), *Meimad* (1998): 16–19.

and unnoticeably, Leibowitz and other Orthodox intellectuals initiated a revolutionary change in the 1950s. Never in two millennia had Esau been a symbol for Arabs or Muslims (traditionally regarded as Ishmael's descendants). Now typological Esau reached beyond his Christian provenance into Islam to unify divergent enemies, as ancient Edom had done. Yosef Dov Soloveitchik identified the Arabs with Amaleq.[20] Shakh and the Ultra-Orthodox followed suit. The new locution has become commonplace. In November 2014, Israel's Sephardic chief rabbi, Yiẓḥaq Yosef, inveighed against Jews going up the Temple Mount: "Stop inciting Esau's descendants and provoking our Arab enemies."[21] During the 2015 Israeli election campaign, Moshe Gafni, political leader of the Lithuanian wing of the Torah Jewry Party, opined that "it is, indeed, a maxim that Esau hates Jacob but we do not wish for war with the Arabs to continue endlessly and must make peace efforts together with the U.S."[22] The quiet revolution begun in the 1950s was now complete.

These were the limits of innovation in the first two decades of Israel's existence. Israel's advocates and critics alike extended the Jacob & Esau typology to the Arabs, but the typology remained traditional. A sense of fragility still pervaded Jewish life almost everywhere. A generation of Cold War liberals, Isaiah Berlin most prominently, endeavored to pluralize the European nation-state so as to make it inhabitable for Jews, but the task was daunting: The nationalizing state left exceedingly narrow space for Jewish life.[23] European liberals could also not imagine that in the long run, the North American Diaspora would prove any different. "It cannot happen in Scarsdale? I am not sure, not completely," said George Steiner as late as 1965. "America is no more immune than any other nationalistic, professedly Christian society from the contagion of anti-Semitism."[24] Twenty years later, historian Stephen Whitfield suggested that American culture did put the lid on antisemitism. Biblical culture, he wrote, at once enhanced and constrained Jacob's new voice, that of

---

[20] Joseph B. Soloveitchik, *Kol Dodi Dofek: Listen, My Beloved Knocks* [1956], trans. David Z. Gordon from the Hebrew (New York: Ktav, 2006). For additional examples, see: Elliott Horowitz, *Reckless Rites* (Princeton, NJ: Princeton University Press, 2006), esp. pp. 144–46.

[21] Reported in *Haaretz* (7 November 2014).

[22] *Haaretz* (9 February 2015). He was responding to questions of *Haaretz* browsers.

[23] Malachi Hacohen, "'The Strange Fact That the State of Israel Exists': The Cold War Liberals Between Cosmopolitanism and Nationalism," *Jewish Social Studies* 15:2 (2009): 37–81.

[24] An observation all the more remarkable for Steiner's U.S. upbringing and affirmation of the Jewish Diaspora. "A Kind of Survivor," in his *George Steiner: A Reader* (New York: Oxford University Press, 1984), pp. 225, 224.

critical modernism.[25] The Jews have become an American success story, model immigrants, a symbol of national ideals and proof of their viability.

The anxiety about Israel and the future, and the predominant ethno-national perspective, were also reflected in the postwar Israeli imagination of imperialism. Book series for children highlighted the prestate national struggle against the British, finding nothing to commend in the Commonwealth.[26] In contrast, Hebrew literature witnessed the last wave of nostalgia toward the Austrian Empire, which was viewed as the victim of nationalism. In 1949, Asher Barash published a collection of stories on Galician Jewish life, permeated with a sense of doom and failure. The lead story, "Embroidery" (רקמה), tied together the declining fortunes of the imperial family and Jewish life.[27] The year after, Rabi Binyamin published his memoirs, which likewise highlighted Austrian Galicia.[28] Haim Be'er's *Feathers* (1979) closed the postwar era, describing the vestiges of fin-de-siècle Viennese culture in 1950s Jerusalem. A half insane follower of the progressive thinker Joseph Popper-Lynkeus was cast as a major character, and it turns out at the end of the book that his son died in the Yom Kippur War (1973). The empire's end and Israel's crisis converged.[29] Hebrew literature marked Israel's independence and survival with visions of a beloved empire's doom. Well into the State era, the cultural universe shaping Jacob & Esau seemed regulated by prestate traditions.

Jacob the Liar, 1968–2000

The 1967 war and the 1968 student revolution occurred as if in different worlds, yet both signaled political changes that shifted Israeli and European dispositions, respectively, toward the Holocaust, thereby undermining the Jacob & Esau typology. The Holocaust novel *Jakob der Lügner* (1969, *Jacob the Liar*), by East German–Jewish screenwriter Jurek Becker (1937–1997), marked an epochal change. Becker survived the Holocaust as a child, first with his parents in the Lodz ghetto, then in

---

[25] *Voices of Jacob, Hands of Esau: Jews in American Life and Thought* (Hamden, CT: Archon Books, 1984).

[26] Eitan Bar-Yosef, "The Nostalgic Return to Mandatory Palestine in Israeli Culture," paper presented at the North Carolina Jewish Studies Seminar, March 29, 2015.

[27] *In the Shadow of Good People: Short Stories* (in Hebrew) (Jerusalem: Bialik institute, 1949).

[28] Rabi Binyamin, *From Zborov to Kineret* (in Hebrew) (Tel Aviv: Devir, 1950). Almost two-thirds of the book is devoted to the Galician shtetl Zborov. The early chapters, published in 1940–42, evoked enthusiastic response among the Hebrew writers' community (pp. 7–10).

[29] Haim Be'er, *Feathers*, trans. Hillel Halkin (Lebanon, NH: University Press of New England, 2004).

a German concentration camp, where he lost his mother in 1945.[30] The Beckers had spoken Polish until after the war, when the father decided to settle in Berlin and abruptly shifted to German. Becker received a socialist education and grew up atheist and anti-Zionist, a Jew defined solely by the Holocaust. In East Germany, Jewishness conferred recognition as a victim of fascism but could become a liability if avowed as a national identity. Important Holocaust films had been produced in Eastern Europe before *Jakob der Lügner*, but to make a film in which the murder of Jews was central and a Jew the hero was tantamount to crossing a minefield. After the film script had passed the East German censor in 1965, Jurek found that the Polish authorities were torpedoing the filming in Cracow, and the East Germans canceled the production the next year.[31]

Becker, a master of the subterfuges of dissent, transmuted the film script into a Holocaust "comic" novel (surmising that novels were less carefully scrutinized than films).[32] *Jakob der Lügner*'s success was immediate, and it won several West German and Swiss prizes. One result was that the official East German film and television agencies joined together to produce another film (1974) with a new screenplay by Becker.[33] It became the first East German film to be shown at the Berlin Film Festival, and the only one ever to be nominated for an Academy Award. It also received East Germany's National Prize (1975). The Holocaust finally broke through the Iron Curtain and became a medium for European self-definition and internationalization.[34]

Situated in a World War II Polish ghetto, *Jacob the Liar* tells of a lower-middle-class Jew, Jakob Heym, formerly a tiny restaurant's owner, who, while being detained at the ghetto's headquarters for violating the curfew, overhears a radio broadcast about the Russians advancing. Apprehensive that his friend Mischa would carry out a suicidal act of escape, he reveals

---

[30] Becker had no memory of the Holocaust years. His father had survived Auschwitz and claimed him after the war, apparently in Sachsenhausen. *"Wenn ich auf meine bisheriges zurückblicke, dann muß ich leider sagen": Jurek Becker 1937–1997: Dokumente zum Leben und Werk ausdem Jurek-Becker-Archiv*, ed. Karin Kiwus (Berlin: Akademie der Künste, 2002), pp. 10–23; Sander Gilman, *Jurek Becker: A Life in Five Worlds* (Chicago: University of Chicago Press, 2003), pp. 17–21, and nn. 30–31, p. 235.

[31] Sander Gilman, *Jurek Becker*, pp. 60–67.

[32] Jurek Becker, *Jakob der Lügner* (Darmstadt: Luchterhand, 1970), and *Jacob the Liar*, trans. Leila Vennewitz (New York: Arcade Pub., 1996).

[33] DEFA Studio für Spielfilme, Gruppe Johannisthal und Fernsehen der DDR; eine Gemeinschaftsproduktion in Zusammenarbeit mit Filmové studio Barrandov; Buch, Jurek Becker; Produktionsleitung, Herbert Ehler; Regie, Frank Beyer, *Jakob der Lügner*, Video-DVD (Northampton, MA: Icestorm International, 1999).

[34] Shai Ginsburg objects: Earlier Polish and Czech Holocaust films, distributed internationally, had already done so. He is right, but they did not have the same impact.

the news to him, and to make it credible, intimates that he has a radio. The "radio" gives renewed hope to the people in the ghetto, who are starving and awaiting deportation to Nazi death camps: Suicides stop, and people begin contemplating a future. Jakob is repeatedly asked for more news and cannot retract it without throwing the ghetto into despair. For Lina, an orphan under his care, he stages mock BBC broadcasts of news and children's stories. The film ends with Jakob, Lina, and their compatriots being transported to an unknown destination, but in the novel, Becker also offered an alternative fantastic ending (the original one), in which Jakob is shot trying to escape but the Russians do arrive and liberate the camp.

Becker's Jacob embodies traditional antisemitic stereotypes, but their meaning is transformed. Jacob's lies, traditionally a means for profiteering, become an act of triumphal imagination, opening up horizons of hope for the ghetto's inmates. Jacob's craftiness and impersonation create a visionary, life-sustaining alternative reality. Traditionally, Jacob's voice gives him away, whereas in the film, the changing voice is constitutive of radio performances that delight and comfort little Lina. Jacob's recollections of his deal with Kowalski, a hairdresser now his friend in the ghetto – free haircuts in exchange for free food – appear not as petty haggling but as dreams of every-dayness and a restoration of humanity. No Leah or Rachel shows up in the film: Jacob is the motherly figure taking care of Lina, and his last name, Heym, connotes "home" in Yiddish and "life" (*Ḥayim*) in Hebrew. With *Jacob the Liar*, the Jewish antihero has become the hero, and the homeless people have reached the point that they can provide a home and sustain the life of a new European culture.

During the same period, the Christian churches, Socialism's major rival, were modifying their teachings about the Jews, and scrutinizing supersessionist typologies that suggested that Christianity had replaced Judaism. In a Catholic Bible picture book from the 1980s, the Jacob & Esau typology was gone, and the narrative underlined that Esau had not been rejected. A 1980 book of Catholic proscriptions on Judaism for instructors was free of Christian typology and sympathetic to Israel. It gave a fair exposition of Jewish views and prohibited the old super-sessionist doctrines. Protestant pedagogy likewise strove to break with Christian anti-Judaism. A 1981 review expressed frustration that the theological change had not yet trickled down to German elementary schools, where schoolbooks still depicted the Jews as sharing in the guilt for the crucifixion. Things changed over the following decades. The Protestant–Jewish dialogue that began seriously in the 1960s and the 1970s has continued ever since, and its effects continue to register in school instruction today.[35]

Post-1967 changes in Jacob & Esau's roles in Israeli culture occurred in a radically different context. Whatever echoes could be heard in Israel of the 1968 events in Europe, they were swallowed up by the canons' roar across the Suez Canal, fighting the War of Attrition. And yet the changes were momentous. Benjamin Tamuz's (1919–1989) novel *Yaakov (Jacob)* signaled a paradigmatic shift in Hebrew literature.[36] Tamuz, a writer, artist and journalist, editor of *Haaretz*'s literary supplement, endeavored to make *Jacob* his masterpiece. Reflective in part of his own biography, the novel tracks the confrontation of its protagonist, Jacob Engelsohn-Malachi, with the meaning of "Israeli" and "Jew" over two decades. Told in multiple voices, it takes Jacob, in four scenes, from the early 1940s Jewish underground in Palestine to the War of Independence and the State's early years to late 1950s Paris and back to early 1960s Israel. *Jacob* signaled Tamuz's break with his Canaanite youth – the endeavor to build a Hebrew nation dissociated from its Jewish past as part of a reawakening Semitic Middle East – and his transition to Jewish Diaspora cosmopolitanism.

Son of a poor émigré, Isaac, who never adjusted to Palestine, and the grandson of Abraham, who is buried in Europe, Jacob remains an outsider to the Israeli establishment, which Tamuz describes in an unflattering fashion. Jacob is a critic of the *Yishuv* and the State's commercial, military, and intellectual elites, and searches for the meaning of the Jewish legacy in Palestine. Leah appears as his early partner whom he declines to marry, and Rachel as his beloved wife who dies during the 1956 Suez War. Esau is nowhere to be seen: The struggle Jacob leads is with himself, and with the compromises that Israeli existence forces on him. Zionist demands consume the space of Esau's challenge. Naturally inclined toward intellectual and artistic inquiry, Jacob, in his childhood and underground days, feels incapacitated by his diasporic origins, but he proves himself both a warrior in Israel's wars and a moneymaker in its

---

[35] Kees de Kort, *Bibelbilderbuch* (Stuttgart: Deutsche Bibelgesellschaft, 1984); Peter Fiedler, *Das Judentum im katholischen Religionsunterricht* (Düsseldorf: Patmos, 1980); Ruth Kastning-Olmesdahl, *Die Juden und der Tod Jesu: Antijüdische Motive in den evangelischen Religionsbüchern für die Grundschule* (Neukirchener-Vluyn: Neukirchener Verlag, 1981); *Menschen suchen – Zugänge finden: Auf dem Weg zum einem Religionpädagogik verantworteten Umgang mit dem Bibel: Festschrift für Christine Reents*, ed. Desmond Bel, Heike Lipski-Melchior, Johannes von Lüpke, and Birgit Ventur (Wuppertal: Foedus, 1999); *Lernen auf Zukunft hin: Einsichten des christlich-jüdischen Gesprächs – 25 Jahre Studium in Israel*, ed. Katja Kriener and Bernd Schröder (Neukirchen-Vluyn: Neukirchener Verlag, 2004).

[36] *Jacob: A Novel* (in Hebrew) (Ramat-Gan: Massada, 1971).

emergent economy. In becoming a fighter and an entrepreneur, he tries to impress the elites and Rachel's relatives into accepting him, yet he feels alienated and repulsed by both.

Jacob endeavors to rid himself of the burden of his ancestor Jacob's triumph over the Angel, and the dubious blessing that consigned Jews to a permanent struggle with God and other nations. Cognizant of the emptiness of Israel's pretension to be a light unto the nations, and of the world's special expectations of Jews, he wishes "that God forget us for a while . . . a few generations without miracles; let everything occurring to us be natural" (p. 149). In an interview with a French journalist, he still articulates the conventional Canaanite-Zionist narrative: The Hebrews (Zionists) are anti-imperialist and friendly to the Palestinians, the Arab states threaten Israel, and the Christians menace the Jewish Diaspora, as demonstrated in the Holocaust (pp. 202–10).

His response to a French-Jewish philanthropist, however, breaks decisively with this narrative and seems a moment of higher truth:

Judaism actually means exile, even voluntary exile. . . . It is as if the entire people chose . . . this most human mode of existence. But the exilic idea is very difficult to realize [and] when the survival instinct stirs, there is a pause: The Jews turn back to their physical homeland and try to settle it. . . . It happened more than once: exile, return, exile, return. . . . Once they stayed long enough [in] the . . . State . . . they go again into exile . . . ostensibly forced to, but, truly, this conforms to the national will. . . . When you talk of your hopes for the . . . new Israeli man . . . you speak merely of a brief pause in the journey (pp. 173–74).

Torn between Israel and the Diaspora – "I have nowhere to rest. Shall I try a different age?" (p. 257) – Jacob's final encounter with the Angel confirms to him that there is no way of escaping its blessing and Jewish destiny: "Whoever has no intention of struggling and triumphing over God has no right to see God or hear his voice" (p. 284). He walks away from the encounter bruised, accepting of the eternal Jewish struggle for universality and authenticity, and becomes a partner of Ruth, a war widow. This suggests tenuous hope for the future.

The questions Tamuz's Jacob posed to the Zionist project were resolved during the next few decades with Jacob's transformation from a national figure into a universal hero. In the background has lurked the growing Palestinian resistance to the post-1967 Israeli occupation and the Lebanon wars, which made Jacob's power and moral dilemmas palatable. The shift often expressed disenchantment with the national project, and yet Jacob remained a favorite poetic subject. Abraham and Isaac could never be relieved of the national burden: The Aqedah remained a major site for negotiating Israeli ambivalence about violence, sacrifice, and death. Earthly Jacob, in contrast, cast a multifarious figure suitable for diverse poetic topoi, dissociated from the nation. His love for Rachel has remained a favorite motif, secure from political critique. Yet the shift from Jacob as a national to a universal symbol dissolved the typology.[37]

Zionist discourse had long been ambivalent about Jacob, and so querying the national myth typically began from within. The War of Independence poet, Ḥayim Guri, expressed exhaustion with war in "On Pillow Stone" (1968): "like Jacob, no ladder, like Jacob, no angels."[38] Moshe Dor's "Hard Water" (1989) recognized that in order to triumph over the angel, Israel renounced gentleness and desire.[39] The anational Israeli national poet Yehuda Amichai dissociated Jacob from the Zionist project in "Jacob and the Angel" (1975) by depicting the struggle as love play between Jacob and Rachel, with a hint of a tragic end: Rachel is called away from the play, and the separation may allude to her death.[40] Dov Chomsky's "Jacob's Dream" (1975) expressed disappointment that "Jacob's dream is no longer dreamt," and in Rina Lee's "Jacob's Ladder" (2000), the ladder turns into an escalator, and desacralized modernity – a "swampy everydayness" (יין החולין) – replaces the biblical magic.[41]

The love story between Jacob and Rachel has become progressively remote from the biblical narrative. For Aryeh Sivan (1969) in "At the Well," and Yoram Beck (1989) in "The Love of Jacob," Jacob is, above all, a lover, and for Beck, also a symbol of creation and death.[42] Equally remote from the Bible are Ḥamutal bar Yosef's "Two Poems on Jacob" (1998), which focus on the loss of Joseph and Jacob's mourning.[43] Recollecting the struggle against the Angel, Leah Senir, in "At the Jabbok Crossing" (1988), introduced the two matriarchs to help Jacob, whereas Ḥavah Pinḥas Cohen's "That Man" (2000) and Admiel Kosman's "At the Jabbok Crossing" (1989) transmuted the fight, respectively, into an overnight struggle of a woman against a man – her call for help remains unanswered, and there is no river to cross and no escape: she is trapped – and Jacob's adventurous night wandering. The national struggle has been privatized and universalized.[44]

---

[37] Hilda Nissimi points out that similar universalization of biblical topoi has become typical of Israeli culture. Jacob is but one obvious exemplar.

[38] Malkah Shaked, *I'll Play You Forever*, 1: 123–24, respectively.   [39] Ibid., 1: 128

[40] Ibid., 1: 127.   [41] Ibid., 1: 126, 1: 134–36, respectively.

[42] Ibid., 1: 124–25: 1: 130–31, respectively.   [43] Ibid., 1:133.

[44] Ibid., 1: 127–28, 1: 133–34, 1: 131–32, respectively. Both Avraham Hus in "Penuel," 1: 132–33, where Jacob struggles with his own anxieties, and Meron Isaacson's "Jacob's Destiny" (1989), 1: 129, in which national and personal fears of war and death converge, are more traditional, but the trend toward denationalization is evident.

Dov Elbaum's *My Life with the Patriarchs* (2001) completed the cycle that Tamuz's *Jacob* began by subverting both rabbinic and nationalist renderings of Jacob.[45] Rebelling against his own Ultra-Orthodox upbringing, Elbaum reshapes the patriarchs as a dysfunctional family living in Hebron. Father–son relations are broken, husband–wife relations are exploitative, and brothers' relations are abusive. The Aqedah looms large: It traumatized Isaac, but Abraham refuses to talk about it. The family's great secret, revealed at the end of the book (yet remaining incomprehensible), is Esau's severed head, which Isaac always carries in his red bag. Abraham appears as an imposing worldly operator, Isaac is a dejected and tormented soul, and Jacob is confused and unstable, a gifted, well-meaning womanizer who, recanting his bad ways in midlife, ends up ludicrously as a yeshivah student.

The patriarchs come into the protagonist's life at crucial junctures, and Abraham tries to help him sort out his troubles. In vain: Progress is only made when the protagonist releases himself from their tutelage and finds an introspective companion who, like him, struggles to confront her legacy and articulate her problems. Revealing the patriarchal family's secrets, and talking about them, he also manages to restore a measure of harmony among the patriarchs. For Elbaum, the Bible and the rabbis remain reference points, but their stories have been so radically rewritten that they are recognizable only to connoisseurs. A therapeutic opening to individual and national traumas, concealed by the biblical and rabbinic stories of the patriarchs, offers the sole chance of overcoming them. Typology must be reinvented to overcome the past.

In the decades that closed the second millennium, European and Israeli culture moved in both parallel and opposite directions in transforming Jacob's image. European culture embraced traditional Jewish Jacob and declared him European, indeed a universal model, whereas Israeli writers distanced themselves from Jewish Jacob, whether rabbinic or Zionist, and converted him into a lover, a mourner, or a lost soul. Both the European and Israeli Jacobs were new and parted ways with Jewish and Christian typology.

The Jewish Esau, 1982–2016

Malka Shaked points out that Jacob's denationalization did not entail demythologization, and that the transformation of Esau's role in Hebrew literature has been far more radical.[46] In the past three decades, Esau has

---

[45] *My Life with the Patriarch* (in Hebrew) (Tel Aviv: Am Oved, 2001).
[46] Malkah Shaked, *I'll Play You Forever*, 1: 179–80.

become a Jewish or, better yet, an Israeli hero. The transformation has occurred across the Israeli political and cultural spectrum, and Esau casts a very different hero for secular and religious, cosmopolitan and nationalist, Palestinian empathic and Greater Israel intellectuals.

Ḥayim Guri's gentle query of the typology in "Smell of the Field" (1985) signaled the trend from within the Zionist mainstream. He was full of sympathy for Esau, the man of the field, the less holy and less sophisticated protagonist, the more open, simple-minded, and stronger one: "Someone must dash and retrieve the plunder. Always. And be less loved, strong and conned and undeserving of mercy."[47] His Esau, "a man of the field," is not a Zionist. Could he be a Palestinian farmer who does the dirty job and seeks to retrieve his plundered land? Unlikely, but Guri's poem reflects the reversal of traditional attitudes toward Jacob & Esau.

Esau's rehabilitation has cut across intellectual currents. Eli Alon and Aharon Amir, the former a Peace Movement activist, the latter a leading Canaanite, are at one about Esau. In Eli's "Esau My Son, My Might and the First Sign of My Strength" (1989), Isaac tells Esau of his love for him. Jacob may be smooth and shrewd, and easily changes forms. A domestic schemer, he knows his way with God and women. Yet Esau is Isaac's beloved man of nature, the rain and wind in the wheat field. Let Jacob have his eloquence and God's blessing – Esau has the earth's blessing.[48] In Amir's "Esau's Epistle" (1986), Esau recognizes that Jacob is a smooth-tongued double-dealer, who is mostly concerned with his historical role – and he laughs at Jacob. He, Esau, is straight and approachable, at peace with his conscience and destiny. He declines to seek the gods' favors with altars, as Jacob does. Let Jacob and his appalling family receive the blessing, and gullible Isaac and pious Rebecca delight in it. He, Esau, is happy enough with his wives and herds on his mountain, enjoying the bountiful red lentil soup. Like Anda Amir-Pinkerfeld in the 1930s, Eli and Amir redeploy Zionist criticism of the traditional Jew, which is not free of antisemitic stereotyping, to adore Esau as the man of the Land. By 1989, however, the New Zionist Man had vanished, and pristine Zionism appears post-Zionist.[49]

Both Yehudit Kafri's "Esau" (1988) and Yoḥai Oppenheimer's "With the Cheated One" (2000) protest against the Bible's focus on Rebecca and Jacob, and its lack of concern for Esau. For Kafri, Esau runs with the deer in the field to ease his pain, and his cry can be heard from near and far, full of hatred and revenge. Then, the love of women consoles him, and when he meets with his brother, he no longer claims the blessing but cries, and the entire world cries with him. Leah Senir's "When Rebecca Died"

---

[47] Ibid., p. 1: 137.   [48] Ibid., p. 1: 138.   [49] Ibid., pp. 1: 138–39.

(1995) reworks the midrash that Esau alone was there to bury Rebecca.[50] She recounts how Rebecca went through an undignified burial at night, in retribution for the human hurt she had caused. Jacob was abroad. Esau returned from the field to search for Rebecca and reburied her, "going to and fro weeping (הלך ילך ובכה) over her bed, as if lamenting his own life."[51] Senir exemplifies recent Hebrew poetry's deployment of biblical and rabbinic material to fashion radically new stories. Esau, the Jewish people's mortal enemy for millennia, is gone, and gone is rabbinic Jacob, too. The enemy has become a subject of love, and the Jewish patriarch a subject of alienation.

If Tamuz's *Jacob* (1971) marked the beginning of the paradigm's reevaluation, Meir Shalev's novel *Esau* (1991), written in the aftermath of the First Lebanon War (1982–85) and the First Intifada (uprising, 1987–91), represented its culmination.[52] Whereas the reputation of *Jacob* remained confined to literary circles, Shalev's novel became a best-seller and was translated into several languages. Shalev was born in 1948 in Nahalal, an agricultural cooperative in the Yizrael Valley acclaimed for raising two generations of Zionist leaders, and he grew up in Jerusalem. He was injured during his military service, studied at the Hebrew University, and became a journalist and a TV and radio producer and host for fifteen years before publishing his first novel in 1988. Since then, he has become one of Israel's most prolific and popular writers. His father, poet and novelist Yizḥak Shalev, was a spokesperson for Greater Israel, but the son is a Left Zionist. His early novels, including *Esau*, tell of Zionist agricultural settlers, founders and sons, their families and communities. As a representative of the grandsons' generation, Meir Shalev, like his protagonists, unravels Zionist Jacob & Esau from within.

Esau is a saga about three generations of a family of bakers in a village near Jerusalem from World War I to the 1970s. The narrator is Esau, brother of Jacob, son of Abraham and Sarah, and uncle of Benjamin (who dies in the army), Romi, and Michael. Three short stories complement his narrative, telling of events that Esau himself could not report. In the aftermath of World War I, Abraham Levy, a descendant of an old Jerusalem Sephardic family who lost his father in the war and saw his family reduced to starvation, marries a powerful, illiterate, beautiful, and generous woman, Sarah, daughter of a Greek Orthodox pilgrim to Jerusalem, Michael Nazaroff, who converted to Judaism. Having lost their holdings in the 1927 earthquake, the family – Abraham, Sarah,

[50] *Midrash Tanḥuma* (ed. Buber), ki-teẓe 4; Naḥmanides on Genesis 35:8.
[51] Ibid., 1: 137 (Kafri), 1: 140 (Oppenheimer), 1: 419 (Senir).
[52] Meir Shalev, *Esau* (Tel Aviv: Am Oved, 1991); *Esau*, trans. Barbara Harshav (New York: Harper Collins, 1994).

and their two sons, Jacob and Esau – leaves Jerusalem for a nearby village, where Abraham establishes a bakery with the aid of a loan from Sarah's family. The twin sons, Jacob and Esau, are both nearsighted, and Jacob monopolizes the single set of eyeglasses. Esau's blurred vision predisposes him to intellectual life, and puts him at a disadvantage in the competition with practical-minded Jacob for both the bakery's inheritance and the heart of beautiful Leah. In 1929, Aunt Miriam, alias Tia Duduch, Abraham's sister, who lost her husband and was raped and maimed by Palestinian rioters in Jerusalem, joins the family with her injured son, Shimeon.

Abraham, an overworked and judgmental father and a spurning husband, prefers Esau to Jacob, whereas Sarah prefers Jacob. Having lost his finger in a bakery accident, the injured Jacob wins Leah, and is about to win the bakery, too, when the disgruntled Esau emigrates, around 1948 (Israel's foundation), to the United States to become a gourmet food columnist. Sarah curses him when he leaves home, telling him that "you will have no family of your own . . . no wife of your own . . . no child of your own . . . no land," which all comes to pass.[53] Esau does not find American life meaningful and remains attached to memories of the family. Sarah dies shortly after his departure, Jacob takes over the bakery, becoming as hardworking, unsociable, and authoritarian as his father was, and, like him, also growing to despise his beloved wife, Leah. Determined to secure the bakery's succession, he imprints his own mutilated hand and that of his eldest son in cement at the bakery's gate: "Abraham Levy and his son Benjamin, bakers, April 1955."[54]

About 1967, however, Benjamin, a soldier, falls to friendly fire. His traumatized mother, Leah, sinks into permanent sleep, and the bereaved Jacob, refusing public sympathy, madly impregnates her to produce Michael, his youngest son. Aging Aunt Duduch breast-feeds Michael, and Jacob, his father, neurotically guards and checks him daily. Yet, Michael is unable to feel pain, his behavior appears otherworldly, and he clings to his sleeping mother, not quite the bakery owner Jacob envisioned. Older sister Romi, reminiscent of grandmother Sarah and uncle Esau in her looks and red complexion, visits her uncle in the United States and develops an intimate relationship with him (and many others). Hearing of the worsening condition of his ailing father Abraham, Esau returns after thirty years for a visit, which gives rise to the story of the Levy family. Jacob bitterly offers Esau both Leah and the bakery – both have become untenable projects. Artistically inclined, enterprising Romi photographs and exhibits the family's story.

---

[53] *Esau* (in Hebrew), p. 311;   [54] Ibid., p. 106.

The biblical narrative of Jacob & Esau serves as a prototype for the family saga, and Shalev repeatedly gestures to it, as if creating a grotesque counterpart. Yet he subverts the narrative, and with it also the Zionist project. The biblical story has moments of horror and grace, and a grand vision of God's people underlies both. The fleeting moments of grace in Shalev's saga reflect natural enjoyment of sun, rain, and the smell of bread; they do not involve human relationships. Love, family and community are an interminable story of misfortune, alienation, jealousy, violence, frustration, and pain. Shalev makes light of his protagonists' misery by portraying their life as grotesque, and leaves them without real hope. The Bible, the rabbis, and Zionism are gone. What is to come is unclear.

The biblical Patriarchs were dignified, successful, devoted to their family and community, at peace with themselves, and in command of life and events. Shalev's patriarchs are lonely, unsociable, tortured souls, overwhelmed by events, and failures. The rabbis idealized the Patriarchs' households and the Matriarchs' happy unions. In Shalev, the matriarchs' marriages are pure hell, Jacob's courtship of beautiful Leah is a parody of the biblical Rachel romance, and Jacob's love toward Leah turns into hatred and virtual rape. God vindicates independent biblical Sarah: Abraham is told to obey her. Shalev's Sarah's strength and free spirit are oddly masculine and animal-like and they are rewarded with Abraham's resentment and rejection. The Zionist ethos elevated collective life in agricultural settlements, returning the Jews to their homeland. Shalev's protagonists are social outcasts leading hard lives, unable to enjoy the fruits of their labor, irreparably damaged by the violence of the Arab–Israeli conflict. The culturally sensitive Esau leaves for a life abroad, yet finds no home there, either. There is no home.

The Bible underlines the Hebrews' foreign origin, and the Patriarchs set a marriage boundary against the Canaanites, but the Patriarchs were, for the most part, welcomed in Canaan, and in the rabbinic story, massive conversion took place in Abraham's household. The conversion of a foreigner into a Jew seemed seamless. Shalev, too, undermines the boundary between foreigner and Jew, the Land and the Diaspora, but the union of foreigner and Jew is unhappy: Sarah comes from a family of converts, and Abraham's family rejects her. Esau and Romi (evocative of Rome) display Sarah's non-Jewish ethnicity and, not coincidentally, they are also intellectually inclined and have extended stays abroad.

Shalev relentlessly parodies the Jacob & Esau paradigm, and subverts the rabbinic typology as well. Rabbinic Jacob, a yeshivah student, becomes an earthy baker, and rabbinic Esau, a warrior, becomes a writer. The brothers' conflict, it turns out, was not about the Jewish people's future but merely about property and a girl. In Genesis, Isaac blesses both his sons, but in Shalev, the mother curses Esau and no one has a blessing. In Genesis, Jacob's limping is a mark of his struggle and triumph over the angel; in Shalev, his mutilated hand is a result of a bakery accident and a pathetic testimony of his love for Leah. The demise of Benjamin is unheroic: He dies of friendly fire. With the loss of Rachel, biblical Jacob finds consolation in her two sons, Joseph and Benjamin, and the loss of Joseph ends up in a joyous reunion and salvation. There is no recovery for Jacob and his family after the death of Benjamin, only Romi's documentation of the family (and Zionism's) losses.

Contrary to some views, *Esau* contains no political critique of the Israeli disinheritance of the Palestinians.[55] Indeed, the Palestinians appear as murderous rioters: The Salomo family's overseer, Ibrahim, turns on it, kills the husband, rapes and maims the wife, and injures the child. (Palestinians who hid Jewish friends during the 1929 riots are nowhere in sight: It would be out of character for the novel.) The Jacob & Esau conflict is internally Jewish: Esau is more the diasporic Jew, and Jacob the Zionist, but there is no solution in Diaspora or Zionism: Diaspora is alienating, and the Zionist project, the work of uncultivated characters, a prolonged misery. Romi, who moves freely between Jacob and Esau, Jewish and non-Jewish, the Land and Diaspora, masculinity and femininity, may represent the most attractive prospect, but hardly one that can sustain a national project. There is no resolution in sight.

Shalev inserts himself into the novel as one of Romi's boyfriends, and *Esau* does what Romi does: document life in disarray. One may not fault an author for choosing the grotesque, decadent, and magically realist to address a tragedy, but it does denigrate Zionism's attractive ideals without helping to rectify the injustice it inflicted on the Palestinians. In sabotaging biblical, rabbinic, and Zionist resources, Shalev leaves Israelis struggling for a future without means.

Orthodox Jews could not dispose of the traditional typology as Shalev did. Instead, in both Israel and the Diaspora, they have reworked the typology in surprising ways, initiating paradigmatic changes while retaining traditional appearances – subversion from within. Improved Jewish–Christian relations and, after September 11, 2001, the putative conflict between "Islam" and "the West" influenced reinterpretation everywhere, but whereas Orthodox leaders in Europe and the United States endeavored to redefine Orthodoxy's place in a multicultural

---

[55] Yosef Oren, *The Writing as a Political Announcement* (in Hebrew) (Rishon Le-Ẓion: Yaḥad, 1992), pp. 57–82.

society, Israeli leaders were most responsive to problems emerging from the Israeli–Palestinian conflict. The former reconfigured Esau as a respected, and even beloved, Christian brother, whereas the latter declared him a lost Jewish brother.

Jonathan Sacks, Chief Rabbi of the British Commonwealth from 1991 to 2013, initially adopted a Taylorite conception of multiculturalism and the self. He argued that Jacob began as an insecure acculturated Jew, not knowing who he was, and ended up finding his Jewish identity as Israel.[56] The blessing that Jacob stole was not his: It was material and not spiritual: "As long as Jacob sought to be Esau there was tension, conflict, rivalry."[57] "Living by someone else's identity creates confusion, anxiety and insecurity," argues Sacks.[58] The struggle with the angel was an internal battle with the fear of Esau, and by conquering the fear and being himself, Jacob could reconcile with Esau. The two-millennia Jewish–Christian feud was unnecessary. Being authentically Jewish in a pluralist society is a prescription for good Jewish–Christian relations. Psychologizing Jacob's wrestling with the angel, Sacks deployed Taylor to vindicate Moses Sofer and illiberal multiculturalism.

Still, attending to Esau's humanity, Sacks moved on to liberalize pluralism, the Torah, and Jewish Orthodoxy. By highlighting Esau's efforts to honor his parents and to win the blessing, and then his bitter cry and pleading, the Torah endeavored, says Sacks, to enlist our sympathies with Esau, and teach us a lesson about love and humanity. Esau was never rejected: Isaac's blessings of the land's fruits to his two sons were virtually identical.[59] Jacob was promised political supremacy, but only as long as his rule was just, and, in fact, Esau's political might would precede his, and Israel would be warned not to touch his territory and not to "abhor an Edomite, since he is your brother." "There is nothing in these commands," continues Sacks, "to remind us of the eternal strife between the two nations predicted before their birth…. During the biblical era

---

[56] Charles Taylor, *Sources of the Self: The Making of the Modern Identity* (Cambridge, MA: Harvard University Press, 1989).

[57] Jonathan Sacks, "Be Thyself" (November 16, 2013), in *Covenant and Conversation*, http://www.rabbisacks.org/vayishlach-5774-thyself/.

[58] Sacks, "This Is Ours", in *A Letter in the Scroll: Understanding Our Jewish Identity and Exploring the Legacy of the World's Oldest Religion* (New York: Free Press, 2000), pp. 204–15; quotation is on p. 207.

[59] The traditional Jewish reading of Esau's blessings (Genesis 27:39) is identical with the King James version – "thy dwelling shall be the fatness of the earth, and of the dew of heaven from above" – and not the modern standard version – "your dwelling will be away from the earth's richness away from the dew of heaven above." Sacks needs to override Malachi 1:2 "but Esau I hated" and interprets "hated" as "less loved," as in Genesis 29:31: "God saw that Leah was hated." ודו״ק

there were periodic tensions ... but normatively, the Israelites were commanded to respect both the Edomites and their land."[60]

Esau was not chosen as an heir to the Abrahamic Covenant because "the twists and turns of covenantal history – exile, slavery, redemption and the wilderness years" – were not for him: When Jacob offered him, on his return from abroad, "please accept my blessing," Esau showed no sign of understanding that the Covenant was at stake. But

> to be chosen does not mean that others are unchosen.... To be secure in one's relationship with G-d does not depend on negating the possibility that others too may have a (different) relationship with Him.... Love is not quantifiable.... All are precious to G-d, each has his or her place in the scheme of things, each has his or her virtues, talents, gifts, and each is precious in the eyes of G-d.... Esau too will have his blessing, his heritage, his land.... There is a humanity here that defies all stereotypes and conventional categorisations. Esau is a child loved by his father and loving him in return.... It is one of the Torah's most profound messages to humanity. How deeply does the world need to hear it today in an age of "the clash of civilizations"![61]

Sacks had to override significant textual and historical resistance, not to mention Midrash, to propound his liberal Orthodox view, and his Esau remains intellectually limited, conforming to traditional stereotypes. Yet he managed to navigate the typology's dissolution and deployed Jacob & Esau to reshape a space for postorthodox Judaism in the unprecedented circumstances that world Jewry faces today. This is no mean accomplishment.

Esau's rehabilitation extended even to Chabad Ḥasidism. The Seventh Lubavitcher Rebbe, Menaḥem Mendel Schneerson (1902–1994), recognized shortly after his arrival in America in 1941 that the United States represented a prospect for the reconstruction of Jewish life destroyed in Europe. He spoke of the United States as a benevolent superpower and a kingdom of grace. In a December 1984 address, commemorating the release of the First Rebbe from a Russian prison, he presented the Chabad celebration, the American holiday of Thanksgiving, and Ḥanukkah as all conveying a single message of religious freedom.[62] He spoke of the partnership of Jews and non-Jews in advancing the observance of the Noaḥide commandments, the Jewish equivalent of Natural Law, and regarded it as preparing the world for the messianic coming, when Jews and non-Jews will worship together. Non-Jewish observers of the Noaḥide commandments were the "righteous among the nations."[63]

---

[60] "Chosenness and its Discontents" (10 November 2007), http://www.rabbisacks.org/covenant-conversation-5768-toldot-chosenness-and-its-discontents/.
[61] Ibid.   [62] http://www.youtube.com/watch?v=bguqj7VaZxk.
[63] *Hitvaadoyut* [1985–86], 2d ed. (Brooklyn, NY: Vaad Hanochos, 1990): 3: 62–65.

Schneerson elided Ḥasidic and kabbalistic traditions, which had established an insurmountable barrier between Jews and non-Jews. He could not leave the image of a bloodthirsty Christian Esau intact. In Chabad weekly homilies, the obscure Og, a legendary giant Amorite king, began taking Esau's place.[64] The First Rebbe had intimated that Esau represented the animal soul, and Jacob the human one.[65] In contrast, in his Saturday afternoon "conversations," Schneerson told his audience that both Jacob and Esau wished to worship God, but whereas Jacob was the perfect righteous ḥasid, who had no evil inclination, Esau was a knowing hunter, who knew how to conquer his instincts. This reflected the virtue of heroism, which he inherited from Isaac. Both strove to inherit this world and the world to come, but Jacob gave priority to the latter, suitable to his mode of worship, and Esau to this one, where his mode is superior.[66] To be sure, Esau did end up going astray and worshipping foreign gods, and the ḥasidim are holier than less observant Jews and Christians, but there is something about the arts of this world for the ḥasidim to learn from their less holy brethren.

Modern Orthodox Israeli rabbis were slower to respond to changing Jewish–Christian relations, but with the growing confrontation between "Islam" and the "West," in the aftermath of 9/11, and the American Christian fundamentalists' support for Israel, the change in Esau's image registered among them, too. In 2009, Benjamin Lau, a moderate National Religious rabbi, surveyed Jacob & Esau's metamorphoses since biblical times. Jewish–Christian relations had a dark past, he said: The seventh stanza of the Ḥanukkah song, Maoz Ẓur, called for the Edomites' destruction and was repressed for fear of the Church. But

our generation seeks reconciliation between the Church and Judaism, and finds itself attacked from the East by a third brother who also carries the single God's name. The seventh encounter of Edom (Esau) and Jacob finds itself in a common front against this brother, the goal of which is reinforcement of man's dignity and stature wherever he is. This is a different sort of encounter, in which God's words to Rebecca "two nations in your womb" are found to be not an invitation to a struggle but an understanding that each one has its fullness and uniqueness, and together we shall need to aim for a life of peace.[67]

---

[64] I heard such homilies delivered in Durham, North Carolina, in 2002–3, using Rashi on Genesis 14:13 and *Genesis Rabah* 53:10; *Deuteronomy Rabah* 1:25.

[65] Schneur Zalman of Liadi, *Liqute Amarim: Tanya* (New York: Qehot Publication Society, 1956), pp. 13b–14a.

[66] Menaḥem Mendel Schneerson, *Liqute Siḥot* (Collected conversations; in Yiddish), 39 vols. (Brooklyn, NY: Qehot, 2001), 20: 108–15.

[67] Benjamin Lau, "Israel vs. Edom – Seventh Round" (in Hebrew), *Haaretz* (4 December 2009), http://www.haaretz.co.il/literature/1.1293204.

Lau's millennial revolution staged Christianity and Judaism against Islam in a war for peace.

Similarly, Isaac Dov Koren, of the Center for Jewish–Christian Understanding and Collaboration in Jerusalem and Efrat, suggests a "New Covenant" between Christianity and Judaism.[68] Koren's mentor, Soloveitchik, limited Jewish–Christian dialogue in the aftermath of Vatican II to nontheological topics. The situation has since changed, says Koren, as both popes and churches have changed their attitudes toward Judaism. They no longer represent Esau and Edom: They are now allies in fighting against Muslim extremists and leftist antisemites.[69] The two brothers have united against their uncle, Ishmael.

Still, there are also other voices in the National Religious camp, ones who wish for the opening to Christian Esau to extend to an understanding with secular Jews and the Palestinians. To be sure, they are not predominant: More common is the evocation of the Palestinians on *Shabbat Zakhor*, before the Purim holiday, when the command to eradicate Amaleq concludes the Torah reading.[70] But like Sacks, these voices articulate exegetical innovation, liberal spirit, and hope, however slim. David Bigman, head of the Maale ha-Gilboa Yeshivah, suggests, following U.S. Orthodox Rabbi Yizḥak Hutner, that Jacob had first to recognize Esau's greatness, to see both his human and divine virtues, before he could reconcile with him: This was the significance of his struggle with Esau's angel. Jacob repented and went through true reconciliation.

Yaakov Nagan, of the West Bank's Tequa and Otniel yeshivot, an activist in the "Jerusalem Peacemakers" and "Interfaith Encounter Association," suggests that the Jacob saga conveys the ambiguous legacy of pain in Jewish history. Nothing came easily to Jacob: His very name connoted struggle, and he had to go through two millennia of exile and struggle with the angels to emerge as a fighter and return to the Land. Understandably, but all the more regrettably, Jacob remained suspicious of Esau, and protective of his identity. His closeness became a hindrance: He missed the chance of marrying Dinah to Esau and was punished for it.

---

[68] "New Covenant" (in Hebrew), trans. Limor Riskin, *Maqor Rishon* (June 26, 2015), http://musaf-shabbat.com/2015/06/26/קורן-דב-יצחק-חדשה-ברית/. The article responded to the arson attack on the ancient Church of the Multiplication of the Loaves and Fish in Capernaum. For this, and many references to contemporary Israeli discourse on Jacob & Esau, I am indebted to my colleague and friend, Hilda Nissimi, Chair of the General History Department at Bar-Ilan University.

[69] Isaac Dov Koren, *Christianity in the Eyes of Judaism: Past, Present and Future* (in Hebrew) (Jerusalem: AJC, 2013).

[70] I have experienced it personally in both the United States and Israel.

Jews should remain open and build good and honest relations with the Other.[71]

On the Religious Left, the Other's identity remains amorphous: Esau could be the nonobservant Jew, the Palestinian, or the Christian. However, the rehabilitation of Esau has extended to the Center and Right, too. In the aftermath of the Israeli disengagement from Gaza, which pitted major segments among the Settlers (residents of the post-1967 Occupied Territories) against the Israeli government, the latter sensed that they had lost the Israeli public. The more thoughtful among them responded by seeking new ways of building bridges to the lost brothers. Esau became a lost Jewish brother, spurred on by Jacob with horrible consequences.

Reem Hacohen, head of the Otniel Yeshivah, overhauled the interpretive tradition by reconfiguring midrashim and kabbalistic homilies favorable to Esau. The Jacob–Esau story could have ended differently, he says, with the two building together, with Rachel and Leah, the House of Israel. Jacob failed the test of brotherly love. Isaac was no dupe for loving Esau: Esau's holiness was greater than Jacob's. He wished to tithe hay and salt because, in the other world, inanimate life is holy, too, and both Isaac and Esau wandered in otherworldly fields. Jacob's theft of the birthright was tantamount to murder, a design on Esau's soul, as it excluded him from the Jewish people. Jacob was punished by exile, and Laban cheated him measure for measure. He committed a second transgression by marrying Leah, who was destined for Esau. Returning to the Land, he sent for Esau, seeking *tiqun*, but failed a third time by refusing him Dinah. The result was the Shekhem rape and massacre, and later Amaleq, and yet later the Temple's destruction. God did not wish it this way, but Jacob was allowed to go the way he wished. In Hacohen, the Jewish-Christian story has vanished. Jacob & Esau has become an internal Jewish story.[72]

Reem Hacohen's message, like that of Nagan and Bigman, is one of peace, reconciliation, and sorrow for the profound loss occasioned by the Jacob & Esau conflict. His Esau is mystical and holy, a product of Kook's kabbalistic tradition, a figure very new and yet recognizably Jewish. In contrast, the Esau emerging from the discourse of former Gush Emunim (Bloc of the faithful) leader Joel Bin Nun, and of the head of the flagship Har-Eẓion *Hesder* Yeshivah (a yeshivah combining advanced Torah study with military service), Yaacov Medan, reflects the profound

---

[71] Yaakov Nagan, "A Blessing Emerges From Pain: Between Jacob & Esau," http://www.kipa.co.il/jew/pash/42/46979.html.

[72] Reem Hacohen, "Contradictions in a Single Womb" (in Hebrew), *Maqor Rishon*, 44 (November 27, 2009), and "How Was the Torah Written?" Lecture at Herzog College (published October 7, 2009), http://www.ynet.co.il/articles/0,7340,L-3786363,00.html, 39:42-53:32.

transformation of Jewish values by religious nationalism. Both are fed up with rabbinic Jacob, the studious yeshivah student whose eyes are set on the world to come, and who, facing the prospect of Esau's attack, prays, offers gifts, and plans to escape in order to save himself. Esau, a warrior and an empire builder (in Nimrod's image), suddenly appears appealing.[73]

No wonder, says Bin Nun, that farmer Isaac, incognizant of Rebecca's oracle, and recognizing the need for household protection, assumed that Jacob, a tent dweller and a Torah student, would need Esau's protection, and that he planned on bestowing political power on Esau. It was Jacob using his voice but offering Esau's hands that opened Isaac's eyes to the successful combination, and to the inferiority of Esau's bloody power politics. But Jacob first needed to learn to fight, and he avoided it until the last minute, attempting to run away from Esau. Encountering the angel and overcoming him, Jacob finally became the synthesis of the two brothers, the way the Jewish State should be, built with Esau's might but with Jacob's justice.[74]

Yaacov Medan goes further. He is exasperated with the secular Israeli intelligentsia, the *belle âme* who supported the disengagement, and with the Ultra-Orthodox yeshivah students shirking military service, and he was horrified by the Jewish State's uprooting of Settler families from Gaza. Israel's actions had biblical precedents, he says: Jacob's sons did not shrink from selling their brother into slavery, and Judean dynasties murdered their siblings. Medan wishes to build bridges to the less acculturated Israelis, even nonreligious ones, who patriotically carry the defense burden – to Israel's Esaus. He points out that the Sages enumerated two great merits of Esau: honoring of parents and love of the Land. Esau wanted the blessing so that he could settle the Land. In contrast, Jacob, who, unlike Abraham and Isaac never fought, escaped abroad. Esau conquered his wish to avenge the blessing's theft out of respect for

---

[73] Genesis 10:8–10 speaks of Nimrod, the King of Shinar, as "mighty on earth" and "a mighty hunter before the Lord." Midrash, *Targum*, and medieval commentators cast Nimrod as Abraham's persecutor (*Bereshit Rabba* 38:13, 42:4), a rebel against God (*Bereshit Rabba* 23:7, 37:2-3; *Pseudo-Jonathan* on 10:8), and an empire builder (Naḥmanides on 10:9 and Radak on 10:8). They coupled the two hunters, Nimrod and Esau, either typologically as tricksters (*Bereshit Rabba* 37:2) or as competitors over Esau's garments: *Bereshit Rabba* 63:13 has Nimrod coveting Esau's garments; *Pirqe de-Rabi Eliezer* 24 has Esau kill Nimrod and take over his garments. Yiẓḥak (Max) Danziger's sculpture Nimrod (1939) became the embodiment of the Canaanite vision of a revival of a secular Semitic culture throughout the Middle East. My thanks to Ari Dubnov, Shai Ginsburg, and Hilda Nissimi for drawing my attention to Bin Nun and Medan's unlikely predecessors.

[74] Joel Bin Nun, "Esau's Hands – Jacob's Voice" (in Hebrew), *Shenaton Amit* [1998]: 13–20, repr. in *Pirqe Avot* (*Alon Shevut*: Tevunot, 2003).

Isaac, and Jacob was never in danger. If family members had an appropriate appreciation of Esau's character, Jacob would not have needed to run abroad. Jacob's sons, in contrast, did not conquer their vengeance, dishonored and hurt their father, and murdered and betrayed a brother. Notwithstanding a two-millennia rabbinic tradition, Esau was an honorable warrior, not unlike King David. Isaac's alliance with him was one of farmer and warrior, the alliance sustaining the Jewish State today.[75]

Moshe Lichtenstein, son of Aharon, the founder of Har-Ezion Yeshivah, and representative of the old guard synthesis of Brisk intellectualism and moderate religious nationalism, responded testily to Medan, reaffirming the two-millennia rabbinic tradition that sees Esau as both Jew and non-Jew, and Jacob as the Covenant and the Land's legitimate inheritor.[76] For all his erudition and firm grasp of rabbinic Esau's ambiguity, Lichtenstein is fighting a rear-guard action against the inexorable logic of religious ethno-nationalism.

Bin Nun and Medan's daring innovation is matched only by their message's appalling character. After two millennia of Jacob's voice crying out over Esau's crimes, the progeny of the Canaanites' Nimrod, the warrior and empire builder, has become the religious national ideal. Jacob has turned into Esau. "Woe, what has become of us!"[77]

---

[75] Yaacov Medan, "Esau's Merit," *Daf Qesher* 522 (December 2006), http://www .etzion.org.il/he/עשו-של-זכותו-תולדות-פרשת. Ari Geiger of Bar-Ilan University has drawn my attention to Medan's 2016 pronouncement: "Isaac & Rebecca, Jacob & Esau": http:// www.youtube.com/watch?v=JhemCzKWP_4&feature=em-uploademail. Medan strives to reconcile rabbinic Esau with his own: He now faults Esau for having left the Land and for marrying Canaanite women. His identity is once again ambiguous: Medan identifies him with both the Settlers' unruly Hilltop Youth and the non-Jews serving in the Israeli Defense Forces. Harnessing his military virtues, exemplified by Judah and King David, is essential to Jewish power, as Jacob's pacifism will not sustain an Israel extending to the Euphrates and overruling Abraham's multiple descendants. Innovative and dangerous.

[76] Moshe Lichtenstein, "Esau as Brother, Esau as Goy" (in Hebrew) 2006, http://www .etzion.org.il/he/כגוי-עשו-כאח-עשו-וישלח-פרשת.

[77] *The Koren Mesorat Harav Kinot* (in Hebrew and English) (Jerusalem: Koren Publishers, 2011), p. 51. The *Qina*'s first stanza, "Remember, God, what has happened to us" is based on Eikha 5:1.

Epilogue: The End of Postwar Exceptionalism

As Jacob became European and Esau Jewish, the memory of the Austrian Empire in Hebrew literature receded. In post-1967 Israel, its space was replaced by the British Commonwealth. Unlike other anticolonial movements, the Israeli Left never developed an anti-imperial discourse.[1] In the final two decades of the British Mandate over Palestine, plans for a Jewish Dominion emerged among British and philo-British Zionists, with most Labor Zionists cool but not obdurate. The plans died out quickly after Israel's foundation, but with the growing recognition of the irresolvability of the Israeli–Palestinian conflict after 1967, a mild nostalgia for the British Mandate began settling in. It rarely expressed itself openly as imperial sympathy: More commonly, childhood, youth, or romance in multiethnic Jerusalem or other urban settings would be invoked, and the *Yishuv* and Zionist project would be shown flourishing under the Mandate. In different ways, writers such as Shulamith Hareven, Amos Oz, Yoram Qaniuk, Tom Segev, and Nathan Shaham recalled cultural diversity and ethno-religious coexistence, and commemorated imperial cosmopolitanism, extinguished by the triumpth of nationalism. British nostalgia mimicked the Austrian one, and the British Army became a fountain for romance stories. The Israeli Left's political program called for two states and ethno-national separation, but writers on the Left imagined a pluralist imperial alternative.[2] As postnational Europe was reclaiming the Jewish intelligentsia's idealized vision of Central European culture, their Israeli compatriots were dreaming of imperial British cosmopolitanism.

---

[1] Arie Dubnov suggests that this is due to the Zionist Left's abiding concern with developing a European image, set first against the East, then the Third World.

[2] Eitan Bar-Yosef, "The Nostalgic Return to Mandatory Palestine in Israeli Culture," provides detailed references; Hadara Lazar, *Ha-Mandatorim: Ereẓ Yisrael, 1940–1948* (in Hebrew) (Jerusalem: Keter, 1990), translated by Lazar as *Out of Palestine: The Making of Modern Israel* (New York: Atlas & Co., 2011). I thank Yaakov Ariel of UNC, Chapel Hill, for literary references.

This book began with Jewish hatred for the Roman Empire, symbolized by Esau, and ends with Jewish nostalgia for empire, and with the Jewish Jacob becoming Esau. Such an ironic and dramatic turn is the product of world Jewry's novel situation in the past half century. Nowadays, Jews have the option of "national" life in Israel, a thriving Jewish life in the United States, and acceptance as European throughout the continent. Jewish national power and American and European integration have undermined the traditional typology. They reflect primarily nation-state experiences, albeit divergent ones, but the Jewish love affair with the nation-state is recent: The majority of European Jews retained imperial sympathies into the early interwar years. Jewish life in empires is millennia old, and appreciation for the Roman Empire has enjoyed gradual growth since the Middle Ages. For traditional Jews, Austria-Hungary was the Roman Empire's last embodiment, and life between nation and empire in Austria-Hungary created unique opportunities for Jewish national life, which made the Dual Monarchy the most beloved empire in Jewish history. Imperial Austrian socialist ideas, like personal national autonomy, federalism, and the transnational intelligentsia, have offered models for mediation of national differences that proved applicable to other settings. Zionists, who disparaged the European nation-state, envisioned federalist arrangements for Palestine along Austrian lines. Paradoxically, Israelis nowadays seek to legitimize the nation-state.

Do recent revolutionary changes mark a long-term transformation in Jewish history or a respite? Ambivalence about Judaism may be constitutive of Christianity, but the post-Holocaust Christian recognition of Judaism as a sister religion seems to have become entrenched. When Christians recognize Jews as elder brothers, Jews cease to think of them as Esau: Esau can become Jewish. The Middle East conflict has foregrounded Jewish–Muslim hostility, historically secondary to Jewish–Christian enmity: The Jews, rejected earlier by the Europeans as Oriental, have now become, in the antisemitic imagination, the European colonial exemplar par excellence. The Jew's global image as the quintessential white imperialist will probably outlast the Jewish State. In turn, Ishmael has become a center of Jewish hatred. As the historical resources supporting Ishmael's new status are limited, Israel's enemies have quickly been converted from Ishmael into Amaleq. If the Jacob & Esau typology resurges, it will be in a form discontinuous with the traditional ones.

The post–World War II Jewish Golden Age may well have passed its peak. Confrontation with the Holocaust's legacy was crucial to European identity in the aftermath of the European Union's formation, and it has foregrounded the Jewish intelligentsia, and Jews in general, as European. The Christian–Jewish dialogue did the same, and conceptions of Judeo-Christian Europe have become popular. Europe's confrontation with the increased role of Muslim communities and other migratory groups has shifted European concerns. The Jews are not an immediate target for mainstream hostility: Muslim, Roma, and immigrant communities are. Yet, historically, wherever and whenever ethnic tensions have arisen in European history, the Jews, already a target for Muslim hostility today, have found themselves victims in the end. Memory of the Holocaust still constitutes a barrier to antisemitism, but it will progressively erode. There are no grounds to believe that antisemitic discourse, ever adaptable and persistent, and now global, will not resurface.

The United States may suggest a more promising trajectory. Repeated historical efforts to ethnicize American identity have shattered against its ethno-cultural diversity, and one hopes the fate of the present one will be no different. Philosemitic Christian traditions continue to counterbalance American nativism. Representatives of other ethnic groups may soon supplant the Jew's image as the ideal immigrant, and Jewish holiday celebrations in the White House may diminish in time, but, notwithstanding the best efforts of the American Israel Public Affairs Committee (AIPAC), antisemitism may remain contained. "My Master was a Jewish carpenter" read the sign on a car on its way from Durham to Chapel Hill the other day. Such a sign would be inconceivable and incomprehensible in Europe. In the context of American nonantisemitic biblical culture, Jacob and Esau are freed from millennial Christian and Jewish typology, and become again free signifiers, open for reinterpretation. A Kingdom of Grace!

Having begun a decade after Israel's foundation, my own lifespan would probably correspond to that of the Jewish State. If history offers any instruction, it is that the ethno-national conflict in Israel-Palestine will run its course, and the second Hasmonean state will have reached its end in my own daughters' lifetime. A catastrophic end is not impossible, but more likely it will be an implosion, the ethnically and religiously diverse population in the Land between the Mediterranean and the Jordan River claiming, albeit not necessarily receiving, their citizenship rights (or their equivalent). The Land's historical diversity will reemerge with no empire yet in sight to impose order. The worst scenarios of ethnic massacres may be exaggerated, but Israeli–Palestinian relations give no grounds for hope of peaceful coexistence either, and one recalls that Jewish–Hellenic confrontation in Caesarea ignited the Jewish–Roman war that ended in Jerusalem's destruction תותבבא". Many a Jacob will then again be crossing the Jordan River with their staffs, hoping to rebuild a community abroad and, yet again, return.

The Jacob & Esau typology will no longer address their queries. Jewry will need to fashion new paradigms to explain the Holocaust and the Jewish State's place in Jewish history. The Spanish expulsion – the greatest *Ḥurban* between the Second Temple's destruction and the Holocaust – generated major new spiritual movements in less than a century. One does not see them yet today, perhaps because the miraculous Jewish State has delayed them. That Hebrew culture – Zionism's greatest achievement – can be sustained with a diminishing Jewish Palestinian community is questionable. Those who point hopefully to the birth of rabbinic Judaism from the Ḥurban's ashes forget that it took the rabbis several centuries to invent "grant me Yavneh and its sages," the strategy that has sustained Jewish life for millennia. Indeed, rabbinic Judaism was implicated in the disastrous Bar-Kokhba Rebellion that gave rise to the Jacob & Esau typology, with Esau and Edom becoming Rome: "A star shall rise from Jacob," said Rabbi Aqiva, refers to Bar-Kokhba.

Unlike some of my friends, pained and ashamed as I am by the injustice that Jewish power has inflicted on the Palestinians, and its gross insensitivity to the humanity of others, I am thankful to have lived my life in this most extraordinary period of Jewish history when Jews have multiple choices for "national" and diasporic life, as opposed to none. The recognition that this unusual historical conjuncture may be nearing its end was among the motives for writing this book. Let it be remembered that there was a moment in history when a postorthodox Jew could imagine European culture accepting traditional Jews, and, indeed, recognizing them as an important marker of its history and culture.

At the end of his "Science as a Vocation," German sociologist Max Weber (1862–1920), an intellectual giant and a cultivated brute, bid his audience attend to the tasks of the day and not be misguided by utopian calls for redemption, which masquerade as secular but are hopelessly religious. He illustrated his call through "the beautiful Edomite watchman's song" in Isaiah (21:11–12), enjoining the Jewish people to "come again and inquire once more": "The people to whom this was said," opined Weber, "has enquired and waited for much more than two millennia, and we are familiar with its deeply distressing fate."[3] Poisoned by ethno-nationalism and *Realpolitik*, Weber could not sense the power and grandeur of Christian and Jewish civilizations coexisting for two millennia in a state of expectation. In his disenchantment, he opted for the modern wager – of which emancipation and the nation-state, Zionism and the

---

[3] *The Vocation Lectures*, ed. with an introduction by David Owen and Tracy Strong, trans. Rodney Livingstone (Indianapolis, IN: Hackett, 2004), p. 31.

Holocaust, are all part – and counterposed open-eyed modern responsibility to a life of expectation in vain.

The jury on modernity is still out, but this book has been guided by a loving postmodern exploration of premodern traditions, calling on them to support a disenchanted life, and show that, *pace* Weber, it is possible to live and die "old and fulfilled by life." My daughters, Hadas and Lilach, and their (future) children will need to recover the experience of Jewish life in a state of expectation and relearn to wait. They may derive some encouragement from the knowledge that at the end of his three-millennia tour, their father, like his ancestor Jacob, "arrived safely in the city": ויבא יעקב שלם.[4]

---

[4] Genesis 33:18. This book has explored four senses of "shalem" (שלם), and all apply: 1. Literally, safely; 2. Midrash (and Rashi), whole (or perfect): whole in his body, his property, and his Torah; 3. Ultra-Orthodox counterintegrationist use – name (שם), language (לשון), and dress (מלבוש): I have retained all three, only added others, so I reckon my perfection superior; 4. Shalem is also a name for Jerusalem, the only Jerusalem that will never be taken away from us, if we do not take it away from ourselves.

Bibliography

Primary Sources

Archives

Carnap Collection. Archives for Scientific Philosophy. University of Pittsburgh, Pittsburgh, PA.

Emergency Committee in Aid of Displaced Foreign Scholars. Manuscripts and Archives Division. New York Public Library. New York, NY.

Erich Auerbach Collection. Deutsches Literaturarchiv. Marbach, Germany.

Friedrich Adler Collection. Verein für Geschichte der Arbeiterbewegung (VGA). Vienna, Austria.

Friedrich Torberg Collection. Wienbibliothek im Rathaus. Vienna, Austria.

Hebrew MS. Bodleian Library. Oxford University. Oxford, UK.

Hebrew MS. Jewish National and University Library. Jerusalem, Israel.

International Association for Cultural Freedom Papers. Joseph Regenstein Library (Special Collections). University of Chicago. Chicago, IL.

Israelitische Kultusgemeinde Wien (IKG, Vienna) Archives. Central Archives for the History of the Jewish People. Hebrew University. Jerusalem, Israel.

Karl Polanyi Digital Archives, Concordia University. Montreal, Quebec, Canada. http://kpolanyi.scoolaid.net:8080/xmlui/handle/10694/718.

Karl Popper Collection. Hoover Institute Archives, Stanford University, Stanford, CA.

Lavinia Mazzucchetti Collection. Fondazione Arnoldo e Alberto Mondadori. Milan, Italy.

Manès Sperber Collection. Österreichisches Literaturarchiv. Vienna, Austria.

Meldearchiv. Vienna, Austria.

Rabbinic and Christian Literature: Biblical, Talmudic, Midrashic, Kabbalistic, Homiletic, Theological, and Scholarly

Abravanel, Yiẓḥak. *Maayane ha-Yeshuah: Perush al Daniel.* Stettin: R. Grossmann, 1860.

Migdal Yeshuot. Koenigsberg: Albert Rosbach, 1860.

Perush al ha-Torah. Jerusalem: Bnei Arabel, 1964

Perush al Neviim Aḥaronim. Jerusalem: Torah va-Daat, 1956.

Perush al Neviim u-Ketuvim. Jerusalem: Abarbanel, 1960.

Albo, Yosef. *Sefer ha-Iqarim*. Ed. Yehoshua Aharonson. Tel Aviv: Sifriati, 1959.

Alighieri, Dante. "Dante's Letter to Can Grande." Trans. Nancy Howe. In *Essays on Dante*, ed. Mark Musa. Bloomington: Indiana University Press, 1964, pp. 32–47.

Alter, Yehudah Leib. *Sefer Sefat Emet*. 5 vols. Piotrków: N.p., 1905.

Ambrose, St. "Isaac, or the Soul" and "Jacob and the Happy Life." In *Seven Exegetical Works*, trans. Michael P. McHugh. Washington, DC: Catholic University of America Press, 1972, pp. 9–68, 117–84.

Anon. *Altercatio Ecclesiae et Synagogae* (Notitia Clavis Patrum Latinorum 577). Library of Latin Texts – Series A. Turnhout: Brepolis Publishers, 2005.

Anon. "The Historie of Jacob and Esau." [1568] In *The Cambridge History of English and American Literature*, ed. A. W. Ward, A. R. Waller, W. P. Trent, J. Erskine, S. P. Sherman, and C. Van Doren. 18 vols. New York: G.P. Putnam's Sons, 1907–21: 5: 125–26.

Ascher, Saul. *Leviathan oder über Religion in Rücksicht des Judentums*. Berlin: Franck, 1792.

Ashkenazi, Jacob ben Isaac. *Tz'enah Ur'enah*. Trans. from the Yiddish by Miriam Stark Zakon. 3 vols. New York: Masorah Publications, 1983.

Athanasius, Bishop of Alexandria. *Select Writings and Letters of Athanasius, Bishop of Alexandria*. Ed. Archibald Robertson. Vol. 4 of *Nicene and Post-Nicene Fathers of the Christian Church*, ed. Philip Schaff and Henry Wace. 14 vols. New York: Christian Literature Company, 1892.

"Aufruf an unsere deutschen Glaubensbrüder," quoted in Samuel Holdheim, *Geschichte der Entstehung und Entwickelung der Jüdischen Reformgemeinde in Berlin*. Berlin: Julius Springer, 1857, pp. 49–52.

Augustine of Hippo. *Concerning the City of God against the Pagans*. Trans. Henry Bettenson. Harmondsworth, UK: Penguin Books, 1985.

De civitate Dei: The City of God Against the Pagans (in English and Latin). 7 vols. Cambridge, MA: Harvard University Press, 1957–72.

Avner of Burgos. *Mostrador de Justicia*. Ed. Walter Mettmann. 2 vols. Opladen: Westdeutscher Verlag, 1994–96.

Baeck, Leo. *Die Pharisäer: Ein Kapitel Jüdischer Geschichte*. Berlin: Schocken, 1934.

Judaism and Christianity. Trans. with an introduction by Walter Kaufmann. Philadelphia: Jewish Publication Society, 1964.

The Essence of Judaism. [1905] Rev. ed. New York: Schocken Books, 1948.

This People Israel: The Meaning of Jewish Existence. Trans. with an introduction by Albert Friedlander. New York: Holt, Rinehart and Winston, 1964.

Barth, Karl. *Church Dogmatics I.2*. [1938] Trans. G. T. Thomson. London: T&T Clark International, 2004.

Homiletics. Trans. Geoffrey W. Bromiley and Donald E. Daniels. Louisville, KY: Westminster/J. Knox Press, 1991.

Beer, Peter. *Dat Yisrael oder Das Judenthum: Das ist einer Versuch einder Darstellung aller wesentlichen Glaubens- Sitten- und Ceremoniallehren heutiger Juden zum Gebrauche bey den Elementarreligionsunterrichte ihrer Jugend nebst einem Anhange fuer Lehrer*. Prague: Karl Barth, 1810.

Die Mosaischen Schriften. Prague: N.p., 1815.

Handbuch der Mosaischen Religion. Vienna: Karl Haas, 1821.

Beermann, Max. *Festpredigten.* Frankfurt am Main: J. Kauffmann, 1909.

Ben Asher, Baḥya. *Kad ha-Qemah.* 2 vols. New York: Kelilat Yofi Pub., 1960.

Perush Rabbenu Baḥya al ha-Torah. 5 vols. in 2. Jerusalem: Mishor, 1994.

ben Nathan, Joseph Official. *Sefer Yosef ha-Meqane.* Ed. Yehudah Rozental. Jerusalem: Meqiẓe Nirdamim, 1970.

Ben Shmuel, Yehudah. *Sefer Ḥasidim.* Ed. Yehudah Hakohen Vistineẓqi. Berlin: Mekiẓe Nirdamim, 1891.

Ben Yosef, Saadiah (Gaon). *Saadia's Polemic against Ḥiwi al-Balkhi.* Ed. Israel Davidson. New York: The Jewish Theological Seminary, 1915.

Sefer Emunot ve-Deot. Trans. Yehudah ben Shaul ibn Tibon from Arabic. Jerusalem: Maqor, 1972.

Berlin, Naphtali Ẓevi Yehudah. *Ḥumash Haameq Davar, Sefer Bereshit.* [1879] Jerusalem: Yeshivat Volozhin, 1999.

Berlin, Shaul ben Ẓevi Hirsch. *Sefer Shelot u-Teshuvot Besamim Rosh.* Berlin: Verlag der Jüdischen Freyschule, 1793.

Bible in Aramaic, The. Ed. Alexander Sperber. 5 vols. Leiden: Brill, 1959.

Bible Moralisée: Codex Vindobonensis 2554, Vienna, Österreichische Nationalbibliothek. Trans. with commentary by Gerald Guest. London: Harvey Miller, 1995.

Bible of the Poor (Biblia Pauperum), The: Facsimile and Edition of the British Library Blockbook C.9 d.2. Trans. Albert Labriola and John Smeltz with commentary. Pittsburgh, PA: Duquesne University Press, 1990.

Biblia Sacra cum glossis, interlineari et ordinaria: Nicolai Lyrani postilla, ac mor-alitatibus, Burgensis additationibus & Thoringi replicis. 6 vols. Venice: N.p., 1588.

Bin Gorion (Berdyczewski), Micha Josef, ed. *Die Sagen der Juden.* 5 vols. Frankfurt am Main: Rütten und Loening, 1913–27.

Joseph und seine Brüder. Berlin: Schocken, 1933.

Bin Nun, Joel. "Esau's Hands–Jacob's Voice" (in Hebrew). *Shenaton Amit* (1998): 13–20; reprinted in *Pirqe Avot.* Alon Shvut: Tevunot, 2003.

Book Bahir, The. Ed. Daniel Abrams with introduction by Moshe Idel. Los Angeles: Cherub Press, 1994.

Brinke, G. R. *Abraham: Der Freund Gottes.* Bern: Ährenlese-Verlag, 1957.

Der Erzvater Jabob: Ein Lebensbild in Skizzen. Bern: Ährenlese-Verlag, 1959.

Buber, Martin, and Franz Rosenzweig. *Die Schrift und ihre Verdeutschung.* Berlin: Schocken, 1936.

Bunyan, John. *The Pilgrim's Progress from This World to That Which Is to Come.* [1678] Chapel Hill, NC: Yesterday's Classics, 2007.

Chorin, Aaron. *Davar Be-Ito; Ein Wort zu seiner Zeit über die Nächstenliebe und den Gottesdienst* (in Hebrew and German). Vienna: Anton Strauß, 1820.

Chrysostom, John. *Discourses against Judaizing Christians.* Trans. Paul W. Harkins. Washington, DC: Catholic University of America Press, 1979.

Cohen, Hermann. *Der Begriff der Religion im System der Philosophie.* Giessen: A. Töpelmann, 1915.

"Der Prophetismus und die Soziologie." In *Hermann Cohens Jüdische Schriften,* ed. Bruno Strauss. 3 vols. Berlin: C. A. Schwetschke, 1924: 2: 398–401.

"Die Nächstenliebe in Talmud." [1888] In *Hermann Cohens Jüdische Schriften*, ed. Bruno Strauss. 3 vols. Berlin: C. A. Schwetschke, 1924: 1: 145–74.

"Innere Beziehungen der Kantischen Philosophie zum Judentum." [1910] In *Hermann Cohens Jüdische Schriften*, ed. Bruno Strauss. 3 vols. Berlin: C. A. Schwetschke, 1924: 1: 284–305.

Cordovero, Moses. *Sefer ha-Zohar im Perush Or Yaqar*. 23 vols. Jerusalem: "Or Yakor" Organization, 1989.

Sefer Shiur Qomah. Warsaw: Yiẓhak Goldmann, 1882.

Crescas, Ḥasdai. *Bittul Iqarei ha-Noẓerim*. Jerusalem: Maqor, 1972.

Culi, Jacob. *The Torah Anthology: MeAm Lo'ez*. Trans. Aryeh Kaplan. 19 vols. New York: Moznayim, 1977.

Cyprian. *Books of Testimonies*. Trans. Ernest Wallis. In *The Ante-Nicene Fathers*, ed. and trans. Alexander Roberts and James Donaldson, rev. by A. Cleveland Coxe. 10 vols. New York: Charles Scribner's Sons, 1903: 5: 508.

Cyril, St., of Alexandria. *Commentary on the Twelve Prophets*. Trans. Robert C. Hill. 2 vols. Washington, DC: Catholic University of America Press, 2008.

Das Alte Testament im Lichte des Alten Orients. 3d ed. Leipzig: J.C. Hinrichsche Buchhandlung, 1916.

Das Buch Exodus. Ed. Shlomo Mayer in collaboration with Joachim Hahn and Almuth Jürgensen. Stuttgart: Calwer, 1997.

Das erste Buch der Tora: Genesis. Trans. and interpreted by B. Jacob. Berlin: Schocken Verlag, 1934.

Deharbe, Joseph. *Katholischer Katechismus, oder, Lehrbegriff, nebst einem kurzen Abrisse der religions-Geschichte von Anbeginn der Welt bis auf unsere Zeit*. Cincinnati, OH: Verlag bei Kreuzburg und Nurre, 1850.

Delitzsch, Friedrich. *Babel und Bibel*. Leipzig: J.C. Hinrichs, 1902.

Babel und Bibel Dritter Schluß(-) Vortrag. Stuttgart: Deutsche Verlags-Anstalt, 1905.

Zweiter Vortrag über Babel und Bibel. Stuttgart: Deutsche Verlags-Anstalt, 1904.

Der Pentateuch. Ed. Salomon Herxheimer. 2d ed. Bernburg: Gröning, 1854.

Der Pentateuch. Trans. and interpreted by Samson Raphael Hirsch. Part I: *Die Genesis*. [1867] 3d ed. Frankfurt am Main: J. Kaufmann, 1899.

De Wette, W. M. L. *Beiträge zur Einleitung in das Alte Testament: Kritik der Israelitischen Geschichte*. 2 vols. Halle: Schimmelpfennig, 1807.

Die israelitische Bibel – Der Pentateuch. Ed. Ludwig Philippson. Leipzig: Baumgärtner, 1844.

Dietlein, O. W. *Die Berliner Erklärung vom 15. August 1845 und deren Literatur*. Berlin: F. A. Herbig, 1846.

Edels, Samuel Eliezer (Maharsha). *Sefer Hidushe Agadot*. Frankfurt, 1682.

Ehrenreich, Shlomo Zalman. *Derashot leḥem Shlomo*. Brooklyn, NY: Joshua Katz, 1976.

Eibeschütz, Jonathan. *And I Came This Day unto the Fountain* (in Hebrew). 2d ed. Ed. and introduced by Pawel Maciejko, with additional studies by Noam Lefler, Jonatan Benarroch, and Shai Alleson Gerberg. Los Angeles: Cherub Press, 2016.

Tiferet Yehonatan. Yozifov, 1873, p. 170.

Yaarot Devash. 2 vols. Józefów: Setzer and Reiner, 1866.

Eisenmenger, Johann Andreas. *Entdecktes Judenthum.* Königsberg, 1711.

Eleh Divre ha-Berit. [1819] Farnborough, UK: Gregg International Publishers, 1969.

Epistle of Barnabas. Trans. Alexander Roberts and James Donaldson. http://www .earlychristianwritings.com/text/barnabas-roberts.html.

Eschelbacher, Joseph. *Das Judentum und das Wesen des Christentums.* Berlin: M. Poppelauer, 1908.

Ettlinger, Jacob. *Shelome Emune Yisrael = Treue Gläubige in Israel! Erklärung gegen die Beschlüsse der Braunschweiger Rabbiner-Versammlung* 1844. N.p., 1845.

Even-Shmuel, Yehudah, ed. *Nistarot shel Rabbi Shimon bar Yoḥai.* In *Midreshe Geula.* Tel Aviv: Bialik Institute & Masada, 1943, p. 188.

Eẓ Ḥayim. Ed. Meir Poppers. Vols. 1–2 of *Kol Kitve ha-ARI.* Ashlag-Brandwein ed. 15 vols. Jerusalem: N.p., 1988.

Faulhaber, Cardinal Michael von. "Judaism, Christianity and Germany." In *Germany: Advent Sermons Preached in St. Michael's, Munich, in 1933*, trans. George D. Smith. New York: Macmillan, 1934.

Fayvush, Shmuel. *Beit Shmuel.* Fürth, 1689.

Feinstein, David. *Kol Dodi on the Torah.* Brooklyn, NY: Masorah Publications, 1992.

Feinstein, Moshe.*Igrot Moshe.* Benei Beraq: Moshe Feinstein, 1985.

Feldman, Louis, James Kugel, and Lawrence Schiffman, eds. *Outside of the Bible: Ancient Jewish Writings Related to Scripture.* 3 vols. Philadelphia: Jewish Publication Society, 2013.

Flekles, Eliezer. "Kesut Einayim." In *Teshuvah me-Ahavah.* [1809] New York: Yisrael Zeev, 1966.

Formstecher, Salomon. "Der Werth des elterlichen Segens." In *Zwölf Predigten.* Würzburg: Etlinger'schen Buchhandlung, 1833, pp. 162–75.

    "Wie können Wir Gott verehren?" In *Zwölf Predigten.* Würzburg: Etlinger'schen Buchhandlung, 1833, pp. 176–92.

Frank, Jacob, *Zbiór Słów Pańskich* (The words of the Lord). Ed., trans., and annotated by Harris Lenowitz. http://archive.org/stream/TheCollectionOfT heWordsOfTheLordJacobFrank/TheCollectionOfTheWordsOfTheLordJa cobFrank_djvu.txt.

Fuhlrott, Joseph. "Das heute geborne Kind ist der Sohn Gottes." In *Predigten auf alle Sonn- und Festtage des Kirchenjahres.* Regensburg: Georg Joseph Maus, 1869, pp. 48-55.

Geiger, Abraham. "Der Kampf christlicher Theologen gegen die bürgerliche Gleichstellung der Juden." *Wissenschaftliche Zeitschrift für jüdische Theologie* 1:3 (1835): 52–67, 340–57.

    Judaism and Its History. Trans. Maurice Mayer. New York: M. Thalmessinger, 1865.

Genesis. Trans. and interpreted by Hermann Gunkel. Göttingen: Vandenhoeck & Ruprecht, 1901.

Genesis. Trans. and interpreted by Hermann Gunkel. 3d ed. [1910] Trans. Mark E. Biddle from German. Macon, GA: Mercer University Press, 1997.

Genesis: Die fünf Bücher der Weisung: Fünf Bücher des Moses. Trans. (*verdeutscht*) Martin Buber with Franz Rosenzweig. Berlin: Lambert Schneider, 1930.

Geon ha-Geonim. Ed. Shlomo Wertheimer. Jerusalem: N.p., 1925.

Gersonides (Levi ben Gershom, Ralbag). *Perush Daniel*. Rome: Obadiah, Menasseh and Benjamin of Rome, 1470.

Güdemann, Moritz. *Jüdische Apologetik*. Glogau: C. Flemming, 1906.

Gunkel, Hermann. *The Legends of Genesis*. Trans. W. H. Carruth. Chicago: Open Court, 1901.

"What Is Left of the Old Testament." [1914] In *What Remains of the Old Testament and Other Essays*, trans. A. K. Dallas. London: Macmillan, 1928, pp. 13–56.

Hacohen, Reem. "Contradictions in a Single Womb" (in Hebrew). *Maqor Rishon* 44 (November 27, 2009).

"How Was the Torah Written?" Lecture at Herzog College, published October 7, 2009. http://www.ynet.co.il/articles/0,7340,L-3786363,00.html, 39:42–53:32.

Hacohen, Ẓadoq.*Divre Sofrim*. Lublin: N.p., 1939.

Poqed Aqarim. Lublin: N.p., 1922.

Resisei Layla. Lublin: N.p., 1926.

Yisrael Qedoshim. Lublin: N.p., 1928.

Ẓidqat ha-Ẓadiq. Lublin: N.p., 1913.

Hacohen-Heller, Aryeh Leib. *Avnei Miluim*. New York: Yisrael Zeev, 1966.

Ha-Kalir, Elazar. "Oto ha-Yom." In *Midreshe Geula*, ed. Yehudah Even-Shmuel. Tel Aviv: Bialik Institute and Masada, 1943, p. 160.

Hakohen, Yiẓḥak. "Al ha-Aẓilut ha-semalit." In *Kabbalot Rabbi Yaakov ve-Rabbi Yiẓḥak benei Rabbi Yaakov Hakohen*, ed. Gershom Scholem. Jerusalem: Ha-Madpis, 1926, pp. 31–35, 82–102.

Halevi, Judah. *Kitab al Khazari: The Kuzari: An Argument for the Faith of Israel*. Trans. Hartwig Hirschfeld. New York: Schocken Books, 1964.

Ha-Meiri, Menaḥem. *Beit ha-Beḥirah al Baba Matẓia*. Ed. Kalman Schlesinger. Jerusalem: Meqitẓe Nirdamim, 1972.

Harnack, Adolph von. *Das Wesen des Christentums: Sechzehn Vorlesungen vor Studierenden aller Fakultäten im Wintersemester 1899/1900 an der Universität Berlin*. Ed. Claus-Dieter Osthövener. Tübingen: Mohr Siebeck, 2005.

Haselbauer, Franz. *Gründlicher Bericht von dem Christenthum* (in German and Judendeutsch). 2 vols. Prague: Colleg. S.I., 1719–22.

Heim, Franz-Anton. "Trauer-Rede" and "Wie und um was wir beten sollen." *Predigt-Magazin in Verbindung mit mehreren Katholischen Gelehrten, predigern und Seelsorgern* 6 (1841): 172 and 128–29, respectively.

Hengstenberg, Ernst Wilhelm. *Christology of the Old Testament*. Trans. Theodore Meyer. 2 vols. Edinburgh: T&T Clark, 1854.

Dissertations on the Genuineness of the Pentateuch. Trans. J. E. Ryland. 2 vols. Edinburgh: John D. Lowe, 1847.

Herder, Johann Gottfried. *Adrastea*. Ed. Günter Arnold. In *Johann Gottfried Herder: Werke*. 10 vols. Frankfurt: Deutscher Klassiker Verlag, 2000: 10: 629–42.

"Bekehrung der Juden." [1803] In *Sämmtliche Werke*, ed. Bernhard Suphan. 33 vols. Berlin: Weidmann, 1877–1913: 24: 61–74.

Briefe, das Studium der Theologie betreffend. [1780–81] In *Theologische Schriften*, ed. Christof Bultmann and Thomas Zippert. Vol 9, part 1, of *Johann Gottfried Herder: Werke.* 10 vols. Frankfurt: Deutscher Klassiker Verlag, 2000.

Ideen zur Philosophie der Geschichte der Menschheit. Vol. 14 of *Sämmtliche Werke*, ed. Bernhard Suphan. 33 vols. Berlin: Weidmann, 1877–1913.

Sämmtliche Werke. Ed. Bernhard Suphan. 33 vols. Berlin: Weidmann, 1877–1913.

Schriften zum Alten Testament. Ed. Rudolf Smend. Vol. 5 of *Johann Gottfried Herder: Werke.* 10 vols. Frankfurt: Deutscher Klassiker Verlag, 2000: 5: 9–178.

Vom Geist der ebräischen Poesie. Vol. 12 of *Sämmtliche Werke.*, ed. Bernhard Suphan. 33 vols. Berlin: Weidmann, 1877–1913.

Hildebrand, Dietrich von. "Die Juden und das Christliche Abendland." In *Die Menschheit am Scheideweg.* Regensburg: Verlag Josef Habbel, 1955, pp. 312–40.

Hirsch, Mendel. *Seder ha-Haftarot.* [1896] Trans. Isaac Levi. New York: Judaica Press, 1966.

Hirsch, Samson Raphael [Ben Usiel]. *Ḥamishah Ḥumshe Torah* (in Hebrew). Trans. Mordechai Breuer. Jerusalem: Mosad Yiẓḥak Breuer, 1966.

Horev: Versuche über Jissroels Pflichten in der Zerstreuung, zunächst für Jissroels denkende Jünglinge und Jungfrauen. Frankfurt am Main: J. Kaufmann, 1909.

"Lessons from Jacob and Esau." In *Collected Writings of Rabbi Samson Raphael Hirsch.* 8 vols. New York, Feldheim, 1997: 7: 319–32.

Neunzehn Briefe über Judentum. Frankfurt am Main: J. Kaufmann, 1911.

"Pädagogische Plaudereien." *Jeschurun* 8:4 (1862): 153–65.

The Hirsch Chumash. Trans. Daniel Haberman. New York: Feldheim, 2000.

The Origin of the Oral Law. Vol. 5 of *Collected Writings of Rabbi Samson Raphael Hirsch.* 8 vols. New York, Feldheim, 1997.

The Pentateuch. Trans. Isaac Levy. 2d rev. ed. London: I. Levy, 1963.

Holdheim, Samuel. "Der Kampf der jüngern mit der ältern Richtung im Judenthum." In *Neue Sammlung jüdischer Predigten.* 3 vols. in 1. Berlin: Carl David, 1852: 1: 290–300.

"Der Name Israel." In *Predigten über die jüdische Religion.* 3 vols. Berlin: Carl David, 1853: 2: 1–12.

"Die verschiedenen Auffassungsweisens des jüdischen Alterthums und unsere Stellung zu demselben." In *Predigten über die jüdische Religion.* 3 vols. Berlin: Julius Springer, 1855: 3: 1–10.

"Gotteshaus." In *Predigten über die jüdische Religion.* 3 vols. Berlin: Julius Springer, 1855: 3: 56–65.

"Höre Israel, der Ewige unser Gott ist einzig!" In *Predigten über die jüdische Religion.* 3 vols. Berlin: Carl David, 1853: 2: 13–21.

Jakob und Israel: Predigt. Schwerin: Kürschner'schen Buchhandlung, 1841.

Horovitz, Jakob. *Die Josephserzählung.* Frankfurt am Main: Kauffmann, 1921.

Horowitz, Isaiah Halevi. *Sefer Shenei Luḥot ha-Berit ha-Shalem.* 4 vols. Haifa: Mekhon Yad Ramah, 1992.

Horowitz, Naftali Ẓevi (Ropshitser). *Zera Qodesh.* 2 vols. Jerusalem: Y. T. Horowitz, 1970.

Horowitz, Pinḥas Eliahu. *Sefer ha-Berit.* Brünn: J. K. Neumanns, 1797.

Hübner, Johann. *Zweymal zwey und funffzig Auserlesene Biblische Historien, der Jugend zum Besten abgefasset.* [1714] 1st U.S. ed. Harrisburg, PA: Wm. Wheit und Wm. Boyer, 1826.

Hugh of St. Victor. *The Didascalicon of Hugh of St. Victor.* Trans. Jerome Taylor. New York: Columbia University Press, 1961.

Ḥumash Haameq Davar, Sefer Bereshit. [1879] Jerusalem: Yeshivat Volozhin, 1999.

Humboldt, Wilhelm von. "Über den Entwurf zu einer neuen Konstitution für die Juden." [1809] In *Werke.* 5 vols. Darmstadt: Wissenschaftliche Buchgesellschaft, 1964): 4: 95–12.

    "Wilhelm von Humboldt on the Principles of Jewish Emancipation Legislation and His Relations to the Jews." Trans. of "Über den Entwurf zu einer neuen Konstitution für die Juden." In *Jewish Rights at the Congresses of Vienna (1814–1815) and Aix-la-Chapelle (1818),* by Max J. Kohler. New York: The American Jewish Committee, 1918, pp. 71–83.

Ibn Ezra, Abraham. *Perush ha-Torah.* Istanbul [Kushtandina], 1514.

    Perush ha-Torah. Vatican MS Ebr. 38. Jerusalem: Maqor, 1974.

Ibn Kaspi, Yosef. *Mishne Kesef.* Ed. Yiẓḥak Halevi Last. Jerusalem: Meqorot, 1970.

Irenaeus. *Against Heresies.* In *The Ante-Nicene Fathers,* ed. and trans. Alexander Roberts and James Donaldson, rev. by A. Cleveland Coxe. 10 vols. New York: Charles Scribner's Sons, 1903: 1: 493.

Isserlein, Yisrael. *Trumat ha-Deshen.* Benei Beraq, Israel: N.p. 1971.

"Jacob." In *The Towneley Mysteries.* London: J. B. Nichols; William Pickering, 1836, pp. 45–48.

Jacob, Benno. *Die Thora Moses.* Frankfurt am Main: Kauffmann, 1912/13.

    The First Book of the Bible: Genesis. Benno Jacob interpretation and commentary abridged, edited, and translated by Ernst Jacob and Walter Jacob. New York: Ktav, 1974.

Jacob ben Reuben. *Sefer Milḥamot Hashem.* Ed. Yehudah Rozental. Jerusalem: Mosad Ha-Rav Kook, 1963.

Jacobson, Jacob H. "Die Nennung Jisrael." In *Eine Auswahl Jisraelitischen Kanzlervorträge.* Leipzig: Fritzsche, 1854, pp. 41–53.

Jacobson, Jacob H., ed. *Abtalion, Deutscher Theil.* [1842] 3d ed. Breslau: Leuckart, 1862.

    Rimonim: Ein deutsches Lesebuch fuer Israeliten in Schule und Haus. Leipzig: Friedrich Brandstetter, 1859.

Jacobson, Moses. *Bischlômâh schel malkhûth: Reden über des Staates, Führer Dinge und Fragen: Gehalten in der Synagoge.* Breslau: W. Jacobsohn, 1900.

"Jakob." In *Lexikon der christlichen Ikonographie,* ed. Engelbert Kirschbaum. 8 vols. Rome: Herder, 1974: 2: 367–83.

Jellinek, Adolf. "Balaam." In *Predigten.* 3 vols. Vienna: Carl Gerold's Sohn, 1862–66: 1: 47–62.

    "Die Einheit und die Mannigfaltigkeit des Völkerslebens." In *Predigten.* 3 vols. Vienna: Carl Gerold's Sohn, 1862–66: 2: 73–84.

    "Esau." In *Predigten.* 3 vols. Vienna: Carl Gerold's Sohn, 1862–66: 2: 203–14.

"Israel's Lehre über die Beziehungen von Juden zu Nichtjuden." In *Predigten*. 3 vols. Vienna: Carl Gerold's Sohn, 1862–66: 2: 139.

"Lo tischkach, oder: Israelit, vergiß nicht!" In *Aus der Wiener israelitischen Cultusgemeinde, 5624: 7 Zeit-Predigten*. Vienna: Herzfeld & Bauer, 1864, pp. 12–24.

Predigten. 3 vols. in 1. Vienna: Carl Gerold's Sohn, 1862–66.

"Schir ha-Schirim." In *Predigten*. 3 vols. Vienna: Carl Gerold's Sohn, 1862–66: 1: 13–30.

"Wajehi ha-mischkan echad, oder die Einheit und Einigkeit Israels." In *Aus der Wiener israelitischen Cultusgemeinde, 5624: 7 Zeit-Predigten*. Vienna: Herzfeld & Bauer, 1864, pp. 1–11.

"Zion (erste Rede)"; "Zion (zweite Rede)." In *Predigten*. 3 vols. Vienna: Carl Gerold's Sohn, 1862–66: 2: 155–66; 167–78.

Jeremias, Alfred. *Das Alte Testament im Lichte des Alten Orients*. 3d ed. Leipzig: J.C. Hinrichsche Buchhandlung, 1916.

Jerome, St. *Commentary on Isaiah* (Notitia Clavis Patrum Latinorum 584). Library of Latin Texts – Series A. Turnhout: Brepolis Publishers, 2005.

Commentary on the Minor Prophets (Notitia Clavis Patrum Latinorum 589). Library of Latin Texts – Series A. Turnhout: Brepolis Publishers, 2005.

Saint Jerome's Hebrew Questions on Genesis. Trans. with introduction and commentary by C. T. R. Hayward. Oxford: Clarendon Press, 1995.

Jonas, Hermann. "Die erkaufte Erstgeburt" and "Die Gelübde." In *Nib Sefataim: Dreissig Predigten*. Hamburg: Frederking & Graf, 1870, pp. 141–49, 149–56, respectively.

JPS Hebrew-English Tanakh: The Traditional Hebrew Text and the New JPS Translation. 2d ed. Philadelphia: Jewish Publication Society, 1999.

Kanter, Felix. *Homiletische Essays*. Frankfurt am Main: J. Kauffmann, 1910.

Kastning-Olmesdahl, Ruth. *Die Juden und der Tod Jesu: Antijüdische Motive in den evangelischen Religionsbüchern für die Grundschule*. Neukirchen-Vluyn: Neukirchener Verlag, 1981.

Lernen auf Zukunft hin: Einsichten des christlich-jüdischen Gesprächs – 25 Jahre Studium in Israel. Ed. Katja Kriener and Bernd Schröder. Neukirchen-Vluyn: Neukirchener Verlag, 2004.

Menschen suchen–Zugänge finden: Auf dem Weg zum einem Religionpädagogik verantworteten Umgang mit dem Bibel: Festschrift für Christine Reents. Ed. Desmond Bel, Heike Lipski-Melchior, Johannes von Lüpke, and Birgit Ventur. Wuppertal: Foedus, 1999.

Katz, Reuven. "Amaleq Transmigration through the Generations." In *Wrestling with God: Jewish Theological Responses during and after the Holocaust*, ed. Steven T. Katz with Shlomo Biderman and Gershon Greenberg. Oxford: Oxford University Press, 2007, pp. 101–4.

Keinz, Friedrich, and K. Bartsch. "Mittheilungen aus der Münchener Kön. Bibliothek." *Germania* 31 (1886): 57–62.

Kimḥi, David. *Perush Radak al Yeshayah*. Ed. Eliezer Aryeh Finkelstein. New York: N.p., 1926.

Sefer ha-Berit u-vikuḥei Radak im ha-Naẓrut. Ed. Frank Talmage. Jerusalem: Bialik Institute, 1974.

Kley, Eduard. "On Honoring God." In *Predigten*. Hamburg: Hoffmann und Campe, 1819, pp. 99–114.

Predigt-Skizzen: Beiträge zu einer künftige Homiletik. Grünberg and Leipzig: Levysohn, 1844.

"The Wishes of the Pious." In *Predigten in dem neuen Israelitischen Temple gehalten von Eduard Kley.* Hamburg: I. Ahrons, 1827, pp. 169–82.

Kobak, Joseph. "Jacob of Venice's Epistle of Polemics" (in Hebrew). *Jeschurun* 6 (1868): 1–34.

Koidanover, Zevi Hirsh. *Kav ha-Yashar.* [1709] Jerusalem: Haktav Institute, 1982.

Koren, Isaac Dov. *Christianity in the Eyes of Judaism: Past, Present and Future* (in Hebrew). Jerusalem: American Jewish Congress, 2013.

"New Covenant" (in Hebrew). Trans. Limor Riskin. *Maqor Rishon* (June 26, 2015). http://musaf-shabbat.com/2015/06/26/קורן-דב-יצחק-חדשה-ברית/.

Koren Mesorat Harav Kinot, The (in Hebrew and English). Jerusalem: Koren Publishers, 2011.

Koren Siddur, The (in Hebrew and English). Jerusalem: Koren Publishers, 2009.

Kort, Kees de. *Bibelbilderbuch.* Stuttgart: Deutsche Bibelgesellschaft, 1984.

Kracauer, Siegfried. "The Bible in German." In *The Mass Ornament: Weimar Essays*, trans. and ed. Thomas Levin. Cambridge, MA: Harvard University Press, 1995, pp. 189–201.

Kuntze, Eduard W. T. *Predigt [on Rom. xvi. 17, 18) über die Pflichten des Christen in dieser so bewegten Zeit, gehalten am 15. Sonntage nach Trinitatis 1845.* 2d ed. Berlin: Bethge, 1845.

Küster, Samuel Christian Gottfried. *Zweimal zwei und fünfzig auserlesene Biblische Erzählungen aus dem Alten und Neuen Testamente [nach Johann Hübner mit Fragen zum Nachdenken, nüzlichen Lehren, gottseligen Gedanken und Bibelsprüchen].* Berlin: Enslin, 1819.

Landau, Ezekiel. *Noda bi-Yehudah.* New York: Halakhah Berurah, 1960.

Lau, Binyamin. "Israel vs. Edom – Seventh Round" (in Hebrew). *Haaretz* (4 December 2009). http://www.haaretz.co.il/literature/1.1293204.

Lechner, Anton. "Die Kirche – Vorbild des Himmels und Thüres zum Himmel." [1828] *Predigt-Magazin in Verbindung mit mehreren Katholischen Gelehrten, predigern und Seelsorgern* 10 (1843): 304–10.

Leibowitz, Nehama. "Accept the Truth from Wherever It Comes" (in Hebrew). *Alon Shvut-Bogrim* 13 (1999): 71–92. http://www.library.yctorah.org/files/2016/09/Accept-the-Truth-from-wherever-it-Comes.pdf.

Studies in the Book of Genesis in the Context of Ancient and Modern Jewish Bible Commentary. Trans. and adapted from the Hebrew by Aryeh Newman. Jerusalem: World Zionist Organization, 1972.

Liberman, Eliezer. *Or Nogah.* Dessau: Schlieder, 1818.

Library of Latin Texts – Series A. Turnhout: Brepolis Publishers, 2005.

Lichtenstein, Moshe. "Esau as Brother, Esau as Goy" (in Hebrew). 2006. http://www.etzion.org.il/he/כגוי-עשו-כאח-עשו-וישלח-פרשת.

Lockshin, Martin. *Rabbi Samuel Ben Meir's Commentary on Geneses: An Annotated Translation.* Lewiston, NY: Edwin Mellen, 1989.

Lopez (Lupis), Issac. *Kur meẓaref ha-Emunot u-mareh ha-Emet.* [1695] Metz: J. Mayer Samuel, 1847.

Luther, Martin. *Luther's Commentary on Genesis.* Trans. J. Theodore Mueller. 2 vols. Grand Rapids, MI: Zondervan, 1958.

Maayana shel Torah. Trans. M. Ẓevi. 5 vols. Tel Aviv: Peer, 1956: 1: 153.

Maharam of Rothenburg (Meir ben Barukh). *Shut Maharam be-rabi Barukh.* Ed. Moshe Aryeh Bloch. Budapest: Sternberg & Comp, 1895.

Maimonides (Moshe ben Maimon). *Epistles of Maimonides: Crisis and Leadership.* Trans. with notes by Abraham Halkin. Philadelphia: Jewish Publication Society, 1993.

Mannheimer, Isaak Noah. *Gottesdienstliche Vorträge.* Vienna: Carl Gerold, 1835. "Warnung an Väter in Israel." In *Gottesdienstliche Vorträge.* 2 vols. in 1. Vienna: Brüder Winter, 1876: 2: 1–19.

Martini, Raymond, Joseph de Voisin, and Johann Benedict Carpzov. *Pugio Fidei adversus Mauros et Judaeos, Raymundi Martini.* [1687] Reprint: Farnborough, UK: Gregg Press, 1967. http://judaica-frankfurt.de/urn/urn:nbn:de:hebis:30-180010008006.

Maybaum, Sigmund. *Jüdische Homiletik.* Berlin: Ferd. Dümmlers Verlagsbuchhandlung, 1890. *Predigten.* 6 vols. Berlin: [imprint varies], 1892–1910.

Mechilta d'Rabbi Ismael cum variis lectionibus et adnotationibus. Ed. and Introduction by S. Horovitz and I. A. Rabin. Jerusalem: Bamberger & Wahrmann, 1960.

Medan, Yaacov. "Esau's Merit." *Daf Qesher* 522 (December 2006). http://www.etzion.org.il/he/פרשת-תולדות-זכותו-של-עשו.

"Isaac & Rebecca, Jacob & Esau," https://www.youtube.com/watch?v=JhemCzKWP_4&feature=em-uploademail.

Menaḥem Man Shakh, Elazar. *Mikhtavim U-maamarim.* 2d ed. 6 vols. in 5. Benei Beraq: E.M.M. Shakh, 1986.

Mendelssohn, Moses. *Jerusalem, or: On Religious Power and Judaism.* Trans. Allan Arkush. Introduction and commentary by Alexander Altmann. Hanover, NH: University Press of New England, 1983. *Sefer Netivot ha-Shalom.* 9 vols. Vienna: Anton Schmid, 1818.

Midrash Bereshit Rabbati. Ed. Chanoch Albeck. Jerusalem: Meqiẓe Nirdamim, 1940.

Midrash Devarim Rabbah. Ed. Saul Lieberman. Jerusalem: Bamberger and Wahrman, 1940.

Midrash Eichah Rabbah. Ed. Shlomo Buber. Vilnius: Romm, 1899.

Midrash Eichah Rabbah. Vilnius and Grodno, 1829.

Midrash Ele Eskerá. Ed. Adolph Jellinek. Leipzig: A. M. Colditz, 1853.

Midrash Esther Rabbah. Ed. Joseph Tabory and Arnon Atzmon. Jerusalem: Schechter Institute, 2014.

Midrash Ha-Gadol. Ed. S. Schechter. Cambridge: Cambridge University Press, 1902.

Midrash Rabbah: Genesis. Ed. Chanoch Albeck and J. Theodor. 3 vols. Jerusalem: Wahrmann Books, 1965.

Midrash Shemot Rabbah: Parashot 1–14. Ed. Avigdor Shinan. Jerusalem: Devir, 1984.

Midrash Sifre. Jerusalem: Mosad Ha-Rav Kook, 1948.

Midrash Tanḥuma. Ed. Solomon Buber. Vilnius: Romm, 1913.

Midrash Tanḥuma. Jerusalem: Makor, 1971.

Midrash Tehilim Known as Shoḥer Tov. Ed. Shlomo Buber. Vilnius: Romm, 1891.

Midrash Va-yiqra Rabbah. Ed. Mordechai Margaliot. 5 vols. Jerusalem: Ministry of Education, 1953–60.

Miqraot Gedolot ha-Keter. Ed. Menaḥem Kohen. Ramat-Gan: Bar-Ilan University Press, 1992–2013.

Nagan, Yaakov. "A Blessing Emerges From Pain: Between Jacob & Esau." http://www.kipa.co.il/jew/pash/42/46979.html.

Naḥmanides (Moshe ben Naḥman). *Commentary on the Torah.* Trans. Charles B. Chavel. 5 vols. New York: Shilo Press, 1971–76.

　Perush ha-Torah. 2 vols. Jerusalem: Mosad Ha-Rav Kook, 1969.

　Sefer ha-Geula. Ed. Yehoshua Aharonson. Tel Aviv: Sifriati, 1959.

"Naḥmanides' Hebrew Account of the Barcelona Disputation" and "The Latin Account of the Barcelona Disputation." In *Debating Truth: The Barcelona Disputation of 1263: A Graphic History,* by Nina Caputo. New York: Oxford University Press, 2017, pp. 90–114, 114–33, respectively.

New Oxford Annotated Bible, The: New Revised Standard Version: with the Apocrypha: An Ecumenical Study Bible. Ed. Michael D. Coogan, Marc Z. Brettler, Carol A. Newsom, and Pheme Perkins. 4th ed. Oxford: Oxford University Press, 2010.

Old Testament Pseudepigrapha, The. Ed. James Charlesworth. 2 vols. Garden City, NY: Doubleday, 1985.

Origen.*Homilies on Genesis and Exodus.* Trans. Ronald E. Heine. Washington, DC: Catholic University of America Press, 1982.

Orth, Ernst. *Jakob und Esau: Drei Predigten nebst einem offnen Schreiben an Herrn Prediger Kuntze, als Antwort auf dessen am 15. Sonntage nach Trinitatis gehaltene Predigt.* Berlin: Oehmigkes Buchhandlung, 1845.

Ozar ha-Geonim. Ed. B. M. Levin. 13 vols. Jerusalem, 1928–43.

Paalzow, Christian Ludwig. *Tractatus historico-politicus de civitate judaeorum.* Berolini: C.G. Schoene, 1803.

Paulus, H. E. G. *Die jüdische Nationalabsonderung nach Ursprung, Folgen und Besserungsmitteln.* Heidelberg: Winter, 1831.

Penet, Yeḥezqel. *Sefer Mareh Yeḥezqel.* Benei Beraq: Benei Shileshim, 2003.

Pesikta de-Rav Kahana. Ed. Bernard Mandelbaum. 2 vols. New York: Jewish Theological Seminary, 1962.

Pesikta Rabbati. Ed. Meir Ish-Shalom. Vienna: Kaiser, 1880.

Pesiqta rabbati: A Synoptic Edition. Ed. Rivka Ulmer. Atlanta: Scholars Press, 1997.

Philippson, Ludwig. *The Development of the Religious Idea in Judaism, Christianity and Mahomedanism.* London: Longman, Brown, Green and Longmans, 1855.

　Die Entwickelung der religiösen Idee im Judenthume, Christenthume und Islam. Leipzig: Baumgärtner, 1847.

Shiloah: Eine Auswahl von Predigten. 2 vols. 2d ed. Leipzig: Baumgärtner's Buchhandlung, 1843–45.

Pirqe de-Rabbi Eliezer. Ed. C. M. Horowitz. Jerusalem: Maqor, 1972.

Plessner, Salomon. "The Silent Observer." In *Sabbath-Predigten für allen Wochenabschnitte*, ed. Elias Plessner. Frankfurt am Main: I. Kaufmann, 1888, pp. 51–60.

———. "The Strict Responsibility." In *Sabbath-Predigten für allen Wochenabschnitte*, ed. Elias Plessner. Frankfurt am Main: I. Kaufmann, 1888, pp. 73–81.

Präger, Moses. *Gebet- und Erbauungsbuch für Israeliten.* 2d rev. ed. Brilon: M. Friedländer, 1860.

Prayer Book for the Days of Awe. Ed. Jules Harlow. New York: Rabbinic Assembly, 1972.

Pulqar, Yiẓḥak (Isaac Pollegar). *Sepher Ezer ha-Dat.* Ed. George S. Belasco. London: J. Jacobs, 1906.

Qolon Yosef. *Shut u-Fisqe Mahariq he-ḥadashim.* Ed. Eliahu Dov Pines. Jerusalem: Or ha-Mizraḥ, 1984.

Rabinovitz, Zvi Meir, ed. *The Liturgical Poems of Rabbi Yannai* (in Hebrew). 2 vols. Jerusalem: Bialik Institute, 1987.

Rashi (Shlomo ben Yiẓḥak). *Teshuvot Rashi.* Ed. Israel Elfenbein. New York: Schulsinger Bros., 1943.

Rath, Meshuluam. *Responsa Mevaser Qol.* Jerusalem: Mosad Ha-Rav Kook, 1956.

Reimarus, Hermann Samuel. *Fragmente des Wolfenbüttelschen Ungenannten.* Ed. Gotthold Ephraim Lessing. 4th ed. Berlin: C.M. Eichhoff, 1835.

Rienecker, Georg. "Am Feste der Heiligen Drei Koenige." In *Predigten auf die Sonn- und Festtage des katholischen Kirchenjahres*, ed. Franz Keller. Nuremberg: Fried. Korn'schen Buchhandlung, 1868, pp. 85–94.

Roberts, Alexander, and James Donaldson, eds. *The Ante-Nicene Fathers.* Trans. Alexander Roberts and James Donaldson, rev. by A. Cleveland Coxe. 10 vols. New York: Charles Scribner's Sons, 1903.

Rosenzweig, Franz. *The Star of Redemption.* [1921] Trans. William W. Hallo. New York: Holt, Rinehart and Winston, 1971.

Rozental, Yehudah. "Chapters of Polemics" (in Hebrew). In *Salo Wittmayer Baron Jubilee.* 3 vols. Jerusalem: American Academy for Jewish Research, 1974: 3: 353–95.

———. "Mi-Tokh 'Sefer Alfonso.'" In *Studies and Essays in Honor of Abraham A. Neuman*, ed. Meir Ben-Horin, Bernard D. Weinryb, and Solomon Zeitlin. Leiden: Brill, 1962, pp. 588–619.

———. "Sefer Teshuvot ha-Meshuvot: Mi-Tokh Ketavav ha-Ivriym shel ha-Mumar Avner mi-Burgos." In *Meḥqarim u-meqorot.* 2 vols. Jerusalem: Reuven Mas, 1967: 1: 324-67.

Sacks, Jonathan. "Be Thyself." *Covenant and Conversation* (November 16, 2013). http://rabbisacks.org/vayishlach-5774-thyself.

———. "Chosenness and Its Discontents," November 10, 2007. http://www.rabbi sacks.org/covenant-conversation-5768-toldot-chosenness-and-its-discon tents/.

"This Is Ours." In *A Letter in the Scroll: Understanding Our Jewish Identity and Exploring the Legacy of the World's Oldest Religion*. New York: Free Press, 2000, pp. 204–15.

Salomon, Gotthold. "Das väterliche Segen." In *Predigten in dem neuen Israelitischen Temple*. 3 vols. Hamburg: I. Ahrons, 1826: 3: 167–80.

"Jakobs Sterne und Israels Scepter." In *Predigten in dem neuen Israelitischen Temple*. 3 vols. Hamburg: I. Ahrons, 1826: 1: 223–38.

Schleiermacher, Friedrich. "The Christian Training of Children." In *Selected Sermons of Schleiermacher*, trans. Mary F. Wilson. London: Hodder and Stoughton, 1890, pp. 146–67.

Schneerson, Menaḥem Mendel. *Hitvaadoyut*. [1985–86] 2d ed. Brooklyn, NY: Vaad Hanochos, 1990.

Liqute Siḥot (in Yiddish). 39 vols. Brooklyn, NY: Qehot, 2001.

Schneur Zalman of Liadi. "Igeret ha-Qodesh." In *Liqute Amarim: Tanya*. New York: Qehot Publication Society, 1956, pp. 102–53.

"Quntras Aharon." In *Liqute Amarim: Tanya*. New York: Qehot Publication Society, 1956, pp. 153–63.

Schoneveld, J. *The Bible in Israeli Education*. Amsterdam: Van Gorcum, 1976.

Schweitzer, Albert. *The Quest for the Historical Jesus: A Critical Study of Its Progress from Reimarus to Wrede*. London: A. and C. Black, 1910.

Sefer Eẓ ha-Daat Tov. 2 vols. Jerusalem: Ahavat Shalom, 2000.

Sefer Gematriot of R. Judah the Pious. Introduced by Daniel Abrams and Israel Ta-Shema. Los Angeles: Cherub Press, 1998.

Sefer ha-Liqutim. Ed. Meir Poppers. Vol. 15 of *Kol Kitve ha-ARI*. 15 vols. Jerusalem: N.p., 1988.

Sefer ha-Yashar. Ed. Joseph Dan with introduction. Jerusalem: Bialik Institute, 1986.

Sefer ha-Zohar im perush ha-Sulam (in Aramaic and Hebrew). Trans. and with commentary by Yehudah Ashlag. 10 vols. London: Shlomoh Dazyeleyski, 1970–71.

Sefer Mevo Shearim. Ed. Yaakov Ẓemaḥ and Natan Shapira. Vol. 4 of *Kol Kitve ha-ARI*. 15 vols. Jerusalem: N.p., 1988.

Sefer Midrash Rabbah. 2 vols. Vilnius: Romm, 1884.

Sefer Nogah ha-Ẓedeq. Dessau: Schliede, 1818.

Sefer Tosafot ha-Shalem. Ed. Yaakov Gelis. 10 vols. Jerusalem: Mifal Tosafot ha-Shalem, 1984.

Sefer Yeẓira. Ed. and trans. with text-critical commentary by A. Peter Hayman. Tübingen: Mohr Siebeck, 2004.

Shemonah Shearim. Ed. Shmuel Vital. Vols. 5–11 of *Kol Kitve ha-ARI*. Ashlag-Brandwein ed. 15 vols. Jerusalem: N.p., 1988.

Siddur ha-Yaavaẓ: Amudei Shamayim, Beit Yaaqov. Compendium composed by Joseph Emden. 2 vols. Jerusalem: Eshkol, 1993.

Sifre. Ed. H. S. Horovitz. Frankfurt am Main: J. Kauffmann, 1917.

Sifre de-ve Rav. Ed. Ḥayim Shaul Horovits. Jerusalem: Sifre Varman, 1966–69.

Sofer, Moses. *Ḥatam Sofer al ha-Torah*. Ed. Yosef Naftali Shtern. 5 vols. Jerusalem: Ḥatam Sofer Institute, 1987.

Qoveẓ Teshuvot. Jerusalem: Ḥatam Sofer Institute, 1973.

Sefer Ḥatam Sofer: Derashot (Sermons). Ed. Yosef Naftali Shtern. 3 vols. in 2. Jerusalem: Ḥatam Sofer Institute, 1989.

Sefer Torat Moshe. [1881] Ed. Shimeon Sofer. Jerusalem: Ḥatam Sofer Institute, 1967.

Shut Ḥatam Sofer ha-ḥadashot. Ed. S. E. Shtern. Jerusalem: Ḥatam Sofer Institute, 1989.

Teshuvot Ḥatam Sofer (Responsa). Nussenzweig ed. 8 vols. Jerusalem: Ḥatam Sofer Institute, 2000–2008.

Teshuvot Ḥatam Sofer ha-ḥadashot. Ed. S. E. Shtern. Jerusalem: Ḥatam Sofer Institute, 1989.

Sofer, Shlomo. *Ḥut ha-Meshulash.* Beregszász: S. Schreiber, 1894.

Soloveitchik, Joseph B. *Kol Dodi Dofek: Listen, My Beloved Knocks.* [1956] Trans. David Z. Gordon from the Hebrew. New York: Ktav, 2006.

Soloveitchik, Yosef Dov. "Jacob and Esau" (in Hebrew). In *Divre Hashqafa,* trans. Moshe Crone from the Yiddish. Jerusalem: World Zionist Organization, 1992, pp. 20–27.

Stahl, Friedrich Julius. *Zwei Sendschreiben an die Unterzeichner der Erklärung vom 15., beziehungsweise 26 Aug. 1845.* Berlin: E. H. Schroeder, 1845.

Stein, Leopold. "Homiletische Beilage." *Der Israelitische Volkslehrer* 5 (1855): 126–28.

Strauss, D. F. *The Life of Jesus Critically Examined.* [1835] Trans. George Eliot. Cambridge: Cambridge University Press, 2010.

Talmud Bavli: English and Hebrew: The Schottenstein Edition: The Gemara: The Classic Vilna Edition, with an Annotated, Interpretive Elucidation as an Aid to Talmud Study. Ed. Hersh Goldwurm, Nosson Scherman, Yisroel Simcha Schorr, and Chaim Malinowitz. 73 vols. Brooklyn, NY: Mesorah Publications, 1990–.

Talmud Bavli: Hebrew-English Edition of the Babylonian Talmud. Ed. Isidore Epstein and Judah J. Slotki. Rev. ed. 30 vols. London: Soncino Press, 1990.

Talmud of the Land of Israel, The: A Preliminary Translation and Explanation. Ed. Jacob Neusner. 35 vols. Chicago: University of Chicago Press, 1982–94.

Targum Pseudo-Jonathan of the Pentateuch: Text and Concordance. Ed. E. G. Clarke. Hoboken, NJ: Ktav Pub. House,1984.

Taubes, Jacob. *Die politische Theologie des Paulus.* Munich: Wilhelm Fink, 1993.

Teichthal, Yissakhar Shlomo. *Em ha-Banim Semeḥa.* Budapest: S. Katzburg, 1943.

Em Habanim Semeha: Restoration of Zion as a Response during the Holocaust. Ed. and trans. Pesach Schindler. Hoboken, NJ: Ktav Pub. House, 1999.

Tertullian. *Adversus Judaeos* (I). Trans. S. Thelwall. In *The Ante-Nicene Fathers,* ed. and trans. Alexander Roberts and James Donaldson, rev. by A. Cleveland Coxe. 10 vols. New York: Charles Scribner's Sons, 1903: 3: 151.

Five Books Against Marcion. Trans. Holmes. In *The Ante-Nicene Fathers,* ed. and trans. Alexander Roberts and James Donaldson, rev. by A. Cleveland Coxe. 10 vols. New York: Charles Scribner's Sons, 1903: 3: 343.

Toledot Yeshu. Ed. and trans. Michael Meerson and Peter Schäfer. Tübingen: Mohr Siebeck, 2014.

Treuenfels, Abraham. "Die Stimme Jakobs." *Predigt Magazin: Homiletische Monatsschrift* 1 (1874–75): 95–102.

Troeltsch, Ernst. "Glaube und Ethos der Habräischen Propheten." [1916] In *Gesammelte Schriften.* 4 vols. Tübingen: J.C.B. Mohr, 1925: 4: 34–65.

"Schlußabschnitt über der Fortwirkung des Haebraismus auf dem Abendland." In *Gesammelte Schriften.* 4 vols. Tübingen: J.C.B. Mohr, 1925: 4: 818–21.

The Social Teaching of the Christian Churches. Trans. Olive Wyon. 2 vols. Chicago: University of Chicago Press, 1976.

Vital, Ḥayim. *Kol Kitve ha-ARI.* Ashlag-Brandwein ed. 15 vols. Jerusalem: N.p., 1988.

Sefer Eẓ ha-Daat Tov. 2 vols. Jerusalem: Ahavat Shalom, 2000.

Wagenseil, Johann Christoph. *Tela ignea Satanae: hoc est arcani, & horribiles Judaeorum adversus Christum Deum, & Christianam religionem libri Aneklotoi.* Altdorf: J. H. Schönnerstaedt, 1681. http://books.google.com/books?id=0x MtAAAAYAAJ&printsec=frontcover&dq=Tela+ignea+Satanae&hl=en&e i=7B64TdC9KMLTgAfpw-Rz&sa=X&oi=bookresult&ct=result&resnu m=2&sqi=2&ved=0CC0Q6AEwAQ#v=onepage&q&f=false.

Wasserman, Elḥanan. *Omer Ani Maasai la-Melekh.* Vilnius: N.p., 1936.

Weiss, Yiẓḥaq. *Avnei Beit ha-Yoẓer.* Jerusalem: Ḥatam Sofer Institute, 1970.

Wellhausen, Julius. *Geschichte Israels.* 2 vols. Berlin: G. Reimer, 1878.

Werman, Cana. *The Book of Jubilees: Introduction, Translation, and Interpretation* (in Hebrew). Jerusalem: Yad Izhak ben-Zvi Press, 2015.

Wessely, Naphtali Herz. *Divre Shalom ve-Emet.* Berlin: Ḥinukh Naarim/Jüdische Freyschule, 1782.

Wessely, Naphtali Herz, and David Friedländer. *Worte der Wahrheit und des Friedens an die gesamte jüdische Nation.* Vienna: J. F. Edlen von Schönfeld, 1782.

Williams, Roger. "A Letter from Roger Williams to Major Mason, 22 June 1670." *Collections of the Massachusetts Historical Society* 1 (1792): 275–83.

Wolfsohn, Aaron. *Abtalion.* 3d ed. Vienna: Anton Schmid, 1814.

Yahuda, Abraham Shalom. *Die Sprache des Pentateuch in ihren Beziehungen zum Aegyptischen.* Berlin: Walter de Gruyter, 1929.

The Language of the Pentateuch in Its Relations to Egyptian. Oxford: Oxford University Press, 1932.

Zamosc, David. *Nahar me-Eden.* Breslau: H. Zultsbakh, 1836.

Zohar, The. Trans. Daniel C. Matt and with commentary. 12 vols. Stanford, CA: Stanford University Press, 2004–17.

Zohar: The Book of Enlightenment. Trans. Daniel Matt and with introduction. New York: Paulist Press, 1983.

Zunz, Leopold. "Etwas über die rabbinische Literatur." In *Gesammelte Schriften.* 3 vols. Berlin: Gerschel, 1875: 1: 1–31.

Gottesdienstliche Vorträge der Juden. [1832] Frankfurt am Main: J. Kauffmann, 1892.

Zur Geschichte und Literatur. Berlin: Veit und Comp, 1845.

Histories

Basnage, Jacques. *The History of the Jews, from Jesus Christ to the Present Time.* London: N.p., 1708.

Ben Natan Faydl, Shmuel Fayvush. "Sefer Tit ha-Yaven." [1649] In *Le-Qorot ha-Gezerot al Yisrael*, ed. Hayim Yonah Gurland. 5 vols. Odessa: Aba Dukhno, 1892: 4: 17–28.

Ben Gorion, Yosef. *Sefer Yosifon.* Ed. with an introduction, commentary, and notes by David Flusser. 2 vols. Jerusalem: Bialik Institute, 1980–81.
   The Arabic Josippon. Trans. Shulamit Sela with introduction. 2 vols. Jerusalem: Ben-Zvi Institute and Tel Aviv University, 2009.

Ber (Birkenthal) of Bolechów. "Sefer Divre Binah." MS Hebrew 8° 7507, Jewish National Library.
   The Memoirs of Ber of Bolechow (1723–1805). Trans. M. Vishnitzer. Humphrey Milford, UK: Oxford University Press, 1922.

Bleichrode, Avraham Moshe. *Toldot Rabenu Aqiva Eger.* Berlin: N.p. 1862.

Cohen, Gerson. *A Critical Edition with a Translation and Notes of The Book of Tradition (Sefer Ha-Qabbalah) by Abraham ibn Daud.* Philadelphia: Jewish Publication Society of America, 1967.

Dan, Joseph, ed. and introd. *Sefer ha-Yashar.* Jerusalem: Bialik Institute, 1986.

Edom: Berichte jüdischer Zeugen und Zeitgenossen über die Judenverfolgungen während der Kreuzzüge. Trans. Nathan Birnbaum und Hugo Herrmann. Berlin: Jüdischer Verlag, 1919.

Flavius Josephus. *Antiquitates Judaicae* (in English and Greek). Trans. H. St. J. Thackeray. 9 vols. Cambridge, MA: Harvard University Press, 1930–98.

Flusser, David. *The History of al-Ṭabarī.* Trans. Franz Rosenthal. 40 vols. Albany: State University of New York Press, 1984–2007.

Ganz, David ben Shlomo. *Sefer Ẓemaḥ David.* Ed. Mordechai Breuer. Jerusalem: Magnes, 1982.

Graetz, Heinrich. *Geschichte der Juden von den ältesten Zeiten bis auf die Gegenwart.* 11 vols. Leipzig: Oskar Leiner, 1853–74.
   Popular History of the Jews. 5 vols. New York: Hebrew Publishing Company, 1919.

Güdemann, Moritz. *Geschichte des Erziehungswesens und der Cultur der abendländischen Juden, während des Mittelalters und der neueren Zeit.* 3 vols. Vienna: Hölder, 1880–88.

Hanover, Natan Neta. *Sefer Yeven Meẓulah.* [1653] Tel Aviv: Ha-Qibutz Ha-Meuḥad, 1945.

Hirsch, Samson Raphael. "Geschichte der Juden: Vom Untergang des jüdischen Staats bis zum Abschluß des Thalmuds." *Jeschurun* 2: (1855–56): 47–69, 89–103, 156–76, 198–214, 315–25, 424–42, 529–49; 3 (1856–57): 63–78, 229–54, 396–413, 557–71; 4 (1857–58): 289–307.

Ibn Daud, Abraham. "Divre Malkhe Yisrael be-Yeme Bayit Sheni." In *Seder Olam Rabbah ve-Seder Olam Zuta u-Megilat Taanit ve-Sefer Ha-Kabbalah le-ha-Ravad.* Basel, 1580, pp. 83b–132b.
   "Zikhron Divre Romi." In *Seder Olam Rabbah ve-Seder Olam Zuta u-Megilat Taanit ve-Sefer Ha-Kabbalah le-ha-Ravad.* Basel, 1580, pp. 80a–83b.

Ibn Virgah, Shmuel. *Sefer Shevet Yehudah.* Ed. Azriel Shoḥet and Yiẓḥak Baer. Jerusalem: Bialik Institute, 1946.

Prinz, Joachim. *Illustrierte Jüdische Geschichte.* 2d ed. Berlin: Brandussche Verlagsbuchhandlung, 1933.

Jüdische Geschichte. Berlin: Verlag für Kulturpolitik, 1931.

Schröckh, Johann Matthias. *Lehrbuch der allgemeinen Weltgeschichte für katolische Schulen.* Stuttgart: Stoppani, 1845.

Literature, Philosophy, and Political Writing

Agnon, Shmuel Yosef. *A Guest for the Night.* Trans. Misha Louvish. New York: Schocken Books, 1968.

Temol Shilshom. Tel Aviv: Schocken, 1968.

Alighieri, Dante. *De Vulgari Eloquentia* (in Latin and English). Ed. Warman Welliver. Ravenna: Longo, 1981.

Inferno: Divina Commedia. Ed. Giorgio Petrocchi. Milan: Mondadori, 1966–67.

Opere. Florence: Bemporad and Figlio, 1921.

Purgatorio: Divina Commedia. Ed. Giorgio Petrocchi. Milan: Mondadori, 1966–67.

The Banquet (Il Convivio). Trans. Katherine Hillard. London: Kegan Paul, 1889.

Amir-Pinkerfeld, Anda. "Esau." In *Gitit: Poems.* Tel Aviv: Ha-Qibuẓ ha-Meuḥad, 1937, pp. 18–24.

Anon [Karl Wilhelm Friedrich Grattenauer]. *Wider die Juden: Ein Wort der Warnung an alle unsere christliche Mitbürger.* 4th ed. Berlin: Schmidt, 1803.

Ascher, Saul. *Die Germanomanie: Skizze zu einem Zeitgemälde.* Berlin: Achenwall, 1815.

Auerbach, Clemens. "Summer 1937." In *Erich Auerbach: Geschichte und Aktualität eines europäischen Philologen,* ed. Martin Treml and Karlheinz Barck. Berlin: Kulturverlag Kadmos, 2007, pp. 495–500.

Auerbach, Erich. *Dante als Poet der irdischen Welt.* Berlin: Walter de Gruyter, 1929.

Dante: Poet of the Secular World. Trans. Ralph Manheim. New York: New York Review of Books, 2007.

Das französische Publikum des 17. Jahrhunderts. Münchener romanistische Arbeiten 3. Munich: Hueber, 1933.

"Der Schriftsteller Montaigne." [1932] In *Gesammelte Aufsätze zur romanischen Philologie,* ed. Fritz Schalk. Bern: Francke, 1967, pp. 184–95.

"Die Entdeckung Dantes in der Romantik." In *Gesammelte Aufsätze zur romanischen Philologie,* ed. Fritz Schalk. Bern: Francke, 1967, pp. 176–83.

"Die Entstehung der Nationalsprachen im Europa des 16. Jahrhunderts." [1930] In *Kultur als Politik: Aufsätze aus dem Exil zur Geschichte und Zukunft Europas (1938–1947),* ed. Christian Rivoletti. Konstanz: Konstanz University Press, 2014, pp. 51–66.

"Epilegomena zu Mimesis." *Romanische Forschungen* 65 (1954): 1–18. Reprinted in *Erich Auerbach: Geschichte und Aktualität eines europäischen Philologen,* ed. Martin Treml and Karlheinz Barck. Berlin: Kulturverlag Kadmos, 2007, pp. 466–79.

"Erich Auerbach: Briefe an Paul Binswanger und Fritz Schalk, Teil I (1930–1937)." Ed. Isolde Burr and Hans Rothe. *Romanistiches Jahrbuch* 59 (2009): 145–90.

"Figura." *Archivum Romanicum* 22 (1938): 436–89.

"Figura." Rev. ed. in *Neue Dantestudien*. Istanbul: I. Horoz basimevi, 1944, pp. 11–71.

"Figura." Trans. Ralph Manheim in *Scenes from the Drama of European Literature*. Minneapolis: University of Minnesota Press, 1984, pp. 11–76.

Gesammelte Aufsätze zur romanischen Philologie. Ed. Fritz Schalk. Bern: Francke, 1967.

"Introduction: Purpose and Method." In *Literary Language and Its Public in Late Latin Antiquity and in the Middle Ages* [1958], trans. Ralph Manheim. Princeton, NJ: Princeton University Press, 1993, pp. 3–24.

Kultur als Politik: Aufsätze aus dem Exil zur Geschichte und Zukunft Europas (1938–1947). Ed. Christian Rivoletti. Konstanz: Konstanz University Press, 2014.

"La Cour et la Ville." [1951] In *Scenes from the Drama of European Literature*, trans. Ralph Manheim. Minneapolis: University of Minnesota Press, 1984, pp. 133–79.

Literary Language and Its Public in Late Latin Antiquity and in the Middle Ages. [1958] Trans. Ralph Manheim. Princeton, NJ: Princeton University Press, 1993.

"Marcel Proust: Der Roman von der verlorenen Zeit." [1927] In *Gesammelte Aufsätze zur romanischen Philologie*, ed. Fritz Schalk. Bern: Francke, 1967, pp. 296–300.

Mimesis: Dargestellte Wirklichkeit in der abendländischen Literatur. [1946] 2d ed. Bern: Francke, 1959.

Mimesis (in Hebrew). Trans. Barukh Karo, with an introduction by Dov Sadan. Jerusalem: Bialik Institute, 1958.

Mimesis: The Representation of Reality in Western Literature. Trans. Willard R. Trask. Princeton, NJ: Princeton University Press, 1953.

"On the Political Theory of Pascal." In *Scenes from the Drama of European Literature*, trans. Ralph Manheim. Minneapolis: University of Minnesota Press, 1984, pp. 101–32.

"'Passio' as Passion." *Proceedings of the Modern Language Association* 56 (1941): 1179–96.

"Philology and 'Weltliteratur." [1952] Trans. Maire and Edward Said. *Centennial Review* 13:1 (1969): 1–17.

"Racine und die Leidenschaften." [1926] In *Gesammelte Aufsätze zur romanischen Philologie*, ed. Fritz Schalk. Bern: Francke, 1967, pp. 196–203.

"Romantik und Realismus." In *Erich Auerbach: Geschichte und Aktualität eines europäischen Philologen*, ed. Martin Treml and Karlheinz Barck. Berlin: Kulturverlag Kadmos, 2007, pp. 426–38.

"Sacrae scripturae sermo humilis." [1941] In *Neue Dantestudien*. Istanbul: I. Horoz basimevi, 1944, pp. 1–10. Rev. and expanded ed. "Sermo humilis." *Romanische Forschungen* 64:3/4 (1952): 304–64.

"Scholarship in Times of Extremes: Letters of Erich Auerbach (1933–46), on the Fiftieth Anniversary of His Death." Trans. Martin Elsky, Martin Vialon, and Robert Stein, with introduction. *Proceedings of the Modern Language Association* 122:3 (2007): 742–62.

"Sermo humilis." In *Literary Language and Its Public*, trans. Ralph Manheim. Princeton, NJ: Princeton University Press, 1993, pp. 25–67.

"Stefan Georges Danteübertragung." *Cultura Italiana e Tedesca* 2:1 (1924): 17–20.

"The Triumph of Evil in Pascal." *Hudson Review* 4:1 (1951): 58–79.

"The Western Public and Its Language." In *Literary Language and Its Public*. [1958] Trans. Ralph Manheim. Princeton, NJ: Princeton University Press, 1993, pp. 235–339.

"Über das Persönliche in der Wirkung des hl. Franz von Assisi." [1927] In *Gesammelte Aufsätze zur romanischen Philologie*, ed. Fritz Schalk. Bern: Francke, 1967, pp. 33–42.

"Über die ernste Nachahmung des Alltäglichen." [1937] In *Erich Auerbach: Geschichte und Aktualität eines europäischen Philologen*, ed. Martin Treml and Karlheinz Barck. Berlin: Kulturverlag Kadmos, 2007, pp. 437–65.

"Vico und Herder." *Deutsche Vierteljahrsschrift für Literaturwissenschaft und Geistesgeschichte* 10:4 (1932): 671–86.

"Zur Dante-Feier." *Neue Rundschau* 23 (1921): 1005–6.

Zur Technik der Frührenaissancenovelle in Italien und Frankreich. Heidelberg: C. Winter, 1921.

Baeck, Leo. *Briefe, Reden, Aufsätze.* Ed. Michael Meyer. Vol. 6 of *Leo Baeck Werke*, ed. Albert H. Friedlander et al. 6 vols. Gütersloh: Gütersloh Verlagshaus, 2006.

This People Israel: The Meaning of Jewish Existence. [1955] Trans. and introduction by Albert Friedlander. New York: Holt, Rinehart and Winston, 1964.

"The Writing of History." [June 15, 1944] *Synagogue Review* (November 1962): 51–59.

Barash, Asher. *Ahavah Zarah.* [1938] In *Kitve Asher Barash* (in Hebrew). 3 vols. Tel Aviv: Massada, 1952: 1: 253–353.

In the Shadow of Good People: Short Stories (in Hebrew). Jerusalem: Bialik Institute, 1949.

Kitve Asher Barash (in Hebrew). 3 vols. Tel Aviv: Massada, 1952.

"Me-Ḥaye Barukh Vilder" (in Hebrew). In *Kitve Asher Barash*. 3 vols. Tel Aviv: Massada, 1952: 1: 393–409.

Pictures from a Brewery. Trans. Katie Kaplan. New York: Bobbs-Merrill, 1971.

"Riqmah." [1949] In *Kitve Asher Barash*. 3 vols. Tel Aviv: Massada, 1952: 1: 167–89.

"The Bones of Reb Shimshon Shapiro." In *Though He Slay Me*, trans. M. Reston. Tel Aviv: Massadah, 1963, pp. 218–85.

Barck, Karlheinz, and Anthony Reynolds. "Walter Benjamin and Erich Auerbach: Fragments of a Correspondence." *Diacritic* 22:3/4 (1992): 81–83.

Basil, Otto, Herbert Eisenrech, and Ivar Ivask. *Die Grosse Erbe: Aufsätze zur österreichischen Literatur.* Graz: Stiasny-Verlag, 1962.

Bauer, Bruno. *Die Judenfrage.* Braunschweig: Friedrich Otto, 1843.

Bauer, Otto. *Die Nationalitätenfrage und die Sozialdemokratie.* Vienna: Wiener Volksbuchhandlung Ignaz Brani, 1907.

Die österreichische Revolution. Vienna: Volksbuchhandlung, 1923.

The Question of Nationalities and Social Democracy. [1907] Ed. Ephraim J. Nimni, trans. Joseph O'Donnell. Minneapolis: University of Minnesota Press, 2000.

Bäumler, Alfred. "Einleitung: Bachofen der Mythologue der Romantik." In *J. J. Bachofen: Der Mythus von Orient und Occident*, ed. Manfred Schroeter. Munich: Beck, 1926, pp. xxiii–ccxciv.

Becker, Jurek. *Jacob the Liar.* Trans. Leila Vennewitz. New York: Arcade Pub. 1996.

Jakob der Lügner. Darmstadt: Luchterhand, 1970.

"Wenn ich auf meine bisheriges zurückblicke, dann muß ich leider sagen": Jurek Becker 1937–1997: Dokumente zum Leben und Werk ausdem Jurek-Becker-Archiv. Ed. Karin Kiwus. Berlin: Akademie der Künste, 2002.

Be'er, Haim. *Feathers.* Trans. Hillel Halkin. Lebanon, NH: University Press of New England, 2004.

Beer-Hofmann, Richard. *Jaákobs Traum: Ein Vorspiel.* Berlin: S. Fischer, 1919.

Jacob's Dream. Trans. Ida Bension Wynn. Philadelphia: Jewish Publication Society, 1946.

Vorspiel auf dem Theater zu König David. Vienna: Johannes-Presse, 1936.

Benjamin, Walter. *Berlin Childhood Around 1900.* Trans. Howard Eiland. Cambridge, MA: Belknap Press of Harvard University Press, 2006.

The Origin of German Tragic Drama. Trans. John Osborne. London: NLR, 1977.

Ben Moses Moellin, Jacob. *Sheelot u-Teshuvot Maharil* (in Hebrew). Cracow: Fischer & Deutscher, 1881.

Bettauer, Hugo. *Die Stadt ohne Juden.* Vienna: Gloriette, 1922.

Bialik, Chaim Nachman. *Collected Poems – Critical Edition* (in Hebrew). Ed. Dan Miron et al. 3 vols. Tel Aviv: Devir, 1983–90.

"Jacob & Esau: A Folk Legend." In *Collected Poems – Critical Edition.* Ed. Dan Miron et al. 3 vols. Tel Aviv: Devir, 1983–90: 1: 172–77.

Birnbaum, Nathan. *Ausgewälte Schriften zur jüdischen Frage.* Czernowitz: Verlag der Buchhandlung Dr. Birnbaum & Dr. Kohut, 1910.

"Die Principien des Zionismus." *Selbst-Emancipation* 5:3, 5:5, 5:6/7 (1892): 27–28, 52–54, 57–58, respectively.

"Die Zionistische Partei." *Selbst-Emancipation* 5:4 (1892): 40.

Gottes Volk. Vienna: R. Löwit, 1918.

"Ostjüdische Aufgaben." *Bukowinär Post*, July 1905. Reprinted in *Ausgewälte Schriften zur jüdischen Frage.* Czernowitz: Verlag der Buchhandlung Dr. Birnbaum & Dr. Kohut, 1910, pp. 260–75.

Selected Works (in Hebrew). Trans. M. Shonfeld. Tel Aviv: Neẓaḥ, 1942.

"The Task of Eastern European Jews." Trans. Joshua Fishman. *International Journal of the Sociology of Language* 226 (2014): 83–99.

"Zu den Reichsrathwahlen." *Selbst-Emancipation* 4:4 (1891): 2–3.

Birnbaum, Nathan, ed. *Der Aufstieg: Eine jüdische Monatsschrift* 1–12 (1930–32).

Blake, William. "On the Marriage of Heaven and Hell." In *Complete Writings.* Oxford: Oxford University Press, 1966.

Bloch, Joseph. *Der national Zwist und die Juden in Österreich*. Vienna: M. Gottlieb, 1886.

Erinnerungen aus meinem Leben. Vienna: Löwit, 1922.

Israel and the Nations. Berlin: B. Harz, 1927.

"Nichts gelernt und nichts vergessen." *Österreichische Wochenschrift* (22 June 1917).

Braun, Felix. *Herbst des Reiches*. Olten: Walter-Verlag, 1957. First published as *Agnes Altkirchner*. Leipzig: Insel-verlag, 1927.

Celan, Paul. "Jakobsstimme." In *Sprachgitter*. Frankfurt am Main: S. Fischer Verlag. 1959.

Chajes, Hirsch Perez. *Reden und Vorträge*. Vienna: Moritz Rosenfeld, 1933.

Speeches and Lectures (in Hebrew). Boston: Beit ha-Midrash le-Morim, 1953.

Charmatz, Richard. *Adolf Fischhof*. Vienna: J.G. Cotta, 1910, pp. 270–73.

Chaucer, Geoffrey. *Canterbury Tales*. Rendered into modern English by J. U. Nicolson. Mineola, NY: Dover, 2004.

Cohen, Hermann. "Antwort auf das offene Schreiben des Herrn Dr. Martin Buber." In *Hermann Cohens Jüdische Schriften*, ed. Bruno Strauss. 3 vols. Berlin: C. A. Schwetschke, 1924: 2: 328–40.

Der Begriff der Religion im System der Philosophie. Giessen: A. Töpelmann, 1915.

"Der Prophetismus und die Soziologie." In *Hermann Cohens Jüdische Schriften*, ed. Bruno Strauss. 3 vols. Berlin: C. A. Schwetschke, 1924: 2: 398–401.

"Deutschtum und Judentum I." In *Hermann Cohens Jüdische Schriften*, ed. Bruno Strauss. 3 vols. Berlin: C. A. Schwetschke, 1924: 2: 237–30.

"Deutschtum und Judentum II." In *Hermann Cohens Jüdische Schriften*, ed. Bruno Strauss, 3 vols. Berlin: C. A. Schwetschke, 1924: 2: 302–18.

"Die Nächstenliebe in Talmud." *Jüdische Schriften* 1 (1888): 145–74.

"Innere Beziehungen der Kantischen Philosophie zum Judentum." In *Hermann Cohens Jüdische Schriften*, ed. Bruno Strauss. 3 vols. Berlin: C. A. Schwetschke, 1924: 1: 284–305.

"Religion und Zionismus." In *Hermann Cohens Jüdische Schriften*, ed. Bruno Strauss, 3 vols. Berlin: C. A. Schwetschke, 1924, 2: 319–27.

Cohn-Bendit, Daniel. "Ein Abend mit Joschka Fischer." *Frankfurter Allgemeine Sonntagszeitung* (20 February 2005).

"Gesprächsrunde über jüdisches Leben im Nachkriegsdeutschland." *Münchener Beiträge zur Jüdischen Geschichte und Kultur* 6:1 (2012): 41–60.

Coleridge, Samuel Taylor. *Specimens of the Table Talk*. 2d ed. London: John Murray, 1836.

Coreth, Anna. *Pietas Austriaca: Ursprung und Entwicklung barocker Frömmigkeit in Österreich*. Vienna: Verlag für Geschichte und Politik, 1959.

Coudenhove-Kalergi, Richard N. *Judenhass von Heute: Das Wesen des Antisemitismus*. Ed. and introduction by R. N. Coudenhove-Kalergi. Vienna: Europa Verlag, 1935.

Paneuropa. Vienna: Paneuropa Verlag, 1923.

Csokor, Franz Theodor. *Europäische Trilogie: Erstes Stück, 3. November 1918; zweites Stück, Besetztes Gebiet; drittes Stück, Der verlorene Sohn*. Vienna: P. Zsolnay, 1952.

Curtius, Ernst Robert. *Deutscher Geist in Gefahr.* Stuttgart: Deutsche verlags-anstalt, 1932.

"Die geistige Bewegung in Deutschland und der französische Geist." *Westdeutsche Wochenschrift* (31 October 1919).

"Die Lehre von den drei Stilen in Altertum und Mittelalter zu Auerbachs *Mimesis.*" *Romanische Forschungen* 64 (1952): 57–70.

Doderer, Heimito von. *Die Dämonen: Roman.* Munich: Biederstein, 1956.

Die Strudlhofstiege; oder, Melzer und die Tiefe der Jahre: Roman. Vienna: Luckmann, 1951.

"Österreichs national Bewußtsein ist übernational." *Die kleine Zeitung* (20 June 1964). Reprinted as "Athenerrede: Von der Wiederkehr Österreichs." In *Die Wiederkehr der Drachen,* ed. Wendelin Schmidt-Dengler. Munich: Biderstein Verlag, 1970, pp. 239–47.

Dohm, Christian Wilhelm von. *Über die bürgerliche Verbesserung der Juden.* 2 vols. Berlin: Friedrich Nicolai, 1781–83.

Elbaum, Dov. *My Life with the Patriarch* (in Hebrew). Tel Aviv: Am Oved, 2001.

Elias, Norbert. "Die Ballade von armen Jakob." In *Los der Menschen.* Frankfurt am Main: Suhrkamp, 1987, pp. 87–98.

Die höfische Gesellschaft: Untersuchungen zur Soziologie des Königtums und der höfischen Aristokratie. [1933] Neuwied: Luchterhand, 1969.

Fichte, Johann Gottlieb. *Beiträge zur Berechtigung der Urteile des Publikums über die Französische Revolution: Zur Beurteilung ihrer Rechtmäßigkeit.* Danzig: Verlag Ferdinand Troschel, 1793.

Fischer, Ernst. *Von Grillparzer zu Kafka.* Vienna: Globus Verlag, 1962.

Fischhof, Adolf. *Die Sprachenrechte in den Staaten gemischter Nationalität.* Vienna: Manz, 1885.

Österreich und die Bürgschaften seines Bestandes. Vienna: Wallishausser, 1869.

Forvm: Internationale Zeitschrift für kulturelle Freiheit, politische Gleichheit und solidarische Arbeit, 1980–95

Forvm: Österreichische Monatsblätter für kulturelle Freiheit, 1954–65. Title changed to *Neues Forum,* 1966–79. Alternative title: *Forum.* Reprinted as *Forvm.* 28 vols. + index vol. Vienna: Ueberreuter, 2002–4.

Freud, Sigmund. *The Interpretation of Dreams.* Trans. James Strachey. New York: Avon Books, 1965.

Fried, Alfred H. *Der Völkerbund: Ein Sammelbuch.* Leipzig: E. P. Tal & Co., 1919.

The Restoration of Europe. New York: Macmillan, 1916.

Friedländer, David. *Sendschreiben an Seine hochwürden, herrn Oberconsistorialrath und Probst Teller zu Berlin von einigen hausvätern jüdischer Religion.* Berlin: August Mylius, 1799.

Friedländer, Salomon. "Das Bewußsein unsres Werthes, II: Als Israeliten." In *Predigten: Gehalten im Tempel der Genossenschaft für Reform im Judenthume zu Berlin.* Leipzig: Wigand, 1847, pp. 105–16.

Fries, Jakob. "Über die Gefährdung des Wohlstandes und Charakteres der Deutschen durch die Juden." *Heidelberger Jahrbücher* 16/17 (1816): 241–64.

Von deutschem Bund und deutscher Staatsverfassung. Heidelberg: Mohr und Winter, 1816.

Geiger, Ludwig. "Herder und das Judentum." In *Deutsche Literatur und die Juden*. Berlin: Georg Reimer, 1910, pp. 63–80. Reprinted in *Herder Today*, ed. Kurt Mueller-Vollmer. Berlin: Walter de Gruyter, 1990, pp. 382–401.

Gladstein, Jacob. "1919" (in Yiddish and English). Trans. Cynthia Ozick. In *The Penguin Book of Modern Yiddish Verse*, ed. Irving Howe, Ruth R. Wisse, and Khone Shmeruk. New York: Viking, 1987, pp. 425–27.

Goethe, Johann Wolfgang von. *Autobiography: Truth and Fiction Relating to My Life*. Trans. John Oxenford. Boston: S. E. Cassino, 1882.

Goldberg, Oskar. *Die Wirklichkeit der Hebräer*. [1925] Wiesbaden: Harrassowitz, 2005.

Goldstein Moritz. "Deutsch-jüdischer Parnass." *Der Kunstwart* 25:11 (March 1, 1912): 281–94.

Greenberg, Uri Zvi. "In the Kingdom of the Cross" (in Yiddish). *Collected Yiddish Works*. 2 vols. Jerusalem: Magnes Press, 1979: 2: 457–72.

In the Kingdom of the Cross (in Hebrew and Yiddish). Trans. Bejamin Harshav. Tel Aviv: Beit Moereshet Uri Zvi Greenberg, 2007.

Kol Ketavav. 19 vols. Jerusalem: Bialik Institute, 1990.

"Vision of a Legionnaire" (in Hebrew). In *Kol Ketavav*, 19 vols. Jerusalem: Bialik Institute, 1990: 2: 7–31.

Groethuysen, Bernard. *Origines de l'esprit bourgeois en France: 1, L'Eglise et la bourgeoisie*. [1927] Paris: Gallimard, 1977.

Gronemann, Sammy. *Reminiscences of a Yeqe* (in Hebrew). Trans. Dov Stock (Sadan) from German. Tel Aviv: Am Oved, 1946.

Güdemann, Moritz. *Nationaljudentum*. Leipzig: Breitenstein, 1897.

Gundolf, Friedrich. *Goethe*. Berlin: G. Bondi, 1916.

Shakespeare und der deutsche Geist. Berlin: G. Bondi, 1914.

Habermas, Jürgen. "Begegnungen mit Gershom Scholem." *Münchener Beiträge zur Jüdischen Geschichte und Kultur* 2 (2007): 9–18.

"Der deutsche Idealismus der jüdischen Philosophen." In *Philosophisch-Politische Profile*. Frankfurt: Suhrkamp, 1971, pp. 37–66.

"Grossherzige Remigranten: Über jüdische Philosophen in der frühen Bundesrepublik: Eine persönliche Erinnerung." *Neue Zürcher Zeitung* (2 July 2011).

"Interview mit Angelo Bolaffi." [1988] In *Die Nachholende Revolution. Kleine politische Schriften 7*. Frankfurt am Main: Suhrkamp, 1990, pp. 21–28.

Habermas, Jürgen, ed. *Stichworte zur geistigen Situation der Zeit*. 2 vols. Frankfurt: Suhrkamp, 1979.

Hainisch, Michael. *Die Zukunft der Deutsch-Österreicher*. Vienna: F. Deuticke, 1892.

Heine, Heinrich. "An Edom." In *Werke und Briefe*. 10 vols. Berlin: Aufbau Verlag, 1972: 8: 166–72.

Briefe 1815–1831. Ed. Fritz Eisner. Vol. 20 of Säkularausgabe. 27 vols. Berlin: Akademie Verlag, 1970–86.

Der Rabbi von Bacherach: Ein Fragment. Ed. Erich Loewenthal. Berlin: Schocken Verlag, 1937.

Florentine Nights. Trans. C. G. Leland. New York: John W. Lovell Company, 1891.

The Rabbi of Bacherach: A Fragment. Trans. E. B. Ashton. New York: Schocken, 1947.

Hertz, Frederick (Friedrich Otto). *The Economic Problem of the Danubian States: A Study in Economic Nationalism.* London: V. Gollancz, 1947.

Hertz, Friedrich Otto. *Nationalgeist und Politik: Beiträge zur Erforschung der tieferen Ursachen des Weltkrieges.* Zurich: Europa-verlag, 1937.

Rasse und Kultur: Eine kritische Untersuchung der Rassentheorien. Leipzig: A. Kröner, 1915.

Hertzka, Theodor. *Freiland: Ein soziales Zukunftsbild.* Leipzig: Duncker & Humblot, 1890.

Herzl, Theodor Herzl. *Der Judenstaat.* Leipzig: M. Breitenstein, 1896.

The Jewish State. Trans. Sylvie d'Avigdor. London: Nutt, 1896.

Hescheles, Jeremiah. "Esau on a visit" (in Yiddish). In *Soneten fun Tohu Vavohu: Poems.* New York: Eigenweg, 1957, pp. 84–86.

Hofmannsthal, Hugo von. "Die Idee Europa: Notizen zu einer Rede." In *Reden und Aufsätze II, vol. 9 of Gesammelte Werke*, ed. Bernd Schoeller and Rudolf Hirsch. 10 vols. Frankfurt am Main: Fischer Taschenbuch, 1979: 9: 43–54.

"Die österreichische Idee." *Reden und Aufsätze II, vol. 9 of Gesammelte Werke*, ed. Bernd Schoeller and Rudolf Hirsch. 10 vols. Frankfurt am Main: Fischer Taschenbuch, 1979: 9: 454–58.

Holdheim, Samuel. *Stahl's Christliche Toleranz beleuchtet.* Berlin: Julius Abelsdorff, 1856.

Horace. *Ars Poetica des Horaz.* Trans. and interpreted by Th. Kayser. Stuttgart: Liebioh, 1888.

Jacob, Benno. *Die Wissenschaft des Judentums: Ihr Einfluß auf die Emanzipation.* Berlin: Poppelhauer, 1907.

Krieg, Revolution und Judentum. Dortmund: N.p., 1919.

Jellinek, Adolph. *Der jüdische Stamm in nichtjüdischen Sprichwörtern.* Vienna: Löwn Buchhandlung, 1881.

"Gedächtnisrede auf Se. Majestät Ferdinand Maximilian Josef, Kaiser von Mexico (14. Juli 1867)." In *Reden bei verschiedenen Gelegenheiten.* Vienna: Brüder Winter, 1874, pp. 67–71.

"Jüdisch-Deutsch." *Die Neuzeit* (15 July 1883).

"Jüdisch-österreichisch," *Die Neuzeit* (15 June 1883).

Studien und Skizzen: Erster Theil: Der jüdische Stamm: Ethnographische Studien. Vienna: Herzfeld & Bauer, 1869.

"Zur Wahlkampagne." *Die Neuzeit* (6 June 1879).

Jelski, Julius. "Judenhaß" and "Alte und neue Heimat." In *Im Wandel der Zeiten: Predigten.* 2 vols. Berlin: Philo-Verlag, 1930: 2: 88–95, 96–100, respectively.

Jollos, Waldemar. *Arte tedesca fra le due guerre.* Ed. with an introduction by Luigi Rognoni. Milan: Mondadori, 1955.

Esau und Jakob. Berlin: S. Fischer, 1919.

Russische Gestalten und Ereignisse. Zurich: Neue Zürcher Zeitung, 1953.

"Untersuchungen über die wirtschaftliche und soziale Lage der Berliner Metallarbeiter." Ph.D. diss., Friedrich-Wilhelms-Universität, Berlin, 1910.

"Juif." In *Encyclopédie ou dictionnaire raisonné des sciences, des arts et des métiers* [1772], ed. Denis Diderot, 9:25. http://encyclopedie.uchicago.edu.

Kafka, Franz. *Briefe 1902–1924*. Frankfurt am Main: S. Fischer, 1966.

Kanter, Felix. *Gleichniße für Reden über jüdische Angelegenheiten*. Frankfurt am Main: J. Kauffmann, 1911.

Kantorowicz, Ernst. *Kaiser Friedrich der Zweite*. Berlin: G. Bondi, 1927.

Kerényi, Károly. *Romandichtung und Mythologie: Ein Briefwechsel mit Thomas Mann*. Zurich: Rhein-Verlag, 1945.

Kewall, Benjamin. *Erlebte Revolution 1848/49: Das Wiener Tagebuch des jüdischen Journalisten Benjamin Kewall*. Ed. Wolfgang Gasser in collaboration with Gottfried Glassner. Vienna: Böhlau, 2010.

Klahr, Alfred [Rudolf]. "Zur Entwicklung der deutschen Nation." [1944] In *Zum 100. Geburtstag und zum 60. Todestag: Der theoretische Begründer der "österreichischen Nation", Dr. Alfred Klahr, 1904–1944*. http://www.antifa-inf o.at/archiv/KLAHR.PDF.

"Zur nationalen Frage in Österreich." *Weg und Ziel* 2:3/4 (1937): 126–33, 173–81.

Kohler, Max J. *Jewish Rights at the Congresses of Vienna (1814–1815) and Aix-la-Chapelle (1818)*. New York: The American Jewish Committee, 1918.

Kohn, Hans. *The Idea of Nationalism*. New York: Macmillan, 1944.

Kolnai, Auriel. *The War Against the West*. New York: Viking Press, 1938.

Kreisky, Bruno. "Kreisky: Keine Politik des Terrors!" *Arbeiter-Zeitung*, (20 April 1968).

Kvitko, Leib. "Esau" (in Yiddish and English). Trans. Allen Mandelbaum and Harold Rabinowitz. In *The Penguin Book of Modern Yiddish Verse*, ed. Irving Howe, Ruth R. Wisse, and Khone Shmeruk. New York: Viking, 1987, pp. 296–99.

Lamdan, Yiẓḥak. *Masadah*. Tel Aviv: Hedim, 1927.

Landau, Ezekiel. "Derush Hesped al Mitat ha-Qesarit Maria Theresa." In *"Your Voice Like a Ram's Horn": Themes and Texts in Traditional Jewish Preaching*, by Marc Saperstein. Cincinnati, OH: Hebrew Union College, 1996, pp. 147–61, 445–68.

Landauer, Gustav. "Sind das Ketzergedanken?" In *Gustav Landauer: Dichter, Ketzer, Außenseiter: Essays und Reden zur Literatur, Philosophie, Judentum*, ed. Hannah Delf. Berlin: Akademie Verlag, 1997, pp. 170–74.

Lasker-Schüler, Else. *Das Hebräerland*. Zurich: Verlag Oprecht, 1937.

"Hebräische Balladen." In *Gedichte 1902–1943*, ed. Friedhelm Kemp. Vol. 1 of *Gesammelte Werke*. 3 vols. Munich: Kösel Verlag, 1961: 1: 289ff.

Hebrew Ballads and Other Poems (in German and English). Trans. and ed. Audri Durchslag and Jeanette Litman-Demeestère. Philadelphia: The Jewish Publication Society, 1980.

"Jakob und Esau" and "Jakob." In *Gesammelte Werke*. 3 vols. Munich: Kösel Verlag, 1961: 1: 296, 1: 297, respectively.

Your Diamond Dreams Cut Open My Arteries: Poems by Else Lasker-Schüler. Trans. and with an introduction by Robert P. Newton. Chapel Hill: University of North Carolina Press, 1982.

Lazarus, Moritz. *Was heißt National? Ein Vortrag*. Berlin: Ferd. Dümmlers Verlagsbuchhandlung, 1880.

Lernet-Holenia, Alexander. *Der Graf Luna: Roman*. Vienna: P. Zsolnay, 1955.

Der Graf von Saint-Germain. Zurich: Morgarten Verlag [Conzett & Huber], 1948.

Levi, Primo.*Survival in Auschwitz*. New York: Touchstone, 1996.

Levinsky, E. L. *Kitve E. L. Levinsky*. 3 vols. Odessa: Yavneh, 1911.

Łódź Ghetto. Produced by Alan Adelson, directed by Kathryn Taverna and Alan Adelson. Jewish Heritage Project, Westport, CT, 1992. Videorecording.

Luft, David. *Hugo von Hofmannsthal and the Austrian Idea: Selected Essays and Addresses, 1906–1927*. West Lafayette, IN: Purdue University Press, 2011.

Manger, Itzik. *Medresh Itsik*. Ed. Chone Shemruk, introduction by Dov Sadan. 2d ed. Jerusalem: Hebrew University, 1969.

Mann, Thomas. *A Sketch of My Life*. Trans. H. T. Lowe-Porter. New York: A. Knopf, 1960.

——— . *Der Junge Joseph*. Berlin: S. Fischer, 1934.

——— . *Die Geschichten Jaakobs*. Berlin: S. Fischer, 1933.

——— . *Doctor Faustus: The Life of the German Composer Adrian Leverkühn as Told by a Friend*. Trans. H. T. Lowe-Porter. New York: A. Knopf, 1948.

——— . *Joseph and His Brothers*. Trans. H. T. Lowe-Porter. New York: Alfred A. Knopf, 1948.

——— . *Joseph and His Brothers*. Translation of *Die Geschichten Jaakobs* by H. T. Lowe-Porter. New York: A. Knopf, 1934.

——— . *Joseph, der Ernährer*. Stockholm: Bermann-Fischer, 1943.

——— . *Joseph in Ägypten*. Vienna: Bermann-Fischer, 1936.

——— . *Joseph in Egypt*. Trans. H. T. Lowe-Porter. 2 vols. New York: A. Knopf, 1938.

——— . *Joseph the Provider*. Trans. H. T. Lowe-Porter. New York: A. Knopf, 1944.

——— . "Joseph und seine Brüder: Ein Vortrag." In *Gesammelte Werke*. 13 vols. Frankfurt am Main: S. Fischer, 1960: 11: 654–69.

——— . *Letters of Thomas Mann, 1889–1955*. Selected and trans. by Richard and Clara Winston. Berkeley: University of California Press, 1990.

——— . "Pariser Rechenschaft." [1926] In *Gesammelte Werke*. 13 vols. Frankfurt am Main: S. Fischer, 1960: 11: 9–97.

——— . "The Dangers Facing Democracy." [1940] In *Gesammelte Werke*. 13 vols. Frankfurt am Main: S. Fischer, 1960: 11: 491–98.

——— . *The Magic Mountain*. Trans. H. T. Lowe-Porter. New York: A. Knopf, 1927.

——— . "The Theme of the Joseph Novels." [1942] In *Thomas Mann's Addresses Delivered at the Library of Congress, 1942–1949*. Washington, DC: Library of Congress, 1963, pp. 1–19.

——— . *Young Joseph*. Trans. H. T. Lowe-Porter. New York: A. Knopf, 1935.

Marchais, Georges. "'Le Mouvement du 22 mars Nanterre' dirigé par l'anarchiste allemand Cohn-Bendit" ("De faux revolutionaries à démasquer"). *L'Humanité* (3 May 1968).

Marr, Wilhelm. *Wählet keinen Juden! Der Weg zum Siege des Germanenthums über das Judenthum: Ein Mahnwort an die Wähler nichtjüdischen Stammes aller Confessionen*. Berlin: Hentze, 1879.

Marx, Karl. "Zur Judenfrage." In *Werke*, by Karl Marx/Friedrich Engels. 41 vols. Berlin: Dietz Verlag, 1959–68: 1 (1976): 347–77.

——— . "Zur Kritik der Hegelschen Rechtsphilosophie. Einleitung." In *Werke*. 41 vols. Berlin: Dietz, 1959–68: 1 (1976): 378–91.

Matejka, Viktor. *Was ist österreichische Kultur?* Vienna: Selbstverlag des Verfassers, 1945.

Mendele Mocher Sefarim. *Kol Kitve Mendele Mocher Sefarim.* Tel Aviv: Devir, 1947.

Mendelssohn, Moses. *Menasseh ben Israel Rettung der Juden.* In *Über die bürgerliche Verbesserung der Juden*, by Christian Wilhelm von Dohm. 2 vols. Berlin: Friedrich Nicolai, 1781–83.

Menger, Anton. *Neue Staatslehre.* Jena: G. Fischer, 1904.

Mommsen, Theodor. *Auch ein Wort über unser Judenthum.* Berlin: Weidmannsche Buchhandlung, 1880.

Morgenstern, Soma. "A Conversation with Dr. Soma Morgenstern." Radio interview (September 30, 1973). In *Kritiken, Berichte, Tagebücher*, ed. Ingolf Schulte. Lüneburg: Zu Klampen, 2001. http://soma-morgenstern.at/user files/file/Materialien/The%20Eternal%20Light.pdf.

Der Sohn des verlorenen Sohnes. Berlin: Erich Reiss, 1935.

Der Sohn des verlorenen Sohnes: Erster Roman der Trilogie Funken im Abgrund; Idyll im Exil: Zweiter Roman der Trilogie Funken im Abgrund; Das Vermächtnis des verlorenen Sohnes: Dritter Roman der Trilogie Funken im Abgrund. Ed. with postscript by Ingolf Schulte. Lüneburg: Zu Klampen, 1996.

Die Blutsäule: Zeichen und Wunder am Sereth. Vienna: Hans Deutsch Verlag, 1964.

Flucht in Frankreich: Ein Romanbericht. Ed. with postscript by Ingolf Schulte. Lüneburg: Zu Klampen, 1998.

In My Father's Pastures. Trans. Ludwig Lewisohn. Philadelphia: Jewish Publication Society, 1947.

The Son of the Lost Son. Trans. Joseph Leftwich and Peter Gross. Philadelphia: Jewish Publication Society, 1946.

The Testament of the Lost Son. Trans. Jacob Sloan and Maurice Samuel. Philadelphia: Jewish Publication Society, 1950.

The Third Pillar. Trans. Ludwig Lewisohn. New York: Farrar, Straus and Cudahy, 1955.

Werke in Einzelbänden. Ed. Ingolf Schulte. 11 vols. Lüneburg: Zu Klampen, 1994–2001.

Nenning, Günther. "Blockade!!!" *Kronen Zeitung* (3 November 2003).

"Die Ballade von armen F. T. Gesungen zu Friedrich Torbergs 90. und Bertolt Brechts 100." In *Wien oder Der Unterschied, Ein Lesebuch*, ed. David Axmann and Marietta Torberg. Munich: Langen Müller, 1998, pp. 269–76.

"Lieber kalter Krieger: Zum Tod Friedrich Torbergs, Begründer des FORVM." In *FORVM*, ed. Günther Nenning. Vienna: Amalthea, 1998, p. 206.

"Unser Wasser," *Kronen Zeitung* (29 January 2003).

Neurath, Otto. "Une encyclopédie internationale de la science unitaire." In *Actes du congrès international de philosophie scientifique.* 8 vols. Paris: Hermann, 1936: 2:54–59.

"L'encyclopédie comme 'modèle.'" *Revue de Synthèse* 12 (1936): 187–201.

Musil, Robert. *The Man Without Qualities.* Trans. Sophie Wilkins from German. 2 vols. New York: Knopf, 1995.

Nenning, Günther, ed. *FORVM: Die berühmsten Beiträge zur Zukunft von einst von Arrabal bis Zuckmayer.* Vienna: Amalthea, 1998.

Nenning, Günther, and Milo Dor, eds. *Landvermessung.* 21 vols. St. Pölten: Residenz, 2005.

Peretz, Y. L. *Kol Kitve Y. L. Peretz* (in Hebrew). Trans. Shimshon Meltzer from Yiddish. 10 vols. Tel Aviv: Devir, 1961.

Philippson, Ludwig. "Anibaueriana: Noch ein Artikel." *Allgemeine Zeitung des Judenthums* (5 August 1844): 445–49.

Polanyi, Karl. "Extramural Lectures: Report No. 1." In *Institute of International Education: Seventeenth Annual Report of the Director.* New York: Institute of International Education, 1936.

The Great Transformation: The Political and Economic Origins of Our Time. New York: Rinehart, 1944.

Popper. Karl. "Epistemology and Industrialization." In *The Myth of the Framework.* London: Routledge, 1994, pp. 185–209.

"Kant's Critique and Cosmology." In *Conjectures and Refutations.* New York: Basic Books, 1963, pp. 175–83.

Logik der Forschung: Zur Erkenntnistheorie der modernen Naturwissenschaft. Vienna: Springer, 1935.

Offene Geswellschaft–offenes Universum: Franz Kreuzer im Gespräch mit Karl R. Popper. Vienna: F. Deuticke, 1982.

"On Culture Clash." In *In Search of a Better World.* London: Routledge, 1992, pp. 117–25.

"Prague Lecture." https://www.lf3.cuni.cz/3LFEN-255.html.

The Logic of Scientific Discovery. Trans. Karl Popper. London: Hutchinson, 1959.

The Open Society and Its Enemies. 2 vols. London: Routledge, 1945.

The Open Society and Its Enemies. 2d ed. Princeton, NJ: Princeton University Press, 1950.

"Toleration and Intellectual Responsibility." In *In Search of a Better World.* London: Routledge, 1992, pp. 188–203.

Unended Quest: An Intellectual Autobiography. LaSalle, IL: Open Court, 1976.

"Zur Philosophie des Heimatgedankens." *Die Quelle* 77 (1927): 899–908.

Popper-Lynkeus, Joseph. *Die allgemeine Nährpflicht als Lösung der sozialen Frage.* Dresden: Carl Reissner, 1912.

Prinz, Joachim. *Helden und Abenteurer der Bibel: Ein Kinderbuch.* Berlin: Paul Baumann-Verlag, 1930.

Wir Juden. Berlin: Erich Reiss, 1934.

Prinz, Joachim, and Louis Pincus. *Israel and the Diaspora: Two Points of View.* Geneva: World Jewish Congress, 1973.

Rabi Binyamin. *From Zborov to Kineret* (in Hebrew). Tel Aviv: Devir, 1950.

Rawidowicz, Simon. "Between Jew and Arab." In *Between Jew and Arab: The Lost Voice of Simon Rawidowicz*, ed. David N. Myers. Hanover, NH: Brandeis University Press, 2008, pp. 135–80.

Renan, Ernest. *Qu'est-ce qu'une nation?* Paris: Calmann Lévy, 1882.

Renner, Karl. *Die Nation als Rechtsidee und die Internationale.* Vienna: Verlag des Vereines in Kommisssion bei Ignaz Brand, 1914.

Marxismus, Krieg und Internationale. Stuttgart: J. H. W. Dietz, 1918.

Österreichs Erneuerung: Politisch-programmatische Aufsätze. 3 vols. Vienna: Ignaz Brand and Co., 1916.

[Rudolf Springer]. *Der Kampf der Österreichischen Nationen um den Staat.* Leipzig: Franz Deuticke, 1902.

[Synopticus]. *Staat und Nation: Staatsrechtliche Untersuchung über die möglichen Principien einer Lösung und die juristischen Voraussetzungen eines Nationalitäten-Gesetzes.* Vienna: Josef Dietl, 1899.

Riesser, Gabriel. "Die Judenfrage: Gegen Bruno Bauer." *Konstitutionelle Jahrbücher* 2/3 (1843): 1–42, 14–57, 172–236.

Gesammelte Schrifte. 4 vols. Frankfurt am Main: Riesser-Stiftung, 1867: 3: 366–67.

Über die Stellung der Bekenner des mosaischen Glaubens in Deutschland. 2d ed. Altona: Hammerich, 1831.

Vertheidigung der Bürgerlichen Gleichstellung der Juden Gegen die Einwürfe des Herrn Dr. Paulus. Altona: Hammerich, 1831.

Rosenberg, Alfred. *Race and Race History and Other Essays.* Ed. Robert Pois. New York: Harper and Row, 1971.

Rosenzweig, Franz. *Zweistromland: Kleinere Schriften zur Religion und Philosophie.* Berlin: Philo Verlag, 1926.

Roth, Joseph. *Hiob: Roman eines einfachen Mannes.* Frankfurt am Main: Suhrkamp, 2011.

Juden auf Wanderschaft. Berlin: Die Schmiede, 1927.

Radetskymarsch. Berlin: Kiepenheuer and Witshe, 1932.

Sachs, Hans. "Comedia: Jacob mit seinem Bruder Esaw." In *Hans Sachs*, ed. Adelbert von Keller. 26 vols. Stuttgart: Literarischer Verein, 1870: 1: 88–110.

"Der Teuffel nam ein Weib." [1557] In *Hans Sachs: Eine Auswahl für Freunde der älteren vaterländischen Dichtungkunst*, ed. Johann Adam Göz. 4 vols. Nuremburg: Bauer und Raspe, 1829: 1: 197–219.

Schäfer, Wilhelm. *Jakob und Esau.* Berlin: Schuster & Loeffler, 1896.

Scheler, Max. *Die Stellung des Menschen im Kosmos.* Darmstadt: Reichl, 1928.

The Human Place in the Cosmos. Trans. Manfred S. Frings. Evanston IL: Northwestern University Press, 2009.

Schlegel, Friedrich. *Kritische Friedrich-Schlegel-Ausgabe.* 36 vols. Munich: Schöningh, 1964.

Schlesinger, Aqiva Yosef. "Letter to Montefiore in August or September 1874." Quoted in "Alliance of the Hebrews, 1863–1875: The Diaspora Roots of an Ultra-Orthodox Proto-Zionist Utopia in Palestine," by Michael K. Silber. *Journal of Israeli History* 27:2 (2008): 146–47.

Scholem, Gerschom. "Against the Myth of the German-Jewish Dialogue." [1964] In *On Jews and Judaism in Crisis*, ed. Werner Dannhauser. New York: Schocken, 1976, pp. 61–64.

The Correspondence of Walter Benjamin and Gershom Scholem, 1932–1940. Cambridge MA: Harvard University Press, 1980.

Schwietering, Julius. "Typologisches in mittelalterlicher Dichtung." In *Vom Werden des deutschen Geistes*, ed. Paul Merker and Wolfgang Stammler. Berlin: De Gruyter, 1925, pp. 40–55.

Seipel, Ignaz. *Nation und Staat*. Vienna: Wilhelm Braumüller, 1916.

Shaked, Malkah. *I'll Play You Forever: The Bible in Modern Hebrew Poetry*. 2 vols. Tel Aviv: Yediot Aḥaronot, 2005.

Shakespeare, William. *The Merchant of Venice*. London: Oxford University Press, 1914.

Shalev, Meir. *Esau*. Tel Aviv: Am Oved, 1991.

Esau. Trans. Barbara Harshav. New York: Harper Collins, 1994.

Sholem Aleichem. *Ḥaye Adam* (in Hebrew). Trans. Y. D. Berkowitz from Yiddish. 3 vols. New York: Shtibel, 1920.

The Complete Tevye the Dairyman (in Hebrew). Trans. Dan Miron from Yiddish. Jerusalem: Keter, 2005.

Spengler, Oswald. *Der Untergang des Abendlandes: Umrisse einer Morphologie der Weltgeschichte*. [1918–23] 2 vols. Munich: C. H. Beck'sche Verlagsbuchhandlung, 1927.

Sperber, Manès. *All das Vergangene . . .* Vienna: Europaverlag, 1983.

"Petit memorial." [1952] In *Être Juif*. Paris: Éditions Odile Jacob, 1994, pp. 113–26.

Spiel, Hilde, ed. *Die zeitgenössische Literatur Österreichs*. Zurich/Munich: Kindler, 1976.

Vienna's Golden Autumn 1866–1938. New York: Weidenfeld and Nicolson, 1987.

Steiner, George. "A Kind of Survivor." In *George Steiner: A Reader*. New York: Oxford University Press, 1984, pp. 220–33.

"Our Homeland, the Text." [1985] In *No Passion Spent: Essays 1978–1995*. New Haven, CT: Yale University Press, 1996, pp. 304–27.

The Portage to San Cristóbal of A.H. New York: Simon and Schuster, 1981.

"Through That Glass Darkly." [1991] In *No Passion Spent: Essays 1978–1995*. New Haven, CT: Yale University Press, 1996, pp. 328–47.

Stoecker, Adolf. *Ein Wort über unser Judenthum: Seperatabdruck aus der 44. und 45. Bande der Preußischen Jahrbücher (1879–1880)*. Berlin: G. Reimer, 1880.

"Unsere Forderungen an das moderne Judenthum." In *Das moderne Judenthum in Deutschland, besonders in Berlin: Zwei Reden in der christl-socialen Arbeiterpartei gehalten*. Berlin: Wiegandt und Grieben, 1880, pp. 4–20.

Swarsensky, Manfred. *Die Chanukah-Geschichte*. Berlin: Jüdischer Buchverlag Erwin Löwe, 1938.

Tamuz, Benjamin. *Jacob: A Novel* (in Hebrew). Ramat-Gan: Massada, 1971.

Torberg, Friedrich. *Auch das war Wien*. Munich: Langen Müller, 1984.

"Austrian Literature Since 1927." *Books Abroad* 28 (1954): 15–20.

"Der Herr Qualtinger." *Forum* 8 (December 1961): 456.

Der Schüler Gerber hat absolviert: Roman. Berlin: P. Zsolnay, 1930.

Die Tante Jolesch oder Der Untergang des Abendlandes in Anekdoten. Munich: Langen-Müller, 1975.

Die zweite Begegnung: Roman. [1950] Munich: Langen Müller, 1963.

Hier bin ich, mein Vater: Roman. Stockholm: Bermann-Fischer, 1948.

In diesem Sinne. . . . Briefe an Freunde und Zeitgenossen. Munich: Langen-Müller, 1981.

"Internal and External Emigration: An Imaginary Dialogue." [1947] Trans. Scott Denham. *New England Review* 20:4 (1999): 38–56.

"Ist Karl Kraus vorlesbar? Helmut Qualtinger und 'Die letzten Tage der Menschheit.'" *Forum* 10 (May 1963): 301.

Kaffehaus war überal. Ed. David Axmann and Marietta Torberg. Munich: Langen Müller, 1982.

Mein ist die Rache. Los Angeles: Pazifische Presse, 1943.

"Motivenbericht zu einem Freispruch." *Forum* 10 (June 1963): 321.

"Sehnsucht nach Alt Aussee." In *Wien oder Der Unterschied: Ein Lesebuch,* ed. David Axmann and Marietta Torberg. Munich: Langen Müller, 1998, pp. 71–87.

Süsskind von Trimberg: Roman. Frankfurt: S. Fischer, 1972.

"Was ist des Dichters Vaterland?" [1948] In *Voreingenommen wie ich bin,* ed. David Axmann and Marietta Torberg. Munich: Langen Müller, 1991, pp. 187–96.

Wien oder Der Unterschied, Ein Lesebuch. Ed. David Axmann and Marietta Torberg. Munich: Langen Müller, 1998.

Treitschke, Heinrich von. "Unser Aussichten." In *Preussische Jahrbücher* [November 15, 1879], trans. Helen Lederer and reprinted in part in *The State, the Nation, and the Jews: Liberalism and the Antisemitism Dispute in Bismarck's Germany,* by Marcel Stoetzler. Lincoln: University of Nebraska Press, 2008, pp. 309–16.

Troeltsch, Ernst. *Der Historismus und seine Probleme.* [1922] Ed. Friedrich Wilhelm Graf and Matthias Schlossberger. 2 vols. Berlin: Walter de Gruyter, 2008.

Gesammelte Schriften. 4 vols. Tübingen: J.C.B. Mohr, 1925.

Historismus und seine Überwindung. [1924] Ed. Gangolf Hübinger and Andreas Terwey. Berlin: Walter de Gruyter, 2006.

"Vorherrschaft des Judentums?" [1920] In *Spectator-Briefe und Berliner Briefe (1919–1922),* ed. Gangolf Hübinger. Vol. 14 of *Ernst Troeltsch kritische Gesamtausgabe.* 20 vols. Berlin: Walter de Gruyter, 2015: 14: 209–17.

Trotsky, Leon. *My Life: An Attempt at an Autobiography.* New York: Pathfinder, 1970.

Unger, Joachim Jacob. *Gesammelte Aufsätze.* Prague: Jakob Brandeis, 1908.

"Mallinckrodt und die Judenfrage in Preußen." *Die neue Zeit* 14:30 (1874): 254–55.

Patriotische Casual-Reden. 2d ed. Prague: Jakob B. Brandeis, 1899.

Vialon, Martin. "Die Stimme Dantes und ihre Resonanz." In *Erich Auerbach: Geschichte und Aktualität eines europäischen Philologen,* ed. Martin Treml and Karlheinz Barck. Berlin: Kulturverlag Kadmos, 2007, pp. 46–56.

Erich Auerbachs Briefe an Martin Hellweg (1939–1950): Edition und historisch-philologischer Kommentar. Tübingen: Francke, 1997.

"Erich Auerbach und Rudolf Bultmann: Probleme abendländischer Geschichtsdeutung." In *Marburger Hermeneutik zwischen Tradition und*

Krise, ed. Matthias Bormuth and Ulrich von Bülow. Göttingen: Wallstein Verlag, 2008, pp. 176–206.

"Helle und Trost für eine 'neue Menschlichkeit' – Erich Auerbachs türkisches Exilbriefwerk." *Deutsche Akademie für Sprache und Dichtung: Jahrbuch 2010.* Göttingen: Wallstein Verlag, 2011, pp. 18–47.

"Passion und Prophetie: Eine Entdeckung: Thomas Manns Dankesbrief an Erich Auerbach für das Buch 'Mimesis.'" *Süddeutsche Zeitung* (27–28 May 2006).

"The Scars of Exile: Paralipomena concerning the Relationship between History, Literature and Politics – Demonstrated in the Examples of Erich Auerbach, Traugott Fuchs and Their Circle in Istanbul." *Yeditepe'de felsefe* 2 (2003): 191–246.

Und wirst erfahren wie das Brot der Fremde so salzig schmeckt: Eric Auerbachs Briefe an Karl Vossler, 1926–1938. Warmbronn: Keicher, 2007.

"Wie haben Sie es geschafft, in Deutschland zu überleben? Zum fünfzigsten Todestag des großen Romanisten erstmals publiziert: Erich Auerbachs Brief an Victor Klemperer vom 7. Mai 1949." *Süddeutsche Zeitung* (13 October 2007).

Vico, Giambattista. *Die neue Wissenschaft über die gemeinschaftliche Natur der Völker.* [*Principi di una scienza nuova*, 3d ed., 1744] Trans. Erich Auerbach. Munich: Allgemeine Verlagsanstalt, 1924.

New Science: Principles of the New Science Concerning the Common Nature of Nations. Trans. David Marsh. London: Penguin, 1999.

Voltaire [François Marie Arouet]. *Oeuvres completes de Voltaire.* 35 vols. Paris: Hachette, 1859.

Weigall, Arthur. *Echnaton, König von Ägypten und seine Zeit.* Trans. Hermann Kees. Basel: B. Schwabe, 1923.

The Life and Time of Akhnaton, Pharaoh of Egypt. Edinburgh: W. Blackwood and Sons, 1910.

Weigel, Hans. *Flucht vor der Grösse: Beiträge zur Erkenntnis und Selbsterkenntnis Österreichs.* Vienna: Wollzeilen Verlag, 1960.

Werfel, Franz. *Twilight of a World.* New York: Viking Press, 1937.

Wiener, Max. *Jüdische Religion im Zeitalter der Emanzipation.* Berlin: Philo, 1933.

Winter, Ernst Karl. "Deutschtum und Judentum." *Wiener Politische Blätter* (3 December 1933). Reprinted in *E.K. Winter: Ein Katholik zwischen Österreichs Fronten, 1933–1938*, ed. K. H. Heinz. Vienna: Hermann Böhlau, 1984, pp. 122–27.

"Die Judenfrage." *Wiener Politische Blätter* (24 May 1936). Reprinted (in part) in *Ernst Karl Winter: Bahnbrecher des Dialogs*, ed. with introduction by Alfred Missong. Vienna: Europa Verlag, 1969, pp. 178–85.

"Die Österreichische Idee." *Wiener Politische Blätter* (27 August 1933). Reprinted in *E.K. Winter: Ein Katholik zwischen Österreichs Fronten, 1933–1938*, ed. K. H. Heinz. Vienna: Hermann Böhlau, 1984, pp. 88–111.

"Die Staatskrise in Österreich." Wiener Politische Blätter (16 April 1933).

Wittelshöfer, Otto. *Politische und wirtschaftliche Gesichtspunkte in der österreichischen Nationalitätenfrage, Preußische Jahrbücher* 76:3. Berlin: Walther, 1894.

Witzany, Günther, ed. *Verraten und verkauft.* Salzburg: Unipress-Verlag, 1993.

Zukunft Österreich: EU-Anschluss und die Folgen. Salzburg: Unipress-Verlag, 1998

Zimmern, Alfred. *The Greek Commonwealth: Politics and Economics in Fifth Century Athens.* London: Oxford University Press, 1911.

The Third British Empire. 3d ed. London: Oxford University Press, 1934.

Zweig, Stefan. *Jeremias.* Leipzig: Insel-verlag, 1917.

The World of Yesterday. New York: Viking, 1943.

Triumph und Tragik des Erasmus von Rotterdam. Vienna: Reichner, 1934.

Secondary Sources

Contemporary Literature and Scholarship

Adler, Emil. "Herder und das Judentums." In *Herder Today: Contributions from the International Herder Conference*, ed. Kurt Mueller-Vollmer. Berlin: Walter de Gruyter, 1990, pp. 382–401.

Adunka, Evelyn. "Der deutschen Sprache letzter 'Jud vom Dienst.' Friedrich Torberg und sein Judentum." In *Die "Gefahren der Vielseitigkeit": Friedrich Torberg 1908–1979.* Vienna: Holzhausen, 2008, pp. 143–62.

"Friedrich Torberg und Hans Weigel – Zwei jüdische Schriftsteller im Nachkriegsösterreich." *Modern Austrian Literature* 27 (1994): 213–37.

Agamben, Giorgio. *The Time That Remains: A Commentary on the Letter to the Romans.* Stanford, CA: Stanford University Press, 2005.

Ages, Arnold. "Montesquieu and the Jews." *Romanische Forschungen* 81:1/2 (1969): 214–19.

Agnon, Shmuel Yosef. "Samuel Holdheim." In *A Shroud of Stories* (in Hebrew). Jerusalem: Schocken, 1984, p. 160.

Altmann, Alexander. *Moses Mendelssohn: A Biographical Study.* Philadelphia: Jewish Publication Society of America, 1973.

"The New Style of Preaching in Nineteenth-Century German Jewry." In *Studies in Nineteenth-Century Jewish Intellectual History*, ed. Alexander Altmann. Cambridge, MA: Harvard University Press, 1964, pp. 65–116.

"Zur Frühgeschichte der Jüdischen Predigt in Deutschland: Leopold Zunz als Prediger." *Leo Baeck Institute Yearbook* 6 (1961): 3–59.

Amichai, Yehuda. "Preface." In *Hebrew Ballads and Other Poems* (in German and English), by Else Lasker-Schüler, trans. and ed. Audri Durchslag and Jeanette Litman-Demeestère. Philadelphia: The Jewish Publication Society, 1980.

Amishai-Maisels, Ziva. "Steinhardt in the Land of Israel." In *Jacob and Israel: Homeland and Identity in the Work of Jakob Steinhardt* (in Hebrew and English), ed. Gabriel Ma'anit, Ruthi Ofek, and Avraham Hai. Tefen: Open Museum, 1998, pp. 70–126 in Hebrew, pp. 197–230 in English.

Anckaert, Luc, Martin Brasser, and Norbert Samuelson, eds. *The Legacy of Franz Rosenzweig.* Leuven, Belgium: Leuven University Press, 2004.

Andics, Hellmut. *Insel der Seligen: Österreich von der Moskauer Deklaration bis zur Gegenwart.* Vienna: Molden-Taschenbuch-Verlag, 1976.

Angerer, Thomas. "De l''Autriche germanique' à l''Autriche européenne'? Identités nationales et internationales de l'Autriche depuis 1918." In *Le rôle et la place des petits pays en Europe au XXe siècle*, ed. Gilbert Trausch. Brüssels: Bruylant, 2005, pp. 407–64.

Antonello, Anna. *La rivista come agente letterario tra Italia e Germania (1921– 1944)*. Pisa: Pacini Editore, 2012.

"*Tra l'agro e il dolce. Note biografiche su Lavinia Mazzucchetti.*" In *"Come il cavaliere sul lago di Costanza": Lavinia Mazzucchetti e la cultura tedesca in Italia*, ed. Anna Antonello. Milan: Fondazione Arnoldo e Alberto Mondadori, 2015, pp. 7–28.

Appelgate, Celia. *Bach in Berlin: Nation and Culture in Mendelssohn's Revival of the St. Matthew Passion*. Ithaca, NY: Cornell University Press, 2005.

Appiah, Kwame Anthony. *In My Father's House: Africa in the Philosophy of Culture*. New York: Oxford University Press, 1992.

"Liberalism, Individuality, and Identity." *Critical Inquiry* 27 (Winter 2001): 305–32.

Apter, Emily. "Global *Translatio*: The 'Invention' of Comparative Literature, Istanbul, 1933." *Critical Inquiry* 29:2 (2003): 253–81.

Arad, Lili. "Her Beauty Your Eyes Shall See." In *High above High* (in Hebrew), ed. Yochai ben Gedalia, Uriel Gelman, and Reuven Gafni. Jerusalem: Yad Ben-Ẓevi, 2016, pp. 133–66.

Arendt, Hannah. *On Violence*. New York: Harcourt, Brace, Jovanovich, 1970.

The Origins of Totalitarianism. New York: Harcourt, Brace & Co., 1951.

Aschheim, Steven. *Beyond the Border: The German-Jewish Legacy Abroad*. Princeton, NJ: Princeton University Press, 2007.

Aspetsberger, Friedbert, Norbert Frei, and Huber Lengauer, eds. *Literatur der Nachkriegszeit und der fünfiger Jahren in Österreich*. Vienna: ÖBV, 1984.

Atze, Marcel. "'Einen, der Unfaßbares verübt, kann man nicht fassen.' Friedrich Torberg und die justizielle Aufarbeitung nationalsozialistischer Gewaltbrechen." In *Die "Gefahren der Vielseitigkeit": Friedrich Torberg 1908–1979*. Vienna: Holzhausen, 2008, pp. 181–99.

Atze, Marcel, and Marcus G. Patka, eds. *Die "Gefahren der Vielseitigkeit": Friedrich Torberg 1908–1979*. Vienna: Holzhausen, 2008.

Avemarie, Friedrich. "Esaus Hände, Jakobs Stimme: Edom als Sinnbild Roms in der frühen rabbinischen Literatur." In *Die Heiden: Juden, Christen und das Problem des Fremden*, ed. Reinhard Feldmeier and Ulrich Heckel. Tübingen: J.C.B. Mohr, 1994, pp. 177–208.

Avivi, Yosef. *Binyan Ariel*. Jerusalem: Misgav Yerushalayim, 1987.

Kabbalat ha-Ari (Kabbala Luriana). 3 vols. Jerusalem: Ben-Zvi Institute, 2008.

Avni, Haim. *Spain, the Jews, and Franco*. Philadelphia: The Jewish Publication Society of America, 1974.

Axmann, David. *Friedrich Torberg: Die Biographie*. Munich: Langen Müller, 2008.

Bach, Ulrich. *Tropics of Vienna: Colonial Utopias of the Habsburg Empire*. New York: Berghahn, 2016.

Bacharach, Walter Zvi. *Anti-Jewish Prejudices in German-Catholic Sermons*. Trans. Chaya Galai. Lewiston. NY: Edwin Mellen Press, 1993.

Baer, Yiẓḥak. "Rashi and the Historical Reality of His Time" (in Hebrew). *Ẓiyon* 15 (1950): 320–32.

"The Hebrew Jossipon." In *Studies and Essays in Jewish History* (in Hebrew). 2 vols. Jerusalem: Israel Historical Society, 1986.

Bakhos, Carol. "Figuring (out) Esau: The Rabbis and Their Others." *Journal of Jewish Studies* 58:2 (2007): 250–62.

Ishmael on the Border: Rabbinic Portrayals of the First Arab. Albany: State University of New York Press, 2006.

Bałaban, Majer. *Le-Toldot ha-Tenuah ha-Frankit.* 2 vols. in 1. Tel Aviv: Dvir, 1934–35.

Bankier, David. "The 'Return of the Jews' in French Jansenism." In *Israel and the Nations.* Jerusalem: Historical Society of Israel and Zalman Shazar Center, 1987, pp. 71–86.

Barck, Karlheinz. "Eine unveröffentliche Korrespondenz: Erich Auerbach/ Werner Krauss." *Beiträge zur Romanischen Philologie* 26:2 (1987): 301–26 and 27:1 (1988): 161–86.

"Erich Auerbach in Berlin: Spurensicherung und ein Porträt." In *Erich Auerbach: Geschichte und Aktualität eines europäischen Philologen,* ed. Martin Treml and Karlheinz Barck. Berlin: Kulturverlag Kadmos, 2007, pp. 195–214.

"5 Briefe Erich Auerbachs an Walter Benjamin in Paris." *Zeitschrift für Germanistik* 6 (1988): 688–94.

Barker, Andrew. *Fictions from an Orphan State: Literary Reflections of Austria between Habsburg and Hitler.* Rochester, NY: Camden House, 2012.

"Tiefe der Zeit, Untiefen der Jahre: Heimito von Doderers 'österreichische Idee' und die 'Athener Rede.'" In *"Excentrische Einsätze,"* ed. Kai Luehrs. Berlin: Walter de Gruyter, 1998, pp. 263–72.

Barnard, F. M. "Herder and Israel." *Jewish Social Studies* 28 (1966): 25–33.

Herder's Social and Political Thought: From Enlightenment to Nationalism. Oxford: Clarendon Press, 1965.

"Introduction." In *J. G. Herder on Social and Political Culture.* Cambridge: Cambridge University Press, 1969, pp. 3–60.

"The Hebrews and Herder's Political Creed." *Modern Language Review* 54 (1959): 533–46.

Baron, Salo. "Ghetto and Emancipation: Shall We Revise the Traditional View?" *Menorah Journal* 14 (1928): 515–26.

"Nationalism and Intolerance." *Menorah Journal* 16 (1929): 503–14 and 17 (1929): 148–58.

Barrett, Charles K. "The Allegory of Abraham, Sarah, and Hagar in Galatians." In *Rechtfertigung: Festschrift für Ernst Käsemann zum 70. Geburtstag,* ed. Johannes Friedrich, Wolfgang Pöhlmann, and Peter Stuhlmacher. Tübingen: Mohr, 1976, pp. 1–16.

Barrière, Hélène, Thomas Eicher, and Manfred Müller, eds. *Schuld-Komplexe: Das Werk Alexander Lernet-Holenias im Nachkriegskontext.* Oberhausen: Athena, 2004.

Bartal, Israel. "Non-Jews and Gentile Society in East European Hebrew and Yiddish Literature, 1856–1914" (in Hebrew). Ph.D. diss., The Hebrew University, 1980.

Bartlett, John. *Edom and the Edomites*. Sheffield, UK: JSOT Press, 1989.

Bar-Yosef, Eitan. "The Nostalgic Return to Mandatory Palestine in Israeli Culture." Paper presented at the North Carolina Jewish Studies Seminar, March 29, 2015.

Bauerkämper, Arnd. "Americanisation as Globalization? Remigrés to West Germany After 1945 and Conceptions of Democracy: The Cases of Hans Rothfels, Ernst Fraenkel and Hans Rosenberg." *Leo Baeck Institute Yearbook* 49:1 (2004): 153–70.

Bein, Alex. "The Jewish Parasite." *Leo Baeck Institute Yearbook* (1964): 3–40.

Belke, Ingrid. *Die sozialreformerischen Ideen von Joseph Popper-Lynkeus (1838–1921)*. In *Zusammenhang mit allgemeinen Reformbestrebungen des Wiener Bürgertums um die Jahrhundertwende*. Tübingen: Mohr, 1978.

Beller, Steven. "Patriotism and the National Identity of Habsburg Jewry, 1860–1914." *Leo Baeck Institute Yearbook* 41 (1996): 215–38.

— *Vienna and the Jews: A Cultural History, 1867–1938*. New York: Cambridge University Press, 1989.

Bellot, Christoph. "Schönfeld, Johann Heinrich." In *Neue deutsche Biographie*. 25 vols. Berlin: Schinzel-Schwarz, 2007: 23: 408–9.

Benbassa, Esther, and Aron Rodrigue. *Sephardi Jewry: A History of the Judeo-Spanish Community, 14th–20th Centuries*. Berkeley: University of California Press, 2000, pp. 60–64.

Benjamin, Mara. *Rosenzweig's Bible: Reinventing Scripture for Jewish Modernity*. Cambridge: Cambridge University Press, 2009.

Ben Shalom, Ram. *Facing Christian Culture: Historical Consciousness and Images of the Past among the Jews of Spain and Southern France during the Middle Ages* (in Hebrew). Jerusalem: Ben-Zvi Institute and the Hebrew University, 2006.

Berger, David. "The Jewish-Christian Debate in the High Middle Ages." In *Essential Papers on Judaism and Christianity in Conflict*, ed. Jeremy Cohen. New York: New York University Press, 1991, pp. 484–513.

— *The Jewish-Christian Debate in the High Middle Ages: A Critical Edition of the Nizzahon Vetus*. Philadelphia: Jewish Publication Society of America, 1979.

— "The Morality of the Patriarchs in Jewish Polemics and Exegesis." In *Cultures in Collision and Conversation*. Boston: Academic Studies Press, 2011, pp. 236–50.

Berger, Stefan, and Alexei Miller, eds. *Nationalizing Empires*. Budapest: Central European University Press, 2014.

Berkovitz, Jay R. *The Shaping of Jewish Identity in Nineteenth-Century France*. Detroit: Wayne State University Press, 1989.

Berlin, Isaiah. "Herder and the Enlightenment." [1965] In *Three Critics of the Enlightenment: Vico, Hamann, Herder*, ed. Henry Hardy. Princeton, NJ: Princeton University Press, 2000, pp. 168–242.

— "The Birth of the Russian Intelligentsia." [1955] In *Russian Thinkers*, ed. Henry Hardy and Aileen Kelly. London: Penguin Books, 1994, pp. 114–35.

"The Counter-Enlightenment." [1973] In *Against the Current: Essays in the History of Ideas*, ed. Henry Hardy. New York: Viking Press, 1980, pp. 1–24.

Bessner, Daniel. *Democracy in Exile: Hans Speier and the Rise of the Defense Intellectual*. Ithaca, NY: Cornell University Press, 2018.

Best, Renate. "Juden und Judenbilder in der gesellschaftlichen Konstruktion der deutsche Nation (1781–1804)." In *Nation und Religion in der deutschen Geschichte*, ed. Heinz-Gerhard Haupt and Dieter Langewiesche. Frankfurt: Campus Verlag, 2001, pp. 170–214.

"Between Religion and Ethnicity: Twentieth-Century Jewish Émigrés and the Shaping of Postwar Culture." Special issue of *Religions* 3:2/3 (2012).

Biddick, Kathleen. *The Typological Imaginary: Circumcision, Technology, History*. Philadelphia: University of Pennsylvania Press, 2003.

Bienkowski, Piotr. "*New Evidence on Edom in the Neo-Babylonian and Persian Periods.*" In *The Land That I Will Show You: Essays on the History and Archaeology of the Ancient Near East in Honor of J. Maxwell Miller*, ed. J. Andrew Dearman and M. Patrick Graham. Sheffield, UK: Sheffield Academic Press, 2001, pp. 198–213.

Birnbaum, Solomon A. "Nathan Birnbaum and National Autonomy." In *The Jews of Austria*, ed. Joseph Fraenkel. London: Vallentine, Mitchell, 1967, pp. 131–46.

Blastenbrei, Peter. *Johann Christoph Wagenseil und seine Stellung zum Judenthum*. Erlangen: Harald Fischer Verlag, 2004.

Blau, Eve. "Supranational Principle as Urban Model: Otto Wagner's *Großstadt* and City Making in Central Europe." In *Histoire de l'art du XIXe siècle (1848–1918)*, ed. Claire Barbillon, Catherine Chevillot, and François-René Martin. Paris: Collections des Rencontre de l'Ecole de Louvre, pp. 501–14.

Blowers, Paul. "Origen, the Rabbis, and the Bible." In *Christianity in Relation to Jews, Greeks, and Romans*, ed. Everett Ferguson. New York: Garland Pubs., 1999, pp. 2–22.

Bock, Hans Manfred. *Kulturelle Wegbereiter politischer Konfliktlösung*. Tübingen: Gunter Narr Verlag, 2005.

Bohn, Volker, ed. *Typologie*. Frankfurt: Suhrkamp, 1988.

Bölke, Peter. "Erbschein aus dem KZ." *Der Spiegel* (19 May 1997).

Bollacher, Martin. "'Feines, scharfsinniges Volk, ein Wunder der Zeiten!' – Herders Verhältnis zum Judentum und zur jüdischen Welt." In *Hebräische Poesie und Jüdischer Volkgeist*, ed. Christoph Schulte. Hildesheim: Georg Olms, 2003, pp. 17–33.

Bonnifield, Lisa. "Modern Jewish Art and Zionism." B.A. thesis, Duke University, 2008.

Bormuth, Matthias. "Meaning and Progress in History – A Comparison between Karl Löwith and Erich Auerbach." *Religions* 3:2 (2012): 151–62.

"Menschenkunde zwischen Meistern – Auerbach und Löwith." In *Erich Auerbach: Geschichte und Aktualität eines europäischen Philologen*, ed. Martin Treml and Karlheinz Barck. Berlin: Kulturverlag Kadmos, 2007, pp. 82–104.

Mimesis und der christliche Gentleman: Erich Auerbach schreibt an Karl Löwith. Warmbronn: Verlag Ulrich Keicher, 2006.

Boyarin, Daniel. "Beyond Judaisms." *Journal for the Study of Judaism* 41:3 (2010): 323–65.

Dying for God. Stanford, CA: Stanford University Press, 1999.

Boyer, John W. *Culture and Political Crisis in Vienna: Christian Socialism in Power, 1897–1918*. Chicago: University of Chicago Press, 1995.

"Freud, Marriage, and Late Viennese Liberalism: A Commentary from 1905." *Journal of Modern History* 50 (March 1978): 72–102.

Braiterman, Zachary. *The Shape of Revelation: Aesthetics and Modern Jewish Thought*. Stanford, CA: Stanford University Press, 2007.

Brawer, A. Y. *Studies in Galician Jewry* (in Hebrew). Jerusalem: Bialik Institute, 1956.

Bregman, Marc. "Pseudepigraphy in Rabbinic Literature." In *Pseudepigraphic Perspectives*, ed. Esther Chazon and Michael Stone. Leiden: Brill, 1999, pp. 27–47.

Breitenbach, Heike. "Thomas Mann und die jüdische Tradition: Untersuchungen zu Joseph und seine Brüder unter besonderer Berücksichtigung der Schriftauslegung des Midrasch." Ph.D. diss., Rheinisch-Westfälischen Technischen Hochschule Aachen, 2009.

Breitenstein, M. Leipzig. *A Jewish State*. Trans. Sylvie d'Avigdor. London: Nutt, 1896.

Brenner, Michael. "Religion, Nation oder Stamm: Zum Wandel der Selbstdefinition unter deutschen Juden." In *Nation und Religion in der deutschen Geschichte*, ed. Heinz-Gerhard Haupt and Dieter Langewiesche. Frankfurt: Campus Verlag, 2001, pp. 587–601.

The Renaissance of Jewish Culture in Weimar Germany. New Haven, CT: Yale University Press, 1996.

Brenner, Michael, Vicki Caron, and Uri R. Kaufmann, eds. *Jewish Emancipation Reconsidered: The French and German Models*, Tübingen: Mohr Siebeck, 2003.

Brettler, Marc. "The Copenhagen School: The Historiographical Issues." *AJS Review* 27:1 (2003): 1–22.

The Creation of History in Ancient Israel. London: Routledge, 1998.

Breuer, Mordechai. "Emancipation and the Rabbis" (in Hebrew). In *Asif*. Jerusalem: Rimonim, 1999, pp. 166–71.

"Orthodoxy and Change" (in Hebrew). In *Torah im Derekh Eretz Movement*, ed. Mordechai Breuer. Ramat-Gan: Bar-Ilan University, 1987, pp. 85–95.

"The Torah with *Derekh Erez* Principle in Samson Raphael Hirsch's Teaching" (in Hebrew). In *Asif*. Jerusalem: Rimonim, 1999, pp. 312–52.

Breuer, Mordechai, ed. *The Torah im Derekh Eretz Movement* (in Hebrew). Ramat-Gan: Bar-Ilan University, 1987.

Brubaker, Rogers. *Ethnicity Without Groups*. Cambridge, MA: Harvard University Press, 2004.

Nationalism Reframed. New York: Cambridge University Press, 1996.

Brubaker, Rogers, Margit Feischmidt, Jon Fox, and Liana Grancea. *Nationalist Politics and Everyday Ethnicity in a Transylvanian Town*. Princeton, NJ: Princeton University Press, 2006.

Buchmayr, Friedrich. "Stufen der Entfremdung: Franz Werfels letzte Jahre in Österreich." *Chilufim: Zeitschrift für Jüdische Kulturgeschichte* 2 (2007): 51–97.

Bude, Heinz, and Bernd Greiner, eds. *Westbindungen: Amerika in der Bundesrepublik*. Hamburg: Hamburger Edition, 1999.

Bunzl, Matti. "The Poetics of Politics and the Politics of Poetics: Richard Beer-Hofmann and Theodor Herzl Reconsidered." *German Quarterly* 69 (Summer 1996): 277–304.

Burbank, Jane, and Frederick Cooper. *Empires in World History: Power and the Politics of Difference*. Princeton, NJ: Princeton University Press, 2010.

Burckhardt, Jacob. *Die Kultur der Renaissance in Italien*. 2d ed. Leipzig: Seemann, 1869.

Burnett, Stephen. *Christian Hebraism in the Reformation Era (1500–1660): Authors, Books, and Jewish Learning*. Leiden: Brill, 2012.

———. *From Christian Hebraism to Jewish Studies: Johannes Buxtorf (1564–1629) and Hebrew Learning in the Seventeenth-Century*. Leiden: Brill, 1996.

Buschmann, Nikolaus. "Auferstehung der Nation." In *Nation und Religion in der deutschen Geschichte*, ed. Heinz-Gerhard Haupt and Dieter Langewiesche. Frankfurt: Campus Verlag, 2001, pp. 333–88.

Cahnman, Werner. "Adolf Fischhof and His Jewish Followers." *Leo Baeck Institute Year Book IV* (1959): 111–40.

———. "Friedrich Wilhelm Schelling and the Thinking of New Judaism." In *German Jewry: Its History and Sociology*. New Brunswick, NJ: Transactions Books, 1989, pp. 209–48.

Calin, William. *The Twentieth-Century Humanist Critics: From Spitzer to Frye*. Toronto: University of Toronto Press, 2007.

Campbell, Douglas Patrick. "The Shadow of the Habsburgs: Memory and National Identity in Austrian Politics and Education, 1918–1955." Ph.D. diss., University of Maryland, 2006.

Carlsson, Eric Wilhelm. "Johann Salomo Semler, the German Enlightenment, and Protestant Theology's Historical Turn." Ph.D. diss., University of Wisconsin–Madison, 2006.

Caron, Vicki. "Comment." In *Jewish Emancipation Reconsidered: The French and German Models*, ed. Michael Brenner, Vicki Caron, and Uri R. Kaufmann. Tübingen: Mohr Siebeck, 2003, pp. 147–53.

Chappel, James. *Catholic Modern: The Challenge of Totalitarianism and the Remaking of the Church*. Cambridge, MA: Harvard University Press, 2018.

Clark, Elizabeth. "Interpretive Fate amid the Church Fathers." In *Hagar, Sarah, and Their Children: Jewish, Christian, and Muslim Perspectives*, ed. Phyllis Trible and Letty M. Russell. Louisville, KY: Westminster John Knox Press, 2006, pp. 127–47.

Cohen, Gerson. "Esau as Symbol in Early Medieval Thought." In *Medieval and Renaissance Studies*, ed. Alexander Altmann. Cambridge, MA: Harvard University Press, 1967, pp. 19–48.

Cohen, Jeremy. *Be Fertile and Increase, Fill the Earth and Master It: The Ancient and Medieval Career of a Biblical Text*. Ithaca, NY: Cornell University Press, 1989.

"Scholarship and Intolerance in the Medieval Academy." *American Historical Review* 91 (1986): 601–4.

"The Second Paris Disputation and Thirteenth-Century Jewish-Christian Polemics" (in Hebrew). *Tarbiz* 68:4 (1999): 557–78.

Cohen, Julia Phillips. *Becoming Ottomans: Sephardi Jews and Imperial Citizenship in the Modern Era*. New York: Oxford University Press, 2014.

Cohen, Shaye J. D. "Antipodal Texts: B. Eruvin 21b–22a and Mark 7:1–23 on the Tradition of the Elders and the Commandment of God." In *Envisioning Judaism*, ed. Ra'anan S. Boustan et al. 2 vols. Tübingen: Mohr Siebeck, 2013: 2: 965–83.

"Does Rashi's Torah Commentary Respond to Christianity? A Comparison of Rashi with Rashbam and Bekhor Shor." In *The Idea of Biblical Interpretation*, ed. Hindy Najman and Judith H. Newman. Leiden: Brill, 2004, pp. 449–72.

"Sabbath Law and Mishnah Shabbat in Origen *De Principiis*." *Jewish Studies Quarterly* 17 (2010): 160–89.

The Beginnings of Jewishness: Boundaries, Varieties, Uncertainties. Berkeley: University of California Press, 1999.

Cole, Laurence, and Daniel Unowsky, eds. *The Limits of Loyalty: Imperial Symbolism, Popular Allegiances, and State Patriotism in the Late Habsburg Monarchy*. New York: Berghahn Books, 2007.

Coleman, Peter. *The Liberal Conspiracy: The Congress for Cultural Freedom and the Struggle for the Mind of Postwar Europe*. New York: Free Press, 1989.

Confino, Alon. *A World without Jews: The Nazi Imagination from Persecution to Genocide*. New Haven, CT: Yale University Press, 2014.

Connelly, John. *From Enemy to Brother: The Revolution in Catholic Teaching on the Jews, 1933–1965*. Cambridge, MA: Harvard University Press, 2012.

Conze, Vanessa. *Das Europa der Deutschen: Ideen von Europa in Deutschland zwischen Reichstradition und Westorientierung (1920–1970)*. Munich: Oldenbourg 2005.

Corbin, Anne-Marie. "Die österreichische Identität in Friedrich Torbergs Forum." *Österreich in Geschichte und Literatur* 46:1 (2002): 2–16.

Corbin-Schuffels, Anne-Marie. *L'image de l'Europe à l'ombre de la guerre froide: La revue Forum de Friedrich Torberg à Vienne (1954–1961)*. Paris: Harmattan, 2001.

Creizenach, Wilhelm. *Geschichte des Neueren Dramas*. 2d ed. 3 vols. Halle: Max Niemeyer, 1911.

"Daniel Cohn-Bendit im Gespräch mit Norbert Frei." In *Münchener Beiträge zur Jüdischen Geschichte und Kultur* 6:1 (2012): 19–40.

Danneberg, Bärbel, Fritz Keller, Aly Machalicky, and Julius Mende, eds. *Die 68ers: Eine Generation und ihre Erbe*. Vienna: Döcker, 1998.

Darmaun, Jacques. *Thomas Mann et les juifs*. Basel: Peter Lang, 1995.

Dassanowsky, Robert. "'Mon Cousin de Liernut': France as a Code for Idealized Personal Political Identity in the 'Austrian' Novels of Alexander Lernet-Holenia." *Austrian Studies* 13 (2005): 173–90.

Phantom Empires: The Novels of Alexander Lernet-Holenia and the Question of Postimperial Austrian Identity. Riverside, CA: Ariadne Press, 1996.

Deák, István. *Beyond Nationalism: The Social and Political History of the Habsburg Officer Corps, 1848–1918*. New York: Oxford University Press, 1990.

Deák, John. *Forging a Multinational State*. Stanford, CA: Stanford University Press, 2015.

De Lange, N. R. M. *Origen and the Jews*. Cambridge: Cambridge University Press, 1976.

Deutsch, Yaakov. *Judaism in Christian Eyes: Ethnographic Descriptions of Jews and Judaism in Early Modern Europe*. Oxford: Oxford University Press, 2012.

Dicou, Bert.*Edom, Israel's Brother and Antagonist: The Role of Edom in Biblical Prophecy and Story*. Sheffield, UK: JSOT Press, 1994.

Diner, Dan. "Geschichte der Juden: Paradigma einer europäischen Geschichtsschreibung." In *Gedächtniszeiten: Über jüdische und andere Geschichten München*. Munich: Beck, 2003, pp. 246–62.

"Vom Stau zur Zeit: Neutralisierung und Latenz zwischen Nachkrieg und Achtundsechzig." In *Latenz: Blinde Passagiere in den Geisteswissenschaften*, ed. Hans Ulrich Gumbrecht and Florian Klinger. Göttingen: Vandenhoeck & Ruprecht, 2011, pp. 165–72.

Diner, Dan, ed. *Enzyklopädie jüdischer Geschichte und Kultur*. 7 vols. Stuttgart: JB Metzler, 2011–17.

Synchrone Welten: Zeiträume jüdischer Geschichte. Göttingen: Vandenhoeck & Ruprecht, 2005.

Dönitz, Saskia. "Historiography Among Byzantine Jews: The Case of Sefer Yosippon." In *Jews in Byzantium: Dialectics of Minority and Majority Cultures*, ed. Robert Bonfil, Oded Irshai, Guy G. Stroumza, and Rina Talgam. Leiden: Brill, 2012, pp. 951–68.

Doron, Avraham. "Nationalism and Judaism in the Conservative Thought of Friedrich Julius Stahl" (in Hebrew). *Ziyon* 77 (2012): 67–94.

Drunen, H. F. van. "'A Sanguine Bunch': Regional Identification in Habsburg Bukovina, 1774–1919." Ph.D. diss., University of Amsterdam, 2013.

Dubin, Lois. "Between Toleration and 'Equalities': Jewish Status and Community in Pre-Revolutionary Europe." *Jahrbuch des Simon-Dubnow-Instituts* 1 (2002): 219–34.

Dubnov, Arie. "Dreaming of the Seventh Dominion in Oxford: Palestine and the British Commonwealth." Lecture presented October 20, 2016, at St. John's College, Oxford.

Ebner, Paulus, and Karl Vocelka. *Die Zahme Revolution: '68 und was davon blieb*. Vienna: Ueberreuter, 1998.

Echternkamp, Joerg. "'Religioeses Nationalgefuehl' oder 'Froemmelei der Deutschtümler'?" In *Nation und Religion in der deutschen Geschichte*, ed. Heinz-Gerhard Haupt and Dieter Langewiesche. Frankfurt: Campus Verlag, 2001, pp. 142–69.

Egyptien, Jürgen. "Die unvollendete Symphonie: Das Konzept einer österreichischen Identität und nationalen Souveränität in den Schriften von Ernst Fischer." In *Österreich-Konzeptionen und jüdisches Selbstverständnis: Identitäts-Transfigurationen im 19. und 20. Jahrhundert*, ed. Hanni Mittelmann and Armin A. Wallas. Tübingen: Max Niemeyer Verlag, 2001, pp. 249–62.

Ehrenfreund, Jacques. *Mémoire Juive et Nationalité Allemande: Les Juifs Berlinois à la Belle Epoque.* Paris: Presses Universitaires de France, 2000.

Eidherr, Armin. "Ejssev – das Gegenüber im Goleß." In *Sonnenuntergang auf eisigblauen Wegen: Zur Thematisierung von Diaspora und Sprache in der jiddischen Literatur des 20. Jahrhunderts.* Vienna: Vienna University Press, 2012, pp. 242–63.

Elazar, Daniel, ed.*Kinship and Consent: The Jewish Political Tradition and Its Contemporary Uses.* 2d ed. New Brunswick, NJ: Transactions Publishers, 1997.

Elior, Rachel. "'Sefer Divre ha-Adon' le-Yaakov Frank." *Meḥqerei Yerushalayim be-Maḥshevet Yisrael* 16/17 (2001): 471–548.

Ellenson, David. *Rabbi Esriel Hildesheimer and the Creation of a Modern Jewish Orthodoxy.* Tuscaloosa: University of Alabama Press, 1990.

"The Orthodox Rabbinate and Apostasy in Nineteenth-Century Germany and Hungary." In *Jewish Apostasy in the Modern World*, ed. Todd M. Endelman. London: Holmes & Meier, 1987, pp. 165–88.

Elsky, Martin. "Erich Auerbach and Walter Benjamin in Flight: *Figura* and Allegory." Paper presented at the Exile and Interpretation Conference, Wake Forest University, November 16–18, 2012.

Elukin, Jonathan. *Living Together/Living Apart: Rethinking Jewish-Christian Relations in the Middle Ages.* Princeton, NJ: Princeton University Press, 2007.

Endelman, Todd. "The Englishness of Jewish Modernity in England." In *Towards Modernity: The European Jewish Model*, ed. Jacob Katz. New Brunswick, NJ: Rutgers University Press, 1987, pp. 225–46.

Engel, David. "Crisis and Lachrymosity: On Salo Baron, Neobaronianism, and the Study of Modern European Jewish History." *Jewish History* 20 (2006): 243–64.

Erben, Tino, Historisches Museum der Stadt Wien, and Robert Waissenberger. *Traum und Wirklichkeit: Wien 1870–1930.* Kataloggestaltung und Plakatserie Tino Erben. Vienna: Eigenverlag der Museen der Stadt Wien, 1985.

Etkes, Immanuel. *Ba'al Ha-Tanya: Rabbi Shneur Zalman of Liady and the Origins of Habad Hasidism.* Jerusalem: Zalman Shazar Center, 2011.

Ettinger, Shmuel. "The Beginnings of the Change in the Attitude of European Society towards the Jews." *Scripta Hierosolymitana* 7 (1961): 193–219.

Fehrenbach, Heidi, and Uta G. Poiger, eds. *Transactions, Transgressions, Transformations: American Culture in Western Europe and Japan.* New York: Berghahn, 2000.

Feigl, Herbert. "The 'Wiener Kreis' in America." In *The Intellectual Migration: Europe and America, 1930–1960*, ed. Donald Fleming and Bernard Bailyn. Cambridge, MA: Harvard University Press, 1969, pp. 630–73.

Feiner, Shmuel. *The Jewish Enlightenment (Jewish Culture and Contexts).* Trans. Chaya Naor. Philadelphia: University of Pennsylvania Press, 2002.

Feldman, Louis. "Josephus' Portrait of Jacob." *Jewish Quarterly Review* 79: 2–3 (1988–89): 101–51.

Feldman, Yael. *Glory and Agony: Isaac's Sacrifice and National Narrative.* Stanford, CA: Stanford University Press, 2010.

Fiedler, Peter. *Das Judentum im katholischen Religionsunterricht.* Düsseldorf: Patmos, 1980.

Fine, Laurence. *Physician of the Soul, Healer of the Cosmos: Isaac Luria and His Kabbalistic Fellowship.* Stanford, CA: Stanford University Press, 2003.

Fink, Carole. *Defending the Rights of Others: The Great Powers, the Jews, and International Minority Protection.* New York: Cambridge University Press, 2004.

Fink, Carole, Philipp Gassert, and Detlef Junker, eds. *1968: The World Transformed.* Cambridge: Cambridge University Press, 1998.

Firestone, Reuven. *Journeys in Holy Lands: The Evolution of the Abraham-Ishmael Legends in Islamic Exegesis.* Albany: State University of New York Press, 1990.

Fishbane, Michael. *Biblical Interpretation in Ancient Israel.* Oxford: Oxford University Press, 1988.

Fishman, Talya. "Forging Jewish Memory: *Besamim Rosh* and the Invention of Pre-Emancipation Jewish Culture." In *Jewish History and Jewish Memory: Essays in Honor of Yosef Hayim Yerushalmi,* ed. Elisheva Carlebach, John Efron, and David Myers. Hanover, NH: University Press of New England, 1998, pp. 70–88.

Fitzgerald, Robert. *Enlarging the Change: The Princeton Seminars in Literary Criticism, 1949–1951.* Boston: Northeastern University Press, 1985.

Fleischer, Wolfgang. *Das verleugnete Leben: Die Biographie des Heimito von Doderer.* Vienna: Kremayr & Scheriau, 1996.

Folz, Robert. *The Concept of Empire in Western Europe from the Fifth to the Fourteenth Century.* Trans. Sheila Ann Ogilvie. London: Edward Arnold, 1969.

Fradde, Steven. *From Tradition to Commentary.* Binghamton: State University of New York Press, 1991.

Fredrickson, George. *Racism: A Short History.* Princeton, NJ: Princeton University Press, 2002.

Frei, Hans. *The Eclipse of Biblical Narrative: A Study in Eighteenth and Nineteenth Century Hermeneutics.* New Haven, CT: Yale University Press, 1974.

Freidenreich. Harriet Pass. *Jewish Politics in Vienna, 1918–1938.* Bloomington: Indiana University Press, 1991.

Freinschlag, Andreas, and Amandine Schneebichler. "Esau in der deutsch-sprachigen Literatur." In *Esau: Bruder und Feind,* ed. Gerhard Langer. Göttingen: Vandenhoeck & Ruprecht, 2009, pp. 273–92.

Frojmovic, Eva. "Blood as a Symbol Between Jews and Christians: The Case of the Laud Maḥzor." Paper presented at Oxford Seminar in Jewish Studies, November 30, 2016.

Fuchs, Albert. *Geistige Strömungen in Österreich, 1867–1918.* Vienna: Löcker, 1949.

Funkenstein, Amos. *Perceptions of Jewish History.* Los Angeles: University of California Press, 1993.

Gager, John. "Simon Peter, Founder of Christianity or Saviour of Israel?" In *Toledot Yeshu ("The Life Story of Jesus") Revisited,* ed. Peter Schäfer, Michael Meerson, and Yaacov Deutsch. Tübingen: Mohr Siebeck, 2011, pp. 221–45.

Garb, Jonathan. "The Cult of the Saints in Lurianic Kabbalah." *Jewish Quarterly Review* 98:2 (2008): 203–29.

Geiger, Ari. "Ha-Perush shel Nicholas de Lyra al Vayikra, Bamidbar u-Devarim." Ph.D. diss., Bar-Ilan University, Ramat-Gan, 2006.

"Jewish Sources of Nicholas of Lyra's Literal Commentary on Lamentations" (in Hebrew). Master's thesis, Bar-Ilan University, Ramat-Gan, 2002.

"Nicholas of Lyra's Literal Commentary on Lamentations and Jewish Exegesis: A Comparative Study." *Medieval Encounters* 16 (2010): 1–22.

Gellen, Kata. "'One Should Have Two Homelands': Discord and Hope in Soma Morgenstern's Sparks in the Abyss." *Religions* 8:2 (2017). http://www.mdpi.com/2077-1444/8/2/26.

Gellner, Ernest. *Language and Solitude: Wittgenstein, Malinowski and the Habsburg Dilemma.* Cambridge: Cambridge University Press, 1998.

Geyer, Michael. "The Subject(s) of Europe." In *Conflicted Memories: Europeanizing Contemporary Histories*, ed. Konrad H. Jarausch and Thomas Lindenberger. New York: Berghahn Books, 2007, pp. 254–80.

Gienow-Hecht, Jessica, and Frank Schumacher, eds. *Culture and International History.* New York: Berghahn Books, 2003.

Giller, Pinchas. *Reading the Zohar.* New York: Oxford University Press, 2001.

Gillman, Abigail. "Between Religion and Culture: Mendelssohn, Buber, Rosenzweig and the Enterprise of Biblical Translation." In *Biblical Translation in Context*, ed. Frederick Knobloch. Bethesda: University Press of Maryland, 2002, pp. 93–114.

Gilman, Sander. *Jurek Becker: A Life in Five Worlds.* Chicago: University of Chicago Press, 2003.

Ginsburg, Shai. "The City and the Body: Jerusalem in Uri Tsvi Greenberg's *Vision of One of the Legions.*" In *Jerusalem: Conflict and Cooperation in a Contested City*, ed. Madelaine Adelman and Miriam Fendius Elma. Syracuse NY: Syracuse University Press, 2014, pp. 143–71.

Ginzberg, Louis. "Die Haggada bei den Kirchenvätern VI." In *Jewish Studies in Memory of George A. Kohut*, ed. Salo W. Baron and Alexander Marx. New York: The Alexander Kohut Memorial Foundation, 1935, pp. 289–314.

Glatt-Gilad, David A. "The Re-Interpretation of the Edomite-Israelite Encounter in Deuteronomy II." *Vetus Testamentum* 47:4 (1997): 441–55.

Goldenberg, Robert. "Did the Amoraim See Christianity as Something New?" In *Pursuing the Text*, ed. John C. Reeves and John Kampen. Sheffield, UK: Sheffield Academic Press, 1994, pp. 293–302.

Gordon, Adi. "The Ideological Convert and the 'Mythology of Coherence': The Contradictory Hans Kohn and his Multiple Metamorphoses." *Leo Baeck Institute Year Book* 55 (2010): 273–93.

Toward Nationalism's End: An Intellectual Biography of Hans Kohn. Waltham, MA: Brandeis University Press, 2017.

Gordon, Adi. ed. *Brith Shalom and Bi-National Zionism* (in Hebrew). Jerusalem: Carmel, 2008.

Gordon, Adi, and Udi Greenberg. "*The City of Man*, European Émigrés, and the Genesis of Postwar Conservative Thought." *Religions* 3:3 (2012): 681–98.

Gordon, Peter Eli. *Rosenzweig and Heidegger: Between Judaism and German Philosophy.* Berkeley: University of California Press, 2003.

Goshen-Goldstein, M. H. "Christianity, Judaism and Modern Bible Study." *Vetus Testamentum Supplements* 28 (1975): 69–88.

Gotzmann, Andreas. "Der Geiger-Tiktin Streit: Trennungskrise und Publizität." In *In Breslau zuhause? Juden in einer mitteleuropäischen Metropole der Neuzeit,* ed. Manfred Hettling, Andreas Reinke, and Norberg Conrads. Hamburg: Dölling und Galitz, 2003, pp. 81–98.

"From Nationality to Religion: Samuel Holdheim's Path to the Extreme Side of Religious Judaism." In *Redefining Judaism in an Age of Emancipation,* ed. Christian Wiese. Leiden: Brill, 2007, pp. 23–62.

Jüdisches Recht im kulturellen Prozess: Die Wahrnehmung der Halacha im Deutschland des 19. Jahrhunderts. Tübingen: Mohr Siebeck, 1997.

"On the Confrontation of Maskilim and Rabbis at the End of the Eighteenth-Century" (in Hebrew). In *"The German-Jewish History We Have Inherited": Young Germans Write Jewish History,* ed. Henry Wassermann. Jerusalem: Magness Press, 2004, pp. 11–35.

"The Dissociation of Religion and Law in Nineteenth-Century German-Jewish Education." *Leo Baeck Institute Yearbook* 43 (1998): 103–26.

Graf Reventlow, Henning, *The Authority of the Bible and the Rise of the Modern World.* Trans. John Bowden. Philadelphia: Fortress Press, 1985.

"The Role of the Old Testament in Liberal Protestant Theology of the Nineteenth-Century." In *Biblical Studies and the Shifting of Paradigms, 1850–1914,* ed. Henning Graf Reventlow and William Farmer. Sheffield, UK: Sheffield Academic Press, 1995, pp. 132–48.

Graf Reventlow, Henning, Walter Sparn, and John Woodbridge, eds. *Historische Kritik und biblischer Kanon in der deutschen Aufklärung.* Wiesbaden: Otto Harrassowitz, 1988.

Green, Abigail. "Intervening in the Jewish Question, 1840–1878." In *Humanitarian Intervention: A History,* ed. Brendan Simms and D. J. B. Trim. Cambridge: Cambridge University Press, 2011, pp. 139–58.

"Religious Internationalisms." In *Internationalisms: A Twentieth-Century History,* ed. Glenda Sluga and Patricia Calvin. Cambridge: Cambridge University Press, 2017, pp. 15–37.

Green, Abigail, and Vincent Viaene, eds. *Religious Internationals in the Modern World.* Basingstoke, UK: Palgrave Macmillan, 2012.

Greenberg, Gershon. "Amaleq in the Holocaust Period" (in Hebrew). In *Derekh ha-Ruah: Festschrift for Eliezer Schweid,* ed. Yehoyada Amir. 2 vols. Jerusalem: Van Leer Institute, 2005: 2: 891–913.

"Introduction: Ultra-Orthodox Responses during and following the War." In *Wrestling with God: Jewish Theological Responses during and after the Holocaust,* ed. Steven T. Katz with Shlomo Biderman and Gershon Greenberg. Oxford: Oxford University Press, 2007, pp. 11–26.

Greenberg, Udi. "The Limits of Dictatorship and the Origins of Democracy: The Political Theory of Carl J. Friedrich from Weimar to the Cold War." In *The Weimar Moment,* ed. Rudy Koshar. New York: Rowman & Littlefield, 2012, pp. 443–64.

The Weimar Century: German Émigrés and the Ideological Foundations of the Cold War. Princeton, NJ: Princeton University Press, 2015.

Grémion, Pierre. *Intelligence de l'anticommunisme: Le Congrès pour la liberté de la culture à Paris (1950–1975)*. Paris: Fayard, 1995.

Griesmayer, Norbert. "Die Zeitschrift 'Tagebuch.' Ergänzende Beobachtungen zur kulturpolitischen Situation in den fünfiger Jahren." In *Literatur der Nachkriegszeit und der fünfiger Jahren in Österreich*. Vienna: ÖBV, 1984, pp. 75–111.

Gruber, Helmut. *Red Vienna: Experiments in Working Class Culture, 1919–1934*. New York: Oxford University Press, 1991.

Gumbrecht, Hans-Ulrich. "Everyday-World and Life-World as Philosophical Concepts: A Genealogical Approach." *New Literary History* 24:4 (1993): 745–61.

— "'Pathos of Earthly Progress': Erich Auerbach's Everydays." In *Literary History and the Challenge of Philology: The Legacy of Erich Auerbach*, ed. Seth Lerer. Stanford, CA: Stanford University Press, 1996, pp. 13–35.

Ha-Am, Aḥad. "Imitation and Assimilation." In *Selected Essays of Ahad Ha'Am*, trans. and ed. Leon Simon. Philadelphia: Jewish Publication Society, 1912, pp. 107-22.

Hacohen, Aviad. "Does Esau Hate Jacob?" (in Hebrew). *Meimad* (1998): 16–19.

Hacohen, Malachi. "Berlin and Popper Between Nation and Empire: Diaspora, Cosmopolitanism, and Jewish Life." *Jewish Historical Studies* 44 (2012): 51–74.

— "Das Kaiserreich, die Sozialdemokratie und die Juden: Ein Versuch, die k. und k. Monarchie wieder in die österreichische Geschichte einzuschreiben." In "1914–2014 – Monarchie als Integrationsmodell?" *Wiener Journal Beilage* (March 12, 2014): 12–13.

— "Dilemmas of Cosmopolitanism: Karl Popper, Jewish Identity and 'Central European Culture.'" *Journal of Modern History* 71:1 (1999): 105–49.

— "From Empire to Cosmopolitanism: The Central-European Jewish Intelligentsia, 1867–1968." In *Jahrbuch des Simon-Dubnow-Instituts* 5 (2006): 117–34.

— "Karl Popper in Exile: The Viennese Progressive Imagination and the Making of The Open Society." *Philosophy of the Social Sciences* 26 (1996): 452–92.

— *Karl Popper – The Formative Years, 1902–1945: Politics and Philosophy in Interwar Vienna*. New York: Cambridge University Press, 2000.

— "Kongress für kulturelle Freiheit." *Enzyklopädie jüdischer Geschichte und Kultur*, ed. Dan Diner. 7 vols. Stuttgart: J. B. Metzler'sche Verlagsbuchhandlung, 2012: 2: 22–28.

— "La città celeste di Popper: Platone, Atene e la società aperta." In *Karl R. Popper, 1902–2002: Ripensando il razionalismo critico (Nuova Civiltà delle Macchine*, 20: 2), ed. and trans. Stefano Gattei. 2 vols. Bologna: Analisi-Trend, 2002: 2: 12–33.

— "Leonard Krieger: Historicization and Political Engagement in Intellectual History." *History and Theory* 35:1 (1996): 80–130.

— "The Congress for Cultural Freedom in Austria: *Forum*, the Rémigrés and Postwar Culture." *Storiografia* 11 (2007): 135–45.

"'The Strange Fact That the State of Israel Exists': The Cold War Liberals Between Cosmopolitanism and Nationalism." *Jewish Social Studies* 15:2 (2009): 37–81.

"Typology and the Holocaust: Erich Auerbach and Judeo-Christian Europe." *Religions* 3:3 (2012): 600–645.

Hacohen, Ran. "Bible Stories for Jewish Children in the German Haskalah" (in Hebrew). Master's thesis., Tel Aviv University, 1994.

"Die Bibel kehrt Heim: Biblische Gedichte für jüdische Kinder." In *Kinder und Jugendliteraturforschung 1996/7*, ed. Hans Eino-Ewers, Ulrich Nassen, Karin Richter, and Rüdiger Steinlein. Stuttgart: Metzler, 1997, pp. 9–21.

Reclaiming the Hebrew Bible: German-Jewish Reception of Biblical Criticism. Berlin: Walter de Gruyter, 2010.

Hadas-Lebel, Mireille. *Jerusalem Against Rome.* Trans. Robyn Fréchet. Leuven, Belgium: Peeters, 2006.

Hailperin, Herman. *Rashi and the Christian Scholars.* Pittsburgh, PA: University of Pittsburgh Press, 1963.

Hall, John A. *Ernest Gellner: An Intellectual Biography.* London: Verso, 2010.

Halperin, David. "Sabbatianism and Kabbalistic Heresy." Unpublished MS written for *The Cambridge Companion to the Kabbalah*, ed. Elliot Wolfson.

"Some Themes in the Book *Va-Avo Ha-Yom el Ha-ʿAyin.*" Paper presented at the Duke-UNC Jewish Studies Seminar, November 24, 2013.

The Faces of the Chariot. Tübingen: J.C.B. Mohr [Paul Siebeck], 1988.

"The Hole in the Sheet, and Other Topics in Sabbatian Kabbalah." Paper presented at the Association for Jewish Studies conference, Los Angeles, 2009.

Hanisch, Ernst. *Der kranke Mann an der Donau: Marx und Engels über Österreich.* Vienna: Europaverlag, 1978.

Hardt, Michael, and Antonio Negri. *Empire.* Cambridge, MA: Harvard University Press, 2000.

Ḥarif, Ḥanan. "'Revival of the East,' Pan-Semitism and Pan-Asianism in Zionist Discourse" (in Hebrew). Ph.D. diss., Hebrew University of Jerusalem, 2013.

Ḥarlap, Yair. "'The Patriarchs' Deeds Are a Sign for Their Descendants' as Typological Exegesis in the *Rishonim* (medieval exegetes)" (in Hebrew). *Megadim* 41 (2005): 65–92.

Härle, Andrea, Cornelia Kogoj, Werner Michael Schwarz, Michael Weese, and Susanne Winkler, eds. *Romane Thana: Orte der Roma und Sinti.* Vienna: Czernin Verlag, 2015.

Har-Shefi, Avishar. *The Myth of the Edomite Kings in Zoharic Literature: Creation and Revelation in the Idrot Texts of the Zohar* (in Hebrew). Los Angeles: Cherub Press, 2014.

Hart, Mitchell. *Social Science and the Politics of Modern Jewish Identity.* Stanford, CA: Stanford University Press, 2000.

Hartmann, Geoffrey. "Preface." In *The Third Pillar: Essays in Jewish Studies.* Philadelphia: University of Pennsylvania Press, 2011, pp. 1–14.

Haupt, Heinz-Gerhard, and Dieter Langewiesche. "Nation und Religion zur Einfuehrung." In *Nation und Religion in der deutschen Geschichte*, ed. Heinz-

Gerhard Haupt and Dieter Langewiesche. Frankfurt: Campus Verlag, 2001, pp. 11–29.

Hautmann, Hans. *Die verlorene Räterepublik: Am Beispiel der Kommunistischen Partei Deutschösterreichs.* Vienna: Europa Verlag, 1971.

Haym, Rudolf. *Herder nach seinem Leben und seinen Werken dargestellt.* 2 vols. Berlin: R. Gaertner, 1880–85.

Hayward, C. T. R. "A Portrait of the Wicked Esau in the Targum of Codex Neofiti 1." In *The Aramaic Bible: Targums in Their Historical Context,* ed. D. R. G. Beattie and M. J. McNamara. Sheffield, UK: JSOT Press, 1994, pp. 291–309.

Hecht, Jonathan. "The Polemical Exchange Between Isaac Pollegar and Abner of Burgos/Alfonso of Valladolid according to Parma MS 2440: Iggeret Teshuvat Apikoros (Epistle to the Apostate) and Teshuvot la-Maheref (Response to the Blasphemer)." Ph.D. diss., New York University, 1993.

Hecht, Louise. *Ein jüdischer Aufklärer in Böhmen: Peter Beer.* Vienna: Böhlau, 2008.

Heinemann, Joseph. *Agadot ve-Toldotehen.* Jerusalem: Keter, 1974.

Heinz, K. H., ed. *E.K. Winter: Ein Katholik zwischen Österreichs Fronten, 1933–1938.* Vienna: Hermann Böhlau, 1984.

Herr, M. D. "Edom." *Encyclopedia Judaica.* Jerusalem: Ketter, 1971: 6:379.

Heschel, Susannah. *Abraham Geiger and the Jewish Jesus.* Chicago: University of Chicago Press, 1998.

The Aryan Jesus: Christian Theologians and the Bible in Nazi Germany. Princeton, NJ: Princeton University Press, 2008.

Hess, Jonathan. *Germans, Jews and the Claims of Modernity.* New Haven, CT: Yale University Press, 2002.

Hever, Hanan. *Poets and Zealots* (in Hebrew). Jerusalem: Bialik Institute, 1994.

Hochgeschwender, Michael. *Freiheit in der Offensive? Der Kongress für Kulturelle Freiheit und die Deutschen.* Munich: Oldenbourg, 1998.

"The Intellectual as Propagandist: *Der Monat*, the Congress for Cultural Freedom and the Process of Westernizastion in Germany." Paper presented at German Historical Institute, Washington, DC, March 1999. http://web .archive.org/web/20000917091401/www.ghi-dc.org/conpotweb/westernpa pers/hochgeschwender.pdf.

Holleis, Eva. *Die Sozialpolitische Partei: Sozialliberale Bestrebungen in Wien um 1900.* Munich: Oldenbourg, 1978.

Hollinger, David. "Communalist and Dispersionist Approaches to American Jewish History in an Increasingly Post-Jewish Era." *American Jewish History,* 95:1 (2009): 1–32.

Science, Jews, and Secular Culture: Studies in Mid-Twentieth-Century American Intellectual History. Princeton, NJ: Princeton University Press, 1996.

Holmes, Deborah. *Langweile ist Gift: Das Leben der Eugenie Schwarzwald.* Vienna: Residenz Verlag, 2013.

Holo, Joshua. "Byzantine Jewish Ethnography." In *Jews in Byzantium,* ed. Robert Bonfil, Oded Irshai, Guy G. Stroumza, and Rina Talgam. Leiden: Brill, 2012, pp. 923–49.

Horn, Gerd-Rainer. *The Spirit of '68.* Oxford: Oxford University Press, 2007.

Horn, Gerd-Rainer, and Padraic Kenney. "Bibliographic Essay." In *Transnational Moments of Change: Europe 1945, 1968, 1989*, ed. Gerd-Rainer Horn and Padraic Kenney. Lanham, MD: Rowman & Littlefield, 2004, pp. 229–33.

Horowitz, Elliot. *Reckless Rites: Purim and the Legacy of Jewish Violence*. Princeton, NJ: Princeton University Press, 2006.

Howard, Thomas Albert. *Religion and the Rise of Historicism: W. M. L. de Wette, Jacob Burckhardt and the Theological Origins of Nineteenth-Century Historical Consciousness*. Cambridge: Cambridge University Press, 2000.

Hubert, Rainer. "Freimaurerei in Österreich 1871 bis 1938." In *Zirkel und Winkelmass*. Vienna: Eigenverlag der Museen der Stadt Wien, 1984, pp. 31–46.

Hubert, Rainer, and Ferdinand Zörrer. "Die östereichischen Grenzlogen." *Quator Coronati Jahrbuch* (1983): 143–66.

Hübinger, Gangolf. *Kulturprotestantismus und Politik: Zum Verhältnis von Liberalismus und Protestantismus in wilhelmischen Deutschland*. Tübingen: Mohr, 1994.

Hubman, Franz, Heimito von Doderer, Herbert Eisenreich, Alexander Lernet-Holenia, Helmut Qualtinger, Friedrich Torberg, and Hans Weigel. *Wien: Vorstadt Europas*. Zurich: Artemis, 1963.

Hülshörster, Christian. *Thomas Mann und Oskar Goldbergs "Wirklichkeit der Hebräer."* Frankfurt am Main: V. Klostermann, 1999.

Humboldt, Wilhelm von. "Über den Entwurf zu einer neuen Konstitution für die Juden." In *Werke*. 5 vols. Darmstadt: Wissenschaftliche Buchgesellschaft, 1964: 4: 95–112.

Hundert, Gerson David. "Re(de)fining Modernity in Jewish History." In *Rethinking European Jewish History*, ed. Jeremy Cohen and Moshe Rosman. Oxford: The Litman Library, 2009, pp. 133–45.

The Jews of Poland-Lithuania in the Eighteenth-Century: A Genealogy of Modernity. Berkeley: University of California Press, 2004.

Huss, Boaz. *Like the Radiance of the Sky: Chapters in the Reception History of the Zohar and the Construction of Its Symbolic Value* (in Hebrew). Jerusalem: Bialik Institute and Ben-Zvi Institute, 2008.

Idel, Moshe. "Ha-Maḥashavah ha-raah shel ha-El (God's Evil Thought)." *Tarbiz* 49:304 (1980): 356–64.

"On Mobility, Individuals, and Groups: Prolegomenon for a Sociological Approach to Sixteenth-Century Kabbalah." *Kabbalah* 3 (1998): 145–73.

Inglehart, Ronald. *Culture Shift in Advanced Industrial Society*. Princeton, NJ.: Princeton University Press, 1990.

The Silent Revolution: Changing Values and Political Styles among Western Publics. Princeton, NJ: Princeton University Press, 1977.

Jacob, Walter. "Benno Jacob's Concept of a Wissenschaft des Judentums." In *Die Exegese hat das erste Wort: Beiträge zu Leben und Werk Benno Jacobs*, ed. Almuth Jürgensen. Stuttgart: Calwer, 2002, pp. 85–97.

"The Life and Work of Benno Jacob." In *Die Exegese hat das erste Wort: Beiträge zu Leben und Werk Benno Jacobs*, ed. Almuth Jürgensen. Stuttgart: Calwer, 2002, pp. 11–31.

Jászi, Oscar. *The Dissolution of the Habsburg Monarchy*. [1929] Chicago: University of Chicago Press, 1961.

Jay, Martin. "The Politics of Translation: Siegfried Kracauer and Walter Benjamin on the Buber-Rosenzweig Bible." *Leo Baeck Institute Yearbook* 21 (1976): 3–24.

Joskowicz, Ari. "Jewish Anticlericalism and the Making of Modern Jewish Politics in Late Enlightenment Prussia and France." *Jewish Social Studies* 17:3 (2011): 40–77.

   The Modernity of Others: Jewish Anti-Catholicism in Germany and France. Stanford, CA: Stanford University Press, 2014.

Judson, Pieter. *Guardians of the Nation: Activists on the Language Frontiers of Imperial Austria*. Cambridge, MA: Harvard University Press, 2007.

   "L'Autriche-Hongrie était-elle un empire?" *Annales: Histoire, Sciences Sociales* 63:3 (2008): 563–96.

   The Habsburg Empire. Cambridge, MA: Harvard University Press, 2016.

   "Jürgen Habermas im Gespräch mit Rachel Salamander." *Münchener Beiträge zur Jüdischen Geschichte und Kultur* 6:1 (2012): 7–18.

Jürgensen, Almuth. "Die Exegese hat das erste Wort: Zu Benno Jacobs Bibelauslegung." In *Die Exegese hat das erste Wort: Beiträge zu Leben und Werk Benno Jacobs*, ed. Almuth Jürgensen. Stuttgart: Calwer, 2002, pp. 124–47.

Kahana, Maoz. *From the Noda BeYehuda to the Chatam Sofer: Halakha and Thought in Their Historical Moment* (in Hebrew). Jerusalem: Zalman Shazar Center, 2015.

   "How Did the Hatam-Sofer Wish to Trump Spinoza? Text, Hermeneutics, and Romanticism in the Writings of R. Moses Sofer" (in Hebrew). *Tarbits* 79:3 (2011): 557–85.

   "The Chatam Sofer: A Decisor in His Own Eyes" (in Hebrew). *Tarbits* 76:3 (2007): 519–56.

Kaiser, Wolfram. *Christian Democracy and the Origins of European Union*. Cambridge: Cambridge University Press, 2007.

   "Transnational Mobilization and Cultural Representation: Political Transfer in an Age of Proto-Globalization, Democratization and Nationalism 1848–1914." *European Review of History* 12:2 (2005): 403–24.

Kalik, Judith. "Christian Kabbalah and Polish Jews: Attitudes of the Church to Jewish Conversion and the Idea of 'Jacob's Return' in the Polish-Lithuanian Commonwealth in the 18th Century." *Jewish History Quarterly* (2004): 492–501.

Kalita, Thomas. "The Influence of Nicholas of Lyra on Martin Luther's *Commentary on Genesis*." Th.D. diss., Catholic University of America, 1985.

Kallus, Menachem. "Pneumatic Mystical Possession and the Eschatology of the Soul in Lurianic Kabbalah." In *Spirit Possession in Judaism: Cases and Contexts from the Middle Ages to the Present*, ed. Matt Goldfish. Detroit: Wayne State University Press, 2003, pp. 159–85.

Kam, Matya. *Israel and the Nations via the Jacob and Esau Story* (in Hebrew). Tel Aviv: Center for Educational Technology, 1996.

Kamer, Christian. *Negotiating National Identities: Between Globalization, the Past and 'the Other.'* Farnham, UK: Ashgate, 2011.

Kamin, Sarah. "Rashi's Commentary on the Song of Songs and the Jewish-Christian Polemic." In *Jews and Christians Interpret the Bible* (in Hebrew). Jerusalem: The Magnes Press, 2008, pp. 31–60.

Kann, Robert A. *The Multinational Empire: Nationalism and National Reform in the Habsburg Empire.* New York: Columbia University Press, 1950.

Kaplan, Marion A. *The Making of the Jewish Middle Class: Women, Family, and Identity in Imperial Germany.* Oxford: Oxford University Press, 1991.

Kasher, Aryeh. *Jews, Idumaeans, and Ancient Arabs: Relations of the Jews in Erez-Israel with the Nations of the Frontier and the Desert during the Hellenistic and Roman Era (332 BCE–70 CE).* Tübingen: J.C.B. Mohr [Paul Siebeck], 1988.

Katz, Jacob. *A House Divided: Orthodoxy and Schism in Nineteenth-Century Central European Jewry.* Trans. Ziporah Brody. Hanover, NH: New England University Press, 1998.

"A State Within a State: The History of an Anti-Semitic Slogan." In *Emancipation and Assimilation: Studies in Modern Jewish History.* Farnborough, UK: Gregg International Publishers, 1972, pp. 56–64.

Between Jews and Gentiles (in Hebrew). Jerusalem: Bialik Institute, 1960.

"Die Entstehung der Judenassimilation in Deutschland und derren Ideologie." [1935] In *Emancipation and Assimilation: Studies in Modern Jewish History.* Farnborough, UK: Gregg International Publishers, 1972, pp. 195–276.

Emancipation and Assimilation: Studies in Modern Jewish History. Farnborough, UK: Gregg International Publishers, 1972.

"Even Though He Has Sinned, He Is Still a Jew" (in Hebrew). *Tarbiz* 27:2/3 (1958): 203–17.

From Prejudice to Destruction: Anti-Semitism, 1700–1933. Cambridge, MA: Harvard University Press, 1980.

Halacha in Straits (in Hebrew). Jerusalem: Magnes Presss, 1992.

Jews and Freemasons in Europe, 1723–1939. Trans. Leonard Oschry. Cambridge, MA: Harvard University Press, 1970.

"Orthodoxy in Historical Perspective." *Studies in Contemporary Jewry* 2 (1986): 3–17.

Out of the Ghetto: The Social Background of Jewish Emancipation, 1770–1870. Cambridge, MA: Harvard University Press, 1973.

"The German Jewish Utopia of Social Emancipation." In *Emancipation and Assimilation: Studies in Modern Jewish History.* Farnborough, UK: Gregg International Publishers, 1972, pp. 91–110.

"The Suggested Relationship between Sabbatianism, Haskalah, and Reform." In *Divine Law in Human Hands.* Jerusalem: Magnes Press, 1998, pp. 504–30.

"The Term 'Jewish Emancipation.'" In *Emancipation and Assimilation: Studies in Modern Jewish History.* Farnborough, UK: Gregg International Publishers, 1972, pp. 21–46.

"The Vicissitudes of Three Apologetic Statements" (in Hebrew). *Ziyon* 23/24 (1958–59): 174–93.

"Towards a Biography of the Hatam Sofer." In *Profiles in Diversity*, ed. Frances Malino and David Sorkin. Detroit: Wayne University Press, 1998, pp. 223–66.

Tradition and Crisis: Jewish Society at the End of the Middle Ages. New York: New York University Press, 1993.

Keller, Fritz. *Wien, Mai 68: Eine heiße Viertelstunde.* Vienna: Mandelbaum Verlag, 2008.

Kempter, Klaus. *Die Jellineks 1820–1955: Eine familienbiographische Studie zum deutschjüdischen Bildungsbürgertum.* Düsseldorf: Droste Verlag, 1998.

Keneally, Thomas. *Schindler's Ark.* London: Hodder and Stoughton, 1982.

Kieval, Hillel. *Languages of Community: The Jewish Experience in the Czech Lands.* Berkeley: University of California Press, 2000.

The Making of Czech Jewry. New York: Oxford University Press, 1988.

King, Jeremy. *Budweisers into Czechs and Germans: A Local History of Bohemian Politics, 1848–1948.* Princeton, NJ: Princeton University Press, 2002.

Klausner, Joseph. *Yehudah ve-Romi.* Tel Aviv: Umah u-Moledet, 1946.

Klein, Mordechai, and Elḥanan Molner. "Ha-Ravad as Historian, II" (in Hebrew). *Hazofeh Quartalis Hebraica* 8 (1924): 24–35.

Klemperer, Klemens von. *Ignaz Seipel: Christian Statesman in a Time of Crisis.* Princeton, NJ: Princeton University Press, 1972.

Klemperer, Victor. *Ich will Zeugnis ablegen bis zum letzten.* 2 vols. Berlin: Aufbau-Verlag, 1995.

Klepper, Deeana Copeland. "Nicholas of Lyra and Franciscan Interest in Hebrew Scholarship." In *Nicholas of Lyra: The Senses of Scripture*, ed. Philip D. W. Krey and Lesley Smith. Leiden: Brill, 2000, pp. 287–311.

The Insight of Unbelievers: Nicholas of Lyra and Christian Reading of Jewish Text in the Later Middle Ages. Philadelphia: University of Pennsylvania Press, 2007.

Klimke, Martin. *The Other Alliance: Student Protest in West Germany and the United States in the Global Sixties.* Princeton, NJ: Princeton University Press, 2010.

Klimke, Martin, and Joachim Scharloth. "1968 in Europe." In *1968 in Europe: A History of Protest and Activism, 1956–1977*, ed. Martin Klimke and Joachim Scharloth. New York: Palgrave Macmillan, 2008, pp. 1–9.

Knoll, August M., Alfred Missong, Wilhelm Schmid, Ernst Karl Winter, and H. K. Zeßner-Spitzenberg. *Die Österreichische Aktion.* Vienna: Selbstverlag der Verfasser [Ernst Karl Winter], 1927.

Koebner, Richard. *Empire.* Cambridge: Cambridge University Press, 1961.

Kogman-Appel, Katrin. "Coping with Christian Pictorial Sources: What Did Jewish Miniaturists *Not* Paint?" *Speculum* 75:4 (2000): 816–58.

Kohl, Katrin, and Ritchie Robertson, eds. *A History of Austrian Literature 1918–2000.* Rochester, NY: Camden House, 2006.

Konrad, Helmut, and Wolfgang Maderthaner, eds. *Das Werden der Ersten Republik: . . . der Rest ist Österreich.* 2 vols. Vienna: Gerold, 2008.

Kontje, Todd. *The Cambridge Introduction to Thomas Mann.* Cambridge: Cambridge University Press, 2011.

Konuk, Kader. *East West Mimesis: Auerbach in Turkey.* Stanford, CA: Stanford University Press, 2010.

"Jewish-German Philologists in Turkish Exile: Leo Spitzer and Erich Auerbach." In *Exile and Otherness: New Approaches to the Experience of the Nazi Refugees*, ed. Alexander Stephan. Bern: Peter Lang, 2005, pp. 31–47.

Kos, Wolfgang. *Eigenheim Österreich: Zu Politik, Kultur und Alltag nach 1945.* Vienna: Sonderzahl, 1994.

Kożuchowski, Adam. *The Afterlife of Austria-Hungary.* Pittsburgh, PA: University of Pittsburgh Press, 2013.

Kraus, Hans Joachim. "Herders Alttestamentliche Forschungen." In *Bückeburger Gespräche über Johann Gottfried Herder*, ed. Johann Gottfried Maltusch. Bückeburg: Verlag Grimme Bückeburger, 1973, pp. 59–75.

Kraushar, Alexander. *Frank i frankisci polscy, 1726–1816* (in Polish). [1895] 2 vols. Now available in English: *Jacob Frank: The End to the Sabbataian Heresy.* Trans. Herbert Levy. Lanham, MD: University Press of America, 2001.

Krauss, Marita. "Jewish Remigration: An Overview of an Emerging Discipline." *Leo Baeck Institute Yearbook* 49:1 (2004): 107–20.

Krauss, Samuel. *Die Wiener Geserah vom Jahre 1421.* Vienna: Braumüller, 1920.

Krawcowicz, Barbara. "Covenantal Theodicy Among Haredi and Modern Jewish Thinkers During and After the Holocaust." Ph.D. diss., University of Indiana, Bloomington, 2013.

"Paradigmatic Thinking and Holocaust Theology." *Journal of Jewish Thought & Philosophy* 22 (2014): 164–89.

Kuéss, Gustav, and Bernhard Scheichelbauer. *200 Jahre Freimaurerei in Österreich.* Vienna: O. Kerry, 1959.

Kuhn, Helmut. "Literaturgeschichte als Geschichtsphilosophie." *Philosophische Rundschau* 11 (1963): 222–48.

Kühne, Jan. "'Wer ist wer?!' Sammy Gronemanns *Jakob und Christian.*" *Pardes* 19 (2013): 191–206.

Kurzke, Hermann. *Thomas Mann: Epoche, Werk, Wirkung.* Munich: C.H. Beck, 1985.

Thomas Mann: Life as a Work of Art: A Biography. Trans. Leslie Willson. Princeton NJ: Princeton University Press, 2002.

Lajarrige, Jacques, ed. *Soma Morgenstern – Von Galizien ins amerikanische Exil.* Berlin: Frank & Timme, 2015.

Landauer, Carl. "Auerbach's Performance and the American Academy." In *Literary History and the Challenge of Philology: The Legacy of Erich Auerbach*, ed. Seth Lerer. Stanford, CA: Stanford University Press, 1996, pp. 179–94.

"'Mimesis' and Erich Auerbach's Self-Mythologizing." *German Studies Review* 11:1 (1988): 83–96.

Lang, Birgit. "Ein Aufenthalt der Dauer: Walter A. Berendsohn und Exilforschung." *Leipziger Beiträge zur jüdischen Geschichte und Kultur* 3 (2005): 61–79.

Langer, Gerhard. "Wer ein lebendiges Wesen tötet, der tötet die ganze Welt: Soma Morgensterns Bezügezur jüdischen Tradition, zu Judentum und Christentum." *Chilufim* 9 (2010): 19–35.

Langer, Ruth. *Cursing the Christians? A History of Birkat HaMinim.* New York: Oxford University Press, 2012.

Lapin, Hayim. "Jewish and Christian Academies in Roman Palestine: Some Preliminary Observations." In *Caesarea Martima: A Retrospective After Two Millennia*, ed. Avner Rabsan and Kenneth G. Holum. Leiden: E. J. Brill, 1996, pp. 496–512.

Lappin, Eleonore, ed. *Jewish Voices, German Words: Growing Up Jewish in Postwar Germany and Austria*. Trans. Krishna Winston. North Haven, CT: Catbird Press, 1994.

Lasch, Christopher. "The Cultural Cold War: A Short History of the Congress for Cultural Freedom." In *The Agony of the American Left*. New York: Vintage, 1968, pp. 61–112.

Lazar, Hadara. *Ha-Mandatorim: Erez Yisrael, 1940–1948* (in Hebrew). Jerusalem: Keter, 1990. Trans. Hadara Lazar as *Out of Palestine: The Making of Modern Israel*. New York: Atlas & Co., 2011.

Lazarom, Ilse. *The Grace of Misery: Joseph Roth and the Politics of Exile, 1919–1939*. Leiden: Brill, 2013.

Lazier, Benjamin. *God Interrupted: Heresy and the European Imagination Between the World Wars*. Princeton, NJ: Princeton University Press, 2008.

Lebovics, Nitzan. "The Jerusalem School: The Theopolitical Hour." *New German Critique* 35 (2008): 97–120.

Lebow, Richard Ned, Wulf Kansteiner, and Claudio Fogu, eds. *The Politics of Memory in Postwar Europe*. Durham, NC: Duke University Press, 2006.

Leff, Lisa. *Sacred Bonds of Solidarity: The Rise of Jewish Internationalism in Nineteenth-Century France*. Stanford, CA: Stanford University Press, 2006.

Leiter, Philomena. "Assimilation, Antisemitismus und NS-Verfolgung: Austritte aus der Jüdischen Gemeinde in Wien 1900–1944." Ph.D. diss., University of Vienna, 2003.

Leonard, Robert. *Von Neumann, Morgenstern, and the Creation of Game Theory: From Chess to Social Science, 1900–1960*. New York: Cambridge University Press, 2012.

Lerner, Warren. *Karl Radek: The Last Internationalist*. Stanford, CA: Stanford University Press, 1970.

Leser, Norbert. *Zwischen Reformismus und Bolschewismus: Der Austromarxismus als Theorie und Praxis*. 2d ed. Vienna: Böhlau, 1985.

Lernet-Holenia, Alexander, et al. *Wien: Vorstadt Europas*. Photos by Franz Hubmann. Zurich: Artemis, 1963.

Lestition, Steven, and Robert Norton. An exchange on "The Counter-Enlightenment." *Journal of the History of Ideas* 68:4 (2007): 635–81; 69:2 (2008): 339–47.

Liberles, Robert. "Dohm's Treatise on the Jews: A Defense of the Enlightenment." *Leo Baeck Institute Year Book* 33 (1988): 29–42.

Lieber, Laura. "'You Have Skirted This Hill Long Enough': The Tension between Rhetoric and History in a Byzantine Piyut." *Hebrew Union College Annual* 80 (2009): 63–114.

Lieberman, Saul. *Hellenism in Jewish Palestine*. 2d ed. New York: Jewish Theological Seminary, 1962.

"Redifat dat Yisrael." In *Salo Wittmayer Baron Jubilee Volume*. 3 vols. Jerusalem: American Academy for Jewish Research, 1974: 3: 213–45.

Shkiin: A Few Words on Some Jewish Legends, Customs and Literary Sources Found in Karaite and Christian Work. 2d ed. Jerusalem: Wahrmann Books, 1970.

"The Martyrs of Caesarea." *Annuaire de l'Institut de philology et d'histoire orientales et slaves* 7 (1939–40): 395–446.

Liebes, Esther. "Cordovero and Luria: A Reexamination of the Myth of the Kings of Edom's Death." In *Maayan Eyn Yaaqov*, ed. Bracha Sack. Beer-Sheva: Ben-Gurion University in the Negev Press, 2009, pp. 32–60.

Liebes, Yehudah. "How the *Zohar* Was Written." In *Studies in the Zohar*. Albany: State University of New York Press, 1993, pp. 85–138.

"New Writings in Sabbatean Kabbalah Originating in Rabbi Jonathan Eibeschütz's Circle" (in Hebrew). *Meḥqerei Yerushalayim be-Maḥshevet Yisrael* 5 (1986): 191–348.

Studies in Jewish Myth and Jewish Messianism. Trans. Batya Stein. Albany: State University of New York Press, 1993.

Studies in the Zohar. Albany: State University of New York Press, 1993.

"The Messiah of the Zohar." In *Studies in the Zohar*. Albany: State University of New York Press, 1993, pp. 1–84.

Liebich, André. *From the Other Shore: Russian Social Democracy After 1921.* Cambridge, MA: Harvard University Press, 1997.

Lindenberger, Herbert. "On the Reception of Mimesis." In *Literary History and the Challenge of Philology: The Legacy of Erich Auerbach*, ed. Seth Lerer. Stanford, CA: Stanford University Press, 1996, pp. 195–213.

Lindner, Amnon. "*Deus venerunt gentes:* Psalms: 78 (79) in the Liturgical Commemoration of the Destruction of Latin Jerusalem." In *Medieval Studies in Honor of Avrom Saltman*, ed. Bat-Sheva Albert, Yvonne Friedman, and Simon Schwarzfuchs. Ramat-Gan: Bar-Ilan University Press, 1995, pp. 145–71.

Lindsay, John. "Edomite Westward Expansion: The Biblical Evidence." *Ancient Near Eastern Studies* 36 (1999): 48–89.

Lipton, Sara. *Images of Intolerance: The Representation of Jews and Judaism in the Bible Moralisée.* Berkeley: University of California Press, 1999.

Lorenz, Dagmar C. G., ed. and trans. *Contemporary Jewish Writing in Austria: An Anthology.* Lincoln: University of Nebraska Press, 1999.

Lowenstein, Steven. *The Berlin Jewish Community: Enlightenment, Family, and Crisis, 1770–1830.* New York: Oxford University Press, 1994.

Lowenthal, Richard. *Der romantische Rückfall.* Stuttgart: W. Kohlhammer, 1970.

Lubich, Ronen. "Jacob & Esau and Rashi's Interpretive Method" (in Hebrew). *Shaanan* 13 (2008): 71–107. http://app.shaanan.ac.il/shnaton/13/4.pdf.

Luft, David. "Cultural Memory and Intellectual History: Locating Austrian Culture." *Studies in Twentieth and Twenty-First Century Literature* 31:1 (2007): 30–51.

Lukàcs, Georg. *Die Theorie des Romans: Ein geschichts-philosophischer Versuch über die Formen der grossen Epik.* [1916] Neuwied am Rhein: Luchterhand, 1963.

Die Zerstörung der Vernunft: Der Weg des Irrationalismus von Schelling zu Hitler. Berlin: Aufbau-Verlag, 1954.

Essays on Realism. Ed. and with introduction by Rodney Livingstone. Trans. David Fernbach. Cambridge, MA: MIT Press, 1981.

MacArtney, C. A. *The Habsburg Empire 1790–1918.* London: Weidenfeld & Nicholson, 1968.

Maciejko, Pawel. "Controverse sur la crypto-chrétienté de Rabbi Jonathan Eibeschütz." *Les cahiers du judaïsme* 29 (2010): 130–34.

"Sabbatian Jesus: Nathan of Gaza and Jacob Frank." Unpublished MS.

"The Dangers (and Pleasures) of Religious Syncretism." Unpublished MS.

"The Literary Character and Doctrine of Jacob Frank's *The Words of the Lord.*" *Kabbalah* 9 (2003): 175–210.

The Mixed Multitude: Jacob Frank and the Frankist Movement, 1755–1816. Philadelphia: University of Pennsylvania Press, 2011.

Maderthaner, Wolfgang. "Das revolutionäre Prinzip: Arbeiterbewegung und Krieg (2)." In *Im Epizentrum des Zusammenbruchs Wien im Ersten Weltkrieg,* ed. Alfred Pfoser and Andreas Weigl. Vienna: Metroverlag, 2013, pp. 566–71.

Maderthaner, Wolfgang, and Lutz Musner. *Unruly Masses: The Other Side of Fin-de-siècle Vienna.* New York: Berghahn Books, 2008.

Magris, Claudio. *Der habsburgische Mythos in der modernen österreichische Literatur.* [1963] Vienna: Paul Zsolnay Verlag, 2000.

Maier, Michaela. "Jew, Madonna and Socialist: Emma Braun-Adler (1858–1935)." *Religions.* Forthcoming.

Manor, Dalia. *Art in Zion: The Genesis of Modern National Art in Jewish Palestine.* London: Routledge, 2005.

Maor, Zohar. "Between Anti-Colonialism and Postcolonialism: *Berit Shalom*'s Critique of Nationalism and Secularization" (in Hebrew). *Theory and Criticism* 10 (2007): 12–28.

"Identity and Confusion: One More Glance at the Whirlpool of Identities in Prague." *Ziyon* 71 (2006): 457–72.

Martin Buber (in Hebrew). Jerusalem: Zalman Shazar Center, 2016.

New Secret Doctrine: Spirituality, Creativity and Nationalism in the Prague Circle (in Hebrew). Jerusalem: Shazar Center, 2010.

Martin, John D. "The Depiction of Jews in the Carnival Plays and Comedies of Hans Folz and Hans Sachs in Early Modern Nuremberg." *Baylor Journal of Theatre and Performance* 3:2 (2006): 43–65.

Martin, Terry. *The Affirmative Action Empire: Nations and Nationalism in the Soviet Union, 1923–1939.* Ithaca, NY: Cornell University Press, 2001.

Mattl, Siegfried. "Art and Revolution in the Austrian 1968." Paper presented in a panel on "1968: Student Revolutions in America and Europe," March 7, 2005, Duke University.

Mazower, Mark. *No Enchanted Palace: The End of Empire and the Ideological Origins of the United Nations.* Princeton, NJ: Princeton University Press, 2008.

McGuckin, John A. "Origen on the Jews." In *Christianity in Relation to Jews, Greeks, and Romans,* ed. Everett Ferguson. New York: Garland Pub., 1999, pp. 23–36.

McGuire, Marilyn. "The Mature Luther's Revision of Marriage Theology: Preference for Patriarchs over Saints in his Commentary on Genesis." Ph.D. diss., St. Louis University, 1999.

Meier, Heinrich. *Leo Strauss and the Theologico-Political Problem.* Cambridge: Cambridge University Press, 2006.

Mell, Julie. "Geteilte Urbanität: Die befestigte Stadt in der deutsch-jüdischen Kunst in der Zeit vor der Entstehung des Ghettos." *Wiener Jahrbuch für Jüdische Geschichte Kultur und Museumswesen* 5 (2001): 25–41.

The Myth of the Medieval Jewish Moneylender. 2 vols. New York: Palgrave Macmillan, 2017.

Mell, Julie, and Malachi Hacohen, eds. *Central European Jewish Émigrés and the Shaping of Postwar Culture: Studies in Memory of Lilian Furst (1931–2009).* Basel: MDPI, 2014.

Menasse, Robert. "Die sozialpartnerschaftliche Ästhetik: Das Österreichische an der österreichischen Literatur der Zweiten Republik." In *Die sozialpartnerschaftliche Ästhetik.* Vienna: Sonderzahl, 1996, pp. 13–124.

Mendelsohn, Ezra. *Painting a People: Maurycy Gottlieb and Jewish Art.* Lebanon, NH: Brandeis University Press, 2002.

Mendes-Flohr, Paul. *German Jews: A Dual Identity.* New Haven, CT: Yale University Press, 1999.

"Martin Buber as a Habsburg Intellectual." In *Jüdische Geschichte als Allgemeine Geschichte: Festschrift für Dan Diner zum 60. Geburtstag,* ed. Raphael Gross and Yfaat Weiss. Gottingen: Vandenhoeck & Ruprecht, 2006, pp. 13–29.

Menges, Karl. "Integration oder Assimilation? Herders Äußerungen über die Juden im Kontext der klassischen Emanzipationsdebatte." *Euphorion* 90 (1996): 394–415.

Merchavia, Chen. *Ha-Talmud Biryi Ha-Naẓrut (500–1248).* Jerusalem: Bialik Institute, 1970.

"On the Hebrew Citations of *Pugio Fidei* in the Saint Genevieve MS" (in Hebrew). *Qiryat Sefer* 51 (1976): 283–88.

"The Talmud in the *Additiones* of Paul of Burgos." *Journal of Jewish Studies* 16: 3/4 (1965): 115–34.

Meron, Guy. *The Waning of the Emancipation: Jewish History, Memory, and the Rise of Fascism in Germany, France, and Hungary.* Detroit: Wayne State University Press, 2011.

Meroz, Ronit. "Geula be-Torat ha-ARI." Ph.D. diss., Hebrew University of Jerusalem, 1988.

Meyer, Michael A. "Jewish Identity in the Decades After 1848." In *Emancipation and Acculturation, 1780–1871,* by Stefi Jersch-Wenzel. Vol. 2 of *German-Jewish History in Modern Times,* ed. Michael A. Meyer and Michael Brenner. 4 vols. New York: Columbia University Press, 1997: 2: 319–47.

Judaism Within Modernity: Essays on Jewish History and Religion. Detroit: Wayne State University Press, 2001.

"'Most of My Brethren Find Me Unacceptable': The Controversial Career of Rabbi Samuel Holdheim." In *Redefining Judaism in an Age of Emancipation,* ed. Christian Wiese. Leiden: Brill, 2007, pp. 3–22.

Response to Modernity: A History of the Reform Movement in Judaism. New York: Oxford University Press, 1988.

Meyer, Thomas. *Vom Ende der Emanzipation: Jüdische Philosophie und Theologie nach 1933.* Göttingen: Vandenhoeck & Ruprecht, 2008.

Michman, Dan. "The Impact of the Holocaust on Religious Jewry." In *Major Changes within the Jewish People in the Wake of the Holocaust*. Jerusalem: Yad Vashem, 1996, pp. 659–707.

Miller, Michael. *Rabbis and Revolutionaries*. Stanford, CA: Stanford University Press, 2011.

Mintz-Manor, Ofir. "Why Are You Giving an Opening to the *Minim*?" (in Hebrew). *Tarbiz* 70:3/4 (2001): 637–44.

Miron, Dan. *Ha-Adam Eno Ela. . . .* Tel Aviv: Zemorah-Bitan, 1999.

Mittelmann, Hanni, and Armin A. Wallas, eds. *Österreich-Konzeptionen und jüdisches Selbstverständnis: Identitäts-Transfigurationen im 19. und 20. Jahrhundert*. Tübingen: Max Niemeyer Verlag, 2001.

Mommsen, Hans. *Die Sozialdemokratie und die Nationalitätenfrage im habsburgischen Vielvölkerstaat*. Vienna: Europa-Verlag, 1963.

Moraw, Peter, Karl Otmar Freiherr von Aretin, Notker Hammerstein, Werner Conze, and Elisabeth Fehrenbach. "Reich." In *Geschichtliche Grundbegriffe*. 8 vols. Stuttgart: Klett-Cotta, 1972–97: 5: 423–508.

Morgenstern, Matthias. "Between the Noahide Laws and Israelite Edomite Brotherhood: Paradigms of Humanity in Modern Jewish Orthodoxy." In *The Quest for a Common Humanity: Human Dignity and Otherness in the Religious Traditions of the Mediterranean*, ed. Katell Berthelot and Matthias Morgenstern. Leiden: Brill, 2011, pp. 101–21.

"Vom 'Götzenzerstörer' zum Protagonisten des Dialogs – Der Erzvater Abraham in 1800 Jahren jüdischer Tradition." In *Interreligiöser Dialog: Chancen abrahamischer Initiativen*, ed. Reinhard Möller and Hanns Christoph Goßmann. Berlin: Lit, 2006, pp. 101–26.

Moritsch, Andreas. ed. *Der Austroslavismus*. Vienna: Böhlau, 1996.

Moses, A. Dirk. "*Das römische Gespräch* in a New Key: Hannah Arendt, Genocide, and the Defense of Republican Civilization." *Journal of Modern History* 85:4 (2013): 867–913.

German Intellectuals and the Nazi Past. New York: Cambridge University Press, 2007.

Moss, Kenneth. *Jewish Renaissance in the Russian Revolution*. Cambridge, MA: Harvard University Press, 2009.

"Negotiating Jewish Nationalism in Interwar Warsaw." In *Warsaw: The Jewish Metropolis*, ed. Glenn Dynner and Francois Guesnet. Leiden: Brill, 2015, pp. 390–434.

Mosse, Geroge. "Jewish Emancipation." In *The Jewish Response to German Culture*, ed. Jehudah Reinhartz and Walter Schatzberg. Hanover, NH: University Press of New England, 1985, pp. 1–16.

Moyn, Samuel. *Origins of the Other: Emmanuel Levinas Between Revelation and Ethics*. Ithaca, NY: Cornell University Press, 2005.

Muchitsch, Wolfgang. "The Cultural Policy of Austrian Refugee Organizations in Great Britain." *Austrian Studies* 6 (1995): 22–40.

Vienna's Golden Autumn 1866–1938. New York: Weidenfeld and Nicolson, 1987.

Mueller-Vollmer, Kurt, ed. *Herder Today: Contributions from the International Herder Conference*. Berlin: Walter de Gruyter, 1990.

Mufti, Amir. "Auerbach in Istanbul: Edward Said, Secular Criticism, and the Question of Minority Culture." *Critical Inquiry*, 25:1 (1998): 95–125.

Müller, Guido. *Europäische Gesellschaftsbeziehungen nach dem Ersten Weltkrieg: Das Deutsch-Französische Studienkomitee und der Europäische Kulturbund.* Munich: R. Oldenbourg, 2005.

Murdoch, Brian. *The Medieval Popular Bible: Expansions of Genesis in the Middle Ages.* Cambridge: D. S. Brewer, 2003.

Musner, Lutz. "Ist Wien Anders? Zur Kulturgeschichte der Stadt nach 1945." In *Wien: Geschichte einer Stadt*, ed. Peter Csendes and Ferdinand Opll. 3 vols. Vienna: Böhlau, 2006: 3: 739–819.

Myers, David. "Hermann Cohen and the Quest for Protestant Judaism." *Leo Baeck Institute Yearbook* 46 (2001): 195–214.

Resisting History. Princeton, NJ: Princeton University Press, 2002.

Nehrlich, Michael. "Romanistik und Anti-Kommunismus." *Das Argument* 4:3/4 (1972): 276–313.

Nesemann, Frank. "Leo Motzkin (1867–1933): Zionist Engagement and Minority Diplomacy." *Central and Eastern European Review* 1 (2007): 1–24.

Neusner, Jacob. "From Enemy to Sibling: Rome and Israel in the First Century of Western Civilization." In *Neusner on Judaism.* 3 vols. Aldershot, UK: Ashgate, 2004–5: 1: 435–63.

Nichols, Stephen G. "Philology on Auerbach's Drama of (Literary) History." In *Literary History and the Challenge of Philology: The Legacy of Erich Auerbach*, ed. Seth Lerer. Stanford, CA: Stanford University Press, 1996, pp. 63–77.

Niehoff, Maren Ruth. "Benno Jacob's Concept of a Wissenschaft des Judentums." In *Die Exegese hat das erste Wort: Beiträge zu Leben und Werk Benno Jacobs*, ed. Almuth Jürgensen. Stuttgart: Calwer, 2002, pp. 85–97.

Nirenberg, David. *Anti-Judaism: The Western Tradition.* New York: W. W. Norton, 2013.

"Hope's Mistakes." *The New Republic* (February 13, 2008): 46–50.

Nisbet, H. B. "Zur Revision des Herder-Bildes im Lichte der neuen Forschung." In *Bückeburger Gespräche über Johann Gottfried Herder 1971*, ed. J. G. Maltusch. Bückeburg: Grimme Bückeburg, 1973, pp. 101–17.

Nord, Philip. *The Republican Moment: Struggles for Democracy in Nineteenth-Century France.* Cambridge, MA: Harvard University Press, 1995.

Nossig, Alfred. *Die Politik des Weltfriedens: Die deutsch-französische Annäherung und die Kontinentalunion.* Berlin: Hermann Walther, 1900.

Nowak, Kurt. *Kulturprotestantismus und Judentum in der Weimarer Republik.* Göttingen: Wallstein, 1993.

Ofrat, Gideon. *One Hundred Years of Art in Israel.* Trans. Peretz Kidron. Boulder, CO: Westview Press, 1998.

Ohly, Friedrich. *Sensus Spiritualis: Studies in Medieval Significs and the Philology of Culture.* Chicago: University of Chicago Press, 2005.

Olson, Jess. *Nathan Birnbaum and Jewish Modernity: Architect of Zionism, Yiddishism, and Orthodoxy.* Stanford, CA: Stanford University Press, 2013.

Oren, Yosef. *The Writing as a Political Announcement* (in Hebrew). Rishon Le-Zion: Yaḥad, 1992.

Osterhammel, Jürgen. *Die Verwandlung der Welt: Eine Geschichte des 19. Jahrhunderts.* Munich: Beck, 2009.

Parkes, James. *The Conflict of the Church and the Synagogue: A Study in the Origins of Antisemitism.* [1934] New York: Atheneum, 1969.

Pasto, James. "W. M. L. De Wette and the Invention of Post-Exilic Judaism." In *Jews, Antiquity and the Nineteenth-Century Imagination*, ed. Hayim Lapin and Dale Martin. Bethesda: University Press of Maryland, 2003, pp. 33–52.

Patka, Marcus. *Freimaurerei und Sozialreform: Der Kampf für Menschenrechte, Pazifismus und Zivilgesellschaft in Österreich 1869–1938.* Vienna: Löcker, 2011.

——— "'Ich möchte am liebsten in Jerusalem begraben sein.' Der Zionist Friedrich Torberg." In *Die "Gefahren der Vielseitigkeit": Friedrich Torberg 1908–1979.* Vienna: Holzhausen, 2008, pp. 163–79.

——— *Österreichische Freimaurer im Nationalsozialismus: Treue und Verrat.* Vienna: Böhlau, 2010.

Patka, Marcus, and Mirjana Stančić, eds. *Die Analyse der Tyrannis: Manès Sperber, 1905–1984.* Vienna: Holzhausen Verlag, 2005.

Pée, Herbert. *Johann Heinrich Schönfeld: Die Gemälde.* Berlin: Deutscher Verlag für Kunstwissenschaft, 1971.

Pelinka, Anton. "Die Studentenbewegung der 60er Jahre in Österreich: 8 Thesen aus politikwissenschaftlicher Sicht." In *Wendepunkte und Kontinuitäten*, ed. Forum Politische Bildung. Innsbruck: Studien Verlag, 1998, pp. 148–57.

——— "The Impact of American Scholarship on Austrian Political Science: The Making of a Discipline." In *The Americanization/Westernization of Austria*, ed. Günter Bischof and Anton Pelinka. New Brunswick, NJ: Transaction Publishers, 2003, pp. 226–34.

Pepin, Craig K. "The Holy Grail of Pure Wissenschaft: University Ideal and University Reform in Post World War II Germany." Ph.D. diss., Duke University, 2001.

Perlmuter, Moshe Arie. *Rabbi Jonathan Eibeschuetz and His Attitude Toward Sabbatianism* (in Hebrew). Jerusalem: Schocken, 1947.

Peyre, Henri. "Erich Auerbach (1892–1957)/Romanist" (in French.) In *Marburger Gelehrte in der ersten Hälfte des 20. Jahrhunderts*, ed. Ingeborg Schnack. Marburg: N. G. Elwert Verlag, 1977, pp. 10–21.

Pfoser, Alfred, and Andreas Weigl, eds. *Im Epizentrum des Zusammenbruchs Wien im Ersten Weltkrieg.* Vienna: Metroverlag, 2013.

Pianko, Noam. *Zionism and the Roads Not Taken: Rawidowicz, Kaplan, Kohn.* Bloomington: University of Indiana Press, 2010.

Polanyi, Karl, Conrad M. Arensberg, and Harry W. Pearson, eds. *Trade and Market in the Early Empires: Economies in History and Theory.* Glencoe, IL: Free Press, 1957.

Polanyi, Michael. "The Republic of Science." [1962] In *Knowing and Being.* Chicago: University of Chicago Press, 1969.

Polliack, Meira. "Medieval Oriental Exegesis on the Character of Jacob in Hosea 12." In *Jewish Studies at the Turn of the Twentieth Century*, ed. Judit Targarona Borrás and Ángel Sáenz-Badillos. 2 vols. Leiden: Brill, 1999: 1: 177–87.

Porter, James. "Erich Auerbach and the Judaizing of Philology." *Critical Inquiry* 35:1 (2008): 115–47.

Pribram, A. F., ed., *Urkunden und Akten zur Geschichte der Juden in Wien.* Vienna: Wilhem Bräumüller, 1918.

Price, David. *Johannes Reuchlin and the Campaign to Destroy Jewish Books.* Oxford: Oxford University Press, 2011.

Prinz, Joachim. *Joachim Prinz, Rebellious Rabbi: An Autobiography: The German and Early American Years.* Ed. and with introduction by Michael A. Meyer. Bloomington: Indiana University Press, 2008.

Qualtinger, Helmut. *Der Herr Karl und andere Texte fürs Theater.* Vienna: Deuticke, 1995.

Rabinbach, Anson. *The Crisis of Austrian Socialism: From Red Vienna to Civil War, 1927–1934.* Chicago: University of Chicago Press, 1983.

Raeff, Marc. *Russia Abroad: A Cultural History of Russian Emigration 1919–1939.* New York: Oxford University Press, 1990.

Rapoport-Albert, Ada. *Women and the Messianic Heresy of Sabbatai Zevi: 1666–1816.* Oxford: Littman Library of Jewish Civilization, 2011.

Ravitzky, Aviezer. *Messianism, Zionism, and Jewish Religious Radicalism.* Trans. Michael Swirsky and Jonathan Chipman from Hebrew. Chicago: University of Chicago Press, 1996.

Raviv, Rivka. "The Shaping of Daniel's Four Empires Prophecies in Rabbinic Literature" (in Hebrew). *JSIJ* 5 (2006): 1–20. http://www.biu.ac.il/JS/JSIJ/5–2006/Raviv.pdf.

Raz-Krakotzkin, Amnon. *The Censor, the Editor, and the Text: The Catholic Church and the Shaping of the Jewish Canon in the Sixteenth Century.* Trans. Jackie Feldman. Philadelphia: University of Pennsylvania Press, 2007.

Rechter, David. "A Nationalism of Small Things: Jewish Autonomy in Late Habsburg Austria." *Leo Baeck Institute Year Book* 52 (2007): 87–109.

Becoming Habsburg: The Jews of Austrian Bukovina, 1774–1918. Oxford: The Littman Library of Jewish Civilization, 2013.

The Jews of Vienna and the First World War. London: The Littman Library of Jewish Civilization, 2001.

Redlich, Joseph. *Emperor Francis Joseph of Austria.* New York: The Macmillan Company, 1929.

Reents, Christine. *Die Bibel als Schul- und Hausbuch für Kinder.* Göttingen: Vandenhoeck & Ruprecht, 1984.

Reich-Ranicki, Marcel. "Außenseiter und Provokateure." In *Über Ruhestörer: Juden in der deutschen Literatur.* Rev. ed. Stuttgart: DVA, 1989, pp. 13–36.

Reifowitz, Ian. *Imagining an Austrian Nation: J.S. Bloch and the Search for a Multiethnic Austrian Identity, 1846–1919.* New York: Columbia University Press, 2003.

"Threads Intertwined: German National Egoism and Liberalism in Adolf Fischhof's Vision for Austria." *Nationalities Papers* 29:3 (2001): 441–58.

Reiner, Avraham (Rami). "'Fragment to Fragment (shever qarev el shever)': Discoveries in the Wuerzburg Jewish Cemetery" (in Hebrew). *Zemanim* 95 (2006): 52–57.

"From the 'Garden of Eden' to the 'Bundle of the Living': The Blessing for the Dead on Medieval Ashkenazi Grave Stones" (in Hebrew). *Ziyon* 76 (2011): 5–28.

Reinhartz, Adele, and Miriam-Simma Walfish. "Conflict and Coexistence in Jewish Interpretation." In *Hagar, Sarah, and Their Children: Jewish, Christian, and Muslim Perspectives*, ed. Phyllis Trible and Letty M. Russell. Louisville, KY: Westminster John Knox Press, 2006, pp. 101–25.

Reinharz, Jehuda. *Fatherland or Promised Land? The Dilemma of the German Jew, 1893–1914.* Ann Arbor: University of Michigan Press, 1975.

Reiter, Wolfgang. "Naturwissenschaften und Remigration." In *Vom Weggehen: Zum Exil von Kunst und Wissenschaft*, ed. Sandra Wiesinger-Stock, Erika Weinzierl, and Konstantin Kaiser. Vienna: Mandelbaum, 2006, pp. 177–218.

Richards, Earl Jeffrey. "Erich Auerbach's *Mimesis* as a Meditation on the Shoah." *German Politics and Society* 19:59 (2001): 62–91.

Ringer, Fritz. *The Decline of the German Mandarins: The German Academic Community, 1890–1933.* Cambridge, MA: Harvard University Press, 1969.

Roemer, Nils. *German City, Jewish Memory: The Story of Worms.* Hanover, NH: University Press of New England, 2010.

Rogerson, John. *Old Testament Criticism in the Nineteenth-Century: England and Germany.* Philadelphia: Fortress Press, 1985.

Rose, Paul. *Revolutionary Antisemitism in Germany: From Kant to Wagner.* Princeton, NJ: Princeton University Press, 1990.

Rosenmann, Moses. *Dr. Adolf Jellinek: Sein Leben und Schaffen.* Vienna: Schlesinger, 1931.

Rosenson, Israel. "Edom – Poetry, Sermons and History" (in Hebrew). *Masoret ha-Piyut* 3 (2002): 45–75.

Rosenthal, Erwin. "Anti-Christian Polemic in Medieval Bible Commentaries." *Journal of Jewish Studies* 11 (1960): 115–35.

Rosenthal, Judah. "The Talmud on Trial I-II." *Jewish Quarterly Review* 47 (1956–57): 58–76, 145–69.

Rosman, Moshe. *Founder of Hasidism: A Quest for the Historical Ba'al Shem Tov.* Berkeley: University of California Press, 1996.

    How Jewish Is Jewish History? Oxford: The Littman Library of Jewish Civilization, 2007.

Rozenblit, Marsha. "Jewish Assimilation in Habsburg Vienna." In *Assimilation and Community: The Jews in Nineteenth-Century Europe*, ed. Jonathan Frankel and Steven Zipperstein. Cambridge: Cambridge University Press, 1992, pp. 225–45.

    Reconstructing a National Identity: The Jews of Habsburg Austria during World War I. New York: Oxford University Press, 2001.

    The Jews of Vienna: Identity and Assimilation, 1867–1914. Albany: State University of New York Press, 1983.

Rozental, Yehudah. "Anti-Christian Polemical Literature Until the End of the Eighteenth-Century" (in Hebrew). *Aresheth* 2 (1960): 130–79; 3 (1961): 433–39.

    "Ribit min ha-Nokhri II." *Talpiyot* 6:2 (1953): 139–52.

"Ribit min ha-Nokhri III." In *Meḥqarim u-Meqorot*. 2 vols. Jerusalem: Reuven Mas, 1967: 1: 299–311.

Rubin, Gil. "From Minority Protection to 'National Dissimilation': German and Jewish Minority Politicians and the Rise of National Socialism, April–September 1933." B.A. thesis, School of History, Hebrew University of Jerusalem, 2010.

Ruderman, David. *Early Modern Jewry: A New Cultural History*. Princeton, NJ: Princeton University Press, 2010.

Rymatzki, Christoph. *Hallischer Pietismus und Judenmission: Johann Heinrich Callenbergs Institutum Judaicum und dessen Freundenkreis (1728–1736)*. Tübingen: Max Niemeyer, 2004.

Sadowski, Dirk. "Maskilisches Bildungsideal und josephinische Erziehungspolitik – Herz Homberg und die jüdisch-deutschen Schulen in Galizien 1787–1806." *Leipziger Beiträge fuer Jüdischen Geschichte und Kultur* 1 (2003): 145–68.

Said, Edward. "Erich Auerbach, Critic of the Earthly World." *Boundary 2* 31:2 (2004): 11–34.

The World, the Text, and the Critic. Cambridge, MA: Harvard University Press, 1983.

Samet, Moshe. "Besamim Rosh by Rabbi Saul Berlin" (in Hebrew). In *He-Ḥadash asur min ha-Torah: Chapters in the History of Orthodoxy*. Jerusalem: Carmel, 2005, pp. 45–66.

He-Ḥadash asur min ha-Torah: Chapters in the History of Orthodoxy (in Hebrew). Jerusalem: Carmel, 2005.

"Moses Mendelssohn, Naphtali Herz Wessely and Their Generation's Rabbis" (in Hebrew). In *He-Ḥadash asur min ha-Torah: Chapters in the History of Orthodoxy*. Jerusalem: Merkaz Dinur, 2005, pp. 67–92.

Saperstein, Marc. "Jewish Typological Exegesis After Nachmanides." *Jewish Studies Quarterly* 1:2 (1993–94): 158–70.

"Your Voice Like a Ram's Horn." Themes and Texts in Traditional Jewish Preaching. Cincinnati, OH: Hebrew Union College, 1996.

Saunders, Frances Stonor. *Who Paid the Piper? The CIA and the Cultural Cold War*. London: Granata, 1999.

Schäfer, Peter. *Jesus in the Talmud*. Princeton, NJ: Princeton University Press, 2007.

The Bar Kokhba War Reconsidered: New Perspectives on the Second Jewish Revolt Against Rome. Ed. Peter Schäfer. Tübingen: J.C.B. Mohr, 2003.

Schäfer, Peter, ed. *Synopse zur Hekhalot-Literatur*. Tübingen: J.C.B. Mohr [Paul Siebeck], 1981.

Schechter, Ronald. *Obstinate Hebrews: Representations of Jews in France, 1715–1815*. Berkeley: University of California Press, 2003.

Scheichl, Paul Sigurd "Why and How Friedrich Torberg's *Forum* Did Not Confront the Past." *New German Critique* 93 (2004): 87–102.

Schildt, Axel. "Reise zurück aus der Zukunft: Beiträge von intellektuellen USA-Remigranten zur atlantischen Allianz, zum westdeutschen Amerikabild und zur 'Amerikanisierung' in den fünfizger Jahren." *Exilforschung* 9 (1991): 25–45.

Zwischen Abendland und Amerika: Studien zur westdeutschen Ideenlandschaft der 50er Jahre. Munich: Oldenbourg, 1999.

Schildt, Axel, and Detlef Sigfried, eds. *Between Marx and Coca-Cola: Youth Cultures in Changing European Societies, 1960–1980.* New York: Berghahn Books, 2006.

Schöffler, Herbert. "Johann Gottfried Herder aus Mohrungen." In *Deutscher Geist im 18. Jahrhundert,* ed. Götz von Selle. Göttingen: Vandenhoeck und Ruprecht, 1956, pp. 61–85.

Scholder, Klaus. "Herder und die Anfänge der historischen Theologie." *Evangelische Theologie* 22 (1962): 425–40.

The Birth of Modern Critical Theology. [1966] Trans. John Bowden. London: SCM Press, 1990.

Scholem, Gershom. "Die Erforschung der Kabbala von Reuchlin bis zur Gegenwart." In *Judaica III: Studien zur jüdischen Mystik.* Frankfurt: Suhrkamp, 1973, pp. 247–63.

"Die Stellung der Kabbala in der europäischen Geistesgeschichte." In *Judaica IV,* ed. Rolf Tiedemann. Frankfurt: Suhrkamp, 1984, pp. 7–18.

Major Trends in Jewish Mysticism. [1941] New York: Schocken Books, 1995.

"Redemption through Sin." In *The Messianic Idea in Judaism.* New York: Schocken Books, 1971, pp. 78–141.

"Reflections on Modern Jewish Studies." [1944] In *On the Possibility of Jewish Mysticism in Our Time & Other Essays,* ed. Avraham Shapira, trans. Jonathan Chipman. Philadelphia: The Jewish Publication Society, 1997, pp. 51–71.

Schorsch, Ismar. *From Text to Context: The Turn to History in Modern Judaism.* Hanover, NH: University Press of New England, 1994.

"The Myth of Sephardic Supremacy." In *From Text to Context: The Turn to History in Modern Judaism.* Hanover, NH: University Press of New England, 1994, pp. 71–92.

Schorske, Carl. *Fin-de-Siècle Vienna: Politics and Culture.* New York: Vintage, 1980.

Schreckenberg, Heinz. *Die christlichen Adversus-Judaeos-Texte und ihr literarisches und historisches Umfeld (1.–11.Jh).* Frankfurt am Main: Peter Lang, 1982.

Schremer, Adiel. *Brothers Estranged: Heresy, Christianity, and Jewish Identity in Late Antiquity.* Oxford: Oxford University Press, 2010.

Schröder, Klaus Albrecht, and Antonia Hoerschelmann, eds. *Gustav Klimt bis Paul Klee: Wotruba und die Moderne.* Vienna: Edition Minerva, 2003.

Schuchard, Marsha Keith. "From Poland to London: Sabbatean Influences on the Mystical Underworld of Zinzendorf, Swedenborg, and Blake." In *Holy Dissent: Jewish and Christian Mystics in Eastern Europe,* ed. Glenn Dynner. Detroit: Wayne University Press, 2011, pp. 250–80.

Schulte, Christoph. "Saul Ascher's *Leviathan,* or: The Invention of Jewish Orthodoxy in 1792." *Leo Baeck Institute Yearbook* 33 (1988): 27–34.

Schulte, Ingolf. "Nachwort des Herausgebers." In *Die Blutsäule.* Lüneburg: Zu Klampen, 1997, pp. 175–93.

Schwartz, Seth. *Imperialism and Jewish Society, 200 B.C.E to 640 C.E.* Princeton, NJ: Princeton University, Press, 2001.

"The Political Geography of Rabbinic Texts." In *The Cambridge Companion to the Talmud and Rabbinic Literature*, ed. Charlotte Elisheva Fonrobert and Martin S. Jaffee. New York: Cambridge University Press, 2007, pp. 75–96.

Were the Jews a Mediterranean Society? Reciprocity and Solidarity in Ancient Judaism. Princeton, NJ: Princeton University Press, 2010.

Schwarzfuchs, Simon. "Religion populaire et polémique savante: Le tournant de la polémique judéo-chrétienne au 12ᵉ siècle." In *Medieval Studies in Honor of Avrom Saltman*, ed. Bat-Sheva Albert, Yvonne Friedman, and Simon Schwarzfuchs. Ramat-Gan, Israel: Bar-Ilan University Press, 1995, pp. 189–206.

Schwarzschild, Steven. "The Theologico-Political Basis of Liberal Christian–Jewish Relations in Modernity." In *Das deutsche Judentum und der Liberalismus*, ed. Friedrich–Naumann–Stiftung and Leo Baeck Institute. Sankt Augustin: COMDOK, 1986, pp. 70–95.

Scott-Smith, Giles. *The Politics of Apolitical Culture: The Congress for Cultural Freedom, the CIA, and Post-War American Hegemony*. London: Routledge, 2002.

Segal, Alan. *Rebecca's Children: Judaism and Christianity in the Roman World*. Cambridge, MA: Harvard University Press, 1986.

Sehan, Azade. "German Academic Exiles in Istanbul: Translation as the *Bildung* of the Other." In *Nation, Language, and the Ethics of Translation*, ed. Sandra Bermann and Michael Wood. Princeton, NJ: Princeton University Press, 2005, pp. 274–88.

Septimus, Dov. "'Under Edom and Not under Ishmael' – Genealogy of a Phrase" (in Hebrew). *Ziyon* 47:2 (1982): 103–11.

Shaked, Malkah. *I'll Play You Forever: The Bible in Modern Hebrew Poetry*. 2 vols. Tel Aviv: Yediot Aḥaronot, 2005.

Shamir, Yehuda. *Rabbi Moses ha-Cohen of Tordesillas and his Book "Ezer ha-Emunah" – A Chapter in the History of the Judeo-Christian Controversy*. Coconut Grove, FL: Field Research Projects, 1972.

Shanes, Joshua. *Diaspora Nationalism and Jewish Identity in Habsburg Galicia*. Cambridge: Cambridge University Press, 2012.

Shapiro, Marc B. *Between the Yeshiva World and Modern Orthodoxy: The Life and Works of Rabbi Jehiel Jacob Weinberg, 1884–1966*. London: Littman Library. 1999.

Shatzmiller, Joseph. "Did the Convert Nicholas Donin Allege the Blood Libel?" (in Hebrew). In vol. 4 of *Studies in the History of the Jewish People and the Land of Israel*, ed. Uriel Rappaport. 5 vols. Haifa: University of Haifa Press, 1970–80: 4 (1978): 173–82.

Le deuxième controverse de Paris: Un chapitre dans la polémique entre Chrétiens et Juifs au Moyen Age. Paris: E. Peeters, 1994.

Shaul, Michal. *Beauty for Ashes: Holocaust Memory and the Rehabilitation of Ashkenazi Haredi Society in Israel, 1945–1961* (in Hebrew). Jerusalem: Yad Vamhem; Yad Izhak ben-Zvi, 2014.

Shavit, Zohar. "From Friedländer's Lesebuch to the Jewish Campe: The Beginnings of Children's Literature in Germany." *Leo Baeck Institute Yearbook* 33 (1988): 385–415.

Shedel, James. *"Fin de siècle* or *Jahrhundertwende:* The Question of an Austrian *Sonderweg."* In *Rethinking Vienna 1900*, ed. Steven Beller. New York: Berghahn, 2001, pp. 80–104.

"The Elusive Fatherland: Dynasty, State, Identity and the Kronprinzenwerk." In *Inszenierungen des kollektiven Gedächtnises: Eigenbilder, Fremdbilder*, ed. Moritz Csáky and Klaus Zeyringer. Innsbruck: StudienVerlag, 2002, pp. 70–82.

"The Problem of Being Austrian: Religion, Law, and Nation from Empire to *Anschluß."* In *Pluralitäten, Religionen und kulturelle Codes*, ed. Moritz Csáky and Klaus Zeyringer. Innsbruck: Studien Verlag, 2001, pp. 117–29.

Sheehan, Jonathan. *The Enlightenment Bible: Translation, Scholarship, Culture.* Princeton, NJ: Princeton University Press, 2005.

Sheppard, Eugene R. *Leo Strauss and the Politics of Exile: The Making of a Political Philosopher.* Waltham, MA: Brandeis University Press, 2006.

Shereshevsky, Esra. "Rashi's and Christian Interpretations." *Jewish Quarterly Review* N.S. 61:1 (1970): 76–86.

Shinan, Avigdor. *The Aggadah in the Aramaic Targums to the Pentateuch* (in Hebrew). 2 vols. Jerusalem: Maqor, 1979: 2: 345–52.

Shmeruk, Chone. *The Illustrations in Yiddish Books of the Sixteenth and Seventeenth Centuries* (in Hebrew). Jerusalem: Akademon Press, 1986.

Shumsky, Dimitry. "Brith Shalom's Uniqueness Reconsidered: Hans Kohn and Autonomist Zionism." *Jewish History* 25 (2011): 339–53.

"Historiography, Nationalism and Bi-Nationalism: Czech-German Jewry, the Prague Zionism and the Origins of the Bi-National Approach of Hugo Bergmann." *Ziyon* 69 (2004): 45–80.

"Leon Pinsker and 'Autoemancipation!': A Reevaluation." *Jewish Social Studies* 18:1 (2011): 33–62.

"On Ethno-Centrism and Its Limits – Czecho-German Jewry in Fin-de-Siècle Prague and the Origins of Zionist Bi-Nationalism." *Jahrbuch des Simon-Dubnow-Instituts* 5 (2006): 173–88.

Signer, Michael A. "Nicholas of Lyra on the Prophet Ezekiel." *Nicholas of Lyra: The Senses of Scripture*, ed. Philip D. W. Krey and Lesley Smith. Leiden: Brill, 2000, pp. 147–71.

Signer, Michael A., and John Van Engen, eds. *Jews and Christians in Twelfth-Century Europe.* Notre Dame, IN: University of Notre Dame Press, 2001.

Silber, Marcos. *Different Nationality, Equal Citizenship: Efforts to Achieve Autonomy for Polish Jewry during the First World War* (in Hebrew). Tel Aviv: Tel Aviv University, 2014.

"Lithuania? But Which? The Changing Political Attitude of the Jewish Political Elite in East Central Europe toward Emerging Lithuania, 1915–1919." In *A Pragmatic Alliance: Jewish-Lithuanian Political Cooperation at the Beginning of the 20th Century*, ed. Vladas Sirutavičius and Darius Staliūnas. Budapest: Central European University Press, 2011, pp. 119–57.

"The Development of a Joint Political Program for the Jews of Poland During World War I – Success and Failure." *Jewish History* 19 (2005): 211–26.

"The Metamorphosis of Pre-Dubnovian Autonomism into Diaspora Jewish-Nationalism." In *Homelands and Diasporas: Greeks, Jews and Their Migrations*, ed. Minna Rozen. London: I. B. Tauris, 2008, pp. 235–55, 391–400.

Silber, Michael K. "From Tolerated Aliens to Citizen-Soldiers: Jewish Military Service in the Era of Joseph II." In *Constructing Nationalities in East Central Europe*, ed. Pieter Judson and Marsha Rozenblit. New York: Berghahn Books, 2005, pp. 19–36.

"Orthodoxy." In *The YIVO Encyclopedia of Jews in Eastern Europe*, ed. Gershon David Hundert. New Haven, CT: Yale University Press, 2008, pp. 1292–97.

"Roots of the Schism in Hungarian Jewry." Ph.D. diss., The Hebrew University of Jerusalem," 1985.

"The Emergence of Ultra-Orthodoxy: The Invention of a Tradition." In *The Uses of Tradition: Jewish Continuity in the Modern Era*, ed. Jack Wertheimer. New York: Jewish Theological Seminary, 1992, pp. 23–84.

"The Historical Experience of German Jewry and Its Impact on Haskalah and Reform in Hungary." In *Toward Modernity*, ed. Jacob Katz. New Brunswick: NJ: Transactions Books, 1987, pp. 107–57.

Silk, Mark. "Notes on the Judeo-Christian Tradition in America." *American Quarterly* 36:1 (1984): 65–85.

Silverman, Lisa. *Becoming Austrians: Jews and Culture Between the World Wars*. Oxford: Oxford University Press, 2012.

Silverman, Paul. "Law and Economics in Interwar Vienna: Kelsen, Mises and the Regeneration of Austrian Liberalism." Ph.D. diss., University of Chicago, 1984.

Simkin, Colin. "The Birth of *The Open* Society." In *Popper's Views on Natural and Social Science*. Leiden: Brill, 1993, pp. 183–90.

Simon, Marcel. *Verus Israel: A Study of the Relations Between Christian and Jews in the Roman Empire AD 135–425*. [1948] London: The Littman Library of Jewish Civilization, 1996.

Sivertsev, Alexei. *Judaism and Imperial Ideology in Late Antiquity*. New York: Cambridge University Press, 2011.

Slezkine, Yuri. *The Jewish Century*. Princeton, NJ: Princeton University Press, 2004.

Sluga, Glenda, and Patricia Calvin. "Rethinking the History of Internationalism." In *Internationalisms: A Twentieth-Century History*, ed. Glenda Sluga and Patricia Calvin. Cambridge: Cambridge University Press, 2017, pp. 3–14.

Smalley, Beryl. *The Study of the Bible in the Middle Ages*. 3d ed. Oxford: Basil Blackwell, 1983.

Smith, Helmut Walser. *The Continuities of German History: Nation, Religion, and Race across the Long Nineteenth Century*. Cambridge: Cambridge University Press, 2008.

Smith, Jonathan Z. "The Prayer of Joseph." In *Religions in Antiquity*, ed. J. Neusner. Leiden: Brill, 1968, pp. 253–94.

Söllner, Alfons. "Normative Westernization? – The Impact of Remigres on the Foundation of Political Thought in Post-War Germany." In *German Ideologies Since 1945*, ed. Jan-Werner Müller. New York: Palgrave Macmillan, 2003, pp. 40–60.

"Soma Morgenstern Dies at 85." *New York Times* (19 April 1976).

Sommer, Benjamin. "Revelation at Sinai in the Hebrew Bible and in Jewish Theology." *Journal of Religion* 79:3 (1999): 422–51.

Sorkin, David. *The Berlin Haskalah and German Religious Thought.* London: Vallentine Mitchell, 2000.

———. *The Count Stanislas de Clermont-Tonnerre's "To the Jews as a Nation … ": The Career of a Quotation.* Jerusalem: Leo Baeck Institute, 2012.

———. "The Impact of Emancipation on German Jewry: A Reconsideration." In *Assimilation and Community: The Jews in Nineteenth-Century Europe,* ed. Jonathan Frankel and Steven Zipperstein. Cambridge: Cambridge University Press, 1992, pp. 177–98.

———. *The Religious Enlightenment: Protestants, Jews, and Catholics from London to Vienna.* Princeton, NJ: Princeton University Press, 2008.

Sorrels, Katherine. *Cosmopolitan Outsiders: Imperial Inclusion, National Exclusion, and the Pan-European Idea, 1900–1930.* New York: Palgrave Macmillan, 2016.

Specter, Matthew. *Jürgen Habermas: An Intellectual Biography.* New York: Cambridge University Press, 2010.

Spector, Scott. *Prague Territories: National Conflict and Cultural Innovation in Kafka's Fin de Siècle.* Berkeley: University of California Press, 2000.

Spiegel, Shalom. *The Last Trial: On the Legends and Lore of the Command to Abraham to Offer Isaac as a Sacrifice: The Akedah.* Trans. from the Hebrew and with introduction by Judah Goldin. New York: Pantheon Books, 1967.

Stachowitsch, Saskia, and Eva Kreisky, eds. *Jüdische Identitäten und antisemitische Politiken im österreichischen Parlament 1861–1933.* Vienna: Böhlau, 2017.

Stadler, Friedrich. "Spätaufklärung und Sozialdemokratie in Wien 1918–1938." In *Aufbruch und Untergang: Österreichische Kultur zwischen 1918 und 1938,* ed. Franz Kadrnoska. Vienna: Europaverlag, 1981, pp. 441–74.

———. *Studien zum Wiener Kreis.* Frankfurt am Main: Suhrkamp, 1997.

———. *Vom Positivismus zur "Wissenschaftliche Weltauffassung."* Vienna: Löcker, 1982.

Stahl, Neta. "'Man's Red Soup': Blood and the Art of Esau in the Poetry of Uri Zvi Greenberg." In *Jewish Blood,* ed. Mitchell Hart. London: Routledge, 2009, pp. 160–71.

Stein, Abraham. *Die Geschichte der Juden in Böhmen.* Brünn: Jüdischer Buch- und Kunstverlag, 1904.

Steinberg, Michael. *The Meaning of the Salzburg Festival.* Ithaca, NY: Cornell University Press, 1990.

Steinmetz, David. "Luther und Calvin am Jabbokufer." *Evangelische Theologie* 57:6 (1997): 522–36.

Stoetzler, Marcel. *The State, the Nation, & the Jews: Liberalism and the Antisemitism Dispute in Bismarck's Germany.* Lincoln: University of Nebraska Press, 2008.

Stourzh, Gerald. "Deutsche Geschichtsschreibung über Österreich." *Forum* 2 (October 1955): 358–60.

———. *Die Gleichberechtigung der Nationalitäten in der Verfassung und Verwaltung Österreichs 1848–1918.* Vienna: Verlag der österreichischen Akademie der Wissenschaft, 1985.

"Ethnic Attribution in Late Imperial Austria: Good Intentions, Evil Consequences." *Austrian Studies* 5 (1994): 67–83.

"Unterrichtsfach 'Gesellschaft.'" *Forum* 1 (September 1954): 12–13.

Stow, Kenneth. "Jewish Pre-Emancipation: 'Ius Commune,' the Roman 'Comunità,' and Marriage in the Early Modern Papal State." In *Tov Elem: Memory, Community and Gender in Medieval and Early Modern Jewish Societies: Essays in Honor of Robert Bonfil*, ed. Elisheva Baumgarten, Amnon Raz-Krakotzkin, and Roni Weinstein. Jerusalem: The Bialik Institute, 2011, pp. 79–102.

Strelka, Josef. ed. *Der Weg war schon das Ziel: Festschrift für Friedrich Torberg zum 70. Geburtstag.* Munich: Langen Müller, 1978.

Sysling, Harry. *Teḥiyyat Ha-Metim* (in English and Hebrew). Tübingen: J.C.B. Mohr, 1996.

Tal, Uriel. *Political Theology and the Third Reich* (in Hebrew). Tel Aviv: Sifriat Poalim, 1989.

Religion, Politics, and Ideology in the Second Reich, 1870–1914. Trans. Noah Jonathan Jacobs. Ithaca, NY: Cornell University Press, 1975.

Taschwer, Klaus. *Hochburg des Antisemitismus: Der Niedergang der Universität Wien im 20. Jahrhundert.* Vienna: Czernin Verlag, 2015.

Taylor, Charles. *Sources of the Self: The Making of the Modern Identity.* Cambridge, MA: Harvard University Press, 1989.

"The Importance of Herder." In *Philosophical Arguments.* Cambridge, MA: Harvard University Press, 1995, pp. 79–99.

Taylor, A. J. P. *The Habsburg Monarchy 1809–1918.* [1941] Chicago: University of Chicago Press, 1976.

Thraede, Klaus. "Jakob und Esau." In *Reallexikon für Antike und Christentum*, ed. Theodor Klauser et al. 26 vols. Stuttgart: A. Hiersmann, 1994: 14: 1118–217.

Tichy, Frank. *Friedrich Torberg: Ein Leben in Widersprüchen.* Vienna: O. Müller, 1995.

Tishbi, Isaiah. *Torat ha-Ra ve-ha-Qelippah be-Kabbalat ha-ARI.* Jerusalem: Aqademon, 1965.

Todeschini, Giacomo. "Franciscan Economics and the Jews in the Middle Ages." In *Friars and Jews in the Middle Ages and Renaissance*, ed. Susan Myers and Steven McMichael. Leiden: Brill, 2004, pp. 99–118.

Tolan, John. *Saracens: Islam in the Medieval European Imagination.* New York: Columbia University Press, 2002.

Touitou, Elazar. "Rashi and His School." In *Medieval Studies in Honor of Avrom Saltman*, ed. Bat-Sheva Albert, Yvonne Friedman, and Simon Schwarzfuchs. Ramat-Gan: Bar-Ilan University Press, 1995, pp. 231–51.

Toury, Jacob. "The Jewish Question – A Semantic Approach." *Leo Baeck Institute Yearbook* 10 (1966): 85–106.

Tov, Emanuel. *Textual Criticism of the Hebrew Bible.* 3d ed. Minneapolis, MN: Fortress Press, 2012.

Trautner-Kromann, Hanne. *Shield and Sword: Jewish Polemics against Christianity and the Christians in France and Spain from 1100–1500.* Tübingen: Mohr, 1993.

Treml, Martin, and Karlheinz Barck, eds. *Erich Auerbach: Geschichte und Aktualität eines europäischen Philologen.* Berlin: Kulturverlag Kadmos, 2007.

Trop, Gabriel. "Politik der Vertriebenen: Hannah Arendt im Schatten des Zweiten Weltkriegs." Paper presented at the *Atempause: Intellektuelle Nachkriegskonzeptionen 1943–1947* conference, April 24, 2014, Ludwig Boltzmann Institut, Vienna.

Turgeman, Asaf. "Mein Bruder ist ein Einzelkind: Die Esau-Darstellung in jüdischen Schriften des Mittelalters." In *Esau: Bruder und Feind*, ed. Gerhard Langer. Göttingen: Vandenhoeck & Ruprecht, 2009, pp. 135–54.

Turniansky, Chava. "A *Haskalah* Version of *Ẓenah u-Renah*" (in Hebrew). *Ha-Sifrut* 2 (1971): 835–41.

Tweraser, Felix W. "Paris Calling Vienna: The Congress for Cultural Freedom and Friedrich Torberg's Editorship of Forum." *Austrian Studies* 13 (2005): 158–72.

Ultes-Nitsche, Heidrun. *"Ich bin eine feine Monarchiemischung": Identitätskonstruktionen in Friedrich Torbergs nichtfiktionalen Texten.* Hamburg: Verlag Dr. Kovač, 2005.

Urbanitsch, Peter. "Pluralist Myth and Nationalist Realities: The Dynastic Myth of the Habsburg Monarchy – a Futile Exercise in the Creation of Identity?" *Austrian History Yearbook* 35 (2004): 101–41.

Vandehooft, David, ed. "In Conversation with Oded Lipschits, *The Fall and Rise of Jerusalem* (Winona Lake, IN: Eisenbrauns, 2005)." *Journal of Hebrew Scriptures* 7:2 (2007): 1–49.

Van Kley, Dale. *The Religious Origins of the French Revolution: From Calvin to the Civil Constitution, 1560–1791.* New Haven, CT: Yale University Press, 1996.

Van Rahden, Till. "Germans of the Jewish *Stamm*: Visions of Community Between Nationalism and Particularism, 1850–1933." In *German History from the Margins*, ed. Nils Roemer and Neil Gregor. Bloomington: Indiana University Press, 2005, pp. 27–48.

——. *Jews and Other Germans: Civil Society, Religious Diversity, and Urban Politics in Breslau, 1860–1925.* Trans. Marcus Brainard. Madison: University of Wisconsin Press, 2008.

——. "Jews and the Ambivalences of German Civil Society: Assessment and Reassessment." *Journal of Modern History* 77 (2005): 1024–47.

——. "Situational Ethnic Affiliation vs. Milieu-Based Identity: The Making of the Jewish Public and Catholic Public in the German Empire" (in Hebrew). In *"The German-Jewish History We Have Inherited": Young Germans Write Jewish History*, ed. Henry Wassermann. Jerusalem: Magnes Press, 2004, pp. 214–41.

Visotzky, Burton. *Fathers of the World: Essays in Rabbinic and Patristic Literatures.* Tübingen: Mohr, 1995.

——. *Golden Bells and Pomegranates: Studies in Midrash Leviticus Rabbah.* Tübingen: Mohr Siebeck, 2003.

Voigt, Sebastian. "'Nous sommes tous des Juifs allemands': Daniel Cohn-Bendit, Pierre Goldman und der Pariser Mai 1968." *Medaon—Magazin für jüdisches*

Leben in Forschung und Bildung 4:7 (2010): 1–18. http://medaon.de/pdf/AV oigt-7–2010.pdf.

Volkov, Shulamit. "Antisemitism as a Cultural Code: Reflections on the History and Historiography of Antisemitism in Imperial Germany." *Leo Baeck Institute Yearbook* 23:1 (1978): 25–46.

Voss, Hermann. *Johann Heinrich Schönfeld: Ein Schwäbischer Maler des 17. Jahrhunderts.* Biberach an der Riß: Biberacher Verlagsdruckerei, 1964.

Wagnleitner, Reinhold. *Coca-Colonization and the Cold War.* Trans. Diana M. Wolf. Chapel Hill: University of North Carolina Press, 1994.

Walicki, Andrzej. "Polish Conceptions of the Intelligentsia and Its Calling." In *Words, Deeds and Values: The Intelligentsias in Russia and Poland during the Nineteenth and Twentieth Centuries*, ed. Fiona Björling and Alexander Pereswetoff-Morath. Lund: Department of East and Central European Studies, 2005, pp. 1–22.

Walser Smith, Helmut. *The Continuities of German History: Nation, Religion, and Race across the Long Nineteenth Century.* Cambridge: Cambridge University Press, 2008.

Walzer, Michael, Menachem Lorberbaum, Noam J. Zohar, and Yair Lorberbaum, eds. *The Jewish Political Tradition.* 2 vols. New Haven, CT: Yale University Press, 2000–2003.

Warner, Michael. "Origins of the Congress for Cultural Freedom, 1949–50." *Studies in Intelligence* 38:5 (1995): 89–98.

Wasserman, Janek. *Black Vienna: The Radical Right in the Red City, 1918–1938.* Ithaca, NY: Cornell University Press, 2014.

Weber, Mathias. "Ein Modell fuer Europa? Die Nationalitätenpolitik in der Habsburger Monarchie Österreich und Ungarn 1867–1914 im Vergleich." *Geschichte in Wissenschaft und Kultur* 47 (1996): 651–72.

Weber, Max. "Science as a Vocation." In *The Vocation Lectures*, ed. with introduction by David S. Owen and Tracy B. Strong, trans. Rodney Livingstone. Indianapolis, IN: Hackett, 2004, pp. 1–31.

Weber, Toni. *Die Praefigurationen im geistlichen Drama Deutschlands.* Marburg: Werner u. Winter, 1919.

Weidner, Daniel. "Secularization, Scripture and the Theory of Reading: J. G. Herder and the Old Testament." *New German Critique* 94 (2005): 169–93.

Weir, Todd H. *Secularism and Religion in Nineteenth-Century Germany: The Rise of the Fourth Confession.* New York: Cambridge University Press, 2014.

"The Specter of 'Godless Jewry': Secularism and the 'Jewish Questions' in Late Nineteenth-Century Germany." *Central European History* 46 (2014): 815–49.

Weiss, Yfaat. "Central European Ethnonationalism and Zionist Binationalism." *Jewish Social Studies* 11 (Fall 2004): 93–117.

Weissberg, Liliane. "Juden oder Hebräer? Religiöse und politische Bekehrung bei Herder." In *Johann Gottfried Herder: Geschichte und Kultur*, ed. Martin Bollacher. Würzburg: Königshausen & Neumann, 1994, pp. 191–212.

"Ortswechsel: Hannah Arendts Suche nach dem "asiatischen Volk." In *Hebräische Poesie und Jüdischer Volkgeist,* ed. Christoph Schulte. Hildesheim: Georg Olms, 2003, pp. 245–56.

Weiss-Wendt, Anton, ed. *The Nazi Genocide of the Roma: Reassessment and Commemoration.* New York: Berghahn Books, 2013.

Wellek, René. "Auerbach's Special Realism." *Kenyon Review* 16 (1954): 299–307.

Wenzel, Edith, ed. "Grenzen und Grenzüberschreitungen: Kulturelle Kontakte zwischen Juden und Christen im Mittelalter." *Aschkenas* 14:1 (2004): 1–7.

Werckmeister, O. K. *The Making of Paul Klee's Career, 1914–1920.* Chicago: University of Chicago Press, 1984.

Wette, W. M. L. de. *Jacob Burckhardt and the Theological Origins of Nineteenth-Century Historical Consciousness.* Cambridge: Cambridge University Press, 2000.

White, Hayden. *Metahistory.* Baltimore: Johns Hopkins University Press, 1973.

Whitfield, Stephen.*Voices of Jacob, Hands of Esau: Jews in American Life and Thought.* Hamden, CT: Archon Books, 1984.

Wiese, Christian. *Challenging Colonial Discourse: Jewish Studies and Protestant Theology in Wilhelmine Germany.* Leiden: Brill, 2005.

"Modern Antisemitism and Jewish Responses in Germany and France, 1880–1914." In *Jewish Emancipation Reconsidered: The French and German Models,* ed. Michael Brenner, Vicki Caron, and Uri R. Kaufmann. Tübingen: Mohr Siebeck, 2003, pp. 129–47.

"Struggling for Normality: The Apologetics of *Wissenschaft des Judentums* in Wilhelmine Germany as an Anti-Colonial Intellectual Revolt against the Protestant Construction of Judaism." In *"Towards Normality?" Acculturation of Modern German Jewry,* ed. Rainer Liedtke and David Rechter. Tübingen: Mohr Siebeck, 2003, pp. 80–89.

"'The Best Antidote against Anti-Semitism'? *Wissenschaft des Judentums,* Protestant Biblical Scholarship, and Anti-Semitism in Germany before 1933." In *Modern Judaism and Historical Consciousness,* ed. Andreas Gotzmann and Christian Wiese. Leiden: Brill, 2007, pp. 177–80.

Wilford, Hugh. *The Mighty Wurlitzer: How the CIA Played America.* Cambridge, MA: Harvard University Press, 2008.

Willi, Thomas. "Die Metamorphose der Bibelwissenschaft in Herders Umgang mit dem Alten Testament." In *Johann Gottfried Herder: Geschichte und Kultur,* ed. Martin Bollacher. Würzburg: Königshausen & Neumann, 1994, pp. 239–56.

Herders Beitrag zum Verstehen des Alten Testament. Tübingen: J.C.B. Moher, 1971.

Williams, A. Lukyn. *Adversus Judaeos: A Bird's-Eye View of Christian Apologiae until the Renaissance.* Cambridge: Cambridge University Press, 1935.

Wingfield, Nancy. "Statutes of Emperor Joseph II as Sites of German Identity." In *Staging the Past,* ed. Nancy Wingfield and Maria Bucur. West Lafayette, IN: Purdue University Press, 2001, pp. 178–204.

Wistrich, Robert. *Socialism and the Jews: The Dilemmas of Assimilation in Germany and Austria-Hungary.* London: Associated University Presses, 1982, chap. 8.

The Jews of Vienna in the Age of Franz Joseph. Oxford: Oxford University Press, 1988.

"The Strange Odyssey of Nathan Birnbaum." In *Laboratory for World Destruction: Germans and Jews in Central Europe*. Lincoln: University of Nebraska Press, 2007, pp. 118–53.

Wolfson, Elliot R. "The Image of Jacob Engraved Upon the Throne: Further Reflections on the Esoteric Doctrine of the German Pietists." In *Along the Path*. Albany: State University of New York Press, 1995, pp. 1–62.

Venturing Beyond: Law and Morality in Kabbalistic Mysticism. New York: Oxford University Press, 2006.

Wolin, Richard. *Heidegger's Children: Hannah Arendt, Karl Löwith, Hans Jonas, and Herbert Marcuse*. Princeton, NJ: Princeton University Press, 2001.

Yarḥi, Yosi. "Maamar 'Aseret Haruge Malkhut u-Mot ha-Melakhim' she-mi-Ketivat Yad ha-ARI: Hebetim shel Torat ha-Gilgul ba-Meot ha-13-16." Master's thesis, The Hebrew University of Jerusalem, 1995.

Yerushalmi, Hayim Yosef. *"Servants of Kings and Not Servants of Servants": Some Aspects of the Political History of the Jews*. Atlanta: Tam Institute for Jewish Studies, 2005.

The Lisbon Massacre of 1506 and the Royal Image in the Shebet Yehudah. Cincinnati, OH: Hebrew Union College, 1976.

Young, Karl. *The Drama of the Medieval Church*. Oxford: Clarendon Press, 1933.

Young-Bruehl, Elisabeth. *Hannah Arendt: For the Love of the World*. New Haven, CT: Yale University Press, 2004.

Yuval, Israel. *Two Nations in Your Womb: Perceptions of Jews and Christians in Late Antiquity and the Middle Ages*. Trans. Barbara Harshav and Jonathan Chipman. Berkeley: University of California Press, 2006.

Zadoff, Noam. "Gershom Scholem: A German Returnee?" Paper presented at the Jewish Studies Seminar, Duke University, May 3, 2012.

Gershom Scholem: From Berlin to Jerusalem and Back. Trans. Jeffrey Green. Waltham, MA: Brandeis University Press, 2017.

Zahra, Tara. *Kidnapped Souls: National Indifference and the Battle for Children in the Bohemian Lands, 1900–1948*. Ithaca, NY: Cornell University Press, 2008.

Zakai, Avihu. *Erich Auerbach and the Crisis of German Philology*. Cham, Switzerland: Springer, 2017.

Zakovitch, Yair. *Jacob: Unexpected Patriarch*. New Haven, CT: Yale University Press, 2012.

Zammito, John H., Karl Menges, and Ernest A. Menze. "Johann Gottfried Herder Revisited: The Revolution in Scholarship in the Last Quarter Century." *Journal of the History of Ideas* 71:4 (2010): 661–84.

Zeman, Herbert, ed. *Literaturgeschichte Österreichs von den Anfängen im Mittelalter bis zur Gegenwart*. Graz: Akademische Druck- u. Verlaganstalt, 1996.

Zerubavel, Yael. *Recovered Roots: Collective Memory and the Making of Israeli National Tradition*. Chicago: University of Chicago Press, 1995.

Ziak, Karl, ed. *Wiedergeburt einer Weltstadt: Wien, 1945–1965*. Vienna: Verlag für Jugend und Volk, 1965.

Ziegerhofer, Anita. *Botschafter Europas: Richard Nikolaus Coudenhove-Kalergi und die Paneuropa-Bewegung in den zwanziger und dreißiger Jahren.* Vienna: Böhlau, 2004.

Zoppel, Christina. "Linientreue und Liberalität: Die Rezeption der zeitgenössischen österreichischen Literatur im kommunistischen 'Tagebuch', 1950–1960." Master's thesis, University of Vienna, 1995.

Index